CONGRESSIONAL VOTING GUIDE

A TEN YEAR COMPILATION OF THE 99TH CONGRESS

Victor W. Bosnich

Printed by arrangement with Kissel Printing
Published by the author
Library of Congress Catalog Card Number: 87-91609
ISBN: 0-9618958-0-2

Bosnich, Victor W.
Congressional Voting Guide.

Questions or comments?
Congressional Voting Guide
Suite 236
3220 N Street, N.W. Georgetown
Washington, D. C. 20007

Typography by Nini Hall, Oak Cliff Word Processing, Dallas, Texas
Printed in the United States of America
First Edition

CONTENTS

CONTENTS

Use Of This Book

The Congressional Voting Guide is a quick reference to the voting records of members finishing the 99th Congress. The information was reproduced with permission, from Congressional Quarterly Inc. and from public records. The measures chosen were deemed "major votes" by the author over the ten-year period 1977-1986.

The house and senate measures, included before the voting records, are presented in the way they were voted upon. Along with these measures is a breakdown of how Republicans and Democrats voted. Democrats are also separated into Northern and Southern states because of the disparity in their voting patterns. Southern Democrats are members from: Alabama, Arkansas, Florida, Georgia, Kentucky, Louisiana, Mississippi, North Carolina, Oklahoma, South Carolina, Tennessee, Texas, and Virginia.

Along with each member of Congress is a biographical background as released by that congressperson. Abbreviated forms of the measures follow the biographical information because of space limitations. They are presented as they were written in the bill and intended to stand alone as an explanation of the measure; however, the entire measure should be reviewed. For example, a measure to "Kill-AIDS ins dscriminatn" is a vote to end a bill that would allow insurance companies to discriminate against persons testing positive for AIDS.

The majority of the bills were taken from 1985-1986 to more thoroughly show the positions of recently elected members. Some issues were included more than once because they were more important than others or because the voting positions changed so often. This is designed to show who were "swing votes" on issues such as: Nicaraguan Aid, South Africa sanctions, MX missile, and Textile Import Quotas. For the period 1977-1984, the bills taken were not voted upon in 1985-1986 except in a few cases.

Presidential Support Scores are from the years 1985-1986 to indicate the congresspersons' alliance with President Reagan's position. These scores are taken from all votes where the President made his position known not just ones included in the Congressional Voting Guide. Opposition scores were not included simply because they are the difference, within a few points, of the PSS and 100.

The Congressional Voting Guide is assumed to be free of error, but if further information is needed on a particular bill or amendment, I would recommend The Congressional Quarterly Weekly Report.

Below are descriptions of the vote abbreviations:

Y Voted for (yea)

Paired for (Agreement, with an opposing member, not to vote)

+ Announced for

C Voted "present" to avoid possible conflict of interest

P Voted "present"

N Voted against (nay)

X Paired against (Agreement, with an opposing member, not to vote)

- Announced against

? Did not vote or otherwise make a position known

Use Of This Book

HOUSE

MEASURES

HOUSE MEASURES

1. **HR 3810. Immigration Reform.** Passage of the bill to overhaul the nation's immigration laws by creating a new system of penalties against employers who knowingly hire illegal aliens, providing legal status to millions of illegal aliens already in the United States, and creating a special program for foreigners to gain legal status if they have a history of working in U.S. agriculture. Passed 230-166: R 62-105; D 168-61 [ND 126-29; SD 42-32], Oct. 9, 1986. (The House subsequently moved to strike the provisions of S 1200, the Senate-passed version of the bill, and insert the provisions of HR 3810. The House then passed S 1200 by voice vote.)

2. **HR 3810. Immigration Reform.** De la Garza, D-Texas, amendment to require Immigration and Naturalization Service employees to obtain warrants before searching open fields for violations of immigration laws. Adopted 221-170: R 85-79; D 136-91 [ND 98-58; SD 38-33], Oct. 9, 1986. A "nay" was a vote supporting the president's position.

3. **HR 3810. Immigration Reform.** Bartlett, R-Texas, amendment to allow only civil rather than criminal penalties for engaging in a pattern or practice of knowingly hiring illegal aliens. Rejected 137-264: R 71-97; D 66-167 [ND 48-110; SD 18-57], Oct. 9, 1986.

4. **HR 4868. South African Sanctions.** Passage, over President Reagan's Sept. 26 veto, of the bill to impose economic sanctions against South Africa. Passed 313-83: R 81-79; D 232-4 [ND 163-0; SD 69-4], Sept. 29, 1986. A two-thirds majority of those present and voting (264 in this case) of both houses is required to override a veto. A "nay" was a vote supporting the president's position.

5. **HR 3838. Tax Overhaul.** Adoption of the conference report on the bill to revise the federal income tax system by reducing individual and corporate tax rates, eliminating or curtailing many deductions, credits and exclusions, repealing the investment tax credit, taxing capital gains as regular income and making other changes. Adopted 292-136: R 116-62; D 176-74 [ND 132-36; SD 44-38], Sept. 25, 1986. A "yea" was a vote supporting the president's position.

6. **HR 4868. South Africa Sanctions.** Fascell, D-Fla., motion to concur in the Senate amendment to the bill to set policy goals to encourage South Africa to end its racial apartheid system and impose economic sanctions, among them barring importation of South African coal, steel and agricultural products, ending U.S. landing rights for South African airliners, and -- with some exceptions -- barring new U.S.

loans to South African businesses or the South African government. Motion agreed to 308-77: R 90-73; D 218-4 [ND 150-0; SD 68-4], Sept. 12, 1986. A "nay" was a vote supporting the president's position.

7. **HR 5484. Omnibus Drug Bill.** Gekas, R-Pa., amendment to authorize imposition of the death penalty on anyone who knowingly causes the death of another individual during the course of a continuing criminal enterprise. Adopted 296-112: R 160-10; D 136-102 [ND 69-93; SD 67-9], Sept. 11, 1986.

8. **HR 5484. Omnibus Drug Bill.** Lungren, R-Calif., amendment to permit the introduction in court of evidence obtained in a warrantless search if the search or seizure was undertaken "in a reasonable, good faith belief that it was in conformity with the Fourth Amendment to the Constitution." Adopted 259-153: R 163-8; D 96-145 [ND 38-127; SD 58-18], Sept. 11, 1986.

9. **HR 5484. Omnibus Drug Bill.** Kramer, R-Colo., amendment to impose a mandatory life sentence for a person aged 21 or older convicted of a second offense of selling a controlled substance to a person under age 21. Adopted 355-54: R 172-1; D 183-53 [ND 112-48; SD 71-5], Sept. 11, 1986.

10. **HR 5484. Omnibus Drug Bill.** Hunter, R-Calif., amendment to the Bennett, D-Fla., amendment, to require that the president deploy the armed forces to halt substantially, within 45 days, the unlawful entry of aircraft and vessels carrying narcotics. Adopted 237-177: R 145-29; D 92-148 [ND 55-108; SD 37-40], Sept. 11, 1986. (The Bennett amendment, to allow the use of members of the armed services to assist drug enforcement officials outside the United States, as amended by the Hunter amendment, subsequently was adopted. A "nay" was a vote supporting the president's position.

11. **HR 4428. Defense Authorization, Fiscal 1987.** Schroeder, D-Colo., amendment to require the withdrawal over a five-year period of one-half the U.S. ground troops currently stationed in Europe and one-third of the U.S. ground troops currently stationed elsewhere abroad and to demobilize half the forces withdrawn. Rejected 90-322: R 14-159; D 76-163 [ND 65-98; SD 11-65], Aug. 13, 1986. A "nay" was a vote supporting the president's position.

12. **HR 4428. Defense Authorization, Fiscal 1987.** Porter, R-Ill., amendment to prohibit the production of binary chemical weapons before Oct. 1, 1987. Adopted 210-209: R 38-137; D 172-72 [ND 142-23; SD 30-49], Aug. 13, 1986. A "nay" was a vote supporting the president's position.

13. **HR 4428. Defense Authorization, Fiscal 1987.** Brown, D-Calif., amendment to bar tests against an object in space of the anti-satellite (ASAT) missile provided the Soviet Union abstains from testing its own version of the weapon. Adopted 222-197: R 28-148; D 194-49 [ND 153-10, SD 41-39], Aug. 13, 1986. A "nay" was a vote supporting the president's position.

14. **HR 4428. Defense Authorization, Fiscal 1987.** Dicks, D-Wash., amendment to prohibit the use of funds to deploy any weapons inconsistent with certain limits contained in the SALT II arms control treaty, provided the Soviet Union continues to observe those limits. Adopted 225-186: R 19-154; D 206-32 [ND 155-6; SD 51-26], Aug. 12, 1986.

15. **HR 4428. Defense Authorization, Fiscal 1987.** Broomfield, R-Mich., amendment to prohibit the use of funds to deploy any weapons inconsistent with the SALT II arms control treaty at such time as the Soviet Union comes into full compliance with the treaty. Rejected 199-214: R 162-13; D 37-201 [ND 8-153; SD 29-48], Aug. 12, 1986. A "yea" was a vote supporting the president's position.

16. **HR 4428. Defense Authorization, Fiscal 1987.** Dellums, D-Calif., amendment to reduce from $3.4 billion to $1 billion the amount authorized for research on the strategic defense initiative, or "star wars." Rejected 114-302: R 1-173; D 113-129 [ND 104-59; SD 9-70], Aug. 12, 1986.

17. **HR 4428. Defense Authorization, Fiscal 1987.** Dornan, R-Calif., amendment to increase from $3.4 billion to $4.8 billion the amount authorized for research on the strategic defense initiative, or "star wars." Rejected 94-324: R 82-93; D 12-231 [ND 2-162; SD 10-69], Aug. 12, 1986.

18. **HR 4428. Defense Authorization, Fiscal 1987.** Gejdenson, D-Conn., amendment to add $1.5 billion to purchase a Trident missile-launching submarine. Rejected 188-211: R 22-146; D 166-65 [ND 122-35; SD 44-30], Aug. 11, 1986.

19. **HR 4428. Defense Authorization, Fiscal 1987.** Bennett, D-Fla., amendment to delete $1.1 billion for 12 MX missiles and add $250 million for various conventional weapons. Rejected 178-210: R 23-144; D 155-66 [ND 129-18; SD 26-48], Aug. 11, 1986.

20. **HR 3129. Omnibus Highway Bill.** McCurdy, D-Okla., amendment to establish a five-year test program permitting states to raise the speed limit from 55 mph to 65 mph on rural sections of the Interstate system. Rejected 198-218: R 117-57; D 81-161 [ND 45-120; SD 36-41], Aug. 6, 1986.

21. **HR 1562. Textile Import Quotas.** Passage, over President Reagan's Dec. 17, 1985, veto, of the bill to place import restrictions on textile and apparel goods. Rejected 276-149: R 71-106; D 205-43 [ND 132-36; SD 73-7], Aug. 6, 1986. A two-thirds majority of those present and voting (284 in this case) of both houses is required to override a veto. A "nay" was a vote supporting the president's position.

22. **HR 4428. Department of Defense Authorization, Fiscal 1987.** Traficant, D-Ohio, amendment to the Mavroules, D-Mass., amendment, to require the Pentagon to buy U.S.-built goods rather than competing foreign-built goods if the price of the U.S. items is not more than 5 percent higher than the foreign items. Adopted 241-163: R 74-100; D 167-63 [ND 115-39; SD 52-24], Aug. 5, 1986. (The Mavroules amendment later was adopted.)

23. **HR 5175. District of Columbia Appropriations, Fiscal 1987.** Dixon, D-Calif., motion that the Committee of the Whole rise and report the bill back to the House. Motion agreed to 241-173: R 23-152; D 218-21 [ND 156-7, SD 62-14], July 24, 1986. (The effect of the vote was to prevent consideration of amendments limiting spending on the appropriations bill, in this case the Dannemeyer, R-Calif., amendment to kill a District law barring insurers from refusing coverage to persons who test positive for acquired immune deficiency syndrome (AIDS). Such amendments are in order only following a defeated motion to rise and report.)

24. **HR 5052. Military Construction Appropriations, Fiscal 1987/Aid to Nicaraguan Rebels.** Hamilton, D-Ind., substitute for title II of the bill as amended by the Edwards, R-Okla., substitute, to provide $27 million for Nicaraguan refugees and $5 million to promote peace negotiations in Central America. Rejected 183-245: R 7-173; D 176-72 [ND 152-15, SD 24-57], June 25, 1986. A "nay" was a vote supporting the president's position.

25. **HR 5052. Military Construction Appropriations, Fiscal 1987/Aid to Nicaraguan Rebels.** Edwards, R-Okla., substitute for title II of the bill, to provide $70 million in military aid and $30 million in non-military aid to the "contra" guerrillas in Nicaragua and $300 million in economic aid to Costa Rica, El Salvador, Guatemala and Honduras. Adopted 221-209: R 170-11; D 51-198 [ND 8-159; SD 43-39], June 25, 1986. A "yea" was a vote supporting the president's position.

26. **H Con Res 350. Adherence to SALT II Agreements.** Broomfield, R-Mich., amendment to provide that the United States should abide by all provisions of the SALT II nuclear arms treaty as long as the Soviet Union does likewise. Rejected 187-222: R 152-15; D 35-207 [ND 7-158, SD 28-49], June 19, 1986. A "yea" was a vote supporting the president's position.

27. **H J Res 589. Saudi Arms Sale.** Passage of the joint resolution to prohibit the administration's proposed $354 million sale of missiles to Saudi Arabia. Passed 356-62: R 131-45; D 225-17 [ND 155-8; SD 70-9], May 7, 1986. A "nay" was a vote supporting the president's position.

28. **HR 4420. Military Retirement Reform.** Passage of the bill to reduce the annuities paid to military personnel who join the armed services after enactment of the bill and retire after less than 30 years of active service. Passed 399-7: R 173-1; D 226-6 [ND 155-4; SD 71-2], April 22, 1986. A "nay" was a vote supporting the president's position.

29. **H J Res 601. Aid to Nicaraguan Rebels.** Hamilton, D-Ind., substitute to provide $27 million in humanitarian aid to Nicaraguan refugees. Adopted 361-66: R 177-1; D 184-65 [ND 154-14; SD 30-51], April 16, 1986. (Republicans voted "yea" on this amendment as a procedural move to prevent consideration of a subsequent amendment by Dave McCurdy, D-Okla.)

30. **HR 4332. Firearms Law Reform.** Passage of the bill to revise the 1968 Gun Control Act to allow the interstate sales

of rifles and shotguns and the interstate transportation of all types of firearms, to ease record-keeping requirements for firearms transactions and to limit federal agents to one unannounced inspection per year of a gun dealer's premises. Passed 292-130: R 161-15; D 131-115 [ND 62-103, SD 69-12], April 10, 1986. (The House subsequently moved to strike the language of S 49, the Senate-passed version of the bill, and insert instead the language of HR 4332.) A "yea" was a vote supporting the president's position.

31. **HR 4332. Firearms Law Reform.** Hughes, D-N.J., amendment to the Volkmer, D-Mo., substitute for the Judiciary Committee substitute, to bar the interstate transportation of handguns. Rejected 177-242: R 40-136; D 137-106 [ND 115-48; SD 22-58], April 9, 1986.

32. **HR 4332. Firearms Law Reform.** Hughes, D-N.J., amendment to the Volkmer, D-Mo., substitute for the Judiciary Committee substitute, to continue the ban on interstate sales of handguns, bar interstate transportation of handguns, retain existing record-keeping requirements and ban silencers. Rejected 176-248: R 40-138; D 136-110 [ND 119-46; SD 17-64], April 9, 1986. (The Volkmer substitute subsequently was adopted, after which the Judiciary Committee substitute was adopted by voice vote.)

33. **H J Res 540. Aid to Nicaraguan Rebels.** Passage of the joint resolution to approve President Reagan's Feb. 25 request for $100 million in military and non-military aid to the "contra" guerrillas in Nicaragua, and to lift restrictions on CIA and Defense Department assistance to the contras. Rejected 210-222: R 164-16; D 46-206 [ND 7-163; SD 39-43], March 20, 1986. A "yea" was a vote supporting the president's position.

34. **HR 1524. Employee Polygraph Protection.** Passage of the bill to prohibit polygraph (lie detector) testing by private employers, with certain exceptions. Passed 236-173: R 39-132; D 197-41 [ND 156-5; SD 41-36], March 12, 1986. A "nay" was a vote supporting the president's position.

35. **HR 3838. Tax Overhaul.** Adoption of the rule (H Res 343) to provide for House floor consideration of the bill to revise the federal income tax system by: lowering individual and corporate tax rates; increasing the personal exemption and standard deduction; eliminating the investment tax credit; eliminating or curtailing a variety of other deductions and credits; creating a new alternative minimum tax for individuals and corporations; and making other changes. Adopted 258-168: R 70-110; D 188-58 [ND 138-28; SD 50-30], Dec. 17, 1985. A "yea" was a vote supporting the president's position.

36. **HR 3132. Armor-Piercing Ammunition.** Hughes, D-N.J., motion to suspend the rules and pass the bill to bar the manufacture or importation of armor-piercing ammunition. Motion agreed to 400-21: R 158-19; D 242-2 [ND 165-1; SD 77-1], Dec. 17, 1985. A two-thirds majority vote of those present and voting (281 in this case) is required for passage under suspension of the rules.

37. **HR 3838. Tax Overhaul.** Adoption of the rule (H Res 336) to provide for House floor consideration of the bill to restructure the income tax laws; reduce tax rates for individuals and corporations; increase the personal exemption and standard deduction; eliminate the investment tax credit; eliminate or curtail a variety of other deductions and credits; create a new alternative minimum tax for individuals and corporations; and make other changes. Rejected 202-223: R 14-164; D 188-59 [ND 135-33; SD 53-26], Dec. 11, 1985. A "yea" was a vote supporting the president's position.

38. **HR 2817. Superfund Reauthorization, Fiscal 1986-90.** Edgar, D-Pa., amendment to require companies to make public an inventory of their emissions of chemicals known to cause or suspected of causing cancer, birth defects or other chronic diseases. Adopted 212-211: R 34-143; D 178-68 [ND 146-22, SD 32-46], Dec. 10, 1985. (The Edgar amendment previously had been adopted in the Committee of the Whole.)

39. **HR 2817. Superfund Reauthorization, Fiscal 1986-90.** Frank, D-Mass., amendment to permit persons injured by the release of toxic substances to sue responsible parties in federal court, except for damages incurred and discovered before enactment. Rejected 162-261: R 20-157; D 142-104 [ND 117-50; SD 25-54], Dec. 10, 1985.

40. **HR 2817. Superfund Reauthorization, Fiscal 1986-90.** Downey, D-N.Y., amendment to strike provisions for a broad-based or "value-added" tax and to provide $10 billion over five years for the "superfund" hazardous-waste cleanup program through increased taxes on chemical feedstocks, petroleum and hazardous-waste disposal and through general revenues. Adopted 220-206: R 73-105; D 147-101 [ND 127-42; SD 20-59], Dec. 10, 1985.

41. **HR 1616. Plant Closing Notification.** Passage of the bill to require employers of at least 50 full-time employees to give workers 90 days' notice of any plant shutdown or layoff involving at least 100 employees or 30 percent of the work force. Rejected 203-208: R 20-154; D 183-54 [ND 153-5; SD 30-49], Nov. 21, 1985.

42. **HR 1616. Plant Closing Notification.** Bartlett, R-Texas, amendment to the Ford, D-Mich., substitute, to delete a provision requiring plant owners to consult with employees before closing a plant in an effort to find alternatives to the shutdown. Adopted 215-193: R 159-15; D 56-178 [ND 6-151; SD 50-27], Nov. 14, 1985.

43. **HR 3128. Deficit-Reduction Amendments.** Passage of the bill to reduce the deficit $19.5 billion over fiscal 1986-88 through spending reductions in the Medicare program; tax increases on tobacco products, imports, coal manufacturers and employers participating in a federal pension plan; and user fees for Customs inspections. The bill would also make changes in the Aid to Families with Dependent Children program and reauthorize the Trade Adjustment Assistance program and related trade agencies. Passed 245-174: R 24-150; D 221-24 [ND 151-15; SD 70-9], Oct. 31, 1985. A "nay" was a vote supporting the president's position.

44. **HR 3629. Department of Defense Appropriations, Fiscal 1986.** Frank, D-Mass., amendment to delete from the bill $1.7 billion for procurement of 12 MX missiles. Rejected 210-214: R 34-144; D 176-70 [ND 149-16; SD 27-54], Oct. 30, 1985. (The Frank amendment had been previously adopted in the Committee of the Whole.) A "nay" was a vote supporting the president's position.

45. **HR 3500. Omnibus Budget Reconciliation, Fiscal 1986.** Passage of the bill to make changes in law to reduce spending by $60.9 billion over fiscal years 1986-88, to conform with the fiscal 1986 budget resolution (S Con Res 32) that called for $276 billion in spending cuts and higher revenues over three years. Passed 228-199: R 15-166; D 213-33 [ND 141-24, SD 72-9], Oct. 24, 1985. A "nay" was a vote supporting the president's position.

46. **HR 1562. Textile Import Quotas.** Passage of the bill to impose new quota restrictions on textile imports. Passed 262-159: R 75-97; D 187-62 [ND 118-49; SD 69-13], Oct. 10, 1985. A "nay" was a vote supporting the president's position.

47. **HR 7. School Lunch and Child Nutrition Act.** Armey, R-Texas, substitute for the Bartlett, R-Texas, amendment, to eliminate the cash and commodity subsidy for lunches for children from families with incomes above 250 percent of the poverty line. Rejected 146-279: R 133-48; D 13-231 [ND 1-165, SD 12-66], Sept. 18, 1985. (The Bartlett amendment was subsequently rejected by voice vote.)

48. **HR 8. Clean Water Act Amendments.** Stangeland, R-Minn., amendment to authorize the Environmental Protection Agency, in a five-year demonstration project, to allow up to 40 localities to operate their own programs for "pre-treatment" of industrial wastes, provided the programs achieve results at least as good as those required under national pre-treatment standards. Rejected 167-257: R 143-38; D 24-219 [ND 8-158; SD 16-61], July 23, 1985.

49. **HR 99. American Conservation Corps.** Passage of the bill to authorize such sums as Congress considers necessary in fiscal 1986-88 to establish an American Conservation Corps to put unemployed youths to work on conservation projects. Passed 193-191: R 18-148; D 175-43 [ND 137-13; SD 38-30], July 11, 1985. A "nay" was a vote supporting the president's position.

50. **HR 1555. Foreign Assistance Authorization, Fiscal 1986.** Stratton, D-N.Y., amendment to repeal the so-called "Clark amendment" to the International Security and Development Cooperation Act of 1980, prohibiting assistance for military or paramilitary operations in Angola. Adopted 236-185: R 176-6; D 60-179 [ND 14-150; SD 46-29], July 10, 1985. A "yea" was a vote supporting the president's position.

51. **HR 1872. Department of Defense Authorization, Fiscal 1986.** Burton, R-Ind., amendment to the Foley, D-Wash., amendment, to permit the introduction of U.S. combat troops into Nicaragua if the president determined that Nicaragua was

supporting, directly or indirectly, military or terrorist operations in El Salvador, Honduras or Costa Rica. Rejected 186-235: R 151-28; D 35-207 [ND 5-160, SD 30-47], June 27, 1985.

52. **HR 1872. Department of Defense Authorization, Fiscal 1986.** Dickinson, R-Ala., amendment to direct the Pentagon to use random polygraph examinations to screen Pentagon and contractor employees with access to classified information. Adopted 333-71: R 172-2; D 161-69 [ND 96-60; SD 65-9], June 26, 1985.

53. **HR 1872. Department of Defense Authorization, Fiscal 1986.** Brown, D-Calif., amendment to bar any test of the anti-satellite (ASAT) missile against a target in space during fiscal 1986 unless the president certifies to Congress that the Soviet Union has tested an ASAT. The amendment also increases by $20 million the fiscal 1986 authorization to carry out the satellite survivability project of the Air Force Space Survivability Program. Adopted 229-193: R 31-148; D 198-45 [ND 157-8; SD 41-37], June 26, 1985. A "nay" was a vote supporting the president's position.

54. **HR 1872. Department of Defense Authorization, Fiscal 1986.** Hertel, D-Mich., amendment to empower the inspector general of the Defense Department to suspend payments to a contractor or debar a contractor if he finds waste, fraud and abuse in connection with the contract. Rejected 176-240: R 24-153; D 152-87 [ND 134-27; SD 18-60], June 25, 1985.

55. **HR 1872. Department of Defense Authorization, Fiscal 1986.** Bennett, D-Fla., substitute for the Spratt, D-S.C., amendment, to bar Pentagon officials who had "significant responsibility" for procurement with a specific defense contractor from accepting employment for two years after leaving the Defense Department from that contractor. Adopted 397-19: R 161-15; D 236-4 [ND 163-1; SD 73-3], June 25, 1985. A "nay was a vote supporting the president's position. (The effect of the amendment was to eliminate the provision in the Spratt amendment that would permit the secretary of defense to waive certain positions from the prohibition. The Spratt amendment, as modified by the Bennett substitute, was subsequently adopted by voice vote.)

56. **HR 1872. Department of Defense Authorization, Fiscal 1986.** Courter, R-N.J., amendment to the Holt, R-Md., substitute for the Price, D-Ill., amendment, to increase from $2.5 billion to $3.7 billion the authorization for the strategic defense initiative. Rejected 104-315: R 97-83; D 7-232 [ND 0-161; SD 7-71], June 20, 1985. A "yea" was a vote supporting the president's position. (The Holt substitute subsequently was rejected.)

57. **HR 1872. Department of Defense Authorization, Fiscal 1986.** Dellums, D-Calif., amendment to the Price, D-Ill., amendment to reduce from $2.5 billion to $954 million the authorization for the strategic defense initiative. Rejected 102-320: R 3-176; D 99-144 [ND 92-71; SD 7-73], June 20, 1985. A "nay" was a vote supporting the president's position.

58. **HR 1872. Department of Defense Authorization, Fiscal 1986.** Skelton, D-Mo., amendment to the Porter, R-Ill., amendment, to authorize the appropriation of $124 million to produce binary chemical weapons subject to certain conditions. Adopted 229-196: R 143-34; D 86-162 [ND 30-138; SD 56-24], June 19, 1985. A "yea" was a vote supporting the president's position.

59. **HR 2577. Supplemental Appropriations, Fiscal 1985.** Boland, D-Mass., amendment to the McDade, R-Pa., amendment, to continue indefinitely the prohibition of any funding by U.S. intelligence agencies that would support, directly or indirectly, military or paramilitary operations in Nicaragua. Rejected 196-232: R 7-174; D 189-58 [ND 156-11; SD 33-47], June 12, 1985. A "nay" was a vote supporting the president's position.

60. **HR 1460. Anti-Apartheid Act.** Passage of the bill to impose sanctions immediately against South Africa, including a ban on bank loans to the South African government, and prohibitions against the sale of computer goods and nuclear power equipment and supplies to that country. Subject to review by the president and Congress, the bill also would bar new U.S. business investment in South Africa and prohibit the importation into the United States of South African gold coins, called Krugerrands. Passed 295-127: R 56-121; D 239-6 [ND 166-0; SD 73-6], June 5, 1985. A "nay" was a vote supporting the president's position.

61. **H Con Res 152. First Budget Resolution, Fiscal 1986.** Leath, D-Texas, amendment to reduce the deficit by $75 billion in fiscal 1986, and by $350 billion over fiscal 1986-88, by eliminating increases in cost-of-living adjustments for recipients of Social Security and other federal retirement programs and by raising $12 billion in new taxes, in combination with spending cuts outlined in the concurrent resolution. Rejected 56-372: R 15-165; D 41-207 [ND 18-150; SD 23-57], May 23, 1985.

62. **HR 1460. Anti-Apartheid Act.** Zschau, R-Calif., amendment to let U.S. firms continue investing in South Africa if their South African units comply with a code of worker rights. Rejected 148-256: R 145-29; D 3-227 [ND 1-156; SD 2-71], May 21, 1985.

63. **S J Res 71. MX Missile Authorization.** Passage of the joint resolution to approve authorization of $1.5 billion to procure 21 MX missiles in fiscal 1985. Passed 219-213: R 158-24; D 61-189 [ND 15-154; SD 46-35], March 26, 1985. A "yea" was a vote supporting the president's position.

64. **HR 1035. Emergency Farm Credit.** Passage of the bill to authorize advance Commodity Credit Corporation crop loans to farmers, to authorize $3 billion in Farmers Home Administration (FmHA) loan guarantees for restructured private loans to farmers, to revise rules for the FmHA loan guarantees and to authorize low-interest federal disaster loans to farmers in certain circumstances. Passed 318-103: R 84-93; D 234-10 [ND 158-6; SD 76-4], Feb. 27, 1985. A "nay" was a vote supporting the president's position.

65. **HR 607. Cost-Savings Disclosure Awards.** Schroeder, D-Colo., motion to suspend the rules and pass the bill to authorize the president and agency inspectors general to grant cash awards to employees who disclose waste, fraud and abuse. Motion agreed to 413-1: R 174-1; D 239-0 [ND 161-0; SD 78-0], Feb. 26, 1985. A two-thirds majority of those present and voting (276 in this case) is required for passage under suspension of the rules.

66. **HR 1096. African Relief.** Wolpe, D-Mich., motion to suspend the rules and pass the bill to authorize $175 million in fiscal year 1985 for disaster and refugee aid for African countries affected by drought and famine. Motion agreed to 391-25: R 151-24; D 240-1 [ND 163-0; SD 77-1], Feb. 26, 1985. A two-thirds majority of those present and voting (278 in this case) is required for passage under suspension of the rules.

67. **HR 4230. Export Administration Act.** Fascell, D-Fla., motion to concur in the Senate amendment with an amendment to ban U.S. commercial bank loans to the government of South Africa. Motion agreed to 269-62: R 96-50; D 173-12 [ND 121-2; SD 52-10], Oct. 11, 1984.

68. **HR 6023. Generalized System of Preferences Renewal Act.** Gephardt, D-Mo., amendment to remove Taiwan, Hong Kong and South Korea from the list of countries eligible for duty-free treatment under the generalized system of preferences. Rejected 174-233: R 14-142; D 160-91 [ND 128-38; SD 32-53], Oct. 3, 1984. A "nay" was a vote supporting the president's position. (The bill subsequently was passed by voice vote.)

69. **HR 6301. Steel Import Stabilization.** Passage of the bill to request that the president negotiate a voluntary agreement with steel-producing nations to limit shipments to the United States to 17 percent of the U.S. market. The agreement would be contingent on domestic steel producers' willingness to modernize plants and aid unemployed or laid-off workers. The bill also would extend for two years the Trade Adjustment Assistance Program, which provides government help to workers whose jobs are eliminated because of foreign competition. Passed 285-134: R 63-98; D 222-36 [ND 156-16; SD 66-20], Oct. 3, 1984.

70. **HR 6299. Social Security Cost-of-Living Adjustment.** Rostenkowski, D-Ill., motion to suspend the rules and pass the bill to provide a cost-of-living adjustment equal to the rate of inflation in January 1985 to Social Security, disability and Supplemental Security income beneficiaries and instructing the Social Security Administration to conduct a study of the cost-of-living adjustment. Motion agreed to 417-4: R 162-2; D 255-2 [ND 170-2; SD 85-0], Oct. 2, 1984. A two-thirds majority of those present and voting (281 in this case) is required for passage under suspension of the rules. A "yea" was a vote supporting the president's position.

71. **HR 5640. Superfund Expansion.** Sawyer, R-Mich., amendment to delete from the bill a section giving citizens the right to sue in federal court for damages caused by hazardous

waste dumping. Adopted 208-200: R 135-22; D 73-178 [ND 23-146; SD 50-32], Aug. 9, 1984.

72. **HR 5399. Intelligence Agencies, Authorizations.** Passage of the bill to make authorizations in fiscal 1985 for the CIA and other intelligence agencies and to prohibit any form of U.S. aid to military or paramilitary groups in Nicaragua. Passed 294-118: R 65-96; D 229-22 [ND 164-3; SD 65-19], Aug. 2, 1984.

73. **HR 11. Education Amendments/School Prayer.** Walker, R-Pa., amendment to the Coats, R-Ind., amendment, to cut off federal education assistance to states and school districts with policies that prohibit silent or vocal prayer in public schools. Rejected 194-215: R 121-33; D 73-182 [ND 18-153; SD 55-29], July 26, 1984.

74. **HR 4170. Deficit Reduction.** Adoption of the conference report on the bill to raise $50 billion in new taxes and to cut Medicare and other spending by about $13 billion through fiscal year 1987. Adopted 268-155: R 76-86; D 192-69 [ND 126-46; SD 66-23], June 27, 1984. A "yea" was a vote supporting the president's position.

75. **HR 1510. Immigration Reform and Control Act.** Wright, D-Texas, amendment to authorize the attorney general to grant temporary resident status to aliens who could show they had arrived in the United States prior to Jan. 1, 1982. Such aliens could seek permanent resident status after two years, providing they could demonstrate an understanding of English and of U.S. history and government, or were enrolled in a course of study to learn these subjects. Adopted 247-170: R 119-39; D 128-131 [ND 67-102; SD 61-29], June 19, 1984.

76. **HR 1510. Immigration Reform and Control Act.** Lungren, R-Calif., amendment to authorize the attorney general to grant temporary resident status to aliens who could show they arrived in the United States prior to Jan. 1, 1980, and permanent resident status to aliens who could show they had arrived in the United States prior to Jan. 1, 1977. Rejected 181-245: R 133-29; D 48-216 [ND 12-163; SD 36-53], June 19, 1984. A "yea" was a vote supporting the president's position.

77. **HR 1510. Immigration Reform and Control Act.** Education and Labor Committee amendment (offered by Hawkins, D-Calif.) to restructure provisions penalizing employers who knowingly hire illegal aliens, deleting the criminal sanctions and increasing the fines. The amendment also included a new procedure for handling cases of alleged employment discrimination. Rejected 166-253: R 9-152; D 157-101 [ND 132-38; SD 25-63], June 12, 1984. A "nay" was a vote supporting the president's position.

78. **HR 5167. Department of Defense Authorization.** Dellums, D-Calif., amendment to prohibit, during fiscal 1985, further deployment in Europe of Pershing II or ground-launched cruise missiles unless the North Atlantic Treaty Organization (NATO) notified the United States that there was a NATO consensus that further deployments should be made. Rejected 104-291:

R 2-154; D 102-137 [ND 98-66; SD 4-71], May 31, 1984. A "nay" was a vote supporting the president's position.

79. **HR 5167.** **Department of Defense Authorization.** Dellums, D-Calif., amendment to delete $7.1 billion for procurement of 34 B-1 bombers. Rejected 163-254: R 19-142; D 144-112 [ND 130-40; SD 14-72], May 23, 1984. A "nay" was a vote supporting the president's position.

80. **HR 5167.** **Department of Defense Authorization.** Lowry, D-Wash., amendment to bar the purchase of additional Pershing II missiles until April 1, 1985, allowing such purchases after that date only if the president certified to Congress that the Soviet Union showed no willingness to limit such weapons and if the Congress thereafter approved resumption of Pershing II purchases by joint resolution. Rejected 122-294: R 7-156; D 115-138 [ND 110-57; SD 5-81], May 23, 1984. A "nay" was a vote supporting the president's position.

81. **HR 5167.** **Department of Defense Authorization.** Smith, D-Fla., amendment to bar the use of funds to purchase Sergeant York anti-aircraft guns (also called DIVADs) until certain test results have been reported to Congress. Rejected 157-229: R 32-123; D 125-106 [ND 112-40; SD 13-66], May 17, 1984. A "nay" was a vote supporting the president's position.

82. **HR 5167.** **Department of Defense Authorization.** Weiss, D-N.Y., amendment to delete funds for production of the Trident II missile. Rejected 93-319: R 3-159; D 90-160 [ND 86-82; SD 4-78], May 17, 1984. A "nay" was a vote supporting the president's position.

83. **HR 5167.** **Department of Defense Authorization.** Dickinson, R-Ala., amendment to the Mavroules, D-Mass., substitute to the Bennett, D-Fla., amendment, to allow the production of 15 MX missiles subject to certain conditions. Adopted 229-199: R 146-17; D 83-182 [ND 22-154; SD 61-28], May 16, 1984. (The Mavroules substitute, as amended, subsequently was adopted by voice vote.) A "yea" was a vote supporting the president's position.

84. **HR 5167.** **Department of Defense Authorization.** Mavroules, D-Mass., amendment to the Bennett, D-Fla., amendment, to bar procurement of MX missiles in fiscal 1985. Rejected 212-218: R 18-146; D 194-72 [ND 161-16; SD 33-56], May 16, 1984. A "nay" was a vote supporting the president's position.

85. **HR 5345.** **Equal Access Act.** Perkins, D-Ky., motion to suspend the rules and pass the bill to allow student religious groups to meet in public secondary schools during non-class hours if other groups do so. Motion rejected 270-151: R 147-17; D 123-134 [ND 47-122; SD 76-12], May 15, 1984. A two-thirds majority of those present and voting (281 in this case) is required for passage under suspension of the rules. A "yea" was a vote supporting the president's position.

86. **HR 5119. Foreign Assistance Authorization.** Broomfield, R-Mich., amendment to authorize President Reagan's requests for military, economic and development aid for Central American countries in fiscal 1984-1985, and to allow military aid for El Salvador in fiscal 1985 if the president certified to Congress that the government had made "demonstrated progress" on human rights and other issues. Adopted 212-208: R 156-8; D 56-200 [ND 7-167; SD 49-33], May 10, 1984. A "yea" was a vote supporting the president's position.

87. **H Con Res 290. Mining of Nicaraguan Waters.** Adoption of the concurrent resolution stating the sense of Congress that no appropriated funds should be used for planning, directing, executing or supporting the mining of ports or territorial waters of Nicaragua. Adopted 281-111: R 57-96; D 224-15 [ND 158-3; SD 66-12), April 12, 1984.

88. **HR 5394. Omnibus Budget Reconciliation Act.** Moore, R-La., motion to recommit the bill to the House Ways and Means Committee with instructions to include provisions imposing a one-year physician fee freeze for Medicare services and to strike provisions in the measure that increased spending. Motion rejected 172-242: R 157-2; D 15-240 [ND 3-170; SD 12-70], April 12, 1984.

89. **HR 4170. Deficit Reduction.** Passage of the bill to raise $49.2 billion in new taxes through fiscal 1987 by closing a wide range of tax loopholes; increasing taxes on distilled liquor, cigarettes and telephones; revamping taxation of the life insurance industry; and making other changes. Passed 318-97: R 95-66; D 223-31 [ND 155-14; SD 68-17], April 11, 1984. A "yea" was a vote supporting the president's position.

90. **HR 3020. Small Business Authorization.** Bliley, R-Va., amendment to eliminate Small Business Administration direct loans, except loans to the handicapped and to minority businesses. Rejected 72-331: R 70-89; D 2-242 [ND 0-161; SD 2-81], March 14, 1984. A "yea" was a vote supporting the president's position.

91. **HR 3648. Amtrak Improvement Act.** Broyhill, R-N.C., amendment to permit the Department of Transportation to sell Conrail unless Congress passes a law disapproving the sale. The bill would require Congress to approve any sale for it to take effect. Rejected 147-254: R 129-26; D 18-228 [ND 3-158; SD 15-70], March 6, 1984. A "yea" was a vote supporting the president's position.

92. **H J Res 1. Equal Rights Amendment.** Rodino, D-N.J., motion to suspend the rules and pass the joint resolution to propose an amendment to the Constitution declaring, "Equality of rights under the law shall not be denied or abridged by the United States or by any state on account of sex." Motion rejected 278-147: R 53-109; D 225-38 [ND 164-13; SD 61-25], Nov. 15, 1983. A two-thirds majority of those present and voting (284 in this case) is required for passage under suspension of the rules. A "nay" was a vote supporting the president's position.

93. **H J Res 364. Multinational Force in Lebanon.** Passage of the joint resolution to provide statutory authorization under the War Powers Resolution for continued U.S. participation in the multinational peacekeeping force in Lebanon for up to 18 months after the enactment of the resolution. Passed 270-161: R 140-27; D 130-134 [ND 70-105; SD 60-29], Sept. 28, 1983. A "yea" was a vote supporting the president's position.

94. **HR 1010. Coal Pipeline Act.** Passage of the bill to grant federal power of eminent domain to certified coal slurry pipeline companies. Rejected 182-235: R 85-75; D 97-160 [ND 52-120; SD 45-40], Sept. 27, 1983.

95. **HR 3133. Department of Housing and Urban Development Appropriations, Fiscal 1984.** Dannemeyer, R-Calif., amendment to prohibit the Environmental Protection Agency from using any funds provided by the bill to impose sanctions during fiscal 1984 on any area for failing to attain any national ambient air quality standard established under the Clean Air Act. Adopted 227-136: R 89-50; D 138-86 [ND 88-58; SD 50-28], June 2, 1983.

96. **HR 1900. Social Security Act Amendments.** Pickle, D-Texas, amendment to gradually raise the normal Social Security retirement age from 65 to 67 after the year 2000, and to delete provisions of the Ways and Means Committee bill that would reduce initial benefit levels beginning in the year 2000 and raise payroll taxes beginning in the year 2015. Adopted 228-202: R 152-14; D 76-188 [ND 23-152; SD 53-36], March 9, 1983. A "yea" was a vote supporting the president's position.

97. **HR 5133. Automobile Domestic Content Requirements.** Passage of the bill to require automakers to use set percentages of U.S. labor and parts in automobiles they sell in the United States. Passed 215-188: R 44-130; D 171-58 [ND 132-20; SD 39-38], Dec. 15, 1982. A "nay" was a vote supporting the president's position.

98. **H J Res 631. Continuing Appropriations, Fiscal 1983/Jobs.** Conte, R-Mass., motion to recommit the joint resolution to the Appropriations Committee with instructions to delete jobs program funding (Title II) and add $44 million in funding for Radio Liberty. Motion rejected 191-215: R 171-7; D 20-208 [ND 2-150; SD 18-58], Dec. 14, 1982. A "yea" was a vote supporting the president's position.

99. **HR 6211. Transportation Assistance Act of 1982.** Adoption of the rule (H Res 620) providing for House floor consideration of the bill to authorize funds for highway and mass transit programs for fiscal 1983-1986 and to increase gasoline and other highway taxes. Adopted 197-194: R 59-114; D 138-80 [ND 112-34; SD 26-46], Dec. 6, 1982.

100. **H Con Res 345. First Budget Resolution, Fiscal 1983.** Oakar, D-Ohio, amendment, to the Latta, R-Ohio, substitute, to increase budget authority by $400 million and outlays by $4.85 billion for health programs in fiscal 1983 to accommodate Medicare funding at current services levels, and to make

corresponding reductions in defense programs. Adopted 228-196: R 64-125; D 164-71 [ND 136-20; SD 28-51], May 27, 1982.

101. **HR 5922. Urgent Supplemental Appropriations, Fiscal 1982.** Boland, D-Mass., amendment to provide $1 billion to the Department of Housing and Urban Development for mortgage interest subsidy payments to home buyers with family income not exceeding 130 percent of the median income for their area. Adopted 343-67: R 128-52; D 215-15 [ND 149-6; SD 66-9], May 12, 1982.

102. **HR 4242. Tax Cuts.** Conable, R-N.Y., substitute amendment to the bill to reduce individual income tax rates by 25 percent across-the-board over three years, to index tax rates beginning in 1985 and to provide business and investment tax incentives. Adopted 238-195: R 190-1; D 48-194 [ND 12-151; SD 36-43], July 29, 1981. A "yea" was a vote supporting the president's position.

103. **H Con Res 115. Fiscal 1982 Budget Targets.** Latta, R-Ohio, substitute, to the resolution as reported by the Budget Committee, to decrease budget authority by $23.1 billion, outlays by $25.7 billion and revenues by $31.1 billion, resulting in a $31 billion deficit for fiscal 1982. Adopted 253-176: R 190-0; D 63-176 (ND 17-144; SD 46-32), May 7, 1981. A "yea" was a vote supporting the president's position.

104. **HR 4995. Defense Department Appropriations, Fiscal 1982.** Addabbo, D-N.Y., amendment to delete $1.801 billion from Air Force procurement intended for the B-1 bomber. Rejected 142-263: R 21-157; D 121-106 [ND 111-42; SD 10-64], Nov. 18, 1981. A "nay" was a vote supporting the president's position.

105. **H Con Res 194. Disapproving AWACS Sale.** Adoption of the concurrent resolution disapproving the sale to Saudi Arabia of Airborne Warning and Control System (AWACS) radar planes, conformal fuel tanks for F-15 aircraft, AIM-9L Sidewinder missiles and KC-707 aerial refueling aircraft. Adopted 301-111: R 108-78; D 193-33 [ND 149-5; SD 44-28], Oct. 14, 1981. A "nay" was a vote supporting the president's position.

106. **HR 7428. Oil Import Fee/Debt Limit.** Passage, over the president's June 5 veto, of the bill to extend through June 30, 1980, the existing debt limit of $879 billion and to disapprove the $4.62 fee per barrel of imported oil that President Carter imposed effective March 15. Passed 335-34: R 142-0; D 193-34 [ND 130-26; SD 63-8], June 5, 1980. A two-thirds majority vote (246 in this case) is required for passage over a veto. A "nay" was a vote supporting the president's position.

107. **HR 7235. Rail Deregulation.** Eckhardt, D-Texas, substitute amendment, to the Staggers, D-W.Va., amendment, to expedite procedures for Interstate Commerce Commission resolution of joint rate division disputes, delete language providing for joint rate surcharge procedures and provide

assistance to the Rock Island and Milwaukee Railroads. Rejected 83-296: R 17-125; D 66-171 [ND 30-132; SD 36-39], Sept. 9, 1980. A "nay" was a vote supporting the president's position.

108. **H Con Res 367. India Nuclear Fuel.** Adoption of the resolution disapproving the shipment to India by the United States of enriched nuclear fuel. Adopted 298-98: R 118-30; D 180-68 [ND 135-34; SD 45-34], Sept. 18, 1980. A "nay" was a vote supporting the president's position.

109. **H J Res 521. Draft Registration Funding.** Appropriations Committee amendment to transfer $13.3 million from the Air Force to the Selective Service System, an independent agency, to start draft registration of 19-and 20-year-old males in 1980. Adopted 218-188: R 83-66; D 135-122 [ND 66-113; SD 69-9], April 22, 1980. A "yea" was a vote supporting the president's position.

110. **HR 5860. Chrysler Loan Guarantees.** Passage of the bill, as amended to authorize $1.5 billion in federal loan guarantees, for the Chrysler Corp. to be matched by $1.93 billion from other sources, including $400 million in wage concessions by the company's unionized workers and $100 million by other employees. Passed 271-136: R 62-88; D 209-48 [ND 154-21; SD 55-27], Dec. 18, 1979. A "yea" was a vote supporting the president's position.

111. **H J Res 74. School Busing Amendment.** Passage of the joint resolution to propose an amendment to the Constitution to prohibit compelling students to attend a school other than the one nearest their home to achieve racial desegregation. Rejected 209-216: R 114-40; D 95-176 [ND 48-138; SD 47-38], July 24, 1979. A two-thirds majority vote (284 in this case) is required for passage of a joint resolution proposing an amendment to the Constitution. A "nay" was a vote supporting the president's position.

112. **HR 2608. Nuclear Regulatory Commission.** Markey, D-Mass., amendment to put a moratorium on NRC issuance of new nuclear plant construction permits through April 1, 1980 (the first six months of fiscal 1980). Rejected 135-254: R 23-121; D 112-133 [ND 105-60; SD 7-73], Nov. 29, 1979.

113. **HR 3000. Energy Department Authorization -- Civilian Programs.** Moffett, D-Conn., amendment to prohibit use of funds appropriated by the bill for expenditures related to lifting price controls on certain types of domestic crude oil. Rejected 135-257: R 7-137; D 128-120 [ND 119-53; SD 9-67], Oct. 11, 1979. A "nay" was a vote supporting the president's position.

114. **HR 12050. Tuition Tax Credits.** Gradison, R-Ohio, motion to recommit the conference report on the bill to provide income tax credits for college and vocational school tuitions to the conference committee, with instructions that House conferees insist on a provision making tuitions paid to private elementary and secondary schools eligible for a credit. Motion agreed to 207-185: R 100-33; D 107-152 [ND

91-86; SD 16-66], Oct. 12, 1978. A "nay" was a vote supporting the president's position.

115. **HR 6805. Consumer Protection Agency.** Passage of the bill to establish an independent Office of Consumer Representation within the Executive Branch to represent the interests of consumers before federal agencies and courts. Rejected 189-227: R 17-126; D 172-101 [ND 147-40; SD 25-61], Feb. 8, 1978. A "yea" was a vote supporting the president's position.

116. **HR 9375. Fiscal 1978 Supplemental Appropriations.** Mahon, D-Texas, motion that the House recede and concur in the Senate amendment, to the bill, rescinding $462 million appropriated in fiscal 1977 for the Defense Department for production of three B-1 bombers. Motion agreed to 234-182: R 30-106; D 204-76 [ND 155-38; SD 49-38], Feb. 22, 1978. A "yea" was a vote supporting the president's position.

117. **HR 3744. Minimum Wage.** Cornell, D-Wis., amendment to permit employers to pay only 85 percent of the minimum wage to young workers under age 18 during their first six months on a job. Rejected 210-211: R 130-12; D 80-199 [ND 33-156; SD 47-43], Sept. 15, 1977. A "nay" was a vote supporting the president's position.

118. **HR 8444. National Energy Policy.** Steiger, R-Wis., motion to recommit the bill to the ad hoc committee on energy with instructions to report it with an amendment deleting the proposed crude oil equalization tax. Motion to recommit rejected 203-219: R 137-3; D 66-216 [ND 16-178; SD 50-38], Aug. 5, 1977. A "nay" was a vote supporting the president's position.

119. **HR 8444. National Energy Policy.** Brown, R-Ohio, amendment to end federal controls on the price of new onshore natural gas retroactive to April 20, 1977, and on new offshore natural gas beginning April 20, 1982, and to extend the Emergency Natural Gas Act of 1977 for three years. Rejected 199-227: R 127-17; D 72-210 [ND 25-169; SD 47-41], Aug. 3, 1977. A "nay" was a vote supporting the president's position.

HOUSE

VOTING RECORDS

ALABAMA

CALLAHAN, H. L. (Sonny) -- Alabama 1st District [Republican]. Counties of Baldwin, Clarke, Escambia, Mobile, Monroe, Washington and Wilcox. Prior Terms: 1985-86. Military Service: U.S. Navy, 1952-54. Occupation: Businessman; Alabama legislator (1970-78); Alabama senator.

1. Immigration Reform N
2. Open fld-search warrants Y
3. Civil pnty-hire ill alien Y
4. So Afr sanc-veto override N
5. Tax Overhaul Y
6. South Africa sanctions N
7. Death penalty-drug bill Y
8. Evidence-warrantless srch Y
9. Life term-second drug off Y
10. Military use in drug war Y
11. Troop reduction in Europe N
12. Prohibit chemical weapons N
13. Bar ASAT testing N
14. Abide SALT II weapons ban N
15. Follow SALT II-Soviets do Y
16. Reduce SDI funding N
17. Increase SDI funding Y
18. Purchase Trident sub N
19. Delete 12 MX;Add conv wpn N
20. Raise speed limit N
21. Textile Import Quotas(*) Y
22. Req Pentagon buy US goods Y
23. AIDS ins anti-dscriminatn N
24. Nicaraguan refugee aid N
25. Nicaraguan contra aid Y
26. US abide by SALT II Y
27. Prohibit Saudi arms sale Y
28. Military Retiremnt Reform Y
29. Nicaraguan refugee aid Y
30. Ease '68 Gun Control Act Y
31. Bar intrstat handgun tran N
32. Keep '68 Gun Control Act N
33. Nicaraguan contra aid Y
34. Bar emp polygraph testing N
35. Tax Overhaul consideratn Y
36. Bar armor-piercing ammo Y
37. Tax Overhaul consideratn N
38. Make comp emissions known N
39. Allow toxic victims suits N
40. Strike Superfund "VAT" N
41. Notify emp-plant closing N
42. Bar emp consult-plant clo Y
43. Medicare cuts;Tax incres' N
44. Delete 12 MX missiles N
45. Spending cuts;Tax incres' N
46. Textile Import Quotas Y
47. Cut some school lunch fds Y
48. Clean Water Act Amendmnts Y
49. Youth work projects N
50. Assist military in Angola Y
51. Allow US troops-Nicaragua Y
52. Pentagon polygraph exams Y
53. Bar ASAT testing N
54. Suspend def pmt for abuse N
55. Bar Pentagon-contr emplmt Y
56. Increase SDI funding Y
57. Reduce SDI funding N
58. Produce chemical weapons Y
59. Bar CIA fndg in Nicaragua N
60. South Africa sanctions N
61. Cut SS COLAs; Raise taxes N
62. Let US invest-So Africa Y
63. Approve 21 MX for 1985 Y
64. Emergency Farm Credit N
65. Awards to whistle blowers Y
66. African disaster relief Y

Presidential Support Score: 1986 - 74% 1985 - 74%

DICKINSON, WILLIAM L. -- Alabama 2nd District [Republican]. Counties of Barbour, Bullock, Butler, Coffee, Conecuh, Covington, Crenshaw, Dale, Geneva, Henry, Houston, Montgomery and Pike. Prior Terms: House: 1965-86. Born: June 5, 1925; Opelika, Ala. Education: University of Alabama Law School. Military Service: U.S. Navy, WW II. Occupation: Judge.

1. Immigration Reform N
2. Open fld-search warrants N
3. Civil pnty-hire ill alien N
4. So Afr sanc-veto override N
5. Tax Overhaul Y
6. South Africa sanctions N
7. Death penalty-drug bill Y
8. Evidence-warrantless srch Y
9. Life term-second drug off Y
10. Military use in drug war N
11. Troop reduction in Europe N
12. Prohibit chemical weapons N
13. Bar ASAT testing N
14. Abide SALT II weapons ban N
15. Follow SALT II-Soviets do Y
16. Reduce SDI funding N
17. Increase SDI funding Y
18. Purchase Trident sub N

DICKINSON, WILLIAM L. (Cont.)

19. Delete 12 MX;Add conv wpn N
20. Raise speed limit Y
21. Textile Import Quotas(*) Y
22. Req Pentagon buy US goods N
23. AIDS ins anti-dscriminatn N
24. Nicaraguan refugee aid N
25. Nicaraguan contra aid Y
26. US abide by SALT II Y
27. Prohibit Saudi arms sale N
28. Military Retiremnt Reform Y
29. Nicaraguan refugee aid Y
30. Ease '68 Gun Control Act Y
31. Bar intrstat handgun tran N
32. Keep '68 Gun Control Act N
33. Nicaraguan contra aid Y
34. Bar emp polygraph testing Y
35. Tax Overhaul consideratn N
36. Bar armor-piercing ammo Y
37. Tax Overhaul consideratn N
38. Make comp emissions known N
39. Allow toxic victims suits N
40. Strike Superfund "VAT" N
41. Notify emp-plant closing N
42. Bar emp consult-plant clo Y
43. Medicare cuts;Tax incres' N
44. Delete 12 MX missiles N
45. Spending cuts;Tax incres' N
46. Textile Import Quotas Y
47. Cut some school lunch fds Y
48. Clean Water Act Amendmnts Y
49. Youth work projects N
50. Assist military in Angola Y
51. Allow US troops-Nicaragua Y
52. Pentagon polygraph exams Y
53. Bar ASAT testing N
54. Suspend def pmt for abuse N
55. Bar Pentagon-contr emplmt N
56. Increase SDI funding N
57. Reduce SDI funding N
58. Produce chemical weapons Y
59. Bar CIA fndg in Nicaragua N
60. South Africa sanctions N
61. Cut SS COLAs; Raise taxes Y
62. Let US invest-So Africa Y
63. Approve 21 MX for 1985 Y
64. Emergency Farm Credit Y
65. Awards to whistle blowers Y
66. African disaster relief Y
67. Ban bank loans to So Afr ?
68. Bar coun duty-free trtmt N
69. Steel import limits N
70. Soc Sec COLAs=inflation Y
71. Bar haz waste vctms suits Y
72. Prohibit aid to Nicaragua ?
73. Cut $-Schs bar sch prayer Y
74. Raise taxes; Cut Medicare N
75. Alien residncy-prior 1982 Y
76. Alien residncy-prior 1980 Y
77. Pen emp-hire illgl aliens X
78. Lmt Persh II/cruse-Europe N
79. Delete 34 B-1 bombers N
80. Bar purch of Pershing II N
81. Bar purchase of Sgt York N
82. Delete $ for Trident II N
83. Allow 15 MX missiles Y
84. Bar MX procurement-1985 N
85. Equal Access Act Y
86. Aid to El Salvador Y
87. Bar Nicarag water mining X
88. Physician/Medicare freeze #
89. Increase "sin" taxes N
90. End SBA direct loans Y
91. Sell Conrail N
92. Equal Rights Amendment N
93. Marines in Lebanon Y
94. Eminent domain-Coal comps N
95. Prohibit EPA sanctions ?
96. SS age increase/Reforms Y
97. Auto domestic content req N
98. Delete jobs program fundg Y
99. Highway-Gas tax bill N
100. Raise Medicare;Cut defnse N
101. Emergency housing aid Y
102. Across-the-board tax cuts Y
103. Gramm-Latta II targets Y
104. Delete B-1 bomber funds N
105. Dsapprov Saudi AWACS sale N
106. Disapprove oil import fee Y
107. Rail Deregulation N
108. Dsapp India nuc fuel sale N
109. Mil draft registration Y
110. Chrysler Loan Guarantees N
111. Prohibit school busing Y
112. Nuclear plant moratorium ?
113. Oil price controls N
114. Tuition Tax Credits N
115. Est Consumer Protect Agcy N
116. Eliminate B-1 bomber fnds N
117. Subminimum wage for youth Y
118. Delete crude oil tax Y
119. Natural gas deregulation Y

Presidential Support Score: 1986 - 72% 1985 - 63%

NICHOLS, BILL -- Alabama 3rd District [Democrat]. Counties of Autauga, Calhoun, Chambers, Clay, Cleburne, Coosa, Elmore, Lee, Macon, Randolph, Russell, Talladega and Tallapoosa. Prior Terms: House: 1967-86. Born: October 16, 1918; Becker,

NICHOLS, BILL (Cont.)

Miss. Education: Auburn University (B.S., M.A.). Military Service: 1942-47. Occupation: businessman; Alabama representative; Alabama senator.

1.	Immigration Reform	X	56.	Increase SDI funding	N
2.	Open fld-search warrants	N	57.	Reduce SDI funding	N
3.	Civil pnty-hire ill alien	N	58.	Produce chemical weapons	Y
4.	So Afr sanc-veto override	Y	59.	Bar CIA fndg in Nicaragua	N
5.	Tax Overhaul	Y	60.	South Africa sanctions	N
6.	South Africa sanctions	Y	61.	Cut SS COLAs;Raise taxes	N
7.	Death penalty-drug bill	Y	62.	Let US invest-So Africa	N
8.	Evidence-warrantless srch	Y	63.	Approve 21 MX for 1985	Y
9.	Life term-second drug off	Y	64.	Emergency Farm Credit	Y
10.	Military use in drug war	N	65.	Awards to whistle blowers	Y
11.	Troop reduction in Europe	N	66.	African disaster relief	Y
12.	Prohibit chemical weapons	N	67.	Ban bank loans to So Afr	N
13.	Bar ASAT testing	N	68.	Bar coun duty-free trtmt	N
14.	Abide SALT II weapons ban	N	69.	Steel import limits	Y
15.	Follow SALT II-Soviets do	Y	70.	Soc Sec COLAs=inflation	Y
16.	Reduce SDI funding	N	71.	Bar haz waste vctms suits	Y
17.	Increase SDI funding	Y	72.	Prohibit aid to Nicaragua	N
18.	Purchase Trident sub	N	73.	Cut $-Schs bar sch prayer	Y
19.	Delete 12 MX;Add conv wpn	N	74.	Raise taxes; Cut Medicare	N
20.	Raise speed limit	N	75.	Alien residncy-prior 1982	N
21.	Textile Import Quotas(*)	Y	76.	Alien residncy-prior 1980	N
22.	Req Pentagon buy US goods	Y	77.	Pen emp-hire illgl aliens	N
23.	AIDS ins anti-dscriminatn	Y	78.	Lmt Persh II/cruse-Europe	N
24.	Nicaraguan refugee aid	N	79.	Delete 34 B-1 bombers	N
25.	Nicaraguan contra aid	Y	80.	Bar purch of Pershing II	N
26.	US abide by SALT II	Y	81.	Bar purchase of Sgt York	N
27.	Prohibit Saudi arms sale	?	82.	Delete $ for Trident II	N
28.	Military Retiremnt Reform	?	83.	Allow 15 MX missiles	Y
29.	Nicaraguan refugee aid	?	84.	Bar MX procurement-1985	N
30.	Ease '68 Gun Control Act	#	85.	Equal Access Act	Y
31.	Bar intrstat handgun tran	?	86.	Aid to El Salvador	Y
32.	Keep '68 Gun Control Act	?	87.	Bar Nicarag water mining	#
33.	Nicaraguan contra aid	Y	88.	Physician/Medicare freeze	?
34.	Bar emp polygraph testing	Y	89.	Increase "sin" taxes	Y
35.	Tax Overhaul consideratn	Y	90.	End SBA direct loans	?
36.	Bar armor-piercing ammo	Y	91.	Sell Conrail	?
37.	Tax Overhaul consideratn	Y	92.	Equal Rights Amendment	N
38.	Make comp emissions known	N	93.	Marines in Lebanon	N
39.	Allow toxic victims suits	N	94.	Eminent domain-Coal comps	N
40.	Strike Superfund "VAT"	N	95.	Prohibit EPA sanctions	Y
41.	Notify emp-plant closing	N	96.	SS age increase/Reforms	N
42.	Bar emp consult-plant clo	Y	97.	Auto domestic content req	Y
43.	Medicare cuts;Tax incres'	Y	98.	Delete jobs program fundg	Y
44.	Delete 12 MX missiles	N	99.	Highway-Gas tax bill	N
45.	Spending cuts;Tax incres'	Y	100.	Raise Medicare;Cut defnse	N
46.	Textile Import Quotas	Y	101.	Emergency housing aid	N
47.	Cut some school lunch fds	N	102.	Across-the-board tax cuts	Y
48.	Clean Water Act Amendmnts	Y	103.	Gramm-Latta II targets	Y
49.	Youth work projects	N	104.	Delete B-1 bomber funds	N
50.	Assist military in Angola	Y	105.	Dsapprov Saudi AWACS sale	N
51.	Allow US troops-Nicaragua	Y	106.	Disapprove oil import fee	Y
52.	Pentagon polygraph exams	Y	107.	Rail Deregulation	N
53.	Bar ASAT testing	N	108.	Dsapp India nuc fuel sale	Y
54.	Suspend def pmt for abuse	N	109.	Mil draft registration	Y
55.	Bar Pentagon-contr emplmt	Y	110.	Chrysler Loan Guarantees	N

NICHOLS, BILL (Cont.)

111. Prohibit school busing Y
112. Nuclear plant moratorium N
113. Oil price controls Y
114. Tuition Tax Credits N
115. Est Consumer Protect Agcy N
116. Eliminate B-1 bomber fnds N
117. Subminimum wage for youth Y
118. Delete crude oil tax Y
119. Natural gas deregulation N

Presidential Support Score: 1986 - 48% 1985 - 61%

BEVILL, TOM -- Alabama 4th District [Democrat] Counties of Blount, Cherokee, Cullman, De Kalb, Etowah, Fayette, Franklin, Lamar, Marion, Marshall, Pickens, St. Clair (pt.), Walker and Winston. Prior Terms: House: 1967-86. Born: March 27, 1921; Townley, Ala. Education: University of Alabama (B.S. LL.B.). Military Service: U.S. Army, 1943-46. Occupation: Attorney; Alabama representative (1958-66).

1. Immigration Reform N
2. Open fld-search warrants N
3. Civil pnty-hire ill alien N
4. So Afr sanc-veto override Y
5. Tax Overhaul Y
6. South Africa sanctions Y
7. Death penalty-drug bill Y
8. Evidence-warrantless srch Y
9. Life term-second drug off Y
10. Military use in drug war N
11. Troop reduction in Europe N
12. Prohibit chemical weapons N
13. Bar ASAT testing N
14. Abide SALT II weapons ban N
15. Follow SALT II-Soviets do Y
16. Reduce SDI funding N
17. Increase SDI funding Y
18. Purchase Trident sub N
19. Delete 12 MX;Add conv wpn N
20. Raise speed limit Y
21. Textile Import Quotas(*) Y
22. Req Pentagon buy US goods Y
23. AIDS ins anti-dscriminatn Y
24. Nicaraguan refugee aid N
25. Nicaraguan contra aid Y
26. US abide by SALT II N
27. Prohibit Saudi arms sale Y
28. Military Retiremnt Reform Y
29. Nicaraguan refugee aid N
30. Ease '68 Gun Control Act Y
31. Bar intrstat handgun tran N
32. Keep '68 Gun Control Act N
33. Nicaraguan contra aid Y
34. Bar emp polygraph testing Y
35. Tax Overhaul consideratn Y
36. Bar armor-piercing ammo Y
37. Tax Overhaul consideratn Y
38. Make comp emissions known N
39. Allow toxic victims suits N
40. Strike Superfund "VAT" N
41. Notify emp-plant closing Y
42. Bar emp consult-plant clo N
43. Medicare cuts;Tax incres' N
44. Delete 12 MX missiles N
45. Spending cuts;Tax incres' Y
46. Textile Import Quotas Y
47. Cut some school lunch fds ?
48. Clean Water Act Amendmnts N
49. Youth work projects N
50. Assist military in Angola Y
51. Allow US troops-Nicaragua Y
52. Pentagon polygraph exams Y
53. Bar ASAT testing N
54. Suspend def pmt for abuse N
55. Bar Pentagon-contr emplmt Y
56. Increase SDI funding N
57. Reduce SDI funding N
58. Produce chemical weapons Y
59. Bar CIA fndg in Nicaragua N
60. South Africa sanctions Y
61. Cut COLAs; Raise taxes N
62. Let US invest-So Africa N
63. Approve 21 MX for 1985 Y
64. Emergency Farm Credit Y
65. Awards to whistle blowers Y
66. African disaster relief Y
67. Ban bank loans to So Afr Y
68. Bar coun duty-free trtmt N
69. Steel import limits Y
70. Soc Sec COLAs=inflation Y
71. Bar haz waste vctms suits Y
72. Prohibit aid to Nicaragua Y
73. Cut $-Schs bar sch prayer Y
74. Raise taxes; Cut Medicare N
75. Alien residncy-prior 1982 Y
76. Alien residncy-prior 1980 N
77. Pen emp-hire illgl aliens N
78. Lmt Persh II/cruse-Europe N
79. Delete 34 B-1 bombers N
80. Bar purch of Pershing II N
81. Bar purchase of Sgt York N
82. Delete $ for Trident II N
83. Allow 15 MX missiles Y
84. Bar MX procurement-1985 N
85. Equal Access Act Y
86. Aid to El Salvador ?

BEVILL, TOM (Cont.)

87. Bar Nicarag water mining Y
88. Physician/Medicare freeze N
89. Increase "sin" taxes Y
90. End SBA direct loans N
91. Sell Conrail N
92. Equal Rights Amendment Y
93. Marines in Lebanon Y
94. Eminent domain-Coal comps N
95. Prohibit EPA sanctions Y
96. SS age increase/Reforms N
97. Auto domestic content req Y
98. Delete jobs program fundg N
99. Highway-Gas tax bill ?
100. Raise Medicare;Cut defnse Y
101. Emergency housing aid Y
102. Across-the-board tax cuts N
103. Gramm-Latta II targets Y
104. Delete B-1 bomber funds N
105. Dsapprov Saudi AWACS sale Y
106. Disapprove oil import fee Y
107. Rail Deregulation N
108. Dsapp India nuc fuel sale Y
109. Mil draft registration Y
110. Chrysler Loan Guarantees N
111. Prohibit school busing Y
112. Nuclear plant moratorium N
113. Oil price controls ?
114. Tuition Tax Credits N
115. Est Consumer Protect Agcy N
116. Eliminate B-1 bomber fnds Y
117. Subminimum wage for youth N
118. Delete crude oil tax Y
119. Natural gas deregulation N

Presidential Support Score: 1986 - 40% 1985 - 54%

FLIPPO, RONNIE G. -- Alabama 5th District [Democrat]. Counties of Colbert, Jackson, Lauderdale, Lawrence, Limestone, Madison and Morgan. Prior Terms: House: 1977-86. Born: August 15, 1937; Florence, Ala. Education: University of North Alabama (B.S.); University of Alabama (M.A.). Occupation: Certified public accountant; partner, Flippo & Robbins; Alabama representative (1971-75); Alabama senator (1975-77).

1. Immigration Reform N
2. Open fld-search warrants N
3. Civil pnty-hire ill alien N
4. So Afr sanc-veto override Y
5. Tax Overhaul Y
6. South Africa sanctions Y
7. Death penalty-drug bill Y
8. Evidence-warrantless srch Y
9. Life term-second drug off Y
10. Military use in drug war N
11. Troop reduction in Europe ?
12. Prohibit chemical weapons ?
13. Bar ASAT testing ?
14. Abide SALT II weapons ban ?
15. Follow SALT II-Soviets do ?
16. Reduce SDI funding N
17. Increase SDI funding Y
18. Purchase Trident sub ?
19. Delete 12 MX;Add conv wpn ?
20. Raise speed limit Y
21. Textile Import Quotas(*) Y
22. Req Pentagon buy US goods Y
23. AIDS ins anti-dscriminatn Y
24. Nicaraguan refugee aid N
25. Nicaraguan contra aid Y
26. US abide by SALT II Y
27. Prohibit Saudi arms sale Y
28. Military Retiremnt Reform Y
29. Nicaraguan refugee aid N
30. Ease '68 Gun Control Act Y
31. Bar intrstat handgun tran N
32. Keep '68 Gun Control Act N
33. Nicaraguan contra aid Y
34. Bar emp polygraph testing Y
35. Tax Overhaul consideratn Y
36. Bar armor-piercing ammo Y
37. Tax Overhaul consideratn Y
38. Make comp emissions known Y
39. Allow toxic victims suits N
40. Strike Superfund "VAT" N
41. Notify emp-plant closing N
42. Bar emp consult-plant clo Y
43. Medicare cuts;Tax incres' Y
44. Delete 12 MX missiles N
45. Spending cuts;Tax incres' Y
46. Textile Import Quotas Y
47. Cut some school lunch fds N
48. Clean Water Act Amendmnts N
49. Youth work projects N
50. Assist military in Angola ?
51. Allow US troops-Nicaragua Y
52. Pentagon polygraph exams Y
53. Bar ASAT testing N
54. Suspend def pmt for abuse N
55. Bar Pentagon-contr emplmt Y
56. Increase SDI funding N
57. Reduce SDI funding N
58. Produce chemical weapons Y

FLIPPO, RONNIE G. (Cont.)

59. Bar CIA fndg in Nicaragua N
60. South Africa sanctions Y
61. Cut SS COLAs; Raise taxes N
62. Let US invest-So Africa N
63. Approve 21 MX for 1985 Y
64. Emergency Farm Credit Y
65. Awards to whistle blowers Y
66. African disaster relief Y
67. Ban bank loans to So Afr Y
68. Bar coun duty-free trtmt Y
69. Steel import limits Y
70. Soc Sec COLAs=inflation Y
71. Bar haz waste vctms suits Y
72. Prohibit aid to Nicaragua N
73. Cut $-Schs bar sch prayer Y
74. Raise taxes; Cut Medicare Y
75. Alien residncy-prior 1982 Y
76. Alien residncy-prior 1980 Y
77. Pen emp-hire illgl aliens N
78. Lmt Persh II/cruse-Europe N
79. Delete 34 B-1 bombers N
80. Bar purch of Pershing II N
81. Bar purchase of Sgt York N
82. Delete $ for Trident II N
83. Allow 15 MX missiles Y
84. Bar MX procurement-1985 N
85. Equal Access Act Y
86. Aid to El Salvador Y
87. Bar Nicarag water mining Y
88. Physician/Medicare freeze N
89. Increase "sin" taxes Y
90. End SBA direct loans N
91. Sell Conrail N
92. Equal Rights Amendment Y
93. Marines in Lebanon N
94. Eminent domain-Coal comps N
95. Prohibit EPA sanctions Y
96. SS age increase/Reforms Y
97. Auto domestic content req Y
98. Delete jobs program fundg N
99. Highway-Gas tax bill Y
100. Raise Medicare;Cut defnse Y
101. Emergency housing aid Y
102. Across-the-board tax cuts N
103. Gramm-Latta II targets Y
104. Delete B-1 bomber funds N
105. Dsapprov Saudi AWACS sale N
106. Disapprove oil import fee Y
107. Rail Deregulation N
108. Dsapp India nuc fuel sale N
109. Mil draft registration Y
110. Chrysler Loan Guarantees Y
111. Prohibit school busing Y
112. Nuclear plant moratorium N
113. Oil price controls N
114. Tuition Tax Credits N
115. Est Consumer Protect Agcy N
116. Eliminate B-1 bomber fnds Y
117. Subminimum wage for youth Y
118. Delete crude oil tax ?
119. Natural gas deregulation ?

Presidential Support Score: 1986 - 33% 1985 - 45%

ERDREICH, BEN -- Alabama 6th District [Democrat]. County of Jefferson (pt.) Prior Terms: House: 1983-86. Born: December 9, 1938; Birmingham, Ala. Education: Yale University (B.A.); University of Alabama School of Law (J.D.). Military Service: U.S. Army, 1963-65. Occupation: Attorney; Alabama representative (1970); county commissioner (1974-82).

1. Immigration Reform N
2. Open fld-search warrants N
3. Civil pnty-hire ill alien N
4. So Afr sanc-veto override Y
5. Tax Overhaul Y
6. South Africa sanctions Y
7. Death penalty-drug bill Y
8. Evidence-warrantless srch Y
9. Life term-second drug off Y
10. Military use in drug war Y
11. Troop reduction in Europe N
12. Prohibit chemical weapons Y
13. Bar ASAT testing N
14. Abide SALT II weapons ban Y
15. Follow SALT II-Soviets do Y
16. Reduce SDI funding N
17. Increase SDI funding N
18. Purchase Trident sub N
19. Delete 12 MX;Add conv wpn N
20. Raise speed limit Y
21. Textile Import Quotas(*) Y
22. Req Pentagon buy US goods Y
23. AIDS ins anti-dscriminatn N
24. Nicaraguan refugee aid N
25. Nicaraguan contra aid Y
26. US abide by SALT II Y
27. Prohibit Saudi arms sale Y
28. Military Retiremnt Reform Y
29. Nicaraguan refugee aid N
30. Ease '68 Gun Control Act Y
31. Bar intrstat handgun tran N
32. Keep '68 Gun Control Act N

ERDREICH, BEN (Cont.)

33. Nicaraguan contra aid Y	65. Awards to whistle blowers Y
34. Bar emp polygraph testing Y	66. African disaster relief Y
35. Tax Overhaul consideratn Y	67. Ban bank loans to So Afr Y
36. Bar armor-piercing ammo Y	68. Bar coun duty-free trtmt Y
37. Tax Overhaul consideratn Y	69. Steel import limits Y
38. Make comp emissions known Y	70. Soc Sec COLAs=inflation Y
39. Allow toxic victims suits N	71. Bar haz waste vctms suits Y
40. Strike Superfund "VAT" N	72. Prohibit aid to Nicaragua N
41. Notify emp-plant closing N	73. Cut $-Schs bar sch prayer Y
42. Bar emp consult-plant clo Y	74. Raise taxes; Cut Medicare N
43. Medicare cuts;Tax incres' N	75. Alien residncy-prior 1982 Y
44. Delete 12 MX missiles N	76. Alien residncy-prior 1980 Y
45. Spending cuts;Tax incres' Y	77. Pen emp-hire illgl aliens N
46. Textile Import Quotas Y	78. Lmt Persh II/cruse-Europe -
47. Cut some school lunch fds N	79. Delete 34 B-1 bombers N
48. Clean Water Act Amendmnts N	80. Bar purch of Pershing II N
49. Youth work projects Y	81. Bar purchase of Sgt York N
50. Assist military in Angola Y	82. Delete $ for Trident II N
51. Allow US troops-Nicaragua Y	83. Allow 15 MX missiles Y
52. Pentagon polygraph exams Y	84. Bar MX procurement-1985 N
53. Bar ASAT testing N	85. Equal Access Act Y
54. Suspend def pmt for abuse N	86. Aid to El Salvador Y
55. Bar Pentagon-contr emplmt Y	87. Bar Nicarag water mining Y
56. Increase SDI funding N	88. Physician/Medicare freeze N
57. Reduce SDI funding N	89. Increase "sin" taxes Y
58. Produce chemical weapons N	90. End SBA direct loans N
59. Bar CIA fndg in Nicaragua N	91. Sell Conrail N
60. South Africa sanctions Y	92. Equal Rights Amendment Y
61. Cut SS COLAs; Raise taxes N	93. Marines in Lebanon Y
62. Let US invest-So Africa N	94. Eminent domain-Coal comps N
63. Approve 21 MX for 1985 Y	95. Prohibit EPA sanctions Y
64. Emergency Farm Credit Y	96. SS age increase/Reforms N

Presidential Support Score: 1986 - 40% 1985 - 52%

SHELBY, RICHARD C. -- Alabama 7th District [Democrat]. Counties of Bibb, Chilton, Choctaw, Dallas, Greene, Hale, Jefferson (pt.), Lowndes, Marengo, Perry, St. Clair (pt.), Shelby, Sumter and Tuscaloosa. Prior Terms: House: 1979-86. Born: May 6, 1934; Birmingham, Ala. Education: University of Alabama (A.B., LL.B.). Occupation: Prosecuting attorney; U.S. commissioner; special assistant attorney; Alabama senator (1970-78).

1. Immigration Reform N	15. Follow SALT II-Soviets do Y
2. Open fld-search warrants N	16. Reduce SDI funding N
3. Civil pnty-hire ill alien N	17. Increase SDI funding Y
4. So Afr sanc-veto override Y	18. Purchase Trident sub X
5. Tax Overhaul Y	19. Delete 12 MX;Add conv wpn N
6. South Africa sanctions Y	20. Raise speed limit ?
7. Death penalty-drug bill Y	21. Textile Import Quotas(*) Y
8. Evidence-warrantless srch Y	22. Req Pentagon buy US goods Y
9. Life term-second drug off Y	23. AIDS ins anti-dscriminatn N
10. Military use in drug war Y	24. Nicaraguan refugee aid N
11. Troop reduction in Europe N	25. Nicaraguan contra aid Y
12. Prohibit chemical weapons N	26. US abide by SALT II Y
13. Bar ASAT testing N	27. Prohibit Saudi arms sale Y
14. Abide SALT II weapons ban N	28. Military Retiremnt Reform Y

SHELBY, RICHARD C. (Cont.)

29. Nicaraguan refugee aid Y
30. Ease '68 Gun Control Act Y
31. Bar intrstat handgun tran N
32. Keep '68 Gun Control Act N
33. Nicaraguan contra aid Y
34. Bar emp polygraph testing Y
35. Tax Overhaul consideratn N
36. Bar armor-piercing ammo Y
37. Tax Overhaul consideratn N
38. Make comp emissions known N
39. Allow toxic victims suits N
40. Strike Superfund "VAT" N
41. Notify emp-plant closing N
42. Bar emp consult-plant clo Y
43. Medicare cuts;Tax incres' Y
44. Delete 12 MX missiles N
45. Spending cuts;Tax incres' N
46. Textile Import Quotas Y
47. Cut some school lunch fds N
48. Clean Water Act Amendmnts Y
49. Youth work projects Y
50. Assist military in Angola Y
51. Allow US troops-Nicaragua Y
52. Pentagon polygraph exams Y
53. Bar ASAT testing N
54. Suspend def pmt for abuse N
55. Bar Pentagon-contr emplmt Y
56. Increase SDI funding Y
57. Reduce SDI funding N
58. Produce chemical weapons Y
59. Bar CIA fndg in Nicaragua N
60. South Africa sanctions Y
61. Cut SS COLAs; Raise taxes N
62. Let US invest-So Africa N
63. Approve 21 MX for 1985 Y
64. Emergency Farm Credit Y
65. Awards to whistle blowers Y
66. African disaster relief Y
67. Ban bank loans to So Afr Y
68. Bar coun duty-free trtmt Y
69. Steel import limits Y
70. Soc Sec COLAs=inflation Y
71. Bar haz waste vctms suits ?
72. Prohibit aid to Nicaragua N
73. Cut $-Schs bar sch prayer Y
74. Raise taxes; Cut Medicare N
75. Alien residncy-prior 1982 Y
76. Alien residncy-prior 1980 Y
77. Pen emp-hire illgl aliens N
78. Lmt Persh II/cruse-Europe N
79. Delete 34 B-1 bombers N
80. Bar purch of Pershing II N
81. Bar purchase of Sgt York N
82. Delete $ for Trident II N
83. Allow 15 MX missiles Y
84. Bar MX procurement-1985 N
85. Equal Access Act Y
86. Aid to El Salvador Y
87. Bar Nicarag water mining ?
88. Physician/Medicare freeze Y
89. Increase "sin" taxes N
90. End SBA direct loans N
91. Sell Conrail Y
92. Equal Rights Amendment N
93. Marines in Lebanon N
94. Eminent domain-Coal comps N
95. Prohibit EPA sanctions N
96. SS age increase/Reforms Y
97. Auto domestic content req Y
98. Delete jobs program fundg N
99. Highway-Gas tax bill N
100. Raise Medicare;Cut defnse N
101. Emergency housing aid Y
102. Across-the-board tax cuts Y
103. Gramm-Latta II targets Y
104. Delete B-1 bomber funds N
105. Dsapprov Saudi AWACS sale Y
106. Disapprove oil import fee Y
107. Rail Deregulation N
108. Dsapp India nuc fuel sale N
109. Mil draft registration Y
110. Chrysler Loan Guarantees N
111. Prohibit school busing Y
112. Nuclear plant moratorium N
113. Oil price controls N

Presidential Support Score: 1986 - 44% 1985 - 52%

A L A S K A

YOUNG, DON -- Representative at Large [Republican]. Prior Terms: House: 1973 (Special Election)-1986. Born: June 9, 1933; Meridian, Calif. Education: Chico State College. Occupation: River boat captain; educator, city councilman; mayor; Alaska representative (1966-70); Alaska senator (1970-73).

1. Immigration Reform N
2. Open fld-search warrants Y
3. Civil pnty-hire ill alien Y
4. So Afr sanc-veto override Y
5. Tax Overhaul N
6. South Africa sanctions ?

YOUNG, DON (Cont.)

7. Death penalty-drug bill ?
8. Evidence-warrantless srch ?
9. Life term-second drug off ?
10. Military use in drug war ?
11. Troop reduction in Europe N
12. Prohibit chemical weapons N
13. Bar ASAT testing N
14. Abide SALT II weapons ban N
15. Follow SALT II-Soviets do Y
16. Reduce SDI funding N
17. Increase SDI funding N
18. Purchase Trident sub N
19. Delete 12 MX;Add conv wpn N
20. Raise speed limit Y
21. Textile Import Quotas(*) N
22. Req Pentagon buy US goods Y
23. AIDS ins anti-dscriminatn N
24. Nicaraguan refugee aid N
25. Nicaraguan contra aid Y
26. US abide by SALT II Y
27. Prohibit Saudi arms sale N
28. Military Retiremnt Reform Y
29. Nicaraguan refugee aid Y
30. Ease '68 Gun Control Act Y
31. Bar intrstat handgun tran N
32. Keep '68 Gun Control Act N
33. Nicaraguan contra aid Y
34. Bar emp polygraph testing Y
35. Tax Overhaul consideratn N
36. Bar armor-piercing ammo Y
37. Tax Overhaul consideratn N
38. Make comp emissions known N
39. Allow toxic victims suits N
40. Strike Superfund "VAT" N
41. Notify emp-plant closing Y
42. Bar emp consult-plant clo N
43. Medicare cuts;Tax incres' N
44. Delete 12 MX missiles N
45. Spending cuts;Tax incres' Y
46. Textile Import Quotas Y
47. Cut some school lunch fds N
48. Clean Water Act Amendmnts Y
49. Youth work projects Y
50. Assist military in Angola Y
51. Allow US troops-Nicaragua Y
52. Pentagon polygraph exams Y
53. Bar ASAT testing N
54. Suspend def pmt for abuse N
55. Bar Pentagon-contr emplmt Y
56. Increase SDI funding N
57. Reduce SDI funding N
58. Produce chemical weapons Y
59. Bar CIA fndg in Nicaragua N
60. South Africa sanctions Y
61. Cut SS COLAs; Raise taxes N
62. Let US invest-So Africa Y
63. Approve 21 MX for 1985 Y
64. Emergency Farm Credit N
65. Awards to whistle blowers Y
66. African disaster relief Y
67. Ban bank loans to So Afr Y
68. Bar coun duty-free trtmt ?
69. Steel import limits N
70. Soc Sec COLAs=inflation Y
71. Bar haz waste vctms suits Y
72. Prohibit aid to Nicaragua Y
73. Cut $-Schs bar sch prayer Y
74. Raise taxes; Cut Medicare Y
75. Alien residncy-prior 1982 Y
76. Alien residncy-prior 1980 Y
77. Pen emp-hire illgl aliens N
78. Lmt Persh II/cruse-Europe N
79. Delete 34 B-1 bombers N
80. Bar purch of Pershing II N
81. Bar purchase of Sgt York N
82. Delete $ for Trident II N
83. Allow 15 MX missiles Y
84. Bar MX procurement-1985 N
85. Equal Access Act Y
86. Aid to El Salvador Y
87. Bar Nicarag water mining Y
88. Physician/Medicare freeze Y
89. Increase "sin" taxes N
90. End SBA direct loans N
91. Sell Conrail N
92. Equal Rights Amendment Y
93. Marines in Lebanon Y
94. Eminent domain-Coal comps Y
95. Prohibit EPA sanctions ?
96. SS age increase/Reforms Y
97. Auto domestic content req ?
98. Delete jobs program fundg Y
99. Highway-Gas tax bill N
100. Raise Medicare;Cut defnse N
101. Emergency housing aid N
102. Across-the-board tax cuts Y
103. Gramm-Latta II targets Y
104. Delete B-1 bomber funds N
105. Dsapprov Saudi AWACS sale Y
106. Disapprove oil import fee ?
107. Rail Deregulation ?
108. Dsapp India nuc fuel sale N
109. Mil draft registration N
110. Chrysler Loan Guarantees Y
111. Prohibit school busing N
112. Nuclear plant moratorium N
113. Oil price controls N
114. Tuition Tax Credits N
115. Est Consumer Protect Agcy N
116. Eliminate B-1 bomber fnds N
117. Subminimum wage for youth N
118. Delete crude oil tax ?
119. Natural gas deregulation Y

Presidential Support Score: 1986 - 63% 1985 - 51%

ARIZONA

McCAIN, JOHN -- Arizona 1st District [Republican]. County of Maricopa (pt.) Prior Terms: House: 1983-86. Born: August 29, 1936, Panama Canal Zone. Education: U.S. Naval Academy; National War College. Military Service: U.S. Navy. Occupation: Director, Navy Liaison Office (1977-81).

1.	Immigration Reform	N	49.	Youth work projects	N
2.	Open fld-search warrants	Y	50.	Assist military in Angola	Y
3.	Civil pnty-hire ill alien	Y	51.	Allow US troops-Nicaragua	Y
4.	So Afr sanc-veto override	Y	52.	Pentagon polygraph exams	Y
5.	Tax Overhaul	Y	53.	Bar ASAT testing	N
6.	South Africa sanctions	Y	54.	Suspend def pmt for abuse	N
7.	Death penalty-drug bill	Y	55.	Bar Pentagon-contr emplmt	N
8.	Evidence-warrantless srch	Y	56.	Increase SDI funding	Y
9.	Life term-second drug off	Y	57.	Reduce SDI funding	N
10.	Military use in drug war	Y	58.	Produce chemical weapons	Y
11.	Troop reduction in Europe	N	59.	Bar CIA fndg in Nicaragua	N
12.	Prohibit chemical weapons	N	60.	South Africa sanctions	N
13.	Bar ASAT testing	N	61.	Cut SS COLAs; Raise taxes	N
14.	Abide SALT II weapons ban	N	62.	Let US invest-So Africa	Y
15.	Follow SALT II-Soviets do	Y	63.	Approve 21 MX for 1985	Y
16.	Reduce SDI funding	N	64.	Emergency Farm Credit	Y
17.	Increase SDI funding	Y	65.	Awards to whistle blowers	Y
18.	Purchase Trident sub	N	66.	African disaster relief	Y
19.	Delete 12 MX;Add conv wpn	N	67.	Ban bank loans to So Afr	Y
20.	Raise speed limit	+	68.	Bar coun duty-free trtmt	N
21.	Textile Import Quotas(*)	N	69.	Steel import limits	Y
22.	Req Pentagon buy US goods	N	70.	Soc Sec COLAs=inflation	Y
23.	AIDS ins anti-dscriminatn	N	71.	Bar haz waste vctms suits	Y
24.	Nicaraguan refugee aid	N	72.	Prohibit aid to Nicaragua	N
25.	Nicaraguan contra aid	Y	73.	Cut $-Schs bar sch prayer	Y
26.	US abide by SALT II	Y	74.	Raise taxes; Cut Medicare	N
27.	Prohibit Saudi arms sale	Y	75.	Alien residncy-prior 1982	N
28.	Military Retiremnt Reform	Y	76.	Alien residncy-prior 1980	N
29.	Nicaraguan refugee aid	Y	77.	Pen emp-hire illgl aliens	N
30.	Ease '68 Gun Control Act	Y	78.	Lmt Persh II/cruse-Europe	N
31.	Bar intrstat handgun tran	N	79.	Delete 34 B-1 bombers	N
32.	Keep '68 Gun Control Act	N	80.	Bar purch of Pershing II	N
33.	Nicaraguan contra aid	Y	81.	Bar purchase of Sgt York	N
34.	Bar emp polygraph testing	N	82.	Delete $ for Trident II	N
35.	Tax Overhaul consideratn	N	83.	Allow 15 MX missiles	Y
36.	Bar armor-piercing ammo	Y	84.	Bar MX procurement-1985	N
37.	Tax Overhaul consideratn	N	85.	Equal Access Act	Y
38.	Make comp emissions known	N	86.	Aid to El Salvador	Y
39.	Allow toxic victims suits	N	87.	Bar Nicarag water mining	N
40.	Strike Superfund "VAT"	Y	88.	Physician/Medicare freeze	Y
41.	Notify emp-plant closing	N	89.	Increase "sin" taxes	N
42.	Bar emp consult-plant clo	Y	90.	End SBA direct loans	N
43.	Medicare cuts;Tax incres'	N	91.	Sell Conrail	Y
44.	Delete 12 MX missiles	?	92.	Equal Rights Amendment	N
45.	Spending cuts;Tax incres'	N	93.	Marines in Lebanon	N
46.	Textile Import Quotas	N	94.	Eminent domain-Coal comps	Y
47.	Cut some school lunch fds	Y	95.	Prohibit EPA sanctions	?
48.	Clean Water Act Amendmnts	Y	96.	SS age increase/Reforms	Y

Presidential Support Score: 1986 - 69% 1985 - 68%

UDALL, MORRIS K. -- Arizona 2nd District [Democrat]. Counties of Maricopa (pt.), Pima (pt.), Pinal (pt.), Santa Cruz (pt.) and Yuma (pt.). Prior Terms: House 1961 (Special Election)-1986. Born: June 15, 1922; St. Johns, Ariz. Education: University of Arizona (LL.B.). Military Service: U.S. Army, 1942-46. Occupation: Professional basketball player (1948-49); county attorney (1952-54); attorney, Udall & Udall (1949-61); vice president, State Bar Assn. (1961); author.

1. Immigration Reform Y
2. Open fld-search warrants Y
3. Civil pnty-hire ill alien Y
4. So Afr sanc-veto override Y
5. Tax Overhaul Y
6. South Africa sanctions Y
7. Death penalty-drug bill N
8. Evidence-warrantless srch N
9. Life term-second drug off N
10. Military use in drug war N
11. Troop reduction in Europe Y
12. Prohibit chemical weapons Y
13. Bar ASAT testing Y
14. Abide SALT II weapons ban Y
15. Follow SALT II-Soviets do N
16. Reduce SDI funding Y
17. Increase SDI funding N
18. Purchase Trident sub Y
19. Delete 12 MX;Add conv wpn Y
20. Raise speed limit Y
21. Textile Import Quotas(*) Y
22. Req Pentagon buy US goods N
23. AIDS ins anti-dscriminatn Y
24. Nicaraguan refugee aid Y
25. Nicaraguan contra aid N
26. US abide by SALT II N
27. Prohibit Saudi arms sale Y
28. Military Retiremnt Reform Y
29. Nicaraguan refugee aid Y
30. Ease '68 Gun Control Act Y
31. Bar intrstat handgun tran Y
32. Keep '68 Gun Control Act N
33. Nicaraguan contra aid N
34. Bar emp polygraph testing Y
35. Tax Overhaul consideratn Y
36. Bar armor-piercing ammo Y
37. Tax Overhaul consideratn Y
38. Make comp emissions known Y
39. Allow toxic victims suits Y
40. Strike Superfund "VAT" N
41. Notify emp-plant closing Y
42. Bar emp consult-plant clo ?
43. Medicare cuts;Tax incres' Y
44. Delete 12 MX missiles Y
45. Spending cuts;Tax incres' Y
46. Textile Import Quotas N
47. Cut some school lunch fds N
48. Clean Water Act Amendmnts N
49. Youth work projects Y
50. Assist military in Angola N
51. Allow US troops-Nicaragua N
52. Pentagon polygraph exams Y
53. Bar ASAT testing Y
54. Suspend def pmt for abuse Y
55. Bar Pentagon-contr emplmt Y
56. Increase SDI funding N
57. Reduce SDI funding ?
58. Produce chemical weapons ?
59. Bar CIA fndg in Nicaragua Y
60. South Africa sanctions Y
61. Cut SS COLAs; Raise taxes Y
62. Let US invest-So Africa ?
63. Approve 21 MX for 1985 N
64. Emergency Farm Credit Y
65. Awards to whistle blowers Y
66. African disaster relief Y
67. Ban bank loans to So Afr ?
68. Bar coun duty-free trtmt ?
69. Steel import limits Y
70. Soc Sec COLAs=inflation Y
71. Bar haz waste vctms suits N
72. Prohibit aid to Nicaragua Y
73. Cut $-Schs bar sch prayer N
74. Raise taxes; Cut Medicare Y
75. Alien residncy-prior 1982 N
76. Alien residncy-prior 1980 N
77. Pen emp-hire illgl aliens Y
78. Lmt Persh II/cruse-Europe N
79. Delete 34 B-1 bombers Y
80. Bar purch of Pershing II Y
81. Bar purchase of Sgt York N
82. Delete $ for Trident II N
83. Allow 15 MX missiles N
84. Bar MX procurement-1985 Y
85. Equal Access Act N
86. Aid to El Salvador N
87. Bar Nicarag water mining Y
88. Physician/Medicare freeze N
89. Increase "sin" taxes ?
90. End SBA direct loans N
91. Sell Conrail N
92. Equal Rights Amendment Y
93. Marines in Lebanon N
94. Eminent domain-Coal comps Y
95. Prohibit EPA sanctions Y
96. SS age increase/Reforms Y
97. Auto domestic content req Y
98. Delete jobs program fundg N
99. Highway-Gas tax bill Y
100. Raise Medicare;Cut defnse Y
101. Emergency housing aid Y
102. Across-the-board tax cuts N

UDALL, MORRIS (Cont.)

103. Gramm-Latta II targets N
104. Delete B-1 bomber funds Y
105. Dsapprov Saudi AWACS sale Y
106. Disapprove oil import fee N
107. Rail Deregulation ?
108. Dsapp India nuc fuel sale Y
109. Mil draft registration N
110. Chrysler Loan Guarantees Y
111. Prohibit school busing N
112. Nuclear plant moratorium Y
113. Oil price controls N
114. Tuition Tax Credits N
115. Est Consumer Protect Agcy Y
116. Eliminate B-1 bomber fnds Y
117. Subminimum wage for youth N
118. Delete crude oil tax N
119. Natural gas deregulation N

Presidential Support Score: 1986 - 19% 1985 - 16%

STUMP, BOB -- Arizona 3rd District [Republican]. Counties of Coconino, La Paz, Maricopa (pt.), Mohave, Yavapai and Yuma (pt.). Prior Terms: House: 1977-86. Born: April 4, 1927; Phoenix, Ariz. Education: Arizona State University (B.S.). Military Service: WW II. Occupation: Arizona representative (1959-1967); Arizona senator (1967-76).

1. Immigration Reform N
2. Open fld-search warrants Y
3. Civil pnty-hire ill alien Y
4. So Afr sanc-veto override N
5. Tax Overhaul Y
6. South Africa sanctions N
7. Death penalty-drug bill Y
8. Evidence-warrantless srch Y
9. Life term-second drug off Y
10. Military use in drug war Y
11. Troop reduction in Europe N
12. Prohibit chemical weapons N
13. Bar ASAT testing N
14. Abide SALT II weapons ban N
15. Follow SALT II-Soviets do Y
16. Reduce SDI funding N
17. Increase SDI funding Y
18. Purchase Trident sub N
19. Delete 12 MX;Add conv wpn N
20. Raise speed limit Y
21. Textile Import Quotas(*) N
22. Req Pentagon buy US goods N
23. AIDS ins anti-dscriminatn N
24. Nicaraguan refugee aid N
25. Nicaraguan contra aid Y
26. US abide by SALT II Y
27. Prohibit Saudi arms sale N
28. Military Retiremnt Reform Y
29. Nicaraguan refugee aid Y
30. Ease '68 Gun Control Act Y
31. Bar intrstat handgun tran N
32. Keep '68 Gun Control Act N
33. Nicaraguan contra aid Y
34. Bar emp polygraph testing N
35. Tax Overhaul consideratn N
36. Bar armor-piercing ammo N
37. Tax Overhaul consideratn N
38. Make comp emissions known N
39. Allow toxic victims suits N
40. Strike Superfund "VAT" N
41. Notify emp-plant closing N
42. Bar emp consult-plant clo Y
43. Medicare cuts;Tax incres' N
44. Delete 12 MX missiles N
45. Spending cuts;Tax incres' N
46. Textile Import Quotas N
47. Cut some school lunch fds Y
48. Clean Water Act Amendmnts Y
49. Youth work projects N
50. Assist military in Angola Y
51. Allow US troops-Nicaragua Y
52. Pentagon polygraph exams Y
53. Bar ASAT testing N
54. Suspend def pmt for abuse N
55. Bar Pentagon-contr emplmt N
56. Increase SDI funding Y
57. Reduce SDI funding N
58. Produce chemical weapons Y
59. Bar CIA fndg in Nicaragua N
60. South Africa sanctions N
61. Cut SS COLAs; Raise taxes Y
62. Let US invest-So Africa Y
63. Approve 21 MX for 1985 Y
64. Emergency Farm Credit N
65. Awards to whistle blowers Y
66. African disaster relief N
67. Ban bank loans to So Afr N
68. Bar coun duty-free trtmt N
69. Steel import limits N
70. Soc Sec COLAs=inflation Y
71. Bar haz waste vctms suits Y
72. Prohibit aid to Nicaragua Y
73. Cut $-Schs bar sch prayer ?
74. Raise taxes; Cut Medicare N
75. Alien residncy-prior 1982 ?
76. Alien residncy-prior 1980 N

STUMP, BOB (Cont.)

77. Pen emp-hire illgl aliens N
78. Lmt Persh II/cruse-Europe N
79. Delete 34 B-1 bombers N
80. Bar purch of Pershing II N
81. Bar purchase of Sgt York ?
82. Delete $ for Trident II N
83. Allow 15 MX missiles Y
84. Bar MX procurement-1985 N
85. Equal Access Act N
86. Aid to El Salvador Y
87. Bar Nicarag water mining N
88. Physician/Medicare freeze Y
89. Increase "sin" taxes N
90. End SBA direct loans Y
91. Sell Conrail Y
92. Equal Rights Amendment N
93. Marines in Lebanon Y
94. Eminent domain-Coal comps N
95. Prohibit EPA sanctions Y
96. SS age increase/Reforms Y
97. Auto domestic content req N
98. Delete jobs program fundg Y
99. Highway-Gas tax bill N
100. Raise Medicare;Cut defnse N
101. Emergency housing aid N
102. Across-the-board tax cuts Y
103. Gramm-Latta II targets Y
104. Delete B-1 bomber funds N
105. Dsapprov Saudi AWACS sale N
106. Disapprove oil import fee Y
107. Rail Deregulation N
108. Dsapp India nuc fuel sale N
109. Mil draft registration Y
110. Chrysler Loan Guarantees N
111. Prohibit school busing Y
112. Nuclear plant moratorium N
113. Oil price controls N
114. Tuition Tax Credits N
115. Est Consumer Protect Agcy N
116. Eliminate B-1 bomber fnds N
117. Subminimum wage for youth Y
118. Delete crude oil tax Y
119. Natural gas deregulation Y

Presidential Support Score: 1986 - 89% 1985 - 84%

RUDD, ELDON -- Arizona 4th District [Republican]. Counties of Apache (pt.) Gila, Graham (pt.), Maricopa (pt.), Navajo and Pinal (pt.) Prior Terms: House: 1977-86. Born: July 15, 1920; Camp Verda, Ariz. Education: Arizona State University (B.A.); University of Arizona (J.D.). Military Service: U.S. Marine Corps, 1942-46. Occupation: FBI special agent (1950-1970); member, Maricopa County Board of Supervisors (1972); member, Governor's Advisory Council on Intergovernmental Relations (1975-76); member, Scottsdale Sister City Commission (1973-76).

1. Immigration Reform ?
2. Open fld-search warrants ?
3. Civil pnty-hire ill alien ?
4. So Afr sanc-veto override N
5. Tax Overhaul Y
6. South Africa sanctions ?
7. Death penalty-drug bill ?
8. Evidence-warrantless srch ?
9. Life term-second drug off ?
10. Military use in drug war ?
11. Troop reduction in Europe N
12. Prohibit chemical weapons N
13. Bar ASAT testing N
14. Abide SALT II weapons ban N
15. Follow SALT II-Soviets do Y
16. Reduce SDI funding N
17. Increase SDI funding Y
18. Purchase Trident sub N
19. Delete 12 MX;Add conv wpn N
20. Raise speed limit Y
21. Textile Import Quotas(*) N
22. Req Pentagon buy US goods N
23. AIDS ins anti-dscriminatn N
24. Nicaraguan refugee aid N
25. Nicaraguan contra aid Y
26. US abide by SALT II ?
27. Prohibit Saudi arms sale N
28. Military Retiremnt Reform Y
29. Nicaraguan refugee aid Y
30. Ease '68 Gun Control Act Y
31. Bar intrstat handgun tran N
32. Keep '68 Gun Control Act N
33. Nicaraguan contra aid Y
34. Bar emp polygraph testing X
35. Tax Overhaul consideratn N
36. Bar armor-piercing ammo N
37. Tax Overhaul consideratn N
38. Make comp emissions known N
39. Allow toxic victims suits N
40. Strike Superfund "VAT" Y
41. Notify emp-plant closing N
42. Bar emp consult-plant clo #
43. Medicare cuts;Tax incres' N
44. Delete 12 MX missiles N

RUDD, ELDON (Cont.)

45.	Spending cuts;Tax incres'	N	83.	Allow 15 MX missiles	Y
46.	Textile Import Quotas	?	84.	Bar MX procurement-1985	N
47.	Cut some school lunch fds	Y	85.	Equal Access Act	Y
48.	Clean Water Act Amendmnts	Y	86.	Aid to El Salvador	Y
49.	Youth work projects	N	87.	Bar Nicarag water mining	X
50.	Assist military in Angola	Y	88.	Physician/Medicare freeze	#
51.	Allow US troops-Nicaragua	Y	89.	Increase "sin" taxes	N
52.	Pentagon polygraph exams	Y	90.	End SBA direct loans	Y
53.	Bar ASAT testing	N	91.	Sell Conrail	?
54.	Suspend def pmt for abuse	N	92.	Equal Rights Amendment	N
55.	Bar Pentagon-contr emplmt	N	93.	Marines in Lebanon	Y
56.	Increase SDI funding	Y	94.	Eminent domain-Coal comps	N
57.	Reduce SDI funding	N	95.	Prohibit EPA sanctions	Y
58.	Produce chemical weapons	Y	96.	SS age increase/Reforms	Y
59.	Bar CIA fndg in Nicaragua	N	97.	Auto domestic content req	N
60.	South Africa sanctions	N	98.	Delete jobs program fundg	Y
61.	Cut SS COLAs; Raise taxes	Y	99.	Highway-Gas tax bill	N
62.	Let US invest-So Africa	#	100.	Raise Medicare;Cut defnse	N
63.	Approve 21 MX for 1985	Y	101.	Emergency housing aid	N
64.	Emergency Farm Credit	N	102.	Across-the-board tax cuts	Y
65.	Awards to whistle blowers	Y	103.	Gramm-Latta II targets	Y
66.	African disaster relief	N	104.	Delete B-1 bomber funds	N
67.	Ban bank loans to So Afr	?	105.	Dsapprov Saudi AWACS sale	Y
68.	Bar coun duty-free trtmt	?	106.	Disapprove oil import fee	Y
69.	Steel import limits	?	107.	Rail Deregulation	N
70.	Soc Sec COLAs=inflation	Y	108.	Dsapp India nuc fuel sale	Y
71.	Bar haz waste vctms suits	Y	109.	Mil draft registration	Y
72.	Prohibit aid to Nicaragua	N	110.	Chrysler Loan Guarantees	N
73.	Cut $-Schs bar sch prayer	Y	111.	Prohibit school busing	Y
74.	Raise taxes; Cut Medicare	N	112.	Nuclear plant moratorium	N
75.	Alien residncy-prior 1982	Y	113.	Oil price controls	N
76.	Alien residncy-prior 1980	Y	114.	Tuition Tax Credits	#
77.	Pen emp-hire illgl aliens	N	115.	Est Consumer Protect Agcy	N
78.	Lmt Persh II/cruse-Europe	N	116.	Eliminate B-1 bomber fnds	N
79.	Delete 34 B-1 bombers	N	117.	Subminimum wage for youth	Y
80.	Bar purch of Pershing II	N	118.	Delete crude oil tax	Y
81.	Bar purchase of Sgt York	N	119.	Natural gas deregulation	Y
82.	Delete $ for Trident II	N			

Presidential Support Score: 1986 - 66% 1985 - 79%

KOLBE, JIM -- Arizona 5th District [Republican]. Counties of Apache (pt.), Cochise, Graham (pt.), Greenlee, Pima (pt.), Pinal (pt.) and Santa Cruz (pt.). Prior Terms: House: 1985-86. Education: Northwestern University; Stanford University (M.B.A.). Occupation: Professional consultant; Arizona senator.

1.	Immigration Reform	N	10.	Military use in drug war	Y
2.	Open fld-search warrants	Y	11.	Troop reduction in Europe	N
3.	Civil pnty-hire ill alien	Y	12.	Prohibit chemical weapons	Y
4.	So Afr sanc-veto override	Y	13.	Bar ASAT testing	N
5.	Tax Overhaul	Y	14.	Abide SALT II weapons ban	N
6.	South Africa sanctions	Y	15.	Follow SALT II-Soviets do	Y
7.	Death penalty-drug bill	Y	16.	Reduce SDI funding	N
8.	Evidence-warrantless srch	Y	17.	Increase SDI funding	N
9.	Life term-second drug off	Y	18.	Purchase Trident sub	N

KOLBE, JIM (Cont.)

19.	Delete 12 MX;Add conv wpn	N	43.	Medicare cuts;Tax incres'	N
20.	Raise speed limit	Y	44.	Delete 12 MX missiles	N
21.	Textile Import Quotas(*)	N	45.	Spending cuts;Tax incres'	N
22.	Req Pentagon buy US goods	N	46.	Textile Import Quotas	N
23.	AIDS ins anti-dscriminatn	Y	47.	Cut some school lunch fds	Y
24.	Nicaraguan refugee aid	N	48.	Clean Water Act Amendmnts	N
25.	Nicaraguan contra aid	Y	49.	Youth work projects	N
26.	US abide by SALT II	Y	50.	Assist military in Angola	Y
27.	Prohibit Saudi arms sale	Y	51.	Allow US troops-Nicaragua	Y
28.	Military Retiremnt Reform	Y	52.	Pentagon polygraph exams	Y
29.	Nicaraguan refugee aid	Y	53.	Bar ASAT testing	N
30.	Ease '68 Gun Control Act	Y	54.	Suspend def pmt for abuse	N
31.	Bar intrstat handgun tran	N	55.	Bar Pentagon-contr emplmt	Y
32.	Keep '68 Gun Control Act	N	56.	Increase SDI funding	N
33.	Nicaraguan contra aid	Y	57.	Reduce SDI funding	N
34.	Bar emp polygraph testing	N	58.	Produce chemical weapons	Y
35.	Tax Overhaul consideratn	N	59.	Bar CIA fndg in Nicaragua	N
36.	Bar armor-piercing ammo	N	60.	South Africa sanctions	N
37.	Tax Overhaul consideratn	N	61.	Cut SS COLAs; Raise taxes	N
38.	Make comp emissions known	Y	62.	Let US invest-So Africa	Y
39.	Allow toxic victims suits	N	63.	Approve 21 MX for 1985	Y
40.	Strike Superfund "VAT"	N	64.	Emergency Farm Credit	N
41.	Notify emp-plant closing	N	65.	Awards to whistle blowers	Y
42.	Bar emp consult-plant clo	Y	66.	African disaster relief	Y

Presidential Support Score: 1986 - 70% 1985 - 78%

ARKANSAS

ALEXANDER, BILL -- Arkansas 1st District [Democrat]. Counties of Arkansas, Clay, Cleburne, Craighead, Critenden, Cross, Fulton, Greene, Independence, Izard, Jackson, Lawrence, Lee, Mississippi, Monroe, Phillips, Poinsett, Prairie, Randolph, St. Francis, Sharp, Stone, Van Buren and Woodruff. Prior Terms: House: 1971-86. Born: January 16, 1934; Memphis, Tenn. Education: University of Arkansas; Southwestern University (B.A.); Venderbilt University (LL.B.). Military Service: U.S. Army, 1951-53. Occupation: Legal research assistant; attorney; Arkansas Waterways commissioner; Port Authority secretary; attorney, Mississippi County Urban Renewal Agency.

1.	Immigration Reform	Y	17.	Increase SDI funding	N
2.	Open fld-search warrants	N	18.	Purchase Trident sub	N
3.	Civil pnty-hire ill alien	N	19.	Delete 12 MX;Add conv wpn	?
4.	So Afr sanc-veto override	Y	20.	Raise speed limit	N
5.	Tax Overhaul	Y	21.	Textile Import Quotas(*)	Y
6.	South Africa sanctions	Y	22.	Req Pentagon buy US goods	Y
7.	Death penalty-drug bill	Y	23.	AIDS ins anti-dscriminatn	Y
8.	Evidence-warrantless srch	Y	24.	Nicaraguan refugee aid	Y
9.	Life term-second drug off	Y	25.	Nicaraguan contra aid	N
10.	Military use in drug war	N	26.	US abide by SALT II	N
11.	Troop reduction in Europe	Y	27.	Prohibit Saudi arms sale	Y
12.	Prohibit chemical weapons	N	28.	Military Retiremnt Reform	?
13.	Bar ASAT testing	Y	29.	Nicaraguan refugee aid	Y
14.	Abide SALT II weapons ban	Y	30.	Ease '68 Gun Control Act	Y
15.	Follow SALT II-Soviets do	N	31.	Bar intrstat handgun tran	N
16.	Reduce SDI funding	N	32.	Keep '68 Gun Control Act	N

ALEXANDER, BILL (Cont.)

33. Nicaraguan contra aid N
34. Bar emp polygraph testing Y
35. Tax Overhaul consideratn Y
36. Bar armor-piercing ammo Y
37. Tax Overhaul consideratn Y
38. Make comp emissions known Y
39. Allow toxic victims suits Y
40. Strike Superfund "VAT" N
41. Notify emp-plant closing Y
42. Bar emp consult-plant clo N
43. Medicare cuts;Tax incres' Y
44. Delete 12 MX missiles N
45. Spending cuts;Tax incres' Y
46. Textile Import Quotas Y
47. Cut some school lunch fds N
48. Clean Water Act Amendmnts N
49. Youth work projects Y
50. Assist military in Angola N
51. Allow US troops-Nicaragua N
52. Pentagon polygraph exams Y
53. Bar ASAT testing ?
54. Suspend def pmt for abuse N
55. Bar Pentagon-contr emplmt Y
56. Increase SDI funding N
57. Reduce SDI funding N
58. Produce chemical weapons Y
59. Bar CIA fndg in Nicaragua Y
60. South Africa sanctions Y
61. Cut SS COLAs; Raise taxes N
62. Let US invest-So Africa X
63. Approve 21 MX for 1985 N
64. Emergency Farm Credit Y
65. Awards to whistle blowers Y
66. African disaster relief Y
67. Ban bank loans to So Afr ?
68. Bar coun duty-free trtmt Y
69. Steel import limits Y
70. Soc Sec COLAs=inflation ?
71. Bar haz waste vctms suits N
72. Prohibit aid to Nicaragua Y
73. Cut $-Schs bar sch prayer ?
74. Raise taxes; Cut Medicare Y
75. Alien residncy-prior 1982 Y
76. Alien residncy-prior 1980 N
77. Pen emp-hire illgl aliens Y
78. Lmt Persh II/cruse-Europe ?
79. Delete 34 B-1 bombers N
80. Bar purch of Pershing II N
81. Bar purchase of Sgt York N
82. Delete $ for Trident II N
83. Allow 15 MX missiles Y
84. Bar MX procurement-1985 N
85. Equal Access Act Y
86. Aid to El Salvador N
87. Bar Nicarag water mining Y
88. Physician/Medicare freeze N
89. Increase "sin" taxes Y
90. End SBA direct loans N
91. Sell Conrail N
92. Equal Rights Amendment Y
93. Marines in Lebanon Y
94. Eminent domain-Coal comps Y
95. Prohibit EPA sanctions ?
96. SS age increase/Reforms Y
97. Auto domestic content req #
98. Delete jobs program fundg N
99. Highway-Gas tax bill ?
100. Raise Medicare;Cut defnse N
101. Emergency housing aid Y
102. Across-the-board tax cuts N
103. Gramm-Latta II targets N
104. Delete B-1 bomber funds N
105. Dsapprov Saudi AWACS sale N
106. Disapprove oil import fee Y
107. Rail Deregulation ?
108. Dsapp India nuc fuel sale N
109. Mil draft registration Y
110. Chrysler Loan Guarantees ?
111. Prohibit school busing N
112. Nuclear plant moratorium N
113. Oil price controls N
114. Tuition Tax Credits N
115. Est Consumer Protect Agcy N
116. Eliminate B-1 bomber fnds N
117. Subminimum wage for youth Y
118. Delete crude oil tax N
119. Natural gas deregulation N

Presidential Support Score: 1986 - 22% 1985 - 25%

ROBINSON, TOMMY -- Arkansas 2nd District [Democrat]. Counties of Conway, Faulkner, Lonoke, Perry, Pulaski, Saline, White and Yell. Prior Terms: 1985-86. Born: March 7, 1942. Education: University of Arkansas (B.A.). Military Service: U.S. Navy, 1959-63. Occupation: Sheriff, state director of public safety; police chief.

1. Immigration Reform N
2. Open fld-search warrants N
3. Civil pnty-hire ill alien N
4. So Afr sanc-veto override Y
5. Tax Overhaul N
6. South Africa sanctions Y

ROBINSON, TOMMY (Cont.)

7. Death penalty-drug bill Y
8. Evidence-warrantless srch Y
9. Life term-second drug off Y
10. Military use in drug war Y
11. Troop reduction in Europe Y
12. Prohibit chemical weapons N
13. Bar ASAT testing N
14. Abide SALT II weapons ban N
15. Follow SALT II-Soviets do Y
16. Reduce SDI funding N
17. Increase SDI funding Y
18. Purchase Trident sub Y
19. Delete 12 MX;Add conv wpn N
20. Raise speed limit N
21. Textile Import Quotas(*) Y
22. Req Pentagon buy US goods Y
23. AIDS ins anti-dscriminatn N
24. Nicaraguan refugee aid N
25. Nicaraguan contra aid Y
26. US abide by SALT II N
27. Prohibit Saudi arms sale Y
28. Military Retiremnt Reform ?
29. Nicaraguan refugee aid N
30. Ease '68 Gun Control Act Y
31. Bar intrstat handgun tran N
32. Keep '68 Gun Control Act N
33. Nicaraguan contra aid Y
34. Bar emp polygraph testing Y
35. Tax Overhaul consideratn N
36. Bar armor-piercing ammo Y
37. Tax Overhaul consideratn N
38. Make comp emissions known Y
39. Allow toxic victims suits Y
40. Strike Superfund "VAT" Y
41. Notify emp-plant closing Y
42. Bar emp consult-plant clo N
43. Medicare cuts;Tax incres' Y
44. Delete 12 MX missiles N
45. Spending cuts;Tax incres' N
46. Textile Import Quotas Y
47. Cut some school lunch fds N
48. Clean Water Act Amendmnts N
49. Youth work projects ?
50. Assist military in Angola Y
51. Allow US troops-Nicaragua Y
52. Pentagon polygraph exams Y
53. Bar ASAT testing N
54. Suspend def pmt for abuse Y
55. Bar Pentagon-contr emplmt Y
56. Increase SDI funding Y
57. Reduce SDI funding N
58. Produce chemical weapons Y
59. Bar CIA fndg in Nicaragua N
60. South Africa sanctions Y
61. Cut SS COLAs; Raise taxes N
62. Let US invest-So Africa N
63. Approve 21 MX for 1985 Y
64. Emergency Farm Credit Y
65. Awards to whistle blowers Y
66. African disaster relief Y

Presidential Support Score: 1986 - 44% 1985 - 45%

HAMMERSCHMIDT, JOHN PAUL -- Arkansas 3rd District [Republican]. Counties of Baxter, Benton, Boone, Carroll, Crawford, Franklin, Howard, Johnson, Logan, Madison, Marion, Montgomery, Newton, Polk, Pope, Scott, Searcy, Sebastion, Sevier and Washington. Prior Terms: House: 1967-86. Born: May 4, 1922; Harrison, Ark. Education: The Citadel; Oklahoma A & M College; University of Arkansas. Military Service: U.S. Army Air Corps, WW II; Air Force Reserve. Occupation: Board chairman, Hammerschmidt Lumber Co.; board member, Harrison Federal Savings and Loan Assn.; boardmember, National Lumber and Building Material Dealers; president, Boone County Industrial Development Corp.; chairman, City Planning Commission; Harrison city councilman.

1. Immigration Reform N
2. Open fld-search warrants Y
3. Civil pnty-hire ill alien N
4. So Afr sanc-veto override N
5. Tax Overhaul N
6. South Africa sanctions N
7. Death penalty-drug bill Y
8. Evidence-warrantless srch Y
9. Life term-second drug off Y
10. Military use in drug war Y
11. Troop reduction in Europe N
12. Prohibit chemical weapons N
13. Bar ASAT testing N
14. Abide SALT II weapons ban N
15. Follow SALT II-Soviets do Y
16. Reduce SDI funding N
17. Increase SDI funding Y
18. Purchase Trident sub N
19. Delete 12 MX;Add conv wpn N
20. Raise speed limit N

HAMMERSCHMIDT, JOHN PAUL (Cont.)

21. Textile Import Quotas(*) Y
22. Req Pentagon buy US goods N
23. AIDS ins anti-dscriminatn N
24. Nicaraguan refugee aid N
25. Nicaraguan contra aid Y
26. US abide by SALT II Y
27. Prohibit Saudi arms sale Y
28. Military Retiremnt Reform Y
29. Nicaraguan refugee aid Y
30. Ease '68 Gun Control Act Y
31. Bar intrstat handgun tran N
32. Keep '68 Gun Control Act N
33. Nicaraguan contra aid Y
34. Bar emp polygraph testing N
35. Tax Overhaul consideratn Y
36. Bar armor-piercing ammo Y
37. Tax Overhaul consideratn N
38. Make comp emissions known N
39. Allow toxic victims suits N
40. Strike Superfund "VAT" N
41. Notify emp-plant closing N
42. Bar emp consult-plant clo Y
43. Medicare cuts;Tax incres' Y
44. Delete 12 MX missiles N
45. Spending cuts;Tax incres' N
46. Textile Import Quotas Y
47. Cut some school lunch fds N
48. Clean Water Act Amendmnts Y
49. Youth work projects N
50. Assist military in Angola Y
51. Allow US troops-Nicaragua Y
52. Pentagon polygraph exams Y
53. Bar ASAT testing N
54. Suspend def pmt for abuse N
55. Bar Pentagon-contr emplmt Y
56. Increase SDI funding Y
57. Reduce SDI funding N
58. Produce chemical weapons Y
59. Bar CIA fndg in Nicaragua N
60. South Africa sanctions N
61. Cut SS COLAs; Raise taxes N
62. Let US invest-So Africa Y
63. Approve 21 MX for 1985 Y
64. Emergency Farm Credit Y
65. Awards to whistle blowers Y
66. African disaster relief Y
67. Ban bank loans to So Afr ?
68. Bar coun duty-free trtmt N
69. Steel import limits N
70. Soc Sec COLAs=inflation Y
71. Bar haz waste vctms suits Y
72. Prohibit aid to Nicaragua N
73. Cut $-Schs bar sch prayer Y
74. Raise taxes; Cut Medicare N
75. Alien residncy-prior 1982 N
76. Alien residncy-prior 1980 N
77. Pen emp-hire illgl aliens N
78. Lmt Persh II/cruse-Europe N
79. Delete 34 B-1 bombers N
80. Bar purch of Pershing II N
81. Bar purchase of Sgt York N
82. Delete $ for Trident II N
83. Allow 15 MX missiles Y
84. Bar MX procurement-1985 N
85. Equal Access Act Y
86. Aid to El Salvador Y
87. Bar Nicarag water mining N
88. Physician/Medicare freeze Y
89. Increase "sin" taxes N
90. End SBA direct loans N
91. Sell Conrail Y
92. Equal Rights Amendment N
93. Marines in Lebanon Y
94. Eminent domain-Coal comps N
95. Prohibit EPA sanctions Y
96. SS age increase/Reforms Y
97. Auto domestic content req N
98. Delete jobs program fundg Y
99. Highway-Gas tax bill N
100. Raise Medicare;Cut defnse N
101. Emergency housing aid Y
102. Across-the-board tax cuts Y
103. Gramm-Latta II targets Y
104. Delete B-1 bomber funds N
105. Dsapprov Saudi AWACS sale N
106. Disapprove oil import fee Y
107. Rail Deregulation N
108. Dsapp India nuc fuel sale Y
109. Mil draft registration ?
110. Chrysler Loan Guarantees N
111. Prohibit school busing Y
112. Nuclear plant moratorium Y
113. Oil price controls N
114. Tuition Tax Credits N
115. Est Consumer Protect Agcy N
116. Eliminate B-1 bomber fnds N
117. Subminimum wage for youth Y
118. Delete crude oil tax Y
119. Natural gas deregulation Y

Presidential Support Score: 1986 - 69% 1985 - 64%

ANTHONY, BERYL, Jr. -- Arkansas 4th District [Democrat]. Counties of Ashley, Bradley, Calhoun, Chicot, Clark, Cleveland, Columbia, Dallas, Desha, Drew, Garland, Grant, Hempstead, Hot Spring, Jefferson, Lafayette, Lincoln, Little River, Miller,

ANTHONY, BERYL, Jr. (Cont.)
Nevada, Ouachita, Pike and Union. Prior Terms: House: 1979-86. Born: February 21, 1938; El Dorado, Ark. Education: University of Arkansas (B.S., B.A., J.D.). Occupation: Attorney; assistant attorney general (1964-65); deputy prosecuting attorney (1966-70); prosecuting attorney (1971-76); legal counsel, Anthony Forest Products Co. (1977).

1. Immigration Reform Y
2. Open fld-search warrants N
3. Civil pnty-hire ill alien Y
4. So Afr sanc-veto override #
5. Tax Overhaul Y
6. South Africa sanctions Y
7. Death penalty-drug bill Y
8. Evidence-warrantless srch Y
9. Life term-second drug off Y
10. Military use in drug war N
11. Troop reduction in Europe N
12. Prohibit chemical weapons N
13. Bar ASAT testing Y
14. Abide SALT II weapons ban Y
15. Follow SALT II-Soviets do N
16. Reduce SDI funding N
17. Increase SDI funding N
18. Purchase Trident sub ?
19. Delete 12 MX;Add conv wpn Y
20. Raise speed limit N
21. Textile Import Quotas(*) Y
22. Req Pentagon buy US goods N
23. AIDS ins anti-dscriminatn Y
24. Nicaraguan refugee aid N
25. Nicaraguan contra aid N
26. US abide by SALT II X
27. Prohibit Saudi arms sale Y
28. Military Retiremnt Reform ?
29. Nicaraguan refugee aid Y
30. Ease '68 Gun Control Act Y
31. Bar intrstat handgun tran Y
32. Keep '68 Gun Control Act Y
33. Nicaraguan contra aid N
34. Bar emp polygraph testing Y
35. Tax Overhaul consideratn Y
36. Bar armor-piercing ammo Y
37. Tax Overhaul consideratn Y
38. Make comp emissions known N
39. Allow toxic victims suits N
40. Strike Superfund "VAT" N
41. Notify emp-plant closing N
42. Bar emp consult-plant clo Y
43. Medicare cuts;Tax incres' Y
44. Delete 12 MX missiles Y
45. Spending cuts;Tax incres' Y
46. Textile Import Quotas Y
47. Cut some school lunch fds N
48. Clean Water Act Amendmnts N
49. Youth work projects Y
50. Assist military in Angola Y
51. Allow US troops-Nicaragua N
52. Pentagon polygraph exams N
53. Bar ASAT testing Y
54. Suspend def pmt for abuse N
55. Bar Pentagon-contr emplmt Y
56. Increase SDI funding N
57. Reduce SDI funding N
58. Produce chemical weapons Y
59. Bar CIA fndg in Nicaragua Y
60. South Africa sanctions Y
61. Cut SS COLAs; Raise taxes Y
62. Let US invest-So Africa N
63. Approve 21 MX for 1985 N
64. Emergency Farm Credit Y
65. Awards to whistle blowers Y
66. African disaster relief Y
67. Ban bank loans to So Afr Y
68. Bar coun duty-free trtmt N
69. Steel import limits N
70. Soc Sec COLAs=inflation Y
71. Bar haz waste vctms suits ?
72. Prohibit aid to Nicaragua ?
73. Cut $-Schs bar sch prayer N
74. Raise taxes; Cut Medicare Y
75. Alien residncy-prior 1982 Y
76. Alien residncy-prior 1980 N
77. Pen emp-hire illgl aliens N
78. Lmt Persh II/cruse-Europe X
79. Delete 34 B-1 bombers N
80. Bar purch of Pershing II N
81. Bar purchase of Sgt York ?
82. Delete $ for Trident II ?
83. Allow 15 MX missiles N
84. Bar MX procurement-1985 Y
85. Equal Access Act Y
86. Aid to El Salvador N
87. Bar Nicarag water mining Y
88. Physician/Medicare freeze N
89. Increase "sin" taxes Y
90. End SBA direct loans N
91. Sell Conrail N
92. Equal Rights Amendment +
93. Marines in Lebanon Y
94. Eminent domain-Coal comps N
95. Prohibit EPA sanctions N
96. SS age increase/Reforms Y
97. Auto domestic content req N
98. Delete jobs program fundg N
99. Highway-Gas tax bill Y
100. Raise Medicare;Cut defnse Y
101. Emergency housing aid Y
102. Across-the-board tax cuts N

ANTHONY, BERYL, Jr. (Cont.)

103. Gramm-Latta II targets Y
104. Delete B-1 bomber funds N
105. Dsapprov Saudi AWACS sale N
106. Disapprove oil import fee Y
107. Rail Deregulation N
108. Dsapp India nuc fuel sale N
109. Mil draft registration ?
110. Chrysler Loan Guarantees N
111. Prohibit school busing N
112. Nuclear plant moratorium X
113. Oil price controls N

Presidential Support Score: 1986 - 26% 1985 - 28%

C A L I F O R N I A

BOSCO, DOUGLAS H. -- California 1st District [Democrat]. Counties of Del Norte, Glenn, Humboldt, Mendocino, Sonoma and Trinity. Prior Terms: House: 1983-86. Born: July 28, 1946; New York. Education: Willamette University (B.A.). Occupation: California ssemblyman; attorney; cofounded Northern California's Emeritus College for Senior Citizens.

1. Immigration Reform Y
2. Open fld-search warrants Y
3. Civil pnty-hire ill alien ?
4. So Afr sanc-veto override Y
5. Tax Overhaul N
6. South Africa sanctions Y
7. Death penalty-drug bill Y
8. Evidence-warrantless srch N
9. Life term-second drug off N
10. Military use in drug war N
11. Troop reduction in Europe ?
12. Prohibit chemical weapons N
13. Bar ASAT testing Y
14. Abide SALT II weapons ban Y
15. Follow SALT II-Soviets do N
16. Reduce SDI funding N
17. Increase SDI funding N
18. Purchase Trident sub N
19. Delete 12 MX;Add conv wpn Y
20. Raise speed limit N
21. Textile Import Quotas(*) Y
22. Req Pentagon buy US goods ?
23. AIDS ins anti-dscriminatn Y
24. Nicaraguan refugee aid Y
25. Nicaraguan contra aid N
26. US abide by SALT II N
27. Prohibit Saudi arms sale Y
28. Military Retiremnt Reform Y
29. Nicaraguan refugee aid Y
30. Ease '68 Gun Control Act Y
31. Bar intrstat handgun tran N
32. Keep '68 Gun Control Act N
33. Nicaraguan contra aid N
34. Bar emp polygraph testing Y
35. Tax Overhaul consideratn Y
36. Bar armor-piercing ammo Y
37. Tax Overhaul consideratn Y
38. Make comp emissions known Y
39. Allow toxic victims suits N
40. Strike Superfund "VAT" N
41. Notify emp-plant closing Y
42. Bar emp consult-plant clo Y
43. Medicare cuts;Tax incres' Y
44. Delete 12 MX missiles Y
45. Spending cuts;Tax incres' Y
46. Textile Import Quotas N
47. Cut some school lunch fds N
48. Clean Water Act Amendmnts N
49. Youth work projects ?
50. Assist military in Angola N
51. Allow US troops-Nicaragua N
52. Pentagon polygraph exams Y
53. Bar ASAT testing Y
54. Suspend def pmt for abuse Y
55. Bar Pentagon-contr emplmt Y
56. Increase SDI funding N
57. Reduce SDI funding N
58. Produce chemical weapons Y
59. Bar CIA fndg in Nicaragua ?
60. South Africa sanctions Y
61. Cut SS COLAs; Raise taxes Y
62. Let US invest-So Africa N
63. Approve 21 MX for 1985 N
64. Emergency Farm Credit N
65. Awards to whistle blowers ?
66. African disaster relief Y
67. Ban bank loans to So Afr Y
68. Bar coun duty-free trtmt Y
69. Steel import limits Y
70. Soc Sec COLAs=inflation Y
71. Bar haz waste vctms suits Y
72. Prohibit aid to Nicaragua Y
73. Cut $-Schs bar sch prayer N
74. Raise taxes; Cut Medicare Y
75. Alien residncy-prior 1982 N
76. Alien residncy-prior 1980 N

BOSCO, DOUGLAS H. (Cont.)

77. Pen emp-hire illgl aliens N
78. Lmt Persh II/cruse-Europe N
79. Delete 34 B-1 bombers Y
80. Bar purch of Pershing II Y
81. Bar purchase of Sgt York ?
82. Delete $ for Trident II Y
83. Allow 15 MX missiles N
84. Bar MX procurement-1985 Y
85. Equal Access Act N
86. Aid to El Salvador N
87. Bar Nicarag water mining Y
88. Physician/Medicare freeze N
89. Increase "sin" taxes Y
90. End SBA direct loans N
91. Sell Conrail N
92. Equal Rights Amendment Y
93. Marines in Lebanon N
94. Eminent domain-Coal comps Y
95. Prohibit EPA sanctions N
96. SS age increase/Reforms N

Presidential Support Score: 1986 - 22% 1985 - 26%

CHAPPIE, GENE -- California 2nd District [Republican]. Counties of Butte, Colusa, Lake, Napa, Shasta (pt.), Sutter, Tehama and Yuba. Prior Terms: House: 1981-86. Born: March 28, 1920; Sacramento, Calif. Military Service: U.S. Army. Occupation: Rancher; El Dorado county supervisor (1950-64); California assemblyman (1965-80).

1. Immigration Reform N
2. Open fld-search warrants Y
3. Civil pnty-hire ill alien Y
4. So Afr sanc-veto override N
5. Tax Overhaul N
6. South Africa sanctions ?
7. Death penalty-drug bill ?
8. Evidence-warrantless srch ?
9. Life term-second drug off ?
10. Military use in drug war ?
11. Troop reduction in Europe N
12. Prohibit chemical weapons N
13. Bar ASAT testing N
14. Abide SALT II weapons ban N
15. Follow SALT II-Soviets do Y
16. Reduce SDI funding N
17. Increase SDI funding Y
18. Purchase Trident sub N
19. Delete 12 MX;Add conv wpn N
20. Raise speed limit Y
21. Textile Import Quotas(*) N
22. Req Pentagon buy US goods N
23. AIDS ins anti-dscriminatn ?
24. Nicaraguan refugee aid N
25. Nicaraguan contra aid Y
26. US abide by SALT II Y
27. Prohibit Saudi arms sale Y
28. Military Retiremnt Reform Y
29. Nicaraguan refugee aid Y
30. Ease '68 Gun Control Act Y
31. Bar intrstat handgun tran N
32. Keep '68 Gun Control Act N
33. Nicaraguan contra aid Y
34. Bar emp polygraph testing N
35. Tax Overhaul consideratn N
36. Bar armor-piercing ammo Y
37. Tax Overhaul consideratn ?
38. Make comp emissions known ?
39. Allow toxic victims suits ?
40. Strike Superfund "VAT" X
41. Notify emp-plant closing X
42. Bar emp consult-plant clo Y
43. Medicare cuts;Tax incres' N
44. Delete 12 MX missiles N
45. Spending cuts;Tax incres' N
46. Textile Import Quotas N
47. Cut some school lunch fds Y
48. Clean Water Act Amendmnts Y
49. Youth work projects ?
50. Assist military in Angola Y
51. Allow US troops-Nicaragua Y
52. Pentagon polygraph exams Y
53. Bar ASAT testing N
54. Suspend def pmt for abuse N
55. Bar Pentagon-contr emplmt Y
56. Increase SDI funding N
57. Reduce SDI funding N
58. Produce chemical weapons Y
59. Bar CIA fndg in Nicaragua N
60. South Africa sanctions N
61. Cut SS COLAs; Raise taxes N
62. Let US invest-So Africa Y
63. Approve 21 MX for 1985 Y
64. Emergency Farm Credit Y
65. Awards to whistle blowers Y
66. African disaster relief Y
67. Ban bank loans to So Afr N
68. Bar coun duty-free trtmt N
69. Steel import limits N
70. Soc Sec COLAs=inflation Y
71. Bar haz waste vctms suits Y
72. Prohibit aid to Nicaragua Y
73. Cut $-Schs bar sch prayer ?
74. Raise taxes; Cut Medicare N

CHAPPIE, GENE (Cont.)

75. Alien residncy-prior 1982 Y
76. Alien residncy-prior 1980 Y
77. Pen emp-hire illgl aliens N
78. Lmt Persh II/cruse-Europe N
79. Delete 34 B-1 bombers N
80. Bar purch of Pershing II N
81. Bar purchase of Sgt York N
82. Delete $ for Trident II N
83. Allow 15 MX missiles Y
84. Bar MX procurement-1985 N
85. Equal Access Act Y
86. Aid to El Salvador Y
87. Bar Nicarag water mining ?
88. Physician/Medicare freeze Y
89. Increase "sin" taxes Y
90. End SBA direct loans N
91. Sell Conrail Y
92. Equal Rights Amendment Y
93. Marines in Lebanon Y
94. Eminent domain-Coal comps Y
95. Prohibit EPA sanctions ?
96. SS age increase/Reforms Y
97. Auto domestic content req N
98. Delete jobs program fundg #
99. Highway-Gas tax bill N
100. Raise Medicare;Cut defnse N
101. Emergency housing aid N
102. Across-the-board tax cuts Y
103. Gramm-Latta II targets Y
104. Delete B-1 bomber funds N
105. Dsapprov Saudi AWACS sale Y

Presidential Support Score: 1986 - 64% 1985 - 59%

MATSUI, ROBERT T. -- California 3rd District [Democrat]. County of Sacramento (pt.) Prior Terms: House: 1979-86. Born: September 17, 1941; Sacramento, Calif. Education: University of California (A.B.); Hastings College of Law (J.D.). Occupation: Attorney; city councilman (1971-78); vice mayor (1977).

1. Immigration Reform Y
2. Open fld-search warrants Y
3. Civil pnty-hire ill alien Y
4. So Afr sanc-veto override Y
5. Tax Overhaul Y
6. South Africa sanctions Y
7. Death penalty-drug bill N
8. Evidence-warrantless srch N
9. Life term-second drug off Y
10. Military use in drug war N
11. Troop reduction in Europe N
12. Prohibit chemical weapons Y
13. Bar ASAT testing Y
14. Abide SALT II weapons ban Y
15. Follow SALT II-Soviets do N
16. Reduce SDI funding Y
17. Increase SDI funding N
18. Purchase Trident sub Y
19. Delete 12 MX;Add conv wpn Y
20. Raise speed limit N
21. Textile Import Quotas(*) N
22. Req Pentagon buy US goods N
23. AIDS ins anti-dscriminatn Y
24. Nicaraguan refugee aid Y
25. Nicaraguan contra aid N
26. US abide by SALT II N
27. Prohibit Saudi arms sale Y
28. Military Retiremnt Reform Y
29. Nicaraguan refugee aid Y
30. Ease '68 Gun Control Act N
31. Bar intrstat handgun tran Y
32. Keep '68 Gun Control Act Y
33. Nicaraguan contra aid N
34. Bar emp polygraph testing Y
35. Tax Overhaul consideratn Y
36. Bar armor-piercing ammo Y
37. Tax Overhaul consideratn Y
38. Make comp emissions known Y
39. Allow toxic victims suits Y
40. Strike Superfund "VAT" Y
41. Notify emp-plant closing Y
42. Bar emp consult-plant clo N
43. Medicare cuts;Tax incres' Y
44. Delete 12 MX missiles Y
45. Spending cuts;Tax incres' Y
46. Textile Import Quotas N
47. Cut some school lunch fds N
48. Clean Water Act Amendmnts N
49. Youth work projects Y
50. Assist military in Angola N
51. Allow US troops-Nicaragua N
52. Pentagon polygraph exams N
53. Bar ASAT testing Y
54. Suspend def pmt for abuse Y
55. Bar Pentagon-contr emplmt Y
56. Increase SDI funding N
57. Reduce SDI funding Y
58. Produce chemical weapons N
59. Bar CIA fndg in Nicaragua Y
60. South Africa sanctions Y
61. Cut SS COLAs; Raise taxes N
62. Let US invest-So Africa N
63. Approve 21 MX for 1985 N
64. Emergency Farm Credit Y

MATSUI, ROBERT T. (Cont.)

65. Awards to whistle blowers Y
66. African disaster relief Y
67. Ban bank loans to So Afr Y
68. Bar coun duty-free trtmt Y
69. Steel import limits Y
70. Soc Sec COLAs=inflation Y
71. Bar haz waste vctms suits N
72. Prohibit aid to Nicaragua Y
73. Cut $-Schs bar sch prayer N
74. Raise taxes; Cut Medicare Y
75. Alien residncy-prior 1982 N
76. Alien residncy-prior 1980 N
77. Pen emp-hire illgl aliens Y
78. Lmt Persh II/cruse-Europe Y
79. Delete 34 B-1 bombers N
80. Bar purch of Pershing II Y
81. Bar purchase of Sgt York N
82. Delete $ for Trident II N
83. Allow 15 MX missiles N
84. Bar MX procurement-1985 Y
85. Equal Access Act N
86. Aid to El Salvador N
87. Bar Nicarag water mining Y
88. Physician/Medicare freeze N
89. Increase "sin" taxes Y
90. End SBA direct loans N
91. Sell Conrail N
92. Equal Rights Amendment Y
93. Marines in Lebanon Y
94. Eminent domain-Coal comps N
95. Prohibit EPA sanctions Y
96. SS age increase/Reforms Y
97. Auto domestic content req Y
98. Delete jobs program fundg N
99. Highway-Gas tax bill Y
100. Raise Medicare;Cut defnse Y
101. Emergency housing aid Y
102. Across-the-board tax cuts N
103. Gramm-Latta II targets N
104. Delete B-1 bomber funds N
105. Dsapprov Saudi AWACS sale Y
106. Disapprove oil import fee N
107. Rail Deregulation N
108. Dsapp India nuc fuel sale Y
109. Mil draft registration N
110. Chrysler Loan Guarantees Y
111. Prohibit school busing N
112. Nuclear plant moratorium Y
113. Oil price controls Y

Presidential Support Score: 1986 - 20% 1985 - 20%

FAZIO, VIC -- California 4th District [Democrat]. Counties of Sacramento (pt), Solano (pt.) and Yolo. Prior Terms: House: 1979-86. Born: October 11, 1942; Winchester, Mass. Education: Union College; California State University. Occupation: Cofounder, California Journal magazine; congressional and legislative consultant (1966-75); California assemblyman (1975-78).

1. Immigration Reform Y
2. Open fld-search warrants Y
3. Civil pnty-hire ill alien Y
4. So Afr sanc-veto override Y
5. Tax Overhaul N
6. South Africa sanctions Y
7. Death penalty-drug bill N
8. Evidence-warrantless srch N
9. Life term-second drug off Y
10. Military use in drug war N
11. Troop reduction in Europe N
12. Prohibit chemical weapons N
13. Bar ASAT testing Y
14. Abide SALT II weapons ban Y
15. Follow SALT II-Soviets do N
16. Reduce SDI funding N
17. Increase SDI funding N
18. Purchase Trident sub Y
19. Delete 12 MX;Add conv wpn N
20. Raise speed limit Y
21. Textile Import Quotas(*) Y
22. Req Pentagon buy US goods N
23. AIDS ins anti-dscriminatn Y
24. Nicaraguan refugee aid Y
25. Nicaraguan contra aid N
26. US abide by SALT II N
27. Prohibit Saudi arms sale Y
28. Military Retiremnt Reform Y
29. Nicaraguan refugee aid Y
30. Ease '68 Gun Control Act N
31. Bar intrstat handgun tran Y
32. Keep '68 Gun Control Act Y
33. Nicaraguan contra aid N
34. Bar emp polygraph testing Y
35. Tax Overhaul consideratn N
36. Bar armor-piercing ammo Y
37. Tax Overhaul consideratn N
38. Make comp emissions known Y
39. Allow toxic victims suits N
40. Strike Superfund "VAT" N
41. Notify emp-plant closing Y
42. Bar emp consult-plant clo N

FAZIO, VIC (Cont.)

No.	Issue	Vote
43.	Medicare cuts;Tax incres'	Y
44.	Delete 12 MX missiles	N
45.	Spending cuts;Tax incres'	Y
46.	Textile Import Quotas	Y
47.	Cut some school lunch fds	N
48.	Clean Water Act Amendmnts	N
49.	Youth work projects	#
50.	Assist military in Angola	N
51.	Allow US troops-Nicaragua	N
52.	Pentagon polygraph exams	Y
53.	Bar ASAT testing	Y
54.	Suspend def pmt for abuse	N
55.	Bar Pentagon-contr emplmt	Y
56.	Increase SDI funding	N
57.	Reduce SDI funding	N
58.	Produce chemical weapons	Y
59.	Bar CIA fndg in Nicaragua	Y
60.	South Africa sanctions	Y
61.	Cut SS COLAs; Raise taxes	Y
62.	Let US invest-So Africa	N
63.	Approve 21 MX for 1985	Y
64.	Emergency Farm Credit	Y
65.	Awards to whistle blowers	Y
66.	African disaster relief	Y
67.	Ban bank loans to So Afr	Y
68.	Bar coun duty-free trtmt	Y
69.	Steel import limits	Y
70.	Soc Sec COLAs=inflation	Y
71.	Bar haz waste vctms suits	N
72.	Prohibit aid to Nicaragua	Y
73.	Cut $-Schs bar sch prayer	N
74.	Raise taxes; Cut Medicare	Y
75.	Alien residncy-prior 1982	N
76.	Alien residncy-prior 1980	N
77.	Pen emp-hire illgl aliens	Y
78.	Lmt Persh II/cruse-Europe	N
79.	Delete 34 B-1 bombers	Y
80.	Bar purch of Pershing II	Y
81.	Bar purchase of Sgt York	Y
82.	Delete $ for Trident II	N
83.	Allow 15 MX missiles	Y
84.	Bar MX procurement-1985	N
85.	Equal Access Act	?
86.	Aid to El Salvador	N
87.	Bar Nicarag water mining	Y
88.	Physician/Medicare freeze	N
89.	Increase "sin" taxes	Y
90.	End SBA direct loans	N
91.	Sell Conrail	N
92.	Equal Rights Amendment	Y
93.	Marines in Lebanon	Y
94.	Eminent domain-Coal comps	N
95.	Prohibit EPA sanctions	Y
96.	SS age increase/Reforms	N
97.	Auto domestic content req	Y
98.	Delete jobs program fundg	N
99.	Highway-Gas tax bill	Y
100.	Raise Medicare;Cut defnse	Y
101.	Emergency housing aid	Y
102.	Across-the-board tax cuts	N
103.	Gramm-Latta II targets	N
104.	Delete B-1 bomber funds	Y
105.	Dsapprov Saudi AWACS sale	Y
106.	Disapprove oil import fee	N
107.	Rail Deregulation	N
108.	Dsapp India nuc fuel sale	Y
109.	Mil draft registration	Y
110.	Chrysler Loan Guarantees	Y
111.	Prohibit school busing	N
112.	Nuclear plant moratorium	Y
113.	Oil price controls	N

Presidential Support Score: 1986 - 20% 1985 - 26%

BURTON, SALA -- California 5th District [Democrat]. County of San Francisco (pt.) Prior Terms: House: 1983-86. Born: April 1, 1925; Bialystok, Poland. Education: San Francisco State University.

No.	Issue	Vote
1.	Immigration Reform	?
2.	Open fld-search warrants	?
3.	Civil pnty-hire ill alien	?
4.	So Afr sanc-veto override	?
5.	Tax Overhaul	?
6.	South Africa sanctions	?
7.	Death penalty-drug bill	?
8.	Evidence-warrantless srch	?
9.	Life term-second drug off	?
10.	Military use in drug war	?
11.	Troop reduction in Europe	?
12.	Prohibit chemical weapons	?
13.	Bar ASAT testing	?
14.	Abide SALT II weapons ban	?
15.	Follow SALT II-Soviets do	X
16.	Reduce SDI funding	?
17.	Increase SDI funding	?
18.	Purchase Trident sub	?
19.	Delete 12 MX;Add conv wpn	?
20.	Raise speed limit	N
21.	Textile Import Quotas(*)	Y
22.	Req Pentagon buy US goods	Y
23.	AIDS ins anti-dscriminatn	Y
24.	Nicaraguan refugee aid	Y
25.	Nicaraguan contra aid	N
26.	US abide by SALT II	X

BURTON, SALA (Cont.)

27. Prohibit Saudi arms sale Y
28. Military Retiremnt Reform Y
29. Nicaraguan refugee aid Y
30. Ease '68 Gun Control Act N
31. Bar intrstat handgun tran Y
32. Keep '68 Gun Control Act Y
33. Nicaraguan contra aid N
34. Bar emp polygraph testing Y
35. Tax Overhaul consideratn Y
36. Bar armor-piercing ammo Y
37. Tax Overhaul consideratn Y
38. Make comp emissions known Y
39. Allow toxic victims suits Y
40. Strike Superfund "VAT" Y
41. Notify emp-plant closing Y
42. Bar emp consult-plant clo N
43. Medicare cuts;Tax incres' Y
44. Delete 12 MX missiles Y
45. Spending cuts;Tax incres' Y
46. Textile Import Quotas Y
47. Cut some school lunch fds N
48. Clean Water Act Amendmnts N
49. Youth work projects Y
50. Assist military in Angola N
51. Allow US troops-Nicaragua N
52. Pentagon polygraph exams N
53. Bar ASAT testing Y
54. Suspend def pmt for abuse Y
55. Bar Pentagon-contr emplmt Y
56. Increase SDI funding N
57. Reduce SDI funding Y
58. Produce chemical weapons N
59. Bar CIA fndg in Nicaragua Y
60. South Africa sanctions Y
61. Cut SS COLAs; Raise taxes N
62. Let US invest-So Africa N
63. Approve 21 MX for 1985 N
64. Emergency Farm Credit Y
65. Awards to whistle blowers Y
66. African disaster relief Y
67. Ban bank loans to So Afr Y
68. Bar coun duty-free trtmt Y
69. Steel import limits Y
70. Soc Sec COLAs=inflation Y
71. Bar haz waste vctms suits ?
72. Prohibit aid to Nicaragua Y
73. Cut $-Schs bar sch prayer N
74. Raise taxes; Cut Medicare Y
75. Alien residncy-prior 1982 N
76. Alien residncy-prior 1980 N
77. Pen emp-hire illgl aliens Y
78. Lmt Persh II/cruse-Europe Y
79. Delete 34 B-1 bombers Y
80. Bar purch of Pershing II Y
81. Bar purchase of Sgt York Y
82. Delete $ for Trident II Y
83. Allow 15 MX missiles N
84. Bar MX procurement-1985 Y
85. Equal Access Act N
86. Aid to El Salvador N
87. Bar Nicarag water mining Y
88. Physician/Medicare freeze N
89. Increase "sin" taxes Y
90. End SBA direct loans N
91. Sell Conrail N
92. Equal Rights Amendment Y
93. Marines in Lebanon Y
94. Eminent domain-Coal comps N

Presidential Support Score: 1986 - 11% 1985 - 15%

BOXER, BARBARA -- California 6th District [Democrat]. Counties of Marin, San Francisco (pt.), San Mateo (pt.) and Solano (pt.). Prior Terms: House: 1983-86. Born: November 11, 1940; Brooklyn, N.Y. Education: Brooklyn College (B.A.). Occupation: Stockbroker and economic researcher (1962-65); journalist and associate editor (1972-74); congressional aid (1974-76); member, Marin County Board of Supervisors (1976-82).

1. Immigration Reform Y
2. Open fld-search warrants Y
3. Civil pnty-hire ill alien N
4. So Afr sanc-veto override Y
5. Tax Overhaul Y
6. South Africa sanctions ?
7. Death penalty-drug bill Y
8. Evidence-warrantless srch N
9. Life term-second drug off N
10. Military use in drug war N
11. Troop reduction in Europe Y
12. Prohibit chemical weapons Y
13. Bar ASAT testing Y
14. Abide SALT II weapons ban Y
15. Follow SALT II-Soviets do N
16. Reduce SDI funding Y
17. Increase SDI funding N
18. Purchase Trident sub Y
19. Delete 12 MX;Add conv wpn Y
20. Raise speed limit N
21. Textile Import Quotas(*) Y
22. Req Pentagon buy US goods Y

BOXER, BARBARA (Cont.)

23. AIDS ins anti-dscriminatn Y
24. Nicaraguan refugee aid Y
25. Nicaraguan contra aid N
26. US abide by SALT II N
27. Prohibit Saudi arms sale Y
28. Military Retiremnt Reform Y
29. Nicaraguan refugee aid Y
30. Ease '68 Gun Control Act N
31. Bar intrstat handgun tran Y
32. Keep '68 Gun Control Act Y
33. Nicaraguan contra aid N
34. Bar emp polygraph testing Y
35. Tax Overhaul consideratn Y
36. Bar armor-piercing ammo Y
37. Tax Overhaul consideratn Y
38. Make comp emissions known Y
39. Allow toxic victims suits Y
40. Strike Superfund "VAT" Y
41. Notify emp-plant closing Y
42. Bar emp consult-plant clo X
43. Medicare cuts;Tax incres' Y
44. Delete 12 MX missiles Y
45. Spending cuts;Tax incres' Y
46. Textile Import Quotas Y
47. Cut some school lunch fds N
48. Clean Water Act Amendmnts N
49. Youth work projects ?
50. Assist military in Angola N
51. Allow US troops-Nicaragua N
52. Pentagon polygraph exams Y
53. Bar ASAT testing Y
54. Suspend def pmt for abuse Y
55. Bar Pentagon-contr emplmt Y
56. Increase SDI funding N
57. Reduce SDI funding Y
58. Produce chemical weapons N
59. Bar CIA fndg in Nicaragua Y
60. South Africa sanctions Y
61. Cut SS COLAs; Raise taxes N
62. Let US invest-So Africa N
63. Approve 21 MX for 1985 N
64. Emergency Farm Credit Y
65. Awards to whistle blowers Y
66. African disaster relief Y
67. Ban bank loans to So Afr Y
68. Bar coun duty-free trtmt Y
69. Steel import limits Y
70. Soc Sec COLAs=inflation Y
71. Bar haz waste vctms suits N
72. Prohibit aid to Nicaragua Y
73. Cut $-Schs bar sch prayer N
74. Raise taxes; Cut Medicare Y
75. Alien residncy-prior 1982 N
76. Alien residncy-prior 1980 N
77. Pen emp-hire illgl aliens Y
78. Lmt Persh II/cruse-Europe Y
79. Delete 34 B-1 bombers Y
80. Bar purch of Pershing II Y
81. Bar purchase of Sgt York ?
82. Delete $ for Trident II Y
83. Allow 15 MX missiles N
84. Bar MX procurement-1985 Y
85. Equal Access Act N
86. Aid to El Salvador N
87. Bar Nicarag water mining Y
88. Physician/Medicare freeze N
89. Increase "sin" taxes Y
90. End SBA direct loans N
91. Sell Conrail N
92. Equal Rights Amendment Y
93. Marines in Lebanon N
94. Eminent domain-Coal comps N
95. Prohibit EPA sanctions Y
96. SS age increase/Reforms N

Presidential Support Score: 1986 - 14% 1985 - 11%

MILLER, GEORGE -- California 7th District [Democrat]. County of Contra Costa (pt.). Prior Terms: House: 1975-86. Born: May 17, 1945; Richmond, Calif. Education: Diablo Valley College; San Francisco State College; University of California Law School (J.D.). Occupation: Attorney; senator's legislative assistant.

1. Immigration Reform Y
2. Open fld-search warrants Y
3. Civil pnty-hire ill alien N
4. So Afr sanc-veto override ?
5. Tax Overhaul Y
6. South Africa sanctions Y
7. Death penalty-drug bill N
8. Evidence-warrantless srch N
9. Life term-second drug off Y
10. Military use in drug war N
11. Troop reduction in Europe Y
12. Prohibit chemical weapons Y
13. Bar ASAT testing Y
14. Abide SALT II weapons ban Y
15. Follow SALT II-Soviets do N
16. Reduce SDI funding Y
17. Increase SDI funding N
18. Purchase Trident sub Y
19. Delete 12 MX;Add conv wpn #
20. Raise speed limit Y

MILLER, GEORGE (Cont.)

21. Textile Import Quotas(*) N
22. Req Pentagon buy US goods Y
23. AIDS ins anti-dscriminatn Y
24. Nicaraguan refugee aid Y
25. Nicaraguan contra aid N
26. US abide by SALT II N
27. Prohibit Saudi arms sale Y
28. Military Retiremnt Reform Y
29. Nicaraguan refugee aid Y
30. Ease '68 Gun Control Act N
31. Bar intrstat handgun tran Y
32. Keep '68 Gun Control Act Y
33. Nicaraguan contra aid N
34. Bar emp polygraph testing Y
35. Tax Overhaul consideratn Y
36. Bar armor-piercing ammo Y
37. Tax Overhaul consideratn Y
38. Make comp emissions known Y
39. Allow toxic victims suits Y
40. Strike Superfund "VAT" N
41. Notify emp-plant closing Y
42. Bar emp consult-plant clo N
43. Medicare cuts;Tax incres' Y
44. Delete 12 MX missiles Y
45. Spending cuts;Tax incres' Y
46. Textile Import Quotas N
47. Cut some school lunch fds N
48. Clean Water Act Amendmnts N
49. Youth work projects ?
50. Assist military in Angola N
51. Allow US troops-Nicaragua N
52. Pentagon polygraph exams Y
53. Bar ASAT testing Y
54. Suspend def pmt for abuse Y
55. Bar Pentagon-contr emplmt Y
56. Increase SDI funding N
57. Reduce SDI funding Y
58. Produce chemical weapons N
59. Bar CIA fndg in Nicaragua Y
60. South Africa sanctions ?
61. Cut SS COLAs; Raise taxes N
62. Let US invest-So Africa N
63. Approve 21 MX for 1985 N
64. Emergency Farm Credit Y
65. Awards to whistle blowers Y
66. African disaster relief Y
67. Ban bank loans to So Afr Y
68. Bar coun duty-free trtmt Y
69. Steel import limits Y
70. Soc Sec COLAs=inflation Y
71. Bar haz waste vctms suits N
72. Prohibit aid to Nicaragua Y
73. Cut $-Schs bar sch prayer N
74. Raise taxes; Cut Medicare Y
75. Alien residncy-prior 1982 N
76. Alien residncy-prior 1980 N
77. Pen emp-hire illgl aliens Y
78. Lmt Persh II/cruse-Europe Y
79. Delete 34 B-1 bombers Y
80. Bar purch of Pershing II ?
81. Bar purchase of Sgt York Y
82. Delete $ for Trident II Y
83. Allow 15 MX missiles N
84. Bar MX procurement-1985 Y
85. Equal Access Act N
86. Aid to El Salvador N
87. Bar Nicarag water mining Y
88. Physician/Medicare freeze N
89. Increase "sin" taxes Y
90. End SBA direct loans N
91. Sell Conrail N
92. Equal Rights Amendment Y
93. Marines in Lebanon N
94. Eminent domain-Coal comps N
95. Prohibit EPA sanctions Y
96. SS age increase/Reforms N
97. Auto domestic content req Y
98. Delete jobs program fundg N
99. Highway-Gas tax bill Y
100. Raise Medicare;Cut defnse Y
101. Emergency housing aid Y
102. Across-the-board tax cuts N
103. Gramm-Latta II targets N
104. Delete B-1 bomber funds Y
105. Dsapprov Saudi AWACS sale Y
106. Disapprove oil import fee Y
107. Rail Deregulation N
108. Dsapp India nuc fuel sale Y
109. Mil draft registration N
110. Chrysler Loan Guarantees Y
111. Prohibit school busing N
112. Nuclear plant moratorium Y
113. Oil price controls Y
114. Tuition Tax Credits ?
115. Est Consumer Protect Agcy Y
116. Eliminate B-1 bomber fnds Y
117. Subminimum wage for youth N
118. Delete crude oil tax N
119. Natural gas deregulation N

Presidential Support Score: 1986 - 15% 1985 - 16%

DELLUMS, RONALD V. -- California 8th District [Democrat]. Counties of Alameda (pt.) and Contra Costa (pt.). Prior Terms: House: 1971-86. Born: November 24, 1935; Oakland, Calif. Education: San Francisco State College (B.S.); University of California (M.S.W.). Military Service: U.S. Marine Corps. Occupation:

DELLUMS, RONALD V. (Cont.)

Senior consultant, Social Dynamics, Inc.; city councilman (1967-71); psychiatric social worker (1962-64); associate director and director, Hunter's Point Youth Opportunities Center (1965-66); planning consultant (1966-67); director, Concentrated Employment Program (1967-68); lecturer.

1. Immigration Reform N
2. Open fld-search warrants Y
3. Civil pnty-hire ill alien Y
4. So Afr sanc-veto override Y
5. Tax Overhaul Y
6. South Africa sanctions Y
7. Death penalty-drug bill N
8. Evidence-warrantless srch N
9. Life term-second drug off N
10. Military use in drug war N
11. Troop reduction in Europe Y
12. Prohibit chemical weapons Y
13. Bar ASAT testing Y
14. Abide SALT II weapons ban Y
15. Follow SALT II-Soviets do N
16. Reduce SDI funding Y
17. Increase SDI funding N
18. Purchase Trident sub N
19. Delete 12 MX;Add conv wpn Y
20. Raise speed limit N
21. Textile Import Quotas(*) Y
22. Req Pentagon buy US goods N
23. AIDS ins anti-dscriminatn Y
24. Nicaraguan refugee aid Y
25. Nicaraguan contra aid N
26. US abide by SALT II N
27. Prohibit Saudi arms sale Y
28. Military Retiremnt Reform Y
29. Nicaraguan refugee aid Y
30. Ease '68 Gun Control Act N
31. Bar intrstat handgun tran Y
32. Keep '68 Gun Control Act Y
33. Nicaraguan contra aid N
34. Bar emp polygraph testing Y
35. Tax Overhaul consideratn Y
36. Bar armor-piercing ammo Y
37. Tax Overhaul consideratn N
38. Make comp emissions known Y
39. Allow toxic victims suits Y
40. Strike Superfund "VAT" Y
41. Notify emp-plant closing Y
42. Bar emp consult-plant clo N
43. Medicare cuts;Tax incres' Y
44. Delete 12 MX missiles Y
45. Spending cuts;Tax incres' Y
46. Textile Import Quotas Y
47. Cut some school lunch fds N
48. Clean Water Act Amendmnts N
49. Youth work projects Y
50. Assist military in Angola N
51. Allow US troops-Nicaragua N
52. Pentagon polygraph exams N
53. Bar ASAT testing Y
54. Suspend def pmt for abuse Y
55. Bar Pentagon-contr emplmt Y
56. Increase SDI funding N
57. Reduce SDI funding Y
58. Produce chemical weapons N
59. Bar CIA fndg in Nicaragua Y
60. South Africa sanctions Y
61. Cut SS COLAs; Raise taxes N
62. Let US invest-So Africa N
63. Approve 21 MX for 1985 N
64. Emergency Farm Credit Y
65. Awards to whistle blowers Y
66. African disaster relief Y
67. Ban bank loans to So Afr P
68. Bar coun duty-free trtmt Y
69. Steel import limits Y
70. Soc Sec COLAs=inflation Y
71. Bar haz waste vctms suits N
72. Prohibit aid to Nicaragua Y
73. Cut $-Schs bar sch prayer N
74. Raise taxes; Cut Medicare N
75. Alien residncy-prior 1982 N
76. Alien residncy-prior 1980 N
77. Pen emp-hire illgl aliens Y
78. Lmt Persh II/cruse-Europe Y
79. Delete 34 B-1 bombers Y
80. Bar purch of Pershing II Y
81. Bar purchase of Sgt York Y
82. Delete $ for Trident II Y
83. Allow 15 MX missiles N
84. Bar MX procurement-1985 Y
85. Equal Access Act N
86. Aid to El Salvador N
87. Bar Nicarag water mining Y
88. Physician/Medicare freeze N
89. Increase "sin" taxes Y
90. End SBA direct loans N
91. Sell Conrail N
92. Equal Rights Amendment Y
93. Marines in Lebanon N
94. Eminent domain-Coal comps N
95. Prohibit EPA sanctions Y
96. SS age increase/Reforms N
97. Auto domestic content req Y
98. Delete jobs program fundg N
99. Highway-Gas tax bill Y
100. Raise Medicare;Cut defnse Y
101. Emergency housing aid Y
102. Across-the-board tax cuts N
103. Gramm-Latta II targets N
104. Delete B-1 bomber funds Y
105. Dsapprov Saudi AWACS sale Y
106. Disapprove oil import fee Y

DELLUMS, RONALD V. (Cont.)

107. Rail Deregulation N
108. Dsapp India nuc fuel sale Y
109. Mil draft registration N
110. Chrysler Loan Guarantees Y
111. Prohibit school busing N
112. Nuclear plant moratorium Y
113. Oil price controls Y
114. Tuition Tax Credits N
115. Est Consumer Protect Agcy Y
116. Eliminate B-1 bomber fnds Y
117. Subminimum wage for youth N
118. Delete crude oil tax N
119. Natural gas deregulation N

Presidential Support Score: 1986 - 13% 1985 - 16%

STARK, FORTNEY H. (PETE) -- California 9th District [Democrat]. County of Alameda (pt.). Prior Terms: House: 1973-86. Born: November 11, 1940; Parkersburg, W. Va. Education: Massachusetts Institute of Technology (B.S.); University of California (M.B.A.). Military Service: U.S. Air Force, 1955-57. Occupation: Principal, Skaife and Co. Securities; founder, Beacon S&L Assn. (1961-63); founder and president, Security National Bank of California (1963-72).

1. Immigration Reform Y
2. Open fld-search warrants N
3. Civil pnty-hire ill alien N
4. So Afr sanc-veto override Y
5. Tax Overhaul Y
6. South Africa sanctions Y
7. Death penalty-drug bill N
8. Evidence-warrantless srch N
9. Life term-second drug off N
10. Military use in drug war N
11. Troop reduction in Europe Y
12. Prohibit chemical weapons Y
13. Bar ASAT testing ?
14. Abide SALT II weapons ban Y
15. Follow SALT II-Soviets do N
16. Reduce SDI funding Y
17. Increase SDI funding N
18. Purchase Trident sub Y
19. Delete 12 MX;Add conv wpn Y
20. Raise speed limit Y
21. Textile Import Quotas(*) N
22. Req Pentagon buy US goods N
23. AIDS ins anti-dscriminatn Y
24. Nicaraguan refugee aid Y
25. Nicaraguan contra aid N
26. US abide by SALT II N
27. Prohibit Saudi arms sale Y
28. Military Retiremnt Reform Y
29. Nicaraguan refugee aid Y
30. Ease '68 Gun Control Act N
31. Bar intrstat handgun tran Y
32. Keep '68 Gun Control Act Y
33. Nicaraguan contra aid N
34. Bar emp polygraph testing Y
35. Tax Overhaul consideratn Y
36. Bar armor-piercing ammo Y
37. Tax Overhaul consideratn Y
38. Make comp emissions known Y
39. Allow toxic victims suits Y
40. Strike Superfund "VAT" Y
41. Notify emp-plant closing Y
42. Bar emp consult-plant clo N
43. Medicare cuts;Tax incres' Y
44. Delete 12 MX missiles Y
45. Spending cuts;Tax incres' N
46. Textile Import Quotas N
47. Cut some school lunch fds N
48. Clean Water Act Amendmnts N
49. Youth work projects Y
50. Assist military in Angola ?
51. Allow US troops-Nicaragua N
52. Pentagon polygraph exams N
53. Bar ASAT testing ?
54. Suspend def pmt for abuse Y
55. Bar Pentagon-contr emplmt Y
56. Increase SDI funding N
57. Reduce SDI funding Y
58. Produce chemical weapons N
59. Bar CIA fndg in Nicaragua Y
60. South Africa sanctions Y
61. Cut SS COLAs; Raise taxes ?
62. Let US invest-So Africa N
63. Approve 21 MX for 1985 N
64. Emergency Farm Credit Y
65. Awards to whistle blowers Y
66. African disaster relief +
67. Ban bank loans to So Afr Y
68. Bar coun duty-free trtmt Y
69. Steel import limits Y
70. Soc Sec COLAs=inflation Y
71. Bar haz waste vctms suits N
72. Prohibit aid to Nicaragua Y
73. Cut $-Schs bar sch prayer N
74. Raise taxes; Cut Medicare Y
75. Alien residncy-prior 1982 N
76. Alien residncy-prior 1980 N
77. Pen emp-hire illgl aliens Y
78. Lmt Persh II/cruse-Europe ?
79. Delete 34 B-1 bombers Y
80. Bar purch of Pershing II Y

STARK, FORTNEY H. (PETE) (Cont.)

81. Bar purchase of Sgt York ?
82. Delete $ for Trident II ?
83. Allow 15 MX missiles N
84. Bar MX procurement-1985 Y
85. Equal Access Act N
86. Aid to El Salvador N
87. Bar Nicarag water mining Y
88. Physician/Medicare freeze N
89. Increase "sin" taxes Y
90. End SBA direct loans ?
91. Sell Conrail ?
92. Equal Rights Amendment Y
93. Marines in Lebanon N
94. Eminent domain-Coal comps N
95. Prohibit EPA sanctions N
96. SS age increase/Reforms Y
97. Auto domestic content req Y
98. Delete jobs program fundg N
99. Highway-Gas tax bill Y
100. Raise Medicare;Cut defnse Y
101. Emergency housing aid Y
102. Across-the-board tax cuts N
103. Gramm-Latta II targets N
104. Delete B-1 bomber funds Y
105. Dsapprov Saudi AWACS sale Y
106. Disapprove oil import fee ?
107. Rail Deregulation Y
108. Dsapp India nuc fuel sale Y
109. Mil draft registration N
110. Chrysler Loan Guarantees X
111. Prohibit school busing N
112. Nuclear plant moratorium Y
113. Oil price controls Y
114. Tuition Tax Credits N
115. Est Consumer Protect Agcy Y
116. Eliminate B-1 bomber fnds Y
117. Subminimum wage for youth N
118. Delete crude oil tax N
119. Natural gas deregulation N

Presidential Support Score: 1986 - 17% 1985 - 18%

EDWARDS, DON -- California 10th District [Democrat]. Counties of Alameda (pt.) and Santa Clara (pt.). Prior Terms: House: 1963-86. Born: January 6, 1915; San Jose, Calif. Education: Stanford University; Stanford Law School. Military Service: U.S. Navy, 1942-45. Occupation: Agent, F.B.I. (1940-41); president, Valley Title Co.

1. Immigration Reform N
2. Open fld-search warrants Y
3. Civil pnty-hire ill alien Y
4. So Afr sanc-veto override Y
5. Tax Overhaul Y
6. South Africa sanctions Y
7. Death penalty-drug bill N
8. Evidence-warrantless srch N
9. Life term-second drug off N
10. Military use in drug war N
11. Troop reduction in Europe Y
12. Prohibit chemical weapons Y
13. Bar ASAT testing Y
14. Abide SALT II weapons ban Y
15. Follow SALT II-Soviets do N
16. Reduce SDI funding Y
17. Increase SDI funding N
18. Purchase Trident sub Y
19. Delete 12 MX;Add conv wpn Y
20. Raise speed limit N
21. Textile Import Quotas(*) Y
22. Req Pentagon buy US goods Y
23. AIDS ins anti-dscriminatn Y
24. Nicaraguan refugee aid Y
25. Nicaraguan contra aid N
26. US abide by SALT II N
27. Prohibit Saudi arms sale Y
28. Military Retiremnt Reform Y
29. Nicaraguan refugee aid Y
30. Ease '68 Gun Control Act N
31. Bar intrstat handgun tran Y
32. Keep '68 Gun Control Act Y
33. Nicaraguan contra aid N
34. Bar emp polygraph testing Y
35. Tax Overhaul consideratn Y
36. Bar armor-piercing ammo Y
37. Tax Overhaul consideratn Y
38. Make comp emissions known Y
39. Allow toxic victims suits Y
40. Strike Superfund "VAT" Y
41. Notify emp-plant closing Y
42. Bar emp consult-plant clo N
43. Medicare cuts;Tax incres' Y
44. Delete 12 MX missiles Y
45. Spending cuts;Tax incres' Y
46. Textile Import Quotas Y
47. Cut some school lunch fds N
48. Clean Water Act Amendmnts N
49. Youth work projects Y
50. Assist military in Angola N
51. Allow US troops-Nicaragua N
52. Pentagon polygraph exams N
53. Bar ASAT testing Y
54. Suspend def pmt for abuse Y
55. Bar Pentagon-contr emplmt Y
56. Increase SDI funding N
57. Reduce SDI funding Y
58. Produce chemical weapons N

EDWARDS, DON (Cont.)

59. Bar CIA fndg in Nicaragua	Y	90. End SBA direct loans	N
60. South Africa sanctions	Y	91. Sell Conrail	N
61. Cut SS COLAs; Raise taxes	N	92. Equal Rights Amendment	Y
62. Let US invest-So Africa	N	93. Marines in Lebanon	N
63. Approve 21 MX for 1985	N	94. Eminent domain-Coal comps	N
64. Emergency Farm Credit	Y	95. Prohibit EPA sanctions	Y
65. Awards to whistle blowers	Y	96. SS age increase/Reforms	N
66. African disaster relief	Y	97. Auto domestic content req	Y
67. Ban bank loans to So Afr	Y	98. Delete jobs program fundg	N
68. Bar coun duty-free trtmt	Y	99. Highway-Gas tax bill	Y
69. Steel import limits	Y	100. Raise Medicare;Cut defnse	Y
70. Soc Sec COLAs=inflation	Y	101. Emergency housing aid	Y
71. Bar haz waste vctms suits	N	102. Across-the-board tax cuts	N
72. Prohibit aid to Nicaragua	Y	103. Gramm-Latta II targets	N
73. Cut $-Schs bar sch prayer	N	104. Delete B-1 bomber funds	Y
74. Raise taxes; Cut Medicare	Y	105. Dsapprov Saudi AWACS sale	Y
75. Alien residncy-prior 1982	N	106. Disapprove oil import fee	Y
76. Alien residncy-prior 1980	N	107. Rail Deregulation	N
77. Pen emp-hire illgl aliens	Y	108. Dsapp India nuc fuel sale	Y
78. Lmt Persh II/cruse-Europe	Y	109. Mil draft registration	N
79. Delete 34 B-1 bombers	Y	110. Chrysler Loan Guarantees	?
80. Bar purch of Pershing II	Y	111. Prohibit school busing	N
81. Bar purchase of Sgt York	Y	112. Nuclear plant moratorium	Y
82. Delete $ for Trident II	Y	113. Oil price controls	Y
83. Allow 15 MX missiles	N	114. Tuition Tax Credits	?
84. Bar MX procurement-1985	Y	115. Est Consumer Protect Agcy	Y
85. Equal Access Act	N	116. Eliminate B-1 bomber fnds	Y
86. Aid to El Salvador	N	117. Subminimum wage for youth	N
87. Bar Nicarag water mining	Y	118. Delete crude oil tax	N
88. Physician/Medicare freeze	N	119. Natural gas deregulation	N
89. Increase "sin" taxes	Y		

Presidential Support Score: 1986 - 16% 1985 - 20%

LANTOS, TOM -- California 11th District [Democrat]. Counties of San Mateo (pt.) and Santa Clara (pt.). Prior Terms: House: 1981-86. Born: Feb. 1, 1928; Budapest. Education: University of Washington (B.A., M.A.); University of California. Occupation: Teacher; senior economic and foreign policy advisor; Presidential task force member, defense and foreign policy.

1. Immigration Reform	Y	19. Delete 12 MX;Add conv wpn	Y
2. Open fld-search warrants	Y	20. Raise speed limit	N
3. Civil pnty-hire ill alien	N	21. Textile Import Quotas(*)	Y
4. So Afr sanc-veto override	Y	22. Req Pentagon buy US goods	Y
5. Tax Overhaul	Y	23. AIDS ins anti-dscriminatn	Y
6. South Africa sanctions	Y	24. Nicaraguan refugee aid	Y
7. Death penalty-drug bill	Y	25. Nicaraguan contra aid	N
8. Evidence-warrantless srch	Y	26. US abide by SALT II	N
9. Life term-second drug off	Y	27. Prohibit Saudi arms sale	Y
10. Military use in drug war	Y	28. Military Retiremnt Reform	Y
11. Troop reduction in Europe	N	29. Nicaraguan refugee aid	Y
12. Prohibit chemical weapons	Y	30. Ease '68 Gun Control Act	Y
13. Bar ASAT testing	Y	31. Bar intrstat handgun tran	Y
14. Abide SALT II weapons ban	Y	32. Keep '68 Gun Control Act	Y
15. Follow SALT II-Soviets do	N	33. Nicaraguan contra aid	N
16. Reduce SDI funding	N	34. Bar emp polygraph testing	Y
17. Increase SDI funding	N	35. Tax Overhaul consideratn	Y
18. Purchase Trident sub	Y	36. Bar armor-piercing ammo	Y

LANTOS, TOM (Cont.)

37. Tax Overhaul consideratn Y
38. Make comp emissions known Y
39. Allow toxic victims suits Y
40. Strike Superfund "VAT" Y
41. Notify emp-plant closing Y
42. Bar emp consult-plant clo N
43. Medicare cuts;Tax incres' Y
44. Delete 12 MX missiles Y
45. Spending cuts;Tax incres' Y
46. Textile Import Quotas Y
47. Cut some school lunch fds N
48. Clean Water Act Amendmnts ?
49. Youth work projects Y
50. Assist military in Angola N
51. Allow US troops-Nicaragua N
52. Pentagon polygraph exams Y
53. Bar ASAT testing Y
54. Suspend def pmt for abuse Y
55. Bar Pentagon-contr emplmt Y
56. Increase SDI funding N
57. Reduce SDI funding N
58. Produce chemical weapons N
59. Bar CIA fndg in Nicaragua Y
60. South Africa sanctions Y
61. Cut SS COLAs; Raise taxes N
62. Let US invest-So Africa N
63. Approve 21 MX for 1985 N
64. Emergency Farm Credit Y
65. Awards to whistle blowers ?
66. African disaster relief #
67. Ban bank loans to So Afr Y
68. Bar coun duty-free trtmt Y
69. Steel import limits Y
70. Soc Sec COLAs=inflation Y
71. Bar haz waste vctms suits N
72. Prohibit aid to Nicaragua Y
73. Cut $-Schs bar sch prayer N
74. Raise taxes; Cut Medicare Y
75. Alien residncy-prior 1982 N
76. Alien residncy-prior 1980 N
77. Pen emp-hire illgl aliens Y
78. Lmt Persh II/cruse-Europe N
79. Delete 34 B-1 bombers Y
80. Bar purch of Pershing II N
81. Bar purchase of Sgt York N
82. Delete $ for Trident II N
83. Allow 15 MX missiles N
84. Bar MX procurement-1985 Y
85. Equal Access Act N
86. Aid to El Salvador N
87. Bar Nicarag water mining ?
88. Physician/Medicare freeze X
89. Increase "sin" taxes ?
90. End SBA direct loans N
91. Sell Conrail N
92. Equal Rights Amendment Y
93. Marines in Lebanon Y
94. Eminent domain-Coal comps N
95. Prohibit EPA sanctions Y
96. SS age increase/Reforms N
97. Auto domestic content req Y
98. Delete jobs program fundg N
99. Highway-Gas tax bill ?
100. Raise Medicare;Cut defnse Y
101. Emergency housing aid Y
102. Across-the-board tax cuts N
103. Gramm-Latta II targets N
104. Delete B-1 bomber funds Y
105. Dsapprov Saudi AWACS sale Y

Presidential Support Score: 1986 - 24% 1985 - 19%

ZSCHAU, ED -- California 12th District [Republican]. Counties of San Mateo (pt.), Santa Clara (pt.) and Stanislaus (pt.). Prior Terms: House: 1983-86. Born: January 6, 1940; Omaha, Neb. Education: Princeton University (A.B.); Stanford University (M.B.A., M.S., Ph.D.). Occupation: Assistant professor (1965-69); visiting assistant professor (1967-68); founder and president, System Industries, Inc. (1968-82); electronics executive (1974-79).

1. Immigration Reform Y
2. Open fld-search warrants Y
3. Civil pnty-hire ill alien N
4. So Afr sanc-veto override ?
5. Tax Overhaul Y
6. South Africa sanctions Y
7. Death penalty-drug bill Y
8. Evidence-warrantless srch Y
9. Life term-second drug off Y
10. Military use in drug war Y
11. Troop reduction in Europe N
12. Prohibit chemical weapons N
13. Bar ASAT testing Y
14. Abide SALT II weapons ban N
15. Follow SALT II-Soviets do Y
16. Reduce SDI funding N
17. Increase SDI funding N
18. Purchase Trident sub ?
19. Delete 12 MX;Add conv wpn ?
20. Raise speed limit Y
21. Textile Import Quotas(*) N
22. Req Pentagon buy US goods N
23. AIDS ins anti-dscriminatn N
24. Nicaraguan refugee aid N

ZSCHAU, ED (Cont.)

25. Nicaraguan contra aid Y
26. US abide by SALT II Y
27. Prohibit Saudi arms sale N
28. Military Retiremnt Reform ?
29. Nicaraguan refugee aid Y
30. Ease '68 Gun Control Act Y
31. Bar intrstat handgun tran Y
32. Keep '68 Gun Control Act Y
33. Nicaraguan contra aid Y
34. Bar emp polygraph testing N
35. Tax Overhaul consideratn N
36. Bar armor-piercing ammo Y
37. Tax Overhaul consideratn N
38. Make comp emissions known N
39. Allow toxic victims suits N
40. Strike Superfund "VAT" Y
41. Notify emp-plant closing N
42. Bar emp consult-plant clo Y
43. Medicare cuts;Tax incres' N
44. Delete 12 MX missiles Y
45. Spending cuts;Tax incres' N
46. Textile Import Quotas N
47. Cut some school lunch fds Y
48. Clean Water Act Amendmnts Y
49. Youth work projects N
50. Assist military in Angola Y
51. Allow US troops-Nicaragua Y
52. Pentagon polygraph exams Y
53. Bar ASAT testing Y
54. Suspend def pmt for abuse N
55. Bar Pentagon-contr emplmt Y
56. Increase SDI funding N
57. Reduce SDI funding N
58. Produce chemical weapons Y
59. Bar CIA fndg in Nicaragua N
60. South Africa sanctions N
61. Cut SS COLAs; Raise taxes N
62. Let US invest-So Africa Y
63. Approve 21 MX for 1985 N
64. Emergency Farm Credit N
65. Awards to whistle blowers Y
66. African disaster relief Y
67. Ban bank loans to So Afr Y
68. Bar coun duty-free trtmt N
69. Steel import limits N
70. Soc Sec COLAs=inflation Y
71. Bar haz waste vctms suits Y
72. Prohibit aid to Nicaragua Y
73. Cut $-Schs bar sch prayer N
74. Raise taxes; Cut Medicare Y
75. Alien residncy-prior 1982 Y
76. Alien residncy-prior 1980 Y
77. Pen emp-hire illgl aliens N
78. Lmt Persh II/cruse-Europe N
79. Delete 34 B-1 bombers N
80. Bar purch of Pershing II N
81. Bar purchase of Sgt York Y
82. Delete $ for Trident II N
83. Allow 15 MX missiles N
84. Bar MX procurement-1985 Y
85. Equal Access Act N
86. Aid to El Salvador Y
87. Bar Nicarag water mining Y
88. Physician/Medicare freeze Y
89. Increase "sin" taxes Y
90. End SBA direct loans Y
91. Sell Conrail Y
92. Equal Rights Amendment Y
93. Marines in Lebanon Y
94. Eminent domain-Coal comps Y
95. Prohibit EPA sanctions Y
96. SS age increase/Reforms Y

Presidential Support Score: 1986 - 53% 1985 - 70%

MINETA, NORMAN Y. -- California 13th District [Democrat]. County of Santa Clara (pt.). Prior Terms: House: 1975-86. Born: November 12, 1931; San Jose, Calif. Education: University of California (B.S.). Military Service: U.S. Army, 1953-56. Occupation: Owner/agent, Mineta Insurance Agency; commissioner, Human Relations Committee (1962-64); commissioner, Housing Authority (1966-67); city councilman (1967-72); mayor (1971-74).

1. Immigration Reform Y
2. Open fld-search warrants Y
3. Civil pnty-hire ill alien N
4. So Afr sanc-veto override Y
5. Tax Overhaul Y
6. South Africa sanctions Y
7. Death penalty-drug bill N
8. Evidence-warrantless srch N
9. Life term-second drug off Y
10. Military use in drug war N
11. Troop reduction in Europe Y
12. Prohibit chemical weapons Y
13. Bar ASAT testing Y
14. Abide SALT II weapons ban Y
15. Follow SALT II-Soviets do N
16. Reduce SDI funding Y
17. Increase SDI funding N
18. Purchase Trident sub Y
19. Delete 12 MX;Add conv wpn Y
20. Raise speed limit N
21. Textile Import Quotas(*) N
22. Req Pentagon buy US goods N
23. AIDS ins anti-dscriminatn Y
24. Nicaraguan refugee aid Y

MINETA, NORMAN Y. (Cont.)

25. Nicaraguan contra aid N
26. US abide by SALT II N
27. Prohibit Saudi arms sale Y
28. Military Retiremnt Reform Y
29. Nicaraguan refugee aid Y
30. Ease '68 Gun Control Act N
31. Bar intrstat handgun tran Y
32. Keep '68 Gun Control Act Y
33. Nicaraguan contra aid N
34. Bar emp polygraph testing Y
35. Tax Overhaul consideratn Y
36. Bar armor-piercing ammo Y
37. Tax Overhaul consideratn Y
38. Make comp emissions known Y
39. Allow toxic victims suits Y
40. Strike Superfund "VAT" Y
41. Notify emp-plant closing Y
42. Bar emp consult-plant clo N
43. Medicare cuts;Tax incres' Y
44. Delete 12 MX missiles Y
45. Spending cuts;Tax incres' N
46. Textile Import Quotas N
47. Cut some school lunch fds N
48. Clean Water Act Amendmnts N
49. Youth work projects Y
50. Assist military in Angola N
51. Allow US troops-Nicaragua N
52. Pentagon polygraph exams N
53. Bar ASAT testing Y
54. Suspend def pmt for abuse Y
55. Bar Pentagon-contr emplmt Y
56. Increase SDI funding N
57. Reduce SDI funding N
58. Produce chemical weapons N
59. Bar CIA fndg in Nicaragua Y
60. South Africa sanctions Y
61. Cut SS COLAs; Raise taxes N
62. Let US invest-So Africa N
63. Approve 21 MX for 1985 N
64. Emergency Farm Credit Y
65. Awards to whistle blowers Y
66. African disaster relief Y
67. Ban bank loans to So Afr Y
68. Bar coun duty-free trtmt Y
69. Steel import limits Y
70. Soc Sec COLAs=inflation Y
71. Bar haz waste vctms suits N
72. Prohibit aid to Nicaragua Y
73. Cut $-Schs bar sch prayer N
74. Raise taxes; Cut Medicare Y
75. Alien residncy-prior 1982 N
76. Alien residncy-prior 1980 N
77. Pen emp-hire illgl aliens Y
78. Lmt Persh II/cruse-Europe Y
79. Delete 34 B-1 bombers Y
80. Bar purch of Pershing II Y
81. Bar purchase of Sgt York Y
82. Delete $ for Trident II N
83. Allow 15 MX missiles N
84. Bar MX procurement-1985 Y
85. Equal Access Act N
86. Aid to El Salvador N
87. Bar Nicarag water mining Y
88. Physician/Medicare freeze N
89. Increase "sin" taxes Y
90. End SBA direct loans N
91. Sell Conrail N
92. Equal Rights Amendment Y
93. Marines in Lebanon N
94. Eminent domain-Coal comps Y
95. Prohibit EPA sanctions Y
96. SS age increase/Reforms N
97. Auto domestic content req Y
98. Delete jobs program fundg N
99. Highway-Gas tax bill Y
100. Raise Medicare;Cut defnse N
101. Emergency housing aid Y
102. Across-the-board tax cuts N
103. Gramm-Latta II targets N
104. Delete B-1 bomber funds Y
105. Dsapprov Saudi AWACS sale Y
106. Disapprove oil import fee N
107. Rail Deregulation N
108. Dsapp India nuc fuel sale Y
109. Mil draft registration N
110. Chrysler Loan Guarantees Y
111. Prohibit school busing N
112. Nuclear plant moratorium N
113. Oil price controls N
114. Tuition Tax Credits N
115. Est Consumer Protect Agcy Y
116. Eliminate B-1 bomber fnds Y
117. Subminimum wage for youth N
118. Delete crude oil tax N
119. Natural gas deregulation N

Presidential Support Score: 1986 - 23% 1985 - 21%

SHUMWAY, NORMAN D. -- California 14th District [Republican]. Counties of Alpine, Amador, El Dorado, Lassen, Modoc, Nevada, Placer, Plumas, San Joaquin (pt.), Shasta (pt.), Sierra and Siskiyou. Prior Terms: House: 1979-86. Born: July 28, 1934; Phoenix, Ariz. Education: University of Utah (B.S.); Hastings College of Law (J.D.). Occupation: Attorney, Cavalero, Bray, Shumway and Geiger; member, San Joaquin County Board of Supervisors (1974-78).

SHUMWAY, NORMAN D. (Cont.)

1. Immigration Reform N
2. Open fld-search warrants Y
3. Civil pnty-hire ill alien Y
4. So Afr sanc-veto override N
5. Tax Overhaul N
6. South Africa sanctions N
7. Death penalty-drug bill Y
8. Evidence-warrantless srch Y
9. Life term-second drug off Y
10. Military use in drug war Y
11. Troop reduction in Europe N
12. Prohibit chemical weapons N
13. Bar ASAT testing N
14. Abide SALT II weapons ban N
15. Follow SALT II-Soviets do Y
16. Reduce SDI funding N
17. Increase SDI funding Y
18. Purchase Trident sub N
19. Delete 12 MX;Add conv wpn N
20. Raise speed limit Y
21. Textile Import Quotas(*) N
22. Req Pentagon buy US goods N
23. AIDS ins anti-dscriminatn N
24. Nicaraguan refugee aid N
25. Nicaraguan contra aid Y
26. US abide by SALT II Y
27. Prohibit Saudi arms sale N
28. Military Retiremnt Reform Y
29. Nicaraguan refugee aid Y
30. Ease '68 Gun Control Act Y
31. Bar intrstat handgun tran N
32. Keep '68 Gun Control Act N
33. Nicaraguan contra aid Y
34. Bar emp polygraph testing N
35. Tax Overhaul consideratn N
36. Bar armor-piercing ammo N
37. Tax Overhaul consideratn N
38. Make comp emissions known N
39. Allow toxic victims suits N
40. Strike Superfund "VAT" N
41. Notify emp-plant closing N
42. Bar emp consult-plant clo Y
43. Medicare cuts;Tax incres' N
44. Delete 12 MX missiles N
45. Spending cuts;Tax incres' N
46. Textile Import Quotas N
47. Cut some school lunch fds Y
48. Clean Water Act Amendmnts Y
49. Youth work projects N
50. Assist military in Angola Y
51. Allow US troops-Nicaragua Y
52. Pentagon polygraph exams ?
53. Bar ASAT testing N
54. Suspend def pmt for abuse ?
55. Bar Pentagon-contr emplmt ?
56. Increase SDI funding Y
57. Reduce SDI funding N
58. Produce chemical weapons Y
59. Bar CIA fndg in Nicaragua N
60. South Africa sanctions N
61. Cut SS COLAs; Raise taxes N
62. Let US invest-So Africa Y
63. Approve 21 MX for 1985 Y
64. Emergency Farm Credit N
65. Awards to whistle blowers Y
66. African disaster relief Y
67. Ban bank loans to So Afr N
68. Bar coun duty-free trtmt N
69. Steel import limits N
70. Soc Sec COLAs=inflation Y
71. Bar haz waste vctms suits Y
72. Prohibit aid to Nicaragua N
73. Cut $-Schs bar sch prayer Y
74. Raise taxes; Cut Medicare N
75. Alien residncy-prior 1982 Y
76. Alien residncy-prior 1980 Y
77. Pen emp-hire illgl aliens N
78. Lmt Persh II/cruse-Europe N
79. Delete 34 B-1 bombers N
80. Bar purch of Pershing II N
81. Bar purchase of Sgt York N
82. Delete $ for Trident II N
83. Allow 15 MX missiles Y
84. Bar MX procurement-1985 N
85. Equal Access Act Y
86. Aid to El Salvador Y
87. Bar Nicarag water mining N
88. Physician/Medicare freeze Y
89. Increase "sin" taxes N
90. End SBA direct loans Y
91. Sell Conrail Y
92. Equal Rights Amendment N
93. Marines in Lebanon Y
94. Eminent domain-Coal comps Y
95. Prohibit EPA sanctions Y
96. SS age increase/Reforms Y
97. Auto domestic content req N
98. Delete jobs program fundg Y
99. Highway-Gas tax bill N
100. Raise Medicare;Cut defnse N
101. Emergency housing aid N
102. Across-the-board tax cuts Y
103. Gramm-Latta II targets Y
104. Delete B-1 bomber funds N
105. Dsapprov Saudi AWACS sale N
106. Disapprove oil import fee Y
107. Rail Deregulation N
108. Dsapp India nuc fuel sale Y
109. Mil draft registration Y
110. Chrysler Loan Guarantees N
111. Prohibit school busing Y
112. Nuclear plant moratorium N
113. Oil price controls N

Presidential Support Score: 1986 - 86% 1985 - 79%

COELHO, TONY -- California 15th District [Democrat]. Counties of Fresno (pt.), Madera, Mariposa, Merced and Stanislaus (pt.). Prior Terms: House: 1979-86. Born: June 15, 1942; Los Banos, Calif. Education: Loyola University (B.A.). Occupation: Congressional administrative assistant (1965-78).

1.	Immigration Reform	Y	55.	Bar Pentagon-contr emplmt	Y
2.	Open fld-search warrants	Y	56.	Increase SDI funding	N
3.	Civil pnty-hire ill alien	N	57.	Reduce SDI funding	Y
4.	So Afr sanc-veto override	Y	58.	Produce chemical weapons	N
5.	Tax Overhaul	Y	59.	Bar CIA fndg in Nicaragua	Y
6.	South Africa sanctions	?	60.	South Africa sanctions	Y
7.	Death penalty-drug bill	Y	61.	Cut SS COLAs; Raise taxes	N
8.	Evidence-warrantless srch	Y	62.	Let US invest-So Africa	N
9.	Life term-second drug off	Y	63.	Approve 21 MX for 1985	N
10.	Military use in drug war	N	64.	Emergency Farm Credit	Y
11.	Troop reduction in Europe	Y	65.	Awards to whistle blowers	Y
12.	Prohibit chemical weapons	Y	66.	African disaster relief	Y
13.	Bar ASAT testing	Y	67.	Ban bank loans to So Afr	?
14.	Abide SALT II weapons ban	Y	68.	Bar coun duty-free trtmt	Y
15.	Follow SALT II-Soviets do	N	69.	Steel import limits	Y
16.	Reduce SDI funding	N	70.	Soc Sec COLAs=inflation	Y
17.	Increase SDI funding	N	71.	Bar haz waste vctms suits	N
18.	Purchase Trident sub	Y	72.	Prohibit aid to Nicaragua	Y
19.	Delete 12 MX;Add conv wpn	Y	73.	Cut $-Schs bar sch prayer	N
20.	Raise speed limit	Y	74.	Raise taxes; Cut Medicare	Y
21.	Textile Import Quotas(*)	Y	75.	Alien residncy-prior 1982	N
22.	Req Pentagon buy US goods	Y	76.	Alien residncy-prior 1980	N
23.	AIDS ins anti-dscriminatn	Y	77.	Pen emp-hire illgl aliens	Y
24.	Nicaraguan refugee aid	Y	78.	Lmt Persh II/cruse-Europe	N
25.	Nicaraguan contra aid	N	79.	Delete 34 B-1 bombers	N
26.	US abide by SALT II	N	80.	Bar purch of Pershing II	N
27.	Prohibit Saudi arms sale	Y	81.	Bar purchase of Sgt York	?
28.	Military Retiremnt Reform	Y	82.	Delete $ for Trident II	?
29.	Nicaraguan refugee aid	Y	83.	Allow 15 MX missiles	N
30.	Ease '68 Gun Control Act	Y	84.	Bar MX procurement-1985	Y
31.	Bar intrstat handgun tran	N	85.	Equal Access Act	N
32.	Keep '68 Gun Control Act	Y	86.	Aid to El Salvador	N
33.	Nicaraguan contra aid	N	87.	Bar Nicarag water mining	Y
34.	Bar emp polygraph testing	Y	88.	Physician/Medicare freeze	N
35.	Tax Overhaul consideratn	Y	89.	Increase "sin" taxes	Y
36.	Bar armor-piercing ammo	Y	90.	End SBA direct loans	N
37.	Tax Overhaul consideratn	Y	91.	Sell Conrail	N
38.	Make comp emissions known	N	92.	Equal Rights Amendment	Y
39.	Allow toxic victims suits	N	93.	Marines in Lebanon	?
40.	Strike Superfund "VAT"	N	94.	Eminent domain-Coal comps	Y
41.	Notify emp-plant closing	Y	95.	Prohibit EPA sanctions	Y
42.	Bar emp consult-plant clo	N	96.	SS age increase/Reforms	N
43.	Medicare cuts;Tax incres'	Y	97.	Auto domestic content req	Y
44.	Delete 12 MX missiles	Y	98.	Delete jobs program fundg	N
45.	Spending cuts;Tax incres'	?	99.	Highway-Gas tax bill	Y
46.	Textile Import Cuotas	Y	100.	Raise Medicare;Cut defnse	Y
47.	Cut some school lunch fds	N	101.	Emergency housing aid	Y
48.	Clean Water Act Amendmnts	?	102.	Across-the-board tax cuts	N
49.	Youth work projects	Y	103.	Gramm-Latta II targets	N
50.	Assist military in Angola	N	104.	Delete B-1 bomber funds	N
51.	Allow US troops-Nicaragua	N	105.	Dsapprov Saudi AWACS sale	Y
52.	Pentagon polygraph exams	Y	106.	Disapprove oil import fee	?
53.	Bar ASAT testing	Y	107.	Rail Deregulation	N
54.	Suspend def pmt for abuse	Y	108.	Dsapp India nuc fuel sale	Y

COELHO, TONY (Cont.)

109. Mil draft registration	N		112. Nuclear plant moratorium	?
110. Chrysler Loan Guarantees	Y		113. Oil price controls	N
111. Prohibit school busing	N			

Presidential Support Score: 1986 - 22% 1985 - 20%

PANETTA, LEON E. -- California 16th District [Democrat]. Counties of Monterey, San Benito, San Luis Obispo (pt.) and Santa Cruz. Prior Terms: House: 1977-86. Born: June 28, 1938; Monterey, Calif. Education: University of Santa Clara (B.A., J.D.). Military Service: U.S. Army, 1963-65. Occupation: Law Review editor; legislative assistant, U.S. Senate (1966-69); director, Office of Civil Rights, HEW; executive assistant, New York mayor (1970-71).

1. Immigration Reform	Y		45. Spending cuts;Tax incres'	Y
2. Open fld-search warrants	Y		46. Textile Import Quotas	N
3. Civil pnty-hire ill alien	N		47. Cut some school lunch fds	N
4. So Afr sanc-veto override	#		48. Clean Water Act Amendmnts	N
5. Tax Overhaul	Y		49. Youth work projects	Y
6. South Africa sanctions	Y		50. Assist military in Angola	N
7. Death penalty-drug bill	Y		51. Allow US troops-Nicaragua	N
8. Evidence-warrantless srch	N		52. Pentagon polygraph exams	Y
9. Life term-second drug off	Y		53. Bar ASAT testing	Y
10. Military use in drug war	N		54. Suspend def pmt for abuse	Y
11. Troop reduction in Europe	N		55. Bar Pentagon-contr emplmt	Y
12. Prohibit chemical weapons	Y		56. Increase SDI funding	N
13. Bar ASAT testing	Y		57. Reduce SDI funding	N
14. Abide SALT II weapons ban	Y		58. Produce chemical weapons	N
15. Follow SALT II-Soviets do	N		59. Bar CIA fndg in Nicaragua	Y
16. Reduce SDI funding	Y		60. South Africa sanctions	Y
17. Increase SDI funding	N		61. Cut SS COLAs; Raise taxes	Y
18. Purchase Trident sub	Y		62. Let US invest-So Africa	N
19. Delete 12 MX;Add conv wpn	Y		63. Approve 21 MX for 1985	N
20. Raise speed limit	Y		64. Emergency Farm Credit	Y
21. Textile Import Quotas(*)	N		65. Awards to whistle blowers	Y
22. Req Pentagon buy US goods	N		66. African disaster relief	Y
23. AIDS ins anti-dscriminatn	Y		67. Ban bank loans to So Afr	Y
24. Nicaraguan refugee aid	Y		68. Bar coun duty-free trtmt	Y
25. Nicaraguan contra aid	N		69. Steel import limits	N
26. US abide by SALT II	N		70. Soc Sec COLAs=inflation	Y
27. Prohibit Saudi arms sale	Y		71. Bar haz waste vctms suits	Y
28. Military Retiremnt Reform	Y		72. Prohibit aid to Nicaragua	Y
29. Nicaraguan refugee aid	Y		73. Cut $-Schs bar sch prayer	N
30. Ease '68 Gun Control Act	N		74. Raise taxes; Cut Medicare	Y
31. Bar intrstat handgun tran	Y		75. Alien residncy-prior 1982	N
32. Keep '68 Gun Control Act	Y		76. Alien residncy-prior 1980	N
33. Nicaraguan contra aid	N		77. Pen emp-hire illgl aliens	Y
34. Bar emp polygraph testing	Y		78. Lmt Persh II/cruse-Europe	Y
35. Tax Overhaul consideratn	Y		79. Delete 34 B-1 bombers	Y
36. Bar armor-piercing ammo	Y		80. Bar purch of Pershing II	Y
37. Tax Overhaul consideratn	Y		81. Bar purchase of Sgt York	Y
38. Make comp emissions known	Y		82. Delete $ for Trident II	N
39. Allow toxic victims suits	N		83. Allow 15 MX missiles	N
40. Strike Superfund "VAT"	Y		84. Bar MX procurement-1985	Y
41. Notify emp-plant closing	Y		85. Equal Access Act	N
42. Bar emp consult-plant clo	N		86. Aid to El Salvador	N
43. Medicare cuts;Tax incres'	Y		87. Bar Nicarag water mining	Y
44. Delete 12 MX missiles	Y		88. Physician/Medicare freeze	N

PANETTA, LEON E. (Cont.)

89. Increase "sin" taxes Y
90. End SBA direct loans N
91. Sell Conrail N
92. Equal Rights Amendment Y
93. Marines in Lebanon Y
94. Eminent domain-Coal comps Y
95. Prohibit EPA sanctions +
96. SS age increase/Reforms N
97. Auto domestic content req N
98. Delete jobs program fundg N
99. Highway-Gas tax bill Y
100. Raise Medicare;Cut defnse N
101. Emergency housing aid Y
102. Across-the-board tax cuts N
103. Gramm-Latta II targets N
104. Delete B-1 bomber funds Y
105. Dsapprov Saudi AWACS sale Y
106. Disapprove oil import fee Y
107. Rail Deregulation N
108. Dsapp India nuc fuel sale Y
109. Mil draft registration N
110. Chrysler Loan Guarantees N
111. Prohibit school busing N
112. Nuclear plant moratorium Y
113. Oil price controls N
114. Tuition Tax Credits N
115. Est Consumer Protect Agcy N
116. Eliminate B-1 bomber fnds Y
117. Subminimum wage for youth N
118. Delete crude oil tax N
119. Natural gas deregulation N

Presidential Support Score: 1986 - 20% 1985 - 20%

PASHAYAN, CHARLES, Jr. -- California 17th District [Republican]. Counties of Fresno (pt.), Kern (pt.), Kings and Tulare. Prior Terms: House: 1979-86. Born: March 27, 1941; Fresno, Calif. Education: Pomona College (B.A.); University of California (J.D.); Oxford University. Military Service: U.S. Army, 1968-70. Occupation: Attorney; special assistant to general counsel, HEW (1973-75).

1. Immigration Reform Y
2. Open fld-search warrants Y
3. Civil pnty-hire ill alien Y
4. So Afr sanc-veto override Y
5. Tax Overhaul Y
6. South Africa sanctions Y
7. Death penalty-drug bill Y
8. Evidence-warrantless srch Y
9. Life term-second drug off Y
10. Military use in drug war Y
11. Troop reduction in Europe N
12. Prohibit chemical weapons N
13. Bar ASAT testing N
14. Abide SALT II weapons ban N
15. Follow SALT II-Soviets do Y
16. Reduce SDI funding N
17. Increase SDI funding N
18. Assist military in Angola N
19. Delete 12 MX;Add conv wpn N
20. Raise speed limit N
21. Textile Import Quotas(*) Y
22. Req Pentagon buy US goods Y
23. AIDS ins anti-dscriminatn N
24. Nicaraguan refugee aid N
25. Nicaraguan contra aid Y
26. US abide by SALT II Y
27. Prohibit Saudi arms sale Y
28. Military Retiremnt Reform Y
29. Nicaraguan refugee aid Y
30. Ease '68 Gun Control Act Y
31. Bar intrstat handgun tran N
32. Keep '68 Gun Control Act N
33. Nicaraguan contra aid Y
34. Bar emp polygraph testing Y
35. Tax Overhaul consideratn N
36. Bar armor-piercing ammo Y
37. Tax Overhaul consideratn N
38. Make comp emissions known N
39. Allow toxic victims suits N
40. Strike Superfund "VAT" Y
41. Notify emp-plant closing N
42. Bar emp consult-plant clo Y
43. Medicare cuts;Tax incres' N
44. Delete 12 MX missiles N
45. Spending cuts;Tax incres' N
46. Textile Import Quotas Y
47. Cut some school lunch fds N
48. Clean Water Act Amendmnts Y
49. Youth work projects N
50. Assist military in Angola Y
51. Allow US troops-Nicaragua Y
52. Pentagon polygraph exams Y
53. Bar ASAT testing N
54. Suspend def pmt for abuse N
55. Bar Pentagon-contr emplmt Y
56. Increase SDI funding Y
57. Reduce SDI funding N
58. Produce chemical weapons Y
59. Bar CIA fndg in Nicaragua N
60. South Africa sanctions N
61. Cut SS COLAs; Raise taxes N
62. Let US invest-So Africa Y
63. Approve 21 MX for 1985 Y
64. Emergency Farm Credit Y

PASHAYAN, CHARLES, Jr. (Cont.)

65. Awards to whistle blowers Y
66. African disaster relief Y
67. Ban bank loans to So Afr Y
68. Bar coun duty-free trtmt N
69. Steel import limits N
70. Soc Sec COLAs=inflation Y
71. Bar haz waste vctms suits Y
72. Prohibit aid to Nicaragua Y
73. Cut $-Schs bar sch prayer Y
74. Raise taxes; Cut Medicare N
75. Alien residncy-prior 1982 Y
76. Alien residncy-prior 1980 Y
77. Pen emp-hire illgl aliens N
78. Lmt Persh II/cruse-Europe N
79. Delete 34 B-1 bombers N
80. Bar purch of Pershing II N
81. Bar purchase of Sgt York N
82. Delete $ for Trident II N
83. Allow 15 MX missiles Y
84. Bar MX procurement-1985 N
85. Equal Access Act Y
86. Aid to El Salvador Y
87. Bar Nicarag water mining N
88. Physician/Medicare freeze Y
89. Increase "sin" taxes N
90. End SBA direct loans N
91. Sell Conrail Y
92. Equal Rights Amendment N
93. Marines in Lebanon Y
94. Eminent domain-Coal comps ?
95. Prohibit EPA sanctions ?
96. SS age increase/Reforms Y
97. Auto domestic content req N
98. Delete jobs program fundg Y
99. Highway-Gas tax bill Y
100. Raise Medicare;Cut defnse Y
101. Emergency housing aid Y
102. Across-the-board tax cuts Y
103. Gramm-Latta II targets Y
104. Delete B-1 bomber funds N
105. Dsapprov Saudi AWACS sale Y
106. Disapprove oil import fee ?
107. Rail Deregulation N
108. Dsapp India nuc fuel sale ?
109. Mil draft registration Y
110. Chrysler Loan Guarantees Y
111. Prohibit school busing Y
112. Nuclear plant moratorium N
113. Oil price controls N

Presidential Support Score: 1986 - 59% 1985 - 59%

LEHMAN, RICHARD H. -- California 18th District [Democrat]. Counties of Calaveras, Fresno (pt.), Mono, San Joaquin (pt.) and Tuolumne. Prior Terms: House: 1983-86. Born: July 20, 1948; Sanger, Calif. Education: Fresno City College; California State University; University of California. Military Service: U.S. Army National Guard, 1970-76. Occupation: Administrative aide (1969-76); California assemblyman (1976-82).

1. Immigration Reform Y
2. Open fld-search warrants Y
3. Civil pnty-hire ill alien Y
4. So Afr sanc-veto override Y
5. Tax Overhaul N
6. South Africa sanctions Y
7. Death penalty-drug bill Y
8. Evidence-warrantless srch N
9. Life term-second drug off Y
10. Military use in drug war Y
11. Troop reduction in Europe N
12. Prohibit chemical weapons Y
13. Bar ASAT testing Y
14. Abide SALT II weapons ban Y
15. Follow SALT II-Soviets do N
16. Reduce SDI funding Y
17. Increase SDI funding N
18. Purchase Trident sub Y
19. Delete 12 MX;Add conv wpn Y
20. Raise speed limit Y
21. Textile Import Quotas(*) Y
22. Req Pentagon buy US goods Y
23. AIDS ins anti-dscriminatn Y
24. Nicaraguan refugee aid Y
25. Nicaraguan contra aid N
26. US abide by SALT II N
27. Prohibit Saudi arms sale +
28. Military Retiremnt Reform Y
29. Nicaraguan refugee aid Y
30. Ease '68 Gun Control Act Y
31. Bar intrstat handgun tran Y
32. Keep '68 Gun Control Act Y
33. Nicaraguan contra aid N
34. Bar emp polygraph testing Y
35. Tax Overhaul consideratn Y
36. Bar armor-piercing ammo Y
37. Tax Overhaul consideratn Y
38. Make comp emissions known N
39. Allow toxic victims suits Y
40. Strike Superfund "VAT" Y
41. Notify emp-plant closing Y
42. Bar emp consult-plant clo N
43. Medicare cuts;Tax incres' Y
44. Delete 12 MX missiles Y
45. Spending cuts;tax incres' Y
46. Textile Import Quotas Y

LEHMAN, RICHARD H. (Cont.)

47. Cut some school lunch fds ?
48. Clean Water Act Amendmnts N
49. Youth work projects ?
50. Assist military in Angola N
51. Allow US troops-Nicaragua N
52. Pentagon polygraph exams Y
53. Bar ASAT testing Y
54. Suspend def pmt for abuse Y
55. Bar Pentagon-contr emplmt Y
56. Increase SDI funding N
57. Reduce SDI funding Y
58. Produce chemical weapons N
59. Bar CIA fndg in Nicaragua Y
60. South Africa sanctions Y
61. Cut SS COLAs; Raise taxes N
62. Let US invest-So Africa N
63. Approve 21 MX for 1985 N
64. Emergency Farm Credit Y
65. Awards to whistle blowers Y
66. African disaster relief Y
67. Ban bank loans to So Afr Y
68. Bar coun duty-free trtmt Y
69. Steel import limits Y
70. Soc Sec COLAs=inflation Y
71. Bar haz waste vctms suits N
72. Prohibit aid to Nicaragua Y
73. Cut $-Schs bar sch prayer N
74. Raise taxes; Cut Medicare Y
75. Alien residncy-prior 1982 Y
76. Alien residncy-prior 1980 N
77. Pen emp-hire illgl aliens N
78. Lmt Persh II/cruse-Europe Y
79. Delete 34 B-1 bombers Y
80. Bar purch of Pershing II Y
81. Bar purchase of Sgt York ?
82. Delete $ for Trident II N
83. Allow 15 MX missiles N
84. Bar MX procurement-1985 Y
85. Equal Access Act N
86. Aid to El Salvador N
87. Bar Nicarag water mining Y
88. Physician/Medicare freeze N
89. Increase "sin" taxes Y
90. End SBA direct loans N
91. Sell Conrail N
92. Equal Rights Amendment Y
93. Marines in Lebanon Y
94. Eminent domain-Coal comps N
95. Prohibit EPA sanctions Y
96. SS age increase/Reforms N

Presidential Support Score: 1986 - 20% 1985 - 16%

LAGOMARSINO, ROBERT J. -- California 19th District [Republican]. Counties of Santa Barbara and Ventura (pt.). Prior Terms: House: 1974 (Special Election)-1986. Born: September 4, 1926; Ventura, Calif. Education: University of California; University of Santa Clara Law School (LL.B.). Military Service: U.S. Navy, WW II. Occupation: Attorney; Ojai city councilman (1958); mayor (1959-60); California senator (1961, 1964, 1966, 1970).

1. Immigration Reform Y
2. Open fld-search warrants Y
3. Civil pnty-hire ill alien Y
4. So Afr sanc-veto override Y
5. Tax Overhaul Y
6. South Africa sanctions Y
7. Death penalty-drug bill Y
8. Evidence-warrantless srch Y
9. Life term-second drug off Y
10. Military use in drug war Y
11. Troop reduction in Europe N
12. Prohibit chemical weapons N
13. Bar ASAT testing N
14. Abide SALT II weapons ban N
15. Follow SALT II-Soviets do Y
16. Reduce SDI funding N
17. Increase SDI funding Y
18. Purchase Trident sub N
19. Delete 12 MX;Add conv wpn N
20. Raise speed limit Y
21. Textile Import Quotas(*) N
22. Req Pentagon buy US goods N
23. AIDS ins anti-dscriminatn N
24. Nicaraguan refugee aid N
25. Nicaraguan contra aid Y
26. US abide by SALT II Y
27. Prohibit Saudi arms sale N
28. Military Retiremnt Reform Y
29. Nicaraguan refugee aid Y
30. Ease '68 Gun Control Act Y
31. Bar intrstat handgun tran N
32. Keep '68 Gun Control Act N
33. Nicaraguan contra aid Y
34. Bar emp polygraph testing N
35. Tax Overhaul consideratn Y
36. Bar armor-piercing ammo Y
37. Tax Overhaul consideratn Y
38. Make comp emissions known N
39. Allow toxic victims suits N
40. Strike Superfund "VAT" N
41. Notify emp-plant closing N
42. Bar emp consult-plant clo Y
43. Medicare cuts;Tax incres' N
44. Delete 12 MX missiles N

LAGOMARSINO, ROBERT J. (Cont.)

45. Spending cuts;Tax incres' N
46. Textile Import Quotas N
47. Cut some school lunch fds Y
48. Clean Water Act Amendmts Y
49. Youth work projects Y
50. Assist military in Angola Y
51. Allow US troops-Nicaragua Y
52. Pentagon polygraph exams Y
53. Bar ASAT testing N
54. Suspend def pmt for abuse N
55. Bar Pentagon-contr emplmt Y
56. Increase SDI funding Y
57. Reduce SDI funding N
58. Produce chemical weapons Y
59. Bar CIA fndg in Nicaragua N
60. South Africa sanctions N
61. Cut SS COLAs; Raise taxes N
62. Let US invest-So Africa Y
63. Approve 21 MX for 1985 Y
64. Emergency Farm Credit N
65. Awards to whistle blowers Y
66. African disaster relief Y
67. Ban bank loans to So Afr N
68. Bar coun duty-free trtmt N
69. Steel import limits N
70. Soc Sec COLAs=inflation Y
71. Bar haz waste vctms suits Y
72. Prohibit aid to Nicaragua N
73. Cut $-Schs bar sch prayer Y
74. Raise taxes; Cut Medicare N
75. Alien residncy-prior 1982 Y
76. Alien residncy-prior 1980 Y
77. Pen emp-hire illgl aliens N
78. Lmt Persh II/cruse-Europe N
79. Delete 34 B-1 bombers N
80. Bar purch of Pershing II N
81. Bar purchase of Sgt York N
82. Delete $ for Trident II N
83. Allow 15 MX missiles Y
84. Bar MX procurement-1985 N
85. Equal Access Act Y
86. Aid to El Salvador Y
87. Bar Nicarag water mining Y
88. Physician/Medicare freeze Y
89. Increase "sin" taxes N
90. End SBA direct loans N
91. Sell Conrail Y
92. Equal Rights Amendment N
93. Marines in Lebanon Y
94. Eminent domain-Coal comps Y
95. Prohibit EPA sanctions Y
96. SS age increase/Reforms Y
97. Auto domestic content req N
98. Delete jobs program fundg Y
99. Highway-Gas tax bill Y
100. Raise Medicare;Cut defnse N
101. Emergency housing aid Y
102. Across-the-board tax cuts Y
103. Gramm-Latta II targets Y
104. Delete B-1 bomber funds N
105. Dsapprov Saudi AWACS sale N
106. Disapprove oil import fee Y
107. Rail Deregulation N
108. Dsapp India nuc fuel sale Y
109. Mil draft registration N
110. Chrysler Loan Guarantees N
111. Prohibit school busing Y
112. Nuclear plant moratorium Y
113. Oil price controls N
114. Tuition Tax Credits Y
115. Est Consumer Protect Agcy N
116. Eliminate B-1 bomber fnds N
117. Subminimum wage for youth Y
118. Delete crude oil tax Y
119. Natural gas deregulation Y

Presidential Support Score: 1986 - 82% 1985 -- 80%

THOMAS, WILLIAM M. -- California 20th District [Republican]. Counties of Kern (pt.), Los Angeles (pt.) and San Luis Obispo (pt.). Prior Terms: House: 1979-86. Born: December 6, 1941; Wallace, Idaho. Education: San Francisco State University (M.A.). Occupation: Professor (1965-74); California state legislator (1974-78).

1. Immigration Reform N
2. Open fld-search warrants Y
3. Civil pnty-hire ill alien N
4. So Afr sanc-veto override ?
5. Tax Overhaul N
6. South Africa sanctions ?
7. Death penalty-drug bill Y
8. Evidence-warrantless srch Y
9. Life term-second drug off Y
10. Military use in drug war Y
11. Troop reduction in Europe N
12. Prohibit chemical weapons N
13. Bar ASAT testing N
14. Abide SALT II weapons ban N
15. Follow SALT II-Soviets do Y
16. Reduce SDI funding N
17. Increase SDI funding N
18. Purchase Trident sub N
19. Delete 12 MX;Add conv wpn N
20. Raise speed limit Y
21. Textile Import Quotas(*) Y
22. Req Pentagon buy US goods N

THOMAS, WILLIAM M. (Cont.)

23. AIDS ins anti-dscriminatn N
24. Nicaraguan refugee aid N
25. Nicaraguan contra aid Y
26. US abide by SALT II N
27. Prohibit Saudi arms sale N
28. Military Retiremnt Reform Y
29. Nicaraguan refugee aid Y
30. Ease '68 Gun Control Act Y
31. Bar intrstat handgun tran N
32. Keep '68 Gun Control Act N
33. Nicaraguan contra aid Y
34. Bar emp polygraph testing N
35. Tax Overhaul consideratn N
36. Bar armor-piercing ammo Y
37. Tax Overhaul consideratn N
38. Make comp emissions known N
39. Allow toxic victims suits N
40. Strike Superfund "VAT" N
41. Notify emp-plant closing N
42. Bar emp consult-plant clo Y
43. Medicare cuts;Tax incres' N
44. Delete 12 MX missiles N
45. Spending cuts;Tax incres' N
46. Textile Import Quotas Y
47. Cut some school lunch fds Y
48. Clean Water Act Amendmnts Y
49. Youth work projects N
50. Assist military in Angola Y
51. Allow US troops-Nicaragua Y
52. Pentagon polygraph exams Y
53. Bar ASAT testing N
54. Suspend def pmt for abuse N
55. Bar Pentagon-contr emplmt Y
56. Increase SDI funding Y
57. Reduce SDI funding N
58. Produce chemical weapons Y
59. Bar CIA fndg in Nicaragua N
60. South Africa sanctions -
61. Cut SS COLAs; Raise taxes N
62. Let US invest-So Africa Y
63. Approve 21 MX for 1985 Y
64. Emergency Farm Credit Y
65. Awards to whistle blowers Y
66. African disaster relief Y
67. Ban bank loans to So Afr Y
68. Bar coun duty-free trtmt N
69. Steel import limits N
70. Soc Sec COLAs=inflation Y
71. Bar haz waste vctms suits ?
72. Prohibit aid to Nicaragua N
73. Cut $-Schs bar sch prayer N
74. Raise taxes; Cut Medicare Y
75. Alien residncy-prior 1982 Y
76. Alien residncy-prior 1980 Y
77. Pen emp-hire illgl aliens N
78. Lmt Persh II/cruse-Europe N
79. Delete 34 B-1 bombers N
80. Bar purch of Pershing II N
81. Bar purchase of Sgt York Y
82. Delete $ for Trident II N
83. Allow 15 MX missiles Y
84. Bar MX procurement-1985 N
85. Equal Access Act Y
86. Aid to El Salvador Y
87. Bar Nicarag water mining Y
88. Physician/Medicare freeze Y
89. Increase "sin" taxes Y
90. End SBA direct loans Y
91. Sell Conrail Y
92. Equal Rights Amendment Y
93. Marines in Lebanon Y
94. Eminent domain-Coal comps Y
95. Prohibit EPA sanctions Y
96. SS age increase/Reforms Y
97. Auto domestic content req N
98. Delete jobs program fundg #
99. Highway-Gas tax bill Y
100. Raise Medicare;Cut defnse N
101. Emergency housing aid Y
102. Across-the-board tax cuts Y
103. Gramm-Latta II targets Y
104. Delete B-1 bomber funds N
105. Dsapprov Saudi AWACS sale N
106. Disapprove oil import fee Y
107. Rail Deregulation N
108. Dsapp India nuc fuel sale Y
109. Mil draft registration Y
110. Chrysler Loan Guarantees N
111. Prohibit school busing Y
112. Nuclear plant moratorium N
113. Oil price controls N

Presidential Support Score: 1986 - 77% 1985 - 61%

FIEDLER, BOBBI -- California 21st District [Republican]. Counties of Los Angeles (pt.) and Ventura (pt.). Prior Terms: House: 1981-86. Born: April 22, 1937; Santa Monica, Calif. Education: Santa Monica City College; Santa Monica Technical School. Occupation: Owned and operated two pharmacies; Los Angeles board of education member.

1. Immigration Reform N
2. Open fld-search warrants Y
3. Civil pnty-hire ill alien N
4. So Afr sanc-veto override ?
5. Tax Overhaul Y
6. South Africa sanctions Y

FIEDLER, BOBBI (Cont.)

7. Death penalty-drug bill	Y	57. Reduce SDI funding	N
8. Evidence-warrantless srch	Y	58. Produce chemical weapons	Y
9. Life term-second drug off	Y	59. Bar CIA fndg in Nicaragua	N
10. Military use in drug war	Y	60. South Africa sanctions	N
11. Troop reduction in Europe	N	61. Cut SS COLAs; Raise taxes	N
12. Prohibit chemical weapons	N	62. Let US invest-So Africa	Y
13. Bar ASAT testing	N	63. Approve 21 MX for 1985	Y
14. Abide SALT II weapons ban	N	64. Emergency Farm Credit	N
15. Follow SALT II-Soviets do	Y	65. Awards to whistle blowers	Y
16. Reduce SDI funding	N	66. African disaster relief	Y
17. Increase SDI funding	Y	67. Ban bank loans to So Afr	Y
18. Purchase Trident sub	N	68. Bar coun duty-free trtmt	N
19. Delete 12 MX;Add conv wpn	N	69. Steel import limits	N
20. Raise speed limit	Y	70. Soc Sec COLAs=inflation	Y
21. Textile Import Quotas(*)	N	71. Bar haz waste vctms suits	Y
22. Req Pentagon buy US goods	N	72. Prohibit aid to Nicaragua	N
23. AIDS ins anti-dscriminatn	N	73. Cut $-Schs bar sch prayer	N
24. Nicaraguan refugee aid	N	74. Raise taxes; Cut Medicare	N
25. Nicaraguan contra aid	Y	75. Alien residncy-prior 1982	N
26. US abide by SALT II	Y	76. Alien residncy-prior 1980	N
27. Prohibit Saudi arms sale	Y	77. Pen emp-hire illgl aliens	N
28. Military Retiremnt Reform	?	78. Lmt Persh II/cruse-Europe	N
29. Nicaraguan refugee aid	Y	79. Delete 34 B-1 bombers	N
30. Ease '68 Gun Control Act	Y	80. Bar purch of Pershing II	N
31. Bar intrstat handgun tran	N	81. Bar purchase of Sgt York	?
32. Keep '68 Gun Control Act	N	82. Delete $ for Trident II	N
33. Nicaraguan contra aid	Y	83. Allow 15 MX missiles	Y
34. Bar emp polygraph testing	N	84. Bar MX procurement-1985	N
35. Tax Overhaul consideratn	N	85. Equal Access Act	Y
36. Bar armor-piercing ammo	Y	86. Aid to El Salvador	Y
37. Tax Overhaul consideratn	N	87. Bar Nicarag water mining	Y
38. Make comp emissions known	N	88. Physician/Medicare freeze	Y
39. Allow toxic victims suits	N	89. Increase "sin" taxes	N
40. Strike Superfund "VAT"	N	90. End SBA direct loans	N
41. Notify emp-plant closing	N	91. Sell Conrail	Y
42. Bar emp consult-plant clo	Y	92. Equal Rights Amendment	Y
43. Medicare cuts;Tax incres'	N	93. Marines in Lebanon	Y
44. Delete 12 MX missiles	N	94. Eminent domain-Coal comps	Y
45. Spending cuts;Tax incres'	N	95. Prohibit EPA sanctions	Y
46. Textile Import Quotas	Y	96. SS age increase/Reforms	Y
47. Cut some school lunch fds	Y	97. Auto domestic content req	N
48. Clean Water Act Amendmnts	Y	98. Delete jobs program fundg	Y
49. Youth work projects	N	99. Highway-Gas tax bill	N
50. Assist military in Angola	Y	100. Raise Medicare;Cut defnse	N
51. Allow US troops-Nicaragua	Y	101. Emergency housing aid	Y
52. Pentagon polygraph exams	Y	102. Across-the-board tax cuts	Y
53. Bar ASAT testing	N	103. Gramm-Latta II targets	Y
54. Suspend def pmt for abuse	N	104. Delete B-1 bomber funds	N
55. Bar Pentagon-contr emplmt	Y	105. Dsapprov Saudi AWACS sale	Y
56. Increase SDI funding	Y		

Presidential Support Score: 1986 - 66% 1985 - 74%

MOORHEAD, CARLOS J. -- California 22nd District [Republican]. County of Los Angeles (pt.). Prior Terms: House: 1973-86. Born: May 6, 1922; Long Beach, Calif. Education: University of California (B.A.); University of Southern California (J.D.). Military Service: U.S. Army WW II. Occupation: Attorney; director, Lawyer's Reference Service, Blendale Bar Assn.; president, Glendale Bar Assn.; California assemblyman.

MOORHEAD, CARLOS J. (Cont.)

1. Immigration Reform Y
2. Open fld-search warrants Y
3. Civil pnty-hire ill alien N
4. So Afr sanc-veto override N
5. Tax Overhaul N
6. South Africa sanctions N
7. Death penalty-drug bill Y
8. Evidence-warrantless srch Y
9. Life term-second drug off Y
10. Military use in drug war Y
11. Troop reduction in Europe N
12. Prohibit chemical weapons N
13. Bar ASAT testing N
14. Abide SALT II weapons ban N
15. Follow SALT II-Soviets do Y
16. Reduce SDI funding N
17. Increase SDI funding Y
18. Purchase Trident sub N
19. Delete 12 MX;Add conv wpn N
20. Raise speed limit Y
21. Textile Import Quotas(*) N
22. Req Pentagon buy US goods N
23. AIDS ins anti-dscriminatn N
24. Nicaraguan refugee aid N
25. Nicaraguan contra aid Y
26. US abide by SALT II Y
27. Prohibit Saudi arms sale Y
28. Military Retiremnt Reform Y
29. Nicaraguan refugee aid Y
30. Ease '68 Gun Control Act Y
31. Bar intrstat handgun tran N
32. Keep '68 Gun Control Act N
33. Nicaraguan contra aid Y
34. Bar emp polygraph testing N
35. Tax Overhaul consideratn N
36. Bar armor-piercing ammo N
37. Tax Overhaul consideratn N
38. Make comp emissions known N
39. Allow toxic victims suits N
40. Strike Superfund "VAT" N
41. Notify emp-plant closing N
42. Bar emp consult-plant clo Y
43. Medicare cuts;Tax incres' N
44. Delete 12 MX missiles N
45. Spending cuts;Tax incres' N
46. Textile Import Quotas N
47. Cut some school lunch fds Y
48. Clean Water Act Amendmnts Y
49. Youth work projects N
50. Assist military in Angola Y
51. Allow US troops-Nicaragua Y
52. Pentagon polygraph exams Y
53. Bar ASAT testing N
54. Suspend def pmt for abuse N
55. Bar Pentagon-contr emplmt Y
56. Increase SDI funding Y
57. Reduce SDI funding N
58. Produce chemical weapons Y
59. Bar CIA fndg in Nicaragua N
60. South Africa sanctions N
61. Cut SS COLAs; Raise taxes N
62. Let US invest-So Africa Y
63. Approve 21 MX for 1985 Y
64. Emergency Farm Credit N
65. Awards to whistle blowers Y
66. African disaster relief Y
67. Ban bank loans to So Afr N
68. Bar coun duty-free trtmt N
69. Steel import limits N
70. Soc Sec COLAs=inflation Y
71. Bar haz waste vctms suits Y
72. Prohibit aid to Nicaragua N
73. Cut $-Schs bar sch prayer Y
74. Raise taxes; Cut Medicare N
75. Alien residncy-prior 1982 Y
76. Alien residncy-prior 1980 Y
77. Pen emp-hire illgl aliens N
78. Lmt Persh II/cruse-Europe N
79. Delete 34 B-1 bombers N
80. Bar purch of Pershing II N
81. Bar purchase of Sgt York N
82. Delete $ for Trident II N
83. Allow 15 MX missiles Y
84. Bar MX procurement-1985 N
85. Equal Access Act Y
86. Aid to El Salvador Y
87. Bar Nicarag water mining N
88. Physician/Medicare freeze Y
89. Increase "sin" taxes N
90. End SBA direct loans Y
91. Sell Conrail Y
92. Equal Rights Amendment N
93. Marines in Lebanon Y
94. Eminent domain-Coal comps Y
95. Prohibit EPA sanctions Y
96. SS age increase/Reforms Y
97. Auto domestic content req N
98. Delete jobs program fundg Y
99. Highway-Gas tax bill N
100. Raise Medicare;Cut defnse N
101. Emergency housing aid N
102. Across-the-board tax cuts Y
103. Gramm-Latta II targets Y
104. Delete B-1 bomber funds N
105. Dsapprov Saudi AWACS sale N
106. Disapprove oil import fee Y
107. Rail Deregulation N
108. Dsapp India nuc fuel sale Y
109. Mil draft registration N
110. Chrysler Loan Guarantees Y
111. Prohibit school busing Y
112. Nuclear plant moratorium N
113. Oil price controls N
114. Tuition Tax Credits Y
115. Est Consumer Protect Agcy N
116. Eliminate B-1 bomber fnds N
117. Subminimum wage for youth Y
118. Delete crude oil tax Y

MOORHEAD, CARLOS J. (Cont.)
119. Natural gas deregulation Y

Presidential Support Score: 1986 - 83% 1985 - 80%

BEILENSON, ANTHONY C. -- California 23rd District [Democrat]. County of Los Angeles (pt.). Prior Terms: House: 1977-86. Born: October 26, 1932; New Rochelle, N.Y. Education: Harvard University (A.B., LL.B.). Occupation: California assemblyman (1963-66); California senator (1967-77).

1. Immigration Reform Y
2. Open fld-search warrants Y
3. Civil pnty-hire ill alien N
4. So Afr sanc-veto override Y
5. Tax Overhaul Y
6. South Africa sanctions Y
7. Death penalty-drug bill Y
8. Evidence-warrantless srch N
9. Life term-second drug off N
10. Military use in drug war N
11. Troop reduction in Europe Y
12. Prohibit chemical weapons Y
13. Bar ASAT testing Y
14. Abide SALT II weapons ban Y
15. Follow SALT II-Soviets do N
16. Reduce SDI funding Y
17. Increase SDI funding N
18. Purchase Trident sub Y
19. Delete 12 MX;Add conv wpn Y
20. Raise speed limit N
21. Textile Import Quotas(*) N
22. Req Pentagon buy US goods N
23. AIDS ins anti-dscriminatn Y
24. Nicaraguan refugee aid Y
25. Nicaraguan contra aid N
26. US abide by SALT II N
27. Prohibit Saudi arms sale Y
28. Military Retiremnt Reform Y
29. Nicaraguan refugee aid Y
30. Ease '68 Gun Control Act N
31. Bar intrstat handgun tran Y
32. Keep '68 Gun Control Act Y
33. Nicaraguan contra aid N
34. Bar emp polygraph testing Y
35. Tax Overhaul consideratn Y
36. Bar armor-piercing ammo Y
37. Tax Overhaul consideratn ?
38. Make comp emissions known Y
39. Allow toxic victims suits Y
40. Strike Superfund "VAT" Y
41. Notify emp-plant closing Y
42. Bar emp consult-plant clo N
43. Medicare cuts;Tax incres' Y
44. Delete 12 MX missiles Y
45. Spending cuts;Tax incres' Y
46. Textile Import Quotas N
47. Cut some school lunch fds N
48. Clean Water Act Amendmnts N
49. Youth work projects Y
50. Assist military in Angola N
51. Allow US troops-Nicaragua N
52. Pentagon polygraph exams ?
53. Bar ASAT testing Y
54. Suspend def pmt for abuse Y
55. Bar Pentagon-contr emplmt Y
56. Increase SDI funding N
57. Reduce SDI funding Y
58. Produce chemical weapons N
59. Bar CIA fndg in Nicaragua Y
60. South Africa sanctions Y
61. Cut SS COLAs; Raise taxes N
62. Let US invest-So Africa N
63. Approve 21 MX for 1985 N
64. Emergency Farm Credit Y
65. Awards to whistle blowers Y
66. African disaster relief Y
67. Ban bank loans to So Afr Y
68. Bar coun duty-free trtmt Y
69. Steel import limits N
70. Soc Sec COLAs=inflation N
71. Bar haz waste vctms suits Y
72. Prohibit aid to Nicaragua Y
73. Cut $-Schs bar sch prayer N
74. Raise taxes; Cut Medicare Y
75. Alien residncy-prior 1982 N
76. Alien residncy-prior 1980 N
77. Pen emp-hire illgl aliens Y
78. Lmt Persh II/cruse-Europe Y
79. Delete 34 B-1 bombers Y
80. Bar purch of Pershing II Y
81. Bar purchase of Sgt York Y
82. Delete $ for Trident II Y
83. Allow 15 MX missiles N
84. Bar MX procurement-1985 Y
85. Equal Access Act N
86. Aid to El Salvador N
87. Bar Nicarag water mining Y
88. Physician/Medicare freeze N
89. Increase "sin" taxes Y
90. End SBA direct loans N
91. Sell Conrail N
92. Equal Rights Amendment Y
93. Marines in Lebanon Y
94. Eminent domain-Coal comps Y
95. Prohibit EPA sanctions N
96. SS age increase/Reforms Y
97. Auto domestic content req N
98. Delete jobs program fundg ?

BEILENSON, ANTHONY C. (Cont.)

99. Highway-Gas tax bill Y
100. Raise Medicare;Cut defnse N
101. Emergency housing aid N
102. Across-the-board tax cuts N
103. Gramm-Latta II targets N
104. Delete B-1 bomber funds Y
105. Dsapprov Saudi AWACS sale Y
106. Disapprove oil import fee X
107. Rail Deregulation N
108. Dsapp India nuc fuel sale Y
109. Mil draft registration N
110. Chrysler Loan Guarantees N
111. Prohibit school busing N
112. Nuclear plant moratorium Y
113. Oil price controls N
114. Tuition Tax Credits N
115. Est Consumer Protect Agcy Y
116. Eliminate B-1 bomber fnds Y
117. Subminimum wage for youth N
118. Delete crude oil tax N
119. Natural gas deregulation N

Presidential Support Score: 1986 - 18% 1985 - 23%

WAXMAN, HENRY A. -- California 24th District [Democrat]. County of Los Angeles (pt.). Prior Terms: House: 1975-86. Born: September 12, 1939; Los Angeles, Calif. Education: University of California (B.A., LL.B.). Occupation: Attorney; California assemblyman.

1. Immigration Reform Y
2. Open fld-search warrants Y
3. Civil pnty-hire ill alien N
4. So Afr sanc-veto override Y
5. Tax Overhaul Y
6. South Africa sanctions Y
7. Death penalty-drug bill N
8. Evidence-warrantless srch N
9. Life term-second drug off N
10. Military use in drug war Y
11. Troop reduction in Europe N
12. Prohibit chemical weapons Y
13. Bar ASAT testing Y
14. Abide SALT II weapons ban Y
15. Follow SALT II-Soviets do N
16. Reduce SDI funding Y
17. Increase SDI funding N
18. Purchase Trident sub Y
19. Delete 12 MX;Add conv wpn Y
20. Raise speed limit N
21. Textile Import Quotas(*) N
22. Req Pentagon buy US goods ?
23. AIDS ins anti-dscriminatn Y
24. Nicaraguan refugee aid Y
25. Nicaraguan contra aid N
26. US abide by SALT II N
27. Prohibit Saudi arms sale Y
28. Military Retiremnt Reform Y
29. Nicaraguan refugee aid Y
30. Ease '68 Gun Control Act N
31. Bar intrstat handgun tran Y
32. Keep '68 Gun Control Act Y
33. Nicaraguan contra aid N
34. Bar emp polygraph testing Y
35. Tax Overhaul consideratn Y
36. Bar armor-piercing ammo Y
37. Tax Overhaul consideratn Y
38. Make comp emissions known Y
39. Allow toxic victims suits Y
40. Strike Superfund "VAT" Y
41. Notify emp-plant closing Y
42. Bar emp consult-plant clo N
43. Medicare cuts;Tax incres' Y
44. Delete 12 MX missiles Y
45. Spending cuts;Tax incres' Y
46. Textile Import Quotas N
47. Cut some school lunch fds N
48. Clean Water Act Amendmnts N
49. Youth work projects Y
50. Assist military in Angola ?
51. Allow US troops-Nicaragua N
52. Pentagon polygraph exams N
53. Bar ASAT testing Y
54. Suspend def pmt for abuse Y
55. Bar Pentagon-contr emplmt Y
56. Increase SDI funding N
57. Reduce SDI funding Y
58. Produce chemical weapons N
59. Bar CIA fndg in Nicaragua Y
60. South Africa sanctions Y
61. Cut SS COLAs; Raise taxes N
62. Let US invest-So Africa N
63. Approve 21 MX for 1985 N
64. Emergency Farm Credit Y
65. Awards to whistle blowers Y
66. African disaster relief Y
67. Ban bank loans to So Afr ?
68. Bar coun duty-free trtmt N
69. Steel import limits N
70. Soc Sec COLAs=inflation Y
71. Bar haz waste vctms suits N
72. Prohibit aid to Nicaragua Y
73. Cut $-Schs bar sch prayer N
74. Raise taxes; Cut Medicare Y
75. Alien residncy-prior 1982 N
76. Alien residncy-prior 1980 N
77. Pen emp-hire illgl aliens Y
78. Lmt Persh II/cruse-Europe Y

WAXMAN, HENRY A. (Cont.)

79. Delete 34 B-1 bombers Y
80. Bar purch of Pershing II Y
81. Bar purchase of Sgt York Y
82. Delete $ for Trident II Y
83. Allow 15 MX missiles N
84. Bar MX procurement-1985 Y
85. Equal Access Act N
86. Aid to El Salvador N
87. Bar Nicarag water mining Y
88. Physician/Medicare freeze N
89. Increase "sin" taxes Y
90. End SBA direct loans N
91. Sell Conrail N
92. Equal Rights Amendment Y
93. Marines in Lebanon N
94. Eminent domain-Coal comps N
95. Prohibit EPA sanctions Y
96. SS age increase/Reforms N
97. Auto domestic content req N
98. Delete jobs program fundg N
99. Highway-Gas tax bill Y
100. Raise Medicare;Cut defnse Y
101. Emergency housing aid Y
102. Across-the-board tax cuts N
103. Gramm-Latta II targets N
104. Delete B-1 bomber funds Y
105. Dsapprov Saudi AWACS sale Y
106. Disapprove oil import fee Y
107. Rail Deregulation N
108. Dsapp India nuc fuel sale Y
109. Mil draft registration N
110. Chrysler Loan Guarantees Y
111. Prohibit school busing N
112. Nuclear plant moratorium Y
113. Oil price controls Y
114. Tuition Tax Credits N
115. Est Consumer Protect Agcy Y
116. Eliminate B-1 bomber fnds Y
117. Subminimum wage for youth N
118. Delete crude oil tax N
119. Natural gas deregulation N

Presidential Support Score: 1986 - 13% 1985 - 28%

ROYBAL, EDWARD R. -- California 25th District [Democrat]. County of Los Angeles (pt.). Prior Terms: House: 1963-86. Born: February 10, 1916; Albuquerque, N.M. Education: University of California; Southwestern University. Military Service: U.S. Army, 1944-45. Occupation: Member, Civilian Conservation Corps (1934-35); social worker, public health educator, California Tuberculosis Assn.; director, health education, Los Angeles County Tuberculosis and Health Assn. (1942-49); Los Angeles City councilman (1949-62).

1. Immigration Reform N
2. Open fld-search warrants Y
3. Civil pnty-hire ill alien Y
4. So Afr sanc-veto override Y
5. Tax Overhaul Y
6. South Africa sanctions Y
7. Death penalty-drug bill N
8. Evidence-warrantless srch N
9. Life term-second drug off N
10. Military use in drug war N
11. Troop reduction in Europe Y
12. Prohibit chemical weapons Y
13. Bar ASAT testing Y
14. Abide SALT II weapons ban Y
15. Follow SALT II-Soviets do N
16. Reduce SDI funding Y
17. Increase SDI funding N
18. Purchase Trident sub Y
19. Delete 12 MX;Add conv wpn ?
20. Raise speed limit Y
21. Textile Import Quotas(*) Y
22. Req Pentagon buy US goods N
23. AIDS ins anti-dscriminatn Y
24. Nicaraguan refugee aid Y
25. Nicaraguan contra aid N
26. US abide by SALT II N
27. Prohibit Saudi arms sale Y
28. Military Retiremnt Reform Y
29. Nicaraguan refugee aid Y
30. Ease '68 Gun Control Act N
31. Bar intrstat handgun tran Y
32. Keep '68 Gun Control Act Y
33. Nicaraguan contra aid N
34. Bar emp polygraph testing Y
35. Tax Overhaul consideratn N
36. Bar armor-piercing ammo Y
37. Tax Overhaul consideratn Y
38. Make comp emissions known Y
39. Allow toxic victims suits Y
40. Strike Superfund "VAT" Y
41. Notify emp-plant closing Y
42. Bar emp consult-plant clo N
43. Medicare cuts;Tax incres' Y
44. Delete 12 MX missiles Y
45. Spending cuts;Tax incres' Y
46. Textile Import Quotas N
47. Cut some school lunch fds N
48. Clean Water Act Amendmnts N
49. Youth work projects ?
50. Assist military in Angola N

ROYBAL, EDWARD R. (Cont.)

51. Allow US troops-Nicaragua N
52. Pentagon polygraph exams N
53. Bar ASAT testing Y
54. Suspend def pmt for abuse Y
55. Bar Pentagon-contr emplmt Y
56. Increase SDI funding N
57. Reduce SDI funding Y
58. Produce chemical weapons N
59. Bar CIA fndg in Nicaragua Y
60. South Africa sanctions Y
61. Cut SS COLAs; Raise taxes N
62. Let US invest-So Africa N
63. Approve 21 MX for 1985 N
64. Emergency Farm Credit Y
65. Awards to whistle blowers Y
66. African disaster relief Y
67. Ban bank loans to So Afr ?
68. Bar coun duty-free trtmt Y
69. Steel import limits Y
70. Soc Sec COLAs=inflation Y
71. Bar haz waste vctms suits N
72. Prohibit aid to Nicaragua Y
73. Cut $-Schs bar sch prayer N
74. Raise taxes; Cut Medicare N
75. Alien residncy-prior 1982 N
76. Alien residncy-prior 1980 N
77. Pen emp-hire illgl aliens Y
78. Lmt Persh II/cruse-Europe Y
79. Delete 34 B-1 bombers Y
80. Bar purch of Pershing II Y
81. Bar purchase of Sgt York Y
82. Delete $ for Trident II Y
83. Allow 15 MX missiles N
84. Bar MX procurement-1985 Y
85. Equal Access Act N
86. Aid to El Salvador N
87. Bar Nicarag water mining Y
88. Physician/Medicare freeze N
89. Increase "sin" taxes Y
90. End SBA direct loans ?
91. Sell Conrail ?
92. Equal Rights Amendment Y
93. Marines in Lebanon N
94. Eminent domain-Coal comps N
95. Prohibit EPA sanctions N
96. SS age increase/Reforms N
97. Auto domestic content req Y
98. Delete jobs program fundg N
99. Highway-Gas tax bill Y
100. Raise Medicare;Cut defnse Y
101. Emergency housing aid Y
102. Across-the-board tax cuts N
103. Gramm-Latta II targets N
104. Delete B-1 bomber funds Y
105. Dsapprov Saudi AWACS sale Y
106. Disapprove oil import fee Y
107. Rail Deregulation N
108. Dsapp India nuc fuel sale Y
109. Mil draft registration N
110. Chrysler Loan Guarantees Y
111. Prohibit school busing N
112. Nuclear plant moratorium Y
113. Oil price controls Y
114. Tuition Tax Credits N
115. Est Consumer Protect Agcy Y
116. Eliminate B-1 bomber fnds Y
117. Subminimum wage for youth N
118. Delete crude oil tax N
119. Natural gas deregulation N

Presidential Support Score: 1986 - 16% 1985 - 16%

BERMAN, HOWARD L. -- California 26th District [Democrat]. County of Los Angeles (pt.). Prior Terms: House: 1983-86. Born: April 15, 1941; Los Angeles, Calif. Education: University of California (B.A., LL.B.). Occupation: Attorney (1966-72); California assemblyman (1972).

1. Immigration Reform Y
2. Open fld-search warrants Y
3. Civil pnty-hire ill alien N
4. So Afr sanc-veto override Y
5. Tax Overhaul Y
6. South Africa sanctions Y
7. Death penalty-drug bill N
8. Evidence-warrantless srch N
9. Life term-second drug off Y
10. Military use in drug war N
11. Troop reduction in Europe Y
12. Prohibit chemical weapons Y
13. Bar ASAT testing Y
14. Abide SALT II weapons ban Y
15. Follow SALT II-Soviets do N
16. Reduce SDI funding Y
17. Increase SDI funding N
18. Purchase Trident sub Y
19. Delete 12 MX;Add conv wpn Y
20. Raise speed limit N
21. Textile Import Quotas(*) N
22. Req Pentagon buy US goods ?
23. AIDS ins anti-dscriminatn Y
24. Nicaraguan refugee aid Y
25. Nicaraguan contra aid N
26. US abide by SALT II N
27. Prohibit Saudi arms sale Y
28. Military Retiremnt Reform Y
29. Nicaraguan refugee aid Y
30. Ease '68 Gun Control Act N

BERMAN, HOWARD L. (Cont.)

31. Bar intrstat handgun tran Y
32. Keep '68 Gun Control Act Y
33. Nicaraguan contra aid N
34. Bar emp polygraph testing Y
35. Tax Overhaul consideratn Y
36. Bar armor-piercing ammo Y
37. Tax Overhaul consideratn Y
38. Make comp emissions known Y
39. Allow toxic victims suits Y
40. Strike Superfund "VAT" Y
41. Notify emp-plant closing Y
42. Bar emp consult-plant clo N
43. Medicare cuts;Tax incres' Y
44. Delete 12 MX missiles Y
45. Spending cuts;Tax incres' Y
46. Textile Import Quotas N
47. Cut some school lunch fds N
48. Clean Water Act Amendmnts N
49. Youth work projects Y
50. Assist military in Angola N
51. Allow US troops-Nicaragua N
52. Pentagon polygraph exams N
53. Bar ASAT testing Y
54. Suspend def pmt for abuse Y
55. Bar Pentagon-contr emplmt Y
56. Increase SDI funding N
57. Reduce SDI funding Y
58. Produce chemical weapons N
59. Bar CIA fndg in Nicaragua Y
60. South Africa sanctions Y
61. Cut SS COLAs; Raise taxes N
62. Let US invest-So Africa N
63. Approve 21 MX for 1985 N
64. Emergency Farm Credit Y
65. Awards to whistle blowers Y
66. African disaster relief Y
67. Ban bank loans to So Afr Y
68. Bar coun duty-free trtmt N
69. Steel import limits N
70. Soc Sec COLAs=inflation ?
71. Bar haz waste vctms suits N
72. Prohibit aid to Nicaragua Y
73. Cut $-Schs bar sch prayer N
74. Raise taxes; Cut Medicare Y
75. Alien residncy-prior 1982 N
76. Alien residncy-prior 1980 N
77. Pen emp-hire illgl aliens Y
78. Lmt Persh II/cruse-Europe Y
79. Delete 34 B-1 bombers Y
80. Bar purch of Pershing II Y
81. Bar purchase of Sgt York Y
82. Delete $ for Trident II Y
83. Allow 15 MX missiles N
84. Bar MX procurement-1985 Y
85. Equal Access Act N
86. Aid to El Salvador N
87. Bar Nicarag water mining Y
88. Physician/Medicare freeze N
89. Increase "sin" taxes Y
90. End SBA direct loans N
91. Sell Conrail ?
92. Equal Rights Amendment Y
93. Marines in Lebanon Y
94. Eminent domain-Coal comps N
95. Prohibit EPA sanctions ?
96. SS age increase/Reforms N

Presidential Support Score: 1986 - 18% 1985 - 24%

LEVINE, MEL -- California 27th District [Democrat]. County of Los Angeles (pt.). Prior Terms: House: 1983-86. Born: June 7, 1943; Los Angeles, Calif. Education: University of California; Princeton University (M.S.); Harvard Law School (J.D.). Occupation: Attorney; Senate legislative assistant; California assemblyman.

1. Immigration Reform Y
2. Open fld-search warrants Y
3. Civil pnty-hire ill alien N
4. So Afr sanc-veto override Y
5. Tax Overhaul Y
6. South Africa sanctions Y
7. Death penalty-drug bill N
8. Evidence-warrantless srch N
9. Life term-second drug off Y
10. Military use in drug war N
11. Troop reduction in Europe Y
12. Prohibit chemical weapons Y
13. Bar ASAT testing Y
14. Abide SALT II weapons ban Y
15. Follow SALT II-Soviets do ?
16. Reduce SDI funding Y
17. Increase SDI funding N
18. Purchase Trident sub Y
19. Delete 12 MX;Add conv wpn Y
20. Raise speed limit N
21. Textile Import Quotas*) N
22. Req Pentagon buy US goods N
23. AIDS ins anti-dscriminatn Y
24. Nicaraguan refugee aid Y
25. Nicaraguan contra aid N
26. US abide by SALT II N
27. Prohibit Saudi arms sale Y
28. Military Retiremnt Reform Y
29. Nicaraguan refugee aid Y
30. Ease '68 Gun Control Act N
31. Bar intrstat handgun tran Y
32. Keep '68 Gun Control Act Y

LEVINE, MEL (Cont.)

33. Nicaraguan contra aid N
34. Bar emp polygraph testing Y
35. Tax Overhaul consideratn Y
36. Bar armor-piercing ammo Y
37. Tax Overhaul consideratn Y
38. Make comp emissions known Y
39. Allow toxic victims suits Y
40. Strike Superfund "VAT" Y
41. Notify emp-plant closing Y
42. Bar emp consult-plant clo N
43. Medicare cuts;Tax incres' Y
44. Delete 12 MX missiles Y
45. Spending cuts;Tax incres' Y
46. Textile Import Quotas N
47. Cut some school lunch fds N
48. Clean Water Act Amendmnts N
49. Youth work projects Y
50. Assist military in Angola N
51. Allow US troops-Nicaragua N
52. Pentagon polygraph exams N
53. Bar ASAT testing Y
54. Suspend def pmt for abuse Y
55. Bar Pentagon-contr emplmt Y
56. Increase SDI funding N
57. Reduce SDI funding Y
58. Produce chemical weapons N
59. Bar CIA fndg in Nicaragua Y
60. South Africa sanctions Y
61. Cut SS COLAs; Raise taxes N
62. Let US invest-So Africa N
63. Approve 21 MX for 1985 N
64. Emergency Farm Credit Y
65. Awards to whistle blowers Y
66. African disaster relief Y
67. Ban bank loans to So Afr Y
68. Bar coun duty-free trtmt Y
69. Steel import limits N
70. Soc Sec COLAs=inflation Y
71. Bar haz waste vctms suits N
72. Prohibit aid to Nicaragua Y
73. Cut $-Schs bar sch prayer X
74. Raise taxes; Cut Medicare Y
75. Alien residncy-prior 1982 N
76. Alien residncy-prior 1980 N
77. Pen emp-hire illgl aliens Y
78. Lmt Persh II/cruse-Europe Y
79. Delete 34 B-1 bombers N
80. Bar purch of Pershing II Y
81. Bar purchase of Sgt York Y
82. Delete $ for Trident II Y
83. Allow 15 MX missiles N
84. Bar MX procurement-1985 Y
85. Equal Access Act N
86. Aid to El Salvador N
87. Bar Nicarag water mining Y
88. Physician/Medicare freeze N
89. Increase "sin" taxes Y
90. End SBA direct loans N
91. Sell Conrail N
92. Equal Rights Amendment Y
93. Marines in Lebanon Y
94. Eminent domain-Coal comps Y
95. Prohibit EPA sanctions +
96. SS age increase/Reforms N

Presidential Support Score: 1986 - 16% 1985 - 24%

DIXON, JULIAN C. -- California 28th District [Democrat]. County of Los Angeles (pt.). Prior Terms: House: 1979-86. Born: August 8, 1934; Washington, D.C. Education: Los Angeles State College (B.S.); Southwestern University (LL.B.). Military Service: U.S. Army 1957-60. Occupation: California state assemblyman (1972-78).

1. Immigration Reform Y
2. Open fld-search warrants Y
3. Civil pnty-hire ill alien N
4. So Afr sanc-veto override Y
5. Tax Overhaul N
6. South Africa sanctions Y
7. Death penalty-drug bill N
8. Evidence-warrantless srch N
9. Life term-second drug off Y
10. Military use in drug war N
11. Troop reduction in Europe Y
12. Prohibit chemical weapons Y
13. Bar ASAT testing Y
14. Abide SALT II weapons ban ?
15. Follow SALT II-Soviets do ?
16. Reduce SDI funding ?
17. Increase SDI funding ?
18. Purchase Trident sub #
19. Delete 12 MX;Add conv wpn ?
20. Raise speed limit N
21. Textile Import Quotas(*) Y
22. Req Pentagon buy US goods Y
23. AIDS ins anti-dscriminatn Y
24. Nicaraguan refugee aid Y
25. Nicaraguan contra aid N
26. US abide by SALT II N
27. Prohibit Saudi arms sale Y
28. Military Retiremnt Reform Y
29. Nicaraguan refugee aid Y
30. Ease '68 Gun Control Act N
31. Bar intrstat handgun tran Y
32. Keep '68 Gun Control Act Y
33. Nicaraguan contra aid N
34. Bar emp polygraph testing Y

DIXON, JULIAN C. (Cont.)

35. Tax Overhaul consideratn Y
36. Bar armor-piercing ammo Y
37. Tax Overhaul consideratn Y
38. Make comp emissions known Y
39. Allow toxic victims suits Y
40. Strike Superfund "VAT" Y
41. Notify emp-plant closing Y
42. Bar emp consult-plant clo X
43. Medicare cuts;Tax incres' Y
44. Delete 12 MX missiles Y
45. Spending cuts;Tax incres' Y
46. Textile Import Quotas Y
47. Cut some school lunch fds N
48. Clean Water Act Amendmnts N
49. Youth work projects Y
50. Assist military in Angola N
51. Allow US troops-Nicaragua N
52. Pentagon polygraph exams ?
53. Bar ASAT testing Y
54. Suspend def pmt for abuse Y
55. Bar Pentagon-contr emplmt Y
56. Increase SDI funding ?
57. Reduce SDI funding #
58. Produce chemical weapons X
59. Bar CIA fndg in Nicaragua Y
60. South Africa sanctions Y
61. Cut SS COLAs; Raise taxes N
62. Let US invest-So Africa N
63. Approve 21 MX for 1985 N
64. Emergency Farm Credit Y
65. Awards to whistle blowers Y
66. African disaster relief Y
67. Ban bank loans to So Afr P
68. Bar coun duty-free trtmt N
69. Steel import limits Y
70. Soc Sec COLAs=inflation Y
71. Bar haz waste vctms suits N
72. Prohibit aid to Nicaragua Y
73. Cut $-Schs bar sch prayer N
74. Raise taxes; Cut Medicare Y
75. Alien residncy-prior 1982 N
76. Alien residncy-prior 1980 N
77. Pen emp-hire illgl aliens Y
78. Lmt Persh II/cruse-Europe #
79. Delete 34 B-1 bombers N
80. Bar purch of Pershing II #
81. Bar purchase of Sgt York Y
82. Delete $ for Trident II Y
83. Allow 15 MX missiles N
84. Bar MX procurement-1985 Y
85. Equal Access Act N
86. Aid to El Salvador N
87. Bar Nicarag water mining Y
88. Physician/Medicare freeze N
89. Increase "sin" taxes Y
90. End SBA direct loans N
91. Sell Conrail ?
92. Equal Rights Amendment Y
93. Marines in Lebanon N
94. Eminent domain-Coal comps N
95. Prohibit EPA sanctions ?
96. SS age increase/Reforms N
97. Auto domestic content req Y
98. Delete jobs program fundg N
99. Highway-Gas tax bill Y
100. Raise Medicare;Cut defnse Y
101. Emergency housing aid Y
102. Across-the-board tax cuts N
103. Gramm-Latta II targets N
104. Delete B-1 bomber funds X
105. Dsapprov Saudi AWACS sale Y
106. Disapprove oil import fee Y
107. Rail Deregulation N
108. Dsapp India nuc fuel sale N
109. Mil draft registration N
110. Chrysler Loan Guarantees Y
111. Prohibit school busing N
112. Nuclear plant moratorium Y
113. Oil price controls Y

Presidential Support Score: 1986 - 14% 1985 - 18%

HAWKINS, AUGUSTUS F. -- California 29th District [Democrat]. County of Los Angeles (pt.). Prior Terms: House: 1963-86. Born: August 31, 1907; Shreveport, La. Education: University of California (A.B.); Institute of Government, University of Southern California. Occupation: Juvenile delinquency prevention worker; realtor; California assemblyman (1934-62).

1. Immigration Reform N
2. Open fld-search warrants Y
3. Civil pnty-hire ill alien Y
4. So Afr sanc-veto override Y
5. Tax Overhaul Y
6. South Africa sanctions Y
7. Death penalty-drug bill N
8. Evidence-warrantless srch N
9. Life term-second drug off N
10. Military use in drug war N
11. Troop reduction in Europe Y
12. Prohibit chemical weapons Y
13. Bar ASAT testing Y
14. Abide SALT II weapons ban Y
15. Follow SALT II-Soviets do N
16. Reduce SDI funding Y
17. Increase SDI funding N
18. Purchase Trident sub Y

HAWKINS, AUGUSTUS F. (Cont.)

19. Delete 12 MX;Add conv wpn Y
20. Raise speed limit N
21. Textile Import Quotas(*) Y
22. Req Pentagon buy US goods Y
23. AIDS ins anti-dscriminatn Y
24. Nicaraguan refugee aid Y
25. Nicaraguan contra aid ?
26. US abide by SALT II N
27. Prohibit Saudi arms sale ?
28. Military Retiremnt Reform Y
29. Nicaraguan refugee aid Y
30. Ease '68 Gun Control Act N
31. Bar intrstat handgun tran Y
32. Keep '68 Gun Control Act Y
33. Nicaraguan contra aid N
34. Bar emp polygraph testing Y
35. Tax Overhaul consideratn Y
36. Bar armor-piercing ammo Y
37. Tax Overhaul consideratn N
38. Make comp emissions known Y
39. Allow toxic victims suits Y
40. Strike Superfund "VAT" Y
41. Notify emp-plant closing #
42. Bar emp consult-plant clo X
43. Medicare cuts;Tax incres' Y
44. Delete 12 MX missiles Y
45. Spending cuts;Tax incres' Y
46. Textile Import Quotas Y
47. Cut some school lunch fds N
48. Clean Water Act Amendmnts N
49. Youth work projects Y
50. Assist military in Angola N
51. Allow US troops-Nicaragua N
52. Pentagon polygraph exams N
53. Bar ASAT testing Y
54. Suspend def pmt for abuse Y
55. Bar Pentagon-contr emplmt Y
56. Increase SDI funding N
57. Reduce SDI funding Y
58. Produce chemical weapons N
59. Bar CIA fndg in Nicaragua ?
60. South Africa sanctions Y
61. Cut SS COLAs; Raise taxes N
62. Let US invest-So Africa N
63. Approve 21 MX for 1985 N
64. Emergency Farm Credit Y
65. Awards to whistle blowers ?
66. African disaster relief Y
67. Ban bank loans to So Afr P
68. Bar coun duty-free trtmt Y
69. Steel import limits Y
70. Soc Sec COLAs=inflation Y
71. Bar haz waste vctms suits N
72. Prohibit aid to Nicaragua Y
73. Cut $-Schs bar sch prayer N
74. Raise taxes; Cut Medicare N
75. Alien residncy-prior 1982 ?
76. Alien residncy-prior 1980 N
77. Pen emp-hire illgl aliens Y
78. Lmt Persh II/cruse-Europe ?
79. Delete 34 B-1 bombers N
80. Bar purch of Pershing II Y
81. Bar purchase of Sgt York #
82. Delete $ for Trident II #
83. Allow 15 MX missiles N
84. Bar MX procurement-1985 Y
85. Equal Access Act N
86. Aid to El Salvador N
87. Bar Nicarag water mining Y
88. Physician/Medicare freeze N
89. Increase "sin" taxes Y
90. End SBA direct loans ?
91. Sell Conrail N
92. Equal Rights Amendment Y
93. Marines in Lebanon Y
94. Eminent domain-Coal comps Y
95. Prohibit EPA sanctions ?
96. SS age increase/Reforms N
97. Auto domestic content req Y
98. Delete jobs program fundg N
99. Highway-Gas tax bill Y
100. Raise Medicare;Cut defnse Y
101. Emergency housing aid ?
102. Across-the-board tax cuts N
103. Gramm-Latta II targets N
104. Delete B-1 bomber funds N
105. Dsapprov Saudi AWACS sale Y
106. Disapprove oil import fee Y
107. Rail Deregulation N
108. Dsapp India nuc fuel sale Y
109. Mil draft registration N
110. Chrysler Loan Guarantees Y
111. Prohibit school busing N
112. Nuclear plant moratorium #
113. Oil price controls Y
114. Tuition Tax Credits N
115. Est Consumer Protect Agcy Y
116. Eliminate B-1 bomber fnds ?
117. Subminimum wage for youth N
118. Delete crude oil tax N
119. Natural gas deregulation N

Presidential Support Score: 1986 - 19% 1985 - 14%

MARTINEZ, MATTHEW G. -- California 30th District [Democrat]. County of Los Angeles (pt.). Prior Terms: House: 1982 (Special Election)-1986. Born: February 14, 1929; Walsenburg, Colo. Military Service: U.S. Marine Corps. Occupation: Small businessman; member, Monterey Park Planning Commission; city councilman (1974-80); mayor; California assemblyman (1980-82).

MARTINEZ, MATTHEW G. (Cont.)

1. Immigration Reform N
2. Open fld-search warrants Y
3. Civil pnty-hire ill alien Y
4. So Afr sanc-veto override Y
5. Tax Overhaul Y
6. South Africa sanctions Y
7. Death penalty-drug bill Y
8. Evidence-warrantless srch Y
9. Life term-second drug off Y
10. Military use in drug war N
11. Troop reduction in Europe Y
12. Prohibit chemical weapons Y
13. Bar ASAT testing Y
14. Abide SALT II weapons ban Y
15. Follow SALT II-Soviets do N
16. Reduce SDI funding N
17. Increase SDI funding N
18. Purchase Trident sub Y
19. Delete 12 MX;Add conv wpn ?
20. Raise speed limit N
21. Textile Import Quotas(*) Y
22. Req Pentagon buy US goods Y
23. AIDS ins anti-dscriminatn Y
24. Nicaraguan refugee aid Y
25. Nicaraguan contra aid N
26. US abide by SALT II N
27. Prohibit Saudi arms sale Y
28. Military Retiremnt Reform Y
29. Nicaraguan refugee aid Y
30. Ease '68 Gun Control Act N
31. Bar intrstat handgun tran ?
32. Keep '68 Gun Control Act ?
33. Nicaraguan contra aid N
34. Bar emp polygraph testing Y
35. Tax Overhaul consideratn Y
36. Bar armor-piercing ammo Y
37. Tax Overhaul consideratn Y
38. Make comp emissions known Y
39. Allow toxic victims suits Y
40. Strike Superfund "VAT" Y
41. Notify emp-plant closing Y
42. Bar emp consult-plant clo N
43. Medicare cuts;Tax incres' Y
44. Delete 12 MX missiles Y
45. Spending cuts;Tax incres' Y
46. Textile Import Quotas Y
47. Cut some school lunch fds N
48. Clean Water Act Amendmnts N
49. Youth work projects Y
50. Assist military in Angola N
51. Allow US troops-Nicaragua N
52. Pentagon polygraph exams Y
53. Bar ASAT testing Y
54. Suspend def pmt for abuse Y
55. Bar Pentagon-contr emplmt Y
56. Increase SDI funding N
57. Reduce SDI funding N
58. Produce chemical weapons N
59. Bar CIA fndg in Nicaragua Y
60. South Africa sanctions Y
61. Cut SS COLAs; Raise taxes N
62. Let US invest-So Africa N
63. Approve 21 MX for 1985 N
64. Emergency Farm Credit Y
65. Awards to whistle blowers Y
66. African disaster relief Y
67. Ban bank loans to So Afr Y
68. Bar coun duty-free trtmt N
69. Steel import limits Y
70. Soc Sec COLAs=inflation Y
71. Bar haz waste vctms suits N
72. Prohibit aid to Nicaragua Y
73. Cut $-Schs bar sch prayer N
74. Raise taxes; Cut Medicare Y
75. Alien residncy-prior 1982 N
76. Alien residncy-prior 1980 N
77. Pen emp-hire illgl aliens Y
78. Lmt Persh II/cruse-Europe Y
79. Delete 34 B-1 bombers Y
80. Bar purch of Pershing II Y
81. Bar purchase of Sgt York Y
82. Delete $ for Trident II Y
83. Allow 15 MX missiles N
84. Bar MX procurement-1985 Y
85. Equal Access Act N
86. Aid to El Salvador N
87. Bar Nicarag water mining Y
88. Physician/Medicare freeze N
89. Increase "sin" taxes N
90. End SBA direct loans N
91. Sell Conrail N
92. Equal Rights Amendment Y
93. Marines in Lebanon N
94. Eminent domain-Coal comps Y
95. Prohibit EPA sanctions ?
96. SS age increase/Reforms N
97. Auto domestic content req Y
98. Delete jobs program fundg N
99. Highway-Gas tax bill Y

Presidential Support Score: 1986 - 18% 1985 - 19%

DYMALLY, MERVYN M. -- California 31st District [Democrat]. County of Los Angeles (pt.). Prior Terms: House: 1981-86. Born: May 12, 1926; Cedron, Trinidad, W.I. Education: California State University (B.A., M.A.); United States International University (Ph.D.). Occupation: Teacher; California state assemblyman; California senator (1966-75); lieutenant governor (1975-79); goodwill ambassador in Africa and West Indies.

DYMALLY, MERVYN M. (Cont.)

1. Immigration Reform N
2. Open fld-search warrants Y
3. Civil pnty-hire ill alien Y
4. So Afr sanc-veto override Y
5. Tax Overhaul N
6. South Africa sanctions Y
7. Death penalty-drug bill N
8. Evidence-warrantless srch N
9. Life term-second drug off N
10. Military use in drug war N
11. Troop reduction in Europe Y
12. Prohibit chemical weapons Y
13. Bar ASAT testing Y
14. Abide SALT II weapons ban Y
15. Follow SALT II-Soviets do N
16. Reduce SDI funding Y
17. Increase SDI funding N
18. Purchase Trident sub Y
19. Delete 12 MX;Add conv wpn Y
20. Raise speed limit N
21. Textile Import Quotas(*) Y
22. Req Pentagon buy US goods Y
23. AIDS ins anti-dscriminatn Y
24. Nicaraguan refugee aid Y
25. Nicaraguan contra aid N
26. US abide by SALT II N
27. Prohibit Saudi arms sale Y
28. Military Retiremnt Reform Y
29. Nicaraguan refugee aid Y
30. Ease '68 Gun Control Act N
31. Bar intrstat handgun tran Y
32. Keep '68 Gun Control Act Y
33. Nicaraguan contra aid N
34. Bar emp polygraph testing Y
35. Tax Overhaul consideratn X
36. Bar armor-piercing ammo ?
37. Tax Overhaul consideratn Y
38. Make comp emissions known N
39. Allow toxic victims suits N
40. Strike Superfund "VAT" Y
41. Notify emp-plant closing ?
42. Bar emp consult-plant clo X
43. Medicare cuts;Tax incres' Y
44. Delete 12 MX missiles Y
45. Spending cuts;Tax incres' Y
46. Textile Import Quotas N
47. Cut some school lunch fds N
48. Clean Water Act Amendmnts N
49. Youth work projects Y
50. Assist military in Angola N
51. Allow US troops-Nicaragua N
52. Pentagon polygraph exams N
53. Bar ASAT testing Y
54. Suspend def pmt for abuse Y
55. Bar Pentagon-contr emplmt Y
56. Increase SDI funding N
57. Reduce SDI funding Y
58. Produce chemical weapons N
59. Bar CIA fndg in Nicaragua Y
60. South Africa sanctions Y
61. Cut SS COLAs; Raise taxes N
62. Let US invest-So Africa N
63. Approve 21 MX for 1985 N
64. Emergency Farm Credit Y
65. Awards to whistle blowers Y
66. African disaster relief Y
67. Ban bank loans to So Afr ?
68. Bar coun duty-free trtmt N
69. Steel import limits Y
70. Soc Sec COLAs=inflation ?
71. Bar haz waste vctms suits N
72. Prohibit aid to Nicaragua P
73. Cut $-Schs bar sch prayer N
74. Raise taxes; Cut Medicare X
75. Alien residncy-prior 1982 ?
76. Alien residncy-prior 1980 X
77. Pen emp-hire illgl aliens Y
78. Lmt Persh II/cruse-Europe ?
79. Delete 34 B-1 bombers N
80. Bar purch of Pershing II Y
81. Bar purchase of Sgt York Y
82. Delete $ for Trident II Y
83. Allow 15 MX missiles N
84. Bar MX procurement-1985 Y
85. Equal Access Act N
86. Aid to El Salvador N
87. Bar Nicarag water mining ?
88. Physician/Medicare freeze N
89. Increase "sin" taxes Y
90. End SBA direct loans N
91. Sell Conrail N
92. Equal Rights Amendment Y
93. Marines in Lebanon N
94. Eminent domain-Coal comps Y
95. Prohibit EPA sanctions Y
96. SS age increase/Reforms N
97. Auto domestic content req Y
98. Delete jobs program fundg N
99. Highway-Gas tax bill Y
100. Raise Medicare;Cut defnse Y
101. Emergency housing aid ?
102. Across-the-board tax cuts N
103. Gramm-Latta II targets N
104. Delete B-1 bomber funds N
105. Dsapprov Saudi AWACS sale Y

Presidential Support Score: 1986 - 14% 1985 - 15%

ANDERSON, GLENN M. -- California 32rd District [Democrat]. County of Los Angeles (pt.). Prior Terms: House: 1969-86. Born: February 21, 1913; Hawthorne, Calif. Education: University of

ANDERSON, GLENN M. (Cont.)
California (B.A.). Military Service: U.S. Army. Occupation: Mayor (1940); California state assemblyman (1943-51); lieutenant governor (1958, 1962); regent, University of California (1959-67); trustee, California State Colleges (1961-67); State Lands commissioner (1959-67).

1. Immigration Reform Y
2. Open fld-search warrants Y
3. Civil pnty-hire ill alien N
4. So Afr sanc-veto override Y
5. Tax Overhaul Y
6. South Africa sanctions Y
7. Death penalty-drug bill Y
8. Evidence-warrantless srch Y
9. Life term-second drug off Y
10. Military use in drug war Y
11. Troop reduction in Europe Y
12. Prohibit chemical weapons Y
13. Bar ASAT testing Y
14. Abide SALT II weapons ban Y
15. Follow SALT II-Soviets do N
16. Reduce SDI funding Y
17. Increase SDI funding N
18. Purchase Trident sub N
19. Delete 12 MX;Add conv wpn N
20. Raise speed limit N
21. Textile Import Quotas(*) N
22. Req Pentagon buy US goods Y
23. AIDS ins anti-dscriminatn Y
24. Nicaraguan refugee aid Y
25. Nicaraguan contra aid N
26. US abide by SALT II N
27. Prohibit Saudi arms sale Y
28. Military Retiremnt Reform Y
29. Nicaraguan refugee aid Y
30. Ease '68 Gun Control Act Y
31. Bar intrstat handgun tran Y
32. Keep '68 Gun Control Act Y
33. Nicaraguan contra aid N
34. Bar emp polygraph testing N
35. Tax Overhaul consideratn Y
36. Bar armor-piercing ammo Y
37. Tax Overhaul consideratn Y
38. Make comp emissions known Y
39. Allow toxic victims suits Y
40. Strike Superfund "VAT" N
41. Notify emp-plant closing Y
42. Bar emp consult-plant clo N
43. Medicare cuts;Tax incres' Y
44. Delete 12 MX missiles N
45. Spending cuts;Tax incres' N
46. Textile Import Quotas N
47. Cut some school lunch fds N
48. Clean Water Act Amendmnts N
49. Youth work projects Y
50. Assist military in Angola Y
51. Allow US troops-Nicaragua N
52. Pentagon polygraph exams Y
53. Bar ASAT testing Y
54. Suspend def pmt for abuse Y
55. Bar Pentagon-contr emplmt Y
56. Increase SDI funding N
57. Reduce SDI funding N
58. Produce chemical weapons Y
59. Bar CIA fndg in Nicaragua Y
60. South Africa sanctions Y
61. Cut SS COLAs; Raise taxes N
62. Let US invest-So Africa N
63. Approve 21 MX for 1985 Y
64. Emergency Farm Credit Y
65. Awards to whistle blowers Y
66. African disaster relief Y
67. Ban bank loans to So Afr Y
68. Bar coun duty-free trtmt N
69. Steel import limits Y
70. Soc Sec COLAs=inflation Y
71. Bar haz waste vctms suits N
72. Prohibit aid to Nicaragua Y
73. Cut $-Schs bar sch prayer N
74. Raise taxes; Cut Medicare N
75. Alien residncy-prior 1982 Y
76. Alien residncy-prior 1980 N
77. Pen emp-hire illgl aliens Y
78. Lmt Persh II/cruse-Europe N
79. Delete 34 B-1 bombers N
80. Bar purch of Pershing II N
81. Bar purchase of Sgt York N
82. Delete $ for Trident II N
83. Allow 15 MX missiles Y
84. Bar MX procurement-1985 N
85. Equal Access Act N
86. Aid to El Salvador N
87. Bar Nicarag water mining Y
88. Physician/Medicare freeze N
89. Increase "sin" taxes N
90. End SBA direct loans N
91. Sell Conrail N
92. Equal Rights Amendment Y
93. Marines in Lebanon Y
94. Eminent domain-Coal comps Y
95. Prohibit EPA sanctions Y
96. SS age increase/Reforms N
97. Auto domestic content req N
98. Delete jobs program fundg N
99. Highway-Gas tax bill Y
100. Raise Medicare;Cut defnse Y
101. Emergency housing aid Y
102. Across-the-board tax cuts N
103. Gramm-Latta II targets N
104. Delete B-1 bomber funds N
105. Dsapprov Saudi AWACS sale Y
106. Disapprove oil import fee Y

ANDERSON, GLENN M. (Cont.)

107. Rail Deregulation Y
108. Dsapp India nuc fuel sale Y
109. Mil draft registration N
110. Chrysler Loan Guarantees Y
111. Prohibit school busing Y
112. Nuclear plant moratorium N
113. Oil price controls ?
114. Tuition Tax Credits N
115. Est Consumer Protect Agcy Y
116. Eliminate B-1 bomber fnds N
117. Subminimum wage for youth N
118. Delete crude oil tax N
119. Natural gas deregulation N

Presidential Support Score: 1986 - 23% 1985 - 39%

DREIER, DAVID -- California 33rd District [Republican]. County of Los Angeles (pt.). Prior Terms: House: 1981-86. Born: July 5, 1952; Kansas City, Mo. Education: Claremont Men's College (B.A., M.A.). Occupation: Director, corporate relations and assistant director, college relations, Claremont Men's College (1975-79).

1. Immigration Reform N
2. Open fld-search warrants Y
3. Civil pnty-hire ill alien N
4. So Afr sanc-veto override N
5. Tax Overhaul N
6. South Africa sanctions N
7. Death penalty-drug bill Y
8. Evidence-warrantless srch Y
9. Life term-second drug off Y
10. Military use in drug war Y
11. Troop reduction in Europe N
12. Prohibit chemical weapons N
13. Bar ASAT testing N
14. Abide SALT II weapons ban N
15. Follow SALT II-Soviets do Y
16. Reduce SDI funding N
17. Increase SDI funding Y
18. Purchase Trident sub N
19. Delete 12 MX;Add conv wpn N
20. Raise speed limit Y
21. Textile Import Quotas(*) N
22. Req Pentagon buy US goods N
23. AIDS ins anti-dscriminatn N
24. Nicaraguan refugee aid N
25. Nicaraguan contra aid Y
26. US abide by SALT II Y
27. Prohibit Saudi arms sale Y
28. Military Retiremnt Reform Y
29. Nicaraguan refugee aid Y
30. Ease '68 Gun Control Act Y
31. Bar intrstat handgun tran N
32. Keep '68 Gun Control Act N
33. Nicaraguan contra aid Y
34. Bar emp polygraph testing N
35. Tax Overhaul consideratn N
36. Bar armor-piercing ammo N
37. Tax Overhaul consideratn N
38. Make comp emissions known N
39. Allow toxic victims suits N
40. Strike Superfund "VAT" N
41. Notify emp-plant closing N
42. Bar emp consult-plant clo Y
43. Medicare cuts;Tax incres' N
44. Delete 12 MX missiles N
45. Spending cuts;Tax incres' N
46. Textile Import Quotas N
47. Cut some school lunch fds Y
48. Clean Water Act Amendmnts Y
49. Youth work projects N
50. Assist military in Angola Y
51. Allow US troops-Nicaragua Y
52. Pentagon polygraph exams Y
53. Bar ASAT testing N
54. Suspend def pmt for abuse N
55. Bar Pentagon-contr emplmt Y
56. Increase SDI funding Y
57. Reduce SDI funding N
58. Produce chemical weapons Y
59. Bar CIA fndg in Nicaragua N
60. South Africa sanctions N
61. Cut SS COLAs; Raise taxes N
62. Let US invest-So Africa Y
63. Approve 21 MX for 1985 Y
64. Emergency Farm Credit N
65. Awards to whistle blowers Y
66. African disaster relief Y
67. Ban bank loans to So Afr N
68. Bar coun duty-free trtmt N
69. Steel import limits N
70. Soc Sec COLAs=inflation Y
71. Bar haz waste vctms suits Y
72. Prohibit aid to Nicaragua N
73. Cut $-Schs bar sch prayer Y
74. Raise taxes; Cut Medicare N
75. Alien residncy-prior 1982 Y
76. Alien residncy-prior 1980 Y
77. Pen emp-hire illgl aliens N
78. Lmt Persh II/cruse-Europe N
79. Delete 34 B-1 bombers N
80. Bar purch of Pershing II N
81. Bar purchase of Sgt York N
82. Delete $ for Trident II N
83. Allow 15 MX missiles Y
84. Bar MX procurement-1985 N

DREIER, DAVID (Cont.)

85. Equal Access Act	Y		96. SS age increase/Reforms	Y
86. Aid to El Salvador	Y		97. Auto domestic content req	N
87. Bar Nicarag water mining	N		98. Delete jobs program fundg	Y
88. Physician/Medicare freeze	Y		99. Highway-Gas tax bill	N
89. Increase "sin" taxes	N		100. Raise Medicare;Cut defnse	N
90. End SBA direct loans	Y		101. Emergency housing aid	?
91. Sell Conrail	Y		102. Across-the-board tax cuts	Y
92. Equal Rights Amendment	N		103. Gramm-Latta II targets	Y
93. Marines in Lebanon	Y		104. Delete B-1 bomber funds	N
94. Eminent domain-Coal comps	Y		105. Dsapprov Saudi AWACS sale	Y
95. Prohibit EPA sanctions	Y			

Presidential Support Score: 1986 - 84% 1985 - 84%

TORRES, ESTEBAN EDWARD -- California 34th District [Democrat]. County of Los Angeles (pt.). Prior Terms: House: 1983-86. Born: January 27, 1930; Miami, Ariz. Military Service: U.S. Army. Occupation: Chief Steward, Local 230, United Auto Workers (1961); International Representative, Region 6, UAW (1963-64); Inter-American Representative in Washington, D.C. for UAW (1965-68); assistant director, International Affairs Department, UAW (1974-77); Ambassador to UNESCO (1977-79); White House aide.

1. Immigration Reform	Y		36. Bar armor-piercing ammo	Y
2. Open fld-search warrants	Y		37. Tax Overhaul consideratn	Y
3. Civil pnty-hire ill alien	Y		38. Make comp emissions known	Y
4. So Afr sanc-veto override	Y		39. Allow toxic victims suits	Y
5. Tax Overhaul	Y		40. Strike Superfund "VAT"	Y
6. South Africa sanctions	Y		41. Notify emp-plant closing	Y
7. Death penalty-drug bill	Y		42. Bar emp consult-plant clo	N
8. Evidence-warrantless srch	N		43. Medicare cuts;Tax incres'	Y
9. Life term-second drug off	Y		44. Delete 12 MX missiles	Y
10. Military use in drug war	N		45. Spending cuts;Tax incres'	Y
11. Troop reduction in Europe	Y		46. Textile Import Quotas	Y
12. Prohibit chemical weapons	Y		47. Cut some school lunch fds	N
13. Bar ASAT testing	Y		48. Clean Water Act Amendmnts	N
14. Abide SALT II weapons ban	?		49. Youth work projects	Y
15. Follow SALT II-Soviets do	?		50. Assist military in Angola	N
16. Reduce SDI funding	Y		51. Allow US troops-Nicaragua	N
17. Increase SDI funding	N		52. Pentagon polygraph exams	Y
18. Purchase Trident sub	Y		53. Bar ASAT testing	Y
19. Delete 12 MX;Add conv wpn	Y		54. Suspend def pmt for abuse	Y
20. Raise speed limit	N		55. Bar Pentagon-contr emplmt	Y
21. Textile Import Quotas(*)	Y		56. Increase SDI funding	N
22. Req Pentagon buy US goods	Y		57. Reduce SDI funding	N
23. AIDS ins anti-dscriminatn	Y		58. Produce chemical weapons	N
24. Nicaraguan refugee aid	Y		59. Bar CIA fndg in Nicaragua	Y
25. Nicaraguan contra aid	N		60. South Africa sanctions	Y
26. US abide by SALT II	N		61. Cut SS COLAs; Raise taxes	N
27. Prohibit Saudi arms sale	Y		62. Let US invest-So Africa	N
28. Military Retiremnt Reform	Y		63. Approve 21 MX for 1985	N
29. Nicaraguan refugee aid	Y		64. Emergency Farm Credit	Y
30. Ease '68 Gun Control Act	N		65. Awards to whistle blowers	Y
31. Bar intrstat handgun tran	+		66. African disaster relief	Y
32. Keep '68 Gun Control Act	+		67. Ban bank loans to So Afr	Y
33. Nicaraguan contra aid	N		68. Bar coun duty-free trtmt	Y
34. Bar emp polygraph testing	Y		69. Steel import limits	Y
35. Tax Overhaul consideratn	Y		70. Soc Sec COLAs=inflation	Y

TORRES, ESTEBAN EDWARD (Cont.)

71. Bar haz waste vctms suits N	84. Bar MX procurement-1985 Y
72. Prohibit aid to Nicaragua Y	85. Equal Access Act N
73. Cut $-Schs bar sch prayer N	86. Aid to El Salvador N
74. Raise taxes; Cut Medicare Y	87. Bar Nicarag water mining Y
75. Alien residncy-prior 1982 N	88. Physician/Medicare freeze N
76. Alien residncy-prior 1980 N	89. Increase "sin" taxes Y
77. Pen emp-hire illgl aliens Y	90. End SBA direct loans N
78. Lmt Persh II/cruse-Europe Y	91. Sell Conrail N
79. Delete 34 B-1 bombers N	92. Equal Rights Amendment Y
80. Bar purch of Pershing II Y	93. Marines in Lebanon Y
81. Bar purchase of Sgt York Y	94. Eminent domain-Coal comps N
82. Delete $ for Trident II Y	95. Prohibit EPA sanctions +
83. Allow 15 MX missiles N	96. SS age increase/Reforms N

Presidential Support Score: 1986 - 18% 1985 - 18%

LEWIS, JERRY -- California 35th District [Republican]. Counties of Inyo, Los Angeles (pt.) and San Bernardino (pt.). Prior Terms: House: 1979-86. Born: October 21, 1934; Seattle, Wash. Education: University of California (B.A.). Occupation: Life underwriter; California assemblyman (1968-78).

1. Immigration Reform Y	38. Make comp emissions known N
2. Open fld-search warrants Y	39. Allow toxic victims suits N
3. Civil pnty-hire ill alien N	40. Strike Superfund "VAT" N
4. So Afr sanc-veto override N	41. Notify emp-plant closing N
5. Tax Overhaul Y	42. Bar emp consult-plant clo Y
6. South Africa sanctions Y	43. Medicare cuts;Tax incres' N
7. Death penalty-drug bill Y	44. Delete 12 MX missiles N
8. Evidence-warrantless srch Y	45. Spending cuts;Tax incres' N
9. Life term-second drug off Y	46. Textile Import Quotas N
10. Military use in drug war Y	47. Cut some school lunch fds Y
11. Troop reduction in Europe N	48. Clean Water Act Amendmnts Y
12. Prohibit chemical weapons N	49. Youth work projects N
13. Bar ASAT testing N	50. Assist military in Angola Y
14. Abide SALT II weapons ban X	51. Allow US troops-Nicaragua Y
15. Follow SALT II-Soviets do #	52. Pentagon polygraph exams Y
16. Reduce SDI funding X	53. Bar ASAT testing N
17. Increase SDI funding #	54. Suspend def pmt for abuse N
18. Purchase Trident sub X	55. Bar Pentagon-contr emplmt Y
19. Delete 12 MX;add conv wpn X	56. Increase SDI funding Y
20. Raise speed limit Y	57. Reduce SDI funding N
21. Textile Import Quotas(*) N	58. Produce chemical weapons Y
22. Req Pentagon buy US goods N	59. Bar CIA fndg in Nicaragua N
23. AIDS ins anti-dscriminatn N	60. South Africa sanctions Y
24. Nicaraguan refugee aid N	61. Cut SS COLAs; Raise taxes N
25. Nicaraguan contra aid Y	62. Let US invest-So Africa #
26. US abide by SALT II ?	63. Approve 21 MX for 1985 Y
27. Prohibit Saudi arms sale Y	64. Emergency Farm Credit N
28. Military Retiremnt Reform Y	65. Awards to whistle blowers Y
29. Nicaraguan refugee aid Y	66. African disaster relief Y
30. Ease '68 Gun Control Act Y	67. Ban bank loans to So Afr Y
31. Bar intrstat handgun tran N	68. Bar coun duty-free trtmt N
32. Keep '68 Gun Control Act N	69. Steel import limits N
33. Nicaraguan contra aid Y	70. Soc Sec COLAs=inflation Y
34. Bar emp polygraph testing N	71. Bar haz waste vctms suits Y
35. Tax Overhaul consideratn N	72. Prohibit aid to Nicaragua N
36. Bar armor-piercing ammo N	73. Cut $-Schs bar sch prayer Y
37. Tax Overhaul consideratn N	74. Raise taxes; Cut Medicare N

LEWIS, JERRY (Cont.)

75. Alien residncy-prior 1982 Y
76. Alien residncy-prior 1980 Y
77. Pen emp-hire illgl aliens N
78. Lmt Persh II/cruse-Europe N
79. Delete 34 B-1 bombers N
80. Bar purch of Pershing II N
81. Bar purchase of Sgt York N
82. Delete $ for Trident II N
83. Allow 15 MX missiles Y
84. Bar MX procurement-1985 N
85. Equal Access Act Y
86. Aid to El Salvador Y
87. Bar Nicarag water mining N
88. Physician/Medicare freeze Y
89. Increase "sin" taxes N
90. End SBA direct loans Y
91. Sell Conrail Y
92. Equal Rights Amendment ?
93. Marines in Lebanon Y
94. Eminent domain-Coal comps N
95. Prohibit EPA sanctions Y
96. SS age increase/Reforms Y
97. Auto domestic content req N
98. Delete jobs program fundg Y
99. Highway-Gas tax bill Y
100. Raise Medicare;Cut defnse N
101. Emergency housing aid Y
102. Across-the-board tax cuts Y
103. Gramm-Latta II targets Y
104. Delete B-1 bomber funds N
105. Dsapprov Saudi AWACS sale Y
106. Disapprove oil import fee Y
107. Rail Deregulation N
108. Dsapp India nuc fuel sale Y
109. Mil draft registration N
110. Chrysler Loan Guarantees N
111. Prohibit school busing Y
112. Nuclear plant moratorium N
113. Oil price controls N

Presidential Support Score: 1986 - 64% 1985 - 65%

BROWN, GEORGE E., Jr. -- California 36th District [Democrat]. Counties of Riverside (pt.) and San Bernardino (pt.). Prior Terms: House: 1963-70; 1973-86. Born: March 6, 1920; Holtville, Calif. Education: University of California (B.A.). Military Service: U.S. Army, WW II. Occupation: Management consultant in engineering and personnel (1957-61); city councilman and mayor (1954-58); California assemblyman (1959-62).

1. Immigration Reform Y
2. Open fld-search warrants Y
3. Civil pnty-hire ill alien Y
4. So Afr sanc-veto override Y
5. Tax Overhaul Y
6. South Africa sanctions ?
7. Death penalty-drug bill N
8. Evidence-warrantless srch N
9. Life term-second drug off ?
10. Military use in drug war N
11. Troop reduction in Europe Y
12. Prohibit chemical weapons Y
13. Bar ASAT testing Y
14. Abide SALT II weapons ban Y
15. Follow SALT II-Soviets do N
16. Reduce SDI funding Y
17. Increase SDI funding N
18. Purchase Trident sub Y
19. Delete 12 MX;Add conv wpn Y
20. Raise speed limit N
21. Textile Import Quotas(*) Y
22. Req Pentagon buy US goods ?
23. AIDS ins anti-dscriminatn Y
24. Nicaraguan refugee aid Y
25. Nicaraguan contra aid N
26. US abide by SALT II N
27. Prohibit Saudi arms sale Y
28. Military Retiremnt Reform Y
29. Nicaraguan refugee aid Y
30. Ease '68 Gun Control Act N
31. Bar intrstat handgun tran Y
32. Keep '68 Gun Control Act Y
33. Nicaraguan contra aid N
34. Bar emp polygraph testing #
35. Tax Overhaul consideratn Y
36. Bar armor-piercing ammo Y
37. Tax Overhaul consideratn Y
38. Make comp emissions known Y
39. Allow toxic victims suits Y
40. Strike Superfund "VAT" Y
41. Notify emp-plant closing ?
42. Bar emp consult-plant clo N
43. Medicare cuts;Tax incres' Y
44. Delete 12 MX missiles Y
45. Spending cuts;Tax incres' ?
46. Textile Import Quotas Y
47. Cut some school lunch fds N
48. Clean Water Act Amendmnts N
49. Youth work projects ?
50. Assist military in Angola N
51. Allow US troops-Nicaragua ?
52. Pentagon polygraph exams ?
53. Bar ASAT testing Y
54. Suspend def pmt for abuse Y
55. Bar Pentagon-contr emplmt Y
56. Increase SDI funding N

BROWN, GEORGE E., Jr. (Cont.)

57. Reduce SDI funding Y
58. Produce chemical weapons N
59. Bar CIA fndg in Nicaragua Y
60. South Africa sanctions Y
61. Cut SS COLAs; Raise taxes N
62. Let US invest-So Africa N
63. Approve 21 MX for 1985 N
64. Emergency Farm Credit Y
65. Awards to whistle blowers Y
66. African disaster relief Y
67. Ban bank loans to So Afr ?
68. Bar coun duty-free trtmt ?
69. Steel import limits Y
70. Soc Sec COLAs=inflation Y
71. Bar haz waste vctms suits N
72. Prohibit aid to Nicaragua Y
73. Cut $-Schs bar sch prayer N
74. Raise taxes; Cut Medicare Y
75. Alien residncy-prior 1982 N
76. Alien residncy-prior 1980 N
77. Pen emp-hire illgl aliens ?
78. Lmt Persh II/cruse-Europe Y
79. Delete 34 B-1 bombers N
80. Bar purch of Pershing II Y
81. Bar purchase of Sgt York N
82. Delete $ for Trident II N
83. Allow 15 MX missiles N
84. Bar MX procurement-1985 Y
85. Equal Access Act N
86. Aid to El Salvador N
87. Bar Nicarag water mining Y
88. Physician/Medicare freeze N
89. Increase "sin" taxes Y
90. End SBA direct loans N
91. Sell Conrail N
92. Equal Rights Amendment Y
93. Marines in Lebanon Y
94. Eminent domain-Coal comps Y
95. Prohibit EPA sanctions Y
96. SS age increase/Reforms N
97. Auto domestic content req ?
98. Delete jobs program fundg N
99. Highway-Gas tax bill Y
100. Raise Medicare;Cut defnse Y
101. Emergency housing aid Y
102. Across-the-board tax cuts N
103. Gramm-Latta II targets N
104. Delete B-1 bomber funds N
105. Dsapprov Saudi AWACS sale Y
106. Disapprove oil import fee N
107. Rail Deregulation N
108. Dsapp India nuc fuel sale Y
109. Mil draft registration N
110. Chrysler Loan Guarantees Y
111. Prohibit school busing N
112. Nuclear plant moratorium Y
113. Oil price controls N
114. Tuition Tax Credits N
115. Est Consumer Protect Agcy Y
116. Eliminate B-1 bomber fnds N
117. Subminimum wage for youth N
118. Delete crude oil tax N
119. Natural gas deregulation N

Presidential Support Score: 1986 - 18% 1985 - 20%

McCANDLESS, ALFRED A. (AL) -- California 37th District [Republican] County of Riverside (pt.). Prior Terms: House: 1983-86. Born: July 23, 1927; Brawley, Calif. Education: University of California (B.A.). Military Service: U.S. Marine Corps, 1945-46. Occupation: Business executive, General Motors, auto-truck dealership (1953-75); county supervisor (1971-82); member, county housing authority; founding member, Sunline Transit Agency.

1. Immigration Reform Y
2. Open fld-search warrants Y
3. Civil pnty-hire ill alien Y
4. So Afr sanc-veto override N
5. Tax Overhaul N
6. South Africa sanctions N
7. Death penalty-drug bill Y
8. Evidence-warrantless srch Y
9. Life term-second drug off Y
10. Military use in drug war Y
11. Troop reduction in Europe N
12. Prohibit chemical weapons N
13. Bar ASAT testing N
14. Abide SALT II weapons ban N
15. Follow SALT II-Soviets do Y
16. Reduce SDI funding N
17. Increase SDI funding N
18. Purchase Trident sub N
19. Delete 12 MX;Add conv wpn N
20. Raise speed limit Y
21. Textile Import Quotas(*) N
22. Req Pentagon buy US goods N
23. AIDS ins anti-dscriminatn N
24. Nicaraguan refugee aid N
25. Nicaraguan contra aid Y
26. US abide by SALT II Y
27. Prohibit Saudi arms sale N
28. Military Retiremnt Reform Y
29. Nicaraguan refugee aid Y
30. Ease '68 Gun Control Act Y

McCANDLESS, ALFRED A. (Cont.)

31. Bar intrstat handgun tran N
32. Keep '68 Gun Control Act N
33. Nicaraguan contra aid Y
34. Bar emp polygraph testing N
35. Tax Overhaul consideratn N
36. Bar armor-piercing ammo Y
37. Tax Overhaul consideratn N
38. Make comp emissions known N
39. Allow toxic victims suits N
40. Strike Superfund "VAT" N
41. Notify emp-plant closing N
42. Bar emp consult-plant clo Y
43. Medicare cuts;Tax incres' N
44. Delete 12 MX missiles N
45. Spending cuts;Tax incres' N
46. Textile Import Quotas N
47. Cut some school lunch fds Y
48. Clean Water Act Amendmnts Y
49. Youth work projects N
50. Assist military in Angola Y
51. Allow US troops-Nicaragua Y
52. Pentagon polygraph exams Y
53. Bar ASAT testing N
54. Suspend def pmt for abuse N
55. Bar Pentagon-contr emplmt Y
56. Increase SDI funding Y
57. Reduce SDI funding N
58. Produce chemical weapons Y
59. Bar CIA fndg in Nicaragua N
60. South Africa sanctions N
61. Cut SS COLAs; Raise taxes N
62. Let US invest-So Africa Y
63. Approve 21 MX for 1985 Y
64. Emergency Farm Credit N
65. Awards to whistle blowers Y
66. African disaster relief Y
67. Ban bank loans to So Afr N
68. Bar coun duty-free trtmt N
69. Steel import limits N
70. Soc Sec COLAs=inflation Y
71. Bar haz waste vctms suits Y
72. Prohibit aid to Nicaragua N
73. Cut $-Schs bar sch prayer Y
74. Raise taxes; Cut Medicare N
75. Alien residncy-prior 1982 Y
76. Alien residncy-prior 1980 Y
77. Pen emp-hire illgl aliens N
78. Lmt Persh II/cruse-Europe N
79. Delete 34 B-1 bombers N
80. Bar purch of Pershing II N
81. Bar purchase of Sgt York N
82. Delete $ for Trident II N
83. Allow 15 MX missiles Y
84. Bar MX procurement-1985 N
85. Equal Access Act Y
86. Aid to El Salvador Y
87. Bar Nicarag water mining Y
88. Physician/Medicare freeze Y
89. Increase "sin" taxes N
90. End SBA direct loans Y
91. Sell Conrail Y
92. Equal Rights Amendment N
93. Marines in Lebanon Y
94. Eminent domain-Coal comps Y
95. Prohibit EPA sanctions Y
96. SS age increase/Reforms Y

Presidential Support Score: 1986 - 77% 1985 - 74%

DORNAN, ROBERT K. -- California 38th District [Republican]. County of Orange (pt.) Prior Terms: House: 1977-82, 1985-86. Occupation: TV talk show host.

1. Immigration Reform Y
2. Open fld-search warrants Y
3. Civil pnty-hire ill alien N
4. So Afr sanc-veto override N
5. Tax Overhaul Y
6. South Africa sanctions N
7. Death penalty-drug bill Y
8. Evidence-warrantless srch Y
9. Life term-second drug off Y
10. Military use in drug war Y
11. Troop reduction in Europe N
12. Prohibit chemical weapons N
13. Bar ASAT testing N
14. Abide SALT II weapons ban N
15. Follow SALT II-Soviets do Y
16. Reduce SDI funding N
17. Increase SDI funding Y
18. Purchase Trident sub N
19. Delete 12 MX;Add conv wpn N
20. Raise speed limit Y
21. Textile Import Quotas(*) N
22. Req Pentagon buy US goods N
23. AIDS ins anti-dscriminatn N
24. Nicaraguan refugee aid N
25. Nicaraguan contra aid Y
26. US abide by SALT II Y
27. Prohibit Saudi arms sale Y
28. Military Retiremnt Reform Y
29. Nicaraguan refugee aid Y
30. Ease '68 Gun Control Act Y
31. Bar intrstat handgun tran N
32. Keep '68 Gun Control Act N
33. Nicaraguan contra aid Y
34. Bar emp polygraph testing ?
35. Tax Overhaul consideratn Y
36. Bar armor-piercing ammo Y

DORNAN, ROBERT K. (Cont.)

37. Tax Overhaul consideratn N
38. Make comp emissions known N
39. Allow toxic victims suits N
40. Strike Superfund "VAT" N
41. Notify emp-plant closing N
42. Bar emp consult-plant clo Y
43. Medicare cuts;Tax incres' N
44. Delete 12 MX missiles N
45. Spending cuts;Tax incres' N
46. Textile Import Quotas N
47. Cut some school lunch fds Y
48. Clean Water Act Amendmnts Y
49. Youth work projects N
50. Assist military in Angola Y
51. Allow US troops-Nicaragua Y
52. Pentagon polygraph exams Y
53. Bar ASAT testing N
54. Suspend def pmt for abuse N
55. Bar Pentagon-contr emplmt N
56. Increase SDI funding Y
57. Reduce SDI funding N
58. Produce chemical weapons Y
59. Bar CIA fndg in Nicaragua N
60. South Africa sanctions N
61. Cut SS COLAs; Raise taxes N
62. Let US invest-So Africa Y
63. Approve 21 MX for 1985 Y
64. Emergency Farm Credit N
65. Awards to whistle blowers Y
66. African disaster relief Y
97. Auto domestic content req N
98. Delete jobs program fundg Y
99. Highway-Gas tax bill Y
100. Raise Medicare;Cut defnse N
101. Emergency housing aid N
102. Across-the-board tax cuts Y
103. Gramm-Latta II targets Y
104. Delete B-1 bomber funds ?
105. Dsapprov Saudi AWACS sale Y
106. Disapprove oil import fee Y
107. Rail Deregulation N
108. Dsapp India nuc fuel sale Y
109. Mil draft registration N
110. Chrysler Loan Guarantees N
111. Prohibit school busing Y
112. Nuclear plant moratorium N
113. Oil price controls N
114. Tuition Tax Credits Y
115. Est Consumer Protect Agcy N
116. Eliminate B-1 bomber fnds N
117. Subminimum wage for youth Y
118. Delete crude oil tax Y
119. Natural gas deregulation Y

Was not in office for votes 67-96.
Presidential Support Score: 1986 - 82% 1985 - 80%

DANNEMEYER, WILLIAM E. -- California 39th District [Republican]. County of Orange (pt.). Prior Terms: House: 1979-86. Born: September 22, 1929; Los Angeles, Calif. Education: Santa Maria Junior College; Valparaiso University (B.A.); Hastings Law School (J.D.). Military Service: U.S. Army. Occupation: Deputy district attorney; assistant district attorney; Municipal Court judge pro tem; Superior Court judge pro tem; member, Orange County Criminal Justice Council; California legislator (1963-66); California general assemblyman (1976).

1. Immigration Reform Y
2. Open fld-search warrants Y
3. Civil pnty-hire ill alien Y
4. So Afr sanc-veto override N
5. Tax Overhaul N
6. South Africa sanctions N
7. Death penalty-drug bill Y
8. Evidence-warrantless srch Y
9. Life term-second drug off Y
10. Military use in drug war Y
11. Troop reduction in Europe N
12. Prohibit chemical weapons N
13. Bar ASAT testing N
14. Abide SALT II weapons ban N
15. Follow SALT II-Soviets do Y
16. Reduce SDI funding N
17. Increase SDI funding Y
18. Purchase Trident sub N
19. Delete 12 MX;Add conv wpn N
20. Raise speed limit Y
21. Textile Import Quotas(*) N
22. Req Pentagon buy US goods N
23. AIDS ins anti-dscriminatn N
24. Nicaraguan refugee aid N
25. Nicaraguan contra aid Y
26. US abide by SALT II Y
27. Prohibit Saudi arms sale N
28. Military Retiremnt Reform Y
29. Nicaraguan refugee aid Y
30. Ease '68 Gun Control Act Y
31. Bar intrstat handgun tran N
32. Keep '68 Gun Control Act N
33. Nicaraguan contra aid Y
34. Bar emp polygraph testing N

DANNEMEYER, WILLIAM E. (Cont.)

35. Tax Overhaul consideratn N
36. Bar armor-piercing ammo Y
37. Tax Overhaul consideratn N
38. Make comp emissions known N
39. Allow toxic victims suits N
40. Strike Superfund "VAT" N
41. Notify emp-plant closing N
42. Bar emp consult-plant clo Y
43. Medicare cuts;Tax incres' N
44. Delete 12 MX missiles N
45. Spending cuts;Tax incres' N
46. Textile Import Quotas N
47. Cut some school lunch fds Y
48. Clean Water Act Amendmnts Y
49. Youth work projects N
50. Assist military in Angola Y
51. Allow US troops-Nicaragua Y
52. Pentagon polygraph exams Y
53. Bar ASAT testing N
54. Suspend def pmt for abuse N
55. Bar Pentagon-contr emplmt Y
56. Increase SDI funding Y
57. Reduce SDI funding N
58. Produce chemical weapons Y
59. Bar CIA fndg in Nicaragua N
60. South Africa sanctions N
61. Cut SS COLAs; Raise taxes N
62. Let US invest-So Africa Y
63. Approve 21 MX for 1985 Y
64. Emergency Farm Credit N
65. Awards to whistle blowers Y
66. African disaster relief N
67. Ban bank loans to So Afr N
68. Bar coun duty-free trtmt N
69. Steel import limits N
70. Soc Sec COLAs=inflation Y
71. Bar haz waste vctms suits Y
72. Prohibit aid to Nicaragua N
73. Cut $-Schs bar sch prayer +
74. Raise taxes; Cut Medicare N
75. Alien residncy-prior 1982 Y
76. Alien residncy-prior 1980 Y
77. Pen emp-hire illgl aliens N
78. Lmt Persh II/cruse-Europe N
79. Delete 34 B-1 bombers N
80. Bar purch of Pershing II N
81. Bar purchase of Sgt York Y
82. Delete $ for Trident II N
83. Allow 15 MX missiles Y
84. Bar MX procurement-1985 N
85. Equal Access Act Y
86. Aid to El Salvador Y
87. Bar Nicarag water mining N
88. Physician/Medicare freeze Y
89. Increase "sin" taxes N
90. End SBA direct loans Y
91. Sell Conrail Y
92. Equal Rights Amendment N
93. Marines in Lebanon N
94. Eminent domain-Coal comps Y
95. Prohibit EPA sanctions Y
96. SS age increase/Reforms Y
97. Auto domestic content req N
98. Delete jobs program fundg Y
99. Highway-Gas tax bill N
100. Raise Medicare;Cut defnse N
101. Emergency housing aid N
102. Across-the-board tax cuts Y
103. Gramm-Latta II targets Y
104. Delete B-1 bomber funds N
105. Dsapprov Saudi AWACS sale N
106. Disapprove oil import fee Y
107. Rail Deregulation N
108. Dsapp India nuc fuel sale N
109. Mil draft registration Y
110. Chrysler Loan Guarantees N
111. Prohibit school busing Y
112. Nuclear plant moratorium N
113. Oil price controls N

Presidential Support Score: 1986 - 83% 1985 - 78%

BADHAM, ROBERT E. -- California 40th District [Republican]. County of Orange (pt.). Prior Terms: House: 1977-86. Born: June 9, 1929; Los Angeles, Calif. Education: Occidental College; Stanford University (B.A.). Military Service: U.S. Navy, 1951-54. Occupation: California legislator (1963-76); officer and director, Hoffman Hardware Co. (1952-69).

1. Immigration Reform Y
2. Open fld-search warrants Y
3. Civil pnty-hire ill alien N
4. So Afr sanc-veto override ?
5. Tax Overhaul N
6. South Africa sanctions N
7. Death penalty-drug bill Y
8. Evidence-warrantless srch Y
9. Life term-second drug off Y
10. Military use in drug war Y

BADHAM, ROBERT E. (Cont.)

11. Troop reduction in Europe N
12. Prohibit chemical weapons N
13. Bar ASAT testing N
14. Abide SALT II weapons ban N
15. Follow SALT II-Soviets do Y
16. Reduce SDI funding N
17. Increase SDI funding Y
18. Purchase Trident sub N
19. Delete 12 MX;Add conv wpn N
20. Raise speed limit Y
21. Textile Import Quotas(*) N
22. Req Pentagon buy US goods N
23. AIDS ins anti-dscriminatn N
24. Nicaraguan refugee aid N
25. Nicaraguan contra aid Y
26. US abide by SALT II #
27. Prohibit Saudi arms sale X
28. Military Retiremnt Reform Y
29. Nicaraguan refugee aid Y
30. Ease '68 Gun Control Act Y
31. Bar intrstat handgun tran N
32. Keep '68 Gun Control Act N
33. Nicaraguan contra aid Y
34. Bar emp polygraph testing N
35. Tax Overhaul consideratn Y
36. Bar armor-piercing ammo Y
37. Tax Overhaul consideratn N
38. Make comp emissions known N
39. Allow toxic victims suits N
40. Strike Superfund "VAT" N
41. Notify emp-plant closing N
42. Bar emp consult-plant clo ?
43. Medicare cuts;Tax incres' N
44. Delete 12 MX missiles N
45. Spending cuts;Tax incres' N
46. Textile Import Quotas N
47. Cut some school lunch fds Y
48. Clean Water Act Amendmnts Y
49. Youth work projects N
50. Assist military in Angola Y
51. Allow US troops-Nicaragua Y
52. Pentagon polygraph exams Y
53. Bar ASAT testing N
54. Suspend def pmt for abuse N
55. Bar Pentagon-contr emplmt Y
56. Increase SDI funding Y
57. Reduce SDI funding N
58. Produce chemical weapons Y
59. Bar CIA fndg in Nicaragua N
60. South Africa sanctions N
61. Cut SS COLAs; Raise taxes N
62. Let US invest-So Africa Y
63. Approve 21 MX for 1985 Y
64. Emergency Farm Credit ?
65. Awards to whistle blowers Y
66. African disaster relief N
67. Ban bank loans to So Afr Y
68. Bar coun duty-free trtmt N
69. Steel import limits N
70. Soc Sec COLAs=inflation Y
71. Bar haz waste vctms suits Y
72. Prohibit aid to Nicaragua N
73. Cut $-Schs bar sch prayer Y
74. Raise taxes; Cut Medicare N
75. Alien residncy-prior 1982 Y
76. Alien residncy-prior 1980 Y
77. Pen emp-hire illgl aliens N
78. Lmt Persh II/cruse-Europe N
79. Delete 34 B-1 bombers N
80. Bar purch of Pershing II N
81. Bar purchase of Sgt York N
82. Delete $ for Trident II N
83. Allow 15 MX missiles Y
84. Bar MX procurement-1985 N
85. Equal Access Act Y
86. Aid to El Salvador Y
87. Bar Nicarag water mining N
88. Physician/Medicare freeze Y
89. Increase "sin" taxes Y
90. End SBA direct loans ?
91. Sell Conrail Y
92. Equal Rights Amendment N
93. Marines in Lebanon Y
94. Eminent domain-Coal comps Y
95. Prohibit EPA sanctions ?
96. SS age increase/Reforms Y
97. Auto domestic content req X
98. Delete jobs program fundg Y
99. Highway-Gas tax bill N
100. Raise Medicare;Cut defnse N
101. Emergency housing aid N
102. Across-the-board tax cuts Y
103. Gramm-Latta II targets Y
104. Delete B-1 bomber funds N
105. Dsapprov Saudi AWACS sale ?
106. Disapprove oil import fee Y
107. Rail Deregulation N
108. Dsapp India nuc fuel sale N
109. Mil draft registration Y
110. Chrysler Loan Guarantees N
111. Prohibit school busing Y
112. Nuclear plant moratorium N
113. Oil price controls ?
114. Tuition Tax Credits ?
115. Est Consumer Protect Agcy N
116. Eliminate B-1 bomber fnds X
117. Subminimum wage for youth Y
118. Delete crude oil tax Y
119. Natural gas deregulation Y

Presidential Support Score: 1986 - 65% 1985 - 61%

LOWERY, BILL -- California 41st District [Republican]. County of San Diego (pt.). Prior Terms: House: 1981-86. Born: May 2, 1947; San Diego, Calif. Education: San Diego State College. Occupation: San Diego city councilman (1977); council liaison, San Diego Unified Port District; deputy mayor (1979).

1. Immigration Reform Y
2. Open fld-search warrants Y
3. Civil pnty-hire ill alien N
4. So Afr sanc-veto override Y
5. Tax Overhaul Y
6. South Africa sanctions Y
7. Death penalty-drug bill Y
8. Evidence-warrantless srch Y
9. Life term-second drug off Y
10. Military use in drug war Y
11. Troop reduction in Europe N
12. Prohibit chemical weapons N
13. Bar ASAT testing N
14. Abide SALT II weapons ban N
15. Follow SALT II-Soviets do Y
16. Reduce SDI funding N
17. Increase SDI funding Y
18. Purchase Trident sub Y
19. Delete 12 MX;Add conv wpn N
20. Raise speed limit Y
21. Textile Import Quotas(*) N
22. Req Pentagon buy US goods N
23. AIDS ins anti-dscriminatn N
24. Nicaraguan refugee aid N
25. Nicaraguan contra aid Y
26. US abide by SALT II Y
27. Prohibit Saudi arms sale Y
28. Military Retiremnt Reform Y
29. Nicaraguan refugee aid Y
30. Ease '68 Gun Control Act Y
31. Bar intrstat handgun tran N
32. Keep '68 Gun Control Act N
33. Nicaraguan contra aid Y
34. Bar emp polygraph testing N
35. Tax Overhaul consideratn N
36. Bar armor-piercing ammo Y
37. Tax Overhaul consideratn N
38. Make comp emissions known N
39. Allow toxic victims suits N
40. Strike Superfund "VAT" N
41. Notify emp-plant closing N
42. Bar emp consult-plant clo Y
43. Medicare cuts;Tax incres' N
44. Delete 12 MX missiles N
45. Spending cuts;Tax incres' N
46. Textile Import Quotas N
47. Cut some school lunch fds Y
48. Clean Water Act Amendmnts Y
49. Youth work projects N
50. Assist military in Angola Y
51. Allow US troops-Nicaragua Y
52. Pentagon polygraph exams Y
53. Bar ASAT testing N
54. Suspend def pmt for abuse N
55. Bar Pentagon-contr emplmt Y
56. Increase SDI funding Y
57. Reduce SDI funding N
58. Produce chemical weapons Y
59. Bar CIA fndg in Nicaragua N
60. South Africa sanctions N
61. Cut SS COLAs; Raise taxes N
62. Let US invest-So Africa #
63. Approve 21 MX for 1985 Y
64. Emergency Farm Credit N
65. Awards to whistle blowers Y
66. African disaster relief Y
67. Ban bank loans to So Afr Y
68. Bar coun duty-free trtmt N
69. Steel import limits N
70. Soc Sec COLAs=inflation Y
71. Bar haz waste vctms suits Y
72. Prohibit aid to Nicaragua N
73. Cut $-Schs bar sch prayer Y
74. Raise taxes; Cut Medicare Y
75. Alien residncy-prior 1982 Y
76. Alien residncy-prior 1980 Y
77. Pen emp-hire illgl aliens N
78. Lmt Persh II/cruse-Europe N
79. Delete 34 B-1 bombers N
80. Bar purch of Pershing II N
81. Bar purchase of Sgt York N
82. Delete $ for Trident II N
83. Allow 15 MX missiles Y
84. Bar MX procurement-1985 N
85. Equal Access Act Y
86. Aid to El Salvador Y
87. Bar Nicarag water mining N
88. Physician/Medicare freeze Y
89. Increase "sin" taxes N
90. End SBA direct loans N
91. Sell Conrail Y
92. Equal Rights Amendment N
93. Marines in Lebanon Y
94. Eminent domain-Coal comps Y
95. Prohibit EPA sanctions Y
96. SS age increase/Reforms Y
97. Auto domestic content req N
98. Delete jobs program fundg Y
99. Highway-Gas tax bill Y
100. Raise Medicare;Cut defnse N
101. Emergency housing aid Y
102. Across-the-board tax cuts Y
103. Gramm-Latta II targets Y
104. Delete B-1 bomber funds N
105. Dsapprov Saudi AWACS sale Y

Presidential Support Score: 1986 - 76% 1985 - 71%

LUNGREN, DAN -- California 42nd District [Republican]. Counties of Los Angeles (pt.) and Orange (pt.). Prior Terms: House: 1979-86. Born: September 22, 1946; Long Beach, Calif. Education: Notre Dame University; University of Southern California Law School; Georgetown University Law Center (J.D.). Occupation: Senate staff member (1969-71); law partner, Ball, Hunt, Hart, Brown and Baerwitz (1973-78).

1.	Immigration Reform	Y	53.	Bar ASAT testing	N
2.	Open fld-search warrants	Y	54.	Suspend def pmt for abuse	N
3.	Civil pnty-hire ill alien	N	55.	Bar Pentagon-contr emplmt	Y
4.	So Afr sanc-veto override	N	56.	Increase SDI funding	Y
5.	Tax Overhaul	Y	57.	Reduce SDI funding	N
6.	South Africa sanctions	N	58.	Produce chemical weapons	Y
7.	Death penalty-drug bill	Y	59.	Bar CIA fndg in Nicaragua	N
8.	Evidence-warrantless srch	Y	60.	South Africa sanctions	N
9.	Life term-second drug off	Y	61.	Cut SS COLAs; Raise taxes	N
10.	Military use in drug war	N	62.	Let US invest-So Africa	Y
11.	Troop reduction in Europe	N	63.	Approve 21 MX for 1985	Y
12.	Prohibit chemical weapons	N	64.	Emergency Farm Credit	N
13.	Bar ASAT testing	N	65.	Awards to whistle blowers	Y
14.	Abide SALT II weapons ban	N	66.	African disaster relief	Y
15.	Follow SALT II-Soviets do	Y	67.	Ban bank loans to So Afr	Y
16.	Reduce SDI funding	N	68.	Bar coun duty-free trtmt	N
17.	Increase SDI funding	Y	69.	Steel import limits	N
18.	Purchase Trident sub	N	70.	Soc Sec COLAs=inflation	Y
19.	Delete 12 MX;Add conv wpn	N	71.	Bar haz waste vctms suits	Y
20.	Raise speed limit	Y	72.	Prohibit aid to Nicaragua	N
21.	Textile Import Quotas(*)	N	73.	Cut $-Schs bar sch prayer	Y
22.	Req Pentagon buy US goods	N	74.	Raise taxes; Cut Medicare	N
23.	AIDS ins anti-dscriminatn	N	75.	Alien residncy-prior 1982	Y
24.	Nicaraguan refugee aid	N	76.	Alien residncy-prior 1980	Y
25.	Nicaraguan contra aid	Y	77.	Pen emp-hire iligl aliens	N
26.	US abide by SALT II	Y	78.	Lmt Persh II/cruse-Europe	N
27.	Prohibit Saudi arms sale	N	79.	Delete 34 B-1 bombers	N
28.	Military Retiremnt Reform	Y	80.	Bar purch of Pershing II	N
29.	Nicaraguan refugee aid	Y	81.	Bar purchase of Sgt York	Y
30.	Ease '68 Gun Control Act	Y	82.	Delete $ for Trident II	N
31.	Bar intrstat handgun tran	Y	83.	Allow 15 MX missiles	Y
32.	Keep '68 Gun Control Act	Y	84.	Bar MX procurement-1985	N
33.	Nicaraguan contra aid	Y	85.	Equal Access Act	Y
34.	Bar emp polygraph testing	N	86.	Aid to El Salvador	Y
35.	Tax Overhaul consideratn	N	87.	Bar Nicarag water mining	N
36.	Bar armor-piercing ammo	Y	88.	Physician/Medicare freeze	Y
37.	Tax Overhaul consideratn	N	89.	Increase "sin" taxes	N
38.	Make comp emissions known	N	90.	End SBA direct loans	Y
39.	Allow toxic victims suits	N	91.	Sell Conrail	Y
40.	Strike Superfund "VAT"	Y	92.	Equal Rights Amendment	N
41.	Notify emp-plant closing	N	93.	Marines in Lebanon	Y
42.	Bar emp consult-plant clo	Y	94.	Eminent domain-Coal comps	Y
43.	Medicare cuts;Tax incres'	N	95.	Prohibit EPA sanctions	Y
44.	Delete 12 MX missiles	N	96.	SS age increase/Reforms	Y
45.	Spending cuts;Tax incres'	N	97.	Auto domestic content req	N
46.	Textile Import Quotas	?	98.	Delete jobs program fundg	Y
47.	Cut some school lunch fds	Y	99.	Highway-Gas tax bill	Y
48.	Clean Water Act Amendmnts	Y	100.	Raise Medicare;Cut defnse	N
49.	Youth work projects	N	101.	Emergency housing aid	N
50.	Assist military in Angola	Y	102.	Across-the-board tax cuts	Y
51.	Allow US troops-Nicaragua	Y	103.	Gramm-Latta II targets	Y
52.	Pentagon polygraph exams	Y	104.	Delete B-1 bomber funds	N

LUNGREN, DAN (Cont.)

105. Dsapprov Saudi AWACS sale N
106. Disapprove oil import fee Y
107. Rail Deregulation N
108. Dsapp India nuc fuel sale Y
109. Mil draft registration Y
110. Chrysler Loan Guarantees N
111. Prohibit school busing Y
112. Nuclear plant moratorium N
113. Oil price controls N

Presidential Support Score: 1986 - 86% 1985 - 80%

PACKARD, RONALD C. -- California 43rd District [Republican]. Counties of Orange (pt.) and San Diego (pt.). Prior Terms: House: 1983-86. Born: January 19, 1931; Meridian, Idaho. Education: Brigham Young University; Portland State University; University of Oregon Dental School. Military Service: U.S. Navy. Occupation: Dentist, U.S. Navy Dental Corps (1957-59); Board of Trustees, Carlsbad Unified School District (1962-74); member, Carlsbad city council; director, North County Transit District; mayor (1978-82); dentist, Packard Dental Clinic (since 1959); officer, Packard Development Corp. (since 1965); vice chairman, board of directors, First National Bank of North County (since 1981).

1. Immigration Reform Y
2. Open fld-search warrants Y
3. Civil pnty-hire ill alien N
4. So Afr sanc-veto override N
5. Tax Overhaul Y
6. South Africa sanctions N
7. Death penalty-drug bill Y
8. Evidence-warrantless srch Y
9. Life term-second drug off Y
10. Military use in drug war Y
11. Troop reduction in Europe N
12. Prohibit chemical weapons N
13. Bar ASAT testing N
14. Abide SALT II weapons ban N
15. Follow SALT II-Soviets do Y
16. Reduce SDI funding N
17. Increase SDI funding Y
18. Purchase Trident sub N
19. Delete 12 MX;Add conv wpn N
20. Raise speed limit N
21. Textile Import Quotas(*) N
22. Req Pentagon buy US goods N
23. AIDS ins anti-dscriminatn N
24. Nicaraguan refugee aid N
25. Nicaraguan contra aid Y
26. US abide by SALT II Y
27. Prohibit Saudi arms sale N
28. Military Retiremnt Reform Y
29. Nicaraguan refugee aid Y
30. Ease '68 Gun Control Act Y
31. Bar intrstat handgun tran N
32. Keep '68 Gun Control Act N
33. Nicaraguan contra aid Y
34. Bar emp polygraph testing N
35. Tax Overhaul consideratn N
36. Bar armor-piercing ammo Y
37. Tax Overhaul consideratn N
38. Make comp emissions known N
39. Allow toxic victims suits N
40. Strike Superfund "VAT" N
41. Notify emp-plant closing N
42. Bar emp consult-plant clo Y
43. Medicare cuts;Tax incres' N
44. Delete 12 MX missiles N
45. Spending cuts;Tax incres' N
46. Textile Import Quotas N
47. Cut some school lunch fds Y
48. Clean Water Act Amendmnts Y
49. Youth work projects N
50. Assist military in Angola Y
51. Allow US troops-Nicaragua Y
52. Pentagon polygraph exams Y
53. Bar ASAT testing N
54. Suspend def pmt for abuse N
55. Bar Pentagon-contr emplmt Y
56. Increase SDI funding Y
57. Reduce SDI funding N
58. Produce chemical weapons Y
59. Bar CIA fndg in Nicaragua N
60. South Africa sanctions N
61. Cut SS COLAs; Raise taxes N
62. Let US invest-So Africa Y
63. Approve 21 MX for 1985 Y
64. Emergency Farm Credit Y
65. Awards to whistle blowers Y
66. African disaster relief Y
67. Ban bank loans to So Afr ?
68. Bar coun duty-free trtmt N
69. Steel import limits N
70. Soc Sec COLAs=inflation Y
71. Bar haz waste vctms suits Y
72. Prohibit aid to Nicaragua N
73. Cut $-Schs bar sch prayer Y
74. Raise taxes; Cut Medicare Y
75. Alien residncy-prior 1982 Y
76. Alien residncy-prior 1980 Y

PACKARD, RONALD C. (Cont.)

77. Pen emp-hire illgl aliens N
78. Lmt Persh II/cruse-Europe N
79. Delete 34 B-1 bombers N
80. Bar purch of Pershing II N
81. Bar purchase of Sgt York N
82. Delete $ for Trident II N
83. Allow 15 MX missiles Y
84. Bar MX procurement-1985 N
85. Equal Access Act Y
86. Aid to El Salvador Y
87. Bar Nicarag water mining N
88. Physician/Medicare freeze Y
89. Increase "sin" taxes Y
90. End SBA direct loans Y
91. Sell Conrail Y
92. Equal Rights Amendment N
93. Marines in Lebanon Y
94. Eminent domain-Coal comps Y
95. Prohibit EPA sanctions Y
96. SS age increase/Reforms Y

Presidential Support Score: 1986 - 84% 1985 - 75%

BATES, JIM -- California 44th District [Democrat]. County of San Diego (pt.). Prior Terms: House: 1983-86. Born: July 21, 1941; Denver, Colo. Education: San Diego University (B.A.). Military Service: U.S. Marine Corps. Occupation: Member, Metropolitan Transit Development Board; chairman, Health Systems Agency; San Diego councilman (1971-74); San Diego Board of Supervisors (1974-80).

1. Immigration Reform Y
2. Open fld-search warrants Y
3. Civil pnty-hire ill alien N
4. So Afr sanc-veto override Y
5. Tax Overhaul Y
6. South Africa sanctions Y
7. Death penalty-drug bill N
8. Evidence-warrantless srch N
9. Life term-second drug off Y
10. Military use in drug war Y
11. Troop reduction in Europe Y
12. Prohibit chemical weapons Y
13. Bar ASAT testing Y
14. Abide SALT II weapons ban Y
15. Follow SALT II-Soviets do N
16. Reduce SDI funding Y
17. Increase SDI funding N
18. Purchase Trident sub N
19. Delete 12 MX;Add conv wpn Y
20. Raise speed limit N
21. Textile Import Quotas(*) Y
22. Req Pentagon buy US goods Y
23. AIDS ins anti-dscriminatn Y
24. Nicaraguan refugee aid Y
25. Nicaraguan contra aid N
26. US abide by SALT II N
27. Prohibit Saudi arms sale Y
28. Military Retiremnt Reform Y
29. Nicaraguan refugee aid Y
30. Ease '68 Gun Control Act N
31. Bar intrstat handgun tran Y
32. Keep '68 Gun Control Act Y
33. Nicaraguan contra aid N
34. Bar emp polygraph testing N
35. Tax Overhaul consideratn Y
36. Bar armor-piercing ammo Y
37. Tax Overhaul consideratn Y
38. Make comp emissions known Y
39. Allow toxic victims suits Y
40. Strike Superfund "VAT" Y
41. Notify emp-plant closing Y
42. Bar emp consult-plant clo N
43. Medicare cuts;Tax incres' Y
44. Delete 12 MX missiles Y
45. Spending cuts;Tax incres' Y
46. Textile Import Quotas Y
47. Cut some school lunch fds N
48. Clean Water Act Amendmnts N
49. Youth work projects Y
50. Assist military in Angola N
51. Allow US troops-Nicaragua N
52. Pentagon polygraph exams Y
53. Bar ASAT testing Y
54. Suspend def pmt for abuse Y
55. Bar Pentagon-contr emplmt Y
56. Increase SDI funding N
57. Reduce SDI funding Y
58. Produce chemical weapons Y
59. Bar CIA fndg in Nicaragua Y
60. South Africa sanctions Y
61. Cut SS COLAs; Raise taxes Y
62. Let US invest-So Africa N
63. Approve 21 MX for 1985 N
64. Emergency Farm Credit N
65. Awards to whistle blowers Y
66. African disaster relief Y
67. Ban bank loans to So Afr ?
68. Bar coun duty-free trtmt Y
69. Steel import limits Y
70. Soc Sec COLAs=inflation Y
71. Bar haz waste vctms suits N
72. Prohibit aid to Nicaragua Y
73. Cut $-Schs bar sch prayer N
74. Raise taxes; Cut Medicare Y
75. Alien residncy-prior 1982 Y
76. Alien residncy-prior 1980 N

BATES, JIM (Cont.)

77. Pen emp-hire illgl aliens Y
78. Lmt Persh II/cruse-Europe Y
79. Delete 34 B-1 bombers Y
80. Bar purch of Pershing II Y
81. Bar purchase of Sgt York Y
82. Delete $ for Trident II Y
83. Allow 15 MX missiles N
84. Bar MX procurement-1985 Y
85. Equal Access Act ?
86. Aid to El Salvador N
87. Bar Nicarag water mining Y
88. Physician/Medicare freeze N
89. Increase "sin" taxes Y
90. End SBA direct loans N
91. Sell Conrail Y
92. Equal Rights Amendment Y
93. Marines in Lebanon N
94. Eminent domain-Coal comps Y
95. Prohibit EPA sanctions Y
96. SS age increase/Reforms Y

Presidential Support Score: 1986 - 19% 1985 - 30%

HUNTER, DUNCAN -- California 45th District [Republican]. Counties of Imperial and San Diego (pt.). Prior Terms: House: 1981-86. Born: May 31, 1948; Riverside, Calif. Education: University of Montana; University of California; Western State University's College of Law (J.D.). Military Service: U.S. Army, 1969-71. Occupation: Attorney.

1. Immigration Reform N
2. Open fld-search warrants N
3. Civil pnty-hire ill alien Y
4. So Afr sanc-veto override N
5. Tax Overhaul Y
6. South Africa sanctions N
7. Death penalty-drug bill Y
8. Evidence-warrantless srch Y
9. Life term-second drug off Y
10. Military use in drug war Y
11. Troop reduction in Europe N
12. Prohibit chemical weapons N
13. Bar ASAT testing N
14. Abide SALT II weapons ban N
15. Follow SALT II-Soviets do Y
16. Reduce SDI funding N
17. Increase SDI funding Y
18. Purchase Trident sub N
19. Delete 12 MX;Add conv wpn N
20. Raise speed limit N
21. Textile Import Quotas(*) Y
22. Req Pentagon buy US goods Y
23. AIDS ins anti-dscriminatn N
24. Nicaraguan refugee aid N
25. Nicaraguan contra aid Y
26. US abide by SALT II Y
27. Prohibit Saudi arms sale Y
28. Military Retiremnt Reform Y
29. Nicaraguan refugee aid Y
30. Ease '68 Gun Control Act Y
31. Bar intrstat handgun tran N
32. Keep '68 Gun Control Act N
33. Nicaraguan contra aid Y
34. Bar emp polygraph testing N
35. Tax Overhaul consideratn N
36. Bar armor-piercing ammo Y
37. Tax Overhaul consideratn N
38. Bar emp consult-plant clo N
39. Allow toxic victims suits N
40. Strike Superfund "VAT" N
41. Notify emp-plant closing N
42. Bar emp consult-plant clo Y
43. Medicare cuts;Tax incres' N
44. Delete 12 MX missiles N
45. Spending cuts;Tax incres' N
46. Textile Import Quotas Y
47. Cut some school lunch fds Y
48. Clean Water Act Amendmnts Y
49. Youth work projects N
50. Assist military in Angola Y
51. Allow US troops-Nicaragua Y
52. Pentagon polygraph exams Y
53. Bar ASAT testing N
54. Suspend def pmt for abuse N
55. Bar Pentagon-contr emplmt Y
56. Increase SDI funding Y
57. Reduce SDI funding N
58. Produce chemical weapons Y
59. Bar CIA fndg in Nicaragua N
60. South Africa sanctions N
61. Cut SS COLAs; Raise taxes N
62. Let US invest-So Africa Y
63. Approve 21 MX for 1985 Y
64. Emergency Farm Credit ?
65. Awards to whistle blowers Y
66. African disaster relief Y
67. Ban bank loans to So Afr N
68. Bar coun duty-free trtmt N
69. Steel import limits Y
70. Soc Sec COLAs=inflation Y
71. Bar haz waste vctms suits Y
72. Prohibit aid to Nicaragua N
73. Cut $-Schs bar sch prayer Y
74. Raise taxes; Cut Medicare N
75. Alien residncy-prior 1982 N
76. Alien residncy-prior 1980 Y
77. Pen emp-hire illgl aliens Y
78. Lmt Persh II/cruse-Europe N

HUNTER, DUNCAN (Cont.)

79.	Delete 34 B-1 bombers	N	93.	Marines in Lebanon	Y
80.	Bar purch of Pershing II	N	94.	Eminent domain-Coal comps	Y
81.	Bar purchase of Sgt York	N	95.	Prohibit EPA sanctions	Y
82.	Delete $ for Trident II	N	96.	SS age increase/Reforms	Y
83.	Allow 15 MX missiles	Y	97.	Auto domestic content req	Y
84.	Bar MX procurement-1985	N	98.	Delete jobs program fundg	Y
85.	Equal Access Act	Y	99.	Highway-Gas tax bill	Y
86.	Aid to El Salvador	Y	100.	Raise Medicare;Cut defnse	N
87.	Bar Nicarag water mining	N	101.	Emergency housing aid	N
88.	Physician/Medicare freeze	Y	102.	Across-the-board tax cuts	Y
89.	Increase "sin" taxes	N	103.	Gramm-Latta II targets	Y
90.	End SBA direct loans	Y	104.	Delete B-1 bomber funds	N
91.	Sell Conrail	Y	105.	Dsapprov Saudi AWACS sale	Y
92.	Equal Rights Amendment	N			

Presidential Support Score: 1986 - 77% 1985 - 74%

COLORADO

SCHROEDER, PATRICIA -- Colorado 1st District [Democrat]. Counties of Adams (pt.), Arapahoe (pt.) and Denver (pt.). Prior Terms: House: 1973-86. Born: July 30, 1940; Portland, Ore. Education: University of Minnesota (B.A.); Harvard University (J.D.). Occupation: Field attorney, National Labor Relations Board (1964-66); law instructor, Community College of Denver (1969-70), University of Colorado (1969), and Regis College (1970-72); legal counsel, Planned Parenthood; hearing officer, Colorado State Department of Personnel (1971-72).

1.	Immigration Reform	N	30.	Ease '68 Gun Control Act	N
2.	Open fld-search warrants	Y	31.	Bar intrstat handgun tran	Y
3.	Civil pnty-hire ill alien	N	32.	Keep '68 Gun Control Act	Y
4.	So Afr sanc-veto override	Y	33.	Nicaraguan contra aid	N
5.	Tax Overhaul	N	34.	Bar emp polygraph testing	Y
6.	South Africa sanctions	?	35.	Tax Overhaul consideratn	N
7.	Death penalty-drug bill	N	36.	Bar armor-piercing ammo	Y
8.	Evidence-warrantless srch	N	37.	Tax Overhaul consideratn	N
9.	Life term-second drug off	Y	38.	Make comp emissions known	Y
10.	Military use in drug war	N	39.	Allow toxic victims suits	Y
11.	Troop reduction in Europe	Y	40.	Strike Superfund "VAT"	Y
12.	Prohibit chemical weapons	Y	41.	Notify emp-plant closing	N
13.	Bar ASAT testing	Y	42.	Bar emp consult-plant clo	Y
14.	Abide SALT II weapons ban	Y	43.	Medicare cuts;Tax incres'	Y
15.	Follow SALT II-Soviets do	N	44.	Delete 12 MX missiles	Y
16.	Reduce SDI funding	Y	45.	Spending cuts;Tax incres'	Y
17.	Increase SDI funding	N	46.	Textile Import Quotas	N
18.	Purchase Trident sub	N	47.	Cut some school lunch fds	N
19.	Delete 12 MX;Add conv wpn	Y	48.	Clean Water Act Amendmnts	N
20.	Raise speed limit	Y	49.	Youth work projects	Y
21.	Textile Import Quotas(*)	Y	50.	Assist military in Angola	N
22.	Req Pentagon buy US goods	N	51.	Allow US troops-Nicaragua	N
23.	AIDS ins anti-dscriminatn	Y	52.	Pentagon polygraph exams	Y
24.	Nicaraguan refugee aid	Y	53.	Bar ASAT testing	Y
25.	Nicaraguan contra aid	N	54.	Suspend def pmt for abuse	Y
26.	US abide by SALT II	N	55.	Bar Pentagon-contr emplmt	Y
27.	Prohibit Saudi arms sale	Y	56.	Increase SDI funding	N
28.	Military Retiremnt Reform	Y	57.	Reduce SDI funding	Y
29.	Nicaraguan refugee aid	Y	58.	Produce chemical weapons	N

SCHROEDER, PATRICIA (Cont.)

59. Bar CIA fndg in Nicaragua Y
60. South Africa sanctions Y
61. Cut SS COLAs; Raise taxes N
62. Let US invest-So Africa N
63. Approve 21 MX for 1985 N
64. Emergency Farm Credit N
65. Awards to whistle blowers Y
66. African disaster relief Y
67. Ban bank loans to So Afr Y
68. Bar coun duty-free trtmt N
69. Steel import limits N
70. Soc Sec COLAs=inflation Y
71. Bar haz waste vctms suits N
72. Prohibit aid to Nicaragua Y
73. Cut $-Schs bar sch prayer N
74. Raise taxes; Cut Medicare N
75. Alien residncy-prior 1982 N
76. Alien residncy-prior 1980 N
77. Pen emp-hire illgl aliens Y
78. Lmt Persh II/cruse-Europe Y
79. Delete 34 B-1 bombers Y
80. Bar purch of Pershing II Y
81. Bar purchase of Sgt York Y
82. Delete $ for Trident II N
83. Allow 15 MX missiles N
84. Bar MX procurement-1985 Y
85. Equal Access Act N
86. Aid to El Salvador N
87. Bar Nicarag water mining Y
88. Physician/Medicare freeze N
89. Increase "sin" taxes N
90. End SBA direct loans N
91. Sell Conrail N
92. Equal Rights Amendment Y
93. Marines in Lebanon N
94. Eminent domain;Coal comps N
95. Prohibit EPA sanctions Y
96. SS age increase/Reforms N
97. Auto domestic content req ?
98. Delete jobs program fundg ?
99. Highway-Gas tax bill N
100. Raise Medicare;Cut defnse Y
101. Emergency housing aid Y
102. Across-the-board tax cuts N
103. Gramm-Latta II targets N
104. Delete B-1 bomber funds Y
105. Dsapprov Saudi AWACS sale Y
106. Disapprove oil import fee Y
107. Rail Deregulation N
108. Dsapp India nuc fuel sale Y
109. Mil draft registration N
110. Chrysler Loan Guarantees N
111. Prohibit school busing N
112. Nuclear plant moratorium Y
113. Oil price controls N
114. Tuition Tax Credits N
115. Est Consumer Protect Agcy N
116. Eliminate B-1 bomber fnds Y
117. Subminimum wage for youth N
118. Delete crude oil tax Y
119. Natural gas deregulation Y

Presidential Support Score: 1986 - 19% 1985 - 30%

WIRTH, TIMOTHY E. -- Colorado 2nd District [Democrat]. Counties of Adams (pt.), Boulder, Clear Creek, Gilpin and Jefferson (pt.). Prior Terms: House: 1975-86. Born: September 22, 1939; Santa Fe, N.M. Education: Harvard College (A.B., M.Ed.); Stanford University (Ph.D.). Military Service: U.S. Army Reserve, 1961-67. Occupation: Special assistant, secretary, HEW; deputy assistant, secretary of education, HEW (1969-70); member, governor's task force on returned Vietnam veterans.

1. Immigration Reform N
2. Open fld-search warrants Y
3. Civil pnty-hire ill alien N
4. So Afr sanc-veto override Y
5. Tax Overhaul Y
6. South Africa sanctions Y
7. Death penalty-drug bill N
8. Evidence-warrantless srch N
9. Life term-second drug off Y
10. Military use in drug war N
11. Troop reduction in Europe N
12. Prohibit chemical weapons Y
13. Bar ASAT testing Y
14. Abide SALT II weapons ban Y
15. Follow SALT II-Soviets do N
16. Reduce SDI funding N
17. Increase SDI funding N
18. Purchase Trident sub Y
19. Delete 12 MX;Add conv wpn Y
20. Raise speed limit Y
21. Textile Import Quotas(*) N
22. Req Pentagon buy US goods Y
23. AIDS ins anti-dscriminatn Y
24. Nicaraguan refugee aid Y
25. Nicaraguan contra aid N
26. US abide by SALT II N
27. Prohibit Saudi arms sale Y
28. Military Retiremnt Reform Y
29. Nicaraguan refugee aid Y
30. Ease '68 Gun Control Act Y

WIRTH, TIMOTHY E. (Cont.)

31. Bar intrstat handgun tran Y
32. Keep '68 Gun Control Act Y
33. Nicaraguan contra aid N
34. Bar emp polygraph testing Y
35. Tax Overhaul consideratn Y
36. Bar armor-piercing ammo Y
37. Tax Overhaul consideratn Y
38. Make comp emissions known Y
39. Allow toxic victims suits N
40. Strike Superfund "VAT" N
41. Notify emp-plant closing Y
42. Bar emp consult-plant clo N
43. Medicare cuts;Tax incres' Y
44. Delete 12 MX missiles Y
45. Spending cuts;Tax incres' Y
46. Textile Import Quotas N
47. Cut some school lunch fds N
48. Clean Water Act Amendmnts N
49. Youth work projects Y
50. Assist military in Angola N
51. Allow US troops-Nicaragua N
52. Pentagon polygraph exams ?
53. Bar ASAT testing Y
54. Suspend def pmt for abuse Y
55. Bar Pentagon-contr emplmt Y
56. Increase SDI funding N
57. Reduce SDI funding N
58. Produce chemical weapons N
59. Bar CIA fndg in Nicaragua Y
60. South Africa sanctions Y
61. Cut SS COLAs; Raise taxes N
62. Let US invest-So Africa N
63. Approve 21 MX for 1985 N
64. Emergency Farm Credit Y
65. Awards to whistle blowers Y
66. African disaster relief Y
67. Ban bank loans to So Afr Y
68. Bar coun duty-free trtmt N
69. Steel import limits Y
70. Soc Sec COLAs=inflation Y
71. Bar haz waste vctms suits N
72. Prohibit aid to Nicaragua Y
73. Cut $-Schs bar sch prayer N
74. Raise taxes; Cut Medicare Y
75. Alien residncy-prior 1982 ?
76. Alien residncy-prior 1980 N
77. Pen emp-hire illgl aliens Y
78. Lmt Persh II/cruse-Europe Y
79. Delete 34 B-1 bombers Y
80. Bar purch of Pershing II Y
81. Bar purchase of Sgt York ?
82. Delete $ for Trident II N
83. Allow 15 MX missiles N
84. Bar MX procurement-1985 Y
85. Equal Access Act N
86. Aid to El Salvador N
87. Bar Nicarag water mining Y
88. Physician/Medicare freeze N
89. Increase "sin" taxes Y
90. End SBA direct loans N
91. Sell Conrail N
92. Equal Rights Amendment Y
93. Marines in Lebanon N
94. Eminent domain-Coal comps N
95. Prohibit EPA sanctions Y
96. SS age increase/Reforms N
97. Auto domestic content req Y
98. Delete jobs program fundg N
99. Highway-Gas tax bill Y
100. Raise Medicare;Cut defnse N
101. Emergency housing aid Y
102. Across-the-board tax cuts N
103. Gramm-Latta II targets N
104. Delete B-1 bomber funds Y
105. Dsapprov Saudi AWACS sale Y
106. Disapprove oil import fee N
107. Rail Deregulation N
108. Dsapp India nuc fuel sale Y
109. Mil draft registration Y
110. Chrysler Loan Guarantees N
111. Prohibit school busing N
112. Nuclear plant moratorium Y
113. Oil price controls N
114. Tuition Tax Credits N
115. Est Consumer Protect Agcy Y
116. Eliminate B-1 bomber fnds Y
117. Subminimum wage for youth Y
118. Delete crude oil tax N
119. Natural gas deregulation Y

Presidential Support Score: 1986 - 27% 1985 - 21%

STRANG, MICHAEL L. -- Colorado 3rd District [Republican]. Counties of Alamosa, Archuleta, Conejos, Costilla, Custer, Delta, Dolores, Eagle, Fremont (pt.), Garfield, Grand, Gunnison, Hinsdale, Huerfano, Jackson, La Plata, Mesa, Mineral, Moffat, Montezuma, Montrose, Ouray, Pitkin, Pueblo, Rio Blanco, Rio Grande, Routt, Saguache, San Juan, San Miguel and Summit. Prior Terms: 1985-86. Occupation: Rancher; stockbroker; Colorado representative.

1. Immigration Reform Y
2. Open fld-search warrants Y
3. Civil pnty-hire ill alien Y
4. So Afr sanc-veto override N

STRANG, MICHAEL L. (Cont.)

5.	Tax Overhaul	Y	36.	Bar armor-piercing ammo	N
6.	South Africa sanctions	N	37.	Tax Overhaul consideratn	N
7.	Death penalty-drug bill	Y	38.	Make comp emissions known	N
8.	Evidence-warrantless srch	Y	39.	Allow toxic victims suits	N
9.	Life term-second drug off	Y	40.	Strike Superfund "VAT"	N
10.	Military use in drug war	Y	41.	Notify emp-plant closing	N
11.	Troop reduction in Europe	Y	42.	Bar emp consult-plant clo	Y
12.	Prohibit chemical weapons	N	43.	Medicare cuts;Tax incres'	N
13.	Bar ASAT testing	N	44.	Delete 12 MX missiles	N
14.	Abide SALT II weapons ban	N	45.	Spending cuts;Tax incres'	N
15.	Follow SALT II-Soviets do	Y	46.	Textile Import Quotas	-
16.	Reduce SDI funding	N	47.	Cut some school lunch fds	Y
17.	Increase SDI funding	Y	48.	Clean Water Act Amendmnts	Y
18.	Purchase Trident sub	N	49.	Youth work projects	N
19.	Delete 12 MX;Add conv wpn	N	50.	Assist military in Angola	Y
20.	Raise speed limit	Y	51.	Allow US troops-Nicaragua	Y
21.	Textile Import Quotas(*)	N	52.	Pentagon polygraph exams	Y
22.	Req Pentagon buy US goods	N	53.	Bar ASAT testing	N
23.	AIDS ins anti-dscriminatn	N	54.	Suspend def pmt for abuse	N
24.	Nicaraguan refugee aid	N	55.	Bar Pentagon-contr emplmt	Y
25.	Nicaraguan contra aid	Y	56.	Increase SDI funding	+
26.	US abide by SALT II	Y	57.	Reduce SDI funding	-
27.	Prohibit Saudi arms sale	Y	58.	Produce chemical weapons	+
28.	Military Retiremnt Reform	Y	59.	Bar CIA fndg in Nicaragua	N
29.	Nicaraguan refugee aid	Y	60.	South Africa sanctions	N
30.	Ease '68 Gun Control Act	Y	61.	Cut SS COLAs; Raise taxes	N
31.	Bar intrstat handgun tran	N	62.	Let US invest-So Africa	Y
32.	Keep '68 Gun Control Act	N	63.	Approve 21 MX for 1985	Y
33.	Nicaraguan contra aid	Y	64.	Emergency Farm Credit	N
34.	Bar emp polygraph testing	N	65.	Awards to whistle blowers	Y
35.	Tax Overhaul consideratn	N	66.	African disaster relief	Y

Presidential Support Score: 1986 - 76% 1985 - 63%

BROWN, HANK -- Colorado 4th District [Republican]. Counties of Adams (pt.), Arapahoe (pt.), Baca, Bent, Cheyenne, Crowley, Kiowa, Kit Carson, Larimer, Las Animas, Lincoln, Logan, Morgan, Otero, Phillips, Prowers, Sedgwick, Washington, Weld and Yuma. Prior Terms: House: 1981-86. Born: February 12, 1940; Denver, Colo. Education: University of Colorado (B.S., J.D.). Military Service: U.S. Navy, 1962-66. Occupation: Vice-president, Monfort of Colorado, Inc. (1969-80); Colorado senator (1972-76).

1.	Immigration Reform	N	16.	Reduce SDI funding	N
2.	Open fld-search warrants	Y	17.	Increase SDI funding	N
3.	Civil pnty-hire ill alien	Y	18.	Purchase Trident sub	N
4.	So Afr sanc-veto override	Y	19.	Delete 12 MX;Add conv wpn	N
5.	Tax Overhaul	Y	20.	Raise speed limit	Y
6.	South Africa sanctions	Y	21.	Textile Import Quotas(*)	N
7.	Death penalty-drug bill	Y	22.	Req Pentagon buy US goods	N
8.	Evidence-warrantless srch	Y	23.	AIDS ins anti-dscriminatn	N
9.	Life term-second drug off	Y	24.	Nicaraguan refugee aid	N
10.	Military use in drug war	Y	25.	Nicaraguan contra aid	Y
11.	Troop reduction in Europe	Y	26.	US abide by SALT II	Y
12.	Prohibit chemical weapons	Y	27.	Prohibit Saudi arms sale	Y
13.	Bar ASAT testing	N	28.	Military Retiremnt Reform	Y
14.	Abide SALT II weapons ban	N	29.	Nicaraguan refugee aid	Y
15.	Follow SALT II-Soviets do	Y	30.	Ease '68 Gun Control Act	Y

BROWN, HANK (Cont.)

31. Bar intrstat handgun tran N
32. Keep '68 Gun Control Act N
33. Nicaraguan contra aid Y
34. Bar emp polygraph testing N
35. Tax Overhaul consideratn N
36. Bar armor-piercing ammo Y
37. Tax Overhaul consideratn N
38. Make comp emissions known N
39. Allow toxic victims suits N
40. Strike Superfund "VAT" N
41. Notify emp-plant closing N
42. Bar emp consult-plant clo Y
43. Medicare cuts;Tax incres' N
44. Delete 12 MX missiles N
45. Spending cuts;Tax incres' N
46. Textile Import Quotas N
47. Cut some school lunch fds Y
48. Clean Water Act Amendmnts Y
49. Youth work projects N
50. Assist military in Angola Y
51. Allow US troops-Nicaragua Y
52. Pentagon polygraph exams Y
53. Bar ASAT testing N
54. Suspend def pmt for abuse N
55. Bar Pentagon-contr emplmt Y
56. Increase SDI funding N
57. Reduce SDI funding N
58. Produce chemical weapons N
59. Bar CIA fndg in Nicaragua N
60. South Africa sanctions Y
61. Cut SS COLAs; Raise taxes Y
62. Let US invest-So Africa Y
63. Approve 21 MX for 1985 Y
64. Emergency Farm Credit N
65. Awards to whistle blowers Y
66. African disaster relief N
67. Ban bank loans to So Afr Y
68. Bar coun duty-free trtmt N
69. Steel import limits N
70. Soc Sec COLAs=inflation Y
71. Bar haz waste vctms suits Y
72. Prohibit aid to Nicaragua N
73. Cut $-Schs bar sch prayer Y
74. Raise taxes; Cut Medicare N
75. Alien residncy-prior 1982 Y
76. Alien residncy-prior 1980 Y
77. Pen emp-hire illgl aliens N
78. Lmt Persh II/cruse-Europe N
79. Delete 34 B-1 bombers Y
80. Bar purch of Pershing II N
81. Bar purchase of Sgt York Y
82. Delete $ for Trident II N
83. Allow 15 MX missiles Y
84. Bar MX procurement-1985 N
85. Equal Access Act Y
86. Aid to El Salvador Y
87. Bar Nicarag water mining Y
88. Physician/Medicare freeze Y
89. Increase "sin" taxes N
90. End SBA direct loans Y
91. Sell Conrail Y
92. Equal Rights Amendment Y
93. Marines in Lebanon N
94. Eminent domain-Coal comps Y
95. Prohibit EPA sanctions N
96. SS age increase/Reforms Y
97. Auto domestic content req N
98. Delete jobs program fundg Y
99. Highway-Gas tax bill N
100. Raise Medicare;Cut defnse Y
101. Emergency housing aid N
102. Across-the-board tax cuts Y
103. Gramm-Latta II targets Y
104. Delete B-1 bomber funds Y
105. Dsapprov Saudi AWACS sale Y

Presidential Support Score: 1986 - 67% 1985 - 70%

KRAMER, KEN -- Colorado 5th District [Republican]. Counties of Arapahoe (pt.), Chaffee, Douglas, Elbert, El Paso, Fremont (pt.), Jefferson (pt.), Lake, Park and Teller. Prior Terms: House: 1979-86. Born: February 19, 1942; Chicago, Ill. Education: University of Illinois (B.A.); Harvard Law School (J.D.). Military Service: U.S. Army, 1967-70. Occupation: Deputy district attorney (1970-72); attorney, Holme, Roberts and Owne (1972-74); partner, Floyd, Kramer and Lambrecht (1975-78); Colorado representative (1973-78).

1. Immigration Reform N
2. Open fld-search warrants Y
3. Civil pnty-hire ill alien Y
4. So Afr sanc-veto override ?
5. Tax Overhaul Y
6. South Africa sanctions N
7. Death penalty-drug bill Y
8. Evidence-warrantless srch Y
9. Life term-second drug off Y
10. Military use in drug war Y
11. Troop reduction in Europe N
12. Prohibit chemical weapons N
13. Bar ASAT testing N
14. Abide SALT II weapons ban N
15. Follow SALT II-Soviets do Y
16. Reduce SDI funding N

KRAMER, KEN (Cont.)

17. Increase SDI funding Y
18. Purchase Trident sub Y
19. Delete 12 MX;Add conv wpn N
20. Raise speed limit Y
21. Textile Import Quotas(*) N
22. Req Pentagon buy US goods N
23. AIDS ins anti-dscriminatn N
24. Nicaraguan refugee aid N
25. Nicaraguan contra aid Y
26. US abide by SALT II Y
27. Prohibit Saudi arms sale Y
28. Military Retiremnt Reform ?
29. Nicaraguan refugee aid Y
30. Ease '68 Gun Control Act Y
31. Bar intrstat handgun tran N
32. Keep '68 Gun Control Act N
33. Nicaraguan contra aid Y
34. Bar emp polygraph testing N
35. Tax Overhaul consideratn N
36. Bar armor-piercing ammo N
37. Tax Overhaul consideratn N
38. Make comp emissions known N
39. Allow toxic victims suits N
40. Strike Superfund "VAT" N
41. Notify emp-plant closing ?
42. Bar emp consult-plant clo Y
43. Medicare cuts;Tax incres' N
44. Delete 12 MX missiles N
45. Spending cuts;Tax incres' N
46. Textile Import Quotas N
47. Cut some school lunch fds Y
48. Clean Water Act Amendmnts Y
49. Youth work projects N
50. Assist military in Angola Y
51. Allow US troops-Nicaragua Y
52. Pentagon polygraph exams Y
53. Bar ASAT testing N
54. Suspend def pmt for abuse N
55. Bar Pentagon-contr emplmt Y
56. Increase SDI funding Y
57. Reduce SDI funding N
58. Produce chemical weapons Y
59. Bar CIA fndg in Nicaragua N
60. South Africa sanctions N
61. Cut SS COLAs; Raise taxes N
62. Let US invest-So Africa Y
63. Approve 21 MX for 1985 Y
64. Emergency Farm Credit N
65. Awards to whistle blowers Y
66. African disaster relief Y
67. Ban bank loans to So Afr Y
68. Bar coun duty-free trtmt N
69. Steel import limits N
70. Soc Sec COLAs=inflation Y
71. Bar haz waste vctms suits Y
72. Prohibit aid to Nicaragua N
73. Cut $-Schs bar sch prayer Y
74. Raise taxes; Cut Medicare N
75. Alien residncy-prior 1982 Y
76. Alien residncy-prior 1980 Y
77. Pen emp-hire illgl aliens N
78. Lmt Persh II/cruse-Europe N
79. Delete 34 B-1 bombers N
80. Bar purch of Pershing II N
81. Bar purchase of Sgt York N
82. Delete $ for Trident II N
83. Allow 15 MX missiles Y
84. Bar MX procurement-1985 N
85. Equal Access Act Y
86. Aid to El Salvador Y
87. Bar Nicarag water mining Y
88. Physician/Medicare freeze Y
89. Increase "sin" taxes N
90. End SBA direct loans Y
91. Sell Conrail Y
92. Equal Rights Amendment N
93. Marines in Lebanon Y
94. Eminent domain-Coal comps N
95. Prohibit EPA sanctions Y
96. SS age increase/Reforms Y
97. Auto domestic content req N
98. Delete jobs program fundg Y
99. Highway-Gas tax bill N
100. Raise Medicare;Cut defnse N
101. Emergency housing aid N
102. Across-the-board tax cuts Y
103. Gramm-Latta II targets Y
104. Delete B-1 bomber funds N
105. Dsapprov Saudi AWACS sale Y
106. Disapprove oil import fee Y
107. Rail Deregulation ?
108. Dsapp India nuc fuel sale Y
109. Mil draft registration Y
110. Chrysler Loan Guarantees Y
111. Prohibit school busing Y
112. Nuclear plant moratorium N
113. Oil price controls N

Presidential Support Score: 1986 - 66% 1985 - 80%

SCHAEFER, DAN -- Colorado 6th District [Republican]. Counties of Adams (pt.), Arapahoe (pt.) and Jefferson (pt.). Prior Terms: House: 1983 (Special Election)-1986. Born: January 25, 1936; Gutenberg, Iowa. Education: Niagara University (B.A.). Occupation: Public relations consultant (1967-83); Colorado assemblyman (1977-78); Colorado senator (1979-83).

SCHAEFER, DAN (Cont.)

1. Immigration Reform	Y	49. Youth work projects	N
2. Open fld-search warrants	Y	50. Assist military in Angola	Y
3. Civil pnty-hire ill alien	N	51. Allow US troops-Nicaragua	Y
4. So Afr sanc-veto override	N	52. Pentagon polygraph exams	Y
5. Tax Overhaul	N	53. Bar ASAT testing	N
6. South Africa sanctions	N	54. Suspend def pmt for abuse	N
7. Death penalty-drug bill	Y	55. Bar Pentagon-contr emplmt	Y
8. Evidence-warrantless srch	Y	56. Increase SDI funding	N
9. Life term-second drug off	Y	57. Reduce SDI funding	N
10. Military use in drug war	Y	58. Produce chemical weapons	?
11. Troop reduction in Europe	N	59. Bar CIA fndg in Nicaragua	N
12. Prohibit chemical weapons	N	60. South Africa sanctions	N
13. Bar ASAT testing	N	61. Cut SS COLAs; Raise taxes	N
14. Abide SALT II weapons ban	N	62. Let US invest-So Africa	Y
15. Follow SALT II-Soviets do	Y	63. Approve 21 MX for 1985	Y
16. Reduce SDI funding	N	64. Emergency Farm Credit	N
17. Increase SDI funding	N	65. Awards to whistle blowers	Y
18. Purchase Trident sub	N	66. African disaster relief	Y
19. Delete 12 MX;Add conv wpn	N	67. Ban bank loans to So Afr	N
20. Raise speed limit	Y	68. Bar coun duty-free trtmt	N
21. Textile Import Quotas(*)	N	69. Steel import limits	N
22. Req Pentagon buy US goods	Y	70. Soc Sec COLAs=inflation	Y
23. AIDS ins anti-dscriminatn	N	71. Bar haz waste vctms suits	Y
24. Nicaraguan refugee aid	N	72. Prohibit aid to Nicaragua	N
25. Nicaraguan contra aid	Y	73. Cut $-Schs bar sch prayer	Y
26. US abide by SALT II	Y	74. Raise taxes; Cut Medicare	N
27. Prohibit Saudi arms sale	Y	75. Alien residncy-prior 1982	Y
28. Military Retiremnt Reform	Y	76. Alien residncy-prior 1980	Y
29. Nicaraguan refugee aid	Y	77. Pen emp-hire illgl aliens	N
30. Ease '68 Gun Control Act	Y	78. Lmt Persh II/cruse-Europe	N
31. Bar intrstat handgun tran	N	79. Delete 34 B-1 bombers	N
32. Keep '68 Gun Control Act	N	80. Bar purch of Pershing II	N
33. Nicaraguan contra aid	Y	81. Bar purchase of Sgt York	Y
34. Bar emp polygraph testing	N	82. Delete $ for Trident II	N
35. Tax Overhaul consideratn	N	83. Allow 15 MX missiles	Y
36. Bar armor-piercing ammo	Y	84. Bar MX procurement-1985	N
37. Tax Overhaul consideratn	N	85. Equal Access Act	Y
38. Make comp emissions known	N	86. Aid to El Salvador	Y
39. Allow toxic victims suits	N	87. Bar Nicarag water mining	N
40. Strike Superfund "VAT"	N	88. Physician/Medicare freeze	Y
41. Notify emp-plant closing	N	89. Increase "sin" taxes	N
42. Bar emp consult-plant clo	Y	90. End SBA direct loans	N
43. Medicare cuts;Tax incres'	N	91. Sell Conrail	Y
44. Delete 12 MX missiles	N	92. Equal Rights Amendment	N
45. Spending cuts;Tax incres'	N	93. Marines in Lebanon	Y
46. Textile Import Quotas	N	94. Eminent domain-Coal comps	Y
47. Cut some school lunch fds	Y	95. Prohibit EPA sanctions	Y
48. Clean Water Act Amendmnts	Y		

Presidential Support Score: 1986 - 76% 1985 - 76%

CONNECTICUT

KENNELLY, BARBARA B. -- Connecticut 1st District [Democrat]. Counties of Hartford (pt.), Middlesex (pt.) and Tolland (pt.). Prior Terms: House: 1982 (Special Election)-1986. Born: July 10, 1936; Hartford, Conn. Education: Trinity College (B.A., M.A.). Occupation: Vice chairwoman, Hartford Commission on

KENNELLY, BARBARA B. (Cont.)

Aging (1971-75); member, Hartford Court of Common Council (1975-79); secretary, State of Connecticut (1979-82); member, Boards of Trustees, Trinity College and Hartford College for Women; director, Hartford Architecture Conservation and Riverfront Recapture, Inc.

1. Immigration Reform Y
2. Open fld-search warrants N
3. Civil pnty-hire ill alien Y
4. So Afr sanc-veto override Y
5. Tax Overhaul Y
6. South Africa sanctions Y
7. Death penalty-drug bill N
8. Evidence-warrantless srch N
9. Life term-second drug off Y
10. Military use in drug war N
11. Troop reduction in Europe N
12. Prohibit chemical weapons Y
13. Bar ASAT testing Y
14. Abide SALT II weapons ban Y
15. Follow SALT II-Soviets do N
16. Reduce SDI funding N
17. Increase SDI funding N
18. Purchase Trident sub Y
19. Delete 12 MX;Add conv wpn Y
20. Raise speed limit N
21. Textile Import Quotas(*) Y
22. Req Pentagon buy US goods Y
23. AIDS ins anti-dscriminatn Y
24. Nicaraguan refugee aid Y
25. Nicaraguan contra aid N
26. US abide by SALT II N
27. Prohibit Saudi arms sale Y
28. Military Retiremnt Reform Y
29. Nicaraguan refugee aid Y
30. Ease '68 Gun Control Act N
31. Bar intrstat handgun tran Y
32. Keep '68 Gun Control Act Y
33. Nicaraguan contra aid N
34. Bar emp polygraph testing Y
35. Tax Overhaul consideratn Y
36. Bar armor-piercing ammo Y
37. Tax Overhaul consideratn Y
38. Make comp emissions known Y
39. Allow toxic victims suits Y
40. Strike Superfund "VAT" Y
41. Notify emp-plant closing Y
42. Bar emp consult-plant clo N
43. Medicare cuts;Tax incres' Y
44. Delete 12 MX missiles Y
45. Spending cuts;Tax incres' Y
46. Textile Import Quotas Y
47. Cut some school lunch fds N
48. Clean Water Act Amendmnts N
49. Youth work projects Y
50. Assist military in Angola N
51. Allow US troops-Nicaragua N
52. Pentagon polygraph exams Y
53. Bar ASAT testing Y
54. Suspend def pmt for abuse N
55. Bar Pentagon-contr emplmt Y
56. Increase SDI funding N
57. Reduce SDI funding N
58. Produce chemical weapons N
59. Bar CIA fndg in Nicaragua Y
60. South Africa sanctions Y
61. Cut SS COLAs; Raise taxes N
62. Let US invest-So Africa N
63. Approve 21 MX for 1985 N
64. Emergency Farm Credit Y
65. Awards to whistle blowers Y
66. African disaster relief Y
67. Ban bank loans to So Afr Y
68. Bar coun duty-free trtmt Y
69. Steel import limits Y
70. Soc Sec COLAs=inflation Y
71. Bar haz waste vctms suits Y
72. Prohibit aid to Nicaragua Y
73. Cut $-Schs bar sch prayer N
74. Raise taxes; Cut Medicare Y
75. Alien residncy-prior 1982 ?
76. Alien residncy-prior 1980 N
77. Pen emp-hire illgl aliens Y
78. Lmt Persh II/cruse-Europe Y
79. Delete 34 B-1 bombers Y
80. Bar purch of Pershing II Y
81. Bar purchase of Sgt York N
82. Delete $ for Trident II Y
83. Allow 15 MX missiles N
84. Bar MX procurement-1985 Y
85. Equal Access Act N
86. Aid to El Salvador N
87. Bar Nicarag water mining Y
88. Physician/Medicare freeze N
89. Increase "sin" taxes Y
90. End SBA direct loans N
91. Sell Conrail N
92. Equal Rights Amendment Y
93. Marines in Lebanon N
94. Eminent domain-Coal comps N
95. Prohibit EPA sanctions N
96. SS age increase/Reforms N
97. Auto domestic content req Y
98. Delete jobs program fundg N
99. Highway-Gas tax bill Y
100. Raise Medicare;Cut defnse Y
101. Emergency housing aid Y

Presidential Support Score: 1986 - 19% 1985 - 23%

GEJDENSON, SAM -- Connecticut 2nd District [Democrat]. Counties of Middlesex (pt.), New London, Tolland (pt.) and Windham. Prior Terms: House: 1981-86. Born: May 20, 1948; Eschwege, Germany. Education: Mitchell College (A.S.); University of Connecticut (B.A.). Occupation: Farmer; broker; town chairman; deputy sheriff; Connecticut representative (1974-78).

1. Immigration Reform Y
2. Open fld-search warrants Y
3. Civil pnty-hire ill alien Y
4. So Afr sanc-veto override Y
5. Tax Overhaul N
6. South Africa sanctions Y
7. Death penalty-drug bill N
8. Evidence-warrantless srch N
9. Life term-second drug off Y
10. Military use in drug war N
11. Troop reduction in Europe N
12. Prohibit chemical weapons Y
13. Bar ASAT testing Y
14. Abide SALT II weapons ban Y
15. Follow SALT II-Soviets do N
16. Reduce SDI funding Y
17. Increase SDI funding N
18. Purchase Trident sub Y
19. Delete 12 MX;Add conv wpn Y
20. Raise speed limit N
21. Textile Import Quotas(*) Y
22. Req Pentagon buy US goods Y
23. AIDS ins anti-dscriminatn Y
24. Nicaraguan refugee aid Y
25. Nicaraguan contra aid N
26. US abide by SALT II N
27. Prohibit Saudi arms sale Y
28. Military Retiremnt Reform Y
29. Nicaraguan refugee aid Y
30. Ease '68 Gun Control Act N
31. Bar intrstat handgun tran Y
32. Keep '68 Gun Control Act Y
33. Nicaraguan contra aid N
34. Bar emp polygraph testing Y
35. Tax Overhaul consideratn Y
36. Bar armor-piercing ammo Y
37. Tax Overhaul consideratn Y
38. Make comp emissions known Y
39. Allow toxic victims suits Y
40. Strike Superfund "VAT" Y
41. Notify emp-plant closing Y
42. Bar emp consult-plant clo N
43. Medicare cuts;Tax incres' Y
44. Delete 12 MX missiles Y
45. Spending cuts;Tax incres' Y
46. Textile Import Quotas Y
47. Cut some school lunch fds N
48. Clean Water Act Amendmnts N
49. Youth work projects Y
50. Assist military in Angola N
51. Allow US troops-Nicaragua N
52. Pentagon polygraph exams Y
53. Bar ASAT testing Y
54. Suspend def pmt for abuse Y
55. Bar Pentagon-contr emplmt Y
56. Increase SDI funding N
57. Reduce SDI funding Y
58. Produce chemical weapons N
59. Bar CIA fndg in Nicaragua Y
60. South Africa sanctions Y
61. Cut SS COLAs; Raise taxes N
62. Let US invest-So Africa N
63. Approve 21 MX for 1985 N
64. Emergency Farm Credit Y
65. Awards to whistle blowers Y
66. African disaster relief Y
67. Ban bank loans to So Afr Y
68. Bar coun duty-free trtmt Y
69. Steel import limits Y
70. Soc Sec COLAs=inflation Y
71. Bar haz waste vctms suits N
72. Prohibit aid to Nicaragua Y
73. Cut $-Schs bar sch prayer N
74. Raise taxes; Cut Medicare Y
75. Alien residncy-prior 1982 N
76. Alien residncy-prior 1980 N
77. Pen emp-hire illgl aliens Y
78. Lmt Persh II/cruse-Europe Y
79. Delete 34 B-1 bombers Y
80. Bar purch of Pershing II Y
81. Bar purchase of Sgt York Y
82. Delete $ for Trident II Y
83. Allow 15 MX missiles N
84. Bar MX procurement-1985 Y
85. Equal Access Act N
86. Aid to El Salvador N
87. Bar Nicarag water mining Y
88. Physician/Medicare freeze N
89. Increase "sin" taxes Y
90. End SBA direct loans N
91. Sell Conrail N
92. Equal Rights Amendment Y
93. Marines in Lebanon Y
94. Eminent domain-Coal comps N
95. Prohibit EPA sanctions N
96. SS age increase/Reforms N
97. Auto domestic content req Y
98. Delete jobs program fundg N
99. Highway-Gas tax bill N
100. Raise Medicare;Cut defnse Y
101. Emergency housing aid Y
102. Across-the-board tax cuts N
103. Gramm-Latta II targets N
104. Delete B-1 bomber funds Y

GEJDENSON, SAM (Cont.)
105. Dsapprov Saudi AWACS sale Y

Presidential Support Score: 1986 - 14% 1985 - 23%

MORRISON, BRUCE A. -- Connecticut 3rd District [Democrat]. Counties of Fairfield (pt.), Middlesex (pt.) and New Haven (pt.). Prior Terms: House: 1983-86. Born: October 8, 1944; New York, N.Y. Education: Massachusetts Institute of Technology (B.S.); University of Illinois (M.S.); Yale Law School (J.D.). Occupation: Attorney; staff attorney, executive director of New Haven Legal Assistance Association (1973-81); chairman, Board of Directors of the National Social Science and Law Center.

1. Immigration Reform Y
2. Open fld-search warrants Y
3. Civil pnty-hire ill alien N
4. So Afr sanc-veto override Y
5. Tax Overhaul Y
6. South Africa sanctions Y
7. Death penalty-drug bill N
8. Evidence-warrantless srch N
9. Life term-second drug off N
10. Military use in drug war N
11. Troop reduction in Europe ?
12. Prohibit chemical weapons ?
13. Bar ASAT testing #
14. Abide SALT II weapons ban #
15. Follow SALT II-Soviets do X
16. Reduce SDI funding #
17. Increase SDI funding X
18. Purchase Trident sub #
19. Delete 12 MX;Add conv wpn #
20. Raise speed limit N
21. Textile Import Quotas(*) Y
22. Req Pentagon buy US goods Y
23. AIDS ins anti-dscriminatn Y
24. Nicaraguan refugee aid Y
25. Nicaraguan contra aid N
26. US abide by SALT II N
27. Prohibit Saudi arms sale Y
28. Military Retiremnt Reform Y
29. Nicaraguan refugee aid Y
30. Ease '68 Gun Control Act N
31. Bar intrstat handgun tran Y
32. Keep '68 Gun Control Act Y
33. Nicaraguan contra aid N
34. Bar emp polygraph testing Y
35. Tax Overhaul consideratn Y
36. Bar armor-piercing ammo Y
37. Tax Overhaul consideratn Y
38. Make comp emissions known Y
39. Allow toxic victims suits Y
40. Strike Superfund "VAT" Y
41. Notify emp-plant closing Y
42. Bar emp consult-plant clo N
43. Medicare cuts;Tax incres' Y
44. Delete 12 MX missiles Y
45. Spending cuts;Tax incres' Y
46. Textile Import Quotas Y
47. Cut some school lunch fds N
48. Clean Water Act Amendmnts N
49. Youth work projects Y
50. Assist military in Angola N
51. Allow US troops-Nicaragua N
52. Pentagon polygraph exams N
53. Bar ASAT testing Y
54. Suspend def pmt for abuse Y
55. Bar Pentagon-contr emplmt Y
56. Increase SDI funding N
57. Reduce SDI funding Y
58. Produce chemical weapons N
59. Bar CIA fndg in Nicaragua Y
60. South Africa sanctions Y
61. Cut SS COLAs; Raise taxes N
62. Let US invest-So Africa X
63. Approve 21 MX for 1985 N
64. Emergency Farm Credit Y
65. Awards to whistle blowers Y
66. African disaster relief Y
67. Ban bank loans to So Afr ?
68. Bar coun duty-free trtmt Y
69. Steel import limits Y
70. Soc Sec COLAs=inflation +
71. Bar haz waste vctms suits Y
72. Prohibit aid to Nicaragua Y
73. Cut $-Schs bar sch prayer N
74. Raise taxes; Cut Medicare Y
75. Alien residncy-prior 1982 N
76. Alien residncy-prior 1980 N
77. Pen emp-hire illgl aliens Y
78. Lmt Persh II/cruse-Europe Y
79. Delete 34 B-1 bombers Y
80. Bar purch of Pershing II Y
81. Bar purchase of Sgt York N
82. Delete $ for Trident II Y
83. Allow 15 MX missiles N
84. Bar MX procurement-1985 Y
85. Equal Access Act N
86. Aid to El Salvador N
87. Bar Nicarag water mining Y
88. Physician/Medicare freeze N
89. Increase "sin" taxes Y
90. End SBA direct loans N

MORRISON, BRUCE A. (Cont.)

91. Sell Conrail	N	94. Eminent domain-Coal comps	N
92. Equal Rights Amendment	Y	95. Prohibit EPA sanctions	N
93. Marines in Lebanon	N	96. SS age increase/Reforms	N

Presidential Support Score: 1986 - 16% 1985 - 28%

McKINNEY, STEWART B. -- Connecticut 4th District [Republican]. County of Fairfield (pt.). Prior Terms: House: 1971-86. Born: January 30, 1931; Pittsburgh, Pa. Education: Princeton University; Yale University (B.A.). Military Service: U.S. Air Force, 1951-55. Occupation: Connecticut representative (1966-70).

1. Immigration Reform	Y	47. Cut some school lunch fds	N
2. Open fld-search warrants	N	48. Clean Water Act Amendmnts	N
3. Civil pnty-hire ill alien	N	49. Youth work projects	Y
4. So Afr sanc-veto override	Y	50. Assist military in Angola	N
5. Tax Overhaul	N	51. Allow US troops-Nicaragua	N
6. South Africa sanctions	#	52. Pentagon polygraph exams	Y
7. Death penalty-drug bill	N	53. Bar ASAT testing	Y
8. Evidence-warrantless srch	N	54. Suspend def pmt for abuse	N
9. Life term-second drug off	Y	55. Bar Pentagon-contr emplmt	Y
10. Military use in drug war	Y	56. Increase SDI funding	N
11. Troop reduction in Europe	N	57. Reduce SDI funding	Y
12. Prohibit chemical weapons	Y	58. Produce chemical weapons	N
13. Bar ASAT testing	Y	59. Bar CIA fndg in Nicaragua	N
14. Abide SALT II weapons ban	?	60. South Africa sanctions	Y
15. Follow SALT II-Soviets do	N	61. Cut SS COLAs; Raise taxes	N
16. Reduce SDI funding	N	62. Let US invest-So Africa	N
17. Increase SDI funding	N	63. Approve 21 MX for 1985	N
18. Purchase Trident sub	Y	64. Emergency Farm Credit	Y
19. Delete 12 MX;Add conv wpn	Y	65. Awards to whistle blowers	Y
20. Raise speed limit	Y	66. African disaster relief	Y
21. Textile Import Quotas(*)	Y	67. Ban bank loans to So Afr	Y
22. Req Pentagon buy US goods	Y	68. Bar coun duty-free trtmt	N
23. AIDS ins anti-dscriminatn	Y	69. Steel import limits	Y
24. Nicaraguan refugee aid	N	70. Soc Sec COLAs=inflation	Y
25. Nicaraguan contra aid	N	71. Bar haz waste vctms suits	N
26. US abide by SALT II	X	72. Prohibit aid to Nicaragua	Y
27. Prohibit Saudi arms sale	Y	73. Cut $-Schs bar sch prayer	N
28. Military Retiremnt Reform	Y	74. Raise taxes; Cut Medicare	Y
29. Nicaraguan refugee aid	Y	75. Alien residncy-prior 1982	N
30. Ease '68 Gun Control Act	N	76. Alien residncy-prior 1980	N
31. Bar intrstat handgun tran	Y	77. Pen emp-hire illgl aliens	N
32. Keep '68 Gun Control Act	Y	78. Lmt Persh II/cruse-Europe	?
33. Nicaraguan contra aid	N	79. Delete 34 B-1 bombers	Y
34. Bar emp polygraph testing	Y	80. Bar purch of Pershing II	Y
35. Tax Overhaul consideratn	?	81. Bar purchase of Sgt York	N
36. Bar armor-piercing ammo	?	82. Delete $ for Trident II	N
37. Tax Overhaul consideratn	?	83. Allow 15 MX missiles	N
38. Make comp emissions known	?	84. Bar MX procurement-1985	Y
39. Allow toxic victims suits	?	85. Equal Access Act	N
40. Strike Superfund "VAT"	?	86. Aid to El Salvador	N
41. Notify emp-plant closing	?	87. Bar Nicarag water mining	Y
42. Bar emp consult-plant clo	?	88. Physician/Medicare freeze	Y
43. Medicare cuts;Tax incres'	Y	89. Increase "sin" taxes	Y
44. Delete 12 MX missiles	Y	90. End SBA direct loans	N
45. Spending cuts;Tax incres'	Y	91. Sell Conrail	N
46. Textile Import Quotas	Y	92. Equal Rights Amendment	Y

McKINNEY, STEWART B. (Cont.)

93. Marines in Lebanon Y
94. Eminent domain-Coal comps N
95. Prohibit EPA sanctions N
96. SS age increase/Reforms Y
97. Auto domestic content req Y
98. Delete jobs program fundg Y
99. Highway-Gas tax bill N
100. Raise Medicare;Cut defnse Y
101. Emergency housing aid Y
102. Across-the-board tax cuts Y
103. Gramm-Latta II targets Y
104. Delete B-1 bomber funds Y
105. Dsapprov Saudi AWACS sale Y
106. Disapprove oil import fee ?
107. Rail Deregulation N
108. Dsapp India nuc fuel sale Y
109. Mil draft registration N
110. Chrysler Loan Guarantees Y
111. Prohibit school busing N
112. Nuclear plant moratorium N
113. Oil price controls N
114. Tuition Tax Credits N
115. Est Consumer Protect Agcy Y
116. Eliminate B-1 bomber fnds Y
117. Subminimum wage for youth N
118. Delete crude oil tax ?
119. Natural gas deregulation ?

Presidential Support Score: 1986 - 31% 1985 - 28%

ROWLAND, JOHN G. -- Connecticut 5th District [Republican]. Counties of Fairfield (pt.) and New Haven (pt.). Prior Terms: 1985-86. Occupation: Insurance businessman; Connecticut representative.

1. Immigration Reform Y
2. Open fld-search warrants N
3. Civil pnty-hire ill alien Y
4. So Afr sanc-veto override Y
5. Tax Overhaul Y
6. South Africa sanctions Y
7. Death penalty-drug bill Y
8. Evidence-warrantless srch Y
9. Life term-second drug off Y
10. Military use in drug war Y
11. Troop reduction in Europe N
12. Prohibit chemical weapons N
13. Bar ASAT testing N
14. Abide SALT II weapons ban N
15. Follow SALT II-Soviets do Y
16. Reduce SDI funding N
17. Increase SDI funding N
18. Purchase Trident sub Y
19. Delete 12 MX;Add conv wpn N
20. Raise speed limit N
21. Textile Import Quotas(*) N
22. Req Pentagon buy US goods Y
23. AIDS ins anti-dscriminatn N
24. Nicaraguan refugee aid N
25. Nicaraguan contra aid Y
26. US abide by SALT II Y
27. Prohibit Saudi arms sale Y
28. Military Retiremnt Reform Y
29. Nicaraguan refugee aid Y
30. Ease '68 Gun Control Act Y
31. Bar intrstat handgun tran Y
32. Keep '68 Gun Control Act N
33. Nicaraguan contra aid N
34. Bar emp polygraph testing Y
35. Tax Overhaul consideratn Y
36. Bar armor-piercing ammo Y
37. Tax Overhaul consideratn N
38. Make comp emissions known Y
39. Allow toxic victims suits N
40. Strike Superfund "VAT" Y
41. Notify emp-plant closing N
42. Bar emp consult-plant clo Y
43. Medicare cuts;Tax incres' N
44. Delete 12 MX missiles N
45. Spending cuts;Tax incres' N
46. Textile Import Quotas N
47. Cut some school lunch fds Y
48. Clean Water Act Amendmnts Y
49. Youth work projects N
50. Assist military in Angola Y
51. Allow US troops-Nicaragua N
52. Pentagon polygraph exams Y
53. Bar ASAT testing N
54. Suspend def pmt for abuse N
55. Bar Pentagon-contr emplmt Y
56. Increase SDI funding N
57. Reduce SDI funding N
58. Produce chemical weapons Y
59. Bar CIA fndg in Nicaragua N
60. South Africa sanctions Y
61. Cut SS COLAs; Raise taxes N
62. Let US invest-So Africa Y
63. Approve 21 MX for 1985 Y
64. Emergency Farm Credit N
65. Awards to whistle blowers Y
66. African disaster relief Y

Presidential Support Score: 1986 - 60% 1985 - 71%

JOHNSON, NANCY L. -- Connecticut 6th District [Republican]. Counties of Fairfield (pt.), Hartford (pt.), Litchfield, New Haven (pt.) and Tolland (pt.). Prior Terms: House: 1983-86. Born: January 5, 1935; Chicago, Ill. Education: University of Chicago; Radcliffe College; University of London on an English Speaking Union Scholarship. Occupation: President, Sheldon Community Guidance Clinic; member, board of directors, New Britain Bank and Trust; professor; Connecticut senator (1976-82).

1.	Immigration Reform	Y
2.	Open fld-search warrants	N
3.	Civil pnty-hire ill alien	Y
4.	So Afr sanc-veto override	Y
5.	Tax Overhaul	Y
6.	South Africa sanctions	Y
7.	Death penalty-drug bill	Y
8.	Evidence-warrantless srch	Y
9.	Life term-second drug off	Y
10.	Military use in drug war	N
11.	Troop reduction in Europe	N
12.	Prohibit chemical weapons	N
13.	Bar ASAT testing	Y
14.	Abide SALT II weapons ban	Y
15.	Follow SALT II-Soviets do	N
16.	Reduce SDI funding	N
17.	Increase SDI funding	N
18.	Purchase Trident sub	+
19.	Delete 12 MX;Add conv wpn	Y
20.	Raise speed limit	N
21.	Textile Import Quotas(*)	N
22.	Req Pentagon buy US goods	Y
23.	AIDS ins anti-dscriminatn	Y
24.	Nicaraguan refugee aid	N
25.	Nicaraguan contra aid	Y
26.	US abide by SALT II	N
27.	Prohibit Saudi arms sale	Y
28.	Military Retiremnt Reform	Y
29.	Nicaraguan refugee aid	Y
30.	Ease '68 Gun Control Act	Y
31.	Bar intrstat handgun tran	Y
32.	Keep '68 Gun Control Act	Y
33.	Nicaraguan contra aid	Y
34.	Bar emp polygraph testing	Y
35.	Tax Overhaul consideratn	Y
36.	Bar armor-piercing ammo	Y
37.	Tax Overhaul consideratn	Y
38.	Make comp emissions known	N
39.	Allow toxic victims suits	N
40.	Strike Superfund "VAT"	Y
41.	Notify emp-plant closing	N
42.	Bar emp consult-plant clo	Y
43.	Medicare cuts;Tax incres'	Y
44.	Delete 12 MX missiles	Y
45.	Spending cuts;Tax incres'	N
46.	Textile Import Quotas	N
47.	Cut some school lunch fds	Y
48.	Clean Water Act Amendmnts	Y
49.	Youth work projects	N
50.	Assist military in Angola	Y
51.	Allow US troops-Nicaragua	N
52.	Pentagon polygraph exams	Y
53.	Bar ASAT testing	Y
54.	Suspend def pmt for abuse	N
55.	Bar Pentagon-contr emplmt	Y
56.	Increase SDI funding	N
57.	Reduce SDI funding	N
58.	Produce chemical weapons	Y
59.	Bar CIA fndg in Nicaragua	N
60.	South Africa sanctions	Y
61.	Cut SS COLAs; Raise taxes	N
62.	Let US invest-So Africa	Y
63.	Approve 21 MX for 1985	N
64.	Emergency Farm Credit	N
65.	Awards to whistle blowers	Y
66.	African disaster relief	Y
67.	Ban bank loans to So Afr	Y
68.	Bar coun duty-free trtmt	N
69.	Steel import limits	Y
70.	Soc Sec COLAs=inflation	Y
71.	Bar haz waste vctms suits	Y
72.	Prohibit aid to Nicaragua	Y
73.	Cut $-Schs bar sch prayer	N
74.	Raise taxes; Cut Medicare	Y
75.	Alien residncy-prior 1982	Y
76.	Alien residncy-prior 1980	N
77.	Pen emp-hire illgl aliens	N
78.	Lmt Persh II/cruse-Europe	N
79.	Delete 34 B-1 bombers	N
80.	Bar purch of Pershing II	N
81.	Bar purchase of Sgt York	N
82.	Delete $ for Trident II	N
83.	Allow 15 MX missiles	N
84.	Bar MX procurement-1985	?
85.	Equal Access Act	N
86.	Aid to El Salvador	Y
87.	Bar Nicarag water mining	Y
88.	Physician/Medicare freeze	Y
89.	Increase "sin" taxes	Y
90.	End SBA direct loans	N
91.	Sell Conrail	Y
92.	Equal Rights Amendment	Y
93.	Marines in Lebanon	Y
94.	Eminent domain-Coal comps	Y
95.	Prohibit EPA sanctions	N
96.	SS age increase/Reforms	N

Presidential Support Score: 1986 - 52% 1985 - 50%

DELAWARE

CARPER, THOMAS R. -- Representative at Large [Democrat]. Prior Terms: House: 1983-86. Born: January 23, 1947; Beckley, W. Va. Education: Ohio State University (B.A.); University of Delaware (M.A.). Military Service: U.S. Navy; Naval Reserves. Occupation: Industrial development specialist for the state division of Economic Development (1975-76): Delaware state treasurer (1976-82).

1.	Immigration Reform	Y
2.	Open fld-search warrants	N
3.	Civil pnty-hire ill alien	N
4.	So Afr sanc-veto override	Y
5.	Tax Overhaul	Y
6.	South Africa sanctions	Y
7.	Death penalty-drug bill	Y
8.	Evidence-warrantless srch	Y
9.	Life term-second drug off	Y
10.	Military use in drug war	Y
11.	Troop reduction in Europe	N
12.	Prohibit chemical weapons	N
13.	Bar ASAT testing	Y
14.	Abide SALT II weapons ban	Y
15.	Follow SALT II-Soviets do	N
16.	Reduce SDI funding	N
17.	Increase SDI funding	N
18.	Purchase Trident sub	Y
19.	Delete 12 MX;Add conv wpn	Y
20.	Raise speed limit	N
21.	Textile Import Quotas(*)	Y
22.	Req Pentagon buy US goods	Y
23.	AIDS ins anti-dscriminatn	Y
24.	Nicaraguan refugee aid	N
25.	Nicaraguan contra aid	N
26.	US abide by SALT II	N
27.	Prohibit Saudi arms sale	Y
28.	Military Retiremnt Reform	Y
29.	Nicaraguan refugee aid	Y
30.	Ease '68 Gun Control Act	N
31.	Bar intrstat handgun tran	Y
32.	Keep '68 Gun Control Act	Y
33.	Nicaraguan contra aid	N
34.	Bar emp polygraph testing	Y
35.	Tax Overhaul consideratn	Y
36.	Bar armor-piercing ammo	Y
37.	Tax Overhaul consideratn	Y
38.	Make comp emissions known	Y
39.	Allow toxic victims suits	N
40.	Strike Superfund "VAT"	N
41.	Notify emp-plant closing	Y
42.	Bar emp consult-plant clo	N
43.	Medicare cuts;Tax incres'	Y
44.	Delete 12 MX missiles	Y
45.	Spending cuts;Tax incres'	Y
46.	Textile Import Quotas	Y
47.	Cut some school lunch fds	N
48.	Clean Water Act Amendmnts	N
49.	Youth work projects	N
50.	Assist military in Angola	Y
51.	Allow US troops-Nicaragua	N
52.	Pentagon polygraph exams	Y
53.	Bar ASAT testing	Y
54.	Suspend def pmt for abuse	N
55.	Bar Pentagon-contr emplmt	Y
56.	Increase SDI funding	N
57.	Reduce SDI funding	N
58.	Produce chemical weapons	N
59.	Bar CIA fndg in Nicaragua	Y
60.	South Africa sanctions	Y
61.	Cut SS COLAs; Raise taxes	Y
62.	Let US invest-So Africa	N
63.	Approve 21 MX for 1985	N
64.	Emergency Farm Credit	N
65.	Awards to whistle blowers	Y
66.	African disaster relief	Y
67.	Ban bank loans to So Afr	Y
68.	Bar coun duty-free trtmt	Y
69.	Steel import limits	Y
70.	Soc Sec COLAs=inflation	Y
71.	Bar haz waste vctms suits	N
72.	Prohibit aid to Nicaragua	Y
73.	Cut $-Schs bar sch prayer	N
74.	Raise taxes; Cut Medicare	Y
75.	Alien residncy-prior 1982	Y
76.	Alien residncy-prior 1980	N
77.	Pen emp-hire illgl aliens	N
78.	Lmt Persh II/cruse-Europe	N
79.	Delete 34 B-1 bombers	Y
80.	Bar purch of Pershing II	N
81.	Bar purchase of Sgt York	N
82.	Delete $ for Trident II	N
83.	Allow 15 MX missiles	N
84.	Bar MX procurement-1985	Y
85.	Equal Access Act	Y
86.	Aid to El Salvador	N
87.	Bar Nicarag water mining	Y
88.	Physician/Medicare freeze	N
89.	Increase "sin" taxes	Y
90.	End SBA direct loans	N
91.	Sell Conrail	N
92.	Equal Rights Amendment	Y
93.	Marines in Lebanon	N
94.	Eminent domain-Coal comps	N
95.	Prohibit EPA sanctions	N
96.	SS age increase/Reforms	Y

Presidential Support Score: 1986 - 30% 1985 - 43%

FLORIDA

HUTTO, EARL -- Florida 1st District [Democrat]. Counties of Bay (pt.), Escombia, Okaloosa, Santa Rosa and Walton. Prior Terms: House: 1979-86. Born: May 12, 1926; Midland City, Ala. Education: Troy State University (B.S.); Northwestern University. Military Service: U.S. Navy, 1944-46. Occupation: Owner and president, Earl Hutto Advertising Agency; founder, WPEX-FM; sports director, WEAR-TV, WSFA-TV, WJHG-TV; Florida representative (1972-78).

1. Immigration Reform Y
2. Open fld-search warrants N
3. Civil pnty-hire ill alien N
4. So Afr sanc-veto override N
5. Tax Overhaul N
6. South Africa sanctions Y
7. Death penalty-drug bill Y
8. Evidence-warrantless srch Y
9. Life term-second drug off Y
10. Military use in drug war N
11. Troop reduction in Europe N
12. Prohibit chemical weapons N
13. Bar ASAT testing N
14. Abide SALT II weapons ban N
15. Follow SALT II-Soviets do Y
16. Reduce SDI funding N
17. Increase SDI funding Y
18. Purchase Trident sub Y
19. Delete 12 MX;Add conv wpn N
20. Raise speed limit N
21. Textile Import Quotas(*) Y
22. Req Pentagon buy US goods N
23. AIDS ins anti-dscriminatn N
24. Nicaraguan refugee aid N
25. Nicaraguan contra aid Y
26. US abide by SALT II Y
27. Prohibit Saudi arms sale Y
28. Military Retiremnt Reform Y
29. Nicaraguan refugee aid N
30. Ease '68 Gun Control Act Y
31. Bar intrstat handgun tran Y
32. Keep '68 Gun Control Act N
33. Nicaraguan contra aid Y
34. Bar emp polygraph testing N
35. Tax Overhaul consideratn N
36. Bar armor-piercing ammo Y
37. Tax Overhaul consideratn N
38. Make comp emissions known N
39. Allow toxic victims suits N
40. Strike Superfund "VAT" N
41. Notify emp-plant closing N
42. Bar emp consult-plant clo Y
43. Medicare cuts;Tax incres' Y
44. Delete 12 MX missiles N
45. Spending cuts;Tax incres' Y
46. Textile Import Quotas Y
47. Cut some school lunch fds N
48. Clean Water Act Amendmnts Y
49. Youth work projects ?
50. Assist military in Angola Y
51. Allow US troops-Nicaragua Y
52. Pentagon polygraph exams Y
53. Bar ASAT testing N
54. Suspend def pmt for abuse N
55. Bar Pentagon-contr emplmt Y
56. Increase SDI funding Y
57. Reduce SDI funding N
58. Produce chemical weapons Y
59. Bar CIA fndg in Nicaragua N
60. South Africa sanctions N
61. Cut SS COLAs; Raise taxes Y
62. Let US invest-So Africa Y
63. Approve 21 MX for 1985 Y
64. Emergency Farm Credit Y
65. Awards to whistle blowers Y
66. African disaster relief Y
67. Ban bank loans to So Afr N
68. Bar coun duty-free trtmt N
69. Steel import limits N
70. Soc Sec COLAs=inflation Y
71. Bar haz waste vctms suits Y
72. Prohibit aid to Nicaragua Y
73. Cut $-Schs bar sch prayer Y
74. Raise taxes; Cut Medicare Y
75. Alien residncy-prior 1982 Y
76. Alien residncy-prior 1980 Y
77. Pen emp-hire illgl aliens N
78. Lmt Persh II/cruse-Europe N
79. Delete 34 B-1 bombers N
80. Bar purch of Pershing II N
81. Bar purchase of Sgt York ?
82. Delete $ for Trident II N
83. Allow 15 MX missiles Y
84. Bar MX procurement-1985 N
85. Equal Access Act Y
86. Aid to El Salvador Y
87. Bar Nicarag water mining N
88. Physician/Medicare freeze Y
89. Increase "sin" taxes Y
90. End SBA direct loans N
91. Sell Conrail N
92. Equal Rights Amendment N
93. Marines in Lebanon Y
94. Eminent domain-Coal comps Y
95. Prohibit EPA sanctions Y
96. SS age increase/Reforms Y
97. Auto domestic content req N
98. Delete jobs program fundg N

HUTTO, EARL (Cont.)

99. Highway-Gas tax bill N
100. Raise Medicare;Cut defnse N
101. Emergency housing aid Y
102. Across-the-board tax cuts Y
103. Gramm-Latta II targets Y
104. Delete B-1 bomber funds N
105. Dsapprov Saudi AWACS sale Y
106. Disapprove oil import fee Y
107. Rail Deregulation Y
108. Dsapp India nuc fuel sale Y
109. Mil draft registration Y
110. Chrysler Loan Guarantees Y
111. Prohibit school busing Y
112. Nuclear plant moratorium N
113. Oil price controls N

Presidential Support Score: 1986 - 56% 1985 - 56%

FUQUA, DON -- Florida 2nd District [Democrat]. Counties of Baker, Bay (pt.), Bradford, Calhoun, Clay (pt.), Columbia, Dixie, Franklin, Gadsen, Gilchrist, Gulf, Hamilton, Holmes, Jackson, Jefferson, Lafayette, Leon, Levy, Liberty, Madison, Suwannee, Taylor, Union, Wakulla, and Washington. Prior Terms: House: 1963-86. Born: August 20, 1933; Jacksonville, Fla. Education: University of Florida. Military Service: Army Medical Corps, 1953-55. Occupation: Florida representative (1958-62).

1. Immigration Reform Y
2. Open fld-search warrants Y
3. Civil pnty-hire ill alien N
4. So Afr sanc-veto override Y
5. Tax Overhaul Y
6. South Africa sanctions Y
7. Death penalty-drug bill Y
8. Evidence-warrantless srch Y
9. Life term-second drug off Y
10. Military use in drug war N
11. Troop reduction in Europe N
12. Prohibit chemical weapons N
13. Bar ASAT testing N
14. Abide SALT II weapons ban Y
15. Follow SALT II-Soviets do Y
16. Reduce SDI funding N
17. Increase SDI funding N
18. Purchase Trident sub N
19. Delete 12 MX;Add conv wpn N
20. Raise speed limit Y
21. Textile Import Quotas(*) Y
22. Req Pentagon buy US goods N
23. AIDS ins anti-dscriminatn ?
24. Nicaraguan refugee aid N
25. Nicaraguan contra aid Y
26. US abide by SALT II ?
27. Prohibit Saudi arms sale Y
28. Military Retiremnt Reform Y
29. Nicaraguan refugee aid N
30. Ease '68 Gun Control Act Y
31. Bar intrstat handgun tran N
32. Keep '68 Gun Control Act N
33. Nicaraguan contra aid Y
34. Bar emp polygraph testing N
35. Tax Overhaul consideratn Y
36. Bar armor-piercing ammo ?
37. Tax Overhaul consideratn Y
38. Make comp emissions known N
39. Allow toxic victims suits N
40. Strike Superfund "VAT" N
41. Notify emp-plant closing N
42. Bar emp consult-plant clo Y
43. Medicare cuts;Tax incres' Y
44. Delete 12 MX missiles N
45. Spending cuts;Tax incres' Y
46. Textile Import Quotas Y
47. Cut some school lunch fds N
48. Clean Water Act Amendmnts N
49. Youth work projects ?
50. Assist military in Angola Y
51. Allow US troops-Nicaragua N
52. Pentagon polygraph exams Y
53. Bar ASAT testing N
54. Suspend def pmt for abuse N
55. Bar Pentagon-contr emplmt Y
56. Increase SDI funding N
57. Reduce SDI funding N
58. Produce chemical weapons Y
59. Bar CIA fndg in Nicaragua N
60. South Africa sanctions Y
61. Cut SS COLAs; Raise taxes N
62. Let US invest-So Africa N
63. Approve 21 MX for 1985 Y
64. Emergency Farm Credit Y
65. Awards to whistle blowers Y
66. African disaster relief Y
67. Ban bank loans to So Afr ?
68. Bar coun duty-free trtmt N
69. Steel import limits Y
70. Soc Sec COLAs=inflation Y
71. Bar haz waste vctms suits Y
72. Prohibit aid to Nicaragua Y
73. Cut $-Schs bar sch prayer Y
74. Raise taxes; Cut Medicare Y
75. Alien residncy-prior 1982 Y
76. Alien residncy-prior 1980 N
77. Pen emp-hire illgl aliens N
78. Lmt Persh II/cruse-Europe N

FUQUA, DON (Cont.)

79. Delete 34 B-1 bombers N
80. Bar purch of Pershing II N
81. Bar purchase of Sgt York N
82. Delete $ for Trident II N
83. Allow 15 MX missiles Y
84. Bar MX procurement-1985 N
85. Equal Access Act Y
86. Aid to El Salvador Y
87. Bar Nicarag water mining Y
88. Physician/Medicare freeze N
89. Increase "sin" taxes Y
90. End SBA direct loans N
91. Sell Conrail N
92. Equal Rights Amendment N
93. Marines in Lebanon Y
94. Eminent domain-Coal comps Y
95. Prohibit EPA sanctions N
96. SS age increase/Reforms Y
97. Auto domestic content req N
98. Delete jobs program fundg N
99. Highway-Gas tax bill N
100. Raise Medicare;Cut defnse N
101. Emergency housing aid Y
102. Across-the-board tax cuts Y
103. Gramm-Latta II targets Y
104. Delete B-1 bomber funds N
105. Dsapprov Saudi AWACS sale Y
106. Disapprove oil import fee Y
107. Rail Deregulation Y
108. Dsapp India nuc fuel sale N
109. Mil draft registration Y
110. Chrysler Loan Guarantees Y
111. Prohibit school busing Y
112. Nuclear plant moratorium N
113. Oil price controls N
114. Tuition Tax Credits N
115. Est Consumer Protect Agcy N
116. Eliminate B-1 bomber fnds N
117. Subminimum wage for youth N
118. Delete crude oil tax Y
119. Natural gas deregulation Y

Presidential Support Score: 1986 - 41% 1985 - 52%

BENNETT, CHARLES E. -- Florida 3rd District [Democrat]. Counties of Duval (pt.) and Nassau. Prior Terms: House: 1949-86. Born: December 2, 1910; Jacksonville, Fla. Education: University of Florida (B.A., J.D.). Military Service: U.S. Army, 1942. Occupation: Attorney; Florida representative (1941); author.

1. Immigration Reform Y
2. Open fld-search warrants N
3. Civil pnty-hire ill alien N
4. So Afr sanc-veto override Y
5. Tax Overhaul Y
6. South Africa sanctions Y
7. Death penalty-drug bill Y
8. Evidence-warrantless srch Y
9. Life term-second drug off Y
10. Military use in drug war Y
11. Troop reduction in Europe N
12. Prohibit chemical weapons Y
13. Bar ASAT testing Y
14. Abide SALT II weapons ban Y
15. Follow SALT II-Soviets do N
16. Reduce SDI funding N
17. Increase SDI funding N
18. Purchase Trident sub Y
19. Delete 12 MX;Add conv wpn Y
20. Raise speed limit N
21. Textile Import Quotas(*) N
22. Req Pentagon buy US goods Y
23. AIDS ins anti-dscriminatn Y
24. Nicaraguan refugee aid N
25. Nicaraguan contra aid Y
26. US abide by SALT II N
27. Prohibit Saudi arms sale Y
28. Military Retiremnt Reform N
29. Nicaraguan refugee aid N
30. Ease '68 Gun Control Act N
31. Bar intrstat handgun tran Y
32. Keep '68 Gun Control Act Y
33. Nicaraguan contra aid Y
34. Bar emp polygraph testing N
35. Tax Overhaul consideratn N
36. Bar armor-piercing ammo Y
37. Tax Overhaul consideratn N
38. Make comp emissions known Y
39. Allow toxic victims suits Y
40. Strike Superfund "VAT" Y
41. Notify emp-plant closing Y
42. Bar emp consult-plant clo N
43. Medicare cuts;Tax incres' Y
44. Delete 12 MX missiles Y
45. Spending cuts;Tax incres' Y
46. Textile Import Quotas N
47. Cut some school lunch fds Y
48. Clean Water Act Amendmnts N
49. Youth work projects Y
50. Assist military in Angola N
51. Allow US troops-Nicaragua N
52. Pentagon polygraph exams Y
53. Bar ASAT testing Y
54. Suspend def pmt for abuse Y
55. Bar Pentagon-contr emplmt Y
56. Increase SDI funding N

BENNETT, CHARLES E. (Cont.)

57. Reduce SDI funding N
58. Produce chemical weapons Y
59. Bar CIA fndg in Nicaragua Y
60. South Africa sanctions Y
61. Cut SS COLAs; Raise taxes N
62. Let US invest-So Africa N
63. Approve 21 MX for 1985 N
64. Emergency Farm Credit Y
65. Awards to whistle blowers Y
66. African disaster relief Y
67. Ban bank loans to So Afr Y
68. Bar coun duty-free trtmt N
69. Steel import limits N
70. Soc Sec COLAs=inflation Y
71. Bar haz waste vctms suits Y
72. Prohibit aid to Nicaragua Y
73. Cut $-Schs bar sch prayer Y
74. Raise taxes; Cut Medicare Y
75. Alien residncy-prior 1982 Y
76. Alien residncy-prior 1980 Y
77. Pen emp-hire illgl aliens N
78. Lmt Persh II/cruse-Europe N
79. Delete 34 B-1 bombers N
80. Bar purch of Pershing II N
81. Bar purchase of Sgt York N
82. Delete $ for Trident II N
83. Allow 15 MX missiles N
84. Bar MX procurement-1985 Y
85. Equal Access Act Y
86. Aid to El Salvador Y
87. Bar Nicarag water mining Y
88. Physician/Medicare freeze Y
89. Increase "sin" taxes Y
90. End SBA direct loans N
91. Sell Conrail N
92. Equal Rights Amendment N
93. Marines in Lebanon N
94. Eminent domain-Coal comps N
95. Prohibit EPA sanctions N
96. SS age increase/Reforms Y
97. Auto domestic content req N
98. Delete jobs program fundg N
99. Highway-Gas tax bill Y
100. Raise Medicare;Cut defnse N
101. Emergency housing aid Y
102. Across-the-board tax cuts N
103. Gramm-Latta II targets Y
104. Delete B-1 bomber funds N
105. Dsapprov Saudi AWACS sale Y
106. Disapprove oil import fee N
107. Rail Deregulation Y
108. Dsapp India nuc fuel sale Y
109. Mil draft registration Y
110. Chrysler Loan Guarantees N
111. Prohibit school busing Y
112. Nuclear plant moratorium N
113. Oil price controls N
114. Tuition Tax Credits N
115. Est Consumer Protect Agcy N
116. Eliminate B-1 bomber fnds N
117. Subminimum wage for youth N
118. Delete crude oil tax N
119. Natural gas deregulation N

Presidential Support Score: 1986 - 33% 1985 - 35%

CHAPPELL, BILL, Jr. -- Florida 4th District [Democrat]. Counties of Clay (pt.), Duval (pt.), Flagler, Putnam (pt.), St. Johns and Volusia. Prior Terms: House: 1969-86. Born: February 3, 1922; Kendrick Fla. Education: University of Florida (B.A., LL.B., J.D.). Military Service: Naval Reserve. Occupation: Prosecuting attorney (1950-54); Florida representative (1954-64).

1. Immigration Reform Y
2. Open fld-search warrants ?
3. Civil pnty-hire ill alien N
4. So Afr sanc-veto override Y
5. Tax Overhaul N
6. South Africa sanctions Y
7. Death penalty-drug bill Y
8. Evidence-warrantless srch Y
9. Life term-second drug off Y
10. Military use in drug war N
11. Troop reduction in Europe N
12. Prohibit chemical weapons N
13. Bar ASAT testing N
14. Abide SALT II weapons ban Y
15. Follow SALT II-Soviets do N
16. Reduce SDI funding N
17. Increase SDI funding N
18. Purchase Trident sub N
19. Delete 12 MX;Add conv wpn N
20. Raise speed limit Y
21. Textile Import Quotas(*) Y
22. Req Pentagon buy US goods N
23. AIDS ins anti-dscriminatn N
24. Nicaraguan refugee aid N
25. Nicaraguan contra aid Y
26. US abide by SALT II Y
27. Prohibit Saudi arms sale Y
28. Military Retiremnt Reform Y
29. Nicaraguan refugee aid N
30. Ease '68 Gun Control Act Y
31. Bar intrstat handgun tran N
32. Keep '68 Gun Control Act N

CHAPPELL, BILL, Jr. (Cont.)

33. Nicaraguan contra aid Y
34. Bar emp polygraph testing N
35. Tax Overhaul consideratn Y
36. Bar armor-piercing ammo Y
37. Tax Overhaul consideratn Y
38. Make comp emissions known N
39. Allow toxic victims suits N
40. Strike Superfund "VAT" N
41. Notify emp-plant closing N
42. Bar emp consult-plant clo Y
43. Medicare cuts;Tax incres' Y
44. Delete 12 MX missiles N
45. Spending cuts;Tax incres' Y
46. Textile Import Quotas Y
47. Cut some school lunch fds N
48. Clean Water Act Amendmnts Y
49. Youth work projects N
50. Assist military in Angola Y
51. Allow US troops-Nicaragua Y
52. Pentagon polygraph exams Y
53. Bar ASAT testing N
54. Suspend def pmt for abuse N
55. Bar Pentagon-contr emplmt ?
56. Increase SDI funding Y
57. Reduce SDI funding N
58. Produce chemical weapons Y
59. Bar CIA fndg in Nicaragua N
60. South Africa sanctions Y
61. Cut SS COLAs; Raise taxes N
62. Let US invest-So Africa N
63. Approve 21 MX for 1985 Y
64. Emergency Farm Credit Y
65. Awards to whistle blowers Y
66. African disaster relief Y
67. Ban bank loans to So Afr Y
68. Bar coun duty-free trtmt N
69. Steel import limits Y
70. Soc Sec COLAs=inflation Y
71. Bar haz waste vctms suits Y
72. Prohibit aid to Nicaragua Y
73. Cut $-Schs bar sch prayer Y
74. Raise taxes; Cut Medicare Y
75. Alien residncy-prior 1982 Y
76. Alien residncy-prior 1980 N
77. Pen emp-hire illgl aliens N
78. Lmt Persh II/cruse-Europe N
79. Delete 34 B-1 bombers N
80. Bar purch of Pershing II N
81. Bar purchase of Sgt York N
82. Delete $ for Trident II N
83. Allow 15 MX missiles Y
84. Bar MX procurement-1985 N
85. Equal Access Act Y
86. Aid to El Salvador Y
87. Bar Nicarag water mining Y
88. Physician/Medicare freeze N
89. Increase "sin" taxes Y
90. End SBA direct loans N
91. Sell Conrail N
92. Equal Rights Amendment N
93. Marines in Lebanon Y
94. Eminent domain-Coal comps N
95. Prohibit EPA sanctions Y
96. SS age increase/Reforms Y
97. Auto domestic content req N
98. Delete jobs program fundg N
99. Highway-Gas tax bill N
100. Raise Medicare;Cut defnse N
101. Emergency housing aid Y
102. Across-the-board tax cuts Y
103. Gramm-Latta II targets Y
104. Delete B-1 bomber funds N
105. Dsapprov Saudi AWACS sale Y
106. Disapprove oil import fee Y
107. Rail Deregulation Y
108. Dsapp India nuc fuel sale Y
109. Mil draft registration Y
110. Chrysler Loan Guarantees Y
111. Prohibit school busing Y
112. Nuclear plant moratorium N
113. Oil price controls N
114. Tuition Tax Credits X
115. Est Consumer Protect Agcy N
116. Eliminate B-1 bomber fnds N
117. Subminimum wage for youth Y
118. Delete crude oil tax Y
119. Natural gas deregulation Y

Presidential Support Score: 1986 - 44% 1985 - 52%

McCOLLUM, BILL -- Florida 5th District [Republican]. Counties of Lake (pt.), Orange (pt.) and Seminole. Prior Terms: House: 1981-86. Born: July 12, 1944; Brooksville, Fla. Education: University of Florida (B.A., J.D.). Military Service: U.S. Navy, 1969. Occupation: Attorney, Pitts,Eubanks and Ross, P.A.

1. Immigration Reform N
2. Open fld-search warrants N
3. Civil pnty-hire ill alien N
4. So Afr sanc-veto override N
5. Tax Overhaul Y
6. South Africa sanctions N
7. Death penalty-drug bill Y
8. Evidence-warrantless srch Y
9. Life term-second drug off Y
10. Military use in drug war N
11. Troop reduction in Europe N
12. Prohibit chemical weapons N

McCOLLUM, BILL (Cont.)

13. Bar ASAT testing N
14. Abide SALT II weapons ban N
15. Follow SALT II-Soviets do Y
16. Reduce SDI funding N
17. Increase SDI funding Y
18. Purchase Trident sub N
19. Delete 12 MX;Add conv wpn N
20. Raise speed limit Y
21. Textile Import Quotas(*) N
22. Req Pentagon buy US goods N
23. AIDS ins anti-dscriminatn N
24. Nicaraguan refugee aid N
25. Nicaraguan contra aid Y
26. US abide by SALT II Y
27. Prohibit Saudi arms sale Y
28. Military Retiremnt Reform Y
29. Nicaraguan refugee aid Y
30. Ease '68 Gun Control Act Y
31. Bar intrstat handgun tran N
32. Keep '68 Gun Control Act N
33. Nicaraguan contra aid Y
34. Bar emp polygraph testing N
35. Tax Overhaul consideratn N
36. Bar armor-piercing ammo Y
37. Tax Overhaul consideratn N
38. Make comp emissions known N
39. Allow toxic victims suits N
40. Strike Superfund "VAT" N
41. Notify emp-plant closing N
42. Bar emp consult-plant clo Y
43. Medicare cuts;Tax incres' X
44. Delete 12 MX missiles N
45. Spending cuts;Tax incres' N
46. Textile Import Quotas N
47. Cut some school lunch fds Y
48. Clean Water Act Amendmnts Y
49. Youth work projects N
50. Assist military in Angola Y
51. Allow US troops-Nicaragua Y
52. Pentagon polygraph exams Y
53. Bar ASAT testing N
54. Suspend def pmt for abuse N
55. Bar Pentagon-contr emplmt Y
56. Increase SDI funding Y
57. Reduce SDI funding N
58. Produce chemical weapons Y
59. Bar CIA fndg in Nicaragua N
60. South Africa sanctions N
61. Cut SS COLAs; Raise taxes N
62. Let US invest-So Africa Y
63. Approve 21 MX for 1985 Y
64. Emergency Farm Credit N
65. Awards to whistle blowers Y
66. African disaster relief Y
67. Ban bank loans to So Afr N
68. Bar coun duty-free trtmt N
69. Steel import limits N
70. Soc Sec COLAs=inflation Y
71. Bar haz waste vctms suits Y
72. Prohibit aid to Nicaragua N
73. Cut $-Schs bar sch prayer Y
74. Raise taxes; Cut Medicare N
75. Alien residncy-prior 1982 Y
76. Alien residncy-prior 1980 Y
77. Pen emp-hire illgl aliens N
78. Lmt Persh II/cruse-Europe N
79. Delete 34 B-1 bombers N
80. Bar purch of Pershing II N
81. Bar purchase of Sgt York N
82. Delete $ for Trident II N
83. Allow 15 MX missiles Y
84. Bar MX procurement-1985 N
85. Equal Access Act N
86. Aid to El Salvador Y
87. Bar Nicarag water mining N
88. Physician/Medicare freeze Y
89. Increase "sin" taxes N
90. End SBA direct loans N
91. Sell Conrail Y
92. Equal Rights Amendment N
93. Marines in Lebanon Y
94. Eminent domain-Coal comps Y
95. Prohibit EPA sanctions Y
96. SS age increase/Reforms Y
97. Auto domestic content req N
98. Delete jobs program fundg Y
99. Highway-Gas tax bill N
100. Raise Medicare;Cut defnse N
101. Emergency housing aid Y
102. Across-the-board tax cuts Y
103. Gramm-Latta II targets Y
104. Delete B-1 bomber funds N
105. Dsapprov Saudi AWACS sale Y

Presidential Support Score: 1986 - 84% 1985 - 80%

MacKAY, BUDDY -- Florida 6th District [Democrat]. Counties of Alachua, Citrus, Hernando, Lake (pt.), Marion, Pasco (pt.), Putnam (pt.) and Sumter. Prior Terms: House: 1983-86. Born: March 22, 1933; Ocala, Fla. Education: University of Florida; University of Florida Law School (J.D.). Military Service: U.S. Air Force, Air Force Reserve. Occupation: Farmer; rancher; attorney; Florida representative (1968-74); Florida senator (1974-80).

MacKAY, BUDDY (Cont.)

1. Immigration Reform Y
2. Open fld-search warrants N
3. Civil pnty-hire ill alien N
4. So Afr sanc-veto override Y
5. Tax Overhaul Y
6. South Africa sanctions Y
7. Death penalty-drug bill Y
8. Evidence-warrantless srch Y
9. Life term-second drug off Y
10. Military use in drug war Y
11. Troop reduction in Europe N
12. Prohibit chemical weapons Y
13. Bar ASAT testing Y
14. Abide SALT II weapons ban Y
15. Follow SALT II-Soviets do N
16. Reduce SDI funding N
17. Increase SDI funding N
18. Purchase Trident sub Y
19. Delete 12 MX;Add conv wpn Y
20. Raise speed limit N
21. Textile Import Quotas(*) N
22. Req Pentagon buy US goods N
23. AIDS ins anti-dscriminatn Y
24. Nicaraguan refugee aid N
25. Nicaraguan contra aid N
26. US abide by SALT II N
27. Prohibit Saudi arms sale N
28. Military Retiremnt Reform Y
29. Nicaraguan refugee aid N
30. Ease '68 Gun Control Act Y
31. Bar intrstat handgun tran N
32. Keep '68 Gun Control Act N
33. Nicaraguan contra aid N
34. Bar emp polygraph testing N
35. Tax Overhaul consideratn Y
36. Bar armor-piercing ammo Y
37. Tax Overhaul consideratn Y
38. Make comp emissions known Y
39. Allow toxic victims suits Y
40. Strike Superfund "VAT" Y
41. Notify emp-plant closing N
42. Bar emp consult-plant clo #
43. Medicare cuts;Tax incres' Y
44. Delete 12 MX missiles Y
45. Spending cuts;Tax incres' Y
46. Textile Import Quotas N
47. Cut some school lunch fds N
48. Clean Water Act Amendmnts N
49. Youth work projects N
50. Assist military in Angola N
51. Allow US troops-Nicaragua N
52. Pentagon polygraph exams Y
53. Bar ASAT testing Y
54. Suspend def pmt for abuse Y
55. Bar Pentagon-contr emplmt Y
56. Increase SDI funding N
57. Reduce SDI funding N
58. Produce chemical weapons N
59. Bar CIA fndg in Nicaragua Y
60. South Africa sanctions Y
61. Cut SS COLAs; Raise taxes Y
62. Let US invest-So Africa N
63. Approve 21 MX for 1985 N
64. Emergency Farm Credit Y
65. Awards to whistle blowers Y
66. African disaster relief Y
67. Ban bank loans to So Afr ?
68. Bar coun duty-free trtmt N
69. Steel import limits N
70. Soc Sec COLAs=inflation Y
71. Bar haz waste vctms suits N
72. Prohibit aid to Nicaragua Y
73. Cut $-Schs bar sch prayer Y
74. Raise taxes; Cut Medicare Y
75. Alien residncy-prior 1982 Y
76. Alien residncy-prior 1980 Y
77. Pen emp-hire illgl aliens N
78. Lmt Persh II/cruse-Europe N
79. Delete 34 B-1 bombers Y
80. Bar purch of Pershing II N
81. Bar purchase of Sgt York Y
82. Delete $ for Trident II N
83. Allow 15 MX missiles N
84. Bar MX procurement-1985 Y
85. Equal Access Act Y
86. Aid to El Salvador N
87. Bar Nicarag water mining Y
88. Physician/Medicare freeze N
89. Increase "sin" taxes Y
90. End SBA direct loans N
91. Sell Conrail N
92. Equal Rights Amendment Y
93. Marines in Lebanon Y
94. Eminent domain-Coal comps Y
95. Prohibit EPA sanctions Y
96. SS age increase/Reforms Y

Presidential Support Score: 1986 - 28% 1985 - 40%

GIBBONS, SAM -- Florida 7th District [Democrat]. County of Hillsborough (pt.). Prior Terms: House: 1963-86. Born: January 20, 1920; Tampa, Fla. Education: University of Florida (J.D.). Military Service: U.S. Army, WW II. Occupation: Attorney; Florida representative (1952-58); Florida senator (1958-62).

1. Immigration Reform Y
2. Open fld-search warrants Y

GIBBONS, SAM (Cont.)

3. Civil pnty-hire ill alien Y
4. So Afr sanc-veto override Y
5. Tax Overhaul Y
6. South Africa sanctions Y
7. Death penalty-drug bill Y
8. Evidence-warrantless srch Y
9. Life term-second drug off Y
10. Military use in drug war N
11. Troop reduction in Europe N
12. Prohibit chemical weapons N
13. Bar ASAT testing Y
14. Abide SALT II weapons ban Y
15. Follow SALT II-Soviets do N
16. Reduce SDI funding N
17. Increase SDI funding N
18. Purchase Trident sub ?
19. Delete 12 MX;Add conv wpn Y
20. Raise speed limit N
21. Textile Import Quotas(*) N
22. Req Pentagon buy US goods N
23. AIDS ins anti-dscriminatn Y
24. Nicaraguan refugee aid N
25. Nicaraguan contra aid Y
26. US abide by SALT II N
27. Prohibit Saudi arms sale Y
28. Military Retiremnt Reform Y
29. Nicaraguan refugee aid N
30. Ease '68 Gun Control Act N
31. Bar intrstat handgun tran Y
32. Keep '68 Gun Control Act Y
33. Nicaraguan contra aid Y
34. Bar emp polygraph testing N
35. Tax Overhaul consideratn Y
36. Bar armor-piercing ammo Y
37. Tax Overhaul consideratn Y
38. Make comp emissions known Y
39. Allow toxic victims suits Y
40. Strike Superfund "VAT" N
41. Notify emp-planC closing N
42. Bar emp consult-plant clo Y
43. Medicare cuts;Tax incres' Y
44. Delete 12 MX missiles Y
45. Spending cuts;Tan incres' N
46. Textile Import Quotas N
47. Cut some school lunch fds Y
48. Clean Water Act Amendmnts N
49. Youth work projects Y
50. Assist military in Angola N
51. Allow US troops-Nicaragua N
52. Pentagon polygraph exams Y
53. Bar ASAT testing Y
54. Suspend def pmt for abuse Y
55. Bar Pentagon-contr emplmt Y
56. Increase SDI funding N
57. Reduce SDI funding N
58. Produce chemical weapons Y
59. Bar CIA fndg in Nicaragua N
60. South Africa sanctions Y
61. Cut SS COLAs; Raise taxes Y
62. Let US invest-So Africa N
63. Approve 21 MX for 1985 N
64. Emergency Farm Credit N
65. Awards to whistle blowers Y
66. African disaster relief Y
67. Ban bank loans to So Afr Y
68. Bar coun duty-free trtmt N
69. Steel import limits ?
70. Soc Sec COLAs=inflation Y
71. Bar haz waste vctms suits N
72. Prohibit aid to Nicaragua Y
73. Cut $-Schs bar sch prayer Y
74. Raise taxes; Cut Medicare Y
75. Alien residncy-prior 1982 Y
76. Alien residncy-prior 1980 N
77. Pen emp-hire illgl aliens Y
78. Lmt Persh II/cruse-Europe ?
79. Delete 34 B-1 bombers Y
80. Bar purch of Pershing II Y
81. Bar purchase of Sgt York N
82. Delete $ for Trident II N
83. Allow 15 MX missiles N
84. Bar MX procurement-1985 Y
85. Equal Access Act N
86. Aid to El Salvador N
87. Bar Nicarag water mining Y
88. Physician/Medicare freeze N
89. Increase "sin" taxes Y
90. End SBA direct loans N
91. Sell Conrail N
92. Equal Rights Amendment Y
93. Marines in Lebanon N
94. Eminent domain-Coal comps ?
95. Prohibit EPA sanctions Y
96. SS age increase/Reforms Y
97. Auto domestic content req N
98. Delete jobs program fundg N
99. Highway-Gas tax bill Y
100. Raise Medicare;Cut defnse N
101. Emergency housing aid N
102. Across-the-board tax cuts N
103. Gramm-Latta II targets Y
104. Delete B-1 bomber funds Y
105. Dsapprov Saudi AWACS sale Y
106. Disapprove oil import fee N
107. Rail Deregulation Y
108. Dsapp India nuc fuel sale N
109. Mil draft registration Y
110. Chrysler Loan Guarantees N
111. Prohibit school busing Y
112. Nuclear plant moratorium ?
113. Oil price controls N
114. Tuition Tax Credits Y
115. Est Consumer Protect Agcy N
116. Eliminate B-1 bomber fnds Y
117. Subminimum wage for youth Y
118. Delete crude oil tax N
119. Natural gas deregulation N

GIBBONS, SAM (Cont.)
Presidential Support Score: 1986 - 34% 1985 - 50%

YOUNG, C. W. BILL -- Florida 8th District [Republican]. County of Pinellas (pt.). Prior Terms: House: 1971-86. Born: December 16, 1930; Harmarville, Pa. Military Service: National Guard, 1948-57. Occupation: Florida senator (1960, 1964-70).

1. Immigration Reform N
2. Open fld-search warrants Y
3. Civil pnty-hire ill alien N
4. So Afr sanc-veto override N
5. Tax Overhaul Y
6. South Africa sanctions N
7. Death penalty-drug bill Y
8. Evidence-warrantless srch Y
9. Life term-second drug off Y
10. Military use in drug war N
11. Troop reduction in Europe N
12. Prohibit chemical weapons N
13. Bar ASAT testing N
14. Abide SALT II weapons ban N
15. Follow SALT II-Soviets do Y
16. Reduce SDI funding N
17. Increase SDI funding Y
18. Purchase Trident sub Y
19. Delete 12 MX;Add conv wpn N
20. Raise speed limit Y
21. Textile Import Quotas(*) N
22. Req Pentagon buy US goods N
23. AIDS ins anti-dscriminatn N
24. Nicaraguan refugee aid N
25. Nicaraguan contra aid Y
26. US abide by SALT II Y
27. Prohibit Saudi arms sale Y
28. Military Retiremnt Reform Y
29. Nicaraguan refugee aid Y
30. Ease '68 Gun Control Act Y
31. Bar intrstat handgun tran Y
32. Keep '68 Gun Control Act N
33. Nicaraguan contra aid Y
34. Bar emp polygraph testing N
35. Tax Overhaul consideratn Y
36. Bar armor-piercing ammo Y
37. Tax Overhaul consideratn N
38. Make comp emissions known N
39. Allow toxic victims suits N
40. Strike Superfund "VAT" Y
41. Notify emp-plant closing N
42. Bar emp consult-plant clo Y
43. Medicare cuts;Tax incres' N
44. Delete 12 MX missiles N
45. Spending cuts;Tax incres' N
46. Textile Import Quotas N
47. Cut some school lunch fds N
48. Clean Water Act Amendmnts Y
49. Youth work projects N
50. Assist military in Angola Y
51. Allow US troops-Nicaragua N
52. Pentagon polygraph exams Y
53. Bar ASAT testing N
54. Suspend def pmt for abuse N
55. Bar Pentagon-contr emplmt Y
56. Increase SDI funding N
57. Reduce SDI funding N
58. Produce chemical weapons Y
59. Bar CIA fndg in Nicaragua N
60. South Africa sanctions N
61. Cut SS COLAs; Raise taxes N
62. Let US invest-So Africa Y
63. Approve 21 MX for 1985 Y
64. Emergency Farm Credit N
65. Awards to whistle blowers Y
66. African disaster relief Y
67. Ban bank loans to So Afr Y
68. Bar coun duty-free trtmt N
69. Steel import limits Y
70. Soc Sec COLAs=inflation Y
71. Bar haz waste vctms suits Y
72. Prohibit aid to Nicaragua Y
73. Cut $-Schs bar sch prayer Y
74. Raise taxes; Cut Medicare N
75. Alien residncy-prior 1982 Y
76. Alien residncy-prior 1980 Y
77. Pen emp-hire illgl aliens N
78. Lmt Persh II/cruse-Europe N
79. Delete 34 B-1 bombers N
80. Bar purch of Pershing II N
81. Bar purchase of Sgt York N
82. Delete $ for Trident II N
83. Allow 15 MX missiles Y
84. Bar MX procurement-1985 N
85. Equal Access Act Y
86. Aid to El Salvador Y
87. Bar Nicarag water mining N
88. Physician/Medicare freeze Y
89. Increase "sin" taxes N
90. End SBA direct loans N
91. Sell Conrail N
92. Equal Rights Amendment N
93. Marines in Lebanon N
94. Eminent domain-Coal comps Y
95. Prohibit EPA sanctions Y
96. SS age increase/Reforms Y
97. Auto domestic content req N
98. Delete jobs program fundg Y
99. Highway-Gas tax bill N
100. Raise Medicare;Cut defnse N
101. Emergency housing aid Y
102. Across-the-board tax cuts Y
103. Gramm-Latta II targets Y
104. Delete B-1 bomber funds N

YOUNG, C. W. BILL (Cont.)

105. Dsapprov Saudi AWACS sale Y
106. Disapprove oil import fee Y
107. Rail Deregulation Y
108. Dsapp India nuc fuel sale Y
109. Mil draft registration Y
110. Chrysler Loan Guarantees N
111. Prohibit school busing Y
112. Nuclear plant moratorium N
113. Oil price controls N
114. Tuition Tax Credits N
115. Est Consumer Protect Agcy N
116. Eliminate B-1 bomber fnds N
117. Subminimum wage for youth Y
118. Delete crude oil tax Y
119. Natural gas deregulation Y

Presidential Support Score: 1986 - 73% 1985 - 74%

BILIRAKIS, MICHAEL -- Florida 9th District [Republican]. Counties of Hillsborough (pt.), Pasco (pt.) and Pinellas (pt.). Prior Terms: House: 1983-86. Born: July 16, 1930; Tarpon Springs, Fla. Education: University of Pittsburgh (B.S.); University of Florida (J.D.). Military Service: U.S. Air Force, 1951-55. Occupation: Attorney; petroleum engineer; geophysical engineer; government contract negotiator; steel worker; county and municipal judge.

1. Immigration Reform N
2. Open fld-search warrants Y
3. Civil pnty-hire ill alien Y
4. So Afr sanc-veto override N
5. Tax Overhaul Y
6. South Africa sanctions N
7. Death penalty-drug bill Y
8. Evidence-warrantless srch Y
9. Life term-second drug off Y
10. Military use in drug war Y
11. Troop reduction in Europe N
12. Prohibit chemical weapons N
13. Bar ASAT testing N
14. Abide SALT II weapons ban N
15. Follow SALT II-Soviets do Y
16. Reduce SDI funding N
17. Increase SDI funding N
18. Purchase Trident sub N
19. Delete 12 MX;Add conv wpn N
20. Raise speed limit Y
21. Textile Import Quotas(*) Y
22. Req Pentagon buy US goods N
23. AIDS ins anti-dscriminatn N
24. Nicaraguan refugee aid N
25. Nicaraguan contra aid Y
26. US abide by SALT II Y
27. Prohibit Saudi arms sale Y
28. Military Retiremnt Reform Y
29. Nicaraguan refugee aid Y
30. Ease '68 Gun Control Act Y
31. Bar intrstat handgun tran N
32. Keep '68 Gun Control Act N
33. Nicaraguan contra aid Y
34. Bar emp polygraph testing N
35. Tax Overhaul consideratn Y
36. Bar armor-piercing ammo Y
37. Tax Overhaul consideratn N
38. Make comp emissions known N
39. Allow toxic victims suits N
40. Strike Superfund "VAT" Y
41. Notify emp-plant closing N
42. Bar emp consult-plant clo Y
43. Medicare cuts;Tax incres' N
44. Delete 12 MX missiles N
45. Spending cuts;Tax incres' N
46. Textile Import Quotas Y
47. Cut some school lunch fds Y
48. Clean Water Act Amendmnts Y
49. Youth work projects N
50. Assist military in Angola Y
51. Allow US troops-Nicaragua Y
52. Pentagon polygraph exams Y
53. Bar ASAT testing N
54. Suspend def pmt for abuse N
55. Bar Pentagon-contr emplmt Y
56. Increase SDI funding N
57. Reduce SDI funding N
58. Produce chemical weapons Y
59. Bar CIA fndg in Nicaragua N
60. South Africa sanctions N
61. Cut SS COLAs; Raise taxes N
62. Let US invest-So Africa Y
63. Approve 21 MX for 1985 Y
64. Emergency Farm Credit N
65. Awards to whistle blowers Y
66. African disaster relief Y
67. Ban bank loans to So Afr N
68. Bar coun duty-free trtmt N
69. Steel import limits Y
70. Soc Sec COLAs=inflation Y
71. Bar haz waste vctms suits Y
72. Prohibit aid to Nicaragua N
73. Cut $-Schs bar sch prayer Y
74. Raise taxes; Cut Medicare N
75. Alien residncy-prior 1982 Y
76. Alien residncy-prior 1980 Y
77. Pen emp-hire illgl aliens N
78. Lmt Persh II/cruse-Europe N

BILIRAKIS, MICHAEL (Cont.)

79. Delete 34 B-1 bombers N
80. Bar purch of Pershing II N
81. Bar purchase of Sgt York Y
82. Delete $ for Trident II N
83. Allow 15 MX missiles Y
84. Bar MX procurement-1985 N
85. Equal Access Act Y
86. Aid to El Salvador Y
87. Bar Nicarag water mining N
88. Physician/Medicare freeze Y
89. Increase "sin" taxes N
90. End SBA direct loans N
91. Sell Conrail Y
92. Equal Rights Amendment N
93. Marines in Lebanon Y
94. Eminent domain-Coal comps Y
95. Prohibit EPA sanctions Y
96. SS age increase/Reforms Y

Presidential Support Score: 1986 - 78% 1985 - 75%

IRELAND, ANDY -- Florida 10th District [Republican]. Counties of DeSoto, Hardee, Manatee, Osceola (pt.) and Polk. Prior Terms: House: 1977-86. Born: August 23, 1930; Cincinnati, Ohio. Education: Yale University (B.S.); Columbia University; Louisiana State University. Occupation: City commissioner (1966-68); banker.

1. Immigration Reform N
2. Open fld-search warrants ?
3. Civil pnty-hire ill alien ?
4. So Afr sanc-veto override Y
5. Tax Overhaul Y
6. South Africa sanctions Y
7. Death penalty-drug bill Y
8. Evidence-warrantless srch Y
9. Life term-second drug off Y
10. Military use in drug war Y
11. Troop reduction in Europe ?
12. Prohibit chemical weapons N
13. Bar ASAT testing N
14. Abide SALT II weapons ban N
15. Follow SALT II-Soviets do Y
16. Reduce SDI funding N
17. Increase SDI funding Y
18. Purchase Trident sub N
19. Delete 12 MX;Add conv wpn N
20. Raise speed limit Y
21. Textile Import Quotas(*) N
22. Req Pentagon buy US goods ?
23. AIDS ins anti-dscriminatn N
24. Nicaraguan refugee aid N
25. Nicaraguan contra aid Y
26. US abide by SALT II Y
27. Prohibit Saudi arms sale Y
28. Military Retiremnt Reform Y
29. Nicaraguan refugee aid Y
30. Ease '68 Gun Control Act #
31. Bar intrstat handgun tran N
32. Keep '68 Gun Control Act N
33. Nicaraguan contra aid Y
34. Bar emp polygraph testing N
35. Tax Overhaul consideratn Y
36. Bar armor-piercing ammo Y
37. Tax Overhaul consideratn N
38. Make comp emissions known N
39. Allow toxic victims suits N
40. Strike Superfund "VAT" Y
41. Notify emp-plant closing N
42. Bar emp consult-plant clo Y
43. Medicare cuts;Tax incres' N
44. Delete 12 MX missiles N
45. Spending cuts;Tax incres' N
46. Textile Import Quotas N
47. Cut some school lunch fds Y
48. Clean Water Act Amendmnts Y
49. Youth work projects N
50. Assist military in Angola Y
51. Allow US troops-Nicaragua Y
52. Pentagon polygraph exams Y
53. Bar ASAT testing N
54. Suspend def pmt for abuse N
55. Bar Pentagon-contr emplmt Y
56. Increase SDI funding Y
57. Reduce SDI funding N
58. Produce chemical weapons Y
59. Bar CIA fndg in Nicaragua N
60. South Africa sanctions N
61. Cut SS COLAs; Raise taxes N
62. Let US invest-So Africa Y
63. Approve 21 MX for 1985 Y
64. Emergency Farm Credit N
65. Awards to whistle blowers Y
66. African disaster relief Y
67. Ban bank loans to So Afr N
68. Bar coun duty-free trtmt N
69. Steel import limits Y
70. Soc Sec COLAs=inflation Y
71. Bar haz waste vctms suits Y
72. Prohibit aid to Nicaragua Y
73. Cut $-Schs bar sch prayer Y
74. Raise taxes; Cut Medicare Y
75. Alien residncy-prior 1982 Y
76. Alien residncy-prior 1980 Y
77. Pen emp-hire illgl aliens N
78. Lmt Persh II/cruse-Europe N
79. Delete 34 B-1 bombers N
80. Bar purch of Pershing II N

IRELAND, ANDY (Cont.)

81. Bar purchase of Sgt York N
82. Delete $ for Trident II N
83. Allow 15 MX missiles Y
84. Bar MX procurement-1985 N
85. Equal Access Act Y
86. Aid to El Salvador Y
87. Bar Nicarag water mining ?
88. Physician/Medicare freeze Y
89. Increase "sin" taxes Y
90. End SBA direct loans N
91. Sell Conrail Y
92. Equal Rights Amendment N
93. Marines in Lebanon Y
94. Eminent domain-Coal comps Y
95. Prohibit EPA sanctions Y
96. SS age increase/Reforms Y
97. Auto domestic content req N
98. Delete jobs program fundg Y
99. Highway-Gas tax bill N
100. Raise Medicare;Cut defnse N
101. Emergency housing aid Y
102. Across-the-board tax cuts Y
103. Gramm-Latta II targets Y
104. Delete B-1 bomber funds N
105. Dsapprov Saudi AWACS sale Y
106. Disapprove oil import fee Y
107. Rail Deregulation Y
108. Dsapp India nuc fuel sale ?
109. Mil draft registration Y
110. Chrysler Loan Guarantees Y
111. Prohibit school busing Y
112. Nuclear plant moratorium N
113. Oil price controls N
114. Tuition Tax Credits ?
115. Est Consumer Protect Agcy N
116. Eliminate B-1 bomber fnds Y
117. Subminimum wage for youth Y
118. Delete crude oil tax N
119. Natural gas deregulation Y

Presidential Support Score: 1986 - 75% 1985 - 80%

NELSON, BILL -- Florida 11th District [Democrat]. Counties of Brevard, Indian River (pt.), Orange (pt.) and Osceola (pt.). Prior Terms: House: 1979-86. Born: September 29, 1942; Miami, Fla. Education: Yale University (B.A.); University of Virginia (J.D.). Military Service: U.S. Army Reserve, 1965-71. Occupation: Attorney; Florida representative (1972-78).

1. Immigration Reform Y
2. Open fld-search warrants N
3. Civil pnty-hire ill alien N
4. So Afr sanc-veto override Y
5. Tax Overhaul Y
6. South Africa sanctions Y
7. Death penalty-drug bill Y
8. Evidence-warrantless srch Y
9. Life term-second drug off Y
10. Military use in drug war +
11. Troop reduction in Europe N
12. Prohibit chemical weapons N
13. Bar ASAT testing N
14. Abide SALT II weapons ban N
15. Follow SALT II-Soviets do Y
16. Reduce SDI funding N
17. Increase SDI funding Y
18. Purchase Trident sub Y
19. Delete 12 MX;Add conv wpn N
20. Raise speed limit N
21. Textile Import Quotas(*) N
22. Req Pentagon buy US goods Y
23. AIDS ins anti-dscriminatn N
24. Nicaraguan refugee aid N
25. Nicaraguan contra aid Y
26. US abide by SALT II Y
27. Prohibit Saudi arms sale Y
28. Military Retiremnt Reform Y
29. Nicaraguan refugee aid N
30. Ease '68 Gun Control Act Y
31. Bar intrstat handgun tran N
32. Keep '68 Gun Control Act N
33. Nicaraguan contra aid Y
34. Bar emp polygraph testing N
35. Tax Overhaul consideratn #
36. Bar armor-piercing ammo +
37. Tax Overhaul consideratn +
38. Make comp emissions known +
39. Allow toxic victims suits +
40. Strike Superfund "VAT" #
41. Notify emp-plant closing X
42. Bar emp consult-plant clo #
43. Medicare cuts;Tax incres' #
44. Delete 12 MX missiles X
45. Spending cuts;Tax incres' #
46. Textile Import Quotas N
47. Cut some school lunch fds N
48. Clean Water Act Amendmnts N
49. Youth work projects Y
50. Assist military in Angola #
51. Allow US troops-Nicaragua Y
52. Pentagon polygraph exams Y
53. Bar ASAT testing N
54. Suspend def pmt for abuse Y
55. Bar Pentagon-contr emplmt Y
56. Increase SDI funding Y
57. Reduce SDI funding N
58. Produce chemical weapons Y

NELSON, BILL (Cont.)

59. Bar CIA fndg in Nicaragua N
60. South Africa sanctions Y
61. Cut SS COLAs; Raise taxes Y
62. Let US invest-So Africa N
63. Approve 21 MX for 1985 Y
64. Emergency Farm Credit N
65. Awards to whistle blowers Y
66. African disaster relief Y
67. Ban bank loans to So Afr Y
68. Bar coun duty-free trtmt N
69. Steel import limits N
70. Soc Sec COLAs=inflation Y
71. Bar haz waste vctms suits Y
72. Prohibit aid to Nicaragua Y
73. Cut $-Schs bar sch prayer Y
74. Raise taxes; Cut Medicare Y
75. Alien residncy-prior 1982 Y
76. Alien residncy-prior 1980 Y
77. Pen emp-hire illgl aliens N
78. Lmt Persh II/cruse-Europe N
79. Delete 34 B-1 bombers N
80. Bar purch of Pershing II N
81. Bar purchase of Sgt York Y
82. Delete $ for Trident II N
83. Allow 15 MX missiles Y
84. Bar MX procurement-1985 N
85. Equal Access Act Y
86. Aid to El Salvador Y
87. Bar Nicarag water mining Y
88. Physician/Medicare freeze N
89. Increase "sin" taxes Y
90. End SBA direct loans N
91. Sell Conrail N
92. Equal Rights Amendment Y
93. Marines in Lebanon Y
94. Eminent domain-Coal comps Y
95. Prohibit EPA sanctions N
96. SS age increase/Reforms N
97. Auto domestic content req N
98. Delete jobs program fundg N
99. Highway-Gas tax bill Y
100. Raise Medicare;Cut defnse N
101. Emergency housing aid Y
102. Across-the-board tax cuts Y
103. Gramm-Latta II targets Y
104. Delete B-1 bomber funds N
105. Dsapprov Saudi AWACS sale Y
106. Disapprove oil import fee Y
107. Rail Deregulation Y
108. Dsapp India nuc fuel sale Y
109. Mil draft registration Y
110. Chrysler Loan Guarantees Y
111. Prohibit school busing N
112. Nuclear plant moratorium N
113. Oil price controls N

Presidential Support Score: 1986 - 43% 1985 - 55%

LEWIS, TOM -- Florida 12th District [Republican]. Counties of Collier (pt.), Glades, Hendry, Highlands, Indian River (pt.), Martin, Okeechobee, Palm Beach (pt.) and St. Lucie. Prior Terms: House: 1983-86. Born: October 26, 1924; Philadelphia, Pa. Education: University of Florida. Military Service: U.S. Air Force, WW II, Korean Conflict. Occupation: Corporate executive (1957-73); mayor and councilman (1964-71); realtor (1972-82); Florida representative (1972-80); Florida senator (1980-82).

1. Immigration Reform N
2. Open fld-search warrants Y
3. Civil pnty-hire ill alien N
4. So Afr sanc-veto override Y
5. Tax Overhaul N
6. South Africa sanctions Y
7. Death penalty-drug bill Y
8. Evidence-warrantless srch Y
9. Life term-second drug off Y
10. Military use in drug war Y
11. Troop reduction in Europe N
12. Prohibit chemical weapons Y
13. Bar ASAT testing N
14. Abide SALT II weapons ban N
15. Follow SALT II-Soviets do Y
16. Reduce SDI funding N
17. Increase SDI funding N
18. Purchase Trident sub N
19. Delete 12 MX;Add conv wpn N
20. Raise speed limit Y
21. Textile Import Quotas(*) N
22. Req Pentagon buy US goods N
23. AIDS ins anti-dscriminatn N
24. Nicaraguan refugee aid N
25. Nicaraguan contra aid Y
26. US abide by SALT II Y
27. Prohibit Saudi arms sale Y
28. Military Retiremnt Reform Y
29. Nicaraguan refugee aid Y
30. Ease '68 Gun Control Act Y
31. Bar intrstat handgun tran N
32. Keep '68 Gun Control Act N
33. Nicaraguan contra aid Y
34. Bar emp polygraph testing N
35. Tax Overhaul consideratn N
36. Bar armor-piercing ammo Y

LEWIS, TOM (Cont.)

37. Tax Overhaul consideratn N
38. Make comp emissions known N
39. Allow toxic victims suits N
40. Strike Superfund "VAT" N
41. Notify emp-plant closing N
42. Bar emp consult-plant clo #
43. Medicare cuts;Tax incres' N
44. Delete 12 MX missiles N
45. Spending cuts;Tax incres' N
46. Textile Import Quotas N
47. Cut some school lunch fds Y
48. Clean Water Act Amendmnts Y
49. Youth work projects N
50. Assist military in Angola Y
51. Allow US troops-Nicaragua Y
52. Pentagon polygraph exams Y
53. Bar ASAT testing N
54. Suspend def pmt for abuse N
55. Bar Pentagon-contr emplmt Y
56. Increase SDI funding Y
57. Reduce SDI funding N
58. Produce chemical weapons N
59. Bar CIA fndg in Nicaragua N
60. South Africa sanctions N
61. Cut SS COLAs; Raise taxes N
62. Let US invest-So Africa Y
63. Approve 21 MX for 1985 Y
64. Emergency Farm Credit Y
65. Awards to whistle blowers Y
66. African disaster relief Y
67. Ban bank loans to So Afr N
68. Bar coun duty-free trtmt N
69. Steel import limits N
70. Soc Sec COLAs=inflation Y
71. Bar haz waste vctms suits Y
72. Prohibit aid to Nicaragua N
73. Cut $-Schs bar sch prayer Y
74. Raise taxes; Cut Medicare N
75. Alien residncy-prior 1982 Y
76. Alien residncy-prior 1980 Y
77. Pen emp-hire illgl aliens N
78. Lmt Persh II/cruse-Europe N
79. Delete 34 B-1 bombers N
80. Bar purch of Pershing II N
81. Bar purchase of Sgt York N
82. Delete $ for Trident II N
83. Allow 15 MX missiles Y
84. Bar MX procurement-1985 N
85. Equal Access Act Y
86. Aid to El Salvador Y
87. Bar Nicarag water mining N
88. Physician/Medicare freeze Y
89. Increase "sin" taxes Y
90. End SBA direct loans N
91. Sell Conrail Y
92. Equal Rights Amendment Y
93. Marines in Lebanon Y
94. Eminent domain-Coal comps Y
95. Prohibit EPA sanctions Y
96. SS age increase/Reforms N

Presidential Support Score: 1986 - 72% 1985 - 66%

MACK, CONNIE -- Florida 13th District [Republican]. Counties of Charlotte, Collier (pt.), Lee and Sarasota. Prior Terms: House: 1983-86. Born: October 29, 1940; Philadelphia, Pa. Occupation: Vice-president, First National Bank of Ft. Myers; senior vice-president, Sun Bank (1971); president and director, Florida National Bank (1975); appointed, Miami Branch of Federal Reserve Board (1981); board of directors, Cape Coral Hospital.

1. Immigration Reform N
2. Open fld-search warrants Y
3. Civil pnty-hire ill alien N
4. So Afr sanc-veto override N
5. Tax Overhaul Y
6. South Africa sanctions N
7. Death penalty-drug bill Y
8. Evidence-warrantless srch Y
9. Life term-second drug off Y
10. Military use in drug war Y
11. Troop reduction in Europe N
12. Prohibit chemical weapons N
13. Bar ASAT testing N
14. Abide SALT II weapons ban N
15. Follow SALT II-Soviets do Y
16. Reduce SDI funding N
17. Increase SDI funding Y
18. Purchase Trident sub N
19. Delete 12 MX;Add conv wpn N
20. Raise speed limit Y
21. Textile Import Quotas(*) N
22. Req Pentagon buy US goods N
23. AIDS ins anti-dscriminatn N
24. Nicaraguan refugee aid N
25. Nicaraguan contra aid Y
26. US abide by SALT II Y
27. Prohibit Saudi arms sale Y
28. Military Retiremnt Reform Y
29. Nicaraguan refugee aid Y
30. Ease '68 Gun Control Act Y
31. Bar intrstat handgun tran N
32. Keep '68 Gun Control Act N
33. Nicaraguan contra aid Y
34. Bar emp polygraph testing N

MACK, CONNIE (Cont.)

35. Tax Overhaul consideratn N
36. Bar armor-piercing ammo Y
37. Tax Overhaul consideratn N
38. Make comp emissions known N
39. Allow toxic victims suits N
40. Strike Superfund "VAT" Y
41. Notify emp-plant closing N
42. Bar emp consult-plant clo Y
43. Medicare cuts;Tax incres' N
44. Delete 12 MX missiles N
45. Spending cuts;Tax incres' N
46. Textile Import Quotas N
47. Cut some school lunch fds Y
48. Clean Water Act Amendmnts Y
49. Youth work projects N
50. Assist military in Angola Y
51. Allow US troops-Nicaragua Y
52. Pentagon polygraph exams Y
53. Bar ASAT testing N
54. Suspend def pmt for abuse N
55. Bar Pentagon-contr emplmt Y
56. Increase SDI funding Y
57. Reduce SDI funding N
58. Produce chemical weapons Y
59. Bar CIA fndg in Nicaragua N
60. South Africa sanctions N
61. Cut SS COLAs; Raise taxes N
62. Let US invest-So Africa #
63. Approve 21 MX for 1985 Y
64. Emergency Farm Credit N
65. Awards to whistle blowers Y
66. African disaster relief Y
67. Ban bank loans to So Afr N
68. Bar coun duty-free trtmt N
69. Steel import limits N
70. Soc Sec COLAs=inflation Y
71. Bar haz waste vctms suits Y
72. Prohibit aid to Nicaragua N
73. Cut $-Schs bar sch prayer Y
74. Raise taxes; Cut Medicare N
75. Alien residncy-prior 1982 Y
76. Alien residncy-prior 1980 Y
77. Pen emp-hire illgl aliens N
78. Lmt Persh II/cruse-Europe N
79. Delete 34 B-1 bombers N
80. Bar purch of Pershing II N
81. Bar purchase of Sgt York N
82. Delete $ for Trident II N
83. Allow 15 MX missiles Y
84. Bar MX procurement-1985 N
85. Equal Access Act Y
86. Aid to El Salvador Y
87. Bar Nicarag water mining N
88. Physician/Medicare freeze Y
89. Increase "sin" taxes N
90. End SBA direct loans Y
91. Sell Conrail Y
92. Equal Rights Amendment Y
93. Marines in Lebanon Y
94. Eminent domain-Coal comps Y
95. Prohibit EPA sanctions N
96. SS age increase/Reforms Y

Presidential Support Score: 1986 - 86% 1985 - 85%

MICA, DAN -- Florida 14th District [Democrat]. Counties of Broward (pt.) and Palm Beach (pt.). Prior Terms: House: 1979-86. Born: February 4, 1944; Binghamtown, N.Y. Education: University of Florida; Florida Atlantic University. Occupation: Teacher; congressional administrative assistant (1968-78).

1. Immigration Reform Y
2. Open fld-search warrants X
3. Civil pnty-hire ill alien N
4. So Afr sanc-veto override Y
5. Tax Overhaul N
6. South Africa sanctions Y
7. Death penalty-drug bill Y
8. Evidence-warrantless srch Y
9. Life term-second drug off Y
10. Military use in drug war Y
11. Troop reduction in Europe N
12. Prohibit chemical weapons Y
13. Bar ASAT testing Y
14. Abide SALT II weapons ban Y
15. Follow SALT II-Soviets do N
16. Reduce SDI funding N
17. Increase SDI funding N
18. Purchase Trident sub Y
19. Delete 12 MX;Add conv wpn Y
20. Raise speed limit N
21. Textile Import Quotas(*) N
22. Req Pentagon buy US goods N
23. AIDS ins anti-dscriminatn Y
24. Nicaraguan refugee aid N
25. Nicaraguan contra aid Y
26. US abide by SALT II N
27. Prohibit Saudi arms sale Y
28. Military Retiremnt Reform Y
29. Nicaraguan refugee aid N
30. Ease '68 Gun Control Act N
31. Bar intrstat handgun tran Y
32. Keep '68 Gun Control Act Y
33. Nicaraguan contra aid Y
34. Bar emp polygraph testing Y
35. Tax Overhaul consideratn Y
36. Bar armor-piercing ammo ?
37. Tax Overhaul consideratn Y
38. Make comp emissions known Y

MICA, DAN (Cont.)

39. Allow toxic victims suits N
40. Strike Superfund "VAT" Y
41. Notify emp-plant closing N
42. Bar emp consult-plant clo Y
43. Medicare cuts;Tax incres' Y
44. Delete 12 MX missiles N
45. Spending cuts;Tax incres' Y
46. Textile Import Quotas N
47. Cut some school lunch fds N
48. Clean Water Act Amendmnts ?
49. Youth work projects N
50. Assist military in Angola Y
51. Allow US troops-Nicaragua N
52. Pentagon polygraph exams Y
53. Bar ASAT testing Y
54. Suspend def pmt for abuse N
55. Bar Pentagon-contr emplmt Y
56. Increase SDI funding N
57. Reduce SDI funding N
58. Produce chemical weapons Y
59. Bar CIA fndg in Nicaragua N
60. South Africa sanctions Y
61. Cut SS COLAs; raise taxes N
62. Let US invest-So Africa N
63. Approve 21 MX for 1985 N
64. Emergency Farm Credit Y
65. Awards to whistle blowers Y
66. African disaster relief Y
67. Ban bank loans to So Afr Y
68. Bar coun duty-free trtmt N
69. Steel import limits N
70. Soc Sec COLAs=inflation Y
71. Bar haz waste vctms suits Y
72. Prohibit aid to Nicaragua Y
73. Cut $-Schs bar sch prayer N
74. Raise taxes; Cut Medicare Y
75. Alien residncy-prior 1982 Y
76. Alien residncy-prior 1980 Y
77. Pen emp-hire illgl aliens N
78. Lmt Persh II/cruse-Europe N
79. Delete 34 B-1 bombers N
80. Bar purch of Pershing II N
81. Bar purchase of Sgt York ?
82. Delete $ for Trident II ?
83. Allow 15 MX missiles N
84. Bar MX procurement-1985 Y
85. Equal Access Act Y
86. Aid to El Salvador Y
87. Bar Nicarag water mining Y
88. Physician/Medicare freeze N
89. Increase "sin" taxes Y
90. End SBA direct loans N
91. Sell Conrail N
92. Equal Rights Amendment Y
93. Marines in Lebanon Y
94. Eminent domain-Coal comps Y
95. Prohibit EPA sanctions ?
96. SS age increase/Reforms N
97. Auto domestic content req Y
98. Delete jobs program fundg N
99. Highway-Gas tax bill Y
100. Raise Medicare;Cut defnse Y
101. Emergency housing aid Y
102. Across-the-board tax cuts Y
103. Gramm-Latta II targets Y
104. Delete B-1 bomber funds N
105. Dsapprov Saudi AWACS sale Y
106. Disapprove oil import fee Y
107. Rail Deregulation Y
108. Dsapp India nuc fuel sale Y
109. Mil draft registration Y
110. Chrysler Loan Guarantees N
111. Prohibit school busing Y
112. Nuclear plant moratorium N
113. Oil price controls N

Presidential Support Score: 1986 - 26% 1985 - 41%

SHAW, E. CLAY, Jr. -- Florida 15th District [Republican]. County of Broward (pt). Prior Terms: House: 1981-86. Born: April 19, 1939; Miami, Fla. Education: Stetson University (B.A., J.D.); University of Alabama (M.A.). Occupation: Owner, wholesale nursery; assistant city attorney (1968); mayor, Fort Lauderdale (1975-81); city prosecutor (1968-69); judge (1969-71); city commissioner (1971-73); vice-mayor (1973-75); ambassador, Papua, New Guinea.

1. Immigration Reform Y
2. Open fld-search warrants N
3. Civil pnty-hire ill alien N
4. So Afr sanc-veto override N
5. Tax Overhaul Y
6. South Africa sanctions N
7. Death penalty-drug bill Y
8. Evidence-warrantless srch Y
9. Life term-second drug off Y
10. Military use in drug war Y
11. Troop reduction in Europe N
12. Prohibit chemical weapons N
13. Bar ASAT testing N
14. Abide SALT II weapons ban N
15. Follow SALT II-Soviets do Y
16. Reduce SDI funding N
17. Increase SDI funding N
18. Purchase Trident sub N

SHAW, E. CLAY, Jr. (Cont.)

19. Delete 12 MX;Add conv wpn N
20. Raise speed limit Y
21. Textile Import Quotas(*) N
22. Req Pentagon buy US goods N
23. AIDS ins anti-dscriminatn N
24. Nicaraguan refugee aid N
25. Nicaraguan contra aid Y
26. US abide by SALT II Y
27. Prohibit Saudi arms sale Y
28. Military Retiremnt Reform Y
29. Nicaraguan refugee aid Y
30. Ease '68 Gun Control Act Y
31. Bar intrstat handgun tran N
32. Keep '68 Gun Control Act N
33. Nicaraguan contra aid Y
34. Bar emp polygraph testing N
35. Tax Overhaul consideratn N
36. Bar armor-piercing ammo Y
37. Tax Overhaul consideratn N
38. Make comp emissions known N
39. Allow toxic victims suits N
40. Strike Superfund "VAT" Y
41. Notify emp-plant closing N
42. Bar emp consult-plant clo Y
43. Medicare cuts;Tax incres' N
44. Delete 12 MX missiles N
45. Spending cuts;Tax incres' N
46. Textile Import Quotas N
47. Cut some school lunch fds Y
48. Clean Water Act Amendmnts N
49. Youth work projects N
50. Assist military in Angola Y
51. Allow US troops-Nicaragua Y
52. Pentagon polygraph exams Y
53. Bar ASAT testing N
54. Suspend def pmt for abuse N
55. Bar Pentagon-contr emplmt Y
56. Increase SDI funding N
57. Reduce SDI funding N
58. Produce chemical weapons Y
59. Bar CIA fndg in Nicaragua N
60. South Africa sanctions N
61. Cut SS COLAs; raise taxes N
62. Let US invest-So Africa Y
63. Approve 21 MX for 1985 Y
64. Emergency Farm Credit Y
65. Awards to whistle blowers Y
66. African disaster relief Y
67. Ban bank loans to So Afr ?
68. Bar coun duty-free trtmt N
69. Steel import limits N
70. Soc Sec COLAs=inflation Y
71. Bar haz waste vctms suits Y
72. Prohibit aid to Nicaragua N
73. Cut $-Schs bar sch prayer ?
74. Raise taxes; Cut Medicare Y
75. Alien residncy-prior 1982 Y
76. Alien residncy-prior 1980 Y
77. Pen emp-hire illgl aliens N
78. Lmt Persh II/cruse-Europe N
79. Delete 34 B-1 bombers N
80. Bar purch of Pershing II N
81. Bar purchase of Sgt York ?
82. Delete $ for Trident II N
83. Allow 15 MX missiles Y
84. Bar MX procurement-1985 N
85. Equal Access Act Y
86. Aid to El Salvador Y
87. Bar Nicarag water mining N
88. Physician/Medicare freeze Y
89. Increase "sin" taxes Y
90. End SBA direct loans N
91. Sell Conrail Y
92. Equal Rights Amendment N
93. Marines in Lebanon Y
94. Eminent domain-Coal comps Y
95. Prohibit EPA sanctions Y
96. SS age increase/Reforms Y
97. Auto domestic content req N
98. Delete jobs program fundg Y
99. Highway-Gas tax bill Y
100. Raise Medicare;Cut defnse N
101. Emergency housing aid N
102. Across-the-board tax cuts Y
103. Gramm-Latta II targets Y
104. Delete B-1 bomber funds N
105. Dsapprov Saudi AWACS sale Y

Presidential Support Score: 1986 - 78% 1985 - 70%

SMITH, LAWRENCE J. -- Florida 16th District [Democrat]. Counties of Broward (pt.) and Dade (pt.). Prior Terms: House: 1983-1986. Born: April 25, 1941; Brooklyn, N.Y. Education: New York University; Brooklyn Law School (LL.B., J.D.). Occupation: Member, Hollywood Planning and Zoning Board (1974-77); county advisory board (1978); Florida representative (1978-82); Governors Task Force on Criminal Justice Systems (1980-1981).

1. Immigration Reform Y
2. Open fld-search warrants N
3. Civil pnty-hire ill alien N
4. So Afr sanc-veto override Y
5. Tax Overhaul Y
6. South Africa sanctions Y

SMITH, LAWRENCE J. (Cont.)

7.	Death penalty-drug bill	Y	52.	Pentagon polygraph exams	Y
8.	Evidence-warrantless srch	Y	53.	Bar ASAT testing	Y
9.	Life term-second drug off	Y	54.	Suspend def pmt for abuse	Y
10.	Military use in drug war	Y	55.	Bar Pentagon-contr emplmt	Y
11.	Troop reduction in Europe	N	56.	Increase SDI funding	?
12.	Prohibit chemical weapons	Y	57.	Reduce SDI funding	N
13.	Bar ASAT testing	Y	58.	Produce chemical weapons	N
14.	Abide SALT II weapons ban	Y	59.	Bar CIA fndg in Nicaragua	Y
15.	Follow SALT II-Soviets do	N	60.	South Africa sanctions	Y
16.	Reduce SSI funding	N	61.	Cut SS COLAs; Raise taxes	N
17.	Increase SDI funding	N	62.	Let US invest-So Africa	N
18.	Purchase Trident sub	Y	63.	Approve 21 MX for 1985	N
19.	Delete 12 MX;Add conv wpn	Y	64.	Emergency Farm Credit	Y
20.	Raise speed limit	N	65.	Awards to whistle blowers	Y
21.	Textile Import Quotas(*)	Y	66.	African disaster relief	Y
22.	Req Pentagon buy US goods	Y	67.	Ban bank loans to So Afr	Y
23.	AIDS ins anti-dscriminatn	Y	68.	Bar coun duty-free trtmt	Y
24.	Nicaraguan refugee aid	N	69.	Steel import limits	Y
25.	Nicaraguan contra aid	Y	70.	Soc Sec COLAs=inflation	Y
26.	US abide by SALT II	N	71.	Bar haz waste vctms suits	N
27.	Prohibit Saudi arms sale	Y	72.	Prohibit aid to Nicaragua	Y
28.	Military Retiremnt Reform	Y	73.	Cut $-Schs bar sch prayer	N
29.	Nicaraguan refugee aid	N	74.	Raise taxes; Cut Medicare	Y
30.	Ease '68 Gun Control Act	N	75.	Alien residncy-prior 1982	N
31.	Bar intrstat handgun tran	Y	76.	Alien residncy-prior 1980	N
32.	Keep '68 Gun Control Act	Y	77.	Pen emp-hire illgl aliens	N
33.	Nicaraguan contra aid	Y	78.	Lmt Persh II/cruse-Europe	N
34.	Bar emp polygraph testing	Y	79.	Delete 34 B-1 bombers	Y
35.	Tax Overhaul consideratn	Y	80.	Bar purch of Pershing II	N
36.	Bar armor-piercing ammo	Y	81.	Bar purchase of Sgt York	Y
37.	Tax Overhaul consideratn	Y	82.	Delete $ for Trident II	Y
38.	Make comp emissions known	Y	83.	Allow 15 MX missiles	N
39.	Allow toxic victims suits	Y	84.	Bar MX procurement-1985	Y
40.	Strike Superfund "VAT"	Y	85.	Equal Access Act	N
41.	Notify emp-plant closing	Y	86.	Aid to El Salvador	N
42.	Bar emp consult-plant clo	N	87.	Bar Nicarag water mining	Y
43.	Medicare cuts;Tax incres'	Y	88.	Physician/Medicare freeze	N
44.	Delete 12 MX missiles	Y	89.	Increase "sin" taxes	Y
45.	Spending cuts;Tax incres'	Y	90.	End SBA direct loans	N
46.	Textile Import Quotas	Y	91.	Sell Conrail	N
47.	Cut some school lunch fds	N	92.	Equal Rights Amendment	Y
48.	Clean Water Act Amendmnts	N	93.	Marines in Lebanon	Y
49.	Youth work projects	?	94.	Eminent domain-Coal comps	Y
50.	Assist military in Angola	Y	95.	Prohibit EPA sanctions	?
51.	Allow US troops-Nicaragua	N	96.	SS age increase/Reforms	N

Presidential Support Score: 1986 - 26% 1085 - 30%

LEHMAN, WILLIAM -- Florida 17th District [Democrat]. County of Dade (pt.). Prior Terms: House: 1973-1986. Born: October 5, 1913; Selma, Ala. Education: University of Alabama (B.S.). Occupation: Member, Dade County school board (1966-72).

1.	Immigration Reform	Y	7.	Death penalty-drug bill	N
2.	Open fld-search warrants	Y	8.	Evidence-warrantless srch	N
3.	Civil pnty-hire ill alien	N	9.	Life term-second drug off	N
4.	So Afr sanc-veto override	Y	10.	Military use in drug war	N
5.	Tax Overhaul	Y	11.	Troop reduction in Europe	Y
6.	South Africa sanctions	Y	12.	Prohibit chemical weapons	Y

LEHMAN, WILLIAM (Cont.)

13. Bar ASAT testing Y
14. Abide SALT II weapons ban Y
15. Follow SALT II-Soviets do N
16. Reduce SDI funding Y
17. Increase SDI funding N
18. Purchase Trident sub Y
19. Delete 12 MX;Add conv wpn Y
20. Raise speed limit N
21. Textile Import Quotas(*) Y
22. Req Pentagon buy US goods N
23. AIDS ins anti-dscriminatn Y
24. Nicaraguan refugee aid Y
25. Nicaraguan contra aid N
26. US abide by SALT II N
27. Prohibit Saudi arms sale Y
28. Military Retiremnt Reform Y
29. Nicaraguan refugee aid Y
30. Ease '68 Gun Control Act N
31. Bar intrstat handgun tran Y
32. Keep '68 Gun Control Act Y
33. Nicaraguan contra aid N
34. Bar emp polygraph testing Y
35. Tax Overhaul consideratn Y
36. Bar armor-piercing ammo Y
37. Tax Overhaul consideratn Y
38. Make comp emissions known Y
39. Allow toxic victims suits Y
40. Strike Superfund "VAT" Y
41. Notify emp-plant closing Y
42. Bar emp consult-plant clo N
43. Medicare cuts;Tax incres' Y
44. Delete 12 MX missiles Y
45. Spending cuts;Tax incres' Y
46. Textile Import Quotas Y
47. Cut some school lunch fds N
48. Clean Water Act Amendmnts N
49. Youth work projects Y
50. Assist military in Angola N
51. Allow US troops-Nicaragua N
52. Pentagon polygraph exams N
53. Bar ASAT testing Y
54. Suspend def pmt for abuse Y
55. Bar Pentagon-contr emplmt Y
56. Increase SDI funding N
57. Reduce SDI funding Y
58. Produce chemical weapons N
59. Bar CIA fndg in Nicaragua Y
60. South Africa sanctions Y
61. Cut SS COLAs; Raise taxes N
62. Let US invest-So Africa N
63. Approve 21 MX for 1985 N
64. Emergency Farm Credit Y
65. Awards to whistle blowers Y
66. African disaster relief Y
67. Ban bank loans to So Afr Y
68. Bar coun duty-free trtmt Y
69. Steel import limits Y
70. Soc Sec COLAs=inflation Y
71. Bar haz waste vctms suits N
72. Prohibit aid to Nicaragua Y
73. Cut $-Schs bar sch prayer N
74. Raise taxes; Cut Medicare Y
75. Alien residncy-prior 1982 Y
76. Alien residncy-prior 1980 N
77. Pen emp-hire illgl aliens Y
78. Lmt Persh II/cruse-Europe Y
79. Delete 34 B-1 bombers Y
80. Bar purch of Pershing II Y
81. Bar purchase of Sgt York ?
82. Delete $ for Trident II Y
83. Allow 15 MX missiles N
84. Bar MX procurement-1985 Y
85. Equal Access Act N
86. Aid to El Salvador N
87. Bar Nicarag water mining Y
88. Physician/Medicare freeze N
89. Increase "sin" taxes Y
90. End SBA direct loans N
91. Sell Conrail N
92. Equal Rights Amendment Y
93. Marines in Lebanon Y
94. Eminent domain-Coal comps Y
95. Prohibit EPA sanctions ?
96. SS age increase/Reforms N
97. Auto domestic content req ?
98. Delete jobs program fundg ?
99. Highway-Gas tax bill ?
100. Raise Medicare;Cut defnse Y
101. Emergency housing aid Y
102. Across-the-board tax cuts N
103. Gramm-Latta II targets N
104. Delete B-1 bomber funds Y
105. Dsapprov Saudi AWACS sale Y
106. Disapprove oil import fee N
107. Rail Deregulation ?
108. Dsapp India nuc fuel sale Y
109. Mil draft registration Y
110. Chrysler Loan Guarantees ?
111. Prohibit school busing N
112. Nuclear plant moratorium N
113. Oil price controls N
114. Tuition Tax Credits N
115. Est Consumer Protect Agcy Y
116. Eliminate B-1 bomber fnds Y
117. Subminimum wage for youth N
118. Delete crude oil tax N
119. Natural gas deregulation N

Presidential Support Score: 1986 - 21% 1985 - 23%

PEPPER, CLAUDE -- Florida 18th District [Democrat]. County of Dade (pt.). Prior Terms: Senate: 1936 (Special Election)-1950;

PEPPER, CLAUDE (Cont.)

House: 1963-86. Born: September 8, 1900; Dudleyville, Ala. Education: University of Alabama (A.B.); Harvard Law School (LL.B.). Military Service: Students' Army Training Corps, 1918. Occupation: Teacher; attorney; Florida representative (1929-30); member, Florida State Board of Public Welfare (1931-32); member, Florida State Board of Law Examiners (1933-1934).

1. Immigration Reform Y
2. Open fld-search warrants Y
3. Civil pnty-hire ill alien N
4. So Afr sanc-veto override Y
5. Tax Overhaul Y
6. South Africa sanctions +
7. Death penalty-drug bill N
8. Evidence-warrantless srch N
9. Life term-second drug off Y
10. Military use in drug war N
11. Troop reduction in Europe N
12. Prohibit chemical weapons Y
13. Bar ASAT testing Y
14. Abide SALT II weapons ban Y
15. Follow SALT II-Soviets do N
16. Reduce SDI funding N
17. Increase SDI funding N
18. Purchase Trident sub Y
19. Delete 12 MX;Add conv wpn X
20. Raise speed limit N
21. Textile Import Quotas(*) #
22. Req Pentagon buy US goods ?
23. AIDS ins anti-dscriminatn Y
24. Nicaraguan refugee aid N
25. Nicaraguan contra aid Y
26. US abide by SALT II N
27. Prohibit Saudi arms sale Y
28. Military Retiremnt Reform Y
29. Nicaraguan refugee aid N
30. Ease '68 Gun Control Act N
31. Bar intrstat handgun tran Y
32. Keep '68 Gun Control Act Y
33. Nicaraguan contra aid Y
34. Bar emp polygraph testing Y
35. Tax Overhaul consideratn Y
36. Bar armor-piercing ammo Y
37. Tax Overhaul consideratn Y
38. Make comp emissions known Y
39. Allow toxic victims suits Y
40. Strike Superfund "VAT" Y
41. Notify emp-plant closing Y
42. Bar emp consult-plant clo N
43. Medicare cuts;Tax incres' Y
44. Delete 12 MX missiles N
45. Spending cuts;Tax incres' Y
46. Textile Import Quotas Y
47. Cut some school lunch fds N
48. Clean Water Act Amendmnts N
49. Youth work projects Y
50. Assist military in Angola Y
51. Allow US troops-Nicaragua N
52. Pentagon polygraph exams +
53. Bar ASAT testing Y
54. Suspend def pmt for abuse Y
55. Bar Pentagon-contr emplmt +
56. Increase SDI funding -
57. Reduce SDI funding X
58. Produce chemical weapons #
59. Bar CIA fndg in Nicaragua Y
60. South Africa sanctions Y
61. Cut SS COLAs; Raise taxes N
62. Let US invest-So Africa N
63. Approve 21 MX for 1985 Y
64. Emergency Farm Credit Y
65. Awards to whistle blowers Y
66. African disaster relief Y
67. Ban bank loans to So Afr Y
68. Bar coun duty-free trtmt Y
69. Steel import limits Y
70. Soc Sec COLAs=inflation Y
71. Bar haz waste vctms suits N
72. Prohibit aid to Nicaragua Y
73. Cut $-Schs bar sch prayer N
74. Raise taxes; Cut Medicare Y
75. Alien residncy-prior 1982 N
76. Alien residncy-prior 1980 N
77. Pen emp-hire illgl aliens Y
78. Lmt Persh II/cruse-Europe N
79. Delete 34 B-1 bombers N
80. Bar purch of Pershing II N
81. Bar purchase of Sgt York X
82. Delete $ for Trident II N
83. Allow 15 MX missiles Y
84. Bar MX procurement-1985 N
85. Equal Access Act N
86. Aid to El Salvador N
87. Bar Nicarag water mining Y
88. Physician/Medicare freeze N
89. Increase "sin" taxes Y
90. End SBA direct loans N
91. Sell Conrail N
92. Equal Rights Amendment Y
93. Marines in Lebanon Y
94. Eminent domain-Coal comps N
95. Prohibit EPA sanctions N
96. SS age increase/Reforms N
97. Auto domestic content req Y
98. Delete jobs program fundg N
99. Highway-Gas tax bill Y
100. Raise Medicare;Cut defnse Y
101. Emergency housing aid Y
102. Across-the-board tax cuts N

PEPPER, CLAUDE (Cont.)

103. Gramm-Latta II targets N
104. Delete B-1 bomber funds X
105. Dsapprov Saudi AWACS sale #
106. Disapprove oil import fee Y
107. Rail Deregulation X
108. Dsapp India nuc fuel sale ?
109. Mil draft registration ?
110. Chrysler Loan Guarantees Y
111. Prohibit school busing N
112. Nuclear plant moratorium N
113. Oil price controls N
114. Tuition Tax Credits N
115. Est Consumer Protect Agcy Y
116. Eliminate B-1 bomber fnds Y
117. Subminimum wage for youth N
118. Delete crude oil tax N
119. Natural gas deregulation N

Presidential Support Score: 1986 - 31% 1985 - 26%

FASCELL, DANTE B. -- Florida 19th District [Democrat]. Counties of Dade (pt.) and Monroe. Prior Terms: House: 1955-86. Born: March 9, 1917; Bridgehampton, Long Island, N.Y. Education: University of Miami (J.D.). Military Service: Florida National Guard, 1941-46; U.S. Armed Forces. Occupation: Florida representative (1950-54).

1. Immigration Reform Y
2. Open fld-search warrants Y
3. Civil pnty-hire ill alien N
4. So Afr sanc-veto override Y
5. Tax Overhaul Y
6. South Africa sanctions Y
7. Death penalty-drug bill Y
8. Evidence-warrantless srch Y
9. Life term-second drug off Y
10. Military use in drug war N
11. Troop reduction in Europe N
12. Prohibit chemical weapons Y
13. Bar ASAT testing Y
14. Abide SALT II weapons ban Y
15. Follow SALT II-Soviets do N
16. Reduce SDI funding N
17. Increase SDI funding N
18. Purchase Trident sub Y
19. Delete 12 MX;Add conv wpn Y
20. Raise speed limit N
21. Textile Import Quotas(*) Y
22. Req Pentagon buy US goods N
23. AIDS ins anti-dscriminatn Y
24. Nicaraguan refugee aid N
25. Nicaraguan contra aid Y
26. US abide by SALT II N
27. Prohibit Saudi arms sale Y
28. Military Retiremnt Reform Y
29. Nicaraguan refugee aid N
30. Ease '68 Gun Control Act N
31. Bar intrstat handgun tran Y
32. Keep '68 Gun Control Act Y
33. Nicaraguan contra aid Y
34. Bar emp polygraph testing Y
35. Tax Overhaul consideratn Y
36. Bar armor-piercing ammo Y
37. Tax Overhaul consideratn Y
38. Make comp emissions known Y
39. Allow toxic victims suits Y
40. Strike Superfund "VAT" Y
41. Notify emp-plant closing Y
42. Bar emp consult-plant clo N
43. Medicare cuts;Tax incres' Y
44. Delete 12 MX missiles N
45. Spending cuts;Tax incres' Y
46. Textile Import Quotas Y
47. Cut some school lunch fds N
48. Clean Water Act Amendmnts N
49. Youth work projects Y
50. Assist military in Angola Y
51. Allow US troops-Nicaragua N
52. Pentagon polygraph exams Y
53. Bar ASAT testing Y
54. Suspend def pmt for abuse N
55. Bar Pentagon-contr emplmt Y
56. Increase SDI funding N
57. Reduce SDI funding N
58. Produce chemical weapons N
59. Bar CIA fndg in Nicaragua N
60. South Africa sanctions Y
61. Cut SS COLAs; Raise taxes N
62. Let US invest-So Africa N
63. Approve 21 MX for 1985 N
64. Emergency Farm Credit Y
65. Awards to whistle blowers ?
66. African disaster relief ?
67. Ban bank loans to So Afr Y
68. Bar coun duty-free trtmt Y
69. Steel import limits Y
70. Soc Sec COLAs=inflation Y
71. Bar haz waste vctms suits N
72. Prohibit aid to Nicaragua Y
73. Cut $-Schs bar sch prayer N
74. Raise taxes; Cut Medicare Y
75. Alien residncy-prior 1982 Y
76. Alien residncy-prior 1980 N
77. Pen emp-hire illgl aliens N
78. Lmt Persh II/cruse-Europe N
79. Delete 34 B-1 bombers Y
80. Bar purch of Pershing II N

FASCELL, DANTE B. (Cont.)

81. Bar purchase of Sgt York Y
82. Delete $ for Trident II N
83. Allow 15 MX missiles N
84. Bar MX procurement-1985 Y
85. Equal Access Act N
86. Aid to El Salvador N
87. Bar Nicarag water mining Y
88. Physician/Medicare freeze N
89. Increase "sin" taxes Y
90. End SBA direct loans N
91. Sell Conrail N
92. Equal Rights Amendment Y
93. Marines in Lebanon Y
94. Eminent domain-Coal comps Y
95. Prohibit EPA sanctions Y
96. SS age increase/Reforms N
97. Auto domestic content req Y
98. Delete jobs program fundg N
99. Highway-Gas tax bill ?
100. Raise Medicare;Cut defnse Y
101. Emergency housing aid N
102. Across-the-board tax cuts N
103. Gramm-Latta II targets N
104. Delete B-1 bomber funds Y
105. Dsapprov Saudi AWACS sale Y
106. Disapprove oil import fee N
107. Rail Deregulation Y
108. Dsapp India nuc fuel sale Y
109. Mil draft registration Y
110. Chrysler Loan Guarantees Y
111. Prohibit school busing N
112. Nuclear plant moratorium ?
113. Oil price controls ?
114. Tuition Tax Credits N
115. Est Consumer Protect Agcy Y
116. Eliminate B-1 bomber fnds Y
117. Subminimum wage for youth N
118. Delete crude oil tax N
119. Natural gas deregulation N

Presidential Support Score: 1986 - 28% 1985 - 34%

GEORGIA

THOMAS, ROBERT LINDSAY -- Georgia 1st District [Democrat]. Counties of Brantley, Bryan, Bulloch, Burke, Camden, Candler, Chatham, Effingham, Emanuel, Evans, Glynn, Jenkins, Liberty, Long, McIntosh, Montgomery, Screven, Tattnall, Toombs and Wayne. Prior Terms: House: 1983-86. Born: November 20, 1943; Patterson, Ga. Education: University of Georgia. Military Service: Georgia Air National Guard. Occupation: Banker (1965-73); farmer; vice president and member, Wayne County Farm Bureau.

1. Immigration Reform Y
2. Open fld-search warrants Y
3. Civil pnty-hire ill alien N
4. So Afr sanc-veto override Y
5. Tax Overhaul N
6. South Africa sanctions Y
7. Death penalty-drug bill Y
8. Evidence-warrantless srch Y
9. Life term-second drug off Y
10. Military use in drug war Y
11. Troop reduction in Europe N
12. Prohibit chemical weapons N
13. Bar ASAT testing N
14. Abide SALT II weapons ban N
15. Follow SALT II-Soviets do Y
16. Reduce SDI funding N
17. Increase SDI funding N
18. Purchase Trident sub Y
19. Delete 12 MX;Add conv wpn N
20. Raise speed limit N
21. Textile Import Quotas(*) Y
22. Req Pentagon buy US goods N
23. AIDS ins anti-dscriminatn Y
24. Nicaraguan refugee aid N
25. Nicaraguan contra aid Y
26. US abide by SALT II Y
27. Prohibit Saudi arms sale Y
28. Military Retiremnt Reform Y
29. Nicaraguan refugee aid N
30. Ease '68 Gun Control Act Y
31. Bar intrstat handgun tran N
32. Keep '68 Gun Control Act N
33. Nicaraguan contra aid Y
34. Bar emp polygraph testing N
35. Tax Overhaul consideratn Y
36. Bar armor-piercing ammo Y
37. Tax Overhaul consideratn Y
38. Make comp emissions known Y
39. Allow toxic victims suits N
40. Strike Superfund "VAT" N
41. Notify emp-plant closing N
42. Bar emp consult-plant clo Y
43. Medicare cuts;Tax incres' Y
44. Delete 12 MX missiles N
45. Spending cuts;Tax incres' Y
46. Textile Import Quotas Y

THOMAS, ROBERT LINDSAY (Cont.)

47. Cut some school lunch fds N
48. Clean Water Act Amendmnts N
49. Youth work projects N
50. Assist military in Angola Y
51. Allow US troops-Nicaragua Y
52. Pentagon polygraph exams Y
53. Bar ASAT testing N
54. Suspend def pmt for abuse N
55. Bar Pentagon-contr emplmt Y
56. Increase SDI funding N
57. Reduce SDI funding N
58. Produce chemical weapons Y
59. Bar CIA fndg in Nicaragua N
60. South Africa sanctions Y
61. Cut SS COLAs; Raise taxes Y
62. Let US invest-So Africa N
63. Approve 21 MX for 1985 Y
64. Emergency Farm Credit Y
65. Awards to whistle blowers Y
66. African disaster relief Y
67. Ban bank loans to So Afr Y
68. Bar coun duty-free trtmt N
69. Steel import limits Y
70. Soc Sec COLAs=inflation Y
71. Bar haz waste vctms suits N
72. Prohibit aid to Nicaragua Y
73. Cut $-Schs bar sch prayer Y
74. Raise taxes; Cut Medicare Y
75. Alien residncy-prior 1982 Y
76. Alien residncy-prior 1980 Y
77. Pen emp-hire illgl aliens N
78. Lmt Persh II/cruse-Europe N
79. Delete 34 B-1 bombers N
80. Bar purch of Pershing II N
81. Bar purchase of Sgt York N
82. Delete $ for Trident II N
83. Allow 15 MX missiles Y
84. Bar MX procurement-1985 N
85. Equal Access Act Y
86. Aid to El Salvador Y
87. Bar Nicarag water mining Y
88. Physician/Medicare freeze N
89. Increase "sin" taxes Y
90. End SBA direct loans N
91. Sell Conrail N
92. Equal Rights Amendment N
93. Marines in Lebanon Y
94. Eminent domain-Coal comps N
95. Prohibit EPA sanctions N
96. SS age increase/Reforms Y

Presidential Support Score: 1986 - 47% 1985 - 50%

HATCHER, CHARLES -- Georgia 2nd District [Democrat]. Counties of Baker, Ben Hill, Berrien, Brooks, Calhoun, Clay, Colquitt, Cook, Criso, Daugherty, Decatur, Early, Echols, Grady, Irwin, Lanier, Lee, Lowndes, Miller, Mitchell, Quitman, Randolph, Seminole, Stewart, Terrell, Thomas, Tift, Turner, Webster and Worth. Prior Terms: House: 1981-86. Born: July 1, 1939; Doerun, Ga. Education: Georgia Southern College (B.S.); University of Georgia (J.D.). Military Service: U.S. Air Force, 1958-62. Occupation: Attorney; teacher; Georgia representative (1973-80); governor's assistant.

1. Immigration Reform Y
2. Open fld-search warrants Y
3. Civil pnty-hire ill alien Y
4. So Afr sanc-veto override ?
5. Tax Overhaul Y
6. South Africa sanctions Y
7. Death penalty-drug bill Y
8. Evidence-warrantless srch Y
9. Life term-second drug off Y
10. Military use in drug war Y
11. Troop reduction in Europe ?
12. Prohibit chemical weapons N
13. Bar ASAT testing N
14. Abide SALT II weapons ban N
15. Follow SALT II-Soviets do Y
16. Reduce SDI funding N
17. Increase SDI funding N
18. Purchase Trident sub N
19. Delete 12 MX;Add conv wpn N
20. Raise speed limit Y
21. Textile Import Quotas(*) Y
22. Req Pentagon buy US goods N
23. AIDS ins anti-dscriminatn Y
24. Nicaraguan refugee aid N
25. Nicaraguan contra aid Y
26. US abide by SALT II ?
27. Prohibit Saudi arms sale Y
28. Military Retiremnt Reform Y
29. Nicaraguan refugee aid N
30. Ease '68 Gun Control Act Y
31. Bar intrstat handgun tran Y
32. Keep '68 Gun Control Act Y
33. Nicaraguan contra aid Y
34. Bar emp polygraph testing ?
35. Tax Overhaul consideratn Y
36. Bar armor-piercing ammo Y
37. Tax Overhaul consideratn Y
38. Make comp emissions known N
39. Allow toxic victims suits N
40. Strike Superfund "VAT" N

HATCHER, CHARLES (Cont.)

41. Notify emp-plant closing N
42. Bar emp consult-plant clo Y
43. Medicare cuts;Tax incres' Y
44. Delete 12 MX missiles N
45. Spending cuts;Tax incres' Y
46. Textile Import Quotas Y
47. Cut some school lunch fds N
48. Clean Water Act Amendmnts ?
49. Youth work projects ?
50. Assist military in Angola Y
51. Allow US troops-Nicaragua Y
52. Pentagon polygraph exams ?
53. Bar ASAT testing N
54. Suspend def pmt for abuse N
55. Bar Pentagon-contr emplmt Y
56. Increase SDI funding N
57. Reduce SDI funding N
58. Produce chemical weapons Y
59. Bar CIA fndg in Nicaragua N
60. South Africa sanctions Y
61. Cut SS COLAs; Raise taxes N
62. Let US invest-So Africa N
63. Approve 21 MX for 1985 Y
64. Emergency Farm Credit Y
65. Awards to whistle blowers ?
66. African disaster relief ?
67. Ban bank loans to So Afr Y
68. Bar coun duty-free trtmt Y
69. Steel import limits Y
70. Soc Sec COLAs=inflation Y
71. Bar haz waste vctms suits ?
72. Prohibit aid to Nicaragua Y
73. Cut $-Schs bar sch prayer ?
74. Raise taxes; Cut Medicare Y
75. Alien residncy-prior 1982 Y
76. Alien residncy-prior 1980 Y
77. Pen emp-hire illgl aliens N
78. Lmt Persh II/cruse-Europe ?
79. Delete 34 B-1 bombers N
80. Bar purch of Pershing II N
81. Bar purchase of Sgt York N
82. Delete $ for Trident II N
83. Allow 15 MX missiles Y
84. Bar MX procurement-1985 N
85. Equal Access Act Y
86. Aid to El Salvador Y
87. Bar Nicarag water mining Y
88. Physician/Medicare freeze N
89. Increase "sin" taxes Y
90. End SBA direct loans N
91. Sell Conrail N
92. Equal Rights Amendment Y
93. Marines in Lebanon Y
94. Eminent domain-Coal comps N
95. Prohibit EPA sanctions N
96. SS age increase/Reforms Y
97. Auto domestic content req Y
98. Delete jobs program fundg N
99. Highway-Gas tax bill N
100. Raise Medicare;Cut defnse N
101. Emergency housing aid Y
102. Across-the-board tax cuts Y
103. Gramm-Latta II targets Y
104. Delete B-1 bomber funds N
105. Dsapprov Saudi AWACS sale Y

Presidential Support Score: 1986 - 34% 1985 - 49%

RAY, RICHARD -- Georgia 3rd District [Democrat]. Counties of Bleckley, Butts, Chattahoochee, Crawford, Dooly, Harris, Houston, Lamar, Macon, Marion, Meriwether, Muscogee, Peach, Pike, Pulaski, Schley, Sumter, Talbot, Taylor, Troup and Upson. Prior Terms: House: 1983-86. Born: February 27, 1927; Fort Valley, Ga. Military Service: U.S. Navy. Occupation: Worked family farm; established painting, pest control, and professional consulting service; councilman (1962); mayor (1964, 1966 and 1968); Senate administrative assistant (1972-1982.)

1. Immigration Reform N
2. Open fld-search warrants Y
3. Civil pnty-hire ill alien N
4. So Afr sanc-veto override Y
5. Tax Overhaul N
6. South Africa sanctions Y
7. Death penalty-drug bill Y
8. Evidence-warrantless srch Y
9. Life term-second drug off Y
10. Military use in drug war N
11. Troop reduction in Europe N
12. Prohibit chemical weapons N
13. Bar ASAT testing N
14. Abide SALT II weapons ban N
15. Follow SALT II-Soviets do Y
16. Reduce SDI funding N
17. Increase SDI funding N
18. Purchase Trident sub N
19. Delete 12 MX;Add conv wpn N
20. Raise speed limit N
21. Textile Import Quotas(*) Y
22. Req Pentagon buy US goods N
23. AIDS ins anti-dscriminatn N
24. Nicaraguan refugee aid N

RAY, RICHARD (Cont.)

25. Nicaraguan contra aid Y
26. US abide by SALT II Y
27. Prohibit Saudi arms sale N
28. Military Retiremnt Reform Y
29. Nicaraguan refugee aid N
30. Ease '68 Gun Control Act Y
31. Bar intrstat handgun tran N
32. Keep '68 Gun Control Act N
33. Nicaraguan contra aid N
34. Bar emp polygraph testing N
35. Tax Overhaul consideratn N
36. Bar armor-piercing ammo Y
37. Tax Overhaul consideratn N
38. Make comp emissions known N
39. Allow toxic victims suits N
40. Strike Superfund "VAT" N
41. Notify emp-plant closing N
42. Bar emp consult-plant clo Y
43. Medicare cuts;Tax incres' Y
44. Delete 12 MX missiles N
45. Spending cuts;Tax incres' Y
46. Textile Import Quotas Y
47. Cut some school lunch fds Y
48. Clean Water Act Amendmnts Y
49. Youth work projects N
50. Assist military in Angola Y
51. Allow US troops-Nicaragua Y
52. Pentagon polygraph exams Y
53. Bar ASAT testing N
54. Suspend def pmt for abuse N
55. Bar Pentagon-contr emplmt Y
56. Increase SDI funding N
57. Reduce SDI funding N
58. Produce chemical weapons Y
59. Bar CIA fndg in Nicaragua N
60. South Africa sanctions Y
61. Cut SS COLAs; Raise taxes Y
62. Let US invest-So Africa N
63. Approve 21 MX for 1985 Y
64. Emergency Farm Credit Y
65. Awards to whistle blowers Y
66. African disaster relief Y
67. Ban bank loans to So Afr Y
68. Bar coun duty-free trtmt N
69. Steel import limits N
70. Soc Sec COLAs=inflation Y
71. Bar haz waste vctms suits Y
72. Prohibit aid to Nicaragua N
73. Cut $-Schs bar sch prayer Y
74. Raise taxes; Cut Medicare Y
75. Alien residncy-prior 1982 Y
76. Alien residncy-prior 1980 Y
77. Pen emp-hire illgl aliens N
78. Lmt Persh II/cruse-Europe N
79. Delete 34 B-1 bombers N
80. Bar purch of Pershing II X
81. Bar purchase of Sgt York N
82. Delete $ for Trident II N
83. Allow 15 MX missiles Y
84. Bar MX procurement-1985 N
85. Equal Access Act Y
86. Aid to El Salvador Y
87. Bar Nicarag water mining N
88. Physician/Medicare freeze N
89. Increase "sin" taxes Y
90. End SBA direct loans Y
91. Sell Conrail N
92. Equal Rights Amendment N
93. Marines in Lebanon N
94. Eminent domain-Coal comps N
95. Prohibit EPA sanctions Y
96. SS age increase/Reforms Y

Presidential Support Score: 1986 - 56% 1985 - 56%

SWINDALL, PAT -- Georgia 4th District [Republican]. Counties of De Kalb (pt.), Fulton (pt.), Newton and Rockdale. Prior Terms: House: 1985-86. Education: University of Georgia (J.D.). Occupation: Attorney; owner, furniture company.

1. Immigration Reform N
2. Open fld-search warrants N
3. Civil pnty-hire ill alien N
4. So Afr sanc-veto override N
5. Tax Overhaul N
6. South Africa sanctions N
7. Death penalty-drug bill Y
8. Evidence-warrantless srch Y
9. Life term-second drug off Y
10. Military use in drug war Y
11. Troop reduction in Europe N
12. Prohibit chemical weapons N
13. Bar ASAT testing N
14. Abide SALT II weapons ban N
15. Follow SALT II-Soviets do Y
16. Reduce SDI funding N
17. Increase SDI funding Y
18. Purchase Trident sub N
19. Delete 12 MX;Add conv wpn N
20. Raise speed limit Y
21. Textile Import Quotas(*) Y
22. Req Pentagon buy US goods N
23. AIDS ins anti-dscriminatn N
24. Nicaraguan refugee aid N
25. Nicaraguan contra aid Y
26. US abide by SALT II Y
27. Prohibit Saudi arms sale Y
28. Military Retiremnt Reform Y
29. Nicaraguan refugee aid Y
30. Ease '68 Gun Control Act Y

SWINDALL, PAT (Cont.)

31. Bar intrstat handgun tran N
32. Keep '68 Gun Control Act N
33. Nicaraguan contra aid Y
34. Bar emp polygraph testing N
35. Tax Overhaul consideratn N
36. Bar armor-piercing ammo Y
37. Tax Overhaul consideratn N
38. Make comp emissions known N
39. Allow toxic victims suits N
40. Strike Superfund "VAT" N
41. Notify emp-plant closing N
42. Bar emp consult-plant clo Y
43. Medicare cuts;Tax incres' N
44. Delete 12 MX missiles N
45. Spending cuts;Tax incres' N
46. Textile Import Quotas Y
47. Cut some school lunch fds Y
48. Clean Water Act Amendmnts Y
49. Youth work projects N
50. Assist military in Angola Y
51. Allow US troops-Nicaragua Y
52. Pentagon polygraph exams Y
53. Bar ASAT testing N
54. Suspend def pmt for abuse N
55. Bar Pentagon-contr emplmt Y
56. Increase SDI funding Y
57. Reduce SDI funding N
58. Produce chemical weapons Y
59. Bar CIA fndg in Nicaragua N
60. South Africa sanctions N
61. Cut SS COLAs; Raise taxes N
62. Let US invest-So Africa Y
63. Approve 21 MX for 1985 Y
64. Emergency Farm Credit N
65. Awards to whistle blowers Y
66. African disaster relief N

Presidential Support Score: 1986 - 82% 1985 - 79%

FOWLER, WYCHE, Jr. -- Georgia 5th District [Democrat]. Counties of De Kalb (pt.) and Fulton (pt.). Prior Terms: House: 1977 (Special Election)-1986. Born: October 6, 1940; Atlanta, Ga. Education: Davidson College (A.B.); Emory University (J.D.). Military Service: U.S. Army, 1962-63. Occupation: Attorney; Atlanta alderman (1970-74); president, Atlanta City Council.

1. Immigration Reform ?
2. Open fld-search warrants ?
3. Civil pnty-hire ill alien ?
4. So Afr sanc-veto override ?
5. Tax Overhaul Y
6. South Africa sanctions Y
7. Death penalty-drug bill Y
8. Evidence-warrantless srch Y
9. Life term-second drug off Y
10. Military use in drug war ?
11. Troop reduction in Europe ?
12. Prohibit chemical weapons ?
13. Bar ASAT testing ?
14. Abide SALT II weapons ban ?
15. Follow SALT II-Soviets do ?
16. Reduce SDI funding ?
17. Increase SDI funding ?
18. Purchase Trident sub ?
19. Delete 12 MX;Add conv wpn ?
20. Raise speed limit ?
21. Textile Import Quotas(*) Y
22. Req Pentagon buy US goods ?
23. AIDS ins anti-dscriminatn ?
24. Nicaraguan refugee aid Y
25. Nicaraguan contra aid N
26. US abide by SALT II N
27. Prohibit Saudi arms sale Y
28. Military Retiremnt Reform Y
29. Nicaraguan refugee aid Y
30. Ease '68 Gun Control Act Y
31. Bar intrstat handgun tran Y
32. Keep '68 Gun Control Act N
33. Nicaraguan contra aid N
34. Bar emp polygraph testing N
35. Tax Overhaul consideratn Y
36. Bar armor-piercing ammo Y
37. Tax Overhaul consideratn N
38. Make comp emissions known Y
39. Allow toxic victims suits N
40. Strike Superfund "VAT" N
41. Notify emp-plant closing N
42. Bar emp consult-plant clo ?
43. Medicare cuts;Tax incres' Y
44. Delete 12 MX missiles Y
45. Spending cuts;Tax incres' Y
46. Textile Import Quotas Y
47. Cut some school lunch fds N
48. Clean Water Act Amendmnts N
49. Youth work projects Y
50. Assist military in Angola Y
51. Allow US troops-Nicaragua N
52. Pentagon polygraph exams Y
53. Bar ASAT testing Y
54. Suspend def pmt for abuse N
55. Bar Pentagon-contr emplmt Y
56. Increase SDI funding N
57. Reduce SDI funding N
58. Produce chemical weapons N
59. Bar CIA fndg in Nicaragua Y
60. South Africa sanctions Y
61. Cut SS COLAs; Raise taxes N
62. Let US invest-So Africa N

FOWLER, WYCHE, Jr. (Cont.)

63. Approve 21 MX for 1985 N
64. Emergency Farm Credit Y
65. Awards to whistle blowers Y
66. African disaster relief Y
67. Ban bank loans to So Afr Y
68. Bar coun duty-free trtmt N
69. Steel import limits Y
70. Soc Sec COLAs=inflation ?
71. Bar haz waste vctms suits N
72. Prohibit aid to Nicaragua Y
73. Cut $-Schs bar sch prayer Y
74. Raise taxes; Cut Medicare Y
75. Alien residncy-prior 1982 Y
76. Alien residncy-prior 1980 Y
77. Pen emp-hire illgl aliens Y
78. Lmt Persh II/cruse-Europe N
79. Delete 34 B-1 bombers Y
80. Bar purch of Pershing II ?
81. Bar purchase of Sgt York N
82. Delete $ for Trident II N
83. Allow 15 MX missiles N
84. Bar MX procurement-1985 Y
85. Equal Access Act Y
86. Aid to El Salvador N
87. Bar Nicarag water mining Y
88. Physician/Medicare freeze N
89. Increase "sin" taxes Y
90. End SBA direct loans ?
91. Sell Conrail N
92. Equal Rights Amendment Y
93. Marines in Lebanon Y
94. Eminent domain-Coal comps N
95. Prohibit EPA sanctions N
96. SS age increase/Reforms N
97. Auto domestic content req Y
98. Delete jobs program fundg Y
99. Highway-Gas tax bill Y
100. Raise Medicare;Cut defnse Y
101. Emergency housing aid Y
102. Across-the-board tax cuts N
103. Gramm-Latta II targets N
104. Delete B-1 bomber funds Y
105. Dsapprov Saudi AWACS sale #
106. Disapprove oil import fee ?
107. Rail Deregulation N
108. Dsapp India nuc fuel sale Y
109. Mil draft registration Y
110. Chrysler Loan Guarantees Y
111. Prohibit school busing N
112. Nuclear plant moratorium Y
113. Oil price controls N
114. Tuition Tax Credits N
115. Est Consumer Protect Agcy Y
116. Eliminate B-1 bomber fnds Y
117. Subminimum wage for youth N
118. Delete crude oil tax N
119. Natural gas deregulation N

Presidential Support Score: 1986 - 17% 1985 - 24%

GINGRICH, NEWT -- Georgia 6th District [Republican]. Counties of Carroll, Clayton, Coweta, Douglas, Fayette, Fulton (pt.), Haralson, Heard, Henry, Paulding, Polk and Spalding. Prior Terms: House: 1979-86. Born: June 7, 1943; Harrisburg, Pa. Education: Emory University (B.A.); Tulane University (M.A., Ph.D.). Occupation: Assistant professor, West Georgia College.

1. Immigration Reform Y
2. Open fld-search warrants Y
3. Civil pnty-hire ill alien N
4. So Afr sanc-veto override Y
5. Tax Overhaul Y
6. South Africa sanctions Y
7. Death penalty-drug bill Y
8. Evidence-warrantless srch Y
9. Life term-second drug off Y
10. Military use in drug war Y
11. Troop reduction in Europe N
12. Prohibit chemical weapons N
13. Bar ASAT testing N
14. Abide SALT II weapons ban ?
15. Follow SALT II-Soviets do Y
16. Reduce SDI funding N
17. Increase SDI funding Y
18. Purchase Trident sub N
19. Delete 12 MX;Add conv wpn N
20. Raise speed limit Y
21. Textile Import Quotas(*) Y
22. Req Pentagon buy US goods N
23. AIDS ins anti-dscriminatn N
24. Nicaraguan refugee aid N
25. Nicaraguan contra aid Y
26. US abide by SALT II Y
27. Prohibit Saudi arms sale Y
28. Military Retiremnt Reform Y
29. Nicaraguan refugee aid Y
30. Ease '68 Gun Control Act Y
31. Bar intrstat handgun tran N
32. Keep '68 Gun Control Act N
33. Nicaraguan contra aid Y
34. Bar emp polygraph testing N
35. Tax Overhaul consideratn N
36. Bar armor-piercing ammo Y
37. Tax Overhaul consideratn N
38. Make Comp emissions known N

GINGRICH, NEWT (Cont).

39. Allow toxic victims suits N
40. Strike Superfund "VAT" N
41. Notify emp-plant closing N
42. Bar emp consult-plant clo Y
43. Medicare cuts;Tax incres' N
44. Delete 12 MX missiles N
45. Spending cuts;Tax incres' N
46. Textile Import Quotas Y
47. Cut some school lunch fds Y
48. Clean Water Act Amendmnts Y
49. Youth work projects N
50. Assist military in Angola Y
51. Allow US troops-Nicaragua Y
52. Pentagon polygraph exams Y
53. Bar ASAT testing N
54. Suspend def pmt for abuse N
55. Bar Pentagon-contr emplmt Y
56. Increase SDI funding Y
57. Reduce SDI funding N
58. Produce chemical weapons Y
59. Bar CIA fndg in Nicaragua N
60. South Africa sanctions N
61. Cut SS COLAs; Raise taxes N
62. Let US invest-So Africa Y
63. Approve 21 MX for 1985 Y
64. Emergency Farm Credit Y
65. Awards to whistle blowers Y
66. African disaster relief Y
67. Ban bank loans to So Afr N
68. Bar coun duty-free trtmt N
69. Steel import limits N
70. Soc Sec COLAs=inflation Y
71. Bar haz waste vctms suits Y
72. Prohibit aid to Nicaragua N
73. Cut $-Schs bar sch prayer Y
74. Raise taxes; Cut Medicare ?
75. Alien residncy-prior 1982 Y
76. Alien residncy-prior 1980 Y
77. Pen emp-hire illgl aliens N
78. Lmt Persh II/cruse-Europe N
79. Delete 34 B-1 bombers N
80. Bar purch of Pershing II N
81. Bar purchase of Sgt York Y
82. Delete $ for Trident II N
83. Allow 15 MX missiles Y
84. Bar MX procurement-1985 N
85. Equal Access Act Y
86. Aid to El Salvador Y
87. Bar Nicarag water mining N
88. Physician/Medicare freeze Y
89. Increase "sin" taxes Y
90. End SBA direct loans Y
91. Sell Conrail Y
92. Equal Rights Amendment N
93. Marines in Lebanon Y
94. Eminent domain-Coal comps Y
95. Prohibit EPA sanctions Y
96. SS age increase/Reforms Y
97. Auto domestic content req Y
98. Delete jobs program fundg Y
99. Highway-Gas tax bill N
100. Raise Medicare;Cut defnse N
101. Emergency housing aid Y
102. Across-the-board tax cuts Y
103. Gramm-Latta II targets Y
104. Delete B-1 bomber funds N
105. Dsapprov Saudi AWACS sale N
106. Disapprove oil import fee Y
107. Rail Deregulation N
108. Dsapp India nuc fuel sale ?
109. Mil draft registration Y
110. Chrysler Loan Guarantees N
111. Prohibit school busing Y
112. Nuclear plant moratorium N
113. Oil price controls N

Presidential Support Score: 1986 - 73% 1985 - 68%

DARDEN, GEORGE (Buddy) -- Georgia 7th District [Democrat]. Counties of Bartow, Catoosa, Chatooga, Cobb, Dade, Floyd and Walker. Prior Terms: House: 1983-86. Born: November 22, 1943. Education: University of Georgia. Occupation: Attorney; congressional aide; district attorney; Georgia representative.

1. Immigration Reform Y
2. Open fld-search warrants N
3. Civil pnty-hire ill alien N
4. So Afr sanc-veto override Y
5. Tax Overhaul N
6. South Africa sanctions Y
7. Death penalty-drug bill Y
8. Evidence-warrantless srch Y
9. Life term-second drug off Y
10. Military use in drug war Y
11. Troop reduction in Europe N
12. Prohibit chemical weapons N
13. Bar ASAT testing N
14. Abide SALT II weapons ban N
15. Follow SALT II-Soviets do Y
16. Reduce SDI funding N
17. Increase SDI funding N
18. Purchase Trident sub #
19. Delete 12 MX;Add conv wpn X
20. Raise speed limit Y
21. Textile Import Quotas(*) Y
22. Req Pentagon buy US goods N

DARDEN, GEORGE (Buddy) (Cont.)

23. AIDS ins anti-dscriminatn Y
24. Nicaraguan refugee aid N
25. Nicaraguan contra aid Y
26. US abide by SALT II Y
27. Prohibit Saudi arms sale Y
28. Military Retiremnt Reform Y
29. Nicaraguan refugee aid N
30. Ease '68 Gun Control Act Y
31. Bar intrstat handgun tran N
32. Keep '68 Gun Control Act N
33. Nicaraguan contra aid Y
34. Bar emp polygraph testing N
35. Tax Overhaul consideratn N
36. Bar armor-piercing ammo Y
37. Tax Overhaul consideratn N
38. Make comp emissions known N
39. Allow toxic victims suits N
40. Strike Superfund "VAT" Y
41. Notify emp-plant closing N
42. Bar emp consult-plant clo Y
43. Medicare cuts;Tax incres' Y
44. Delete 12 MX missiles N
45. Spending cuts;Tax incres' Y
46. Textile Import Quotas Y
47. Cut some school lunch fds N
48. Clean Water Act Amendmnts N
49. Youth work projects Y
50. Assist military in Angola Y
51. Allow US troops-Nicaragua Y
52. Pentagon polygraph exams Y
53. Bar ASAT testing N
54. Suspend def pmt for abuse N
55. Bar Pentagon-contr emplmt Y
56. Increase SDI funding N
57. Reduce SDI funding N
58. Produce chemical weapons Y
59. Bar CIA fndg in Nicaragua N
60. South Africa sanctions Y
61. Cut SS COLAs; Raise taxes N
62. Let US invest-So Africa N
63. Approve 21 MX for 1985 Y
64. Emergency Farm Credit Y
65. Awards to whistle blowers Y
66. African disaster relief Y
67. Ban bank loans to So Afr Y
68. Bar coun duty-free trtmt N
69. Steel import limits Y
70. Soc Sec COLAs=inflation Y
71. Bar haz waste vctms suits N
72. Prohibit aid to Nicaragua Y
73. Cut $-Schs bar sch prayer Y
74. Raise taxes; Cut Medicare N
75. Alien residncy-prior 1982 Y
76. Alien residncy-prior 1980 Y
77. Pen emp-hire illgl aliens N
78. Lmt Persh II/cruse-Europe N
79. Delete 34 B-1 bombers N
80. Bar purch of Pershing II N
81. Bar purchase of Sgt York N
82. Delete $ for Trident II N
83. Allow 15 MX missiles Y
84. Bar MX procurement-1985 N
85. Equal Access Act Y
86. Aid to El Salvador Y
87. Bar Nicarag water mining N
88. Physician/Medicare freeze N
89. Increase "sin" taxes Y
90. End SBA direct loans N
91. Sell Conrail N
92. Equal Rights Amendment Y

Presidential Support Score: 1986 - 48% 1985 - 51%

ROWLAND, J. ROY -- Georgia 8th District [Democrat]. Counties of Appling, Atkinson, Bacon, Baldwin, Bibb, Charlton, Clinch, Coffee, Dodge, Glascock, Greene, Hancock, Jasper, Jeff Davis, Jefferson, Johnson, Jones, Laurens, Monroe, Pierce, Putnam, Taliaferro, Telfair, Treutlen, Twiggs, Ware, Washington, Wheeler, Wilcox and Wilkinson. Prior Terms: House: 1983-86. Born: February 3, 1926; Wrightville, Ga. Education: Emory University; South Georgia College; University of Georgia; Medical College of Georgia. Military Service: U.S. Army. Occupation: Family physician; Georgia representative (1976-82).

1. Immigration Reform Y
2. Open fld-search warrants N
3. Civil pnty-hire ill alien N
4. So Afr sanc-veto override Y
5. Tax Overhaul N
6. South Africa sanctions Y
7. Death penalty-drug bill Y
8. Evidence-warrantless srch Y
9. Life term-second drug off Y
10. Military use in drug war Y
11. Troop reduction in Europe N
12. Prohibit chemical weapons N
13. Bar ASAT testing N
14. Abide SALT II weapons ban N
15. Follow SALT II-Soviets do Y
16. Reduce SDI funding N
17. Increase SDI funding N
18. Purchase Trident sub Y
19. Delete 12 MX;Add conv wpn N
20. Raise speed limit N

ROWLAND, J. ROY (Cont.)

21. Textile Import Quotas(*) Y
22. Req Pentagon buy US goods N
23. AIDS ins anti-dscriminatn Y
24. Nicaraguan refugee aid N
25. Nicaraguan contra aid Y
26. US abide by SALT II Y
27. Prohibit Saudi arms sale Y
28. Military Retiremnt Reform Y
29. Nicaraguan refugee aid N
30. Ease '68 Gun Control Act Y
31. Bar intrstat handgun tran N
32. Keep '68 Gun Control Act N
33. Nicaraguan contra aid Y
34. Bar emp polygraph testing N
35. Tax Overhaul consideratn Y
36. Bar armor-piercing ammo Y
37. Tax Overhaul consideratn Y
38. Make comp emissions known N
39. Allow toxic victims suits N
40. Strike Superfund "VAT" N
41. Notify emp-plant closing N
42. Bar emp consult-plant clo Y
43. Medicare cuts;Tax incres' Y
44. Delete 12 MX missiles N
45. Spending cuts;Tax incres' Y
46. Textile Import Quotas Y
47. Cut some school lunch fds N
48. Clean Water Act Amendmnts N
49. Youth work projects N
50. Assist military in Angola Y
51. Allow US troops-Nicaragua Y
52. Pentagon polygraph exams Y
53. Bar ASAT testing N
54. Suspend def pmt for abuse N
55. Bar Pentagon-contr emplmt Y
56. Increase SDI funding N
57. Reduce SDI funding N
58. Produce chemical weapons Y
59. Bar CIA fndg in Nicaragua N
60. South Africa sanctions Y
61. Cut COLAs; Raise taxes Y
62. Let US invest-So Africa N
63. Approve 21 MX for 1985 Y
64. Emergency Farm Credit Y
65. Awards to whistle blowers Y
66. African disaster relief Y
67. Ban bank loans to So Afr Y
68. Bar coun duty-free trtmt N
69. Steel import limits Y
70. Soc Sec COLAs=inflation Y
71. Bar haz waste vctms suits N
72. Prohibit aid to Nicaragua Y
73. Cut $-Schs bar sch prayer Y
74. Raise taxes; Cut Medicare Y
75. Alien residncy-prior 1982 Y
76. Alien residncy-prior 1980 Y
77. Pen emp-hire illgl aliens N
78. Lmt Persh II/cruse-Europe N
79. Delete 34 B-1 bombers N
80. Bar purch of Pershing II N
81. Bar purchase of Sgt York N
82. Delete $ for Trident II N
83. Allow 15 MX missiles Y
84. Bar MX procurement-1985 N
85. Equal Access Act Y
86. Aid to El Salvador Y
87. Bar Nicarag water mining Y
88. Physician/Medicare freeze N
89. Increase "sin" taxes Y
90. End SBA direct loans N
91. Sell Conrail N
92. Equal Rights Amendment N
93. Marines in Lebanon Y
94. Eminent domain-Coal comps N
95. Pronibit EPA sanctions ?
96. SS age increase/Reforms Y

Presidential Support Score: 1986 - 44% 1985 - 50%

JENKINS, ED -- Georgia 9th District [Democrat]. Counties of Banks, Cherokee, Dawson, Fannin, Forsyth, Franklin, Gilmer, Gordon, Gwinnett (pt.), Habersham, Hall, Hart, Jackson, Lumpkin, Murray, Pickens, Rabun, Stephens, Towns, Union, White and Whitfield. Prior Terms: House: 1977-86. Born: January 4, 1933; Young Harris, Ga. Education: Young Harris College (A.A.); University of Georgia (LL.B.). Occupation: Attorney, assistant U.S. attorney; county and city attorney.

1. Immigration Reform Y
2. Open fld-search warrants N
3. Civil pnty-hire ill alien N
4. So Afr sanc-veto override Y
5. Tax Overhaul Y
6. South Africa sanctions Y
7. Death penalty-drug bill Y
8. Evidence-warrantless srch Y
9. Life term-second drug off Y
10. Military use in drug war Y
11. Troop reduction in Europe N
12. Prohibit chemical weapons Y
13. Bar ASAT testing N
14. Abide SALT II weapons ban ?
15. Follow SALT II-Soviets do ?
16. Reduce SDI funding ?
17. Increase SDI funding ?
18. Purchase Trident sub ?
19. Delete 12 MX;Add conv wpn ?
20. Raise speed limit Y

JENKINS, ED (Cont.)

21. Textile Import Quotas(*) Y
22. Req Pentagon buy US goods Y
23. AIDS ins anti-dscriminatn Y
24. Nicaraguan refugee aid N
25. Nicaraguan contra aid Y
26. US abide by SALT II Y
27. Prohibit Saudi arms sale Y
28. Military Retiremnt Reform Y
29. Nicaraguan refugee aid N
30. Ease '68 Gun Control Act Y
31. Bar intrstat handgun tran N
32. Keep '68 Gun Control Act N
33. Nicaraguan contra aid Y
34. Bar emp polygraph testing N
35. Tax Overhaul consideratn Y
36. Bar armor-piercing ammo Y
37. Tax Overhaul consideratn Y
38. Make comp emissions known Y
39. Allow toxic victims suits N
40. Strike Superfund "VAT" N
41. Notify emp-plant closing N
42. Bar emp consult-plant clo Y
43. Medicare cuts;Tax incres' Y
44. Delete 12 MX miCoal comps Y
45. Spending cuts;Tax incres' Y
46. Textile Import Quotas Y
47. Cut some school lunch fds N
48. Clean Water Act Amendmnts N
49. Youth work projects Y
50. Assist military in Angola Y
51. Allow US troops-Nicaragua Y
52. Pentagon polygraph exams Y
53. Bar ASAT testing N
54. Suspend def pmt for abuse N
55. Bar Pentagon-contr emplmt Y
56. Increase SDI funding N
57. Reduce SDI funding N
58. Produce chemical weapons Y
59. Bar CIA fndg in Nicaragua N
60. South Africa sanctions Y
61. Cut SS COLAs; Raise taxes N
62. Let US invest-So Africa ?
63. Approve 21 MX for 1985 N
64. Emergency Farm Credit Y
65. Awards to whistle blowers Y
66. African disaster relief Y
67. Ban bank loans to So Afr ?
68. Bar coun duty-free trtmt Y
69. Steel import limits Y
70. Soc Sec COLAs=inflation Y
71. Bar haz waste vctms suits Y
72. Prohibit aid to Nicaragua Y
73. Cut $-Schs bar sch prayer Y
74. Raise taxes; Cut Medicare Y
75. Alien residncy-prior 1982 Y
76. Alien residncy-prior 1980 Y
77. Pen emp-hire illgl aliens N
78. Lmt Persh II/cruse-Europe ?
79. Delete 34 B-1 bombers ?
80. Bar purch of Pershing II N
81. Bar purchase of Sgt York N
82. Delete $ for Trident II N
83. Allow 15 MX missiles Y
84. Bar MX procurement-1985 Y
85. Equal Access Act Y
86. Aid to El Salvador Y
87. Bar Nicarag water mining Y
88. Physician/Medicare freeze N
89. Increase "sin" taxes Y
90. End SBA direct loans N
91. Sell Conrail Y
92. Equal Rights Amendment ?
93. Marines in Lebanon Y
94. Eminent domain-Coal comps N
95. Prohibit EPA sanctions N
96. SS age increase/Reforms Y
97. Auto domestic content req Y
98. Delete jobs program fundg Y
99. Highway-Gas tax bill Y
100. Raise Medicare;Cut defnse N
101. Emergency housing aid Y
102. Across-the-board tax cuts N
103. Gramm-Latta II targets Y
104. Delete B-1 bomber funds N
105. Dsapprov Saudi AWACS sale N
106. Disapprove oil import fee ?
107. Rail Deregulation Y
108. Dsapp India nuc fuel sale Y
109. Mil draft registration Y
110. Chrysler Loan Guarantees Y
111. Prohibit school busing Y
112. Nuclear plant moratorium N
113. Oil price controls N
114. Tuition Tax Credits N
115. Est Consumer Protect Agcy N
116. Eliminate B-1 bomber fnds Y
117. Subminimum wage for youth Y
118. Delete crude oil tax N
119. Natural gas deregulation N

Presidential Support Score: 1986 - 40% 1985 - 48%

BARNARD, DOUG, Jr. -- Georgia 10th District [Democrat]. Counties of Barrow, Clarke, Columbia, Elbert, Gwinnett (pt.), Lincoln, McDuffie, Madison, Morgan, Oconee, Oglethorpe, Richmond, Walton, Warren and Wilkes. Prior Terms: House: 1977-86. Born: March 20, 1922; Augusta, Ga. Education: Mercer University (B.A., LL.B.). Military Service: U.S. Army. Occupation:

BARNARD, DOUG, Jr. (Cont.)

Executive secretary to the governor (1963-66); employee, Georgia Railroad Bank and Trust Co. (1948-49, 1950-62, 1966-76); employee, Federal Reserve Bank of America (1949-50); board member, Georgia Department of Transportation (1966-76); member, Augusta Transportation Authority (1973-76).

1. Immigration Reform X
2. Open fld-search warrants #
3. Civil pnty-hire ill alien X
4. So Afr sanc-veto override Y
5. Tax Overhaul Y
6. South Africa sanctions Y
7. Death penalty-drug bill Y
8. Evidence-warrantless srch Y
9. Life term-second drug off Y
10. Military use in drug war Y
11. Troop reduction in Europe N
12. Prohobit chemical weapons N
13. Bar ASAT testing N
14. Abide SALT II weapons ban N
15. Follow SALT II-Soviets do Y
16. Reduce SDI funding N
17. Increase SDI funding Y
18. Purchase Trident sub Y
19. Delete 12 MX;Add conv wpn N
20. Raise speed limit Y
21. Textile Import Quotas(*) Y
22. Req Pentagon buy US goods N
23. AIDS ins anti-dscriminatn Y
24. Nicaraguan refugee aid N
25. Nicaraguan contra aid Y
26. US abide by SALT II Y
27. Prohibit Saudi arms asle Y
28. Military Retiremnt Reform ?
29. Nicaraguan refugee aid N
30. Ease '68 Gun Control Act Y
31. Bar intrstat handgun tran N
32. Keep '68 Gun Control Act N
33. Nicaraguan contra aid Y
34. Bar emp polygraph testing N
35. Tax Overhaul consideratn Y
36. Bar armor-piercing ammo Y
37. Tax Overhaul consideratn Y
38. Make comp emissions known N
39. Allow toxic victims suits N
40. Strike Superfund "VAT" Y
41. Notify emp-plant closing N
42. Bar emp consult-plant clo Y
43. Medicare cuts;Tax incres' Y
44. Delete 12 MX missiles N
45. Spending cuts;Tax incres' Y
46. Textile IMport Quotas Y
47. Cut some school lunch fds N
48. Clean Water Act Amendmnts N
49. Youth work projects N
50. Assist military in Angola Y
51. Allow US troops-Nicaragua Y
52. Pentagon polygraph exams Y
53. Bar ASAT testing N
54. Suspend def pmt for abuse N
55. Bar Pentagon-contr emplmt Y
56. Increase SDI funding N
57. Reduce SDI funding N
58. Produce chemical weapons Y
59. Bar CIA fndg in Nicaragua N
60. South Africa sanctions Y
61. Cut SS COLAs; Raise taxes Y
62. Let US invest-So Africa N
63. Approve 21 MX for 1985 Y
64. Emergency Farm Credit Y
65. Awards to whistle blowers Y
66. African disaster relief Y
67. Ban bank loans to So Afr N
68. Bar coun duty-free trtmt ?
69. Steel import limits Y
70. Soc Sec COLAs-inflation Y
71. Bar haz waste vctms suits N
72. Prohobit aid to Nicaragua Y
73. Cut $-Schs bar sch prayer Y
74. Raise taxes; Cut Medicare N
75. Alien residncy-prior 1982 Y
76. Alien residncy-prior 1980 Y
77. Pen emp-hire illgl aliens N
78. Lmt Persh II/cruse-Europe ?
79. Delete 34 B-1 bombers ?
80. Bar purch of Pershing II N
81. Bar purchase of Sgt York ?
82. Delete $ for Trident II ?
83. Allow 15 MX missiles Y
84. Bar MX procurement-1985 N
85. Equal Access Act Y
86. Aid to El Salvador Y
87. Bar Nicarag water mining ?
88. Physician/Medicare freeze N
89. Increase "sin" taxes Y
90. End SBA direct loans N
91. Sell Conrail N
92. Equal Rights Amendment N
93. Marines in Lebanon Y
94. Eminent domain-Coal comps N
95. Prohibit EPA sanctions N
96. SS age increase/Reforms Y
97. Auto domestic content req N
98. Delete jobs program fundg N
99. Highway-Gas tax bill N
100. Raise Medicare;Cut defnse N
101. Emergency housing aid Y
102. Across-the-board tax cuts Y
103. Gramm-Latta II targets Y
104. Delete B-1 bomber funds N
105. Dsapprov Saudi AWACS sale X
106. Disapprove oil import fee Y

BARNARD, DOUG, Jr. (Cont.)

107. Rail Deregulation N
108. Dsapp India nuc fuel sale N
109. Mil draft registration Y
110. Chrysler Loan Guarantees N
111. Prohibit school busing Y
112. Nuclear plant moratorium N
113. Oil price controls N
114. Tuition Tax Credits Y
115. Est Consumer Protect Agcy N
116. Eliminate B-1 bomber fnds Y
117. Subminimum wage for youth Y
118. Delete crude oil tax N
119. Natural gas deregulation Y

Presidential Support Score: 1986 - 56% 1985 - 54%

HAWAII

ABERCROMBIE, NEIL -- Hawaii 1st District [Democrat]. County of Honolulu (pt.). Prior Terms: House: 1986 (Special Election)-1986. Sworn in September 23, 1986, to fill the vacancy created when Cecil Heftel resigned.

1. Immigration Reform Y
2. Open fld-search warrants Y
3. Civil Pnty-hire ill alien N
4. So Afr sanc-veto override Y
5. Tax Overhaul Y

Presidential Support Score: 1986 - 33%

AKAKA, DANIEL K. -- Hawaii 2nd District [Democrat]. Counties of Hawaii, Honolulu (pt.), Kalawao, Kauai and Maui. Prior Terms: House: 1977-86. Born: September 11, 1924; Honolulu, Hawaii. Education: University of Hawaii. Military Service: U.S. Army, 1945-47. Occupation: Teacher (1953-60); vice-principal (1960); principal (1963-71); program specialist (1968-71); director (1971-74); director, Hawaii Office of Economic Opportunity; special assistant, Human Resources, and director, Progressive Neighborhoods Program (1975-76).

1. Immigration Reform N
2. Open fld-search warrants Y
3. Civil pnty-hire ill alien Y
4. So Afr sanc-veto override Y
5. Tax Overhaul N
6. South Africa sanctions Y
7. Death penalty-drug bill N
8. Evidence-warrantless srch N
9. Life term-second drug off Y
10. Military use in drug war N
11. Troop reduction in Europe N
12. Prohibit chemical weapons Y
13. Bar ASAT testing Y
14. Abide SALT II weapons ban Y
15. Follow SALT II-Soviets do N
16. Reduce SDI funding N
17. Increase SDI funding N
18. Purchase Trident sub N
19. Delete 12 MX;Add conv wpn Y
20. Raise speed limit N
21. Textile Import Quotas(*) N
22. Req Pentagon buy US goods Y
23. AIDS ins anti-dscriminatn Y
24. Nicaraguan refugee aid Y
25. Nicaraguan contra aid N
26. US abide by SALT II N
27. Prohibit Saudi arms sale Y
28. Military Retiremnt Reform ?
29. Nicaraguan refugee aid Y
30. Ease '68 Gun Control Act N
31. Bar intrstat handgun tran Y
32. Keep '68 Gun Control Act Y
33. Nicaraguan contra aid N
34. Bar emp polygraph testing Y
35. Tax Overhaul consideratn Y
36. Bar armor-piercing ammo Y
37. Tax Overhaul consideratn Y
38. Make comp emissions known Y
39. Allow toxic victims suits Y
40. Strike Superfund "VAT" Y
41. Notify emp-plant closing Y
42. Bar emp consult-plant clo X
43. Medicare cuts;Tax incres' Y
44. Delete 12 MX missiles ?
45. Spending cuts;Tax incres' Y
46. Textile Import Quotas N
47. Cut some school lunch fds N
48. Clean Water Act Amendmnts N
49. Youth work projects Y
50. Assist military in Angola N
51. Allow US troops-Nicaragua N
52. Pentagon polygraph exams N
53. Bar ASAT testing Y
54. Suspend def pmt for abuse N

AKAKA, DANIEL K. (Cont.)

55. Bar Pentagon-contr emplmt ?
56. Increase SDI funding N
57. Reduce SDI funding Y
58. Produce chemical weapons Y
59. Bar VIA fndg in Nicaragua Y
60. South Africa sanctions Y
61. Cut SS COLAs; Raise taxes N
62. Let US invest-So Africa N
63. Approve 21 MX for 1985 N
64. Emergency Farm Credit Y
65. Awards to whistle blowers Y
66. African disaster relief Y
67. Ban bank loans to So Afr Y
68. Bar coun duty-free trtmt Y
69. Steel import limits Y
70. Soc Sec COLAs=inflation Y
71. Bar haz waste vctms suits N
72. Prohibit aid to Nicaragua Y
73. Cut $-Schs bar sch prayer N
74. Raise taxes; Cut Medicare #
75. Alien residncy-prior 1982 N
76. Alien residncy-prior 1980 N
77. Pen emp-hire illgl aliens Y
78. Lmt Persh II/cruse-Europe N
79. Delete 34 B-1 bombers N
80. Bar purch of Pershing II N
81. Bar purchase of Sgt York Y
82. Delete $ for Trident II N
83. Allow 15 MX missiles N
84. Bar MX procurement-1985 Y
85. Equal Access Act N
86. Aid to El Salvador N
87. Bar Nicarag water mining ?
88. Physician/Medicare freeze N
89. Increase "sin" taxes Y
90. End SBA direct loans ?
91. Sell Conrail N
92. Equal Rights Amendment Y
93. Marines in Lebanon Y
94. Eminent domain-Coal comps Y
95. Prohibit EPA sanctions N
96. SS age increase/Reforms N
97. Auto domestic content req Y
98. Delete jobs program fundg N
99. Highway-Gas tax bill Y
100. Raise Medicare;Cut defnse Y
101. Emergency housing aid Y
102. Across-the-board tax cuts N
103. Gramm-Latta II targets N
104. Delete B-1 bomber funds N
105. Dsapprov Saudi AWACS sale Y
106. Disapprove oil import fee Y
107. Rail Deregulation N
108. Dsapp India nuc fuel sale N
109. Mil draft registration Y
110. Chrysler Loan Guarantees #
111. Prohibit school busing N
112. Nuclear plant moratorium Y
113. Oil price controls N
114. Tuition Tax Credits N
115. Est Consumer Protect Agcy Y
116. Eliminate B-1 bomber fnds N
117. Subminimum wage for youth N
118. Delete crude oil tax N
119. Natural gas deregulation N

Presidential Support Score: 1986 - 18% 1985 - 26%

I D A H O

CRAIG, LARRY E. -- Idaho 1st District [Republican]. Counties of Ada (pt.), Adams, Benewah, Boise, Bonner, Boundary, Canyon, Clearwater, Gem, Idaho, Kootenai, Latah, Lewis, Nez Perce, Owyhee, Payette, Shoshone, Valley and Washington. Prior Terms: House: 1981-86. Born: July 20, 1945; Council, Idaho. Education: University of Idaho (B.A.). Occupation: Farmer-rancher; Idaho senator.

1. Immigration Reform N
2. Open fld-search warrants Y
3. Civil pnty-hire ill alien Y
4. So Afr sanc-veto override N
5. Tax Overhaul N
6. South Africa sanctions N
7. Death penalty-drug bill Y
8. Evidence-warrantless srch Y
9. Life term-second drug off Y
10. Military use in drug war Y
11. Troop reduction in Europe N
12. Prohibit chemical weapons N
13. Bar ASAT testing N
14. Abide SALT II weapons ban N
15. Follow SALT II-Soviets do Y
16. Reduce SDI funding N
17. Increase SDI funding Y
18. Purchase Trident sub N
19. Delete 12 MX;Add conv wpn N
20. Raise speed limit Y
21. Textile Import Quotas(*) N
22. Req Pentagon buy US goods Y
23. AIDS ins anti-dscriminatn N
24. Nicaraguan refugee aid N
25. Nicaraguan contra aid Y
26. US abiCe by SALT II Y
27. Prohibit Saudi arms sale Y
28. Military Retiremnt Reform Y

CRAIG, LARRY E. (Cont.)

29. Nicaraguan refugee aid Y
30. Ease '68 Gun Control Act Y
31. Bar intrstat handgun tran N
32. Keep '68 Gun Control Act N
33. Nicaraguan contra aid Y
34. Bar emp polygraph testing N
35. Tax Overhaul consideratn N
36. Bar armor-piercing ammo N
37. Tax Overhaul consideratn N
38. Make comp emissions known N
39. Allow toxic victims suits N
40. Strike Superfund "VAT" N
41. Notify emp-plant closing N
42. Bar emp consult-plant clo Y
43. Medicare cuts;Tax incres' N
44. Delete 12 MX missiles N
45. Spending cuts;Tax incres' N
46. Textile Import Quotas N
47. Cut some school lunch fds Y
48. Clean Water Act Amendmnts Y
49. Youth work projects N
50. Assist military in Angola Y
51. Allow US troops-Nicaragua Y
52. Pentagon polygraph exams Y
53. Bar ASAT testing N
54. Suspend def pmt for abuse N
55. Bar Pentagon-contr emplmt Y
56. Increase SDI funding Y
57. Reduce SDI funding N
58. Produce chemical weapons Y
59. Bar CIA fndg in Nicaragua N
60. South Africa sanctions N
61. Cut SS COLAs; Raise taxes N
62. Let US invest-So Africa Y
63. Approve 21 MX for 1985 Y
64. Emergency Farm Credit N
65. Awards to whistle blowers Y
66. African disaster relief N
67. Ban bank loans to So Afr Y
68. Bar coun duty-free trtmt N
69. Steel import limits N
70. Soc Sec COLAs=inflation Y
71. Bar haz waste vctms suits Y
72. Prohibit aid to Nicaragua N
73. Cut $-Schs bar sch prayer Y
74. Raise taxes; Cut Medicare N
75. Alien residncy-prior 1982 Y
76. Alien residncy-prior 1980 Y
77. Pen emp-hire illgl aliens N
78. Lmt Persh II/cruse-Europe N
79. Delete 34 B-1 bombers N
80. Bar purch of Pershing II N
81. Bar purchase of Sgt York N
82. Delete $ for Trident II N
83. Allow 15 MX missiles Y
84. Bar MX procurement-1985 N
85. Equal Access Act Y
86. Aid to El Salvador Y
87. Bar Nicarag water mining X
88. Physician/Medicare freeze #
89. Increase "sin" taxes N
90. End SBA direct loans Y
91. Sell Conrail Y
92. Equal Rights Amendment N
93. Marines in Lebanon Y
94. Eminent domain-Coal comps N
95. Prohibit EPA sanctions ?
96. SS age increase/Reforms Y
97. Auto domestic content req N
98. Delete jobs program fundg Y
99. Highway-Gas tax bill N
100. Raise Medicare;Cut defnse N
101. Emergency housing aid Y
102. Across-the-board tax cuts Y
103. Gramm-Latta II targets Y
104. Delete B-1 bomber funds N
105. Dsapprov Saudi AWACS sale N

Presidential Support Score: 1986 - 80% 1985 - 75%

STALLINGS, RICHARD -- Idaho 2nd District [Democrat]. Counties of Ada (pt.), Bannock, Bear Lake, Bingham, Blaune, Booneville, Butte, Camas, Caribou, Cassia, Clark, Custer, Elmore, Franklin, Fremont, Gooding, Jefferson, Jerome, Lemhi, Lincoln, Madison, Minidoka, Oneida, Power, Teton and Twin Falls. Prior Terms: 1985-86. Born: October 7, 1940. Education: Weber State University (B.S.); Utah State University (M.A.). Occupation: Professor.

1. Immigration Reform Y
2. Open fld-search warrants Y
3. Civil pnty-hire ill alien Y
4. So Afr sanc-veto override Y
5. Tax Overhaul Y
6. South Africa sanctions Y
7. Death penalty-drug bill Y
8. Evidence-warrantless srch Y
9. Life term-second drug off Y
10. Military use in drug war Y
11. Troop reduction in Europe N
12. Prohibit chemical weapons Y
13. Bar ASAT testing Y
14. Abide SALT II weapons ban Y
15. Follow SALT II-Soviets do N
16. Reduce SDI funding N

STALLINGS, RICHARD (Cont.)

17. Increase SDI funding N
18. Purchase Trident sub Y
19. Delete 12 MX;Add conv wpn Y
20. Raise speed limit Y
21. Textile Import Quotas(*) N
22. Req Pentagon buy US goods Y
23. AIDS ins anti-dscriminatn Y
24. Nicaraguan refugee aid N
25. Nicaraguan contra aid N
26. US abide by SALT II Y
27. Prohibit Saudi arms sale Y
28. Military Retiremnt Reform Y
29. Nicaraguan refugee aid Y
30. Ease '68 Gun Control Act Y
31. Bar intrstat handgun tran N
32. Keep '68 Gun Control Act N
33. Nicaraguan contra aid N
34. Bar emp polygraph testing Y
35. Tax Overhaul consideratn Y
36. Bar armor-piercing ammo Y
37. Tax Overhaul consideratn Y
38. Make comp emissions known Y
39. Allow toxic victims suits N
40. Strike Superfund "VAT" Y
41. Notify emp-plant closing #
42. Bar emp consult-plant clo N
43. Medicare cuts;Tax incres' Y
44. Delete 12 MX missiles Y
45. Spending cuts;Tax incres' Y
46. Textile Import Quotas N
47. Cut some school lunch fds N
48. Clean Water Act Amendmnts Y
49. Youth work projects N
50. Assist military in Angola N
51. Allow US troops-Nicaragua N
52. Pentagon polygraph exams Y
53. Bar ASAT testing Y
54. Suspend def pmt for abuse Y
55. Bar Pentagon-contr emplmt Y
56. Increase SDI funding N
57. Reduce SDI funding N
58. Produce chemical weapons N
59. Bar CIA fndg in Nicaragua Y
60. South Africa sanctions ?
61. Cut SS COLAs; Raise taxes N
62. Let US invest-So Africa N
63. Approve 21 MX for 1985 N
64. Emergency Farm Credit Y
65. Awards to whistle blowers Y
66. African disaster relief Y

Presidential Support Score: 1986 - 42% 1985 - 41%

I L L I N O I S

HAYES, CHARLES A. -- Illinois 1st District [Democrat]. County of Cook (pt.). Prior Terms: House: 1983 (Special Election)-1986. Born: February 17, 1918; Cairo, Ill. Occupation: Civilian Conservation Corps worker; woodworker; International Vice President and Director of the United Food and Commercial Workers Union.

1. Immigration Reform N
2. Open fld-search warrants N
3. Civil pnty-hire ill alien Y
4. So Afr sanc-veto override Y
5. Tax Overhaul Y
6. South Africa sanctions Y
7. Death penalty-drug bill N
8. Evidence-warrantless srch N
9. Life term-second drug off N
10. Military use in drug war N
11. Troop reduction in Europe Y
12. Prohibit chemical weapons Y
13. Bar ASAT testing Y
14. Abide SALT II weapons ban Y
15. Follow SALT II-Soviets do N
16. Reduce SDI funding Y
17. Increase SDI funding N
18. Purchase Trident sub Y
19. Delete 12 MX;Add conv wpn Y
20. Raise speed limit Y
21. Textile Import Quotas(*) Y
22. Req Pentagon buy US goods Y
23. AIDS ins anti-dscriminatn Y
24. Nicaraguan refugee aid Y
25. Nicaraguan contra aid N
26. US abide by SALT II N
27. Prohibit Saudi arms sale Y
28. Military Retiremnt Reform Y
29. Nicaraguan refugee aid Y
30. Ease '68 Gun Control Act N
31. Bar intrstat handgun tran Y
32. Keep '68 Gun Control Act Y
33. Nicaraguan contra aid N
34. Bar emp polygraph testing Y
35. Tax Overhaul consideratn Y
36. Bar armor-piercing ammo Y
37. Tax Overhaul consideratn Y
38. Make comp emissions known Y
39. Allow toxic victims suits Y
40. Strike Superfund "VAT" Y
41. Notify emp-plant closing Y
42. Bar emp consult-plant clo N

HAYES, CHARLES A. (Cont.)

43. Medicare cuts;Tax incres' Y
44. Delete 12 MX missiles Y
45. Spending cuts;Tax incres' Y
46. Textile Import Quotas Y
47. Cut some school lunch fds N
48. Clean Water Act Amendmnts N
49. Youth work projects Y
50. Assist military in Angola N
51. Allow US troops-Nicaragua N
52. Pentagon polygraph exams N
53. Bar ASAT testing Y
54. Suspend def pmt for abuse Y
55. Bar Pentagon-contr emplmt Y
56. Increase SDI funding N
57. Reduce SDI funding Y
58. Produce chemical weapons N
59. Bar CIA fndg in Nicaragua Y
60. South Africa sanctions Y
61. Cut SS COLAs; Raise taxes N
62. Let US invest-So Africa N
63. Approve 21 MX for 1985 N
64. Emergency Farm Credit Y
65. Awards to whistle blowers Y
66. African disaster relief Y
67. Ban bank loans to So Afr P
68. Bar coun duty-free trtmt Y
69. Steel import limits Y
70. Soc Sec COLAs=inflation Y
71. Bar haz waste vctms suits N
72. Prohibit aid to Nicaragua Y
73. Cut $-Schs bar sch prayer N
74. Raise taxes; Cut Medicare N
75. Alien residncy-prior 1982 N
76. Alien residncy-prior 1980 N
77. Pen emp-hire illgl aliens Y
78. Lmt Persh II/cruse-Europe Y
79. Delete 34 B-1 bombers Y
80. Bar purch of Pershing II Y
81. Bar purchase of Sgt York Y
82. Delete $ for Trident II Y
83. Allow 15 MX missiles N
84. Bar MX procurement-1985 Y
85. Equal Access Act N
86. Aid to El Salvador N
87. Bar Nicarag water mining ?
88. Physician/Medicare freeze N
89. Increase "sin" taxes Y
90. End SBA direct loans N
91. Sell Conrail N
92. Equal Rights Amendment Y
93. Marines in Lebanon N
94. Eminent domain-Coal comps Y

Presidential Support Score: 1986 - 13% 1985 - 15%

SAVAGE, GUS -- Illinois 2nd District [Democrat]. County of Cook (pt.). Prior Terms: House: 1981-86. Born: October 30, 1925; Detroit, Mich. Education: Roosevelt University (B.A.); Chicago-Kent College of Law. Military Service: WW II, 1943-46. Occupation: Editor.

1. Immigration Reform N
2. Open fld-search warrants Y
3. Civil pnty-hire ill alien Y
4. So Afr sanc-veto override Y
5. Tax Overhaul Y
6. South Africa sanctions Y
7. Death penalty-drug bill N
8. Evidence-warrantless srch N
9. Life term-second drug off N
10. Military use in drug war N
11. Troop reduction in Europe Y
12. Prohibit chemical weapons Y
13. Bar ASAT testing ?
14. Abide SALT II weapons ban Y
15. Follow SALT II-Soviets do N
16. Reduce SDI funding Y
17. Increase SDI funding N
18. Purchase Trident sub N
19. Delete 12 MX;Add conv wpn ?
20. Raise speed limit N
21. Textile Import Quotas(*) Y
22. Req Pentagon buy US goods Y
23. AIDS ins anti-dscriminatn Y
24. Nicaraguan refugee aid Y
25. Nicaraguan contra aid N
26. US abide by SALT II N
27. Prohibit Saudi arms sale Y
28. Military Retiremnt Reform Y
29. Nicaraguan refugee aid Y
30. Ease '68 Gun Control Act N
31. Bar intrstat handgun tran Y
32. Keep '68 Gun Control Act Y
33. Nicaraguan contra aid N
34. Bar emp polygraph testing Y
35. Tax Overhaul consideratn Y
36. Bar armor-piercing ammo Y
37. Tax Overhaul consideratn N
38. Make comp emissions known Y
39. Allow toxic victims suits Y
40. Strike Superfund "VAT" Y
41. Notify emp-plant closing Y
42. Bar emp consult-plant clo N
43. Medicare cuts;Tax incres' Y
44. Delete 12 MX missiles Y
45. Spending cuts;Tax incres' Y
46. Textile Import Quotas Y
47. Cut some school lunch fds N
48. Clean Water Act Amendmnts N

SAVAGE, GUS (Cont.)

49. Youth work projects	Y		78. Lmt Persh II/cruse-Europe	Y
50. Assist military in Angola	N		79. Delete 34 B-1 bombers	Y
51. Allow US troops-Nicaragua	N		80. Bar purch of Pershing II	Y
52. Pentagon polygraph exams	N		81. Bar purchase of Sgt York	Y
53. Bar ASAT testing	Y		82. Delete $ for Trident II	Y
54. Suspend def pmt for abuse	Y		83. Allow 15 MX missiles	N
55. Bar Pentagon-contr emplmt	Y		84. Bar MX procurement-1985	Y
56. Increase SDI funding	?		85. Equal Access Act	N
57. Reduce SDI funding	Y		86. Aid to El Salvador	N
58. Produce chemical weapons	N		87. Bar Nicarag water mining	Y
59. Bar CIA fndg in Nicaragua	Y		88. Physician/Medicare freeze	N
60. South Africa sanctions	Y		89. Increase "sin" taxes	Y
61. Cut SS COLAs; Raise taxes	N		90. End SBA direct loans	?
62. Let US invest-So Africa	N		91. Sell Conrail	N
63. Approve 21 MX for 1985	N		92. Equal Rights Amendment	Y
64. Emergency Farm Credit	Y		93. Marines in Lebanon	N
65. Awards to whistle blowers	Y		94. Eminent domain-Coal comps	N
66. African disaster relief	Y		95. Prohibit EPA sanctions	Y
67. Ban bank loans to So Afr	P		96. SS age increase/Reforms	N
68. Bar coun duty-free trtmt	Y		97. Auto domestic content req	Y
69. Steel import limits	Y		98. Delete jobs program fundg	N
70. Soc Sec COLAs=inflation	Y		99. Highway-Gas tax bill	?
71. Bar haz waste vctms suits	N		100. Raise Medicare;Cut defnse	Y
72. Prohibit aid to Nicaragua	Y		101. Emergency housing aid	Y
73. Cut $-Schs bar sch prayer	N		102. Across-the-board tax cuts	N
74. Raise taxes; Cut Medicare	N		103. Gramm-Latta II targets	N
75. Alien residncy-prior 1982	N		104. Delete B-1 bomber funds	Y
76. Alien residncy-prior 1980	N		105. Dsapprov Saudi AWACS sale	?
77. Pen emp-hire illgl aliens	Y			

Presidential Support Score: 1986 - 15% 1985 - 13%

RUSSO, MARTY -- Illinois 3rd District [Democrat]. County of Cook (pt.). Prior Terms: House: 1975-86. Born: January 23, 1944; CHicago, Ill. Education: De Paul University (B.A., J.D.). Occupation: Law clerk, Illinois Appellate Court (1967-68); assistant state's attorney (1971-73).

1. Immigration Reform	?		22. Req Pentagon buy US goods	Y
2. Open fld-search warrants	?		23. AIDS ins anti-dscriminatn	N
3. Civil pnty-hire ill alien	?		24. Nicaraguan refugee aid	Y
4. So Afr sanc-veto override	Y		25. Nicaraguan contra aid	N
5. Tax Overhaul	Y		26. US abide by SALT II	N
6. South Africa sanctions	Y		27. Prohibit Saudi arms sale	Y
7. Death penalty-drug bill	Y		28. Military Retiremnt Reform	Y
8. Evidence-warrantless srch	Y		29. Nicaraguan refugee aid	Y
9. Life term-second drug off	Y		30. Ease '68 Gun Control Act	N
10. Military use in drug war	Y		31. Bar intrstat handgun tran	Y
11. Troop reduction in Europe	N		32. Keep '68 Gun Control Act	Y
12. Prohibit chemical weapons	Y		33. Nicaraguan contra aid	N
13. Bar ASAT testing	Y		34. Bar emp polygraph testing	Y
14. Abide SALT II weapons ban	Y		35. Tax Overhaul consideratn	Y
15. Follow SALT II-Soviets do	N		36. Bar armor-piercing ammo	Y
16. Reduce SDI funding	Y		37. Tax Overhaul consideratn	Y
17. Increase SDI funding	N		38. Make comp emissions known	Y
18. Purchase Trident sub	N		39. Allow toxic victims suits	N
19. Delete 12 MX;Add conv wpn	Y		40. Strike Superfund "VAT"	N
20. Raise speed limit	N		41. Notify emp-plant closing	Y
21. Textile Import Quotas(*)	Y		42. Bar emp consult-plant clo	N

RUSSO, MARTY (Cont.)

43. Medicare cuts;Tax incres'	Y	82. Delete $ for Trident II	Y
44. Delete 12 MX missiles	Y	83. Allow 15 MX missiles	N
45. Spending cuts;Tax incres'	Y	84. Bar MX procurement-1985	Y
46. Textile Import Quotas	Y	85. Equal Access Act	N
47. Cut some school lunch fds	N	86. Aid to El Salvador	N
48. Clean Water Act Amendmnts	N	87. Bar Nicarag water mining	#
49. Youth work projects	Y	88. Physician/Medicare freeze	N
50. Assist military in Angola	N	89. Increase "sin" taxes	Y
51. Allow US troops-Nicaragua	N	90. End SBA direct loans	N
52. Pentagon polygraph exams	Y	91. Sell Conrail	N
53. Bar ASAT testing	Y	92. Equal Rights Amendment	N
54. Suspend def pmt for abuse	Y	93. Marines in Lebanon	N
55. Bar Pentagon-contr emplmt	Y	94. Eminent domain-Coal comps	N
56. Increase SDI funding	N	95. Prohibit EPA sanctions	N
57. Reduce SDI funding	Y	96. SS age increase/Reforms	N
58. Produce chemical weapons	N	97. Auto domestic content req	Y
59. Bar CIA fndg in Nicaragua	Y	98. Delete jobs program fundg	N
60. South Africa sanctions	Y	99. Highway-Gas tax bill	Y
61. Cut SS COLAs; Raise taxes	N	100. Raise Medicare;Cut defnse	Y
62. Let US invest-So Africa	N	101. Emergency housing aid	Y
63. Approve 21 MX for 1985	N	102. Across-the-board tax cuts	N
64. Emergency Farm Credit	Y	103. Gramm-Latta II targets	N
65. Awards to whistle blowers	Y	104. Delete B-1 bomber funds	Y
66. African disaster relief	Y	105. Dsapprov Saudi AWACS sale	Y
67. Ban bank loans to So Afr	Y	106. Disapprove oil import fee	Y
68. Bar coun duty-free trtmt	Y	107. Rail Deregulation	?
69. Steel import limits	Y	108. Dsapp India nuc fuel sale	Y
70. Soc Sec COLAs=inflation	Y	109. Mil draft registration	Y
71. Bar haz waste vctms suits	N	110. Chrysler Loan Guarantees	Y
72. Prohibit aid to Nicaragua	Y	111. Prohibit school busing	Y
73. Cut $-Schs bar sch prayer	N	112. Nuclear plant moratorium	N
74. Raise taxes; Cut Medicare	Y	113. Oil price controls	Y
75. Alien residncy-prior 1982	Y	114. Tuition Tax Credits	Y
76. Alien residncy-prior 1980	N	115. Est Consumer Protect Agcy	Y
77. Pen emp-hire illgl aliens	N	116. Eliminate B-1 bomber fnds	Y
78. Lmt Persh II/cruse-Europe	Y	117. Subminimum wage for youth	N
79. Delete 34 B-1 bombers	?	118. Delete crude oil tax	N
80. Bar purch of Pershing II	?	119. Natural gas deregulation	N
81. Bar purchase of Sgt York	Y		

Presidential Support Score: 1986 - 18% 1985 - 23%

O'BRIEN, GEORGE M. -- Illinois 4th District [Republican]. Counties of Cook (pt.), Kane, Kendall (pt.) and Will. Prior Terms: House: 1973-86. Born: June 17, 1917; Chicago, Ill. Education: Northwestern University (A.B.); Yale University (J.D.). Military Service: U.S. Air Force, 1941-45. Occupation: Attorney; member, Will County Board of Supervisors (1956-64).

George O'Brien died July 17, 1986 and his seat was left vacant for the remainder of the year.

LIPINSKI, WILLIAM O. -- Illinois 5th District [Democrat]. County of Cook (pt.). Prior Terms: House: 1983-86. Born: December 22, 1937; Chicago, Ill. Education: Loras College. Occupation: Precinct captain; alderman (1975-83); president, Greater Midway Economic and Community Development Committee.

LIPINSKI, WILLIAM O. (Cont.)

1. Immigration Reform Y
2. Open fld-search warrants N
3. Civil pnty-hire ill alien N
4. So Afr sanc-veto override Y
5. Tax Overhaul Y
6. South Africa sanctions Y
7. Death penalty-drug bill Y
8. Evidence-warrantless srch Y
9. Life term-second drug off Y
10. Military use in drug war Y
11. Troop reduction in Europe N
12. Prohibit chemical weapons N
13. Bar ASAT testing N
14. Abide SALT II weapons ban Y
15. Follow SALT II-Soviets do Y
16. Reduce SDI funding N
17. Increase SDI funding N
18. Purchase Trident sub N
19. Delete 12 MX;Add conv wpn N
20. Raise speed limit N
21. Textile Import Quotas(*) Y
22. Req Pentagon buy US goods Y
23. AIDS ins anti-dscriminatn Y
24. Nicaraguan refugee aid N
25. Nicaraguan contra aid Y
26. US abide by SALT II Y
27. Prohibit Saudi arms sale N
28. Military Retiremnt Reform Y
29. Nicaraguan refugee aid N
30. Ease '68 Gun Control Act N
31. Bar intrstat handgun tran Y
32. Keep '68 Gun Control Act Y
33. Nicaraguan contra aid Y
34. Bar emp polygraph testing Y
35. Tax Overhaul consideratn Y
36. Bar armor-piercing ammo Y
37. Tax Overhaul consideratn Y
38. Make comp emissions known Y
39. Allow toxic victims suits Y
40. Strike Superfund "VAT" Y
41. Notify emp-plant closing Y
42. Bar emp consult-plant clo N
43. Medicare cuts;Tax incres' Y
44. Delete 12 MX missiles Y
45. Spending cuts;Tax incres' Y
46. Textile Import Quotas Y
47. Cut some school lunch fds N
48. Clean Water Act Amendmnts N
49. Youth work projects Y
50. Assist military in Angola N
51. Allow US troops-Nicaragua N
52. Pentagon polygraph exams Y
53. Bar ASAT testing Y
54. Suspend def pmt for abuse Y
55. Bar Pentagon-contr emplmt Y
56. Increase SDI funding N
57. Reduce SDI funding N
58. Produce chemical weapons Y
59. Bar CIA fndg in Nicaragua N
60. South Africa sanctions Y
61. Cut SS COLAs; Raise taxes N
62. Let US invest-So Africa N
63. Approve 21 MX for 1985 Y
64. Emergency Farm Credit Y
65. Awards to whistle blowers Y
66. African disaster relief Y
67. Ban bank loans to So Afr ?
68. Bar coun duty-free trtmt Y
69. Steel import limits Y
70. Soc Sec COLAs=inflation Y
71. Bar haz waste vctms suits N
72. Prohibit aid to Nicaragua Y
73. Cut $-Schs bar sch prayer Y
74. Raise taxes; Cut Medicare Y
75. Alien residncy-prior 1982 Y
76. Alien residncy-prior 1980 N
77. Pen emp-hire illgl aliens Y
78. Lmt Persh II/cruse-Europe N
79. Delete 34 B-1 bombers Y
80. Bar purch of Pershing II N
81. Bar purchase of Sgt York Y
82. Delete $ for Trident II N
83. Allow 15 MX missiles Y
84. Bar MX procurement-1985 N
85. Equal Access Act Y
86. Aid to El Salvador N
87. Bar Nicarag water mining ?
88. Physician/Medicare freeze N
89. Increase "sin" taxes Y
90. End SBA direct loans N
91. Sell Conrail N
92. Equal Rights Amendment N
93. Marines in Lebanon N
94. Eminent domain-Coal comps N
95. Prohibit EPA sanctions N
96. SS age increase/Reforms Y

Presidential Support Score: 1986 - 42% 1985 - 36%

HYDE, HENRY J. -- Illinois 6th District [Republican]. Counties of Cook (pt.) and Du Page (pt.). Prior Terms: House: 1975-86. Born: April 18, 1924; Chicago, Ill. Education: Georgetown University (B.S.S.); Loyola University (J.D.). Military Service: U.S. Navy, WW II. Occupation: Attorney; Illinois legislator (1967-74).

1. Immigration Reform N
2. Open fld-search warrants N
3. Civil pnty-hire ill alien N
4. So Afr sanc-veto override N

HYDE, HENRY J. (Cont.)

5. Tax Overhaul Y
6. South Africa sanctions N
7. Death penalty-drug bill Y
8. Evidence-warrantless srch Y
9. Life term-second drug off Y
10. Military use in drug war Y
11. Troop reduction in Europe N
12. Prohibit chemical weapons N
13. Bar ASAT testing N
14. Abide SALT II weapons ban N
15. Follow SALT II-Soviets do Y
16. Reduce SDI funding N
17. Increase SDI funding Y
18. Purchase Trident sub N
19. Delete 12 MX;Add conv wpn N
20. Raise speed limit Y
21. Textile Import Quotas(*) N
22. Req Pentagon buy US goods N
23. AIDS ins anti-dscriminatn N
24. Nicaraguan refugee aid N
25. Nicaraguan contra aid Y
26. US abide by SALT II Y
27. Prohibit Saudi arms sale N
28. Military Retiremnt Reform Y
29. Nicaraguan refugee aid Y
30. Ease '68 Gun Control Act Y
31. Bar intrstat handgun tran N
32. Keep '68 Gun Control Act Y
33. Nicaraguan contra aid Y
34. Bar emp polygraph testing N
35. Tax Overhaul consideratn Y
36. Bar armor-piercing ammo Y
37. Tax Overhaul consideratn N
38. Make comp emissions known N
39. Allow toxic victims suits ?
40. Strike Superfund "VAT" Y
41. Notify emp-plant closing N
42. Bar emp consult-plant clo Y
43. Medicare cuts;Tax incres' N
44. Delete 12 MX missiles N
45. Spending cuts;Tax incres' N
46. Textile Import Quotas X
47. Cut some school lunch fds Y
48. Clean Water Act Amendmnts Y
49. Youth work projects N
50. Assist military in Angola Y
51. Allow US troops-Nicaragua Y
52. Pentagon polygraph exams Y
53. Bar ASAT testing N
54. Suspend def pmt for abuse N
55. Bar Pentagon-contr emplmt Y
56. Increase SDI funding Y
57. Reduce SDI funding N
58. Produce chemical weapons Y
59. Bar CIA fndg in Nicaragua N
60. South Africa sanctions N
61. Cut SS COLAs; Raise taxes N
62. Let US invest-So Africa Y
63. Approve 21 MX for 1985 Y
64. Emergency Farm Credit N
65. Awards to whistle blowers Y
66. African disaster relief Y
67. Ban bank loans to So Afr N
68. Bar coun duty-free trtmt N
69. Steel import limits N
70. Soc Sec COLAs=inflation Y
71. Bar haz waste vctms suits Y
72. Prohibit aid to Nicaragua N
73. Cut $-Schs bar sch prayer Y
74. Raise taxes; Cut Medicare N
75. Alien residncy-prior 1982 Y
76. Alien residncy-prior 1980 Y
77. Pen emp-hire illgl aliens N
78. Lmt Persh II/cruse-Europe N
79. Delete 34 B-1 bombers N
80. Bar purch of Pershing II N
81. Bar purchase of Sgt York N
82. Delete $ for Trident II N
83. Allow 15 MX missiles Y
84. Bar MX procurement-1985 N
85. Equal Access Act Y
86. Aid to El Salvador Y
87. Bar Nicarag water mining N
88. Physician/Medicare freeze Y
89. Increase "sin" taxes Y
90. End SBA direct loans N
91. Sell Conrail Y
92. Equal Rights Amendment N
93. Marines in Lebanon Y
94. Eminent domain-Coal comps N
95. Prohibit EPA sanctions Y
96. SS age increase/Reforms Y
97. Auto domestic content req N
98. Delete jobs program fundg Y
99. Highway-Gas tax bill N
100. Raise Medicare;Cut defnse N
101. Emergency housing aid Y
102. Across-the-board tax cuts Y
103. Gramm-Latta II targets Y
104. Delete B-1 bomber funds N
105. Dsapprov Saudi AWACS sale N
106. Disapprove oil import fee Y
107. Rail Deregulation N
108. Dsapp India nuc fuel sale Y
109. Mil draft registration Y
110. Chrysler Loan Guarantees Y
111. Prohibit school busing Y
112. Nuclear plant moratorium N
113. Oil price controls N
114. Tuition Tax Credits Y
115. Est Consumer Protect Agcy N
116. Eliminate B-1 bomber fnds N
117. Subminimum wage for youth Y
118. Delete crude oil tax Y
119. Natural gas deregulation Y

Presidential Support Score: 1986 - 76% 1985 - 71%

COLLINS, CARDISS -- Illinois 7th District [Democrat]. County of Cook (pt.). Prior Terms: House: 1973 (Special Election)-1986. Born: September 24, 1931; St. Lois, Mo. Education: Northwestern University. Occupation: Stenographer; secretary; accountant; revenue auditor.

1. Immigration Reform Y
2. Open fld-search warrants N
3. Civil pnty-hire ill alien N
4. So Afr sanc-veto override Y
5. Tax Overhaul Y
6. South Africa sanctions Y
7. Death penalty-drug bill N
8. Evidence-warrantless srch N
9. Life term-second drug off N
10. Military use in drug war N
11. Troop reduction in Europe Y
12. Prohibit chemical weapons Y
13. Bar ASAT testing Y
14. Abide SALT II weapons ban Y
15. Follow SALT II-Soviets do N
16. Reduce SDI funding Y
17. Increase SDI funding N
18. Purchase Trident sub N
19. Delete 12 MX;Add conv wpn Y
20. Raise speed limit Y
21. Textile Import Quotas(*) Y
22. Req Pentagon buy US goods Y
23. AIDS ins anti-dscriminatn Y
24. Nicaraguan refugee aid Y
25. Nicaraguan contra aid N
26. US abide by SALT II N
27. Prohibit Saudi arms sale Y
28. Military Retiremnt Reform Y
29. Nicaraguan refugee aid Y
30. Ease '68 Gun Control Act N
31. Bar intrstat handgun tran Y
32. Keep '68 Gun Control Act Y
33. Nicaraguan contra aid N
34. Bar emp polygraph testing #
35. Tax Overhaul consideratn Y
36. Bar armor-piercing ammo Y
37. Tax Overhaul consideratn Y
38. Make comp emissions known Y
39. Allow toxic victims suits Y
40. Strike Superfund "VAT" Y
41. Notify emp-plant closing Y
42. Bar emp consult-plant clo N
43. Medicare cuts;Tax incres' Y
44. Delete 12 MX missiles #
45. Spending cuts;Tax incres' Y
46. Textile Import Quotas Y
47. Cut some school lunch fds N
48. Clean Water Act Amendmnts N
49. Youth work projects ?
50. Assist military in Angola N
51. Allow US troops-Nicaragua N
52. Pentagon polygraph exams N
53. Bar ASAT testing Y
54. Suspend def pmt for abuse Y
55. Bar Pentagon-contr emplmt Y
56. Increase SDI funding N
57. Reduce SDI funding Y
58. Produce chemical weapons N
59. Bar CIA fndg in Nicaragua Y
60. South Africa sanctions Y
61. Cut SS COLAs; Raise taxes N
62. Let US invest-So Africa N
63. Approve 21 MX for 1985 N
64. Emergency Farm Credit Y
65. Awards to whistle blowers Y
66. African disaster relief Y
67. Ban bank loans to So Afr P
68. Bar coun duty-free trtmt Y
69. Steel import limits Y
70. Soc Sec COLAs=inflation Y
71. Bar haz waste vctms suits N
72. Prohibit aid to Nicaragua Y
73. Cut \$-Schs bar sch prayer N
74. Raise taxes; Cut Medicare N
75. Alien residncy-prior 1982 N
76. Alien residncy-prior 1980 N
77. Pen emp-hire illgl aliens Y
78. Lmt Persh II/cruse-Europe Y
79. Delete 34 B-1 bombers Y
80. Bar purch of Pershing II ?
81. Bar purchase of Sgt York Y
82. Delete $ for Trident II Y
83. Allow 15 MX missiles N
84. Bar MX procurement-1985 Y
85. Equal Access Act N
86. Aid to El Salvador N
87. Bar Nicarag water mining Y
88. Physician/Medicare freeze N
89. Increase "sin" taxes Y
90. End SBA direct loans ?
91. Sell Conrail ?
92. Equal Rights Amendment Y
93. Marines in Lebanon N
94. Eminent domain-Coal comps N
95. Prohibit EPA sanctions ?
96. SS age increase/Reforms N
97. Auto domestic content req Y
98. Delete jobs program fundg N
99. Highway-Gas tax bill Y
100. Raise Medicare;Cut defnse Y
101. Emergency housing aid Y
102. Across-the-board tax cuts N
103. Gramm-Latta II targets N
104. Delete B-1 bomber funds Y
105. Dsapprov Saudi AWACS sale Y
106. Disapprove oil import fee Y
107. Rail Deregulation N
108. Dsapp India nuc fuel sale Y

COLLINS, CARDISS (Cont.)

109. Mil draft registration N
110. Chrysler Loan Guarantees Y
111. Prohibit school busing N
112. Nuclear plant moratorium Y
113. Oil price controls ?
114. Tuition Tax Credits N
115. Est Consumer Protect Agcy #
116. Eliminate B-1 bomber fnds #
117. Subminimum wage for youth N
118. Delete crude oil tax N
119. Natural gas deregulation N

Presidential Support Score: 1986 - 11% 1985 - 16%

ROSTENKOWSKI, DAN -- Illinois 8th District [Democrat]. County of Cook (pt.). Prior Terms: House: 1959-86. Born: January 2, 1928; Chicago, Ill. Education: St. John's Military Academy; Loyola University. Military Service: U.S. Army, Korean War. Occupation: Illinois representative; Illinois senator.

1. Immigration Reform Y
2. Open fld-search warrants Y
3. Civil pnty-hire ill alien N
4. So Afr sanc-veto override ?
5. Tax Overhaul Y
6. South Africa sanctions Y
7. Death penalty-drug bill Y
8. Evidence-warrantless srch Y
9. Life term-second drug off Y
10. Military use in drug war ?
11. Troop reduction in Europe N
12. Prohibit chemical weapons Y
13. Bar ASAT testing Y
14. Abide SALT II weapons ban Y
15. Follow SALT II-Soviets do N
16. Reduce SDI funding N
17. Increase SDI funding N
18. Purchase Trident sub Y
19. Delete 12 MX;Add conv wpn Y
20. Raise speed limit N
21. Textile Import Quotas(*) N
22. Req Pentagon buy US goods Y
23. AIDS ins anti-dscriminatn Y
24. Nicaraguan refugee aid Y
25. Nicaraguan contra aid N
26. US abide by SALT II ?
27. Prohibit Saudi arms sale Y
28. Military Retiremnt Reform Y
29. Nicaraguan refugee aid Y
30. Ease '68 Gun Control Act N
31. Bar intrstat handgun tran Y
32. Keep '68 Gun Control Act Y
33. Nicaraguan contra aid N
34. Bar emp polygraph testing Y
35. Tax Overhaul consideratn Y
36. Bar armor-piercing ammo Y
37. Tax Overhaul consideratn Y
38. Make comp emissions known Y
39. Allow toxic victims suits N
40. Strike Superfund "VAT" Y
41. Notify emp-plant closing Y
42. Bar emp consult-plant clo N
43. Medicare cuts;Tax incres' ?
44. Delete 12 MX missiles Y
45. Spending cuts;Tax incres' Y
46. Textile Import Quotas N
47. Cut some school lunch fds N
48. Clean Water Act Amendmnts N
49. Youth work projects ?
50. Assist military in Angola N
51. Allow US troops-Nicaragua N
52. Pentagon polygraph exams Y
53. Bar ASAT testing Y
54. Suspend def pmt for abuse Y
55. Bar Pentagon-contr emplmt Y
56. Increase SDI funding ?
57. Reduce SDI funding ?
58. Produce chemical weapons N
59. Bar CIA fndg in Nicaragua Y
60. South Africa sanctions Y
61. Cut SS COLAs; Raise taxes N
62. Let US invest-So Africa N
63. Approve 21 MX for 1985 N
64. Emergency Farm Credit Y
65. Awards to whistle blowers Y
66. African disaster relief Y
67. Ban bank loans to So Afr Y
68. Bar coun duty-free trtmt Y
69. Steel import limits Y
70. Soc Sec COLAs=inflation Y
71. Bar haz waste vctms suits N
72. Prohibit aid to Nicaragua Y
73. Cut $-Schs bar sch prayer ?
74. Raise taxes; Cut Medicare Y
75. Alien residncy-prior 1982 N
76. Alien residncy-prior 1980 N
77. Pen emp-hire illgl aliens Y
78. Lmt Persh II/cruse-Europe N
79. Delete 34 B-1 bombers N
80. Bar purch of Pershing II N
81. Bar purchase of Sgt York N
82. Delete $ for Trident II Y
83. Allow 15 MX missiles N
84. Bar MX procurement-1985 Y
85. Equal Access Act ?
86. Aid to El Salvador ?
87. Bar Nicarag water mining Y
88. Physician/Medicare freeze N

ROSTENKOWSKI, DAN (Cont.)

89. Increase "sin" taxes Y
90. End SBA direct loans N
91. Sell Conrail N
92. Equal Rights Amendment Y
93. Marines in Lebanon Y
94. Eminent domain-Coal comps N
95. Prohibit EPA sanctions N
96. SS age increase/Reforms Y
97. Auto domestic content req N
98. Delete jobs program fundg N
99. Highway-Gas tax bill Y
100. Raise Medicare;Cut defnse Y
101. Emergency housing aid Y
102. Across-the-board tax cuts N
103. Gramm-Latta II targets N
104. Delete B-1 bomber funds Y
105. Dsapprov Saudi AWACS sale Y
106. Disapprove oil import fee N
107. Rail Deregulation Y
108. Dsapp India nuc fuel sale N
109. Mil draft registration Y
110. Chrysler Loan Guarantees Y
111. Prohibit school busing N
112. Nuclear plant moratorium ?
113. Oil price controls N
114. Tuition Tax Credits Y
115. Est Consumer Protect Agcy #
116. Eliminate B-1 bomber fnds Y
117. Subminimum wage for youth N
118. Delete crude oil tax N
119. Natural gas deregulation N

Presidential Support Score: 1986 - 19% 1985 - 28%

YATES, SIDNEY R. -- Illinois 9th District [Democrat]. County of Cook (pt.). Prior Terms: House: 1949-62; 1965-86. Born: August 27, 1909; Chicago, Ill. Education: University of Chicago (Ph.D., J.D.). Military Service: U.S. Navy. Occupation: Assistant attorney, Illinois state bank receiver (1935-37); assistant attorney general (1937-40); editor, law bulletin (1947); U.S. representative, Trusteeship Council, U.N. (1963-64).

1. Immigration Reform ?
2. Open fld-search warrants ?
3. Civil pnty-hire ill alien N
4. So Afr sanc-veto override Y
5. Tax Overhaul Y
6. South Africa sanctions Y
7. Death penalty-drug bill N
8. Evidence-warrantless srch N
9. Life term-second drug off N
10. Military use in drug war N
11. Troop reduction in Europe ?
12. Prohibit chemical weapons Y
13. Bar ASAT testing Y
14. Abide SALT II weapons ban #
15. Follow SALT II-Soviets do ?
16. Reduce SDI funding Y
17. Increase SDI funding N
18. Purchase Trident sub X
19. Delete 12 MX;Add conv wpn +
20. Raise speed limit N
21. Textile Import Quotas(*) Y
22. Req Pentagon buy US goods N
23. AIDS ins anti-dscriminatn Y
24. Nicaraguan refugee aid Y
25. Nicaraguan contra aid N
26. US abide by SALT II N
27. Prohibit Saudi arms sale Y
28. Military Retiremnt Reform Y
29. Nicaraguan refugee aid Y
30. Ease '68 Gun Control Act N
31. Bar intrstat handgun tran Y
32. Keep '68 Gun Control Act Y
33. Nicaraguan contra aid N
34. Bar emp polygraph testing Y
35. Tax Overhaul consideratn Y
36. Bar armor-piercing ammo Y
37. Tax Overhaul consideratn Y
38. Make comp emissions known Y
39. Allow toxic victims suits Y
40. Strike Superfund "VAT" Y
41. Notify emp-plant closing Y
42. Bar emp consult-plant clo N
43. Medicare cuts;Tax incres' Y
44. Delete 12 MX missiles Y
45. Spending cuts;Tax incres' Y
46. Textile Import Quotas N
47. Cut some school lunch fds N
48. Clean Water Act Amendmnts N
49. Youth work projects Y
50. Assist military in Angola N
51. Allow US troops-Nicaragua N
52. Pentagon polygraph exams N
53. Bar ASAT testing Y
54. Suspend def pmt for abuse Y
55. Bar Pentagon-contr emplmt Y
56. Increase SDI funding N
57. Reduce SDI funding Y
58. Produce chemical weapons N
59. Bar CIA fndg in Nicaragua Y
60. South Africa sanctions Y
61. Cut SS COLAs; Raise taxes N
62. Let US invest-So Africa N

YATES, SIDNEY R. (Cont.)

63. Approve 21 MX for 1985 N
64. Emergency Farm Credit Y
65. Awards to whistle blowers Y
66. African disaster relief Y
67. Ban bank loans to So Afr Y
68. Bar coun duty-free trtmt Y
69. Steel import limits Y
70. Soc Sec COLAs=inflation Y
71. Bar haz waste vctms suits N
72. Prohibit aid to Nicaragua Y
73. Cut $-Schs bar sch prayer N
74. Raise taxes; cut Medicare Y
75. Alien residncy-prior 1982 N
76. Alien residncy-prior 1980 N
77. Pen emp-hire illgl aliens Y
78. Lmt Persh II/cruse-Europe Y
79. Delete 34 B-1 bombers Y
80. Bar purch of Pershing II Y
81. Bar purchase of Sgt York Y
82. Delete $ for Trident II Y
83. Allow 15 MX missiles N
84. Bar MX procurement-1985 Y
85. Equal Access Act N
86. Aid to El Salvador N
87. Bar Nicarag water mining Y
88. Physician/Medicare freeze N
89. Increase "sin" taxes Y
90. End SBA direct loans N
91. Sell Conrail N
92. Equal Rights Amendment Y
93. Marines in Lebanon N
94. Eminent domain-Coal comps N
95. Prohibit EPA sanctions Y
96. SS age increase/Reforms N
97. Auto domestic content req ?
98. Delete jobs program fundg N
99. Highway-Gas tax bill Y
100. Raise Medicare;Cut defnse Y
101. Emergency housing aid Y
102. Across-the-board tax cuts N
103. Gramm-Latta IC targets N
104. Delete B-1 bomber funds Y
105. Dsapprov Saudi AWACS sale Y
106. Disapprove oil import fee Y
107. Rail Deregulation Y
108. Dsapp India nuc fuel sale Y
109. Mil draft registration N
110. Chrysler Loan Guarantees ?
111. Prohibit school busing N
112. Nuclear plant moratorium Y
113. Oil price controls Y
114. Tuition Tax Credits N
115. Est Consumer Protect Agcy Y
116. Eliminate B-1 bomber fnds Y
117. Subminimum wage for youth N
118. Delete crude oil tax Y
119. Natural gas deregulation N

Presidential Support Score: 1986 - 18% 1985 - 31%

PORTER, JOHN EDWARD -- Illinois 10th District [Republican]. Counties of Cook (pt.) and Lake (pt.). Prior Terms: House: 1980 (Special Election)-1986. Born: June 1, 1935; Evanston, Ill. Education: Massachusetts Institute of Technology; Northwestern University (B.S., B.A.); University of Michigan (J.D.). Military Service: U.S. Army Reserves, 1958-64. Occupation: Illinois representative (1973-79); attorney.

1. Immigration Reform Y
2. Open fld-search warrants N
3. Civil pnty-hire ill alien N
4. So Afr sanc-veto override N
5. Tax Overhaul Y
6. South Africa sanctions N
7. Death penalty-drug bill Y
8. Evidence-warrantless srch Y
9. Life term-second drug off Y
10. Military use in drug war Y
11. Troop reduction in Europe N
12. Prohibit chemical weapons Y
13. Bar ASAT testing Y
14. Abide SALT II weapons ban N
15. Follow SALT II-Soviets do Y
16. Reduce SDI funding N
17. Increase SDI funding N
18. Purchase Trident sub N
19. Delete 12 MX;Add conv wpn N
20. Raise speed limit Y
21. Textile Import Quotas(*) N
22. Req Pentagon buy US goods N
23. AIDS ins anti-dscriminatn N
24. Nicaraguan refugee aid N
25. Nicaraguan contra aid Y
26. US abide by SALT II Y
27. Prohibit Saudi arms sale Y
28. Military Retiremnt Reform Y
29. Nicaraguan refugee aid Y
30. Ease '68 Gun Control Act N
31. Bar intrstat handgun tran Y
32. Keep '68 Gun Control Act Y
33. Nicaraguan contra aid Y
34. Bar emp polygraph testing N
35. Tax Overhaul consideratn Y
36. Bar armor-piercing ammo Y
37. Tax Overhaul consideratn N
38. Make comp emissions known N

PORTER, JOHN EDWARD (Cont.)

39. Allow toxic victims suits N
40. Strike Superfund "VAT" Y
41. Notify emp-plant closing N
42. Bar emp consult-plant clo Y
43. Medicare cuts;Tax incres' Y
44. Delete 12 MX missiles N
45. Spending cuts;Tax incres' Y
46. Textile Import Quotas -
47. Cut some school lunch fds Y
48. Clean Water Act Amendmnts Y
49. Youth work projects N
50. Assist military in Angola Y
51. Allow US troops-Nicaragua Y
52. Pentagon polygraph exams Y
53. Bar ASAT testing Y
54. Suspend def pmt for abuse N
55. Bar Pentagon-contr emplmt Y
56. Increase SDI funding N
57. Reduce SDI funding N
58. Produce chemical weapons N
59. Bar CIA fndg in Nicaragua N
60. South Africa sanctions Y
61. Cut SS COLAs; Raise taxes Y
62. Let US invest-So Africa Y
63. Approve 21 MX for 1985 Y
64. Emergency Farm Credit N
65. Awards to whistle blowers Y
66. African disaster relief Y
67. Ban bank loans to So Afr Y
68. Bar coun duty-free trtmt N
69. Steel import limits N
70. Soc Sec COLAs=inflation Y
71. Bar haz waste vctms suits Y
72. Prohibit aid to Nicaragua Y
73. Cut $-Schs bar sch prayer N
74. Raise taxes; Cut Medicare Y
75. Alien residncy-prior 1982 Y
76. Alien residncy-prior 1980 Y
77. Pen emp-hire illgl aliens N
78. Lmt Persh II/cruse-Europe N
79. Delete 34 B-1 bombers N
80. Bar purch of Pershing II N
81. Bar purchase of Sgt York Y
82. Delete $ for Trident II N
83. Allow 15 MX missiles Y
84. Bar MX procurement-1985 N
85. Equal Access Act N
86. Aid to El Salvador Y
87. Bar Nicarag water mining N
88. Physician/Medicare freeze Y
89. Increase "sin" taxes Y
90. End SBA direct loans Y
91. Sell Conrail Y
92. Equal Rights Amendment Y
93. Marines in Lebanon Y
94. Eminent domain-Coal comps Y
95. Prohibit EPA sanctions N
96. SS age increase/Reforms Y
97. Auto domestic content req N
98. Delete jobs program fundg Y
99. Highway-Gas tax bill N
100. Raise Medicare;Cut defnse Y
101. Emergency housing aid Y
102. Across-the-board tax cuts Y
103. Gramm-Latta II targets Y
104. Delete B-1 bomber funds N
105. Dsapprov Saudi AWACS sale Y
106. Disapprove oil import fee Y
107. Rail Deregulation N
108. Dsapp India nuc fuel sale Y
109. Mil draft registration N

Presidential Support Score: 1986 - 58% 1985 - 68%

ANNUNZIO, FRANK -- Illinois 11th District [Democrat]. County of Cook (pt.). Prior Terms: House: 1965-86. Born: January 12, 1915; Chicago, Ill. Education: DePaul University (B.S., M.S.). Occupation: Teacher (1936-42); assistant supervisor, National Defense Program (1942-43); educational and legislative representative, United States Steelworkers of America (1943-48); Illinois director of labor (1948-52).

1. Immigration Reform Y
2. Open fld-search warrants Y
3. Civil pnty-hire ill alien N
4. So Afr sanc-veto override Y
5. Tax Overhaul Y
6. South Africa sanctions Y
7. Death penalty-drug bill Y
8. Evidence-warrantless srch N
9. Life term-second drug off Y
10. Military use in drug war Y
11. Troop reduction in Europe N
12. Prohibit chemical weapons Y
13. Bar ASAT testing Y
14. Abide SALT II weapons ban Y
15. Follow SALT II-Soviets do N
16. Reduce SDI funding N
17. Increase SDI funding N
18. Purchase Trident sub Y
19. Delete 12 MX;Add conv wpn Y
20. Raise speed limit N
21. Textile Import Quotas(*) Y
22. Req Pentagon buy US goods Y
23. AIDS ins anti-dscriminatn Y
24. Nicaraguan refugee aid Y

ANNUNZIO, FRANK (Cont.)

25. Nicaraguan contra aid N
26. US abide by SALT II N
27. Prohibit Saudi arms sale Y
28. Military Retiremnt Reform Y
29. Nicaraguan refugee aid Y
30. Ease '68 Gun Control Act N
31. Bar intrstat handgun tran Y
32. Keep '68 Gun Control Act Y
33. Nicaraguan contra aid N
34. Bar emp polygraph testing Y
35. Tax Overhaul consideratn Y
36. Bar armor-piercing ammo Y
37. Tax Overhaul consideratn Y
38. Make comp emissions known Y
39. Allow toxic victims suits Y
40. Strike Superfund "VAT" Y
41. Notify emp-plant closing Y
42. Bar emp consult-plant clo N
43. Medicare cuts;Tax incres' Y
44. Delete 12 MX missiles Y
45. Spending cuts;Tax incres' Y
46. Textile Import Quotas Y
47. Cut some school lunch fds N
48. Clean Water Act Amendmnts N
49. Youth work projects Y
50. Assist military in Angola N
51. Allow US troops-Nicaragua N
52. Pentagon polygrCph exams ?
53. Bar ASAT testing Y
54. Suspend def pmt for abuse N
55. Bar Pentagon-contr emplmt Y
56. Increase SDI funding N
57. Reduce SDI funding N
58. Produce chemical weapons N
59. Bar CIA fndg in Nicaragua Y
60. South Africa sanctions Y
61. Cut SS COLAs; Raise taxes N
62. Let US invest-So Africa N
63. Approve 21 MX for 1985 N
64. Emergency Farm Credit Y
65. Awards to whistle blowers Y
66. African disaster relief Y
67. Ban bank loans to So Afr Y
68. Bar coun duty-free trtmt Y
69. Steel import limits Y
70. Soc Sec COLAs=inflation Y
71. Bar haz waste vctms suits N
72. Prohibit aid to Nicaragua Y
73. Cut $-Schs bar sch prayer N
74. Raise taxes; Cut Medicare Y
75. Alien residncy-prior 1982 N
76. Alien residncy-prior 1980 N
77. Pen emp-hire illgl aliens Y
78. Lmt Persh II/cruse-Europe N
79. Delete 34 B-1 bombers N
80. Bar purch of Pershing II N
81. Bar purchase of Sgt York N
82. Delete $ for Trident II N
83. Allow 15 MX missiles N
84. Bar MX procurement-1985 Y
85. Equal Access Act N
86. Aid to El Salvador N
87. Bar Nicarag water mining Y
88. Physician/Medicare freeze N
89. Increase "sin" taxes Y
90. End SBA direct loans N
91. Sell Conrail N
92. Equal Rights Amendment Y
93. Marines in Lebanon Y
94. Eminent domain-Coal comps Y
95. Prohibit EPA sanctions N
96. SS age increase/Reforms Y
97. Auto domestic content req Y
98. Delete jobs program fundg N
99. Highway-Gas tax bill Y
100. Raise Medicare;cut defnse Y
101. Emergency housing aid Y
102. Across-the-board tax cuts N
103. Gramm-Latta II targets N
104. Delete B-1 bomber funds N
105. Dsapprov Saudi AWACS sale Y
106. Disapprove oil import fee ?
107. Rail Deregulation Y
108. Dsapp India nuc fuel sale N
109. Mil draft registration N
110. Chrysler Loan Guarantees Y
111. Prohibit school busing Y
112. Nuclear plant moratorium N
113. Oil price controls Y
114. Tuition Tax Credits Y
115. Est Consumer Protect Agcy Y
116. Eliminate B-1 bomber fnds Y
117. Subminimum wage for youth N
118. Delete crude oil tax N
119. Natural gas deregulation N

Presidential Support Score: 1986 - 24% 1985 - 29%

CRANE, PHILIP M. -- Illinois 12th District [Republican]. Counties of Cook (pt.), Lake (pt.) and McHenry (pt.). Prior Terms: House: 1969 (Special Election)-1986. Born: November 3, 1930; Chicago, Ill. Education: DePauw University; Hillsdale College; University of Michigan; University of Vienna; Indiana University (M.A., Ph.D.). Occupation: Teacher; director of schools; trustee; director, Intercollegiate Studies Institute; chairman, American Conservative Union; author.

CRANE, PHILIP M. (Cont.)

1.	Immigration Reform	N	60.	South Africa sanctions	N
2.	Open fld-search warrants	Y	61.	Cut SS COLAs; Raise taxes	N
3.	Civil pnty-hire ill alien	Y	62.	Let US invest-So Africa	Y
4.	So Afr sanc-veto override	N	63.	Approve 21 MX for 1985	Y
5.	Tax Overhaul	N	64.	Emergency Farm Credit	N
6.	South Africa sanctions	N	65.	Awards to whistle blowers	?
7.	Death penalty-drug bill	Y	66.	African disaster relief	X
8.	Evidence-warrantless srch	Y	67.	Ban bank loans to So Afr	N
9.	Life term-second drug off	Y	68.	Bar coun duty-free trtmt	N
10.	Military use in drug war	Y	69.	Steel import limits	N
11.	Troop reduction in Europe	N	70.	Soc Sec COLAs=inflation	N
12.	Prohibit chemical weapons	N	71.	Bar haz waste vctms suits	Y
13.	Bar ASAT testing	N	72.	Prohibit aid to Nicaragua	N
14.	Abide SALT II weapons ban	N	73.	Cut $-Schs bar sch prayer	Y
15.	Follow SALT II-Soviets do	Y	74.	Raise taxes; Cut Medicare	N
16.	Reduce SDI funding	N	75.	Alien residncy-prior 1982	Y
17.	Increase SDI funding	Y	76.	Alien residncy-prior 1980	Y
18.	Purchase Trident sub	N	77.	Pen emp-hire illgl aliens	N
19.	Delete 12 MX;Add conv wpn	N	78.	Lmt Persh II/cruse-Europe	N
20.	Raise speed limit	Y	79.	Delete 34 B-1 bombers	N
21.	Textile Import Quotas(*)	N	80.	Bar purch of Pershing II	N
22.	Req Pentagon buy US goods	N	81.	Bar purchase of Sgt York	N
23.	AIDS ins anti-dscriminatn	N	82.	Delete $ for Trident II	N
24.	Nicaraguan refugee aid	N	83.	Allow 15 MX missiles	Y
25.	Nicaraguan contra aid	Y	84.	Bar MX procurement-1985	N
26.	US abide by SALT II	Y	85.	Equal Access Act	Y
27.	Prohibit Saudi arms sale	Y	86.	Aid to El Salvador	Y
28.	Military Retiremnt Reform	Y	87.	Bar Nicarag water mining	N
29.	Nicaraguan refugee aid	Y	88.	Physician/Medicare freeze	Y
30.	Ease '68 Gun Control Act	Y	89.	Increase "sin" taxes	N
31.	Bar intrstat handgun tran	N	90.	End SBA direct loans	Y
32.	Keep '68 Gun Control Act	N	91.	Sell Conrail	Y
33.	Nicaraguan contra aid	Y	92.	Equal Rights Amendment	N
34.	Bar emp polygraph testing	N	93.	Marines in Lebanon	N
35.	Tax Overhaul consideratn	N	94.	Eminent domain-Coal comps	Y
36.	Bar armor-piercing ammo	N	95.	Prohibit EPA sanctions	Y
37.	Tax Overhaul consideratn	N	96.	SS age increase/Reforms	Y
38.	Make comp emissions known	N	97.	Auto domestic content req	N
39.	Allow toxic victims suits	N	98.	Delete jobs program fundg	Y
40.	Strike Superfund "VAT"	N	99.	Highway-Gas tax bill	N
41.	Notify emp-plant closing	X	100.	Raise Medicare;Cut defnse	N
42.	Bar emp consult-plant clo	Y	101.	Emergency housing aid	N
43.	Medicare cuts;Tax incres'	N	102.	Across-the-board tax cuts	Y
44.	Delete 12 MX missiles	N	103.	Gramm-Latta II targets	Y
45.	Spending cuts;Tax incres'	N	104.	Delete B-1 bomber funds	N
46.	Textile Import Quotas	N	105.	Dsapprov Saudi AWACS sale	?
47.	Cut some school lunch fds	Y	106.	Disapprove oil import fee	Y
48.	Clean Water Act Amendmnts	N	107.	Rail Deregulation	N
49.	Youth work projects	N	108.	Dsapp India nuc fuel sale	Y
50.	Assist military in Angola	Y	109.	Mil draft registration	N
51.	Allow US troops-Nicaragua	Y	110.	Chrysler Loan Guarantees	X
52.	Pentagon polygraph exams	Y	111.	Prohibit school busing	Y
53.	Bar ASAT testing	N	112.	Nuclear plant moratorium	?
54.	Suspend def pmt for abuse	N	113.	Oil price controls	?
55.	Bar Pentagon-contr emplmt	Y	114.	Tuition Tax Credits	#
56.	Increase SDI funding	Y	115.	Est Consumer Protect Agcy	N
57.	Reduce SDI funding	N	116.	Eliminate B-1 bomber fnds	N
58.	Produce chemical weapons	Y	117.	Subminimum wage for youth	Y
59.	Bar CIA fndg in Nicaragua	N	118.	Delete crude oil tax	Y

CRANE, PHILIP M. (Cont.)
119. Natural gas deregulation Y

Presidential Support Score: 1986 - 83% 1985 - 80%

FAWELL, HARRIS W. -- Illinois 13th District [Republican]. Counties of Cook (pt.), Du Page (pt.) and Will (pt.). Prior Terms: 1985-86. Occupation: Attorney; Illinois senator.

1. Immigration Reform N
2. Open fld-search warrants N
3. Civil pnty-hire ill alien N
4. So Afr sanc-veto override Y
5. Tax Overp emissions known Y
6. South Africa sanctions Y
7. Death penalty-drug bill Y
8. Evidence-warrantless srch Y
9. Bar emp consult-plant clo Y
10. Military use in drug war Y
11. Troop reduction in Europe N
12. Prohibit chemical weapons N
13. Bar ASAT testing N
14. Abide SALT II weapons ban N
15. Follow SALT II-Soviets do Y
16. Reduce SDI funding N
17. Increase SDI funding N
18. Purchase Trident sub N
19. Delete 12 MX;Add conv wpn N
20. Raise speed limit N
21. Textile Import Quotas(*) N
22. Req Pentagon buy US goods N
23. AIDS ins anti-dscriminatn N
24. Nicaraguan refugee aid N
25. Nicaraguan contra aid Y
26. US abide by SALT II Y
27. Prohibit Saudi arms sale N
28. Military Retiremnt Reform Y
29. Nicaraguan refugee aid Y
30. Ease '68 Gun Control Act N
31. Bar intrstat handgun tran Y
32. Keep '68 Gun Control Act Y
33. Nicaraguan contra aid Y
34. Bar emp polygraph testing N
35. Tax Overhaul consideratn Y
36. Bar armor-piercing ammo Y
37. Tax Overhaul consideratn N
38. Make comp emissions known Y
39. Allow toxic victims suits N
40. Strike Superfund "VAT" Y
41. Notify emp-plant closing N
42. Bar emp consult-plant clo Y
43. Medicare cuts;Tax incres' N
44. Delete 12 MX missiles N
45. Spending cuts;Tax incres' N
46. Textile Import Quotas N
47. Cut some school lunch fds Y
48. Clean Water Act Amendmnts Y
49. Youth work projects N
50. Assist military in Angola Y
51. Allow US troops-Nicaragua Y
52. Pentagon polygraph exams Y
53. Bar ASAT testing N
54. Suspend def pmt for abuse Y
55. Bar Pentagon-contr emplmt Y
56. Increase SDI funding Y
57. Reduce SDI funding N
58. Produce chemical weapons Y
59. Bar CIA fndg in Nicaragua N
60. South Africa sanctions N
61. Cut SS COLAs; Raise taxes N
62. Let US invest-So Africa Y
63. Approve 21 MX for 1985 Y
64. Emergency Farm Credit N
65. Awards to whistle blowers Y
66. African disaster relief Y

Presidential Support Score: 1986 - 68% 1985 - 85%

GROTBERG, JOHN E. -- Illinois 14th District [Republican]. Counties of Boone (pt.), Cook (pt.), De Kalb, Du Page (pt.), Kane (pt.), Kendall (pt.), La Salle (pt.), McHenry (pt.) and Marshall (pt.). Prior Terms: 1985-86. Occupation: Management consultant; Illinois legislator; Illinois senator.

John Grotberg died November 16, 1986 and had not voted in 1986 because of illness.

MADIGAN, EDWARD R. -- Illinois 15th District [Republican]. Counties of Champaign (pt.), De Witt, Ford, Grundy, Iroquois, Kankakee, La Salle (pt.), Livingston, Logan (pt.), McLean, Platt, Will (pt.) and Woodford (pt.). Prior Terms: House: 1973-86. Born: January 13, 1936; Lincoln, Ill. Education: Lincoln College. Occupation: Member, Board of Zoning Appeals;

MADIGAN, EDWARD R. (Cont.)
owner, taxicab fleet and car leasing firm; Illinois assembly (1967-73).

1. Immigration Reform N
2. Open fld-search warrants Y
3. Civil pnty-hire ill alien N
4. So Afr sanc-veto override Y
5. Tax Overhaul N
6. South Africa sanctions Y
7. Death penalty-drug bill Y
8. Evidence-warrantless srch Y
9. Life term-second drug off Y
10. Military use in drug war Y
11. Troop reduction in Europe N
12. Prohibit chemical weapons N
13. Bar ASAT testing N
14. Abide SALT II weapons ban N
15. Follow SALT II-Soviets do Y
16. Reduce SDI funding N
17. Increase SDI funding N
18. Purchase Trident sub N
19. Delete 12 MX;Add conv wpn N
20. Raise speed limit Y
21. Textile Import Quotas(*) N
22. Req Pentagon buy US goods Y
23. AIDS ins anti-dscriminatn N
24. Nicaraguan refugee aid N
25. Nicaraguan contra aid Y
26. US abide by SALT II Y
27. Prohibit Saudi arms sale N
28. Military Retiremnt Reform Y
29. Nicaraguan refugee aid Y
30. Ease '68 Gun Control Act Y
31. Bar intrstat handgun tran Y
32. Keep '68 Gun Control Act N
33. Nicaraguan contra aid Y
34. Bar emp polygraph testing ?
35. Tax Overhaul consideratn N
36. Bar armor-piercing ammo Y
37. Tax Overhaul consideratn N
38. Make comp emissions known N
39. Allow toxic victims suits N
40. Strike Superfund "VAT" Y
41. Notify emp-plant closing Y
42. Bar emp consult-plant clo N
43. Medicare cuts;Tax incres' N
44. Delete 12 MX missiles N
45. Spending cuts;Tax incres' N
46. Textile Import Quotas N
47. Cut some school lunch fds N
48. Clean Water Act Amendmnts Y
49. Youth work projects N
50. Assist military in Angola Y
51. Allow US troops-Nicaragua Y
52. Pentagon polygraph exams Y
53. Bar ASAT testing N
54. Suspend def pmt for abuse Y
55. Bar Pentagon-contr emplmt Y
56. Increase SDI funding N
57. Reduce SDI funding N
58. Produce chemical weapons Y
59. Bar CIA fndg in Nicaragua N
60. South Africa sanctions Y
61. Cut SS COLAs; Raise taxes N
62. Let US invest-So Africa Y
63. Approve 21 MX for 1985 Y
64. Emergency Farm Credit ?
65. Awards to whistle blowers ?
66. African disaster relief ?
67. Ban bank loans to So Afr Y
68. Bar coun duty-free trtmt N
69. Steel import limits Y
70. Soc Sec COLAs=inflation Y
71. Bar haz waste vctms suits N
72. Prohibit aid to Nicaragua Y
73. Cut $-Schs bar sch prayer Y
74. Raise taxes; Cut Medicare Y
75. Alien residncy-prior 1982 ?
76. Alien residncy-prior 1980 Y
77. Pen emp-hire illgl aliens N
78. Lmt Persh II/cruse-Europe N
79. Delete 34 B-1 bombers N
80. Bar purch of Pershing II N
81. Bar purchase of Sgt York N
82. Delete $ for Trident II N
83. Allow 15 MX missiles Y
84. Bar MX procurement-1985 N
85. Equal Access Act Y
86. Aid to El Salvador Y
87. Bar Nicarag water mining Y
88. Physician/Medicare freeze Y
89. Increase "sin" taxes N
90. End SBA direct loans N
91. Sell Conrail N
92. Equal Rights Amendment N
93. Marines in Lebanon Y
94. Eminent domain-Coal comps N
95. Prohibit EPA sanctions Y
96. SS age increase/Reforms Y
97. Auto domestic content req Y
98. Delete jobs program fundg Y
99. Highway-Gas tax bill N
100. Raise Medicare;Cut defnse N
101. Emergency housing aid Y
102. Across-the-board tax cuts Y
103. Gramm-Latta II targets Y
104. Delete B-1 bomber funds ?
105. Dsapprov Saudi AWACS sale Y
106. Disapprove oil import fee Y
107. Rail Deregulation N
108. Dsapp India nuc fuel sale N
109. Mil draft registration N
110. Chrysler Loan Guarantees Y
111. Prohibit school busing N
112. Nuclear plant moratorium N

MADIGAN, EDWARD R. (Cont.)

113. Oil price controls N
114. Tuition Tax Credits ?
115. Est Consumer Protect Agcy N
116. Eliminate B-1 bomber fnds N
117. Subminimum wage for youth Y
118. Delete crude oil tax Y
119. Natural gas deregulation Y

Presidential Support Score: 1986 - 67% 1985 - 60%

MARTIN, LYNN -- Illinois 16th District [Republican]. Counties of Boone (pt.), Carroll, Jo Daviess, Lee, Ogle, Stephenson, Whiteside and Winnebago. Prior Terms: House: 1981-86. Born: December 26, 1939; Chicago, Ill. Education: University of Illinois (B.A.). Occupation: Teacher; Illinois representative (1977-79); Illinois senator (1979).

1. Immigration Reform Y
2. Open fld-search warrants Y
3. Civil pnty-hire ill alien N
4. So Afr sanc-veto override Y
5. Tax Overhaul Y
6. South Africa sanctions Y
7. Death penalty-drug bill Y
8. Evidence-warrantless srch Y
9. Life term-second drug off Y
10. Military use in drug war Y
11. Troop reduction in Europe Y
12. Prohibit chemical weapons Y
13. Bar ASAT testing N
14. Abide SALT II weapons ban N
15. Follow SALT II-Soviets do Y
16. Reduce SDI funding N
17. Increase SDI funding N
18. Purchase Trident sub N
19. Delete 12 MX;Add conv wpn N
20. Raise speed limit N
21. Textile Import Quotas(*) N
22. Req Pentagon buy US goods Y
23. AIDS ins anti-dscriminatn N
24. Nicaraguan refugee aid N
25. Nicaraguan contra aid Y
26. US abide by SALT II Y
27. Prohibit Saudi arms sale Y
28. Military Retiremnt Reform Y
29. Nicaraguan refugee aid Y
30. Ease '68 Gun Control Act Y
31. Bar intrstat handgun tran ?
32. Keep '68 Gun Control Act Y
33. Nicaraguan contra aid Y
34. Bar emp polygraph testing Y
35. Tax Overhaul consideratn N
36. Bar armor-piercing ammo Y
37. Tax Overhaul consideratn N
38. Make comp emissions known N
39. Allow toxic victims suits N
40. Strike Superfund "VAT" Y
41. Notify emp-plant closing N
42. Bar emp consult-plant clo Y
43. Medicare cuts;Tax incres' N
44. Delete 12 MX missiles N
45. Spending cuts;Tax incres' N
46. Textile Import Quotas ?
47. Cut some school lunch fds Y
48. Clean Water Act Amendmnts Y
49. Youth work projects N
50. Assist military in Angola Y
51. Allow US troops-Nicaragua Y
52. Pentagon polygraph exams Y
53. Bar ASAT testing N
54. Suspend def pmt for abuse N
55. Bar Pentagon-contr emplmt Y
56. Increase SDI funding Y
57. Reduce SDI funding N
58. Produce chemical weapons N
59. Bar CIA fndg in Nicaragua N
60. South Africa sanctions Y
61. Cut SS COLAs; Raise taxes N
62. Let US invest-So Africa N
63. Approve 21 MX for 1985 Y
64. Emergency Farm Credit ?
65. Awards to whistle blowers ?
66. African disaster relief ?
67. Ban bank loans to So Afr Y
68. Bar coun duty-free trtmt N
69. Steel import limits Y
70. Soc Sec COLAs=inflation Y
71. Bar haz waste vctms suits Y
72. Prohibit aid to Nicaragua Y
73. Cut $-Schs bar sch prayer N
74. Raise taxes; Cut Medicare N
75. Alien residncy-prior 1982 N
76. Alien residncy-prior 1980 Y
77. Pen emp-hire illgl aliens Y
78. Lmt Persh II/cruse-Europe N
79. Delete 34 B-1 bombers N
80. Bar purch of Pershing II N
81. Bar purchase of Sgt York ?
82. Delete $ for Trident II N
83. Allow 15 MX missiles Y
84. Bar MX procurement-1985 N
85. Equal Access Act Y
86. Aid to El Salvador Y
87. Bar Nicarag water mining Y
88. Physician/Medicare freeze Y
89. Increase "sin" taxes N
90. End SBA direct loans Y

MARTIN, LYNN (Cont.)

91.	Sell Conrail	N	99.	Highway-Gas tax bill	Y
92.	Equal Rights Amendment	Y	100.	Raise Medicare;Cut defnse	N
93.	Marines in Lebanon	Y	101.	Emergency housing aid	N
94.	Eminent domain-Coal comps	N	102.	Across-the-board tax cuts	Y
95.	Prohibit EPA sanctions	N	103.	Gramm-Latta II targets	Y
96.	SS age increase/Reforms	Y	104.	Delete B-1 bomber funds	N
97.	Auto domestic content req	Y	105.	Dsapprov Saudi AWACS sale	Y
98.	Delete jobs program fundg	Y			

Presidential Support Score: 1986 - 75% 1985 - 61%

EVANS, LANE -- Illinois 17th District [Democrat]. Counties of Bureau, Fulton (pt.), Henderson, Henry, Knox, La Salle (pt.), McDonough (pt.), Marshall (pt.), Mercer, Peoria (pt.), Putnam, Rock Island, Stark and Warren. Prior Terms: House: 1983-86. Born: August 4, 1951; Rock Island, Ill. Education: Augustana College (B.A.); Georgetown University Law Center. Military Service: U.S. Marine Corps. Occupation: Partner, Community Legal Clinic; legal counsel, National Association for the Advancement of Colored People and American Civil Liberties Union.

1.	Immigration Reform	N	38.	Make comp emissions known	Y
2.	Open fld-search warrants	Y	39.	Allow toxic victims suits	Y
3.	Civil pnty-hire ill alien	Y	40.	Strike Superfund "VAT"	Y
4.	So Afr sanc-veto override	Y	41.	Notify emp-plant closing	Y
5.	Tax Overhaul	Y	42.	Bar emp consult-plant clo	N
6.	South Africa sanctions	Y	43.	Medicare cuts;Tax incres'	Y
7.	Death penalty-drug bill	N	44.	Delete 12 MX missiles	Y
8.	Evidence-warrantless srch	N	45.	Spending cuts;Tax incres'	Y
9.	Life term-second drug off	N	46.	Textile Import Quotas	Y
10.	Military use in drug war	N	47.	Cut some school lunch fds	N
11.	Troop reduction in Europe	Y	48.	Clean Water Act Amendmnts	N
12.	Prohibit chemical weapons	Y	49.	Youth work projects	Y
13.	Bar ASAT testing	Y	50.	Assist military in Angola	N
14.	Abide SALT II weapons ban	Y	51.	Allow US troops-Nicaragua	N
15.	Follow SALT II-Soviets do	N	52.	Pentagon polygraph exams	Y
16.	Reduce SDI funding	Y	53.	Bar ASAT testing	Y
17.	Increase SDI funding	N	54.	Suspend def pmt for abuse	Y
18.	Purchase Trident sub	N	55.	Bar Pentagon-contr emplmt	Y
19.	Delete 12 MX;Add conv wpn	?	56.	Increase SDI funding	N
20.	Raise speed limit	N	57.	Reduce SDI funding	Y
21.	Textile Import Quotas(*)	Y	58.	Produce chemical weapons	N
22.	Req Pentagon buy US goods	Y	59.	Bar CIA fndg in Nicaragua	Y
23.	AIDS ins anti-dscriminatn	Y	60.	South Africa sanctions	Y
24.	Nicaraguan refugee aid	Y	61.	Cut SS COLAs; Raise taxes	N
25.	Nicaraguan contra aid	N	62.	Let US invest-So Africa	N
26.	US abide by SALT II	N	63.	Approve 21 MX for 1985	N
27.	Prohibit Saudi arms sale	Y	64.	Emergency Farm Credit	Y
28.	Military Retiremnt Reform	Y	65.	Awards to whistle blowers	Y
29.	Nicaraguan refugee aid	Y	66.	African disaster relief	Y
30.	Ease '68 Gun Control Act	N	67.	Ban bank loans to So Afr	Y
31.	Bar intrstat handgun tran	Y	68.	Bar coun duty-free trtmt	Y
32.	Keep '68 Gun Control Act	Y	69.	Steel import limits	Y
33.	Nicaraguan contra aid	N	70.	Soc Sec COLAs=inflation	Y
34.	Bar emp polygraph testing	Y	71.	Bar haz waste vctms suits	N
35.	Tax Overhaul consideratn	Y	72.	Prohibit aid to Nicaragua	Y
36.	Bar armor-piercing ammo	Y	73.	Cut $-Schs bar sch prayer	N
37.	Tax Overhaul consideratn	Y	74.	Raise taxes; Cut Medicare	Y

EVANS, LANE (Cont.)

75. Alien residncy-prior 1982 N
76. Alien residncy-prior 1980 N
77. Pen emp-hire illgl aliens Y
78. Lmt Persh II/cruse-Europe Y
79. Delete 34 B-1 bombers Y
80. Bar purch of Pershing II Y
81. Bar purchase of Sgt York Y
82. Delete $ for Trident II Y
83. Allow 15 MX missiles N
84. Bar MX procurement-1985 Y
85. Equal Access Act N
86. Aid to El Salvador N
87. Bar Nicarag water mining Y
88. Physician/Medicare freeze N
89. Increase "sin" taxes Y
90. End SBA direct loans N
91. Sell Conrail N
92. Equal Rights Amendment Y
93. Marines in Lebanon N
94. Eminent domain-Coal comps N
95. Prohibit EPA sanctions Y
96. SS age increase/Reforms N

Presidential Support Score: 1986 - 14% 1985 - 14%

MICHEL, ROBERT H. -- Illinois 18th District [Republican]. Counties of Brown, Cass, Fulton (pt.), Hancock, Logan (pt.), McDonough (pt.), Macon (pt.), Mason, Menard, Morgan, Peoria (pt.), Sangamon (pt.), Schuyler (pt.), Scott, Tazewell and Woodford (pt.). Prior Terms: House: 1957-86. Born: March 2, 1923; Peoria, Ill. Education: Bradley University (B.S.). Military Service: U.S. Army. Occupation: Congressional administrative assistant (1949-56).

1. Immigration Reform Y
2. Open fld-search warrants N
3. Civil pnty-hire ill alien N
4. So Afr sanc-veto override N
5. Tax Overhaul Y
6. South Africa sanctions ?
7. Death penalty-drug bill Y
8. Evidence-warrantless srch Y
9. Life term-second drug off Y
10. Military use in drug war Y
11. Troop reduction in Europe N
12. Prohibit chemical weapons N
13. Bar ASAT testing N
14. Abide SALT II weapons ban N
15. Follow SALT II-Soviets do Y
16. Reduce SDI funding N
17. Increase SDI funding Y
18. Purchase Trident sub N
19. Delete 12 MX;Add conv wpn N
20. Raise speed limit Y
21. Textile Import Quotas(*) N
22. Req Pentagon buy US goods N
23. AIDS ins anti-dscriminatn N
24. Nicaraguan refugee aid N
25. Nicaraguan contra aid Y
26. US abide by SALT II Y
27. Prohibit Saudi arms sale N
28. Military Retiremnt Reform Y
29. Nicaraguan refugee aid Y
30. Ease '68 Gun Control Act Y
31. Bar intrstat handgun tran N
32. Keep '68 Gun Control Act N
33. Nicaraguan contra aid Y
34. Bar emp polygraph testing N
35. Tax Overhaul consideratn Y
36. Bar armor-piercing ammo Y
37. Tax Overhaul consideratn N
38. Make comp emissions known N
39. Allow toxic victims suits N
40. Strike Superfund "VAT" Y
41. Notify emp-plant closing N
42. Bar emp consult-plant clo Y
43. Medicare cuts;Tax incres' N
44. Delete 12 MX missiles N
45. Spending cuts;Tax incres' N
46. Textile Import Quotas N
47. Cut some school lunch fds ?
48. Clean Water Act Amendmnts Y
49. Youth work projects N
50. Assist military in Angola Y
51. Allow US troops-Nicaragua Y
52. Pentagon polygraph exams Y
53. Bar ASAT testing N
54. Suspend def pmt for abuse N
55. Bar Pentagon-contr emplmt Y
56. Increase SDI funding Y
57. Reduce SDI funding N
58. Produce chemical weapons Y
59. Bar CIA fndg in Nicaragua N
60. South Africa sanctions N
61. Cut SS COLAs; Raise taxes N
62. Let US invest-So Africa ?
63. Approve 21 MX for 1985 Y
64. Emergency Farm Credit N
65. Awards to whistle blowers Y
66. African disaster relief Y
67. Ban bank loans to So Afr Y
68. Bar coun duty-free trtmt N
69. Steel import limits N
70. Soc Sec COLAs=inflation Y
71. Bar haz waste vctms suits Y
72. Prohibit aid to Nicaragua N

MICHEL, ROBERT H. (Cont.)

73. Cut $-Schs bar sch prayer Y
74. Raise taxes; Cut Medicare Y
75. Alien residncy-prior 1982 Y
76. Alien residncy-prior 1980 Y
77. Pen emp-hire illgl aliens N
78. Lmt Persh II/cruse-Europe N
79. Delete 34 B-1 bombers N
80. Bar purch of Pershing II N
81. Bar purchase of Sgt York N
82. Delete $ for Trident II N
83. Allow 15 MX missiles Y
84. Bar MX procurement-1985 N
85. Equal Access Act Y
86. Aid to El Salvador Y
87. Bar Nicarag water mining N
88. Physician/Medicare freeze Y
89. Increase "sin" taxes Y
90. End SBA direct loans N
91. Sell Conrail Y
92. Equal Rights Amendment N
93. Marines in Lebanon Y
94. Eminent domain-Coal comps Y
95. Prohibit EPA sanctions Y
96. SS age increase/Reforms Y
97. Auto domestic content req N
98. Delete jobs program fundg Y
99. Highway-Gas tax bill Y
100. Raise Medicare;Cut defnse N
101. Emergency housing aid N
102. Across-the-board tax cuts Y
103. Gramm-Latta II targets Y
104. Delete B-1 bomber funds N
105. Dsapprov Saudi AWACS sale N
106. Disapprove oil import fee Y
107. Rail Deregulation Y
108. Dsapp India nuc fuel sale Y
109. Mil draft registration X
110. Chrysler Loan Guarantees N
111. Prohibit school busing N
112. Nuclear plant moratorium N
113. Oil price controls X
114. Tuition Tax Credits Y
115. Est Consumer Protect Agcy N
116. Eliminate B-1 bomber fnds N
117. Subminimum wage for youth Y
118. Delete crude oil tax #
119. Natural gas deregulation Y

Presidential Support Score: 1986 - 75% 1985 - 85%

BRUCE, TERRY L. -- Illinois 19th District [Democrat]. Counties of Champaign (pt.), Clark, Clay, Coles, Crawford, Cumberland, Douglas, Edgar, Edwards, Effingham, Hamilton, Jasper, Lawrence, Richland, Vermilion, Wabash, Wayne and White. Prior Terms: 1985-86. Born: March 25, 1944. Education: University of Illinois (B.S., J.D.). Occupation: Attorney; Illinois senator.

1. Immigration Reform Y
2. Open fld-search warrants Y
3. Civil pnty-hire ill alien Y
4. So Afr sanc-veto override Y
5. Tax Overhaul N
6. South Africa sanctions Y
7. Death penalty-drug bill Y
8. Evidence-warrantless srch N
9. Life term-second drug off Y
10. Military use in drug war N
11. Troop reduction in Europe Y
12. Prohibit chemical weapons Y
13. Bar ASAT testing Y
14. Abide SALT II weapons ban Y
15. Follow SALT II-Soviets do N
16. Reduce SDI funding Y
17. Increase SDI funding N
18. Purchase Trident sub Y
19. Delete 12 MX;Add conv wpn Y
20. Raise speed limit N
21. Textile Import Quotas(*) Y
22. Req Pentagon buy US goods Y
23. AIDS ins anti-dscriminatn Y
24. Nicaraguan refugee aid Y
25. Nicaraguan contra aid N
26. US abide by SALT II N
27. Prohibit Saudi arms sale Y
28. Military Retiremnt Reform Y
29. Nicaraguan refugee aid Y
30. Ease '68 Gun Control Act Y
31. Bar intrstat handgun tran N
32. Keep '68 Gun Control Act N
33. Nicaraguan contra aid N
34. Bar emp polygraph testing Y
35. Tax Overhaul consideratn Y
36. Bar armor-piercing ammo Y
37. Tax Overhaul consideratn Y
38. Make comp emissions known Y
39. Allow toxic victims suits Y
40. Strike Superfund "VAT" N
41. Notify emp-plant closing Y
42. Bar emp consult-plant clo N
43. Medicare cuts;Tax incres' Y
44. Delete 12 MX missiles Y
45. Spending cuts;Tax incres' Y
46. Textile Import Quotas Y
47. Cut some school lunch fds N
48. Clean Water Act Amendmnts N

BRUCE, TERRY L. (Cont.)

49. Youth work projects Y
50. Assist military in Angola N
51. Allow US troops-Nicaragua N
52. Pentagon polygraph exams Y
53. Bar ASAT testing Y
54. Suspend def pmt for abuse Y
55. Bar Pentagon-contr emplmt Y
56. Increase SDI funding N
57. Reduce SDI funding Y
58. Produce chemical weapons N
59. Bar CIA fndg in Nicaragua Y
60. South Africa sanctions Y
61. Cut SS COLAs; Raise taxes N
62. Let US invest-So Africa N
63. Approve 21 MX for 1985 N
64. Emergency Farm Credit Y
65. Awards to whistle blowers Y
66. African disaster relief Y

Presidential Support Score: 1986 - 20% 1985 - 29%

DURBIN, RICHARD J. -- Illinois 20th District [Democrat]. Counties of Adams, Calhoun, Christian, Fayette (pt.), Green, Jersey, Macon (pt.), Macoupin, Montgomery (pt.), Moultrie, Pike, Sangamon (pt.), Schuyler (pt.) and Shelby. Prior Terms: House: 1983-86. Born: November 21, 1944; East St. Louis, Ill. Education: Georgetown University (B.A., J.D.). Occupation: U.S. Senate staff member; attorney; Illinois senator (1969-72, 1977-78); associate professor of Medical Humanities at Southern Illinois University.

1. Immigration Reform Y
2. Open fld-search warrants Y
3. Civil pnty-hire ill alien Y
4. So Afr sanc-veto override Y
5. Tax Overhaul Y
6. South Africa sanctions Y
7. Death penalty-drug bill Y
8. Evidence-warrantless srch Y
9. Life term-second drug off Y
10. Military use in drug war N
11. Troop reduction in Europe Y
12. Prohibit chemical weapons Y
13. Bar ASAT testing Y
14. Abide SALT II weapons ban Y
15. Follow SALT II-Soviets do N
16. Reduce SDI funding Y
17. Increase SDI funding N
18. Purchase Trident sub Y
19. Delete 12 MX;Add conv wpn Y
20. Raise speed limit Y
21. Textile Import Quotas(*) Y
22. Req Pentagon buy US goods Y
23. AIDS ins anti-dscriminatn Y
24. Nicaraguan refugee aid Y
25. Nicaraguan contra aid N
26. US abide by SALT II N
27. Prohibit Saudi arms sale Y
28. Military Retiremnt Reform Y
29. Nicaraguan refugee aid Y
30. Ease '68 Gun Control Act N
31. Bar intrstat handgun tran N
32. Keep '68 Gun Control Act Y
33. Nicaraguan contra aid N
34. Bar emp polygraph testing Y
35. Tax Overhaul consideratn Y
36. Bar armor-piercing ammo Y
37. Tax Overhaul consideratn Y
38. Make comp emissions known Y
39. Allow toxic victims suits Y
40. Strike Superfund "VAT" Y
41. Notify emp-plant closing Y
42. Bar emp consult-plant clo N
43. Medicare cuts;Tax incres' Y
44. Delete 12 MX missiles Y
45. Spending cuts;Tax incres' Y
46. Textile Import Quotas Y
47. Cut some school lunch fds N
48. Clean Water Act Amendmnts N
49. Youth work projects Y
50. Assist military in Angola N
51. Allow US troops-Nicaragua N
52. Pentagon polygraph exams Y
53. Bar ASAT testing Y
54. Suspend def pmt for abuse Y
55. Bar Pentagon-contr emplmt Y
56. Increase SDI funding N
57. Reduce SDI funding Y
58. Produce chemical weapons N
59. Bar CIA fndg in Nicaragua Y
60. South Africa sanctions Y
61. Cut SS COLAs; Raise taxes N
62. Let US invest-So Africa N
63. Approve 21 MX for 1985 N
64. Emergency Farm Credit Y
65. Awards to whistle blowers Y
66. African disaster relief Y
67. Ban bank loans to So Afr Y
68. Bar coun duty-free trtmt Y
69. Steel import limits Y
70. Soc Sec COLAs=inflation Y
71. Bar haz waste vctms suits N
72. Prohibit aid to Nicaragua Y
73. Cut $-Schs bar sch prayer N
74. Raise taxes; Cut Medicare Y

DURBIN, RICHARD J. (Cont.)

75. Alien residncy-prior 1982 Y
76. Alien residncy-prior 1980 Y
77. Pen emp-hire illgl aliens Y
78. Lmt Persh II/cruse-Europe N
79. Delete 34 B-1 bombers Y
80. Bar purch of Pershing II Y
81. Bar purchase of Sgt York Y
82. Delete $ for Trident II N
83. Allow 15 MX missiles N
84. Bar MX procurement-1985 Y
85. Equal Access Act N
86. Aid to El Salvador N
87. Bar Nicarag water mining Y
88. Physician/Medicare freeze N
89. Increase "sin" taxes Y
90. End SBA direct loans N
91. Sell Conrail N
92. Equal Rights Amendment Y
93. Marines in Lebanon N
94. Eminent domain-Coal comps N
95. Prohibit EPA sanctions Y
96. SS age increase/Reforms N

Presidential Support Score: 1986 - 17% 1985 - 28%

PRICE, MELVIN -- Illinois 21st District [Democrat]. Counties of Bond, Clinton (pt.), Madison, Montgomery (pt.) and St. Clair (pt.). Prior Terms: House: 1945-86. Born: January 1, 1905; East St. Louis, Ill. Education: St. Louis University. Occupation: Newspaper correspondent; member, St. Clair County Board of Sueprvisors (1929-31); congressional secretary (1933-43).

1. Immigration Reform Y
2. Open fld-search warrants Y
3. Civil pnty-hire ill alien N
4. So Afr sanc-veto override Y
5. Tax Overhaul Y
6. South Africa sanctions Y
7. Death penalty-drug bill Y
8. Evidence-warrantless srch N
9. Life term-second drug off Y
10. Military use in drug war N
11. Troop reduction in Europe N
12. Prohibit chemical weapons N
13. Bar ASAT testing Y
14. Abide SALT II weapons ban Y
15. Follow SALT II-Soviets do N
16. Reduce SDI funding N
17. Increase SDI funding N
18. Purchase Trident sub Y
19. Delete 12 MX;Add conv wpn N
20. Raise speed limit Y
21. Textile Import Quotas(*) Y
22. Req Pentagon buy US goods Y
23. AIDS ins anti-dscriminatn Y
24. Nicaraguan refugee aid Y
25. Nicaraguan contra aid N
26. US abide by SALT II N
27. Prohibit Saudi arms sale Y
28. Military Retiremnt Reform Y
29. Nicaraguan refugee aid Y
30. Ease '68 Gun Control Act Y
31. Bar intrstat handgun tran Y
32. Keep '68 Gun Control Act N
33. Nicaraguan contra aid N
34. Bar emp polygraph testing Y
35. Tax Overhaul consideratn ?
36. Bar armor-piercing ammo ?
37. Tax Overhaul consideratn ?
38. Make comp emissions known ?
39. Allow toxic victims suits ?
40. Strike Superfund "VAT" ?
41. Notify emp-plant closing ?
42. Bar emp consult-plant clo ?
43. Medicare cuts;Tax incres' N
44. Delete 12 MX missiles N
45. Spending cuts;Tax incres' Y
46. Textile Import Quotas Y
47. Cut some school lunch fds N
48. Clean Water Act Amendmnts Y
49. Youth work projects Y
50. Assist military in Angola N
51. Allow US troops-Nicaragua N
52. Pentagon polygraph exams Y
53. Bar ASAT testing Y
54. Suspend def pmt for abuse N
55. Bar Pentagon-contr emplmt Y
56. Increase SDI funding N
57. Reduce SDI funding N
58. Produce chemical weapons Y
59. Bar CIA fndg in Nicaragua Y
60. South Africa sanctions Y
61. Cut SS COLAs; Raise taxes N
62. Let US invest-So Africa N
63. Approve 21 MX for 1985 Y
64. Emergency Farm Credit Y
65. Awards to whistle blowers Y
66. African disaster relief Y
67. Ban bank loans to So Afr Y
68. Bar coun duty-free trtmt Y
69. Steel import limits Y
70. Soc Sec COLAs=inflation Y
71. Bar haz waste vctms suits N
72. Prohibit aid to Nicaragua Y
73. Cut $-Schs bar sch prayer N
74. Raise taxes; Cut Medicare Y

PRICE, MELVIN (Cont.)

75. Alien residncy-prior 1982 N
76. Alien residncy-prior 1980 N
77. Pen emp-hire illgl aliens Y
78. Lmt Persh II/cruse-Europe N
79. Delete 34 B-1 bombers N
80. Bar purch of Pershing II N
81. Bar purchase of Sgt York N
82. Delete $ for Trident II N
83. Allow 15 MX missiles Y
84. Bar MX procurement-1985 N
85. Equal Access Act Y
86. Aid to El Salvador N
87. Bar Nicarag water mining ?
88. Physician/Medicare freeze N
89. Increase "sin" taxes Y
90. End SBA direct loans N
91. Sell Conrail N
92. Equal Rights Amendment Y
93. Marines in Lebanon Y
94. Eminent domain-Coal comps N
95. Prohibit EPA sanctions ?
96. SS age increase/Reforms N
97. Auto domestic content req Y
98. Delete jobs program fundg N
99. Highway-Gas tax bill Y
100. Raise Medicare;Cut defnse N
101. Emergency housing aid Y
102. Across-the-board tax cuts N
103. Gramm-Latta II targets N
104. Delete B-1 bomber funds N
105. Dsapprov Saudi AWACS sale N
106. Disapprove oil import fee Y
107. Rail Deregulation N
108. Dsapp India nuc fuel sale N
109. Mil draft registration Y
110. Chrysler Loan Guarantees Y
111. Prohibit school busing N
112. Nuclear plant moratorium N
113. Oil price controls Y
114. Tuition Tax Credits Y
115. Est Consumer Protect Agcy Y
116. Eliminate B-1 bomber fnds Y
117. Subminimum wage for youth N
118. Delete crude oil tax N
119. Natural gas deregulation N

Presidential Support Score: 1986 - 27% 1985 - 33%

GRAY, KENNETH J. -- Illinois 22nd District [Democrat]. Counties of Alexander, Clinton (pt.), Fayette (pt.), Franklin, Gallatin, Hardin, Jackson, Jefferson, Johnson, Marion, Massac, Monroe, Perry, Pope, Pulaski, Randolph, St. Clair (pt.), Saline, Union, Washington and Williamson. Prior Terms: House: 1954-74, 1985-86. Born: West Frankfort, Ill. Education: West Frankfort Community High School; Army Advanced School. Military Service: U.S. Army and Air Force. Occupation: Pilot, president, business consultants; owner, Antique Car Museum.

1. Immigration Reform Y
2. Open fld-search warrants Y
3. Civil pnty-hire ill alien Y
4. So Afr sanc-veto override Y
5. Tax Overhaul Y
6. South Africa sanctions Y
7. Death penalty-drug bill Y
8. Evidence-warrantless srch N
9. Life term-second drug off Y
10. Military use in drug war N
11. Troop reduction in Europe N
12. Prohibit chemical weapons N
13. Bar ASAT testing Y
14. Abide SALT II weapons ban Y
15. Follow SALT II-Soviets do N
16. Reduce SDI funding N
17. Increase SDI funding N
18. Purchase Trident sub Y
19. Delete 12 MX;Add conv wpn Y
20. Raise speed limit Y
21. Textile Import Quotas(*) Y
22. Req Pentagon buy US goods Y
23. AIDS ins anti-dscriminatn Y
24. Nicaraguan refugee aid Y
25. Nicaraguan contra aid N
26. US abide by SALT II N
27. Prohibit Saudi arms sale Y
28. Military Retiremnt Reform Y
29. Nicaraguan refugee aid Y
30. Ease '68 Gun Control Act Y
31. Bar intrstat handgun tran N
32. Keep '68 Gun Control Act N
33. Nicaraguan contra aid N
34. Bar emp polygraph testing Y
35. Tax Overhaul consideratn ?
36. Bar armor-piercing ammo ?
37. Tax Overhaul consideratn Y
38. Make comp emissions known Y
39. Allow toxic victims suits N
40. Strike Superfund "VAT" N
41. Notify emp-plant closing Y
42. Bar emp consult-plant clo N
43. Medicare cuts;Tax incres' N
44. Delete 12 MX missiles +
45. Spending cuts;Tax incres' Y
46. Textile Import Quotas Y

GRAY, KENNETH J. (Cont.)

47. Cut some school lunch fds	N		57. Reduce SDI funding	N
48. Clean Water Act Amendmnts	?		58. Produce chemical weapons	Y
49. Youth work projects	Y		59. Bar CIA fndg in Nicaragua	Y
50. Assist military in Angola	X		60. South Africa sanctions	Y
51. Allow US troops-Nicaragua	N		61. Cut SS COLAs; Raise taxes	N
52. Pentagon polygraph exams	Y		62. Let US invest-So Africa	N
53. Bar ASAT testing	Y		63. Approve 21 MX for 1985	N
54. Suspend def pmt for abuse	Y		64. Emergency Farm Credit	Y
55. Bar Pentagon-contr emplmt	Y		65. Awards to whistle blowers	?
56. Increase SDI funding	N		66. African disaster relief	?

Presidential Support Score: 1986 - 28% 1985 - 26%

INDIANA

VISCLOSKY, PETER J. -- Indiana 1st District [Democrat]. Counties of Lake (pt.), La Porte (pt.) and Porter (pt.). Prior Terms: 1985-86. Born: August 13, 1949. Education: Indiana University (B.S.); University of Notre Dame (J.D.); Georgetown University (LL.M.). Occupation: Attorney; congressional aide.

1. Immigration Reform	Y		34. Bar emp polygraph testing	Y
2. Open fld-search warrants	N		35. Tax Overhaul consideratn	Y
3. Civil pnty-hire ill alien	Y		36. Bar armor-piercing ammo	Y
4. So Afr sanc-veto override	Y		37. Tax Overhaul consideratn	Y
5. Tax Overhaul	Y		38. Make comp emissions known	Y
6. South Africa sanctions	Y		39. Allow toxic victims suits	N
7. Death penalty-drug bill	N		40. Strike Superfund "VAT"	N
8. Evidence-warrantless srch	N		41. Notify emp-plant closing	Y
9. Life term-second drug off	N		42. Bar emp consult-plant clo	N
10. Military use in drug war	N		43. Medicare cuts;Tax incres'	Y
11. Troop reduction in Europe	N		44. Delete 12 MX missiles	Y
12. Prohibit chemical weapons	Y		45. Spending cuts;Tax incres'	Y
13. Bar ASAT testing	Y		46. Textile Import Quotas	Y
14. Abide SALT II weapons ban	Y		47. Cut some school lunch fds	N
15. Follow SALT II-Soviets do	N		48. Clean Water Act Amendmnts	N
16. Reduce SDI funding	N		49. Youth work projects	Y
17. Increase SDI funding	N		50. Assist military in Angola	N
18. Purchase Trident sub	Y		51. Allow US troops-Nicaragua	N
19. Delete 12 MX;Add conv wpn	Y		52. Pentagon polygraph exams	N
20. Raise speed limit	N		53. Bar ASAT testing	Y
21. Textile Import Quotas(*)	Y		54. Suspend def pmt for abuse	N
22. Req Pentagon buy US goods	Y		55. Bar Pentagon-contr emplmt	Y
23. AIDS ins anti-dscriminatn	Y		56. Increase SDI funding	N
24. Nicaraguan refugee aid	Y		57. Reduce SDI funding	N
25. Nicaraguan contra aid	N		58. Produce chemical weapons	N
26. US abide by SALT II	N		59. Bar CIA fndg in Nicaragua	Y
27. Prohibit Saudi arms sale	Y		60. South Africa sanctions	Y
28. Military Retiremnt Reform	Y		61. Cut SS COLAs; Raise taxes	Y
29. Nicaraguan refugee aid	Y		62. Let US invest-So Africa	N
30. Ease '68 Gun Control Act	N		63. Approve 21 MX for 1985	N
31. Bar intrstat handgun tran	Y		64. Emergency Farm Credit	Y
32. Keep '68 Gun Control Act	Y		65. Awards to whistle blowers	Y
33. Nicaraguan contra aid	N		66. African disaster relief	Y

Presidential Support Score: 1986 - 18% 1985 - 30%

SHARP, PHILIP R. -- Indiana 2nd District [Democrat]. Counties of Bartholomew (pt.), Decatur, Delaware (pt.), Fayette (pt.), Henry (pt.), Johnson, Marion (pt.), Randolph, Rush (pt.), Shelby and Wayne. Prior Terms: House: 1975-86. Born: July 15, 1942; Baltimore, Md. Education: Georgetown University (B.S., Ph.D.); Oxford University. Occupation: Associate professor, Ball State University; legislative assistant (1964-69).

1. Immigration Reform Y
2. Open fld-search warrants N
3. Civil pnty-hire ill alien N
4. So Afr sanc-veto override Y
5. Tax Overhaul Y
6. South Africa sanctions Y
7. Death penalty-drug bill N
8. Evidence-warrantless srch N
9. Life term-second drug off Y
10. Military use in drug war N
11. Troop reduction in Europe N
12. Prohibit chemical weapons ?
13. Bar ASAT testing Y
14. Abide SALT II weapons ban Y
15. Follow SALT II-Soviets do N
16. Reduce SDI funding N
17. Increase SDI funding N
18. Purchase Trident sub Y
19. Delete 12 MX;Add conv wpn Y
20. Raise speed limit Y
21. Textile Import Quotas(*) Y
22. Req Pentagon buy US goods Y
23. AIDS ins anti-dscriminatn N
24. Nicaraguan refugee aid Y
25. Nicaraguan contra aid N
26. US abide by SALT II N
27. Prohibit Saudi arms sale Y
28. Military Retiremnt Reform Y
29. Nicaraguan refugee aid Y
30. Ease '68 Gun Control Act Y
31. Bar intrstat handgun tran N
32. Keep '68 Gun Control Act N
33. Nicaraguan contra aid N
34. Bar emp polygraph testing Y
35. Tax Overhaul consideratn Y
36. Bar armor-piercing ammo Y
37. Tax Overhaul consideratn Y
38. Make comp emissions known Y
39. Allow toxic victims suits Y
40. Strike Superfund "VAT" Y
41. Notify emp-plant closing Y
42. Bar emp consult-plant clo N
43. Medicare cuts;Tax incres' Y
44. Delete 12 MX missiles Y
45. Spending cuts;Tax incres' N
46. Textile Import Quotas N
47. Cut some school lunch fds N
48. Clean Water Act Amendmnts N
49. Youth work projects N
50. Assist military in Angola Y
51. Allow US troops-Nicaragua N
52. Pentagon polygraph exams Y
53. Bar ASAT testing Y
54. Suspend def pmt for abuse Y
55. Bar Pentagon-contr emplmt Y
56. Increase SDI funding N
57. Reduce SDI funding N
58. Produce chemical weapons N
59. Bar CIA fndg in Nicaragua Y
60. South Africa sanctions Y
61. Cut SS COLAs; Raise taxes N
62. Let US invest-So Africa N
63. Approve 21 MX for 1985 N
64. Emergency Farm Credit Y
65. Awards to whistle blowers Y
66. African disaster relief Y
67. Ban bank loans to So Afr Y
68. Bar coun duty-free trtmt N
69. Steel import limits Y
70. Soc Sec COLAs=inflation Y
71. Bar haz waste vctms suits N
72. Prohibit aid to Nicaragua ?
73. Cut $-Schs bar sch prayer Y
74. Raise taxes; Cut Medicare Y
75. Alien residncy-prior 1982 Y
76. Alien residncy-prior 1980 N
77. Pen emp-hire illgl aliens N
78. Lmt Persh II/cruse-Europe N
79. Delete 34 B-1 bombers +
80. Bar purch of Pershing II -
81. Bar purchase of Sgt York -
82. Delete $ for Trident II -
83. Allow 15 MX missiles N
84. Bar MX procurement-1985 Y
85. Equal Access Act Y
86. Aid to El Salvador N
87. Bar Nicarag water mining Y
88. Physician/Medicare freeze N
89. Increase "sin" taxes Y
90. End SBA direct loans N
91. Sell Conrail N
92. Equal Rights Amendment Y
93. Marines in Lebanon N
94. Eminent domain-Coal comps Y
95. Prohibit EPA sanctions Y
96. SS age increase/Reforms N
97. Auto domestic content req Y
98. Delete jobs program fundg N
99. Highway-Gas tax bill N
100. Raise Medicare;Cut defnse Y
101. Emergency housing aid Y
102. Across-the-board tax cuts N

SHARP, PHILIP R. (Cont.)

103. Gramm-Latta II targets N
104. Delete B-1 bomber funds Y
105. Dsapprov Saudi AWACS sale Y
106. Disapprove oil import fee Y
107. Rail Deregulation N
108. Dsapp India nuc fuel sale Y
109. Mil draft registration N
110. Chrysler Loan Guarantees Y
111. Prohibit school busing N
112. Nuclear plant moratorium N
113. Oil price controls N
114. Tuition Tax Credits N
115. Est Consumer Protect Agcy Y
116. Eliminate B-1 bomber fnds Y
117. Subminimum wage for youth Y
118. Delete crude oil tax N
119. Natural gas deregulation N

Presidential Support Score: 1986 - 24% 1985 - 43%

HILER, JOHN -- Indiana 3rd District [Republican]. Counties of Elkhart, Kosciusko (pt.), La Porte (pt.), Marshall, St. Joseph and Starke. Prior Terms: House: 1981-86. Born: April 24, 1953; Chicago, Ill. Education: Williams College (B.A.); University of Chicago (MBA). Occupation: Marketing director, Charles O. Hiler and Son, Inc., and Accurate Castings, Inc. (1977-81); LaLumiere school trustee.

1. Immigration Reform N
2. Open fld-search warrants N
3. Civil pnty-hire ill alien Y
4. So Afr sanc-veto override Y
5. Tax Overhaul Y
6. South Africa sanctions Y
7. Death penalty-drug bill Y
8. Evidence-warrantless srch Y
9. Life term-second drug off Y
10. Military use in drug war Y
11. Troop reduction in Europe N
12. Prohibit chemical weapons N
13. Bar ASAT testing N
14. Abide SALT II weapons ban N
15. Follow SALT II-Soviets do Y
16. Reduce SDI funding N
17. Increase SDI funding Y
18. Purchase Trident sub Y
19. Delete 12 MX;Add conv wpn N
20. Raise speed limit Y
21. Textile Import Quotas(*) N
22. Req Pentagon buy US goods N
23. AIDS ins anti-dscriminatn N
24. Nicaraguan refugee aid N
25. Nicaraguan contra aid Y
26. US abide by SALT II Y
27. Prohibit Saudi arms sale N
28. Military Retiremnt Reform Y
29. Nicaraguan refugee aid Y
30. Ease '68 Gun Control Act Y
31. Bar intrstat handgun tran N
32. Keep '68 Gun Control Act N
33. Nicaraguan contra aid Y
34. Bar emp polygraph testing N
35. Tax Overhaul consideratn N
36. Bar armor-piercing ammo Y
37. Tax Overhaul consideratn N
38. Make comp emissions known N
39. Allow toxic victims suits N
40. Strike Superfund "VAT" Y
41. Notify emp-plant closing N
42. Bar emp consult-plant clo Y
43. Medicare cuts;Tax incres' N
44. Delete 12 MX missiles N
45. Spending cuts;Tax incres' N
46. Textile Import Quotas N
47. Cut some school lunch fds Y
48. Clean Water Act Amendmnts Y
49. Youth work projects N
50. Assist military in Angola Y
51. Allow US troops-Nicaragua Y
52. Pentagon polygraph exams Y
53. Bar ASAT testing N
54. Suspend def pmt for abuse N
55. Bar Pentagon-contr emplmt Y
56. Increase SDI funding Y
57. Reduce SDI funding N
58. Produce chemical weapons Y
59. Bar CIA fndg in Nicaragua N
60. South Africa sanctions Y
61. Cut SS COLAs; Raise taxes N
62. Let US invest-So Africa Y
63. Approve 21 MX for 1985 Y
64. Emergency Farm Credit N
65. Awards to whistle blowers Y
66. African disaster relief Y
67. Ban bank loans to So Afr ?
68. Bar coun duty-free trtmt N
69. Steel import limits N
70. Soc Sec COLAs=inflation Y
71. Bar haz waste vctms suits Y
72. Prohibit aid to Nicaragua N
73. Cut $-Schs bar sch prayer Y
74. Raise taxes; Cut Medicare N
75. Alien residncy-prior 1982 +
76. Alien residncy-prior 1980 Y
77. Pen emp-hire illgl aliens N
78. Lmt Persh II/cruse-Europe N

HILER, JOHN (Cont.)

79. Delete 34 B-1 bombers N
80. Bar purch of Pershing II N
81. Bar purchase of Sgt York ?
82. Delete $ for Trident II N
83. Allow 15 MX missiles Y
84. Bar MX procurement-1985 N
85. Equal Access Act Y
86. Aid to El Salvador Y
87. Bar Nicarag water mining N
88. Physician/Medicare freeze Y
89. Increase "sin" taxes N
90. End SBA direct loans Y
91. Sell Conrail Y
92. Equal Rights Amendment N
93. Marines in Lebanon Y
94. Eminent domain-Coal comps Y
95. Prohibit EPA sanctions Y
96. SS age increase/Reforms Y
97. Auto domestic content req N
98. Delete jobs program fundg Y
99. Highway-Gas tax bill N
100. Raise Medicare;Cut defnse N
101. Emergency housing aid Y
102. Across-the-board tax cuts Y
103. Gramm-Latta II targets Y
104. Delete B-1 bomber funds N
105. Dsapprov Saudi AWACS sale N

Presidential Support Score: 1986 - 77% 1985 - 80%

COATS, DAN -- Indiana 4th District [Republican]. Counties of Adams, Allen, De Kalb, Huntington, Jay, Lagrange, Noble, Steuben, Wells and Whitley. Prior Terms: House: 1981-86. Born: May 16, 1943; Jackson, Mich. Education: Wheaton College (B.A.); Indiana University Law School (J.D.). Occupation: Assistant vice-president and counsel, Mutual Security Life Insurance Co.; congressional staff member (1976-80); board member, Anthony Wayne Rehabilitation Center, Historic River Cruises.

1. Immigration Reform N
2. Open fld-search warrants N
3. Civil pnty-hire ill alien N
4. So Afr sanc-veto override Y
5. Tax Overhaul Y
6. South Africa sanctions Y
7. Death penalty-drug bill Y
8. Evidence-warrantless srch Y
9. Life term-second drug off Y
10. Military use in drug war Y
11. Troop reduction in Europe N
12. Prohibit chemical weapons Y
13. Bar ASAT testing N
14. Abide SALT II weapons ban N
15. Follow SALT II-Soviets do Y
16. Reduce SDI funding N
17. Increase SDI funding N
18. Purchase Trident sub Y
19. Delete 12 MX;Add conv wpn N
20. Raise speed limit Y
21. Textile Import Quotas(*) N
22. Req Pentagon buy US goods Y
23. AIDS ins anti-dscriminatn N
24. Nicaraguan refugee aid N
25. Nicaraguan contra aid Y
26. US abide by SALT II Y
27. Prohibit Saudi arms sale Y
28. Military Retiremnt Reform Y
29. Nicaraguan refugee aid Y
30. Ease '68 Gun Control Act Y
31. Bar intrstat handgun tran N
32. Keep '68 Gun Control Act N
33. Nicaraguan contra aid Y
34. Bar emp polygraph testing N
35. Tax Overhaul consideratn Y
36. Bar armor-piercing ammo Y
37. Tax Overhaul consideratn N
38. Make comp emissions known N
39. Allow toxic victims suits N
40. Strike Superfund "VAT" Y
41. Notify emp-plant closing N
42. Bar emp consult-plant clo Y
43. Medicare cuts;Tax incres' N
44. Delete 12 MX missiles N
45. Spending cuts;Tax incres' N
46. Textile Import Quotas N
47. Cut some school lunch fds Y
48. Clean Water Act Amendmnts Y
49. Youth work projects N
50. Assist military in Angola Y
51. Allow US troops-Nicaragua Y
52. Pentagon polygraph exams Y
53. Bar ASAT testing N
54. Suspend def pmt for abuse N
55. Bar Pentagon-contr emplmt Y
56. Increase SDI funding Y
57. Reduce SDI funding N
58. Produce chemical weapons N
59. Bar CIA fndg in Nicaragua N
60. South Africa sanctions Y
61. Cut SS COLAs; Raise taxes N
62. Let US invest-So Africa Y
63. Approve 21 MX for 1985 Y
64. Emergency Farm Credit Y

COATS, DAN (Cont.)

65. Awards to whistle blowers Y
66. African disaster relief Y
67. Ban bank loans to So Afr Y
68. Bar coun duty-free trtmt N
69. Steel import limits N
70. Soc Sec COLAs=inflation Y
71. Bar haz waste vctms suits Y
72. Prohibit aid to Nicaragua N
73. Cut $-Schs bar sch prayer Y
74. Raise taxes; Cut Medicare N
75. Alien residncy-prior 1982 Y
76. Alien residncy-prior 1980 Y
77. Pen emp-hire illgl aliens N
78. Lmt Persh II/cruse-Europe N
79. Delete 34 B-1 bombers N
80. Bar purch of Pershing II N
81. Bar purchase of Sgt York N
82. Delete $ for Trident II N
83. Allow 15 MX missiles Y
84. Bar MX procurement-1985 N
85. Equal Access Act Y
86. Aid to El Salvador Y
87. Bar Nicarag water mining N
88. Physician/Medicare freeze Y
89. Increase "sin" taxes N
90. End SBA direct loans N
91. Sell Conrail Y
92. Equal Rights Amendment N
93. Marines in Lebanon Y
94. Eminent domain-Coal comps Y
95. Prohibit EPA sanctions N
96. SS age increase/Reforms Y
97. Auto domestic content req N
98. Delete jobs program fundg Y
99. Highway-Gas tax bill N
100. Raise Medicare;Cut defnse N
101. Emergency housing aid Y
102. Across-the-board tax cuts Y
103. Gramm-Latta II targets Y
104. Delete B-1 bomber funds N
105. Dsapprov Saudi AWACS sale Y

Presidential Support Score: 1986 - 69% 1985 - 74%

HILLIS, ELWOOD -- Indiana 5th District [Republican]. Counties of Carroll, Cass, Fulton, Grant, Howard, Jasper, Kosciusko (pt.), Lake (pt.), Miami, Newton, Porter (pt.), Pulaski, Wabash and White. Prior Terms: House: 1971-86. Born: March 6, 1926; Kokomo, Ind. Education: Culver Military Academy; Indiana University (B.S., LL.B.). Military Service: U.S. Army, WW II. Occupation: Indiana representative; attorney.

1. Immigration Reform ?
2. Open fld-search warrants ?
3. Civil pnty-hire ill alien N
4. So Afr sanc-veto override Y
5. Tax Overhaul Y
6. South Africa sanctions Y
7. Death penalty-drug bill Y
8. Evidence-warrantless srch Y
9. Life term-second drug off Y
10. Military use in drug war N
11. Troop reduction in Europe ?
12. Prohibit chemical weapons ?
13. Bar ASAT testing ?
14. Abide SALT II weapons ban ?
15. Follow SALT II-Soviets do ?
16. Reduce SDI funding ?
17. Increase SDI funding ?
18. Purchase Trident sub ?
19. Delete 12 MX;Add conv wpn ?
20. Raise speed limit ?
21. Textile Import Quotas(*) Y
22. Req Pentagon buy US goods ?
23. AIDS ins anti-dscriminatn N
24. Nicaraguan refugee aid N
25. Nicaraguan contra aid Y
26. US abide by SALT II ?
27. Prohibit Saudi arms sale N
28. Military Retiremnt Reform Y
29. Nicaraguan refugee aid Y
30. Ease '68 Gun Control Act Y
31. Bar intrstat handgun tran Y
32. Keep '68 Gun Control Act Y
33. Nicaraguan contra aid Y
34. Bar emp polygraph testing N
35. Tax Overhaul consideratn ?
36. Bar armor-piercing ammo ?
37. Tax Overhaul consideratn N
38. Make comp emissions known ?
39. Allow toxic victims suits N
40. Strike Superfund "VAT" N
41. Notify emp-plant closing ?
42. Bar emp consult-plant clo Y
43. Medicare cuts;Tax incres' N
44. Delete 12 MX missiles N
45. Spending cuts;Tax incres' N
46. Textile Import Quotas Y
47. Cut some school lunch fds Y
48. Clean Water Act Amendmnts Y
49. Youth work projects ?
50. Assist military in Angola Y
51. Allow US troops-Nicaragua Y
52. Pentagon polygraph exams Y
53. Bar ASAT testing N
54. Suspend def pmt for abuse N

HILLIS, ELWOOD (Cont.)

55. Bar Pentagon-contr emplmt Y
56. Increase SDI funding Y
57. Reduce SDI funding N
58. Produce chemical weapons Y
59. Bar CIA fndg in Nicaragua N
60. South Africa sanctions N
61. Cut SS COLAs; Raise taxes N
62. Let US invest-So Africa Y
63. Approve 21 MX for 1985 Y
64. Emergency Farm Credit N
65. Awards to whistle blowers Y
66. African disaster relief Y
67. Ban bank loans to So Afr ?
68. Bar coun duty-free trtmt N
69. Steel import limits Y
70. Soc Sec COLAs=inflation Y
71. Bar haz waste vctms suits Y
72. Prohibit aid to Nicaragua Y
73. Cut $-Schs bar sch prayer Y
74. Raise taxes; Cut Medicare Y
75. Alien residncy-prior 1982 Y
76. Alien residncy-prior 1980 Y
77. Pen emp-hire illgl aliens N
78. Lmt Persh II/cruse-Europe N
79. Delete 34 B-1 bombers N
80. Bar purch of Pershing II N
81. Bar purchase of Sgt York N
82. Delete $ for Trident II N
83. Allow 15 MX missiles Y
84. Bar MX procurement-1985 N
85. Equal Access Act Y
86. Aid to El Salvador Y
87. Bar Nicarag water mining N
88. Physician/Medicare freeze Y
89. Increase "sin" taxes Y
90. End SBA direct loans Y
91. Sell Conrail Y
92. Equal Rights Amendment N
93. Marines in Lebanon N
94. Eminent domain-Coal comps N
95. Prohibit EPA sanctions Y
96. SS age increase/Reforms Y
97. Auto domestic content req Y
98. Delete jobs program fundg Y
99. Highway-Gas tax bill ?
100. Raise Medicare;Cut defnse N
101. Emergency housing aid Y
102. Across-the-board tax cuts Y
103. Gramm-Latta II targets Y
104. Delete B-1 bomber funds N
105. Dsapprov Saudi AWACS sale Y
106. Disapprove oil import fee Y
107. Rail Deregulation N
108. Dsapp India nuc fuel sale Y
109. Mil draft registration Y
110. Chrysler Loan Guarantees Y
111. Prohibit school busing Y
112. Nuclear plant moratorium N
113. Oil price controls N
114. Tuition Tax Credits ?
115. Est Consumer Protect Agcy N
116. Eliminate B-1 bomber fnds N
117. Subminimum wage for youth Y
118. Delete crude oil tax Y
119. Natural gas deregulation Y

Presidential Support Score: 1986 - 44% 1985 - 65%

BURTON, DAN -- Indiana 6th District [Republican]. Counties of Blackford, Boone, Clinton, Delaware (pt.), Hamilton, Hancock, Henry (pt.), Madison, Marion (pt.), Rush (pt.) and Tipton. Prior Terms: House: 1983-86. Born: June 21, 1938; Indianapolis, Ind. Education: Indiana University. Military Service: U.S. Army, 1956-57. Occupation: Indiana representative (1967, 1977-79); Indiana senator (1968-76, 1980-82).

1. Immigration Reform N
2. Open fld-search warrants Y
3. Civil pnty-hire ill alien Y
4. So Afr sanc-veto override N
5. Tax Overhaul N
6. South Africa sanctions N
7. Death penalty-drug bill Y
8. Evidence-warrantless srch Y
9. Life term-second drug off Y
10. Military use in drug war Y
11. Troop reduction in Europe N
12. Prohibit chemical weapons N
13. Bar ASAT testing N
14. Abide SALT II weapons ban N
15. Follow SALT II-Soviets do Y
16. Reduce SDI funding N
17. Increase SDI funding Y
18. Purchase Trident sub N
19. Delete 12 MX;Add conv wpn N
20. Raise speed limit Y
21. Textile Import Quotas(*) N
22. Req Pentagon buy US goods N
23. AIDS ins anti-dscriminatn N
24. Nicaraguan refugee aid N
25. Nicaraguan contra aid Y
26. US abide by SALT II Y
27. Prohibit Saudi arms sale Y
28. Military Retiremnt Reform Y
29. Nicaraguan refugee aid Y
30. Ease '68 Gun Control Act Y

BURTON, DAN (Cont.)

31. Bar intrstat handgun tran N
32. Keep '68 Gun Control Act N
33. Nicaraguan contra aid Y
34. Bar emp polygraph testing N
35. Tax Overhaul consideratn N
36. Bar armor-piercing ammo Y
37. Tax Overhaul consideratn N
38. Make comp emissions known N
39. Allow toxic victims suits N
40. Strike Superfund "VAT" N
41. Notify emp-plant closing N
42. Bar emp consult-plant clo Y
43. Medicare cuts;Tax incres' N
44. Delete 12 MX missiles N
45. Spending cuts;Tax incres' N
46. Textile Import Quotas N
47. Cut some school lunch fds Y
48. Clean Water Act Amendmnts Y
49. Youth work projects ?
50. Assist military in Angola Y
51. Allow US troops-Nicaragua Y
52. Pentagon polygraph exams Y
53. Bar ASAT testing N
54. Suspend def pmt for abuse N
55. Bar Pentagon-contr emplmt Y
56. Increase SDI funding Y
57. Reduce SDI funding N
58. Produce chemical weapons Y
59. Bar CIA fndg in Nicaragua N
60. South Africa sanctions N
61. Cut SS COLAs; Raise taxes N
62. Let US invest-So Africa Y
63. Approve 21 MX for 1985 Y
64. Emergency Farm Credit N
65. Awards to whistle blowers Y
66. African disaster relief Y
67. Ban bank loans to So Afr N
68. Bar coun duty-free trtmt N
69. Steel import limits Y
70. Soc Sec COLAs=inflation Y
71. Bar haz waste vctms suits Y
72. Prohibit aid to Nicaragua N
73. Cut $-Schs bar sch prayer Y
74. Raise taxes; Cut Medicare N
75. Alien residncy-prior 1982 Y
76. Alien residncy-prior 1980 Y
77. Pen emp-hire illgl aliens N
78. Lmt Persh II/cruse-Europe N
79. Delete 34 B-1 bombers N
80. Bar purch of Pershing II N
81. Bar purchase of Sgt York N
82. Delete $ for Trident II N
83. Allow 15 MX missiles Y
84. Bar MX procurement-1985 N
85. Equal Access Act Y
86. Aid to El Salvador Y
87. Bar Nicarag water mining N
88. Physician/Medicare freeze Y
89. Increase "sin" taxes Y
90. End SBA direct loans Y
91. Sell Conrail Y
92. Equal Rights Amendment N
93. Marines in Lebanon Y
94. Eminent domain-Coal comps Y
95. Prohibit EPA sanctions Y
96. SS age increase/Reforms Y

Presidential Support Score: 1986 - 82% 1985 - 80%

MYERS, JOHN T. -- Indiana 7th District [Republican]. Counties of Benton, Clay, Fountain, Hendricks, Montgomery, Morgan, Owen, Parke, Putnam, Sullivan, Tippecanoe, Vermillion, Vigo and Warren. Prior Terms: House: 1967-86. Born: February 8, 1927; Covington, Ind. Education: Indiana State University (B.S.). Military Service: U.S. Army. Occupation: Cashier and trust officer, The Fountain Trust Co.

1. Immigration Reform N
2. Open fld-search warrants N
3. Civil pnty-hire ill alien N
4. So Afr sanc-veto override N
5. Tax Overhaul N
6. South Africa sanctions N
7. Death penalty-drug bill Y
8. Evidence-warrantless srch Y
9. Life term-second drug off Y
10. Military use in drug war N
11. Troop reduction in Europe N
12. Prohibit chemical weapons N
13. Bar ASAT testing N
14. Abide SALT II weapons ban N
15. Follow SALT II-Soviets do Y
16. Reduce SDI funding N
17. Increase SDI funding Y
18. Purchase Trident sub N
19. Delete 12 MX;Add conv wpn N
20. Raise speed limit Y
21. Textile Import Quotas(*) N
22. Req Pentagon buy US goods Y
23. AIDS ins anti-dscriminatn Y
24. Nicaraguan refugee aid N
25. Nicaraguan contra aid Y
26. US abide by SALT II Y
27. Prohibit Saudi arms sale N
28. Military Retiremnt Reform Y
29. Nicaraguan refugee aid Y
30. Ease '68 Gun Control Act Y

MYERS, JOHN T. (Cont.)

31. Bar intrstat handgun tran N
32. Keep '68 Gun Control Act N
33. Nicaraguan contra aid Y
34. Bar emp polygraph testing N
35. Tax Overhaul consideratn N
36. Bar armor-piercing ammo Y
37. Tax Overhaul consideratn N
38. Make comp emissions known N
39. Allow toxic victims suits N
40. Strike Superfund "VAT" N
41. Notify emp-plant closing N
42. Bar emp consult-plant clo Y
43. Medicare cuts;Tax incres' N
44. Delete 12 MX missiles N
45. Spending cuts;Tax incres' N
46. Textile Import Quotas N
47. Cut some school lunch fds Y
48. Clean Water Act Amendmnts Y
49. Youth work projects N
50. Assist military in Angola Y
51. Allow US troops-Nicaragua Y
52. Pentagon polygraph exams Y
53. Bar ASAT testing N
54. Suspend def pmt for abuse N
55. Bar Pentagon-contr emplmt N
56. Increase SDI funding N
57. Reduce SDI funding N
58. Produce chemical weapons Y
59. Bar CIA fndg in Nicaragua N
60. South Africa sanctions N
61. Cut SS COLAs; Raise taxes N
62. Let US invest-So Africa #
63. Approve 21 MX for 1985 Y
64. Emergency Farm Credit Y
65. Awards to whistle blowers Y
66. African disaster relief Y
67. Ban bank loans to So Afr Y
68. Bar coun duty-free trtmt N
69. Steel import limits Y
70. Soc Sec COLAs=inflation Y
71. Bar haz waste vctms suits Y
72. Prohibit aid to Nicaragua Y
73. Cut $-Schs bar sch prayer Y
74. Raise taxes; Cut Medicare N
75. Alien residncy-prior 1982 Y
76. Alien residncy-prior 1980 Y
77. Pen emp-hire illgl aliens N
78. Lmt Persh II/cruse-Europe N
79. Delete 34 B-1 bombers N
80. Bar purch of Pershing II N
81. Bar purchase of Sgt York N
82. Delete $ for Trident II N
83. Allow 15 MX missiles Y
84. Bar MX procurement-1985 N
85. Equal Access Act Y
86. Aid to El Salvador Y
87. Bar Nicarag water mining N
88. Physician/Medicare freeze Y
89. Increase "sin" taxes N
90. End SBA direct loans N
91. Sell Conrail Y
92. Equal Rights Amendment N
93. Marines in Lebanon N
94. Eminent domain-Coal comps ?
95. Prohibit EPA sanctions Y
96. SS age increase/Reforms Y
97. Auto domestic content req N
98. Delete jobs program fundg Y
99. Highway-Gas tax bill N
100. Raise Medicare;Cut defnse N
101. Emergency housing aid Y
102. Across-the-board tax cuts Y
103. Gramm-Latta II targets Y
104. Delete B-1 bomber funds N
105. Dsapprov Saudi AWACS sale N
106. Disapprove oil import fee Y
107. Rail Deregulation N
108. Dsapp India nuc fuel sale N
109. Mil draft registration N
110. Chrysler Loan Guarantees Y
111. Prohibit school busing Y
112. Nuclear plant moratorium N
113. Oil price controls N
114. Tuition Tax Credits Y
115. Est Consumer Protect Agcy N
116. Eliminate B-1 bomber fnds N
117. Subminimum wage for youth Y
118. Delete crude oil tax Y
119. Natural gas deregulation Y

Presidential Support Score: 1986 - 67% 1985 - 69%

McCLOSKEY, FRANK -- Indiana 8th District [Democrat]. Counties of Crawford (pt.), Daviess, Gibson, Greene, Knox, Lawrence, Martin, Monroe (pt.), Orange, Pike, Posey, Spencer, Vanderburgh, Warrick and Washington (pt.). Prior Terms: House: 1982 (Special Election)-1986. Born: June 12, 1939; Philadelphia, Pa. Education: Indiana University (A.B., J.D.). Military Service: U.S. Air Force, 4 years. Occupation: Newspaperman; mayor of Bloomington, Indiana (1971-82).

1. Immigration Reform Y
2. Open fld-search warrants N
3. Civil pnty-hire ill alien N
4. So Afr sanc-veto override Y

McCLOSKEY, FRANK (Cont.)

5. Tax Overhaul Y
6. South Africa sanctions Y
7. Death penalty-drug bill Y
8. Evidence-warrantless srch N
9. Life term-second drug off Y
10. Military use in drug war Y
11. Troop reduction in Europe N
12. Prohibit chemical weapons N
13. Bar ASAT testing Y
14. Abide SALT II weapons ban Y
15. Follow SALT II-Soviets do N
16. Reduce SDI funding N
17. Increase SDI funding N
18. Purchase Trident sub Y
19. Delete 12 MX;Add conv wpn Y
20. Raise speed limit Y
21. Textile Import Quotas(*) Y
22. Req Pentagon buy US goods Y
23. AIDS ins anti-dscriminatn N
24. Nicaraguan refugee aid Y
25. Nicaraguan contra aid N
26. US abide by SALT II N
27. Prohibit Saudi arms sale Y
28. Military Retiremnt Reform Y
29. Nicaraguan refugee aid Y
30. Ease '68 Gun Control Act Y
31. Bar intrstat handgun tran N
32. Keep '68 Gun Control Act N
33. Nicaraguan contra aid N
34. Bar emp polygraph testing Y
35. Tax Overhaul consideratn Y
36. Bar armor-piercing ammo Y
37. Tax Overhaul consideratn Y
38. Make comp emissions known Y
39. Allow toxic victims suits Y
40. Strike Superfund "VAT" Y
41. Notify emp-plant closing Y
42. Bar emp consult-plant clo N
43. Medicare cuts;Tax incres' Y
44. Delete 12 MX missiles Y
45. Spending cuts;Tax incres' Y
46. Textile Import Quotas Y
47. Cut some school lunch fds N
48. Clean Water Act Amendmnts N
49. Youth work projects Y
50. Assist military in Angola Y
51. Allow US troops-Nicaragua N
52. Pentagon polygraph exams Y
53. Bar ASAT testing Y
54. Suspend def pmt for abuse Y
55. Bar Pentagon-contr emplmt Y
56. Increase SDI funding N
57. Reduce SDI funding N
58. Produce chemical weapons N
59. Bar CIA fndg in Nicaragua Y
60. South Africa sanctions Y
61. Cut SS COLAs; Raise taxes N
62. Let US invest-So Africa N
63. Approve 21 MX for 1985
64. Emergency Farm Credit
65. Awards to whistle blowers
66. African disaster relief
67. Ban bank loans to So Afr Y
68. Bar coun duty-free trtmt Y
69. Steel import limits Y
70. Soc Sec COLAs=inflation Y
71. Bar haz waste vctms suits N
72. Prohibit aid to Nicaragua Y
73. Cut $-Schs bar sch prayer N
74. Raise taxes; Cut Medicare Y
75. Alien residncy-prior 1982 N
76. Alien residncy-prior 1980 N
77. Pen emp-hire illgl aliens Y
78. Lmt Persh II/cruse-Europe N
79. Delete 34 B-1 bombers Y
80. Bar purch of Pershing II N
81. Bar purchase of Sgt York N
82. Delete $ for Trident II N
83. Allow 15 MX missiles N
84. Bar MX procurement-1985 Y
85. Equal Access Act Y
86. Aid to El Salvador N
87. Bar Nicarag water mining Y
88. Physician/Medicare freeze N
89. Increase "sin" taxes Y
90. End SBA direct loans N
91. Sell Conrail N
92. Equal Rights Amendment Y
93. Marines in Lebanon N
94. Eminent domain-Coal comps N
95. Prohibit EPA sanctions N
96. SS age increase/Reforms N

Votes 63-66 were missed because of an election dispute.

Presidential Support Score: 1986 - 24% 1985 - 29%

HAMILTON, LEE H. -- Indiana 9th District [Democrat]. Counties of Bartholomew (pt.), Brown, Clark, Crawford (pt.), Dearborn, Dubois, Fayette (pt.), Floyd, Franklin, Harrison, Jackson, Jefferson, Jennings, Monroe (pt.), Ohio, Perry, Ripley, Scott, Switzerland, Union and Washington (pt.). Prior Terms: House: 1965-86. Born: April 20, 1931; Daytona Beach, Fla. Education: DePauw University (A.B.); Goethe University, Indiana University (J.D.). Occupation: Attorney; instructor, American Banking Institute.

HAMILTON, LEE H. (Cont.)

1. Immigration Reform	Y	60. South Africa sanctions	Y
2. Open fld-search warrants	N	61. Cut SS COLAs; Raise taxes	N
3. Civil pnty-hire ill alien	N	62. Let US invest-So Africa	N
4. So Afr sanc-veto override	Y	63. Approve 21 MX for 1985	N
5. Tax Overhaul	Y	64. Emergency Farm Credit	Y
6. South Africa sanctions	Y	65. Awards to whistle blowers	Y
7. Death penalty-drug bill	N	66. African disaster relief	Y
8. Evidence-warrantless srch	N	67. Ban bank loans to So Afr	Y
9. Life term-second drug off	Y	68. Bar coun duty-free trtmt	N
10. Military use in drug war	N	69. Steel import limits	Y
11. Troop reduction in Europe	N	70. Soc Sec COLAs=inflation	Y
12. Prohibit chemical weapons	N	71. Bar haz waste vctms suits	N
13. Bar ASAT testing	Y	72. Prohibit aid to Nicaragua	Y
14. Abide SALT II weapons ban	Y	73. Cut $-Schs bar sch prayer	Y
15. Follow SALT II-Soviets do	N	74. Raise taxes; Cut Medicare	Y
16. Reduce SDI funding	N	75. Alien residncy-prior 1982	N
17. Increase SDI funding	N	76. Alien residncy-prior 1980	N
18. Purchase Trident sub	Y	77. Pen emp-hire illgl aliens	N
19. Delete 12 MX;Add conv wpn	Y	78. Lmt Persh II/cruse-Europe	N
20. Raise speed limit	Y	79. Delete 34 B-1 bombers	Y
21. Textile Import Quotas(*)	N	80. Bar purch of Pershing II	N
22. Req Pentagon buy US goods	Y	81. Bar purchase of Sgt York	N
23. AIDS ins anti-dscriminatn	Y	82. Delete $ for Trident II	N
24. Nicaraguan refugee aid	Y	83. Allow 15 MX missiles	N
25. Nicaraguan contra aid	N	84. Bar MX procurement-1985	Y
26. US abide by SALT II	N	85. Equal Access Act	Y
27. Prohibit Saudi arms sale	N	86. Aid to El Salvador	N
28. Military Retiremnt Reform	Y	87. Bar Nicarag water mining	Y
29. Nicaraguan refugee aid	Y	88. Physician/Medicare freeze	N
30. Ease '68 Gun Control Act	Y	89. Increase "sin" taxes	Y
31. Bar intrstat handgun tran	N	90. End SBA direct loans	N
32. Keep '68 Gun Control Act	N	91. Sell Conrail	N
33. Nicaraguan contra aid	N	92. Equal Rights Amendment	Y
34. Bar emp polygraph testing	Y	93. Marines in Lebanon	Y
35. Tax Overhaul consideratn	N	94. Eminent domain-Coal comps	N
36. Bar armor-piercing ammo	Y	95. Prohibit EPA sanctions	Y
37. Tax Overhaul consideratn	N	96. SS age increase/Reforms	Y
38. Make comp emissions known	Y	97. Auto domestic content req	Y
39. Allow toxic victims suits	?	98. Delete jobs program fundg	N
40. Strike Superfund "VAT"	Y	99. Highway-Gas tax bill	N
41. Notify emp-plant closing	Y	100. Raise Medicare;Cut defnse	Y
42. Bar emp consult-plant clo	N	101. Emergency housing aid	Y
43. Medicare cuts;Tax incres'	Y	102. Across-the-board tax cuts	N
44. Delete 12 MX missiles	Y	103. Gramm-Latta II targets	N
45. Spending cuts;Tax incres'	N	104. Delete B-1 bomber funds	Y
46. Textile Import Quotas	N	105. Dsapprov Saudi AWACS sale	Y
47. Cut some school lunch fds	N	106. Disapprove oil import fee	Y
48. Clean Water Act Amendmnts	N	107. Rail Deregulation	N
49. Youth work projects	N	108. Dsapp India nuc fuel sale	N
50. Assist military in Angola	Y	109. Mil draft registration	Y
51. Allow US troops-Nicaragua	N	110. Chrysler Loan Guarantees	Y
52. Pentagon polygraph exams	Y	111. Prohibit school busing	N
53. Bar ASAT testing	Y	112. Nuclear plant moratorium	N
54. Suspend def pmt for abuse	N	113. Oil price controls	N
55. Bar Pentagon-contr emplmt	Y	114. Tuition Tax Credits	N
56. Increase SDI funding	N	115. Est Consumer Protect Agcy	N
57. Reduce SDI funding	N	116. Eliminate B-1 bomber fnds	Y
58. Produce chemical weapons	Y	117. Subminimum wage for youth	Y
59. Bar CIA fndg in Nicaragua	Y	118. Delete crude oil tax	N

HAMILTON, LEE H. (Cont.)
119. Natural gas deregulation N

Presidential Support Score: 1986 - 33% 1985 - 38%

JACOBS, ANDREW, Jr. -- Indiana 10th District [Democrat]. County of Marion (pt.). Prior Terms: House: 1965-72; 1975-86. Born: February 24, 1932; Indianapolis, Ind. Education: Indiana University (B.S., LL.B.). Military Service: U.S. Marine Corps, 1950-52. Occupation: Attorney; Indiana representative (1959-60).

1. Immigration Reform N
2. Open fld-search warrants N
3. Civil pnty-hire ill alien Y
4. So Afr sanc-veto override Y
5. Tax Overhaul N
6. South Africa sanctions Y
7. Death penalty-drug bill N
8. Evidence-warrantless srch N
9. Life term-second drug off Y
10. Military use in drug war Y
11. Troop reduction in Europe Y
12. Prohibit chemical weapons Y
13. Bar ASAT testing Y
14. Abide SALT II weapons ban Y
15. Follow SALT II-Soviets do N
16. Reduce SDI funding Y
17. Increase SDI funding N
18. Purchase Trident sub Y
19. Delete 12 MX;Add conv wpn Y
20. Raise speed limit N
21. Textile Import Quotas(*) Y
22. Req Pentagon buy US goods Y
23. AIDS ins anti-dscriminatn Y
24. Nicaraguan refugee aid Y
25. Nicaraguan contra aid N
26. US abide by SALT II N
27. Prohibit Saudi arms sale Y
28. Military Retiremnt Reform Y
29. Nicaraguan refugee aid Y
30. Ease '68 Gun Control Act N
31. Bar intrstat handgun tran Y
32. Keep '68 Gun Control Act Y
33. Nicaraguan contra aid N
34. Bar emp polygraph testing Y
35. Tax Overhaul consideratn N
36. Bar armor-piercing ammo Y
37. Tax Overhaul consideratn N
38. Make comp emissions known Y
39. Allow toxic victims suits Y
40. Strike Superfund "VAT" N
41. Notify emp-plant closing Y
42. Bar emp consult-plant clo N
43. Medicare cuts;Tax incres' Y
44. Delete 12 MX missiles Y
45. Spending cuts;Tax incres' N
46. Textile Import Quotas N
47. Cut some school lunch fds N
48. Clean Water Act Amendmnts Y
49. Youth work projects N
50. Assist military in Angola N
51. Allow US troops-Nicaragua N
52. Pentagon polygraph exams N
53. Bar ASAT testing Y
54. Suspend def pmt for abuse Y
55. Bar Pentagon-contr emplmt Y
56. Increase SDI funding N
57. Reduce SDI funding Y
58. Produce chemical weapons N
59. Bar CIA fndg in Nicaragua Y
60. South Africa sanctions Y
61. Cut SS COLAs; Raise taxes N
62. Let US invest-So Africa N
63. Approve 21 MX for 1985 N
64. Emergency Farm Credit Y
65. Awards to whistle blowers Y
66. African disaster relief Y
67. Ban bank loans to So Afr Y
68. Bar coun duty-free trtmt Y
69. Steel import limits Y
70. Soc Sec COLAs=inflation Y
71. Bar haz waste vctms suits N
72. Prohibit aid to Nicaragua N
73. Cut $-Schs bar sch prayer Y
74. Raise taxes; Cut Medicare Y
75. Alien residncy-prior 1982 N
76. Alien residncy-prior 1980 N
77. Pen emp-hire illgl aliens Y
78. Lmt Persh II/cruse-Europe Y
79. Delete 34 B-1 bombers Y
80. Bar purch of Pershing II Y
81. Bar purchase of Sgt York Y
82. Delete $ for Trident II N
83. Allow 15 MX missiles N
84. Bar MX procurement-1985 Y
85. Equal Access Act Y
86. Aid to El Salvador N
87. Bar Nicarag water mining Y
88. Physician/Medicare freeze N
89. Increase "sin" taxes Y
90. End SBA direct loans N
91. Sell Conrail N
92. Equal Rights Amendment Y
93. Marines in Lebanon N
94. Eminent domain-Coal comps N
95. Prohibit EPA sanctions Y
96. SS age increase/Reforms N
97. Auto domestic content req Y
98. Delete jobs program fundg N

JACOBS, ANDREW, Jr. (Cont.)

99. Highway-Gas tax bill N
100. Raise Medicare;Cut defnse Y
101. Emergency housing aid Y
102. Across-the-board tax cuts N
103. Gramm-Latta II targets Y
104. Delete B-1 bomber funds Y
105. Dsapprov Saudi AWACS sale Y
106. Disapprove oil import fee Y
107. Rail Deregulation Y
108. Dsapp India nuc fuel sale Y
109. Mil draft registration N
110. Chrysler Loan Guarantees Y
111. Prohibit school busing Y
112. Nuclear plant moratorium Y
113. Oil price controls N
114. Tuition Tax Credits ?
115. Est Consumer Protect Agcy N
116. Eliminate B-1 bomber fnds Y
117. Subminimum wage for youth Y
118. Delete crude oil tax Y
119. Natural gas deregulation N

Presidential Support Score: 1986 - 16% 1985 - 35%

IOWA

LEACH, JIM -- Iowa 1st District [Republican]. Counties of Appanoose, Davis, Des Moines, Henry, Jefferson, Keokuk, Lee, Louisa, Lucas, Mahaska, Monroe, Muscatine, Scott, Van Buren, Wapello and Washington. Prior Terms: House: 1977-86. Born: October 15, 1942; Davenport, Iowa. Education: Princeton University (B.A.); Johns Hopkins University (M.A.); London School of Economics. Occupation: President, Flamegas Co., Inc.; administative assistant to the director, Office of Economic Opportunity; Foreign Service Officer; director, Federal Home Loan Bank Board.

1. Immigration Reform Y
2. Open fld-search warrants N
3. Civil pnty-hire ill alien N
4. So Afr sanc-veto override Y
5. Tax Overhaul Y
6. South Africa sanctions Y
7. Death penalty-drug bill N
8. Evidence-warrantless srch N
9. Life term-second drug off Y
10. Military use in drug war N
11. Troop reduction in Europe N
12. Prohibit chemical weapons Y
13. Bar ASAT testing Y
14. Abide SALT II weapons ban Y
15. Follow SALT II-Soviets do N
16. Reduce SDI funding Y
17. Increase SDI funding N
18. Purchase Trident sub N
19. Delete 12 MX;Add conv wpn Y
20. Raise speed limit N
21. Textile Import Quotas(*) N
22. Req Pentagon buy US goods N
23. AIDS ins anti-dscriminatn Y
24. Nicaraguan refugee aid Y
25. Nicaraguan contra aid N
26. US abide by SALT II N
27. Prohibit Saudi arms sale Y
28. Military Retiremnt Reform Y
29. Nicaraguan refugee aid Y
30. Ease '68 Gun Control Act Y
31. Bar intrstat handgun tran Y
32. Keep '68 Gun Control Act Y
33. Nicaraguan contra aid N
34. Bar emp polygraph testing Y
35. Tax Overhaul consideratn Y
36. Bar armor-piercing ammo Y
37. Tax Overhaul consideratn Y
38. Make comp emissions known Y
39. Allow toxic victims suits Y
40. Strike Superfund "VAT" Y
41. Notify emp-plant closing Y
42. Bar emp consult-plant clo N
43. Medicare cuts;Tax incres' Y
44. Delete 12 MX missiles Y
45. Spending cuts;Tax incres' N
46. Textile Import Quotas N
47. Cut some school lunch fds N
48. Clean Water Act Amendmnts N
49. Youth work projects Y
50. Assist military in Angola N
51. Allow US troops-Nicaragua N
52. Pentagon polygraph exams N
53. Bar ASAT testing Y
54. Suspend def pmt for abuse Y
55. Bar Pentagon-contr emplmt Y
56. Increase SDI funding N
57. Reduce SDI funding Y
58. Produce chemical weapons N
59. Bar CIA fndg in Nicaragua Y
60. South Africa sanctions Y
61. Cut SS COLAs; Raise taxes N
62. Let US invest-So Africa N

LEACH, JIM (Cont.)

63. Approve 21 MX for 1985 N
64. Emergency Farm Credit Y
65. Awards to whistle blowers Y
66. African disaster relief Y
67. Ban bank loans to So Afr Y
68. Bar coun duty-free trtmt N
69. Steel import limits N
70. Soc Sec COLAs=inflation Y
71. Bar haz waste vctms suits Y
72. Prohibit aid to Nicaragua Y
73. Cut $-Schs bar sch prayer N
74. Raise taxes; Cut Medicare Y
75. Alien residncy-prior 1982 Y
76. Alien residncy-prior 1980 Y
77. Pen emp-hire illgl aliens N
78. Lmt Persh II/cruse-Europe Y
79. Delete 34 B-1 bombers Y
80. Bar purch of Pershing II Y
81. Bar purchase of Sgt York N
82. Delete $ for Trident II Y
83. Allow 15 MX missiles N
84. Bar MX procurement-1985 Y
85. Equal Access Act N
86. Aid to El Salvador N
87. Bar Nicarag water mining Y
88. Physician/Medicare freeze Y
89. Increase "sin" taxes Y
90. End SBA direct loans Y
91. Sell Conrail Y
92. Equal Rights Amendment Y
93. Marines in Lebanon Y
94. Eminent domain-Coal comps N
95. Prohibit EPA sanctions ?
96. SS age increase/Reforms Y
97. Auto domestic content req Y
98. Delete jobs program fundg Y
99. Highway-Gas tax bill N
100. Raise Medicare;Cut defnse Y
101. Emergency housing aid Y
102. Across-the-board tax cuts Y
103. Gramm-Latta II targets Y
104. Delete B-1 bomber funds Y
105. Dsapprov Saudi AWACS sale Y
106. Disapprove oil import fee Y
107. Rail Deregulation ?
108. Dsapp India nuc fuel sale Y
109. Mil draft registration N
110. Chrysler Loan Guarantees Y
111. Prohibit school busing N
112. Nuclear plant moratorium ?
113. Oil price controls N
114. Tuition Tax Credits Y
115. Est Consumer Protect Agcy N
116. Eliminate B-1 bomber fnds Y
117. Subminimum wage for youth Y
118. Delete crude oil tax Y
119. Natural gas deregulation N

Presidential Support Score: 1986 - 47% 1985 - 34%

TAUKE, THOMAS J. -- Iowa 2nd District [Republican]. Counties of Allamakee, Buchanan, Cedar, Clayton, Clinton, Delaware, Dubuque, Fayette, Jackson, Jones and Linn. Prior Terms: House: 1979-86. Born: October 11, 1950; Dubuque, Iowa. Education: University of Iowa College of Law (J.D.). Occupation: Attorney, Curnan, Fitzsimmons, Schilling and Tauke; Iowa assemblyman (1975).

1. Immigration Reform ?
2. Open fld-search warrants ?
3. Civil pnty-hire ill alien ?
4. So Afr sanc-veto override Y
5. Tax Overhaul Y
6. South Africa sanctions Y
7. Death penalty-drug bill N
8. Evidence-warrantless srch Y
9. Life term-second drug off Y
10. Military use in drug war Y
11. Troop reduction in Europe Y
12. Prohibit chemical weapons Y
13. Bar ASAT testing Y
14. Abide SALT II weapons ban Y
15. Follow SALT II-Soviets do Y
16. Reduce SDI funding N
17. Increase SDI funding N
18. Purchase Trident sub N
19. Delete 12 MX;Add conv wpn Y
20. Raise speed limit Y
21. Textile Import Quotas(*) N
22. Req Pentagon buy US goods Y
23. AIDS ins anti-dscriminatn N
24. Nicaraguan refugee aid Y
25. Nicaraguan contra aid N
26. US abide by SALT II N
27. Prohibit Saudi arms sale N
28. Military Retiremnt Reform Y
29. Nicaraguan refugee aid Y
30. Ease '68 Gun Control Act Y
31. Bar intrstat handgun tran N
32. Keep '68 Gun Control Act Y
33. Nicaraguan contra aid N
34. Bar emp polygraph testing Y
35. Tax Overhaul consideratn N
36. Bar armor-piercing ammo Y
37. Tax Overhaul consideratn N
38. Make comp emissions known N

TAUKE, THOMAS J. (Cont.)

39. Allow toxic victims suits N
40. Strike Superfund "VAT" Y
41. Notify emp-plant closing N
42. Bar emp consult-plant clo Y
43. Medicare cuts;Tax incres' Y
44. Delete 12 MX missiles Y
45. Spending cuts;Tax incres' N
46. Textile Import Quotas N
47. Cut some school lunch fds N
48. Clean Water Act Amendmnts N
49. Youth work projects N
50. Assist military in Angola Y
51. Allow US troops-Nicaragua N
52. Pentagon polygraph exams Y
53. Bar ASAT testing Y
54. Suspend def pmt for abuse N
55. Bar Pentagon-contr emplmt Y
56. Increase SDI funding N
57. Reduce SDI funding N
58. Produce chemical weapons N
59. Bar CIA fndg in Nicaragua N
60. South Africa sanctions Y
61. Cut SS COLAs; Raise taxes N
62. Let US invest-So Africa Y
63. Approve 21 MX for 1985 N
64. Emergency Farm Credit Y
65. Awards to whistle blowers Y
66. African disaster relief Y
67. Ban bank loans to So Afr Y
68. Bar coun duty-free trtmt ?
69. Steel import limits N
70. Soc Sec COLAs=inflation Y
71. Bar haz waste vctms suits Y
72. Prohibit aid to Nicaragua Y
73. Cut $-Schs bar sch prayer N
74. Raise taxes; Cut Medicare Y
75. Alien residncy-prior 1982 Y
76. Alien residncy-prior 1980 Y
77. Pen emp-hire illgl aliens N
78. Lmt Persh II/cruse-Europe N
79. Delete 34 B-1 bombers Y
80. Bar purch of Pershing II N
81. Bar purchase of Sgt York Y
82. Delete $ for Trident II N
83. Allow 15 MX missiles N
84. Bar MX procurement-1985 Y
85. Equal Access Act Y
86. Aid to El Salvador Y
87. Bar Nicarag water mining Y
88. Physician/Medicare freeze Y
89. Increase "sin" taxes Y
90. End SBA direct loans Y
91. Sell Conrail Y
92. Equal Rights Amendment N
93. Marines in Lebanon N
94. Eminent domain-Coal comps ?
95. Prohibit EPA sanctions N
96. SS age increase/Reforms Y
97. Auto domestic content req X
98. Delete jobs program fundg Y
99. Highway-Gas tax bill N
100. Raise Medicare;Cut defnse Y
101. Emergency housing aid Y
102. Across-the-board tax cuts Y
103. Gramm-Latta II targets Y
104. Delete B-1 bomber funds Y
105. Dsapprov Saudi AWACS sale N
106. Disapprove oil import fee Y
107. Rail Deregulation N
108. Dsapp India nuc fuel sale Y
109. Mil draft registration N
110. Chrysler Loan Guarantees N
111. Prohibit school busing N
112. Nuclear plant moratorium N
113. Oil price controls ?

Presidential Support Score: 1986 - 55% 1985 - 52%

EVANS, COOPER -- Iowa 3rd District [Republican]. Counties of Benton, Black Hawk, Bremer, Butler, Chickasaw, Floyd, Grundy, Howard, Iowa, Johnson, Marshall, Mitchell, Poweshiek, Toma, Winneshiek and Worth. Prior Terms: House: 1981-86. Born: May 26, 1924; Cedar Rapids, Iowa. Education: Iowa State University (B.S., M.S.). U.S. Army Command and General Staff College; Oak Ridge School of Reactor Technology. Military Service: U.S. Army, 1943-46, 1949-65. Occupation: Staff, Atomic Energy Commission (1956-58); NASA director (1963-65); Iowa representative (1975-79); commissioner, Grundy County Memorial Hospital; director, Hawkeye Institute of Technology; assistant commissioner, Grundy County Soil Conservation District; president, Community Development Corp.

1. Immigration Reform Y
2. Open fld-search warrants Y
3. Civil pnty-hire ill alien N
4. So Afr sanc-veto override Y
5. Tax Overhaul Y
6. South Africa sanctions Y
7. Death penalty-drug bill Y
8. Evidence-warrantless srch Y

EVANS, COOPER (Cont.)

9. Life term-second drug off Y
10. Military use in drug war Y
11. Troop reduction in Europe N
12. Prohibit chemical weapons N
13. Bar ASAT testing Y
14. Abide SALT II weapons ban N
15. Follow SALT II-Soviets do Y
16. Reduce SDI funding N
17. Increase SDI funding N
18. Purchase Trident sub N
19. Delete 12 MX;Add conv wpn Y
20. Raise speed limit Y
21. Textile Import Quotas(*) N
22. Req Pentagon buy US goods N
23. AIDS ins anti-dscriminatn N
24. Nicaraguan refugee aid N
25. Nicaraguan contra aid Y
26. US abide by SALT II Y
27. Prohibit Saudi arms sale Y
28. Military Retiremnt Reform Y
29. Nicaraguan refugee aid Y
30. Ease '68 Gun Control Act Y
31. Bar intrstat handgun tran N
32. Keep '68 Gun Control Act N
33. Nicaraguan contra aid ?
34. Bar emp polygraph testing N
35. Tax Overhaul consideratn Y
36. Bar armor-piercing ammo Y
37. Tax Overhaul consideratn N
38. Make comp emissions known N
39. Allow toxic victims suits Y
40. Strike Superfund "VAT" Y
41. Notify emp-plant closing N
42. Bar emp consult-plant clo Y
43. Medicare cuts;Tax incres' Y
44. Delete 12 MX missiles Y
45. Spending cuts;Tax incres' N
46. Textile Import Quotas N
47. Cut some school lunch fds N
48. Clean Water Act Amendmnts Y
49. Youth work projects N
50. Assist military in Angola N
51. Allow US troops-Nicaragua N
52. Pentagon polygraph exams Y
53. Bar ASAT testing Y
54. Suspend def pmt for abuse Y
55. Bar Pentagon-contr emplmt Y
56. Increase SDI funding N
57. Reduce SDI funding N
58. Produce chemical weapons Y
59. Bar CIA fndg in Nicaragua N
60. South Africa sanctions Y
61. Cut SS COLAs; Raise taxes N
62. Let US invest-So Africa Y
63. Approve 21 MX for 1985 N
64. Emergency Farm Credit Y
65. Awards to whistle blowers Y
66. African disaster relief Y
67. Ban bank loans to So Afr Y
68. Bar coun duty-free trtmt N
69. Steel import limits N
70. Soc Sec COLAs=inflation Y
71. Bar haz waste vctms suits Y
72. Prohibit aid to Nicaragua N
73. Cut $-Schs bar sch prayer N
74. Raise taxes; Cut Medicare Y
75. Alien residncy-prior 1982 Y
76. Alien residncy-prior 1980 Y
77. Pen emp-hire illgl aliens N
78. Lmt Persh II/cruse-Europe N
79. Delete 34 B-1 bombers N
80. Bar purch of Pershing II N
81. Bar purchase of Sgt York Y
82. Delete $ for Trident II N
83. Allow 15 MX missiles N
84. Bar MX procurement-1985 Y
85. Equal Access Act Y
86. Aid to El Salvador Y
87. Bar Nicarag water mining Y
88. Physician/Medicare freeze Y
89. Increase "sin" taxes Y
90. End SBA direct loans N
91. Sell Conrail Y
92. Equal Rights Amendment Y
93. Marines in Lebanon Y
94. Eminent domain-Coal comps N
95. Prohibit EPA sanctions N
96. SS age increase/Reforms Y
97. Auto domestic content req N
98. Delete jobs program fundg Y
99. Highway-Gas tax bill N
100. Raise Medicare;Cut defnse Y
101. Emergency housing aid Y
102. Across-the-board tax cuts Y
103. Gramm-Latta II targets Y
104. Delete B-1 bomber funds N
105. Dsapprov Saudi AWACS sale Y

Presidential Support Score: 1986 - 56% 1985 - 41%

SMITH, NEAL -- Iowa 4th District [Democrat]. Counties of Boone, Dallas, Hamilton, Jasper, Polk and Story. Prior Terms: House: 1959-86. Born: March 23, 1920; Hedrick, Iowa. Education: Drake University Law School; Missouri University; Syracuse University. Military Service: W W II. Occupation: Attorney.

1. Immigration Reform Y
2. Open fld-search warrants Y

SMITH, NEAL (Cont.)
3. Civil pnty-hire ill alien N
4. So Afr sanc-veto override Y
5. Tax Overhaul Y
6. South Africa sanctions Y
7. Death penalty-drug bill N
8. Evidence-warrantless srch Y
9. Life term-second drug off Y
10. Military use in drug war Y
11. Troop reduction in Europe N
12. Prohibit chemical weapons Y
13. Bar ASAT testing Y
14. Abide SALT II weapons ban Y
15. Follow SALT II-Soviets do N
16. Reduce SDI funding N
17. Increase SDI funding N
18. Purchase Trident sub N
19. Delete 12 MX;Add conv wpn ?
20. Raise speed limit Y
21. Textile Import Quotas(*) N
22. Req Pentagon buy US goods Y
23. AIDS ins anti-dscriminatn Y
24. Nicaraguan refugee aid Y
25. Nicaraguan contra aid N
26. US abide by SALT II N
27. Prohibit Saudi arms sale Y
28. Military Retiremnt Reform Y
29. Nicaraguan refugee aid N
30. Ease '68 Gun Control Act Y
31. Bar intrstat handgun tran N
32. Keep '68 Gun Control Act N
33. Nicaraguan contra aid N
34. Bar emp polygraph testing Y
35. Tax Overhaul consideratn Y
36. Bar armor-piercing ammo Y
37. Tax Overhaul consideratn Y
38. Make comp emissions known Y
39. Allow toxic victims suits Y
40. Strike Superfund "VAT" Y
41. Notify emp-plant closing ?
42. Bar emp consult-plant clo N
43. Medicare cuts;Tax incres' Y
44. Delete 12 MX missiles Y
45. Spending cuts;Tax incres' N
46. Textile Import Quotas N
47. Cut some school lunch fds N
48. Clean Water Act Amendmnts N
49. Youth work projects Y
50. Assist military in Angola N
51. Allow US troops-Nicaragua N
52. Pentagon polygraph exams Y
53. Bar ASAT testing Y
54. Suspend def pmt for abuse N
55. Bar Pentagon-contr emplmt Y
56. Increase SDI funding N
57. Reduce SDI funding N
58. Produce chemical weapons N
59. Bar CIA fndg in Nicaragua Y
60. South Africa sanctions Y
61. Cut SS COLAs; Raise taxes N
62. Let US invest-So Africa N
63. Approve 21 MX for 1985 N
64. Emergency Farm Credit Y
65. Awards to whistle blowers Y
66. African disaster relief Y
67. Ban bank loans to So Afr Y
68. Bar coun duty-free trtmt Y
69. Steel import limits N
70. Soc Sec COLAs=inflation Y
71. Bar haz waste vctms suits N
72. Prohibit aid to Nicaragua Y
73. Cut $-Schs bar sch prayer N
74. Raise taxes; Cut Medicare Y
75. Alien residncy-prior 1982 Y
76. Alien residncy-prior 1980 N
77. Pen emp-hire illgl aliens N
78. Lmt Persh II/cruse-Europe N
79. Delete 34 B-1 bombers Y
80. Bar purch of Pershing II N
81. Bar purchase of Sgt York ?
82. Delete $ for Trident II N
83. Allow 15 MX missiles N
84. Bar MX procurement-1985 Y
85. Equal Access Act N
86. Aid to El Salvador N
87. Bar Nicarag water mining Y
88. Physician/Medicare freeze N
89. Increase "sin" taxes Y
90. End SBA direct loans N
91. Sell Conrail N
92. Equal Rights Amendment Y
93. Marines in Lebanon N
94. Eminent domain-Coal comps Y
95. Prohibit EPA sanctions N
96. SS age increase/Reforms N
97. Auto domestic content req N
98. Delete jobs program fundg N
99. Highway-Gas tax bill Y
100. Raise Medicare;Cut defnse Y
101. Emergency housing aid Y
102. Across-the-board tax cuts N
103. Gramm-Latta II targets N
104. Delete B-1 bomber funds Y
105. Dsapprov Saudi AWACS sale Y
106. Disapprove oil import fee Y
107. Rail Deregulation N
108. Dsapp India nuc fuel sale Y
109. Mil draft registration N
110. Chrysler Loan Guarantees Y
111. Prohibit school busing N
112. Nuclear plant moratorium N
113. Oil price controls N
114. Tuition Tax Credits N
115. Est Consumer Protect Agcy Y
116. Eliminate B-1 bomber fnds N
117. Subminimum wage for youth ?
118. Delete crude oil tax N

SMITH, NEAL (Cont.)
119. Natural gas deregulation N

Presidential Support Score: 1986 - 23% 1985 - 30%

LIGHTFOOT, JAMES ROSS -- Iowa 5th District [Republican]. Counties of Adair, Adams, Audubon, Calhoun, Carroll, Cass, Clarke, Crawford, Decatur, Fremont, Greene, Guthrie, Harrison, Madison, Marion, Mills, Montgomery, Page, Pottawattomie, Ringgold, Sac, Shelby, Taylor, Union, Warren, Wayne and Webster. Prior Terms: 1985-86. Occupation: Broadcaster; businessman.

1. Immigration Reform Y
2. Open fld-search warrants N
3. Civil pnty-hire ill alien Y
4. So Afr sanc-veto override Y
5. Tax Overhaul Y
6. South Africa sanctions Y
7. Death penalty-drug bill Y
8. Evidence-warrantless srch Y
9. Life term-second drug off Y
10. Military use in drug war Y
11. Troop reduction in Europe N
12. Prohibit chemical weapons N
13. Bar ASAT testing N
14. Abide SALT II weapons ban N
15. Follow SALT II-Soviets do Y
16. Reduce SDI funding N
17. Increase SDI funding N
18. Purchase Trident sub N
19. Delete 12 MX;add conv wpn Y
20. Raise speed limit Y
21. Textile Import Quotas(*) N
22. Req Pentagon buy US goods Y
23. AIDS ins anti-dscriminatn N
24. Nicaraguan refugee aid N
25. Nicaraguan contra aid N
26. US abide by SALT II Y
27. Prohibit Saudi arms sale Y
28. Military Retiremnt Reform Y
29. Nicaraguan refugee aid Y
30. Ease '68 Gun Control Act Y
31. Bar intrstat handgun tran N
32. Keep '68 Gun Control Act N
33. Nicaraguan contra aid N
34. Bar emp polygraph testing N
35. Tax Overhaul consideratn N
36. Bar armor-piercing ammo Y
37. Tax Overhaul consideratn N
38. Make comp emissions known N
39. Allow toxic victims suits N
40. Strike Superfund "VAT" Y
41. Notify emp-plant closing N
42. Bar emp consult-plant clo Y
43. Medicare cuts;Tax incres' N
44. Delete 12 MX missiles Y
45. Spending cuts;Tax incres' N
46. Textile Import Quotas N
47. Cut some school lunch fds N
48. Clean Water Act Amendmnts Y
49. Youth work projects N
50. Assist military in Angola Y
51. Allow US troops-Nicaragua Y
52. Pentagon polygraph exams Y
53. Bar ASAT testing N
54. Suspend def pmt for abuse N
55. Bar Pentagon-contr emplmt Y
56. Increase SDI funding N
57. Reduce SDI funding N
58. Produce chemical weapons Y
59. Bar CIA fndg in Nicaragua N
60. South Africa sanctions Y
61. Cut SS COLAs; Raise taxes N
62. Let US invest-So Africa Y
63. Approve 21 MX for 1985 Y
64. Emergency Farm Credit Y
65. Awards to whistle blowers Y
66. African disaster relief Y

Presidential Support Score: 1986 - 69% 1985 - 63%

BEDELL, BERKLEY -- Iowa 6th District [Democrat]. Counties of Buena Vista, Cerro Gordo, Cherokee, Clay, Dickinson, Emmet, Franklin, Hancock, Hardin, Humboldt, Ida, Kossuth, Lyon, Monona, O'Brien, Osceola, Palo Alto, Plymouth, Pocahontas, Sioux, Winnebago, Woodbury and Wright. Prior Terms: House: 1975-86. Born: March 5, 1921; Spirit Lake, Iowa. Education: Iowa State University. Military Service: U.S. Army Air Force, 1942-45. Occupation: Founder and chairman, Berkley & Co.; member, Spirit Lake Board of Education (1957-62).

1. Immigration Reform Y
2. Open fld-search warrants Y
3. Civil pnty-hire ill alien N
4. So Afr sanc-veto override Y

BEDELL, BERKLEY (Cont.)

5. Tax Overhaul Y
6. South Africa sanctions Y
7. Death penalty-drug bill N
8. Evidence-warrantless srch N
9. Life term-second drug off Y
10. Military use in drug war N
11. Troop reduction in Europe Y
12. Prohibit chemical weapons Y
13. Bar ASAT testing Y
14. Abide SALT II weapons ban Y
15. Follow SALT II-Soviets do N
16. Reduce SDI funding Y
17. Increase SDI funding N
18. Purchase Trident sub N
19. Delete 12 MX;Add conv wpn Y
20. Raise speed limit N
21. Textile Import Quotas(*) C
22. Req Pentagon buy US goods Y
23. AIDS ins anti-dscriminatn Y
24. Nicaraguan refugee aid Y
25. Nicaraguan contra aid N
26. US abide by SALT II N
27. Prohibit Saudi arms sale Y
28. Military Retiremnt Reform Y
29. Nicaraguan refugee aid Y
30. Ease '68 Gun Control Act N
31. Bar intrstat handgun tran Y
32. Keep '68 Gun Control Act Y
33. Nicaraguan contra aid N
34. Bar emp polygraph testing Y
35. Tax Overhaul consideratn Y
36. Bar armor-piercing ammo Y
37. Tax Overhaul consideratn Y
38. Make comp emissions known Y
39. Allow toxic victims suits Y
40. Strike Superfund "VAT" Y
41. Notify emp-plant closing Y
42. Bar emp consult-plant clo N
43. Medicare cuts;Tax incres' Y
44. Delete 12 MX missiles Y
45. Spending cuts;Tax incres' Y
46. Textile Import Quotas C
47. Cut some school lunch fds N
48. Clean Water Act Amendmnts N
49. Youth work projects Y
50. Assist military in Angola N
51. Allow US troops-Nicaragua N
52. Pentagon polygraph exams N
53. Bar ASAT testing Y
54. Suspend def pmt for abuse Y
55. Bar Pentagon-contr emplmt Y
56. Increase SDI funding N
57. Reduce SDI funding Y
58. Produce chemical weapons N
59. Bar CIA fndg in Nicaragua Y
60. South Africa sanctions Y
61. Cut SS COLAs; Raise taxes Y
62. Let US invest-So Africa N
63. Approve 21 MX for 1985 N
64. Emergency Farm Credit Y
65. Awards to whistle blowers Y
66. African disaster relief Y
67. Ban bank loans to So Afr Y
68. Bar coun duty-free trtmt P
69. Steel import limits N
70. Soc Sec COLAs=inflation Y
71. Bar haz waste vctms suits N
72. Prohibit aid to Nicaragua Y
73. Cut $-Schs bar sch prayer N
74. Raise taxes; Cut Medicare Y
75. Alien residncy-prior 1982 Y
76. Alien residncy-prior 1980 N
77. Pen emp-hire illgl aliens N
78. Lmt Persh II/cruse-Europe Y
79. Delete 34 B-1 bombers Y
80. Bar purch of Pershing II Y
81. Bar purchase of Sgt York Y
82. Delete $ for Trident II Y
83. Allow 15 MX missiles N
84. Bar MX procurement-1985 Y
85. Equal Access Act Y
86. Aid to El Salvador N
87. Bar Nicarag water mining ?
88. Physician/Medicare freeze N
89. Increase "sin" taxes Y
90. End SBA direct loans N
91. Sell Conrail N
92. Equal Rights Amendment N
93. Marines in Lebanon N
94. Eminent domain-Coal comps N
95. Prohibit EPA sanctions N
96. SS age increase/Reforms Y
97. Auto domestic content req N
98. Delete jobs program fundg N
99. Highway-Gas tax bill N
100. Raise Medicare;Cut defnse Y
101. Emergency housing aid Y
102. Across-the-board tax cuts N
103. Gramm-Latta II targets N
104. Delete B-1 bomber funds ?
105. Dsapprov Saudi AWACS sale Y
106. Disapprove oil import fee Y
107. Rail Deregulation N
108. Dsapp India nuc fuel sale Y
109. Mil draft registration N
110. Chrysler Loan Guarantees Y
111. Prohibit school busing N
112. Nuclear plant moratorium Y
113. Oil price controls N
114. Tuition Tax Credits N
115. Est Consumer Protect Agcy N
116. Eliminate B-1 bomber fnds Y
117. Subminimum wage for youth N
118. Delete crude oil tax N
119. Natural gas deregulation N

Presidential Support Score: 1986 - 16% 1985 - 21%

KANSAS

ROBERTS, PAT -- Kansas 1st District [Republican]. Counties of Barber, Barton, Cheyenne, Clark, Cloud, Comanche, Decatur, Dickinson, Edwards, Ellis, Ellsworth, Finney, Ford, Gove, Graham, Grant, Gray, Greeley, Hamilton, Haskell, Hodgeman, Jewell, Kearny, Kiowa, Lane, Lincoln, Logan, Marshall, Meade, Mitchell, Morton, Ness, Norton, Osborne, Ottawa, Pawnee, Phillips, Pratt, Rawlins, Republic, Rice, Rooks, Rush, Russell, Saline, Scott, Seward, Sheridan, Sherman, Smith, Stafford, Stanton, Stevens, Thomas, Trego, Wallace, Washington and Wichita. Prior Terms: House: 1981-86. Born: April 23, 1936; Topeka, Kan. Education: Kansas State University (B.A.). Military Service: U.S. Marine Corps, 1958-62. Occupation: Newspaper owner and editor; congressional press secretary; congressional administrative assistant.

1. Immigration Reform N
2. Open fld-search warrants Y
3. Civil pnty-hire ill alien Y
4. So Afr sanc-veto override Y
5. Tax Overhaul N
6. South Africa sanctions Y
7. Death penalty-drug bill Y
8. Evidence-warrantless srch Y
9. Life term-second drug off Y
10. Military use in drug war Y
11. Troop reduction in Europe N
12. Prohibit chemical weapons N
13. Bar ASAT testing N
14. Abide SALT II weapons ban N
15. Follow SALT II-Soviets do Y
16. Reduce SDI funding N
17. Increase SDI funding N
18. Purchase Trident sub N
19. Delete 12 MX;Add conv wpn N
20. Raise speed limit Y
21. Textile Import Quotas(*) N
22. Req Pentagon buy US goods N
23. AIDS ins anti-dscriminatn N
24. Nicaraguan refugee aid N
25. Nicaraguan contra aid Y
26. US abide by SALT II Y
27. Prohibit Saudi arms sale Y
28. Military Retiremnt Reform Y
29. Nicaraguan refugee aid Y
30. Ease '68 Gun Control Act Y
31. Bar intrstat handgun tran N
32. Keep '68 Gun Control Act N
33. Nicaraguan contra aid Y
34. Bar emp polygraph testing N
35. Tax Overhaul consideratn N
36. Bar armor-piercing ammo Y
37. Tax Overhaul consideratn N
38. Make comp emissions known N
39. Allow toxic victims suits N
40. Strike Superfund "VAT" N
41. Notify emp-plant closing N
42. Bar emp consult-plant clo Y
43. Medicare cuts;Tax incres' N
44. Delete 12 MX missiles Y
45. Spending cuts;Tax incres' N
46. Textile Import Quotas N
47. Cut some school lunch fds Y
48. Clean Water Act Amendmnts Y
49. Youth work projects N
50. Assist military in Angola Y
51. Allow US troops-Nicaragua Y
52. Pentagon polygraph exams Y
53. Bar ASAT testing Y
54. Suspend def pmt for abuse N
55. Bar Pentagon-contr emplmt Y
56. Increase SDI funding N
57. Reduce SDI funding N
58. Produce chemical weapons Y
59. Bar CIA fndg in Nicaragua N
60. South Africa sanctions N
61. Cut SS COLAs; Raise taxes N
62. Let US invest-So Africa Y
63. Approve 21 MX for 1985 N
64. Emergency Farm Credit Y
65. Awards to whistle blowers Y
66. African disaster relief Y
67. Ban bank loans to So Afr Y
68. Bar coun duty-free trtmt N
69. Steel import limits N
70. Soc Sec COLAs=inflation Y
71. Bar haz waste vctms suits Y
72. Prohibit aid to Nicaragua N
73. Cut $-Schs bar sch prayer Y
74. Raise taxes; Cut Medicare N
75. Alien residncy-prior 1982 Y
76. Alien residncy-prior 1980 Y
77. Pen emp-hire illgl aliens N
78. Lmt Persh II/cruse-Europe N
79. Delete 34 B-1 bombers N
80. Bar purch of Pershing II N
81. Bar purchase of Sgt York N
82. Delete $ for Trident II N
83. Allow 15 MX missiles Y
84. Bar MX procurement-1985 N
85. Equal Access Act Y
86. Aid to El Salvador Y

ROBERTS, PAT (Cont.)

87. Bar Nicarag water mining N
88. Physician/Medicare freeze Y
89. Increase "sin" taxes N
90. End SBA direct loans N
91. Sell Conrail Y
92. Equal Rights Amendment N
93. Marines in Lebanon Y
94. Eminent domain-Coal comps N
95. Prohibit EPA sanctions N
96. SS age increase/Reforms Y
97. Auto domestic content req N
98. Delete jobs program fundg Y
99. Highway-Gas tax bill N
100. Raise Medicare;Cut defnse N
101. Emergency housing aid N
102. Across-the-board tax cuts Y
103. Gramm-Latta II targets Y
104. Delete B-1 bomber funds N
105. Dsapprov Saudi AWACS sale N

Presidential Support Score: 1986 - 69% 1985 - 63%

SLATTERY, JIM -- Kansas 2nd District [Democrat]. Counties of Atchison, Brown, Clay, Doniphan, Douglas, Geary, Jackson, Jefferson, Leavenworth, Nemaha, Pottawatomie, Riley and Shawnee. Prior Terms: House: 1983-86. Born: August 4, 1948; Good Intent, Kan. Education: Washburn University (B.S., J.D.). Occupation: Realtor; Kansas representative (1972-78); acting secretary of revenue (1979); member, Board of Directors, Highland Park Bank & Trust; member, Board of Regents, Washburn University.

1. Immigration Reform Y
2. Open fld-search warrants Y
3. Civil pnty-hire ill alien N
4. So Afr sanc-veto override Y
5. Tax Overhaul Y
6. South Africa sanctions Y
7. Death penalty-drug bill Y
8. Evidence-warrantless srch N
9. Life term-second drug off Y
10. Military use in drug war Y
11. Troop reduction in Europe N
12. Prohibit chemical weapons N
13. Bar ASAT testing Y
14. Abide SALT II weapons ban Y
15. Follow SALT II-Soviets do N
16. Reduce SDI funding N
17. Increase SDI funding N
18. Purchase Trident sub Y
19. Delete 12 MX;Add conv wpn Y
20. Raise speed limit Y
21. Textile Import Quotas(*) N
22. Req Pentagon buy US goods N
23. AIDS ins anti-dscriminatn N
24. Nicaraguan refugee aid Y
25. Nicaraguan contra aid N
26. US abide by SALT II N
27. Prohibit Saudi arms sale Y
28. Military Retiremnt Reform Y
29. Nicaraguan refugee aid Y
30. Ease '68 Gun Control Act Y
31. Bar intrstat handgun tran N
32. Keep '68 Gun Control Act N
33. Nicaraguan contra aid N
34. Bar emp polygraph testing Y
35. Tax Overhaul consideratn Y
36. Bar armor-piercing ammo Y
37. Tax Overhaul consideratn Y
38. Make comp emissions known N
39. Allow toxic victims suits N
40. Strike Superfund "VAT" N
41. Notify emp-plant closing Y
42. Bar emp consult-plant clo N
43. Medicare cuts;Tax incres' Y
44. Delete 12 MX missiles Y
45. Spending cuts;Tax incres' N
46. Textile Import Quotas N
47. Cut some school lunch fds N
48. Clean Water Act Amendmnts N
49. Youth work projects N
50. Assist military in Angola Y
51. Allow US troops-Nicaragua N
52. Pentagon polygraph exams Y
53. Bar ASAT testing Y
54. Suspend def pmt for abuse N
55. Bar Pentagon-contr emplmt Y
56. Increase SDI funding N
57. Reduce SDI funding N
58. Produce chemical weapons Y
59. Bar CIA fndg in Nicaragua N
60. South Africa sanctions Y
61. Cut SS COLAs; Raise taxes Y
62. Let US invest-So Africa N
63. Approve 21 MX for 1985 N
64. Emergency Farm Credit Y
65. Awards to whistle blowers Y
66. African disaster relief Y
67. Ban bank loans to So Afr Y
68. Bar coun duty-free trtmt Y
69. Steel import limits N
70. Soc Sec COLAs=inflation Y
71. Bar haz waste vctms suits Y
72. Prohibit aid to Nicaragua Y

SLATTERY, JIM (Cont.)

73.	Cut $-Schs bar sch prayer	N	85.	Equal Access Act	N
74.	Raise taxes; Cut Medicare	N	86.	Aid to El Salvador	N
75.	Alien residncy-prior 1982	Y	87.	Bar Nicarag water mining	Y
76.	Alien residncy-prior 1980	N	88.	Physician/Medicare freeze	N
77.	Pen emp-hire illgl aliens	N	89.	Increase "sin" taxes	Y
78.	Lmt Persh II/cruse-Europe	N	90.	End SBA direct loans	N
79.	Delete 34 B-1 bombers	N	91.	Sell Conrail	N
80.	Bar purch of Pershing II	N	92.	Equal Rights Amendment	Y
81.	Bar purchase of Sgt York	N	93.	Marines in Lebanon	Y
82.	Delete $ for Trident II	N	94.	Eminent domain-Coal comps	N
83.	Allow 15 MX missiles	N	95.	Prohibit EPA sanctions	N
84.	Bar MX procurement-1985	Y	96.	SS age increase/Reforms	Y

Presidential Support Score: 1986 - 35% 1985 - 43%

MEYERS, JAN -- Kansas 3rd District [Republican]. Counties of Johnson, Linn, Miami and Wyandotte. Prior Terms: 1985-86. Occupation: Kansas senator; member, city council.

1.	Immigration Reform	N	34.	Bar emp polygraph testing	N
2.	Open fld-search warrants	N	35.	Tax Overhaul consideratn	Y
3.	Civil pnty-hire ill alien	N	36.	Bar armor-piercing ammo	Y
4.	So Afr sanc-veto override	Y	37.	Tax Overhaul consideratn	Y
5.	Tax Overhaul	Y	38.	Make comp emissions known	N
6.	South Africa sanctions	Y	39.	Allow toxic victims suits	N
7.	Death penalty-drug bill	Y	40.	Strike Superfund "VAT"	Y
8.	Evidence-warrantless srch	Y	41.	Notify emp-plant closing	N
9.	Life term-second drug off	Y	42.	Bar emp consult-plant clo	Y
10.	Military use in drug war	Y	43.	Medicare cuts;Tax incres'	N
11.	Troop reduction in Europe	N	44.	Delete 12 MX missiles	Y
12.	Prohibit chemical weapons	Y	45.	Spending cuts;Tax incres'	N
13.	Bar ASAT testing	Y	46.	Textile Import Quotas	N
14.	Abide SALT II weapons ban	N	47.	Cut some school lunch fds	Y
15.	Follow SALT II-Soviets do	Y	48.	Clean Water Act Amendmnts	Y
16.	Reduce SDI funding	N	49.	Youth work projects	?
17.	Increase SDI funding	N	50.	Assist military in Angola	Y
18.	Purchase Trident sub	N	51.	Allow US troops-Nicaragua	Y
19.	Delete 12 MX;Add conv wpn	N	52.	Pentagon polygraph exams	Y
20.	Raise speed limit	N	53.	Bar ASAT testing	Y
21.	Textile Import Quotas(*)	N	54.	Suspend def pmt for abuse	Y
22.	Req Pentagon buy US goods	N	55.	Bar Pentagon-contr emplmt	Y
23.	AIDS ins anti-dscriminatn	N	56.	Increase SDI funding	N
24.	Nicaraguan refugee aid	N	57.	Reduce SDI funding	N
25.	Nicaraguan contra aid	Y	58.	Produce chemical weapons	Y
26.	US abide by SALT II	Y	59.	Bar CIA fndg in Nicaragua	N
27.	Prohibit Saudi arms sale	Y	60.	South Africa sanctions	N
28.	Military Retiremnt Reform	Y	61.	Cut SS COLAs; Raise taxes	N
29.	Nicaraguan refugee aid	Y	62.	Let US invest-So Africa	Y
30.	Ease '68 Gun Control Act	Y	63.	Approve 21 MX for 1985	Y
31.	Bar intrstat handgun tran	Y	64.	Emergency Farm Credit	Y
32.	Keep '68 Gun Control Act	Y	65.	Awards to whistle blowers	Y
33.	Nicaraguan contra aid	Y	66.	African disaster relief	Y

Presidential Support Score: 1986 - 59% 1985 - 68%

GLICKMAN, DAN -- Kansas 4th District [Democrat]. Counties of Harper, Kingman, Reno, Sedgwick and Sumner. Prior Terms: House: 1977-86. Born: November 24, 1944; Wichita, Kan. Education: University of Michigan (B.A.); George Washington University

GLICKMAN, DAN (Cont.)
(J.D.). Occupation: Attorney; businessman; trial attorney for U.S. Securities and Exchange Commission (1969-70); member, Wichita Board of Education.

1. Immigration Reform Y
2. Open fld-search warrants Y
3. Civil pnty-hire ill alien N
4. So Afr sanc-veto override Y
5. Tax Overhaul Y
6. South Africa sanctions Y
7. Death penalty-drug bill Y
8. Evidence-warrantless srch N
9. Life term-second drug off Y
10. Military use in drug war N
11. Troop reduction in Europe N
12. Prohibit chemical weapons N
13. Bar ASAT testing Y
14. Abide SALT II weapons ban Y
15. Follow SALT II-Soviets do N
16. Reduce SDI funding Y
17. Increase SDI funding N
18. Purchase Trident sub Y
19. Delete 12 MX;Add conv wpn Y
20. Raise speed limit Y
21. Textile Import Quotas(*) N
22. Req Pentagon buy US goods N
23. AIDS ins anti-dscriminatn N
24. Nicaraguan refugee aid Y
25. Nicaraguan contra aid N
26. US abide by SALT II N
27. Prohibit Saudi arms sale Y
28. Military Retiremnt Reform Y
29. Nicaraguan refugee aid Y
30. Ease '68 Gun Control Act Y
31. Bar intrstat handgun tran N
32. Keep '68 Gun Control Act N
33. Nicaraguan contra aid N
34. Bar emp polygraph testing Y
35. Tax Overhaul consideratn Y
36. Bar armor-piercing ammo Y
37. Tax Overhaul consideratn Y
38. Make comp emissions known Y
39. Allow toxic victims suits N
40. Strike Superfund "VAT" N
41. Notify emp-plant closing Y
42. Bar emp consult-plant clo N
43. Medicare cuts;Tax incres' Y
44. Delete 12 MX missiles Y
45. Spending cuts;Tax incres' N
46. Textile Import Quotas N
47. Cut some school lunch fds N
48. Clean Water Act Amendmnts N
49. Youth work projects N
50. Assist military in Angola Y
51. Allow US troops-Nicaragua N
52. Pentagon polygraph exams N
53. Bar ASAT testing Y
54. Suspend def pmt for abuse N
55. Bar Pentagon-contr emplmt Y
56. Increase SDI funding N
57. Reduce SDI funding N
58. Produce chemical weapons Y
59. Bar CIA fndg in Nicaragua Y
60. South Africa sanctions Y
61. Cut SS COLAs; Raise taxes N
62. Let US invest-So Africa N
63. Approve 21 MX for 1985 N
64. Emergency Farm Credit Y
65. Awards to whistle blowers Y
66. African disaster relief Y
67. Ban bank loans to So Afr Y
68. Bar coun duty-free trtmt Y
69. Steel import limits N
70. Soc Sec COLAs=inflation Y
71. Bar haz waste vctms suits Y
72. Prohibit aid to Nicaragua Y
73. Cut $-Schs bar sch prayer N
74. Raise taxes; Cut Medicare Y
75. Alien residncy-prior 1982 Y
76. Alien residncy-prior 1980 N
77. Pen emp-hire illgl aliens N
78. Lmt Persh II/cruse-Europe N
79. Delete 34 B-1 bombers N
80. Bar purch of Pershing II N
81. Bar purchase of Sgt York N
82. Delete $ for Trident II N
83. Allow 15 MX missiles N
84. Bar MX procurement-1985 Y
85. Equal Access Act N
86. Aid to El Salvador N
87. Bar Nicarag water mining Y
88. Physician/Medicare freeze N
89. Increase "sin" taxes Y
90. End SBA direct loans N
91. Sell Conrail Y
92. Equal Rights Amendment Y
93. Marines in Lebanon Y
94. Eminent domain-Coal comps N
95. Prohibit EPA sanctions N
96. SS age increase/Reforms Y
97. Auto domestic content req N
98. Delete jobs program fundg N
99. Highway-Gas tax bill N
100. Raise Medicare;Cut defnse N
101. Emergency housing aid Y
102. Across-the-board tax cuts Y
103. Gramm-Latta II targets N
104. Delete B-1 bomber funds Y
105. Dsapprov Saudi AWACS sale Y
106. Disapprove oil import fee Y
107. Rail Deregulation N
108. Dsapp India nuc fuel sale Y
109. Mil draft registration N
110. Chrysler Loan Guarantees N

GLICKMAN, DAN (Cont.)

111. Prohibit school busing N
112. Nuclear plant moratorium #
113. Oil price controls N
114. Tuition Tax Credits N
115. Est Consumer Protect Agcy N
116. Eliminate B-1 bomber fnds Y
117. Subminimum wage for youth N
118. Delete crude oil tax N
119. Natural gas deregulation Y

Presidential Support Score: 1986 - 28% 1985 - 36%

WHITTAKER, BOB -- Kansas 5th District [Republican]. Counties of Allen, Anderson, Bourbon, Butler, Chase, Chautauqua, Cherokee, Coffey, Cowley, Crawford, Elk, Franklin, Greenwood, Harvey, Labette, Lyon, McPherson, Marion, Montgomery, Morris, Neosho, Osage, Wabaunsee, Wilson and Woodson. Prior Terms: House: 1979-86. Born: September 18, 1939; Eureka, Kan. Education: Illinois College of Optometry (D.O.). Occupation: Optometrist; Kansas representative (1974-77).

1. Immigration Reform N
2. Open fld-search warrants N
3. Civil pnty-hire ill alien N
4. So Afr sanc-veto override N
5. Tax Overhaul N
6. South Africa sanctions N
7. Death penalty-drug bill Y
8. Evidence-warrantless srch Y
9. Life term-second drug off Y
10. Military use in drug war Y
11. Troop reduction in Europe N
12. Prohibit chemical weapons N
13. Bar ASAT testing N
14. Abide SALT II weapons ban N
15. Follow SALT II-Soviets do Y
16. Reduce SDI funding N
17. Increase SDI funding N
18. Purchase Trident sub N
19. Delete 12 MX;Add conv wpn N
20. Raise speed limit Y
21. Textile Import Quotas(*) N
22. Req Pentagon buy US goods Y
23. AIDS ins anti-dscriminatn N
24. Nicaraguan refugee aid N
25. Nicaraguan contra aid Y
26. US abide by SALT II Y
27. Prohibit Saudi arms sale Y
28. Military Retiremnt Reform Y
29. Nicaraguan refugee aid Y
30. Ease '68 Gun Control Act Y
31. Bar intrstat handgun tran N
32. Keep '68 Gun Control Act N
33. Nicaraguan contra aid Y
34. Bar emp polygraph testing N
35. Tax Overhaul consideratn N
36. Bar armor-piercing ammo Y
37. Tax Overhaul consideratn N
38. Make comp emissions known N
39. Allow toxic victims suits N
40. Strike Superfund "VAT" N
41. Notify emp-plant closing N
42. Bar emp consult-plant clo Y
43. Medicare cuts;Tax incres' Y
44. Delete 12 MX missiles Y
45. Spending cuts;Tax incres' N
46. Textile Import Quotas N
47. Cut some school lunch fds Y
48. Clean Water Act Amendmnts Y
49. Youth work projects N
50. Assist military in Angola Y
51. Allow US troops-Nicaragua Y
52. Pentagon polygraph exams Y
53. Bar ASAT testing N
54. Suspend def pmt for abuse N
55. Bar Pentagon-contr emplmt Y
56. Increase SDI funding N
57. Reduce SDI funding N
58. Produce chemical weapons Y
59. Bar CIA fndg in Nicaragua N
60. South Africa sanctions N
61. Cut SS COLAs; Raise taxes N
62. Let US invest-So Africa Y
63. Approve 21 MX for 1985 Y
64. Emergency Farm Credit Y
65. Awards to whistle blowers Y
66. African disaster relief Y
67. Ban bank loans to So Afr Y
68. Bar coun duty-free trtmt N
69. Steel import limits N
70. Soc Sec COLAs=inflation Y
71. Bar haz waste vctms suits Y
72. Prohibit aid to Nicaragua N
73. Cut $-Schs bar sch prayer Y
74. Raise taxes; Cut Medicare Y
75. Alien residncy-prior 1982 Y
76. Alien residncy-prior 1980 Y
77. Pen emp-hire illgl aliens N
78. Lmt Persh II/cruse-Europe N
79. Delete 34 B-1 bombers N
80. Bar purch of Pershing II N
81. Bar purchase of Sgt York N
82. Delete $ for Trident II N
83. Allow 15 MX missiles Y
84. Bar MX procurement-1985 N

WHITTAKER, BOB (Cont.)

85. Equal Access Act Y
86. Aid to El Salvador Y
87. Bar Nicarag water mining Y
88. Physician/Medicare freeze Y
89. Increase "sin" taxes Y
90. End SBA direct loans Y
91. Sell Conrail Y
92. Equal Rights Amendment N
93. Marines in Lebanon Y
94. Eminent domain-Coal comps N
95. Prohibit EPA sanctions N
96. SS age increase/Reforms Y
97. Auto domestic content req N
98. Delete jobs program fundg Y
99. Highway-Gas tax bill N
100. Raise Medicare;Cut defnse N
101. Emergency housing aid N
102. Across-the-board tax cuts Y
103. Gramm-Latta II targets Y
104. Delete B-1 bomber funds N
105. Dsapprov Saudi AWACS sale Y
106. Disapprove oil import fee Y
107. Rail Deregulation N
108. Dsapp India nuc fuel sale Y
109. Mil draft registration Y
110. Chrysler Loan Guarantees N
111. Prohibit school busing Y
112. Nuclear plant moratorium N
113. Oil price controls N

Presidential Support Score: 1986 - 66% 1985 - 58%

KENTUCKY

HUBBARD, CARROLL, Jr. -- Kentucky 1st District [Democrat]. Counties of Ballard, Butler, Caldwell, Calloway, Carlisle, Christian, Crittenden, Fulton, Graves, Henderson, Hickman, Hopkins, Livingston, Logan, Lyon, McCracken, McLean, Marshall, Muhlenberg, Ohio, Todd, Trigg, Union and Webster. Prior Terms: House: 1975-86. Born: July 7, 1937; Murray, Ky. Education: Georgetown College (B.A.); University of Louisville (J.D.). Occupation: Attorney; Kentucky senator (1967-74).

1. Immigration Reform N
2. Open fld-search warrants Y
3. Civil pnty-hire ill alien N
4. So Afr sanc-veto override Y
5. Tax Overhaul N
6. South Africa sanctions Y
7. Death penalty-drug bill Y
8. Evidence-warrantless srch Y
9. Life term-second drug off Y
10. Military use in drug war Y
11. Troop reduction in Europe N
12. Prohibit chemical weapons N
13. Bar ASAT testing N
14. Abide SALT II weapons ban N
15. Follow SALT II-Soviets do Y
16. Reduce SDI funding N
17. Increase SDI funding N
18. Purchase Trident sub N
19. Delete 12 MX;Add conv wpn N
20. Raise speed limit Y
21. Textile Import Quotas(*) Y
22. Req Pentagon buy US goods Y
23. AIDS ins anti-dscriminatn N
24. Nicaraguan refugee aid N
25. Nicaraguan contra aid Y
26. US abide by SALT II Y
27. Prohibit Saudi arms sale Y
28. Military Retiremnt Reform Y
29. Nicaraguan refugee aid Y
30. Ease '68 Gun Control Act Y
31. Bar intrstat handgun tran N
32. Keep '68 Gun Control Act N
33. Nicaraguan contra aid N
34. Bar emp polygraph testing Y
35. Tax Overhaul consideratn N
36. Bar armor-piercing ammo Y
37. Tax Overhaul consideratn N
38. Make comp emissions known N
39. Allow toxic victims suits N
40. Strike Superfund "VAT" N
41. Notify emp-plant closing ?
42. Bar emp consult-plant clo N
43. Medicare cuts;Tax incres' N
44. Delete 12 MX missiles N
45. Spending cuts;Tax incres' N
46. Textile Import Quotas Y
47. Cut some school lunch fds N
48. Clean Water Act Amendmnts Y
49. Youth work projects N
50. Assist military in Angola Y
51. Allow US troops-Nicaragua Y
52. Pentagon polygraph exams Y
53. Bar ASAT testing N
54. Suspend def pmt for abuse N
55. Bar Pentagon-contr emplmt Y
56. Increase SDI funding N
57. Reduce SDI funding N
58. Produce chemical weapons Y

HUBBARD, CARROLL, Jr. (Cont.)

59. Bar CIA fndg in Nicaragua N
60. South Africa sanctions Y
61. Cut SS COLAs; Raise taxes N
62. Let US invest-So Africa N
63. Approve 21 MX for 1985 Y
64. Emergency Farm Credit Y
65. Awards to whistle blowers Y
66. African disaster relief Y
67. Ban bank loans to So Afr N
68. Bar coun duty-free trtmt N
69. Steel import limits Y
70. Soc Sec COLAs=inflation Y
71. Bar haz waste vctms suits Y
72. Prohibit aid to Nicaragua N
73. Cut $-Schs bar sch prayer ?
74. Raise taxes; Cut Medicare N
75. Alien residncy-prior 1982 Y
76. Alien residncy-prior 1980 N
77. Pen emp-hire illgl aliens Y
78. Lmt Persh II/cruse-Europe N
79. Delete 34 B-1 bombers N
80. Bar purch of Pershing II N
81. Bar purchase of Sgt York N
82. Delete $ for Trident II N
83. Allow 15 MX missiles Y
84. Bar MX procurement-1985 N
85. Equal Access Act Y
86. Aid to El Salvador Y
87. Bar Nicarag water mining N
88. Physician/Medicare freeze Y
89. Increase "sin" taxes N
90. End SBA direct loans N
91. Sell Conrail N
92. Equal Rights Amendment N
93. Marines in Lebanon N
94. Eminent domain-Coal comps N
95. Prohibit EPA sanctions Y
96. SS age increase/Reforms N
97. Auto domestic content req Y
98. Delete jobs program fundg Y
99. Highway-Gas tax bill N
100. Raise Medicare;Cut defnse N
101. Emergency housing aid Y
102. Across-the-board tax cuts Y
103. Gramm-Latta II targets N
104. Delete B-1 bomber funds N
105. Dsapprov Saudi AWACS sale N
106. Disapprove oil import fee Y
107. Rail Deregulation N
108. Dsapp India nuc fuel sale N
109. Mil draft registration Y
110. Chrysler Loan Guarantees Y
111. Prohibit school busing Y
112. Nuclear plant moratorium N
113. Oil price controls N
114. Tuition Tax Credits N
115. Est Consumer Protect Agcy N
116. Eliminate B-1 bomber fnds N
117. Subminimum wage for youth N
118. Delete crude oil tax Y
119. Natural gas deregulation Y

Presidential Support Score: 1986 - 53% 1985 - 59%

NATCHER, WILLIAM H. -- Kentucky 2nd District [Democrat]. Counties of Allen, Barren, Breckenridge, Bullitt, Daviess, Edmonson, Grayson, Hancock, Hardin, Hart, Larus, Marion, Meade, Nelson, Simpson, Spencer, Warren and Washington. Prior Terms: House: 1953 (Special Election)-1986. Born: September 11, 1909; Bowling Green, Ky. Education: Western Kentucky State College (A.B.); Ohio State University (LL.B.). Military Service: U.S. Navy, 1942-45. Occupation: Attorney; federal conciliation commissioner (1936-37); Warren County attorney (1937-49); commonwealth attorney (1951-53).

1. Immigration Reform Y
2. Open fld-search warrants Y
3. Civil pnty-hire ill alien N
4. So Afr sanc-veto override Y
5. Tax Overhaul Y
6. South Africa sanctions Y
7. Death penalty-drug bill Y
8. Evidence-warrantless srch Y
9. Life term-second drug off Y
10. Military use in drug war Y
11. Troop reduction in Europe N
12. Prohibit chemical weapons Y
13. Bar ASAT testing Y
14. Abide SALT II weapons ban Y
15. Follow SALT II-Soviets do N
16. Reduce SDI funding N
17. Increase SDI funding N
18. Purchase Trident sub Y
19. Delete 12 MX;Add conv wpn N
20. Raise speed limit N
21. Textile Import Quotas(*) Y
22. Req Pentagon buy US goods Y
23. AIDS ins anti-dscriminatn Y
24. Nicaraguan refugee aid N
25. Nicaraguan contra aid N
26. US abide by SALT II N
27. Prohibit Saudi arms sale Y
28. Military Retiremnt Reform Y

NATCHER, WILLIAM H. (Cont.)

29. Nicaraguan refugee aid Y
30. Ease '68 Gun Control Act Y
31. Bar intrstat handgun tran N
32. Keep '68 Gun Control Act N
33. Nicaraguan contra aid N
34. Bar emp polygraph testing Y
35. Tax Overhaul consideratn Y
36. Bar armor-piercing ammo Y
37. Tax Overhaul consideratn Y
38. Make comp emissions known N
39. Allow toxic victims suits Y
40. Strike Superfund "VAT" N
41. Notify emp-plant closing Y
42. Bar emp consult-plant clo N
43. Medicare cuts;Tax incres' Y
44. Delete 12 MX missiles N
45. Spending cuts;Tax incres' Y
46. Textile Import Quotas Y
47. Cut some school lunch fds N
48. Clean Water Act Amendmnts N
49. Youth work projects Y
50. Assist military in Angola Y
51. Allow US troops-Nicaragua N
52. Pentagon polygraph exams Y
53. Bar ASAT testing Y
54. Suspend def pmt for abuse N
55. Bar Pentagon-contr emplmt Y
56. Increase SDI funding N
57. Reduce SDI funding N
58. Produce chemical weapons N
59. Bar CIA fndg in Nicaragua Y
60. South Africa sanctions Y
61. Cut SS COLAs; Raise taxes N
62. Let US invest-So Africa N
63. Approve 21 MX for 1985 N
64. Emergency Farm Credit Y
65. Awards to whistle blowers Y
66. African disaster relief Y
67. Ban bank loans to So Afr Y
68. Bar coun duty-free trtmt Y
69. Steel import limits Y
70. Soc Sec COLAs=inflation Y
71. Bar haz waste vctms suits Y
72. Prohibit aid to Nicaragua Y
73. Cut $-Schs bar sch prayer Y
74. Raise taxes; Cut Medicare N
75. Alien residncy-prior 1982 N
76. Alien residncy-prior 1980 N
77. Pen emp-hire illgl aliens N
78. Lmt Persh II/cruse-Europe N
79. Delete 34 B-1 bombers N
80. Bar purch of Pershing II N
81. Bar purchase of Sgt York N
82. Delete $ for Trident II N
83. Allow 15 MX missiles N
84. Bar MX procurement-1985 Y
85. Equal Access Act Y
86. Aid to El Salvador N
87. Bar Nicarag water mining Y
88. Physician/Medicare freeze N
89. Increase "sin" taxes N
90. End SBA direct loans N
91. Sell Conrail N
92. Equal Rights Amendment Y
93. Marines in Lebanon N
94. Eminent domain-coal comps N
95. Prohibit EPA sanctions N
96. SS age increase/Reforms N
97. Auto domestic content req Y
98. Delete jobs program fundg N
99. Highway-Gas tax bill Y
100. Raise Medicare;Cut defnse Y
101. Emergency housing aid Y
102. Across-the-board tax cuts N
103. Gramm-Latta II targets Y
104. Delete B-1 bomber funds N
105. Dsapprov Saudi AWACS sale Y
106. Disapprove oil import fee Y
107. Rail Deregulation N
108. Dsapp India nuc fuel sale Y
109. Mil draft registration N
110. Chrysler Loan Guarantees Y
111. Prohibit school busing Y
112. Nuclear plant moratorium N
113. Oil price controls N
114. Tuition Tax Credits Y
115. Est Consumer Protect Agcy N
116. Eliminate B-1 bomber fnds Y
117. Subminimum wage for youth N
118. Delete crude oil tax N
119. Natural gas deregulation Y

Presidential Support Score: 1986 - 30% 1985 - 30%

MAZZOLI, ROMANO L. -- Kentucky 3rd District [Democrat]. County of Jefferson (pt.). Prior Terms: House: 1971-86. Born: November 2, 1932; Louisville, Ky. Education: University of Notre Dame (B.S.); University of Louisville (J.D.). Military Service: U.S. Army, 1954-56. Occupation: Attorney, Louisville & Nashville Railroad Co. (1960-62); attorney (1962-70); lecturer (1963-67); Kentucky senator (1967-70).

1. Immigration Reform Y
2. Open fld-search warrants Y
3. Civil pnty-hire ill alien N
4. So Afr sanc-veto override Y

MAZZOLI, ROMANO L. (Cont.)

5. Tax Overhaul Y
6. South Africa sanctions Y
7. Death penalty-drug bill Y
8. Evidence-warrantless srch Y
9. Life term-second drug off Y
10. Military use in drug war N
11. Troop reduction in Europe N
12. Prohibit chemical weapons Y
13. Bar ASAT testing Y
14. Abide SALT II weapons ban N
15. Follow SALT II-Soviets do Y
16. Reduce SDI funding N
17. Increase SDI funding N
18. Purchase Trident sub N
19. Delete 12 MX;Add conv wpn Y
20. Raise speed limit N
21. Textile Import Quotas(*) N
22. Req Pentagon buy US goods Y
23. AIDS ins anti-dscriminatn N
24. Nicaraguan refugee aid N
25. Nicaraguan contra aid N
26. US abide by SALT II Y
27. Prohibit Saudi arms sale N
28. Military Retiremnt Reform Y
29. Nicaraguan refugee aid N
30. Ease '68 Gun Control Act Y
31. Bar intrstat handgun tran Y
32. Keep '68 Gun Control Act Y
33. Nicaraguan contra aid N
34. Bar emp polygraph testing Y
35. Tax Overhaul consideratn N
36. Bar armor-piercing ammo Y
37. Tax Overhaul consideratn Y
38. Make comp emissions known N
39. Allow toxic victims suits N
40. Strike Superfund "VAT" N
41. Notify emp-plant closing Y
42. Bar emp consult-plant clo N
43. Medicare cuts;Tax incres' Y
44. Delete 12 MX missiles Y
45. Spending cuts;Tax incres' Y
46. Textile Import Quotas N
47. Cut some school lunch fds N
48. Clean Water Act Amendmnts N
49. Youth work projects N
50. Assist military in Angola N
51. Allow US troops-Nicaragua N
52. Pentagon polygraph exams Y
53. Bar ASAT testing Y
54. Suspend def pmt for abuse Y
55. Bar Pentagon-contr emplmt Y
56. Increase SDI funding N
57. Reduce SDI funding N
58. Produce chemical weapons N
59. Bar CIA fndg in Nicaragua N
60. South Africa sanctions Y
61. Cut SS COLAs; Raise taxes N
62. Let US invest-So Africa N
63. Approve 21 MX for 1985 N
64. Emergency Farm Credit N
65. Awards to whistle blowers Y
66. African disaster relief Y
67. Ban bank loans to So Afr Y
68. Bar coun duty-free trtmt N
69. Steel import limits N
70. Soc Sec COLAs=inflation Y
71. Bar haz waste vctms suits Y
72. Prohibit aid to Nicaragua Y
73. Cut $-Schs bar sch prayer N
74. Raise taxes; Cut Medicare Y
75. Alien residncy-prior 1982 N
76. Alien residncy-prior 1980 N
77. Pen emp-hire illgl aliens N
78. Lmt Persh II/cruse-Europe N
79. Delete 34 B-1 bombers Y
80. Bar purch of Pershing II N
81. Bar purchase of Sgt York N
82. Delete $ for Trident II N
83. Allow 15 MX missiles N
84. Bar MX procurement-1985 Y
85. Equal Access Act Y
86. Aid to El Salvador N
87. Bar Nicarag water mining Y
88. Physician/Medicare freeze N
89. Increase "sin" taxes N
90. End SBA direct loans N
91. Sell Conrail +
92. Equal Rights Amendment N
93. Marines in Lebanon N
94. Eminent domain-Coal comps N
95. Prohibit EPA sanctions N
96. SS age increase/Reforms Y
97. Auto domestic content req Y
98. Delete jobs program fundg N
99. Highway-Gas tax bill Y
100. Raise Medicare;Cut defnse N
101. Emergency housing aid Y
102. Across-the-board tax cuts Y
103. Gramm-Latta II targets Y
104. Delete B-1 bomber funds Y
105. Dsapprov Saudi AWACS sale Y
106. Disapprove oil import fee N
107. Rail Deregulation N
108. Dsapp India nuc fuel sale Y
109. Mil draft registration N
110. Chrysler Loan Guarantees Y
111. Prohibit school busing N
112. Nuclear plant moratorium N
113. Oil price controls N
114. Tuition Tax Credits Y
115. Est Consumer Protect Agcy N
116. Eliminate B-1 bomber fnds Y
117. Subminimum wage for youth N
118. Delete crude oil tax N
119. Natural gas deregulation N

Presidential Support Score: 1986 - 41% 1985 - 48%

SNYDER, GENE -- Kentucky 4th District [Republican]. Counties of Boone, Campbell, Carroll, Gallatin, Grant, Henry, Jefferson (pt.), Kenton, Oldham, Owen, Pendleton and Trimble. Prior Terms: House: 1963-86. Born: January 26, 1928; Louisville, Ky. Education: University of Louisville, Jefferson School of Law (LL.B.). Occupation: Attorney; magistrate (1956, 1961).

1.	Immigration Reform	N	54.	Suspend def pmt for abuse	N
2.	Open fld-search warrants	N	55.	Bar Pentagon-contr emplmt	Y
3.	Civil pnty-hire ill alien	N	56.	Increase SDI funding	Y
4.	So Afr sanc-veto override	N	57.	Reduce SDI funding	N
5.	Tax Overhaul	Y	58.	Produce chemical weapons	Y
6.	South Africa sanctions	?	59.	Bar CIA fndg in Nicaragua	N
7.	Death penalty-drug bill	?	60.	South Africa sanctions	N
8.	Evidence-warrantless srch	Y	61.	Cut SS COLAs; Raise taxes	N
9.	Life term-second drug off	Y	62.	Let US invest-So Africa	Y
10.	Military use in drug war	Y	63.	Approve 21 MX for 1985	Y
11.	Troop reduction in Europe	N	64.	Emergency Farm Credit	Y
12.	Prohibit chemical weapons	N	65.	Awards to whistle blowers	Y
13.	Bar ASAT testing	N	66.	African disaster relief	Y
14.	Abide SALT II weapons ban	N	67.	Ban bank loans to So Afr	N
15.	Follow SALT II-Soviets do	Y	68.	Bar coun duty-free trtmt	N
16.	Reduce SDI funding	N	69.	Steel import limits	Y
17.	Increase SDI funding	Y	70.	Soc Sec COLAs=inflation	Y
18.	Purchase Trident sub	N	71.	Bar haz waste vctms suits	Y
19.	Delete 12 MX;Add conv wpn	N	72.	Prohibit aid to Nicaragua	Y
20.	Raise speed limit	N	73.	Cut $-Schs bar sch prayer	Y
21.	Textile Import Quotas(*)	N	74.	Raise taxes; Cut Medicare	Y
22.	Req Pentagon buy US goods	N	75.	Alien residncy-prior 1982	Y
23.	AIDS ins anti-dscriminatn	N	76.	Alien residncy-prior 1980	Y
24.	Nicaraguan refugee aid	N	77.	Pen emp-hire illgl aliens	N
25.	Nicaraguan contra aid	Y	78.	Lmt Persh II/cruse-Europe	N
26.	US abide by SALT II	Y	79.	Delete 34 B-1 bombers	N
27.	Prohibit Saudi arms sale	N	80.	Bar purch of Pershing II	N
28.	Military Retiremnt Reform	Y	81.	Bar purchase of Sgt York	N
29.	Nicaraguan refugee aid	Y	82.	Delete $ for Trident II	N
30.	Ease '68 Gun Control Act	Y	83.	Allow 15 MX missiles	Y
31.	Bar intrstat handgun tran	N	84.	Bar MX procurement-1985	N
32.	Keep '68 Gun Control Act	N	85.	Equal Access Act	Y
33.	Nicaraguan contra aid	Y	86.	Aid to El Salvador	Y
34.	Bar emp polygraph testing	N	87.	Bar Nicarag water mining	N
35.	Tax Overhaul consideratn	Y	88.	Physician/Medicare freeze	Y
36.	Bar armor-piercing ammo	Y	89.	Increase "sin" taxes	Y
37.	Tax Overhaul consideratn	Y	90.	End SBA direct loans	N
38.	Make comp emissions known	N	91.	Sell Conrail	Y
39.	Allow toxic victims suits	N	92.	Equal Rights Amendment	N
40.	Strike Superfund "VAT"	N	93.	Marines in Lebanon	N
41.	Notify emp-plant closing	N	94.	Eminent domain-Coal comps	N
42.	Bar emp consult-plant clo	Y	95.	Prohibit EPA sanctions	Y
43.	Medicare cuts;Tax incres'	Y	96.	SS age increase/Reforms	N
44.	Delete 12 MX missiles	N	97.	Auto domestic content req	Y
45.	Spending cuts;Tax incres'	Y	98.	Delete jobs program fundg	Y
46.	Textile Import Quotas	Y	99.	Highway-Gas tax bill	Y
47.	Cut some school lunch fds	Y	100.	Raise Medicare;Cut defnse	Y
48.	Clean Water Act Amendmnts	Y	101.	Emergency housing aid	N
49.	Youth work projects	N	102.	Across-the-board tax cuts	Y
50.	Assist military in Angola	Y	103.	Gramm-Latta II targets	Y
51.	Allow US troops-Nicaragua	Y	104.	Delete B-1 bomber funds	N
52.	Pentagon polygraph exams	Y	105.	Dsapprov Saudi AWACS sale	N
53.	Bar ASAT testing	N	106.	Disapprove oil import fee	Y

SNYDER, GENE (Cont.)

107. Rail Deregulation N
108. Dsapp India nuc fuel sale Y
109. Mil draft registration N
110. Chrysler Loan Guarantees N
111. Prohibit school busing Y
112. Nuclear plant moratorium N
113. Oil price controls N
114. Tuition Tax Credits Y
115. Est Consumer Protect Agcy N
116. Eliminate B-1 bomber fnds N
117. Subminimum wage for youth Y
118. Delete crude oil tax Y
119. Natural gas deregulation N

Presidential Support Score: 1986 - 73% 1985 - 65%

ROGERS, HAROLD -- Kentucky 5th District [Republican]. Counties of Adair, Bell, Casey, Clay, Clinton, Cumberland, Estill, Garrard, Green, Harlan, Jackson Jessamine, Knox. Laurel, Lee, Leslie, Letcher (pt.), Lincoln, McCreary, Metcalfe, Monroe, Owsley, Pulaski, Rockcastle, Russell, Taylor, Wayne and Whitley. Prior Terms: House: 1981-86. Born: December 31, 1937; Barrier, Ky. Education: University of Kentucky (A.B., LL.B.); Western Kentucky University. Military Service: U.S. National Gaurd, 1957-64. Occupation: Radio newsman and announcer; attorney; commonwealth attorney, Pulaskie and Rockcastle Counties (1969-80).

1. Immigration Reform Y
2. Open fld-search warrants N
3. Civil pnty-hire ill alien N
4. So Afr sanc-veto override N
5. Tax Overhaul Y
6. South Africa sanctions N
7. Death penalty-drug bill Y
8. Evidence-warrantless srch Y
9. Life term-second drug off Y
10. Military use in drug war Y
11. Troop reduction in Europe N
12. Prohibit chemical weapons N
13. Bar ASAT testing N
14. Abide SALT II weapons ban N
15. Follow SALT II-Soviets do Y
16. Reduce SDI funding N
17. Increase SDI funding N
18. Purchase Trident sub N
19. Delete 12 MX;Add conv wpn N
20. Raise speed limit N
21. Textile Import Quotas(*) Y
22. Req Pentagon buy US goods Y
23. AIDS ins anti-dscriminatn N
24. Nicaraguan refugee aid N
25. Nicaraguan contra aid Y
26. US abide by SALT II Y
27. Prohibit Saudi arms sale N
28. Military Retiremnt Reform Y
29. Nicaraguan refugee aid Y
30. Ease '68 Gun Control Act Y
31. Bar intrstat handgun tran N
32. Keep '68 Gun Control Act N
33. Nicaraguan contra aid Y
34. Bar emp polygraph testing N
35. Tax Overhaul consideratn Y
36. Bar armor-piercing ammo Y
37. Tax Overhaul consideratn -
38. Make comp emissions known N
39. Allow toxic victims suits N
40. Strike Superfund "VAT" N
41. Notify emp-plant closing N
42. Bar emp consult-plant clo Y
43. Medicare cuts;Tax incres' Y
44. Delete 12 MX missiles N
45. Spending cuts;Tax incres' N
46. Textile Import Quotas Y
47. Cut some school lunch fds Y
48. Clean Water Act Amendmnts Y
49. Youth work projects N
50. Assist military in Angola Y
51. Allow US troops-Nicaragua Y
52. Pentagon polygraph exams Y
53. Bar ASAT testing N
54. Suspend def pmt for abuse N
55. Bar Pentagon-contr emplmt Y
56. Increase SDI funding Y
57. Reduce SDI funding N
58. Produce chemical weapons Y
59. Bar CIA fndg in Nicaragua N
60. South Africa sanctions N
61. Cut SS COLAs; Raise taxes N
62. Let US invest-So Africa Y
63. Approve 21 MX for 1985 Y
64. Emergency Farm Credit Y
65. Awards to whistle blowers Y
66. African disaster relief Y
67. Ban bank loans to So Afr N
68. Bar coun duty-free trtmt N
69. Steel import limits Y
70. Soc Sec COLAs=inflation Y
71. Bar haz waste vctms suits Y
72. Prohibit aid to Nicaragua Y
73. Cut $-Schs bar sch prayer Y
74. Raise taxes; Cut Medicare N

ROGERS, HAROLD (Cont.)

75. Alien residncy-prior 1982 Y
76. Alien residncy-prior 1980 Y
77. Pen emp-hire illgl aliens N
78. Lmt Persh II/cruse-Europe N
79. Delete 34 B-1 bombers N
80. Bar purch of Pershing II N
81. Bar purchase of Sgt York N
82. Delete $ for Trident II N
83. Allow 15 MX missiles Y
84. Bar MX procurement-1985 N
85. Equal Access Act Y
86. Aid to El Salvador Y
87. Bar Nicarag water mining N
88. Physician/Medicare freeze Y
89. Increase "sin" taxes N
90. End SBA direct loans N
91. Sell Conrail Y
92. Equal Rights Amendment N
93. Marines in Lebanon Y
94. Eminent domain-Coal comps N
95. Prohibit EPA sanctions Y
96. SS age increase/Reforms Y
97. Auto domestic content req Y
98. Delete jobs program fundg Y
99. Highway-Gas tax bill N
100. Raise Medicare;Cut defnse N
101. Emergency housing aid Y
102. Across-the-board tax cuts Y
103. Gramm-Latta II targets Y
104. Delete B-1 bomber funds N
105. Dsapprov Saudi AWACS sale N

Presidential Support Score: 1986 - 69% 1985 - 64%

HOPKINS, LARRY J. -- Kentucky 6th District [Republican]. Counties of Anderson, Bourbon, Boyle, Bracken, Clark, Fayette, Franklin, Harrison, Madison, Mercer, Montgomery, Nicholas, Robertson, Scott, Shelby and Woodford. Prior Terms: House: 1979-86. Born: October 25, 1933; Detroit, Mich. Education: Murray State University; Southern Methodist University; Purdue University. Military Service: U.S. Marine Corps, 1954-56. Occupation: Broker; county clerk (1969); Kentucky representative (1972-77); Kentucky senator (1978).

1. Immigration Reform N
2. Open fld-search warrants N
3. Civil pnty-hire ill alien N
4. So Afr sanc-veto override Y
5. Tax Overhaul Y
6. South Africa sanctions Y
7. Death penalty-drug bill Y
8. Evidence-warrantless srch Y
9. Life term-second drug off Y
10. Military use in drug war Y
11. Troop reduction in Europe N
12. Prohibit chemical weapons N
13. Bar ASAT testing N
14. Abide SALT II weapons ban N
15. Follow SALT II-Soviets do Y
16. Reduce SDI funding N
17. Increase SDI funding N
18. Purchase Trident sub N
19. Delete 12 MX;Add conv wpn N
20. Raise speed limit Y
21. Textile Import Quotas(*) Y
22. Req Pentagon buy US goods Y
23. AIDS ins anti-dscriminatn N
24. Nicaraguan refugee aid N
25. Nicaraguan contra aid Y
26. US abide by SALT II Y
27. Prohibit Saudi arms sale N
28. Military Retiremnt Reform Y
29. Nicaraguan refugee aid Y
30. Ease '68 Gun Control Act Y
31. Bar intrstat handgun tran N
32. Keep '68 Gun Control Act N
33. Nicaraguan contra aid N
34. Bar emp polygraph testing N
35. Tax Overhaul consideratn Y
36. Bar armor-piercing ammo Y
37. Tax Overhaul consideratn ?
38. Make comp emissions known N
39. Allow toxic victims suits N
40. Strike Superfund "VAT" Y
41. Notify emp-plant closing N
42. Bar emp consult-plant clo Y
43. Medicare cuts;Tax incres' N
44. Delete 12 MX missiles Y
45. Spending cuts;Tax incres' N
46. Textile Import Quotas Y
47. Cut some school lunch fds Y
48. Clean Water Act Amendmnts Y
49. Youth work projects N
50. Assist military in Angola Y
51. Allow US troops-Nicaragua Y
52. Pentagon polygraph exams Y
53. Bar ASAT testing Y
54. Suspend def pmt for abuse N
55. Bar Pentagon-contr emplmt Y
56. Increase SDI funding N
57. Reduce SDI funding N
58. Produce chemical weapons Y
59. Bar CIA fndg in Nicaragua N
60. South Africa sanctions Y

HOPKINS, LARRY J. (Cont.)

61. Cut SS COLAs; Raise taxes N
62. Let US invest-So Africa N
63. Approve 21 MX for 1985 Y
64. Emergency Farm Credit Y
65. Awards to whistle blowers Y
66. African disaster relief Y
67. Ban bank loans to So Afr N
68. Bar coun duty-free trtmt N
69. Steel import limits Y
70. Soc Sec COLAs=inflation Y
71. Bar haz waste vctms suits Y
72. Prohibit aid to Nicaragua N
73. Cut $-Schs bar sch prayer Y
74. Raise taxes; Cut Medicare N
75. Alien residncy-prior 1982 N
76. Alien residncy-prior 1980 Y
77. Pen emp-hire illgl aliens N
78. Lmt Persh II/cruse-Europe N
79. Delete 34 B-1 bombers N
80. Bar purch of Pershing II N
81. Bar purchase of Sgt York Y
82. Delete $ for Trident II N
83. Allow 15 MX missiles Y
84. Bar MX procurement-1985 N
85. Equal Access Act Y
86. Aid to El Salvador Y
87. Bar Nicarag water mining N
88. Physician/Medicare freeze Y
89. Increase "sin" taxes N
90. End SBA direct loans Y
91. Sell Conrail Y
92. Equal Rights Amendment Y
93. Marines in Lebanon N
94. Eminent domain-Coal comps #
95. Prohibit EPA sanctions N
96. SS age increase/Reforms Y
97. Auto domestic content req Y
98. Delete jobs program fundg Y
99. Highway-Gas tax bill N
100. Raise Medicare;Cut defnse Y
101. Emergency housing aid Y
102. Across-the-board tax cuts Y
103. Gramm-Latta II targets Y
104. Delete B-1 bomber funds N
105. Dsapprov Saudi AWACS sale N
106. Disapprove oil import fee Y
107. Rail Deregulation -
108. Dsapp India nuc fuel sale Y
109. Mil draft registration Y
110. Chrysler Loan Guarantees N
111. Prohibit school busing Y
112. Nuclear plant moratorium Y
113. Oil price controls ?

Presidential Support Score: 1986 - 73% 1985 - 61%

PERKINS, CARL C. -- Kentucky 7th District [Democrat]. Counties of Bath, Boyd, Breathitt, Carter, Elliott, Fleming, Floyd, Greenup, Johnson, Knott, Lawrence, Letcher (pt.), Lewis, Magoffin, Martin, Mason, Menifee, Morgan, Perry, Pike, Powell, Rowan and Wolfe. Prior Terms: 1985-86. Born: August 6, 1954. Education: Davidson College; University of Louisville (J.D.). Occupation: Law clerk; assistant attorney; partner and practicing attorney, Weinberg, Perkins & Campbell; hosted weekly television talk-show since 1980; farmer.

1. Immigration Reform Y
2. Open fld-search warrants Y
3. Civil pnty-hire ill alien N
4. So Afr sanc-veto override Y
5. Tax Overhaul N
6. South Africa sanctions Y
7. Death penalty-drug bill Y
8. Evidence-warrantless srch N
9. Life term-second drug off Y
10. Military use in drug war Y
11. Troop reduction in Europe N
12. Prohibit chemical weapons Y
13. Bar ASAT testing Y
14. Abide SALT II weapons ban Y
15. Follow SALT II-Soviets do N
16. Reduce SDI funding Y
17. Increase SDI funding N
18. Purchase Trident sub Y
19. Delete 12 MX;Add conv wpn Y
20. Raise speed limit N
21. Textile Import Quotas(*) Y
22. Req Pentagon buy US goods Y
23. AIDS ins anti-dscriminatn Y
24. Nicaraguan refugee aid N
25. Nicaraguan contra aid N
26. US abide by SALT II N
27. Prohibit Saudi arms sale Y
28. Military Retiremnt Reform Y
29. Nicaraguan refugee aid N
30. Ease '68 Gun Control Act Y
31. Bar intrstat handgun tran N
32. Keep '68 Gun Control Act N
33. Nicaraguan contra aid N
34. Bar emp polygraph testing Y
35. Tax Overhaul consideratn Y
36. Bar armor-piercing ammo N
37. Tax Overhaul consideratn Y
38. Make comp emissions known N

PERKINS, CARL C. (Cont.)

39. Allow toxic victims suits N
40. Strike Superfund "VAT" N
41. Notify emp-plant closing Y
42. Bar emp consult-plant clo N
43. Medicare cuts;Tax incres' Y
44. Delete 12 MX missiles Y
45. Spending cuts;Tax incres' Y
46. Textile Import Quotas Y
47. Cut some school lunch fds N
48. Clean Water Act Amendmnts N
49. Youth work projects Y
50. Assist military in Angola N
51. Allow US troops-Nicaragua N
52. Pentagon polygraph exams N
53. Bar ASAT testing Y
54. Suspend def pmt for abuse N
55. Bar Pentagon-contr emplmt Y
56. Increase SDI funding N
57. Reduce SDI funding Y
58. Produce chemical weapons N
59. Bar CIA fndg in Nicaragua Y
60. South Africa sanctions Y
61. Cut SS COLAs; Raise taxes N
62. Let US invest-So Africa N
63. Approve 21 MX for 1985 N
64. Emergency Farm Credit Y
65. Awards to whistle blowers Y
66. African disaster relief Y

Presidential Support Score: 1986 - 23% 1985 - 20%

L O U I S I A N A

LIVINGSTON, BOB -- Louisiana 1st District [Republican]. Counties of Orleans (pt.), Plaquemines, St. Bernard and St. Tammany. Prior Terms: House: 1977 (Special Election)-1986. Born: April 30, 1943; Colorado Springs, Colo. Education: Tulane University (B.A., LL.B.); Loyola University. Military Service: U.S. Navy, 1961-63; U.S. Navy Reserve, 1967. Occupation: Attorney; assistant U.S. attorney (1970-73); chief special prosecutor and chief of the Armed Robbery Division, District Attorney's Office (1974-75); chief prosecutor, Attorney General's Office (1975-76).

1. Immigration Reform Y
2. Open fld-search warrants N
3. Civil pnty-hire ill alien N
4. So Afr sanc-veto override N
5. Tax Overhaul Y
6. South Africa sanctions ?
7. Death penalty-drug bill Y
8. Evidence-warrantless srch Y
9. Life term-second drug off Y
10. Military use in drug war Y
11. Troop reduction in Europe N
12. Prohibit chemical weapons N
13. Bar ASAT testing N
14. Abide SALT II weapons ban N
15. Follow SALT II-Soviets do Y
16. Reduce SDI funding N
17. Increase SDI funding Y
18. Purchase Trident sub Y
19. Delete 12 MX;Add conv wpn N
20. Raise speed limit Y
21. Textile Import Quotas(*) N
22. Req Pentagon buy US goods N
23. AIDS ins anti-dscriminatn N
24. Nicaraguan refugee aid N
25. Nicaraguan contra aid Y
26. US abide by SALT II Y
27. Prohibit Saudi arms sale N
28. Military Retiremnt Reform Y
29. Nicaraguan refugee aid Y
30. Ease '68 Gun Control Act Y
31. Bar intrstat handgun tran N
32. Keep '68 Gun Control Act N
33. Nicaraguan contra aid Y
34. Bar emp polygraph testing N
35. Tax Overhaul consideratn N
36. Bar armor-piercing ammo Y
37. Tax Overhaul consideratn N
38. Make comp emissions known N
39. Allow toxic victims suits N
40. Strike Superfund "VAT" N
41. Notify emp-plant closing N
42. Bar emp consult-plant clo Y
43. Medicare cuts;Tax incres' N
44. Delete 12 MX missiles N
45. Spending cuts;Tax incres' Y
46. Textile Import Quotas ?
47. Cut some school lunch fds Y
48. Clean Water Act Amendmnts Y
49. Youth work projects N
50. Assist military in Angola Y
51. Allow US troops-Nicaragua Y
52. Pentagon polygraph exams Y
53. Bar ASAT testing N
54. Suspend def pmt for abuse N
55. Bar Pentagon-contr emplmt Y
56. Increase SDI funding Y
57. Reduce SDI funding N
58. Produce chemical weapons Y

LIVINGSTON, BOB (Cont.)

59. Bar CIA fndg in Nicaragua N
60. South Africa sanctions Y
61. Cut SS COLAs; Raise taxes N
62. Let US invest-So Africa Y
63. Approve 21 MX for 1985 Y
64. Emergency Farm Credit N
65. Awards to whistle blowers Y
66. African disaster relief Y
67. Ban bank loans to So Afr N
68. Bar coun duty-free trtmt N
69. Steel import limits N
70. Soc Sec COLAs=inflation Y
71. Bar haz waste vctms suits Y
72. Prohibit aid to Nicaragua N
73. Cut $-Schs bar sch prayer Y
74. Raise taxes; Cut Medicare N
75. Alien residncy-prior 1982 Y
76. Alien residncy-prior 1980 Y
77. Pen emp-hire illgl aliens N
78. Lmt Persh II/cruse-Europe N
79. Delete 34 B-1 bombers N
80. Bar purch of Pershing II N
81. Bar purchase of Sgt York N
82. Delete $ for Trident II N
83. Allow 15 MX missiles Y
84. Bar MX procurement-1985 N
85. Equal Access Act Y
86. Aid to El Salvador Y
87. Bar Nicarag water mining N
88. Physician/Medicare freeze Y
89. Increase "sin" taxes N
90. End SBA direct loans Y
91. Sell Conrail ?
92. Equal Rights Amendment N
93. Marines in Lebanon Y
94. Eminent domain-Coal comps Y
95. Prohibit EPA sanctions N
96. SS age increase/Reforms Y
97. Auto domestic content req N
98. Delete jobs program fundg Y
99. Highway-Gas tax bill N
100. Raise Medicare;Cut defnse N
101. Emergency housing aid ?
102. Across-the-board tax cuts Y
103. Gramm-Latta II targets Y
104. Delete B-1 bomber funds N
105. Dsapprov Saudi AWACS sale Y
106. Disapprove oil import fee Y
107. Rail Deregulation N
108. Dsapp India nuc fuel sale Y
109. Mil draft registration Y
110. Chrysler Loan Guarantees N
111. Prohibit school busing Y
112. Nuclear plant moratorium N
113. Oil price controls N
114. Tuition Tax Credits Y
115. Est Consumer Protect Agcy N
116. Eliminate B-1 bomber fnds N
117. Subminimum wage for youth Y

Presidential Support Score: 1986 - 75% 1985 - 74%

BOGGS, LINDY (Mrs. Hale) -- Louisiana 2nd District [Democrat]. Counties of Jefferson (pt.) and Orleans (pt.). Prior Terms: House: 1973 (Special Election)-1986. Born: Brunswick Plantation, Point Conusee Parish, La. Education: Sophie Newcomb College of Tulane University. Occupation: Teacher; regent, Smithsonian Institution.

1. Immigration Reform Y
2. Open fld-search warrants ?
3. Civil pnty-hire ill alien Y
4. So Afr sanc-veto override Y
5. Tax Overhaul Y
6. South Africa sanctions Y
7. Death penalty-drug bill N
8. Evidence-warrantless srch N
9. Life term-second drug off Y
10. Military use in drug war Y
11. Troop reduction in Europe ?
12. Prohibit chemical weapons Y
13. Bar ASAT testing Y
14. Abide SALT II weapons ban Y
15. Follow SALT II-Soviets do N
16. Reduce SDI funding N
17. Increase SDI funding N
18. Purchase Trident sub Y
19. Delete 12 MX;Add conv wpn N
20. Raise speed limit N
21. Textile Import Quotas(*) Y
22. Req Pentagon buy US goods ?
23. AIDS ins anti-dscriminatn Y
24. Nicaraguan refugee aid ?
25. Nicaraguan contra aid N
26. US abide by SALT II N
27. Prohibit Saudi arms sale Y
28. Military Retiremnt Reform Y
29. Nicaraguan refugee aid Y
30. Ease '68 Gun Control Act Y
31. Bar intrstat handgun tran Y
32. Keep '68 Gun Control Act N
33. Nicaraguan contra aid N
34. Bar emp polygraph testing Y
35. Tax Overhaul consideratn Y
36. Bar armor-piercing ammo Y
37. Tax Overhaul consideratn Y
38. Make comp emissions known ?
39. Allow toxic victims suits Y
40. Strike Superfund "VAT" N

BOGGS, LINDY (Mrs. Hale) (Cont.)

41. Notify emp-plant closing Y
42. Bar emp consult-plant clo N
43. Medicare cuts;Tax incres' Y
44. Delete 12 MX missiles Y
45. Spending cuts;Tax incres' Y
46. Textile Import Quotas Y
47. Cut some school lunch fds N
48. Clean Water Act Amendmnts N
49. Youth work projects Y
50. Assist military in Angola Y
51. Allow US troops-Nicaragua N
52. Pentagon polygraph exams Y
53. Bar ASAT testing Y
54. Suspend def pmt for abuse N
55. Bar Pentagon-contr emplmt Y
56. Increase SDI funding N
57. Reduce SDI funding N
58. Produce chemical weapons N
59. Bar CIA fndg in Nicaragua Y
60. South Africa sanctions Y
61. Cut SS COLAs; Raise taxes N
62. Let US invest-So Africa N
63. Approve 21 MX for 1985 N
64. Emergency Farm Credit Y
65. Awards to whistle blowers Y
66. African disaster relief Y
67. Ban bank loans to So Afr P
68. Bar coun duty-free trtmt N
69. Steel import limits Y
70. Soc Sec COLAs=inflation Y
71. Bar haz waste vctms suits N
72. Prohibit aid to Nicaragua Y
73. Cut $-Schs bar sch prayer N
74. Raise taxes; Cut Medicare Y
75. Alien residncy-prior 1982 Y
76. Alien residncy-prior 1980 N
77. Pen emp-hire illgl aliens Y
78. Lmt Persh II/cruse-Europe N
79. Delete 34 B-1 bombers N
80. Bar purch of Pershing II N
81. Bar purchase of Sgt York N
82. Delete $ for Trident II N
83. Allow 15 MX missiles N
84. Bar MX procurement-1985 Y
85. Equal Access Act Y
86. Aid to El Salvador ?
87. Bar Nicarag water mining Y
88. Physician/Medicare freeze N
89. Increase "sin" taxes Y
90. End SBA direct loans N
91. Sell Conrail N
92. Equal Rights Amendment Y
93. Marines in Lebanon Y
94. Eminent domain-Coal comps Y
95. Prohibit EPA sanctions Y
96. SS age increase/Reforms N
97. Auto domestic content req Y
98. Delete jobs program fundg N
99. Highway-Gas tax bill Y
100. Raise Medicare;Cut defnse Y
101. Emergency housing aid Y
102. Across-the-board tax cuts N
103. Gramm-Latta II targets N
104. Delete B-1 bomber funds N
105. Dsapprov Saudi AWACS sale Y
106. Disapprove oil import fee Y
107. Rail Deregulation X
108. Dsapp India nuc fuel sale Y
109. Mil draft registration Y
110. Chrysler Loan Guarantees Y
111. Prohibit school busing N
112. Nuclear plant moratorium N
113. Oil price controls X
114. Tuition Tax Credits Y
115. Est Consumer Protect Agcy Y
116. Eliminate B-1 bomber fnds N
117. Subminimum wage for youth N
118. Delete crude oil tax Y
119. Natural gas deregulation Y

Presidential Support Score: 1986 - 23% 1985 - 28%

TAUZIN, W. J. (BILLY) -- Louisiana 3rd District [Democrat]. Counties of Assumption, Iberia, Jefferson (pt.), Lafourche, St. Charles, St. Martin (pt.), St. Mary and Terrebonne. Prior Terms: House: 1980 (Special Election)-1986. Born: June 14, 1943; Chackbay, La. Education: Nicholls State University (B.A.); Louisiana State University Law School (J.D.). Occupation: Attorney, Marcel, Marcel, Fanquy & Tauzin; Lousiana representative (1971-80).

1. Immigration Reform N
2. Open fld-search warrants N
3. Civil pnty-hire ill alien N
4. So Afr sanc-veto override Y
5. Tax Overhaul Y
6. South Africa sanctions Y
7. Death penalty-drug bill Y
8. Evidence-warrantless srch Y
9. Life term-second drug off Y
10. Military use in drug war Y
11. Troop reduction in Europe N
12. Prohibit chemical weapons N
13. Bar ASAT testing N
14. Abide SALT II weapons ban N

TAUZIN, W. J. (Billy) (Cont.)

15. Follow SALT II-Soviets do Y
16. Reduce SDI funding N
17. Increase SDI funding N
18. Purchase Trident sub N
19. Delete 12 MX;Add conv wpn N
20. Raise speed limit Y
21. Textile Import Quotas(*) Y
22. Req Pentagon buy US goods Y
23. AIDS ins anti-dscriminatn Y
24. Nicaraguan refugee aid N
25. Nicaraguan contra aid Y
26. US abide by SALT II Y
27. Prohibit Saudi arms sale Y
28. Military Retiremnt Reform Y
29. Nicaraguan refugee aid N
30. Ease '68 Gun Control Act Y
31. Bar intrstat handgun tran N
32. Keep '68 Gun Control Act N
33. Nicaraguan contra aid Y
34. Bar emp polygraph testing Y
35. Tax Overhaul consideratn N
36. Bar armor-piercing ammo Y
37. Tax Overhaul consideratn N
38. Make comp emissions known N
39. Allow toxic victims suits N
40. Strike Superfund "VAT" N
41. Notify emp-plant closing N
42. Bar emp consult-plant clo Y
43. Medicare cuts;Tax incres' #
44. Delete 12 MX missiles N
45. Spending cuts;Tax incres' Y
46. Textile Import Quotas Y
47. Cut some school lunch fds Y
48. Clean Water Act Amendmnts N
49. Youth work projects ?
50. Assist military in Angola Y
51. Allow US troops-Nicaragua Y
52. Pentagon polygraph exams Y
53. Bar ASAT testing N
54. Suspend def pmt for abuse N
55. Bar Pentagon-contr emplmt Y
56. Increase SDI funding N
57. Reduce SDI funding N
58. Produce chemical weapons Y
59. Bar CIA fndg in Nicaragua N
60. South Africa sanctions Y
61. Cut SS COLAs; Raise taxes N
62. Let US invest-So Africa N
63. Approve 21 MX for 1985 Y
64. Emergency Farm Credit Y
65. Awards to whistle blowers Y
66. African disaster relief Y
67. Ban bank loans to So Afr Y
68. Bar coun duty-free trtmt Y
69. Steel import limits Y
70. Soc Sec COLAs=inflation Y
71. Bar haz waste vctms suits Y
72. Prohibit aid to Nicaragua N
73. Cut $-Schs bar sch prayer Y
74. Raise taxes; Cut Medicare N
75. Alien residncy-prior 1982 Y
76. Alien residncy-prior 1980 N
77. Pen emp-hire illgl aliens N
78. Lmt Persh II/cruse-Europe N
79. Delete 34 B-1 bombers N
80. Bar purch of Pershing II N
81. Bar purchase of Sgt York Y
82. Delete $ for Trident II N
83. Allow 15 MX missiles Y
84. Bar MX procurement-1985 N
85. Equal Access Act Y
86. Aid to El Salvador Y
87. Bar Nicarag water mining ?
88. Physician/Medicare freeze X
89. Increase "sin" taxes N
90. End SBA direct loans N
91. Sell Conrail Y
92. Equal Rights Amendment Y
93. Marines in Lebanon Y
94. Eminent domain-Coal comps Y
95. Prohibit EPA sanctions N
96. SS age increase/Reforms Y
97. Auto domestic content req Y
98. Delete jobs program fundg Y
99. Highway-Gas tax bill N
100. Raise Medicare;Cut defnse N
101. Emergency housing aid Y
102. Across-the-board tax cuts N
103. Gramm-Latta II targets Y
104. Delete B-1 bomber funds N
105. Dsapprov Saudi AWACS sale Y
106. Disapprove oil import fee Y
107. Rail Deregulation #
108. Dsapp India nuc fuel sale Y

Presidential Support Score: 1986 - 48% 1985 - 54%

ROEMER, BUDDY -- Louisiana 4th District [Democrat]. Counties of Beauregard (pt.), Bossier, Caddo, Claiborne, De Soto, Red River, Sabine, Vernon and Webster. Prior Terms: House: 1981-86. Born: October 4, 1943; Shreveport, La. Education: Harvard University (B.A., M.B.A). Occupation: Businessman; farmer; banker; vice president of sales, Innovative Data Systems, Inc.; partner, Scopena Plantation; director, Bank of the Mid-South.

ROEMER, BUDDY (Cont.)

1. Immigration Reform N
2. Open fld-search warrants N
3. Civil pnty-hire ill alien N
4. So Afr sanc-veto override Y
5. Tax Overhaul Y
6. South Africa sanctions Y
7. Death penalty-drug bill Y
8. Evidence-warrantless srch Y
9. Life term-second drug off Y
10. Military use in drug war Y
11. Troop reduction in Europe N
12. Prohibit chemical weapons N
13. Bar ASAT testing N
14. Abide SALT II weapons ban N
15. Follow SALT II-Soviets do Y
16. Reduce SDI funding N
17. Increase SDI funding N
18. Purchase Trident sub N
19. Delete 12 MX;Add conv wpn N
20. Raise speed limit Y
21. Textile Import Quotas(*) Y
22. Req Pentagon buy US goods Y
23. AIDS ins anti-dscriminatn Y
24. Nicaraguan refugee aid N
25. Nicaraguan contra aid Y
26. US abide by SALT II Y
27. Prohibit Saudi arms sale Y
28. Military Retiremnt Reform Y
29. Nicaraguan refugee aid N
30. Ease '68 Gun Control Act Y
31. Bar intrstat handgun tran N
32. Keep '68 Gun Control Act N
33. Nicaraguan contra aid Y
34. Bar emp polygraph testing Y
35. Tax Overhaul consideratn N
36. Bar armor-piercing ammo Y
37. Tax Overhaul consideratn N
38. Make comp emissions known Y
39. Allow toxic victims suits Y
40. Strike Superfund "VAT" N
41. Notify emp-plant closing N
42. Bar emp consult-plant clo Y
43. Medicare cuts;Tax incres' Y
44. Delete 12 MX missiles Y
45. Spending cuts;Tax incres' Y
46. Textile Import Quotas N
47. Cut some school lunch fds Y
48. Clean Water Act Amendmnts N
49. Youth work projects ?
50. Assist military in Angola Y
51. Allow US troops-Nicaragua Y
52. Pentagon polygraph exams Y
53. Bar ASAT testing N
54. Suspend def pmt for abuse N
55. Bar Pentagon-contr emplmt Y
56. Increase SDI funding N
57. Reduce SDI funding N
58. Produce chemical weapons Y
59. Bar CIA fndg in Nicaragua N
60. South Africa sanctions Y
61. Cut SS COLAs; Raise taxes Y
62. Let US invest-So Africa N
63. Approve 21 MX for 1985 Y
64. Emergency Farm Credit N
65. Awards to whistle blowers Y
66. African disaster relief Y
67. Ban bank loans to So Afr Y
68. Bar coun duty-free trtmt N
69. Steel import limits N
70. Soc Sec COLAs=inflation Y
71. Bar haz waste vctms suits Y
72. Prohibit aid to Nicaragua N
73. Cut $-Schs bar sch prayer Y
74. Raise taxes; Cut Medicare Y
75. Alien residncy-prior 1982 Y
76. Alien residncy-prior 1980 N
77. Pen emp-hire illgl aliens N
78. Lmt Persh II/cruse-Europe N
79. Delete 34 B-1 bombers N
80. Bar purch of Pershing II N
81. Bar purchase of Sgt York Y
82. Delete $ for Trident II N
83. Allow 15 MX missiles Y
84. Bar MX procurement-1985 N
85. Equal Access Act Y
86. Aid to El Salvador Y
87. Bar Nicarag water mining N
88. Physician/Medicare freeze N
89. Increase "sin" taxes N
90. End SBA direct loans N
91. Sell Conrail N
92. Equal Rights Amendment N
93. Marines in Lebanon N
94. Eminent domain-Coal comps Y
95. Prohibit EPA sanctions N
96. SS age increase/Reforms Y
97. Auto domestic content req Y
98. Delete jobs program fundg Y
99. Highway-Gas tax bill N
100. Raise Medicare;Cut defnse N
101. Emergency housing aid N
102. Across-the-board tax cuts Y
103. Gramm-Latta II targets Y
104. Delete B-1 bomber funds N
105. Dsapprov Saudi AWACS sale Y

Presidential Support Score: 1986 - 50% 1985 - 66%

HUCKABY, JERRY -- Louisiana 5th District [Democrat]. Counties of Bienville, Caldwell, Catahoula, Concordia, East Carroll, Franklin, Grant Jackson, La Salle, Lincoln, Madison, Morehouse, Natchitoches, Ouachita, Rapides (pt.), Richland, Ten-

HUCKABY, JERRY (Cont.)
sas, Union, West Carroll and Winn. Prior Terms: House: 1977-1986. Born: July 19, 1941; Hodge, Jackson Parish, La. Education: Louisiana State University (B.S.); Georgia State University (M.B.A.). Occupation: Dairyman; farmer; businessman, Western Electric (1963-73).

1.	Immigration Reform	Y	54.	Suspend def pmt for abuse	N
2.	Open fld-search warrants	Y	55.	Bar Pentagon-contr emplmt	Y
3.	Civil pnty-hire ill alien	Y	56.	Increase SDI funding	N
4.	So Afr sanc-veto override	?	57.	Reduce SDI funding	N
5.	Tax Overhaul	Y	58.	Produce chemical weapons	N
6.	South Africa sanctions	?	59.	Bar CIA fndg in Nicaragua	N
7.	Death penalty-drug bill	?	60.	South Africa sanctions	Y
8.	Evidence-warrantless srch	?	61.	Cut SS COLAs; Raise taxes	N
9.	Life term-second drug off	?	62.	Let US invest-So Africa	N
10.	Military use in drug war	?	63.	Approve 21 MX for 1985	Y
11.	Troop reduction in Europe	N	64.	Emergency Farm Credit	Y
12.	Prohibit chemical weapons	Y	65.	Awards to whistle blowers	Y
13.	Bar ASAT testing	N	66.	African disaster relief	Y
14.	Abide SALT II weapons ban	Y	67.	Ban bank loans to So Afr	Y
15.	Follow SALT II-Soviets do	N	68.	Bar coun duty-free trtmt	N
16.	Reduce SDI funding	N	69.	Steel import limits	N
17.	Increase SDI funding	N	70.	Soc Sec COLAs=inflation	Y
18.	Purchase Trident sub	N	71.	Bar haz waste vctms suits	Y
19.	Delete 12 MX;Add conv wpn	N	72.	Prohibit aid to Nicaragua	Y
20.	Raise speed limit	Y	73.	Cut $-Schs bar sch prayer	Y
21.	Textile Import Quotas(*)	Y	74.	Raise taxes; Cut Medicare	Y
22.	Req Pentagon buy US goods	Y	75.	Alien residncy-prior 1982	N
23.	AIDS ins anti-dscriminatn	?	76.	Alien residncy-prior 1980	N
24.	Nicaraguan refugee aid	N	77.	Pen emp-hire illgl aliens	N
25.	Nicaraguan contra aid	Y	78.	Lmt Persh II/cruse-Europe	N
26.	US abide by SALT II	X	79.	Delete 34 B-1 bombers	N
27.	Prohibit Saudi arms sale	Y	80.	Bar purch of Pershing II	N
28.	Military Retiremnt Reform	Y	81.	Bar purchase of Sgt York	N
29.	Nicaraguan refugee aid	N	82.	Delete $ for Trident II	N
30.	Ease '68 Gun Control Act	Y	83.	Allow 15 MX missiles	Y
31.	Bar intrstat handgun tran	N	84.	Bar MX procurement-1985	N
32.	Keep '68 Gun Control Act	N	85.	Equal Access Act	Y
33.	Nicaraguan contra aid	Y	86.	Aid to El Salvador	Y
34.	Bar emp polygraph testing	N	87.	Bar Nicarag water mining	Y
35.	Tax Overhaul consideratn	N	88.	Physician/Medicare freeze	N
36.	Bar armor-piercing ammo	Y	89.	Increase "sin" taxes	Y
37.	Tax Overhaul consideratn	N	90.	End SBA direct loans	N
38.	Make comp emissions known	Y	91.	Sell Conrail	N
39.	Allow toxic victims suits	N	92.	Equal Rights Amendment	Y
40.	Strike Superfund "VAT"	N	93.	Marines in Lebanon	Y
41.	Notify emp-plant closing	N	94.	Eminent domain-Coal comps	Y
42.	Bar emp consult-plant clo	Y	95.	Prohibit EPA sanctions	N
43.	Medicare cuts;Tax incres'	Y	96.	SS age increase/Reforms	N
44.	Delete 12 MX missiles	N	97.	Auto domestic content req	N
45.	Spending cuts;Tax incres'	Y	98.	Delete jobs program fundg	Y
46.	Textile Import Quotas	Y	99.	Highway-Gas tax bill	N
47.	Cut some school lunch fds	N	100.	Raise Medicare;Cut defnse	N
48.	Clean Water Act Amendmnts	?	101.	Emergency housing aid	Y
49.	Youth work projects	Y	102.	Across-the-board tax cuts	Y
50.	Assist military in Angola	Y	103.	Gramm-Latta II targets	Y
51.	Allow US troops-Nicaragua	?	104.	Delete B-1 bomber funds	N
52.	Pentagon polygraph exams	Y	105.	Dsapprov Saudi AWACS sale	N
53.	Bar ASAT testing	N	106.	Disapprove oil import fee	Y

HUCKABY, JERRY (Cont.)

107. Rail Deregulation Y
108. Dsapp India nuc fuel sale Y
109. Mil draft registration Y
110. Chrysler Loan Guarantees Y
111. Prohibit school busing Y
112. Nuclear plant moratorium N
113. Oil price controls N
114. Tuition Tax Credits N
115. Est Consumer Protect Agcy N
116. Eliminate B-1 bomber fnds N
117. Subminimum wage for youth Y
118. Delete crude oil tax Y
119. Natural gas deregulation Y

Presidential Support Score: 1986 - 41% 1985 - 49%

MOORE, W. HENSON -- Louisiana 6th District [Republican]. Counties of East Baton Rouge (pt.), Livingston, Tangipahoa and Washington. Prior Terms: House: 1975 (Special Election)-1986. Born: October 4, 1939; Lake Charles, La. Education: Louisiana State University (B.A., J.D., M.A.). Military Service: U.S. Army, 1965-67. Occupation: Attorney; teacher; partner, Dale, Owen, Richardson, Taylor and Mathews.

1. Immigration Reform ?
2. Open fld-search warrants ?
3. Civil pnty-hire ill alien ?
4. So Afr sanc-veto override ?
5. Tax Overhaul Y
6. South Africa sanctions ?
7. Death penalty-drug bill Y
8. Evidence-warrantless srch Y
9. Life term-second drug off Y
10. Military use in drug war Y
11. Troop reduction in Europe ?
12. Prohibit chemical weapons ?
13. Bar ASAT testing ?
14. Abide SALT II weapons ban ?
15. Follow SALT II-Soviets do ?
16. Reduce SDI funding ?
17. Increase SDI funding ?
18. Purchase Trident sub ?
19. Delete 12 MX;Add conv wpn ?
20. Raise speed limit ?
21. Textile Import Quotas(*) ?
22. Req Pentagon buy US goods ?
23. AIDS ins anti-dscriminatn N
24. Nicaraguan refugee aid N
25. Nicaraguan contra aid Y
26. US abide by SALT II Y
27. Prohibit Saudi arms sale Y
28. Military Retiremnt Reform Y
29. Nicaraguan refugee aid Y
30. Ease '68 Gun Control Act Y
31. Bar intrstat handgun tran N
32. Keep '68 Gun Control Act N
33. Nicaraguan contra aid Y
34. Bar emp polygraph testing N
35. Tax Overhaul consideratn N
36. Bar armor-piercing ammo Y
37. Tax Overhaul consideratn N
38. Make comp emissions known N
39. Allow toxic victims suits N
40. Strike Superfund "VAT" N
41. Notify emp-plant closing N
42. Bar emp consult-plant clo Y
43. Medicare cuts;Tax incres' N
44. Delete 12 MX missiles N
45. Spending cuts;Tax incres' Y
46. Textile Import Quotas N
47. Cut some school lunch fds Y
48. Clean Water Act Amendmnts Y
49. Youth work projects N
50. Assist military in Angola Y
51. Allow US troops-Nicaragua Y
52. Pentagon polygraph exams Y
53. Bar ASAT testing N
54. Suspend def pmt for abuse N
55. Bar Pentagon-contr emplmt Y
56. Increase SDI funding Y
57. Reduce SDI funding N
58. Produce chemical weapons Y
59. Bar CIA fndg in Nicaragua N
60. South Africa sanctions Y
61. Cut SS COLAs; Raise taxes N
62. Let US invest-So Africa Y
63. Approve 21 MX for 1985 Y
64. Emergency Farm Credit Y
65. Awards to whistle blowers Y
66. African disaster relief Y
67. Ban bank loans to So Afr Y
68. Bar coun duty-free trtmt N
69. Steel import limits N
70. Soc Sec COLAs=inflation Y
71. Bar haz waste vctms suits Y
72. Prohibit aid to Nicaragua Y
73. Cut $-Schs bar sch prayer Y
74. Raise taxes; Cut Medicare Y
75. Alien residncy-prior 1982 Y
76. Alien residncy-prior 1980 Y
77. Pen emp-hire illgl aliens N
78. Lmt Persh II/cruse-Europe N
79. Delete 34 B-1 bombers N
80. Bar purch of Pershing II N
81. Bar purchase of Sgt York N
82. Delete $ for Trident II N
83. Allow 15 MX missiles Y
84. Bar MX procurement-1985 N

MOORE, W. HENSON (Cont.)

85. Equal Access Act Y
86. Aid to El Salvador Y
87. Bar Nicarag water mining N
88. Physician/Medicare freeze Y
89. Increase "sin" taxes Y
90. End SBA direct loans N
91. Sell Conrail Y
92. Equal Rights Amendment N
93. Marines in Lebanon Y
94. Eminent domain-Coal comps Y
95. Prohibit EPA sanctions N
96. SS age increase/Reforms Y
97. Auto domestic content req N
98. Delete jobs program fundg Y
99. Highway-Gas tax bill N
100. Raise Medicare;Cut defnse N
101. Emergency housing aid Y
102. Across-the-board tax cuts Y
103. Gramm-Latta II targets Y
104. Delete B-1 bomber funds N
105. Dsapprov Saudi AWACS sale Y
106. Disapprove oil import fee Y
107. Rail Deregulation N
108. Dsapp India nuc fuel sale Y
109. Mil draft registration N
110. Chrysler Loan Guarantees N
111. Prohibit school busing Y
112. Nuclear plant moratorium N
113. Oil price controls N
114. Tuition Tax Credits Y
115. Est Consumer Protect Agcy N
116. Eliminate B-1 bomber fnds N
117. Subminimum wage for youth Y
118. Delete crude oil tax Y
119. Natural gas deregulation Y

Presidential Support Score: 1986 - 34% 1985 - 68%

BREAUX, JOHN B. -- Louisiana 7th District [Democrat]. Counties of Acadia, Allen (pt.), Beauregard (pt.), Calcasieu, Cameron, Jefferson Davis, Lafayette, St. Martin (pt.) and Vermilion. Prior Terms: House: 1972 (Special Election)-1986. Born: March 1, 1944; Crowley, La. Education: University of Southwestern Louisiana (B.A.); Louisiana State University Law School (J.D.). Occupation: Attorney, Brown, McKernan, Ingram & Breaux (1967-68); congressional assistant (1968-72).

1. Immigration Reform ?
2. Open fld-search warrants ?
3. Civil pnty-hire ill alien ?
4. So Afr sanc-veto override ?
5. Tax Overhaul Y
6. South Africa sanctions ?
7. Death penalty-drug bill ?
8. Evidence-warrantless srch ?
9. Life term-second drug off ?
10. Military use in drug war ?
11. Troop reduction in Europe ?
12. Prohibit chemical weapons ?
13. Bar ASAT testing N
14. Abide SALT II weapons ban ?
15. Follow SALT II-Soviets do ?
16. Reduce SDI funding ?
17. Increase SDI funding ?
18. Purchase Trident sub ?
19. Delete 12 MX;Add conv wpn ?
20. Raise speed limit ?
21. Textile Import Quotas(*) Y
22. Req Pentagon buy US goods ?
23. AIDS ins anti-dscriminatn Y
24. Nicaraguan refugee aid N
25. Nicaraguan contra aid Y
26. US abide by SALT II ?
27. Prohibit Saudi arms sale #
28. Military Retiremnt Reform ?
29. Nicaraguan refugee aid Y
30. Ease '68 Gun Control Act Y
31. Bar intrstat handgun tran N
32. Keep '68 Gun Control Act N
33. Nicaraguan contra aid Y
34. Bar emp polygraph testing Y
35. Tax Overhaul consideratn N
36. Bar armor-piercing ammo Y
37. Tax Overhaul consideratn N
38. Make comp emissions known N
39. Allow toxic victims suits N
40. Strike Superfund "VAT" N
41. Notify emp-plant closing Y
42. Bar emp consult-plant clo Y
43. Medicare cuts;Tax incres' Y
44. Delete 12 MX missiles N
45. Spending cuts;Tax incres' Y
46. Textile Import Quotas Y
47. Cut some school lunch fds N
48. Clean Water Act Amendmnts N
49. Youth work projects N
50. Assist military in Angola Y
51. Allow US troops-Nicaragua Y
52. Pentagon polygraph exams Y
53. Bar ASAT testing N
54. Suspend def pmt for abuse ?
55. Bar Pentagon-contr emplmt ?
56. Increase SDI funding N
57. Reduce SDI funding N
58. Produce chemical weapons Y

BREAUX, JOHN B. (Cont.)

59. Bar CIA fndg in Nicaragua N
60. South Africa sanctions Y
61. Cut SS COLAs; Raise taxes N
62. Let US invest-So Africa X
63. Approve 21 MX for 1985 Y
64. Emergency Farm Credit Y
65. Awards to whistle blowers Y
66. African disaster relief Y
67. Ban bank loans to So Afr ?
68. Bar coun duty-free trtmt N
69. Steel import limits Y
70. Soc Sec COLAs=inflation Y
71. Bar haz waste vctms suits Y
72. Prohibit aid to Nicaragua Y
73. Cut $-Schs bar sch prayer Y
74. Raise taxes; Cut Medicare Y
75. Alien residncy-prior 1982 Y
76. Alien residncy-prior 1980 Y
77. Pen emp-hire illgl aliens N
78. Lmt Persh II/cruse-Europe N
79. Delete 34 B-1 bombers N
80. Bar purch of Pershing II N
81. Bar purchase of Sgt York Y
82. Delete $ for Trident II N
83. Allow 15 MX missiles Y
84. Bar MX procurement-1985 N
85. Equal Access Act Y
86. Aid to El Salvador Y
87. Bar Nicarag water mining Y
88. Physician/Medicare freeze N
89. Increase "sin" taxes Y
90. End SBA direct loans N
91. Sell Conrail Y
92. Equal Rights Amendment Y
93. Marines in Lebanon Y
94. Eminent domain-Coal comps Y
95. Prohibit EPA sanctions N
96. SS age increase/Reforms Y
97. Auto domestic content req N
98. Delete jobs program fundg N
99. Highway-Gas tax bill Y
100. Raise Medicare;Cut defnse N
101. Emergency housing aid Y
102. Across-the-board tax cuts N
103. Gramm-Latta II targets Y
104. Delete B-1 bomber funds X
105. Dsapprov Saudi AWACS sale Y
106. Disapprove oil import fee ?
107. Rail Deregulation N
108. Dsapp India nuc fuel sale Y
109. Mil draft registration Y
110. Chrysler Loan Guarantees Y
111. Prohibit school busing Y
112. Nuclear plant moratorium X
113. Oil price controls N
114. Tuition Tax Credits Y
115. Est Consumer Protect Agcy N
116. Eliminate B-1 bomber fnds N
117. Subminimum wage for youth Y
118. Delete crude oil tax Y
119. Natural gas deregulation Y

Presidential Support Score: 1986 - 22% 1985 - 49%

LONG, CATHY -- Louisiana 8th District [Democrat]. Counties of Allen (pt.), Ascension, Avoyelles, East Baton Rouge (pt.), East Feliciana, Evangeline, Iberville, Pointe Coupee, Rapides (pt.), St. Helena, St. James, St. John the Baptist, St. Landry, West Baton Rouge and West Feliciana. Prior Terms: 1985 (Special Election)-1986. Born: Dayton, Ohio. Education: Louisiana State University (B.A.). Occupation: U.S. Navy, pharmacist's mate; congressional staff assistant.

1. Immigration Reform Y
2. Open fld-search warrants Y
3. Civil pnty-hire ill alien N
4. So Afr sanc-veto override Y
5. Tax Overhaul Y
6. South Africa sanctions Y
7. Death penalty-drug bill N
8. Evidence-warrantless srch N
9. Life term-second drug off N
10. Military use in drug war N
11. Troop reduction in Europe Y
12. Prohibit chemical weapons Y
13. Bar ASAT testing Y
14. Abide SALT II weapons ban Y
15. Follow SALT II-Soviets do N
16. Reduce SDI funding Y
17. Increase SDI funding N
18. Purchase Trident sub Y
19. Delete 12 MX;Add conv wpn Y
20. Raise speed limit ?
21. Textile Import Quotas(*) #
22. Req Pentagon buy US goods ?
23. AIDS ins anti-dscriminatn Y
24. Nicaraguan refugee aid Y
25. Nicaraguan contra aid N
26. US abide by SALT II N
27. Prohibit Saudi arms sale Y
28. Military Retiremnt Reform Y
29. Nicaraguan refugee aid Y
30. Ease '68 Gun Control Act Y
31. Bar intrstat handgun tran N
32. Keep '68 Gun Control Act N

LONG, CATHY (Cont.)

33.	Nicaraguan contra aid	N	48.	Clean Water Act Amendmnts	N
34.	Bar emp polygraph testing	Y	49.	Youth work projects	Y
35.	Tax Overhaul consideratn	N	50.	Assist military in Angola	Y
36.	Bar armor-piercing ammo	Y	51.	Allow US troops-Nicaragua	N
37.	Tax Overhaul consideratn	N	52.	Pentagon polygraph exams	Y
38.	Make comp emissions known	Y	53.	Bar ASAT testing	Y
39.	Allow toxic victims suits	Y	54.	Suspend def pmt for abuse	N
40.	Strike Superfund "VAT"	N	55.	Bar Pentagon-contr emplmt	Y
41.	Notify emp-plant closing	Y	56.	Increase SDI funding	N
42.	Bar emp consult-plant clo	N	57.	Reduce SDI funding	N
43.	Medicare cuts;Tax incres'	Y	58.	Produce chemical weapons	N
44.	Delete 12 MX missiles	Y	59.	Bar CIA fndg in Nicaragua	N
45.	Spending cuts;Tax incres'	Y	60.	South Africa sanctions	Y
46.	Textile Import Quotas	Y	61.	Cut SS COLAs; Raise taxes	N
47.	Cut some school lunch fds	?	62.	Let US invest-So Africa	N

Presidential Support Score: 1986 - 20% 1985 - 33 %

M A I N E

McKERNAN, JOHN R., Jr. -- Maine 1st District [Republican]. Counties of Cumberland, Kennebec, Knox, Lincoln, Sagadahoc, Waldo and York. Prior Terms: House: 1983-86. Born: May 20, 1948; Bangor, Maine. Education: Dartmouth College (A.B.); University of Maine School of Law (J.D.). Military Service: Maine Army National Guard, 1970-73. Occupation: Attorney; Maine representative (1972, re-elected 1974).

1.	Immigration Reform	Y	31.	Bar intrstat handgun tran	N
2.	Open fld-search warrants	Y	32.	Keep '68 Gun Control Act	N
3.	Civil pnty-hire ill alien	N	33.	Nicaraguan contra aid	Y
4.	So Afr sanc-veto override	Y	34.	Bar emp polygraph testing	N
5.	Tax Overhaul	Y	35.	Tax Overhaul consideratn	Y
6.	South Africa sanctions	Y	36.	Bar armor-piercing ammo	Y
7.	Death penalty-drug bill	Y	37.	Tax Overhaul consideratn	N
8.	Evidence-warrantless srch	Y	38.	Make comp emissions known	Y
9.	Life term-second drug off	Y	39.	Allow toxic victims suits	Y
10.	Military use in drug war	Y	40.	Strike Superfund "VAT"	Y
11.	Troop reduction in Europe	N	41.	Notify emp-plant closing	N
12.	Prohibit chemical weapons	Y	42.	Bar emp consult-plant clo	Y
13.	Bar ASAT testing	Y	43.	Medicare cuts;Tax incres'	N
14.	Abide SALT II weapons ban	Y	44.	Delete 12 MX missiles	Y
15.	Follow SALT II-Soviets do	N	45.	Spending cuts;Tax incres'	N
16.	Reduce SDI funding	N	46.	Textile Import Quotas	Y
17.	Increase SDI funding	N	47.	Cut some school lunch fds	N
18.	Purchase Trident sub	N	48.	Clean Water Act Amendmnts	N
19.	Delete 12 MX;Add conv wpn	N	49.	Youth work projects	N
20.	Raise speed limit	Y	50.	Assist military in Angola	Y
21.	Textile Import Quotas(*)	Y	51.	Allow US troops-Nicaragua	N
22.	Req Pentagon buy US goods	Y	52.	Pentagon polygraph exams	Y
23.	AIDS ins anti-dscriminatn	N	53.	Bar ASAT testing	Y
24.	Nicaraguan refugee aid	N	54.	Suspend def pmt for abuse	N
25.	Nicaraguan contra aid	Y	55.	Bar Pentagon-contr emplmt	Y
26.	US abide by SALT II	N	56.	Increase SDI funding	N
27.	Prohibit Saudi arms sale	Y	57.	Reduce SDI funding	N
28.	Military Retiremnt Reform	Y	58.	Produce chemical weapons	N
29.	Nicaraguan refugee aid	Y	59.	Bar CIA fndg in Nicaragua	N
30.	Ease '68 Gun Control Act	Y	60.	South Africa sanctions	Y

McKERNAN, JOHN R., Jr. (Cont.)

61. Cut SS COLAs; Raise taxes N
62. Let US invest-So Africa Y
63. Approve 21 MX for 1985 Y
64. Emergency Farm Credit Y
65. Awards to whistle blowers Y
66. African disaster relief Y
67. Ban bank loans to So Afr Y
68. Bar coun duty-free trtmt Y
69. Steel import limits Y
70. Soc Sec COLAs=inflation Y
71. Bar haz waste vctms suits N
72. Prohibit aid to Nicaragua Y
73. Cut $-Schs bar sch prayer N
74. Raise taxes; Cut Medicare Y
75. Alien residncy-prior 1982 Y
76. Alien residncy-prior 1980 Y
77. Pen emp-hire illgl aliens N
78. Lmt Persh II/cruse-Europe N
79. Delete 34 B-1 bombers N
80. Bar purch of Pershing II N
81. Bar purchase of Sgt York Y
82. Delete $ for Trident II N
83. Allow 15 MX missiles Y
84. Bar MX procurement-1985 N
85. Equal Access Act Y
86. Aid to El Salvador Y
87. Bar Nicarag water mining Y
88. Physician/Medicare freeze Y
89. Increase "sin" taxes Y
90. End SBA direct loans N
91. Sell Conrail Y
92. Equal Rights Amendment Y
93. Marines in Lebanon Y
94. Eminent domain-Coal comps Y
95. Prohibit EPA sanctions N
96. SS age increase/Reforms Y

Presidential Support Score: 1986 - 44% 1985 - 50%

SNOWE, OLYMPIA J. -- Maine 2nd District [Republican]. Counties of Androscoggin, Aroostook, Franklin, Hancock, Oxford, Penobscott, Piscataquis, Somerset and Washington, Prior Terms: House: 1979-86. Born: February 21, 1947; Augusta, Maine. Education: University of Maine (B.A.). Occupation: Maine representative (1973-76); Maine senator (1976-78).

1. Immigration Reform Y
2. Open fld-search warrants Y
3. Civil pnty-hire ill alien N
4. So Afr sanc-veto override Y
5. Tax Overhaul Y
6. South Africa sanctions Y
7. Death penalty-drug bill Y
8. Evidence-warrantless srch Y
9. Life term-second drug off Y
10. Military use in drug war Y
11. Troop reduction in Europe N
12. Prohibit chemical weapons Y
13. Bar ASAT testing Y
14. Abide SALT II weapons ban Y
15. Follow SALT II-Soviets do Y
16. Reduce SDI funding N
17. Increase SDI funding N
18. Purchase Trident sub N
19. Delete 12 MX;Add conv wpn N
20. Raise speed limit N
21. Textile Import Quotas(*) Y
22. Req Pentagon buy US goods Y
23. AIDS ins anti-dscriminatn N
24. Nicaraguan refugee aid N
25. Nicaraguan contra aid Y
26. US abide by SALT II N
27. Prohibit Saudi arms sale Y
28. Military Retiremnt Reform Y
29. Nicaraguan refugee aid Y
30. Ease '68 Gun Control Act Y
31. Bar intrstat handgun tran N
32. Keep '68 Gun Control Act N
33. Nicaraguan contra aid N
34. Bar emp polygraph testing Y
35. Tax Overhaul consideratn Y
36. Bar armor-piercing ammo Y
37. Tax Overhaul consideratn N
38. Make comp emissions known Y
39. Allow toxic victims suits Y
40. Strike Superfund "VAT" Y
41. Notify emp-plant closing N
42. Bar emp consult-plant clo Y
43. Medicare cuts;Tax incres' Y
44. Delete 12 MX missiles Y
45. Spending cuts;Tax incres' N
46. Textile Import Quotas Y
47. Cut some school lunch fds N
48. Clean Water Act Amendmnts N
49. Youth work projects Y
50. Assist military in Angola Y
51. Allow US troops-Nicaragua N
52. Pentagon polygraph exams Y
53. Bar ASAT testing Y
54. Suspend def pmt for abuse N
55. Bar Pentagon-contr emplmt Y
56. Increase SDI funding N
57. Reduce SDI funding N
58. Produce chemical weapons N
59. Bar CIA fndg in Nicaragua N
60. South Africa sanctions Y
61. Cut SS COLAs; Raise taxes N
62. Let US invest-So Africa N

SNOWE, OLYMPIA J. (Cont.)

63. Approve 21 MX for 1985 Y
64. Emergency Farm Credit Y
65. Awards to whistle blowers Y
66. African disaster relief Y
67. Ban bank loans to So Afr Y
68. Bar coun duty-free trtmt Y
69. Steel import limits Y
70. Soc Sec COLAs=inflation Y
71. Bar haz waste vctms suits N
72. Prohibit aid to Nicaragua Y
73. Cut $-Schs bar sch prayer N
74. Raise taxes; Cut Medicare Y
75. Alien residncy-prior 1982 Y
76. Alien residncy-prior 1980 Y
77. Pen emp-hire illgl aliens N
78. Lmt Persh II/cruse-Europe N
79. Delete 34 B-1 bombers N
80. Bar purch of Pershing II N
81. Bar purchase of Sgt York Y
82. Delete $ for Trident II N
83. Allow 15 MX missiles Y
84. Bar MX procurement-1985 N
85. Equal Access Act Y
86. Aid to El Salvador Y
87. Bar Nicarag water mining Y
88. Physician/Medicare freeze Y
89. Increase "sin" taxes Y
90. End SBA direct loans N
91. Sell Conrail Y
92. Equal Rights Amendment Y
93. Marines in Lebanon Y
94. Eminent domain-Coal comps Y
95. Prohibit EPA sanctions N
96. SS age increase/Reforms Y
97. Auto domestic content req N
98. Delete jobs program fundg Y
99. Highway-Gas tax bill N
100. Raise Medicare;Cut defnse Y
101. Emergency housing aid Y
102. Across-the-board tax cuts Y
103. Gramm-Latta II targets Y
104. Delete B-1 bomber funds N
105. Dsapprov Saudi AWACS sale Y
106. Disapprove oil import fee Y
107. Rail Deregulation N
108. Dsapp India nuc fuel sale Y
109. Mil draft registration Y
110. Chrysler Loan Guarantees N
111. Prohibit school busing N
112. Nuclear plant moratorium N
113. Oil price controls N

Presidential Support Score: 1986 - 45% 1985 - 48%

MARYLAND

DYSON, ROY -- Maryland 1st District [Democrat]. Counties of Calvert, Caroline, Cecil, Charles, Dorchester, Harford (pt.), Kent, Queen Anne's, St. Mary's, Somerset, Talbot, Wicomico and Worcester. Prior Terms: House: 1981-86. Born: November 15, 1948; Great Mills, Md. Education: University of Baltimore; University of Maryland. Occupation: Maryland delegate (1974, 1978).

1. Immigration Reform Y
2. Open fld-search warrants Y
3. Civil pnty-hire ill alien N
4. So Afr sanc-veto override Y
5. Tax Overhaul N
6. South Africa sanctions Y
7. Death penalty-drug bill Y
8. Evidence-warrantless srch Y
9. Life term-second drug off Y
10. Military use in drug war Y
11. Troop reduction in Europe N
12. Prohibit chemical weapons N
13. Bar ASAT testing N
14. Abide SALT II weapons ban N
15. Follow SALT II-Soviets do Y
16. Reduce SDI funding N
17. Increase SDI funding N
18. Purchase Trident sub Y
19. Delete 12 MX;Add conv wpn N
20. Raise speed limit Y
21. Textile Import Quotas(*) Y
22. Req Pentagon buy US goods ?
23. AIDS ins anti-dscriminatn Y
24. Nicaraguan refugee aid N
25. Nicaraguan contra aid Y
26. US abide by SALT II Y
27. Prohibit Saudi arms sale Y
28. Military Retiremnt Reform Y
29. Nicaraguan refugee aid N
30. Ease '68 Gun Control Act Y
31. Bar intrstat handgun tran N
32. Keep '68 Gun Control Act N
33. Nicaraguan contra aid Y
34. Bar emp polygraph testing Y
35. Tax Overhaul consideratn N
36. Bar armor-piercing ammo Y
37. Tax Overhaul consideratn N
38. Make comp emissions known Y

DYSON, ROY (Cont.)

39. Allow toxic victims suits N
40. Strike Superfund "VAT" Y
41. Notify emp-plant closing Y
42. Bar emp consult-plant clo N
43. Medicare cuts;Tax incres' Y
44. Delete 12 MX missiles N
45. Spending cuts;Tax incres' Y
46. Textile Import Quotas Y
47. Cut some school lunch fds N
48. Clean Water Act Amendmnts N
49. Youth work projects N
50. Assist military in Angola Y
51. Allow US troops-Nicaragua N
52. Pentagon polygraph exams Y
53. Bar ASAT testing N
54. Suspend def pmt for abuse N
55. Bar Pentagon-contr emplmt Y
56. Increase SDI funding N
57. Reduce SDI funding N
58. Produce chemical weapons Y
59. Bar CIA fndg in Nicaragua N
60. South Africa sanctions Y
61. Cut SS COLAs; Raise taxes N
62. Let US invest-So Africa ?
63. Approve 21 MX for 1985 Y
64. Emergency Farm Credit Y
65. Awards to whistle blowers Y
66. African disaster relief Y
67. Ban bank loans to So Afr ?
68. Bar coun duty-free trtmt Y
69. Steel import limits Y
70. Soc Sec COLAs=inflation Y
71. Bar haz waste vctms suits Y
72. Prohibit aid to Nicaragua Y
73. Cut $-Schs bar sch prayer Y
74. Raise taxes; Cut Medicare N
75. Alien residncy-prior 1982 Y
76. Alien residncy-prior 1980 N
77. Pen emp-hire illgl aliens N
78. Lmt Persh II/cruse-Europe N
79. Delete 34 B-1 bombers N
80. Bar purch of Pershing II N
81. Bar purchase of Sgt York N
82. Delete $ for Trident II N
83. Allow 15 MX missiles N
84. Bar MX procurement-1985 Y
85. Equal Access Act Y
86. Aid to El Salvador Y
87. Bar Nicarag water mining N
88. Physician/Medicare freeze Y
89. Increase "sin" taxes N
90. End SBA direct loans N
91. Sell Conrail N
92. Equal Rights Amendment Y
93. Marines in Lebanon Y
94. Eminent domain-Coal comps N
95. Prohibit EPA sanctions Y
96. SS age increase/Reforms N
97. Auto domestic content req Y
98. Delete jobs program fundg N
99. Highway-Gas tax bill Y
100. Raise Medicare;Cut defnse Y
101. Emergency housing aid Y
102. Across-the-board tax cuts Y
103. Gramm-Latta II targets Y
104. Delete B-1 bomber funds N
105. Dsapprov Saudi AWACS sale Y

Presidential Support Score: 1986 - 53% 1985 - 55%

BENTLEY, H. DELICH -- Maryland 2nd District [Republican]. Counties of Baltimore (pt.) and Harford(pt.). Prior Terms: 1985-86. Education: University of Missouri. Occupation: Business consultant; founder, HDB International; reporter; editor, Baltimore Sun.

1. Immigration Reform N
2. Open fld-search warrants N
3. Civil pnty-hire ill alien N
4. So Afr sanc-veto override Y
5. Tax Overhaul N
6. South Africa sanctions Y
7. Death penalty-drug bill Y
8. Evidence-warrantless srch Y
9. Life term-second drug off Y
10. Military use in drug war Y
11. Troop reduction in Europe N
12. Prohibit chemical weapons N
13. Bar ASAT testing N
14. Abide SALT II weapons ban N
15. Follow SALT II-Soviets do Y
16. Reduce SDI funding N
17. Increase SDI funding N
18. Purchase Trident sub N
19. Delete 12 MX;Add conv wpn N
20. Raise speed limit N
21. Textile Import Quotas(*) Y
22. Req Pentagon buy US goods Y
23. AIDS ins anti-dscriminatn Y
24. Nicaraguan refugee aid N
25. Nicaraguan contra aid Y
26. US abide by SALT II Y
27. Prohibit Saudi arms sale Y
28. Military Retiremnt Reform Y
29. Nicaraguan refugee aid Y
30. Ease '68 Gun Control Act Y
31. Bar intrstat handgun tran N
32. Keep '68 Gun Control Act N

BENTLEY, H. DELICH (Cont.)

33. Nicaraguan contra aid Y
34. Bar emp polygraph testing Y
35. Tax Overhaul consideratn Y
36. Bar armor-piercing ammo Y
37. Tax Overhaul consideratn N
38. Make comp emissions known N
39. Allow toxic victims suits N
40. Strike Superfund "VAT" N
41. Notify emp-plant closing N
42. Bar emp consult-plant clo Y
43. Medicare cuts;Tax incres' N
44. Delete 12 MX missiles N
45. Spending cuts;Tax incres' N
46. Textile Import Quotas Y
47. Cut some school lunch fds Y
48. Clean Water Act Amendmnts Y
49. Youth work projects N
50. Assist military in Angola Y
51. Allow US troops-Nicaragua Y
52. Pentagon polygraph exams Y
53. Bar ASAT testing N
54. Suspend def pmt for abuse N
55. Bar Pentagon-contr emplmt N
56. Increase SDI funding Y
57. Reduce SDI funding N
58. Produce chemical weapons Y
59. Bar CIA fndg in Nicaragua N
60. South Africa sanctions N
61. Cut SS COLAs; Raise taxes N
62. Let US invest-So Africa N
63. Approve 21 MX for 1985 Y
64. Emergency Farm Credit Y
65. Awards to whistle blowers Y
66. African disaster relief Y

Presidential Support Score: 1986 - 56% 1985 - 64%

MIKULSKI, BARBARA A. -- Maryland 3rd District [Democrat]. Counties of Baltimore (pt.), Howard (pt.) and City of Baltimore (pt.). Prior Terms: House: 1977-86. Born: May 17, 1945; Baltimore, Md. Education: Mount Saint Agnes College (B.A.); University of Maryland (M.S.W.). Occupation: City councilwoman (1971-76); adjunct professor, author, lecturer; teacher; social worker.

1. Immigration Reform Y
2. Open fld-search warrants Y
3. Civil pnty-hire ill alien N
4. So Afr sanc-veto override Y
5. Tax Overhaul Y
6. South Africa sanctions Y
7. Death penalty-drug bill N
8. Evidence-warrantless srch Y
9. Life term-second drug off Y
10. Military use in drug war N
11. Troop reduction in Europe ?
12. Prohibit chemical weapons Y
13. Bar ASAT testing Y
14. Abide SALT II weapons ban Y
15. Follow SALT II-Soviets do N
16. Reduce SDI funding Y
17. Increase SDI funding N
18. Purchase Trident sub ?
19. Delete 12 MX;Add conv wpn #
20. Raise speed limit N
21. Textile Import Quotas(*) Y
22. Req Pentagon buy US goods Y
23. AIDS ins anti-dscriminatn ?
24. Nicaraguan refugee aid Y
25. Nicaraguan contra aid N
26. US abide by SALT II N
27. Prohibit Saudi arms sale Y
28. Military Retiremnt Reform Y
29. Nicaraguan refugee aid Y
30. Ease '68 Gun Control Act N
31. Bar intrstat handgun tran Y
32. Keep '68 Gun Control Act Y
33. Nicaraguan contra aid N
34. Bar emp polygraph testing Y
35. Tax Overhaul consideratn N
36. Bar armor-piercing ammo Y
37. Tax Overhaul consideratn N
38. Make comp emissions known Y
39. Allow toxic victims suits Y
40. Strike Superfund "VAT" Y
41. Notify emp-plant closing Y
42. Bar emp consult-plant clo N
43. Medicare cuts;Tax incres' Y
44. Delete 12 MX missiles Y
45. Spending cuts;Tax incres' Y
46. Textile Import Quotas Y
47. Cut some school lunch fds N
48. Clean Water Act Amendmnts N
49. Youth work projects Y
50. Assist military in Angola N
51. Allow US troops-Nicaragua N
52. Pentagon polygraph exams Y
53. Bar ASAT testing Y
54. Suspend def pmt for abuse Y
55. Bar Pentagon-contr emplmt Y
56. Increase SDI funding N
57. Reduce SDI funding N
58. Produce chemical weapons N
59. Bar CIA fndg in Nicaragua Y
60. South Africa sanctions Y
61. Cut SS COLAs; Raise taxes N
62. Let US invest-So Africa N

MIKULSKI, BARBARA A. (Cont.)

63. Approve 21 MX for 1985 N
64. Emergency Farm Credit Y
65. Awards to whistle blowers Y
66. African disaster relief Y
67. Ban bank loans to So Afr ?
68. Bar coun duty-free trtmt Y
69. Steel import limits Y
70. Soc Sec COLAs=inflation Y
71. Bar haz waste vctms suits N
72. Prohibit aid to Nicaragua Y
73. Cut $-Schs bar sch prayer N
74. Raise taxes; Cut Medicare Y
75. Alien residncy-prior 1982 N
76. Alien residncy-prior 1980 N
77. Pen emp-hire illgl aliens Y
78. Lmt Persh II/cruse-Europe Y
79. Delete 34 B-1 bombers Y
80. Bar purch of Pershing II Y
81. Bar purchase of Sgt York N
82. Delete $ for Trident II N
83. Allow 15 MX missiles N
84. Bar MX procurement-1985 Y
85. Equal Access Act N
86. Aid to El Salvador N
87. Bar Nicarag water mining Y
88. Physician/Medicare freeze N
89. Increase "sin" taxes #
90. End SBA direct loans N
91. Sell Conrail ?
92. Equal Rights Amendment Y
93. Marines in Lebanon Y
94. Eminent domain-Coal comps N
95. Prohibit EPA sanctions Y
96. SS age increase/Reforms N
97. Auto domestic content req Y
98. Delete jobs program fundg N
99. Highway-Gas tax bill Y
100. Raise Medicare;Cut defnse Y
101. Emergency housing aid ?
102. Across-the-board tax cuts N
103. Gramm-Latta II targets N
104. Delete B-1 bomber funds Y
105. Dsapprov Saudi AWACS sale Y
106. Disapprove oil import fee Y
107. Rail Deregulation N
108. Dsapp India nuc fuel sale Y
109. Mil draft registration Y
110. Chrysler Loan Guarantees Y
111. Prohibit school busing N
112. Nuclear plant moratorium Y
113. Oil price controls Y
114. Tuition Tax Credits Y
115. Est Consumer Protect Agcy Y
116. Eliminate B-1 bomber fnds Y
117. Subminimum wage for youth N
118. Delete crude oil tax N
119. Natural gas deregulation N

Presidential Support Score: 1986 - 11% 1985 - 18%

HOLT, MARJORIE S. -- Maryland 4th District [Republican]. Counties of Anne Arundel, Howard (pt.) and Prince George's (pt.). Prior Terms: House: 1973-86. Born: September 17, 1920; Birmingham, Ala. Education: University of Florida (LL.B., J.D.). Occupation: County clerk (1966-72).

1. Immigration Reform N
2. Open fld-search warrants N
3. Civil pnty-hire ill alien N
4. So Afr sanc-veto override N
5. Tax Overhaul N
6. South Africa sanctions N
7. Death penalty-drug bill Y
8. Evidence-warrantless srch Y
9. Life term-second drug off Y
10. Military use in drug war ?
11. Troop reduction in Europe N
12. Prohibit chemical weapons N
13. Bar ASAT testing N
14. Abide SALT II weapons ban N
15. Follow SALT II-Soviets do Y
16. Reduce SDI funding N
17. Increase SDI funding Y
18. Purchase Trident sub ?
19. Delete 12 MX;Add conv wpn X
20. Raise speed limit ?
21. Textile Import Quotas(*) N
22. Req Pentagon buy US goods N
23. AIDS ins anti-dscriminatn N
24. Nicaraguan refugee aid N
25. Nicaraguan contra aid Y
26. US abide by SALT II Y
27. Prohibit Saudi arms sale N
28. Military Retiremnt Reform Y
29. Nicaraguan refugee aid Y
30. Ease '68 Gun Control Act Y
31. Bar intrstat handgun tran N
32. Keep '68 Gun Control Act N
33. Nicaraguan contra aid Y
34. Bar emp polygraph testing N
35. Tax Overhaul consideratn Y
36. Bar armor-piercing ammo Y
37. Tax Overhaul consideratn N
38. Make comp emissions known N
39. Allow toxic victims suits N
40. Strike Superfund "VAT" Y
41. Notify emp-plant closing N
42. Bar emp consult-plant clo Y

HOLT MARJORIE S. (Cont.)

43.	Medicare cuts;Tax incres'	N	82.	Delete $ for Trident II	N
44.	Delete 12 MX missiles	N	83.	Allow 15 MX missiles	Y
45.	Spending cuts;Tax incres'	N	84.	Bar MX procurement-1985	N
46.	Textile Import Quotas	N	85.	Equal Access Act	Y
47.	Cut some school lunch fds	Y	86.	Aid to El Salvador	Y
48.	Clean Water Act Amendmnts	N	87.	Bar Nicarag water mining	N
49.	Youth work projects	N	88.	Physician/Medicare freeze	Y
50.	Assist military in Angola	Y	89.	Increase "sin" taxes	Y
51.	Allow US troops-Nicaragua	?	90.	End SBA direct loans	N
52.	Pentagon polygraph exams	?	91.	Sell Conrail	Y
53.	Bar ASAT testing	X	92.	Equal Rights Amendment	Y
54.	Suspend def pmt for abuse	?	93.	Marines in Lebanon	Y
55.	Bar Pentagon-contr emplmt	?	94.	Eminent domain-Coal comps	Y
56.	Increase SDI funding	Y	95.	Prohibit EPA sanctions	?
57.	Reduce SDI funding	N	96.	SS age increase/Reforms	Y
58.	Produce chemical weapons	Y	97.	Auto domestic content req	N
59.	Bar CIA fndg in Nicaragua	N	98.	Delete jobs program fundg	Y
60.	South Africa sanctions	N	99.	Highway-Gas tax bill	N
61.	Cut SS COLAs; Raise taxes	N	100.	Raise Medicare;Cut defnse	Y
62.	Let US invest-So Africa	Y	101.	Emergency housing aid	N
63.	Approve 21 MX for 1985	Y	102.	Across-the-board tax cuts	Y
64.	Emergency Farm Credit	N	103.	Gramm-Latta II targets	Y
65.	Awards to whistle blowers	?	104.	Delete B-1 bomber funds	N
66.	African disaster relief	?	105.	Dsapprov Saudi AWACS sale	N
67.	Ban bank loans to So Afr	Y	106.	Disapprove oil import fee	Y
68.	Bar coun duty-free trtmt	N	107.	Rail Deregulation	N
69.	Steel import limits	Y	108.	Dsapp India nuc fuel sale	Y
70.	Soc Sec COLAs=inflation	Y	109.	Mil draft registration	Y
71.	Bar haz waste vctms suits	Y	110.	Chrysler Loan Guarantees	X
72.	Prohibit aid to Nicaragua	N	111.	Prohibit school busing	Y
73.	Cut $-Schs bar sch prayer	Y	112.	Nuclear plant moratorium	N
74.	Raise taxes; Cut Medicare	Y	113.	Oil price controls	N
75.	Alien residncy-prior 1982	Y	114.	Tuition Tax Credits	Y
76.	Alien residncy-prior 1980	Y	115.	Est Consumer Protect Agcy	N
77.	Pen emp-hire illgl aliens	N	116.	Eliminate B-1 bomber fnds	N
78.	Lmt Persh II/cruse-Europe	N	117.	Subminimum wage for youth	Y
79.	Delete 34 B-1 bombers	N	118.	Delete crude oil tax	?
80.	Bar purch of Pershing II	N	119.	Natural gas deregulation	Y
81.	Bar purchase of Sgt York	N			

Presidential Support Score: 1986 - 63% 1985 - 69%

HOYER, STENY H. -- Maryland 5th District [Democrat]. County of Prince George's (pt.). Prior Terms: House: 1981 (Special Election)-1986. Born: June 14, 1939; New York City, N.Y. Education: University of Maryland (B.S.); Georgetown University Law Center (J.D.). Occupation: Federal employee; executive assistant to a U.S. senator; Maryland senator; attorney; chairman, Joint Commission on Intergovernmental Cooperation; member, State Board for Higher Education.

1.	Immigration Reform	Y	9.	Life term-second drug off	Y
2.	Open fld-search warrants	Y	10.	Military use in drug war	N
3.	Civil pnty-hire ill alien	N	11.	Troop reduction in Europe	N
4.	So Afr sanc-veto override	Y	12.	Prohibit chemical weapons	Y
5.	Tax Overhaul	N	13.	Bar ASAT testing	Y
6.	South Africa sanctions	Y	14.	Abide SALT II weapons ban	Y
7.	Death penalty-drug bill	N	15.	Follow SALT II-Soviets do	N
8.	Evidence-warrantless srch	N	16.	Reduce SDI funding	Y

HOYER, STENY H. (Cont.)

17. Increase SDI funding N
18. Purchase Trident sub Y
19. Delete 12 MX;Add conv wpn N
20. Raise speed limit N
21. Textile Import Quotas(*) Y
22. Req Pentagon buy US goods N
23. AIDS ins anti-dscriminatn Y
24. Nicaraguan refugee aid Y
25. Nicaraguan contra aid N
26. US abide by SALT II N
27. Prohibit Saudi arms sale Y
28. Military Retiremnt Reform Y
29. Nicaraguan refugee aid Y
30. Ease '68 Gun Control Act N
31. Bar intrstat handgun tran ?
32. Keep '68 Gun Control Act Y
33. Nicaraguan contra aid N
34. Bar emp polygraph testing Y
35. Tax Overhaul consideratn N
36. Bar armor-piercing ammo Y
37. Tax Overhaul consideratn N
38. Make comp emissions known N
39. Allow toxic victims suits N
40. Strike Superfund "VAT" Y
41. Notify emp-plant closing Y
42. Bar emp consult-plant clo N
43. Medicare cuts;Tax incres' Y
44. Delete 12 MX missiles N
45. Spending cuts;Tax incres' Y
46. Textile Import Quotas Y
47. Cut some school lunch fds N
48. Clean Water Act Amendmnts N
49. Youth work projects Y
50. Assist military in Angola N
51. Allow US troops-Nicaragua N
52. Pentagon polygraph exams Y
53. Bar ASAT testing Y
54. Suspend def pmt for abuse Y
55. Bar Pentagon-contr emplmt Y
56. Increase SDI funding N
57. Reduce SDI funding N
58. Produce chemical weapons Y
59. Bar CIA fndg in Nicaragua Y
60. South Africa sanctions Y
61. Cut SS COLAs; Raise taxes N
62. Let US invest-So Africa N
63. Approve 21 MX for 1985 Y
64. Emergency Farm Credit Y
65. Awards to whistle blowers Y
66. African disaster relief Y
67. Ban bank loans to So Afr Y
68. Bar coun duty-free trtmt Y
69. Steel import limits Y
70. Soc Sec COLAs=inflation Y
71. Bar haz waste vctms suits ?
72. Prohibit aid to Nicaragua Y
73. Cut $-Schs bar sch prayer N
74. Raise taxes; Cut Medicare Y
75. Alien residncy-prior 1982 N
76. Alien residncy-prior 1980 N
77. Pen emp-hire illgl aliens Y
78. Lmt Persh II/cruse-Europe N
79. Delete 34 B-1 bombers N
80. Bar purch of Pershing II N
81. Bar purchase of Sgt York N
82. Delete $ for Trident II N
83. Allow 15 MX missiles Y
84. Bar MX procurement-1985 N
85. Equal Access Act N
86. Aid to El Salvador N
87. Bar Nicarag water mining Y
88. Physician/Medicare freeze N
89. Increase "sin" taxes Y
90. End SBA direct loans N
91. Sell Conrail N
92. Equal Rights Amendment Y
93. Marines in Lebanon Y
94. Eminent domain-Coal comps N
95. Prohibit EPA sanctions N
96. SS age increase/Reforms N
97. Auto domestic content req Y
98. Delete jobs program fundg N
99. Highway-Gas tax bill Y
100. Raise Medicare;Cut defnse Y
101. Emergency housing aid Y
102. Across-the-board tax cuts N
103. Gramm-Latta II targets
104. Delete B-1 bomber funds N
105. Dsapprov Saudi AWACS sale Y

Sworn in June 23, 1981 and missed vote 103.

Presidential Support Score: 1986 - 22% 1985 - 29%

BYRON, BEVERLY B. -- Maryland 6th District [Democrat]. Counties of Allegany, Carroll, Frederick Garrett, Howard (pt.), Montgomery (pt.) and Washington. Prior Terms: House: 1979-86. Born: July 27, 1932; Baltimore, Md. Education: Hood College. Occupation: Boardmember, American Red Cross; secretary, Frederick Heart Assn.

1. Immigration Reform Y
2. Open fld-search warrants N
3. Civil pnty-hire ill alien N
4. So Afr sanc-veto override Y

BYRON, BEVERLY B. (Cont.)

5. Tax Overhaul Y
6. South Africa sanctions Y
7. Death penalty-drug bill Y
8. Evidence-warrantless srch Y
9. Life term-second drug off Y
10. Military use in drug war N
11. Troop reduction in Europe N
12. Prohibit chemical weapons N
13. Bar ASAT testing N
14. Abide SALT II weapons ban N
15. Follow SALT II-Soviets do Y
16. Reduce SDI funding N
17. Increase SDI funding N
18. Purchase Trident sub Y
19. Delete 12 MX;Add conv wpn N
20. Raise speed limit N
21. Textile Import Quotas(*) Y
22. Req Pentagon buy US goods N
23. AIDS ins anti-dscriminatn Y
24. Nicaraguan refugee aid N
25. Nicaraguan contra aid Y
26. US abide by SALT II N
27. Prohibit Saudi arms sale Y
28. Military Retiremnt Reform Y
29. Nicaraguan refugee aid N
30. Ease '68 Gun Control Act Y
31. Bar intrstat handgun tran N
32. Keep '68 Gun Control Act N
33. Nicaraguan contra aid Y
34. Bar emp polygraph testing Y
35. Tax Overhaul consideratn Y
36. Bar armor-piercing ammo Y
37. Tax Overhaul consideratn N
38. Make comp emissions known N
39. Allow toxic victims suits N
40. Strike Superfund "VAT" Y
41. Notify emp-plant closing N
42. Bar emp consult-plant clo Y
43. Medicare cuts;Tax incres' Y
44. Delete 12 MX missiles N
45. Spending cuts;Tax incres' Y
46. Textile Import Quotas Y
47. Cut some school lunch fds Y
48. Clean Water Act Amendmnts N
49. Youth work projects Y
50. Assist military in Angola Y
51. Allow US troops-Nicaragua N
52. Pentagon polygraph exams Y
53. Bar ASAT testing N
54. Suspend def pmt for abuse N
55. Bar Pentagon-contr emplmt Y
56. Increase SDI funding N
57. Reduce SDI funding N
58. Produce chemical weapons Y
59. Bar CIA fndg in Nicaragua N
60. South Africa sanctions Y
61. Cut SS COLAs; Raise taxes N
62. Let US invest-So Africa Y
63. Approve 21 MX for 1985 Y
64. Emergency Farm Credit Y
65. Awards to whistle blowers Y
66. African disaster relief Y
67. Ban bank loans to So Afr Y
68. Bar coun duty-free trtmt N
69. Steel import limits Y
70. Soc Sec COLAs=inflation Y
71. Bar haz waste vctms suits Y
72. Prohibit aid to Nicaragua Y
73. Cut $-Schs bar sch prayer Y
74. Raise taxes; Cut Medicare N
75. Alien residncy-prior 1982 Y
76. Alien residncy-prior 1980 Y
77. Pen emp-hire illgl aliens N
78. Lmt Persh II/cruse-Europe N
79. Delete 34 B-1 bombers N
80. Bar purch of Pershing II N
81. Bar purchase of Sgt York N
82. Delete $ for Trident II N
83. Allow 15 MX missiles Y
84. Bar MX procurement-1985 N
85. Equal Access Act Y
86. Aid to El Salvador Y
87. Bar Nicarag water mining N
88. Physician/Medicare freeze N
89. Increase "sin" taxes N
90. End SBA direct loans N
91. Sell Conrail N
92. Equal Rights Amendment Y
93. Marines in Lebanon N
94. Eminent domain-Coal comps N
95. Prohibit EPA sanctions Y
96. SS age increase/Reforms Y
97. Auto domestic content req N
98. Delete jobs program fundg N
99. Highway-Gas tax bill ?
100. Raise Medicare;Cut defnse Y
101. Emergency housing aid Y
102. Across-the-board tax cuts Y
103. Gramm-Latta II targets Y
104. Delete B-1 bomber funds N
105. Dsapprov Saudi AWACS sale Y
106. Disapprove oil import fee Y
107. Rail Deregulation N
108. Dsapp India nuc fuel sale Y
109. Mil draft registration Y
110. Chrysler Loan Guarantees Y
111. Prohibit school busing Y
112. Nuclear plant moratorium N
113. Oil price controls N

Presidential Support Score: 1986 - 50% 1985 - 52%

MITCHELL, PARREN J. -- Maryland 7th District [Democrat]. County of Baltimore (pt.) and City of Baltimore (pt.). Prior Terms:

MITCHELL, PARREN J. (Cont.)
House: 1971-86. Born: April 29, 1922; Baltimore, Md. Education: Morgan State College (A.B.); University of Maryland (M.A.). Military Service: U.S. Army, 1942-45. Occupation: Head of Community Action Agency; professor; assistant director, Urban Studies.

1. Immigration Reform X
2. Open fld-search warrants ?
3. Civil pnty-hire ill alien Y
4. So Afr sanc-veto override Y
5. Tax Overhaul N
6. South Africa sanctions Y
7. Death penalty-drug bill N
8. Evidence-warrantless srch N
9. Life term-second drug off ?
10. Military use in drug war N
11. Troop reduction in Europe Y
12. Prohibit chemical weapons Y
13. Bar ASAT testing Y
14. Abide SALT II weapons ban ?
15. Follow SALT II-Soviets do ?
16. Reduce SDI funding #
17. Increase SDI funding X
18. Purchase Trident sub X
19. Delete 12 MX;Add conv wpn Y
20. Raise speed limit ?
21. Textile Import Quotas(*) Y
22. Req Pentagon buy US goods Y
23. AIDS ins anti-dscriminatn Y
24. Nicaraguan refugee aid Y
25. Nicaraguan contra aid N
26. US abide by SALT II N
27. Prohibit Saudi arms sale Y
28. Military Retiremnt Reform Y
29. Nicaraguan refugee aid Y
30. Ease '68 Gun Control Act N
31. Bar intrstat handgun tran Y
32. Keep '68 Gun Control Act Y
33. Nicaraguan contra aid N
34. Bar emp polygraph testing N
35. Tax Overhaul consideratn Y
36. Bar armor-piercing ammo Y
37. Tax Overhaul consideratn N
38. Make comp emissions known Y
39. Allow toxic victims suits Y
40. Strike Superfund "VAT" Y
41. Notify emp-plant closing Y
42. Bar emp consult-plant clo N
43. Medicare cuts;Tax incres' Y
44. Delete 12 MX missiles Y
45. Spending cuts;Tax incres' Y
46. Textile Import Quotas Y
47. Cut some school lunch fds N
48. Clean Water Act Amendmnts N
49. Youth work projects Y
50. Assist military in Angola N
51. Allow US troops-Nicaragua N
52. Pentagon polygraph exams ?
53. Bar ASAT testing Y
54. Suspend def pmt for abuse Y
55. Bar Pentagon-contr emplmt Y
56. Increase SDI funding N
57. Reduce SDI funding Y
58. Produce chemical weapons N
59. Bar CIA fndg in Nicaragua ?
60. South Africa sanctions Y
61. Cut SS COLAs; Raise taxes N
62. Let US invest-So Africa N
63. Approve 21 MX for 1985 N
64. Emergency Farm Credit Y
65. Awards to whistle blowers Y
66. African disaster relief Y
67. Ban bank loans to So Afr P
68. Bar coun duty-free trtmt Y
69. Steel import limits Y
70. Soc Sec COLAs=inflation Y
71. Bar haz waste vctms suits N
72. Prohibit aid to Nicaragua Y
73. Cut $-Schs bar sch prayer N
74. Raise taxes; Cut Medicare N
75. Alien residncy-prior 1982 N
76. Alien residncy-prior 1980 N
77. Pen emp-hire illgl aliens Y
78. Lmt Persh II/cruse-Europe Y
79. Delete 34 B-1 bombers #
80. Bar purch of Pershing II #
81. Bar purchase of Sgt York ?
82. Delete $ for Trident II Y
83. Allow 15 MX missiles N
84. Bar MX procurement-1985 Y
85. Equal Access Act N
86. Aid to El Salvador N
87. Bar Nicarag water mining Y
88. Physician/Medicare freeze N
89. Increase "sin" taxes Y
90. End SBA direct loans N
91. Sell Conrail N
92. Equal Rights Amendment Y
93. Marines in Lebanon N
94. Eminent domain-coal comps N
95. Prohibit EPA sanctions N
96. SS age increase/Reforms N
97. Auto domestic content req Y
98. Delete jobs program fundg N
99. Highway-Gas tax bill Y
100. Raise Medicare;Cut defnse Y
101. Emergency housing aid Y
102. Across-the-board tax cuts N
103. Gramm-Latta II targets N
104. Delete B-1 bomber funds Y
105. Dsapprov Saudi AWACS sale Y
106. Disapprove oil import fee Y

MITCHELL, PARREN J. (Cont.)

107. Rail Deregulation N
108. Dsapp India nuc fuel sale Y
109. Mil draft registration N
110. Chrysler Loan Guarantees Y
111. Prohibit school busing N
112. Nuclear plant moratorium Y
113. Oil price controls Y
114. Tuition Tax Credits ?
115. Est Consumer Protect Agcy Y
116. Eliminate B-1 bomber fnds Y
117. Subminimum wage for youth N
118. Delete crude oil tax N
119. Natural gas deregulation N

Presidential Support Score: 1986 - 11% 1985 - 15%

BARNES, MICHAEL D. -- Maryland 8th District [Democrat]. County of Montgomery (pt.). Prior Terms: House: 1979-86. Born: September 3, 1943; Washington, D.C. Education: University of North Carolina (B.A.); George Washington University (J.D.). Military Service: U.S. Marine Corps, 1967-69. Occupation: Senate staff member (1970-72); attorney, Covington & Burling (1972-75); vice chairman, Washington Metropolitan Area Transit Commission (1976-78); commissioner, Public Service Commission of Maryland (1975-78).

1. Immigration Reform Y
2. Open fld-search warrants Y
3. Civil pnty-hire ill alien N
4. So Afr sanc-veto override Y
5. Tax Overhaul N
6. South Africa sanctions Y
7. Death penalty-drug bill N
8. Evidence-warrantless srch N
9. Life term-second drug off N
10. Military use in drug war N
11. Troop reduction in Europe N
12. Prohibit chemical weapons Y
13. Bar ASAT testing Y
14. Abide SALT II weapons ban Y
15. Follow SALT II-Soviets do N
16. Reduce SDI funding Y
17. Increase SDI funding N
18. Purchase Trident sub Y
19. Delete 12 MX;Add conv wpn Y
20. Raise speed limit N
21. Textile Import Quotas(*) Y
22. Req Pentagon buy US goods ?
23. AIDS ins anti-dscriminatn Y
24. Nicaraguan refugee aid Y
25. Nicaraguan contra aid N
26. US abide by SALT II N
27. Prohibit Saudi arms sale Y
28. Military Retiremnt Reform ?
29. Nicaraguan refugee aid Y
30. Ease '68 Gun Control Act N
31. Bar intrstat handgun tran Y
32. Keep '68 Gun Control Act Y
33. Nicaraguan contra aid N
34. Bar emp polygraph testing #
35. Tax Overhaul consideratn N
36. Bar armor-piercing ammo Y
37. Tax Overhaul consideratn N
38. Make comp emissions known Y
39. Allow toxic victims suits Y
40. Strike Superfund "VAT" Y
41. Notify emp-plant closing Y
42. Bar emp consult-plant clo N
43. Medicare cuts;Tax incres' Y
44. Delete 12 MX missiles Y
45. Spending cuts;Tax incres' Y
46. Textile Import Quotas Y
47. Cut some school lunch fds N
48. Clean Water Act Amendmnts N
49. Youth work projects Y
50. Assist military in Angola N
51. Allow US troops-Nicaragua N
52. Pentagon polygraph exams N
53. Bar ASAT testing Y
54. Suspend def pmt for abuse Y
55. Bar Pentagon-contr emplmt Y
56. Increase SDI funding N
57. Reduce SDI funding N
58. Produce chemical weapons N
59. Bar CIA fndg in Nicaragua Y
60. South Africa sanctions Y
61. Cut SS COLAs; Raise taxes N
62. Let US invest-So Africa N
63. Approve 21 MX for 1985 N
64. Emergency Farm Credit Y
65. Awards to whistle blowers Y
66. African disaster relief Y
67. Ban bank loans to So Afr Y
68. Bar coun duty-free trtmt Y
69. Steel import limits Y
70. Soc Sec COLAs=inflation Y
71. Bar haz waste vctms suits N
72. Prohibit aid to Nicaragua Y
73. Cut $-Schs bar sch prayer N
74. Raise taxes; Cut Medicare Y
75. Alien residncy-prior 1982 N
76. Alien residncy-prior 1980 N
77. Pen emp-hire illgl aliens Y
78. Lmt Persh II/cruse-Europe N

BARNES, MICHAEL D. (Cont.)

79. Delete 34 B-1 bombers Y
80. Bar purch of Pershing II N
81. Bar purchase of Sgt York Y
82. Delete $ for Trident II N
83. Allow 15 MX missiles N
84. Bar MX procurement-1985 Y
85. Equal Access Act N
86. Aid to El Salvador N
87. Bar Nicarag water mining Y
88. Physician/Medicare freeze N
89. Increase "sin" taxes Y
90. End SBA direct loans N
91. Sell Conrail N
92. Equal Rights Amendment Y
93. Marines in Lebanon Y
94. Eminent domain-Coal comps N
95. Prohibit EPA sanctions Y
96. SS age increase/Reforms N
97. Auto domestic content req Y
98. Delete jobs program fundg N
99. Highway-Gas tax bill ?
100. Raise Medicare;Cut defnse Y
101. Emergency housing aid Y
102. Across-the-board tax cuts N
103. Gramm-Latta II targets N
104. Delete B-1 bomber funds Y
105. Dsapprov Saudi AWACS sale Y
106. Disapprove oil import fee Y
107. Rail Deregulation N
108. Dsapp India nuc fuel sale Y
109. Mil draft registration N
110. Chrysler Loan Guarantees N
111. Prohibit school busing N
112. Nuclear plant moratorium Y
113. Oil price controls Y

Presidential Support Score: 1986 - 11% 1985 - 25%

M A S S A C H U S E T T S

CONTE, SILVIO O. -- Massachusetts 1st District [Republican]. Counties of Berkshire, Franklin, Hampden (pt.), Hampshire and Worcester (pt.). Prior Terms: House: 1959-86. Born: November 9, 1921; Pittsfield, Mass. Education: Boston College; Boston College Law School. Military Service: U.S. Navy (Seabee), WW II. Occupation: Machinist, General Electric Co.; Massacusetts senator (1951-58).

1. Immigration Reform Y
2. Open fld-search warrants N
3. Civil pnty-hire ill alien N
4. So Afr sanc-veto override Y
5. Tax Overhaul Y
6. South Africa sanctions Y
7. Death penalty-drug bill Y
8. Evidence-warrantless srch N
9. Life term-second drug off Y
10. Military use in drug war N
11. Troop reduction in Europe N
12. Prohibit chemical weapons Y
13. Bar ASAT testing Y
14. Abide SALT II weapons ban Y
15. Follow SALT II-Soviets do N
16. Reduce SDI funding N
17. Increase SDI funding N
18. Purchase Trident sub Y
19. Delete 12 MX;Add conv wpn +
20. Raise speed limit N
21. Textile Import Quotas(*) Y
22. Req Pentagon buy US goods Y
23. AIDS ins anti-dscriminatn Y
24. Nicaraguan refugee aid Y
25. Nicaraguan contra aid N
26. US abide by SALT II N
27. Prohibit Saudi arms sale Y
28. Military Retiremnt Reform Y
29. Nicaraguan refugee aid Y
30. Ease '68 Gun Control Act Y
31. Bar intrstat handgun tran Y
32. Keep '68 Gun Control Act Y
33. Nicaraguan contra aid N
34. Bar emp polygraph testing Y
35. Tax Overhaul consideratn Y
36. Bar armor-piercing ammo Y
37. Tax Overhaul consideratn N
38. Make comp emissions known Y
39. Allow toxic victims suits Y
40. Strike Superfund "VAT" Y
41. Notify emp-plant closing Y
42. Bar emp consult-plant clo N
43. Medicare cuts;Tax incres' Y
44. Delete 12 MX missiles +
45. Spending cuts;Tax incres' N
46. Textile Import Quotas Y
47. Cut some school lunch fds N
48. Clean Water Act Amendmnts N
49. Youth work projects Y
50. Assist military in Angola N
51. Allow US troops-Nicaragua N
52. Pentagon polygraph exams Y
53. Bar ASAT testing Y
54. Suspend def pmt for abuse N

CONTE, SILVIO O. (Cont.)

55. Bar Pentagon-contr emplmt Y
56. Increase SDI funding N
57. Reduce SDI funding N
58. Produce chemical weapons N
59. Bar CIA fndg in Nicaragua Y
60. South Africa sanctions Y
61. Cut SS COLAs; Raise taxes N
62. Let US invest-So Africa N
63. Approve 21 MX for 1985 N
64. Emergency Farm Credit N
65. Awards to whistle blowers Y
66. African disaster relief Y
67. Ban bank loans to So Afr Y
68. Bar coun duty-free trtmt Y
69. Steel import limits Y
70. Soc Sec COLAs=inflation Y
71. Bar haz waste vctms suits N
72. Prohibit aid to Nicaragua Y
73. Cut $-Schs bar sch prayer N
74. Raise taxes; Cut Medicare Y
75. Alien residncy-prior 1982 N
76. Alien residncy-prior 1980 N
77. Pen emp-hire illgl aliens N
78. Lmt Persh II/cruse-Europe Y
79. Delete 34 B-1 bombers Y
80. Bar purch of Pershing II Y
81. Bar purchase of Sgt York N
82. Delete $ for Trident II Y
83. Allow 15 MX missiles N
84. Bar MX procurement-1985 Y
85. Equal Access Act N
86. Aid to El Salvador N
87. Bar Nicarag water mining Y
88. Physician/Medicare freeze Y
89. Increase "sin" taxes C
90. End SBA direct loans N
91. Sell Conrail N
92. Equal Rights Amendment Y
93. Marines in Lebanon N
94. Eminent domain-Coal comps N
95. Prohibit EPA sanctions ?
96. SS age increase/Reforms N
97. Auto domestic content req Y
98. Delete jobs program fundg Y
99. Highway-Gas tax bill ?
100. Raise Medicare;Cut defnse Y
101. Emergency housing aid Y
102. Across-the-board tax cuts Y
103. Gramm-Latta II targets Y
104. Delete B-1 bomber funds Y
105. Dsapprov Saudi AWACS sale Y
106. Disapprove oil import fee Y
107. Rail Deregulation N
108. Dsapp India nuc fuel sale Y
109. Mil draft registration N
110. Chrysler Loan Guarantees Y
111. Prohibit school busing N
112. Nuclear plant moratorium Y
113. Oil price controls Y
114. Tuition Tax Credits Y
115. Est Consumer Protect Agcy Y
116. Eliminate B-1 bomber fnds Y
117. Subminimum wage for youth Y
118. Delete crude oil tax Y
119. Natural gas deregulation N

Presidential Support Score: 1986 - 26% 1985 - 36%

BOLAND, EDWARD P. -- Massachusetts 2nd District [Democrat]. Counties of Hampden (pt.) and Worcester (pt.). Prior Terms: House: 1953-86. Born: October 1, 1911; Springfield, Mass. Education: Boston College Law School. Military Service: U.S. Army, 1942-46. Occupation: Massachusetts legislator (1934-40); Hampden County registrar of deeds (1946-52); military aid to governor (1949-52).

1. Immigration Reform #
2. Open fld-search warrants ?
3. Civil pnty-hire ill alien ?
4. So Afr sanc-veto override Y
5. Tax Overhaul Y
6. South Africa sanctions Y
7. Death penalty-drug bill Y
8. Evidence-warrantless srch N
9. Life term-second drug off Y
10. Military use in drug war N
11. Troop reduction in Europe N
12. Prohibit chemical weapons Y
13. Bar ASAT testing +
14. Abide SALT II weapons ban Y
15. Follow SALT II-Soviets do N
16. Reduce SDI funding N
17. Increase SDI funding N
18. Purchase Trident sub Y
19. Delete 12 MX;Add conv wpn Y
20. Raise speed limit N
21. Textile Import Quotas(*) Y
22. Req Pentagon buy US goods Y
23. AIDS ins anti-dscriminatn Y
24. Nicaraguan refugee aid Y
25. Nicaraguan contra aid N
26. US abide by SALT II N
27. Prohibit Saudi arms sale Y
28. Military Retiremnt Reform Y
29. Nicaraguan refugee aid Y
30. Ease '68 Gun Control Act N

BOLAND, EDWARD P. (Cont.)

31. Bar intrstat handgun tran Y
32. Keep '68 Gun Control Act Y
33. Nicaraguan contra aid N
34. Bar emp polygraph testing Y
35. Tax Overhaul consideratn Y
36. Bar armor-piercing ammo Y
37. Tax Overhaul consideratn Y
38. Make comp emissions known Y
39. Allow toxic victims suits Y
40. Strike Superfund "VAT" N
41. Notify emp-plant closing Y
42. Bar emp consult-plant clo N
43. Medicare cuts;Tax incres' Y
44. Delete 12 MX missiles Y
45. Spending cuts;Tax incres' Y
46. Textile Import Quotas Y
47. Cut some school lunch fds N
48. Clean Water Act Amendmnts N
49. Youth work projects Y
50. Assist military in Angola N
51. Allow US troops-Nicaragua N
52. Pentagon polygraph exams Y
53. Bar ASAT testing Y
54. Suspend def pmt for abuse Y
55. Bar Pentagon-contr emplmt Y
56. Increase SDI funding N
57. Reduce SDI funding N
58. Produce chemical weapons N
59. Bar CIA fndg in Nicaragua Y
60. South Africa sanctions Y
61. Cut SS COLAs; Raise taxes N
62. Let US invest-So Africa N
63. Approve 21 MX for 1985 N
64. Emergency Farm Credit Y
65. Awards to whistle blowers Y
66. African disaster relief Y
67. Ban bank loans to So Afr Y
68. Bar coun duty-free trtmt Y
69. Steel import limits Y
70. Soc Sec COLAs=inflation Y
71. Bar haz waste vctms suits N
72. Prohibit aid to Nicaragua Y
73. Cut $-Schs bar sch prayer N
74. Raise taxes; Cut Medicare Y
75. Alien residncy-prior 1982 Y
76. Alien residncy-prior 1980 N
77. Pen emp-hire illgl aliens Y
78. Lmt Persh II/cruse-Europe N
79. Delete 34 B-1 bombers Y
80. Bar purch of Pershing II N
81. Bar purchase of Sgt York ?
82. Delete $ for Trident II N
83. Allow 15 MX missiles N
84. Bar MX procurement-1985 Y
85. Equal Access Act N
86. Aid to El Salvador N
87. Bar Nicarag water mining Y
88. Physician/Medicare freeze N
89. Increase "sin" taxes Y
90. End SBA direct loans N
91. Sell Conrail N
92. Equal Rights Amendment Y
93. Marines in Lebanon Y
94. Eminent domain-Coal comps Y
95. Prohibit EPA sanctions N
96. SS age increase/Reforms ?
97. Auto domestic content req Y
98. Delete jobs program fundg N
99. Highway-Gas tax bill Y
100. Raise Medicare;Cut defnse Y
101. Emergency housing aid Y
102. Across-the-board tax cuts N
103. Gramm-Latta II targets N
104. Delete B-1 bomber funds Y
105. Dsapprov Saudi AWACS sale Y
106. Disapprove oil import fee Y
107. Rail Deregulation ?
108. Dsapp India nuc fuel sale Y
109. Mil draft registration Y
110. Chrysler Loan Guarantees Y
111. Prohibit school busing N
112. Nuclear plant moratorium Y
113. Oil price controls Y
114. Tuition Tax Credits Y
115. Est Consumer Protect Agcy Y
116. Eliminate B-1 bomber fnds Y
117. Subminimum wage for youth N
118. Delete crude oil tax N
119. Natural gas deregulation N

Presidential Support Score: 1986 - 20% 1985 - 28%

EARLY, JOSEPH D. -- Massachusetts 3rd District [Democrat]. Counties of Middlesex (pt.), Norfolk (pt.) and Worcester (pt.). Prior Terms: House: 1975-86. Born: January 31, 1933; Worcester, Mass. Education: College of the Holy Cross (B.S.). Military Service: U.S. Navy, 1955-57. Occupation: Prep-school teacher (1959-63); Massachusetts representatiave (1963-74).

1. Immigration Reform Y
2. Open fld-search warrants N
3. Civil pnty-hire ill alien N
4. So Afr sanc-veto override Y
5. Tax Overhaul Y
6. South Africa sanctions ?
7. Death penalty-drug bill Y
8. Evidence-warrantless srch N

EARLY, JOSEPH D. (Cont.)

9. Life term-second drug off N
10. Military use in drug war Y
11. Troop reduction in Europe Y
12. Prohibit chemical weapons Y
13. Bar ASAT testing Y
14. Abide SALT II weapons ban Y
15. Follow SALT II-Soviets do N
16. Reduce SDI funding N
17. Increase SDI funding N
18. Purchase Trident sub Y
19. Delete 12 MX;Add conv wpn Y
20. Raise speed limit N
21. Textile Import Quotas(*) Y
22. Req Pentagon buy US goods N
23. AIDS ins anti-dscriminatn Y
24. Nicaraguan refugee aid Y
25. Nicaraguan contra aid N
26. US abide by SALT II N
27. Prohibit Saudi arms sale Y
28. Military Retiremnt Reform ?
29. Nicaraguan refugee aid Y
30. Ease '68 Gun Control Act N
31. Bar intrstat handgun tran Y
32. Keep '68 Gun Control Act Y
33. Nicaraguan contra aid N
34. Bar emp polygraph testing Y
35. Tax Overhaul consideratn Y
36. Bar armor-piercing ammo Y
37. Tax Overhaul consideratn Y
38. Make comp emissions known Y
39. Allow toxic victims suits Y
40. Strike Superfund "VAT" Y
41. Notify emp-plant closing Y
42. Bar emp consult-plant clo N
43. Medicare cuts;Tax incres' Y
44. Delete 12 MX missiles Y
45. Spending cuts;Tax incres' Y
46. Textile Import Quotas Y
47. Cut some school lunch fds N
48. Clean Water Act Amendmnts N
49. Youth work projects Y
50. Assist military in Angola N
51. Allow US troops-Nicaragua N
52. Pentagon polygraph exams Y
53. Bar ASAT testing Y
54. Suspend def pmt for abuse N
55. Bar Pentagon-contr emplmt Y
56. Increase SDI funding N
57. Reduce SDI funding N
58. Produce chemical weapons N
59. Bar CIA fndg in Nicaragua Y
60. South Africa sanctions Y
61. Cut SS COLAs; Raise taxes N
62. Let US invest-So Africa N
63. Approve 21 MX for 1985 N
64. Emergency Farm Credit Y
65. Awards to whistle blowers Y
66. African disaster relief Y
67. Ban bank loans to So Afr ?
68. Bar coun duty-free trtmt Y
69. Steel import limits Y
70. Soc Sec COLAs=inflation Y
71. Bar haz waste vctms suits N
72. Prohibit aid to Nicaragua Y
73. Cut $-Schs bar sch prayer ?
74. Raise taxes; Cut Medicare N
75. Alien residncy-prior 1982 Y
76. Alien residncy-prior 1980 N
77. Pen emp-hire illgl aliens Y
78. Lmt Persh II/cruse-Europe Y
79. Delete 34 B-1 bombers Y
80. Bar purch of Pershing II Y
81. Bar purchase of Sgt York ?
82. Delete $ for Trident II Y
83. Allow 15 MX missiles N
84. Bar MX procurement-1985 Y
85. Equal Access Act N
86. Aid to El Salvador N
87. Bar Nicarag water mining Y
88. Physician/Medicare freeze N
89. Increase "sin" taxes N
90. End SBA direct loans ?
91. Sell Conrail N
92. Equal Rights Amendment Y
93. Marines in Lebanon N
94. Eminent domain-Coal comps Y
95. Prohibit EPA sanctions N
96. SS age increase/Reforms N
97. Auto domestic content req Y
98. Delete jobs program fundg N
99. Highway-Gas tax bill Y
100. Raise Medicare;Cut defnse Y
101. Emergency housing aid N
102. Across-the-board tax cuts N
103. Gramm-Latta II targets N
104. Delete B-1 bomber funds Y
105. Dsapprov Saudi AWACS sale Y
106. Disapprove oil import fee Y
107. Rail Deregulation N
108. Dsapp India nuc fuel sale Y
109. Mil draft registration N
110. Chrysler Loan Guarantees N
111. Prohibit school busing Y
112. Nuclear plant moratorium Y
113. Oil price controls Y
114. Tuition Tax Credits Y
115. Est Consumer Protect Agcy Y
116. Eliminate B-1 bomber fnds Y
117. Subminimum wage for youth N
118. Delete crude oil tax N
119. Natural gas deregulation N

Presidential Support Score: 1986 - 13% 1985 - 28%

FRANK, BARNEY -- Massachusetts 4th District [Democrat]. Counties of Bristol (pt.), Middlesex (pt.) and Norfolk (pt.). Prior Terms: House: 1981-86. Born: March 31, 1940; Bayonne, N.J. Education: Harvard College (B.A.); Harvard University. Occupation: Teaching fellow, Harvard College (1963-67); assistant to the director, Kennedy Institute of Politics (1966-67); executive assistant to mayor (1968-71); administative assistant to congressman (1971-72); Massachusetts representative (1973-80); lecturer, Kennedy School of Government (1978-80); attorney.

1. Immigration Reform Y
2. Open fld-search warrants N
3. Civil pnty-hire ill alien N
4. So Afr sanc-veto override Y
5. Tax Overhaul Y
6. South Africa sanctions Y
7. Death penalty-drug bill N
8. Evidence-warrantless srch N
9. Life term-second drug off Y
10. Military use in drug war N
11. Troop reduction in Europe Y
12. Prohibit chemical weapons Y
13. Bar ASAT testing Y
14. Abide SALT II weapons ban Y
15. Follow SALT II-Soviets do N
16. Reduce SDI funding Y
17. Increase SDI funding N
18. Purchase Trident sub Y
19. Delete 12 MX;Add conv wpn Y
20. Raise speed limit Y
21. Textile Import Quotas(*) Y
22. Req Pentagon buy US goods N
23. AIDS ins anti-dscriminatn Y
24. Nicaraguan refugee aid Y
25. Nicaraguan contra aid N
26. US abide by SALT II N
27. Prohibit Saudi arms sale Y
28. Military Retiremnt Reform Y
29. Nicaraguan refugee aid Y
30. Ease '68 Gun Control Act N
31. Bar intrstat handgun tran Y
32. Keep '68 Gun Control Act Y
33. Nicaraguan contra aid N
34. Bar emp polygraph testing Y
35. Tax Overhaul consideratn Y
36. Bar armor-piercing ammo Y
37. Tax Overhaul consideratn Y
38. Make comp emissions known Y
39. Allow toxic victims suits Y
40. Strike Superfund "VAT" Y
41. Notify emp-plant closing Y
42. Bar emp consult-plant clo N
43. Medicare cuts;Tax incres' Y
44. Delete 12 MX missiles Y
45. Spending cuts;Tax incres' Y
46. Textile Import Quotas Y
47. Cut some school lunch fds N
48. Clean Water Act Amendmnts N
49. Youth work projects Y
50. Assist military in Angola N
51. Allow US troops-Nicaragua N
52. Pentagon polygraph exams N
53. Bar ASAT testing Y
54. Suspend def pmt for abuse Y
55. Bar Pentagon-contr emplmt Y
56. Increase SDI funding N
57. Reduce SDI funding Y
58. Produce chemical weapons N
59. Bar CIA fndg in Nicaragua Y
60. South Africa sanctions Y
61. Cut SS COLAs; Raise taxes N
62. Let US invest-So Africa N
63. Approve 21 MX for 1985 N
64. Emergency Farm Credit Y
65. Awards to whistle blowers Y
66. African disaster relief Y
67. Ban bank loans to So Afr Y
68. Bar coun duty-free trtmt Y
69. Steel import limits Y
70. Soc Sec COLAs=inflation Y
71. Bar haz waste vctms suits N
72. Prohibit aid to Nicaragua Y
73. Cut $-Schs bar sch prayer N
74. Raise taxes; Cut Medicare ?
75. Alien residncy-prior 1982 N
76. Alien residncy-prior 1980 N
77. Pen emp-hire illgl aliens N
78. Lmt Persh II/cruse-Europe Y
79. Delete 34 B-1 bombers Y
80. Bar purch of Pershing II Y
81. Bar purchase of Sgt York Y
82. Delete $ for Trident II Y
83. Allow 15 MX missiles N
84. Bar MX procurement-1985 Y
85. Equal Access Act N
86. Aid to El Salvador N
87. Bar Nicarag water mining Y
88. Physician/Medicare freeze N
89. Increase "sin" taxes Y
90. End SBA direct loans N
91. Sell Conrail N
92. Equal Rights Amendment Y
93. Marines in Lebanon N
94. Eminent domain-Coal comps Y
95. Prohibit EPA sanctions Y
96. SS age increase/Reforms N
97. Auto domestic content req Y
98. Delete jobs program fundg N

FRANK, BARNEY (Cont.)

99. Highway-Gas tax bill Y
100. Raise Medicare;Cut defnse Y
101. Emergency housing aid Y
102. Across-the-board tax cuts N
103. Gramm-Latta II targets N
104. Delete B-1 bomber funds Y
105. Dsapprov Saudi AWACS sale Y

Presidential Support Score: 1986 - 17% 1985 - 25%

ATKINS, CHESTER G. -- Massachusetts 5th District [Democrat]. Counties of Essex (pt.), Middlesex (pt.) and Worcester (pt.). Prior Terms: 1985-86. Born: April 15, 1948. Education: Antioch College (B.A.). Occupation: State representative; state senator.

1. Immigration Reform Y
2. Open fld-search warrants N
3. Civil pnty-hire ill alien N
4. So Afr sanc-veto override Y
5. Tax Overhaul Y
6. South Africa sanctions ?
7. Death penalty-drug bill N
8. Evidence-warrantless srch N
9. Life term-second drug off Y
10. Military use in drug war N
11. Troop reduction in Europe Y
12. Prohibit chemical weapons Y
13. Bar ASAT testing Y
14. Abide SALT II weapons ban Y
15. Follow SALT II-Soviets do N
16. Reduce SDI funding Y
17. Increase SDI funding N
18. Purchase Trident sub Y
19. Delete 12 MX;Add conv wpn Y
20. Raise speed limit N
21. Textile Import Quotas(*) Y
22. Req Pentagon buy US goods N
23. AIDS ins anti-dscriminatn Y
24. Nicaraguan refugee aid Y
25. Nicaraguan contra aid N
26. US abide by SALT II N
27. Prohibit Saudi arms sale Y
28. Military Retiremnt Reform Y
29. Nicaraguan refugee aid Y
30. Ease '68 Gun Control Act N
31. Bar intrstat handgun tran Y
32. Keep '68 Gun Control Act Y
33. Nicaraguan contra aid N
34. Bar emp polygraph testing Y
35. Tax Overhaul consideratn Y
36. Bar armor-piercing ammo Y
37. Tax Overhaul consideratn Y
38. Make comp emissions known Y
39. Allow toxic victims suits Y
40. Strike Superfund "VAT" Y
41. Notify emp-plant closing ?
42. Bar emp consult-plant clo N
43. Medicare cuts;Tax incres' Y
44. Delete 12 MX missiles Y
45. Spending cuts;Tax incres' Y
46. Textile Import Quotas Y
47. Cut some school lunch fds N
48. Clean Water Act Amendmnts N
49. Youth work projects Y
50. Assist military in Angola N
51. Allow US troops-Nicaragua N
52. Pentagon polygraph exams Y
53. Bar ASAT testing Y
54. Suspend def pmt for abuse Y
55. Bar Pentagon-contr emplmt Y
56. Increase SDI funding N
57. Reduce SDI funding Y
58. Produce chemical weapons N
59. Bar CIA fndg in Nicaragua Y
60. South Africa sanctions Y
61. Cut SS COLAs; Raise taxes N
62. Let US invest-So Africa N
63. Approve 21 MX for 1985 N
64. Emergency Farm Credit Y
65. Awards to whistle blowers Y
66. African disaster relief Y

Presidential Support Score: 1986 - 17% 1985 - 20%

MAVROULES, NICHOLAS -- Massachusetts 6th District [Democrat]. Counties of Essex (pt.) and Middlesex (pt.). Prior Terms: House: 1979-86. Born: November 1, 1929; Peabody, Mass. Education: Massacusetts Institute of Technology. Occupation: Employee, Sylvania Corp. (1949-67); mayor (1967-79).

1. Immigration Reform Y
2. Open fld-search warrants N
3. Civil pnty-hire ill alien N
4. So Afr sanc-veto override Y
5. Tax Overhaul Y
6. South Africa sanctions Y
7. Death penalty-drug bill Y
8. Evidence-warrantless srch N

MAVROULES, NICHOLAS (Cont.)

9. Life term-second drug off Y
10. Military use in drug war N
11. Troop reduction in Europe N
12. Prohibit chemical weapons Y
13. Bar ASAT testing Y
14. Abide SALT II weapons ban Y
15. Follow SALT II-Soviets do N
16. Reduce SDI funding Y
17. Increase SDI funding N
18. Purchase Trident sub Y
19. Delete 12 MX;Add conv wpn Y
20. Raise speed limit N
21. Textile Import Quotas(*) Y
22. Req Pentagon buy US goods N
23. AIDS ins anti-dscriminatn Y
24. Nicaraguan refugee aid Y
25. Nicaraguan contra aid N
26. US abide by SALT II N
27. Prohibit Saudi arms sale Y
28. Military Retiremnt Reform Y
29. Nicaraguan refugee aid Y
30. Ease '68 Gun Control Act N
31. Bar intrstat handgun tran Y
32. Keep '68 Gun Control Act Y
33. Nicaraguan contra aid N
34. Bar emp polygraph testing Y
35. Tax Overhaul consideratn Y
36. Bar armor-piercing ammo Y
37. Tax Overhaul consideratn Y
38. Make comp emissions known Y
39. Allow toxic victims suits Y
40. Strike Superfund "VAT" Y
41. Notify emp-plant closing Y
42. Bar emp consult-plant clo N
43. Medicare cuts;Tax incres' Y
44. Delete 12 MX missiles Y
45. Spending cuts;Tax incres' Y
46. Textile Import Quotas Y
47. Cut some school lunch fds N
48. Clean Water Act Amendmnts N
49. Youth work projects Y
50. Assist military in Angola N
51. Allow US troops-Nicaragua N
52. Pentagon polygraph exams Y
53. Bar ASAT testing Y
54. Suspend def pmt for abuse Y
55. Bar Pentagon-contr emplmt Y
56. Increase SDI funding N
57. Reduce SDI funding Y
58. Produce chemical weapons N
59. Bar CIA fndg in Nicaragua Y
60. South Africa sanctions Y
61. Cut SS COLAs; Raise taxes N
62. Let US invest-So Africa N
63. Approve 21 MX for 1985 N
64. Emergency Farm Credit Y
65. Awards to whistle blowers Y
66. African disaster relief Y
67. Ban bank loans to So Afr Y
68. Bar coun duty-free trtmt Y
69. Steel import limits Y
70. Soc Sec COLAs=inflation Y
71. Bar haz waste vctms suits N
72. Prohibit aid to Nicaragua Y
73. Cut $-Schs bar sch prayer N
74. Raise taxes; Cut Medicare Y
75. Alien residncy-prior 1982 N
76. Alien residncy-prior 1980 N
77. Pen emp-hire illgl aliens Y
78. Lmt Persh II/cruse-Europe Y
79. Delete 34 B-1 bombers Y
80. Bar purch of Pershing II Y
81. Bar purchase of Sgt York N
82. Delete $ for Trident II Y
83. Allow 15 MX missiles N
84. Bar MX procurement-1985 Y
85. Equal Access Act N
86. Aid to El Salvador N
87. Bar Nicarag water mining Y
88. Physician/Medicare freeze N
89. Increase "sin" taxes Y
90. End SBA direct loans N
91. Sell Conrail N
92. Equal Rights Amendment Y
93. Marines in Lebanon Y
94. Eminent domain-Coal comps Y
95. Prohibit EPA sanctions N
96. SS age increase/Reforms N
97. Auto domestic content req Y
98. Delete jobs program fundg N
99. Highway-Gas tax bill Y
100. Raise Medicare;Cut defnse Y
101. Emergency housing aid Y
102. Across-the-board tax cuts N
103. Gramm-Latta II targets N
104. Delete B-1 bomber funds Y
105. Dsapprov Saudi AWACS sale Y
106. Disapprove oil import fee Y
107. Rail Deregulation N
108. Dsapp India nuc fuel sale Y
109. Mil draft registration N
110. Chrysler Loan Guarantees Y
111. Prohibit school busing N
112. Nuclear plant moratorium Y
113. Oil price controls Y

Presidential Support Score: 1986 - 18% 1985 - 20%

MARKEY, EDWARD J. -- Massachusetts 7th District [Democrat]. Counties of Middlesex (pt.)and Suffolk (pt.). Prior Terms: House: 1976 (Special Election) - 1986. Born: July 11, 1946; Malden,

MARKEY, EDWARD J. (Cont.)
Mass. Education: Boston College (B.A., J.D.). Military Service: U.S. Army Reserve, 1968-73. Occupation: Massachusetts representative (1972).

1. Immigration Reform Y
2. Open fld-search warrants ?
3. Civil pnty-hire ill alien N
4. So Afr sanc-veto override Y
5. Tax Overhaul Y
6. South Africa sanctions ?
7. Death penalty-drug bill ?
8. Evidence-warrantless srch ?
9. Life term-second drug off ?
10. Military use in drug war ?
11. Troop reduction in Europe Y
12. Prohibit chemical weapons Y
13. Bar ASAT testing Y
14. Abide SALT II weapons ban Y
15. Follow SALT II-Soviets do N
16. Reduce SDI funding Y
17. Increase SDI funding N
18. Purchase Trident sub Y
19. Delete 12 MX;Add conv wpn Y
20. Raise speed limit N
21. Textile Import Quotas(*) Y
22. Req Pentagon buy US goods N
23. AIDS ins anti-dscriminatn Y
24. Nicaraguan refugee aid Y
25. Nicaraguan contra aid N
26. US abide by SALT II N
27. Prohibit Saudi arms sale Y
28. Military Retiremnt Reform Y
29. Nicaraguan refugee aid Y
30. Ease '68 Gun Control Act N
31. Bar intrstat handgun tran Y
32. Keep '68 Gun Control Act Y
33. Nicaraguan contra aid N
34. Bar emp polygraph testing Y
35. Tax Overhaul consideratn Y
36. Bar armor-piercing ammo Y
37. Tax Overhaul consideratn Y
38. Make comp emissions known Y
39. Allow toxic victims suits Y
40. Strike Superfund "VAT" Y
41. Notify emp-plant closing Y
42. Bar emp consult-plant clo N
43. Medicare cuts;Tax incres' Y
44. Delete 12 MX missiles Y
45. Spending cuts;Tax incres' Y
46. Textile Import Quotas Y
47. Cut some school lunch fds N
48. Clean Water Act Amendmnts N
49. Youth work projects Y
50. Assist military in Angola N
51. Allow US troops-Nicaragua N
52. Pentagon polygraph exams N
53. Bar ASAT testing Y
54. Suspend def pmt for abuse Y
55. Bar Pentagon-contr emplmt Y
56. Increase SDI funding N
57. Reduce SDI funding Y
58. Produce chemical weapons N
59. Bar CIA fndg in Nicaragua Y
60. South Africa sanctions Y
61. Cut SS COLAs; Raise taxes N
62. Let US invest-So Africa N
63. Approve 21 MX for 1985 N
64. Emergency Farm Credit Y
65. Awards to whistle blowers Y
66. African disaster relief Y
67. Ban bank loans to So Afr Y
68. Bar coun duty-free trtmt Y
69. Steel import limits Y
70. Soc Sec COLAs=inflation Y
71. Bar haz waste vctms suits N
72. Prohibit aid to Nicaragua Y
73. Cut $-Schs bar sch prayer N
74. Raise taxes; Cut Medicare N
75. Alien residncy-prior 1982 N
76. Alien residncy-prior 1980 N
77. Pen emp-hire illgl aliens Y
78. Lmt Persh II/cruse-Europe Y
79. Delete 34 B-1 bombers Y
80. Bar purch of Pershing II Y
81. Bar purchase of Sgt York Y
82. Delete $ for Trident II Y
83. Allow 15 MX missiles N
84. Bar MX procurement-1985 Y
85. Equal Access Act N
86. Aid to El Salvador N
87. Bar Nicarag water mining Y
88. Physician/Medicare freeze N
89. Increase "sin" taxes Y
90. End SBA direct loans ?
91. Sell Conrail ?
92. Equal Rights Amendment Y
93. Marines in Lebanon Y
94. Eminent domain-Coal comps N
95. Prohibit EPA sanctions Y
96. SS age increase/Reforms N
97. Auto domestic content req Y
98. Delete jobs program fundg N
99. Highway-Gas tax bill Y
100. Raise Medicare;Cut defnse Y
101. Emergency housing aid Y
102. Across-the-board tax cuts N
103. Gramm-Latta II targets N
104. Delete B-1 bomber funds Y
105. Dsapprov Saudi AWACS sale Y
106. Disapprove oil import fee Y
107. Rail Deregulation N
108. Dsapp India nuc fuel sale Y
109. Mil draft registration N
110. Chrysler Loan Guarantees Y

MARKEY, EDWARD J. (Cont.)

111. Prohibit school busing N
112. Nuclear plant moratorium Y
113. Oil price controls Y
114. Tuition Tax Credits Y
115. Est Consumer Protect Agcy Y
116. Eliminate B-1 bomber fnds Y
117. Subminimum wage for youth N
118. Delete crude oil tax N
119. Natural gas deregulation N

Presidential Support Score: 1986 - 11% 1985 - 23%

O'NEILL, THOMAS P. Jr. -- Massachusetts 8th District [Democrat]. Counties of Middlesex (pt.) and Suffolk (pt.). Prior Terms: House: 1953-1986. Born: December 9, 1912; Cambridge, Mass. Education: Boston College (A.B.). Occupation: Insurance businessman; Massachusetts legislator (1936-52). Speaker of the House.

4. So Afr sanc-veto override Y
21. Textile Import Quotas(*) Y
33. Nicaraguan contra aid N
92. Equal Rights Amendment Y
102. Across-the-board tax cuts N
117. Subminimum wage for youth N

Speaker of the House votes at his discretion and to break ties.

MOAKLEY, JOE -- Massachusetts 9th District [Democrat]. Counties of Bristol (pt.), Norfolk (pt.), Plymouth (pt.) and Suffolk (pt.). Prior Terms: House: 1973-86. Born: April 27, 1927. Education: University of Miami; Suffolk University Law School (LL.B.). Military Service: U.S. Navy, 1943-46. Occupation: Massachusetts representative (1952-64); Massachusetts senator (1964-71); city councilor (1971-72).

1. Immigration Reform Y
2. Open fld-search warrants N
3. Civil pnty-hire ill alien N
4. So Afr sanc-veto override Y
5. Tax Overhaul Y
6. South Africa sanctions Y
7. Death penalty-drug bill Y
8. Evidence-warrantless srch N
9. Life term-second drug off Y
10. Military use in drug war N
11. Troop reduction in Europe N
12. Prohibit chemical weapons Y
13. Bar ASAT testing Y
14. Abide SALT II weapons ban Y
15. Follow SALT II-Soviets do N
16. Reduce SDI funding Y
17. Increase SDI funding N
18. Purchase Trident sub Y
19. Delete 12 MX;Add conv wpn Y
20. Raise speed limit N
21. Textile Import Quotas(*) Y
22. Req Pentagon buy US goods Y
23. AIDS ins anti-dscriminatn Y
24. Nicaraguan refugee aid Y
25. Nicaraguan contra aid N
26. US abide by SALT II N
27. Prohibit Saudi arms sale Y
28. Military Retiremnt Reform Y
29. Nicaraguan refugee aid Y
30. Ease '68 Gun Control Act N
31. Bar intrstat handgun tran Y
32. Keep '68 Gun Control Act Y
33. Nicaraguan contra aid N
34. Bar emp polygraph testing Y
35. Tax Overhaul consideratn Y
36. Bar armor-piercing ammo Y
37. Tax Overhaul consideratn Y
38. Make comp emissions known Y
39. Allow toxic victims suits Y
40. Strike Superfund "VAT" Y
41. Notify emp-plant closing Y
42. Bar emp consult-plant clo N
43. Medicare cuts;Tax incres' Y
44. Delete 12 MX missiles Y
45. Spending cuts;Tax incres' Y
46. Textile Import Quotas Y
47. Cut some school lunch fds N
48. Clean Water Act Amendmnts N
49. Youth work projects Y
50. Assist military in Angola N
51. Allow US troops-Nicaragua N
52. Pentagon polygraph exams Y
53. Bar ASAT testing Y
54. Suspend def pmt for abuse Y
55. Bar Pentagon-contr emplmt Y
56. Increase SDI funding N
57. Reduce SDI funding Y
58. Produce chemical weapons N
59. Bar CIA fndg in Nicaragua Y
60. South Africa sanctions Y

MOAKLEY, JOE (Cont.)

61. Cut SS COLAs; Raise taxes N
62. Let US invest-So Africa N
63. Approve 21 MX for 1985 N
64. Emergency Farm Credit Y
65. Awards to whistle blowers Y
66. African disaster relief Y
67. Ban bank loans to So Afr Y
68. Bar coun duty-free trtmt Y
69. Steel import limits Y
70. Soc Sec COLAs=inflation Y
71. Bar haz waste vctms suits N
72. Prohibit aid to Nicaragua Y
73. Cut $-Schs bar sch prayer N
74. Raise taxes; Cut Medicare Y
75. Alien residncy-prior 1982 Y
76. Alien residncy-prior 1980 N
77. Pen emp-hire illgl aliens Y
78. Lmt Persh II/cruse-Europe Y
79. Delete 34 B-1 bombers Y
80. Bar purch of Pershing II Y
81. Bar purchase of Sgt York ?
82. Delete $ for Trident II ?
83. Allow 15 MX missiles N
84. Bar MX procurement-1985 Y
85. Equal Access Act N
86. Aid to El Salvador N
87. Bar Nicarag water mining Y
88. Physician/Medicare freeze N
89. Increase "sin" taxes Y
90. End SBA direct loans N
91. Sell Conrail N
92. Equal Rights Amendment Y
93. Marines in Lebanon Y
94. Eminent domain-Coal comps N
95. Prohibit EPA sanctions N
96. SS age increase/Reforms N
97. Auto domestic content req Y
98. Delete jobs program fundg N
99. Highway-Gas tax bill Y
100. Raise Medicare;Cut defnse Y
101. Emergency housing aid Y
102. Across-the-board tax cuts N
103. Gramm-Latta II targets N
104. Delete B-1 bomber funds #
105. Dsapprov Saudi AWACS sale Y
106. Disapprove oil import fee Y
107. Rail Deregulation N
108. Dsapp India nuc fuel sale Y
109. Mil draft registration Y
110. Chrysler Loan Guarantees Y
111. Prohibit school busing Y
112. Nuclear plant moratorium Y
113. Oil price controls Y
114. Tuition Tax Credits Y
115. Est Consumer Protect Agcy Y
116. Eliminate B-1 bomber fnds Y
117. Subminimum wage for youth N
118. Delete crude oil tax N
119. Natural gas deregulation N

Presidential Support Score: 1986 - 15% 1985 - 23%

STUDDS, GERRY E. -- Massachusetts 10th District [Democrat]. Counties of Barnstable, Bristol (pt.), Dukes, Nantucket, Norfolk (pt.) and Plymouth (pt.). Prior Terms: House: 1973-86. Born: May 12, 1937; Mineola, N.Y. Education: Yale University (B.A., M.A.T.). Occupation: Foreign service officer, State Department (1961-62); executive director, Domestic Peace Corps; legislative assistant (1964); teacher (1965-69).

1. Immigration Reform Y
2. Open fld-search warrants Y
3. Civil pnty-hire ill alien N
4. So Afr sanc-veto override Y
5. Tax Overhaul Y
6. South Africa sanctions Y
7. Death penalty-drug bill N
8. Evidence-warrantless srch N
9. Life term-second drug off N
10. Military use in drug war N
11. Troop reduction in Europe Y
12. Prohibit chemical weapons Y
13. Bar ASAT testing Y
14. Abide SALT II weapons ban Y
15. Follow SALT II-Soviets do N
16. Reduce SDI funding Y
17. Increase SDI funding N
18. Purchase Trident sub Y
19. Delete 12 MX;Add conv wpn Y
20. Raise speed limit N
21. Textile Import Quotas(*) Y
22. Req Pentagon buy US goods N
23. AIDS ins anti-dscriminatn Y
24. Nicaraguan refugee aid Y
25. Nicaraguan contra aid N
26. US abide by SALT II N
27. Prohibit Saudi arms sale N
28. Military Retiremnt Reform Y
29. Nicaraguan refugee aid Y
30. Ease '68 Gun Control Act N
31. Bar intrstat handgun tran Y
32. Keep '68 Gun Control Act Y
33. Nicaraguan contra aid N
34. Bar emp polygraph testing Y
35. Tax Overhaul consideratn Y
36. Bar armor-piercing ammo Y

STUDDS, GERRY E. (Cont.)

37. Tax Overhaul consideratn Y
38. Make comp emissions known Y
39. Allow toxic victims suits Y
40. Strike Superfund "VAT" Y
41. Notify emp-plant closing Y
42. Bar emp consult-plant clo N
43. Medicare cuts;Tax incres' Y
44. Delete 12 MX missiles Y
45. Spending cuts;Tax incres' Y
46. Textile Import Quotas Y
47. Cut some school lunch fds N
48. Clean Water Act Amendmnts N
49. Youth work projects Y
50. Assist military in Angola N
51. Allow US troops-Nicaragua N
52. Pentagon polygraph exams N
53. Bar ASAT testing Y
54. Suspend def pmt for abuse Y
55. Bar Pentagon-contr emplmt Y
56. Increase SDI funding N
57. Reduce SDI funding Y
58. Produce chemical weapons N
59. Bar CIA fndg in Nicaragua Y
60. South Africa sanctions Y
61. Cut SS COLAs; Raise taxes N
62. Let US invest-So Africa N
63. Approve 21 MX for 1985 N
64. Emergency Farm Credit Y
65. Awards to whistle blowers Y
66. African disaster relief Y
67. Ban bank loans to So Afr Y
68. Bar coun duty-free trtmt Y
69. Steel import limits Y
70. Soc Sec COLAs=inflation Y
71. Bar haz waste vctms suits N
72. Prohibit aid to Nicaragua Y
73. Cut $-Schs bar sch prayer N
74. Raise taxes; Cut Medicare Y
75. Alien residncy-prior 1982 N
76. Alien residncy-prior 1980 N
77. Pen emp-hire illgl aliens Y
78. Lmt Persh II/cruse-Europe Y
79. Delete 34 B-1 bombers Y
80. Bar purch of Pershing II Y
81. Bar purchase of Sgt York Y
82. Delete $ for Trident II Y
83. Allow 15 MX missiles N
84. Bar MX procurement-1985 Y
85. Equal Access Act N
86. Aid to El Salvador N
87. Bar Nicarag water mining Y
88. Physician/Medicare freeze N
89. Increase "sin" taxes Y
90. End SBA direct loans N
91. Sell Conrail N
92. Equal Rights Amendment Y
93. Marines in Lebanon N
94. Eminent domain-Coal comps N
95. Prohibit EPA sanctions N
96. SS age increase/Reforms Y
97. Auto domestic content req Y
98. Delete jobs program fundg N
99. Highway-Gas tax bill N
100. Raise Medicare;Cut defnse Y
101. Emergency housing aid Y
102. Across-the-board tax cuts N
103. Gramm-Latta II targets N
104. Delete B-1 bomber funds Y
105. Dsapprov Saudi AWACS sale Y
106. Disapprove oil import fee Y
107. Rail Deregulation N
108. Dsapp India nuc fuel sale Y
109. Mil draft registration N
110. Chrysler Loan Guarantees Y
111. Prohibit school busing N
112. Nuclear plant moratorium Y
113. Oil price controls Y
114. Tuition Tax Credits N
115. Est Consumer Protect Agcy Y
116. Eliminate B-1 bomber fnds Y
117. Subminimum wage for youth N
118. Delete crude oil tax N
119. Natural gas deregulation N

Presidential Support Score: 1986 - 16% 1985 - 21%

DONNELLY, BRIAN J. -- Massachusetts 11th District [Democrat]. Counties of Norfolk (pt.), Plymouth (pt.) and Suffolk (pt.). Prior Terms: House: 1979-86. Born: March 2, 1946; Dorchester, Mass. Education: Boston University (B.S.). Occupation: Director of Youth Activities, YMCA (1968-70); coach (1969-72); Massachusetts representative (1973-78).

1. Immigration Reform Y
2. Open fld-search warrants N
3. Civil pnty-hire ill alien N
4. So Afr sanc-veto override Y
5. Tax Overhaul Y
6. South Africa sanctions Y
7. Death penalty-drug bill Y
8. Evidence-warrantless srch N
9. Life term-second drug off Y
10. Military use in drug war Y
11. Troop reduction in Europe Y
12. Prohibit chemical weapons Y
13. Bar ASAT testing N
14. Abide SALT II weapons ban Y

DONNELLY, BRIAN J. (Cont.)

15. Follow SALT II-Soviets do Y
16. Reduce SDI funding N
17. Increase SDI funding N
18. Purchase Trident sub Y
19. Delete 12 MX;Add conv wpn Y
20. Raise speed limit N
21. Textile Import Quotas(*) Y
22. Req Pentagon buy US goods Y
23. AIDS ins anti-dscriminatn Y
24. Nicaraguan refugee aid Y
25. Nicaraguan contra aid N
26. US abide by SALT II N
27. Prohibit Saudi arms sale +
28. Military Retiremnt Reform Y
29. Nicaraguan refugee aid Y
30. Ease '68 Gun Control Act N
31. Bar intrstat handgun tran Y
32. Keep '68 Gun Control Act Y
33. Nicaraguan contra aid N
34. Bar emp polygraph testing Y
35. Tax Overhaul consideratn Y
36. Bar armor-piercing ammo Y
37. Tax Overhaul consideratn Y
38. Make comp emissions known Y
39. Allow toxic victims suits Y
40. Strike Superfund "VAT" Y
41. Notify emp-plant closing Y
42. Bar emp consult-plant clo N
43. Medicare cuts;Tax incres' Y
44. Delete 12 MX missiles Y
45. Spending cuts;Tax incres' Y
46. Textile Import Quotas Y
47. Cut some school lunch fds N
48. Clean Water Act Amendmnts N
49. Youth work projects Y
50. Assist military in Angola N
51. Allow US troops-Nicaragua N
52. Pentagon polygraph exams Y
53. Bar ASAT testing Y
54. Suspend def pmt for abuse Y
55. Bar Pentagon-contr emplmt Y
56. Increase SDI funding N
57. Reduce SDI funding N
58. Produce chemical weapons N
59. Bar CIA fndg in Nicaragua Y
60. South Africa sanctions Y
61. Cut SS COLAs; Raise taxes N
62. Let US invest-So Africa N
63. Approve 21 MX for 1985 N
64. Emergency Farm Credit Y
65. Awards to whistle blowers Y
66. African disaster relief Y
67. Ban bank loans to So Afr Y
68. Bar coun duty-free trtmt Y
69. Steel import limits Y
70. Soc Sec COLAs=inflation Y
71. Bar haz waste vctms suits N
72. Prohibit aid to Nicaragua Y
73. Cut $-Schs bar sch prayer N
74. Raise taxes; Cut Medicare Y
75. Alien residncy-prior 1982 Y
76. Alien residncy-prior 1980 N
77. Pen emp-hire illgl aliens Y
78. Lmt Persh II/cruse-Europe N
79. Delete 34 B-1 bombers Y
80. Bar purch of Pershing II N
81. Bar purchase of Sgt York Y
82. Delete $ for Trident II N
83. Allow 15 MX missiles N
84. Bar MX procurement-1985 Y
85. Equal Access Act N
86. Aid to El Salvador N
87. Bar Nicarag water mining Y
88. Physician/Medicare freeze N
89. Increase "sin" taxes Y
90. End SBA direct loans N
91. Sell Conrail N
92. Equal Rights Amendment Y
93. Marines in Lebanon N
94. Eminent domain-Coal comps Y
95. Prohibit EPA sanctions N
96. SS age increase/Reforms N
97. Auto domestic content req N
98. Delete jobs program fundg N
99. Highway-Gas tax bill Y
100. Raise Medicare;Cut defnse N
101. Emergency housing aid N
102. Across-the-board tax cuts N
103. Gramm-Latta II targets N
104. Delete B-1 bomber funds #
105. Dsapprov Saudi AWACS sale Y
106. Disapprove oil import fee Y
107. Rail Deregulation N
108. Dsapp India nuc fuel sale Y
109. Mil draft registration N
110. Chrysler Loan Guarantees Y
111. Prohibit school busing Y
112. Nuclear plant moratorium N
113. Oil price controls Y

Presidential Support Score: 1986 - 17% 1985 - 26%

M I C H I G A N

CONYERS, JOHN Jr. -- Michigan 1st District [Democrat]. County of Wayne (pt.). Prior Terms: House: 1965-86. Born: May 16, 1929; Detroit, Mich. Education: Wayne State University (B.A.,

CONYERS, JOHN Jr. (Cont.)
LL.B.). Military Service: U.S. Army. Occupation: Congressional legislative assistant (1958-61).

1. Immigration Reform X
2. Open fld-search warrants ?
3. Civil pnty-hire ill alien ?
4. So Afr sanc-veto override Y
5. Tax Overhaul N
6. South Africa sanctions Y
7. Death penalty-drug bill X
8. Evidence-warrantless srch N
9. Life term-second drug off N
10. Military use in drug war N
11. Troop reduction in Europe Y
12. Prohibit chemical weapons Y
13. Bar ASAT testing Y
14. Abide SALT II weapons ban Y
15. Follow SALT II-Soviets do N
16. Reduce SDI funding Y
17. Increase SDI funding N
18. Purchase Trident sub Y
19. Delete 12 MX;Add conv wpn Y
20. Raise speed limit N
21. Textile Import Quotas(*) Y
22. Req Pentagon buy US goods ?
23. AIDS ins anti-dscriminatn Y
24. Nicaraguan refugee aid Y
25. Nicaraguan contra aid N
26. US abide by SALT II N
27. Prohibit Saudi arms sale N
28. Military Retiremnt Reform Y
29. Nicaraguan refugee aid Y
30. Ease '68 Gun Control Act N
31. Bar intrstat handgun tran Y
32. Keep '68 Gun Control Act Y
33. Nicaraguan contra aid N
34. Bar emp polygraph testing Y
35. Tax Overhaul consideratn N
36. Bar armor-piercing ammo Y
37. Tax Overhaul consideratn N
38. Make comp emissions known Y
39. Allow toxic victims suits Y
40. Strike Superfund "VAT" Y
41. Notify emp-plant closing ?
42. Bar emp consult-plant clo ?
43. Medicare cuts;Tax incres' Y
44. Delete 12 MX missiles Y
45. Spending cuts;Tax incres' ?
46. Textile Import Quotas Y
47. Cut some school lunch fds N
48. Clean Water Act Amendmnts N
49. Youth work projects Y
50. Assist military in Angola N
51. Allow US troops-Nicaragua N
52. Pentagon polygraph exams ?
53. Bar ASAT testing N
54. Suspend def pmt for abuse ?
55. Bar Pentagon-contr emplmt Y
56. Increase SDI funding N
57. Reduce SDI funding Y
58. Produce chemical weapons N
59. Bar CIA fndg in Nicaragua Y
60. South Africa sanctions Y
61. Cut SS COLAs; Raise taxes N
62. Let US invest-So Africa N
63. Approve 21 MX for 1985 N
64. Emergency Farm Credit Y
65. Awards to whistle blowers Y
66. African disaster relief Y
67. Ban bank loans to So Afr P
68. Bar coun duty-free trtmt Y
69. Steel import limits Y
70. Soc Sec COLAs=inflation Y
71. Bar haz waste vctms suits N
72. Prohibit aid to Nicaragua Y
73. Cut $-Schs bar sch prayer N
74. Raise taxes; Cut Medicare N
75. Alien residncy-prior 1982 N
76. Alien residncy-prior 1980 N
77. Pen emp-hire illgl aliens Y
78. Lmt Persh II/cruse-Europe Y
79. Delete 34 B-1 bombers Y
80. Bar purch of Pershing II Y
81. Bar purchase of Sgt York Y
82. Delete $ for Trident II Y
83. Allow 15 MX missiles N
84. Bar MX procurement-1985 Y
85. Equal Access Act N
86. Aid to El Salvador N
87. Bar Nicarag water mining Y
88. Physician/Medicare freeze N
89. Increase "sin" taxes Y
90. End SBA direct loans N
91. Sell Conrail N
92. Equal Rights Amendment Y
93. Marines in Lebanon N
94. Eminent domain-Coal comps Y
95. Prohibit EPA sanctions ?
96. SS age increase/Reforms N
97. Auto domestic content req Y
98. Delete jobs program fundg N
99. Highway-Gas tax bill N
100. Raise Medicare;Cut defnse Y
101. Emergency housing aid Y
102. Across-the-board tax cuts N
103. Gramm-Latta II targets N
104. Delete B-1 bomber funds Y
105. Dsapprov Saudi AWACS sale Y
106. Disapprove oil import fee Y
107. Rail Deregulation Y
108. Dsapp India nuc fuel sale Y
109. Mil draft registration N
110. Chrysler Loan Guarantees Y
111. Prohibit school busing N
112. Nuclear plant moratorium Y

CONYERS, JOHN Jr. (Cont.)

113. Oil price controls Y
114. Tuition Tax Credits Y
115. Est Consumer Protect Agcy Y
116. Eliminate B-1 bomber fnds Y
117. Subminimum wage for youth N
118. Delete crude oil tax N
119. Natural gas deregulation N

Presidential Support Score: 1986 - 11% 1985 - 13%

PURSELL, CARL D. -- Michigan 2nd District [Republican]. Counties of Branch (pt.), Hillsdale, Jackson (pt.), Lenawee (pt.), Washtenaw (pt.) and Wayne (pt.). Prior Terms: House: 1977-86. Born: December 19, 1932; Imlay City, Mich. Education: Eastern Michigan University (B.A., M.A.). Military Service: U.S. Army, 1957-59. Occupation: Wayne County commissioner (1969-70); Michigan senator (1971-76).

1. Immigration Reform N
2. Open fld-search warrants N
3. Civil pnty-hire ill alien N
4. So Afr sanc-veto override Y
5. Tax Overhaul Y
6. South Africa sanctions Y
7. Death penalty-drug bill Y
8. Evidence-warrantless srch Y
9. Life term-second drug off Y
10. Military use in drug war N
11. Troop reduction in Europe N
12. Prohibit chemical weapons Y
13. Bar ASAT testing Y
14. Abide SALT II weapons ban Y
15. Follow SALT II-Soviets do Y
16. Reduce SDI funding N
17. Increase SDI funding N
18. Purchase Trident sub N
19. Delete 12 MX;Add conv wpn N
20. Raise speed limit N
21. Textile Import Quotas(*) N
22. Req Pentagon buy US goods Y
23. AIDS ins anti-dscriminatn N
24. Nicaraguan refugee aid N
25. Nicaraguan contra aid Y
26. US abide by SALT II Y
27. Prohibit Saudi arms sale Y
28. Military Retiremnt Reform Y
29. Nicaraguan refugee aid Y
30. Ease '68 Gun Control Act N
31. Bar intrstat handgun tran Y
32. Keep '68 Gun Control Act Y
33. Nicaraguan contra aid Y
34. Bar emp polygraph testing N
35. Tax Overhaul consideratn Y
36. Bar armor-piercing ammo Y
37. Tax Overhaul consideratn N
38. Make comp emissions known N
39. Allow toxic victims suits N
40. Strike Superfund "VAT" Y
41. Notify emp-plant closing N
42. Bar emp consult-plant clo Y
43. Medicare cuts;Tax incres' N
44. Delete 12 MX missiles N
45. Spending cuts;Tax incres' N
46. Textile Import Quotas N
47. Cut some school lunch fds N
48. Clean Water Act Amendmnts N
49. Youth work projects X
50. Assist military in Angola Y
51. Allow US troops-Nicaragua N
52. Pentagon polygraph exams Y
53. Bar ASAT testing Y
54. Suspend def pmt for abuse Y
55. Bar Pentagon-contr emplmt Y
56. Increase SDI funding N
57. Reduce SDI funding N
58. Produce chemical weapons Y
59. Bar CIA fndg in Nicaragua N
60. South Africa sanctions ?
61. Cut SS COLAs; Raise taxes N
62. Let US invest-So Africa N
63. Approve 21 MX for 1985 Y
64. Emergency Farm Credit Y
65. Awards to whistle blowers Y
66. African disaster relief Y
67. Ban bank loans to So Afr ?
68. Bar coun duty-free trtmt ?
69. Steel import limits Y
70. Soc Sec COLAs=inflation Y
71. Bar haz waste vctms suits ?
72. Prohibit aid to Nicaragua Y
73. Cut $-Schs bar sch prayer N
74. Raise taxes; Cut Medicare N
75. Alien residncy-prior 1982 N
76. Alien residncy-prior 1980 Y
77. Pen emp-hire illgl aliens N
78. Lmt Persh II/cruse-Europe N
79. Delete 34 B-1 bombers Y
80. Bar purch of Pershing II N
81. Bar purchase of Sgt York N
82. Delete $ for Trident II N
83. Allow 15 MX missiles Y
84. Bar MX procurement-1985 N
85. Equal Access Act Y
86. Aid to El Salvador Y
87. Bar Nicarag water mining Y
88. Physician/Medicare freeze Y

PURSELL, CARL D. (Cont.)

89. Increase "sin" taxes N
90. End SBA direct loans N
91. Sell Conrail Y
92. Equal Rights Amendment Y
93. Marines in Lebanon Y
94. Eminent domain-Coal comps Y
95. Prohibit EPA sanctions ?
96. SS age increase/Reforms Y
97. Auto domestic content req ?
98. Delete jobs program fundg Y
99. Highway-Gas tax bill N
100. Raise Medicare;Cut defnse Y
101. Emergency housing aid Y
102. Across-the-board tax cuts Y
103. Gramm-Latta II targets Y
104. Delete B-1 bomber funds Y
105. Dsapprov Saudi AWACS sale Y
106. Disapprove oil import fee Y
107. Rail Deregulation Y
108. Dsapp India nuc fuel sale Y
109. Mil draft registration N
110. Chrysler Loan Guarantees Y
111. Prohibit school busing Y
112. Nuclear plant moratorium Y
113. Oil price controls N
114. Tuition Tax Credits N
115. Est Consumer Protect Agcy Y
116. Eliminate B-1 bomber fnds Y
117. Subminimum wage for youth Y
118. Delete crude oil tax Y
119. Natural gas deregulation Y

Presidential Support Score: 1986 - 51% 1985 - 56%

WOLPE, HOWARD -- Michigan 3rd District [Democrat]. Counties of Barry (pt.), Calhoun, Eaton, Ingham (pt.) and Kalamazoo (pt.). Prior Terms: House: 1979-86. Born: November 2, 1939; Los Angeles, Calif. Education: Reed College (B.A.); Massachusetts Institute of Technology (Ph.D.). Occupation: Consultant, Peace Corps (1966-67); consultant, Foreign Service Institute (1967-72); professor (1967-72); city commissioner (1969-72); Michigan representative (1972-76); senator's regional representative and state liaison (1976-78).

1. Immigration Reform Y
2. Open fld-search warrants Y
3. Civil pnty-hire ill alien Y
4. So Afr sanc-veto override Y
5. Tax Overhaul Y
6. South Africa sanctions Y
7. Death penalty-drug bill N
8. Evidence-warrantless srch N
9. Life term-second drug off Y
10. Military use in drug war N
11. Troop reduction in Europe N
12. Prohibit chemical weapons Y
13. Bar ASAT testing Y
14. Abide SALT II weapons ban Y
15. Follow SALT II-Soviets do N
16. Reduce SDI funding Y
17. Increase SDI funding N
18. Purchase Trident sub Y
19. Delete 12 MX;Add conv wpn Y
20. Raise speed limit N
21. Textile Import Quotas(*) Y
22. Req Pentagon buy US goods Y
23. AIDS ins anti-dscriminatn Y
24. Nicaraguan refugee aid Y
25. Nicaraguan contra aid N
26. US abide by SALT II N
27. Prohibit Saudi arms sale Y
28. Military Retiremnt Reform Y
29. Nicaraguan refugee aid Y
30. Ease '68 Gun Control Act ?
31. Bar intrstat handgun tran Y
32. Keep '68 Gun Control Act Y
33. Nicaraguan contra aid N
34. Bar emp polygraph testing Y
35. Tax Overhaul consideratn Y
36. Bar armor-piercing ammo Y
37. Tax Overhaul consideratn Y
38. Make comp emissions known Y
39. Allow toxic victims suits Y
40. Strike Superfund "VAT" Y
41. Notify emp-plant closing Y
42. Bar emp consult-plant clo N
43. Medicare cuts;Tax incres' Y
44. Delete 12 MX missiles Y
45. Spending cuts;Tax incres' Y
46. Textile Import Quotas Y
47. Cut some school lunch fds N
48. Clean Water Act Amendmnts N
49. Youth work projects Y
50. Assist military in Angola N
51. Allow US troops-Nicaragua N
52. Pentagon polygraph exams N
53. Bar ASAT testing Y
54. Suspend def pmt for abuse Y
55. Bar Pentagon-contr emplmt Y
56. Increase SDI funding N
57. Reduce SDI funding Y
58. Produce chemical weapons N
59. Bar CIA fndg in Nicaragua Y
60. South Africa sanctions Y

WOLPE, HOWARD (Cont.)

61. Cut SS COLAs; Raise taxes N
62. Let US invest-So Africa N
63. Approve 21 MX for 1985 N
64. Emergency Farm Credit Y
65. Awards to whistle blowers Y
66. African disaster relief Y
67. Ban bank loans to So Afr Y
68. Bar coun duty-free trtmt Y
69. Steel import limits Y
70. Soc Sec COLAs=inflation Y
71. Bar haz waste vctms suits N
72. Prohibit aid to Nicaragua Y
73. Cut $-Schs bar sch prayer N
74. Raise taxes; Cut Medicare Y
75. Alien residncy-prior 1982 N
76. Alien residncy-prior 1980 N
77. Pen emp-hire illgl aliens Y
78. Lmt Persh II/cruse-Europe Y
79. Delete 34 B-1 bombers Y
80. Bar purch of Pershing II Y
81. Bar purchase of Sgt York Y
82. Delete $ for Trident II Y
83. Allow 15 MX missiles N
84. Bar MX procurement-1985 Y
85. Equal Access Act N
86. Aid to El Salvador N
87. Bar Nicarag water mining Y
88. Physician/Medicare freeze N
89. Increase "sin" taxes Y
90. End SBA direct loans N
91. Sell Conrail N
92. Equal Rights Amendment Y
93. Marines in Lebanon N
94. Eminent domain-Coal comps ?
95. Prohibit EPA sanctions Y
96. SS age increase/Reforms N
97. Auto domestic content req Y
98. Delete jobs program fundg N
99. Highway-Gas tax bill Y
100. Raise Medicare;Cut defnse Y
101. Emergency housing aid Y
102. Across-the-board tax cuts N
103. Gramm-Latta II targets N
104. Delete B-1 bomber funds Y
105. Dsapprov Saudi AWACS sale Y
106. Disapprove oil import fee Y
107. Rail Deregulation N
108. Dsapp India nuc fuel sale Y
109. Mil draft registration N
110. Chrysler Loan Guarantees Y
111. Prohibit school busing N
112. Nuclear plant moratorium Y
113. Oil price controls Y

Presidential Support Score: 1986 - 16% 1985 - 21%

SILJANDER, MARK D. -- Michigan 4th District [Republican]. Counties of Allegan (pt.), Berrien, Branch (pt.), Cass, Kalamazoo (pt.), Ottawa (pt.), St. Joseph and Van Buren. Prior Terms: House: 1981 (Special Election)-1986. Born: June 11, 1951; Chicago, Ill. Education: Michigan University (B.S., M.A.). Occupation: Michigan representative (1976-80); member, Fabius Township Board.

1. Immigration Reform N
2. Open fld-search warrants N
3. Civil pnty-hire ill alien N
4. So Afr sanc-veto override ?
5. Tax Overhaul Y
6. South Africa sanctions N
7. Death penalty-drug bill Y
8. Evidence-warrantless srch Y
9. Life term-second drug off Y
10. Military use in drug war Y
11. Troop reduction in Europe N
12. Prohibit chemical weapons N
13. Bar ASAT testing N
14. Abide SALT II weapons ban N
15. Follorw SALT II-Soviets o Y
16. Reduce SDI funding N
17. Increase SDI funding Y
18. Purchase Trident sub N
19. Delete 12 MX;Add conv wpn N
20. Raise speed limit Y
21. Textile Import Quotas(*) ?
22. Req Pentagon buy US goods ?
23. AIDS ins anti-dscriminatn N
24. Nicaraguan refugee aid N
25. Nicaraguan contra aid Y
26. US abide by SALT II Y
27. Prohibit Saudi arms sale Y
28. Military Retiremnt Reform Y
29. Nicaraguan refugee aid Y
30. Ease '68 Gun Control Act Y
31. Bar intrstat handgun tran N
32. Keep '68 Gun Control Act N
33. Nicaraguan contra aid Y
34. Bar emp polygraph testing N
35. Tax Overhaul consideratn N
36. Bar armor-piercing ammo Y
37. Tax Overhaul consideratn N
38. Make comp emissions known N
39. Allow toxic victims suits N
40. Strike Superfund "VAT" N
41. Notify emp-plant closing N
42. Bar emp consult-plant clo Y

SILJANDER, MARK D. (Cont.)

43. Medicare cuts;Tax incres' N
44. Delete 12 MX missiles N
45. Spending cuts;Tax incres' N
46. Textile Import Quotas N
47. Cut some school lunch fds Y
48. Clean Water Act Amendmnts Y
49. Youth work projects X
50. Assist military in Angola Y
51. Allow US troops-Nicaragua Y
52. Pentagon polygraph exams ?
53. Bar ASAT testing N
54. Suspend def pmt for abuse N
55. Bar Pentagon-contr emplmt Y
56. Increase SDI funding Y
57. Reduce SDI funding N
58. Produce chemical weapons Y
59. Bar CIA fndg in Nicaragua N
60. South Africa sanctions N
61. Cut SS COLAs; Raise taxes N
62. Let US invest-So Africa Y
63. Approve 21 MX for 1985 Y
64. Emergency Farm Credit Y
65. Awards to whistle blowers Y
66. African disaster relief Y
67. Ban bank loans to So Afr ?
68. Bar coun duty-free trtmt N
69. Steel import limits N
70. Soc Sec COLAs=inflation Y
71. Bar haz waste vctms suits Y
72. Prohibit aid to Nicaragua N
73. Cut $-Schs bar sch prayer Y
74. Raise taxes; Cut Medicare N
75. Alien residncy-prior 1982 Y
76. Alien residncy-prior 1980 N
77. Pen emp-hire illgl aliens N
78. Lmt Persh II/cruse-Europe N
79. Delete 34 B-1 bombers N
80. Bar purch of Pershing II N
81. Bar purchase of Sgt York N
82. Delete $ for Trident II N
83. Allow 15 MX missiles Y
84. Bar MX procurement-1985 N
85. Equal Access Act Y
86. Aid to El Salvador Y
87. Bar Nicarag water mining N
88. Physician/Medicare freeze Y
89. Increase "sin" taxes N
90. End SBA direct loans Y
91. Sell Conrail ?
92. Equal Rights Amendment N
93. Marines in Lebanon Y
94. Eminent domain-Coal comps N
95. Prohibit EPA sanctions ?
96. SS age increase/Reforms Y
97. Auto domestic content req Y
98. Delete jobs program fundg Y
99. Highway-Gas tax bill N
100. Raise Medicare;Cut defnse N
101. Emergency housing aid Y
102. Across-the-board tax cuts Y
103. Gramm-Latta II targets Y
104. Delete B-1 bomber funds N
105. Dsapprov Saudi AWACS sale Y

Presidential Support Score: 1986 - 73% 1985 - 73%

HENRY, PAUL B. -- Michigan 5th District [Republican]. Counties of Allegan (pt.), Barry (pt.), Ionia (pt.), Kent (pt.) and Newaygo (pt.). Prior Terms: 1985-86. Education: Wheaton College; Duke University (M.A., Ph.D.). Occupation: Educator; Michigan representative; Michigan senator; professor, Calvin College and Duke University; congressional assistant.

1. Immigration Reform Y
2. Open fld-search warrants N
3. Civil pnty-hire ill alien N
4. So Afr sanc-veto override Y
5. Tax Overhaul Y
6. South Africa sanctions Y
7. Death penalty-drug bill Y
8. Evidence-warrantless srch Y
9. Life term-second drug off Y
10. Military use in drug war Y
11. Troop reduction in Europe N
12. Prohibit chemical weapons Y
13. Bar ASAT testing N
14. Abide SALT II weapons ban Y
15. Follow SALT II-Soviets do N
16. Reduce SDI funding N
17. Increase SDI funding N
18. Purchase Trident sub N
19. Delete 12 MX;Add conv wpn Y
20. Raise speed limit Y
21. Textile Import Quotas(*) Y
22. Req Pentagon buy US goods Y
23. AIDS ins anti-dscriminatn N
24. Nicaraguan refugee aid N
25. Nicaraguan contra aid Y
26. US abide by SALT II N
27. Prohibit Saudi arms sale Y
28. Military Retiremnt Reform Y
29. Nicaraguan refugee aid Y
30. Ease '68 Gun Control Act N
31. Bar intrstat handgun tran N
32. Keep '68 Gun Control Act Y

HENRY, PAUL B. (Cont.)

33. Nicaraguan contra aid Y
34. Bar emp polygraph testing N
35. Tax Overhaul consideratn Y
36. Bar armor-piercing ammo Y
37. Tax Overhaul consideratn N
38. Make comp emissions known N
39. Allow toxic victims suits N
40. Strike Superfund "VAT" Y
41. Notify emp-plant closing N
42. Bar emp consult-plant clo Y
43. Medicare cuts;Tax incres' N
44. Delete 12 MX missiles Y
45. Spending cuts;Tax incres' N
46. Textile Import Quotas Y
47. Cut some school lunch fds N
48. Clean Water Act Amendmnts N
49. Youth work projects N
50. Assist military in Angola Y
51. Allow US troops-Nicaragua N
52. Pentagon polygraph exams Y
53. Bar ASAT testing N
54. Suspend def pmt for abuse Y
55. Bar Pentagon-contr emplmt Y
56. Increase SDI funding N
57. Reduce SDI funding N
58. Produce chemical weapons N
59. Bar CIA fndg in Nicaragua N
60. South Africa sanctions N
61. Cut SS COLAs; Raise taxes N
62. Let US invest-So Africa Y
63. Approve 21 MX for 1985 N
64. Emergency Farm Credit Y
65. Awards to whistle blowers Y
66. African disaster relief Y

Presidential Support Score: 1986 - 43% 1985 - 60%

CARR, BOB -- Michigan 6th District [Democrat]. Counties of Clinton (pt.), Genesee (pt.), Ingham (pt.), Jackson (pt.), Livingston (pt.), Oakland (pt.) and Shiawassee (pt.). Prior Terms: House: 1975-80; 1983-86. Born: March 27, 1944. Education: University of Wisconsin Law School. Occupation: Senate staff member (1968-69); assistant attorney general, Michigan (1970-72); counsel, Joint Committee on Legal Education (1971-72).

1. Immigration Reform N
2. Open fld-search warrants Y
3. Civil pnty-hire ill alien N
4. So Afr sanc-veto override Y
5. Tax Overhaul N
6. South Africa sanctions Y
7. Death penalty-drug bill Y
8. Evidence-warrantless srch Y
9. Life term-second drug off Y
10. Military use in drug war Y
11. Troop reduction in Europe N
12. Prohibit chemical weapons Y
13. Bar ASAT testing Y
14. Abide SALT II weapons ban Y
15. Follow SALT II-Soviets do N
16. Reduce SDI funding Y
17. Increase SDI funding N
18. Purchase Trident sub N
19. Delete 12 MX;Add conv wpn Y
20. Raise speed limit Y
21. Textile Import Quotas(*) Y
22. Req Pentagon buy US goods Y
23. AIDS ins anti-dscriminatn Y
24. Nicaraguan refugee aid Y
25. Nicaraguan contra aid N
26. US abide by SALT II N
27. Prohibit Saudi arms sale Y
28. Military Retiremnt Reform Y
29. Nicaraguan refugee aid Y
30. Ease '68 Gun Control Act Y
31. Bar intrstat handgun tran N
32. Keep '68 Gun Control Act N
33. Nicaraguan contra aid N
34. Bar emp polygraph testing Y
35. Tax Overhaul consideratn N
36. Bar armor-piercing ammo Y
37. Tax Overhaul consideratn N
38. Make comp emissions known N
39. Allow toxic victims suits N
40. Strike Superfund "VAT" Y
41. Notify emp-plant closing Y
42. Bar emp consult-plant clo N
43. Medicare cuts;Tax incres' Y
44. Delete 12 MX missiles Y
45. Spending cuts;Tax incres' N
46. Textile Import Quotas Y
47. Cut some school lunch fds N
48. Clean Water Act Amendmnts N
49. Youth work projects Y
50. Assist military in Angola N
51. Allow US troops-Nicaragua N
52. Pentagon polygraph exams Y
53. Bar ASAT testing Y
54. Suspend def pmt for abuse Y
55. Bar Pentagon-contr emplmt Y
56. Increase SDI funding N
57. Reduce SDI funding Y
58. Produce chemical weapons N
59. Bar CIA fndg in Nicaragua Y
60. South Africa sanctions Y
61. Cut SS COLAs; Raise taxes N
62. Let US invest-So Africa ?

CARR, BOB (Cont.)

63. Approve 21 MX for 1985 N
64. Emergency Farm Credit Y
65. Awards to whistle blowers Y
66. African disaster relief Y
67. Ban bank loans to So Afr Y
68. Bar coun duty-free trtmt Y
69. Steel import limits Y
70. Soc Sec COLAs=inflation Y
71. Bar haz waste vctms suits N
72. Prohibit aid to Nicaragua Y
73. Cut $-Schs bar sch prayer Y
74. Raise taxes; Cut Medicare N
75. Alien residncy-prior 1982 Y
76. Alien residncy-prior 1980 N
77. Pen emp-hire illgl aliens Y
78. Lmt Persh II/cruse-Europe N
79. Delete 34 B-1 bombers Y
80. Bar purch of Pershing II Y
81. Bar purchase of Sgt York N
82. Delete $ for Trident II Y
83. Allow 15 MX missiles N
84. Bar MX procurement-1985 Y
85. Equal Access Act Y
86. Aid to El Salvador N
87. Bar Nicarag water mining Y
88. Physician/Medicare freeze N
89. Increase "sin" taxes N
90. End SBA direct loans N
91. Sell Conrail N
92. Equal Rights Amendment Y
93. Marines in Lebanon Y
94. Eminent domain-Coal comps N
95. Prohibit EPA sanctions N
96. SS age increase/Reforms N
106. Disapprove oil import fee Y
107. Rail Deregulation Y
108. Dsapp India nuc fuel sale Y
109. Mil draft registration N
110. Chrysler Loan Guarantees Y
111. Prohibit school busing N
112. Nuclear plant moratorium Y
113. Oil price controls N
114. Tuition Tax Credits N
115. Est Consumer Protect Agcy Y
116. Eliminate B-1 bomber fnds Y
117. Subminimum wage for youth N
118. Delete crude oil tax N
119. Natural gas deregulation N

Was not in office for votes 97-105.
Presidential Support Score: 1986 - 20% 1985 - 29%

KILDEE, DALE E. -- Michigan 7th District [Democrat]. Counties of Genesee (pt.), Lapeer (pt.), Oakland (pt.), Sanilac (pt.) and Shiawassee (pt.). Prior Terms: House: 1977-86. Born: September 16, 1929; Flint, Mich. Education: Sacred Hart Seminary (B.A.); University of Michigan (M.A.). Occupation: Teacher; Michigan representative (1965-74); Michigan senator (1975-77).

1. Immigration Reform Y
2. Open fld-search warrants Y
3. Civil pnty-hire ill alien Y
4. So Afr sanc-veto override Y
5. Tax Overhaul Y
6. South Africa sanctions Y
7. Death penalty-drug bill N
8. Evidence-warrantless srch N
9. Life term-second drug off Y
10. Military use in drug war N
11. Troop reduction in Europe N
12. Prohibit chemical weapons Y
13. Bar ASAT testing Y
14. Abide SALT II weapons ban Y
15. Follow SALT II-Soviets do N
16. Reduce SDI funding Y
17. Increase SDI funding N
18. Purchase Trident sub N
19. Delete 12 MX;Add conv wpn Y
20. Raise speed limit N
21. Textile Import Quotas(*) Y
22. Req Pentagon buy US goods Y
23. AIDS ins anti-dscriminatn Y
24. Nicaraguan refugee aid Y
25. Nicaraguan contra aid N
26. US abide by SALT II N
27. Prohibit Saudi arms sale Y
28. Military Retiremnt Reform Y
29. Nicaraguan refugee aid Y
30. Ease '68 Gun Control Act N
31. Bar intrstat handgun tran Y
32. Keep '68 Gun Control Act Y
33. Nicaraguan contra aid N
34. Bar emp polygraph testing Y
35. Tax Overhaul consideratn N
36. Bar armor-piercing ammo Y
37. Tax Overhaul consideratn N
38. Make comp emissions known Y
39. Allow toxic victims suits Y
40. Strike Superfund "VAT" Y
41. Notify emp-plant closing Y
42. Bar emp consult-plant clo N
43. Medicare cuts;Tax incres' Y
44. Delete 12 MX missiles Y
45. Spending cuts;Tax incres' Y
46. Textile Import Quotas #
47. Cut some school lunch fds N
48. Clean Water Act Amendmnts N
49. Youth work projects Y
50. Assist military in Angola N

KILDEE, DALE E. (Cont.)

51. Allow US troops-Nicaragua N
52. Pentagon polygraph exams N
53. Bar ASAT testing Y
54. Suspend def pmt for abuse Y
55. Bar Pentagon-contr emplmt Y
56. Increase SDI funding N
57. Reduce SDI funding Y
58. Produce chemical weapons N
59. Bar CIA fndg in Nicaragua Y
60. South Africa sanctions Y
61. Cut SS COLAs; Raise taxes N
62. Let US invest-So Africa N
63. Approve 21 MX for 1985 N
64. Emergency Farm Credit Y
65. Awards to whistle blowers Y
66. African disaster relief Y
67. Ban bank loans to So Afr Y
68. Bar coun duty-free trtmt Y
69. Steel import limits Y
70. Soc Sec COLAs=inflation Y
71. Bar haz waste vctms suits N
72. Prohibit aid to Nicaragua Y
73. Cut $-Schs bar sch prayer N
74. Raise taxes; Cut Medicare N
75. Alien residncy-prior 1982 N
76. Alien residncy-prior 1980 N
77. Pen emp-hire illgl aliens Y
78. Lmt Persh II/cruse-Europe Y
79. Delete 34 B-1 bombers Y
80. Bar purch of Pershing II Y
81. Bar purchase of Sgt York Y
82. Delete $ for Trident II Y
83. Allow 15 MX missiles N
84. Bar MX procurement-1985 Y
85. Equal Access Act N
86. Aid to El Salvador N
87. Bar Nicarag water mining Y
88. Physician/Medicare freeze N
89. Increase "sin" taxes Y
90. End SBA direct loans N
91. Sell Conrail N
92. Equal Rights Amendment Y
93. Marines in Lebanon N
94. Eminent domain-Coal comps N
95. Prohibit EPA sanctions N
96. SS age increase/Reforms N
97. Auto domestic content req Y
98. Delete jobs program fundg N
99. Highway-Gas tax bill Y
100. Raise Medicare;Cut defnse Y
101. Emergency housing aid Y
102. Across-the-board tax cuts N
103. Gramm-Latta II targets N
104. Delete B-1 bomber funds Y
105. Dsapprov Saudi AWACS sale Y
106. Disapprove oil import fee Y
107. Rail Deregulation Y
108. Dsapp India nuc fuel sale Y
109. Mil draft registration N
110. Chrysler Loan Guarantees Y
111. Prohibit school busing N
112. Nuclear plant moratorium Y
113. Oil price controls Y
114. Tuition Tax Credits Y
115. Est Consumer Protect Agcy Y
116. Eliminate B-1 bomber fnds Y
117. Subminimum wage for youth N
118. Delete crude oil tax N
119. Natural gas deregulation N

Presidential Support Score: 1986 - 14% 1985 - 18%

TRAXLER, BOB -- Michigan 8th District [Democrat]. Counties of Arenac, Bay. Genesee (pt.), Huron, Lapeer (pt.), Midland (pt.), Saginaw (pt.), St. Clair (pt.), Sanilac (pt.) and Tuscola. Prior Terms: House: 1974 (Special Election)-1986. Born: July 21, 1931; Kawakawlin, Mich. Education: Michigan State University (B.A.); Detroit College of Law (LL.B.). Occupation: Assistant prosecutor (1960-62); Michigan representative (1962-74).

1. Immigration Reform ?
2. Open fld-search warrants ?
3. Civil pnty-hire ill alien ?
4. So Afr sanc-veto override Y
5. Tax Overhaul Y
6. South Africa sanctions Y
7. Death penalty-drug bill N
8. Evidence-warrantless srch N
9. Life term-second drug off Y
10. Military use in drug war N
11. Troop reduction in Europe N
12. Prohibit chemical weapons Y
13. Bar ASAT testing Y
14. Abide SALT II weapons ban Y
15. Follow SALT II-Soviets do N
16. Reduce SDI funding Y
17. Increase SDI funding N
18. Purchase Trident sub Y
19. Delete 12 MX;Add conv wpn Y
20. Raise speed limit Y
21. Textile Import Quotas(*) Y
22. Req Pentagon buy US goods Y
23. AIDS ins anti-dscriminatn Y
24. Nicaraguan refugee aid Y

TRAXLER, BOB (Cont.)

25. Nicaraguan contra aid N
26. US abide by SALT II N
27. Prohibit Saudi arms sale Y
28. Military Retiremnt Reform Y
29. Nicaraguan refugee aid Y
30. Ease '68 Gun Control Act Y
31. Bar intrstat handgun tran N
32. Keep '68 Gun Control Act N
33. Nicaraguan contra aid N
34. Bar emp polygraph testing Y
35. Tax Overhaul consideratn Y
36. Bar armor-piercing ammo Y
37. Tax Overhaul consideratn Y
38. Make comp emissions known Y
39. Allow toxic victims suits N
40. Strike Superfund "VAT" Y
41. Notify emp-plant closing Y
42. Bar emp consult-plant clo N
43. Medicare cuts;Tax incres' Y
44. Delete 12 MX missiles Y
45. Spending cuts;Tax incres' N
46. Textile Import Quotas Y
47. Cut some school lunch fds N
48. Clean Water Act Amendmnts N
49. Youth work projects Y
50. Assist military in Angola N
51. Allow US troops-Nicaragua N
52. Pentagon polygraph exams Y
53. Bar ASAT testing Y
54. Suspend def pmt for abuse Y
55. Bar Pentagon-contr emplmt Y
56. Increase SDI funding N
57. Reduce SDI funding Y
58. Produce chemical weapons N
59. Bar CIA fndg in Nicaragua Y
60. South Africa sanctions Y
61. Cut SS COLAs; Raise taxes N
62. Let US invest-So Africa N
63. Approve 21 MX for 1985 N
64. Emergency Farm Credit Y
65. Awards to whistle blowers Y
66. African disaster relief Y
67. Ban bank loans to So Afr Y
68. Bar coun duty-free trtmt Y
69. Steel import limits Y
70. Soc Sec COLAs=inflation Y
71. Bar haz waste vctms suits N
72. Prohibit aid to Nicaragua ?
73. Cut $-Schs bar sch prayer N
74. Raise taxes; Cut Medicare N
75. Alien residncy-prior 1982 N
76. Alien residncy-prior 1980 N
77. Pen emp-hire illgl aliens N
78. Lmt Persh II/cruse-Europe Y
79. Delete 34 B-1 bombers Y
80. Bar purch of Pershing II N
81. Bar purchase of Sgt York ?
82. Delete $ for Trident II N
83. Allow 15 MX missiles N
84. Bar MX procurement-1985 Y
85. Equal Access Act Y
86. Aid to El Salvador N
87. Bar Nicarag water mining Y
88. Physician/Medicare freeze N
89. Increase "sin" taxes N
90. End SBA direct loans N
91. Sell Conrail N
92. Equal Rights Amendment Y
93. Marines in Lebanon N
94. Eminent domain-Coal comps N
95. Prohibit EPA sanctions ?
96. SS age increase/Reforms N
97. Auto domestic content req Y
98. Delete jobs program fundg N
99. Highway-Gas tax bill Y
100. Raise Medicare;Cut defnse Y
101. Emergency housing aid Y
102. Across-the-board tax cuts N
103. Gramm-Latta II targets N
104. Delete B-1 bomber funds Y
105. Dsapprov Saudi AWACS sale Y
106. Disapprove oil import fee Y
107. Rail Deregulation Y
108. Dsapp India nuc fuel sale Y
109. Mil draft registration N
110. Chrysler Loan Guarantees Y
111. Prohibit school busing Y
112. Nuclear plant moratorium N
113. Oil price controls Y
114. Tuition Tax Credits Y
115. Est Consumer Protect Agcy Y
116. Eliminate B-1 bomber fnds Y
117. Subminimum wage for youth N
118. Delete crude oil tax N
119. Natural gas deregulation N

Presidential Support Score: 1986 - 19% 1985 - 26%

VANDER JAGT, GUY -- Michigan 9th District [Republican]. Counties of Senzie, Grand Traverse (pt.), Ionia (pt.), Kent (pt.), Lake Leelanau, Manistee, Mason, Montcalm, Muskegon, Newaygo (pt.), Oceana and Ottawa (pt.). Prior Terms: House: 1966 (Special Election)-1986. Born: August 26, 1931; Cadillac, Mich. Education: Hope College (B.A.); Yale University (B.D.); Bonn University, Rotary Fellowship (1956); University of Michigan (LL.B.). Occupation: Attorney, Warner, Norcross & Judd (1960-64); Michigan senator (1965-66).

VANDER JAGT, GUY (Cont.)

1. Immigration Reform N
2. Open fld-search warrants Y
3. Civil pnty-hire ill alien Y
4. So Afr sanc-veto override ?
5. Tax Overhaul Y
6. South Africa sanctions N
7. Death penalty-drug bill Y
8. Evidence-warrantless srch Y
9. Life term-second drug off Y
10. Military use in drug war Y
11. Troop reduction in Europe N
12. Prohibit chemical weapons N
13. Bar ASAT testing N
14. Abide SALT II weapons ban N
15. Follow SALT II-Soviets do Y
16. Reduce SDI funding N
17. Increase SDI funding Y
18. Purchase Trident sub ?
19. Delete 12 MX;Add conv wpn ?
20. Raise speed limit Y
21. Textile Import Quotas(*) N
22. Req Pentagon buy US goods Y
23. AIDS ins anti-dscriminatn N
24. Nicaraguan refugee aid N
25. Nicaraguan contra aid Y
26. US abide by SALT II Y
27. Prohibit Saudi arms sale Y
28. Military Retiremnt Reform Y
29. Nicaraguan refugee aid Y
30. Ease '68 Gun Control Act Y
31. Bar intrstat handgun tran N
32. Keep '68 Gun Control Act N
33. Nicaraguan contra aid Y
34. Bar emp polygraph testing N
35. Tax Overhaul consideratn Y
36. Bar armor-piercing ammo Y
37. Tax Overhaul consideratn N
38. Make comp emissions known N
39. Allow toxic victims suits N
40. Strike Superfund "VAT" N
41. Notify emp-plant closing N
42. Bar emp consult-plant clo Y
43. Medicare cuts;Tax incres' N
44. Delete 12 MX missiles N
45. Spending cuts;Tax incres' N
46. Textile Import Quotas N
47. Cut some school lunch fds Y
48. Clean Water Act Amendmnts Y
49. Youth work projects N
50. Assist military in Angola Y
51. Allow US troops-Nicaragua Y
52. Pentagon polygraph exams Y
53. Bar ASAT testing N
54. Suspend def pmt for abuse N
55. Bar Pentagon-contr emplmt Y
56. Increase SDI funding N
57. Reduce SDI funding N
58. Produce chemical weapons Y
59. Bar CIA fndg in Nicaragua N

60. South Africa sanctions N
61. Cut SS COLAs; Raise taxes N
62. Let US invest-So Africa Y
63. Approve 21 MX for 1985 Y
64. Emergency Farm Credit N
65. Awards to whistle blowers Y
66. African disaster relief Y
67. Ban bank loans to So Afr ?
68. Bar coun duty-free trtmt N
69. Steel import limits Y
70. Soc Sec COLAs=inflation Y
71. Bar haz waste vctms suits Y
72. Prohibit aid to Nicaragua N
73. Cut $-Schs bar sch prayer Y
74. Raise taxes; Cut Medicare N
75. Alien residncy-prior 1982 Y
76. Alien residncy-prior 1980 ?
77. Pen emp-hire illgl aliens N
78. Lmt Persh II/cruse-Europe ?
79. Delete 34 B-1 bombers N
80. Bar purch of Pershing II N
81. Bar purchase of Sgt York N
82. Delete $ for Trident II N
83. Allow 15 MX missiles ?
84. Bar MX procurement-1985 N
85. Equal Access Act Y
86. Aid to El Salvador Y
87. Bar Nicarag water mining X
88. Physician/Medicare freeze #
89. Increase "sin" taxes Y
90. End SBA direct loans Y
91. Sell Conrail Y
92. Equal Rights Amendment N
93. Marines in Lebanon Y
94. Eminent domain-Coal comps Y
95. Prohibit EPA sanctions N
96. SS age increase/Reforms Y
97. Auto domestic content req N
98. Delete jobs program fundg Y
99. Highway-Gas tax bill N
100. Raise Medicare;Cut defnse N
101. Emergency housing aid Y
102. Across-the-board tax cuts Y
103. Gramm-Latta II targets Y
104. Delete B-1 bomber funds N
105. Dsapprov Saudi AWACS sale Y
106. Disapprove oil import fee ?
107. Rail Deregulation Y
108. Dsapp India nuc fuel sale Y
109. Mil draft registration N
110. Chrysler Loan Guarantees Y
111. Prohibit school busing Y
112. Nuclear plant moratorium N
113. Oil price controls N
114. Tuition Tax Credits Y
115. Est Consumer Protect Agcy N
116. Eliminate B-1 bomber fnds ?
117. Subminimum wage for youth Y
118. Delete crude oil tax Y

VANDER JAGT, GUY (Cont.)
119. Natural gas deregulation Y

Presidential Support Score: 1986 - 63% 1985 - 65%

SCHUETTE, BILL -- Michigan 10th District [Republican]. Counties of Antrim (pt.), Clare, Clinton (pt.), Crawford (pt.), Gladwin, Grand Traverse (pt.), Gratiot, Iosco (pt.), Isabella, Kalkaska, Mecosta, Midland (pt.), Missaukee, Ogemaw, Osceola, Oscoda (pt.), Rosscommon, Saginaw (pt.), Shiawassee (pt.) and Wexford. Prior Terms: 1985-86. Education: Georgetown University; University of San Francisco (J.D.). Occupation: Attorney.

1.	Immigration Reform	N	34.	Bar emp polygraph testing	N
2.	Open fld-search warrants	Y	35.	Tax Overhaul consideratn	Y
3.	Civil pnty-hire ill alien	Y	36.	Bar armor-piercing ammo	Y
4.	So Afr sanc-veto override	Y	37.	Tax Overhaul consideratn	N
5.	Tax Overhaul	Y	38.	Make comp emissions known	N
6.	South Africa sanctions	Y	39.	Allow toxic victims suits	N
7.	Death penalty-drug bill	Y	40.	Strike Superfund "VAT"	N
8.	Evidence-warrantless srch	Y	41.	Notify emp-plant closing	N
9.	Life term-second drug off	Y	42.	Bar emp consult-plant clo	Y
10.	Military use in drug war	Y	43.	Medicare cuts;Tax incres'	N
11.	Troop reduction in Europe	N	44.	Delete 12 MX missiles	N
12.	Prohibit chemical weapons	N	45.	Spending cuts;Tax incres'	N
13.	Bar ASAT testing	N	46.	Textile Import Quotas	Y
14.	Abide SALT II weapons ban	N	47.	Cut some school lunch fds	N
15.	Follow SALT II-Soviets do	Y	48.	Clean Water Act Amendmnts	Y
16.	Reduce SDI funding	N	49.	Youth work projects	N
17.	Increase SDI funding	N	50.	Assist military in Angola	Y
18.	Purchase Trident sub	N	51.	Allow US troops-Nicaragua	Y
19.	Delete 12 MX;Add conv wpn	N	52.	Pentagon polygraph exams	Y
20.	Raise speed limit	N	53.	Bar ASAT testing	N
21.	Textile Import Quotas(*)	Y	54.	Suspend def pmt for abuse	N
22.	Req Pentagon buy US goods	Y	55.	Bar Pentagon-contr emplmt	Y
23.	AIDS ins anti-dscriminatn	N	56.	Increase SDI funding	N
24.	Nicaraguan refugee aid	N	57.	Reduce SDI funding	N
25.	Nicaraguan contra aid	Y	58.	Produce chemical weapons	Y
26.	US abide by SALT II	Y	59.	Bar CIA fndg in Nicaragua	N
27.	Prohibit Saudi arms sale	Y	60.	South Africa sanctions	N
28.	Military Retiremnt Reform	Y	61.	Cut SS COLAs; Raise taxes	N
29.	Nicaraguan refugee aid	Y	62.	Let US invest-So Africa	Y
30.	Ease '68 Gun Control Act	Y	63.	Approve 21 MX for 1985	Y
31.	Bar intrstat handgun tran	N	64.	Emergency Farm Credit	Y
32.	Keep '68 Gun Control Act	N	65.	Awards to whistle blowers	Y
33.	Nicaraguan contra aid	Y	66.	African disaster relief	Y

Presidential Support Score: 1986 - 60% 1985 - 68%

DAVIS, ROBERT W. -- Michigan 11th District [Republican]. Counties of Alcona, Alger, Alpena, Antrim (pt.), Baraga, Charlevoix, Cheboygan, Chippewa, Crawford (pt.), Delta, Dickinson, Emmet, Gogebic, Grand Traverse (pt.), Houghton, Iosco (pt.), Iron, Keweenaw, Luce, Machinac, Marquette, Menominee, Montmorency, Ontonagon, Oscoda (pt.), Otsego, Presque Isle and Schoolcraft. Prior Terms: House: 1979-86. Born: July 31, 1932; Marquette, Mich. Education: Northern Michigan University; Hillsdale College; Wayne State University (B.S.). Occupation: Funeral director (1954-66); city councilman (1964-66); Michigan representative (1966-70); Michigan senator (1970-78).

DAVIS, ROBERT W. (Cont.)

1. Immigration Reform Y
2. Open fld-search warrants Y
3. Civil pnty-hire ill alien N
4. So Afr sanc-veto override Y
5. Tax Overhaul Y
6. South Africa sanctions Y
7. Death penalty-drug bill Y
8. Evidence-warrantless srch Y
9. Life term-second drug off Y
10. Military use in drug war Y
11. Troop reduction in Europe N
12. Prohibit chemical weapons N
13. Bar ASAT testing N
14. Abide SALT II weapons ban Y
15. Follow SALT II-Soviets do Y
16. Reduce SDI funding N
17. Increase SDI funding N
18. Purchase Trident sub N
19. Delete 12 MX;Add conv wpn N
20. Raise speed limit Y
21. Textile Import Quotas(*) Y
22. Req Pentagon buy US goods Y
23. AIDS ins anti-dscriminatn N
24. Nicaraguan refugee aid N
25. Nicaraguan contra aid Y
26. US abide by SALT II ?
27. Prohibit Saudi arms sale Y
28. Military Retiremnt Reform Y
29. Nicaraguan refugee aid Y
30. Ease '68 Gun Control Act Y
31. Bar intrstat handgun tran N
32. Keep '68 Gun Control Act N
33. Nicaraguan contra aid Y
34. Bar emp polygraph testing Y
35. Tax Overhaul consideratn Y
36. Bar armor-piercing ammo Y
37. Tax Overhaul consideratn N
38. Make comp emissions known N
39. Allow toxic victims suits N
40. Strike Superfund "VAT" Y
41. Notify emp-plant closing Y
42. Bar emp consult-plant clo N
43. Medicare cuts;Tax incres' Y
44. Delete 12 MX missiles N
45. Spending cuts;Tax incres' N
46. Textile Import Quotas Y
47. Cut some school lunch fds N
48. Clean Water Act Amendmnts N
49. Youth work projects Y
50. Assist military in Angola Y
51. Allow US troops-Nicaragua Y
52. Pentagon polygraph exams Y
53. Bar ASAT testing N
54. Suspend def pmt for abuse N
55. Bar Pentagon-contr emplmt ?
56. Increase SDI funding N
57. Reduce SDI funding N
58. Produce chemical weapons Y
59. Bar CIA fndg in Nicaragua N
60. South Africa sanctions Y
61. Cut SS COLAs; Raise taxes N
62. Let US invest-So Africa Y
63. Approve 21 MX for 1985 Y
64. Emergency Farm Credit Y
65. Awards to whistle blowers Y
66. African disaster relief Y
67. Ban bank loans to So Afr Y
68. Bar coun duty-free trtmt N
69. Steel import limits ?
70. Soc Sec COLAs=inflation Y
71. Bar haz waste vctms suits N
72. Prohibit aid to Nicaragua ?
73. Cut $-Schs bar sch prayer N
74. Raise taxes; Cut Medicare N
75. Alien residncy-prior 1982 Y
76. Alien residncy-prior 1980 Y
77. Pen emp-hire illgl aliens N
78. Lmt Persh II/cruse-Europe N
79. Delete 34 B-1 bombers N
80. Bar purch of Pershing II N
81. Bar purchase of Sgt York N
82. Delete $ for Trident II N
83. Allow 15 MX missiles Y
84. Bar MX procurement-1985 N
85. Equal Access Act Y
86. Aid to El Salvador Y
87. Bar Nicarag water mining N
88. Physician/Medicare freeze Y
89. Increase "sin" taxes Y
90. End SBA direct loans N
91. Sell Conrail Y
92. Equal Rights Amendment N
93. Marines in Lebanon Y
94. Eminent domain-Coal comps Y
95. Prohibit EPA sanctions N
96. SS age increase/Reforms N
97. Auto domestic content req Y
98. Delete jobs program fundg N
99. Highway-Gas tax bill N
100. Raise Medicare;Cut defnse Y
101. Emergency housing aid Y
102. Across-the-board tax cuts Y
103. Gramm-Latta II targets Y
104. Delete B-1 bomber funds X
105. Dsapprov Saudi AWACS sale N
106. Disapprove oil import fee ?
107. Rail Deregulation Y
108. Dsapp India nuc fuel sale Y
109. Mil draft registration Y
110. Chrysler Loan Guarantees Y
111. Prohibit school busing Y
112. Nuclear plant moratorium N
113. Oil price controls N

Presidential Support Score: 1986 - 39% 1985 - 49%

BONIOR, DAVID E. -- Michigan 12th District [Democrat]. Counties of Macomb (pt.) and St. Clair (pt.). Prior Terms: House: 1977-86. Born: June 6, 1945; Detroit, Mich. Education: University of Iowa (B.A.); Chapman College (M.A.). Military Service: U.S. Air Force, 1968-72. Occupation: Michigan representative (1973-77).

1. Immigration Reform Y
2. Open fld-search warrants Y
3. Civil pnty-hire ill alien N
4. So Afr sanc-veto override Y
5. Tax Overhaul Y
6. South Africa sanctions Y
7. Death penalty-drug bill N
8. Evidence-warrantless srch N
9. Life term-second drug off Y
10. Military use in drug war N
11. Troop reduction in Europe Y
12. Prohibit chemical weapons Y
13. Bar ASAT testing Y
14. Abide SALT II weapons ban Y
15. Follow SALT II-Soviets do N
16. Reduce SDI funding Y
17. Increase SDI funding N
18. Purchase Trident sub Y
19. Delete 12 MX;Add conv wpn Y
20. Raise speed limit ?
21. Textile Import Quotas(*) Y
22. Req Pentagon buy US goods Y
23. AIDS ins anti-dscriminatn Y
24. Nicaraguan refugee aid Y
25. Nicaraguan contra aid N
26. US abide by SALT II N
27. Prohibit Saudi arms sale N
28. Military Retiremnt Reform Y
29. Nicaraguan refugee aid Y
30. Ease '68 Gun Control Act N
31. Bar intrstat handgun tran Y
32. Keep '68 Gun Control Act Y
33. Nicaraguan contra aid N
34. Bar emp polygraph testing Y
35. Tax Overhaul consideratn Y
36. Bar armor-piercing ammo Y
37. Tax Overhaul consideratn Y
38. Make comp emissions known Y
39. Allow toxic victims suits Y
40. Strike Superfund "VAT" Y
41. Notify emp-plant closing #
42. Bar emp consult-plant clo N
43. Medicare cuts;Tax incres' Y
44. Delete 12 MX missiles Y
45. Spending cuts;Tax incres' Y
46. Textile Import Quotas Y
47. Cut some school lunch fds N
48. Clean Water Act Amendmnts Y
49. Youth work projects Y
50. Assist military in Angola N
51. Allow US troops-Nicaragua N
52. Pentagon polygraph exams N
53. Bar ASAT testing Y
54. Suspend def pmt for abuse ?
55. Bar Pentagon-contr emplmt Y
56. Increase SDI funding N
57. Reduce SDI funding Y
58. Produce chemical weapons N
59. Bar CIA fndg in Nicaragua Y
60. South Africa sanctions Y
61. Cut SS COLAs; Raise taxes N
62. Let US invest-So Africa N
63. Approve 21 MX for 1985 N
64. Emergency Farm Credit Y
65. Awards to whistle blowers Y
66. African disaster relief Y
67. Ban bank loans to So Afr ?
68. Bar coun duty-free trtmt Y
69. Steel import limits Y
70. Soc Sec COLAs=inflation Y
71. Bar haz waste vctms suits ?
72. Prohibit aid to Nicaragua Y
73. Cut $-Schs bar sch prayer N
74. Raise taxes; Cut Medicare Y
75. Alien residncy-prior 1982 N
76. Alien residncy-prior 1980 N
77. Pen emp-hire illgl aliens Y
78. Lmt Persh II/cruse-Europe Y
79. Delete 34 B-1 bombers Y
80. Bar purch of Pershing II Y
81. Bar purchase of Sgt York Y
82. Delete $ for Trident II #
83. Allow 15 MX missiles N
84. Bar MX procurement-1985 Y
85. Equal Access Act N
86. Aid to El Salvador N
87. Bar Nicarag water mining Y
88. Physician/Medicare freeze N
89. Increase "sin" taxes Y
90. End SBA direct loans N
91. Sell Conrail N
92. Equal Rights Amendment Y
93. Marines in Lebanon Y
94. Eminent domain-Coal comps N
95. Prohibit EPA sanctions N
96. SS age increase/Reforms N
97. Auto domestic content req Y
98. Delete jobs program fundg N
99. Highway-Gas tax bill Y
100. Raise Medicare;Cut defnse Y
101. Emergency housing aid Y
102. Across-the-board tax cuts N
103. Gramm-Latta II targets N
104. Delete B-1 bomber funds Y
105. Dsapprov Saudi AWACS sale Y
106. Disapprove oil import fee Y

BONIOR, DAVID E. (Cont.)

107. Rail Deregulation	N		114. Tuition Tax Credits	N
108. Dsapp India nuc fuel sale	Y		115. Est Consumer Protect Agcy	Y
109. Mil draft registration	Y		116. Eliminate B-1 bomber fnds	Y
110. Chrysler Loan Guarantees	Y		117. Subminimum wage for youth	N
111. Prohibit school busing	N		118. Delete crude oil tax	N
112. Nuclear plant moratorium	Y		119. Natural gas deregulation	N
113. Oil price controls	#			

Presidential Support Score: 1986 - 16% 1985 - 19%

CROCKETT, GEORGE W., Jr. -- Michigan 13th District [Democrat]. County of Wayne (pt.). Prior Terms: House: 1980 (Special Election)-1986. Born: August 10, 1909; Jacksonville, Fla. Education: Morehouse College (A.B.); University of Michigan Law School (J.D.). Occupation: Attorney, Goodman, Crockett, Eden & Robb; judge.

1. Immigration Reform	?		43. Medicare cuts;Tax incres'	Y
2. Open fld-search warrants	?		44. Delete 12 MX missiles	Y
3. Civil pnty-hire ill alien	N		45. Spending cuts;Tax incres'	Y
4. So Afr sanc-veto override	Y		46. Textile Import Quotas	N
5. Tax Overhaul	Y		47. Cut some school lunch fds	N
6. South Africa sanctions	?		48. Clean Water Act Amendmnts	N
7. Death penalty-drug bill	N		49. Youth work projects	?
8. Evidence-warrantless srch	N		50. Assist military in Angola	N
9. Life term-second drug off	N		51. Allow US troops-Nicaragua	N
10. Military use in drug war	N		52. Pentagon polygraph exams	N
11. Troop reduction in Europe	Y		53. Bar ASAT testing	Y
12. Prohibit chemical weapons	Y		54. Suspend def pmt for abuse	Y
13. Bar ASAT testing	Y		55. Bar Pentagon-contr emplmt	Y
14. Abide SALT II weapons ban	Y		56. Increase SDI funding	N
15. Follow SALT II-Soviets do	N		57. Reduce SDI funding	Y
16. Reduce SDI funding	Y		58. Produce chemical weapons	N
17. Increase SDI funding	N		59. Bar CIA fndg in Nicaragua	Y
18. Purchase Trident sub	N		60. South Africa sanctions	Y
19. Delete 12 MX;Add conv wpn	#		61. Cut SS COLAs; Raise taxes	N
20. Raise speed limit	Y		62. Let US invest-So Africa	N
21. Textile Import Quotas(*)	Y		63. Approve 21 MX for 1985	N
22. Req Pentagon buy US goods	?		64. Emergency Farm Credit	Y
23. AIDS ins anti-dscriminatn	Y		65. Awards to whistle blowers	Y
24. Nicaraguan refugee aid	Y		66. African disaster relief	Y
25. Nicaraguan contra aid	N		67. Ban bank loans to So Afr	?
26. US abide by SALT II	N		68. Bar coun duty-free trtmt	Y
27. Prohibit Saudi arms sale	Y		69. Steel import limits	Y
28. Military Retiremnt Reform	Y		70. Soc Sec COLAs=inflation	Y
29. Nicaraguan refugee aid	Y		71. Bar haz waste vctms suits	N
30. Ease '68 Gun Control Act	N		72. Prohibit aid to Nicaragua	Y
31. Bar intrstat handgun tran	Y		73. Cut $-Schs bar sch prayer	N
32. Keep '68 Gun Control Act	Y		74. Raise taxes; Cut Medicare	Y
33. Nicaraguan contra aid	N		75. Alien residncy-prior 1982	N
34. Bar emp polygraph testing	Y		76. Alien residncy-prior 1980	N
35. Tax Overhaul consideratn	Y		77. Pen emp-hire illgl aliens	Y
36. Bar armor-piercing ammo	Y		78. Lmt Persh II/cruse-Europe	#
37. Tax Overhaul consideratn	Y		79. Delete 34 B-1 bombers	Y
38. Make comp emissions known	N		80. Bar purch of Pershing II	Y
39. Allow toxic victims suits	Y		81. Bar purchase of Sgt York	Y
40. Strike Superfund "VAT"	Y		82. Delete $ for Trident II	Y
41. Notify emp-plant closing	Y		83. Allow 15 MX missiles	N
42. Bar emp consult-plant clo	?		84. Bar MX procurement-1985	Y

CROCKETT, GEORGE W., Jr. (Cont.)

85. Equal Access Act N
86. Aid to El Salvador N
87. Bar Nicarag water mining Y
88. Physician/Medicare freeze N
89. Increase "sin" taxes Y
90. End SBA direct loans N
91. Sell Conrail N
92. Equal Rights Amendment Y
93. Marines in Lebanon N
94. Eminent domain-Coal comps N
95. Prohibit EPA sanctions ?
96. SS age increase/Reforms N
97. Auto domestic content req Y
98. Delete jobs program fundg N
99. Highway-Gas tax bill Y
100. Raise Medicare;Cut defnse ?
101. Emergency housing aid Y
102. Across-the-board tax cuts N
103. Gramm-Latta II targets N
104. Delete B-1 bomber funds N
105. Dsapprov Saudi AWACS sale Y

Presidential Support Score: 1986 - 13% 1985 - 19%

HERTEL, DENNIS M. -- Michigan 14th District [Democrat]. Counties of Macoma (pt.), Oakland (pt.) and Wayne (pt.). Prior Terms: House: 1981-86. Born: December 7, 1948; Detroit, Mich. Education: Eastern Michigan University (B.A.); Wayne State University (J.D.). Occupation: Attorney; law school teaching assistant; intern, State Attorney General's Office; staff member, Governor's Corrections and Reform Committee; teacher; Michigan representative (1975-80).

1. Immigration Reform Y
2. Open fld-search warrants Y
3. Civil pnty-hire ill alien Y
4. So Afr sanc-veto override Y
5. Tax Overhaul N
6. South Africa sanctions Y
7. Death penalty-drug bill N
8. Evidence-warrantless srch N
9. Life term-second drug off Y
10. Military use in drug war Y
11. Troop reduction in Europe N
12. Prohibit chemical weapons Y
13. Bar ASAT testing Y
14. Abide SALT II weapons ban Y
15. Follow SALT II-Soviets do N
16. Reduce SDI funding N
17. Increase SDI funding N
18. Purchase Trident sub Y
19. Delete 12 MX;Add conv wpn Y
20. Raise speed limit N
21. Textile Import Quotas(*) Y
22. Req Pentagon buy US goods Y
23. AIDS ins anti-dscriminatn Y
24. Nicaraguan refugee aid Y
25. Nicaraguan contra aid N
26. US abide by SALT II N
27. Prohibit Saudi arms sale Y
28. Military Retiremnt Reform Y
29. Nicaraguan refugee aid Y
30. Ease '68 Gun Control Act N
31. Bar intrstat handgun tran Y
32. Keep '68 Gun Control Act Y
33. Nicaraguan contra aid N
34. Bar emp polygraph testing Y
35. Tax Overhaul consideratn Y
36. Bar armor-piercing ammo Y
37. Tax Overhaul consideratn Y
38. Make comp emissions known Y
39. Allow toxic victims suits Y
40. Strike Superfund "VAT" Y
41. Notify emp-plant closing Y
42. Bar emp consult-plant clo N
43. Medicare cuts;Tax incres' N
44. Delete 12 MX missiles Y
45. Spending cuts;Tax incres' N
46. Textile Import Quotas Y
47. Cut some school lunch fds N
48. Clean Water Act Amendmnts N
49. Youth work projects Y
50. Assist military in Angola N
51. Allow US troops-Nicaragua N
52. Pentagon polygraph exams Y
53. Bar ASAT testing Y
54. Suspend def pmt for abuse Y
55. Bar Pentagon-contr emplmt Y
56. Increase SDI funding N
57. Reduce SDI funding Y
58. Produce chemical weapons N
59. Bar CIA fndg in Nicaragua Y
60. South Africa sanctions Y
61. Cut SS COLAs; Raise taxes N
62. Let US invest-So Africa N
63. Approve 21 MX for 1985 N
64. Emergency Farm Credit Y
65. Awards to whistle blowers Y
66. African disaster relief Y
67. Ban bank loans to So Afr Y
68. Bar coun duty-free trtmt Y
69. Steel import limits Y
70. Soc Sec COLAs=inflation Y
71. Bar haz waste vctms suits N
72. Prohibit aid to Nicaragua Y

HERTEL, DENNIS M. (Cont.)

73. Cut $-Schs bar sch prayer N
74. Raise taxes; Cut Medicare N
75. Alien residncy-prior 1982 Y
76. Alien residncy-prior 1980 N
77. Pen emp-hire illgl aliens Y
78. Lmt Persh II/cruse-Europe N
79. Delete 34 B-1 bombers Y
80. Bar purch of Pershing II N
81. Bar purchase of Sgt York ?
82. Delete $ for Trident II N
83. Allow 15 MX missiles N
84. Bar MX procurement-1985 Y
85. Equal Access Act N
86. Aid to El Salvador N
87. Bar Nicarag water mining Y
88. Physician/Medicare freeze N
89. Increase "sin" taxes N
90. End SBA direct loans N
91. Sell Conrail ?
92. Equal Rights Amendment Y
93. Marines in Lebanon N
94. Eminent domain-Coal comps N
95. Prohibit EPA sanctions N
96. SS age increase/Reforms N
97. Auto domestic content req Y
98. Delete jobs program fundg N
99. Highway-Gas tax bill Y
100. Raise Medicare;Cut defnse Y
101. Emergency housing aid Y
102. Across-the-board tax cuts N
103. Gramm-Latta II targets N
104. Delete B-1 bomber funds Y
105. Dsapprov Saudi AWACS sale Y

Presidential Support Score: 1986 - 15% 1985 - 29%

FORD, WILLIAM D. -- Michigan 15th District [Democrat]. Counties of Washtenaw (pt.) and Wayne (pt.). Prior Terms: House: 1965-86. Born: August 6, 1927; Detroit, Mich. Education: Wayne University; University of Denver (B.S., LL.B.). Military Service: U.S. Navy, 1944-46; U.S. Air Force Reserve, 1950-58. Occupation: Attorney; justice of the peace (1955-57); Melvindale city attorney (1957-59); Michigan senator (1962-64).

1. Immigration Reform Y
2. Open fld-search warrants N
3. Civil pnty-hire ill alien Y
4. So Afr sanc-veto override Y
5. Tax Overhaul N
6. South Africa sanctions Y
7. Death penalty-drug bill N
8. Evidence-warrantless srch N
9. Life term-second drug off Y
10. Military use in drug war N
11. Troop reduction in Europe N
12. Prohibit chemical weapons ?
13. Bar ASAT testing Y
14. Abide SALT II weapons ban Y
15. Follow SALT II-Soviets do N
16. Reduce SDI funding Y
17. Increase SDI funding N
18. Purchase Trident sub Y
19. Delete 12 MX;Add conv wpn Y
20. Raise speed limit ?
21. Textile Import Quotas(*) Y
22. Req Pentagon buy US goods Y
23. AIDS ins anti-dscriminatn Y
24. Nicaraguan refugee aid Y
25. Nicaraguan contra aid N
26. US abide by SALT II N
27. Prohibit Saudi arms sale Y
28. Military Retiremnt Reform Y
29. Nicaraguan refugee aid Y
30. Ease '68 Gun Control Act Y
31. Bar intrstat handgun tran Y
32. Keep '68 Gun Control Act N
33. Nicaraguan contra aid N
34. Bar emp polygraph testing Y
35. Tax Overhaul consideratn Y
36. Bar armor-piercing ammo Y
37. Tax Overhaul consideratn Y
38. Make comp emissions known N
39. Allow toxic victims suits Y
40. Strike Superfund "VAT" Y
41. Notify emp-plant closing Y
42. Bar emp consult-plant clo N
43. Medicare cuts;Tax incres' Y
44. Delete 12 MX missiles Y
45. Spending cuts;Tax incres' Y
46. Textile Import Quotas Y
47. Cut some school lunch fds N
48. Clean Water Act Amendmnts N
49. Youth work projects #
50. Assist military in Angola N
51. Allow US troops-Nicaragua N
52. Pentagon polygraph exams N
53. Bar ASAT testing Y
54. Suspend def pmt for abuse Y
55. Bar Pentagon-contr emplmt Y
56. Increase SDI funding N
57. Reduce SDI funding Y
58. Produce chemical weapons N
59. Bar CIA fndg in Nicaragua Y
60. South Africa sanctions ?
61. Cut SS COLAs; Raise taxes N
62. Let US invest-So Africa N

FORD, WILLIAM D. (Cont.)

63. Approve 21 MX for 1985 N
64. Emergency Farm Credit Y
65. Awards to whistle blowers ?
66. African disaster relief Y
67. Ban bank loans to So Afr Y
68. Bar coun duty-free trtmt Y
69. Steel import limits Y
70. Soc Sec COLAs=inflation Y
71. Bar haz waste vctms suits N
72. Prohibit aid to Nicaragua Y
73. Cut $-Schs bar sch prayer N
74. Raise taxes; Cut Medicare Y
75. Alien residncy-prior 1982 N
76. Alien residncy-prior 1980 N
77. Pen emp-hire illgl aliens Y
78. Lmt Persh II/cruse-Europe Y
79. Delete 34 B-1 bombers Y
80. Bar purch of Pershing II Y
81. Bar purchase of Sgt York Y
82. Delete $ for Trident II N
83. Allow 15 MX missiles N
84. Bar MX procurement-1985 Y
85. Equal Access Act N
86. Aid to El Salvador N
87. Bar Nicarag water mining Y
88. Physician/Medicare freeze N
89. Increase "sin" taxes Y
90. End SBA direct loans N
91. Sell Conrail N
92. Equal Rights Amendment Y
93. Marines in Lebanon N
94. Eminent domain-Coal comps N
95. Prohibit EPA sanctions N
96. SS age increase/Reforms N
97. Auto domestic content req Y
98. Delete jobs program fundg N
99. Highway-Gas tax bill Y
100. Raise Medicare;Cut defnse Y
101. Emergency housing aid Y
102. Across-the-board tax cuts N
103. Gramm-Latta II targets N
104. Delete B-1 bomber funds Y
105. Dsapprov Saudi AWACS sale Y
106. Disapprove oil import fee Y
107. Rail Deregulation Y
108. Dsapp India nuc fuel sale Y
109. Mil draft registration N
110. Chrysler Loan Guarantees Y
111. Prohibit school busing Y
112. Nuclear plant moratorium N
113. Oil price controls Y
114. Tuition Tax Credits N
115. Est Consumer Protect Agcy Y
116. Eliminate B-1 bomber fnds Y
117. Subminimum wage for youth N
118. Delete crude oil tax N
119. Natural gas deregulation N

Presidential Support Score: 1986 - 17% 1985 - 16%

DINGELL, JOHN D. -- Michigan 16th District [Democrat]. Counties of Lenawee (pt.), Monroe and Wayne (pt.). Prior Terms: House: 1955 (Special Election)-1986. Born: July 8, 1926; Colorado Springs, Colo. Education: Georgetown University (B.S., J.D.). Military Service: WW II. Occupation: Attorney; research assistant to U.S. district judge; prosecuting attorney (1953-55).

1. Immigration Reform Y
2. Open fld-search warrants Y
3. Civil pnty-hire ill alien N
4. So Afr sanc-veto override Y
5. Tax Overhaul N
6. South Africa sanctions Y
7. Death penalty-drug bill Y
8. Evidence-warrantless srch N
9. Life term-second drug off Y
10. Military use in drug war N
11. Troop reduction in Europe N
12. Prohibit chemical weapons N
13. Bar ASAT testing Y
14. Abide SALT II weapons ban Y
15. Follow SALT II-Soviets do N
16. Reduce SDI funding Y
17. Increase SDI funding N
18. Purchase Trident sub Y
19. Delete 12 MX;Add conv wpn Y
20. Raise speed limit N
21. Textile Import Quotas(*) Y
22. Req Pentagon buy US goods Y
23. AIDS ins anti-dscriminatn Y
24. Nicaraguan refugee aid Y
25. Nicaraguan contra aid N
26. US abide by SALT II N
27. Prohibit Saudi arms sale N
28. Military Retiremnt Reform Y
29. Nicaraguan refugee aid Y
30. Ease '68 Gun Control Act Y
31. Bar intrstat handgun tran N
32. Keep '68 Gun Control Act N
33. Nicaraguan contra aid N
34. Bar emp polygraph testing Y
35. Tax Overhaul consideratn Y
36. Bar armor-piercing ammo Y
37. Tax Overhaul consideratn Y
38. Make comp emissions known N

DINGELL, JOHN D. (Cont.)

39. Allow toxic victims suits N
40. Strike Superfund "VAT" N
41. Notify emp-plant closing Y
42. Bar emp consult-plant clo N
43. Medicare cuts;Tax incres' Y
44. Delete 12 MX missiles Y
45. Spending cuts;Tax incres' Y
46. Textile Import Quotas Y
47. Cut some school lunch fds N
48. Clean Water Act Amendmnts N
49. Youth work projects #
50. Assist military in Angola N
51. Allow US troops-Nicaragua N
52. Pentagon polygraph exams N
53. Bar ASAT testing Y
54. Suspend def pmt for abuse Y
55. Bar Pentagon-contr emplmt Y
56. Increase SDI funding N
57. Reduce SDI funding Y
58. Produce chemical weapons Y
59. Bar CIA fndg in Nicaragua Y
60. South Africa sanctions ?
61. Cut SS COLAs; Raise taxes N
62. Let US invest-So Africa ?
63. Approve 21 MX for 1985 N
64. Emergency Farm Credit Y
65. Awards to whistle blowers Y
66. African disaster relief Y
67. Ban bank loans to So Afr Y
68. Bar coun duty-free trtmt Y
69. Steel import limits Y
70. Soc Sec COLAs=inflation Y
71. Bar haz waste vctms suits N
72. Prohibit aid to Nicaragua Y
73. Cut $-Schs bar sch prayer N
74. Raise taxes; Cut Medicare Y
75. Alien residncy-prior 1982 Y
76. Alien residncy-prior 1980 N
77. Pen emp-hire illgl aliens Y
78. Lmt Persh II/cruse-Europe N
79. Delete 34 B-1 bombers Y
80. Bar purch of Pershing II N
81. Bar purchase of Sgt York Y
82. Delete $ for Trident II N
83. Allow 15 MX missiles N
84. Bar MX procurement-1985 Y
85. Equal Access Act Y
86. Aid to El Salvador N
87. Bar Nicarag water mining Y
88. Physician/Medicare freeze N
89. Increase "sin" taxes Y
90. End SBA direct loans N
91. Sell Conrail N
92. Equal Rights Amendment Y
93. Marines in Lebanon N
94. Eminent domain-Coal comps Y
95. Prohibit EPA sanctions N
96. SS age increase/Reforms N
97. Auto domestic content req Y
98. Delete jobs program fundg N
99. Highway-Gas tax bill Y
100. Raise Medicare;Cut defnse Y
101. Emergency housing aid Y
102. Across-the-board tax cuts N
103. Gramm-Latta II targets N
104. Delete B-1 bomber funds Y
105. Dsapprov Saudi AWACS sale Y
106. Disapprove oil import fee ?
107. Rail Deregulation Y
108. Dsapp India nuc fuel sale N
109. Mil draft registration Y
110. Chrysler Loan Guarantees Y
111. Prohibit school busing Y
112. Nuclear plant moratorium Y
113. Oil price controls N
114. Tuition Tax Credits N
115. Est Consumer Protect Agcy Y
116. Eliminate B-1 bomber fnds Y
117. Subminimum wage for youth N
118. Delete crude oil tax N
119. Natural gas deregulation N

Presidential Support Score: 1986 - 25% 1985 - 23%

LEVIN, SANDER M. -- Michigan 17th District [Democrat]. Counties of Oakland (pt.) and Wayne (pt.). Prior Terms: House: 1983-86. Born: September 6, 1931; Detroit, Mich. Education: University of Chicago (B.A.); Columbia University (M.A.); Harvard University (LL.B.). Occupation: Partner, Schwartz, O'Hare and Levin (1957-64); Oakland County Board of Supervisors (1961-64); Michigan senator (1965-70); adjunct professor of law (1971-74); private law practice (1971-74); fellow, Kennedy School of Government, Institute of Politics, Harvard University (1975); assistant administrator, Agency for International Development (1977-81); counsel for Jaffe, Snider, Raitt, Garrett & Heuer (1981-82).

1. Immigration Reform Y
2. Open fld-search warrants N
3. Civil pnty-hire ill alien Y
4. So Afr sanc-veto override Y

LEVIN, SANDER M. (Cont.)

5. Tax Overhaul Y
6. South Africa sanctions Y
7. Death penalty-drug bill N
8. Evidence-warrantless srch N
9. Life term-second drug off Y
10. Military use in drug war N
11. Troop reduction in Europe N
12. Prohibit chemical weapons Y
13. Bar ASAT testing Y
14. Abide SALT II weapons ban Y
15. Follow SALT II-Soviets do N
16. Reduce SDI funding N
17. Increase SDI funding N
18. Purchase Trident sub Y
19. Delete 12 MX;Add conv wpn ?
20. Raise speed limit N
21. Textile Import Quotas(*) Y
22. Req Pentagon buy US goods Y
23. AIDS ins anti-dscriminatn Y
24. Nicaraguan refugee aid Y
25. Nicaraguan contra aid N
26. US abide by SALT II N
27. Prohibit Saudi arms sale Y
28. Military Retiremnt Reform Y
29. Nicaraguan refugee aid Y
30. Ease '68 Gun Control Act N
31. Bar intrstat handgun tran Y
32. Keep '68 Gun Control Act Y
33. Nicaraguan contra aid N
34. Bar emp polygraph testing Y
35. Tax Overhaul consideratn Y
36. Bar armor-piercing ammo Y
37. Tax Overhaul consideratn Y
38. Make comp emissions known Y
39. Allow toxic victims suits N
40. Strike Superfund "VAT" Y
41. Notify emp-plant closing Y
42. Bar emp consult-plant clo N
43. Medicare cuts;Tax incres' Y
44. Delete 12 MX missiles Y
45. Spending cuts;Tax incres' Y
46. Textile Import Quotas Y
47. Cut some school lunch fds N
48. Clean Water Act Amendmnts N
49. Youth work projects Y
50. Assist military in Angola N
51. Allow US troops-Nicaragua N
52. Pentagon polygraph exams Y
53. Bar ASAT testing Y
54. Suspend def pmt for abuse Y
55. Bar Pentagon-contr emplmt Y
56. Increase SDI funding N
57. Reduce SDI funding N
58. Produce chemical weapons N
59. Bar CIA fndg in Nicaragua Y
60. South Africa sanctions Y
61. Cut SS COLAs; Raise taxes N
62. Let US invest-So Africa N
63. Approve 21 MX for 1985 N
64. Emergency Farm Credit Y
65. Awards to whistle blowers Y
66. African disaster relief Y
67. Ban bank loans to So Afr Y
68. Bar coun duty-free trtmt Y
69. Steel import limits Y
70. Soc Sec COLAs=inflation Y
71. Bar haz waste vctms suits N
72. Prohibit aid to Nicaragua Y
73. Cut $-Schs bar sch prayer N
74. Raise taxes; Cut Medicare C
75. Alien residncy-prior 1982 N
76. Alien residncy-prior 1980 N
77. Pen emp-hire illgl aliens Y
78. Lmt Persh II/cruse-Europe N
79. Delete 34 B-1 bombers Y
80. Bar purch of Pershing II N
81. Bar purchase of Sgt York Y
82. Delete $ for Trident II Y
83. Allow 15 MX missiles N
84. Bar MX procurement-1985 Y
85. Equal Access Act N
86. Aid to El Salvador N
87. Bar Nicarag water mining Y
88. Physician/Medicare freeze N
89. Increase "sin" taxes C
90. End SBA direct loans N
91. Sell Conrail N
92. Equal Rights Amendment Y
93. Marines in Lebanon Y
94. Eminent domain-Coal comps N
95. Prohibit EPA sanctions Y
96. SS age increase/Reforms N

Presidential Support Score: 1986 - 18% 1985 - 23%

BROOMFIELD, WM. S. -- Michigan 18th District [Republican]. Counties of Livingston (pt.), Macomb (pt.) and Oakland (pt.). Prior Terms: House: 1957-86. Born: April 28, 1922; Royal Oak, Mich. Education: Michigan State University. Occupation: Michigan representative (1948-54); Michigan senator (1954).

1. Immigration Reform N
2. Open fld-search warrants N
3. Civil pnty-hire ill alien N
4. So Afr sanc-veto override N
5. Tax Overhaul Y
6. South Africa sanctions Y
7. Death penalty-drug bill Y
8. Evidence-warrantless srch Y

BROOMFIELD, WM. S. (Cont.)

9. Life term-second drug off Y
10. Military use in drug war Y
11. Troop reduction in Europe N
12. Prohibit chemical weapons N
13. Bar ASAT testing N
14. Abide SALT II weapons ban N
15. Follow SALT II-Soviets do Y
16. Reduce SDI funding N
17. Increase SDI funding Y
18. Purchase Trident sub N
19. Delete 12 MX;Add conv wpn N
20. Raise speed limit N
21. Textile Import Quotas(*) N
22. Req Pentagon buy US goods N
23. AIDS ins anti-dscriminatn N
24. Nicaraguan refugee aid N
25. Nicaraguan contra aid Y
26. US abide by SALT II Y
27. Prohibit Saudi arms sale Y
28. Military Retiremnt Reform Y
29. Nicaraguan refugee aid Y
30. Ease '68 Gun Control Act N
31. Bar intrstat handgun tran Y
32. Keep '68 Gun Control Act Y
33. Nicaraguan contra aid Y
34. Bar emp polygraph testing N
35. Tax Overhaul consideratn Y
36. Bar armor-piercing ammo Y
37. Tax Overhaul consideratn N
38. Make comp emissions known N
39. Allow toxic victims suits N
40. Strike Superfund "VAT" Y
41. Notify emp-plant closing N
42. Bar emp consult-plant clo Y
43. Medicare cuts;Tax incres' N
44. Delete 12 MX missiles N
45. Spending cuts;Tax incres' N
46. Textile Import Quotas N
47. Cut some school lunch fds Y
48. Clean Water Act Amendmnts N
49. Youth work projects ?
50. Assist military in Angola Y
51. Allow US troops-Nicaragua Y
52. Pentagon polygraph exams Y
53. Bar ASAT testing N
54. Suspend def pmt for abuse Y
55. Bar Pentagon-contr emplmt Y
56. Increase SDI funding N
57. Reduce SDI funding N
58. Produce chemical weapons Y
59. Bar CIA fndg in Nicaragua N
60. South Africa sanctions N
61. Cut SS COLAs; Raise taxes N
62. Let US invest-So Africa Y
63. Approve 21 MX for 1985 Y
64. Emergency Farm Credit N
65. Awards to whistle blowers Y
66. African disaster relief Y
67. Ban bank loans to So Afr Y
68. Bar coun duty-free trtmt N
69. Steel import limits Y
70. Soc Sec COLAs=inflation Y
71. Bar haz waste vctms suits Y
72. Prohibit aid to Nicaragua N
73. Cut $-Schs bar sch prayer Y
74. Raise taxes; Cut Medicare N
75. Alien residncy-prior 1982 N
76. Alien residncy-prior 1980 N
77. Pen emp-hire illgl aliens N
78. Lmt Persh II/cruse-Europe N
79. Delete 34 B-1 bombers N
80. Bar purch of Pershing II N
81. Bar purchase of Sgt York N
82. Delete $ for Trident II N
83. Allow 15 MX missiles Y
84. Bar MX procurement-1985 N
85. Equal Access Act Y
86. Aid to El Salvador Y
87. Bar Nicarag water mining Y
88. Physician/Medicare freeze Y
89. Increase "sin" taxes Y
90. End SBA direct loans Y
91. Sell Conrail Y
92. Equal Rights Amendment N
93. Marines in Lebanon Y
94. Eminent domain-Coal comps N
95. Prohibit EPA sanctions N
96. SS age increase/Reforms Y
97. Auto domestic content req Y
98. Delete jobs program fundg Y
99. Highway-Gas tax bill N
100. Raise Medicare;Cut defnse N
101. Emergency housing aid Y
102. Across-the-board tax cuts Y
103. Gramm-Latta II targets Y
104. Delete B-1 bomber funds N
105. Dsapprov Saudi AWACS sale Y
106. Disapprove oil import fee Y
107. Rail Deregulation N
108. Dsapp India nuc fuel sale Y
109. Mil draft registration N
110. Chrysler Loan Guarantees Y
111. Prohibit school busing Y
112. Nuclear plant moratorium N
113. Oil price controls N
114. Tuition Tax Credits Y
115. Est Consumer Protect Agcy N
116. Eliminate B-1 bomber fnds N
117. Subminimum wage for youth Y
118. Delete crude oil tax Y
119. Natural gas deregulation Y

Presidential Support Score: 1986 - 69% 1985 - 73%

MINNESOTA

PENNY, TIMOTHY J. -- Minnesota 1st District [Democrat]. Counties of Blue Earth, Dakota (pt.), Dodge, Filmore, Freeborn, Goodhue (pt.), Houston, Le Sueur (pt.), Mower, Olmsted, Rice, Scott (pt.), Steele, Wabasha, Waseca and Winona. Prior Terms: House: 1983-86. Born: November 19, 1951; Freeborn County, Minn. Education: Winona State University. Occupation: Minnesota senator (1976, re-elected 1980).

1.	Immigration Reform	Y	49.	Youth work projects	N
2.	Open fld-search warrants	Y	50.	Assist military in Angola	N
3.	Civil pnty-hire ill alien	N	51.	Allow US troops-Nicaragua	N
4.	So Afr sanc-veto override	Y	52.	Pentagon polygraph exams	Y
5.	Tax Overhaul	Y	53.	Bar ASAT testing	Y
6.	South Africa sanctions	Y	54.	Suspend def pmt for abuse	Y
7.	Death penalty-drug bill	N	55.	Bar Pentagon-contr emplmt	Y
8.	Evidence-warrantless srch	Y	56.	Increase SDI funding	N
9.	Life term-second drug off	Y	57.	Reduce SDI funding	Y
10.	Military use in drug war	Y	58.	Produce chemical weapons	N
11.	Troop reduction in Europe	N	59.	Bar CIA fndg in Nicaragua	Y
12.	Prohibit chemical weapons	Y	60.	South Africa sanctions	Y
13.	Bar ASAT testing	Y	61.	Cut SS COLAs; Raise taxes	Y
14.	Abide SALT II weapons ban	Y	62.	Let US invest-So Africa	N
15.	Follow SALT II-Soviets do	N	63.	Approve 21 MX for 1985	N
16.	Reduce SDI funding	Y	64.	Emergency Farm Credit	Y
17.	Increase SDI funding	N	65.	Awards to whistle blowers	Y
18.	Purchase Trident sub	Y	66.	African disaster relief	Y
19.	Delete 12 MX;Add conv wpn	Y	67.	Ban bank loans to So Afr	Y
20.	Raise speed limit	N	68.	Bar coun duty-free trtmt	N
21.	Textile Import Quotas(*)	N	69.	Steel import limits	N
22.	Req Pentagon buy US goods	Y	70.	Soc Sec COLAs=inflation	Y
23.	AIDS ins anti-dscriminatn	Y	71.	Bar haz waste vctms suits	N
24.	Nicaraguan refugee aid	Y	72.	Prohibit aid to Nicaragua	Y
25.	Nicaraguan contra aid	N	73.	Cut $-Schs bar sch prayer	N
26.	US abide by SALT II	N	74.	Raise taxes; Cut Medicare	Y
27.	Prohibit Saudi arms sale	Y	75.	Alien residncy-prior 1982	Y
28.	Military Retiremnt Reform	Y	76.	Alien residncy-prior 1980	N
29.	Nicaraguan refugee aid	Y	77.	Pen emp-hire illgl aliens	N
30.	Ease '68 Gun Control Act	Y	78.	Lmt Persh II/cruse-Europe	Y
31.	Bar intrstat handgun tran	N	79.	Delete 34 B-1 bombers	Y
32.	Keep '68 Gun Control Act	N	80.	Bar purch of Pershing II	Y
33.	Nicaraguan contra aid	N	81.	Bar purchase of Sgt York	Y
34.	Bar emp polygraph testing	Y	82.	Delete $ for Trident II	Y
35.	Tax Overhaul consideratn	Y	83.	Allow 15 MX missiles	N
36.	Bar armor-piercing ammo	Y	84.	Bar MX procurement-1985	Y
37.	Tax Overhaul consideratn	Y	85.	Equal Access Act	Y
38.	Make comp emissions known	Y	86.	Aid to El Salvador	N
39.	Allow toxic victims suits	Y	87.	Bar Nicarag water mining	Y
40.	Strike Superfund "VAT"	Y	88.	Physician/Medicare freeze	N
41.	Notify emp-plant closing	Y	89.	Increase "sin" taxes	Y
42.	Bar emp consult-plant clo	Y	90.	End SBA direct loans	N
43.	Medicare cuts;Tax incres'	Y	91.	Sell Conrail	N
44.	Delete 12 MX missiles	Y	92.	Equal Rights Amendment	Y
45.	Spending cuts;Tax incres'	Y	93.	Marines in Lebanon	N
46.	Textile Import Quotas	N	94.	Eminent domain-Coal comps	N
47.	Cut some school lunch fds	N	95.	Prohibit EPA sanctions	Y
48.	Clean Water Act Amendmnts	N	96.	SS age increase/Reforms	Y

Presidential Support Score: 1986 - 35% 1985 - 25%

WEBER, VIN -- Minnesota 2nd District [Republican]. Counties of Big Stone, Brown, Chippewa, Cottonwood, Douglas, Faribault, Grant (pt.), Jackson, Kandiyohi, Lac qui Parle, Le Sueur (pt.), Lincoln, Lyon, McLeod, Martin, Meeker, Murray, Nicollet, Nobles, Pipestone, Pope, Redwood, Renville, Rock, Sibley, Stevens, Swift, Traverse, Watonwen, Wright (pt.) and Yellow Medicine. Prior Terms: House: 1981-86. Born: July 24, 1952; Slayton, Minn. Education: University of Minnesota. Occupation: President, Weber Publishing Co.; publisher; congressional press secretary (1974-75); senator's aide (1979-80).

1. Immigration Reform Y
2. Open fld-search warrants Y
3. Civil pnty-hire ill alien N
4. So Afr sanc-veto override Y
5. Tax Overhaul Y
6. South Africa sanctions Y
7. Death penalty-drug bill N
8. Evidence-warrantless srch Y
9. Life term-second drug off Y
10. Military use in drug war Y
11. Troop reduction in Europe N
12. Prohibit chemical weapons Y
13. Bar ASAT testing N
14. Abide SALT II weapons ban N
15. Follow SALT II-Soviets do Y
16. Reduce SDI funding N
17. Increase SDI funding Y
18. Purchase Trident sub N
19. Delete 12 MX;Add conv wpn N
20. Raise speed limit Y
21. Textile Import Quotas(*) N
22. Req Pentagon buy US goods N
23. AIDS ins anti-dscriminatn N
24. Nicaraguan refugee aid N
25. Nicaraguan contra aid Y
26. US abide by SALT II Y
27. Prohibit Saudi arms sale Y
28. Military Retiremnt Reform Y
29. Nicaraguan refugee aid Y
30. Ease '68 Gun Control Act Y
31. Bar intrstat handgun tran N
32. Keep '68 Gun Control Act N
33. Nicaraguan contra aid Y
34. Bar emp polygraph testing Y
35. Tax Overhaul consideratn N
36. Bar armor-piercing ammo ?
37. Tax Overhaul consideratn N
38. Make comp emissions known ?
39. Allow toxic victims suits ?
40. Strike Superfund "VAT" #
41. Notify emp-plant closing N
42. Bar emp consult-plant clo Y
43. Medicare cuts;Tax incres' N
44. Delete 12 MX missiles N
45. Spending cuts;Tax incres' N
46. Textile Import Quotas N
47. Cut some school lunch fds N
48. Clean Water Act Amendmnts N
49. Youth work projects ?
50. Assist military in Angola Y
51. Allow US troops-Nicaragua Y
52. Pentagon polygraph exams Y
53. Bar ASAT testing N
54. Suspend def pmt for abuse Y
55. Bar Pentagon-contr emplmt Y
56. Increase SDI funding Y
57. Reduce SDI funding N
58. Produce chemical weapons N
59. Bar CIA fndg in Nicaragua N
60. South Africa sanctions Y
61. Cut SS COLAs; Raise taxes N
62. Let US invest-So Africa N
63. Approve 21 MX for 1985 Y
64. Emergency Farm Credit Y
65. Awards to whistle blowers Y
66. African disaster relief N
67. Ban bank loans to So Afr Y
68. Bar coun duty-free trtmt N
69. Steel import limits N
70. Soc Sec COLAs=inflation Y
71. Bar haz waste vctms suits N
72. Prohibit aid to Nicaragua N
73. Cut $-Schs bar sch prayer Y
74. Raise taxes; Cut Medicare N
75. Alien residncy-prior 1982 Y
76. Alien residncy-prior 1980 Y
77. Pen emp-hire illgl aliens N
78. Lmt Persh II/cruse-Europe N
79. Delete 34 B-1 bombers Y
80. Bar purch of Pershing II N
81. Bar purchase of Sgt York Y
82. Delete $ for Trident II N
83. Allow 15 MX missiles Y
84. Bar MX procurement-1985 N
85. Equal Access Act Y
86. Aid to El Salvador Y
87. Bar Nicarag water mining N
88. Physician/Medicare freeze Y
89. Increase "sin" taxes N
90. End SBA direct loans Y
91. Sell Conrail Y
92. Equal Rights Amendment N
93. Marines in Lebanon Y
94. Eminent domain-Coal comps N
95. Prohibit EPA sanctions N
96. SS age increase/Reforms Y
97. Auto domestic content req N
98. Delete jobs program fundg Y

WEBER, VIN (Cont.)

99. Highway-Gas tax bill N
100. Raise Medicare;Cut defnse N
101. Emergency housing aid N
102. Across-the-board tax cuts Y
103. Gramm-Latta II targets Y
104. Delete B-1 bomber funds Y
105. Dsapprov Saudi AWACS sale Y

Presidential Support Score: 1986 - 69% 1985 - 64%

FRENZEL, BILL -- Minnesota 3rd District [Republican]. Counties of Carver, Dakota (pt.), Goodhue (pt.), Hennepin (pt.) and Scott (pt.). Prior Terms: House: 1971-86. Born: July 31, 1928; St. Paul, Minn. Education: Dartmouth College (B.A., M.B.A.). Military Service: U.S. Navy, Korean Conflict. Occupation: Minnesota representative (1962-70); president, Minneapolis Terminal Warehouse Co.

1. Immigration Reform Y
2. Open fld-search warrants N
3. Civil pnty-hire ill alien N
4. So Afr sanc-veto override Y
5. Tax Overhaul N
6. South Africa sanctions Y
7. Death penalty-drug bill Y
8. Evidence-warrantless srch Y
9. Life term-second drug off Y
10. Military use in drug war Y
11. Troop reduction in Europe N
12. Prohibit chemical weapons N
13. Bar ASAT testing Y
14. Abide SALT II weapons ban Y
15. Follow SALT II-Soviets do Y
16. Reduce SDI funding N
17. Increase SDI funding N
18. Purchase Trident sub N
19. Delete 12 MX;Add conv wpn N
20. Raise speed limit Y
21. Textile Import Quotas(*) N
22. Req Pentagon buy US goods N
23. AIDS ins anti-dscriminatn Y
24. Nicaraguan refugee aid N
25. Nicaraguan contra aid Y
26. US abide by SALT II Y
27. Prohibit Saudi arms sale Y
28. Military Retiremnt Reform Y
29. Nicaraguan refugee aid Y
30. Ease '68 Gun Control Act Y
31. Bar intrstat handgun tran Y
32. Keep '68 Gun Control Act Y
33. Nicaraguan contra aid N
34. Bar emp polygraph testing N
35. Tax Overhaul consideratn N
36. Bar armor-piercing ammo Y
37. Tax Overhaul consideratn N
38. Make comp emissions known N
39. Allow toxic victims suits N
40. Strike Superfund "VAT" Y
41. Notify emp-plant closing N
42. Bar emp consult-plant clo ?
43. Medicare cuts;Tax incres' N
44. Delete 12 MX missiles N
45. Spending cuts;Tax incres' N
46. Textile Import Quotas N
47. Cut some school lunch fds Y
48. Clean Water Act Amendmnts Y
49. Youth work projects N
50. Assist military in Angola Y
51. Allow US troops-Nicaragua Y
52. Pentagon polygraph exams ?
53. Bar ASAT testing Y
54. Suspend def pmt for abuse N
55. Bar Pentagon-contr emplmt Y
56. Increase SDI funding N
57. Reduce SDI funding N
58. Produce chemical weapons Y
59. Bar CIA fndg in Nicaragua N
60. South Africa sanctions N
61. Cut SS COLAs; Raise taxes Y
62. Let US invest-So Africa Y
63. Approve 21 MX for 1985 Y
64. Emergency Farm Credit Y
65. Awards to whistle blowers ?
66. African disaster relief ?
67. Ban bank loans to So Afr Y
68. Bar coun duty-free trtmt N
69. Steel import limits N
70. Soc Sec COLAs=inflation Y
71. Bar haz waste vctms suits Y
72. Prohibit aid to Nicaragua Y
73. Cut $-Schs bar sch prayer N
74. Raise taxes; Cut Medicare Y
75. Alien residncy-prior 1982 Y
76. Alien residncy-prior 1980 Y
77. Pen emp-hire illgl aliens N
78. Lmt Persh II/cruse-Europe N
79. Delete 34 B-1 bombers Y
80. Bar purch of Pershing II N
81. Bar purchase of Sgt York Y
82. Delete $ for Trident II N
83. Allow 15 MX missiles Y
84. Bar MX procurement-1985 N
85. Equal Access Act Y
86. Aid to El Salvador Y
87. Bar Nicarag water mining Y
88. Physician/Medicare freeze Y

FRENZEL, BILL (Cont.)

89.	Increase "sin" taxes	Y	105.	Dsapprov Saudi AWACS sale	Y
90.	End SBA direct loans	Y	106.	Disapprove oil import fee	Y
91.	Sell Conrail	Y	107.	Rail Deregulation	Y
92.	Equal Rights Amendment	Y	108.	Dsapp India nuc fuel sale	Y
93.	Marines in Lebanon	Y	109.	Mil draft registration	N
94.	Eminent domain-Coal comps	?	110.	Chrysler Loan Guarantees	N
95.	Prohibit EPA sanctions	?	111.	Prohibit school busing	N
96.	SS age increase/Reforms	Y	112.	Nuclear plant moratorium	?
97.	Auto domestic content req	N	113.	Oil price controls	N
98.	Delete jobs program fundg	Y	114.	Tuition Tax Credits	Y
99.	Highway-Gas tax bill	N	115.	Est Consumer Protect Agcy	N
100.	Raise Medicare;Cut defnse	N	116.	Eliminate B-1 bomber fnds	Y
101.	Emergency housing aid	N	117.	Subminimum wage for youth	Y
102.	Across-the-board tax cuts	Y	118.	Delete crude oil tax	Y
103.	Gramm-Latta II targets	Y	119.	Natural gas deregulation	Y
104.	Delete B-1 bomber funds	N			

Presidential Support Score: 1986 - 66% 1985 - 63%

VENTO, BRUCE F. -- Minnesota 4th District [Democrat]. Counties of Dakota (pt.), Ramsey (pt.), and Washington (pt.). Prior Terms: House: 1977-86. Born: October 7, 1940; St. Paul, Minn. Education: University of Minnesota (A.A.); Wisconsin State University (B.S.). Occupation: Teacher; Minnesota representative (1970).

1.	Immigration Reform	Y	34.	Bar emp polygraph testing	Y
2.	Open fld-search warrants	N	35.	Tax Overhaul consideratn	Y
3.	Civil pnty-hire ill alien	N	36.	Bar armor-piercing ammo	Y
4.	So Afr sanc-veto override	Y	37.	Tax Overhaul consideratn	Y
5.	Tax Overhaul	Y	38.	Make comp emissions known	Y
6.	South Africa sanctions	Y	39.	Allow toxic victims suits	Y
7.	Death penalty-drug bill	N	40.	Strike Superfund "VAT"	Y
8.	Evidence-warrantless srch	N	41.	Notify emp-plant closing	Y
9.	Life term-second drug off	N	42.	Bar emp consult-plant clo	N
10.	Military use in drug war	N	43.	Medicare cuts;Tax incres'	Y
11.	Troop reduction in Europe	N	44.	Delete 12 MX missiles	Y
12.	Prohibit chemical weapons	Y	45.	Spending cuts;Tax incres'	Y
13.	Bar ASAT testing	Y	46.	Textile Import Quotas	Y
14.	Abide SALT II weapons ban	Y	47.	Cut some school lunch fds	N
15.	Follow SALT II-Soviets do	N	48.	Clean Water Act Amendmnts	N
16.	Reduce SDI funding	Y	49.	Youth work projects	Y
17.	Increase SDI funding	N	50.	Assist military in Angola	N
18.	Purchase Trident sub	N	51.	Allow US troops-Nicaragua	N
19.	Delete 12 MX;Add conv wpn	Y	52.	Pentagon polygraph exams	?
20.	Raise speed limit	N	53.	Bar ASAT testing	Y
21.	Textile Import Quotas(*)	Y	54.	Suspend def pmt for abuse	Y
22.	Req Pentagon buy US goods	Y	55.	Bar Pentagon-contr emplmt	Y
23.	AIDS ins anti-dscriminatn	Y	56.	Increase SDI funding	N
24.	Nicaraguan refugee aid	Y	57.	Reduce SDI funding	Y
25.	Nicaraguan contra aid	N	58.	Produce chemical weapons	N
26.	US abide by SALT II	N	59.	Bar CIA fndg in Nicaragua	Y
27.	Prohibit Saudi arms sale	Y	60.	South Africa sanctions	Y
28.	Military Retiremnt Reform	Y	61.	Cut SS COLAs; Raise taxes	N
29.	Nicaraguan refugee aid	Y	62.	Let US invest-So Africa	N
30.	Ease '68 Gun Control Act	N	63.	Approve 21 MX for 1985	N
31.	Bar intrstat handgun tran	Y	64.	Emergency Farm Credit	Y
32.	Keep '68 Gun Control Act	Y	65.	Awards to whistle blowers	Y
33.	Nicaraguan contra aid	N	66.	African disaster relief	Y

VENTO, BRUCE F. (Cont.)

67. Ban bank loans to So Afr Y
68. Bar coun duty-free trtmt Y
69. Steel import limits Y
70. Soc Sec COLAs=inflation Y
71. Bar haz waste vctms suits N
72. Prohibit aid to Nicaragua Y
73. Cut $-Schs bar sch prayer N
74. Raise taxes; Cut Medicare Y
75. Alien residncy-prior 1982 N
76. Alien residncy-prior 1980 N
77. Pen emp-hire illgl aliens Y
78. Lmt Persh II/cruse-Europe Y
79. Delete 34 B-1 bombers Y
80. Bar purch of Pershing II Y
81. Bar purchase of Sgt York #
82. Delete $ for Trident II Y
83. Allow 15 MX missiles N
84. Bar MX procurement-1985 Y
85. Equal Access Act N
86. Aid to El Salvador N
87. Bar Nicarag water mining Y
88. Physician/Medicare freeze N
89. Increase "sin" taxes Y
90. End SBA direct loans N
91. Sell Conrail N
92. Equal Rights Amendment Y
93. Marines in Lebanon N
94. Eminent domain-Coal comps N
95. Prohibit EPA sanctions Y
96. SS age increase/Reforms N
97. Auto domestic content req Y
98. Delete jobs program fundg N
99. Highway-Gas tax bill Y
100. Raise Medicare;Cut defnse Y
101. Emergency housing aid Y
102. Across-the-board tax cuts N
103. Gramm-Latta II targets N
104. Delete B-1 bomber funds Y
105. Dsapprov Saudi AWACS sale Y
106. Disapprove oil import fee ?
107. Rail Deregulation Y
108. Dsapp India nuc fuel sale Y
109. Mil draft registration N
110. Chrysler Loan Guarantees Y
111. Prohibit school busing N
112. Nuclear plant moratorium Y
113. Oil price controls Y
114. Tuition Tax Credits Y
115. Est Consumer Protect Agcy Y
116. Eliminate B-1 bomber fnds Y
117. Subminimum wage for youth N
118. Delete crude oil tax N
119. Natural gas deregulation N

Presidential Support Score: 1986 - 18% 1985 - 21%

SABO, MARTIN OLAV -- Minnesota 5th District [Democrat]. County of Hennepin (pt.). Prior Terms: House: 1979-86. Born: February 28, 1938; Crosby, N.D. Education: Augsburg College (B.A.); University of Minnesota. Occupation: Minnesota representative (1960-78).

1. Immigration Reform Y
2. Open fld-search warrants N
3. Civil pnty-hire ill alien N
4. So Afr sanc-veto override Y
5. Tax Overhaul Y
6. South Africa sanctions Y
7. Death penalty-drug bill N
8. Evidence-warrantless srch N
9. Life term-second drug off N
10. Military use in drug war N
11. Troop reduction in Europe N
12. Prohibit chemical weapons Y
13. Bar ASAT testing Y
14. Abide SALT II weapons ban Y
15. Follow SALT II-Soviets do N
16. Reduce SDI funding Y
17. Increase SDI funding N
18. Purchase Trident sub Y
19. Delete 12 MX;Add conv wpn Y
20. Raise speed limit N
21. Textile Import Quotas(*) Y
22. Req Pentagon buy US goods Y
23. AIDS ins anti-dscriminatn Y
24. Nicaraguan refugee aid Y
25. Nicaraguan contra aid N
26. US abide by SALT II N
27. Prohibit Saudi arms sale Y
28. Military Retiremnt Reform Y
29. Nicaraguan refugee aid Y
30. Ease '68 Gun Control Act N
31. Bar intrstat handgun tran Y
32. Keep '68 Gun Control Act Y
33. Nicaraguan contra aid N
34. Bar emp polygraph testing Y
35. Tax Overhaul consideratn Y
36. Bar armor-piercing ammo Y
37. Tax Overhaul consideratn Y
38. Make comp emissions known Y
39. Allow toxic victims suits Y
40. Strike Superfund "VAT" Y
41. Notify emp-plant closing Y
42. Bar emp consult-plant clo N
43. Medicare cuts;Tax incres' Y
44. Delete 12 MX missiles Y
45. Spending cuts;Tax incres' Y
46. Textile Import Quotas N

SABO, MARTIN OLAV (Cont.)

47. Cut some school lunch fds N
48. Clean Water Act Amendmnts N
49. Youth work projects Y
50. Assist military in Angola N
51. Allow US troops-Nicaragua N
52. Pentagon polygraph exams N
53. Bar ASAT testing Y
54. Suspend def pmt for abuse Y
55. Bar Pentagon-contr emplmt Y
56. Increase SDI funding N
57. Reduce SDI funding Y
58. Produce chemical weapons N
59. Bar CIA fndg in Nicaragua Y
60. South Africa sanctions Y
61. Cut SS COLAs; Raise taxes N
62. Let US invest-So Africa N
63. Approve 21 MX for 1985 N
64. Emergency Farm Credit Y
65. Awards to whistle blowers Y
66. African disaster relief Y
67. Ban bank loans to So Afr Y
68. Bar coun duty-free trtmt N
69. Steel import limits Y
70. Soc Sec COLAs=inflation Y
71. Bar haz waste vctms suits N
72. Prohibit aid to Nicaragua Y
73. Cut $-Schs bar sch prayer N
74. Raise taxes; Cut Medicare Y
75. Alien residncy-prior 1982 N
76. Alien residncy-prior 1980 N
77. Pen emp-hire illgl aliens Y
78. Lmt Persh II/cruse-Europe ?
79. Delete 34 B-1 bombers Y
80. Bar purch of Pershing II Y
81. Bar purchase of Sgt York Y
82. Delete $ for Trident II Y
83. Allow 15 MX missiles N
84. Bar MX procurement-1985 Y
85. Equal Access Act N
86. Aid to El Salvador N
87. Bar Nicarag water mining Y
88. Physician/Medicare freeze N
89. Increase "sin" taxes Y
90. End SBA direct loans N
91. Sell Conrail N
92. Equal Rights Amendment Y
93. Marines in Lebanon N
94. Eminent domain-Coal comps N
95. Prohibit EPA sanctions ?
96. SS age increase/Reforms N
97. Auto domestic content req Y
98. Delete jobs program fundg N
99. Highway-Gas tax bill Y
100. Raise Medicare;Cut defnse Y
101. Emergency housing aid Y
102. Across-the-board tax cuts N
103. Gramm-Latta II targets N
104. Delete B-1 bomber funds Y
105. Dsapprov Saudi AWACS sale Y
106. Disapprove oil import fee N
107. Rail Deregulation N
108. Dsapp India nuc fuel sale Y
109. Mil draft registration N
110. Chrysler Loan Guarantees Y
111. Prohibit school busing N
112. Nuclear plant moratorium Y
113. Oil price controls Y

Presidential Support Score: 1986 - 19% 1985 - 16%

SIKORSKI, GERRY -- Minnesota 6th District [Democrat]. Counties of Anoka, Hennepin (pt.), Ramsey (pt.), Sherburne (pt.), Washington (pt.) and Wright (pt.). Prior Terms: House: 1983-86. Born: April 26, 1948; Breckenridge, Minn. Education: University of Minnesota (B.A., J.D.). Occupation: Attorney; township and city attorney; treasurer, Legal Assistance of Minnesota; president, Washington County Legal Assistance; Minnesota senator (1976-82).

1. Immigration Reform N
2. Open fld-search warrants N
3. Civil pnty-hire ill alien N
4. So Afr sanc-veto override Y
5. Tax Overhaul Y
6. South Africa sanctions Y
7. Death penalty-drug bill N
8. Evidence-warrantless srch N
9. Life term-second drug off ?
10. Military use in drug war ?
11. Troop reduction in Europe Y
12. Prohibit chemical weapons Y
13. Bar ASAT testing Y
14. Abide SALT II weapons ban Y
15. Follow SALT II-Soviets do N
16. Reduce SDI funding Y
17. Increase SDI funding N
18. Purchase Trident sub Y
19. Delete 12 MX;Add conv wpn Y
20. Raise speed limit N
21. Textile Import Quotas(*) Y
22. Req Pentagon buy US goods Y
23. AIDS ins anti-dscriminatn Y
24. Nicaraguan refugee aid Y
25. Nicaraguan contra aid N
26. US abide by SALT II N

SIKORSKI, GERRY (Cont.)

27. Prohibit Saudi arms sale	Y		62. Let US invest-So Africa	N
28. Military Retiremnt Reform	Y		63. Approve 21 MX for 1985	N
29. Nicaraguan refugee aid	Y		64. Emergency Farm Credit	Y
30. Ease '68 Gun Control Act	Y		65. Awards to whistle blowers	Y
31. Bar intrstat handgun tran	N		66. African disaster relief	Y
32. Keep '68 Gun Control Act	N		67. Ban bank loans to So Afr	Y
33. Nicaraguan contra aid	N		68. Bar coun duty-free trtmt	Y
34. Bar emp polygraph testing	Y		69. Steel import limits	Y
35. Tax Overhaul consideratn	Y		70. Soc Sec COLAs=inflation	Y
36. Bar armor-piercing ammo	Y		71. Bar haz waste vctms suits	N
37. Tax Overhaul consideratn	Y		72. Prohibit aid to Nicaragua	Y
38. Make comp emissions known	Y		73. Cut $-Schs bar sch prayer	N
39. Allow toxic victims suits	Y		74. Raise taxes; Cut Medicare	N
40. Strike Superfund "VAT"	Y		75. Alien residncy-prior 1982	Y
41. Notify emp-plant closing	Y		76. Alien residncy-prior 1980	N
42. Bar emp consult-plant clo	N		77. Pen emp-hire illgl aliens	Y
43. Medicare cuts;Tax incres'	Y		78. Lmt Persh II/cruse-Europe	Y
44. Delete 12 MX missiles	Y		79. Delete 34 B-1 bombers	Y
45. Spending cuts;Tax incres'	Y		80. Bar purch of Pershing II	Y
46. Textile Import Quotas	Y		81. Bar purchase of Sgt York	Y
47. Cut some school lunch fds	N		82. Delete $ for Trident II	Y
48. Clean Water Act Amendmnts	N		83. Allow 15 MX missiles	N
49. Youth work projects	Y		84. Bar MX procurement-1985	Y
50. Assist military in Angola	N		85. Equal Access Act	Y
51. Allow US troops-Nicaragua	N		86. Aid to El Salvador	N
52. Pentagon polygraph exams	Y		87. Bar Nicarag water mining	Y
53. Bar ASAT testing	Y		88. Physician/Medicare freeze	N
54. Suspend def pmt for abuse	Y		89. Increase "sin" taxes	Y
55. Bar Pentagon-contr emplmt	Y		90. End SBA direct loans	N
56. Increase SDI funding	N		91. Sell Conrail	N
57. Reduce SDI funding	Y		92. Equal Rights Amendment	Y
58. Produce chemical weapons	N		93. Marines in Lebanon	N
59. Bar CIA fndg in Nicaragua	Y		94. Eminent domain-Coal comps	N
60. South Africa sanctions	Y		95. Prohibit EPA sanctions	Y
61. Cut SS COLAs; Raise taxes	N		96. SS age increase/Reforms	N

Presidential Support Score: 1986 - 16% 1985 - 23%

STANGELAND, ARLAN -- Minnesota 7th District [Republican]. Counties of Becker, Beltrami (pt.), Benton, Clay, Clearwater, Grant (pt.), Hubbard (pt.), Kittson, Lake of the Woods, Mahnomen, Marshall, Morrison, Norman, Otter Tail, Pennington, Polk, Red Lake, Roseau, Sherburne (pt.), Sterns, Todd, Wadena and Wilkin. Prior Terms: House: 1977 (Special Election)-1986. Born: February 8, 1930; Fargo, N.D. Occupation: Minnesota representative (1966-74); farmer; member, Board of Education (1976).

1. Immigration Reform	Y		12. Prohibit chemical weapons	N
2. Open fld-search warrants	Y		13. Bar ASAT testing	N
3. Civil pnty-hire ill alien	N		14. Abide SALT II weapons ban	N
4. So Afr sanc-veto override	?		15. Follow SALT II-Soviets do	Y
5. Tax Overhaul	Y		16. Reduce SDI funding	N
6. South Africa sanctions	Y		17. Increase SDI funding	N
7. Death penalty-drug bill	Y		18. Purchase Trident sub	N
8. Evidence-warrantless srch	Y		19. Delete 12 MX;Add conv wpn	N
9. Life term-second drug off	Y		20. Raise speed limit	N
10. Military use in drug war	Y		21. Textile Import Quotas(*)	N
11. Troop reduction in Europe	N		22. Req Pentagon buy US goods	N

STANGELAND, ARLAN (Cont.)

23. AIDS ins anti-dscriminatn N
24. Nicaraguan refugee aid N
25. Nicaraguan contra aid Y
26. US abide by SALT II Y
27. Prohibit Saudi arms sale N
28. Military Retiremnt Reform Y
29. Nicaraguan refugee aid Y
30. Ease '68 Gun Control Act Y
31. Bar intrstat handgun tran N
32. Keep '68 Gun Control Act N
33. Nicaraguan contra aid Y
34. Bar emp polygraph testing Y
35. Tax Overhaul consideratn Y
36. Bar armor-piercing ammo Y
37. Tax Overhaul consideratn Y
38. Make comp emissions known N
39. Allow toxic victims suits N
40. Strike Superfund "VAT" N
41. Notify emp-plant closing N
42. Bar emp consult-plant clo Y
43. Medicare cuts;Tax incres' N
44. Delete 12 MX missiles N
45. Spending cuts;Tax incres' N
46. Textile Import Quotas N
47. Cut some school lunch fds N
48. Clean Water Act Amendmnts Y
49. Youth work projects N
50. Assist military in Angola Y
51. Allow US troops-Nicaragua Y
52. Pentagon polygraph exams Y
53. Bar ASAT testing N
54. Suspend def pmt for abuse N
55. Bar Pentagon-contr emplmt Y
56. Increase SDI funding Y
57. Reduce SDI funding N
58. Produce chemical weapons Y
59. Bar CIA fndg in Nicaragua N
60. South Africa sanctions N
61. Cut SS COLAs; Raise taxes N
62. Let US invest-So Africa Y
63. Approve 21 MX for 1985 Y
64. Emergency Farm Credit Y
65. Awards to whistle blowers Y
66. African disaster relief Y
67. Ban bank loans to So Afr Y
68. Bar coun duty-free trtmt N
69. Steel import limits N
70. Soc Sec COLAs=inflation Y
71. Bar haz waste vctms suits Y
72. Prohibit aid to Nicaragua Y
73. Cut $-Schs bar sch prayer Y
74. Raise taxes; Cut Medicare N
75. Alien residncy-prior 1982 N
76. Alien residncy-prior 1980 Y
77. Pen emp-hire illgl aliens N
78. Lmt Persh II/cruse-Europe N
79. Delete 34 B-1 bombers ?
80. Bar purch of Pershing II N
81. Bar purchase of Sgt York N
82. Delete $ for Trident II N
83. Allow 15 MX missiles Y
84. Bar MX procurement-1985 N
85. Equal Access Act Y
86. Aid to El Salvador Y
87. Bar Nicarag water mining #
88. Physician/Medicare freeze Y
89. Increase "sin" taxes N
90. End SBA direct loans Y
91. Sell Conrail Y
92. Equal Rights Amendment N
93. Marines in Lebanon Y
94. Eminent domain-Coal comps N
95. Prohibit EPA sanctions Y
96. SS age increase/Reforms Y
97. Auto domestic content req N
98. Delete jobs program fundg Y
99. Highway-Gas tax bill N
100. Raise Medicare;Cut defnse Y
101. Emergency housing aid Y
102. Across-the-board tax cuts Y
103. Gramm-Latta II targets Y
104. Delete B-1 bomber funds N
105. Dsapprov Saudi AWACS sale N
106. Disapprove oil import fee Y
107. Rail Deregulation Y
108. Dsapp India nuc fuel sale Y
109. Mil draft registration Y
110. Chrysler Loan Guarantees Y
111. Prohibit school busing Y
112. Nuclear plant moratorium N
113. Oil price controls N
114. Tuition Tax Credits Y
115. Est Consumer Protect Agcy N
116. Eliminate B-1 bomber fnds N
117. Subminimum wage for youth Y
118. Delete crude oil tax Y
119. Natural gas deregulation Y

Presidential Support Score: 1986 - 69% 1985 - 65%

OBERSTAR, JAMES L. -- Minnesota 8th District [Democrat]. Counties of Aitkin, Beltrami (pt.), Carlton, Cass, Chisago, Cook, Crow Wing, Hubbard (pt.), Isanti, Itasca, Kanabec, Koochiching, Lake, Mille Locs, Pine, St. Louis and Sherburne (pt.). Prior Terms: House: 1975-86. Born: September 10, 1934; Chisholm, Minn. Education: St. Thomas College (B.A.); College of Europe, Bruges, Belgium (M.A.); Georgetown University. Occupation: Administrative assistant to congressman (1963-74).

OBERSTAR, JAMES L. (Cont.)

1. Immigration Reform Y
2. Open fld-search warrants N
3. Civil pnty-hire ill alien N
4. So Afr sanc-veto override Y
5. Tax Overhaul Y
6. South Africa sanctions Y
7. Death penalty-drug bill N
8. Evidence-warrantless srch N
9. Life term-second drug off N
10. Military use in drug war N
11. Troop reduction in Europe N
12. Prohibit chemical weapons Y
13. Bar ASAT testing Y
14. Abide SALT II weapons ban Y
15. Follow SALT II-Soviets do N
16. Reduce SDI funding Y
17. Increase SDI funding N
18. Purchase Trident sub Y
19. Delete 12 MX;Add conv wpn Y
20. Raise speed limit N
21. Textile Import Quotas(*) Y
22. Req Pentagon buy US goods Y
23. AIDS ins anti-dscriminatn Y
24. Nicaraguan refugee aid Y
25. Nicaraguan contra aid N
26. US abide by SALT II N
27. Prohibit Saudi arms sale Y
28. Military Retiremnt Reform ?
29. Nicaraguan refugee aid Y
30. Ease '68 Gun Control Act Y
31. Bar intrstat handgun tran N
32. Keep '68 Gun Control Act N
33. Nicaraguan contra aid N
34. Bar emp polygraph testing Y
35. Tax Overhaul consideratn Y
36. Bar armor-piercing ammo Y
37. Tax Overhaul consideratn Y
38. Make comp emissions known Y
39. Allow toxic victims suits Y
40. Strike Superfund "VAT" Y
41. Notify emp-plant closing Y
42. Bar emp consult-plant clo N
43. Medicare cuts;Tax incres' Y
44. Delete 12 MX missiles Y
45. Spending cuts;Tax incres' Y
46. Textile Import Quotas Y
47. Cut some school lunch fds N
48. Clean Water Act Amendmnts N
49. Youth work projects Y
50. Assist military in Angola N
51. Allow US troops-Nicaragua N
52. Pentagon polygraph exams N
53. Bar ASAT testing Y
54. Suspend def pmt for abuse Y
55. Bar Pentagon-contr emplmt Y
56. Increase SDI funding N
57. Reduce SDI funding Y
58. Produce chemical weapons N
59. Bar CIA fndg in Nicaragua Y
60. South Africa sanctions Y
61. Cut SS COLAs; Raise taxes N
62. Let US invest-So Africa N
63. Approve 21 MX for 1985 N
64. Emergency Farm Credit Y
65. Awards to whistle blowers Y
66. African disaster relief Y
67. Ban bank loans to So Afr Y
68. Bar coun duty-free trtmt Y
69. Steel import limits Y
70. Soc Sec COLAs=inflation Y
71. Bar haz waste vctms suits N
72. Prohibit aid to Nicaragua Y
73. Cut $-Schs bar sch prayer N
74. Raise taxes; Cut Medicare Y
75. Alien residncy-prior 1982 N
76. Alien residncy-prior 1980 N
77. Pen emp-hire illgl aliens ?
78. Lmt Persh II/cruse-Europe Y
79. Delete 34 B-1 bombers Y
80. Bar purch of Pershing II Y
81. Bar purchase of Sgt York Y
82. Delete $ for Trident II Y
83. Allow 15 MX missiles N
84. Bar MX procurement-1985 Y
85. Equal Access Act N
86. Aid to El Salvador N
87. Bar Nicarag water mining Y
88. Physician/Medicare freeze N
89. Increase "sin" taxes Y
90. End SBA direct loans N
91. Sell Conrail N
92. Equal Rights Amendment Y
93. Marines in Lebanon N
94. Eminent domain-Coal comps N
95. Prohibit EPA sanctions Y
96. SS age increase/Reforms N
97. Auto domestic content req Y
98. Delete jobs program fundg N
99. Highway-Gas tax bill N
100. Raise Medicare;Cut defnse Y
101. Emergency housing aid Y
102. Across-the-board tax cuts N
103. Gramm-Latta II targets N
104. Delete B-1 bomber funds Y
105. Dsapprov Saudi AWACS sale Y
106. Disapprove oil import fee Y
107. Rail Deregulation Y
108. Dsapp India nuc fuel sale Y
109. Mil draft registration N
110. Chrysler Loan Guarantees Y
111. Prohibit school busing N
112. Nuclear plant moratorium Y
113. Oil price controls Y
114. Tuition Tax Credits N
115. Est Consumer Protect Agcy Y
116. Eliminate B-1 bomber fnds Y
117. Subminimum wage for youth N
118. Delete crude oil tax N

OBERSTAR, JAMES L. (Cont.)
119. Natural gas deregulation N

Presidential Support Score: 1986 - 17% 1985 - 16%

MISSISSIPPI

WHITTEN, JAMIE L. -- Mississippi 1st District [Democrat]. Counties of Alcorn, Benton, Calhoun, Chickasaw, DeSoto, Grenada, Itawamba, Lafayette, Lee, Marshall, Monroe, Panola, Pontotoc, Prentiss, Tallahatchie (pt.), Tate, Tippah, Tishomingo, Union and Yalobusha. Prior Terms: House: 1941 (Special Election)-1986. Born: April 18, 1910; Cascilla, Miss. Education: University of Mississippi. Occupation: Attorney; school princial (1930-31); district attorney; Mississippi representative.

1. Immigration Reform N
2. Open fld-search warrants Y
3. Civil pnty-hire ill alien N
4. So Afr sanc-veto override Y
5. Tax Overhaul Y
6. South Africa sanctions Y
7. Death penalty-drug bill ?
8. Evidence-warrantless srch ?
9. Life term-second drug off ?
10. Military use in drug war ?
11. Troop reduction in Europe ?
12. Prohibit chemical weapons Y
13. Bar ASAT testing Y
14. Abide SALT II weapons ban Y
15. Follow SALT II-Soviets do N
16. Reduce SDI funding N
17. Increase SDI funding N
18. Purchase Trident sub Y
19. Delete 12 MX;Add conv wpn N
20. Raise speed limit N
21. Textile Import Quotas(*) Y
22. Req Pentagon buy US goods Y
23. AIDS ins anti-dscriminatn Y
24. Nicaraguan refugee aid N
25. Nicaraguan contra aid N
26. US abide by SALT II N
27. Prohibit Saudi arms sale Y
28. Military Retiremnt Reform Y
29. Nicaraguan refugee aid N
30. Ease '68 Gun Control Act Y
31. Bar intrstat handgun tran N
32. Keep '68 Gun Control Act N
33. Nicaraguan contra aid N
34. Bar emp polygraph testing N
35. Tax Overhaul consideratn Y
36. Bar armor-piercing ammo Y
37. Tax Overhaul consideratn Y
38. Make comp emissions known ?
39. Allow toxic victims suits ?
40. Strike Superfund "VAT" Y
41. Notify emp-plant closing Y
42. Bar emp consult-plant clo Y
43. Medicare cuts;Tax incres' Y
44. Delete 12 MX missiles N
45. Spending cuts;Tax incres' N
46. Textile Import Quotas Y
47. Cut some school lunch fds N
48. Clean Water Act Amendmnts N
49. Youth work projects Y
50. Assist military in Angola Y
51. Allow US troops-Nicaragua N
52. Pentagon polygraph exams ?
53. Bar ASAT testing N
54. Suspend def pmt for abuse N
55. Bar Pentagon-contr emplmt Y
56. Increase SDI funding N
57. Reduce SDI funding N
58. Produce chemical weapons N
59. Bar CIA fndg in Nicaragua Y
60. South Africa sanctions Y
61. Cut SS COLAs; Raise taxes N
62. Let US invest-So Africa ?
63. Approve 21 MX for 1985 N
64. Emergency Farm Credit Y
65. Awards to whistle blowers Y
66. African disaster relief Y
67. Ban bank loans to So Afr Y
68. Bar coun duty-free trtmt Y
69. Steel import limits Y
70. Soc Sec COLAs=inflation Y
71. Bar haz waste vctms suits Y
72. Prohibit aid to Nicaragua Y
73. Cut $-Schs bar sch prayer Y
74. Raise taxes; Cut Medicare N
75. Alien residncy-prior 1982 N
76. Alien residncy-prior 1980 N
77. Pen emp-hire illgl aliens N
78. Lmt Persh II/cruse-Europe N
79. Delete 34 B-1 bombers N
80. Bar purch of Pershing II N
81. Bar purchase of Sgt York N
82. Delete $ for Trident II N
83. Allow 15 MX missiles N
84. Bar MX procurement-1985 Y
85. Equal Access Act Y
86. Aid to El Salvador N

WHITTEN, JAMIE L. (Cont.)

87. Bar Nicarag water mining Y
88. Physician/Medicare freeze N
89. Increase "sin" taxes N
90. End SBA direct loans N
91. Sell Conrail N
92. Equal Rights Amendment Y
93. Marines in Lebanon Y
94. Eminent domain-Coal comps N
95. Prohibit EPA sanctions N
96. SS age increase/Reforms N
97. Auto domestic content req Y
98. Delete jobs program fundg N
99. Highway-Gas tax bill Y
100. Raise Medicare;Cut defnse Y
101. Emergency housing aid Y
102. Across-the-board tax cuts N
103. Gramm-Latta II targets N
104. Delete B-1 bomber funds N
105. Dsapprov Saudi AWACS sale N
106. Disapprove oil import fee Y
107. Rail Deregulation N
108. Dsapp India nuc fuel sale Y
109. Mil draft registration Y
110. Chrysler Loan Guarantees Y
111. Prohibit school busing Y
112. Nuclear plant moratorium N
113. Oil price controls N
114. Tuition Tax Credits Y
115. Est Consumer Protect Agcy ?
116. Eliminate B-1 bomber fnds N
117. Subminimum wage for youth Y
118. Delete crude oil tax Y
119. Natural gas deregulation N

Presidential Support Score: 1986 - 31% 1985 - 33%

FRANKLIN, WEBB -- Mississippi 2nd District [Republican]. Counties of Attala, Bolivar, Carroll, Choctaw, Coahoma, Holmes, Humphreys, Issaquena, Leake, Leflore, Madison, Montgomery, Quitman, Sharkey, Sunflower, Tallahatchie (pt.), Tunica, Warren, Washington, Webster and Yazoo. Prior Terms: House: 1983-86. Born: December 13, 1941; Greenwood, Miss. Education: Mississippi State University (B.A.); University of Mississippi (J.D.). Military Service: U.S. Army. Occupation: Attorney; assistant district attorney (1972-78); circuit judge (1978-82).

1. Immigration Reform N
2. Open fld-search warrants N
3. Civil pnty-hire ill alien Y
4. So Afr sanc-veto override Y
5. Tax Overhaul Y
6. South Africa sanctions Y
7. Death penalty-drug bill Y
8. Evidence-warrantless srch Y
9. Life term-second drug off Y
10. Military use in drug war Y
11. Troop reduction in Europe N
12. Prohibit chemical weapons N
13. Bar ASAT testing N
14. Abide SALT II weapons ban N
15. Follow SALT II-Soviets do Y
16. Reduce SDI funding N
17. Increase SDI funding Y
18. Purchase Trident sub N
19. Delete 12 MX;Add conv wpn N
20. Raise speed limit Y
21. Textile Import Quotas(*) Y
22. Req Pentagon buy US goods Y
23. AIDS ins anti-dscriminatn N
24. Nicaraguan refugee aid N
25. Nicaraguan contra aid Y
26. US abide by SALT II Y
27. Prohibit Saudi arms sale ?
28. Military Retiremnt Reform Y
29. Nicaraguan refugee aid Y
30. Ease '68 Gun Control Act Y
31. Bar intrstat handgun tran N
32. Keep '68 Gun Control Act N
33. Nicaraguan contra aid Y
34. Bar emp polygraph testing N
35. Tax Overhaul consideratn N
36. Bar armor-piercing ammo Y
37. Tax Overhaul consideratn N
38. Make comp emissions known N
39. Allow toxic victims suits N
40. Strike Superfund "VAT" N
41. Notify emp-plant closing N
42. Bar emp consult-plant clo Y
43. Medicare cuts;Tax incres' N
44. Delete 12 MX missiles N
45. Spending cuts;Tax incres' N
46. Textile Import Quotas Y
47. Cut some school lunch fds Y
48. Clean Water Act Amendmnts Y
49. Youth work projects N
50. Assist military in Angola Y
51. Allow US troops-Nicaragua Y
52. Pentagon polygraph exams Y
53. Bar ASAT testing N
54. Suspend def pmt for abuse ?
55. Bar Pentagon-contr emplmt Y
56. Increase SDI funding Y

FRANKLIN, WEBB (Cont.)

57. Reduce SDI funding	N		77. Pen emp-hire illgl aliens	N
58. Produce chemical weapons	N		78. Lmt Persh II/cruse-Europe	N
59. Bar CIA fndg in Nicaragua	N		79. Delete 34 B-1 bombers	N
60. South Africa sanctions	N		80. Bar purch of Pershing II	N
61. Cut SS COLAs; Raise taxes	N		81. Bar purchase of Sgt York	N
62. Let US invest-So Africa	Y		82. Delete $ for Trident II	N
63. Approve 21 MX for 1985	Y		83. Allow 15 MX missiles	Y
64. Emergency Farm Credit	Y		84. Bar MX procurement-1985	N
65. Awards to whistle blowers	Y		85. Equal Access Act	Y
66. African disaster relief	Y		86. Aid to El Salvador	Y
67. Ban bank loans to So Afr	Y		87. Bar Nicarag water mining	N
68. Bar coun duty-free trtmt	N		88. Physician/Medicare freeze	Y
69. Steel import limits	N		89. Increase "sin" taxes	Y
70. Soc Sec COLAs=inflation	Y		90. End SBA direct loans	Y
71. Bar haz waste vctms suits	Y		91. Sell Conrail	Y
72. Prohibit aid to Nicaragua	N		92. Equal Rights Amendment	N
73. Cut $-Schs bar sch prayer	Y		93. Marines in Lebanon	Y
74. Raise taxes; Cut Medicare	Y		94. Eminent domain-Coal comps	Y
75. Alien residncy-prior 1982	Y		95. Prohibit EPA sanctions	Y
76. Alien residncy-prior 1980	Y		96. SS age increase/Reforms	Y

Presidential Support Score: 1986 - 55% 1985 - 68%

MONTGOMERY, G. V. (Sonny) -- Mississippi 3rd District [Democrat]. Counties of Clarke, Clay, Jasper, Jones, Kemper, Lauderdale, Lownces, Nesnoba, Newton, Noxubee, Oktibbeha, Rankin, Scott, Simpson (pt.), Smith and Winston. Prior Terms: House: 1967-86. Born: Meridian, Miss. Education: Mississippi State University (B.S.). Military Service: U.S. Army. Occupation: Mississippi senator (1956-66).

1. Immigration Reform	N		29. Nicaraguan refugee aid	N
2. Open fld-search warrants	N		30. Ease '68 Gun Control Act	Y
3. Civil pnty-hire ill alien	N		31. Bar intrstat handgun tran	N
4. So Afr sanc-veto override	N		32. Keep '68 Gun Control Act	N
5. Tax Overhaul	N		33. Nicaraguan contra aid	Y
6. South Africa sanctions	N		34. Bar emp polygraph testing	N
7. Death penalty-drug bill	Y		35. Tax Overhaul consideratn	Y
8. Evidence-warrantless srch	Y		36. Bar armor-piercing ammo	Y
9. Life term-second drug off	Y		37. Tax Overhaul consideratn	Y
10. Military use in drug war	N		38. Make comp emissions known	N
11. Troop reduction in Europe	N		39. Allow toxic victims suits	N
12. Prohibit chemical weapons	N		40. Strike Superfund "VAT"	N
13. Bar ASAT testing	N		41. Notify emp-plant closing	N
14. Abide SALT II weapons ban	N		42. Bar emp consult-plant clo	Y
15. Follow SALT II-Soviets do	Y		43. Medicare cuts;Tax incres'	Y
16. Reduce SDI funding	N		44. Delete 12 MX missiles	N
17. Increase SDI funding	N		45. Spending cuts;Tax incres'	Y
18. Purchase Trident sub	N		46. Textile Import Quotas	Y
19. Delete 12 MX;Add conv wpn	N		47. Cut some school lunch fds	Y
20. Raise speed limit	N		48. Clean Water Act Amendmnts	Y
21. Textile Import Quotas(*)	Y		49. Youth work projects	N
22. Req Pentagon buy US goods	N		50. Assist military in Angola	Y
23. AIDS ins anti-dscriminatn	N		51. Allow US troops-Nicaragua	Y
24. Nicaraguan refugee aid	N		52. Pentagon polygraph exams	Y
25. Nicaraguan contra aid	Y		53. Bar ASAT testing	N
26. US abide by SALT II	Y		54. Suspend def pmt for abuse	N
27. Prohibit Saudi arms sale	N		55. Bar Pentagon-contr emplmt	N
28. Military Retiremnt Reform	Y		56. Increase SDI funding	N

MONTGOMERY, G. V. (Sonny) Cont)

57. Reduce SDI funding N
58. Produce chemical weapons Y
59. Bar CIA fndg in Nicaragua N
60. South Africa sanctions N
61. Cut SS COLAs; Raise taxes Y
62. Let US invest-So Africa Y
63. Approve 21 MX for 1985 Y
64. Emergency Farm Credit Y
65. Awards to whistle blowers Y
66. African disaster relief Y
67. Ban bank loans to So Afr ?
68. Bar coun duty-free trtmt Y
69. Steel import limits Y
70. Soc Sec COLAs=inflation Y
71. Bar haz waste vctms suits Y
72. Prohibit aid to Nicaragua N
73. Cut $-Schs bar sch prayer Y
74. Raise taxes; Cut Medicare Y
75. Alien residncy-prior 1982 N
76. Alien residncy-prior 1980 N
77. Pen emp-hire illgl aliens N
78. Lmt Persh II/cruse-Europe N
79. Delete 34 B-1 bombers N
80. Bar purch of Pershing II N
81. Bar purchase of Sgt York N
82. Delete $ for Trident II N
83. Allow 15 MX missiles Y
84. Bar MX procurement-1985 N
85. Equal Access Act Y
86. Aid to El Salvador Y
87. Bar Nicarag water mining N
88. Physician/Medicare freeze Y
89. Increase "sin" taxes Y
90. End SBA direct loans N
91. Sell Conrail Y
92. Equal Rights Amendment N
93. Marines in Lebanon Y
94. Eminent domain-Coal comps Y
95. Prohibit EPA sanctions Y
96. SS age increase/Reforms Y
97. Auto domestic content req N
98. Delete jobs program fundg Y
99. Highway-Gas tax bill Y
100. Raise Medicare;Cut defnse N
101. Emergency housing aid Y
102. Across-the-board tax cuts Y
103. Gramm-Latta II targets Y
104. Delete B-1 bomber funds N
105. Dsapprov Saudi AWACS sale N
106. Disapprove oil import fee Y
107. Rail Deregulation N
108. Dsapp India nuc fuel sale Y
109. Mil draft registration Y
110. Chrysler Loan Guarantees N
111. Prohibit school busing Y
112. Nuclear plant moratorium N
113. Oil price controls N
114. Tuition Tax Credits ?
115. Est Consumer Protect Agcy N
116. Eliminate B-1 bomber fnds N
117. Subminimum wage for youth Y
118. Delete crude oil tax Y
119. Natural gas deregulation Y

Presidential Support Score: 1986 - 57% 1985 - 66%

DOWDY, WAYNE -- Mississippi 4th District [Democrat]. Counties of Adams, Amite, Claiborne, Copiah, Franklin, Hinds, Jefferson, Jefferson Davis, Lawrence, Lincoln, Marion, Pike, Simpson (pt.), Walthall and Wilkinson. Prior Terms: House: 1981 (Special Election)-1986. Born: July 27, 1943; Fitzgerald, Fla. Education: Millsaps College (B.A.); Jackson School of Law (LL.B.). Military Service: Mississippi National Guard; U.S. Army Reserves, 1966-72. Occupation: Radio stations owner; city judge (1970-74); mayor (1978-81).

1. Immigration Reform N
2. Open fld-search warrants N
3. Civil pnty-hire ill alien Y
4. So Afr sanc-veto override Y
5. Tax Overhaul N
6. South Africa sanctions Y
7. Death penalty-drug bill Y
8. Evidence-warrantless srch Y
9. Life term-second drug off Y
10. Military use in drug war Y
11. Troop reduction in Europe N
12. Prohibit chemical weapons N
13. Bar ASAT testing Y
14. Abide SALT II weapons ban Y
15. Follow SALT II-Soviets do N
16. Reduce SDI funding N
17. Increase SDI funding N
18. Purchase Trident sub Y
19. Delete 12 MX;Add conv wpn N
20. Raise speed limit N
21. Textile Import Quotas(*) Y
22. Req Pentagon buy US goods Y
23. AIDS ins anti-dscriminatn Y
24. Nicaraguan refugee aid N
25. Nicaraguan contra aid Y
26. US abide by SALT II N
27. Prohibit Saudi arms sale Y
28. Military Retiremnt Reform Y

DOWDY, WAYNE (Cont.)

29. Nicaraguan refugee aid N
30. Ease '68 Gun Control Act Y
31. Bar intrstat handgun tran N
32. Keep '68 Gun Control Act N
33. Nicaraguan contra aid Y
34. Bar emp polygraph testing N
35. Tax Overhaul consideratn N
36. Bar armor-piercing ammo Y
37. Tax Overhaul consideratn N
38. Make comp emissions known N
39. Allow toxic victims suits N
40. Strike Superfund "VAT" N
41. Notify emp-plant closing N
42. Bar emp consult-plant clo Y
43. Medicare cuts;Tax incres' Y
44. Delete 12 MX missiles N
45. Spending cuts;Tax incres' Y
46. Textile Import Quotas Y
47. Cut some school lunch fds N
48. Clean Water Act Amendmnts N
49. Youth work projects ?
50. Assist military in Angola N
51. Allow US troops-Nicaragua N
52. Pentagon polygraph exams Y
53. Bar ASAT testing Y
54. Suspend def pmt for abuse N
55. Bar Pentagon-contr emplmt Y
56. Increase SDI funding N
57. Reduce SDI funding N
58. Produce chemical weapons Y
59. Bar CIA fndg in Nicaragua N
60. South Africa sanctions Y
61. Cut SS COLAs; Raise taxes N
62. Let US invest-So Africa N
63. Approve 21 MX for 1985 Y
64. Emergency Farm Credit Y
65. Awards to whistle blowers Y
66. African disaster relief Y
67. Ban bank loans to So Afr ?
68. Bar coun duty-free trtmt Y
69. Steel import limits Y
70. Soc Sec COLAs=inflation Y
71. Bar haz waste vctms suits N
72. Prohibit aid to Nicaragua Y
73. Cut $-Schs bar sch prayer Y
74. Cut SS COLAs; Raise taxes Y
75. Alien residncy-prior 1982 N
76. Alien residncy-prior 1980 N
77. Pen emp-hire illgl aliens N
78. Lmt Persh II/cruse-Europe ?
79. Delete 34 B-1 bombers N
80. Bar purch of Pershing II N
81. Bar purchase of Sgt York N
82. Delete $ for Trident II N
83. Allow 15 MX missiles N
84. Bar MX procurement-1985 Y
85. Equal Access Act Y
86. Aid to El Salvador Y
87. Bar Nicarag water mining Y
88. Physician/Medicare freeze N
89. Increase "sin" taxes Y
90. End SBA direct loans N
91. Sell Conrail N
92. Equal Rights Amendment Y
93. Marines in Lebanon N
94. Eminent domain-Coal comps N
95. Prohibit EPA sanctions Y
96. SS age increase/Reforms N
97. Auto domestic content req Y
98. Delete jobs program fundg N
99. Highway-Gas tax bill Y
100. Raise Medicare;Cut defnse Y
101. Emergency housing aid Y
102. Across-the-board tax cuts N
103. Gramm-Latta II targets
104. Delete B-1 bomber funds N
105. Dsapprov Saudi AWACS sale Y

Sworn in July 9, 1981 and missed vote 103.

Presidential Support Score: 1986 - 27% 1985 - 36%

LOTT, TRENT -- Mississippi 5th District [Republican]. Counties of Covington, Forrest, George, Greene, Hancock, Harrison, Jackson, Lamar, Pearl River, Perry, Stone and Wayne. Prior Terms: House: 1973-86. Born: October 9, 1941; Grenada, Miss. Education: University of Mississippi (B.P.A., J.D.). Occupation: Attorney, Bryan and Gordon (1967-68); congressional staff member (1968-72).

1. Immigration Reform Y
2. Open fld-search warrants N
3. Civil pnty-hire ill alien N
4. So Afr sanc-veto override N
5. Tax Overhaul Y
6. South Africa sanctions N
7. Death penalty-drug bill Y
8. Evidence-warrantless srch Y
9. Life term-second drug off Y
10. Military use in drug war Y
11. Troop reduction in Europe ?
12. Prohibit chemical weapons N
13. Bar ASAT testing N
14. Abide SALT II weapons ban N
15. Follow SALT II-Soviets do Y
16. Reduce SDI funding N

LOTT, TRENT (Cont.)

17. Increase SDI funding Y
18. Purchase Trident sub N
19. Delete 12 MX;Add conv wpn N
20. Raise speed limit Y
21. Textile Import Quotas(*) Y
22. Req Pentagon buy US goods N
23. AIDS ins anti-dscriminatn N
24. Nicaraguan refugee aid N
25. Nicaraguan contra aid Y
26. US abide by SALT II Y
27. Prohibit Saudi arms sale Y
28. Military Retiremnt Reform Y
29. Nicaraguan refugee aid Y
30. Ease '68 Gun Control Act Y
31. Bar intrstat handgun tran N
32. Keep '68 Gun Control Act N
33. Nicaraguan contra aid Y
34. Bar emp polygraph testing N
35. Tax Overhaul consideratn N
36. Bar armor-piercing ammo Y
37. Tax Overhaul consideratn N
38. Make comp emissions known N
39. Allow toxic victims suits N
40. Strike Superfund "VAT" N
41. Notify emp-plant closing N
42. Bar emp consult-plant clo Y
43. Medicare cuts;Tax incres' N
44. Delete 12 MX missiles N
45. Spending cuts;Tax incres' N
46. Textile Import Quotas Y
47. Cut some school lunch fds Y
48. Clean Water Act Amendmnts Y
49. Youth work projects N
50. Assist military in Angola Y
51. Allow US troops-Nicaragua Y
52. Pentagon polygraph exams ?
53. Bar ASAT testing N
54. Suspend def pmt for abuse N
55. Bar Pentagon-contr emplmt Y
56. Increase SDI funding Y
57. Reduce SDI funding N
58. Produce chemical weapons Y
59. Bar CIA fndg in Nicaragua N
60. South Africa sanctions N
61. Cut SS COLAs; Raise taxes N
62. Let US invest-So Africa Y
63. Approve 21 MX for 1985 Y
64. Emergency Farm Credit N
65. Awards to whistle blowers Y
66. African disaster relief Y
67. Ban bank loans to So Afr N
68. Bar coun duty-free trtmt N
69. Steel import limits N
70. Soc Sec COLAs=inflation Y
71. Bar haz waste vctms suits Y
72. Prohibit aid to Nicaragua N
73. Cut $-Schs bar sch prayer Y
74. Raise taxes; Cut Medicare N
75. Alien residncy-prior 1982 Y
76. Alien residncy-prior 1980 Y
77. Pen emp-hire illgl aliens N
78. Lmt Persh II/cruse-Europe N
79. Delete 34 B-1 bombers N
80. Bar purch of Pershing II N
81. Bar purchase of Sgt York N
82. Delete $ for Trident II N
83. Allow 15 MX missiles Y
84. Bar MX procurement-1985 N
85. Equal Access Act Y
86. Aid to El Salvador Y
87. Bar Nicarag water mining N
88. Physician/Medicare freeze Y
89. Increase "sin" taxes Y
90. End SBA direct loans N
91. Sell Conrail Y
92. Equal Rights Amendment N
93. Marines in Lebanon Y
94. Eminent domain-coal comps Y
95. Prohibit EPA sanctions Y
96. SS age increase/Reforms Y
97. Auto domestic content req N
98. Delete jobs program fundg Y
99. Highway-Gas tax bill Y
100. Raise Medicare;Cut defnse N
101. Emergency housing aid Y
102. Across-the-board tax cuts Y
103. Gramm-Latta II targets Y
104. Delete B-1 bomber funds N
105. Dsapprov Saudi AWACS sale N
106. Disapprove oil import fee Y
107. Rail Deregulation N
108. Dsapp India nuc fuel sale Y
109. Mil draft registration Y
110. Chrysler Loan Guarantees N
111. Prohibit school busing Y
112. Nuclear plant moratorium N
113. Oil price controls N
114. Tuition Tax Credits ?
115. Est Consumer Protect Agcy N
116. Eliminate B-1 bomber fnds N
117. Subminimum wage for youth Y
118. Delete crude oil tax Y
119. Natural gas deregulation Y

Presidential Support Score: 1986 - 77% 1985 - 73%

MISSOURI

CLAY, WILLIAM (Bill) -- Missouri 1st District [Democrat]. County of St. Louis (pt.), St. Louis City (pt.). Prior Terms: House:

CLAY, WILLIAM (Bill) (Cont.)
1969-86. Born: April 30, 1931; St. Louis, Mo. Education: St. Louis University (B.S.). Occupation: Real estate broker; manager, life insurance co. (1959-61); alderman (1959-64).

1. Immigration Reform Y
2. Open fld-search warrants Y
3. Civil pnty-hire ill alien N
4. So Afr sanc-veto override Y
5. Tax Overhaul N
6. South Africa sanctions Y
7. Death penalty-drug bill N
8. Evidence-warrantless srch N
9. Life term-second drug off N
10. Military use in drug war N
11. Troop reduction in Europe Y
12. Prohibit chemical weapons Y
13. Bar ASAT testing Y
14. Abide SALT II weapons ban ?
15. Follow SALT II-Soviets do ?
16. Reduce SDI funding ?
17. Increase SDI funding ?
18. Purchase Trident sub ?
19. Delete 12 MX;Add conv wpn ?
20. Raise speed limit N
21. Textile Import Quotas(*) Y
22. Req Pentagon buy US goods ?
23. AIDS ins anti-dscriminatn Y
24. Nicaraguan refugee aid Y
25. Nicaraguan contra aid N
26. US abide by SALT II N
27. Prohibit Saudi arms sale Y
28. Military Retiremnt Reform Y
29. Nicaraguan refugee aid Y
30. Ease '68 Gun Control Act N
31. Bar intrstat handgun tran Y
32. Keep '68 Gun Control Act Y
33. Nicaraguan contra aid N
34. Bar emp polygraph testing Y
35. Tax Overhaul consideratn N
36. Bar armor-piercing ammo Y
37. Tax Overhaul consideratn N
38. Make comp emissions known Y
39. Allow toxic victims suits Y
40. Strike Superfund "VAT" Y
41. Notify emp-plant closing Y
42. Bar emp consult-plant clo N
43. Medicare cuts;Tax incres' Y
44. Delete 12 MX missiles Y
45. Spending cuts;Tax incres' Y
46. Textile Import Quotas Y
47. Cut some school lunch fds N
48. Clean Water Act Amendmnts N
49. Youth work projects Y
50. Assist military in Angola N
51. Allow US troops-Nicaragua N
52. Pentagon polygraph exams N
53. Bar ASAT testing Y
54. Suspend def pmt for abuse Y
55. Bar Pentagon-contr emplmt Y
56. Increase SDI funding N
57. Reduce SDI funding Y
58. Produce chemical weapons N
59. Bar CIA fndg in Nicaragua Y
60. South Africa sanctions Y
61. Cut SS COLAs; Raise taxes N
62. Let US invest-So Africa N
63. Approve 21 MX for 1985 N
64. Emergency Farm Credit Y
65. Awards to whistle blowers Y
66. African disaster relief Y
67. Ban bank loans to So Afr P
68. Bar coun duty-free trtmt Y
69. Steel import limits Y
70. Soc Sec COLAs=inflation Y
71. Bar haz waste vctms suits N
72. Prohibit aid to Nicaragua Y
73. Cut $-Schs bar sch prayer N
74. Raise taxes; Cut Medicare N
75. Alien residncy-prior 1982 N
76. Alien residncy-prior 1980 N
77. Pen emp-hire illgl aliens Y
78. Lmt Persh II/cruse-Europe Y
79. Delete 34 B-1 bombers Y
80. Bar purch of Pershing II Y
81. Bar purchase of Sgt York Y
82. Delete $ for Trident II Y
83. Allow 15 MX missiles N
84. Bar MX procurement-1985 Y
85. Equal Access Act N
86. Aid to El Salvador N
87. Bar Nicarag water mining Y
88. Physician/Medicare freeze N
89. Increase "sin" taxes Y
90. End SBA direct loans N
91. Sell Conrail N
92. Equal Rights Amendment Y
93. Marines in Lebanon N
94. Eminent domain-Coal comps N
95. Prohibit EPA sanctions ?
96. SS age increase/Reforms N
97. Auto domestic content req Y
98. Delete jobs program fundg N
99. Highway-Gas tax bill Y
100. Raise Medicare;Cut defnse Y
101. Emergency housing aid Y
102. Across-the-board tax cuts N
103. Gramm-Latta II targets N
104. Delete B-1 bomber funds Y
105. Dsapprov Saudi AWACS sale Y
106. Disapprove oil import fee Y
107. Rail Deregulation N
108. Dsapp India nuc fuel sale ?
109. Mil draft registration N
110. Chrysler Loan Guarantees Y

CLAY, WILLIAM (Bill) (Cont.)

111. Prohibit school busing N
112. Nuclear plant moratorium Y
113. Oil price controls Y
114. Tuition Tax Credits N
115. Est Consumer Protect Agcy Y
116. Eliminate B-1 bomber fnds Y
117. Subminimum wage for youth N
118. Delete crude oil tax N
119. Natural gas deregulation N

Presidential Support Score: 1986 - 8% 1985 - 15%

YOUNG, ROBERT A. -- Missouri 2nd District [Democrat]. Counties of St. Charles (pt.) and St. Louis (pt.). Prior Terms: House: 1977-86. Born: November 27, 1923; St. Louis, Mo. Military Service: U.S. Army, 1943-45. Occupation: Pipefitter; Missouri representative (1957-63); Missouri senator (1963-77).

1. Immigration Reform Y
2. Open fld-search warrants N
3. Civil pnty-hire ill alien N
4. So Afr sanc-veto override Y
5. Tax Overhaul Y
6. South Africa sanctions Y
7. Death penalty-drug bill Y
8. Evidence-warrantless srch Y
9. Life term-second drug off Y
10. Military use in drug war N
11. Troop reduction in Europe N
12. Prohibit chemical weapons N
13. Bar ASAT testing N
14. Abide SALT II weapons ban Y
15. Follow SALT II-Soviets do N
16. Reduce SDI funding N
17. Increase SDI funding N
18. Purchase Trident sub Y
19. Delete 12 MX;Add conv wpn Y
20. Raise speed limit N
21. Textile Import Quotas(*) Y
22. Req Pentagon buy US goods Y
23. AIDS ins anti-dscriminatn ?
24. Nicaraguan refugee aid Y
25. Nicaraguan contra aid N
26. US abide by SALT II N
27. Prohibit Saudi arms sale Y
28. Military Retiremnt Reform Y
29. Nicaraguan refugee aid Y
30. Ease '68 Gun Control Act Y
31. Bar intrstat handgun tran N
32. Keep '68 Gun Control Act N
33. Nicaraguan contra aid N
34. Bar emp polygraph testing Y
35. Tax Overhaul consideratn ?
36. Bar armor-piercing ammo ?
37. Tax Overhaul consideratn N
38. Make comp emissions known N
39. Allow toxic victims suits N
40. Strike Superfund "VAT" N
41. Notify emp-plant closing Y
42. Bar emp consult-plant clo N
43. Medicare cuts;Tax incres' Y
44. Delete 12 MX missiles Y
45. Spending cuts;Tax incres' Y
46. Textile Import Quotas Y
47. Cut some school lunch fds N
48. Clean Water Act Amendmnts N
49. Youth work projects Y
50. Assist military in Angola N
51. Allow US troops-Nicaragua N
52. Pentagon polygraph exams Y
53. Bar ASAT testing N
54. Suspend def pmt for abuse N
55. Bar Pentagon-contr emplmt Y
56. Increase SDI funding N
57. Reduce SDI funding Y
58. Produce chemical weapons Y
59. Bar CIA fndg in Nicaragua Y
60. South Africa sanctions Y
61. Cut SS COLAs; Raise taxes N
62. Let US invest-So Africa N
63. Approve 21 MX for 1985 N
64. Emergency Farm Credit Y
65. Awards to whistle blowers Y
66. African disaster relief Y
67. Ban bank loans to So Afr Y
68. Bar coun duty-free trtmt Y
69. Steel import limits Y
70. Soc Sec COLAs=inflation Y
71. Bar haz waste vctms suits X
72. Prohibit aid to Nicaragua Y
73. Cut $-Schs bar sch prayer N
74. Raise taxes; Cut Medicare Y
75. Alien residncy-prior 1982 N
76. Alien residncy-prior 1980 N
77. Pen emp-hire illgl aliens Y
78. Lmt Persh II/cruse-Europe N
79. Delete 34 B-1 bombers N
80. Bar purch of Pershing II N
81. Bar purchase of Sgt York ?
82. Delete $ for Trident II X
83. Allow 15 MX missiles N
84. Bar MX procurement-1985 Y
85. Equal Access Act N
86. Aid to El Salvador N
87. Bar Nicarag water mining Y
88. Physician/Medicare freeze N

YOUNG, ROBERT A. (Cont.)

89. Increase "sin" taxes Y
90. End SBA direct loans ?
91. Sell Conrail N
92. Equal Rights Amendment N
93. Marines in Lebanon N
94. Eminent domain-coal comps Y
95. Prohibit EPA sanctions Y
96. SS age increase/Reforms N
97. Auto domestic content req Y
98. Delete jobs program fundg N
99. Highway-Gas tax bill Y
100. Raise Medicare;Cut defnse N
101. Emergency housing aid Y
102. Across-the-board tax cuts N
103. Gramm-Latta II targets Y
104. Delete B-1 bomber funds N
105. Dsapprov Saudi AWACS sale Y
106. Disapprove oil import fee Y
107. Rail Deregulation N
108. Dsapp India nuc fuel sale N
109. Mil draft registration Y
110. Chrysler Loan Guarantees Y
111. Prohibit school busing Y
112. Nuclear plant moratorium N
113. Oil price controls Y
114. Tuition Tax Credits Y
115. Est Consumer Protect Agcy N
116. Eliminate B-1 bomber fnds N
117. Subminimum wage for youth N
118. Delete crude oil tax N
119. Natural gas deregulation N

Presidential Support Score: 1986 - 25% 1985 - 26%

GEPHARDT, RICHARD A. -- Missouri 3rd District [Democrat]. Counties of Jefferson and St. Louis (pt.), St. Louis City (pt.). Prior Terms: House: 1977-86. Born: January 31, 1941; St. Louis, Mo. Education: Northwestern University (B.S.); Michigan Law School (J.D.). Military Service: Missouri Air National Guard, 1965-1971. Occupation: Attorney; alderman (1971-77).

1. Immigration Reform #
2. Open fld-search warrants ?
3. Civil pnty-hire ill alien #
4. So Afr sanc-veto override Y
5. Tax Overhaul Y
6. South Africa sanctions ?
7. Death penalty-drug bill ?
8. Evidence-warrantless srch N
9. Life term-second drug off Y
10. Military use in drug war N
11. Troop reduction in Europe N
12. Prohibit chemical weapons Y
13. Bar ASAT testing Y
14. Abide SALT II weapons ban Y
15. Follow SALT II-Soviets do N
16. Reduce SDI funding N
17. Increase SDI funding N
18. Purchase Trident sub Y
19. Delete 12 MX;Add conv wpn Y
20. Raise speed limit N
21. Textile Import Quotas(*) Y
22. Req Pentagon buy US goods Y
23. AIDS ins anti-dscriminatn Y
24. Nicaraguan refugee aid Y
25. Nicaraguan contra aid N
26. US abide by SALT II N
27. Prohibit Saudi arms sale Y
28. Military Retiremnt Reform ?
29. Nicaraguan refugee aid Y
30. Ease '68 Gun Control Act X
31. Bar intrstat handgun tran ?
32. Keep '68 Gun Control Act Y
33. Nicaraguan contra aid N
34. Bar emp polygraph testing ?
35. Tax Overhaul consideratn Y
36. Bar armor-piercing ammo Y
37. Tax Overhaul consideratn Y
38. Make comp emissions known Y
39. Allow toxic victims suits Y
40. Strike Superfund "VAT" N
41. Notify emp-plant closing Y
42. Bar emp consult-plant clo N
43. Medicare cuts;Tax incres' Y
44. Delete 12 MX missiles Y
45. Spending cuts;Tax incres' Y
46. Textile Import Quotas Y
47. Cut some school lunch fds N
48. Clean Water Act Amendmnts N
49. Youth work projects Y
50. Assist military in Angola N
51. Allow US troops-Nicaragua N
52. Pentagon polygraph exams Y
53. Bar ASAT testing Y
54. Suspend def pmt for abuse Y
55. Bar Pentagon-contr emplmt Y
56. Increase SDI funding N
57. Reduce SDI funding N
58. Produce chemical weapons Y
59. Bar CIA fndg in Nicaragua Y
60. South Africa sanctions Y
61. Cut SS COLAs; Raise taxes Y
62. Let US invest-So Africa N
63. Approve 21 MX for 1985 N
64. Emergency Farm Credit Y

GEPHARDT, RICHARD A. (Cont.)

65. Awards to whistle blowers Y
66. African disaster relief Y
67. Ban bank loans to So Afr ?
68. Bar coun duty-free trtmt Y
69. Steel import limits Y
70. Soc Sec COLAs=inflation Y
71. Bar haz waste vctms suits N
72. Prohibit aid to Nicaragua Y
73. Cut $-Schs bar sch prayer N
74. Raise taxes; Cut Medicare Y
75. Alien residncy-prior 1982 N
76. Alien residncy-prior 1980 N
77. Pen emp-hire illgl aliens Y
78. Lmt Persh II/cruse-Europe N
79. Delete 34 B-1 bombers Y
80. Bar purch of Pershing II N
81. Bar purchase of Sgt York N
82. Delete $ for Trident II N
83. Allow 15 MX missiles N
84. Bar MX procurement-1985 Y
85. Equal Access Act N
86. Aid to El Salvador N
87. Bar Nicarag water mining Y
88. Physician/Medicare freeze N
89. Increase "sin" taxes Y
90. End SBA direct loans N
91. Sell Conrail N
92. Equal Rights Amendment Y
93. Marines in Lebanon Y
94. Eminent domain-Coal comps N
95. Prohibit EPA sanctions Y
96. SS age increase/Reforms N
97. Auto domestic content req Y
98. Delete jobs program fundg N
99. Highway-Gas tax bill Y
100. Raise Medicare;Cut defnse N
101. Emergency housing aid N
102. Across-the-board tax cuts N
103. Gramm-Latta II targets N
104. Delete B-1 bomber funds N
105. Dsapprov Saudi AWACS sale Y
106. Disapprove oil import fee N
107. Rail Deregulation N
108. Dsapp India nuc fuel sale ?
109. Mil draft registration Y
110. Chrysler Loan Guarantees Y
111. Prohibit school busing Y
112. Nuclear plant moratorium ?
113. Oil price controls N
114. Tuition Tax Credits Y
115. Est Consumer Protect Agcy N
116. Eliminate B-1 bomber fnds Y
117. Subminimum wage for youth N
118. Delete crude oil tax N
119. Natural gas deregulation N

Presidential Support Score: 1986 - 16% 1985 - 26%

SKELTON, IKE -- Missouri 4th District [Democrat]. Counties of Barton, Bates, Benton, Camden, Cass, Cole, Henry, Hickory, Jackson (pt.), Johnson, Laclede, Lafayette, Maries, Miller, Moniteau, Morgan, Pettis, Pulaski, St. Clair, Texas and Vernon. Prior Terms: House: 1977-86. Born: December 20, 1931; Lexington, Mo. Education: University of Missouri (A.B., LL.B.); University of Edinburgh. Occupation: Prosecuting attorney (1957-60); special assistant, Missouri attorney general (1961-63); Missouri senator (1970-76).

1. Immigration Reform N
2. Open fld-search warrants N
3. Civil pnty-hire ill alien N
4. So Afr sanc-veto override ?
5. Tax Overhaul Y
6. South Africa sanctions Y
7. Death penalty-drug bill Y
8. Evidence-warrantless srch Y
9. Life term-second drug off Y
10. Military use in drug war N
11. Troop reduction in Europe N
12. Prohibit chemical weapons N
13. Bar ASAT testing N
14. Abide SALT II weapons ban N
15. Follow SALT II-Soviets do Y
16. Reduce SDI funding N
17. Increase SDI funding N
18. Purchase Trident sub Y
19. Delete 12 MX;add conv wpn N
20. Raise speed limit Y
21. Textile Import Quotas(*) Y
22. Req Pentagon buy US goods N
23. AIDS ins anti-dscriminatn Y
24. Nicaraguan refugee aid N
25. Nicaraguan contra aid Y
26. US abide by SALT II Y
27. Prohibit Saudi arms sale Y
28. Military Retiremnt Reform Y
29. Nicaraguan refugee aid N
30. Ease '68 Gun Control Act Y
31. Bar intrstat handgun tran N
32. Keep '68 Gun Control Act N
33. Nicaraguan contra aid Y
34. Bar emp polygraph testing Y

SKELTON, IKE (Cont.)

35. Tax Overhaul consideratn N
36. Bar armor-piercing ammo Y
37. Tax Overhaul consideratn N
38. Make comp emissions known N
39. Allow toxic victims suits N
40. Strike Superfund "VAT" Y
41. Notify emp-plant closing Y
42. Bar emp consult-plant clo N
43. Medicare cuts;Tax incres' Y
44. Delete 12 MX missiles N
45. Spending cuts;Tax incres' ?
46. Textile Import Quotas Y
47. Cut some school lunch fds N
48. Clean Water Act Amendmnts N
49. Youth work projects ?
50. Assist military in Angola Y
51. Allow US troops-Nicaragua Y
52. Pentagon polygraph exams Y
53. Bar ASAT testing N
54. Suspend def pmt for abuse N
55. Bar Pentagon-contr emplmt Y
56. Increase SDI funding N
57. Reduce SDI funding N
58. Produce chemical weapons Y
59. Bar CIA fndg in Nicaragua N
60. South Africa sanctions Y
61. Cut SS COLAs; Raise taxes N
62. Let US invest-So Africa N
63. Approve 21 MX for 1985 Y
64. Emergency Farm Credit Y
65. Awards to whistle blowers Y
66. African disaster relief Y
67. Ban bank loans to So Afr ?
68. Bar coun duty-free trtmt Y
69. Steel import limits Y
70. Soc Sec COLAs=inflation Y
71. Bar haz waste vctms suits N
72. Prohibit aid to Nicaragua Y
73. Cut $-Schs bar sch prayer Y
74. Raise taxes; Cut Medicare Y
75. Alien residncy-prior 1982 Y
76. Alien residncy-prior 1980 Y
77. Pen emp-hire illgl aliens N
78. Lmt Persh II/cruse-Europe N
79. Delete 34 B-1 bombers N
80. Bar purch of Pershing II N
81. Bar purchase of Sgt York N
82. Delete $ for Trident II N
83. Allow 15 MX missiles Y
84. Bar MX procurement-1985 N
85. Equal Access Act Y
86. Aid to El Salvador Y
87. Bar Nicarag water mining Y
88. Physician/Medicare freeze N
89. Increase "sin" taxes Y
90. End SBA direct loans N
91. Sell Conrail N
92. Equal Rights Amendment N
93. Marines in Lebanon N
94. Eminent domain-Coal comps N
95. Prohibit EPA sanctions ?
96. SS age increase/Reforms N
97. Auto domestic content req Y
98. Delete jobs program fundg N
99. Highway-Gas tax bill ?
100. Raise Medicare;Cut defnse N
101. Emergency housing aid Y
102. Across-the-board tax cuts N
103. Gramm-Latta II targets Y
104. Delete B-1 bomber funds N
105. Dsapprov Saudi AWACS sale Y
106. Disapprove oil import fee Y
107. Rail Deregulation N
108. Dsapp India nuc fuel sale N
109. Mil draft registration Y
110. Chrysler Loan Guarantees Y
111. Prohibit school busing Y
112. Nuclear plant moratorium N
113. Oil price controls N
114. Tuition Tax Credits N
115. Est Consumer Protect Agcy N
116. Eliminate B-1 bomber fnds N
117. Subminimum wage for youth N
118. Delete crude oil tax N
119. Natural gas deregulation N

Presidential Support Score: 1986 - 47% 1985 - 44%

WHEAT, ALAN -- Missouri 5th District [Democrat]. County of Jackson (pt.). Prior Terms: House: 1983-86. Born: October 16, 1951; San Antonio, Tex. Education: Grinnell College (B.A.). Occupation: Economist; county executive aide; Missouri representative (1976-82).

1. Immigration Reform Y
2. Open fld-search warrants Y
3. Civil pnty-hire ill alien N
4. So Afr sanc-veto override Y
5. Tax Overhaul Y
6. South Africa sanctions Y
7. Death penalty-drug bill N
8. Evidence-warrantless srch N
9. Life term-second drug off Y
10. Military use in drug war N
11. Troop reduction in Europe Y
12. Prohibit chemical weapons Y
13. Bar ASAT testing Y
14. Abide SALT II weapons ban Y

WHEAT, ALAN (Cont.)

15. Follow SALT II-Soviets do N
16. Reduce SDI funding Y
17. Increase SDI funding N
18. Purchase Trident sub Y
19. Delete 12 MX;Add conv wpn Y
20. Raise speed limit N
21. Textile Import Quotas(*) Y
22. Req Pentagon buy US goods Y
23. AIDS ins anti-dscriminatn Y
24. Nicaraguan refugee aid Y
25. Nicaraguan contra aid N
26. US abide by SALT II N
27. Prohibit Saudi arms sale Y
28. Military Retiremnt Reform Y
29. Nicaraguan refugee aid Y
30. Ease '68 Gun Control Act N
31. Bar intrstat handgun tran Y
32. Keep '68 Gun Control Act Y
33. Nicaraguan contra aid N
34. Bar emp polygraph testing Y
35. Tax Overhaul consideratn Y
36. Bar armor-piercing ammo Y
37. Tax Overhaul consideratn Y
38. Make comp emissions known Y
39. Allow toxic victims suits Y
40. Strike Superfund "VAT" Y
41. Notify emp-plant closing Y
42. Bar emp consult-plant clo N
43. Medicare cuts;Tax incres' #
44. Delete 12 MX missiles Y
45. Spending cuts;Tax incres' Y
46. Textile Import Quotas Y
47. Cut some school lunch fds N
48. Clean Water Act Amendmnts N
49. Youth work projects Y
50. Assist military in Angola N
51. Allow US troops-Nicaragua N
52. Pentagon polygraph exams N
53. Bar ASAT testing Y
54. Suspend def pmt for abuse Y
55. Bar Pentagon-contr emplmt Y
56. Increase SDI funding N
57. Reduce SDI funding Y
58. Produce chemical weapons N
59. Bar CIA fndg in Nicaragua Y
60. South Africa sanctions Y
61. Cut SS COLAs; Raise taxes N
62. Let US invest-So Africa N
63. Approve 21 MX for 1985 N
64. Emergency Farm Credit Y
65. Awards to whistle blowers Y
66. African disaster relief Y
67. Ban bank loans to So Afr P
68. Bar coun duty-free trtmt Y
69. Steel import limits Y
70. Soc Sec COLAs=inflation Y
71. Bar haz waste vctms suits N
72. Prohibit aid to Nicaragua Y
73. Cut $-Schs bar sch prayer N
74. Raise taxes; Cut Medicare Y
75. Alien residncy-prior 1982 N
76. Alien residncy-prior 1980 N
77. Pen emp-hire illgl aliens Y
78. Lmt Persh II/cruse-Europe Y
79. Delete 34 B-1 bombers Y
80. Bar purch of Pershing II Y
81. Bar purchase of Sgt York Y
82. Delete $ for Trident II Y
83. Allow 15 MX missiles N
84. Bar MX procurement-1985 Y
85. Equal Access Act N
86. Aid to El Salvador N
87. Bar Nicarag water mining Y
88. Physician/Medicare freeze N
89. Increase "sin" taxes Y
90. End SBA direct loans N
91. Sell Conrail N
92. Equal Rights Amendment Y
93. Marines in Lebanon N
94. Eminent domain-Coal comps N
95. Prohibit EPA sanctions Y
96. SS age increase/Reforms N

Presidential Support Score: 1986 - 15% 1985 - 15%

COLEMAN, E. THOMAS -- Missouri 6th District [Republican]. Counties of Andrew, Atchison, Buchanan, Caldwell, Carroll, Chariton, Clay, Clinton, Cooper, Daviess, De Kalb, Gentry, Grundy, Harrison, Holt, Howard, Jackson (pt.), Linn, Livingston, Mercer, Nodaway, Platte, Putnam, Ray, Saline, Schuyler, Sullivan and Worth. Prior Terms: House: 1976 (Special Election) - 1986. Born: May 29, 1943; Kansas City, Mo. Education: William Jewell College (B.A.); New York University (M.A.); Washington University (J.D.). Occupation: Attorney; assistant attorney general (1969-72); Missouri representative (1972-76).

1. Immigration Reform Y
2. Open fld-search warrants Y
3. Civil pnty-hire ill alien N
4. So Afr sanc-veto override ?
5. Tax Overhaul N
6. South Africa sanctions Y
7. Death penalty-drug bill Y
8. Evidence-warrantless srch Y

COLEMAN, E. THOMAS (Cont.)

9. Life term-second drug off Y
10. Military use in drug war Y
11. Troop reduction in Europe N
12. Prohibit chemical weapons N
13. Bar ASAT testing N
14. Abide SALT II weapons ban N
15. Follow SALT II-Soviets do Y
16. Reduce SDI funding N
17. Increase SDI funding Y
18. Purchase Trident sub N
19. Delete 12 MX;Add conv wpn N
20. Raise speed limit Y
21. Textile Import Quotas(*) Y
22. Req Pentagon buy US goods N
23. AIDS ins anti-dscriminatn N
24. Nicaraguan refugee aid N
25. Nicaraguan contra aid Y
26. US abide by SALT II Y
27. Prohibit Saudi arms sale Y
28. Military Retiremnt Reform Y
29. Nicaraguan refugee aid Y
30. Ease '68 Gun Control Act Y
31. Bar intrstat handgun tran Y
32. Keep '68 Gun Control Act Y
33. Nicaraguan contra aid Y
34. Bar emp polygraph testing N
35. Tax Overhaul consideratn N
36. Bar armor-piercing ammo Y
37. Tax Overhaul consideratn N
38. Make comp emissions known N
39. Allow toxic victims suits N
40. Strike Superfund "VAT" Y
41. Notify emp-plant closing N
42. Bar emp consult-plant clo Y
43. Medicare cuts;Tax incres' N
44. Delete 12 MX missiles N
45. Spending cuts;Tax incres' N
46. Textile Import Quotas N
47. Cut some school lunch fds N
48. Clean Water Act Amendmnts Y
49. Youth work projects N
50. Assist military in Angola Y
51. Allow US troops-Nicaragua Y
52. Pentagon polygraph exams Y
53. Bar ASAT testing N
54. Suspend def pmt for abuse N
55. Bar Pentagon-contr emplmt Y
56. Increase SDI funding N
57. Reduce SDI funding N
58. Produce chemical weapons Y
59. Bar CIA fndg in Nicaragua N
60. South Africa sanctions Y
61. Cut SS COLAs; Raise taxes N
62. Let US invest-So Africa Y
63. Approve 21 MX for 1985 Y
64. Emergency Farm Credit Y
65. Awards to whistle blowers Y
66. African disaster relief Y
67. Ban bank loans to So Afr Y
68. Bar coun duty-free trtmt N
69. Steel import limits N
70. Soc Sec COLAs=inflation Y
71. Bar haz waste vctms suits Y
72. Prohibit aid to Nicaragua N
73. Cut $-Schs bar sch prayer N
74. Raise taxes; Cut Medicare N
75. Alien residncy-prior 1982 N
76. Alien residncy-prior 1980 Y
77. Pen emp-hire illgl aliens N
78. Lmt Persh II/cruse-Europe N
79. Delete 34 B-1 bombers N
80. Bar purch of Pershing II N
81. Bar purchase of Sgt York ?
82. Delete $ for Trident II N
83. Allow 15 MX missiles Y
84. Bar MX procurement-1985 N
85. Equal Access Act N
86. Aid to El Salvador Y
87. Bar Nicarag water mining N
88. Physician/Medicare freeze Y
89. Increase "sin" taxes ?
90. End SBA direct loans N
91. Sell Conrail Y
92. Equal Rights Amendment N
93. Marines in Lebanon Y
94. Eminent domain-Coal comps N
95. Prohibit EPA sanctions N
96. SS age increase/Reforms Y
97. Auto domestic content req Y
98. Delete jobs program fundg Y
99. Highway-Gas tax bill N
100. Raise Medicare;Cut defnse Y
101. Emergency housing aid Y
102. Across-the-board tax cuts Y
103. Gramm-Latta II targets Y
104. Delete B-1 bomber funds N
105. Dsapprov Saudi AWACS sale N
106. Disapprove oil import fee Y
107. Rail Deregulation N
108. Dsapp India nuc fuel sale Y
109. Mil draft registration Y
110. Chrysler Loan Guarantees N
111. Prohibit school busing Y
112. Nuclear plant moratorium N
113. Oil price controls N
114. Tuition Tax Credits Y
115. Est Consumer Protect Agcy N
116. Eliminate B-1 bomber fnds N
117. Subminimum wage for youth Y
118. Delete crude oil tax Y
119. Natural gas deregulation Y

Presidential Support Score: 1986 - 67% 1985 - 56%

TAYLOR, GENE -- Missouri 7th District [Republican]. Counties of Barry, Cedar, Christian, Dade, Dallas, Douglas, Greene, Jasper, Lawrence, McDonald, Newton, Ozark, Polk, Stone, Taney, Webster and Wright. Prior Terms: House: 1973-86. Born: February 10, 1928; Sarcoxie, Mo. Education: Southwest Missouri State College. Military Service: Missouri National Guard, 1948-49. Occupation: Automobile dealer; mayor (1954-60).

1.	Immigration Reform	N	52.	Pentagon polygraph exams	Y
2.	Open fld-search warrants	Y	53.	Bar ASAT testing	N
3.	Civil pnty-hire ill alien	N	54.	Suspend def pmt for abuse	N
4.	So Afr sanc-veto override	N	55.	Bar Pentagon-contr emplmt	Y
5.	Tax Overhaul	N	56.	Increase SDI funding	N
6.	South Africa sanctions	N	57.	Reduce SDI funding	N
7.	Death penalty-drug bill	Y	58.	Produce chemical weapons	Y
8.	Evidence-warrantless srch	Y	59.	Bar CIA fndg in Nicaragua	N
9.	Life term-second drug off	Y	60.	South Africa sanctions	N
10.	Military use in drug war	Y	61.	Cut SS COLAs; Raise taxes	N
11.	Troop reduction in Europe	N	62.	Let US invest-So Africa	Y
12.	Prohibit chemical weapons	N	63.	Approve 21 MX for 1985	Y
13.	Bar ASAT testing	N	64.	Emergency Farm Credit	Y
14.	Abide SALT II weapons ban	N	65.	Awards to whistle blowers	Y
15.	Follow SALT II-Soviets do	Y	66.	African disaster relief	Y
16.	Reduce SDI funding	N	67.	Ban bank loans to So Afr	N
17.	Increase SDI funding	Y	68.	Bar coun duty-free trtmt	N
18.	Purchase Trident sub	N	69.	Steel import limits	N
19.	Delete 12 MX;Add conv wpn	X	70.	Soc Sec COLAs=inflation	Y
20.	Raise speed limit	N	71.	Bar haz waste vctms suits	Y
21.	Textile Import Quotas(*)	Y	72.	Prohibit aid to Nicaragua	N
22.	Req Pentagon buy US goods	N	73.	Cut $-Schs bar sch prayer	#
23.	AIDS ins anti-dscriminatn	N	74.	Raise taxes; Cut Medicare	N
24.	Nicaraguan refugee aid	N	75.	Alien residncy-prior 1982	Y
25.	Nicaraguan contra aid	Y	76.	Alien residncy-prior 1980	Y
26.	US abide by SALT II	Y	77.	Pen emp-hire illgl aliens	N
27.	Prohibit Saudi arms sale	Y	78.	Lmt Persh II/cruse-Europe	N
28.	Military Retiremnt Reform	Y	79.	Delete 34 B-1 bombers	N
29.	Nicaraguan refugee aid	Y	80.	Bar purch of Pershing II	N
30.	Ease '68 Gun Control Act	Y	81.	Bar purchase of Sgt York	N
31.	Bar intrstat handgun tran	N	82.	Delete $ for Trident II	N
32.	Keep '68 Gun Control Act	N	83.	Allow 15 MX missiles	Y
33.	Nicaraguan contra aid	Y	84.	Bar MX procurement-1985	N
34.	Bar emp polygraph testing	X	85.	Equal Access Act	Y
35.	Tax Overhaul consideratn	Y	86.	Aid to El Salvador	Y
36.	Bar armor-piercing ammo	Y	87.	Bar Nicarag water mining	N
37.	Tax Overhaul consideratn	N	88.	Physician/Medicare freeze	Y
38.	Make comp emissions known	N	89.	Increase "sin" taxes	Y
39.	Allow toxic victims suits	N	90.	End SBA direct loans	Y
40.	Strike Superfund "VAT"	Y	91.	Sell Conrail	Y
41.	Notify emp-plant closing	N	92.	Equal Rights Amendment	N
42.	Bar emp consult-plant clo	Y	93.	Marines in Lebanon	Y
43.	Medicare cuts;Tax incres'	N	94.	Eminent domain-Coal comps	N
44.	Delete 12 MX missiles	N	95.	Prohibit EPA sanctions	Y
45.	Spending cuts;Tax incres'	N	96.	SS age increase/Reforms	Y
46.	Textile Import Quotas	Y	97.	Auto domestic content req	N
47.	Cut some school lunch fds	Y	98.	Delete jobs program fundg	Y
48.	Clean Water Act Amendmnts	Y	99.	Highway-Gas tax bill	?
49.	Youth work projects	N	100.	Raise Medicare;Cut defnse	N
50.	Assist military in Angola	Y	101.	Emergency housing aid	N
51.	Allow US troops-Nicaragua	Y	102.	Across-the-board tax cuts	Y

TAYLOR, GENE (Cont.)

103. Gramm-Latta II targets Y
104. Delete B-1 bomber funds N
105. Dsapprov Saudi AWACS sale N
106. Disapprove oil import fee Y
107. Rail Deregulation N
108. Dsapp India nuc fuel sale Y
109. Mil draft registration Y
110. Chrysler Loan Guarantees N
111. Prohibit school busing Y
112. Nuclear plant moratorium N
113. Oil price controls N
114. Tuition Tax Credits N
115. Est Consumer Protect Agcy N
116. Eliminate B-1 bomber fnds N
117. Subminimum wage for youth Y
118. Delete crude oil tax Y
119. Natural gas deregulation Y

Presidential Support Score: 1986 - 68% 1985 - 66%

EMERSON, BILL -- Missouri 8th District [Republican]. Counties of Bollinger, Butler, Cape Girardeau, Carter, Crawford, Dent, Dunklin, Franklin (pt.), Howell, Iron, Madison, Mississippi, New Madrid, Oregon, Pemiscot, Perry, Phelps, Reynolds, Ripley, Ste. Genevieve, St. Francois, Scott, Shannon, Stoddard, Washington and Wayne. Prior Terms: House: 1981-86. Born: January 1, 1938; St. Louis, Mo. Education: Westminster College (B.A.); University of Baltimore (LL.B.). Military Service: U.S. Air Force Reserve. Occupation: Page, U.S. House of Representatives; congressional administrative assistant; director, government relations, Fairchild Industries; director, public affairs, Interstate Natural Gas Assn.; director, federal relations, TRW, Inc.; executive assistant to the chairman of the Federal Election Commission.

1. Immigration Reform N
2. Open fld-search warrants Y
3. Civil pnty-hire ill alien Y
4. So Afr sanc-veto override N
5. Tax Overhaul Y
6. South Africa sanctions N
7. Death penalty-drug bill Y
8. Evidence-warrantless srch Y
9. Life term-second drug off Y
10. Military use in drug war Y
11. Troop reduction in Europe N
12. Prohibit chemical weapons N
13. Bar ASAT testing N
14. Abide SALT II weapons ban N
15. Follow SALT II-Soviets do Y
16. Reduce SDI funding N
17. Increase SDI funding Y
18. Purchase Trident sub N
19. Delete 12 MX;Add conv wpn N
20. Raise speed limit Y
21. Textile Import Quotas(*) Y
22. Req Pentagon buy US goods Y
23. AIDS ins anti-dscriminatn N
24. Nicaraguan refugee aid N
25. Nicaraguan contra aid Y
26. US abide by SALT II Y
27. Prohibit Saudi arms sale Y
28. Military Retiremnt Reform Y
29. Nicaraguan refugee aid Y
30. Ease '68 Gun Control Act Y
31. Bar intrstat handgun tran N
32. Keep '68 Gun Control Act N
33. Nicaraguan contra aid Y
34. Bar emp polygraph testing N
35. Tax Overhaul consideratn N
36. Bar armor-piercing ammo Y
37. Tax Overhaul consideratn N
38. Make comp emissions known N
39. Allow toxic victims suits N
40. Strike Superfund "VAT" N
41. Notify emp-plant closing N
42. Bar emp consult-plant clo Y
43. Medicare cuts;Tax incres' N
44. Delete 12 MX missiles N
45. Spending cuts;Tax incres' N
46. Textile Import Quotas Y
47. Cut some school lunch fds Y
48. Clean Water Act Amendmnts Y
49. Youth work projects N
50. Assist military in Angola Y
51. Allow US troops-Nicaragua Y
52. Pentagon polygraph exams Y
53. Bar ASAT testing N
54. Suspend def pmt for abuse N
55. Bar Pentagon-contr emplmt Y
56. Increase SDI funding N
57. Reduce SDI funding N
58. Produce chemical weapons ?
59. Bar CIA fndg in Nicaragua N
60. South Africa sanctions ?
61. Cut SS COLAs; Raise taxes N
62. Let US invest-So Africa Y

EMERSON, BILL (Cont)

63. Approve 21 MX for 1985 Y
64. Emergency Farm Credit Y
65. Awards to whistle blowers Y
66. African disaster relief Y
67. Ban bank loans to So Afr Y
68. Bar coun duty-free trtmt N
69. Steel import limits N
70. Soc Sec COLAs=inflation Y
71. Bar haz waste vctms suits Y
72. Prohibit aid to Nicaragua N
73. Cut $-Schs bar sch prayer Y
74. Raise taxes; Cut Medicare N
75. Alien residncy-prior 1982 Y
76. Alien residncy-prior 1980 Y
77. Pen emp-hire illgl aliens N
78. Lmt Persh II/cruse-Europe N
79. Delete 34 B-1 bombers N
80. Bar purch of Pershing II N
81. Bar purchase of Sgt York N
82. Delete $ for Trident II N
83. Allow 15 MX missiles Y
84. Bar MX procurement-1985 N
85. Equal Access Act Y
86. Aid to El Salvador Y
87. Bar Nicarag water mining N
88. Physician/Medicare freeze Y
89. Increase "sin" taxes N
90. End SBA direct loans N
91. Sell Conrail Y
92. Equal Rights Amendment N
93. Marines in Lebanon Y
94. Eminent domain-Coal comps N
95. Prohibit EPA sanctions Y
96. SS age increase/Reforms Y
97. Auto domestic content req N
98. Delete jobs program fundg Y
99. Highway-Gas tax bill N
100. Raise Medicare;Cut defnse N
101. Emergency housing aid Y
102. Across-the-board tax cuts Y
103. Gramm-Latta II targets Y
104. Delete B-1 bomber funds N
105. Dsapprov Saudi AWACS sale N

Presidential Support Score: 1986 - 69% 1985 - 60%

VOLKMER, HAROLD L. -- Missouri 9th District [Democrat]. Counties of Adair, Audrain, Boone, Callaway, Clark, Franklin (pt.), Gasconade, Knox, Lewis, Lincoln, Macon, Marion, Monroe, Montgomery, Osage, Pike, Ralls, Randolph, St. Charles (pt.), Scotland, Shelby and Warren. Prior Terms: House: 1977-86. Born: April 4, 1931; Jefferson City, Mo. Education: St. Louis University; University of Missouri (LL.B.). Military Service: U.S. Army, 1955-57. Occupation: Assistant attorney general; prosecuting attorney (1960-66); Missouri representative.

1. Immigration Reform N
2. Open fld-search warrants N
3. Civil pnty-hire ill alien N
4. So Afr sanc-veto override Y
5. Tax Overhaul Y
6. South Africa sanctions Y
7. Death penalty-drug bill Y
8. Evidence-warrantless srch Y
9. Life term-second drug off Y
10. Military use in drug war Y
11. Troop reduction in Europe N
12. Prohibit chemical weapons N
13. Bar ASAT testing Y
14. Abide SALT II weapons ban Y
15. Follow SALT II-Soviets do N
16. Reduce SDI funding N
17. Increase SDI funding N
18. Purchase Trident sub Y
19. Delete 12 MX;Add conv wpn Y
20. Raise speed limit N
21. Textile Import Quotas(*) Y
22. Req Pentagon buy US goods Y
23. AIDS ins anti-dscriminatn Y
24. Nicaraguan refugee aid Y
25. Nicaraguan contra aid N
26. US abide by SALT II N
27. Prohibit Saudi arms sale Y
28. Military Retiremnt Reform Y
29. Nicaraguan refugee aid Y
30. Ease '68 Gun Control Act Y
31. Bar intrstat handgun tran N
32. Keep '68 Gun Control Act N
33. Nicaraguan contra aid N
34. Bar emp polygraph testing Y
35. Tax Overhaul consideratn Y
36. Bar armor-piercing ammo Y
37. Tax Overhaul consideratn Y
38. Make comp emissions known Y
39. Allow toxic victims suits N
40. Strike Superfund "VAT" N
41. Notify emp-plant closing Y
42. Bar emp consult-plant clo N
43. Medicare cuts;Tax incres' N
44. Delete 12 MX missiles Y
45. Spending cuts;Tax incres' N
46. Textile Import Quotas Y
47. Cut some school lunch fds N
48. Clean Water Act Amendmnts N

VOLKMER, HAROLD L. (Cont.)

49. Youth work projects Y
50. Assist military in Angola Y
51. Allow US troops-Nicaragua N
52. Pentagon polygraph exams Y
53. Bar ASAT testing Y
54. Suspend def pmt for abuse N
55. Bar Pentagon-contr emplmt Y
56. Increase SDI funding N
57. Reduce SDI funding N
58. Produce chemical weapons Y
59. Bar CIA fndg in Nicaragua Y
60. South Africa sanctions Y
61. Cut SS COLAs; Raise taxes N
62. Let US invest-So Africa N
63. Approve 21 MX for 1985 N
64. Emergency Farm Credit Y
65. Awards to whistle blowers Y
66. African disaster relief Y
67. Ban bank loans to So Afr Y
68. Bar coun duty-free trtmt Y
69. Steel import limits Y
70. Soc Sec COLAs=inflation Y
71. Bar haz waste vctms suits N
72. Prohibit aid to Nicaragua Y
73. Cut $-Schs bar sch prayer Y
74. Raise taxes; Cut Medicare N
75. Alien residncy-prior 1982 Y
76. Alien residncy-prior 1980 Y
77. Pen emp-hire illgl aliens N
78. Lmt Persh II/cruse-Europe N
79. Delete 34 B-1 bombers N
80. Bar purch of Pershing II N
81. Bar purchase of Sgt York N
82. Delete $ for Trident II N
83. Allow 15 MX missiles N
84. Bar MX procurement-1985 Y
85. Equal Access Act Y
86. Aid to El Salvador N
87. Bar Nicarag water mining Y
88. Physician/Medicare freeze N
89. Increase "sin" taxes Y
90. End SBA direct loans N
91. Sell Conrail N
92. Equal Rights Amendment Y
93. Marines in Lebanon N
94. Eminent domain-Coal comps N
95. Prohibit EPA sanctions Y
96. SS age increase/Reforms N
97. Auto domestic content req Y
98. Delete jobs program fundg N
99. Highway-Gas tax bill N
100. Raise Medicare;Cut defnse Y
101. Emergency housing aid Y
102. Across-the-board tax cuts N
103. Gramm-Latta II targets Y
104. Delete B-1 bomber funds N
105. Dsapprov Saudi AWACS sale Y
106. Disapprove oil import fee Y
107. Rail Deregulation N
108. Dsapp India nuc fuel sale Y
109. Mil draft registration Y
110. Chrysler Loan Guarantees Y
111. Prohibit school busing N
112. Nuclear plant moratorium N
113. Oil price controls N
114. Tuition Tax Credits Y
115. Est Consumer Protect Agcy N
116. Eliminate B-1 bomber fnds Y
117. Subminimum wage for youth N
118. Delete crude oil tax N
119. Natural gas deregulation N

Presidential Support Score: 1986 - 32% 1985 - 30%

M O N T A N A

WILLIAMS, PAT -- Montana 1st District [Democrat]. Counties of Beaverhead, Broadwater, Deer Lodge, Flathead, Gallatin, Glacier, Granite, Jefferson, Lake, Lewis and Clark, Liberty, Lincoln, Madison, Meagher, Mineral, Missoula, Park, Pondera, Powell, Ravalli, Sanders, Silver Bow, Toole and Yellowstone National Park. Prior Terms: House: 1979-86. Born: October 30, 1937; Helena, Mont. Education: University of Montana; University of Denver (B.A.); Western Montana College. Military Service: U.S. Army, 1960-61. Occupation: Teacher (1960-66); Montana representative (1966-68); congressional executive assistant (1969-71); Montana state coordinator, Family Education Program (1971-78); member, State Legislative Reapportionment Commission (1973); member, Montana Employment and Training Council (1972-78).

1. Immigration Reform Y
2. Open fld-search warrants Y
3. Civil pnty-hire ill alien Y
4. So Afr sanc-veto override Y

WILLIAMS, PAT (Cont.)

5. Tax Overhaul N
6. South Africa sanctions Y
7. Death penalty-drug bill N
8. Evidence-warrantless srch N
9. Life term-second drug off N
10. Military use in drug war N
11. Troop reduction in Europe N
12. Prohibit chemical weapons Y
13. Bar ASAT testing Y
14. Abide SALT II weapons ban Y
15. Follow SALT II-Soviets do N
16. Reduce SDI funding Y
17. Increase SDI funding N
18. Purchase Trident sub Y
19. Delete 12 MX;Add conv wpn Y
20. Raise speed limit Y
21. Textile Import Quotas(*) Y
22. Req Pentagon buy US goods Y
23. AIDS ins anti-dscriminatn Y
24. Nicaraguan refugee aid Y
25. Nicaraguan contra aid N
26. US abide by SALT II N
27. Prohibit Saudi arms sale Y
28. Military Retiremnt Reform Y
29. Nicaraguan refugee aid Y
30. Ease '68 Gun Control Act Y
31. Bar intrstat handgun tran N
32. Keep '68 Gun Control Act N
33. Nicaraguan contra aid N
34. Bar emp polygraph testing Y
35. Tax Overhaul consideratn Y
36. Bar armor-piercing ammo Y
37. Tax Overhaul consideratn Y
38. Make comp emissions known Y
39. Allow toxic victims suits Y
40. Strike Superfund "VAT" N
41. Notify emp-plant closing Y
42. Bar emp consult-plant clo N
43. Medicare cuts;Tax incres' Y
44. Delete 12 MX missiles Y
45. Spending cuts;Tax incres' Y
46. Textile Import Quotas Y
47. Cut some school lunch fds N
48. Clean Water Act Amendmnts Y
49. Youth work projects Y
50. Assist military in Angola N
51. Allow US troops-Nicaragua N
52. Pentagon polygraph exams N
53. Bar ASAT testing Y
54. Suspend def pmt for abuse Y
55. Bar Pentagon-contr emplmt Y
56. Increase SDI funding N
57. Reduce SDI funding Y
58. Produce chemical weapons Y
59. Bar CIA fndg in Nicaragua Y
60. South Africa sanctions Y
61. Cut SS COLAs; Raise taxes N
62. Let US invest-So Africa ?
63. Approve 21 MX for 1985 N
64. Emergency Farm Credit Y
65. Awards to whistle blowers Y
66. African disaster relief Y
67. Ban bank loans to So Afr Y
68. Bar coun duty-free trtmt ?
69. Steel import limits Y
70. Soc Sec COLAs=inflation Y
71. Bar haz waste vctms suits N
72. Prohibit aid to Nicaragua Y
73. Cut $-Schs bar sch prayer N
74. Raise taxes; Cut Medicare N
75. Alien residncy-prior 1982 ?
76. Alien residncy-prior 1980 N
77. Pen emp-hire illgl aliens Y
78. Lmt Persh II/cruse-Europe Y
79. Delete 34 B-1 bombers Y
80. Bar purch of Pershing II Y
81. Bar purchase of Sgt York Y
82. Delete $ for Trident II Y
83. Allow 15 MX missiles Y
84. Bar MX procurement-1985 Y
85. Equal Access Act N
86. Aid to El Salvador N
87. Bar Nicarag water mining Y
88. Physician/Medicare freeze N
89. Increase "sin" taxes Y
90. End SBA direct loans N
91. Sell Conrail N
92. Equal Rights Amendment Y
93. Marines in Lebanon Y
94. Eminent domain-Coal comps N
95. Prohibit EPA sanctions Y
96. SS age increase/Reforms N
97. Auto domestic content req Y
98. Delete jobs program fundg N
99. Highway-Gas tax bill N
100. Raise Medicare;Cut defnse Y
101. Emergency housing aid Y
102. Across-the-board tax cuts N
103. Gramm-Latta II targets N
104. Delete B-1 bomber funds Y
105. Dsapprov Saudi AWACS sale Y
106. Disapprove oil import fee Y
107. Rail Deregulation N
108. Dsapp India nuc fuel sale Y
109. Mil draft registration Y
110. Chrysler Loan Guarantees Y
111. Prohibit school busing N
112. Nuclear plant moratorium Y
113. Oil price controls N

Presidential Support Score: 1986 - 13% 1985 - 18%

MARLENEE, RON -- Montana 2nd District [Republican]. Counties of Big Horn, Blaine, Carbon, Carter, Cascade, Chouteau, Custer, Daniels, Dawson, Fallon, Fergus, Garfield, Golden Valley, Hill, Judith Basin, McCone, Musselshell, Petroleum, Phillips, Powder River, Prairie, Richland, Roosevelt, Rosebud, Sheridan, Stillwater, Sweet Grass, Teton, Treasure, Valley, Wheatland, Wibaux and Yellowstone. Prior Terms: House: 1977-86. Born: August 8, 1935; Scobey, Mont. Education: University of Montana; Montana State University. Occupation: Rancher, congressional committeeman (1975-76).

1. Immigration Reform N
2. Open fld-search warrants Y
3. Civil pnty-hire ill alien Y
4. So Afr sanc-veto override N
5. Tax Overhaul N
6. South Africa sanctions N
7. Death penalty-drug bill Y
8. Evidence-warrantless srch Y
9. Life term-second drug off Y
10. Military use in drug war Y
11. Troop reduction in Europe N
12. Prohibit chemical weapons N
13. Bar ASAT testing N
14. Abide SALT II weapons ban N
15. Follow SALT II-Soviets do Y
16. Reduce SDI funding N
17. Increase SDI funding Y
18. Purchase Trident sub N
19. Delete 12 MX;Add conv wpn N
20. Raise speed limit Y
21. Textile Import Quotas(*) N
22. Req Pentagon buy US goods N
23. AIDS ins anti-dscriminatn N
24. Nicaraguan refugee aid N
25. Nicaraguan contra aid Y
26. US abide by SALT II Y
27. Prohibit Saudi arms sale N
28. Military Retiremnt Reform Y
29. Nicaraguan refugee aid Y
30. Ease '68 Gun Control Act Y
31. Bar intrstat handgun tran N
32. Keep '68 Gun Control Act N
33. Nicaraguan contra aid Y
34. Bar emp polygraph testing N
35. Tax Overhaul consideratn N
36. Bar armor-piercing ammo N
37. Tax Overhaul consideratn N
38. Make comp emissions known N
39. Allow toxic victims suits N
40. Strike Superfund "VAT" N
41. Notify emp-plant closing N
42. Bar emp consult-plant clo Y
43. Medicare cuts;Tax incres' ?
44. Delete 12 MX missiles ?
45. Spending cuts;Tax incres' N
46. Textile Import Quotas N
47. Cut some school lunch fds N
48. Clean Water Act Amendmnts Y
49. Youth work projects N
50. Assist military in Angola Y
51. Allow US troops-Nicaragua Y
52. Pentagon polygraph exams Y
53. Bar ASAT testing N
54. Suspend def pmt for abuse N
55. Bar Pentagon-contr emplmt Y
56. Increase SDI funding Y
57. Reduce SDI funding N
58. Produce chemical weapons Y
59. Bar CIA fndg in Nicaragua N
60. South Africa sanctions N
61. Cut SS COLAs; Raise taxes N
62. Let US invest-So Africa Y
63. Approve 21 MX for 1985 Y
64. Emergency Farm Credit Y
65. Awards to whistle blowers Y
66. African disaster relief Y
67. Ban bank loans to So Afr Y
68. Bar coun duty-free trtmt N
69. Steel import limits N
70. Soc Sec COLAs=inflation Y
71. Bar haz waste vctms suits Y
72. Prohibit aid to Nicaragua N
73. Cut $-Schs bar sch prayer Y
74. Raise taxes; Cut Medicare N
75. Alien residncy-prior 1982 Y
76. Alien residncy-prior 1980 Y
77. Pen emp-hire illgl aliens N
78. Lmt Persh II/cruse-Europe N
79. Delete 34 B-1 bombers N
80. Bar purch of Pershing II N
81. Bar purchase of Sgt York N
82. Delete $ for Trident II N
83. Allow 15 MX missiles Y
84. Bar MX procurement-1985 N
85. Equal Access Act Y
86. Aid to El Salvador Y
87. Bar Nicarag water mining N
88. Physician/Medicare freeze Y
89. Increase "sin" taxes N
90. End SBA direct loans N
91. Sell Conrail N
92. Equal Rights Amendment N
93. Marines in Lebanon Y
94. Eminent domain-Coal comps N
95. Prohibit EPA sanctions ?
96. SS age increase/Reforms Y
97. Auto domestic content req N
98. Delete jobs program fundg Y

MARLENEE, RON (Cont.)

99.	Highway-Gas tax bill	?	110.	Chrysler Loan Guarantees	Y
100.	Raise Medicare;Cut defnse	Y	111.	Prohibit school busing	Y
101.	Emergency housing aid	Y	112.	Nuclear plant moratorium	Y
102.	Across-the-board tax cuts	Y	113.	Oil price controls	N
103.	Gramm-Latta II targets	Y	114.	Tuition Tax Credits	N
104.	Delete B-1 bomber funds	N	115.	Est Consumer Protect Agcy	N
105.	Dsapprov Saudi AWACS sale	N	116.	Eliminate B-1 bomber fnds	N
106.	Disapprove oil import fee	Y	117.	Subminimum wage for youth	Y
107.	Rail Deregulation	N	118.	Delete crude oil tax	Y
108.	Dsapp India nuc fuel sale	Y	119.	Natural gas deregulation	Y
109.	Mil draft registration	N			

Presidential Support Score: 1986 - 75% 1985 - 61%

NEBRASKA

BEREUTER, DOUGLAS K. -- Nebraska 1st District [Republican]. Counties of Butler, Cass (pt.), Cedar, Colfax, Cuming, Dakota, Dixon, Dodge, Fillmore, Gage, Jefferson, Johnson, Knox, Lancaster, Madison, Nemaha, Otoe, Pawnee, Pierce, Richardson, Saline, Saunders, Seward, Stanton, Thurston, Wayne and York. Prior Terms: House: 1979-86. Born: October 6, 1939; York, Neb. Education: University of Nebraska (B.A.); Harvard University (M.C.P., M.P.A.); Eagleton Institute of Politics. Military Service: U.S. Army, 1963-65. Occupation: Residential and commercial development consultant; part owner, automobile and hardware dealership; division director, Nebraska Department of Economic Development (1967-68); director, state office of Planning and Programming (1968-71); federal-state relations coordinator, Nebraska (1967-71); Nebraska senator (1975-78).

1.	Immigration Reform	N	28.	Military Retiremnt Reform	Y
2.	Open fld-search warrants	N	29.	Nicaraguan refugee aid	Y
3.	Civil pnty-hire ill alien	N	30.	Ease '68 Gun Control Act	Y
4.	So Afr sanc-veto override	Y	31.	Bar intrstat handgun tran	Y
5.	Tax Overhaul	Y	32.	Keep '68 Gun Control Act	N
6.	South Africa sanctions	Y	33.	Nicaraguan contra aid	Y
7.	Death penalty-drug bill	Y	34.	Bar emp polygraph testing	Y
8.	Evidence-warrantless srch	Y	35.	Tax Overhaul consideratn	N
9.	Life term-second drug off	Y	36.	Bar armor-piercing ammo	Y
10.	Military use in drug war	N	37.	Tax Overhaul consideratn	N
11.	Troop reduction in Europe	N	38.	Make comp emissions known	N
12.	Prohibit chemical weapons	N	39.	Allow toxic victims suits	N
13.	Bar ASAT testing	N	40.	Strike Superfund "VAT"	N
14.	Abide SALT II weapons ban	N	41.	Notify emp-plant closing	N
15.	Follow SALT II-Soviets do	Y	42.	Bar emp consult-plant clo	Y
16.	Reduce SDI funding	N	43.	Medicare cuts;Tax incres'	Y
17.	Increase SDI funding	N	44.	Delete 12 MX missiles	Y
18.	Purchase Trident sub	N	45.	Spending cuts;Tax incres'	N
19.	Delete 12 MX;Add conv wpn	Y	46.	Textile Import Quotas	N
20.	Raise speed limit	Y	47.	Cut some school lunch fds	Y
21.	Textile Import Quotas(*)	N	48.	Clean Water Act Amendmnts	Y
22.	Req Pentagon buy US goods	N	49.	Youth work projects	Y
23.	AIDS ins anti-dscriminatn	N	50.	Assist military in Angola	Y
24.	Nicaraguan refugee aid	N	51.	Allow US troops-Nicaragua	N
25.	Nicaraguan contra aid	Y	52.	Pentagon polygraph exams	Y
26.	US abide by SALT II	Y	53.	Bar ASAT testing	N
27.	Prohibit Saudi arms sale	Y	54.	Suspend def pmt for abuse	N

BEREUTER, DOUGLAS K. (Cont.)

55. Bar Pentagon-contr emplmt Y
56. Increase SDI funding N
57. Reduce SDI funding N
58. Produce chemical weapons Y
59. Bar CIA fndg in Nicaragua N
60. South Africa sanctions N
61. Cut SS COLAs; Raise taxes N
62. Let US invest-So Africa Y
63. Approve 21 MX for 1985 N
64. Emergency Farm Credit Y
65. Awards to whistle blowers Y
66. African disaster relief Y
67. Ban bank loans to So Afr Y
68. Bar coun duty-free trtmt N
69. Steel import limits N
70. Soc Sec COLAs=inflation Y
71. Bar haz waste vctms suits Y
72. Prohibit aid to Nicaragua Y
73. Cut $-Schs bar sch prayer N
74. Raise taxes; Cut Medicare Y
75. Alien residncy-prior 1982 Y
76. Alien residncy-prior 1980 Y
77. Pen emp-hire illgl aliens N
78. Lmt Persh II/cruse-Europe N
79. Delete 34 B-1 bombers N
80. Bar purch of Pershing II N
81. Bar purchase of Sgt York N
82. Delete $ for Trident II N
83. Allow 15 MX missiles N
84. Bar MX procurement-1985 Y
85. Equal Access Act Y
86. Aid to El Salvador Y
87. Bar Nicarag water mining Y
88. Physician/Medicare freeze Y
89. Increase "sin" taxes Y
90. End SBA direct loans N
91. Sell Conrail Y
92. Equal Rights Amendment Y
93. Marines in Lebanon N
94. Eminent domain-Coal comps N
95. Prohibit EPA sanctions N
96. SS age increase/Reforms Y
97. Auto domestic content req N
98. Delete jobs program fundg Y
99. Highway-Gas tax bill N
100. Raise Medicare;Cut defnse Y
101. Emergency housing aid Y
102. Across-the-board tax cuts Y
103. Gramm-Latta II targets Y
104. Delete B-1 bomber funds N
105. Dsapprov Saudi AWACS sale N
106. Disapprove oil import fee Y
107. Rail Deregulation Y
108. Dsapp India nuc fuel sale Y
109. Mil draft registration Y
110. Chrysler Loan Guarantees Y
111. Prohibit school busing N
112. Nuclear plant moratorium Y
113. Oil price controls N

Presidential Support Score: 1986 - 58% 1985 - 58%

DAUB, HAL -- Nebraska 2nd District [Republican]. Counties of Douglas, Sarpy, Washington. Prior Terms: House: 1981-86. Born: April 23, 1941; Fort Bragg, N.C. Education: Washington University (B.S.); University of Nebraska-Lincoln (J.D.). Military Service: U.S. Army, 1966-68. Occupation: Attorney, Fitzgerald, Brown, Leahy, McGill & Strom Associates (1968-71); vice-president and general council, Standard Chemical Manufacturing Co. (1971-81).

1. Immigration Reform N
2. Open fld-search warrants N
3. Civil pnty-hire ill alien N
4. So Afr sanc-veto override Y
5. Tax Overhaul Y
6. South Africa sanctions Y
7. Death penalty-drug bill Y
8. Evidence-warrantless srch Y
9. Life term-second drug off Y
10. Military use in drug war N
11. Troop reduction in Europe N
12. Prohibit chemical weapons N
13. Bar ASAT testing N
14. Abide SALT II weapons ban N
15. Follow SALT II-Soviets do Y
16. Reduce SDI funding N
17. Increase SDI funding N
18. Purchase Trident sub N
19. Delete 12 MX;Add conv wpn N
20. Raise speed limit Y
21. Textile Import Quotas(*) N
22. Req Pentagon buy US goods N
23. AIDS ins anti-dscriminatn N
24. Nicaraguan refugee aid N
25. Nicaraguan contra aid Y
26. US abide by SALT II Y
27. Prohibit Saudi arms sale Y
28. Military Retiremnt Reform Y
29. Nicaraguan refugee aid Y
30. Ease '68 Gun Control Act Y
31. Bar intrstat handgun tran N
32. Keep '68 Gun Control Act N
33. Nicaraguan contra aid Y
34. Bar emp polygraph testing N

DAUB, HAL (Cont.)

35. Tax Overhaul consideratn Y
36. Bar armor-piercing ammo Y
37. Tax Overhaul consideratn Y
38. Make comp emissions known N
39. Allow toxic victims suits N
40. Strike Superfund "VAT" N
41. Notify emp-plant closing N
42. Bar emp consult-plant clo Y
43. Medicare cuts;Tax incres' N
44. Delete 12 MX missiles N
45. Spending cuts;Tax incres' N
46. Textile Import Quotas N
47. Cut some school lunch fds Y
48. Clean Water Act Amendmnts Y
49. Youth work projects N
50. Assist military in Angola Y
51. Allow US troops-Nicaragua Y
52. Pentagon polygraph exams Y
53. Bar ASAT testing Y
54. Suspend def pmt for abuse N
55. Bar Pentagon-contr emplmt Y
56. Increase SDI funding N
57. Reduce SDI funding N
58. Produce chemical weapons Y
59. Bar CIA fndg in Nicaragua N
60. South Africa sanctions Y
61. Cut SS COLAs; Raise taxes N
62. Let US invest-So Africa Y
63. Approve 21 MX for 1985 Y
64. Emergency Farm Credit Y
65. Awards to whistle blowers Y
66. African disaster relief Y
67. Ban bank loans to So Afr Y
68. Bar coun duty-free trtmt N
69. Steel import limits N
70. Soc Sec COLAs=inflation Y
71. Bar haz waste vctms suits Y
72. Prohibit aid to Nicaragua Y
73. Cut $-Schs bar sch prayer Y
74. Raise taxes; Cut Medicare Y
75. Alien residncy-prior 1982 Y
76. Alien residncy-prior 1980 Y
77. Pen emp-hire illgl aliens N
78. Lmt Persh II/cruse-Europe N
79. Delete 34 B-1 bombers N
80. Bar purch of Pershing II N
81. Bar purchase of Sgt York N
82. Delete $ for Trident II N
83. Allow 15 MX missiles Y
84. Bar MX procurement-1985 N
85. Equal Access Act Y
86. Aid to El Salvador Y
87. Bar Nicarag water mining Y
88. Physician/Medicare freeze Y
89. Increase "sin" taxes Y
90. End SBA direct loans N
91. Sell Conrail Y
92. Equal Rights Amendment Y
93. Marines in Lebanon Y
94. Eminent domain-Coal comps N
95. Prohibit EPA sanctions Y
96. SS age increase/Reforms Y
97. Auto domestic content req N
98. Delete jobs program fundg Y
99. Highway-Gas tax bill N
100. Raise Medicare;Cut defnse Y
101. Emergency housing aid Y
102. Across-the-board tax cuts Y
103. Gramm-Latta II targets Y
104. Delete B-1 bomber funds N
105. Dsapprov Saudi AWACS sale N

Presidential Support Score: 1986 - 78% 1985 - 74%

SMITH, VIRGINIA -- Nebraska 3rd District [Republican]. Counties of Adams, Antelope, Arthur, Banner, Blaine, Boone, Box Butte, Boyd, Brown, Buffalo, Chase, Cherry, Cheyenne, Clay, Custer, Dawes, Dawson, Deuel, Dundy, Franklin, Frontier, Furnas, Garden, Garfield, Gosper, Grant, Greeley, Hall, Hamilton, Harlan, Hayes, Hitchcock, Hocker, Holt, Howard, Kearney, Keith, Keya Paha, Kimball, Lincoln, Logan, Loup, McPherson, Merrick, Morrill, Nance, Nuckolls, Perkins, Phelps, Platte, Polk, Red Willow, Rock, Scotts Bluff, Sheridan, Shermon, Sioux, Thayer, Thomas, Valley, Webster and Wheeler. Prior Terms: House: 1975-86. Born: June 30, 1911; Randolph, Iowa. Education: University of Nebraska (B.A.). Occupation: Chairman, American Farm Bureau of Women (1955-74).

1. Immigration Reform Y
2. Open fld-search warrants ?
3. Civil pnty-hire ill alien Y
4. So Afr sanc-veto override Y
5. Tax Overhaul Y
6. South Africa sanctions Y
7. Death penalty-drug bill Y
8. Evidence-warrantless srch Y
9. Life term-second drug off Y
10. Military use in drug war Y

SMITH, VIRGINIA (Cont.)

11.	Troop reduction in Europe	N	66.	African disaster relief	Y
12.	Prohibit chemical weapons	N	67.	Ban bank loans to So Afr	Y
13.	Bar ASAT testing	N	68.	Bar coun duty-free trtmt	N
14.	Abide SALT II weapons ban	N	69.	Steel import limits	N
15.	Follow SALT II-Soviets do	Y	70.	Soc Sec COLAs=inflation	Y
16.	Reduce SDI funding	N	71.	Bar haz waste vctms suits	Y
17.	Increase SDI funding	N	72.	Prohibit aid to Nicaragua	Y
18.	Purchase Trident sub	N	73.	Cut $-Schs bar sch prayer	Y
19.	Delete 12 MX;Add conv wpn	Y	74.	Raise taxes; Cut Medicare	Y
20.	Raise speed limit	Y	75.	Alien residncy-prior 1982	Y
21.	Textile Import Quotas(*)	N	76.	Alien residncy-prior 1980	Y
22.	Req Pentagon buy US goods	N	77.	Pen emp-hire illgl aliens	N
23.	AIDS ins anti-dscriminatn	Y	78.	Lmt Persh II/cruse-Europe	N
24.	Nicaraguan refugee aid	N	79.	Delete 34 B-1 bombers	N
25.	Nicaraguan contra aid	Y	80.	Bar purch of Pershing II	N
26.	US abide by SALT II	Y	81.	Bar purchase of Sgt York	N
27.	Prohibit Saudi arms sale	Y	82.	Delete $ for Trident II	N
28.	Military Retiremnt Reform	Y	83.	Allow 15 MX missiles	N
29.	Nicaraguan refugee aid	Y	84.	Bar MX procurement-1985	Y
30.	Ease '68 Gun Control Act	Y	85.	Equal Access Act	Y
31.	Bar intrstat handgun tran	N	86.	Aid to El Salvador	Y
32.	Keep '68 Gun Control Act	N	87.	Bar Nicarag water mining	Y
33.	Nicaraguan contra aid	Y	88.	Physician/Medicare freeze	Y
34.	Bar emp polygraph testing	N	89.	Increase "sin" taxes	Y
35.	Tax Overhaul consideratn	Y	90.	End SBA direct loans	N
36.	Bar armor-piercing ammo	Y	91.	Sell Conrail	Y
37.	Tax Overhaul consideratn	N	92.	Equal Rights Amendment	Y
38.	Make comp emissions known	N	93.	Marines in Lebanon	Y
39.	Allow toxic victims suits	N	94.	Eminent domain-Coal comps	N
40.	Strike Superfund "VAT"	N	95.	Prohibit EPA sanctions	Y
41.	Notify emp-plant closing	N	96.	SS age increase/Reforms	Y
42.	Bar emp consult-plant clo	Y	97.	Auto domestic content req	N
43.	Medicare cuts;Tax incres'	Y	98.	Delete jobs program fundg	Y
44.	Delete 12 MX missiles	Y	99.	Highway-Gas tax bill	N
45.	Spending cuts;Tax incres'	N	100.	Raise Medicare;Cut defnse	Y
46.	Textile Import Quotas	N	101.	Emergency housing aid	Y
47.	Cut some school lunch fds	Y	102.	Across-the-board tax cuts	Y
48.	Clean Water Act Amendmnts	Y	103.	Gramm-Latta II targets	Y
49.	Youth work projects	N	104.	Delete B-1 bomber funds	N
50.	Assist military in Angola	Y	105.	Dsapprov Saudi AWACS sale	N
51.	Allow US troops-Nicaragua	Y	106.	Disapprove oil import fee	Y
52.	Pentagon polygraph exams	Y	107.	Rail Deregulation	Y
53.	Bar ASAT testing	N	108.	Dsapp India nuc fuel sale	Y
54.	Suspend def pmt for abuse	N	109.	Mil draft registration	Y
55.	Bar Pentagon-contr emplmt	Y	110.	Chrysler Loan Guarantees	N
56.	Increase SDI funding	N	111.	Prohibit school busing	Y
57.	Reduce SDI funding	N	112.	Nuclear plant moratorium	N
58.	Produce chemical weapons	Y	113.	Oil price controls	N
59.	Bar CIA fndg in Nicaragua	N	114.	Tuition Tax Credits	Y
60.	South Africa sanctions	N	115.	Est Consumer Protect Agcy	N
61.	Cut SS COLAs; Raise taxes	N	116.	Eliminate B-1 bomber fnds	N
62.	Let US invest-So Africa	Y	117.	Subminimum wage for youth	Y
63.	Approve 21 MX for 1985	N	118.	Delete crude oil tax	Y
64.	Emergency Farm Credit	Y	119.	Natural gas deregulation	Y
65.	Awards to whistle blowers	Y			

Presidential Support Score: 1986 - 65% 1985 - 58%

NEVADA

REID, HARRY M. -- Nevada 1st District [Democrat]. County of Clark (pt.). Prior Terms: House: 1983-86. Born: December 2, 1939; Searchlight, Nev. Education: Southern Utah State College (A.D.); Utah State University (B.S.); George Washington School of Law (J.D.). Occupation: Attorney, city attorney (1964-66); member, Board of Trustees, Southern Nevada Memorial Hospital (1967-69); Nevada assemblyman (1969-70); Nevada lieutenant governor (1970-74); Nevada gaming commission (1977-81).

1. Immigration Reform N
2. Open fld-search warrants N
3. Civil pnty-hire ill alien Y
4. So Afr sanc-veto override Y
5. Tax Overhaul Y
6. South Africa sanctions Y
7. Death penalty-drug bill Y
8. Evidence-warrantless srch Y
9. Life term-second drug off Y
10. Military use in drug war Y
11. Troop reduction in Europe N
12. Prohibit chemical weapons Y
13. Bar ASAT testing Y
14. Abide SALT II weapons ban Y
15. Follow SALT II-Soviets do N
16. Reduce SDI funding N
17. Increase SDI funding Y
18. Purchase Trident sub Y
19. Delete 12 MX;Add conv wpn N
20. Raise speed limit Y
21. Textile Import Quotas(*) Y
22. Req Pentagon buy US goods Y
23. AIDS ins anti-dscriminatn Y
24. Nicaraguan refugee aid Y
25. Nicaraguan contra aid N
26. US abide by SALT II N
27. Prohibit Saudi arms sale Y
28. Military Retiremnt Reform Y
29. Nicaraguan refugee aid Y
30. Ease '68 Gun Control Act Y
31. Bar intrstat handgun tran N
32. Keep '68 Gun Control Act N
33. Nicaraguan contra aid N
34. Bar emp polygraph testing Y
35. Tax Overhaul consideratn Y
36. Bar armor-piercing ammo Y
37. Tax Overhaul consideratn Y
38. Make comp emissions known Y
39. Allow toxic victims suits Y
40. Strike Superfund "VAT" Y
41. Notify emp-plant closing Y
42. Bar emp consult-plant clo N
43. Medicare cuts;Tax incres' N
44. Delete 12 MX missiles N
45. Spending cuts;Tax incres' Y
46. Textile Import Quotas Y
47. Cut some school lunch fds N
48. Clean Water Act Amendmnts N
49. Youth work projects #
50. Assist military in Angola N
51. Allow US troops-Nicaragua N
52. Pentagon polygraph exams Y
53. Bar ASAT testing Y
54. Suspend def pmt for abuse Y
55. Bar Pentagon-contr emplmt Y
56. Increase SDI funding N
57. Reduce SDI funding N
58. Produce chemical weapons N
59. Bar CIA fndg in Nicaragua Y
60. South Africa sanctions Y
61. Cut SS COLAs; Raise taxes N
62. Let US invest-So Africa N
63. Approve 21 MX for 1985 Y
64. Emergency Farm Credit Y
65. Awards to whistle blowers Y
66. African disaster relief Y
67. Ban bank loans to So Afr ?
68. Bar coun duty-free trtmt Y
69. Steel import limits Y
70. Soc Sec COLAs=inflation Y
71. Bar haz waste vctms suits N
72. Prohibit aid to Nicaragua Y
73. Cut $-Schs bar sch prayer N
74. Raise taxes; Cut Medicare Y
75. Alien residncy-prior 1982 Y
76. Alien residncy-prior 1980 Y
77. Pen emp-hire illgl aliens Y
78. Lmt Persh II/cruse-Europe N
79. Delete 34 B-1 bombers Y
80. Bar purch of Pershing II N
81. Bar purchase of Sgt York Y
82. Delete $ for Trident II N
83. Allow 15 MX missiles Y
84. Bar MX procurement-1985 N
85. Equal Access Act N
86. Aid to El Salvador N
87. Bar Nicarag water mining Y
88. Physician/Medicare freeze N
89. Increase "sin" taxes Y
90. End SBA direct loans N
91. Sell Conrail N
92. Equal Rights Amendment N
93. Marines in Lebanon Y
94. Eminent domain-Coal comps N
95. Prohibit EPA sanctions Y
96. SS age increase/Reforms N

REID, HARRY M. (Cont.)
Presidential Support Score: 1986 - 25% 1985 - 44%

VUCANOVICH, BARBARA F. -- Nevada 2nd District [Republican]. Counties of Churchill, Clark (pt.), Douglas, Elko, Esmeralda, Eureka, Humboldt, Lander, Lincoln, Lyon, Mineral, Nye, Pershing, Storey, Washoe and White Pine. Carson City. Prior Terms: House: 1983-86. Born: June 22, 1921; Camp Dix, N.J. Education: Manhattanville College of the Sacred Heart. Occupation: Operated speed reading school (1965-68); travel agent (1968-74); senator's aide.

1. Immigration Reform Y
2. Open fld-search warrants N
3. Civil pnty-hire ill alien Y
4. So Afr sanc-veto override N
5. Tax Overhaul N
6. South Africa sanctions Y
7. Death penalty-drug bill Y
8. Evidence-warrantless srch Y
9. Life term-second drug off Y
10. Military use in drug war Y
11. Troop reduction in Europe N
12. Prohibit chemical weapons N
13. Bar ASAT testing N
14. Abide SALT II weapons ban N
15. Follow SALT II-Soviets do Y
16. Reduce SDI funding N
17. Increase SDI funding Y
18. Purchase Trident sub N
19. Delete 12 MX;Add conv wpn N
20. Raise speed limit Y
21. Textile Import Quotas(*) N
22. Req Pentagon buy US goods N
23. AIDS ins anti-dscriminatn N
24. Nicaraguan refugee aid N
25. Nicaraguan contra aid Y
26. US abide by SALT II Y
27. Prohibit Saudi arms sale Y
28. Military Retiremnt Reform Y
29. Nicaraguan refugee aid Y
30. Ease '68 Gun Control Act Y
31. Bar intrstat handgun tran N
32. Keep '68 Gun Control Act N
33. Nicaraguan contra aid Y
34. Bar emp polygraph testing N
35. Tax Overhaul consideratn N
36. Bar armor-piercing ammo N
37. Tax Overhaul consideratn N
38. Make comp emissions known N
39. Allow toxic victims suits N
40. Strike Superfund "VAT" Y
41. Notify emp-plant closing N
42. Bar emp consult-plant clo Y
43. Medicare cuts;Tax incres' N
44. Delete 12 MX missiles N
45. Spending cuts;Tax incres' N
46. Textile Import Quotas N
47. Cut some school lunch fds N
48. Clean Water Act Amendmnts Y
49. Youth work projects ?
50. Assist military in Angola Y
51. Allow US troops-Nicaragua Y
52. Pentagon polygraph exams Y
53. Bar ASAT testing N
54. Suspend def pmt for abuse N
55. Bar Pentagon-contr emplmt Y
56. Increase SDI funding Y
57. Reduce SDI funding N
58. Produce chemical weapons Y
59. Bar CIA fndg in Nicaragua N
60. South Africa sanctions N
61. Cut SS COLAs; Raise taxes N
62. Let US invest-So Africa Y
63. Approve 21 MX for 1985 Y
64. Emergency Farm Credit N
65. Awards to whistle blowers Y
66. African disaster relief Y
67. Ban bank loans to So Afr Y
68. Bar coun duty-free trtmt N
69. Steel import limits N
70. Soc Sec COLAs=inflation Y
71. Bar haz waste vctms suits Y
72. Prohibit aid to Nicaragua N
73. Cut $-Schs bar sch prayer Y
74. Raise taxes; Cut Medicare N
75. Alien residncy-prior 1982 N
76. Alien residncy-prior 1980 N
77. Pen emp-hire illgl aliens N
78. Lmt Persh II/cruse-Europe N
79. Delete 34 B-1 bombers N
80. Bar purch of Pershing II N
81. Bar purchase of Sgt York N
82. Delete $ for Trident II N
83. Allow 15 MX missiles Y
84. Bar MX procurement-1985 N
85. Equal Access Act Y
86. Aid to El Salvador Y
87. Bar Nicarag water mining N
88. Physician/Medicare freeze Y
89. Increase "sin" taxes N
90. End SBA direct loans Y
91. Sell Conrail Y
92. Equal Rights Amendment N
93. Marines in Lebanon Y
94. Eminent domain-Coal comps Y
95. Prohibit EPA sanctions +
96. SS age increase/Reforms Y

VUCANOVICH, BARBARA F. (Cont.)
Presidential Support Score: 1986 - 68% 1985 - 70%

NEW HAMPSHIRE

SMITH, ROBERT C. -- New Hampshire 1st District [Republican]. Counties of Belknap, Carroll, Hillsborough (pt.), Merrimack (pt.), Rockingham (pt.) and Strafford. Prior Terms: 1985-86. Occupation: Realtor.

1. Immigration Reform N
2. Open fld-search warrants N
3. Civil pnty-hire ill alien N
4. So Afr sanc-veto override N
5. Tax Overhaul Y
6. South Africa sanctions N
7. Death penalty-drug bill Y
8. Evidence-warrantless srch Y
9. Life term-second drug off Y
10. Military use in drug war Y
11. Troop reduction in Europe N
12. Prohibit chemical weapons N
13. Bar ASAT testing N
14. Abide SALT II weapons ban N
15. Follow SALT II-Soviets do Y
16. Reduce SDI funding N
17. Increase SDI funding Y
18. Purchase Trident sub N
19. Delete 12 MX;Add conv wpn N
20. Raise speed limit Y
21. Textile Import Quotas(*) Y
22. Req Pentagon buy US goods N
23. AIDS ins anti-dscriminatn N
24. Nicaraguan refugee aid N
25. Nicaraguan contra aid Y
26. US abide by SALT II Y
27. Prohibit Saudi arms sale Y
28. Military Retiremnt Reform Y
29. Nicaraguan refugee aid Y
30. Ease '68 Gun Control Act Y
31. Bar intrstat handgun tran N
32. Keep '68 Gun Control Act N
33. Nicaraguan contra aid Y
34. Bar emp polygraph testing N
35. Tax Overhaul consideratn N
36. Bar armor-piercing ammo Y
37. Tax Overhaul consideratn N
38. Make comp emissions known Y
39. Allow toxic victims suits N
40. Strike Superfund "VAT" Y
41. Notify emp-plant closing N
42. Bar emp consult-plant clo Y
43. Medicare cuts;Tax incres' N
44. Delete 12 MX missiles N
45. Spending cuts;Tax incres' N
46. Textile Import Quotas Y
47. Cut some school lunch fds Y
48. Clean Water Act Amendmnts Y
49. Youth work projects N
50. Assist military in Angola Y
51. Allow US troops-Nicaragua Y
52. Pentagon polygraph exams Y
53. Bar ASAT testing N
54. Suspend def pmt for abuse N
55. Bar Pentagon-contr emplmt Y
56. Increase SDI funding Y
57. Reduce SDI funding N
58. Produce chemical weapons Y
59. Bar CIA fndg in Nicaragua N
60. South Africa sanctions N
61. Cut SS COLAs; Raise taxes N
62. Let US invest-So Africa Y
63. Approve 21 MX for 1985 Y
64. Emergency Farm Credit N
65. Awards to whistle blowers Y
66. African disaster relief N

Presidential Support Score: 1986 - 82% 1985 - 84%

GREGG, JUDD -- New Hampshire 2nd District [Republican]. Counties of Cheshire, Coos, Grafton, Hillsborough (pt.), Merrimack (pt.), Rockingham (pt.) amd Sullivan. Prior Terms: House: 1981-86. Born: February 14, 1947; Nashua, N.H. Education: Phillips Exeter Academy; Columbia University (A.B.); Boston University (J.D., LL.M.). Occupation: Attorney; director, Indian Head Banks, Inc.; president, Nashua Community Council; treasurer, Nashua Fresh Air Camp; alternate member, Greenfield Planning Board; president, Crotched Mountain Rehabilitation Foundation.

1. Immigration Reform N
2. Open fld-search warrants N
3. Civil pnty-hire ill alien N
4. So Afr sanc-veto override ?
5. Tax Overhaul Y
6. South Africa sanctions Y
7. Death penalty-drug bill N
8. Evidence-warrantless srch Y
9. Life term-second drug off Y
10. Military use in drug war Y

GREGG, JUDD (Cont.)

11. Troop reduction in Europe N
12. Prohibit chemical weapons Y
13. Bar ASAT testing N
14. Abide SALT II weapons ban N
15. Follow SALT II-Soviets do Y
16. Reduce SDI funding N
17. Increase SDI funding N
18. Purchase Trident sub N
19. Delete 12 MX;Add conv wpn N
20. Raise speed limit Y
21. Textile Import Quotas(*) Y
22. Req Pentagon buy US goods N
23. AIDS ins anti-dscriminatn N
24. Nicaraguan refugee aid N
25. Nicaraguan contra aid Y
26. US abide by SALT II Y
27. Prohibit Saudi arms sale Y
28. Military Retiremnt Reform Y
29. Nicaraguan refugee aid Y
30. Ease '68 Gun Control Act Y
31. Bar intrstat handgun tran N
32. Keep '68 Gun Control Act N
33. Nicaraguan contra aid Y
34. Bar emp polygraph testing Y
35. Tax Overhaul consideratn N
36. Bar armor-piercing ammo Y
37. Tax Overhaul consideratn N
38. Make comp emissions known Y
39. Allow toxic victims suits N
40. Strike Superfund "VAT" Y
41. Notify emp-plant closing N
42. Bar emp consult-plant clo Y
43. Medicare cuts;Tax incres' N
44. Delete 12 MX missiles N
45. Spending cuts;Tax incres' N
46. Textile Import Quotas Y
47. Cut some school lunch fds Y
48. Clean Water Act Amendmnts N
49. Youth work projects N
50. Assist military in Angola Y
51. Allow US troops-Nicaragua Y
52. Pentagon polygraph exams Y
53. Bar ASAT testing N
54. Suspend def pmt for abuse N
55. Bar Pentagon-contr emplmt Y
56. Increase SDI funding Y
57. Reduce SDI funding N
58. Produce chemical weapons N
59. Bar CIA fndg in Nicaragua N
60. South Africa sanctions Y
61. Cut SS COLAs; Raise taxes Y
62. Let US invest-So Africa N
63. Approve 21 MX for 1985 Y
64. Emergency Farm Credit N
65. Awards to whistle blowers Y
66. African disaster relief Y
67. Ban bank loans to So Afr Y
68. Bar coun duty-free trtmt N
69. Steel import limits N
70. Soc Sec COLAs=inflation Y
71. Bar haz waste vctms suits N
72. Prohibit aid to Nicaragua N
73. Cut $-Schs bar sch prayer Y
74. Raise taxes; Cut Medicare Y
75. Alien residncy-prior 1982 Y
76. Alien residncy-prior 1980 Y
77. Pen emp-hire illgl aliens N
78. Lmt Persh II/cruse-Europe N
79. Delete 34 B-1 bombers N
80. Bar purch of Pershing II N
81. Bar purchase of Sgt York ?
82. Delete $ for Trident II N
83. Allow 15 MX missiles Y
84. Bar MX procurement-1985 N
85. Equal Access Act Y
86. Aid to El Salvador Y
87. Bar Nicarag water mining Y
88. Physician/Medicare freeze Y
89. Increase "sin" taxes N
90. End SBA direct loans Y
91. Sell Conrail Y
92. Equal Rights Amendment Y
93. Marines in Lebanon Y
94. Eminent domain-Coal comps Y
95. Prohibit EPA sanctions Y
96. SS age increase/Reforms Y
97. Auto domestic content req N
98. Delete jobs program fundg Y
99. Highway-Gas tax bill Y
100. Raise Medicare;Cut defnse N
101. Emergency housing aid N
102. Across-the-board tax cuts Y
103. Gramm-Latta II targets Y
104. Delete B-1 bomber funds N
105. Dsapprov Saudi AWACS sale Y

Presidential Support Score: 1986 - 74% 1985 - 70%

NEW JERSEY

FLORIO, JAMES J. -- New Jersey 1st District [Democrat]. Counties of Camden (pt.) and Gloucester. Prior Terms: House: 1975-86. Born: August 29, 1937; Brooklyn, N.Y. Education: Trenton State College (B.A.); Columbia University; Rutgers University Law School (LL.D.). Military Service: U.S. Navy, 1955-58; U.S. Naval Reserve, 1958-74. Occupation: New Jersey legislator (1970-74).

FLORIO, JAMES J. (Cont.)

1. Immigration Reform Y
2. Open fld-search warrants N
3. Civil pnty-hire ill alien N
4. So Afr sanc-veto override Y
5. Tax Overhaul Y
6. South Africa sanctions Y
7. Death penalty-drug bill Y
8. Evidence-warrantless srch N
9. Life term-second drug off Y
10. Military use in drug war Y
11. Troop reduction in Europe Y
12. Prohibit chemical weapons Y
13. Bar ASAT testing Y
14. Abide SALT II weapons ban Y
15. Follow SALT II-Soviets do N
16. Reduce SDI funding N
17. Increase SDI funding N
18. Purchase Trident sub Y
19. Delete 12 MX;Add conv wpn Y
20. Raise speed limit N
21. Textile Import Quotas(*) Y
22. Req Pentagon buy US goods Y
23. AIDS ins anti-dscriminatn Y
24. Nicaraguan refugee aid N
25. Nicaraguan contra aid N
26. US abide by SALT II N
27. Prohibit Saudi arms sale Y
28. Military Retiremnt Reform Y
29. Nicaraguan refugee aid N
30. Ease '68 Gun Control Act Y
31. Bar intrstat handgun tran Y
32. Keep '68 Gun Control Act Y
33. Nicaraguan contra aid N
34. Bar emp polygraph testing Y
35. Tax Overhaul consideratn Y
36. Bar armor-piercing ammo Y
37. Tax Overhaul consideratn Y
38. Make comp emissions known Y
39. Allow toxic victims suits Y
40. Strike Superfund "VAT" Y
41. Notify emp-plant closing Y
42. Bar emp consult-plant clo N
43. Medicare cuts;Tax incres' Y
44. Delete 12 MX missiles Y
45. Spending cuts;Tax incres' Y
46. Textile Import Quotas Y
47. Cut some school lunch fds N
48. Clean Water Act Amendmnts N
49. Youth work projects Y
50. Assist military in Angola N
51. Allow US troops-Nicaragua N
52. Pentagon polygraph exams Y
53. Bar ASAT testing Y
54. Suspend def pmt for abuse Y
55. Bar Pentagon-contr emplmt Y
56. Increase SDI funding N
57. Reduce SDI funding N
58. Produce chemical weapons N
59. Bar CIA fndg in Nicaragua Y
60. South Africa sanctions Y
61. Cut SS COLAs; Raise taxes N
62. Let US invest-So Africa N
63. Approve 21 MX for 1985 N
64. Emergency Farm Credit Y
65. Awards to whistle blowers Y
66. African disaster relief Y
67. Ban bank loans to So Afr Y
68. Bar coun duty-free trtmt Y
69. Steel import limits Y
70. Soc Sec COLAs=inflation Y
71. Bar haz waste vctms suits N
72. Prohibit aid to Nicaragua Y
73. Cut $-Schs bar sch prayer N
74. Raise taxes; Cut Medicare N
75. Alien residncy-prior 1982 Y
76. Alien residncy-prior 1980 N
77. Pen emp-hire illgl aliens Y
78. Lmt Persh II/cruse-Europe N
79. Delete 34 B-1 bombers Y
80. Bar purch of Pershing II Y
81. Bar purchase of Sgt York Y
82. Delete $ for Trident II N
83. Allow 15 MX missiles N
84. Bar MX procurement-1985 Y
85. Equal Access Act N
86. Aid to El Salvador N
87. Bar Nicarag water mining Y
88. Physician/Medicare freeze N
89. Increase "sin" taxes N
90. End SBA direct loans N
91. Sell Conrail N
92. Equal Rights Amendment Y
93. Marines in Lebanon N
94. Eminent domain-Coal comps N
95. Prohibit EPA sanctions +
96. SS age increase/Reforms N
97. Auto domestic content req Y
98. Delete jobs program fundg N
99. Highway-Gas tax bill ?
100. Raise Medicare;Cut defnse Y
101. Emergency housing aid Y
102. Across-the-board tax cuts N
103. Gramm-Latta II targets N
104. Delete B-1 bomber funds #
105. Dsapprov Saudi AWACS sale Y
106. Disapprove oil import fee Y
107. Rail Deregulation N
108. Dsapp India nuc fuel sale N
109. Mil draft registration Y
110. Chrysler Loan Guarantees Y
111. Prohibit school busing N
112. Nuclear plant moratorium Y
113. Oil price controls Y
114. Tuition Tax Credits Y
115. Est Consumer Protect Agcy Y
116. Eliminate B-1 bomber fnds Y
117. Subminimum wage for youth N
118. Delete crude oil tax N

FLORIO, JAMES J. (Cont.)
119. Natural gas deregulation N

Presidential Support Score: 1986 - 18% 1985 - 25%

HUGHES, WILLIAM J. -- New Jersey 2nd District [Democrat]. Counties of Atlantic, Burlington (pt.), Cape May, Cumberland, Ocean (pt.) and Salem. Prior Terms: House: 1975-86. Born: October 17, 1932; Salem N.J. Education: Rutgers University (A.B., J.D.). Occupation: Attorney; Cape May County assistant prosecutor (1960-70).

1. Immigration Reform N
2. Open fld-search warrants N
3. Civil pnty-hire ill alien N
4. So Afr sanc-veto override Y
5. Tax Overhaul Y
6. South Africa sanctions Y
7. Death penalty-drug bill Y
8. Evidence-warrantless srch Y
9. Life term-second drug off N
10. Military use in drug war N
11. Troop reduction in Europe N
12. Prohibit chemical weapons Y
13. Bar ASAT testing Y
14. Abide SALT II weapons ban Y
15. Follow SALT II-Soviets do N
16. Reduce SDI funding N
17. Increase SDI funding N
18. Purchase Trident sub Y
19. Delete 12 MX;Add conv wpn Y
20. Raise speed limit N
21. Textile Import Quotas(*) Y
22. Req Pentagon buy US goods Y
23. AIDS ins anti-dscriminatn Y
24. Nicaraguan refugee aid Y
25. Nicaraguan contra aid N
26. US abide by SALT II N
27. Prohibit Saudi arms sale Y
28. Military Retiremnt Reform Y
29. Nicaraguan refugee aid Y
30. Ease '68 Gun Control Act N
31. Bar intrstat handgun tran Y
32. Keep '68 Gun Control Act Y
33. Nicaraguan contra aid N
34. Bar emp polygraph testing Y
35. Tax Overhaul consideratn N
36. Bar armor-piercing ammo Y
37. Tax Overhaul consideratn N
38. Make comp emissions known Y
39. Allow toxic victims suits N
40. Strike Superfund "VAT" Y
41. Notify emp-plant closing Y
42. Bar emp consult-plant clo N
43. Medicare cuts;Tax incres' Y
44. Delete 12 MX missiles Y
45. Spending cuts;Tax incres' N
46. Textile Import Quotas Y
47. Cut some school lunch fds N
48. Clean Water Act Amendmnts N
49. Youth work projects N
50. Assist military in Angola N
51. Allow US troops-Nicaragua N
52. Pentagon polygraph exams Y
53. Bar ASAT testing Y
54. Suspend def pmt for abuse N
55. Bar Pentagon-contr emplmt Y
56. Increase SDI funding N
57. Reduce SDI funding N
58. Produce chemical weapons Y
59. Bar CIA fndg in Nicaragua Y
60. South Africa sanctions Y
61. Cut SS COLAs; Raise taxes N
62. Let US invest-So Africa N
63. Approve 21 MX for 1985 N
64. Emergency Farm Credit Y
65. Awards to whistle blowers Y
66. African disaster relief Y
67. Ban bank loans to So Afr Y
68. Bar coun duty-free trtmt N
69. Steel import limits Y
70. Soc Sec COLAs=inflation Y
71. Bar haz waste vctms suits Y
72. Prohibit aid to Nicaragua Y
73. Cut $-Schs bar sch prayer N
74. Raise taxes; Cut Medicare N
75. Alien residncy-prior 1982 Y
76. Alien residncy-prior 1980 Y
77. Pen emp-hire illgl aliens N
78. Lmt Persh II/cruse-Europe N
79. Delete 34 B-1 bombers Y
80. Bar purch of Pershing II N
81. Bar purchase of Sgt York ?
82. Delete $ for Trident II N
83. Allow 15 MX missiles Y
84. Bar MX procurement-1985 N
85. Equal Access Act Y
86. Aid to El Salvador N
87. Bar Nicarag water mining Y
88. Physician/Medicare freeze N
89. Increase "sin" taxes Y
90. End SBA direct loans N
91. Sell Conrail N
92. Equal Rights Amendment Y
93. Marines in Lebanon Y
94. Eminent domain-Coal comps N
95. Prohibit EPA sanctions N
96. SS age increase/Reforms N

HUGHES, WILLIAM J. (Cont.)

97. Auto domestic content req Y
98. Delete jobs program fundg N
99. Highway-Gas tax bill N
100. Raise Medicare;Cut defnse Y
101. Emergency housing aid Y
102. Across-the-board tax cuts N
103. Gramm-Latta II targets N
104. Delete B-1 bomber funds Y
105. Dsapprov Saudi AWACS sale Y
106. Disapprove oil import fee Y
107. Rail Deregulation N
108. Dsapp India nuc fuel sale Y
109. Mil draft registration Y
110. Chrysler Loan Guarantees Y
111. Prohibit school busing N
112. Nuclear plant moratorium Y
113. Oil price controls Y
114. Tuition Tax Credits Y
115. Est Consumer Protect Agcy Y
116. Eliminate B-1 bomber fnds Y
117. Subminimum wage for youth N
118. Delete crude oil tax Y
119. Natural gas deregulation N

Presidential Support Score: 1986 - 27% 1985 - 30%

HOWARD, JAMES J. -- New Jersey 3rd District [Democrat]. Counties of Middlesex (pt.), Monmouth (pt.) and Ocean (pt.). Prior Terms: House: 1965-86. Born: July 24, 1927; Irvington, N.J. Education: St. Bonaventure University (B.A.); Rutgers University (M.Ed.). Military Service: U.S. Navy, WW II. Occupation: Teacher; acting principal; president, Monmouth County Education Assn.

1. Immigration Reform Y
2. Open fld-search warrants Y
3. Civil pnty-hire ill alien N
4. So Afr sanc-veto override Y
5. Tax Overhaul Y
6. South Africa sanctions Y
7. Death penalty-drug bill Y
8. Evidence-warrantless srch N
9. Life term-second drug off Y
10. Military use in drug war Y
11. Troop reduction in Europe N
12. Prohibit chemical weapons Y
13. Bar ASAT testing Y
14. Abide SALT II weapons ban Y
15. Follow SALT II-Soviets do N
16. Reduce SDI funding Y
17. Increase SDI funding N
18. Purchase Trident sub Y
19. Delete 12 MX;Add conv wpn Y
20. Raise speed limit N
21. Textile Import Quotas(*) Y
22. Req Pentagon buy US goods ?
23. AIDS ins anti-dscriminatn Y
24. Nicaraguan refugee aid Y
25. Nicaraguan contra aid N
26. US abide by SALT II N
27. Prohibit Saudi arms sale Y
28. Military Retiremnt Reform Y
29. Nicaraguan refugee aid Y
30. Ease '68 Gun Control Act N
31. Bar intrstat handgun tran Y
32. Keep '68 Gun Control Act Y
33. Nicaraguan contra aid N
34. Bar emp polygraph testing Y
35. Tax Overhaul consideratn Y
36. Bar armor-piercing ammo Y
37. Tax Overhaul consideratn Y
38. Make comp emissions known Y
39. Allow toxic victims suits Y
40. Strike Superfund "VAT" Y
41. Notify emp-plant closing Y
42. Bar emp consult-plant clo N
43. Medicare cuts;Tax incres' Y
44. Delete 12 MX missiles Y
45. Spending cuts;Tax incres' N
46. Textile Import Quotas Y
47. Cut some school lunch fds N
48. Clean Water Act Amendmnts N
49. Youth work projects Y
50. Assist military in Angola N
51. Allow US troops-Nicaragua N
52. Pentagon polygraph exams Y
53. Bar ASAT testing Y
54. Suspend def pmt for abuse Y
55. Bar Pentagon-contr emplmt Y
56. Increase SDI funding N
57. Reduce SDI funding Y
58. Produce chemical weapons N
59. Bar CIA fndg in Nicaragua Y
60. South Africa sanctions Y
61. Cut SS COLAs; Raise taxes N
62. Let US invest-So Africa N
63. Approve 21 MX for 1985 N
64. Emergency Farm Credit Y
65. Awards to whistle blowers Y
66. African disaster relief Y
67. Ban bank loans to So Afr ?
68. Bar coun duty-free trtmt Y
69. Steel import limits Y
70. Soc Sec COLAs=inflation Y
71. Bar haz waste vctms suits N
72. Prohibit aid to Nicaragua ?

HOWARD, JAMES J. (Cont.)

73. Cut $-Schs bar sch prayer N
74. Raise taxes; Cut Medicare Y
75. Alien residncy-prior 1982 ?
76. Alien residncy-prior 1980 N
77. Pen emp-hire illgl aliens Y
78. Lmt Persh II/cruse-Europe ?
79. Delete 34 B-1 bombers Y
80. Bar purch of Pershing II N
81. Bar purchase of Sgt York ?
82. Delete $ for Trident II Y
83. Allow 15 MX missiles N
84. Bar MX procurement-1985 Y
85. Equal Access Act N
86. Aid to El Salvador N
87. Bar Nicarag water mining Y
88. Physician/Medicare freeze N
89. Increase "sin" taxes Y
90. End SBA direct loans N
91. Sell Conrail N
92. Equal Rights Amendment Y
93. Marines in Lebanon N
94. Eminent domain-Coal comps Y
95. Prohibit EPA sanctions ?
96. SS age increase/Reforms N
97. Auto domestic content req Y
98. Delete jobs program fundg N
99. Highway-Gas tax bill Y
100. Raise Medicare;Cut defnse Y
101. Emergency housing aid Y
102. Across-the-board tax cuts N
103. Gramm-Latta II targets N
104. Delete B-1 bomber funds Y
105. Dsapprov Saudi AWACS sale Y
106. Disapprove oil import fee Y
107. Rail Deregulation ?
108. Dsapp India nuc fuel sale ?
109. Mil draft registration Y
110. Chrysler Loan Guarantees Y
111. Prohibit school busing N
112. Nuclear plant moratorium Y
113. Oil price controls Y
114. Tuition Tax Credits Y
115. Est Consumer Protect Agcy Y
116. Eliminate B-1 bomber fnds Y
117. Subminimum wage for youth N
118. Delete crude oil tax N
119. Natural gas deregulation N

Presidential Support Score: 1986 - 22% 1985 - 21%

SMITH, CHRISTOPHER H. -- New Jersey 4th District [Republican]. Counties of Burlington (pt.), Camden (pt.), Mercer (pt.), Middlesex (pt.) and Monmouth (pt.). Prior Terms: House: 1981-86. Born: March 4, 1953; Rahway, N.J. Education: Trenton State College (B.A.); Worcester College. Occupation: Businessman; executive director, New Jersey Right to Life Committee, Inc. (1976-78); legislative agent, New Jersey state legislature (1979).

1. Immigration Reform Y
2. Open fld-search warrants N
3. Civil pnty-hire ill alien N
4. So Afr sanc-veto override Y
5. Tax Overhaul Y
6. South Africa sanctions Y
7. Death penalty-drug bill N
8. Evidence-warrantless srch Y
9. Life term-second drug off Y
10. Military use in drug war Y
11. Troop reduction in Europe N
12. Prohibit chemical weapons Y
13. Bar ASAT testing N
14. Abide SALT II weapons ban N
15. Follow SALT II-Soviets do Y
16. Reduce SDI funding N
17. Increase SDI funding N
18. Purchase Trident sub N
19. Delete 12 MX;Add conv wpn Y
20. Raise speed limit N
21. Textile Import Quotas(*) Y
22. Req Pentagon buy US goods Y
23. AIDS ins anti-dscriminatn N
24. Nicaraguan refugee aid N
25. Nicaraguan contra aid Y
26. US abide by SALT II Y
27. Prohibit Saudi arms sale Y
28. Military Retiremnt Reform Y
29. Nicaraguan refugee aid Y
30. Ease '68 Gun Control Act Y
31. Bar intrstat handgun tran Y
32. Keep '68 Gun Control Act Y
33. Nicaraguan contra aid Y
34. Bar emp polygraph testing Y
35. Tax Overhaul consideratn N
36. Bar armor-piercing ammo Y
37. Tax Overhaul consideratn N
38. Make comp emissions known Y
39. Allow toxic victims suits Y
40. Strike Superfund "VAT" Y
41. Notify emp-plant closing Y
42. Bar emp consult-plant clo N
43. Medicare cuts;Tax incres' N
44. Delete 12 MX missiles Y
45. Spending cuts;Tax incres' N
46. Textile Import Quotas Y

SMITH, CHRISTOPHER H. (Cont.)

47. Cut some school lunch fds N
48. Clean Water Act Amendmnts N
49. Youth work projects Y
50. Assist military in Angola Y
51. Allow US troops-Nicaragua N
52. Pentagon polygraph exams Y
53. Bar ASAT testing N
54. Suspend def pmt for abuse N
55. Bar Pentagon-contr emplmt Y
56. Increase SDI funding Y
57. Reduce SDI funding N
58. Produce chemical weapons N
59. Bar CIA fndg in Nicaragua N
60. South Africa sanctions Y
61. Cut SS COLAs; Raise taxes N
62. Let US invest-So Africa N
63. Approve 21 MX for 1985 N
64. Emergency Farm Credit Y
65. Awards to whistle blowers Y
66. African disaster relief Y
67. Ban bank loans to So Afr Y
68. Bar coun duty-free trtmt Y
69. Steel import limits Y
70. Soc Sec COLAs=inflation Y
71. Bar haz waste vctms suits N
72. Prohibit aid to Nicaragua N
73. Cut $-Schs bar sch prayer Y
74. Raise taxes; Cut Medicare Y
75. Alien residncy-prior 1982 N
76. Alien residncy-prior 1980 N
77. Pen emp-hire illgl aliens N
78. Lmt Persh II/cruse-Europe N
79. Delete 34 B-1 bombers N
80. Bar purch of Pershing II N
81. Bar purchase of Sgt York N
82. Delete $ for Trident II N
83. Allow 15 MX missiles Y
84. Bar MX procurement-1985 N
85. Equal Access Act Y
86. Aid to El Salvador Y
87. Bar Nicarag water mining Y
88. Physician/Medicare freeze Y
89. Increase "sin" taxes Y
90. End SBA direct loans N
91. Sell Conrail Y
92. Equal Rights Amendment N
93. Marines in Lebanon Y
94. Eminent domain-Coal comps N
95. Prohibit EPA sanctions N
96. SS age increase/Reforms Y
97. Auto domestic content req Y
98. Delete jobs program fundg N
99. Highway-Gas tax bill Y
100. Raise Medicare;Cut defnse Y
101. Emergency housing aid Y
102. Across-the-board tax cuts Y
103. Gramm-Latta II targets Y
104. Delete B-1 bomber funds N
105. Dsapprov Saudi AWACS sale Y

Presidential Support Score: 1986 - 45% 1985 - 45%

ROUKEMA, MARGE -- New Jersey 5th District [Republican]. Counties of Bergen (pt.), Hunterdon (pt.), Mercer (pt.), Morris (pt.), Passaic (pt.), Sussex (pt.) and Warren (pt.). Prior Terms: House: 1981-86. Born: September 19, 1929; Newark, N.J. Education: Montclair State College (B.A.); Rutgers University. Occupation: Teacher (1970-73); chairman, State Legislation Committee; co-founder, Ridgewood Senior Citizens Housing Corp.; member, Mayor's Advisory Charter Study Committee.

1. Immigration Reform N
2. Open fld-search warrants N
3. Civil pnty-hire ill alien N
4. So Afr sanc-veto override Y
5. Tax Overhaul Y
6. South Africa sanctions Y
7. Death penalty-drug bill N
8. Evidence-warrantless srch Y
9. Life term-second drug off Y
10. Military use in drug war Y
11. Troop reduction in Europe N
12. Prohibit chemical weapons Y
13. Bar ASAT testing Y
14. Abide SALT II weapons ban N
15. Follow SALT II-Soviets do Y
16. Reduce SDI funding N
17. Increase SDI funding N
18. Purchase Trident sub N
19. Delete 12 MX;Add conv wpn Y
20. Raise speed limit N
21. Textile Import Quotas(*) Y
22. Req Pentagon buy US goods Y
23. AIDS ins anti-dscriminatn N
24. Nicaraguan refugee aid N
25. Nicaraguan contra aid Y
26. US abide by SALT II N
27. Prohibit Saudi arms sale Y
28. Military Retiremnt Reform Y
29. Nicaraguan refugee aid Y
30. Ease '68 Gun Control Act N
31. Bar intrstat handgun tran Y
32. Keep '68 Gun Control Act Y
33. Nicaraguan contra aid Y
34. Bar emp polygraph testing N

ROUKEMA, MARGE (Cont.)

35. Tax Overhaul consideratn Y
36. Bar armor-piercing ammo Y
37. Tax Overhaul consideratn N
38. Make comp emissions known Y
39. Allow toxic victims suits N
40. Strike Superfund "VAT" N
41. Notify emp-plant closing N
42. Bar emp consult-plant clo Y
43. Medicare cuts;Tax incres' N
44. Delete 12 MX missiles Y
45. Spending cuts;Tax incres' N
46. Textile Import Quotas Y
47. Cut some school lunch fds N
48. Clean Water Act Amendmnts N
49. Youth work projects N
50. Assist military in Angola Y
51. Allow US troops-Nicaragua N
52. Pentagon polygraph exams Y
53. Bar ASAT testing Y
54. Suspend def pmt for abuse N
55. Bar Pentagon-contr emplmt Y
56. Increase SDI funding N
57. Reduce SDI funding N
58. Produce chemical weapons N
59. Bar CIA fndg in Nicaragua Y
60. South Africa sanctions Y
61. Cut SS COLAs; Raise taxes N
62. Let US invest-So Africa Y
63. Approve 21 MX for 1985 N
64. Emergency Farm Credit N
65. Awards to whistle blowers Y
66. African disaster relief Y
67. Ban bank loans to So Afr Y
68. Bar coun duty-free trtmt N
69. Steel import limits N
70. Soc Sec COLAs=inflation Y
71. Bar haz waste vctms suits Y
72. Prohibit aid to Nicaragua Y
73. Cut $-Schs bar sch prayer N
74. Raise taxes; Cut Medicare Y
75. Alien residncy-prior 1982 N
76. Alien residncy-prior 1980 Y
77. Pen emp-hire illgl aliens N
78. Lmt Persh II/cruse-Europe N
79. Delete 34 B-1 bombers N
80. Bar purch of Pershing II N
81. Bar purchase of Sgt York Y
82. Delete $ for Trident II N
83. Allow 15 MX missiles N
84. Bar MX procurement-1985 Y
85. Equal Access Act Y
86. Aid to El Salvador N
87. Bar Nicarag water mining Y
88. Physician/Medicare freeze Y
89. Increase "sin" taxes Y
90. End SBA direct loans N
91. Sell Conrail Y
92. Equal Rights Amendment Y
93. Marines in Lebanon Y
94. Eminent domain-Coal comps Y
95. Prohibit EPA sanctions N
96. SS age increase/Reforms Y
97. Auto domestic content req N
98. Delete jobs program fundg Y
99. Highway-Gas tax bill N
100. Raise Medicare;Cut defnse Y
101. Emergency housing aid N
102. Across-the-board tax cuts Y
103. Gramm-Latta II targets Y
104. Delete B-1 bomber funds N
105. Dsapprov Saudi AWACS sale Y

Presidential Support Score: 1986 - 55% 1985 - 49%

DWYER, BERNARD J. -- New Jersey 6th District [Democrat]. Counties of Middlesex, (pt.) and Union (pt.). Prior Terms: House: 1981-86. Born: January 24, 1921; Perth Amboy, N.J. Education: Rutgers University. Military Service: U.S. Navy, 1940-45. Occupation: Insurance broker-owner, Fraser Bros.; township councilman (1958-70); mayor (1969-73); New Jersey senator (1974-80); trustee, John F. Kennedy Medical Center; member, Chamber of Commerce.

1. Immigration Reform Y
2. Open fld-search warrants N
3. Civil pnty-hire ill alien N
4. So Afr sanc-veto override Y
5. Tax Overhaul Y
6. South Africa sanctions Y
7. Death penalty-drug bill Y
8. Evidence-warrantless srch N
9. Life term-second drug off Y
10. Military use in drug war Y
11. Troop reduction in Europe N
12. Prohibit chemical weapons Y
13. Bar ASAT testing Y
14. Abide SALT II weapons ban Y
15. Follow SALT II-Soviets do N
16. Reduce SDI funding N
17. Increase SDI funding N
18. Purchase Trident sub Y
19. Delete 12 MX;Add conv wpn Y
20. Raise speed limit N
21. Textile Import Quotas(*) Y
22. Req Pentagon buy US goods ?

DWYER, BERNARD J. (Cont.)

23. AIDS ins anti-dscriminatn Y
24. Nicaraguan refugee aid Y
25. Nicaraguan contra aid N
26. US abide by SALT II N
27. Prohibit Saudi arms sale Y
28. Military Retiremnt Reform Y
29. Nicaraguan refugee aid Y
30. Ease '68 Gun Control Act N
31. Bar intrstat handgun tran Y
32. Keep '68 Gun Control Act Y
33. Nicaraguan contra aid N
34. Bar emp polygraph testing Y
35. Tax Overhaul consideratn Y
36. Bar armor-piercing ammo Y
37. Tax Overhaul consideratn Y
38. Make comp emissions known Y
39. Allow toxic victims suits Y
40. Strike Superfund "VAT" Y
41. Notify emp-plant closing Y
42. Bar emp consult-plant clo N
43. Medicare cuts;Tax incres' Y
44. Delete 12 MX missiles Y
45. Spending cuts;Tax incres' Y
46. Textile Import Quotas Y
47. Cut some school lunch fds N
48. Clean Water Act Amendmnts N
49. Youth work projects Y
50. Assist military in Angola N
51. Allow US troops-Nicaragua N
52. Pentagon polygraph exams Y
53. Bar ASAT testing Y
54. Suspend def pmt for abuse Y
55. Bar Pentagon-contr emplmt Y
56. Increase SDI funding N
57. Reduce SDI funding N
58. Produce chemical weapons N
59. Bar CIA fndg in Nicaragua Y
60. South Africa sanctions Y
61. Cut SS COLAs; Raise taxes N
62. Let US invest-So Africa N
63. Approve 21 MX for 1985 N
64. Emergency Farm Credit Y
65. Awards to whistle blowers Y
66. African disaster relief Y
67. Ban bank loans to So Afr Y
68. Bar coun duty-free trtmt Y
69. Steel import limits Y
70. Soc Sec COLAs=inflation Y
71. Bar haz waste vctms suits N
72. Prohibit aid to Nicaragua Y
73. Cut $-Schs bar sch prayer N
74. Raise taxes; Cut Medicare Y
75. Alien residncy-prior 1982 Y
76. Alien residncy-prior 1980 N
77. Pen emp-hire illgl aliens Y
78. Lmt Persh II/cruse-Europe N
79. Delete 34 B-1 bombers Y
80. Bar purch of Pershing II N
81. Bar purchase of Sgt York Y
82. Delete $ for Trident II N
83. Allow 15 MX missiles N
84. Bar MX procurement-1985 Y
85. Equal Access Act N
86. Aid to El Salvador N
87. Bar Nicarag water mining Y
88. Physician/Medicare freeze N
89. Increase "sin" taxes Y
90. End SBA direct loans N
91. Sell Conrail N
92. Equal Rights Amendment Y
93. Marines in Lebanon Y
94. Eminent domain-Coal comps Y
95. Prohibit EPA sanctions N
96. SS age increase/Reforms N
97. Auto domestic content req Y
98. Delete jobs program fundg N
99. Highway-Gas tax bill Y
100. Raise Medicare;Cut defnse Y
101. Emergency housing aid Y
102. Across-the-board tax cuts N
103. Gramm-Latta II targets N
104. Delete B-1 bomber funds Y
105. Dsapprov Saudi AWACS sale Y

Presidential Support Score: 1986 - 18% 1985 - 25%

RINALDO, MATTHEW J. -- New Jersey 7th District [Republican]. Counties of Mercer (pt.), Middlesex (pt.), Monmouth (pt.), Somerset (pt.) and Union (pt.). Prior Terms: House: 1973-86. Born: September 1, 1931; Elizabeth, N.J. Education: Rutgers University (B.S.); Seton Hall University (M.B.A.); New York University. Occupation: Faculty member, Rutgers University; boardmember, Union Center National Bank (1970-72); boardmember, Union County Board of Freeholders (1963-64); president, Township of Union Zoning Board of Adjustment (1962-63); New Jersey senator (1967-72).

1. Immigration Reform N
2. Open fld-search warrants N
3. Civil pnty-hire ill alien Y
4. So Afr sanc-veto override Y
5. Tax Overhaul ?
6. South Africa sanctions Y

RINALDO, MATTHEW J. (Cont.)

7. Death penalty-drug bill Y
8. Evidence-warrantless srch Y
9. Life term-second drug off Y
10. Military use in drug war Y
11. Troop reduction in Europe N
12. Prohibit chemical weapons Y
13. Bar ASAT testing N
14. Abide SALT II weapons ban N
15. Follow SALT II-Soviets do Y
16. Reduce SDI funding N
17. Increase SDI funding N
18. Purchase Trident sub N
19. Delete 12 MX;Add conv wpn N
20. Raise speed limit N
21. Textile Import Quotas(*) Y
22. Req Pentagon buy US goods Y
23. AIDS ins anti-dscriminatn N
24. Nicaraguan refugee aid N
25. Nicaraguan contra aid Y
26. US abide by SALT II Y
27. Prohibit Saudi arms sale Y
28. Military Retiremnt Reform Y
29. Nicaraguan refugee aid Y
30. Ease '68 Gun Control Act Y
31. Bar intrstat handgun tran Y
32. Keep '68 Gun Control Act Y
33. Nicaraguan contra aid Y
34. Bar emp polygraph testing Y
35. Tax Overhaul consideratn N
36. Bar armor-piercing ammo Y
37. Tax Overhaul consideratn N
38. Make comp emissions known Y
39. Allow toxic victims suits Y
40. Strike Superfund "VAT" N
41. Notify emp-plant closing Y
42. Bar emp consult-plant clo N
43. Medicare cuts;Tax incres' Y
44. Delete 12 MX missiles N
45. Spending cuts;Tax incres' N
46. Textile Import Quotas Y
47. Cut some school lunch fds N
48. Clean Water Act Amendmnts N
49. Youth work projects Y
50. Assist military in Angola Y
51. Allow US troops-Nicaragua Y
52. Pentagon polygraph exams Y
53. Bar ASAT testing N
54. Suspend def pmt for abuse N
55. Bar Pentagon-contr emplmt ?
56. Increase SDI funding N
57. Reduce SDI funding N
58. Produce chemical weapons N
59. Bar CIA fndg in Nicaragua N
60. South Africa sanctions Y
61. Cut SS COLAs; Raise taxes N
62. Let US invest-So Africa N
63. Approve 21 MX for 1985 Y
64. Emergency Farm Credit N
65. Awards to whistle blowers Y
66. African disaster relief Y
67. Ban bank loans to So Afr Y
68. Bar coun duty-free trtmt Y
69. Steel import limits Y
70. Soc Sec COLAs=inflation Y
71. Bar haz waste vctms suits N
72. Prohibit aid to Nicaragua Y
73. Cut $-Schs bar sch prayer ?
74. Raise taxes; Cut Medicare N
75. Alien residncy-prior 1982 N
76. Alien residncy-prior 1980 N
77. Pen emp-hire illgl aliens Y
78. Lmt Persh II/cruse-Europe N
79. Delete 34 B-1 bombers N
80. Bar purch of Pershing II N
81. Bar purchase of Sgt York N
82. Delete $ for Trident II N
83. Allow 15 MX missiles Y
84. Bar MX procurement-1985 N
85. Equal Access Act Y
86. Aid to El Salvador Y
87. Bar Nicarag water mining Y
88. Physician/Medicare freeze N
89. Increase "sin" taxes Y
90. End SBA direct loans N
91. Sell Conrail N
92. Equal Rights Amendment Y
93. Marines in Lebanon Y
94. Eminent domain-Coal comps N
95. Prohibit EPA sanctions N
96. SS age increase/Reforms N
97. Auto domestic content req Y
98. Delete jobs program fundg N
99. Highway-Gas tax bill Y
100. Raise Medicare;Cut defnse Y
101. Emergency housing aid Y
102. Across-the-board tax cuts Y
103. Gramm-Latta II targets Y
104. Delete B-1 bomber funds N
105. Dsapprov Saudi AWACS sale Y
106. Disapprove oil import fee Y
107. Rail Deregulation N
108. Dsapp India nuc fuel sale N
109. Mil draft registration N
110. Chrysler Loan Guarantees Y
111. Prohibit school busing N
112. Nuclear plant moratorium N
113. Oil price controls Y
114. Tuition Tax Credits Y
115. Est Consumer Protect Agcy Y
116. Eliminate B-1 bomber fnds N
117. Subminimum wage for youth Y
118. Delete crude oil tax Y
119. Natural gas deregulation N

Presidential Support Score: 1986 - 40% 1985 - 50%

ROE, ROBERT A. -- New Jersey 8th District [Democrat]. Counties of Bergen (pt.), Morris (pt.) and Passaic (pt.). Prior Terms: House: 1969 (Special Election)-1986. Born: February 28, 1924; Wayne, N.J. Education: Oregon State University; Washington State University. Military Service: U.S. Army, WW II. Occupation: Committeeman, Wayne Township (1955-56); mayor, Wayne Township (1956-61); Passaic County Freeholder (1959-63); director of board, Chosen Freeholders (1962-63); commissioner, Conservation and Economic Development New Jersey (1963-69).

1. Immigration Reform Y
2. Open fld-search warrants N
3. Civil pnty-hire ill alien N
4. So Afr sanc-veto override Y
5. Tax Overhaul Y
6. South Africa sanctions Y
7. Death penalty-drug bill Y
8. Evidence-warrantless srch Y
9. Life term-second drug off Y
10. Military use in drug war Y
11. Troop reduction in Europe N
12. Prohibit chemical weapons Y
13. Bar ASAT testing Y
14. Abide SALT II weapons ban Y
15. Follow SALT II-Soviets do N
16. Reduce SDI funding Y
17. Increase SDI funding N
18. Purchase Trident sub Y
19. Delete 12 MX;Add conv wpn Y
20. Raise speed limit N
21. Textile Import Quotas(*) Y
22. Req Pentagon buy US goods Y
23. AIDS ins anti-dscriminatn Y
24. Nicaraguan refugee aid Y
25. Nicaraguan contra aid N
26. US abide by SALT II N
27. Prohibit Saudi arms sale Y
28. Military Retiremnt Reform Y
29. Nicaraguan refugee aid Y
30. Ease '68 Gun Control Act N
31. Bar intrstat handgun tran Y
32. Keep '68 Gun Control Act Y
33. Nicaraguan contra aid N
34. Bar emp polygraph testing Y
35. Tax Overhaul consideratn N
36. Bar armor-piercing ammo Y
37. Tax Overhaul consideratn N
38. Make comp emissions known Y
39. Allow toxic victims suits Y
40. Strike Superfund "VAT" N
41. Notify emp-plant closing Y
42. Bar emp consult-plant clo N
43. Medicare cuts;Tax incres' Y
44. Delete 12 MX missiles Y
45. Spending cuts;Tax incres' Y
46. Textile Import Quotas Y
47. Cut some school lunch fds N
48. Clean Water Act Amendmnts N
49. Youth work projects Y
50. Assist military in Angola ?
51. Allow US troops-Nicaragua N
52. Pentagon polygraph exams ?
53. Bar ASAT testing Y
54. Suspend def pmt for abuse Y
55. Bar Pentagon-contr emplmt Y
56. Increase SDI funding N
57. Reduce SDI funding N
58. Produce chemical weapons N
59. Bar CIA fndg in Nicaragua Y
60. South Africa sanctions Y
61. Cut SS COLAs; Raise taxes N
62. Let US invest-So Africa N
63. Approve 21 MX for 1985 N
64. Emergency Farm Credit Y
65. Awards to whistle blowers Y
66. African disaster relief Y
67. Ban bank loans to So Afr Y
68. Bar coun duty-free trtmt Y
69. Steel import limits Y
70. Soc Sec COLAs=inflation Y
71. Bar haz waste vctms suits Y
72. Prohibit aid to Nicaragua Y
73. Cut $-Schs bar sch prayer N
74. Raise taxes; Cut Medicare Y
75. Alien residncy-prior 1982 Y
76. Alien residncy-prior 1980 N
77. Pen emp-hire illgl aliens Y
78. Lmt Persh II/cruse-Europe ?
79. Delete 34 B-1 bombers Y
80. Bar purch of Pershing II N
81. Bar purchase of Sgt York ?
82. Delete $ for Trident II N
83. Allow 15 MX missiles N
84. Bar MX procurement-1985 Y
85. Equal Access Act N
86. Aid to El Salvador N
87. Bar Nicarag water mining Y
88. Physician/Medicare freeze N
89. Increase "sin" taxes Y
90. End SBA direct loans N
91. Sell Conrail N
92. Equal Rights Amendment Y
93. Marines in Lebanon Y
94. Eminent domain-Coal comps Y
95. Prohibit EPA sanctions N
96. SS age increase/Reforms N
97. Auto domestic content req Y
98. Delete jobs program fundg N
99. Highway-Gas tax bill N
100. Raise Medicare;Cut defnse Y

ROE, ROBERT A. (Cont.)

101. Emergency housing aid Y
102. Across-the-board tax cuts N
103. Gramm-Latta II targets N
104. Delete B-1 bomber funds N
105. Dsapprov Saudi AWACS sale Y
106. Disapprove oil import fee Y
107. Rail Deregulation N
108. Dsapp India nuc fuel sale Y
109. Mil draft registration Y
110. Chrysler Loan Guarantees Y
111. Prohibit school busing N
112. Nuclear plant moratorium N
113. Oil price controls ?
114. Tuition Tax Credits Y
115. Est Consumer Protect Agcy Y
116. Eliminate B-1 bomber fnds N
117. Subminimum wage for youth ?
118. Delete crude oil tax N
119. Natural gas deregulation N

Presidential Support Score: 1986 - 22% 1985 - 18%

TORRICELLI, ROBERT G. -- New Jersey 9th District [Democrat]. County of Bergen (pt.). Prior Terms: House: 1983-86. Born: August 26, 1951; Paterson, N.J. Education: Rutgers University; Rutgers University School of Law (J.D.); Harvard University (M.P.A.). Occupation: Attorney; governor's assistant (1975-78); Vice president's counsel (1978-80).

1. Immigration Reform Y
2. Open fld-search warrants N
3. Civil pnty-hire ill alien N
4. So Afr sanc-veto override Y
5. Tax Overhaul Y
6. South Africa sanctions Y
7. Death penalty-drug bill Y
8. Evidence-warrantless srch N
9. Life term-second drug off Y
10. Military use in drug war Y
11. Troop reduction in Europe N
12. Prohibit chemical weapons Y
13. Bar ASAT testing Y
14. Abide SALT II weapons ban Y
15. Follow SALT II-Soviets do N
16. Reduce SDI funding N
17. Increase SDI funding N
18. Purchase Trident sub Y
19. Delete 12 MX;Add conv wpn Y
20. Raise speed limit N
21. Textile Import Quotas(*) Y
22. Req Pentagon buy US goods Y
23. AIDS ins anti-dscriminatn Y
24. Nicaraguan refugee aid Y
25. Nicaraguan contra aid N
26. US abide by SALT II N
27. Prohibit Saudi arms sale Y
28. Military Retiremnt Reform Y
29. Nicaraguan refugee aid Y
30. Ease '68 Gun Control Act N
31. Bar intrstat handgun tran Y
32. Keep '68 Gun Control Act Y
33. Nicaraguan contra aid N
34. Bar emp polygraph testing Y
35. Tax Overhaul consideratn Y
36. Bar armor-piercing ammo Y
37. Tax Overhaul consideratn Y
38. Make comp emissions known Y
39. Allow toxic victims suits Y
40. Strike Superfund "VAT" Y
41. Notify emp-plant closing Y
42. Bar emp consult-plant clo N
43. Medicare cuts;Tax incres' Y
44. Delete 12 MX missiles Y
45. Spending cuts;Tax incres' Y
46. Textile Import Quotas Y
47. Cut some school lunch fds N
48. Clean Water Act Amendmnts N
49. Youth work projects Y
50. Assist military in Angola N
51. Allow US troops-Nicaragua N
52. Pentagon polygraph exams Y
53. Bar ASAT testing Y
54. Suspend def pmt for abuse Y
55. Bar Pentagon-contr emplmt Y
56. Increase SDI funding N
57. Reduce SDI funding N
58. Produce chemical weapons N
59. Bar CIA fndg in Nicaragua Y
60. South Africa sanctions Y
61. Cut SS COLAs; Raise taxes N
62. Let US invest-So Africa N
63. Approve 21 MX for 1985 N
64. Emergency Farm Credit ?
65. Awards to whistle blowers Y
66. African disaster relief Y
67. Ban bank loans to So Afr Y
68. Bar coun duty-free trtmt Y
69. Steel import limits Y
70. Soc Sec COLAs=inflation Y
71. Bar haz waste vctms suits N
72. Prohibit aid to Nicaragua Y
73. Cut $-Schs bar sch prayer N
74. Raise taxes; Cut Medicare N
75. Alien residncy-prior 1982 Y
76. Alien residncy-prior 1980 Y
77. Pen emp-hire illgl aliens N
78. Lmt Persh II/cruse-Europe Y

TORRICELLI, ROBERT G. (Cont.)

79. Delete 34 B-1 bombers Y
80. Bar purch of Pershing II Y
81. Bar purchase of Sgt York Y
82. Delete $ for Trident II N
83. Allow 15 MX missiles N
84. Bar MX procurement-1985 Y
85. Equal Access Act N
86. Aid to El Salvador N
87. Bar Nicarag water mining Y
88. Physician/Medicare freeze N
89. Increase "sin" taxes Y
90. End SBA direct loans N
91. Sell Conrail N
92. Equal Rights Amendment Y
93. Marines in Lebanon Y
94. Eminent domain-Coal comps N
95. Prohibit EPA sanctions Y
96. SS age increase/Reforms N

Presidential Support Score: 1986 - 18% 1985 - 24%

RODINO, PETER W., Jr. -- New Jersey 10th District [Democrat]. Counties of Essex (pt.), Hudson (pt.) and Union (pt.). Prior Terms: House: 1949-1986. Born: June 7, 1909; Newark, N.J. Education: University of Newark (Rutgers). Military Service: U.S. Army, WW II. Occupation: Attorney; delegate, Intergovernmental Committee for European Migration (1962-72); delegate, North Atlantic Assembly.

1. Immigration Reform Y
2. Open fld-search warrants Y
3. Civil pnty-hire ill alien N
4. So Afr sanc-veto override Y
5. Tax Overhaul Y
6. South Africa sanctions Y
7. Death penalty-drug bill N
8. Evidence-warrantless srch N
9. Life term-second drug off N
10. Military use in drug war N
11. Troop reduction in Europe Y
12. Prohibit chemical weapons Y
13. Bar ASAT testing Y
14. Abide SALT II weapons ban Y
15. Follow SALT II-Soviets do N
16. Reduce SDI funding Y
17. Increase SDI funding N
18. Purchase Trident sub Y
19. Delete 12 MX;Add conv wpn Y
20. Raise speed limit N
21. Textile Import Quotas(*) Y
22. Req Pentagon buy US goods Y
23. AIDS ins anti-dscriminatn Y
24. Nicaraguan refugee aid Y
25. Nicaraguan contra aid N
26. US abide by SALT II X
27. Prohibit Saudi arms sale Y
28. Military Retiremnt Reform Y
29. Nicaraguan refugee aid Y
30. Ease '68 Gun Control Act N
31. Bar intrstat handgun tran Y
32. Keep '68 Gun Control Act Y
33. Nicaraguan contra aid N
34. Bar emp polygraph testing Y
35. Tax Overhaul consideratn Y
36. Bar armor-piercing ammo Y
37. Tax Overhaul consideratn Y
38. Make comp emissions known Y
39. Allow toxic victims suits Y
40. Strike Superfund "VAT" Y
41. Notify emp-plant closing Y
42. Bar emp consult-plant clo N
43. Medicare cuts;Tax incres' Y
44. Delete 12 MX missiles Y
45. Spending cuts;Tax incres' Y
46. Textile Import Quotas Y
47. Cut some school lunch fds N
48. Clean Water Act Amendmnts N
49. Youth work projects ?
50. Assist military in Angola N
51. Allow US troops-Nicaragua N
52. Pentagon polygraph exams N
53. Bar ASAT testing Y
54. Suspend def pmt for abuse N
55. Bar Pentagon-contr emplmt Y
56. Increase SDI funding N
57. Reduce SDI funding Y
58. Produce chemical weapons N
59. Bar CIA fndg in Nicaragua Y
60. South Africa sanctions Y
61. Cut SS COLAs; Raise taxes N
62. Let US invest-So Africa N
63. Approve 21 MX for 1985 N
64. Emergency Farm Credit Y
65. Awards to whistle blowers Y
66. African disaster relief Y
67. Ban bank loans to So Afr Y
68. Bar coun duty-free trtmt Y
69. Steel import limits Y
70. Soc Sec COLAs=inflation Y
71. Bar haz waste vctms suits N
72. Prohibit aid to Nicaragua ?
73. Cut $-Schs bar sch prayer N
74. Raise taxes; Cut Medicare N
75. Alien residncy-prior 1982 N
76. Alien residncy-prior 1980 N
77. Pen emp-hire illgl aliens N
78. Lmt Persh II/cruse-Europe ?

RODINO, PETER W, Jr. (Cont.)

79. Delete 34 B-1 bombers Y
80. Bar purch of Pershing II Y
81. Bar purchase of Sgt York Y
82. Delete $ for Trident II Y
83. Allow 15 MX missiles N
84. Bar MX procurement-1985 Y
85. Equal Access Act N
86. Aid to El Salvador N
87. Bar Nicarag water mining Y
88. Physician/Medicare freeze N
89. Increase "sin" taxes Y
90. End SBA direct loans N
91. Sell Conrail N
92. Equal Rights Amendment Y
93. Marines in Lebanon N
94. Eminent domain-Coal comps Y
95. Prohibit EPA sanctions N
96. SS age increase/Reforms N
97. Auto domestic content req Y
98. Delete jobs program fundg N
99. Highway-Gas tax bill Y
100. Raise Medicare;Cut defnse Y
101. Emergency housing aid Y
102. Across-the-board tax cuts N
103. Gramm-Latta II targets N
104. Delete B-1 bomber funds Y
105. Dsapprov Saudi AWACS sale Y
106. Disapprove oil import fee Y
107. Rail Deregulation N
108. Dsapp India nuc fuel sale Y
109. Mil draft registration N
110. Chrysler Loan Guarantees Y
111. Prohibit school busing N
112. Nuclear plant moratorium Y
113. Oil price controls Y
114. Tuition Tax Credits Y
115. Est Consumer Protect Agcy Y
116. Eliminate B-1 bomber fnds Y
117. Subminimum wage for youth N
118. Delete crude oil tax N
119. Natural gas deregulation N

Presidential Support Score: 1986 - 16% 1985 - 16%

GALLO, DEAN A. -- New Jersey 11th District [Republican]. Counties of Bergen (pt.), Essex (pt.), Hudson (pt.), Morris (pt.)and Possaic (pt.). Prior Terms: 1985-86. Occupation: Businessman; New Jersey assemblyman.

1. Immigration Reform N
2. Open fld-search warrants N
3. Civil pnty-hire ill alien Y
4. So Afr sanc-veto override Y
5. Tax Overhaul Y
6. South Africa sanctions Y
7. Death penalty-drug bill Y
8. Evidence-warrantless srch Y
9. Life term-second drug off Y
10. Military use in drug war Y
11. Troop reduction in Europe N
12. Prohibit chemical weapons N
13. Bar ASAT testing N
14. Abide SALT II weapons ban N
15. Follow SALT II-Soviets do Y
16. Reduce SDI funding N
17. Increase SDI funding N
18. Purchase Trident sub N
19. Delete 12 MX;Add conv wpn N
20. Raise speed limit N
21. Textile Import Quotas(*) N
22. Req Pentagon buy US goods N
23. AIDS ins anti-dscriminatn Y
24. Nicaraguan refugee aid N
25. Nicaraguan contra aid Y
26. US abide by SALT II Y
27. Prohibit Saudi arms sale Y
28. Military Retiremnt Reform Y
29. Nicaraguan refugee aid Y
30. Ease '68 Gun Control Act Y
31. Bar intrstat handgun tran N
32. Keep '68 Gun Control Act N
33. Nicaraguan contra aid Y
34. Bar emp polygraph testing Y
35. Tax Overhaul consideratn N
36. Bar armor-piercing ammo Y
37. Tax Overhaul consideratn N
38. Make comp emissions known Y
39. Allow toxic victims suits Y
40. Strike Superfund "VAT" N
41. Notify emp-plant closing N
42. Bar emp consult-plant clo Y
43. Medicare cuts;Tax incres' N
44. Delete 12 MX missiles N
45. Spending cuts;Tax incres' N
46. Textile Import Quotas N
47. Cut some school lunch fds Y
48. Clean Water Act Amendmnts Y
49. Youth work projects N
50. Assist military in Angola Y
51. Allow US troops-Nicaragua Y
52. Pentagon polygraph exams Y
53. Bar ASAT testing N
54. Suspend def pmt for abuse N
55. Bar Pentagon-contr emplmt Y
56. Increase SDI funding Y
57. Reduce SDI funding N
58. Produce chemical weapons Y
59. Bar CIA fndg in Nicaragua N
60. South Africa sanctions Y

GALLO, DEAN A. (Cont.)

61. Cut SS COLAs; Raise taxes N
62. Let US invest-So Africa Y
63. Approve 21 MX for 1985 Y
64. Emergency Farm Credit N
65. Awards to whistle blowers Y
66. African disaster relief Y

Presidential Support Score: 1986 - 70% 1985 - 63%

COURTER, JIM -- New Jersey 12th District [Republican]. Counties of Essex (pt.), Hunterdon (pt.), Morris (pt.), Somerset (pt.), Sussex (pt.), Union (pt.) and Warren (pt.). Prior Terms: House: 1979-86. Born: October 14, 1941; Montclair, N.J. Education: Colgate University (B.A.); Duke University (J.D.). Occupation: Peace Corps volunteer; assistant corporation counsel for Washington, D.C. (1969-70); attorney, Union County Legal Services (1970-71); assistant prosecutor (1973-77).

1. Immigration Reform N
2. Open fld-search warrants N
3. Civil pnty-hire ill alien Y
4. So Afr sanc-veto override Y
5. Tax Overhaul Y
6. South Africa sanctions Y
7. Death penalty-drug bill Y
8. Evidence-warrantless srch Y
9. Life term-second drug off Y
10. Military use in drug war Y
11. Troop reduction in Europe N
12. Prohibit chemical weapons N
13. Bar ASAT testing N
14. Abide SALT II weapons ban N
15. Follow SALT II-Soviets do Y
16. Reduce SDI funding N
17. Increase SDI funding Y
18. Purchase Trident sub N
19. Delete 12 MX;Add conv wpn N
20. Raise speed limit N
21. Textile Import Quotas(*) N
22. Req Pentagon buy US goods N
23. AIDS ins anti-dscriminatn N
24. Nicaraguan refugee aid N
25. Nicaraguan contra aid Y
26. US abide by SALT II Y
27. Prohibit Saudi arms sale Y
28. Military Retiremnt Reform Y
29. Nicaraguan refugee aid Y
30. Ease '68 Gun Control Act Y
31. Bar intrstat handgun tran Y
32. Keep '68 Gun Control Act Y
33. Nicaraguan contra aid Y
34. Bar emp polygraph testing Y
35. Tax Overhaul consideratn Y
36. Bar armor-piercing ammo Y
37. Tax Overhaul consideratn N
38. Make comp emissions known Y
39. Allow toxic victims suits Y
40. Strike Superfund "VAT" N
41. Notify emp-plant closing N
42. Bar emp consult-plant clo Y
43. Medicare cuts;Tax incres' N
44. Delete 12 MX missiles N
45. Spending cuts;Tax incres' N
46. Textile Import Quotas N
47. Cut some school lunch fds Y
48. Clean Water Act Amendmnts Y
49. Youth work projects N
50. Assist military in Angola Y
51. Allow US troops-Nicaragua Y
52. Pentagon polygraph exams Y
53. Bar ASAT testing N
54. Suspend def pmt for abuse N
55. Bar Pentagon-contr emplmt Y
56. Increase SDI funding Y
57. Reduce SDI funding N
58. Produce chemical weapons Y
59. Bar CIA fndg in Nicaragua N
60. South Africa sanctions Y
61. Cut SS COLAs; Raise taxes N
62. Let US invest-So Africa N
63. Approve 21 MX for 1985 Y
64. Emergency Farm Credit N
65. Awards to whistle blowers Y
66. African disaster relief Y
67. Ban bank loans to So Afr N
68. Bar coun duty-free trtmt N
69. Steel import limits N
70. Soc Sec COLAs=inflation Y
71. Bar haz waste vctms suits Y
72. Prohibit aid to Nicaragua N
73. Cut $-Schs bar sch prayer ?
74. Raise taxes; Cut Medicare N
75. Alien residncy-prior 1982 Y
76. Alien residncy-prior 1980 Y
77. Pen emp-hire illgl aliens N
78. Lmt Persh II/cruse-Europe N
79. Delete 34 B-1 bombers N
80. Bar purch of Pershing II N
81. Bar purchase of Sgt York Y
82. Delete $ for Trident II N
83. Allow 15 MX missiles Y
84. Bar MX procurement-1985 N
85. Equal Access Act Y
86. Aid to El Salvador Y
87. Bar Nicarag water mining N
88. Physician/Medicare freeze Y

COURTER, JIM (Cont.)

89. Increase "sin" taxes N
90. End SBA direct loans N
91. Sell Conrail N
92. Equal Rights Amendment Y
93. Marines in Lebanon Y
94. Eminent domain-coal comps Y
95. Prohibit EPA sanctions N
96. SS age increase/Reforms Y
97. Auto domestic content req N
98. Delete jobs program fundg Y
99. Highway-Gas tax bill N
100. Raise Medicare;Cut defnse Y
101. Emergency housing aid Y
102. Across-the-board tax cuts Y
103. Gramm-Latta II targets Y
104. Delete B-1 bomber funds N
105. Dsapprov Saudi AWACS sale Y
106. Disapprove oil import fee Y
107. Rail Deregulation N
108. Dsapp India nuc fuel sale Y
109. Mil draft registration Y
110. Chrysler Loan Guarantees N
111. Prohibit school busing N
112. Nuclear plant moratorium N
113. Oil price controls N

Presidential Support Score: 1986 - 69% 1985 - 70%

SAXTON, H. JAMES -- New Jersey 13th District [Republican]. Counties of Burlington (pt.), Camden (pt.), Monmouth (pt.) and Ocean (pt.). Prior Terms: 1985-86. Occupation: Realtor; New Jersey assemblyman, New Jersey senator; teacher.

1. Immigration Reform N
2. Open fld-search warrants Y
3. Civil pnty-hire ill alien Y
4. So Afr sanc-veto override Y
5. Tax Overhaul Y
6. South Africa sanctions Y
7. Death penalty-drug bill Y
8. Evidence-warrantless srch Y
9. Life term-second drug off Y
10. Military use in drug war Y
11. Troop reduction in Europe N
12. Prohibit chemical weapons N
13. Bar ASAT testing N
14. Abide SALT II weapons ban N
15. Follow SALT II-Soviets do Y
16. Reduce SDI funding N
17. Increase SDI funding N
18. Purchase Trident sub N
19. Delete 12 MX;Add conv wpn N
20. Raise speed limit N
21. Textile Import Quotas(*) N
22. Req Pentagon buy US goods N
23. AIDS ins anti-dscriminatn N
24. Nicaraguan refugee aid N
25. Nicaraguan contra aid Y
26. US abide by SALT II Y
27. Prohibit Saudi arms sale Y
28. Military Retiremnt Reform Y
29. Nicaraguan refugee aid Y
30. Ease '68 Gun Control Act Y
31. Bar intrstat handgun tran Y
32. Keep '68 Gun Control Act Y
33. Nicaraguan contra aid Y
34. Bar emp polygraph testing Y
35. Tax Overhaul consideratn N
36. Bar armor-piercing ammo Y
37. Tax Overhaul consideratn N
38. Make comp emissions known Y
39. Allow toxic victims suits N
40. Strike Superfund "VAT" N
41. Notify emp-plant closing N
42. Bar emp consult-plant clo Y
43. Medicare cuts;Tax incres' N
44. Delete 12 MX missiles Y
45. Spending cuts;Tax incres' N
46. Textile Import Quotas N
47. Cut some school lunch fds Y
48. Clean Water Act Amendmnts N
49. Youth work projects N
50. Assist military in Angola Y
51. Allow US troops-Nicaragua Y
52. Pentagon polygraph exams Y
53. Bar ASAT testing N
54. Suspend def pmt for abuse Y
55. Bar Pentagon-contr emplmt Y
56. Increase SDI funding N
57. Reduce SDI funding N
58. Produce chemical weapons Y
59. Bar CIA fndg in Nicaragua N
60. South Africa sanctions Y
61. Cut SS COLAs; Raise taxes N
62. Let US invest-So Africa Y
63. Approve 21 MX for 1985 Y
64. Emergency Farm Credit N
65. Awards to whistle blowers Y
66. African disaster relief Y

Presidential Support Score: 1986 - 66% 1985 - 61%

GUARINI, FRANK J. -- New Jersey 14th District [Democrat]. Counties of Bergen (pt.) and Hudson (pt.). Prior Terms: House: 1979-

GUARINI, FRANK J. (Cont.)

86. Born: August 20, 1924; Jersey City, N.J. Education: Dartmouth College; Columbia University; New York University (J.D.); Hague Academy of International Law. Military Service: U.S. Navy, WW II. Occupation: Attorney; New Jersey senator (1965-76).

1. Immigration Reform N
2. Open fld-search warrants N
3. Civil pnty-hire ill alien Y
4. So Afr sanc-veto override Y
5. Tax Overhaul Y
6. South Africa sanctions Y
7. Death penalty-drug bill Y
8. Evidence-warrantless srch Y
9. Life term-second drug off Y
10. Military use in drug war Y
11. Troop reduction in Europe N
12. Prohibit chemical weapons Y
13. Bar ASAT testing Y
14. Abide SALT II weapons ban Y
15. Follow SALT II-Soviets do N
16. Reduce SDI funding N
17. Increase SDI funding N
18. Purchase Trident sub Y
19. Delete 12 MX;Add conv wpn N
20. Raise speed limit N
21. Textile Import Quotas(*) Y
22. Req Pentagon buy US goods N
23. AIDS ins anti-dscriminatn Y
24. Nicaraguan refugee aid N
25. Nicaraguan contra aid N
26. US abide by SALT II N
27. Prohibit Saudi arms sale Y
28. Military Retiremnt Reform Y
29. Nicaraguan refugee aid Y
30. Ease '68 Gun Control Act N
31. Bar intrstat handgun tran Y
32. Keep '68 Gun Control Act Y
33. Nicaraguan contra aid N
34. Bar emp polygraph testing Y
35. Tax Overhaul consideratn Y
36. Bar armor-piercing ammo Y
37. Tax Overhaul consideratn Y
38. Make comp emissions known Y
39. Allow toxic victims suits N
40. Strike Superfund "VAT" Y
41. Notify emp-plant closing Y
42. Bar emp consult-plant clo -
43. Medicare cuts;Tax incres' Y
44. Delete 12 MX missiles Y
45. Spending cuts;Tax incres' Y
46. Textile Import Quotas Y
47. Cut some school lunch fds N
48. Clean Water Act Amendmnts N
49. Youth work projects Y
50. Assist military in Angola N
51. Allow US troops-Nicaragua N
52. Pentagon polygraph exams Y
53. Bar ASAT testing Y
54. Suspend def pmt for abuse Y
55. Bar Pentagon-contr emplmt Y
56. Increase SDI funding N
57. Reduce SDI funding N
58. Produce chemical weapons N
59. Bar CIA fndg in Nicaragua Y
60. South Africa sanctions Y
61. Cut SS COLAs; Raise taxes N
62. Let US invest-So Africa N
63. Approve 21 MX for 1985 N
64. Emergency Farm Credit Y
65. Awards to whistle blowers Y
66. African disaster relief Y
67. Ban bank loans to So Afr Y
68. Bar coun duty-free trtmt Y
69. Steel import limits Y
70. Soc Sec COLAs=inflation Y
71. Bar haz waste vctms suits N
72. Prohibit aid to Nicaragua ?
73. Cut $-Schs bar sch prayer N
74. Raise taxes; Cut Medicare N
75. Alien residncy-prior 1982 N
76. Alien residncy-prior 1980 N
77. Pen emp-hire illgl aliens Y
78. Lmt Persh II/cruse-Europe ?
79. Delete 34 B-1 bombers Y
80. Bar purch of Pershing II N
81. Bar purchase of Sgt York Y
82. Delete $ for Trident II N
83. Allow 15 MX missiles N
84. Bar MX procurement-1985 Y
85. Equal Access Act N
86. Aid to El Salvador N
87. Bar Nicarag water mining Y
88. Physician/Medicare freeze N
89. Increase "sin" taxes Y
90. End SBA direct loans N
91. Sell Conrail N
92. Equal Rights Amendment Y
93. Marines in Lebanon N
94. Eminent domain-coal comps Y
95. Prohibit EPA sanctions N
96. SS age increase/Reforms N
97. Auto domestic content req Y
98. Delete jobs program fundg N
99. Highway-Gas tax bill Y
100. Raise Medicare;Cut defnse Y
101. Emergency housing aid Y
102. Across-the-board tax cuts N
103. Gramm-Latta II targets N
104. Delete B-1 bomber funds Y
105. Dsapprov Saudi AWACS sale Y
106. Disapprove oil import fee Y

GUARINI, FRANK I. (Cont.)

107. Rail Deregulation N
108. Dsapp India nuc fuel sale Y
109. Mil draft registration Y
110. Chrysler Loan Guarantees Y
111. Prohibit school busing N
112. Nuclear plant moratorium Y
113. Oil price controls Y

Presidential Support Score: 1986 - 22% 1985 - 21%

NEW MEXICO

LUJAN, MANUEL, Jr. -- New Mexico 1st District [Republican]. Counties of Bernalillo, De Baca, Guadalupe and Torrance. Prior Terms: House: 1969-86. Born: May 12, 1928; San Ildefonso, N.M. Education: College of Santa Fe (B.A.). Occupation: Partner insurance agency; president, New Mexico Insurance Agents Assn.

1. Immigration Reform N
2. Open fld-search warrants Y
3. Civil pnty-hire ill alien Y
4. So Afr sanc-veto override Y
5. Tax Overhaul Y
6. South Africa sanctions Y
7. Death penalty-drug bill Y
8. Evidence-warrantless srch Y
9. Life term-second drug off Y
10. Military use in drug war Y
11. Troop reduction in Europe N
12. Prohibit chemical weapons N
13. Bar ASAT testing N
14. Abide SALT II weapons ban N
15. Follow SALT II-Soviets do Y
16. Reduce SDI funding N
17. Increase SDI funding N
18. Purchase Trident sub N
19. Delete 12 MX;Add conv wpn N
20. Raise speed limit Y
21. Textile Import Quotas(*) N
22. Req Pentagon buy US goods Y
23. AIDS ins anti-dscriminatn N
24. Nicaraguan refugee aid N
25. Nicaraguan contra aid Y
26. US abide by SALT II Y
27. Prohibit Saudi arms sale ?
28. Military Retiremnt Reform ?
29. Nicaraguan refugee aid ?
30. Ease '68 Gun Control Act ?
31. Bar intrstat handgun tran ?
32. Keep '68 Gun Control Act ?
33. Nicaraguan contra aid Y
34. Bar emp polygraph testing N
35. Tax Overhaul consideratn Y
36. Bar armor-piercing ammo Y
37. Tax Overhaul consideratn N
38. Make comp emissions known N
39. Allow toxic victims suits N
40. Strike Superfund "VAT" N
41. Notify emp-plant closing Y
42. Bar emp consult-plant clo Y
43. Medicare cuts;Tax incres' N
44. Delete 12 MX missiles N
45. Spending cuts;Tax incres' N
46. Textile Import Quotas N
47. Cut some school lunch fds Y
48. Clean Water Act Amendmnts Y
49. Youth work projects N
50. Assist military in Angola Y
51. Allow US troops-Nicaragua Y
52. Pentagon polygraph exams Y
53. Bar ASAT testing N
54. Suspend def pmt for abuse N
55. Bar Pentagon-contr emplmt Y
56. Increase SDI funding N
57. Reduce SDI funding N
58. Produce chemical weapons Y
59. Bar CIA fndg in Nicaragua N
60. South Africa sanctions N
61. Cut SS COLAs; Raise taxes Y
62. Let US invest-So Africa Y
63. Approve 21 MX for 1985 Y
64. Emergency Farm Credit N
65. Awards to whistle blowers Y
66. African disaster relief Y
67. Ban bank loans to So Afr N
68. Bar coun duty-free trtmt N
69. Steel import limits N
70. Soc Sec COLAs=inflation Y
71. Bar haz waste vctms suits Y
72. Prohibit aid to Nicaragua N
73. Cut $-Schs bar sch prayer Y
74. Raise taxes; Cut Medicare N
75. Alien residncy-prior 1982 Y
76. Alien residncy-prior 1980 Y
77. Pen emp-hire illgl aliens Y
78. Lmt Persh II/cruse-Europe N
79. Delete 34 B-1 bombers N
80. Bar purch of Pershing II N
81. Bar purchase of Sgt York N
82. Delete $ for Trident II N
83. Allow 15 MX missiles Y
84. Bar MX procurement-1985 N

LUJAN, MANUEL, Jr. (Cont.)

85. Equal Access Act Y
86. Aid to El Salvador Y
87. Bar Nicarag water mining N
88. Physician/Medicare freeze Y
89. Increase "sin" taxes Y
90. End SBA direct loans N
91. Sell Conrail Y
92. Equal Rights Amendment Y
93. Marines in Lebanon Y
94. Eminent domain-Coal comps Y
95. Prohibit EPA sanctions Y
96. SS age increase/Reforms Y
97. Auto domestic content req N
98. Delete jobs program fundg Y
99. Highway-Gas tax bill N
100. Raise Medicare;Cut defnse Y
101. Emergency housing aid Y
102. Across-the-board tax cuts Y
103. Gramm-Latta II targets Y
104. Delete B-1 bomber funds N
105. Dsapprov Saudi AWACS sale Y
106. Disapprove oil import fee Y
107. Rail Deregulation N
108. Dsapp India nuc fuel sale Y
109. Mil draft registration N
110. Chrysler Loan Guarantees N
111. Prohibit school busing Y
112. Nuclear plant moratorium N
113. Oil price controls N
114. Tuition Tax Credits Y
115. Est Consumer Protect Agcy N
116. Eliminate B-1 bomber fnds N
117. Subminimum wage for youth Y
118. Delete crude oil tax Y
119. Natural gas deregulation Y

Presidential Support Score: 1986 - 58% 1985 - 71%

SKEEN, JOE -- New Mexico 2nd District [Republican]. Counties of Chaves, Curry, Dona Ana, Eddy, Grant, Hidalgo, Lea, Lincoln, Luna, Otero, Quay, Roosevelt, Sierra and Union. Prior Terms: House: 1981-86. Born: June 30, 1927; Roswell, N.M. Education: Texas A&M. Military Service: U.S. Navy. Occupation: Rancher; New Mexico senator.

1. Immigration Reform N
2. Open fld-search warrants Y
3. Civil pnty-hire ill alien Y
4. So Afr sanc-veto override N
5. Tax Overhaul Y
6. South Africa sanctions N
7. Death penalty-drug bill Y
8. Evidence-warrantless srch Y
9. Life term-second drug off Y
10. Military use in drug war Y
11. Troop reduction in Europe N
12. Prohibit chemical weapons N
13. Bar ASAT testing N
14. Abide SALT II weapons ban N
15. Follow SALT II-Soviets do Y
16. Reduce SDI funding N
17. Increase SDI funding N
18. Purchase Trident sub Y
19. Delete 12 MX;Add conv wpn N
20. Raise speed limit Y
21. Textile Import Quotas(*) Y
22. Req Pentagon buy US goods N
23. AIDS ins anti-dscriminatn N
24. Nicaraguan refugee aid N
25. Nicaraguan contra aid Y
26. US abide by SALT II Y
27. Prohibit Saudi arms sale Y
28. Military Retiremnt Reform Y
29. Nicaraguan refugee aid Y
30. Ease '68 Gun Control Act Y
31. Bar intrstat handgun tran N
32. Keep '68 Gun Control Act N
33. Nicaraguan contra aid Y
34. Bar emp polygraph testing N
35. Tax Overhaul consideratn Y
36. Bar armor-piercing ammo Y
37. Tax Overhaul consideratn N
38. Make comp emissions known N
39. Allow toxic victims suits N
40. Strike Superfund "VAT" N
41. Notify emp-plant closing N
42. Bar emp consult-plant clo Y
43. Medicare cuts;Tax incres' N
44. Delete 12 MX missiles N
45. Spending cuts;Tax incres' N
46. Textile Import Quotas Y
47. Cut some school lunch fds Y
48. Clean Water Act Amendmnts Y
49. Youth work projects N
50. Assist military in Angola Y
51. Allow US troops-Nicaragua Y
52. Pentagon polygraph exams Y
53. Bar ASAT testing N
54. Suspend def pmt for abuse N
55. Bar Pentagon-contr emplmt Y
56. Increase SDI funding Y
57. Reduce SDI funding N
58. Produce chemical weapons Y
59. Bar CIA fndg in Nicaragua N
60. South Africa sanctions N
61. Cut SS COLAs; Raise taxes N
62. Let US invest-So Africa Y

SKEEN, JOE (Cont.)

63. Approve 21 MX for 1985 Y
64. Emergency Farm Credit Y
65. Awards to whistle blowers Y
66. African disaster relief Y
67. Ban bank loans to So Afr N
68. Bar coun duty-free trtmt N
69. Steel import limits N
70. Soc Sec COLAs=inflation Y
71. Bar haz waste vctms suits Y
72. Prohibit aid to Nicaragua N
73. Cut $-Schs bar sch prayer Y
74. Raise taxes; Cut Medicare N
75. Alien residncy-prior 1982 N
76. Alien residncy-prior 1980 N
77. Pen emp-hire illgl aliens N
78. Lmt Persh II/cruse-Europe N
79. Delete 34 B-1 bombers N
80. Bar purch of Pershing II N
81. Bar purchase of Sgt York N
82. Delete $ for Trident II N
83. Allow 15 MX missiles Y
84. Bar MX procurement-1985 N
85. Equal Access Act Y
86. Aid to El Salvador Y
87. Bar Nicarag water mining N
88. Physician/Medicare freeze Y
89. Increase "sin" taxes N
90. End SBA direct loans Y
91. Sell Conrail Y
92. Equal Rights Amendment N
93. Marines in Lebanon Y
94. Eminent domain-Coal comps N
95. Prohibit EPA sanctions Y
96. SS age increase/Reforms Y
97. Auto domestic content req N
98. Delete jobs program fundg Y
99. Highway-Gas tax bill N
100. Raise Medicare;Cut defnse N
101. Emergency housing aid N
102. Across-the-board tax cuts Y
103. Gramm-Latta II targets Y
104. Delete B-1 bomber funds N
105. Dsapprov Saudi AWACS sale N

Presidential Support Score: 1986 - 69% 1985 - 68%

RICHARDSON, BILL -- New Mexico 3rd District [Democrat]. Counties of Catron, Cibola, Colfax, Harding, Los Alamos, McKinley, Mora, Rio Arriba, Sandoval, San Juan, San Miguel, Sante Fe, Socorro, Taos and Valencia. Prior Terms: House: 1983-86. Born: November 15, 1947; Pasadena, Calif. Education: Tufts University (B.A.); Fletcher School of Law & Diplomacy (M.A.). Occupation: Office of Congressional Relations, Dept. of State (1973-75); professional staff member and investigator, Senate subcommittee on Foreign Relations assistance (1975-78).

1. Immigration Reform Y
2. Open fld-search warrants Y
3. Civil pnty-hire ill alien Y
4. So Afr sanc-veto override Y
5. Tax Overhaul Y
6. South Africa sanctions Y
7. Death penalty-drug bill Y
8. Evidence-warrantless srch Y
9. Life term-second drug off Y
10. Military use in drug war Y
11. Troop reduction in Europe N
12. Prohibit chemical weapons Y
13. Bar ASAT testing Y
14. Abide SALT II weapons ban Y
15. Follow SALT II-Soviets do N
16. Reduce SDI funding N
17. Increase SDI funding N
18. Purchase Trident sub Y
19. Delete 12 MX;Add conv wpn Y
20. Raise speed limit Y
21. Textile Import Quotas(*) Y
22. Req Pentagon buy US goods Y
23. AIDS ins anti-dscriminatn Y
24. Nicaraguan refugee aid Y
25. Nicaraguan contra aid N
26. US abide by SALT II N
27. Prohibit Saudi arms sale Y
28. Military Retiremnt Reform Y
29. Nicaraguan refugee aid Y
30. Ease '68 Gun Control Act Y
31. Bar intrstat handgun tran N
32. Keep '68 Gun Control Act N
33. Nicaraguan contra aid N
34. Bar emp polygraph testing Y
35. Tax Overhaul consideratn Y
36. Bar armor-piercing ammo Y
37. Tax Overhaul consideratn Y
38. Make comp emissions known Y
39. Allow toxic victims suits N
40. Strike Superfund "VAT" N
41. Notify emp-plant closing Y
42. Bar emp consult-plant clo N
43. Medicare cuts;Tax incres' Y
44. Delete 12 MX missiles Y
45. Spending cuts;Tax incres' Y
46. Textile Import Quotas Y
47. Cut some school lunch fds N
48. Clean Water Act Amendmnts N

RICHARDSON, BILL (Cont.)

49.	Youth work projects	Y	73.	Cut $-Schs bar sch prayer	N
50.	Assist military in Angola	N	74.	Raise taxes; Cut Medicare	Y
51.	Allow US troops-Nicaragua	N	75.	Alien residncy-prior 1982	Y
52.	Pentagon polygraph exams	Y	76.	Alien residncy-prior 1980	N
53.	Bar ASAT testing	Y	77.	Pen emp-hire illgl aliens	Y
54.	Suspend def pmt for abuse	Y	78.	Lmt Persh II/cruse-Europe	N
55.	Bar Pentagon-contr emplmt	Y	79.	Delete 34 B-1 bombers	N
56.	Increase SDI funding	N	80.	Bar purch of Pershing II	N
57.	Reduce SDI funding	N	81.	Bar purchase of Sgt York	?
58.	Produce chemical weapons	N	82.	Delete $ for Trident II	N
59.	Bar CIA fndg in Nicaragua	Y	83.	Allow 15 MX missiles	N
60.	South Africa sanctions	Y	84.	Bar MX procurement-1985	Y
61.	Cut SS COLAs; Raise taxes	N	85.	Equal Access Act	Y
62.	Let US invest-So Africa	N	86.	Aid to El Salvador	N
63.	Approve 21 MX for 1985	N	87.	Bar Nicarag water mining	Y
64.	Emergency Farm Credit	Y	88.	Physician/Medicare freeze	N
65.	Awards to whistle blowers	Y	89.	Increase "sin" taxes	Y
66.	African disaster relief	Y	90.	End SBA direct loans	N
67.	Ban bank loans to So Afr	Y	91.	Sell Conrail	N
68.	Bar coun duty-free trtmt	Y	92.	Equal Rights Amendment	Y
69.	Steel import limits	Y	93.	Marines in Lebanon	N
70.	Soc Sec COLAs=inflation	Y	94.	Eminent domain-Coal comps	N
71.	Bar haz waste vctms suits	N	95.	Prohibit EPA sanctions	Y
72.	Prohibit aid to Nicaragua	Y	96.	SS age increase/Reforms	N

Presidential Support Score: 1986 - 25% 1985 - 25%

NEW YORK

CARNEY, WILLIAM -- New York 1st District [Republican]. County of Suffolk (pt.). Prior Terms: House: 1979-86. Born: July 1, 1942; Brooklyn, N.Y. Education: Florida State University. Military Service: U.S. Army Medical Corps, 1961-64. Occupation: Suffolk county legislator (1976-78).

1.	Immigration Reform	N	24.	Nicaraguan refugee aid	N
2.	Open fld-search warrants	N	25.	Nicaraguan contra aid	Y
3.	Civil pnty-hire ill alien	N	26.	US abide by SALT II	Y
4.	So Afr sanc-veto override	Y	27.	Prohibit Saudi arms sale	Y
5.	Tax Overhaul	N	28.	Military Retiremnt Reform	N
6.	South Africa sanctions	?	29.	Nicaraguan refugee aid	Y
7.	Death penalty-drug bill	?	30.	Ease '68 Gun Control Act	Y
8.	Evidence-warrantless srch	Y	31.	Bar intrstat handgun tran	N
9.	Life term-second drug off	Y	32.	Keep '68 Gun Control Act	N
10.	Military use in drug war	N	33.	Nicaraguan contra aid	Y
11.	Troop reduction in Europe	Y	34.	Bar emp polygraph testing	N
12.	Prohibit chemical weapons	N	35.	Tax Overhaul consideratn	Y
13.	Bar ASAT testing	N	36.	Bar armor-piercing ammo	Y
14.	Abide SALT II weapons ban	N	37.	Tax Overhaul consideratn	N
15.	Follow SALT II-Soviets do	Y	38.	Make comp emissions known	N
16.	Reduce SDI funding	N	39.	Allow toxic victims suits	N
17.	Increase SDI funding	Y	40.	Strike Superfund "VAT"	N
18.	Purchase Trident sub	N	41.	Notify emp-plant closing	N
19.	Delete 12 MX;Add conv wpn	N	42.	Bar emp consult-plant clo	Y
20.	Raise speed limit	Y	43.	Medicare cuts;Tax incres'	N
21.	Textile Import Quotas(*)	N	44.	Delete 12 MX missiles	N
22.	Req Pentagon buy US goods	N	45.	Spending cuts;Tax incres'	N
23.	AIDS ins anti-dscriminatn	N	46.	Textile Import Quotas	Y

CARNEY, WILLIAM (Cont.)

47. Cut some school lunch fds Y
48. Clean Water Act Amendmnts N
49. Youth work projects N
50. Assist military in Angola Y
51. Allow US troops-Nicaragua Y
52. Pentagon polygraph exams Y
53. Bar ASAT testing N
54. Suspend def pmt for abuse N
55. Bar Pentagon-contr emplmt Y
56. Increase SDI funding Y
57. Reduce SDI funding N
58. Produce chemical weapons Y
59. Bar CIA fndg in Nicaragua N
60. South Africa sanctions N
61. Cut SS COLAs; Raise taxes N
62. Let US invest-So Africa N
63. Approve 21 MX for 1985 Y
64. Emergency Farm Credit N
65. Awards to whistle blowers Y
66. African disaster relief Y
67. Ban bank loans to So Afr Y
68. Bar coun duty-free trtmt N
69. Steel import limits N
70. Soc Sec COLAs=inflation Y
71. Bar haz waste vctms suits Y
72. Prohibit aid to Nicaragua N
73. Cut $-Schs bar sch prayer Y
74. Raise taxes; Cut Medicare N
75. Alien residncy-prior 1982 Y
76. Alien residncy-prior 1980 Y
77. Pen emp-hire illgl aliens N
78. Lmt Persh II/cruse-Europe N
79. Delete 34 B-1 bombers N
80. Bar purch of Pershing II N
81. Bar purchase of Sgt York N
82. Delete $ for Trident II N
83. Allow 15 MX missiles Y
84. Bar MX procurement-1985 N
85. Equal Access Act Y
86. Aid to El Salvador Y
87. Bar Nicarag water mining N
88. Physician/Medicare freeze Y
89. Increase "sin" taxes N
90. End SBA direct loans N
91. Sell Conrail ?
92. Equal Rights Amendment N
93. Marines in Lebanon Y
94. Eminent domain-Coal comps Y
95. Prohibit EPA sanctions ?
96. SS age increase/Reforms Y
97. Auto domestic content req N
98. Delete jobs program fundg Y
99. Highway-Gas tax bill ?
100. Raise Medicare;Cut defnse N
101. Emergency housing aid Y
102. Across-the-board tax cuts Y
103. Gramm-Latta II targets Y
104. Delete B-1 bomber funds N
105. Dsapprov Saudi AWACS sale Y
106. Disapprove oil import fee Y
107. Rail Deregulation N
108. Dsapp India nuc fuel sale N
109. Mil draft registration Y
110. Chrysler Loan Guarantees Y
111. Prohibit school busing Y
112. Nuclear plant moratorium ?
113. Oil price controls N

Presidential Support Score: 1986 - 65% 1985 - 68%

DOWNEY, THOMAS J. -- New York 2nd District [Democrat]. County of Suffolk (pt.). Prior Terms: House: 1975-86. Born: January 28, 1949; Ozone Park, N.Y. Education: Cornell University; St. John's University Law School. Occupation: Suffolk County legislator (1971-75).

1. Immigration Reform Y
2. Open fld-search warrants Y
3. Civil pnty-hire ill alien Y
4. So Afr sanc-veto override Y
5. Tax Overhaul Y
6. South Africa sanctions Y
7. Death penalty-drug bill N
8. Evidence-warrantless srch N
9. Life term-second drug off Y
10. Military use in drug war N
11. Troop reduction in Europe N
12. Prohibit chemical weapons Y
13. Bar ASAT testing Y
14. Abide SALT II weapons ban Y
15. Follow SALT II-Soviets do N
16. Reduce SDI funding Y
17. Increase SDI funding N
18. Purchase Trident sub Y
19. Delete 12 MX;Add conv wpn Y
20. Raise speed limit N
21. Textile Import Quotas(*) N
22. Req Pentagon buy US goods N
23. AIDS ins anti-dscriminatn Y
24. Nicaraguan refugee aid Y
25. Nicaraguan contra aid N
26. US abide by SALT II N
27. Prohibit Saudi arms sale Y
28. Military Retiremnt Reform Y
29. Nicaraguan refugee aid Y
30. Ease '68 Gun Control Act N
31. Bar intrstat handgun tran Y
32. Keep '68 Gun Control Act Y

DOWNEY, THOMAS J. (Cont.)

33. Nicaraguan contra aid N
34. Bar emp polygraph testing Y
35. Tax Overhaul consideratn Y
36. Bar armor piercing ammo Y
37. Tax Overhaul consideratn Y
38. Make comp emissions known Y
39. Allow toxic victims suits Y
40. Strike Superfund "VAT" Y
41. Notify emp-plant closing Y
42. Bar emp consult-plant clo N
43. Medicare cuts;Tax incres' Y
44. Delete 12 MX missiles Y
45. Spending cuts;Tax incres' Y
46. Textile Import Quotas N
47. Cut some school lunch fds N
48. Clean Water Act Amendmnts ?
49. Youth work projects Y
50. Assist military in Angola N
51. Allow US troops-Nicaragua N
52. Pentagon polygraph exams N
53. Bar ASAT testing Y
54. Suspend def pmt for abuse Y
55. Bar Pentagon-contr emplmt Y
56. Increase SDI funding N
57. Reduce SDI funding Y
58. Produce chemical weapons N
59. Bar CIA fndg in Nicaragua Y
60. South Africa sanctions Y
61. Cut SS COLAs; Raise taxes N
62. Let US invest-So Africa N
63. Cut SS COLAs; Raise taxes N
64. Emergency Farm Credit Y
65. Awards to whistle blowers Y
66. African disaster relief Y
67. Ban bank loans to So Afr Y
68. Bar coun duty-free trtmt N
69. Steel import limits Y
70. Soc Sec COLAs=inflation Y
71. Bar haz waste vctms suits N
72. Prohibit aid to Nicaragua Y
73. Cut $-Schs bar sch prayer N
74. Raise taxes; Cut Medicare Y
75. Alien residncy-prior 1982 N
76. Alien residncy-prior 1980 N
77. Pen emp-hire illgl aliens Y
78. Lmt Persh II/cruse-Europe Y
79. Delete 34 B-1 bombers Y
80. Bar purch of Pershing II Y
81. Bar purchase of Sgt York Y
82. Delete $ for Trident II Y
83. Allow 15 MX missiles N
84. Bar MX procurement-1985 Y
85. Equal Access Act N
86. Aid to El Salvador N
87. Bar Nicarag water mining Y
88. Physician/Medicare freeze N
89. Increase "sin" taxes Y
90. End SBA direct loans N
91. Sell Conrail N
92. Equal Rights Amendment Y
93. Marines in Lebanon N
94. Eminent domain-Coal comps N
95. Prohibit EPA sanctions N
96. SS age increase/Reforms Y
97. Auto domestic content req Y
98. Delete jobs program fundg N
99. Highway-Gas tax bill Y
100. Raise Medicare;Cut defnse C
101. Emergency housing aid Y
102. Across-the-board tax cuts N
103. Gramm-Latta II targets N
104. Delete B-1 bomber funds Y
105. Dsapprov Saudi AWACS sale Y
106. Disapprove oil import fee Y
107. Rail Deregulation N
108. Dsapp India nuc fuel sale Y
109. Mil draft registration N
110. Chrysler Loan Guarantees Y
111. Prohibit school busing N
112. Nuclear plant moratorium Y
113. Oil price controls Y
114. Tuition Tax Credits N
115. Est Consumer Protect Agcy Y
116. Eliminate B-1 bomber fnds Y
117. Subminimum wage for youth N
118. Delete crude oil tax N
119. Natural gas deregulation N

Presidential Support Score: 1986 - 18% 1985 - 21%

MRAZEK, ROBERT J. -- New York 3rd District [Democrat]. Counties of Nassau (pt.) and Suffolk (pt.). Prior Terms: House: 1983-86. Born: November 6, 1945; Newport, R.I. Education: Cornell University. Military Service: U.S. Navy. Occupation: Writer, small businessman; U.S. senate staff member; county legislator (1975-82).

1. Immigration Reform Y
2. Open fld-search warrants Y
3. Civil pnty-hire ill alien N
4. So Afr sanc-veto override Y
5. Tax Overhaul N
6. South Africa sanctions ?
7. Death penalty-drug bill N
8. Evidence-warrantless srch N
9. Life term-second drug off Y
10. Military use in drug war N

MRAZEK, ROBERT J. (Cont.)

11.	Troop reduction in Europe	Y	54.	Suspend def pmt for abuse	Y
12.	Prohibit chemical weapons	Y	55.	Bar Pentagon-contr emplmt	Y
13.	Bar ASAT testing	Y	56.	Increase SDI funding	N
14.	Abide SALT II weapons ban	Y	57.	Reduce SDI funding	Y
15.	Follow SALT II-Soviets do	N	58.	Produce chemical weapons	N
16.	Reduce SDI funding	Y	59.	Bar CIA fndg in Nicaragua	Y
17.	Increase SDI funding	N	60.	South Africa sanctions	Y
18.	Purchase Trident sub	Y	61.	Cut SS COLAs; Raise taxes	N
19.	Delete 12 MX;Add conv wpn	Y	62.	Let US invest-So Africa	N
20.	Raise speed limit	Y	63.	Approve 21 MX for 1985	N
21.	Textile Import Quotas(*)	Y	64.	Emergency Farm Credit	N
22.	Req Pentagon buy US goods	Y	65.	Awards to whistle blowers	Y
23.	AIDS ins anti-dscriminatn	Y	66.	African disaster relief	Y
24.	Nicaraguan refugee aid	Y	67.	Ban bank loans to So Afr	Y
25.	Nicaraguan contra aid	N	68.	Bar coun duty-free trtmt	Y
26.	US abide by SALT II	N	69.	Steel import limits	Y
27.	Prohibit Saudi arms sale	Y	70.	Soc Sec COLAs=inflation	Y
28.	Military Retiremnt Reform	Y	71.	Bar haz waste vctms suits	N
29.	Nicaraguan refugee aid	Y	72.	Prohibit aid to Nicaragua	Y
30.	Ease '68 Gun Control Act	N	73.	Cut $-Schs bar sch prayer	N
31.	Bar intrstat handgun tran	Y	74.	Raise taxes; Cut Medicare	Y
32.	Keep '68 Gun Control Act	Y	75.	Alien residncy-prior 1982	N
33.	Nicaraguan contra aid	N	76.	Alien residncy-prior 1980	N
34.	Bar emp polygraph testing	Y	77.	Pen emp-hire illgl aliens	Y
35.	Tax Overhaul consideratn	Y	78.	Lmt Persh II/cruse-Europe	Y
36.	Bar armor-piercing ammo	Y	79.	Delete 34 B-1 bombers	Y
37.	Tax Overhaul consideratn	Y	80.	Bar purch of Pershing II	Y
38.	Make comp emissions known	Y	81.	Bar purchase of Sgt York	N
39.	Allow toxic victims suits	N	82.	Delete $ for Trident II	Y
40.	Strike Superfund "VAT"	Y	83.	Allow 15 MX missiles	N
41.	Notify emp-plant closing	Y	84.	Bar MX procurement-1985	Y
42.	Bar emp consult-plant clo	N	85.	Equal Access Act	N
43.	Medicare cuts;Tax incres'	Y	86.	Aid to El Salvador	N
44.	Delete 12 MX missiles	Y	87.	Bar Nicarag water mining	Y
45.	Spending cuts;Tax incres'	Y	88.	Physician/Medicare freeze	N
46.	Textile Import Quotas	Y	89.	Increase "sin" taxes	Y
47.	Cut some school lunch fds	N	90.	End SBA direct loans	N
48.	Clean Water Act Amendmnts	N	91.	Sell Conrail	N
49.	Youth work projects	Y	92.	Equal Rights Amendment	Y
50.	Assist military in Angola	N	93.	Marines in Lebanon	Y
51.	Allow US troops-Nicaragua	N	94.	Eminent domain-Coal comps	N
52.	Pentagon polygraph exams	N	95.	Prohibit EPA sanctions	N
53.	Bar ASAT testing	Y	96.	SS age increase/Reforms	N

Presidential Support Score: 1986 - 17% 1985 - 24%

LENT, NORMAN F. -- New York 4th District [Republican]. County of Nassau (pt.). Prior Terms: House: 1971-86. Born: March 23, 1931; Oceanside, N.Y. Education: Hofstra University (B.A.); Cornell Law School (LL.B.). Military Service: U.S. Navy. Occupation: Associate police justice (1960-62); New York senator (1962-70); attorney, Hill, Lent and Troescher.

1.	Immigration Reform	N	7.	Death penalty-drug bill	Y
2.	Open fld-search warrants	N	8.	Evidence-warrantless srch	Y
3.	Civil pnty-hire ill alien	N	9.	Life term-second drug off	Y
4.	So Afr sanc-veto override	Y	10.	Military use in drug war	Y
5.	Tax Overhaul	N	11.	Troop reduction in Europe	N
6.	South Africa sanctions	Y	12.	Prohibit chemical weapons	N

LENT, NORMAN F. (Cont)

13. Bar ASAT testing N
14. Abide SALT II weapons ban N
15. Follow SALT II-Soviets do Y
16. Reduce SDI funding N
17. Increase SDI funding N
18. Purchase Trident sub N
19. Delete 12 MX;Add conv wpn N
20. Raise speed limit N
21. Textile Import Quotas(*) N
22. Req Pentagon buy US goods Y
23. AIDS ins anti-dscriminatn N
24. Nicaraguan refugee aid N
25. Nicaraguan contra aid Y
26. US abide by SALT II Y
27. Prohibit Saudi arms sale Y
28. Military Retiremnt Reform Y
29. Nicaraguan refugee aid Y
30. Ease '68 Gun Control Act Y
31. Bar intrstat handgun tran Y
32. Keep '68 Gun Control Act Y
33. Nicaraguan contra aid Y
34. Bar emp polygraph testing ?
35. Tax Overhaul consideratn Y
36. Bar armor-piercing ammo Y
37. Tax Overhaul consideratn N
38. Make comp emissions known N
39. Allow toxic victims suits N
40. Strike SuperfunCoal comps N
41. Notify emp-plant closing N
42. Bar emp consult-plant clo Y
43. Medicare cuts;Tax incres' N
44. Delete 12 MX missiles N
45. Spending cuts;Tax incres' N
46. Textile Import Cuotas Y
47. Cut some school lunch fds N
48. Clean Water Act Amendmnts N
49. Youth work projects N
50. Assist military in Angola Y
51. Allow US troops-Nicaragua Y
52. Pentagon polygraph exams Y
53. Bar ASAT testing N
54. Suspend def pmt for abuse N
55. Bar Pentagon-contr emplmt Y
56. Increase SDI funding N
57. Reduce SDI funding N
58. Produce chemical weapons Y
59. Bar CIA fndg in Nicaragua N
60. South Africa sanctions Y
61. Cut SS COLAs; Raise taxes N
62. Let US invest-So Africa Y
63. Approve 21 MX for 1985 Y
64. Emergency Farm Credit N
65. Awards to whistle blowers Y
66. African disaster relief Y
67. Ban bank loans to So Afr N
68. Bar coun duty-free trtmt N
69. Steel import limits Y
70. Soc Sec COLAs=inflation Y
71. Bar haz waste vctms suits N
72. Prohibit aid to Nicaragua N
73. Cut $-Schs bar sch prayer Y
74. Raise taxes; Cut Medicare Y
75. Alien residncy-prior 1982 N
76. Alien residncy-prior 1980 Y
77. Pen emp-hire illgl aliens N
78. Lmt Persh II/cruse-Europe N
79. Delete 34 B-1 bombers N
80. Bar purch of Pershing II N
81. Bar purchase of Sgt York N
82. Delete $ for Trident II N
83. Allow 15 MX missiles Y
84. Bar MX procurement-1985 N
85. Equal Access Act N
86. Aid to El Salvador Y
87. Bar Nicarag water mining Y
88. Physician/Medicare freeze Y
89. Increase "sin" taxes Y
90. End SBA direct loans N
91. Sell Conrail Y
92. Equal Rights Amendment ?
93. Marines in Lebanon Y
94. Eminent domain-Coal comps N
95. Prohibit EPA sanctions N
96. SS age increase/Reforms Y
97. Auto domestic content req N
98. Delete jobs program fundg Y
99. Highway-Gas tax bill Y
100. Raise Medicare;Cut defnse Y
101. Emergency housing aid Y
102. Across-the-board tax cuts Y
103. Gramm-Latta II targets Y
104. Delete B-1 bomber funds N
105. Dsapprov Saudi AWACS sale Y
106. Disapprove oil import fee Y
107. Rail Deregulation ?
108. Dsapp India nuc fuel sale N
109. Mil draft registration Y
110. Chrysler Loan Guarantees Y
111. Prohibit school busing Y
112. Nuclear plant moratorium N
113. Oil price controls N
114. Tuition Tax Credits Y
115. Est Consumer Protect Agcy N
116. Eliminate B-1 bomber fnds N
117. Subminimum wage for youth Y
118. Delete crude oil tax Y
119. Natural gas deregulation Y

Presidential Support Score: 1986 - 61% 1985 - 65%

McGRATH, RAYMOND J. -- New York 5th District [Republican]. County of Nassau (pt.). Prior Terms: House: 1981-86. Born: March

McGRATH, RAYMOND J. (Cont.)
27, 1942; Valley Stream, N.Y. Education: State University, Brockport (B.S.); New York University (M.A.). Occupation: Teacher; lecturer (1969); author; New York assemblyman.

1. Immigration Reform N
2. Open fld-search warrants N
3. Civil pnty-hire ill alien N
4. So Afr sanc-veto override Y
5. Tax Overhaul Y
6. South Africa sanctions Y
7. Death penalty-drug bill Y
8. Evidence-warrantless srch Y
9. Life term-second drug off Y
10. Military use in drug war Y
11. Troop reduction in Europe N
12. Prohibit chemical weapons Y
13. Bar ASAT testing N
14. Abide SALT II weapons ban N
15. Follow SALT II-Soviets do Y
16. Reduce SDI funding N
17. Increase SDI funding N
18. Purchase Trident sub Y
19. Delete 12 MX;Add conv wpn N
20. Raise speed limit N
21. Textile Import Quotas(*) Y
22. Req Pentagon buy US goods N
23. AIDS ins anti-dscriminatn N
24. Nicaraguan refugee aid N
25. Nicaraguan contra aid Y
26. US abide by SALT II Y
27. Prohibit Saudi arms sale Y
28. Military Retiremnt Reform Y
29. Nicaraguan refugee aid Y
30. Ease '68 Gun Control Act Y
31. Bar intrstat handgun tran Y
32. Keep '68 Gun Control Act Y
33. Nicaraguan contra aid Y
34. Bar emp polygraph testing N
35. Tax Overhaul consideratn Y
36. Bar armor-piercing ammo Y
37. Tax Overhaul consideratn Y
38. Make comp emissions known Y
39. Allow toxic victims suits N
40. Strike Superfund "VAT" Y
41. Notify emp-plant closing N
42. Bar emp consult-plant clo Y
43. Medicare cuts;Tax incres' ?
44. Delete 12 MX missiles N
45. Spending cuts;Tax incres' N
46. Textile Import Quotas Y
47. Cut some school lunch fds N
48. Clean Water Act Amendmnts N
49. Youth work projects N
50. Assist military in Angola Y
51. Allow US troops-Nicaragua Y
52. Pentagon polygraph exams Y
53. Bar ASAT testing N
54. Suspend def pmt for abuse N
55. Bar Pentagon-contr emplmt Y
56. Increase SDI funding N
57. Reduce SDI funding N
58. Produce chemical weapons Y
59. Bar CIA fndg in Nicaragua N
60. South Africa sanctions Y
61. Cut SS COLAs; Raise taxes N
62. Let US invest-So Africa ?
63. Approve 21 MX for 1985 Y
64. Emergency Farm Credit ?
65. Awards to whistle blowers Y
66. African disaster relief Y
67. Ban bank loans to So Afr Y
68. Bar coun duty-free trtmt ?
69. Steel import limits ?
70. Soc Sec COLAs=inflation ?
71. Bar haz waste vctms suits N
72. Prohibit aid to Nicaragua N
73. Cut $-Schs bar sch prayer Y
74. Raise taxes; Cut Medicare Y
75. Alien residncy-prior 1982 N
76. Alien residncy-prior 1980 Y
77. Pen emp-hire illgl aliens N
78. Lmt Persh II/cruse-Europe N
79. Delete 34 B-1 bombers N
80. Bar purch of Pershing II N
81. Bar purchase of Sgt York N
82. Delete $ for Trident II N
83. Allow 15 MX missiles Y
84. Bar MX procurement-1985 N
85. Equal Access Act N
86. Aid to El Salvador Y
87. Bar Nicarag water mining Y
88. Physician/Medicare freeze Y
89. Increase "sin" taxes Y
90. End SBA direct loans N
91. Sell Conrail ?
92. Equal Rights Amendment N
93. Marines in Lebanon Y
94. Eminent domain-Coal comps Y
95. Prohibit EPA sanctions N
96. SS age increase/Reforms Y
97. Auto domestic content req N
98. Delete jobs program fundg Y
99. Highway-Gas tax bill Y
100. Raise Medicare;Cut defnse Y
101. Emergency housing aid Y
102. Across-the-board tax cuts Y
103. Gramm-Latta II targets Y
104. Delete B-1 bomber funds N
105. Dsapprov Saudi AWACS sale Y

Presidential Support Score: 1986 - 59% 1985 - 64%

WALDON, ALTON R., Jr. -- New York 6th District [Democrat]. County of Queens (pt.). Prior Terms: House: 1986 (Special Election). Born December 21, 1936; Lakeland, Fla. Education: John Jay College of Criminal Justice; New York Law School. Military Service: U.S. Army. Occupation: Officer (later Captain), New York City Housing Police Department; deputy commissioner, New York State Division of Human Rights (appointed 1975); counsel to New York State Office of Mental Retardation and Developmental Disabilities (appointed 1981); state assemblyman (1982-86).

1.	Immigration Reform	Y	12.	Prohibit chemical weapons	Y
2.	Open fld-search warrants	Y	13.	Bar ASAT testing	Y
3.	Civil pnty-hire ill alien	N	14.	Abide SALT II weapons ban	Y
4.	So Afr sanc-veto override	Y	15.	Follow SALT II-Soviets do	N
5.	Tax Overhaul	N	16.	Reduce SDI funding	Y
6.	South Africa sanctions	Y	17.	Increase SDI funding	N
7.	Death penalty-drug bill	N	18.	Purchase Trident sub	N
8.	Evidence-warrantless srch	N	19.	Delete 12 MX;Add conv wpn	Y
9.	Life term-second drug off	Y	20.	Raise speed limit	N
10.	Military use in drug war	N	21.	Textile Import Quotas(*)	Y
11.	Troop reduction in Europe	N	22.	Req Pentagon buy US goods	Y

Presidential Support Score: 1986 - 15%

ACKERMAN, GARY L. -- New York 7th District [Democrat]. County of Queens (pt.). Prior Terms: House: 1983-86. Born: November 19, 1942; Brooklyn, N.Y. Education: Queens College; St. John's University. Occupation: Public school teacher; newspaper editor; businessman; New York senator (1979-83).

1.	Immigration Reform	Y	30.	Ease '68 Gun Control Act	N
2.	Open fld-search warrants	N	31.	Bar intrstat handgun tran	Y
3.	Civil pnty-hire ill alien	N	32.	Keep '68 Gun Control Act	Y
4.	So Afr sanc-veto override	Y	33.	Nicaraguan contra aid	N
5.	Tax Overhaul	N	34.	Bar emp polygraph testing	Y
6.	South Africa sanctions	?	35.	Tax Overhaul consideratn	Y
7.	Death penalty-drug bill	?	36.	Bar armor-piercing ammo	Y
8.	Evidence-warrantless srch	?	37.	Tax Overhaul consideratn	Y
9.	Life term-second drug off	?	38.	Make comp emissions known	Y
10.	Military use in drug war	N	39.	Allow toxic victims suits	Y
11.	Troop reduction in Europe	N	40.	Strike Superfund "VAT"	Y
12.	Prohibit chemical weapons	Y	41.	Notify emp-plant closing	Y
13.	Bar ASAT testing	Y	42.	Bar emp consult-plant clo	N
14.	Abide SALT II weapons ban	Y	43.	Medicare cuts;Tax incres'	Y
15.	Follow SALT II-Soviets do	N	44.	Delete 12 MX missiles	Y
16.	Reduce SDI funding	Y	45.	Spending cuts;Tax incres'	Y
17.	Increase SDI funding	N	46.	Textile Import Quotas	Y
18.	Purchase Trident sub	Y	47.	Cut some school lunch fds	N
19.	Delete 12 MX;Add conv wpn	Y	48.	Clean Water Act Amendmnts	N
20.	Raise speed limit	N	49.	Youth work projects	Y
21.	Textile Import Quotas(*)	Y	50.	Assist military in Angola	N
22.	Req Pentagon buy US goods	Y	51.	Allow US troops-Nicaragua	N
23.	AIDS ins anti-dscriminatn	Y	52.	Pentagon polygraph exams	?
24.	Nicaraguan refugee aid	Y	53.	Bar ASAT testing	Y
25.	Nicaraguan contra aid	N	54.	Suspend def pmt for abuse	Y
26.	US abide by SALT II	N	55.	Bar Pentagon-contr emplmt	Y
27.	Prohibit Saudi arms sale	Y	56.	Increase SDI funding	N
28.	Military Retiremnt Reform	Y	57.	Reduce SDI funding	Y
29.	Nicaraguan refugee aid	Y	58.	Produce chemical weapons	N

ACKERMAN, GARY L. (Cont.)

59. Bar CIA fndg in Nicaragua Y
60. South Africa sanctions Y
61. Cut SS COLAs; Raise taxes N
62. Let US invest-So Africa N
63. Approve 21 MX for 1985 N
64. Emergency Farm Credit ?
65. Awards to whistle blowers ?
66. African disaster relief ?
67. Ban bank loans to So Afr Y
68. Bar coun duty-free trtmt N
69. Steel import limits Y
70. Soc Sec COLAs=inflation Y
71. Bar haz waste vctms suits N
72. Prohibit aid to Nicaragua Y
73. Cut $-Schs bar sch prayer N
74. Raise taxes; Cut Medicare N
75. Alien residncy-prior 1982 N
76. Alien residncy-prior 1980 N
77. Pen emp-hire illgl aliens Y
78. Lmt Persh II/cruse-Europe Y
79. Delete 34 B-1 bombers Y
80. Bar purch of Pershing II Y
81. Bar purchase of Sgt York Y
82. Delete $ for Trident II Y
83. Allow 15 MX missiles N
84. Bar MX procurement-1985 Y
85. Equal Access Act N
86. Aid to El Salvador N
87. Bar Nicarag water mining Y
88. Physician/Medicare freeze N
89. Increase "sin" taxes Y
90. End SBA direct loans N
91. Sell Conrail -
92. Equal Rights Amendment Y
93. Marines in Lebanon Y
94. Eminent domain-Coal comps Y
95. Prohibit EPA sanctions N
96. SS age increase/Reforms N

Presidential Support Score: 1986 - 11% 1985 - 20%

SCHEUER, JAMES H. -- New York 8th District [Democrat]. Counties of Bronx (pt.), Nassau (pt.) and Queens (pt.). Prior Terms: House: 1964-72; 1974-86. Born: February 6, 1920; New York City, N.Y. Education: Swarthmore College (A.B.); Columbia Law School (LL.B.); Howard Graduate School. Military Service: U.S. Army, 1943-45. Occupation: Economist, U.S. Foreign Economic Administration (1945-46); staff member, Office of Price Stabilization (1951-52); member, Citizens' Housing and Planning Council of New York City.

1. Immigration Reform Y
2. Open fld-search warrants N
3. Civil pnty-hire ill alien N
4. So Afr sanc-veto override Y
5. Tax Overhaul Y
6. South Africa sanctions Y
7. Death penalty-drug bill N
8. Evidence-warrantless srch N
9. Life term-second drug off N
10. Military use in drug war N
11. Troop reduction in Europe Y
12. Prohibit chemical weapons Y
13. Bar ASAT testing Y
14. Abide SALT II weapons ban Y
15. Follow SALT II-Soviets do N
16. Reduce SDI funding Y
17. Increase SDI funding N
18. Purchase Trident sub Y
19. Delete 12 MX;Add conv wpn Y
20. Raise speed limit N
21. Textile Import Quotas(*) Y
22. Req Pentagon buy US goods Y
23. AIDS ins anti-dscriminatn Y
24. Nicaraguan refugee aid Y
25. Nicaraguan contra aid N
26. US abide by SALT II N
27. Prohibit Saudi arms sale Y
28. Military Retiremnt Reform Y
29. Nicaraguan refugee aid Y
30. Ease '68 Gun Control Act N
31. Bar intrstat handgun tran Y
32. Keep '68 Gun Control Act Y
33. Nicaraguan contra aid N
34. Bar emp polygraph testing Y
35. Tax Overhaul consideratn Y
36. Bar armor-piercing ammo Y
37. Tax Overhaul consideratn Y
38. Make comp emissions known Y
39. Allow toxic victims suits Y
40. Strike Superfund "VAT" Y
41. Notify emp-plant closing Y
42. Bar emp consult-plant clo N
43. Medicare cuts;Tax incres' Y
44. Delete 12 MX missiles Y
45. Spending cuts;Tax incres' Y
46. Textile Import Quotas N
47. Cut some school lunch fds N
48. Clean Water Act Amendmnts N
49. Youth work projects Y
50. Assist military in Angola N
51. Allow US troops-Nicaragua N
52. Pentagon polygraph exams N
53. Bar ASAT testing Y
54. Suspend def pmt for abuse Y

SCHEUER, JAMES H. (Cont.)

55. Bar Pentagon-contr emplmt Y
56. Increase SDI funding N
57. Reduce SDI funding Y
58. Produce chemical weapons N
59. Bar CIA fndg in Nicaragua Y
60. South Africa sanctions Y
61. Cut SS COLAs; Raise taxes N
62. Let US invest-So Africa N
63. Approve 21 MX for 1985 N
64. Emergency Farm Credit Y
65. Awards to whistle blowers ?
66. African disaster relief Y
67. Ban bank loans to So Afr Y
68. Bar coun duty-free trtmt N
69. Steel import limits Y
70. Soc Sec COLAs=inflation Y
71. Bar haz waste vctms suits N
72. Prohibit aid to Nicaragua Y
73. Cut $-Schs bar sch prayer N
74. Raise taxes; Cut Medicare Y
75. Alien residncy-prior 1982 Y
76. Alien residncy-prior 1980 N
77. Pen emp-hire illgl aliens N
78. Lmt Persh II/cruse-Europe Y
79. Delete 34 B-1 bombers Y
80. Bar purch of Pershing II Y
81. Bar purchase of Sgt York Y
82. Delete $ for Trident II Y
83. Allow 15 MX missiles N
84. Bar MX procurement-1985 Y
85. Equal Access Act N
86. Aid to El Salvador N
87. Bar Nicarag water mining Y
88. Physician/Medicare freeze N
89. Increase "sin" taxes Y
90. End SBA direct loans N
91. Sell Conrail N
92. Equal Rights Amendment Y
93. Marines in Lebanon Y
94. Eminent domain-Coal comps N
95. Prohibit EPA sanctions Y
96. SS age increase/Reforms N
97. Auto domestic content req Y
98. Delete jobs program fundg N
99. Highway-Gas tax bill Y
100. Raise Medicare;Cut defnse Y
101. Emergency housing aid Y
102. Across-the-board tax cuts N
103. Gramm-Latta II targets N
104. Delete B-1 bomber funds Y
105. Dsapprov Saudi AWACS sale Y
106. Disapprove oil import fee N
107. Rail Deregulation Y
108. Dsapp India nuc fuel sale Y
109. Mil draft registration Y
110. Chrysler Loan Guarantees Y
111. Prohibit school busing N
112. Nuclear plant moratorium Y
113. Oil price controls Y
114. Tuition Tax Credits Y
115. Est Consumer Protect Agcy Y
116. Eliminate B-1 bomber fnds Y
117. Subminimum wage for youth N
118. Delete crude oil tax N
119. Natural gas deregulation N

Presidential Support Score: 1986 - 17% 1985 - 19%

MANTON, THOMAS J. -- New York 9th District [Democrat]. County of Queens (pt.). Prior Terms: 1985-86. Born: November 3, 1932. Education: St. Johns University (B.B.A., J.D.). Military Service: U.S. Marine Corps, 1951-53. Occupation: New York City councilman, New York City policeman.

1. Immigration Reform Y
2. Open fld-search warrants Y
3. Civil pnty-hire ill alien N
4. So Afr sanc-veto override Y
5. Tax Overhaul N
6. South Africa sanctions Y
7. Death penalty-drug bill Y
8. Evidence-warrantless srch Y
9. Life term-second drug off Y
10. Military use in drug war Y
11. Troop reduction in Europe N
12. Prohibit chemical weapons Y
13. Bar ASAT testing Y
14. Abide SALT II weapons ban Y
15. Follow SALT II-Soviets do N
16. Reduce SDI funding N
17. Increase SDI funding N
18. Purchase Trident sub Y
19. Delete 12 MX;Add conv wpn Y
20. Raise speed limit N
21. Textile Import Quotas(*) Y
22. Req Pentagon buy US goods ?
23. AIDS ins anti-dscriminatn Y
24. Nicaraguan refugee aid Y
25. Nicaraguan contra aid N
26. US abide by SALT II N
27. Prohibit Saudi arms sale Y
28. Military Retiremnt Reform Y
29. Nicaraguan refugee aid Y
30. Ease '68 Gun Control Act N
31. Bar intrstat handgun tran Y
32. Keep '68 Gun Control Act Y
33. Nicaraguan contra aid N
34. Bar emp polygraph testing Y

MANTON, THOMAS J. (Cont.)

35. Tax Overhaul consideratn Y
36. Bar armor-piercing ammo Y
37. Tax Overhaul consideratn Y
38. Make comp emissions known Y
39. Allow toxic victims suits N
40. Strike Superfund "VAT" N
41. Notify emp-plant closing Y
42. Bar emp consult-plant clo N
43. Medicare cuts;Tax incres' Y
44. Delete 12 MX missiles Y
45. Spending cuts;Tax incres' Y
46. Textile Import Quotas Y
47. Cut some school lunch fds N
48. Clean Water Act Amendmnts N
49. Youth work projects Y
50. Assist military in Angola N
51. Allow US troops-Nicaragua N
52. Pentagon polygraph exams Y
53. Bar ASAT testing Y
54. Suspend def pmt for abuse Y
55. Bar Pentagon-contr emplmt Y
56. Increase SDI funding N
57. Reduce SDI funding N
58. Produce chemical weapons N
59. Bar CIA fndg in Nicaragua Y
60. South Africa sanctions Y
61. Cut SS COLAs; Raise taxes N
62. Let US invest-So Africa N
63. Approve 21 MX for 1985 N
64. Emergency Farm Credit ?
65. Awards to whistle blowers Y
66. African disaster relief Y

Presidential Support Score: 1986 - 18% 1985 - 23%

SCHUMER, CHARLES E. -- New York 10th District [Democrat]. County of Kings (pt.). Prior Terms: House: 1981-86. Born: November 23, 1950; Brooklyn, N.Y. Education: Harvard College (J.D.). Occupation: New York assemblyman (1974-80).

1. Immigration Reform Y
2. Open fld-search warrants Y
3. Civil pnty-hire ill alien N
4. So Afr sanc-veto override Y
5. Tax Overhaul Y
6. South Africa sanctions Y
7. Death penalty-drug bill N
8. Evidence-warrantless srch N
9. Life term-second drug off Y
10. Military use in drug war Y
11. Troop reduction in Europe N
12. Prohibit chemical weapons Y
13. Bar ASAT testing Y
14. Abide SALT II weapons ban Y
15. Follow SALT II-Soviets do N
16. Reduce SDI funding N
17. Increase SDI funding N
18. Purchase Trident sub Y
19. Delete 12 MX;Add conv wpn Y
20. Raise speed limit N
21. Textile Import Quotas(*) N
22. Req Pentagon buy US goods N
23. AIDS ins anti-dscriminatn ?
24. Nicaraguan refugee aid Y
25. Nicaraguan contra aid N
26. US abide by SALT II N
27. Prohibit Saudi arms sale Y
28. Military Retiremnt Reform Y
29. Nicaraguan refugee aid Y
30. Ease '68 Gun Control Act N
31. Bar intrstat handgun tran Y
32. Keep '68 Gun Control Act Y
33. Nicaraguan contra aid N
34. Bar emp polygraph testing Y
35. Tax Overhaul consideratn Y
36. Bar armor-piercing ammo Y
37. Tax Overhaul consideratn Y
38. Make comp emissions known Y
39. Allow toxic victims suits Y
40. Strike Superfund "VAT" Y
41. Notify emp-plant closing Y
42. Bar emp consult-plant clo N
43. Medicare cuts;Tax incres' Y
44. Delete 12 MX missiles Y
45. Spending cuts;Tax incres' Y
46. Textile Import Quotas N
47. Cut some school lunch fds N
48. Clean Water Act Amendmnts N
49. Youth work projects ?
50. Assist military in Angola N
51. Allow US troops-Nicaragua N
52. Pentagon polygraph exams Y
53. Bar ASAT testing Y
54. Suspend def pmt for abuse Y
55. Bar Pentagon-contr emplmt Y
56. Increase SDI funding N
57. Reduce SDI funding N
58. Produce chemical weapons N
59. Bar CIA fndg in Nicaragua Y
60. South Africa sanctions Y
61. Cut SS COLAs; Raise taxes N
62. Let US invest-So Africa N
63. Approve 21 MX for 1985 N
64. Emergency Farm Credit Y
65. Awards to whistle blowers Y
66. African disaster relief Y
67. Ban bank loans to So Afr Y
68. Bar coun duty-free trtmt Y
69. Steel import limits Y
70. Soc Sec COLAs=inflation Y

SCHUMER, CHARLES E. (Cont.)

71. Bar haz waste vctms suits ?
72. Prohibit aid to Nicaragua Y
73. Cut $-Schs bar sch prayer N
74. Raise taxes; Cut Medicare N
75. Alien residncy-prior 1982 ?
76. Alien residncy-prior 1980 N
77. Pen emp-hire illgl aliens Y
78. Lmt Persh II/cruse-Europe Y
79. Delete 34 B-1 bombers Y
80. Bar purch of Pershing II Y
81. Bar purchase of Sgt York Y
82. Delete $ for Trident II Y
83. Allow 15 MX missiles N
84. Bar MX procurement-1985 Y
85. Equal Access Act N
86. Aid to El Salvador N
87. Bar Nicarag water mining Y
88. Physician/Medicare freeze N
89. Increase "sin" taxes Y
90. End SBA direct loans N
91. Sell Conrail N
92. Equal Rights Amendment Y
93. Marines in Lebanon Y
94. Eminent domain-Coal comps Y
95. Prohibit EPA sanctions Y
96. SS age increase/Reforms N
97. Auto domestic content req Y
98. Delete jobs program fundg N
99. Highway-Gas tax bill Y
100. Raise Medicare;Cut defnse Y
101. Emergency housing aid Y
102. Across-the-board tax cuts N
103. Gramm-Latta II targets N
104. Delete B-1 bomber funds Y
105. Dsapprov Saudi AWACS sale Y

Presidential Support Score: 1986 - 17% 1985 - 28%

TOWNS, EDOLPHUS -- New York 11th District [Democrat]. County of Kings (pt.). Prior Terms: House: 1983-86. Born: July 21, 1934; Chadbourn, N.C. Education: North Carolina A&T State University (B.S.); Adelphi University. Military Service: U.S. Army, 1956-58. Occupation: Teacher; deputy hospital administrator (1965-71); deputy president, Borough of Brooklyn (1976-82).

1. Immigration Reform N
2. Open fld-search warrants Y
3. Civil pnty-hire ill alien Y
4. So Afr sanc-veto override Y
5. Tax Overhaul Y
6. South Africa sanctions ?
7. Death penalty-drug bill N
8. Evidence-warrantless srch N
9. Life term-second drug off N
10. Military use in drug war N
11. Troop reduction in Europe Y
12. Prohibit chemical weapons Y
13. Bar ASAT testing Y
14. Abide SALT II weapons ban Y
15. Follow SALT II-Soviets do N
16. Reduce SDI funding Y
17. Increase SDI funding N
18. Purchase Trident sub N
19. Delete 12 MX;Add conv wpn Y
20. Raise speed limit N
21. Textile Import Quotas(*) Y
22. Req Pentagon buy US goods ?
23. AIDS ins anti-dscriminatn Y
24. Nicaraguan refugee aid Y
25. Nicaraguan contra aid N
26. US abide by SALT II N
27. Prohibit Saudi arms sale Y
28. Military Retiremnt Reform Y
29. Nicaraguan refugee aid Y
30. Ease '68 Gun Control Act N
31. Bar intrstat handgun tran Y
32. Keep '68 Gun Control Act Y
33. Nicaraguan contra aid N
34. Bar emp polygraph testing ?
35. Tax Overhaul consideratn Y
36. Bar armor-piercing ammo Y
37. Tax Overhaul consideratn Y
38. Make comp emissions known Y
39. Allow toxic victims suits N
40. Strike Superfund "VAT" Y
41. Notify emp-plant closing Y
42. Bar emp consult-plant clo N
43. Medicare cuts;Tax incres' Y
44. Delete 12 MX missiles Y
45. Spending cuts;Tax incres' Y
46. Textile Import Quotas Y
47. Cut some school lunch fds N
48. Clean Water Act Amendmnts N
49. Youth work projects ?
50. Assist military in Angola N
51. Allow US troops-Nicaragua N
52. Pentagon polygraph exams N
53. Bar ASAT testing Y
54. Suspend def pmt for abuse ?
55. Bar Pentagon-contr emplmt ?
56. Increase SDI funding ?
57. Reduce SDI funding ?
58. Produce chemical weapons N
59. Bar CIA fndg in Nicaragua Y
60. South Africa sanctions Y

TOWNS, EDOLPHUS (Cont.)

61.	Cut SS COLAs; Raise taxes	N	79.	Delete 34 B-1 bombers	Y
62.	Let US invest-So Africa	N	80.	Bar purch of Pershing II	Y
63.	Approve 21 MX for 1985	N	81.	Bar purchase of Sgt York	?
64.	Emergency Farm Credit	Y	82.	Delete $ for Trident II	Y
65.	Awards to whistle blowers	Y	83.	Allow 15 MX missiles	N
66.	African disaster relief	Y	84.	Bar MX procurement-1985	Y
67.	Ban bank loans to So Afr	P	85.	Equal Access Act	N
68.	Bar coun duty-free trtmt	Y	86.	Aid to El Salvador	N
69.	Steel import limits	Y	87.	Bar Nicarag water mining	Y
70.	Soc Sec COLAs=inflation	Y	88.	Physician/Medicare freeze	N
71.	Bar haz waste vctms suits	N	89.	Increase "sin" taxes	Y
72.	Prohibit aid to Nicaragua	Y	90.	End SBA direct loans	?
73.	Cut $-Schs bar sch prayer	N	91.	Sell Conrail	N
74.	Raise taxes; Cut Medicare	N	92.	Equal Rights Amendment	Y
75.	Alien residncy-prior 1982	N	93.	Marines in Lebanon	N
76.	Alien residncy-prior 1980	N	94.	Eminent domain-Coal comps	Y
77.	Pen emp-hire illgl aliens	Y	95.	Prohibit EPA sanctions	N
78.	Lmt Persh II/cruse-Europe	Y	96.	SS age increase/Reforms	N

Presidential Support Score: 1986 - 15% 1985 - 11%

OWENS, MAJOR R. -- New York 12th District [Democrat]. County of Kings (pt.). Prior Terms: House: 1983-86. Born: June, 1936; Memphis, Tenn. Education: Morehouse College; Atlanta University (M.S.). Occupation: Vice president, Metropolitan Council on Housing (1964); community coordinator, Brooklyn Public Library (1965); executive director, Brownsville Community Council (1966); commissioner, New York City Community Development Agency (1968-73); director, Community Media Library Program (1974); author; lecturer; New York state senator (1974-82).

1.	Immigration Reform	Y	28.	Military Retiremnt Reform	Y
2.	Open fld-search warrants	N	29.	Nicaraguan refugee aid	Y
3.	Civil pnty-hire ill alien	Y	30.	Ease '68 Gun Control Act	N
4.	So Afr sanc-veto override	Y	31.	Bar intrstat handgun tran	Y
5.	Tax Overhaul	Y	32.	Keep '68 Gun Control Act	Y
6.	South Africa sanctions	?	33.	Nicaraguan contra aid	N
7.	Death penalty-drug bill	N	34.	Bar emp polygraph testing	Y
8.	Evidence-warrantless srch	N	35.	Tax Overhaul consideratn	Y
9.	Life term-second drug off	Y	36.	Bar armor-piercing ammo	Y
10.	Military use in drug war	N	37.	Tax Overhaul consideratn	Y
11.	Troop reduction in Europe	Y	38.	Make comp emissions known	Y
12.	Prohibit chemical weapons	Y	39.	Allow toxic victims suits	Y
13.	Bar ASAT testing	Y	40.	Strike Superfund "VAT"	Y
14.	Abide SALT II weapons ban	Y	41.	Notify emp-plant closing	Y
15.	Follow SALT II-Soviets do	N	42.	Bar emp consult-plant clo	N
16.	Reduce SDI funding	Y	43.	Medicare cuts;Tax incres'	Y
17.	Increase SDI funding	N	44.	Delete 12 MX missiles	Y
18.	Purchase Trident sub	Y	45.	Spending cuts;Tax incres'	Y
19.	Delete 12 MX;Add conv wpn	Y	46.	Textile Import Quotas	Y
20.	Raise speed limit	N	47.	Cut some school lunch fds	N
21.	Textile Import Quotas(*)	Y	48.	Clean Water Act Amendmnts	N
22.	Req Pentagon buy US goods	Y	49.	Youth work projects	Y
23.	AIDS ins anti-dscriminatn	Y	50.	Assist military in Angola	N
24.	Nicaraguan refugee aid	Y	51.	Allow US troops-Nicaragua	-
25.	Nicaraguan contra aid	N	52.	Pentagon polygraph exams	-
26.	US abide by SALT II	N	53.	Bar ASAT testing	#
27.	Prohibit Saudi arms sale	Y	54.	Suspend def pmt for abuse	+

OWENS, MAJOR R. (Cont.)

55. Bar Pentagon-contr emplmt +
56. Increase SDI funding N
57. Reduce SDI funding Y
58. Produce chemical weapons N
59. Bar CIA fndg in Nicaragua Y
60. South Africa sanctions Y
61. Cut SS COLAs; Raise taxes N
62. Let US invest-So Africa N
63. Approve 21 MX for 1985 N
64. Emergency Farm Credit Y
65. Awards to whistle blowers Y
66. African disaster relief Y
67. Ban bank loans to So Afr P
68. Bar coun duty-free trtmt Y
69. Steel import limits Y
70. Soc Sec COLAs=inflation Y
71. Bar haz waste vctms suits N
72. Prohibit aid to Nicaragua ?
73. Cut $-Schs bar sch prayer N
74. Raise taxes; Cut Medicare N
75. Alien residncy-prior 1982 N
76. Alien residncy-prior 1980 N
77. Pen emp-hire illgl aliens Y
78. Lmt Persh II/cruse-Europe Y
79. Delete 34 B-1 bombers Y
80. Bar purch of Pershing II Y
81. Bar purchase of Sgt York Y
82. Delete $ for Trident II Y
83. Allow 15 MX missiles N
84. Bar MX procurement-1985 Y
85. Equal Access Act N
86. Aid to El Salvador N
87. Bar Nicarag water mining Y
88. Physician/Medicare freeze N
89. Increase "sin" taxes Y
90. End SBA direct loans N
91. Sell Conrail N
92. Equal Rights Amendment Y
93. Marines in Lebanon N
94. Eminent domain-Coal comps N
95. Prohibit EPA sanctions N
96. SS age increase/Reforms N

Presidential Support Score: 1986 - 10% 1985 - 16%

SOLARZ, STEPHEN J. -- New York 13th District [Democrat]. County of Kings (pt.). Prior Terms: House: 1975-86. Born: September 12, 1940; New York City, N.Y. Education: Brandeis University (A.B.); Columbia University (M.A.). Occupation: Attorney; New York assemblyman (1968-72); trustee, Brandeis University.

1. Immigration Reform #
2. Open fld-search warrants ?
3. Civil pnty-hire ill alien N
4. So Afr sanc-veto override Y
5. Tax Overhaul Y
6. South Africa sanctions Y
7. Death penalty-drug bill N
8. Evidence-warrantless srch N
9. Life term-second drug off N
10. Military use in drug war N
11. Troop reduction in Europe N
12. Prohibit chemical weapons Y
13. Bar ASAT testing Y
14. Abide SALT II weapons ban Y
15. Follow SALT II-Soviets do N
16. Reduce SDI funding Y
17. Increase SDI funding N
18. Purchase Trident sub Y
19. Delete 12 MX;Add conv wpn Y
20. Raise speed limit N
21. Textile Import Quotas(*) N
22. Req Pentagon buy US goods N
23. AIDS ins anti-dscriminatn Y
24. Nicaraguan refugee aid Y
25. Nicaraguan contra aid N
26. US abide by SALT II N
27. Prohibit Saudi arms sale Y
28. Military Retiremnt Reform Y
29. Nicaraguan refugee aid Y
30. Ease '68 Gun Control Act N
31. Bar intrstat handgun tran Y
32. Keep '68 Gun Control Act Y
33. Nicaraguan contra aid N
34. Bar emp polygraph testing Y
35. Tax Overhaul consideratn Y
36. Bar armor-piercing ammo Y
37. Tax Overhaul consideratn Y
38. Make comp emissions known Y
39. Allow toxic victims suits Y
40. Strike Superfund "VAT" Y
41. Notify emp-plant closing Y
42. Bar emp consult-plant clo N
43. Medicare cuts;Tax incres' Y
44. Delete 12 MX missiles Y
45. Spending cuts;Tax incres' Y
46. Textile Import Quotas N
47. Cut some school lunch fds N
48. Clean Water Act Amendmnts N
49. Youth work projects Y
50. Assist military in Angola N
51. Allow US troops-Nicaragua N
52. Pentagon polygraph exams Y
53. Bar ASAT testing Y
54. Suspend def pmt for abuse Y
55. Bar Pentagon-contr emplmt Y
56. Increase SDI funding N
57. Reduce SDI funding N
58. Produce chemical weapons N

SOLARZ, STEPHEN J. (Cont.)

59. Bar CIA fndg in Nicaragua Y
60. South Africa sanctions Y
61. Cut SS COLAs; Raise taxes N
62. Let US invest-So Africa N
63. Approve 21 MX for 1985 N
64. Emergency Farm Credit Y
65. Awards to whistle blowers Y
66. African disaster relief Y
67. Ban bank loans to So Afr Y
68. Bar coun duty-free trtmt N
69. Steel import limits Y
70. Soc Sec COLAs=inflation Y
71. Bar haz waste vctms suits N
72. Prohibit aid to Nicaragua Y
73. Cut $-Schs bar sch prayer N
74. Raise taxes; Cut Medicare Y
75. Alien residncy-prior 1982 N
76. Alien residncy-prior 1980 N
77. Pen emp-hire illgl aliens N
78. Lmt Persh II/cruse-Europe Y
79. Delete 34 B-1 bombers Y
80. Bar purch of Pershing II N
81. Bar purchase of Sgt York Y
82. Delete $ for Trident II Y
83. Allow 15 MX missiles N
84. Bar MX procurement-1985 Y
85. Equal Access Act X
86. Aid to El Salvador N
87. Bar Nicarag water mining ?
88. Physician/Medicare freeze N
89. Increase "sin" taxes Y
90. End SBA direct loans N
91. Sell Conrail N
92. Equal Rights Amendment Y
93. Marines in Lebanon Y
94. Eminent domain-Coal comps Y
95. Prohibit EPA sanctions Y
96. SS age increase/Reforms N
97. Auto domestic content req Y
98. Delete jobs program fundg N
99. Highway-Gas tax bill Y
100. Raise Medicare;Cut defnse Y
101. Emergency housing aid Y
102. Across-the-board tax cuts N
103. Gramm-Latta II targets N
104. Delete B-1 bomber funds Y
105. Dsapprov Saudi AWACS sale Y
106. Disapprove oil import fee N
107. Rail Deregulation N
108. Dsapp India nuc fuel sale Y
109. Mil draft registration Y
110. Chrysler Loan Guarantees Y
111. Prohibit school busing N
112. Nuclear plant moratorium #
113. Oil price controls Y
114. Tuition Tax Credits Y
115. Est Consumer Protect Agcy Y
116. Eliminate B-1 bomber fnds Y
117. Subminimum wage for youth N
118. Delete crude oil tax N
119. Natural gas deregulation N

Presidential Support Score: 1986 - 18% 1985 - 24%

MOLINARI, GUY V. -- New York 14th District [Republican]. Counties of Kings (pt.) and Richmond. Prior Terms: House: 1981-86. Born: November 23, 1928; New York City, N.Y. Education: Wagner College (B.A.); New York Law School. Military Service: U.S. Marine Corps. Occupation: Attorney; New York legislator (1974-80).

1. Immigration Reform N
2. Open fld-search warrants N
3. Civil pnty-hire ill alien Y
4. So Afr sanc-veto override Y
5. Tax Overhaul N
6. South Africa sanctions Y
7. Death penalty-drug bill Y
8. Evidence-warrantless srch Y
9. Life term-second drug off Y
10. Military use in drug war Y
11. Troop reduction in Europe N
12. Prohibit chemical weapons Y
13. Bar ASAT testing N
14. Abide SALT II weapons ban N
15. Follow SALT II-Soviets do Y
16. Reduce SDI funding N
17. Increase SDI funding N
18. Purchase Trident sub N
19. Delete 12 MX;Add conv wpn N
20. Raise speed limit N
21. Textile Import Quotas(*) Y
22. Req Pentagon buy US goods N
23. AIDS ins anti-dscriminatn N
24. Nicaraguan refugee aid N
25. Nicaraguan contra aid Y
26. US abide by SALT II Y
27. Prohibit Saudi arms sale Y
28. Military Retiremnt Reform Y
29. Nicaraguan refugee aid Y
30. Ease '68 Gun Control Act Y
31. Bar intrstat handgun tran Y
32. Keep '68 Gun Control Act Y
33. Nicaraguan contra aid Y
34. Bar emp polygraph testing N
35. Tax Overhaul consideratn N
36. Bar armor-piercing ammo Y

MOLINARI, GUY V. (Cont.)

37. Tax Overhaul consideratn N
38. Make comp emissions known Y
39. Allow toxic victims suits Y
40. Strike Superfund "VAT" Y
41. Notify emp-plant closing N
42. Bar emp consult-plant clo Y
43. Medicare cuts;Tax incres' N
44. Delete 12 MX missiles N
45. Spending cuts;Tax incres' Y
46. Textile Import Quotas N
47. Cut some school lunch fds Y
48. Clean Water Act Amendmnts Y
49. Youth work projects N
50. Assist military in Angola Y
51. Allow US troops-Nicaragua Y
52. Pentagon polygraph exams Y
53. Bar ASAT testing N
54. Suspend def pmt for abuse N
55. Bar Pentagon-contr emplmt Y
56. Increase SDI funding N
57. Reduce SDI funding N
58. Produce chemical weapons N
59. Bar CIA fndg in Nicaragua N
60. South Africa sanctions Y
61. Cut SS COLAs; Raise taxes N
62. Let US invest-So Africa N
63. Approve 21 MX for 1985 Y
64. Emergency Farm Credit N
65. Awards to whistle blowers Y
66. African disaster relief Y
67. Ban bank loans to So Afr Y
68. Bar coun duty-free trtmt N
69. Steel import limits N
70. Soc Sec COLAs=inflation Y
71. Bar haz waste vctms suits N
72. Prohibit aid to Nicaragua N
73. Cut $-Schs bar sch prayer Y
74. Raise taxes; Cut Medicare N
75. Alien residncy-prior 1982 Y
76. Alien residncy-prior 1980 N
77. Pen emp-hire illgl aliens N
78. Lmt Persh II/cruse-Europe N
79. Delete 34 B-1 bombers N
80. Bar purch of Pershing II N
81. Bar purchase of Sgt York N
82. Delete $ for Trident II N
83. Allow 15 MX missiles Y
84. Bar MX procurement-1985 N
85. Equal Access Act Y
86. Aid to El Salvador Y
87. Bar Nicarag water mining N
88. Physician/Medicare freeze Y
89. Increase "sin" taxes N
90. End SBA direct loans N
91. Sell Conrail Y
92. Equal Rights Amendment ?
93. Marines in Lebanon Y
94. Eminent domain-Coal comps N
95. Prohibit EPA sanctions N
96. SS age increase/Reforms N
97. Auto domestic content req N
98. Delete jobs program fundg Y
99. Highway-Gas tax bill ?
100. Raise Medicare;Cut defnse Y
101. Emergency housing aid Y
102. Across-the-board tax cuts Y
103. Gramm-Latta II targets Y
104. Delete B-1 bomber funds N
105. Dsapprov Saudi AWACS sale Y

Presidential Support Score: 1986 - 68% 1985 - 64%

GREEN, BILL -- New York 15th District [Republican]. County of New York (pt.). Prior Terms: House: 1978 (Special Election)-1986. Born: October 16, 1929; New York City, N.Y. Education: Harvard College (B.A.); Harvard Law School (J.D.). Military Service: U.S. Army, 1953-55. Occupation: Attorney; law secretary to judge (1955-56); chief counsel, New York legislative committee (1961-64).

1. Immigration Reform Y
2. Open fld-search warrants N
3. Civil pnty-hire ill alien N
4. So Afr sanc-veto override Y
5. Tax Overhaul N
6. South Africa sanctions Y
7. Death penalty-drug bill Y
8. Evidence-warrantless srch N
9. Life term-second drug off Y
10. Military use in drug war N
11. Troop reduction in Europe N
12. Prohibit chemical weapons Y
13. Bar ASAT testing Y
14. Abide SALT II weapons ban Y
15. Follow SALT II-Soviets do N
16. Reduce SDI funding N
17. Increase SDI funding N
18. Purchase Trident sub N
19. Delete 12 MX;Add conv wpn Y
20. Raise speed limit N
21. Textile Import Quotas(*) N
22. Req Pentagon buy US goods N
23. AIDS ins anti-dscriminatn Y
24. Nicaraguan refugee aid Y
25. Nicaraguan contra aid N
26. US abide by SALT II N

GREEN, BILL (Cont.)

27. Prohibit Saudi arms sale Y
28. Military Retiremnt Reform Y
29. Nicaraguan refugee aid Y
30. Ease '68 Gun Control Act N
31. Bar intrstat handgun tran Y
32. Keep '68 Gun Control Act Y
33. Nicaraguan contra aid N
34. Bar emp polygraph testing Y
35. Tax Overhaul consideratn N
36. Bar armor-piercing ammo Y
37. Tax Overhaul consideratn N
38. Make comp emissions known Y
39. Allow toxic victims suits Y
40. Strike Superfund "VAT" Y
41. Notify emp-plant closing N
42. Bar emp consult-plant clo Y
43. Medicare cuts;Tax incres' Y
44. Delete 12 MX missiles Y
45. Spending cuts;Tax incres' Y
46. Textile Import Quotas N
47. Cut some school lunch fds Y
48. Clean Water Act Amendmnts N
49. Youth work projects N
50. Assist military in Angola Y
51. Allow US troops-Nicaragua N
52. Pentagon polygraph exams N
53. Bar ASAT testing Y
54. Suspend def pmt for abuse N
55. Bar Pentagon-contr emplmt Y
56. Increase SDI funding N
57. Reduce SDI funding N
58. Produce chemical weapons N
59. Bar CIA fndg in Nicaragua Y
60. South Africa sanctions Y
61. Cut SS COLAs; Raise taxes N
62. Let US invest-So Africa Y
63. Approve 21 MX for 1985 N
64. Emergency Farm Credit N
65. Awards to whistle blowers Y
66. African disaster relief Y
67. Ban bank loans to So Afr Y
68. Bar coun duty-free trtmt N
69. Steel import limits N
70. Soc Sec COLAs=inflation Y
71. Bar haz waste vctms suits N
72. Prohibit aid to Nicaragua Y
73. Cut $-Schs bar sch prayer N
74. Raise taxes; Cut Medicare Y
75. Alien residncy-prior 1982 N
76. Alien residncy-prior 1980 N
77. Pen emp-hire illgl aliens Y
78. Lmt Persh II/cruse-Europe N
79. Delete 34 B-1 bombers Y
80. Bar purch of Pershing II N
81. Bar purchase of Sgt York N
82. Delete $ for Trident II N
83. Allow 15 MX missiles ?
84. Bar MX procurement-1985 Y
85. Equal Access Act N
86. Aid to El Salvador N
87. Bar Nicarag water mining Y
88. Physician/Medicare freeze N
89. Increase "sin" taxes Y
90. End SBA direct loans N
91. Sell Conrail Y
92. Equal Rights Amendment Y
93. Marines in Lebanon Y
94. Eminent domain-Coal comps Y
95. Prohibit EPA sanctions N
96. SS age increase/Reforms Y
97. Auto domestic content req N
98. Delete jobs program fundg Y
99. Highway-Gas tax bill Y
100. Raise Medicare;Cut defnse Y
101. Emergency housing aid N
102. Across-the-board tax cuts Y
103. Gramm-Latta II targets Y
104. Delete B-1 bomber funds Y
105. Dsapprov Saudi AWACS sale Y
106. Disapprove oil import fee Y
107. Rail Deregulation N
108. Dsapp India nuc fuel sale Y
109. Mil draft registration N
110. Chrysler Loan Guarantees N
111. Prohibit school busing N
112. Nuclear plant moratorium N
113. Oil price controls N
114. Tuition Tax Credits Y
115. Est Consumer Protect Agcy
116. Eliminate B-1 bomber fnds Y

Sworn in February 21, 1978 and missed vote 115.

Presidential Support Score: 1986 - 38% 1985 - 35%

RANGEL, CHARLES B. -- New York 16th District [Democrat]. County of New York (pt.). Prior Terms: House: 1971-86. Born: June 11, 1930; New York City, N.Y. Education: New York University (B.A.); St. John's Law School (LL.B., J.D.). Military Service: U.S. Army, 1948-52. Occupation: Assistant U.S. attorney; counsel to speaker, New York Assembly; counsel, New York Housing Authority; counsel, presidential Draft Revision Committee; New York assemblyman (1966-70).

RANGEL, CHARLES B. (Cont.)

1. Immigration Reform Y
2. Open fld-search warrants Y
3. Civil pnty-hire ill alien Y
4. So Afr sanc-veto override Y
5. Tax Overhaul Y
6. South Africa sanctions #
7. Death penalty-drug bill N
8. Evidence-warrantless srch N
9. Life term-second drug off N
10. Military use in drug war N
11. Troop reduction in Europe Y
12. Prohibit chemical weapons Y
13. Bar ASAT testing Y
14. Abide SALT II weapons ban Y
15. Follow SALT II-Soviets do N
16. Reduce SDI funding Y
17. Increase SDI funding N
18. Purchase Trident sub N
19. Delete 12 MX;Add conv wpn Y
20. Raise speed limit N
21. Textile Import Quotas(*) Y
22. Req Pentagon buy US goods Y
23. AIDS ins anti-dscriminatn Y
24. Nicaraguan refugee aid Y
25. Nicaraguan contra aid N
26. US abide by SALT II X
27. Prohibit Saudi arms sale Y
28. Military Retiremnt Reform N
29. Nicaraguan refugee aid Y
30. Ease '68 Gun Control Act N
31. Bar intrstat handgun tran Y
32. Keep '68 Gun Control Act Y
33. Nicaraguan contra aid N
34. Bar emp polygraph testing Y
35. Tax Overhaul consideratn Y
36. Bar armor-piercing ammo Y
37. Tax Overhaul consideratn Y
38. Make comp emissions known Y
39. Allow toxic victims suits Y
40. Strike Superfund "VAT" Y
41. Notify emp-plant closing Y
42. Bar emp consult-plant clo N
43. Medicare cuts;Tax incres' Y
44. Delete 12 MX missiles Y
45. Spending cuts;Tax incres' Y
46. Textile Import Quotas Y
47. Cut some school lunch fds ?
48. Clean Water Act Amendmnts N
49. Youth work projects Y
50. Assist military in Angola N
51. Allow US troops-Nicaragua N
52. Pentagon polygraph exams N
53. Bar ASAT testing Y
54. Suspend def pmt for abuse Y
55. Bar Pentagon-contr emplmt Y
56. Increase SDI funding N
57. Reduce SDI funding Y
58. Produce chemical weapons N
59. Bar CIA fndg in Nicaragua Y
60. South Africa sanctions Y
61. Cut SS COLAs; Raise taxes N
62. Let US invest-So Africa N
63. Approve 21 MX for 1985 N
64. Emergency Farm Credit Y
65. Awards to whistle blowers ?
66. African disaster relief Y
67. Ban bank loans to So Afr P
68. Bar coun duty-free trtmt Y
69. Steel import limits Y
70. Soc Sec COLAs=inflation Y
71. Bar haz waste vctms suits N
72. Prohibit aid to Nicaragua Y
73. Cut $-Schs bar sch prayer N
74. Raise taxes; Cut Medicare Y
75. Alien residncy-prior 1982 N
76. Alien residncy-prior 1980 N
77. Pen emp-hire illgl aliens Y
78. Lmt Persh II/cruse-Europe Y
79. Delete 34 B-1 bombers Y
80. Bar purch of Pershing II Y
81. Bar purchase of Sgt York Y
82. Delete $ for Trident II Y
83. Allow 15 MX missiles N
84. Bar MX procurement-1985 Y
85. Equal Access Act N
86. Aid to El Salvador N
87. Bar Nicarag water mining Y
88. Physician/Medicare freeze N
89. Increase "sin" taxes Y
90. End SBA direct loans N
91. Sell Conrail N
92. Equal Rights Amendment Y
93. Marines in Lebanon N
94. Eminent domain-Coal comps Y
95. Prohibit EPA sanctions Y
96. SS age increase/Reforms N
97. Auto domestic content req Y
98. Delete jobs program fundg N
99. Highway-Gas tax bill Y
100. Raise Medicare;Cut defnse Y
101. Emergency housing aid Y
102. Across-the-board tax cuts N
103. Gramm-Latta II targets N
104. Delete B-1 bomber funds Y
105. Dsapprov Saudi AWACS sale Y
106. Disapprove oil import fee N
107. Rail Deregulation N
108. Dsapp India nuc fuel sale Y
109. Mil draft registration N
110. Chrysler Loan Guarantees Y
111. Prohibit school busing N
112. Nuclear plant moratorium Y
113. Oil price controls ?
114. Tuition Tax Credits N
115. Est Consumer Protect Agcy Y
116. Eliminate B-1 bomber fnds Y
117. Subminimum wage for youth N
118. Delete crude oil tax N

RANGEL, CHARLES B. (Cont.)
119. Natural gas deregulation N

Presidential Support Score: 1986 - 17% 1985 - 16%

WEISS, TED -- New York 17th District [Democrat]. Counties of Bronx (pt.) and New York (pt.). Prior Terms: House: 1977-1986. Born: September 17, 1927; Hungary. Education: Syracuse University (B.A., LL.B.). Military Service: U.S. Army, 1946-47. Occupation: Assistant district attorney (1955-59); member, city council (1962-77).

1. Immigration Reform ?
2. Open fld-search warrants ?
3. Civil pnty-hire ill alien ?
4. So Afr sanc-veto override Y
5. Tax Overhaul N
6. South Africa sanctions Y
7. Death penalty-drug bill N
8. Evidence-warrantless srch N
9. Life term-second drug off N
10. Military use in drug war N
11. Troop reduction in Europe N
12. Prohibit chemical weapons Y
13. Bar ASAT testing Y
14. Abide SALT II weapons ban Y
15. Follow SALT II-Soviets do N
16. Reduce SDI funding Y
17. Increase SDI funding N
18. Purchase Trident sub ?
19. Delete 12 MX;Add conv wpn ?
20. Raise speed limit N
21. Textile Import Quotas(*) Y
22. Req Pentagon buy US goods N
23. AIDS ins anti-dscriminatn Y
24. Nicaraguan refugee aid Y
25. Nicaraguan contra aid N
26. US abide by SALT II N
27. Prohibit Saudi arms sale Y
28. Military Retiremnt Reform N
29. Nicaraguan refugee aid Y
30. Ease '68 Gun Control Act N
31. Bar intrstat handgun tran Y
32. Keep '68 Gun Control Act Y
33. Nicaraguan contra aid N
34. Bar emp polygraph testing N
35. Tax Overhaul consideratn Y
36. Bar armor-piercing ammo Y
37. Tax Overhaul consideratn Y
38. Make comp emissions known Y
39. Allow toxic victims suits Y
40. Strike Superfund "VAT" Y
41. Notify emp-plant closing Y
42. Bar emp consult-plant clo N
43. Medicare cuts;Tax incres' Y
44. Delete 12 MX missiles Y
45. Spending cuts;Tax incres' Y
46. Textile Import Quotas Y
47. Cut some school lunch fds N
48. Clean Water Act Amendmnts N
49. Youth work projects Y
50. Assist military in Angola N
51. Allow US troops-Nicaragua N
52. Pentagon polygraph exams N
53. Bar ASAT testing Y
54. Suspend def pmt for abuse Y
55. Bar Pentagon-contr emplmt Y
56. Increase SDI funding N
57. Reduce SDI funding Y
58. Produce chemical weapons N
59. Bar CIA fndg in Nicaragua Y
60. South Africa sanctions Y
61. Cut SS COLAs; Raise taxes N
62. Let US invest-So Africa N
63. Approve 21 MX for 1985 N
64. Emergency Farm Credit Y
65. Awards to whistle blowers Y
66. African disaster relief Y
67. Ban bank loans to So Afr Y
68. Bar coun duty-free trtmt N
69. Steel import limits Y
70. Soc Sec COLAs=inflation Y
71. Bar haz waste vctms suits N
72. Prohibit aid to Nicaragua Y
73. Cut $-Schs bar sch prayer N
74. Raise taxes; Cut Medicare N
75. Alien residncy-prior 1982 N
76. Alien residncy-prior 1980 N
77. Pen emp-hire illgl aliens #
78. Lmt Persh II/cruse-Europe Y
79. Delete 34 B-1 bombers Y
80. Bar purch of Pershing II Y
81. Bar purchase of Sgt York Y
82. Delete $ for Trident II Y
83. Allow 15 MX missiles N
84. Bar MX procurement-1985 Y
85. Equal Access Act N
86. Aid to El Salvador N
87. Bar Nicarag water mining Y
88. Physician/Medicare freeze N
89. Increase "sin" taxes Y
90. End SBA direct loans N
91. Sell Conrail N
92. Equal Rights Amendment Y
93. Marines in Lebanon N
94. Eminent domain-Coal comps Y
95. Prohibit EPA sanctions +
96. SS age increase/Reforms N
97. Auto domestic content req Y
98. Delete jobs program fundg N

WEISS, TED (Cont.)

99. Highway-Gas tax bill N
100. Raise Medicare;Cut defnse Y
101. Emergency housing aid Y
102. Across-the-board tax cuts N
103. Gramm-Latta II targets N
104. Delete B-1 bomber funds Y
105. Dsapprov Saudi AWACS sale Y
106. Disapprove oil import fee Y
107. Rail Deregulation Y
108. Dsapp India nuc fuel sale Y
109. Mil draft registration N
110. Chrysler Loan Guarantees Y
111. Prohibit school busing N
112. Nuclear plant moratorium Y
113. Oil price controls Y
114. Tuition Tax Credits N
115. Est Consumer Protect Agcy Y
116. Eliminate B-1 bomber fnds Y
117. Subminimum wage for youth N
118. Delete crude oil tax N
119. Natural gas deregulation N

Presidential Support Score: 1986 - 13% 1985 - 23%

GARCIA, ROBERT -- New York 18th District [Democrat]. County of Bronx (pt.). Prior Terms: House: 1978 (Special Election)-1986. Born: January 9, 1933; New York City, N.Y. Education: City College of New York; Community College of New York; R.C.A. Institute. Military Service: U.S. Army, Korean Conflict. Occupation: Computer engineer; New York legislator (1965-78); member, State's Temporary Commission to Evaluate the Drug Laws; member, New York City Charter Revision Commission; boardmember, South Bronx Overall Development Corporation; member, Harlem Urban Development Corporation.

1. Immigration Reform N
2. Open fld-search warrants Y
3. Civil pnty-hire ill alien Y
4. So Afr sanc-veto override Y
5. Tax Overhaul Y
6. South Africa sanctions Y
7. Death penalty-drug bill N
8. Evidence-warrantless srch N
9. Life term-second drug off N
10. Military use in drug war N
11. Troop reduction in Europe N
12. Prohibit chemical weapons Y
13. Bar ASAT testing Y
14. Abide SALT II weapons ban Y
15. Follow SALT II-Soviets do N
16. Reduce SDI funding Y
17. Increase SDI funding N
18. Purchase Trident sub Y
19. Delete 12 MX;Add conv wpn #
20. Raise speed limit ?
21. Textile Import Quotas(*) Y
22. Req Pentagon buy US goods Y
23. AIDS ins anti-dscriminatn Y
24. Nicaraguan refugee aid Y
25. Nicaraguan contra aid N
26. US abide by SALT II N
27. Prohibit Saudi arms sale Y
28. Military Retiremnt Reform ?
29. Nicaraguan refugee aid Y
30. Ease '68 Gun Control Act N
31. Bar intrstat handgun tran Y
32. Keep '68 Gun Control Act Y
33. Nicaraguan contra aid N
34. Bar emp polygraph testing Y
35. Tax Overhaul consideratn Y
36. Bar armor-piercing ammo Y
37. Tax Overhaul consideratn Y
38. Make comp emissions known Y
39. Allow toxic victims suits Y
40. Strike Superfund "VAT" Y
41. Notify emp-plant closing Y
42. Bar emp consult-plant clo N
43. Medicare cuts;Tax incres' Y
44. Delete 12 MX missiles Y
45. Spending cuts;Tax incres' Y
46. Textile Import Quotas Y
47. Cut some school lunch fds N
48. Clean Water Act Amendmnts N
49. Youth work projects Y
50. Assist military in Angola N
51. Allow US troops-Nicaragua N
52. Pentagon polygraph exams N
53. Bar ASAT testing Y
54. Suspend def pmt for abuse Y
55. Bar Pentagon-contr emplmt Y
56. Increase SDI funding ?
57. Reduce SDI funding Y
58. Produce chemical weapons N
59. Bar CIA fndg in Nicaragua Y
60. South Africa sanctions Y
61. Cut SS COLAs; Raise taxes N
62. Let US invest-So Africa N
63. Approve 21 MX for 1985 N
64. Emergency Farm Credit Y
65. Awards to whistle blowers Y
66. African disaster relief Y
67. Ban bank loans to So Afr Y
68. Bar coun duty-free trtmt Y

GARCIA, ROBERT (Cont.)

69. Steel import limits Y
70. Soc Sec COLAs=inflation Y
71. Bar haz waste vctms suits N
72. Prohibit aid to Nicaragua Y
73. Cut $-Schs bar sch prayer N
74. Raise taxes; Cut Medicare Y
75. Alien residncy-prior 1982 N
76. Alien residncy-prior 1980 N
77. Pen emp-hire illgl aliens Y
78. Lmt Persh II/cruse-Europe Y
79. Delete 34 B-1 bombers Y
80. Bar purch of Pershing II Y
81. Bar purchase of Sgt York Y
82. Delete $ for Trident II Y
83. Allow 15 MX missiles N
84. Bar MX procurement-1985 Y
85. Equal Access Act N
86. Aid to El Salvador N
87. Bar Nicarag water mining Y
88. Physician/Medicare freeze N
89. Increase "sin" taxes Y
90. End SBA direct loans N
91. Sell Conrail N
92. Equal Rights Amendment #
93. Marines in Lebanon N
94. Eminent domain-Coal comps N
95. Prohibit EPA sanctions N
96. SS age increase/Reforms N
97. Auto domestic content req Y
98. Delete jobs program fundg N
99. Highway-Gas tax bill Y
100. Raise Medicare;Cut defnse ?
101. Emergency housing aid Y
102. Across-the-board tax cuts N
103. Gramm-Latta II targets N
104. Delete B-1 bomber funds Y
105. Dsapprov Saudi AWACS sale ?
106. Disapprove oil import fee N
107. Rail Deregulation #
108. Dsapp India nuc fuel sale Y
109. Mil draft registration N
110. Chrysler Loan Guarantees Y
111. Prohibit school busing N
112. Nuclear plant moratorium Y
113. Oil price controls Y
114. Tuition Tax Credits Y
115. Est Consumer Protect Agcy
116. Eliminate B-1 bomber fnds Y

Sworn in February 21, 1978 and missed vote 115.
Presidential Support Score: 1986 - 14% 1985 - 21%

BIAGGI, MARIO -- New York 19th District [Democrat]. Counties of Bronx (pt.) and Westchester (pt.). Prior Terms: House: 1969-1986. Born: October 26, 1917; New York City, N.Y. Education: New York Law School (LL.B.). Occupation: Community relations specialist, New York State Division of Housing (1961-65); assistant to the Secretary of State, New York State; New York City policeman (1942-65); attorney.

1. Immigration Reform Y
2. Open fld-search warrants N
3. Civil pnty-hire ill alien N
4. So Afr sanc-veto override Y
5. Tax Overhaul Y
6. South Africa sanctions Y
7. Death penalty-drug bill Y
8. Evidence-warrantless srch N
9. Life term-second drug off Y
10. Military use in drug war Y
11. Troop reduction in Europe N
12. Prohibit chemical weapons Y
13. Bar ASAT testing Y
14. Abide SALT II weapons ban Y
15. Follow SALT II-Soviets do N
16. Reduce SDI funding N
17. Increase SDI funding N
18. Purchase TridAnt sub Y
19. Delete 12 MX;Add conv wpn Y
20. Raise speed limit Y
21. Textile Import Quotas(*) Y
22. Req Pentagon buy US goods Y
23. AIDS ins anti-dscriminatn Y
24. Nicaraguan refugee aid N
25. Nicaraguan contra aid Y
26. US abide by SALT II N
27. Prohibit Saudi arms sale Y
28. Military Retiremnt Reform Y
29. Nicaraguan refugee aid Y
30. Ease '68 Gun Control Act N
31. Bar intrstat handgun tran Y
32. Keep '68 Gun Control Act Y
33. Nicaraguan contra aid N
34. Bar emp polygraph testing Y
35. Tax Overhaul consideratn Y
36. Bar armor-piercing ammo Y
37. Tax Overhaul consideratn Y
38. Make comp emissions known Y
39. Allow toxic victims suits Y
40. Strike Superfund "VAT" Y
41. Notify emp-plant closing #
42. Bar emp consult-plant clo ?
43. Medicare cuts;Tax incres' Y
44. Delete 12 MX missiles Y
45. Spending cuts;Tax incres' Y
46. Textile Import Quotas Y
47. Cut some school lunch fds N
48. Clean Water Act Amendmnts N

BIAGGI, MARIO (Cont.)

49. Youth work projects Y
50. Assist military in Angola N
51. Allow US troops-Nicaragua N
52. Pentagon polygraph exams Y
53. Bar ASAT testing Y
54. Suspend def pmt for abuse Y
55. Bar Pentagon-contr emplmt ?
56. Increase SDI funding N
57. Reduce SDI funding N
58. Produce chemical weapons Y
59. Bar CIA fndg in Nicaragua N
60. South Africa sanctions Y
61. Cut SS COLAs; Raise taxes N
62. Let US invest-So Africa N
63. Approve 21 MX for 1985 N
64. Emergency Farm Credit Y
65. Awards to whistle blowers Y
66. African disaster relief Y
67. Ban bank loans to So Afr Y
68. Bar coun duty-free trtmt N
69. Steel import limits Y
70. Soc Sec COLAs=inflation Y
71. Bar haz waste vctms suits N
72. Prohibit aid to Nicaragua Y
73. Cut $-Schs bar sch prayer N
74. Raise taxes; Cut Medicare Y
75. Alien residncy-prior 1982 Y
76. Alien residncy-prior 1980 N
77. Pen emp-hire illgl aliens Y
78. Lmt Persh II/cruse-Europe N
79. Delete 34 B-1 bombers Y
80. Bar purch of Pershing II N
81. Bar purchase of Sgt York ?
82. Delete $ for Trident II N
83. Allow 15 MX missiles N
84. Bar MX procurement-1985 Y
85. Equal Access Act Y
86. Aid to El Salvador N
87. Bar Nicarag water mining #
88. Physician/Medicare freeze N
89. Increase "sin" taxes Y
90. End SBA direct loans N
91. Sell Conrail ?
92. Equal Rights Amendment Y
93. Marines in Lebanon Y
94. Eminent domain-Coal comps ?
95. Prohibit EPA sanctions Y
96. SS age increase/Reforms N
97. Auto domestic content req Y
98. Delete jobs program fundg N
99. Highway-Gas tax bill Y
100. Raise Medicare;Cut defnse Y
101. Emergency housing aid Y
102. Across-the-board tax cuts Y
103. Gramm-Latta II targets N
104. Delete B-1 bomber funds Y
105. Dsapprov Saudi AWACS sale Y
106. Disapprove oil import fee N
107. Rail Deregulation N
108. Dsapp India nuc fuel sale N
109. Mil draft registration Y
110. Chrysler Loan Guarantees Y
111. Prohibit school busing N
112. Nuclear plant moratorium Y
113. Oil price controls Y
114. Tuition Tax Credits Y
115. Est Consumer Protect Agcy Y
116. Eliminate B-1 bomber fnds N
117. Subminimum wage for youth N
118. Delete crude oil tax N
119. Natural gas deregulation N

Presidential Support Score: 1986 - 26% 1985 - 38%

DioGUARDI, JOSEPH -- New York 20th District [Republican]. County of Westchester (pt.). Prior Terms: 1985-86. Occupation: Accountant; partner, Arthur Anderson & Co.

1. Immigration Reform Y
2. Open fld-search warrants N
3. Civil pnty-hire ill alien N
4. So Afr sanc-veto override Y
5. Tax Overhaul Y
6. South Africa sanctions Y
7. Death penalty-drug bill Y
8. Evidence-warrantless srch Y
9. Life term-second drug off Y
10. Military use in drug war Y
11. Troop reduction in Europe N
12. Prohibit chemical weapons N
13. Bar ASAT testing N
14. Abide SALT II weapons ban N
15. Follow SALT II-Soviets do Y
16. Reduce SDI funding N
17. Increase SDI funding N
18. Purchase Trident sub Y
19. Delete 12 MX;Add conv wpn Y
20. Raise speed limit N
21. Textile Import Quotas(*) Y
22. Req Pentagon buy US goods Y
23. AIDS ins anti-dscriminatn N
24. Nicaraguan refugee aid N
25. Nicaraguan contra aid Y
26. US abide by SALT II Y
27. Prohibit Saudi arms sale Y
28. Military Retiremnt Reform Y
29. Nicaraguan refugee aid Y
30. Ease '68 Gun Control Act N
31. Bar intrstat handgun tran Y
32. Keep '68 Gun Control Act N

DioGUARDI, JOSEPH (Cont.)

33. Nicaraguan contra aid Y
34. Bar emp polygraph testing N
35. Tax Overhaul consideratn N
36. Bar armor-piercing ammo Y
37. Tax Overhaul consideratn N
38. Make comp emissions known Y
39. Allow toxic victims suits Y
40. Strike Superfund "VAT" N
41. Notify emp-plant closing N
42. Bar emp consult-plant clo Y
43. Medicare cuts;Tax incres' N
44. Delete 12 MX missiles Y
45. Spending cuts;Tax incres' N
46. Textile Import Quotas Y
47. Cut some school lunch fds Y
48. Clean Water Act Amendmnts Y
49. Youth work projects N
50. Assist military in Angola Y
51. Allow US troops-Nicaragua Y
52. Pentagon polygraph exams Y
53. Bar ASAT testing N
54. Suspend def pmt for abuse N
55. Bar Pentagon-contr emplmt Y
56. Increase SDI funding N
57. Reduce SDI funding N
58. Produce chemical weapons Y
59. Bar CIA fndg in Nicaragua N
60. South Africa sanctions Y
61. Cut SS COLAs; Raise taxes N
62. Let US invest-So Africa N
63. Approve 21 MX for 1985 N
64. Emergency Farm Credit N
65. Awards to whistle blowers Y
66. African disaster relief Y

Presidential Support Score: 1986 - 57% 1985 - 60%

FISH, HAMILTON Jr. -- New York 21st District [Republican]. Counties of Dutchess (pt.), Orange (pt.), Putnam and Westchester (pt.). Prior Terms: House: 1969-86. Born: June 3, 1926; Washington, D.C. Education: Harvard (A.B.); New York University (LL.B.); John F. Kennedy School of Public Administration. Military Service: U.S. Naval Reserve, 1944-46. Occupation: Vice consul, Foreign Service; assistant counsel, New York State Assembly Judiciary Committee.

1. Immigration Reform Y
2. Open fld-search warrants N
3. Civil pnty-hire ill alien N
4. So Afr sanc-veto override Y
5. Tax Overhaul Y
6. South Africa sanctions Y
7. Death penalty-drug bill Y
8. Evidence-warrantless srch Y
9. Life term-second drug off Y
10. Military use in drug war N
11. Troop reduction in Europe N
12. Prohibit chemical weapons Y
13. Bar ASAT testing Y
14. Abide SALT II weapons ban Y
15. Follow SALT II-Soviets do N
16. Reduce SDI funding N
17. Increase SDI funding N
18. Purchase Trident sub N
19. Delete 12 MX;Add conv wpn N
20. Raise speed limit N
21. Textile Import Quotas(*) Y
22. Req Pentagon buy US goods Y
23. AIDS ins anti-dscriminatn N
24. Nicaraguan refugee aid N
25. Nicaraguan contra aid Y
26. US abide by SALT II N
27. Prohibit Saudi arms sale Y
28. Military Retiremnt Reform Y
29. Nicaraguan refugee aid Y
30. Ease '68 Gun Control Act Y
31. Bar intrstat handgun tran N
32. Keep '68 Gun Control Act N
33. Nicaraguan contra aid Y
34. Bar emp polygraph testing N
35. Tax Overhaul consideratn N
36. Bar armor-piercing ammo Y
37. Tax Overhaul consideratn N
38. Make comp emissions known Y
39. Allow toxic victims suits N
40. Strike Superfund "VAT" Y
41. Notify emp-plant closing Y
42. Bar emp consult-plant clo N
43. Medicare cuts;Tax incres' ?
44. Delete 12 MX missiles N
45. Spending cuts;Tax incres' Y
46. Textile Import Quotas Y
47. Cut some school lunch fds N
48. Clean Water Act Amendmnts N
49. Youth work projects N
50. Assist military in Angola Y
51. Allow US troops-Nicaragua ?
52. Pentagon polygraph exams ?
53. Bar ASAT testing #
54. Suspend def pmt for abuse ?
55. Bar Pentagon-contr emplmt ?
56. Increase SDI funding N
57. Reduce SDI funding N
58. Produce chemical weapons N
59. Bar CIA fndg in Nicaragua N
60. South Africa sanctions Y

FISH, HAMILTON Jr. (Cont.)

61. Cut SS COLAs; Raise taxes -
62. Let US invest-So Africa N
63. Approve 21 MX for 1985 Y
64. Emergency Farm Credit Y
65. Awards to whistle blowers Y
66. African disaster relief Y
67. Ban bank loans to So Afr Y
68. Bar coun duty-free trtmt ?
69. Steel import limits Y
70. Soc Sec COLAs=inflation Y
71. Bar haz waste vctms suits Y
72. Prohibit aid to Nicaragua Y
73. Cut $-Schs bar sch prayer N
74. Raise taxes; Cut Medicare Y
75. Alien residncy-prior 1982 N
76. Alien residncy-prior 1980 Y
77. Pen emp-hire illgl aliens N
78. Lmt Persh II/cruse-Europe N
79. Delete 34 B-1 bombers Y
80. Bar purch of Pershing II N
81. Bar purchase of Sgt York Y
82. Delete $ for Trident II N
83. Allow 15 MX missiles Y
84. Bar MX procurement-1985 N
85. Equal Access Act N
86. Aid to El Salvador Y
87. Bar Nicarag water mining N
88. Physician/Medicare freeze Y
89. Increase "sin" taxes Y
90. End SBA direct loans N
91. Sell Conrail N
92. Equal Rights Amendment N
93. Marines in Lebanon Y
94. Eminent domain-Coal comps Y
95. Prohibit EPA sanctions Y
96. SS age increase/Reforms Y
97. Auto domestic content req Y
98. Delete jobs program fundg Y
99. Highway-Gas tax bill Y
100. Raise Medicare;Cut defnse Y
101. Emergency housing aid Y
102. Across-the-board tax cuts Y
103. Gramm-Latta II targets Y
104. Delete B-1 bomber funds N
105. Dsapprov Saudi AWACS sale Y
106. Disapprove oil import fee Y
107. Rail Deregulation ?
108. Dsapp India nuc fuel sale Y
109. Mil draft registration N
110. Chrysler Loan Guarantees Y
111. Prohibit school busing N
112. Nuclear plant moratorium Y
113. Oil price controls N
114. Tuition Tax Credits Y
115. Est Consumer Protect Agcy N
116. Eliminate B-1 bomber fnds N
117. Subminimum wage for youth N
118. Delete crude oil tax Y
119. Natural gas deregulation Y

Presidential Support Score: 1986 - 40% 1985 - 45%

GILMAN, BENJAMIN A. -- New York 22nd District [Republican]. Counties of Orange (pt.), Rockland, Sullivan (pt.) and Westchester (pt.). Prior Terms: House: 1973-86. Born: December 6, 1922; Poughkeepsie, N.Y. Education: Wharton School of Business and Finance; University of Pennsylvania (B.S.); New York Law School (LL.B.). Military Service: U.S. Army Air Corps, WW II. Occupation: New York deputy assistant attorney general; assistant attorney general; attorney; New York representative (1967-72).

1. Immigration Reform Y
2. Open fld-search warrants N
3. Civil pnty-hire ill alien N
4. So Afr sanc-veto override Y
5. Tax Overhaul N
6. South Africa sanctions Y
7. Death penalty-drug bill Y
8. Evidence-warrantless srch Y
9. Life term-second drug off Y
10. Military use in drug war N
11. Troop reduction in Europe N
12. Prohibit chemical weapons N
13. Bar ASAT testing N
14. Abide SALT II weapons ban N
15. Follow SALT II-Soviets do Y
16. Reduce SDI funding N
17. Increase SDI funding N
18. Purchase Trident sub Y
19. Delete 12 MX;Add conv wpn N
20. Raise speed limit N
21. Textile Import Quotas(*) Y
22. Req Pentagon buy US goods Y
23. AIDS ins anti-dscriminatn N
24. Nicaraguan refugee aid N
25. Nicaraguan contra aid Y
26. US abide by SALT II Y
27. Prohibit Saudi arms sale Y
28. Military Retiremnt Reform Y
29. Nicaraguan refugee aid Y
30. Ease '68 Gun Control Act Y
31. Bar intrstat handgun tran N
32. Keep '68 Gun Control Act N
33. Nicaraguan contra aid Y
34. Bar emp polygraph testing Y

GILMAN, BENJAMIN A. (Cont.)

35. Tax Overhaul consideratn Y
36. Bar armor-piercing ammo Y
37. Tax Overhaul consideratn N
38. Make comp emissions known Y
39. Allow toxic victims suits Y
40. Strike Superfund "VAT" N
41. Notify emp-plant closing Y
42. Bar emp consult-plant clo N
43. Medicare cuts;Tax incres' Y
44. Delete 12 MX missiles N
45. Spending cuts;Tax incres' Y
46. Textile Import Quotas Y
47. Cut some school lunch fds N
48. Clean Water Act Amendmnts N
49. Youth work projects Y
50. Assist military in Angola Y
51. Allow US troops-Nicaragua Y
52. Pentagon polygraph exams Y
53. Bar ASAT testing N
54. Suspend def pmt for abuse Y
55. Bar Pentagon-contr emplmt Y
56. Increase SDI funding N
57. Reduce SDI funding N
58. Produce chemical weapons Y
59. Bar CIA fndg in Nicaragua N
60. South Africa sanctions Y
61. Cut SS COLAs; Raise taxes N
62. Let US invest-So Africa N
63. Approve 21 MX for 1985 Y
64. Emergency Farm Credit Y
65. Awards to whistle blowers Y
66. African disaster relief Y
67. Ban bank loans to So Afr Y
68. Bar coun duty-free trtmt Y
69. Steel import limits Y
70. Soc Sec COLAs=inflation Y
71. Bar haz waste vctms suits N
72. Prohibit aid to Nicaragua N
73. Cut $-Schs bar sch prayer N
74. Raise taxes; Cut Medicare N
75. Alien residncy-prior 1982 N
76. Alien residncy-prior 1980 N
77. Pen emp-hire illgl aliens N
78. Lmt Persh II/cruse-Europe N
79. Delete 34 B-1 bombers N
80. Bar purch of Pershing II N
81. Bar purchase of Sgt York N
82. Delete $ for Trident II N
83. Allow 15 MX missiles Y
84. Bar MX procurement-1985 N
85. Equal Access Act N
86. Aid to El Salvador Y
87. Bar Nicarag water mining Y
88. Physician/Medicare freeze Y
89. Increase "sin" taxes Y
90. End SBA direct loans N
91. Sell Conrail N
92. Equal Rights Amendment Y
93. Marines in Lebanon Y
94. Eminent domain-Coal comps N
95. Prohibit EPA sanctions Y
96. SS age increase/Reforms N
97. Auto domestic content req Y
98. Delete jobs program fundg Y
99. Highway-Gas tax bill N
100. Raise Medicare;Cut defnse Y
101. Emergency housing aid Y
102. Across-the-board tax cuts Y
103. Gramm-Latta II targets Y
104. Delete B-1 bomber funds N
105. Dsapprov Saudi AWACS sale Y
106. Disapprove oil import fee ?
107. Rail Deregulation -
108. Dsapp India nuc fuel sale Y
109. Mil draft registration N
110. Chrysler Loan Guarantees Y
111. Prohibit school busing N
112. Nuclear plant moratorium Y
113. Oil price controls #
114. Tuition Tax Credits Y
115. Est Consumer Protect Agcy Y
116. Eliminate B-1 bomber fnds N
117. Subminimum wage for youth N
118. Delete crude oil tax Y
119. Natural gas deregulation N

Presidential Support Score: 1986 - 43% 1985 - 44%

STRATTON, SAMUEL S. -- New York 23rd District [Democrat]. Counties of Albany, Montgomery (pt.), Rensselaer (pt.) and Schenectady. Prior Terms: House: 1959-86. Born: September 27, 1916; Yonkers, N.Y. Education: University of Rochester (A.B.); Haverford College (M.A.); Harvard University (M.A.); Hartwick College (LL.D.). Military Service: U.S. Navy, 1942, 1951-53. Occupation: Congressional Secretary (1940-42); deputy secretary general, Far Eastern Commission (1946-48); city councilman (1950-56); Schenectady mayor (1956-59); college lecturer; radio and TV news commentator.

1. Immigration Reform Y
2. Open fld-search warrants N
3. Civil pnty-hire ill alien N
4. So Afr sanc-veto override Y

STRATTON, SAMUEL S. (Cont.)

5. Tax Overhaul Y
6. South Africa sanctions +
7. Death penalty-drug bill ?
8. Evidence-warrantless srch ?
9. Life term-second drug off ?
10. Military use in drug war ?
11. Troop reduction in Europe N
12. Prohibit chemical weapons N
13. Bar ASAT testing N
14. Abide SALT II weapons ban N
15. Follow SALT II-Soviets do Y
16. Reduce SDI funding N
17. Increase SDI funding Y
18. Purchase Trident sub Y
19. Delete 12 MX;Add conv wpn N
20. Raise speed limit Y
21. Textile Import Quotas(*) Y
22. Req Pentagon buy US goods Y
23. AIDS ins anti-dscriminatn Y
24. Nicaraguan refugee aid N
25. Nicaraguan contra aid Y
26. US abide by SALT II Y
27. Prohibit Saudi arms sale Y
28. Military Retiremnt Reform Y
29. Nicaraguan refugee aid Y
30. Ease '68 Gun Control Act N
31. Bar intrstat handgun tran Y
32. Keep '68 Gun Control Act Y
33. Nicaraguan contra aid Y
34. Bar emp polygraph testing Y
35. Tax Overhaul consideratn Y
36. Bar armor-piercing ammo Y
37. Tax Overhaul consideratn Y
38. Make comp emissions known N
39. Allow toxic victims suits N
40. Strike Superfund "VAT" Y
41. Notify emp-plant closing Y
42. Bar emp consult-plant clo N
43. Medicare cuts;Tax incres' Y
44. Delete 12 MX missiles N
45. Spending cuts;Tax incres' Y
46. Textile Import Quotas Y
47. Cut some school lunch fds N
48. Clean Water Act Amendmnts Y
49. Youth work projects N
50. Assist military in Angola Y
51. Allow US troops-Nicaragua Y
52. Pentagon polygraph exams Y
53. Bar ASAT testing N
54. Suspend def pmt for abuse N
55. Bar Pentagon-contr emplmt N
56. Increase SDI funding N
57. Reduce SDI funding N
58. Produce chemical weapons Y
59. Bar CIA fndg in Nicaragua N
60. South Africa sanctions Y
61. Cut SS COLAs; Raise taxes N
62. Let US invest-So Africa N
63. Approve 21 MX for 1985 Y
64. Emergency Farm Credit Y
65. Awards to whistle blowers Y
66. African disaster relief Y
67. Ban bank loans to So Afr N
68. Bar coun duty-free trtmt N
69. Steel import limits Y
70. Soc Sec COLAs=inflation Y
71. Bar haz waste vctms suits Y
72. Prohibit aid to Nicaragua N
73. Cut $-Schs bar sch prayer Y
74. Raise taxes; Cut Medicare Y
75. Alien residncy-prior 1982 N
76. Alien residncy-prior 1980 N
77. Pen emp-hire illgl aliens Y
78. Lmt Persh II/cruse-Europe N
79. Delete 34 B-1 bombers N
80. Bar purch of Pershing II N
81. Bar purchase of Sgt York N
82. Delete $ for Trident II N
83. Allow 15 MX missiles Y
84. Bar MX procurement-1985 N
85. Equal Access Act Y
86. Aid to El Salvador Y
87. Bar Nicarag water mining N
88. Physician/Medicare freeze N
89. Increase "sin" taxes Y
90. End SBA direct loans N
91. Sell Conrail N
92. Equal Rights Amendment Y
93. Marines in Lebanon N
94. Eminent domain-Coal comps N
95. Prohibit EPA sanctions ?
96. SS age increase/Reforms Y
97. Auto domestic content req Y
98. Delete jobs program fundg N
99. Highway-Gas tax bill Y
100. Raise Medicare;Cut defnse N
101. Emergency housing aid Y
102. Across-the-board tax cuts N
103. Gramm-Latta II targets N
104. Delete B-1 bomber funds N
105. Dsapprov Saudi AWACS sale X
106. Disapprove oil import fee N
107. Rail Deregulation N
108. Dsapp India nuc fuel sale Y
109. Mil draft registration Y
110. Chrysler Loan Guarantees Y
111. Prohibit school busing N
112. Nuclear plant moratorium N
113. Oil price controls N
114. Tuition Tax Credits Y
115. Est Consumer Protect Agcy N
116. Eliminate B-1 bomber fnds N
117. Subminimum wage for youth N
118. Delete crude oil tax N
119. Natural gas deregulation N

Presidential Support Score: 1986 - 50% 1985 - 59%

SOLOMON, GERALD B. H. -- New York 24th District [Republican]. Counties of Columbia, Dutchess (pt.), Greene, Rensselaer (pt.), Saratoga, Warren and Washington. Prior Terms: House: 1979-86. Born: August 14, 1930; Okeechobee, Fla. Education: Siene College; St. Lawrence University. Military Service: U.S. Marines, 1951-52. Occupation: New York assemblyman (1972-78); founding partner, insurance and investments firm.

1. Immigration Reform -
2. Open fld-search warrants ?
3. Civil pnty-hire ill alien Y
4. So Afr sanc-veto override N
5. Tax Overhaul Y
6. South Africa sanctions N
7. Death penalty-drug bill Y
8. Evidence-warrantless srch Y
9. Life term-second drug off Y
10. Military use in drug war Y
11. Troop reduction in Europe N
12. Prohibit chemical weapons N
13. Bar ASAT testing N
14. Abide SALT II weapons ban N
15. Follow SALT II-Soviets do Y
16. Reduce SDI funding N
17. Increase SDI funding Y
18. Purchase Trident sub Y
19. Delete 12 MX;Add conv wpn N
20. Raise speed limit Y
21. Textile Import Quotas(*) Y
22. Req Pentagon buy US goods Y
23. AIDS ins anti-dscriminatn N
24. Nicaraguan refugee aid N
25. Nicaraguan contra aid Y
26. US abide by SALT II Y
27. Prohibit Saudi arms sale N
28. Military Retiremnt Reform Y
29. Nicaraguan refugee aid Y
30. Ease '68 Gun Control Act Y
31. Bar intrstat handgun tran N
32. Keep '68 Gun Control Act N
33. Nicaraguan contra aid Y
34. Bar emp polygraph testing N
35. Tax Overhaul consideratn N
36. Bar armor-piercing ammo Y
37. Tax Overhaul consideratn N
38. Make comp emissions known N
39. Allow toxic victims suits N
40. Strike Superfund "VAT" Y
41. Notify emp-plant closing N
42. Bar emp consult-plant clo Y
43. Medicare cuts;Tax incres' N
44. Delete 12 MX missiles N
45. Spending cuts;Tax incres' N
46. Textile Import Quotas ?
47. Cut some school lunch fds Y
48. Clean Water Act Amendmnts Y
49. Youth work projects N
50. Assist military in Angola Y
51. Allow US troops-Nicaragua Y
52. Pentagon polygraph exams Y
53. Bar ASAT testing N
54. Suspend def pmt for abuse N
55. Bar Pentagon-contr emplmt Y
56. Increase SDI funding Y
57. Reduce SDI funding N
58. Produce chemical weapons Y
59. Bar CIA fndg in Nicaragua N
60. South Africa sanctions N
61. Cut SS COLAs; Raise taxes N
62. Let US invest-So Africa Y
63. Approve 21 MX for 1985 Y
64. Emergency Farm Credit N
65. Awards to whistle blowers Y
66. African disaster relief Y
67. Ban bank loans to So Afr N
68. Bar coun duty-free trtmt Y
69. Steel import limits Y
70. Soc Sec COLAs=inflation Y
71. Bar haz waste vctms suits Y
72. Prohibit aid to Nicaragua N
73. Cut $-Schs bar sch prayer Y
74. Raise taxes; Cut Medicare N
75. Alien residncy-prior 1982 N
76. Alien residncy-prior 1980 Y
77. Pen emp-hire illgl aliens N
78. Lmt Persh II/cruse-Europe N
79. Delete 34 B-1 bombers N
80. Bar purch of Pershing II N
81. Bar purchase of Sgt York N
82. Delete $ for Trident II N
83. Allow 15 MX missiles Y
84. Bar MX procurement-1985 N
85. Equal Access Act Y
86. Aid to El Salvador Y
87. Bar Nicarag water mining N
88. Physician/Medicare freeze Y
89. Increase "sin" taxes N
90. End SBA direct loans ?
91. Sell Conrail Y
92. Equal Rights Amendment N
93. Marines in Lebanon Y
94. Eminent domain-Coal comps N
95. Prohibit EPA sanctions N
96. SS age increase/Reforms Y
97. Auto domestic content req Y
98. Delete jobs program fundg Y
99. Highway-Gas tax bill N
100. Raise Medicare;Cut defnse N
101. Emergency housing aid Y
102. Across-the-board tax cuts Y
103. Gramm-Latta II targets Y
104. Delete B-1 bomber funds N

SOLOMON, GERALD B. H. (Cont.)

105. Dsapprov Saudi AWACS sale N
106. Disapprove oil import fee Y
107. Rail Deregulation N
108. Dsapp India nuc fuel sale Y
109. Mil draft registration Y
110. Chrysler Loan Guarantees N
111. Prohibit school busing Y
112. Nuclear plant moratorium N
113. Oil price controls N

Presidential Support Score: 1986 - 80% 1985 - 70%

BOEHLERT, SHERWOOD L. -- New York 25th District [Republican]. Counties of Chenango, Cortland, Delaware (pt.), Madison (pt.), Montgomery (pt.), Oneida (pt.), Otsego, Schoharie and Tompkins (pt.). Prior Terms: House: 1983-86. Born: September 28, 1936; Utica, N.Y. Education: Utica College (A.B.). Military Service: U.S. Army, 1956-58. Occupation: Chief of Staff (1964-79); Oneida county executive (1979); Board of Directors, Utica College Foundation.

1. Immigration Reform Y
2. Open fld-search warrants N
3. Civil pnty-hire ill alien N
4. So Afr sanc-veto override Y
5. Tax Overhaul Y
6. South Africa sanctions Y
7. Death penalty-drug bill Y
8. Evidence-warrantless srch Y
9. Life term-second drug off Y
10. Military use in drug war Y
11. Troop reduction in Europe N
12. Prohibit chemical weapons N
13. Bar ASAT testing Y
14. Abide SALT II weapons ban Y
15. Follow SALT II-Soviets do N
16. Reduce SDI funding N
17. Increase SDI funding N
18. Purchase Trident sub N
19. Delete 12 MX;Add conv wpn Y
20. Raise speed limit N
21. Textile Import Quotas(*) Y
22. Req Pentagon buy US goods Y
23. AIDS ins anti-dscriminatn N
24. Nicaraguan refugee aid Y
25. Nicaraguan contra aid N
26. US abide by SALT II N
27. Prohibit Saudi arms sale Y
28. Military Retiremnt Reform Y
29. Nicaraguan refugee aid Y
30. Ease '68 Gun Control Act Y
31. Bar intrstat handgun tran N
32. Keep '68 Gun Control Act N
33. Nicaraguan contra aid N
34. Bar emp polygraph testing Y
35. Tax Overhaul consideratn N
36. Bar armor-piercing ammo Y
37. Tax Overhaul consideratn N
38. Make comp emissions known Y
39. Allow toxic victims suits Y
40. Strike Superfund "VAT" Y
41. Notify emp-plant closing Y
42. Bar emp consult-plant clo Y
43. Medicare cuts;Tax incres' Y
44. Delete 12 MX missiles Y
45. Spending cuts;Tax incres' N
46. Textile Import Quotas Y
47. Cut some school lunch fds N
48. Clean Water Act Amendmnts N
49. Youth work projects Y
50. Assist military in Angola Y
51. Allow US troops-Nicaragua N
52. Pentagon polygraph exams Y
53. Bar ASAT testing Y
54. Suspend def pmt for abuse N
55. Bar Pentagon-contr emplmt Y
56. Increase SDI funding Y
57. Reduce SDI funding N
58. Produce chemical weapons Y
59. Bar CIA fndg in Nicaragua N
60. South Africa sanctions Y
61. Cut SS COLAs; Raise taxes N
62. Let US invest-So Africa N
63. Approve 21 MX for 1985 Y
64. Emergency Farm Credit Y
65. Awards to whistle blowers ?
66. African disaster relief ?
67. Ban bank loans to So Afr Y
68. Bar coun duty-free trtmt N
69. Steel import limits Y
70. Soc Sec COLAs=inflation Y
71. Bar haz waste vctms suits N
72. Prohibit aid to Nicaragua Y
73. Cut $-Schs bar sch prayer N
74. Raise taxes; Cut Medicare Y
75. Alien residncy-prior 1982 Y
76. Alien residncy-prior 1980 Y
77. Pen emp-hire illgl aliens N
78. Lmt Persh II/cruse-Europe N
79. Delete 34 B-1 bombers N
80. Bar purch of Pershing II N
81. Bar purchase of Sgt York Y
82. Delete $ for Trident II N
83. Allow 15 MX missiles Y
84. Bar MX procurement-1985 N

BOEHLERT, SHERWOOD L. (Cont.)

85. Equal Access Act Y
86. Aid to El Salvador Y
87. Bar Nicarag water mining Y
88. Physician/Medicare freeze Y
89. Increase "sin" taxes Y
90. End SBA direct loans N
91. Sell Conrail Y
92. Equal Rights Amendment Y
93. Marines in Lebanon Y
94. Eminent domain-Coal comps N
95. Prohibit EPA sanctions N
96. SS age increase/Reforms Y

Presidential Support Score: 1986 - 45% 1985 - 41%

MARTIN, DAVID O'B. -- New York 26th District [Republican]. Counties of Clinton, Essex, Franklin, Fulton, Hamilton, Herkimer, Jefferson, Lewis and St. Lawrence. Prior Terms: House: 1981-86. Born: April 26, 1944; Ogdensburg, N.Y. Education: University of Notre Dame (B.B.A.); Albany Law School. Military Service: U.S. Marine Corps. Occupation: County legislator (1973, 1975); New York state assemblyman (1976, 1978).

1. Immigration Reform N
2. Open fld-search warrants N
3. Civil pnty-hire ill alien Y
4. So Afr sanc-veto override ?
5. Tax Overhaul N
6. South Africa sanctions Y
7. Death penalty-drug bill Y
8. Evidence-warrantless srch Y
9. Life term-second drug off Y
10. Military use in drug war Y
11. Troop reduction in Europe N
12. Prohibit chemical weapons N
13. Bar ASAT testing N
14. Abide SALT II weapons ban N
15. Follow SALT II-Soviets do Y
16. Reduce SDI funding N
17. Increase SDI funding N
18. Purchase Trident sub N
19. Delete 12 MX;Add conv wpn N
20. Raise speed limit Y
21. Textile Import Quotas(*) Y
22. Req Pentagon buy US goods N
23. AIDS ins anti-dscriminatn N
24. Nicaraguan refugee aid N
25. Nicaraguan contra aid Y
26. US abide by SALT II #
27. Prohibit Saudi arms sale Y
28. Military Retiremnt Reform Y
29. Nicaraguan refugee aid Y
30. Ease '68 Gun Control Act Y
31. Bar intrstat handgun tran ?
32. Keep '68 Gun Control Act N
33. Nicaraguan contra aid Y
34. Bar emp polygraph testing N
35. Tax Overhaul consideratn N
36. Bar armor-piercing ammo Y
37. Tax Overhaul consideratn N
38. Make comp emissions known N
39. Allow toxic victims suits N
40. Strike Superfund "VAT" Y
41. Notify emp-plant closing N
42. Bar emp consult-plant clo ?
43. Medicare cuts;Tax incres' N
44. Delete 12 MX missiles N
45. Spending cuts;Tax incres' N
46. Textile Import Quotas Y
47. Cut some school lunch fds N
48. Clean Water Act Amendmnts Y
49. Youth work projects N
50. Assist military in Angola Y
51. Allow US troops-Nicaragua Y
52. Pentagon polygraph exams Y
53. Bar ASAT testing N
54. Suspend def pmt for abuse N
55. Bar Pentagon-contr emplmt Y
56. Increase SDI funding N
57. Reduce SDI funding N
58. Produce chemical weapons Y
59. Bar CIA fndg in Nicaragua N
60. South Africa sanctions Y
61. Cut SS COLAs; Raise taxes N
62. Let US invest-So Africa Y
63. Approve 21 MX for 1985 Y
64. Emergency Farm Credit Y
65. Awards to whistle blowers Y
66. African disaster relief Y
67. Ban bank loans to So Afr Y
68. Bar coun duty-free trtmt N
69. Steel import limits N
70. Soc Sec COLAs=inflation Y
71. Bar haz waste vctms suits Y
72. Prohibit aid to Nicaragua Y
73. Cut $-Schs bar sch prayer Y
74. Raise taxes; Cut Medicare Y
75. Alien residncy-prior 1982 N
76. Alien residncy-prior 1980 Y
77. Pen emp-hire illgl aliens N
78. Lmt Persh II/cruse-Europe N
79. Delete 34 B-1 bombers N
80. Bar purch of Pershing II N
81. Bar purchase of Sgt York N
82. Delete $ for Trident II N
83. Allow 15 MX missiles Y
84. Bar MX procurement-1985 N

MARTIN, DAVID O'B. (Cont.)

85. Equal Access Act Y
86. Aid to El Salvador Y
87. Bar Nicarag water mining N
88. Physician/Medicare freeze Y
89. Increase "sin" taxes Y
90. End SBA direct loans N
91. Sell Conrail Y
92. Equal Rights Amendment N
93. Marines in Lebanon Y
94. Eminent domain-Coal comps Y
95. Prohibit EPA sanctions N
96. SS age increase/Reforms Y
97. Auto domestic content req N
98. Delete jobs program fundg Y
99. Highway-Gas tax bill N
100. Raise Medicare;Cut defnse N
101. Emergency housing aid Y
102. Across-the-board tax cuts Y
103. Gramm-Latta II targets Y
104. Delete B-1 bomber funds ?
105. Dsapprov Saudi AWACS sale N

Presidential Support Score: 1986 - 52% 1985 - 59%

WORTLEY, GEORGE C. -- New York 27th District [Republican]. Counties of Madison (pt.) and Onondaga. Prior Terms: House: 1981-86. Born: December 8, 1926; Syracuse, N.Y. Education: Syracuse University (B.S.). Military Service: U.S. Navy, 1945-46. Occupation: Newspaper publisher.

1. Immigration Reform Y
2. Open fld-search warrants N
3. Civil pnty-hire ill alien N
4. So Afr sanc-veto override Y
5. Tax Overhaul Y
6. South Africa sanctions Y
7. Death penalty-drug bill +
8. Evidence-warrantless srch Y
9. Life term-second drug off Y
10. Military use in drug war Y
11. Troop reduction in Europe N
12. Prohibit chemical weapons Y
13. Bar ASAT testing N
14. Abide SALT II weapons ban N
15. Follow SALT II-Soviets do Y
16. Reduce SDI funding N
17. Increase SDI funding N
18. Purchase Trident sub N
19. Delete 12 MX;Add conv wpn N
20. Raise speed limit N
21. Textile Import Quotas(*) N
22. Req Pentagon buy US goods Y
23. AIDS ins anti-dscriminatn N
24. Nicaraguan refugee aid N
25. Nicaraguan contra aid Y
26. US abide by SALT II Y
27. Prohibit Saudi arms sale Y
28. Military Retiremnt Reform Y
29. Nicaraguan refugee aid Y
30. Ease '68 Gun Control Act Y
31. Bar intrstat handgun tran N
32. Keep '68 Gun Control Act N
33. Nicaraguan contra aid Y
34. Bar emp polygraph testing N
35. Tax Overhaul consideratn N
36. Bar armor-piercing ammo Y
37. Tax Overhaul consideratn N
38. Make comp emissions known N
39. Allow toxic victims suits N
40. Strike Superfund "VAT" Y
41. Notify emp-plant closing N
42. Bar emp consult-plant clo Y
43. Medicare cuts;Tax incres' N
44. Delete 12 MX missiles N
45. Spending cuts;Tax incres' N
46. Textile Import Quotas N
47. Cut some school lunch fds N
48. Clean Water Act Amendmnts Y
49. Youth work projects N
50. Assist military in Angola Y
51. Allow US troops-Nicaragua Y
52. Pentagon polygraph exams ?
53. Bar ASAT testing X
54. Suspend def pmt for abuse ?
55. Bar Pentagon-contr emplmt ?
56. Increase SDI funding Y
57. Reduce SDI funding N
58. Produce chemical weapons N
59. Bar CIA fndg in Nicaragua N
60. South Africa sanctions Y
61. Cut SS COLAs; Raise taxes N
62. Let US invest-So Africa Y
63. Approve 21 MX for 1985 Y
64. Emergency Farm Credit Y
65. Awards to whistle blowers Y
66. African disaster relief Y
67. Ban bank loans to So Afr N
68. Bar coun duty-free trtmt N
69. Steel import limits N
70. Soc Sec COLAs=inflation Y
71. Bar haz waste vctms suits Y
72. Prohibit aid to Nicaragua Y
73. Cut $-Schs bar sch prayer Y
74. Raise taxes; Cut Medicare Y
75. Alien residncy-prior 1982 N
76. Alien residncy-prior 1980 Y
77. Pen emp-hire illgl aliens N
78. Lmt Persh II/cruse-Europe N

WORTLEY, GEORGE C. Cont.)

79. Delete 34 B-1 bombers N
80. Bar purch of Pershing II N
81. Bar purchase of Sgt York N
82. Delete $ for Trident II N
83. Allow 15 MX missiles Y
84. Bar MX procurement-1985 N
85. Equal Access Act Y
86. Aid to El Salvador Y
87. Bar Nicarag water mining N
88. Physician/Medicare freeze Y
89. Increase "sin" taxes Y
90. End SBA direct loans N
91. Sell Conrail Y
92. Equal Rights Amendment Y
93. Marines in Lebanon Y
94. Eminent domain-Coal comps Y
95. Prohibit EPA sanctions Y
96. SS age increase/Reforms Y
97. Auto domestic content req Y
98. Delete jobs program fundg Y
99. Highway-Gas tax bill Y
100. Raise Medicare;Cut defnse N
101. Emergency housing aid Y
102. Across-the-board tax cuts Y
103. Gramm-Latta II targets Y
104. Delete B-1 bomber funds N
105. Dsapprov Saudi AWACS sale Y

Presidential Support Score: 1986 - 64% 1985 - 65%

McHUGH, MATTHEW F. -- New York 28th District [Democrat]. Counties of Broome, Delaware, (pt.), Sullivan (pt.), Tioga, Tompkins (pt.) and Ulster. Prior Terms: House: 1975-86. Born: December 6, 1938; Phildaelphia, Pa. Education: Mount St. Mary's College (B.A.); Villanova Law School (J.D.). Occupation: Attorney; district attorney (1969-72); vice president, Chamber of Commerce.

1. Immigration Reform Y
2. Open fld-search warrants N
3. Civil pnty-hire ill alien N
4. So Afr sanc-veto override Y
5. Tax Overhaul Y
6. South Africa sanctions Y
7. Death penalty-drug bill N
8. Evidence-warrantless srch N
9. Life term-second drug off N
10. Military use in drug war Y
11. Troop reduction in Europe N
12. Prohibit chemical weapons Y
13. Bar ASAT testing Y
14. Abide SALT II weapons ban Y
15. Follow SALT II-Soviets do N
16. Reduce SDI funding N
17. Increase SDI funding N
18. Purchase Trident sub Y
19. Delete 12 MX;Add conv wpn Y
20. Raise speed limit N
21. Textile Import Quotas(*) N
22. Req Pentagon buy US goods N
23. AIDS ins anti-dscriminatn Y
24. Nicaraguan refugee aid Y
25. Nicaraguan contra aid N
26. US abide by SALT II N
27. Prohibit Saudi arms sale Y
28. Military Retiremnt Reform Y
29. Nicaraguan refugee aid Y
30. Ease '68 Gun Control Act N
31. Bar intrstat handgun tran Y
32. Keep '68 Gun Control Act Y
33. Nicaraguan contra aid N
34. Bar emp polygraph testing Y
35. Tax Overhaul consideratn Y
36. Bar armor-piercing ammo Y
37. Tax Overhaul consideratn Y
38. Make comp emissions known Y
39. Allow toxic victims suits Y
40. Strike Superfund "VAT" Y
41. Notify emp-plant closing Y
42. Bar emp consult-plant clo N
43. Medicare cuts;Tax incres' Y
44. Delete 12 MX missiles Y
45. Spending cuts;Tax incres' Y
46. Textile Import Quotas N
47. Cut some school lunch fds N
48. Clean Water Act Amendmnts N
49. Youth work projects Y
50. Assist military in Angola N
51. Allow US troops-Nicaragua N
52. Pentagon polygraph exams Y
53. Bar ASAT testing Y
54. Suspend def pmt for abuse -
55. Bar Pentagon-contr emplmt +
56. Increase SDI funding N
57. Reduce SDI funding N
58. Produce chemical weapons N
59. Bar CIA fndg in Nicaragua Y
60. South Africa sanctions Y
61. Cut SS COLAs; Raise taxes N
62. Let US invest-So Africa N
63. Approve 21 MX for 1985 N
64. Emergency Farm Credit Y
65. Awards to whistle blowers Y
66. African disaster relief Y
67. Ban bank loans to So Afr Y
68. Bar coun duty-free trtmt N
69. Steel import limits N
70. Soc Sec COLAs=inflation Y

McHUGH, MATTHEW F. (Cont)

71. Bar haz waste vctms suits N
72. Prohibit aid to Nicaragua Y
73. Cut $-Schs bar sch prayer N
74. Raise taxes; Cut Medicare Y
75. Alien residncy-prior 1982 N
76. Alien residncy-prior 1980 N
77. Pen emp-hire illgl aliens N
78. Lmt Persh II/cruse-Europe N
79. Delete 34 B-1 bombers Y
80. Bar purch of Pershing II N
81. Bar purchase of Sgt York Y
82. Delete $ for Trident II Y
83. Allow 15 MX missiles N
84. Bar MX procurement-1985 Y
85. Equal Access Act N
86. Aid to El Salvador N
87. Bar Nicarag water mining Y
88. Physician/Medicare freeze N
89. Increase "sin" taxes Y
90. End SBA direct loans N
91. Sell Conrail N
92. Equal Rights Amendment Y
93. Marines in Lebanon N
94. Eminent domain-Coal comps N
95. Prohibit EPA sanctions Y
96. SS age increase/Reforms N
97. Auto domestic content req N
98. Delete jobs program fundg N
99. Highway-Gas tax bill Y
100. Raise Medicare;Cut defnse Y
101. Emergency housing aid Y
102. Across-the-board tax cuts N
103. Gramm-Latta II targets N
104. Delete B-1 bomber funds Y
105. Dsapprov Saudi AWACS sale Y
106. Disapprove oil import fee Y
107. Rail Deregulation N
108. Dsapp India nuc fuel sale Y
109. Mil draft registration N
110. Chrysler Loan Guarantees Y
111. Prohibit school busing N
112. Nuclear plant moratorium Y
113. Oil price controls Y
114. Tuition Tax Credits N
115. Est Consumer Protect Agcy Y
116. Eliminate B-1 bomber fnds Y
117. Subminimum wage for youth N
118. Delete crude oil tax N
119. Natural gas deregulation N

Presidential Support Score: 1986 - 23% 1985 - 25%

HORTON, FRANK -- New York 29th District [Republican]. Counties of Cayuga, Monroe (pt.), Oneida (pt.), Oswego, Seneca and Wayne. Prior Terms: House: 1963-86. Born: December 12, 1919; Cuero, Tex. Education: Louisiana State University (B.A.); Cornell Law School (LL.B.). Military Service: U.S. Army, 1941-45. Occupation: Attorney; Rochester city councilman (1955-61).

1. Immigration Reform N
2. Open fld-search warrants Y
3. Civil pnty-hire ill alien Y
4. So Afr sanc-veto override Y
5. Tax Overhaul N
6. South Africa sanctions Y
7. Death penalty-drug bill Y
8. Evidence-warrantless srch N
9. Life term-second drug off Y
10. Military use in drug war N
11. Troop reduction in Europe N
12. Prohibit chemical weapons Y
13. Bar ASAT testing Y
14. Abide SALT II weapons ban Y
15. Follow SALT II-Soviets do N
16. Reduce SDI funding N
17. Increase SDI funding N
18. Purchase Trident sub ?
19. Delete 12 MX;Add conv wpn ?
20. Raise speed limit Y
21. Textile Import Quotas(*) Y
22. Req Pentagon buy US goods Y
23. AIDS ins anti-dscriminatn Y
24. Nicaraguan refugee aid N
25. Nicaraguan contra aid N
26. US abide by SALT II #
27. Prohibit Saudi arms sale Y
28. Military Retiremnt Reform Y
29. Nicaraguan refugee aid Y
30. Ease '68 Gun Control Act Y
31. Bar intrstat handgun tran N
32. Keep '68 Gun Control Act N
33. Nicaraguan contra aid N
34. Bar emp polygraph testing Y
35. Tax Overhaul consideratn N
36. Bar armor-piercing ammo Y
37. Tax Overhaul consideratn N
38. Make comp emissions known Y
39. Allow toxic victims suits Y
40. Strike Superfund "VAT" Y
41. Notify emp-plant closing #
42. Bar emp consult-plant clo N
43. Medicare cuts;Tax incres' Y
44. Delete 12 MX missiles Y
45. Spending cuts;Tax incres' Y
46. Textile Import Quotas Y
47. Cut some school lunch fds N
48. Clean Water Act Amendmnts N

HORTON, FRANK (Cont.)

49. Youth work projects #
50. Assist military in Angola N
51. Allow US troops-Nicaragua N
52. Pentagon polygraph exams Y
53. Bar ASAT testing Y
54. Suspend def pmt for abuse N
55. Bar Pentagon-contr emplmt Y
56. Increase SDI funding N
57. Reduce SDI funding N
58. Produce chemical weapons N
59. Bar CIA fndg in Nicaragua N
60. South Africa sanctions Y
61. Cut SS COLAs; Raise taxes N
62. Let US invest-So Africa N
63. Approve 21 MX for 1985 Y
64. Emergency Farm Credit Y
65. Awards to whistle blowers Y
66. African disaster relief Y
67. Ban bank loans to So Afr ?
68. Bar coun duty-free trtmt N
69. Steel import limits Y
70. Soc Sec COLAs=inflation Y
71. Bar haz waste vctms suits N
72. Prohibit aid to Nicaragua Y
73. Cut $-Schs bar sch prayer N
74. Raise taxes; Cut Medicare Y
75. Alien residncy-prior 1982 Y
76. Alien residncy-prior 1980 Y
77. Pen emp-hire illgl aliens Y
78. Lmt Persh II/cruse-Europe N
79. Delete 34 B-1 bombers Y
80. Bar purch of Pershing II N
81. Bar purchase of Sgt York N
82. Delete $ for Trident II N
83. Allow 15 MX missiles Y
84. Bar MX procurement-1985 N
85. Equal Access Act Y
86. Aid to El Salvador Y
87. Bar Nicarag water mining Y
88. Physician/Medicare freeze Y
89. Increase "sin" taxes Y
90. End SBA direct loans N
91. Sell Conrail N
92. Equal Rights Amendment Y
93. Marines in Lebanon N
94. Eminent domain-Coal comps N
95. Prohibit EPA sanctions Y
96. SS age increase/Reforms Y
97. Auto domestic content req Y
98. Delete jobs program fundg Y
99. Highway-Gas tax bill N
100. Raise Medicare;Cut defnse Y
101. Emergency housing aid Y
102. Across-the-board tax cuts Y
103. Gramm-Latta II targets Y
104. Delete B-1 bomber funds Y
105. Dsapprov Saudi AWACS sale Y
106. Disapprove oil import fee Y
107. Rail Deregulation N
108. Dsapp India nuc fuel sale Y
109. Mil draft registration N
110. Chrysler Loan Guarantees Y
111. Prohibit school busing N
112. Nuclear plant moratorium N
113. Oil price controls N
114. Tuition Tax Credits Y
115. Est Consumer Protect Agcy Y
116. Eliminate B-1 bomber fnds Y
117. Subminimum wage for youth N
118. Delete crude oil tax Y
119. Natural gas deregulation Y

Presidential Support Score: 1986 - 27% 1985 - 31%

ECKERT, FRED -- New York 30th District [Republican]. Counties of Genesse, Livingston (pt.), Monroe (pt.) and Ontario (pt.). Prior Terms: 1985-86. Education: North Texas State University. Occupation: Ambassador to Fiji; New York senator; town supervisor; president, advertising agency.

1. Immigration Reform N
2. Open fld-search warrants N
3. Civil pnty-hire ill alien N
4. So Afr sanc-veto override N
5. Tax Overhaul Y
6. South Africa sanctions N
7. Death penalty-drug bill Y
8. Evidence-warrantless srch N
9. Life term-second drug off Y
10. Military use in drug war N
11. Troop reduction in Europe Y
12. Prohibit chemical weapons N
13. Bar ASAT testing N
14. Abide SALT II weapons ban N
15. Follow SALT II-Soviets do Y
16. Reduce SDI funding N
17. Increase SDI funding Y
18. Purchase Trident sub N
19. Delete 12 MX;Add conv wpn N
20. Raise speed limit Y
21. Textile Import Quotas(*) N
22. Req Pentagon buy US goods N
23. AIDS ins anti-dscriminatn N
24. Nicaraguan refugee aid N
25. Nicaraguan contra aid Y
26. US abide by SALT II Y
27. Prohibit Saudi arms sale Y
28. Military Retiremnt Reform Y

ECKERT, FRED (Cont.)

29.	Nicaraguan refugee aid	?	48.	Clean Water Act Amendmnts	Y
30.	Ease '68 Gun Control Act	Y	49.	Youth work projects	N
31.	Bar intrstat handgun tran	N	50.	Assist military in Angola	Y
32.	Keep '68 Gun Control Act	N	51.	Allow US troops-Nicaragua	Y
33.	Nicaraguan contra aid	Y	52.	Pentagon polygraph exams	Y
34.	Bar emp polygraph testing	N	53.	Bar ASAT testing	N
35.	Tax Overhaul consideratn	Y	54.	Suspend def pmt for abuse	N
36.	Bar armor-piercing ammo	Y	55.	Bar Pentagon-contr emplmt	N
37.	Tax Overhaul consideratn	N	56.	Increase SDI funding	Y
38.	Make comp emissions known	N	57.	Reduce SDI funding	N
39.	Allow toxic victims suits	N	58.	Produce chemical weapons	Y
40.	Strike Superfund "VAT"	N	59.	Bar CIA fndg in Nicaragua	N
41.	Notify emp-plant closing	N	60.	South Africa sanctions	N
42.	Bar emp consult-plant clo	Y	61.	Cut SS COLAs; Raise taxes	N
43.	Medicare cuts;Tax incres'	N	62.	Let US invest-So Africa	Y
44.	Delete 12 MX missiles	N	63.	Approve 21 MX for 1985	Y
45.	Spending cuts;Tax incres'	N	64.	Emergency Farm Credit	N
46.	Textile Import Quotas	N	65.	Awards to whistle blowers	Y
47.	Cut some school lunch fds	Y	66.	African disaster relief	Y

Presidential Support Score: 1986 - 81% 1985 - 94%

KEMP, JACK F. -- New York 31st District [Republican]. Counties of Cattaraugus (pt.), Erie (pt.), Livingston (pt.), Ontario (pt.) and Wyoming. Prior Terms: House: 1971-86. Born: July 13, 1935; Los Angeles, Calif. Education: Occidental College (B.A.). Military Service: U.S. Army Reserve, 1958-62. Occupation: Professional football player; public relations officer, Marine Midland Bank.

1.	Immigration Reform	N	30.	Ease '68 Gun Control Act	Y
2.	Open fld-search warrants	Y	31.	Bar intrstat handgun tran	N
3.	Civil pnty-hire ill alien	Y	32.	Keep '68 Gun Control Act	N
4.	So Afr sanc-veto override	N	33.	Nicaraguan contra aid	Y
5.	Tax Overhaul	Y	34.	Bar emp polygraph testing	Y
6.	South Africa sanctions	N	35.	Tax Overhaul consideratn	Y
7.	Death penalty-drug bill	Y	36.	Bar armor-piercing ammo	Y
8.	Evidence-warrantless srch	Y	37.	Tax Overhaul consideratn	N
9.	Life term-second drug off	Y	38.	Make comp emissions known	N
10.	Military use in drug war	Y	39.	Allow toxic victims suits	N
11.	Troop reduction in Europe	N	40.	Strike Superfund "VAT"	N
12.	Prohibit chemical weapons	N	41.	Notify emp-plant closing	N
13.	Bar ASAT testing	N	42.	Bar emp consult-plant clo	Y
14.	Abide SALT II weapons ban	N	43.	Medicare cuts;Tax incres'	N
15.	Follow SALT II-Soviets do	Y	44.	Delete 12 MX missiles	N
16.	Reduce SDI funding	N	45.	Spending cuts;Tax incres'	N
17.	Increase SDI funding	Y	46.	Textile Import Quotas	N
18.	Purchase Trident sub	N	47.	Cut some school lunch fds	Y
19.	Delete 12 MX;Add conv wpn	N	48.	Clean Water Act Amendmnts	Y
20.	Raise speed limit	Y	49.	Youth work projects	N
21.	Textile Import Quotas(*)	N	50.	Assist military in Angola	Y
22.	Req Pentagon buy US goods	N	51.	Allow US troops-Nicaragua	Y
23.	AIDS ins anti-dscriminatn	N	52.	Pentagon polygraph exams	Y
24.	Nicaraguan refugee aid	N	53.	Bar ASAT testing	N
25.	Nicaraguan contra aid	Y	54.	Suspend def pmt for abuse	N
26.	US abide by SALT II	Y	55.	Bar Pentagon-contr emplmt	Y
27.	Prohibit Saudi arms sale	Y	56.	Increase SDI funding	Y
28.	Military Retiremnt Reform	Y	57.	Reduce SDI funding	N
29.	Nicaraguan refugee aid	Y	58.	Produce chemical weapons	Y

KEMP, JACK F. (Cont.)

59. Bar CIA fndg in Nicaragua N
60. South Africa sanctions N
61. Cut SS COLAs; Raise taxes N
62. Let US invest-So Africa Y
63. Approve 21 MX for 1985 Y
64. Emergency Farm Credit N
65. Awards to whistle blowers Y
66. African disaster relief Y
67. Ban bank loans to So Afr Y
68. Bar coun duty-free trtmt N
69. Steel import limits N
70. Soc Sec COLAs=inflation Y
71. Bar haz waste vctms suits Y
72. Prohibit aid to Nicaragua N
73. Cut $-Schs bar sch prayer Y
74. Raise taxes; Cut Medicare N
75. Alien residncy-prior 1982 Y
76. Alien residncy-prior 1980 N
77. Pen emp-hire illgl aliens N
78. Lmt Persh II/cruse-Europe N
79. Delete 34 B-1 bombers ?
80. Bar purch of Pershing II N
81. Bar purchase of Sgt York N
82. Delete $ for Trident II N
83. Allow 15 MX missiles Y
84. Bar MX procurement-1985 N
85. Equal Access Act Y
86. Aid to El Salvador Y
87. Bar Nicarag water mining N
88. Physician/Medicare freeze Y
89. Increase "sin" taxes N
90. End SBA direct loans Y
91. Sell Conrail Y
92. Equal Rights Amendment N
93. Marines in Lebanon Y
94. Eminent domain-Coal comps N
95. Prohibit EPA sanctions Y
96. SS age increase/Reforms Y
97. Auto domestic content req N
98. Delete jobs program fundg Y
99. Highway-Gas tax bill N
100. Raise Medicare;Cut defnse N
101. Emergency housing aid N
102. Across-the-board tax cuts Y
103. Gramm-Latta II targets Y
104. Delete B-1 bomber funds N
105. Dsapprov Saudi AWACS sale Y
106. Disapprove oil import fee Y
107. Rail Deregulation N
108. Dsapp India nuc fuel sale Y
109. Mil draft registration Y
110. Chrysler Loan Guarantees N
111. Prohibit school busing Y
112. Nuclear plant moratorium N
113. Oil price controls ?
114. Tuition Tax Credits Y
115. Est Consumer Protect Agcy N
116. Eliminate B-1 bomber fnds N
117. Subminimum wage for youth Y
118. Delete crude oil tax Y
119. Natural gas deregulation Y

Presidential Support Score: 1986 - 70% 1985 -- 79%

LaFALCE, JOHN J. -- New York 32nd District [Democrat]. Counties of Erie (pt.), Monroe (pt.), Niagara and Orleans. Prior Terms: House: 1975-86. Born: October 6, 1939; Buffalo, N.Y. Education: Canisuis College (B.S.); Villanova Law School (J.D.). Military Service: U.S. Army, 1965-67. Occupation: New York senator (1971-72); New York assemblyman (1973-74).

1. Immigration Reform Y
2. Open fld-search warrants N
3. Civil pnty-hire ill alien N
4. So Afr sanc-veto override Y
5. Tax Overhaul Y
6. South Africa sanctions Y
7. Death penalty-drug bill N
8. Evidence-warrantless srch N
9. Life term-second drug off N
10. Military use in drug war Y
11. Troop reduction in Europe N
12. Prohibit chemical weapons Y
13. Bar ASAT testing ?
14. Abide SALT II weapons ban Y
15. Follow SALT II-Soviets do N
16. Reduce SDI funding Y
17. Increase SDI funding N
18. Purchase Trident sub #
19. Delete 12 MX;Add conv wpn #
20. Raise speed limit N
21. Textile Import Quotas(*) N
22. Req Pentagon buy US goods N
23. AIDS ins anti-dscrimInatn N
24. Nicaraguan refugee aid Y
25. Nicaraguan contra aid N
26. US abide by SALT II N
27. Prohibit Saudi arms sale Y
28. Military Retiremnt Reform Y
29. Nicaraguan refugee aid Y
30. Ease '68 Gun Control Act N
31. Bar intrstat handgun tran Y
32. Keep '68 Gun Control Act Y
33. Nicaraguan contra aid N
34. Bar emp polygraph testing Y
35. Tax Overhaul consideratn Y
36. Bar armor-piercing ammo Y

LaFALCE, JOHN J. (Cont.)

37. Tax Overhaul consideratn Y
38. Make comp emissions known Y
39. Allow toxic victims suits Y
40. Strike Superfund "VAT" Y
41. Notify emp-plant closing Y
42. Bar emp consult-plant clo N
43. Medicare cuts;Tax incres' #
44. Delete 12 MX missiles Y
45. Spending cuts;Tax incres' Y
46. Textile Import Quotas N
47. Cut some school lunch fds N
48. Clean Water Act Amendmnts N
49. Youth work projects Y
50. Assist military in Angola N
51. Allow US troops-Nicaragua N
52. Pentagon polygraph exams Y
53. Bar ASAT testing Y
54. Suspend def pmt for abuse N
55. Bar Pentagon-contr emplmt Y
56. Increase SDI funding N
57. Reduce SDI funding N
58. Produce chemical weapons N
59. Bar CIA fndg in Nicaragua Y
60. South Africa sanctions Y
61. Cut SS COLAs; Raise taxes N
62. Let US invest-So Africa N
63. Approve 21 MX for 1985 N
64. Emergency Farm Credit Y
65. Awards to whistle blowers Y
66. African disaster relief Y
67. Ban bank loans to So Afr Y
68. Bar coun duty-free trtmt ?
69. Steel import limits Y
70. Soc Sec COLAs=inflation Y
71. Bar haz waste vctms suits N
72. Prohibit aid to Nicaragua Y
73. Cut $-Schs bar sch prayer N
74. Raise taxes; Cut Medicare Y
75. Alien residncy-prior 1982 Y
76. Alien residncy-prior 1980 N
77. Pen emp-hire illgl aliens N
78. Lmt Persh II/cruse-Europe Y
79. Delete 34 B-1 bombers Y
80. Bar purch of Pershing II Y
81. Bar purchase of Sgt York Y
82. Delete $ for Trident II Y
83. Allow 15 MX missiles N
84. Bar MX procurement-1985 Y
85. Equal Access Act Y
86. Aid to El Salvador N
87. Bar Nicarag water mining Y
88. Physician/Medicare freeze N
89. Increase "sin" taxes Y
90. End SBA direct loans N
91. Sell Conrail N
92. Equal Rights Amendment Y
93. Marines in Lebanon N
94. Eminent domain-Coal comps N
95. Prohibit EPA sanctions N
96. SS age increase/Reforms N
97. Auto domestic content req Y
98. Delete jobs program fundg N
99. Highway-Gas tax bill N
100. Raise Medicare;Cut defnse Y
101. Emergency housing aid Y
102. Across-the-board tax cuts N
103. Gramm-Latta II targets N
104. Delete B-1 bomber funds Y
105. Dsapprov Saudi AWACS sale Y
106. Disapprove oil import fee Y
107. Rail Deregulation N
108. Dsapp India nuc fuel sale Y
109. Mil draft registration Y
110. Chrysler Loan Guarantees Y
111. Prohibit school busing N
112. Nuclear plant moratorium N
113. Oil price controls Y
114. Tuition Tax Credits N
115. Est Consumer Protect Agcy Y
116. Eliminate B-1 bomber fnds Y
117. Subminimum wage for youth N
118. Delete crude oil tax N
119. Natural gas deregulation N

Presidential Support Score: 1986 - 18% 1985 - 30%

NOWAK, HENRY J. -- New York 33rd District [Democrat]. County of Erie (pt.). Prior Terms: House: 1975-86. Born: February 21, 1935; Buffalo, N.Y. Education: Canisius College (B.B.A.); University of Buffalo (J.D.). Military Service: U.S. Army, 1957-58. Occupation: Attorney; confidential secretary to Supreme Court justice; county comptroller (1966-74).

1. Immigration Reform Y
2. Open fld-search warrants N
3. Civil pnty-hire ill alien N
4. So Afr sanc-veto override Y
5. Tax Overhaul Y
6. South Africa sanctions Y
7. Death penalty-drug bill N
8. Evidence-warrantless srch N
9. Life term-second drug off Y
10. Military use in drug war Y
11. Troop reduction in Europe N
12. Prohibit chemical weapons Y
13. Bar ASAT testing Y
14. Abide SALT II-Soviets do Y

NOWAK, HENRY J. (Cont.)

15. Follow SALT II-Soviets do N
16. Reduce SDI funding Y
17. Increase SDI funding N
18. Purchase Trident sub Y
19. Delete 12 MX;Add conv wpn Y
20. Raise speed limit N
21. Textile Import Quotas(*) Y
22. Req Pentagon buy US goods Y
23. AIDS ins anti-dscrimination Y
24. Nicaraguan refugee aid Y
25. Nicaraguan contra aid N
26. US abide by SALT II N
27. Prohibit Saudi arms sale Y
28. Military Retiremnt Reform Y
29. Nicaraguan refugee aid Y
30. Ease '68 Gun Control Act N
31. Bar intrstat handgun tran Y
32. Keep '68 Gun Control Act Y
33. Nicaraguan contra aid N
34. Bar emp polygraph testing Y
35. Tax Overhaul consideratn Y
36. Bar armor-piercing ammo Y
37. Tax Overhaul consideratn Y
38. Make comp emissions known Y
39. Allow toxic victims suits Y
40. Strike Superfund "VAT" Y
41. Notify emp-plant closing Y
42. Bar emp consult-plant clo N
43. Medicare cuts;Tax incres' Y
44. Delete 12 MX missiles Y
45. Spending cuts;Tax incres' Y
46. Textile Import Quotas Y
47. Cut some school lunch fds N
48. Clean Water Act Amendmnts N
49. Youth work projects Y
50. Assist military in Angola N
51. Allow US troops-Nicaragua N
52. Pentagon polygraph exams Y
53. Bar ASAT testing Y
54. Suspend def pmt for abuse Y
55. Bar Pentagon-contr emplmt Y
56. Increase SDI funding N
57. Reduce SDI funding Y
58. Produce chemical weapons N
59. Bar CIA fndg in Nicaragua Y
60. South Africa sanctions Y
61. Cut SS COLAs; Raise taxes N
62. Let US invest-So Africa N
63. Approve 21 MX for 1985 N
64. Emergency Farm Credit Y
65. Awards to whistle blowers Y
66. African disaster relief Y
67. Ban bank loans to So Afr Y
68. Bar coun duty-free trtmt Y
69. Steel import limits Y
70. Soc Sec COLAs=inflation Y
71. Bar haz waste vctms suits N
72. Prohibit aid to Nicaragua Y
73. Cut $-Schs bar sch prayer N
74. Raise taxes; Cut Medicare Y
75. Alien residncy-prior 1982 N
76. Alien residncy-prior 1980 N
77. Pen emp-hire illgl aliens Y
78. Lmt Persh II/cruse-Europe Y
79. Delete 34 B-1 bombers Y
80. Bar purch of Pershing II Y
81. Bar purchase of Sgt York Y
82. Delete $ for Trident II Y
83. Allow 15 MX missiles N
84. Bar MX procurement-1985 Y
85. Equal Access Act Y
86. Aid to El Salvador N
87. Bar Nicarag water mining Y
88. Physician/Medicare freeze N
89. Increase "sin" taxes Y
90. End SBA direct loans N
91. Sell Conrail N
92. Equal Rights Amendment N
93. Marines in Lebanon N
94. Eminent domain-Coal comps N
95. Prohibit EPA sanctions Y
96. SS age increase/Reforms N
97. Auto domestic content req Y
98. Delete jobs program fundg N
99. Highway-Gas tax bill N
100. Raise Medicare;Cut defnse Y
101. Emergency housing aid Y
102. Across-the-board tax cuts N
103. Gramm-Latta II targets N
104. Delete B-1 bomber funds Y
105. Dsapprov Saudi AWACS sale Y
106. Disapprove oil import fee ?
107. Rail Deregulation N
108. Dsapp India nuc fuel sale Y
109. Mil draft registration N
110. Chrysler Loan Guarantees Y
111. Prohibit school busing N
112. Nuclear plant moratorium N
113. Oil price controls Y
114. Tuition Tax Credits Y
115. Est Consumer Protect Agcy Y
116. Eliminate B-1 bomber fnds Y
117. Subminimum wage for youth Y
118. Delete crude oil tax N
119. Natural gas deregulation N

Presidential Support Score: 1986 - 17% 1985 -- 23%

LUNDINE, STAN N. -- New York 34th District [Democrat]. Counties of Allegany, Cattaraugus (pt.), Chautaugua, Chemung, Schuyler, Steuven, Tompkins (pt.) and Yates. Prior Terms: House: 1976

LUNDINE, STAN N. (Cont.)
(Special Election)-1986. Born: February 4, 1939; Jamestown, N.Y. Education: Duke University (A.B.); New York University School of Law (LL.B.). Occupation: Public defender; associate corporation counsel; Planning Commission chairman (1965-69); mayor (1969-76).

1. Immigration Reform Y
2. Open fld-search warrants Y
3. Civil pnty-hire ill alien N
4. So Afr sanc-veto override Y
5. Tax Overhaul Y
6. South Africa sanctions ?
7. Death penalty-drug bill N
8. Evidence-warrantless srch N
9. Life term-second drug off Y
10. Military use in drug war Y
11. Troop reduction in Europe Y
12. Prohibit chemical weapons Y
13. Bar ASAT testing Y
14. Abide SALT II weapons ban Y
15. Follow SALT II-Soviets do N
16. Reduce SDI funding Y
17. Increase SDI funding N
18. Purchase Trident sub ?
19. Delete 12 MX;Add conv wpn ?
20. Raise speed limit N
21. Textile Import Quotas(*) Y
22. Req Pentagon buy US goods ?
23. AIDS ins anti-dscriminatn ?
24. Nicaraguan refugee aid ?
25. Nicaraguan contra aid N
26. US abide by SALT II N
27. Prohibit Saudi arms sale Y
28. Military Retiremnt Reform Y
29. Nicaraguan refugee aid Y
30. Ease '68 Gun Control Act Y
31. Bar intrstat handgun tran N
32. Keep '68 Gun Control Act Y
33. Nicaraguan contra aid N
34. Bar emp polygraph testing Y
35. Tax Overhaul consideratn Y
36. Bar armor-piercing ammo Y
37. Tax Overhaul consideratn Y
38. Make comp emissions known N
39. Allow toxic victims suits Y
40. Strike Superfund "VAT" Y
41. Notify emp-plant closing N
42. Bar emp consult-plant clo N
43. Medicare cuts;Tax incres' Y
44. Delete 12 MX missiles Y
45. Spending cuts;Tax incres' Y
46. Textile Import Quotas Y
47. Cut some school lunch fds N
48. Clean Water Act Amendmnts N
49. Youth work projects Y
50. Assist military in Angola N
51. Allow US troops-Nicaragua N
52. Pentagon polygraph exams N
53. Bar ASAT testing Y
54. Suspend def pmt for abuse Y
55. Bar Pentagon-contr emplmt Y
56. Increase SDI funding N
57. Reduce SDI funding Y
58. Produce chemical weapons N
59. Bar CIA fndg in Nicaragua Y
60. South Africa sanctions Y
61. Cut SS COLAs; Raise taxes N
62. Let US invest-So Africa X
63. Approve 21 MX for 1985 N
64. Emergency Farm Credit Y
65. Awards to whistle blowers Y
66. African disaster relief Y
67. Ban bank loans to So Afr ?
68. Bar coun duty-free trtmt Y
69. Steel import limits Y
70. Soc Sec COLAs=inflation Y
71. Bar haz waste vctms suits N
72. Prohibit aid to Nicaragua Y
73. Cut $-Schs bar sch prayer N
74. Raise taxes; Cut Medicare Y
75. Alien residncy-prior 1982 Y
76. Alien residncy-prior 1980 N
77. Pen emp-hire illgl aliens Y
78. Lmt Persh II/cruse-Europe ?
79. Delete 34 B-1 bombers ?
80. Bar purch of Pershing II ?
81. Bar purchase of Sgt York Y
82. Delete $ for Trident II N
83. Allow 15 MX missiles N
84. Bar MX procurement-1985 Y
85. Equal Access Act Y
86. Aid to El Salvador N
87. Bar Nicarag water mining ?
88. Physician/Medicare freeze N
89. Increase "sin" taxes Y
90. End SBA direct loans N
91. Sell Conrail N
92. Equal Rights Amendment Y
93. Marines in Lebanon N
94. Eminent domain-Coal comps Y
95. Prohibit EPA sanctions Y
96. SS age increase/Reforms Y
97. Auto domestic content req Y
98. Delete jobs program fundg N
99. Highway-Gas tax bill N
100. Raise Medicare;Cut defnse Y
101. Emergency housing aid Y
102. Across-the-board tax cuts Y
103. Gramm-Latta II targets N
104. Delete B-1 bomber funds Y
105. Dsapprov Saudi AWACS sale Y
106. Disapprove oil import fee Y

LUNDINE, STAN N. (Cont.)

107. Rail Deregulation N
108. Dsapp India nuc fuel sale Y
109. Mil draft registration N
110. Chrysler Loan Guarantees Y
111. Prohibit school busing N
112. Nuclear plant moratorium N
113. Oil price controls N
114. Tuition Tax Credits ?
115. Est Consumer Protect Agcy N
116. Eliminate B-1 bomber fnds Y
117. Subminimum wage for youth Y
118. Delete crude oil tax N
119. Natural gas deregulation N

Presidential Support Score: 1986 - 15% 1985 - 23%

NORTH CAROLINA

JONES, WALTER B. -- North Carolina 1st District [Democrat]. Counties of Beaufort, Bertie, Camden, Carteret, Chowan, Craven, Currituck, Dare, Gates, Greene, Hartford, Hyde, Lenoir, Martin, Northhampton, Pamlico, Pasquotank, Perquimans, Pitt, Tyrrell and Washington. Prior Terms: House: 1966 (Special Election)1986. Born: August 19, 1913; Fayetteville, N.C. Education: North Carolina State University (B.S.). Occupation: Office supply businessman (1934-49); mayor of Farmville (1949-53); North Carolina representative (1955, 1957, 1959); North Carolina senator (1965).

1. Immigration Reform N
2. Open fld-search warrants Y
3. Civil pnty-hire ill alien N
4. So Afr sanc-veto override ?
5. Tax Overhaul Y
6. South Africa sanctions Y
7. Death penalty-drug bill Y
8. Evidence-warrantless srch Y
9. Life term-second drug off Y
10. Military use in drug war N
11. Troop reduction in Europe N
12. Prohibit chemical weapons N
13. Bar ASAT testing Y
14. Abide SALT II weapons ban ?
15. Follow SALT II-Soviets do ?
16. Reduce SDI funding N
17. Increase SDI funding N
18. Purchase Trident sub Y
19. Delete 12 MX;Add conv wpn Y
20. Raise speed limit N
21. Textile Import Quotas(*) Y
22. Req Pentagon buy US goods Y
23. AIDS ins anti-dscriminatn Y
24. Nicaraguan refugee aid Y
25. Nicaraguan contra aid N
26. US abide by SALT II N
27. Prohibit Saudi arms sale ?
28. Military Retiremnt Reform Y
29. Nicaraguan refugee aid Y
30. Ease '68 Gun Control Act Y
31. Bar intrstat handgun tran Y
32. Keep '68 Gun Control Act N
33. Nicaraguan contra aid N
34. Bar emp polygraph testing N
35. Tax Overhaul consideratn Y
36. Bar armor-piercing ammo Y
37. Tax Overhaul consideratn Y
38. Make comp emissions known N
39. Allow toxic victims suits N
40. Strike Superfund "VAT" N
41. Notify emp-plant closing N
42. Bar emp consult-plant clo Y
43. Medicare cuts;Tax incres' Y
44. Delete 12 MX missiles Y
45. Spending cuts;Tax incres' Y
46. Textile Import Quotas Y
47. Cut some school lunch fds N
48. Clean Water Act Amendmnts N
49. Youth work projects N
50. Assist military in Angola N
51. Allow US troops-Nicaragua N
52. Pentagon polygraph exams ?
53. Bar ASAT testing Y
54. Suspend def pmt for abuse ?
55. Bar Pentagon-contr emplmt Y
56. Increase SDI funding N
57. Reduce SDI funding Y
58. Produce chemical weapons N
59. Bar CIA fndg in Nicaragua Y
60. South Africa sanctions Y
61. Cut SS COLAs; Raise taxes N
62. Let US invest-So Africa X
63. Approve 21 MX for 1985 N
64. Emergency Farm Credit Y
65. Awards to whistle blowers Y
66. African disaster relief Y
67. Ban bank loans to So Afr Y
68. Bar coun duty-free trtmt ?
69. Steel import limits Y
70. Soc Sec COLAs=inflation Y

JONES, WALTER B. (Cont.)

71. Bar haz waste vctms suits Y
72. Prohibit aid to Nicaragua Y
73. Cut $-Schs bar sch prayer N
74. Raise taxes; Cut Medicare Y
75. Alien residncy-prior 1982 N
76. Alien residncy-prior 1980 N
77. Pen emp-hire illgl aliens Y
78. Lmt Persh II/cruse-Europe N
79. Delete 34 B-1 bombers N
80. Bar purch of Pershing II N
81. Bar purchase of Sgt York N
82. Delete $ for Trident II N
83. Allow 15 MX missiles N
84. Bar MX procurement-1985 Y
85. Equal Access Act Y
86. Aid to El Salvador N
87. Bar Nicarag water mining ?
88. Physician/Medicare freeze ?
89. Increase "sin" taxes ?
90. End SBA direct loans N
91. Sell Conrail N
92. Equal Rights Amendment Y
93. Marines in Lebanon Y
94. Eminent domain-Coal comps Y
95. Prohibit EPA sanctions N
96. SS age increase/Reforms Y
97. Auto domestic content req Y
98. Delete jobs program fundg N
99. Highway-Gas tax bill Y
100. Raise Medicare;Cut defnse Y
101. Emergency housing aid Y
102. Across-the-board tax cuts N
103. Gramm-Latta II targets N
104. Delete B-1 bomber funds ?
105. Dsapprov Saudi AWACS sale ?
106. Disapprove oil import fee N
107. Rail Deregulation N
108. Dsapp India nuc fuel sale N
109. Mil draft registration Y
110. Chrysler Loan Guarantees Y
111. Prohibit school busing Y
112. Nuclear plant moratorium N
113. Oil price controls ?
114. Tuition Tax Credits N
115. Est Consumer Protect Agcy N
116. Eliminate B-1 bomber fnds N
117. Subminimum wage for youth Y
118. Delete crude oil tax N
119. Natural gas deregulation Y

Presidential Support Score: 1986 - 27% 1985 - 20%

VALENTINE, TIM -- North Carolina 2nd District [Democrat]. Counties of Caswell, Durham, Edgecombe, Granville, Halifax, Johnston (pt.), Nash, Person, Vance, Warren and Wilson. Prior Terms: House: 1983-86. Born: March 15, 1926; Nashville, Tenn. Education: The Citadel (A.B.); University of North Carolina, Chapel Hill (LL.B.). Military Service: U.S. Air Force, 1944-46. Occupation: Attorney; North Carolina representative (1955-60); legal advisor to Governor (1965); legislative counsel to Governor (1967).

1. Immigration Reform N
2. Open fld-search warrants N
3. Civil pnty-hire ill alien N
4. So Afr sanc-veto override Y
5. Tax Overhaul Y
6. South Africa sanctions Y
7. Death penalty-drug bill Y
8. Evidence-warrantless srch Y
9. Life term-second drug off Y
10. Military use in drug war N
11. Troop reduction in Europe N
12. Prohibit chemical weapons N
13. Bar ASAT testing N
14. Abide SALT II weapons ban N
15. Follow SALT II-Soviets do Y
16. Reduce SDI funding N
17. Increase SDI funding N
18. Purchase Trident sub N
19. Delete 12 MX;Add conv wpn N
20. Raise speed limit N
21. Textile Import Quotas(*) Y
22. Req Pentagon buy US goods Y
23. AIDS ins anti-dscrimnatn Y
24. Nicaraguan refugee aid Y
25. Nicaraguan contra aid N
26. US abide by SALT II Y
27. Prohibit Saudi arms sale Y
28. Military Retiremnt Reform Y
29. Nicaraguan refugee aid N
30. Ease '68 Gun Control Act Y
31. Bar intrstat handgun tran N
32. Keep '68 Gun Control Act N
33. Nicaraguan contra aid N
34. Bar emp polygraph testing N
35. Tax Overhaul consideratn N
36. Bar armor-piercing ammo Y
37. Tax Overhaul consideratn N
38. Make comp emissions known N
39. Allow toxic victims suits N
40. Strike Superfund "VAT" Y
41. Notify emp-plant closing N
42. Bar emp consult-plant clo Y

VALENTINE, TIM (Cont.)

43. Medicare cuts;Tax incres' Y
44. Delete 12 MX missiles N
45. Spending cuts;Tax incres' Y
46. Textile Import Quotas Y
47. Cut some school lunch fds N
48. Clean Water Act Amendmnts Y
49. Youth work projects N
50. Assist military in Angola Y
51. Allow US troops-Nicaragua Y
52. Pentagon polygraph exams Y
53. Bar ASAT testing N
54. Suspend def pmt for abuse N
55. Bar Pentagon-contr emplmt ?
56. Increase SDI funding N
57. Reduce SDI funding N
58. Produce chemical weapons Y
59. Bar CIA fndg in Nicaragua N
60. South Africa sanctions Y
61. Cut SS COLAs; Raise taxes N
62. Let US invest-So Africa N
63. Approve 21 MX for 1985 Y
64. Emergency Farm Credit Y
65. Awards to whistle blowers Y
66. African disaster relief Y
67. Ban bank loans to So Afr Y
68. Bar coun duty-free trtmt Y
69. Steel import limits N
70. Soc Sec COLAs=inflation Y
71. Bar haz waste vctms suits Y
72. Prohibit aid to Nicaragua ?
73. Cut $-Schs bar sch prayer Y
74. Raise taxes; Cut Medicare Y
75. Alien residncy-prior 1982 N
76. Alien residncy-prior 1980 N
77. Pen emp-hire illgl aliens N
78. Lmt Persh II/cruse-Europe N
79. Delete 34 B-1 bombers N
80. Bar purch of Pershing II N
81. Bar purchase of Sgt York N
82. Delete $ for Trident II N
83. Allow 15 MX missiles Y
84. Bar MX procurement-1985 N
85. Equal Access Act Y
86. Aid to El Salvador Y
87. Bar Nicarag water mining Y
88. Physician/Medicare freeze N
89. Increase "sin" taxes Y
90. End SBA direct loans N
91. Sell Conrail N
92. Equal Rights Amendment N
93. Marines in Lebanon Y
94. Eminent domain-Coal comps Y
95. Prohibit EPA sanctions Y
96. SS age increase/Reforms Y

Presidential Support Score: 1986 - 40% 1985 - 46%

WHITLEY, CHARLES -- North Carolina 3rd District [Democrat]. Counties of Bladen, Duplin, Harnett, Johnston (pt.), Jones, Lee, Moore (pt.), Onslow, Pender, Sampson and Wayne. Prior Terms: House: 1977-86. Born: January 3, 1927; Siler City, N.C. Education: Wake Forest University (B.A., LL.B.); George Washington University (M.A.). Military Service: U.S. Army, 1944-46. Occupation: Attorney; administrative assistant (1961-76).

1. Immigration Reform N
2. Open fld-search warrants Y
3. Civil pnty-hire ill alien N
4. So Afr sanc-veto override Y
5. Tax Overhaul N
6. South Africa sanctions Y
7. Death penalty-drug bill Y
8. Evidence-warrantless srch Y
9. Life term-second drug off Y
10. Military use in drug war N
11. Troop reduction in Europe N
12. Prohibit chemical weapons N
13. Bar ASAT testing Y
14. Abide SALT II weapons ban Y
15. Follow SALT II-Soviets do N
16. Reduce SDI funding N
17. Increase SDI funding N
18. Purchase Trident sub N
19. Delete 12 MX;Add conv wpn N
20. Raise speed limit N
21. Textile Import Quotas(*) Y
22. Req Pentagon buy US goods Y
23. AIDS ins anti-dscrimnatn Y
24. Nicaraguan refugee aid N
25. Nicaraguan contra aid N
26. US abide by SALT II N
27. Prohibit Saudi arms sale Y
28. Military Retiremnt Reform Y
29. Nicaraguan refugee aid N
30. Ease '68 Gun Control Act Y
31. Bar intrstat handgun tran N
32. Keep '68 Gun Control Act N
33. Nicaraguan contra aid N
34. Bar emp polygraph testing N
35. Tax Overhaul consideratn Y
36. Bar armor-piercing ammo Y
37. Tax Overhaul consideratn Y
38. Make comp emissions known N
39. Allow toxic victims suits N
40. Strike Superfund "VAT" Y

WHITLEY, CHARLES (Cont.)

41. Notify emp-plant closing N
42. Bar emp consult-plant clo Y
43. Medicare cuts;Tax incres' Y
44. Delete 12 MX missiles N
45. Spending cuts;Tax incres' Y
46. Textile Import Quotas Y
47. Cut some school lunch fds N
48. Clean Water Act Amendmnts N
49. Youth work projects ?
50. Assist military in Angola Y
51. Allow US troops-Nicaragua N
52. Pentagon polygraph exams Y
53. Bar ASAT testing Y
54. Suspend def pmt for abuse N
55. Bar Pentagon-contr emplmt Y
56. Increase SDI funding N
57. Reduce SDI funding N
58. Produce chemical weapons Y
59. Bar CIA fndg in Nicaragua Y
60. South Africa sanctions Y
61. Cut SS COLAs; Raise taxes N
62. Let US invest-So Africa N
63. Approve 21 MX for 1985 Y
64. Emergency Farm Credit Y
65. Awards to whistle blowers Y
66. African disaster relief Y
67. Ban bank loans to So Afr ?
68. Bar coun duty-free trtmt N
69. Steel import limits Y
70. Soc Sec COLAs=inflation Y
71. Bar haz waste vctms suits Y
72. Prohibit aid to Nicaragua Y
73. Cut $-Schs bar sch prayer Y
74. Raise taxes; Cut Medicare Y
75. Alien residncy-prior 1982 Y
76. Alien residncy-prior 1980 Y
77. Pen emp-hire illgl aliens Y
78. Lmt Persh II/cruse-Europe N
79. Delete 34 B-1 bombers N
80. Bar purch of Pershing II N
81. Bar purchase of Sgt York N
82. Delete $ for Trident II N
83. Allow 15 MX missiles Y
84. Bar MX procurement-1985 N
85. Equal Access Act Y
86. Aid to El Salvador Y
87. Bar Nicarag water mining Y
88. Physician/Medicare freeze N
89. Increase "sin" taxes Y
90. End SBA direct loans N
91. Sell Conrail N
92. Equal Rights Amendment Y
93. Marines in Lebanon Y
94. Eminent domain-Coal comps N
95. Prohibit EPA sanctions Y
96. SS age increase/Reforms Y
97. Auto domestic content req N
98. Delete jobs program fundg N
99. Highway-Gas tax bill N
100. Raise Medicare;Cut defnse N
101. Emergency housing aid Y
102. Across-the-board tax cuts N
103. Gramm-Latta II targets N
104. Delete B-1 bomber funds N
105. Dsapprov Saudi AWACS sale N
106. Disapprove oil import fee Y
107. Rail Deregulation N
108. Dsapp India nuc fuel sale Y
109. Mil draft registration Y
110. Chrysler Loan Guarantees Y
111. Prohibit school busing N
112. Nuclear plant moratorium N
113. Oil price controls N
114. Tuition Tax Credits N
115. Est Consumer Protect Agcy N
116. Eliminate B-1 bomber fnds N
117. Subminimum wage for youth N
118. Delete crude oil tax N
119. Natural gas deregulation N

Presidential Support Score: 1986 - 32% 1985 - 43%

COBEY, WILLIAM W., Jr. -- North Carolina 4th District [Republican]. Counties of Chatham, Franklin, Orange, Randolph and Wake. Prior Terms: 1985-86. Education: Emory University; University of Pennsylvania (M.A.); University of Pittsburgh (M.Ed.). Occupation: President, management and consulting firm; athletic director.

1. Immigration Reform N
2. Open fld-search warrants Y
3. Civil pnty-hire ill alien N
4. So Afr sanc-veto override N
5. Tax Overhaul Y
6. South Africa sanctions N
7. Death penalty-drug bill Y
8. Evidence-warrantless srch Y
9. Life term-second drug off Y
10. Military use in drug war Y
11. Troop reduction in Europe N
12. Prohibit chemical weapons N
13. Bar ASAT testing N
14. Abide SALT II weapons ban N
15. Follow SALT II-Soviets do Y
16. Reduce SDI funding N
17. Increase SDI funding Y
18. Purchase Trident sub N

COBEY, WILLIAM W., Jr. (Cont.)

19. Delete 12 MX;Add conv wpn N
20. Raise speed limit Y
21. Textile Import Quotas(*) Y
22. Req Pentagon buy US goods Y
23. AIDS ins anti-dscriminatn N
24. Nicaraguan refugee aid N
25. Nicaraguan contra aid Y
26. US abide by SALT II Y
27. Prohibit Saudi arms sale Y
28. Military Retiremnt Reform Y
29. Nicaraguan refugee aid Y
30. Ease '68 Gun Control Act Y
31. Bar intrstat handgun tran N
32. Keep '68 Gun Control Act N
33. Nicaraguan contra aid Y
34. Bar emp polygraph testing N
35. Tax Overhaul consideratn N
36. Bar armor-piercing ammo Y
37. Tax Overhaul consideratn N
38. Make comp emissions known N
39. Allow toxic victims suits N
40. Strike Superfund "VAT" N
41. Notify emp-plant closing N
42. Bar emp consult-plant clo Y
43. Medicare cuts;Tax incres' N
44. Delete 12 MX missiles N
45. Spending cuts;Tax incres' N
46. Textile Import Quotas Y
47. Cut some school lunch fds Y
48. Clean Water Act Amendmnts Y
49. Youth work projects N
50. Assist military in Angola Y
51. Allow US troops-Nicaragua Y
52. Pentagon polygraph exams Y
53. Bar ASAT testing N
54. Suspend def pmt for abuse N
55. Bar Pentagon-contr emplmt Y
56. Increase SDI funding Y
57. Reduce SDI funding N
58. Produce chemical weapons Y
59. Bar CIA fndg in Nicaragua N
60. South Africa sanctions N
61. Cut SS COLAs; Raise taxes N
62. Let US invest-So Africa Y
63. Approve 21 MX for 1985 Y
64. Emergency Farm Credit N
65. Awards to whistle blowers Y
66. African disaster relief N

Presidential Support Score: 1986 - 70% 1985 - 80%

NEAL, STEPHEN L. -- North Carolina 5th District [Democrat]. Counties of Alexander, Alleghany, Ashe, Forsyth, Rockingham, Stokes, Surry and Wilkes. Prior Terms: House: 1975-86. Born: November 7, 1934; Winston-Salem, N.C. Education: University of Hawaii. Occupation: Resort businessman; mortgage banker; newspaper publisher.

1. Immigration Reform Y
2. Open fld-search warrants Y
3. Civil pnty-hire ill alien N
4. So Afr sanc-veto override Y
5. Tax Overhaul Y
6. South Africa sanctions Y
7. Death penalty-drug bill Y
8. Evidence-warrantless srch ?
9. Life term-second drug off Y
10. Military use in drug war N
11. Troop reduction in Europe N
12. Prohibit chemical weapons N
13. Bar ASAT testing Y
14. Abide SALT II weapons ban Y
15. Follow SALT II-Soviets do N
16. Reduce SDI funding N
17. Increase SDI funding N
18. Purchase Trident sub Y
19. Delete 12 MX;Add conv wpn N
20. Raise speed limit Y
21. Textile Import Quotas(*) Y
22. Req Pentagon buy US goods Y
23. AIDS ins anti-dscriminatn Y
24. Nicaraguan refugee aid Y
25. Nicaraguan contra aid N
26. US abide by SALT II N
27. Prohibit Saudi arms sale Y
28. Military Retiremnt Reform Y
29. Nicaraguan refugee aid Y
30. Ease '68 Gun Control Act Y
31. Bar intrstat handgun tran N
32. Keep '68 Gun Control Act N
33. Nicaraguan contra aid N
34. Bar emp polygraph testing Y
35. Tax Overhaul consideratn Y
36. Bar armor-piercing ammo Y
37. Tax Overhaul consideratn Y
38. Make comp emissions known Y
39. Allow toxic victims suits N
40. Strike Superfund "VAT" Y
41. Notify emp-plant closing N
42. Bar emp consult-plant clo Y
43. Medicare cuts;Tax incres' Y
44. Delete 12 MX missiles N
45. Spending cuts;Tax incres' Y
46. Textile Import Quotas Y
47. Cut some school lunch fds N
48. Clean Water Act Amendmnts N
49. Youth work projects Y
50. Assist military in Angola N

NEAL, STEPHEN L. (Cont.)

51. Allow US troops-Nicaragua N
52. Pentagon polygraph exams Y
53. Bar ASAT testing Y
54. Suspend def pmt for abuse N
55. Bar Pentagon-contr emplmt Y
56. Increase SDI funding N
57. Reduce SDI funding N
58. Produce chemical weapons Y
59. Bar CIA fndg in Nicaragua Y
60. South Africa sanctions Y
61. Cut SS COLAs; Raise taxes N
62. Let US invest-So Africa N
63. Approve 21 MX for 1985 Y
64. Emergency Farm Credit Y
65. Awards to whistle blowers Y
66. African disaster relief Y
67. Ban bank loans to So Afr Y
68. Bar coun duty-free trtmt N
69. Steel import limits N
70. Soc Sec COLAs=inflation Y
71. Bar haz waste vctms suits N
72. Prohibit aid to Nicaragua Y
73. Cut $-Schs bar sch prayer ?
74. Raise taxes; Cut Medicare Y
75. Alien residncy-prior 1982 Y
76. Alien residncy-prior 1980 Y
77. Pen emp-hire illgl aliens N
78. Lmt Persh II/cruse-Europe N
79. Delete 34 B-1 bombers N
80. Bar purch of Pershing II N
81. Bar purchase of Sgt York N
82. Delete $ for Trident II N
83. Allow 15 MX missiles Y
84. Bar MX procurement-1985 Y
85. Equal Access Act Y
86. Aid to El Salvador N
87. Bar Nicarag water mining Y
88. Physician/Medicare freeze N
89. Increase "sin" taxes Y
90. End SBA direct loans N
91. Sell Conrail N
92. Equal Rights Amendment Y
93. Marines in Lebanon N
94. Eminent domain-Coal comps Y
95. Prohibit EPA sanctions Y
96. SS age increase/Reforms ?
97. Auto domestic content req N
98. Delete jobs program fundg N
99. Highway-Gas tax bill N
100. Raise Medicare;Cut defnse N
101. Emergency housing aid ?
102. Across-the-board tax cuts N
103. Gramm-Latta II targets N
104. Delete B-1 bomber funds N
105. Dsapprov Saudi AWACS sale Y
106. Disapprove oil import fee Y
107. Rail Deregulation N
108. Dsapp India nuc fuel sale Y
109. Mil draft registration Y
110. Chrysler Loan Guarantees N
111. Prohibit school busing Y
112. Nuclear plant moratorium N
113. Oil price controls N
114. Tuition Tax Credits N
115. Est Consumer Protect Agcy N
116. Eliminate B-1 bomber fnds Y
117. Subminimum wage for youth Y
118. Delete crude oil tax N
119. Natural gas deregulation Y

Presidential Support Score: 1986 - 28% 1985 - 36%

COBLE, HOWARD -- North Carolina 6th District [Republican]. Counties of Alamance, Davidson and Guilford. Prior Terms: 1985-86. Education: Guilford College (B.A.); University of North Carolina (J.D.). Occupation: Attorney; North Carolina legislator; assistant U.S. attorney.

1. Immigration Reform N
2. Open fld-search warrants Y
3. Civil pnty-hire ill alien Y
4. So Afr sanc-veto override N
5. Tax Overhaul Y
6. South Africa sanctions N
7. Death penalty-drug bill Y
8. Evidence-warrantless srch Y
9. Life term-second drug off Y
10. Military use in drug war Y
11. Troop reduction in Europe N
12. Prohibit chemical weapons Y
13. Bar ASAT testing N
14. Abide SALT II weapons ban N
15. Follow SALT II-Soviets do Y
16. Reduce SDI funding N
17. Increase SDI funding N
18. Purchase Trident sub N
19. Delete 12 MX;Add conv wpn N
20. Raise speed limit Y
21. Textile Import Quotas(*) Y
22. Req Pentagon buy US goods Y
23. AIDS ins anti-dscriminatn N
24. Nicaraguan refugee aid N
25. Nicaraguan contra aid Y
26. US abide by SALT II Y

COBLE, HOWARD (Cont.)

27. Prohibit Saudi arms sale Y
28. Military Retiremnt Reform Y
29. Nicaraguan refugee aid Y
30. Ease '68 Gun Control Act Y
31. Bar intrstat handgun tran N
32. Keep '68 Gun Control Act N
33. Nicaraguan contra aid Y
34. Bar emp polygraph testing N
35. Tax Overhaul consideratn N
36. Bar armor-piercing ammo Y
37. Tax Overhaul consideratn N
38. Make comp emissions known N
39. Allow toxic victims suits N
40. Strike Superfund "VAT" N
41. Notify emp-plant closing N
42. Bar emp consent-plant clo Y
43. Medicare cuts;Tax incres' N
44. Delete 12 MX missiles N
45. Spending cuts;Tax incres' N
46. Textile Import Quotas Y
47. Cut some school lunch fds Y
48. Clean Water Act Amendmnts Y
49. Youth work projects N
50. Assist military in Angola Y
51. Allow US troops-Nicaragua Y
52. Pentagon polygraph exams Y
53. Bar ASAT testing N
54. Suspend def pmt for abuse Y
55. Bar Pentagon-contr emplmt Y
56. Increase SDI funding N
57. Reduce SDI funding N
58. Produce chemical weapons Y
59. Bar CIA fndg in Nicaragua N
60. South Africa sanctions N
61. Cut SS COLAs; Raise taxes N
62. Let US invest-So Africa Y
63. Approve 21 MX for 1985 Y
64. Emergency Farm Credit N
65. Awards to whistle blowers Y
66. African disaster relief N

Presidential Support Score: 1986 - 68% 1985 - 69%

ROSE, CHARLES -- North Carolina 7th District [Democrat]. Counties of Brunswick, Columbus, Cumberland, New Hanover and Robeson. Prior Terms: House: 1973-86. Born: August 10, 1939; Fayetteville, N.C. Education: Davidson College (A.B.); University of North Carolina (LL.B.). Occupation: Chief district prosdecutor, Cumberland and Hoke Counties (1967-70); boardmember, Lumbee Bank.

1. Immigration Reform Y
2. Open fld-search warrants Y
3. Civil pnty-hire ill alien N
4. So Afr sanc-veto override ?
5. Tax Overhaul Y
6. South Africa sanctions Y
7. Death penalty-drug bill Y
8. Evidence-warrantless srch Y
9. Life term-second drug off Y
10. Military use in drug war N
11. Troop reduction in Europe N
12. Prohibit chemical weapons N
13. Bar ASAT testing Y
14. Abide SALT II weapons ban Y
15. Follow SALT II-Soviets do N
16. Reduce SDI funding N
17. Increase SDI funding N
18. Purchase Trident sub N
19. Delete 12 MX;Add conv wpn N
20. Raise speed limit Y
21. Textile Import Quotas(*) Y
22. Req Pentagon buy US goods Y
23. AIDS ins anti-dscriminatn Y
24. Nicaraguan refugee aid Y
25. Nicaraguan contra aid N
26. US abide by SALT II N
27. Prohibit Saudi arms sale N
28. Military Retiremnt Reform Y
29. Nicaraguan refugee aid Y
30. Ease '68 Gun Control Act Y
31. Bar intrstat handgun tran Y
32. Keep '68 Gun Control Act N
33. Nicaraguan contra aid N
34. Bar emp polygraph testing N
35. Tax Overhaul consideratn Y
36. Bar armor-piercing ammo Y
37. Tax Overhaul consideratn Y
38. Make comp emissions known N
39. Allow toxic victims suits N
40. Strike Superfund "VAT" N
41. Notify emp-plant closing ?
42. Bar emp consult-plant clo Y
43. Medicare cuts;Tax incres' Y
44. Delete 12 MX missiles N
45. Spending cuts;Tax incres' Y
46. Textile Import Quotas Y
47. Cut some school lunch fds N
48. Clean Water Act Amendmnts N
49. Youth work projects N
50. Assist military in Angola ?
51. Allow US troops-Nicaragua N
52. Pentagon polygraph exams Y

ROSE CHARLES (Cont.)

53. Bar ASAT testing N
54. Suspend def pmt for abuse N
55. Bar Pentagon-contr emplmt Y
56. Increase SDI funding N
57. Reduce SDI funding N
58. Produce chemical weapons Y
59. Bar CIA fndg in Nicaragua Y
60. South Africa sanctions Y
61. Cut SS COLAs; Raise taxes N
62. Let US invest-So Africa N
63. Approve 21 MX for 1985 N
64. Emergency Farm Credit Y
65. Awards to whistle blowers Y
66. African disaster relief Y
67. Ban bank loans to So Afr Y
68. Bar coun duty-free trtmt Y
69. Steel import limits Y
70. Soc Sec COLAs=inflation Y
71. Bar haz waste vctms suits Y
72. Prohibit aid to Nicaragua Y
73. Cut $-Schs bar sch prayer Y
74. Raise taxes; Cut Medicare Y
75. Alien residncy-prior 1982 Y
76. Alien residncy-prior 1980 N
77. Pen emp-hire illgl aliens ?
78. Lmt Persh II/cruse-Europe ?
79. Delete 34 B-1 bombers N
80. Bar purch of Pershing II N
81. Bar purchase of Sgt York Y
82. Delete $ for Trident II N
83. Allow 15 MX missiles Y
84. Bar MX procurement-1985 N
85. Equal Access Act Y
86. Aid to El Salvador N
87. Bar Nicarag water mining Y
88. Physician/Medicare freeze N
89. Increase "sin" taxes Y
90. End SBA direct loans N
91. Sell Conrail N
92. Equal Rights Amendment Y
93. Marines in Lebanon Y
94. Eminent domain-Coal comps Y
95. Prohibit EPA sanctions Y
96. SS age increase/Reforms N
97. Auto domestic content req Y
98. Delete jobs program fundg N
99. Highway-Gas tax bill Y
100. Raise Medicare;Cut defnse N
101. Emergency housing aid Y
102. Across-the-board tax cuts N
103. Gramm-Latta II targets N
104. Delete B-1 bomber funds N
105. Dsapprov Saudi AWACS sale N
106. Disapprove oil import fee ?
107. Rail Deregulation ?
108. Dsapp India nuc fuel sale Y
109. Mil draft registration Y
110. Chrysler Loan Guarantees N
111. Prohibit school busing N
112. Nuclear plant moratorium N
113. Oil price controls N
114. Tuition Tax Credits N
115. Est Consumer Protect Agcy N
116. Eliminate B-1 bomber fnds Y
117. Subminimum wage for youth N
118. Delete crude oil tax N
119. Natural gas deregulation N

Presidential Support Score: 1986 - 30% 1985 - 28%

HEFNER, W. G. (Bill) -- North Carolina 8th District [Democrat]. Counties of Anson, Cabarrus, Davie, Hoke, Montgomery, Moore (pt.), Richmond, Rowan, Scotland, Stanly, Union and Yadkin (pt.). Prior Terms: House: 1975-86. Born: April 11, 1930; Elora, Tenn. Occupation: Entertainer and gospel music broadcaster; president, WRKB radio station.

1. Immigration Reform ?
2. Open fld-search warrants ?
3. Civil pnty-hire ill alien ?
4. So Afr sanc-veto override Y
5. Tax Overhaul Y
6. South Africa sanctions Y
7. Death penalty-drug bill Y
8. Evidence-warrantless srch Y
9. Life term-second drug off Y
10. Military use in drug war N
11. Troop reduction in Europe N
12. Prohibit chemical weapons N
13. Bar ASAT testing Y
14. Abide SALT II weapons ban Y
15. Follow SALT II-Soviets do N
16. Reduce SDI funding N
17. Increase SDI funding N
18. Purchase Trident sub Y
19. Delete 12 MX;Add conv wpn N
20. Raise speed limit N
21. Textile Import Quotas(*) Y
22. Req Pentagon buy US goods Y
23. AIDS ins anti-dscriminatn Y
24. Nicaraguan refugee aid Y
25. Nicaraguan contra aid N
26. US abide by SALT II N

HEFNER, W. G. (Bill) (Cont.)

27. Prohibit Saudi arms sale Y
28. Military Retiremnt Reform Y
29. Nicaraguan refugee aid N
30. Ease '68 Gun Control Act Y
31. Bar intrstat handgun tran N
32. Keep '68 Gun Control Act N
33. Nicaraguan contra aid N
34. Bar emp polygraph testing N
35. Tax Overhaul consideratn Y
36. Bar armor-piercing ammo Y
37. Tax Overhaul consideratn Y
38. Make comp emissions known N
39. Allow toxic victims suits N
40. Strike Superfund "VAT" N
41. Notify emp-plant closing N
42. Bar emp consult-plant clo Y
43. Medicare cuts;Tax incres' Y
44. Delete 12 MX missiles N
45. Spending cuts;Tax incres' Y
46. Textile Import Quotas Y
47. Cut some school lunch fds N
48. Clean Water Act Amendmnts ?
49. Youth work projects ?
50. Assist military in Angola ?
51. Allow US troops-Nicaragua ?
52. Pentagon polygraph exams ?
53. Bar ASAT testing ?
54. Suspend def pmt for abuse N
55. Bar Pentagon-contr emplmt Y
56. Increase SDI funding N
57. Reduce SDI funding N
58. Produce chemical weapons Y
59. Bar CIA fndg in Nicaragua Y
60. South Africa sanctions Y
61. Cut SS COLAs; Raise taxes N
62. Let US invest-So Africa N
63. Approve 21 MX for 1985 Y
64. Emergency Farm Credit Y
65. Awards to whistle blowers Y
66. African disaster relief Y
67. Ban bank loans to So Afr ?
68. Bar coun duty-free trtmt N
69. Steel import limits Y
70. Soc Sec COLAs=inflation Y
71. Bar haz waste vctms suits Y
72. Prohibit aid to Nicaragua Y
73. Cut $-Schs bar sch prayer Y
74. Raise taxes; Cut Medicare Y
75. Alien residncy-prior 1982 Y
76. Alien residncy-prior 1980 Y
77. Pen emp-hire illgl aliens N
78. Lmt Persh II/cruse-Europe N
79. Delete 34 B-1 bombers N
80. Bar purch of Pershing II N
81. Bar purchase of Sgt York N
82. Delete $ for Trident II N
83. Allow 15 MX missiles Y
84. Bar MX procurement-1985 N
85. Equal Access Act Y
86. Aid to El Salvador N
87. Bar Nicarag water mining Y
88. Physician/Medicare freeze N
89. Increase "sin" taxes Y
90. End SBA direct loans N
91. Sell Conrail N
92. Equal Rights Amendment Y
93. Marines in Lebanon Y
94. Eminent domain-Coal comps N
95. Prohibit EPA sanctions Y
96. SS age increase/Reforms Y
97. Auto domestic content req N
98. Delete jobs program fundg N
99. Highway-Gas tax bill N
100. Raise Medicare;Cut defnse N
101. Emergency housing aid Y
102. Across-the-board tax cuts N
103. Gramm-Latta II targets N
104. Delete B-1 bomber funds N
105. Dsapprov Saudi AWACS sale Y
106. Disapprove oil import fee Y
107. Rail Deregulation N
108. Dsapp India nuc fuel sale Y
109. Mil draft registration ?
110. Chrysler Loan Guarantees N
111. Prohibit school busing N
112. Nuclear plant moratorium N
113. Oil price controls N
114. Tuition Tax Credits N
115. Est Consumer Protect Agcy N
116. Eliminate B-1 bomber fnds Y
117. Subminimum wage for youth Y
118. Delete crude oil tax Y
119. Natural gas deregulation N

Presidential Support Score: 1986 - 31% 1985 - 35%

McMILLAN, ALEX -- North Carolina 9th District [Republican]. Counties of Iredell, Lincoln, Mecklenburg and Yadkin (pt.). Prior Terms: 1985-86. Education: University of North Carolina; University of Virginia (M.B.A.). Military Service: U.S. Army Intelligence. Occupation: Executive, super market chain; county commissioner.

McMILLAN, ALEX (Cont.)

1. Immigration Reform Y
2. Open fld-search warrants N
3. Civil pnty-hire ill alien N
4. So Afr sanc-veto override N
5. Tax Overhaul Y
6. South Africa sanctions Y
7. Death penalty-drug bill Y
8. Evidence-warrantless srch Y
9. Life term-second drug off Y
10. Military use in drug war Y
11. Troop reduction in Europe N
12. Prohibit chemical weapons N
13. Bar ASAT testing N
14. Abide SALT II weapons ban N
15. Follow SALT II-Soviets do Y
16. Reduce SDI funding N
17. Increase SDI funding N
18. Purchase Trident sub N
19. Delete 12 MX;Add conv wpn N
20. Raise speed limit Y
21. Textile Import Quotas(*) Y
22. Req Pentagon buy US goods Y
23. AIDS ins anti-dscriminatn ?
24. Nicaraguan refugee aid N
25. Nicaraguan contra aid Y
26. US abide by SALT II Y
27. Prohibit Saudi arms sale Y
28. Military Retiremnt Reform Y
29. Nicaraguan refugee aid Y
30. Ease '68 Gun Control Act Y
31. Bar intrstat handgun tran N
32. Keep '68 Gun Control Act N
33. Nicaraguan contra aid Y
34. Bar emp polygraph testing N
35. Tax Overhaul consideratn Y
36. Bar armor-piercing ammo Y
37. Tax Overhaul consideratn N
38. Make comp emissions known N
39. Allow toxic victims suits N
40. Strike Superfund "VAT" N
41. Notify emp-plant closing N
42. Bar emp consult-plant clo Y
43. Medicare cuts;Tax incres' N
44. Delete 12 MX missiles N
45. Spending cuts;Tax incres' N
46. Textile Import Quotas Y
47. Cut some school lunch fds Y
48. Clean Water Act Amendmnts Y
49. Youth work projects N
50. Assist military in Angola Y
51. Allow US troops-Nicaragua Y
52. Pentagon polygraph exams Y
53. Bar ASAT testing N
54. Suspend def pmt for abuse N
55. Bar Pentagon-contr emplmt Y
56. Increase SDI funding N
57. Reduce SDI funding N
58. Produce chemical weapons Y
59. Bar CIA fndg in Nicaragua N
60. South Africa sanctions N
61. Cut SS COLAs; Raise taxes N
62. Let US invest-So Africa Y
63. Approve 21 MX for 1985 Y
64. Emergency Farm Credit N
65. Awards to whistle blowers Y
66. African disaster relief Y

Presidential Support Score: 1986 - 65% 1985 - 79%

VACANT -- North Carolina 10th District was left vacant when James Broyhill resigned to run for the Senate. See Broyhill in the North Carolina Senate.

HENDON, W. M. -- North Carolina 11th District [Republican]. Counties of Avery (pt.), Buncombe, Cherokee, Clay, Graham, Haywood, Henderson, Jackson, McDowell, Macon, Madison, Mitchell, Polk, Rutherford, Swain, Transylvania and Yancy. Prior Terms: House: 1981-82; 1985-86. Born: November 9, 1944; Asheville, N.C. Education: University of Tennessee (B.A., M.A.). Occupation: Business underwriter; teacher.

1. Immigration Reform N
2. Open fld-search warrants N
3. Civil pnty-hire ill alien Y
4. So Afr sanc-veto override N
5. Tax Overhaul Y
6. South Africa sanctions N
7. Death penalty-drug bill Y
8. Evidence-warrantless srch Y
9. Life term-second drug off Y
10. Military use in drug war Y
11. Troop reduction in Europe N
12. Prohibit chemical weapons N
13. Bar ASAT testing N
14. Abide SALT II weapons ban N

HENDON, W. M. (Cont.)

15. Follow SALT II-Soviets do	Y		46. Textile Import Quotas	Y
16. Reduce SDI funding	N		47. Cut some school lunch fds	N
17. Increase SDI funding	Y		48. Clean Water Act Amendmnts	Y
18. Purchase Trident sub	N		49. Youth work projects	N
19. Delete 12 MX;Add conv wpn	N		50. Assist military in Angola	Y
20. Raise speed limit	Y		51. Allow US troops-Nicaragua	Y
21. Textile Import Quotas(*)	Y		52. Pentagon polygraph exams	Y
22. Req Pentagon buy US goods	Y		53. Bar ASAT testing	N
23. AIDS ins anti-dscriminatn	N		54. Suspend def pmt for abuse	Y
24. Nicaraguan refugee aid	N		55. Bar Pentagon-contr emplmt	Y
25. Nicaraguan contra aid	Y		56. Increase SDI funding	N
26. US abide by SALT II	Y		57. Reduce SDI funding	N
27. Prohibit Saudi arms sale	Y		58. Produce chemical weapons	Y
28. Military Retiremnt Reform	Y		59. Bar CIA fndg in Nicaragua	N
29. Nicaraguan refugee aid	Y		60. South Africa sanctions	N
30. Ease '68 Gun Control Act	Y		61. Cut SS COLAs; Raise taxes	N
31. Bar intrstat handgun tran	N		62. Let US invest-So Africa	Y
32. Keep '68 Gun Control Act	N		63. Approve 21 MX for 1985	Y
33. Nicaraguan contra aid	Y		64. Emergency Farm Credit	Y
34. Bar emp polygraph testing	N		65. Awards to whistle blowers	Y
35. Tax Overhaul consideratn	Y		66. African disaster relief	Y
36. Bar armor-piercing ammo	Y		97. Auto domestic content req	N
37. Tax Overhaul consideratn	N		98. Delete jobs program fundg	Y
38. Make comp emissions known	N		99. Highway-Gas tax bill	?
39. Allow toxic victims suits	N		100. Raise Medicare;Cut defnse	N
40. Strike Superfund "VAT"	N		101. Emergency housing aid	Y
41. Notify emp-plant closing	N		102. Across-the-board tax cuts	Y
42. Bar emp consult-plant clo	Y		103. Gramm-Latta II targets	Y
43. Medicare cuts;Tax incres'	N		104. Delete B-1 bomber funds	N
44. Delete 12 MX missiles	N		105. Dsapprov Saudi AWACS sale	Y
45. Spending cuts;Tax incres'	N			

Was not in office for votes 67-96.
Presidential Support Score: 1986 - 61% 1985 - 64%

NORTH DAKOTA

DORGAN, BYRON L. -- Representative at Large [Democrat]. Prior Terms: House: 1981-86. Born: May 14, 1942; Dickinson, N.D. Education: University of North Dakota (B.S.); University of Denver (M.B.A.). Occupation: Employee, executive development program, Martin-Marietta Corp. (1966-67); deputy tax commissioner (1966-69); tax commissioner (1969-76); chairman, multi-state tax commission (1972-74); president, Midwest Assn. of Tax Administrators (1970).

1. Immigration Reform	Y		11. Troop reduction in Europe	Y
2. Open fld-search warrants	N		12. Prohibit chemical weapons	Y
3. Civil pnty-hire ill alien	N		13. Bar ASAT testing	Y
4. So Afr sanc-veto override	Y		14. Abide SALT II weapons ban	Y
5. Tax Overhaul	Y		15. Follow SALT II-Soviets do	N
6. South Africa sanctions	Y		16. Reduce SDI funding	Y
7. Death penalty-drug bill	Y		17. Increase SDI funding	N
8. Evidence-warrantless srch	Y		18. Purchase Trident sub	N
9. Life term-second drug off	Y		19. Delete 12 MX;Add conv wpn	Y
10. Military use in drug war	N		20. Raise speed limit	Y

DORGAN, BYRON L. (Cont.)

21.	Textile Import Quotas(*)	N	64.	Emergency Farm Credit	Y
22.	Req Pentagon buy US goods	Y	65.	Awards to whistle blowers	Y
23.	AIDS ins anti-dscriminatn	Y	66.	African disaster relief	Y
24.	Nicaraguan refugee aid	Y	67.	Ban bank loans to So Afr	Y
25.	Nicaraguan contra aid	N	68.	Bar coun duty-free trtmt	Y
26.	US abide by SALT II	N	69.	Steel import limits	N
27.	Prohibit Saudi arms sale	Y	70.	Soc Sec COLAs=inflation	Y
28.	Military Retiremnt Reform	Y	71.	Bar haz waste vctms suits	N
29.	Nicaraguan refugee aid	Y	72.	Prohibit aid to Nicaragua	Y
30.	Ease '68 Gun Control Act	Y	73.	Cut $-Schs bar sch prayer	N
31.	Bar intrstat handgun tran	N	74.	Raise taxes; Cut Medicare	Y
32.	Keep '68 Gun Control Act	N	75.	Alien residncy-prior 1982	Y
33.	Nicaraguan contra aid	N	76.	Alien residncy-prior 1980	N
34.	Bar emp polygraph testing	Y	77.	Pen emp-hire illgl aliens	N
35.	Tax Overhaul consideratn	Y	78.	Lmt Persh II/cruse-Europe	Y
36.	Bar armor-piercing ammo	Y	79.	Delete 34 B-1 bombers	N
37.	Tax Overhaul consideratn	Y	80.	Bar purch of Pershing II	Y
38.	Make comp emissions known	Y	81.	Bar purchase of Sgt York	Y
39.	Allow toxic victims suits	N	82.	Delete $ for Trident II	Y
40.	Strike Superfund "VAT"	Y	83.	Allow 15 MX missiles	N
41.	Notify emp-plant closing	Y	84.	Bar MX procurement-1985	Y
42.	Bar emp consult-plant clo	N	85.	Equal Access Act	N
43.	Medicare cuts;Tax incres'	Y	86.	Aid to El Salvador	N
44.	Delete 12 MX missiles	Y	87.	Bar Nicarag water mining	Y
45.	Spending cuts;Tax incres'	N	88.	Physician/Medicare freeze	N
46.	Textile Import Quotas	N	89.	Increase "sin" taxes	Y
47.	Cut some school lunch fds	N	90.	End SBA direct loans	N
48.	Clean Water Act Amendmnts	N	91.	Sell Conrail	N
49.	Youth work projects	Y	92.	Equal Rights Amendment	Y
50.	Assist military in Angola	N	93.	Marines in Lebanon	N
51.	Allow US troops-Nicaragua	N	94.	Eminent domain-Coal comps	N
52.	Pentagon polygraph exams	Y	95.	Prohibit EPA sanctions	Y
53.	Bar ASAT testing	Y	96.	SS age increase/Reforms	N
54.	Suspend def pmt for abuse	Y	97.	Auto domestic content req	Y
55.	Bar Pentagon-contr emplmt	Y	98.	Delete jobs program fundg	N
56.	Increase SDI funding	N	99.	Highway-Gas tax bill	Y
57.	Reduce SDI funding	N	100.	Raise Medicare;Cut defnse	Y
58.	Produce chemical weapons	N	101.	Emergency housing aid	Y
59.	Bar CIA fndg in Nicaragua	Y	102.	Across-the-board tax cuts	N
60.	South Africa sanctions	Y	103.	Gramm-Latta II targets	N
61.	Cut SS COLAs; Raise taxes	N	104.	Delete B-1 bomber funds	+
62.	Let US invest-So Africa	N	105.	Dsapprov Saudi AWACS sale	Y
63.	Approve 21 MX for 1985	N			

Presidential Support Score: 1986 - 25% 1985 - 23%

OHIO

LUKEN, THOMAS A. -- Ohio 1st District [Democrat]. County of Hamilton (pt.). Prior Terms: House: 1974 (Special Election)-1986. Born: July 9, 1925; Cincinnati, Ohio. Education: Xavier University; Salmon P. Chase Law School. Military Service: U.S. Marine Corps. Occupation: City solicitor (1955-61); U.S. district attorney (1961-64); city council (1964-67; 1969-73); mayor (1971-72).

1.	Immigration Reform	Y	4.	So Afr sanc-veto override	Y
2.	Open fld-search warrants	Y	5.	Tax Overhaul	Y
3.	Civil pnty-hire ill alien	N	6.	South Africa sanctions	Y

LUKEN, THOMAS A. (Cont.)

7. Death penalty-drug bill N
8. Evidence-warrantless srch Y
9. Life term-second drug off Y
10. Military use in drug war Y
11. Troop reduction in Europe N
12. Prohibit chemical weapons Y
13. Bar ASAT testing Y
14. Abide SALT II weapons ban Y
15. Follow SALT II-Soviets do N
16. Reduce SDI funding Y
17. Increase SDI funding N
18. Purchase Trident sub ?
19. Delete 12 MX;Add conv wpn ?
20. Raise speed limit Y
21. Textile Import Quotas(*) N
22. Req Pentagon buy US goods Y
23. AIDS ins anti-dscriminatn Y
24. Nicaraguan refugee aid Y
25. Nicaraguan contra aid N
26. US abide by SALT II N
27. Prohibit Saudi arms sale Y
28. Military Retiremnt Reform Y
29. Nicaraguan refugee aid Y
30. Ease '68 Gun Control Act Y
31. Bar intrstat handgun tran N
32. Keep '68 Gun Control Act N
33. Nicaraguan contra aid N
34. Bar emp polygraph testing Y
35. Tax Overhaul consideratn Y
36. Bar armor-piercing ammo Y
37. Tax Overhaul consideratn Y
38. Make comp emissions known N
39. Allow toxic victims suits N
40. Strike Superfund "VAT" Y
41. Notify emp-plant closing Y
42. Bar emp consult-plant clo N
43. Medicare cuts;Tax incres' Y
44. Delete 12 MX missiles Y
45. Spending cuts;Tax incres' Y
46. Textile Import Quotas N
47. Cut some school lunch fds N
48. Clean Water Act Amendmnts N
49. Youth work projects Y
50. Assist military in Angola N
51. Allow US troops-Nicaragua ?
52. Pentagon polygraph exams ?
53. Bar ASAT testing ?
54. Suspend def pmt for abuse ?
55. Bar Pentagon-contr emplmt ?
56. Increase SDI funding ?
57. Reduce SDI funding ?
58. Produce chemical weapons N
59. Bar CIA fndg in Nicaragua Y
60. South Africa sanctions Y
61. Cut SS COLAs; Raise taxes Y
62. Let US invest-So Africa N
63. Approve 21 MX for 1985 N
64. Emergency Farm Credit N
65. Awards to whistle blowers Y
66. African disaster relief Y
67. Ban bank loans to So Afr Y
68. Bar coun duty-free trtmt Y
69. Steel import limits Y
70. Soc Sec COLAs=inflation Y
71. Bar haz waste vctms suits Y
72. Prohibit aid to Nicaragua Y
73. Cut $-Schs bar sch prayer N
74. Raise taxes; Cut Medicare Y
75. Alien residncy-prior 1982 N
76. Alien residncy-prior 1980 N
77. Pen emp-hire illgl aliens N
78. Lmt Persh II/cruse-Europe N
79. Delete 34 B-1 bombers N
80. Bar purch of Pershing II N
81. Bar purchase of Sgt York Y
82. Delete $ for Trident II N
83. Allow 15 MX missiles Y
84. Bar MX procurement-1985 Y
85. Equal Access Act Y
86. Aid to El Salvador N
87. Bar Nicarag water mining Y
88. Physician/Medicare freeze N
89. Increase "sin" taxes Y
90. End SBA direct loans N
91. Sell Conrail N
92. Equal Rights Amendment N
93. Marines in Lebanon N
94. Eminent domain-Coal comps ?
95. Prohibit EPA sanctions N
96. SS age increase/Reforms N
97. Auto domestic content req Y
98. Delete jobs program fundg N
99. Highway-Gas tax bill Y
100. Raise Medicare;Cut defnse Y
101. Emergency housing aid Y
102. Across-the-board tax cuts Y
103. Gramm-Latta II targets Y
104. Delete B-1 bomber funds N
105. Dsapprov Saudi AWACS sale Y
106. Disapprove oil import fee Y
107. Rail Deregulation N
108. Dsapp India nuc fuel sale Y
109. Mil draft registration Y
110. Chrysler Loan Guarantees Y
111. Prohibit school busing Y
112. Nuclear plant moratorium N
113. Oil price controls Y
114. Tuition Tax Credits Y
115. Est Consumer Protect Agcy N
116. Eliminate B-1 bomber fnds N
117. Subminimum wage for youth Y
118. Delete crude oil tax N
119. Natural gas deregulation N

Presidential Support Score: 1986 - 22% 1985 - 33%

GRADISON, WILLIS D., Jr. -- Ohio 2nd District [Republican]. Counties of Brown, Clermont (pt.) and Hamilton (pt.). Prior Terms: House: 1975-86. Born: December 28, 1928; Cincinnati, Ohio. Education: Yale University (B.A.); Harvard (M.B.A., D.C.S). Occupation: Investment broker; assistant to under secretary of the Treasury (1953-55); assistant to Secretary of Health, Education and Welfare (1955-57); Cincinnati city councilman (1961-74); member, National Advisory Council on Economic Opportunity (1971-74); member, Tax Policy Advisory Committee, Council on Environmental Quality (1970-72); Cincinnati mayor (1971); board chairman, Federal Home Loan Bank of Cincinnati (1970-74).

1. Immigration Reform N
2. Open fld-search warrants N
3. Civil pnty-hire ill alien N
4. So Afr sanc-veto override Y
5. Tax Overhaul Y
6. South Africa sanctions Y
7. Death penalty-drug bill Y
8. Evidence-warrantless srch Y
9. Life term-second drug off Y
10. Military use in drug war Y
11. Troop reduction in Europe N
12. Prohibit chemical weapons Y
13. Bar ASAT testing Y
14. Abide SALT II weapons ban N
15. Follow SALT II-Soviets do Y
16. Reduce SDI funding N
17. Increase SDI funding N
18. Purchase Trident sub N
19. Delete 12 MX;Add conv wpn Y
20. Raise speed limit Y
21. Textile Import Quotas(*) N
22. Req Pentagon buy US goods N
23. AIDS ins anti-dscriminatn Y
24. Nicaraguan refugee aid N
25. Nicaraguan contra aid Y
26. US abide by SALT II Y
27. Prohibit Saudi arms sale Y
28. Military Retiremnt Reform ?
29. Nicaraguan refugee aid N
30. Ease '68 Gun Control Act N
31. Bar intrstat handgun tran Y
32. Keep '68 Gun Control Act Y
33. Nicaraguan contra aid Y
34. Bar emp polygraph testing N
35. Tax Overhaul consideratn Y
36. Bar armor-piercing ammo Y
37. Tax Overhaul consideratn Y
38. Make comp emissions known N
39. Allow toxic victims suits N
40. Strike Superfund "VAT" N
41. Notify emp-plant closing N
42. Bar emp consult-plant clo Y
43. Medicare cuts;Tax incres' N
44. Delete 12 MX missiles Y
45. Spending cuts;Tax incres' N
46. Textile Import Quotas N
47. Cut some school lunch fds Y
48. Clean Water Act Amendmnts Y
49. Youth work projects N
50. Assist military in Angola Y
51. Allow US troops-Nicaragua Y
52. Pentagon polygraph exams Y
53. Bar ASAT testing Y
54. Suspend def pmt for abuse N
55. Bar Pentagon-contr emplmt Y
56. Increase SDI funding Y
57. Reduce SDI funding N
58. Produce chemical weapons N
59. Bar CIA fndg in Nicaragua N
60. South Africa sanctions ?
61. Cut SS COLAs; Raise taxes ?
62. Let US invest-So Africa Y
63. Approve 21 MX for 1985 N
64. Emergency Farm Credit N
65. Awards to whistle blowers Y
66. African disaster relief Y
67. Ban bank loans to So Afr Y
68. Bar coun duty-free trtmt N
69. Steel import limits N
70. Soc Sec COLAs=inflation Y
71. Bar haz waste vctms suits Y
72. Prohibit aid to Nicaragua Y
73. Cut $-Schs bar sch prayer N
74. Raise taxes; Cut Medicare Y
75. Alien residncy-prior 1982 Y
76. Alien residncy-prior 1980 Y
77. Pen emp-hire illgl aliens N
78. Lmt Persh II/cruse-Europe N
79. Delete 34 B-1 bombers N
80. Bar purch of Pershing II N
81. Bar purchase of Sgt York N
82. Delete $ for Trident II N
83. Allow 15 MX missiles N
84. Bar MX procurement-1985 Y
85. Equal Access Act N
86. Aid to El Salvador Y
87. Bar Nicarag water mining Y
88. Physician/Medicare freeze Y
89. Increase "sin" taxes Y
90. End SBA direct loans ?
91. Sell Conrail Y
92. Equal Rights Amendment Y
93. Marines in Lebanon N
94. Eminent domain-Coal comps Y

GRADISON, WILLIS D. Jr. (Cont.)

95. Prohibit EPA sanctions ?
96. SS age increase/Reforms Y
97. Auto domestic content req N
98. Delete jobs program fundg Y
99. Highway-Gas tax bill Y
100. Raise Medicare;Cut defnse N
101. Emergency housing aid N
102. Across-the-board tax cuts Y
103. Gramm-Latta II targets Y
104. Delete B-1 bomber funds N
105. Dsapprov Saudi AWACS sale Y
106. Disapprove oil import fee Y
107. Rail Deregulation N
108. Dsapp India nuc fuel sale N
109. Mil draft registration Y
110. Chrysler Loan Guarantees C
111. Prohibit school busing Y
112. Nuclear plant moratorium N
113. Oil price controls N
114. Tuition Tax Credits Y
115. Est Consumer Protect Agcy N
116. Eliminate B-1 bomber fnds N
117. Subminimum wage for youth Y
118. Delete crude oil tax Y
119. Natural gas deregulation Y

Presidential Support Score: 1986 - 60% 1985 - 65%

HALL, TONY P. -- Ohio 3rd District [Democrat]. County of Montgomery (pt.). Prior Terms: House: 1979-86. Born: January 16, 1942; Dayton, Ohio. Education: Denison University (A.B.). Occupation: Peace Corps teacher; small businessman; real estate investor; Ohio representative (1969-73); Ohio senator (1973-79).

1. Immigration Reform ?
2. Open fld-search warrants Y
3. Civil pnty-hire ill alien Y
4. So Afr sanc-veto override Y
5. Tax Overhaul N
6. South Africa sanctions Y
7. Death penalty-drug bill Y
8. Evidence-warrantless srch N
9. Life term-second drug off Y
10. Military use in drug war Y
11. Troop reduction in Europe N
12. Prohibit chemical weapons Y
13. Bar ASAT testing Y
14. Abide SALT II weapons ban Y
15. Follow SALT II-Soviets do N
16. Reduce SDI funding Y
17. Increase SDI funding N
18. Purchase Trident sub Y
19. Delete 12 MX;Add conv wpn Y
20. Raise speed limit Y
21. Textile Import Quotas(*) Y
22. Req Pentagon buy US goods Y
23. AIDS ins anti-dscriminatn N
24. Nicaraguan refugee aid Y
25. Nicaraguan contra aid N
26. US abide by SALT II N
27. Prohibit Saudi arms sale Y
28. Military Retiremnt Reform Y
29. Nicaraguan refugee aid N
30. Ease '68 Gun Control Act N
31. Bar intrstat handgun tran Y
32. Keep '68 Gun Control Act Y
33. Nicaraguan contra aid N
34. Bar emp polygraph testing N
35. Tax Overhaul consideratn Y
36. Bar armor-piercing ammo Y
37. Tax Overhaul consideratn Y
38. Make comp emissions known Y
39. Allow toxic victims suits Y
40. Strike Superfund "VAT" Y
41. Notify emp-plant closing Y
42. Bar emp consult-plant clo N
43. Medicare cuts;Tax incres' Y
44. Delete 12 MX missiles Y
45. Spending cuts;Tax incres' Y
46. Textile Import Quotas Y
47. Cut some school lunch fds N
48. Clean Water Act Amendmnts N
49. Youth work projects Y
50. Assist military in Angola ?
51. Allow US troops-Nicaragua N
52. Pentagon polygraph exams Y
53. Bar ASAT testing Y
54. Suspend def pmt for abuse Y
55. Bar Pentagon-contr emplmt Y
56. Increase SDI funding N
57. Reduce SDI funding Y
58. Produce chemical weapons N
59. Bar CIA fndg in Nicaragua Y
60. South Africa sanctions Y
61. Cut SS COLAs; Raise taxes N
62. Let US invest-So Africa ?
63. Approve 21 MX for 1985 N
64. Emergency Farm Credit Y
65. Awards to whistle blowers Y
66. African disaster relief Y
67. Ban bank loans to So Afr Y
68. Bar coun duty-free trtmt Y
69. Steel import limits Y
70. Soc Sec COLAs=inflation Y
71. Bar haz waste vctms suits N
72. Prohibit aid to Nicaragua Y

HALL, TONY P. (Cont.)

73. Cut $-Schs bar sch prayer Y
74. Raise taxes; Cut Medicare N
75. Alien residncy-prior 1982 N
76. Alien residncy-prior 1980 N
77. Pen emp-hire illgl aliens Y
78. Lmt Persh II/cruse-Europe N
79. Delete 34 B-1 bombers N
80. Bar purch of Pershing II Y
81. Bar purchase of Sgt York N
82. Delete $ for Trident II N
83. Allow 15 MX missiles N
84. Bar MX procurement-1985 Y
85. Equal Access Act Y
86. Aid to El Salvador N
87. Bar Nicarag water mining Y
88. Physician/Medicare freeze N
89. Increase "sin" taxes Y
90. End SBA direct loans N
91. Sell Conrail N
92. Equal Rights Amendment Y
93. Marines in Lebanon Y
94. Eminent domain-Coal comps N
95. Prohibit EPA sanctions Y
96. SS age increase/Reforms N
97. Auto domestic content req Y
98. Delete jobs program fundg N
99. Highway-Gas tax bill Y
100. Raise Medicare;Cut defnse Y
101. Emergency housing aid Y
102. Across-the-board tax cuts N
103. Gramm-Latta II targets Y
104. Delete B-1 bomber funds N
105. Dsapprov Saudi AWACS sale Y
106. Disapprove oil import fee Y
107. Rail Deregulation N
108. Dsapp India nuc fuel sale Y
109. Mil draft registration N
110. Chrysler Loan Guarantees Y
111. Prohibit school busing Y
112. Nuclear plant moratorium Y
113. Oil price controls Y

Presidential Support Score: 1986 - 15% 1985 - 29%

OXLEY, MICHAEL G. -- Ohio 4th District [Republican]. Counties of Allen, Auglaize, Crawford, Hancock, Hardin, Knox, Richland (pt.), Shelby and Wyandot. Prior Terms: House: 1981 (Special Election)-1986. Born: February 11, 1944; Findlay, Ohio. Education: Miami University (B.A.); Ohio State University (J.D.). Occupation: Attorney; Ohio representative (1972-79); congressional staff member; staff member, lieutenant governor; staff member, attorney general; special agent, FBI.

1. Immigration Reform N
2. Open fld-search warrants N
3. Civil pnty-hire ill alien Y
4. So Afr sanc-veto override X
5. Tax Overhaul Y
6. South Africa sanctions N
7. Death penalty-drug bill Y
8. Evidence-warrantless srch Y
9. Life term-second drug off Y
10. Military use in drug war N
11. Troop reduction in Europe N
12. Prohibit chemical weapons N
13. Bar ASAT testing N
14. Abide SALT II weapons ban N
15. Follow SALT II-Soviets do Y
16. Reduce SDI funding N
17. Increase SDI funding N
18. Purchase Trident sub N
19. Delete 12 MX;Add conv wpn N
20. Raise speed limit Y
21. Textile Import Quotas(*) N
22. Req Pentagon buy US goods N
23. AIDS ins anti-dscrimінatn N
24. Nicaraguan refugee aid N
25. Nicaraguan contra aid Y
26. US abide by SALT II Y
27. Prohibit Saudi arms sale N
28. Military Retiremnt Reform Y
29. Nicaraguan refugee aid Y
30. Ease '68 Gun Control Act Y
31. Bar intrstat handgun tran Y
32. Keep '68 Gun Control Act Y
33. Nicaraguan contra aid Y
34. Bar emp polygraph testing N
35. Tax Overhaul consideratn N
36. Bar armor-piercing ammo Y
37. Tax Overhaul consideratn N
38. Make comp emissions known N
39. Allow toxic victims suits N
40. Strike Superfund "VAT" N
41. Notify emp-plant closing N
42. Bar emp consult-plant clo Y
43. Medicare cuts;Tax incres' N
44. Delete 12 MX missiles N
45. Spending cuts;Tax incres' N
46. Textile Import Quotas N
47. Cut some school lunch fds Y
48. Clean Water Act Amendmnts Y

OXLEY, MICHAEL G. (Cont.)

49. Youth work projects N
50. Assist military in Angola Y
51. Allow US troops-Nicaragua N
52. Pentagon polygraph exams Y
53. Bar ASAT testing N
54. Suspend def pmt for abuse N
55. Bar Pentagon-contr emplmt Y
56. Increase SDI funding N
57. Reduce SDI funding N
58. Produce chemical weapons Y
59. Bar CIA fndg in Nicaragua N
60. South Africa sanctions N
61. Cut SS COLAs; Raise taxes N
62. Let US invest-So Africa Y
63. Approve 21 MX for 1985 Y
64. Emergency Farm Credit Y
65. Awards to whistle blowers Y
66. African disaster relief Y
67. Ban bank loans to So Afr Y
68. Bar coun duty-free trtmt N
69. Steel import limits N
70. Soc Sec COLAs=inflation Y
71. Bar haz waste vctms suits Y
72. Prohibit aid to Nicaragua N
73. Cut $-Schs bar sch prayer +
74. Raise taxes; Cut Medicare Y
75. Alien residncy-prior 1982 Y
76. Alien residncy-prior 1980 Y
77. Pen emp-hire illgl aliens N
78. Lmt Persh II/cruse-Europe N
79. Delete 34 B-1 bombers N
80. Bar purch of Pershing II N
81. Bar purchase of Sgt York N
82. Delete $ for Trident II N
83. Allow 15 MX missiles Y
84. Bar MX procurement-1985 N
85. Equal Access Act Y
86. Aid to El Salvador Y
87. Bar Nicarag water mining N
88. Physician/Medicare freeze Y
89. Increase "sin" taxes Y
90. End SBA direct loans Y
91. Sell Conrail Y
92. Equal Rights Amendment N
93. Marines in Lebanon Y
94. Eminent domain-Coal comps N
95. Prohibit EPA sanctions Y
96. SS age increase/Reforms Y
97. Auto domestic content req N
98. Delete jobs program fundg Y
99. Highway-Gas tax bill N
100. Raise Medicare;Cut defnse N
101. Emergency housing aid Y
102. Across-the-board tax cuts Y
103. Gramm-Latta II targets
104. Delete B-1 bomber funds N
105. Dsapprov Saudi AWACS sale N

Sworn in July 21, 1981 and missed vote 103.

Presidential Support Score: 1986 - 80% 1985 - 75%

LATTA, DELBERT L. -- Ohio 5th District [Republican]. Counties of Defiance, Erie, Fulton (pt.), Henry, Huron (pt.), Ottawa, Paulding, Putnam, Sandusky, Seneca, Williams and Wood (pt.). Prior Terms: House: 1959-86. Born: March 5, 1920; Weston, Ohio. Education: Ohio Northern University (A.B., LL.B.). Occupation: Attorney; Ohio senator.

1. Immigration Reform N
2. Open fld-search warrants Y
3. Civil pnty-hire ill alien Y
4. So Afr sanc-veto override N
5. Tax Overhaul Y
6. South Africa sanctions N
7. Death penalty-drug bill Y
8. Evidence-warrantless srch Y
9. Life term-second drug off Y
10. Military use in drug war Y
11. Troop reduction in Europe N
12. Prohibit chemical weapons N
13. Bar ASAT testing N
14. Abide SALT II weapons ban N
15. Follow SALT II-Soviets do Y
16. Reduce SDI funding N
17. Increase SDI funding Y
18. Purchase Trident sub N
19. Delete 12 MX;Add conv wpn N
20. Raise speed limit N
21. Textile Import Quotas(*) N
22. Req Pentagon buy US goods Y
23. AIDS ins anti-dscriminatn N
24. Nicaraguan refugee aid N
25. Nicaraguan contra aid Y
26. US abide by SALT II Y
27. Prohibit Saudi arms sale N
28. Military Retiremnt Reform Y
29. Nicaraguan refugee aid Y
30. Ease '68 Gun Control Act Y
31. Bar intrstat handgun tran N
32. Keep '68 Gun Control Act N

LATTA, DELBERT L. (Cont.)

33. Nicaraguan contra aid Y
34. Bar emp polygraph testing ?
35. Tax Overhaul consideratn Y
36. Bar armor-piercing ammo Y
37. Tax Overhaul consideratn N
38. Make comp emissions known N
39. Allow toxic victims suits N
40. Strike Superfund "VAT" Y
41. Notify emp-plant closing N
42. Bar emp consult-plant clo Y
43. Medicare cuts;Tax incres' N
44. Delete 12 MX missiles N
45. Spending cuts;Tax incres' N
46. Textile Import Quotas N
47. Cut some school lunch fds Y
48. Clean Water Act Amendmnts Y
49. Youth work projects N
50. Assist military in Angola Y
51. Allow US troops-Nicaragua Y
52. Pentagon polygraph exams Y
53. Bar ASAT testing N
54. Suspend def pmt for abuse N
55. Bar Pentagon-contr emplmt Y
56. Increase SDI funding Y
57. Reduce SDI funding N
58. Produce chemical weapons Y
59. Bar CIA fndg in Nicaragua N
60. South Africa sanctions N
61. Cut SS COLAs; Raise taxes N
62. Let US invest-So Africa Y
63. Approve 21 MX for 1985 Y
64. Emergency Farm Credit Y
65. Awards to whistle blowers Y
66. African disaster relief Y
67. Ban bank loans to So Afr N
68. Bar coun duty-free trtmt N
69. Steel import limits N
70. Soc Sec COLAs=inflation Y
71. Bar haz waste vctms suits Y
72. Prohibit aid to Nicaragua N
73. Cut $-Schs bar sch prayer Y
74. Raise taxes; Cut Medicare N
75. Alien residncy-prior 1982 Y
76. Alien residncy-prior 1980 Y
77. Pen emp-hire illgl aliens N
78. Lmt Persh II/cruse-Europe N
79. Delete 34 B-1 bombers N
80. Bar purch of Pershing II N
81. Bar purchase of Sgt York ?
82. Delete $ for Trident II N
83. Allow 15 MX missiles Y
84. Bar MX procurement-1985 N
85. Equal Access Act Y
86. Aid to El Salvador Y
87. Bar Nicarag water mining ?
88. Physician/Medicare freeze Y
89. Increase "sin" taxes Y
90. End SBA direct loans N
91. Sell Conrail Y
92. Equal Rights Amendment N
93. Marines in Lebanon Y
94. Eminent domain-Coal comps N
95. Prohibit EPA sanctions Y
96. SS age increase/Reforms Y
97. Auto domestic content req Y
98. Delete jobs program fundg Y
99. Highway-Gas tax bill Y
100. Raise Medicare;Cut defnse N
101. Emergency housing aid N
102. Across-the-board tax cuts Y
103. Gramm-Latta II targets Y
104. Delete B-1 bomber funds N
105. Dsapprov Saudi AWACS sale N
106. Disapprove oil import fee Y
107. Rail Deregulation ?
108. Dsapp India nuc fuel sale Y
109. Mil draft registration N
110. Chrysler Loan Guarantees Y
111. Prohibit school busing Y
112. Nuclear plant moratorium N
113. Oil price controls N
114. Tuition Tax Credits Y
115. Est Consumer Protect Agcy N
116. Eliminate B-1 bomber fnds N
117. Subminimum wage for youth Y
118. Delete crude oil tax Y
119. Natural gas deregulation Y

Presidential Support Score: 1986 - 64% 1985 - 85%

McEWEN, BOB -- Ohio 6th District [Republican]. Counties of Adams, Athens (pt.), Clermont (pt.), Clinton, Fayette (pt.), Highland, Hocking, Jackson, Montgomery (pt.), Pike, Ross, Scioto, Vinton and Warren. Prior Terms: House: 1981-86. Born: January 12, 1950; Hillsboro, Ohio. Education: University of Miami (B.B.A.). Occupation: Ohio representative (1974-80); congressional assistant; vice president, Boebinger, Inc.

1. Immigration Reform #
2. Open fld-search warrants ?
3. Civil pnty-hire ill alien ?
4. So Afr sanc-veto override N

McEWEN, BOB (Cont.)

5.	Tax Overhaul	Y	56.	Increase SDI funding	Y
6.	South Africa sanctions	N	57.	Reduce SDI funding	N
7.	Death penalty-drug bill	Y	58.	Produce chemical weapons	Y
8.	Evidence-warrantless srch	Y	59.	Bar CIA fndg in Nicaragua	N
9.	Life term-second drug off	Y	60.	South Africa sanctions	N
10.	Military use in drug war	N	61.	Cut SS COLAs; Raise taxes	N
11.	Troop reduction in Europe	Y	62.	Let US invest-So Africa	Y
12.	Prohibit chemical weapons	N	63.	Approve 21 MX for 1985	Y
13.	Bar ASAT testing	N	64.	Emergency Farm Credit	Y
14.	Abide SALT II weapons ban	N	65.	Awards to whistle blowers	Y
15.	Follow SALT II-Soviets do	Y	66.	African disaster relief	Y
16.	Reduce SDI funding	N	67.	Ban bank loans to So Afr	?
17.	Increase SDI funding	Y	68.	Bar coun duty-free trtmt	N
18.	Purchase Trident sub	N	69.	Steel import limits	Y
19.	Delete 12 MX;Add conv wpn	N	70.	Soc Sec COLAs=inflation	Y
20.	Raise speed limit	Y	71.	Bar haz waste vctms suits	#
21.	Textile Import Quotas(*)	N	72.	Prohibit aid to Nicaragua	N
22.	Req Pentagon buy US goods	Y	73.	Cut $-Schs bar sch prayer	Y
23.	AIDS ins anti-dscriminatn	N	74.	Raise taxes; Cut Medicare	N
24.	Nicaraguan refugee aid	N	75.	Alien residncy-prior 1982	Y
25.	Nicaraguan contra aid	Y	76.	Alien residncy-prior 1980	Y
26.	US abide by SALT II	Y	77.	Pen emp-hire illgl aliens	N
27.	Prohibit Saudi arms sale	Y	78.	Lmt Persh II/cruse-Europe	N
28.	Military Retiremnt Reform	Y	79.	Delete 34 B-1 bombers	N
29.	Nicaraguan refugee aid	Y	80.	Bar purch of Pershing II	?
30.	Ease '68 Gun Control Act	Y	81.	Bar purchase of Sgt York	N
31.	Bar intrstat handgun tran	N	82.	Delete $ for Trident II	N
32.	Keep '68 Gun Control Act	N	83.	Allow 15 MX missiles	Y
33.	Nicaraguan contra aid	Y	84.	Bar MX procurement-1985	N
34.	Bar emp polygraph testing	N	85.	Equal Access Act	Y
35.	Tax Overhaul consideratn	N	86.	Aid to El Salvador	Y
36.	Bar armor-piercing ammo	Y	87.	Bar Nicarag water mining	N
37.	Tax Overhaul consideratn	N	88.	Physician/Medicare freeze	Y
38.	Make comp emissions known	N	89.	Increase "sin" taxes	N
39.	Allow toxic victims suits	N	90.	End SBA direct loans	N
40.	Strike Superfund "VAT"	Y	91.	Sell Conrail	Y
41.	Notify emp-plant closing	N	92.	Equal Rights Amendment	N
42.	Bar emp consult-plant clo	Y	93.	Marines in Lebanon	Y
43.	Medicare cuts;Tax incres'	N	94.	Eminent domain-Coal comps	N
44.	Delete 12 MX missiles	N	95.	Prohibit EPA sanctions	Y
45.	Spending cuts;Tax incres'	N	96.	SS age increase/Reforms	Y
46.	Textile Import Quotas	N	97.	Auto domestic content req	Y
47.	Cut some school lunch fds	Y	98.	Delete jobs program fundg	Y
48.	Clean Water Act Amendmnts	Y	99.	Highway-Gas tax bill	N
49.	Youth work projects	N	100.	Raise Medicare;Cut defnse	N
50.	Assist military in Angola	Y	101.	Emergency housing aid	Y
51.	Allow US troops-Nicaragua	Y	102.	Across-the-board tax cuts	Y
52.	Pentagon polygraph exams	Y	103.	Gramm-Latta II targets	Y
53.	Bar ASAT testing	N	104.	Delete B-1 bomber funds	N
54.	Suspend def pmt for abuse	Y	105.	Dsapprov Saudi AWACS sale	N
55.	Bar Pentagon-contr emplmt	Y			

Presidential Support Score: 1986 - 68% 1985 - 69%

DeWINE, MICHAEL -- Ohio 7th District [Republican]. Counties of Champaign (pt.), Clark, Fayette (pt.), Greene, Logan, Madison (pt.), Marion, Pickaway and Union. Prior Terms: House: 1983-

DeWINE, MICHAEL (Cont.)

86. Born: January 5, 1947. Education: Miami University (B.S.); Ohio Northern University College of Law (J.D.). Occupation: Attorney; assistant prosecuting attorney (1973-75); prosecuting attorney (1977-81); Ohio senator (1981).

1.	Immigration Reform	Y	49.	Youth work projects	N
2.	Open fld-search warrants	N	50.	Assist military in Angola	Y
3.	Civil pnty-hire ill alien	Y	51.	Allow US troops-Nicaragua	Y
4.	So Afr sanc-veto override	N	52.	Pentagon polygraph exams	Y
5.	Tax Overhaul	Y	53.	Bar ASAT testing	N
6.	South Africa sanctions	Y	54.	Suspend def pmt for abuse	N
7.	Death penalty-drug bill	Y	55.	Bar Pentagon-contr emplmt	Y
8.	Evidence-warrantless srch	Y	56.	Increase SDI funding	Y
9.	Life term-second drug off	Y	57.	Reduce SDI funding	N
10.	Military use in drug war	Y	58.	Produce chemical weapons	Y
11.	Troop reduction in Europe	N	59.	Bar CIA fndg in Nicaragua	N
12.	Prohibit chemical weapons	N	60.	South Africa sanctions	N
13.	Bar ASAT testing	N	61.	Cut SS COLAs; Raise taxes	N
14.	Abide SALT II weapons ban	N	62.	Let US invest-So Africa	Y
15.	Follow SALT II-Soviets do	Y	63.	Approve 21 MX for 1985	Y
16.	Reduce SDI funding	N	64.	Emergency Farm Credit	Y
17.	Increase SDI funding	Y	65.	Awards to whistle blowers	Y
18.	Purchase Trident sub	N	66.	African disaster relief	Y
19.	Delete 12 MX;Add conv wpn	N	67.	Ban bank loans to So Afr	N
20.	Raise speed limit	N	68.	Bar coun duty-free trtmt	N
21.	Textile Import Quotas(*)	N	69.	Steel import limits	Y
22.	Req Pentagon buy US goods	N	70.	Soc Sec COLAs=inflation	Y
23.	AIDS ins anti-dscriminatn	N	71.	Bar haz waste vctms suits	Y
24.	Nicaraguan refugee aid	N	72.	Prohibit aid to Nicaragua	N
25.	Nicaraguan contra aid	Y	73.	Cut $-Schs bar sch prayer	Y
26.	US abide by SALT II	Y	74.	Raise taxes; Cut Medicare	Y
27.	Prohibit Saudi arms sale	N	75.	Alien residncy-prior 1982	Y
28.	Military Retiremnt Reform	Y	76.	Alien residncy-prior 1980	N
29.	Nicaraguan refugee aid	Y	77.	Pen emp-hire illgl aliens	N
30.	Ease '68 Gun Control Act	Y	78.	Lmt Persh II/cruse-Europe	N
31.	Bar intrstat handgun tran	N	79.	Delete 34 B-1 bombers	N
32.	Keep '68 Gun Control Act	Y	80.	Bar purch of Pershing II	N
33.	Nicaraguan contra aid	Y	81.	Bar purchase of Sgt York	N
34.	Bar emp polygraph testing	N	82.	Delete $ for Trident II	N
35.	Tax Overhaul consideratn	Y	83.	Allow 15 MX missiles	Y
36.	Bar armor-piercing ammo	Y	84.	Bar MX procurement-1985	N
37.	Tax Overhaul consideratn	N	85.	Equal Access Act	Y
38.	Make comp emissions known	N	86.	Aid to El Salvador	Y
39.	Allow toxic victims suits	N	87.	Bar Nicarag water mining	N
40.	Strike Superfund "VAT"	Y	88.	Physician/Medicare freeze	Y
41.	Notify emp-plant closing	N	89.	Increase "sin" taxes	Y
42.	Bar emp consult-plant clo	Y	90.	End SBA direct loans	Y
43.	Medicare cuts;Tax incres'	N	91.	Sell Conrail	?
44.	Delete 12 MX missiles	N	92.	Equal Rights Amendment	N
45.	Spending cuts;Tax incres'	N	93.	Marines in Lebanon	Y
46.	Textile Import Quotas	N	94.	Eminent domain-Coal comps	N
47.	Cut some school lunch fds	Y	95.	Prohibit EPA sanctions	N
48.	Clean Water Act Amendmnts	N	96.	SS age increase/Reforms	Y

Presidential Support Score: 1986 - 77% 1985 - 78%

KINDNESS, THOMAS N. -- Ohio 8th District [Republican]. Counties of Butler, Champaign (pt.), Darke, Mercer, Miami, Preble and Van

KINDNESS, THOMAS N. (Cont.)
Wert. Prior Terms: House: 1975-86. Born: August 26, 1929; Knoxville, Tenn. Education: University of Maryland (A.B.); George Washington School of Law. Occupation: City councilman (1964-69); mayor (1964-67); Ohio representative (1971-74); assistant counsel, Champion International Corp.

1. Immigration Reform ?
2. Open fld-search warrants ?
3. Civil pnty-hire ill alien ?
4. So Afr sanc-veto override ?
5. Tax Overhaul N
6. South Africa sanctions N
7. Death penalty-drug bill Y
8. Evidence-warrantless srch Y
9. Life term-second drug off Y
10. Military use in drug war Y
11. Troop reduction in Europe N
12. Prohibit chemical weapons N
13. Bar ASAT testing N
14. Abide SALT II weapons ban N
15. Follow SALT II-Soviets do Y
16. Reduce SDI funding N
17. Increase SDI funding N
18. Purchase Trident sub N
19. Delete 12 MX;Add conv wpn N
20. Raise speed limit Y
21. Textile Import Quotas(*) Y
22. Req Pentagon buy US goods Y
23. AIDS ins anti-dscrimnatn N
24. Nicaraguan refugee aid N
25. Nicaraguan contra aid Y
26. US abide by SALT II Y
27. Prohibit Saudi arms sale Y
28. Military Retiremnt Reform Y
29. Nicaraguan refugee aid Y
30. Ease '68 Gun Control Act Y
31. Bar intrstat handgun tran N
32. Keep '68 Gun Control Act N
33. Nicaraguan contra aid Y
34. Bar emp polygraph testing ?
35. Tax Overhaul consideratn N
36. Bar armor-piercing ammo Y
37. Tax Overhaul consideratn N
38. Make comp emissions known N
39. Allow toxic victims suits N
40. Strike Superfund "VAT" Y
41. Notify emp-plant closing N
42. Bar emp consult-plant clo Y
43. Medicare cuts;Tax incres' N
44. Delete 12 MX missiles N
45. Spending cuts;Tax incres' N
46. Textile Import Quotas Y
47. Cut some school lunch fds Y
48. Clean Water Act Amendmnts Y
49. Youth work projects N
50. Assist military in Angola Y
51. Allow US troops-Nicaragua Y
52. Pentagon polygraph exams Y
53. Bar ASAT testing N
54. Suspend def pmt for abuse N
55. Bar Pentagon-contr emplmt N
56. Increase SDI funding Y
57. Reduce SDI funding N
58. Produce chemical weapons Y
59. Bar CIA fndg in Nicaragua N
60. South Africa sanctions N
61. Cut SS COLAs; Raise taxes N
62. Let US invest-So Africa Y
63. Approve 21 MX for 1985 Y
64. Emergency Farm Credit Y
65. Awards to whistle blowers Y
66. African disaster relief N
67. Ban bank loans to So Afr N
68. Bar coun duty-free trtmt N
69. Steel import limits N
70. Soc Sec COLAs=Inflation Y
71. Bar haz waste vctms suits Y
72. Prohibit aid to Nicaragua N
73. Cut $-Schs bar sch prayer Y
74. Raise taxes; Cut Medicare Y
75. Alien residncy-prior 1982 Y
76. Alien residncy-prior 1980 Y
77. Pen emp-hire illgl aliens N
78. Lmt Persh II/cruse-Europe N
79. Delete 34 B-1 bombers N
80. Bar purch of Pershing II N
81. Bar purchase of Sgt York Y
82. Delete $ for Trident II N
83. Allow 15 MX missiles Y
84. Bar MX procurement-1985 N
85. Equal Access Act Y
86. Aid to El Salvador Y
87. Bar Nicarag water mining X
88. Physician/Medicare freeze Y
89. Increase "sin" taxes Y
90. End SBA direct loans N
91. Sell Conrail ?
92. Equal Rights Amendment N
93. Marines in Lebanon Y
94. Eminent domain-Coal comps N
95. Prohibit EPA sanctions N
96. SS age increase/Reforms Y
97. Auto domestic content req Y
98. Delete jobs program fundg ?
99. Highway-Gas tax bill N
100. Raise Medicare;Cut defnse N
101. Emergency housing aid Y
102. Across-the-board tax cuts Y
103. Gramm-Latta II targets Y
104. Delete B-1 bomber funds N

KINDNESS, THOMAS N. (Cont.)

105. Dsapprov Saudi AWACS sale Y
106. Disapprove oil import fee Y
107. Rail Deregulation N
108. Dsapp India nuc fuel sale Y
109. Mil draft registration Y
110. Chrysler Loan Guarantees N
111. Prohibit school busing Y
112. Nuclear plant moratorium N
113. Oil price controls N
114. Tuition Tax Credits Y
115. Est Consumer Protect Agcy N
116. Eliminate B-1 bomber fnds N
117. Subminimum wage for youth #
118. Delete crude oil tax Y
119. Natural gas deregulation Y

Presidential Support Score: 1986 - 59% 1985 - 73%

KAPTUR, MARCY -- Ohio 9th District [Democrat]. Counties of Fulton (pt.), Lucas and Wood (pt.). Prior Terms: House: 1983-86. Born: June 17, 1946; Toledo, Ohio. Education: University of Wisconsin (B.A.); University of Michigan (M.A.). Occupation: Urban planner; county commissioner (1969-73); self-employed consultant; Director of Planning and Urban Development, National Center for Urban Ethnic Affairs (1975-76); White House aide (1977-79); deputy secretary for Policy, Research, and Operations, National Consumer Cooperative Bank (1979-81).

1. Immigration Reform ?
2. Open fld-search warrants ?
3. Civil pnty-hire ill alien ?
4. So Afr sanc-veto override Y
5. Tax Overhaul N
6. South Africa sanctions Y
7. Death penalty-drug bill Y
8. Evidence-warrantless srch N
9. Life term-second drug off Y
10. Military use in drug war Y
11. Troop reduction in Europe N
12. Prohibit chemical weapons Y
13. Bar ASAT testing Y
14. Abide SALT II weapons ban Y
15. Follow SALT II-Soviets do N
16. Reduce SDI funding N
17. Increase SDI funding N
18. Purchase Trident sub Y
19. Delete 12 MX;Add conv wpn Y
20. Raise speed limit N
21. Textile Import Quotas(*) Y
22. Req Pentagon buy US goods Y
23. AIDS ins anti-dscriminatn Y
24. Nicaraguan refugee aid Y
25. Nicaraguan contra aid N
26. US abide by SALT II N
27. Prohibit Saudi arms sale Y
28. Military Retiremnt Reform Y
29. Nicaraguan refugee aid Y
30. Ease '68 Gun Control Act N
31. Bar intrstat handgun tran Y
32. Keep '68 Gun Control Act Y
33. Nicaraguan contra aid N
34. Bar emp polygraph testing Y
35. Tax Overhaul consideratn N
36. Bar armor-piercing ammo Y
37. Tax Overhaul consideratn N
38. Make comp emissions known Y
39. Allow toxic victims suits Y
40. Strike Superfund "VAT" Y
41. Notify emp-plant closing Y
42. Bar emp consult-plant clo N
43. Medicare cuts;Tax incres' Y
44. Delete 12 MX missiles Y
45. Spending cuts;Tax incres' Y
46. Textile Import Quotas Y
47. Cut some school lunch fds N
48. Clean Water Act Amendmnts N
49. Youth work projects Y
50. Assist military in Angola N
51. Allow US troops-Nicaragua N
52. Pentagon polygraph exams Y
53. Bar ASAT testing Y
54. Suspend def pmt for abuse Y
55. Bar Pentagon-contr emplmt Y
56. Increase SDI funding N
57. Reduce SDI funding N
58. Produce chemical weapons N
59. Bar CIA fndg in Nicaragua Y
60. South Africa sanctions Y
61. Cut SS COLAs; Raise taxes N
62. Let US invest-So Africa N
63. Approve 21 MX for 1985 N
64. Emergency Farm Credit Y
65. Awards to whistle blowers Y
66. African disaster relief Y
67. Ban bank loans to So Afr ?
68. Bar coun duty-free trtmt N
69. Steel import limits Y
70. Soc Sec COLAs=inflation Y
71. Bar haz waste vctms suits N
72. Prohibit aid to Nicaragua Y

KAPTUR, MARCY (Cont.)

73. Cut $-Schs bar sch prayer N
74. Raise taxes; Cut Medicare N
75. Alien residncy-prior 1982 Y
76. Alien residncy-prior 1980 N
77. Pen emp-hire illgl aliens ?
78. Lmt Persh II/cruse-Europe Y
79. Delete 34 B-1 bombers Y
80. Bar purch of Pershing II Y
81. Bar purchase of Sgt York Y
82. Delete $ for Trident II N
83. Allow 15 MX missiles N
84. Bar MX procurement-1985 Y
85. Equal Access Act Y
86. Aid to El Salvador N
87. Bar Nicarag water mining Y
88. Physician/Medicare freeze N
89. Increase "sin" taxes Y
90. End SBA direct loans N
91. Sell Conrail N
92. Equal Rights Amendment Y
93. Marines in Lebanon N
94. Eminent domain-Coal comps N
95. Prohibit EPA sanctions N
96. SS age increase/Reforms N

Presidential Support Score: 1986 - 17% 1985 - 26%

MILLER, CLARENCE E. -- Ohio 10th District [Republican]. Counties of Athens (pt.), Fairfield, Gallia, Guernsey (pt.), Lawrence, Licking (pt.), Meigs, Morgan, Muskingum, Perry and Washington (pt.). Prior Terms: House: 1967-86. Born: November 1, 1917; Lancaster, Ohio. Education: International Correspondence Schools. Occupation: City councilman (1957-63); mayor (1963-65).

1. Immigration Reform N
2. Open fld-search warrants N
3. Civil pnty-hire ill alien N
4. So Afr sanc-veto override N
5. Tax Overhaul N
6. South Africa sanctions N
7. Death penalty-drug bill Y
8. Evidence-warrantless srch Y
9. Life term-second drug off Y
10. Military use in drug war Y
11. Troop reduction in Europe N
12. Prohibit chemical weapons N
13. Bar ASAT testing N
14. Abide SALT II weapons ban N
15. Follow SALT II-Soviets do Y
16. Reduce SDI funding N
17. Increase SDI funding N
18. Purchase Trident sub N
19. Delete 12 MX;Add conv wpn N
20. Raise speed limit Y
21. Textile Import Quotas(*) Y
22. Req Pentagon buy US goods Y
23. AIDS ins anti-dscriminatn N
24. Nicaraguan refugee aid N
25. Nicaraguan contra aid Y
26. US abide by SALT II Y
27. Prohibit Saudi arms sale N
28. Military Retiremnt Reform Y
29. Nicaraguan refugee aid Y
30. Ease '68 Gun Control Act Y
31. Bar intrstat handgun tran N
32. Keep '68 Gun Control Act N
33. Nicaraguan contra aid Y
34. Bar emp polygraph testing N
35. Tax Overhaul consideratn Y
36. Bar armor-piercing ammo Y
37. Tax Overhaul consideratn N
38. Make comp emissions known ?
39. Allow toxic victims suits ?
40. Strike Superfund "VAT" ?
41. Notify emp-plant closing N
42. Bar emp consult-plant clo Y
43. Medicare cuts;Tax incres' N
44. Delete 12 MX missiles N
45. Spending cuts;Tax incres' N
46. Textile Import Quotas Y
47. Cut some school lunch fds Y
48. Clean Water Act Amendmnts Y
49. Youth work projects N
50. Assist military in Angola Y
51. Allow US troops-Nicaragua Y
52. Pentagon polygraph exams Y
53. Bar ASAT testing N
54. Suspend def pmt for abuse Y
55. Bar Pentagon-contr emplmt Y
56. Increase SDI funding Y
57. Reduce SDI funding N
58. Produce chemical weapons Y
59. Bar CIA fndg in Nicaragua N
60. South Africa sanctions N
61. Cut SS COLAs; Raise taxes N
62. Let US invest-So Africa Y
63. Approve 21 MX for 1985 Y
64. Emergency Farm Credit Y
65. Awards to whistle blowers Y
66. African disaster relief Y
67. Ban bank loans to So Afr N
68. Bar coun duty-free trtmt N

MILLER, CLARENCE E. (Cont.)

69. Steel import limits Y
70. Soc Sec COLAs=inflation Y
71. Bar haz waste vctms suits Y
72. Prohibit aid to Nicaragua N
73. Cut $-Schs bar sch prayer Y
74. Raise taxes; Cut Medicare Y
75. Alien residncy-prior 1982 Y
76. Alien residncy-prior 1980 Y
77. Pen emp-hire illgl aliens N
78. Lmt Persh II/cruse-Europe N
79. Delete 34 B-1 bombers N
80. Bar purch of Pershing II N
81. Bar purchase of Sgt York Y
82. Delete $ for Trident II N
83. Allow 15 MX missiles Y
84. Bar MX procurement-1985 N
85. Equal Access Act Y
86. Aid to El Salvador Y
87. Bar Nicarag water mining Y
88. Physician/Medicare freeze Y
89. Increase "sin" taxes Y
90. End SBA direct loans N
91. Sell Conrail Y
92. Equal Rights Amendment N
93. Marines in Lebanon N
94. Eminent domain-Coal comps N
95. Prohibit EPA sanctions Y
96. SS age increase/Reforms N
97. Auto domestic content req Y
98. Delete jobs program fundg Y
99. Highway-Gas tax bill N
100. Raise Medicare;Cut defnse N
101. Emergency housing aid N
102. Across-the-board tax cuts Y
103. Gramm-Latta II targets Y
104. Delete B-1 bomber funds N
105. Dsapprov Saudi AWACS sale N
106. Disapprove oil import fee Y
107. Rail Deregulation N
108. Dsapp India nuc fuel sale N
109. Mil draft registration N
110. Chrysler Loan Guarantees N
111. Prohibit school busing Y
112. Nuclear plant moratorium N
113. Oil price controls N
114. Tuition Tax Credits Y
115. Est Consumer Protect Agcy N
116. Eliminate B-1 bomber fnds N
117. Subminimum wage for youth Y
118. Delete crude oil tax Y
119. Natural gas deregulation Y

Presidential Support Score: 1986 - 76% 1985 - 70%

ECKART, DENNIS E. -- Ohio 11th District [Democrat]. Counties of Ashtabula, Geauga, Lake (pt.), Portage and Trumbull (pt.). Prior Terms: House: 1981-86. Born: April 6, 1950; Cleveland Ohio. Education: Xavier University; Cleveland Marshall Law School. Occupation: Ohio legislator (1975-80).

1. Immigration Reform Y
2. Open fld-search warrants Y
3. Civil pnty-hire ill alien Y
4. So Afr sanc-veto override Y
5. Tax Overhaul Y
6. South Africa sanctions Y
7. Death penalty-drug bill Y
8. Evidence-warrantless srch N
9. Life term-second drug off Y
10. Military use in drug war Y
11. Troop reduction in Europe Y
12. Prohibit chemical weapons Y
13. Bar ASAT testing Y
14. Abide SALT II weapons ban Y
15. Follow SALT II-Soviets do N
16. Reduce SDI funding N
17. Increase SDI funding N
18. Purchase Trident sub Y
19. Delete 12 MX;Add conv wpn Y
20. Raise speed limit N
21. Textile Import Quotas(*) Y
22. Req Pentagon buy US goods Y
23. AIDS ins anti-dscriminatn Y
24. Nicaraguan refugee aid Y
25. Nicaraguan contra aid N
26. US abide by SALT II N
27. Prohibit Saudi arms sale -
28. Military Retiremnt Reform Y
29. Nicaraguan refugee aid Y
30. Ease '68 Gun Control Act Y
31. Bar intrstat handgun tran N
32. Keep '68 Gun Control Act Y
33. Nicaraguan contra aid N
34. Bar emp polygraph testing Y
35. Tax Overhaul consideratn Y
36. Bar armor-piercing ammo Y
37. Tax Overhaul consideratn N
38. Make comp emissions known N
39. Allow toxic victims suits N
40. Strike Superfund "VAT" N
41. Notify emp-plant closing Y
42. Bar emp consult-plant clo N
43. Medicare cuts;Tax incres' Y
44. Delete 12 MX missiles Y

ECKART, DENNIS E. (Cont.)

45. Spending cuts;Tax incres' Y
46. Textile Import Quotas Y
47. Cut some school lunch fds N
48. Clean Water Act Amendmnts N
49. Youth work projects Y
50. Assist military in Angola N
51. Allow US troops-Nicaragua ?
52. Pentagon polygraph exams Y
53. Bar ASAT testing Y
54. Suspend def pmt for abuse Y
55. Bar Pentagon-contr emplmt Y
56. Increase SDI funding N
57. Reduce SDI funding Y
58. Produce chemical weapons N
59. Bar CIA fndg in Nicaragua Y
60. South Africa sanctions Y
61. Cut SS COLAs; Raise taxes N
62. Let US invest-So Africa N
63. Approve 21 MX for 1985 N
64. Emergency Farm Credit Y
65. Awards to whistle blowers Y
66. African disaster relief #
67. Ban bank loans to So Afr Y
68. Bar coun duty-free trtmt Y
69. Steel import limits Y
70. Soc Sec COLAs=inflation Y
71. Bar haz waste vctms suits N
72. Prohibit aid to Nicaragua Y
73. Cut $-Schs bar sch prayer N
74. Raise taxes; Cut Medicare N
75. Alien residncy-prior 1982 Y
76. Alien residncy-prior 1980 N
77. Pen emp-hire illgl aliens Y
78. Lmt Persh II/cruse-Europe Y
79. Delete 34 B-1 bombers N
80. Bar purch of Pershing II Y
81. Bar purchase of Sgt York Y
82. Delete $ for Trident II N
83. Allow 15 MX missiles N
84. Bar MX procurement-1985 Y
85. Equal Access Act Y
86. Aid to El Salvador N
87. Bar Nicarag water mining Y
88. Physician/Medicare freeze N
89. Increase "sin" taxes Y
90. End SBA direct loans N
91. Sell Conrail N
92. Equal Rights Amendment Y
93. Marines in Lebanon N
94. Eminent domain-Coal comps N
95. Prohibit EPA sanctions Y
96. SS age increase/Reforms N
97. Auto domestic content req Y
98. Delete jobs program fundg N
99. Highway-Gas tax bill Y
100. Raise Medicare;Cut defnse Y
101. Emergency housing aid Y
102. Across-the-board tax cuts N
103. Gramm-Latta II targets N
104. Delete B-1 bomber funds N
105. Dsapprov Saudi AWACS sale Y

Presidential Support Score: 1986 - 22% 1985 - 24%

KASICH, JOHN R. -- Ohio 12th District [Republican]. Counties of Delaware, Franklin (pt.), Licking (pt.) and Morrow. Prior Terms: House: 1983-86. Born: May 13, 1952; McKees Rocks, Pa. Education: Ohio State University (B.A.). Occupation: Administrative assistant (1975-77); Ohio senator (1979-82).

1. Immigration Reform N
2. Open fld-search warrants ?
3. Civil pnty-hire ill alien Y
4. So Afr sanc-veto override Y
5. Tax Overhaul Y
6. South Africa sanctions Y
7. Death penalty-drug bill Y
8. Evidence-warrantless srch Y
9. Life term-second drug off Y
10. Military use in drug war Y
11. Troop reduction in Europe N
12. Prohibit chemical weapons N
13. Bar ASAT testing N
14. Abide SALT II weapons ban N
15. Follow SALT II-Soviets do Y
16. Reduce SDI funding N
17. Increase SDI funding Y
18. Purchase Trident sub N
19. Delete 12 MX;Add conv wpn N
20. Raise speed limit Y
21. Textile Import Quotas(*) N
22. Req Pentagon buy US goods Y
23. AIDS ins anti-dscriminatn N
24. Nicaraguan refugee aid N
25. Nicaraguan contra aid Y
26. US abide by SALT II Y
27. Prohibit Saudi arms sale Y
28. Military Retiremnt Reform Y
29. Nicaraguan refugee aid Y
30. Ease '68 Gun Control Act Y
31. Bar intrstat handgun tran N
32. Keep '68 Gun Control Act N
33. Nicaraguan contra aid Y
34. Bar emp polygraph testing N

KASICH, JOHN R. (Cont.)

35. Tax Overhaul consideratn N
36. Bar armor-piercing ammo Y
37. Tax Overhaul consideratn N
38. Make comp emissions known N
39. Allow toxic victims suits N
40. Strike Superfund "VAT" N
41. Notify emp-plant closing N
42. Bar emp consult-plant clo Y
43. Medicare cuts;Tax incres' N
44. Delete 12 MX missiles N
45. Spending cuts;Tax incres' N
46. Textile Import Quotas N
47. Cut some school lunch fds Y
48. Clean Water Act Amendmnts Y
49. Youth work projects N
50. Assist military in Angola Y
51. Allow US troops-Nicaragua Y
52. Pentagon polygraph exams Y
53. Bar ASAT testing N
54. Suspend def pmt for abuse N
55. Bar Pentagon-contr emplmt Y
56. Increase SDI funding Y
57. Reduce SDI funding N
58. Produce chemical weapons Y
59. Bar CIA fndg in Nicaragua N
60. South Africa sanctions Y
61. Cut SS COLAs; Raise taxes N
62. Let US invest-So Africa Y
63. Approve 21 MX for 1985 Y
64. Emergency Farm Credit Y
65. Awards to whistle blowers Y
66. African disaster relief Y
67. Ban bank loans to So Afr N
68. Bar coun duty-free trtmt Y
69. Steel import limits Y
70. Soc Sec COLAs=inflation Y
71. Bar haz waste vctms suits Y
72. Prohibit aid to Nicaragua N
73. Cut $-Schs bar sch prayer Y
74. Raise taxes; Cut Medicare N
75. Alien residncy-prior 1982 Y
76. Alien residncy-prior 1980 Y
77. Pen emp-hire illgl aliens N
78. Lmt Persh II/cruse-Europe N
79. Delete 34 B-1 bombers N
80. Bar purch of Pershing II N
81. Bar purchase of Sgt York N
82. Delete $ for Trident II N
83. Allow 15 MX missiles Y
84. Bar MX procurement-1985 N
85. Equal Access Act Y
86. Aid to El Salvador Y
87. Bar Nicarag water mining N
88. Physician/Medicare freeze Y
89. Increase "sin" taxes Y
90. End SBA direct loans N
91. Sell Conrail Y
92. Equal Rights Amendment N
93. Marines in Lebanon N
94. Eminent domain-Coal comps N
95. Prohibit EPA sanctions Y
96. SS age increase/Reforms Y

Presidential Support Score: 1986 - 70% 1985 - 74%

PEASE, DONALD J. -- Ohio 13th District [Democrat]. Counties of Ashland, Huron (pt.), Loran (pt.), Medina, Richland (pt.) and Summit (pt.). Prior Terms: House: 1977-86. Born: September 26, 1931; Toledo, Ohio. Education: Ohio University (B.S., M.A.); King's College, University of Durham. Military Service: U.S. Army, 1955-57. Occupation: Newspaper editor; Oberlin city councilman (1962-64); Ohio senator (1965-66, 1975-76); Ohio representative (1969-74).

1. Immigration Reform Y
2. Open fld-search warrants N
3. Civil pnty-hire ill alien N
4. So Afr sanc-veto override Y
5. Tax Overhaul Y
6. South Africa sanctions Y
7. Death penalty-drug bill Y
8. Evidence-warrantless srch N
9. Life term-second drug off N
10. Military use in drug war N
11. Troop reduction in Europe N
12. Prohibit chemical weapons Y
13. Bar ASAT testing Y
14. Abide SALT II weapons ban Y
15. Follow SALT II-Soviets do N
16. Reduce SDI funding Y
17. Increase SDI funding N
18. Purchase Trident sub N
19. Delete 12 MX;Add conv wpn Y
20. Raise speed limit N
21. Textile Import Quotas(*) N
22. Req Pentagon buy US goods Y
23. AIDS ins anti-dscriminatn Y
24. Nicaraguan refugee aid Y
25. Nicaraguan contra aid N
26. US abide by SALT II N
27. Prohibit Saudi arms sale Y
28. Military Retiremnt Reform Y

PEASE, DONALD J. (Cont.)

29. Nicaraguan refugee aid Y
30. Ease '68 Gun Control Act Y
31. Bar intrstat handgun tran Y
32. Keep '68 Gun Control Act Y
33. Nicaraguan contra aid N
34. Bar emp polygraph testing Y
35. Tax Overhaul consideratn Y
36. Bar armor-piercing ammo Y
37. Tax Overhaul consideratn Y
38. Make comp emissions known Y
39. Allow toxic victims suits N
40. Strike Superfund "VAT" Y
41. Notify emp-plant closing Y
42. Bar emp consult-plant clo N
43. Medicare cuts;Tax incres' Y
44. Delete 12 MX missiles Y
45. Spending cuts;Tax incres' Y
46. Textile Import Quotas N
47. Cut some school lunch fds N
48. Clean Water Act Amendmnts N
49. Youth work projects Y
50. Assist military in Angola N
51. Allow US troops-Nicaragua N
52. Pentagon polygraph exams N
53. Bar ASAT testing Y
54. Suspend def pmt for abuse N
55. Bar Pentagon-contr emplmt Y
56. Increase SDI funding N
57. Reduce SDI funding Y
58. Produce chemical weapons N
59. Bar CIA fndg in Nicaragua Y
60. South Africa sanctions Y
61. Cut SS COLAs; Raise taxes Y
62. Let US invest-So Africa N
63. Approve 21 MX for 1985 N
64. Emergency Farm Credit Y
65. Awards to whistle blowers Y
66. African disaster relief Y
67. Ban bank loans to So Afr Y
68. Bar coun duty-free trtmt N
69. Steel import limits Y
70. Soc Sec COLAs=inflation Y
71. Bar haz waste vctms suits Y
72. Prohibit aid to Nicaragua Y
73. Cut $-Schs bar sch prayer N
74. Raise taxes; Cut Medicare Y
75. Alien residncy-prior 1982 Y
76. Alien residncy-prior 1980 N
77. Pen emp-hire illgl aliens Y
78. Lmt Persh II/cruse-Europe Y
79. Delete 34 B-1 bombers Y
80. Bar purch of Pershing II N
81. Bar purchase of Sgt York Y
82. Delete $ for Trident II N
83. Allow 15 MX missiles N
84. Bar MX procurement-1985 Y
85. Equal Access Act Y
86. Aid to El Salvador N
87. Bar Nicarag water mining Y
88. Physician/Medicare freeze N
89. Increase "sin" taxes Y
90. End SBA direct loans N
91. Sell Conrail Y
92. Equal Rights Amendment Y
93. Marines in Lebanon N
94. Eminent domain-Coal comps N
95. Prohibit EPA sanctions Y
96. SS age increase/Reforms N
97. Auto domestic content req Y
98. Delete jobs program fundg N
99. Highway-Gas tax bill Y
100. Raise Medicare;Cut defnse Y
101. Emergency housing aid Y
102. Across-the-board tax cuts N
103. Gramm-Latta II targets N
104. Delete B-1 bomber funds Y
105. Dsapprov Saudi AWACS sale Y
106. Disapprove oil import fee Y
107. Rail Deregulation N
108. Dsapp India nuc fuel sale Y
109. Mil draft registration N
110. Chrysler Loan Guarantees Y
111. Prohibit school busing N
112. Nuclear plant moratorium N
113. Oil price controls Y
114. Tuition Tax Credits Y
115. Est Consumer Protect Agcy Y
116. Eliminate B-1 bomber fnds Y
117. Subminimum wage for youth Y
118. Delete crude oil tax N
119. Natural gas deregulation Y

Presidential Support Score: 1986 - 25% 1985 - 28%

SEIBERLING, JOHN F. -- Ohio 14th District [Democrat]. County of Summit (pt.). Prior Terms: House: 1971-86. Born: September 8, 1918; Akron, Ohio. Education: Harvard University (A.B.); Columbia University (LL.B.). Military Service: U.S. Army. Occupation: : Associate, Donovan, Leisure, Newton & Irvine (1949-54); legal staff member, Goodyear Tire Co (1954-70); member, Tri-County Regional Planning Commission (1966-68).

SEIBERLING, JOHN F. (Cont.)

1. Immigration Reform Y
2. Open fld-search warrants Y
3. Civil pnty-hire ill alien N
4. So Afr sanc-veto override Y
5. Tax Overhaul Y
6. South Africa sanctions Y
7. Death penalty-drug bill N
8. Evidence-warrantless srch N
9. Life term-second drug off Y
10. Military use in drug war N
11. Troop reduction in Europe N
12. Prohibit chemical weapons Y
13. Bar ASAT testing Y
14. Abide SALT II weapons ban Y
15. Follow SALT II-Soviets do N
16. Reduce SDI funding Y
17. Increase SDI funding N
18. Purchase Trident sub N
19. Delete 12 MX;Add conv wpn Y
20. Raise speed limit N
21. Textile Import Quotas(*) N
22. Req Pentagon buy US goods Y
23. AIDS ins anti-dscriminatn Y
24. Nicaraguan refugee aid Y
25. Nicaraguan contra aid N
26. US abide by SALT II N
27. Prohibit Saudi arms sale Y
28. Military Retiremnt Reform ?
29. Nicaraguan refugee aid Y
30. Ease '68 Gun Control Act N
31. Bar intrstat handgun tran Y
32. Keep '68 Gun Control Act Y
33. Nicaraguan contra aid N
34. Bar emp polygraph testing Y
35. Tax Overhaul consideratn Y
36. Bar armor-piercing ammo Y
37. Tax Overhaul consideratn Y
38. Make comp emissions known Y
39. Allow toxic victims suits Y
40. Strike Superfund "VAT" Y
41. Notify emp-plant closing Y
42. Bar emp consult-plant clo N
43. Medicare cuts;Tax incres' Y
44. Delete 12 MX missiles Y
45. Spending cuts;Tax incres' Y
46. Textile Import Quotas N
47. Cut some school lunch fds N
48. Clean Water Act Amendmnts N
49. Youth work projects Y
50. Assist military in Angola N
51. Allow US troops-Nicaragua N
52. Pentagon polygraph exams N
53. Bar ASAT testing Y
54. Suspend def pmt for abuse Y
55. Bar Pentagon-contr emplmt Y
56. Increase SDI funding N
57. Reduce SDI funding Y
58. Produce chemical weapons N
59. Bar CIA fndg in Nicaragua Y
60. South Africa sanctions Y
61. Cut SS COLAs; Raise taxes N
62. Let US invest-So Africa N
63. Approve 21 MX for 1985 N
64. Emergency Farm Credit ?
65. Awards to whistle blowers Y
66. African disaster relief Y
67. Ban bank loans to So Afr Y
68. Bar coun duty-free trtmt Y
69. Steel import limits Y
70. Soc Sec COLAs=inflation Y
71. Bar haz waste vctms suits N
72. Prohibit aid to Nicaragua Y
73. Cut $-Schs bar sch prayer N
74. Raise taxes; Cut Medicare Y
75. Alien residncy-prior 1982 N
76. Alien residncy-prior 1980 N
77. Pen emp-hire illgl aliens Y
78. Lmt Persh II/cruse-Europe Y
79. Delete 34 B-1 bombers Y
80. Bar purch of Pershing II Y
81. Bar purchase of Sgt York Y
82. Delete $ for Trident II Y
83. Allow 15 MX missiles N
84. Bar MX procurement-1985 Y
85. Equal Access Act N
86. Aid to El Salvador N
87. Bar Nicarag water mining Y
88. Physician/Medicare freeze N
89. Increase "sin" taxes Y
90. End SBA direct loans N
91. Sell Conrail N
92. Equal Rights Amendment Y
93. Marines in Lebanon Y
94. Eminent domain-Coal comps Y
95. Prohibit EPA sanctions Y
96. SS age increase/Reforms N
97. Auto domestic content req Y
98. Delete jobs program fundg N
99. Highway-Gas tax bill N
100. Raise Medicare;Cut defnse Y
101. Emergency housing aid Y
102. Across-the-board tax cuts N
103. Gramm-Latta II targets N
104. Delete B-1 bomber funds Y
105. Dsapprov Saudi AWACS sale Y
106. Disapprove oil import fee Y
107. Rail Deregulation N
108. Dsapp India nuc fuel sale Y
109. Mil draft registration N
110. Chrysler Loan Guarantees Y
111. Prohibit school busing N
112. Nuclear plant moratorium Y
113. Oil price controls Y
114. Tuition Tax Credits Y
115. Est Consumer Protect Agcy Y
116. Eliminate B-1 bomber fnds Y

SEIBERLING, JOHN F. (Cont.)

117. Subminimum wage for youth N
118. Delete crude oil tax N
119. Natural gas deregulation N

Presidential Support Score: 1986 - 16% 1985 - 19%

WYLIE, CHALMERS P. -- Ohio 15th District [Republican]. Counties of Franklin (pt.) and Madison (pt.). Prior Terms: House: 1967-86. Born: November 23, 1920; Norwich, Ohio. Education: Otterbein College; Ohio State University; Harvard Law School. Military Service: U.S. Army. Occupation: Assistant attorney general (1948, 1951-53); assistant city attorney (1949-50); city attorney (1953); administrator, Bureau of Workmen's Compensation (1957); partner, Gingher & Christensen (1959); Ohio legislator (1961-66).

1. Immigration Reform N
2. Open fld-search warrants N
3. Civil pnty-hire ill alien N
4. So Afr sanc-veto override Y
5. Tax Overhaul Y
6. South Africa sanctions Y
7. Death penalty-drug bill Y
8. Evidence-warrantless srch Y
9. Life term-second drug off Y
10. Military use in drug war Y
11. Troop reduction in Europe N
12. Prohibit chemical weapons N
13. Bar ASAT testing N
14. Abide SALT II weapons ban N
15. Follow SALT II-Soviets do Y
16. Reduce SDI funding N
17. Increase SDI funding N
18. Purchase Trident sub N
19. Delete 12 MX;Add conv wpn N
20. Raise speed limit N
21. Textile Import Quotas(*) N
22. Req Pentagon buy US goods Y
23. AIDS ins anti-dscriminatn N
24. Nicaraguan refugee aid N
25. Nicaraguan contra aid Y
26. US abide by SALT II Y
27. Prohibit Saudi arms sale Y
28. Military Retiremnt Reform Y
29. Nicaraguan refugee aid Y
30. Ease '68 Gun Control Act N
31. Bar intrstat handgun tran Y
32. Keep '68 Gun Control Act Y
33. Nicaraguan contra aid N
34. Bar emp polygraph testing ?
35. Tax Overhaul consideratn Y
36. Bar armor-piercing ammo Y
37. Tax Overhaul consideratn Y
38. Make comp emissions known N
39. Allow toxic victims suits N
40. Strike Superfund "VAT" Y
41. Notify emp-plant closing N
42. Bar emp consult-plant clo Y
43. Medicare cuts;Tax incres' N
44. Delete 12 MX missiles N
45. Spending cuts;Tax incres' N
46. Textile Import Quotas Y
47. Cut some school lunch fds Y
48. Clean Water Act Amendmnts Y
49. Youth work projects N
50. Assist military in Angola Y
51. Allow US troops-Nicaragua Y
52. Pentagon polygraph exams Y
53. Bar ASAT testing N
54. Suspend def pmt for abuse N
55. Bar Pentagon-contr emplmt Y
56. Increase SDI funding N
57. Reduce SDI funding N
58. Produce chemical weapons Y
59. Bar CIA fndg in Nicaragua N
60. South Africa sanctions Y
61. Cut SS COLAs; Raise taxes N
62. Let US invest-So Africa N
63. Approve 21 MX for 1985 Y
64. Emergency Farm Credit N
65. Awards to whistle blowers Y
66. African disaster relief Y
67. Ban bank loans to So Afr Y
68. Bar coun duty-free trtmt N
69. Steel import limits Y
70. Soc Sec COLAs=inflation Y
71. Bar haz waste vctms suits Y
72. Prohibit aid to Nicaragua Y
73. Cut $-Schs bar sch prayer Y
74. Raise taxes; Cut Medicare N
75. Alien residncy-prior 1982 Y
76. Alien residncy-prior 1980 Y
77. Pen emp-hire illgl aliens N
78. Lmt Persh II/cruse-Europe N
79. Delete 34 B-1 bombers N
80. Bar purch of Pershing II N
81. Bar purchase of Sgt York N
82. Delete $ for Trident II ?
83. Allow 15 MX missiles Y
84. Bar MX procurement-1985 N

WYLIE, CHALMERS P. (Cont.)

85. Equal Access Act Y
86. Aid to El Salvador Y
87. Bar Nicarag water mining N
88. Physician/Medicare freeze Y
89. Increase "sin" taxes Y
90. End SBA direct loans N
91. Sell Conrail ?
92. Equal Rights Amendment N
93. Marines in Lebanon Y
94. Eminent domain-Coal comps N
95. Prohibit EPA sanctions N
96. SS age increase/Reforms Y
97. Auto domestic content req Y
98. Delete jobs program fundg Y
99. Highway-Gas tax bill Y
100. Raise Medicare;Cut defnse Y
101. Emergency housing aid Y
102. Across-the-board tax cuts Y
103. Gramm-Latta II targets Y
104. Delete B-1 bomber funds N
105. Dsapprov Saudi AWACS sale N
106. Disapprove oil import fee Y
107. Rail Deregulation N
108. Dsapp India nuc fuel sale Y
109. Mil draft registration N
110. Chrysler Loan Guarantees Y
111. Prohibit school busing Y
112. Nuclear plant moratorium N
113. Oil price controls N
114. Tuition Tax Credits Y
115. Est Consumer Protect Agcy Y
116. Eliminate B-1 bomber fnds N
117. Subminimum wage for youth Y
118. Delete crude oil tax Y
119. Natural gas deregulation Y

Presidential Support Score: 1986 - 63% 1985 - 68%

REGULA, RALPH -- Ohio 16th District [Republican]. Counties of Carroll (pt.), Holmes, Stark and Wayne. Prior Terms: House: 1973-86. Born: December 3, 1924; Beach City, Ohio. Education: Mount Union College (B.A.); William McKinley School of Law (LL.B.). Military Service: U.S. Navy, WW II. Occupation: Attorney; director, Stark County Bar Assn.; member, Ohio Board of Education (1960-64); Ohio representative (1965-66); Ohio senator (1967-72).

1. Immigration Reform N
2. Open fld-search warrants N
3. Civil pnty-hire ill alien N
4. So Afr sanc-veto override Y
5. Tax Overhaul N
6. South Africa sanctions Y
7. Death penalty-drug bill Y
8. Evidence-warrantless srch Y
9. Life term-second drug off Y
10. Military use in drug war Y
11. Troop reduction in Europe N
12. Prohibit chemical weapons Y
13. Bar ASAT testing Y
14. Abide SALT II weapons ban N
15. Follow SALT II-Soviets do Y
16. Reduce SDI funding N
17. Increase SDI funding N
18. Purchase Trident sub N
19. Delete 12 MX;Add conv wpn N
20. Raise speed limit N
21. Textile Import Quotas(*) Y
22. Req Pentagon buy US goods Y
23. AIDS ins anti-dscriminatn N
24. Nicaraguan refugee aid N
25. Nicaraguan contra aid Y
26. US abide by SALT II Y
27. Prohibit Saudi arms sale Y
28. Military Retiremnt Reform Y
29. Nicaraguan refugee aid Y
30. Ease '68 Gun Control Act Y
31. Bar intrstat handgun tran N
32. Keep '68 Gun Control Act N
33. Nicaraguan contra aid Y
34. Bar emp polygraph testing Y
35. Tax Overhaul consideratn Y
36. Bar armor-piercing ammo Y
37. Tax Overhaul consideratn N
38. Make comp emissions known N
39. Allow toxic victims suits N
40. Strike Superfund "VAT" Y
41. Notify emp-plant closing N
42. Bar emp consult-plant clo Y
43. Medicare cuts;Tax incres' N
44. Delete 12 MX missiles N
45. Spending cuts;Tax incres' N
46. Textile Import Quotas Y
47. Cut some school lunch fds Y
48. Clean Water Act Amendmnts N
49. Youth work projects Y
50. Assist military in Angola Y
51. Allow US troops-Nicaragua Y
52. Pentagon polygraph exams Y
53. Bar ASAT testing Y
54. Suspend def pmt for abuse N

REGULA, RALPH (Cont.)

55. Bar Pentagon-contr emplmt Y
56. Increase SDI funding N
57. Reduce SDI funding N
58. Produce chemical weapons N
59. Bar CIA fndg in Nicaragua N
60. South Africa sanctions N
61. Cut SS COLAs; Raise taxes N
62. Let US invest-So Africa Y
63. Approve 21 MX for 1985 Y
64. Emergency Farm Credit Y
65. Awards to whistle blowers Y
66. African disaster relief Y
67. Ban bank loans to So Afr Y
68. Bar coun duty-free trtmt Y
69. Steel import limits Y
70. Soc Sec COLAs=inflation Y
71. Bar haz waste vctms suits Y
72. Prohibit aid to Nicaragua Y
73. Cut $-Schs bar sch prayer Y
74. Raise taxes; Cut Medicare Y
75. Alien residncy-prior 1982 Y
76. Alien residncy-prior 1980 Y
77. Pen emp-hire illgl aliens N
78. Lmt Persh II/cruse-Europe N
79. Delete 34 B-1 bombers N
80. Bar purch of Pershing II N
81. Bar purchase of Sgt York N
82. Delete $ for Trident II N
83. Allow 15 MX missiles Y
84. Bar MX procurement-1985 N
85. Equal Access Act Y
86. Aid to El Salvador Y
87. Bar Nicarag water mining Y
88. Physician/Medicare freeze Y
89. Increase "sin" taxes Y
90. End SBA direct loans N
91. Sell Conrail N
92. Equal Rights Amendment Y
93. Marines in Lebanon Y
94. Eminent domain-Coal comps N
95. Prohibit EPA sanctions N
96. SS age increase/Reforms N
97. Auto domestic content req Y
98. Delete jobs program fundg Y
99. Highway-Gas tax bill N
100. Raise Medicare;Cut defnse N
101. Emergency housing aid Y
102. Across-the-board tax cuts Y
103. Gramm-Latta II targets Y
104. Delete B-1 bomber funds N
105. Dsapprov Saudi AWACS sale N
106. Disapprove oil import fee Y
107. Rail Deregulation N
108. Dsapp India nuc fuel sale Y
109. Mil draft registration Y
110. Chrysler Loan Guarantees N
111. Prohibit school busing Y
112. Nuclear plant moratorium N
113. Oil price controls N
114. Tuition Tax Credits Y
115. Est Consumer Protect Agcy N
116. Eliminate B-1 bomber fnds N
117. Subminimum wage for youth Y
118. Delete crude oil tax Y
119. Natural gas deregulation Y

Presidential Support Score: 1986 - 55% 1985 - 60%

TRAFICANT, JAMES A., Jr. -- Ohio 17th District [Democrat]. Counties of Columbiana (pt.), Mahoning and Trumbull (pt.). Prior Terms: 1985-86. Born: May 8, 1941. Education: University of Pittsburgh (B.S.); Youngstown State (M.S.). Occupation: Sheriff; director, county drug program; consumer finance director.

1. Immigration Reform N
2. Open fld-search warrants Y
3. Civil pnty-hire ill alien N
4. So Afr sanc-veto override Y
5. Tax Overhaul Y
6. South Africa sanctions Y
7. Death penalty-drug bill Y
8. Evidence-warrantless srch Y
9. Life term-second drug off Y
10. Military use in drug war Y
11. Troop reduction in Europe Y
12. Prohibit chemical weapons Y
13. Bar ASAT testing Y
14. Abide SALT II weapons ban Y
15. Follow SALT II-Soviets do N
16. Reduce SDI funding Y
17. Increase SDI funding N
18. Purchase Trident sub Y
19. Delete 12 MX;Add conv wpn Y
20. Raise speed limit N
21. Textile Import Quotas(*) Y
22. Req Pentagon buy US goods Y
23. AIDS ins anti-dscriminatn Y
24. Nicaraguan refugee aid Y
25. Nicaraguan contra aid N
26. US abide by SALT II N
27. Prohibit Saudi arms sale Y
28. Military Retiremnt Reform Y
29. Nicaraguan refugee aid Y
30. Ease '68 Gun Control Act N

TRAFICANT, JAMES A., Jr. (Cont.)

31. Bar intrstat handgun tran Y
32. Keep '68 Gun Control Act Y
33. Nicaraguan contra aid N
34. Bar emp polygraph testing Y
35. Tax Overhaul consideratn N
36. Bar armor-piercing ammo Y
37. Tax Overhaul consideratn N
38. Make comp emissions known Y
39. Allow toxic victims suits Y
40. Strike Superfund "VAT" Y
41. Notify emp-plant closing Y
42. Bar emp consult-plant clo N
43. Medicare cuts;Tax incres' Y
44. Delete 12 MX missiles Y
45. Spending cuts;Tax incres' N
46. Textile Import Quotas Y
47. Cut some school lunch fds N
48. Clean Water Act Amendmnts N
49. Youth work projects Y
50. Assist military in Angola N
51. Allow US troops-Nicaragua N
52. Pentagon polygraph exams N
53. Bar ASAT testing Y
54. Suspend def pmt for abuse Y
55. Bar Pentagon-contr emplmt Y
56. Increase SDI funding N
57. Reduce SDI funding Y
58. Produce chemical weapons N
59. Bar CIA fndg in Nicaragua Y
60. South Africa sanctions Y
61. Cut SS COLAs; Raise taxes N
62. Let US invest-So Africa N
63. Approve 21 MX for 1985 N
64. Emergency Farm Credit Y
65. Awards to whistle blowers Y
66. African disaster relief Y

Presidential Support Score: 1986 - 10% 1985 - 13%

APPLEGATE, DOUGLAS -- Ohio 18th District [Democrat]. Counties of Belmont, Carroll (pt.), Columbiana (pt.), Coshocton, Guernsey (pt.), Harrison, Jefferson, Monroe, Noble and Tuscarawas (pt.). Prior Terms: House: 1977-86. Born: March 27, 1928; Steubenville, Ohio. Occupation: Ohio representative (1961-69) Ohio senator (1969-77); Ohio Constitutional Revision commissioner.

1. Immigration Reform N
2. Open fld-search warrants N
3. Civil pnty-hire ill alien N
4. So Afr sanc-veto override Y
5. Tax Overhaul N
6. South Africa sanctions Y
7. Death penalty-drug bill Y
8. Evidence-warrantless srch Y
9. Life term-second drug off Y
10. Military use in drug war Y
11. Troop reduction in Europe Y
12. Prohibit chemical weapons Y
13. Bar ASAT testing N
14. Abide SALT II weapons ban Y
15. Follow SALT II-Soviets do N
16. Reduce SDI funding N
17. Increase SDI funding N
18. Purchase Trident sub Y
19. Delete 12 MX;Add conv wpn Y
20. Raise speed limit N
21. Textile Import Quotas(*) Y
22. Req Pentagon buy US goods Y
23. AIDS ins anti-dscriminatn Y
24. Nicaraguan refugee aid Y
25. Nicaraguan contra aid N
26. US abide by SALT II N
27. Prohibit Saudi arms sale Y
28. Military Retiremnt Reform Y
29. Nicaraguan refugee aid Y
30. Ease '68 Gun Control Act Y
31. Bar intrstat handgun tran Y
32. Keep '68 Gun Control Act Y
33. Nicaraguan contra aid N
34. Bar emp polygraph testing Y
35. Tax Overhaul consideratn N
36. Bar armor-piercing ammo Y
37. Tax Overhaul consideratn N
38. Make comp emissions known Y
39. Allow toxic victims suits N
40. Strike Superfund "VAT" N
41. Notify emp-plant closing Y
42. Bar emp consult-plant clo N
43. Medicare cuts;Tax incres' N
44. Delete 12 MX missiles Y
45. Spending cuts;Tax incres' N
46. Textile Import Quotas Y
47. Cut some school lunch fds N
48. Clean Water Act Amendmnts N
49. Youth work projects Y
50. Assist military in Angola N
51. Allow US troops-Nicaragua N
52. Pentagon polygraph exams Y
53. Bar ASAT testing Y
54. Suspend def pmt for abuse Y
55. Bar Pentagon-contr emplmt Y
56. Increase SDI funding N

APPLEGATE, DOUGLAS (Cont.)

57. Reduce SDI funding N
58. Produce chemical weapons N
59. Bar CIA fndg in Nicaragua Y
60. South Africa sanctions Y
61. Cut SS COLAs; Raise taxes N
62. Let US invest-So Africa N
63. Approve 21 MX for 1985 N
64. Emergency Farm Credit Y
65. Awards to whistle blowers Y
66. African disaster relief Y
67. Ban bank loans to So Afr N
68. Bar coun duty-free trtmt Y
69. Steel import limits Y
70. Soc Sec COLAs=inflation Y
71. Bar haz waste vctms suits Y
72. Prohibit aid to Nicaragua Y
73. Cut $-Schs bar sch prayer Y
74. Raise taxes; Cut Medicare N
75. Alien residncy-prior 1982 Y
76. Alien residncy-prior 1980 N
77. Pen emp-hire illgl aliens N
78. Lmt Persh II/cruse-Europe N
79. Delete 34 B-1 bombers N
80. Bar purch of Pershing II N
81. Bar purchase of Sgt York N
82. Delete $ for Trident II N
83. Allow 15 MX missiles Y
84. Bar MX procurement-1985 Y
85. Equal Access Act Y
86. Aid to El Salvador N
87. Bar Nicarag water mining Y
88. Physician/Medicare freeze N
89. Increase "sin" taxes Y
90. End SBA direct loans N
91. Sell Conrail N
92. Equal Rights Amendment Y
93. Marines in Lebanon N
94. Eminent domain-Coal comps N
95. Prohibit EPA sanctions Y
96. SS age increase/Reforms N
97. Auto domestic content req Y
98. Delete jobs program fundg N
99. Highway-Gas tax bill Y
100. Raise Medicare;Cut defnse Y
101. Emergency housing aid Y
102. Across-the-board tax cuts N
103. Gramm-Latta II targets N
104. Delete B-1 bomber funds N
105. Dsapprov Saudi AWACS sale Y
106. Disapprove oil import fee Y
107. Rail Deregulation N
108. Dsapp India nuc fuel sale Y
109. Mil draft registration N
110. Chrysler Loan Guarantees Y
111. Prohibit school busing Y
112. Nuclear plant moratorium N
113. Oil price controls Y
114. Tuition Tax Credits Y
115. Est Consumer Protect Agcy Y
116. Eliminate B-1 bomber fnds N
117. Subminimum wage for youth N
118. Delete crude oil tax Y
119. Natural gas deregulation N

Presidential Support Score: 1986 - 24% 1985 - 29%

FEIGHAN, EDWARD F. -- Ohio 19th District [Democrat]. Counties of Cuyahoga (pt.), Lake (pt.) and Lorain (pt.) Prior Terms: House: 1983-86. Born: October 22, 1947; Lakewood, Ohio. Education: Loyola University; Cleveland State University (J.D.). Occupation: Ohio representative (1973-78); county commissioner (1979-82); former member, National Advisory Council on Economic Opportunity.

1. Immigration Reform Y
2. Open fld-search warrants N
3. Civil pnty-hire ill alien N
4. So Afr sanc-veto override Y
5. Tax Overhaul Y
6. South Africa sanctions Y
7. Death penalty-drug bill N
8. Evidence-warrantless srch N
9. Life term-second drug off Y
10. Military use in drug war N
11. Troop reduction in Europe N
12. Prohibit chemical weapons Y
13. Bar ASAT testing Y
14. Abide SALT II weapons ban Y
15. Follow SALT II-Soviets do N
16. Reduce SDI funding Y
17. Increase SDI funding N
18. Purchase Trident sub Y
19. Delete 12 MX;Add conv wpn Y
20. Raise speed limit N
21. Textile Import Quotas(*) Y
22. Req Pentagon buy US goods Y
23. AIDS ins anti-dscriminatn Y
24. Nicaraguan refugee aid Y
25. Nicaraguan contra aid N
26. US abide by SALT II N
27. Prohibit Saudi arms sale Y
28. Military Retiremnt Reform Y

FEIGHAN, EDWARD F. (Cont.)

29. Nicaraguan refugee aid Y
30. Ease '68 Gun Control Act N
31. Bar intrstat handgun tran Y
32. Keep '68 Gun Control Act Y
33. Nicaraguan contra aid N
34. Bar emp polygraph testing Y
35. Tax Overhaul consideratn N
36. Bar armor-piercing ammo Y
37. Tax Overhaul consideratn Y
38. Make comp emissions known N
39. Allow toxic victims suits Y
40. Strike Superfund "VAT" N
41. Notify emp-plant closing Y
42. Bar emp consult-plant clo N
43. Medicare cuts;Tax incres' Y
44. Delete 12 MX missiles Y
45. Spending cuts;Tax incres' Y
46. Textile Import Quotas Y
47. Cut some school lunch fds N
48. Clean Water Act Amendmnts N
49. Youth work projects Y
50. Assist military in Angola N
51. Allow US troops-Nicaragua N
52. Pentagon polygraph exams Y
53. Bar ASAT testing Y
54. Suspend def pmt for abuse Y
55. Bar Pentagon-contr emplmt Y
56. Increase SDI funding N
57. Reduce SDI funding N
58. Produce chemical weapons N
59. Bar CIA fndg in Nicaragua Y
60. South Africa sanctions Y
61. Cut SS COLAs; Raise taxes N
62. Let US invest-So Africa N
63. Approve 21 MX for 1985 N
64. Emergency Farm Credit Y
65. Awards to whistle blowers Y
66. African disaster relief Y
67. Ban bank loans to So Afr Y
68. Bar coun duty-free trtmt Y
69. Steel import limits Y
70. Soc Sec COLAs=inflation Y
71. Bar haz waste vctms suits N
72. Prohibit aid to Nicaragua Y
73. Cut $-Schs bar sch prayer N
74. Raise taxes; Cut Medicare N
75. Alien residncy-prior 1982 Y
76. Alien residncy-prior 1980 N
77. Pen emp-hire illgl aliens Y
78. Lmt Persh II/cruse-Europe Y
79. Delete 34 B-1 bombers Y
80. Bar purch of Pershing II Y
81. Bar purchase of Sgt York Y
82. Delete $ for Trident II Y
83. Allow 15 MX missiles N
84. Bar MX procurement-1985 Y
85. Equal Access Act N
86. Aid to El Salvador N
87. Bar Nicarag water mining Y
88. Physician/Medicare freeze N
89. Increase "sin" taxes Y
90. End SBA direct loans N
91. Sell Conrail N
92. Equal Rights Amendment Y
93. Marines in Lebanon Y
94. Eminent domain-Coal comps N
95. Prohibit EPA sanctions Y
96. SS age increase/Reforms N

Presidential Support Score: 1986 - 16% 1985 - 29%

OAKAR, MARY ROSE -- Ohio 20th District [Democrat]. County of Cuyahoga (pt.). Prior Terms: House: 1977-86. Born: March 5, 1940; Cleveland, Ohio. Education: Ursuline College (B.A.); John Carrol University (M.A.). Occupation: Clerk, Higbee Co. (1956-58); telephone operator (1957-62); instructor, Lourdes Academy (1963-70); assistant professor, English, Cuyahoga Community College (1968-75); Cleveland city councilman (1973-77).

1. Immigration Reform Y
2. Open fld-search warrants Y
3. Civil pnty-hire ill alien Y
4. So Afr sanc-veto override Y
5. Tax Overhaul Y
6. South Africa sanctions Y
7. Death penalty-drug bill Y
8. Evidence-warrantless srch N
9. Life term-second drug off Y
10. Military use in drug war N
11. Troop reduction in Europe Y
12. Prohibit chemical weapons Y
13. Bar ASAT testing Y
14. Abide SALT II weapons ban Y
15. Follow SALT II-Soviets do N
16. Reduce SDI funding Y
17. Increase SDI funding N
18. Purchase Trident sub Y
19. Delete 12 MX;Add conv wpn Y
20. Raise speed limit N
21. Textile Import Quotas(*) Y
22. Req Pentagon buy US goods Y
23. AIDS ins anti-dscriminatn Y
24. Nicaraguan refugee aid Y

OAKAR, MARY ROSE (Cont.)

25. Nicaraguan contra aid N
26. US abide by SALT II N
27. Prohibit Saudi arms sale Y
28. Military Retiremnt Reform Y
29. Nicaraguan refugee aid Y
30. Ease '68 Gun Control Act N
31. Bar intrstat handgun tran Y
32. Keep '68 Gun Control Act Y
33. Nicaraguan contra aid N
34. Bar emp polygraph testing Y
35. Tax Overhaul consideratn N
36. Bar armor-piercing ammo Y
37. Tax Overhaul consideratn Y
38. Make comp emissions known Y
39. Allow toxic victims suits Y
40. Strike Superfund "VAT" N
41. Notify emp-plant closing Y
42. Bar emp consult-plant clo N
43. Medicare cuts;Tax incres' Y
44. Delete 12 MX missiles Y
45. Spending cuts;Tax incres' Y
46. Textile Import Quotas Y
47. Cut some school lunch fds N
48. Clean Water Act Amendmnts N
49. Youth work projects Y
50. Assist military in Angola N
51. Allow US troops-Nicaragua N
52. Pentagon polygraph exams N
53. Bar ASAT testing Y
54. Suspend def pmt for abuse Y
55. Bar Pentagon-contr emplmt Y
56. Increase SDI funding N
57. Reduce SDI funding Y
58. Produce chemical weapons N
59. Bar CIA fndg in Nicaragua Y
60. South Africa sanctions Y
61. Cut SS COLAs; Raise taxes N
62. Let US invest-So Africa N
63. Approve 21 MX for 1985 N
64. Emergency Farm Credit Y
65. Awards to whistle blowers Y
66. African disaster relief Y
67. Ban bank loans to So Afr ?
68. Bar coun duty-free trtmt Y
69. Steel import limits Y
70. Soc Sec COLAs=inflation Y
71. Bar haz waste vctms suits N
72. Prohibit aid to Nicaragua Y
73. Cut $-Schs bar sch prayer N
74. Raise taxes; Cut Medicare Y
75. Alien residncy-prior 1982 N
76. Alien residncy-prior 1980 N
77. Pen emp-hire illgl aliens Y
78. Lmt Persh II/cruse-Europe Y
79. Delete 34 B-1 bombers N
80. Bar purch of Pershing II Y
81. Bar purchase of Sgt York N
82. Delete $ for Trident II Y
83. Allow 15 MX missiles N
84. Bar MX procurement-1985 Y
85. Equal Access Act N
86. Aid to El Salvador N
87. Bar Nicarag water mining Y
88. Physician/Medicare freeze N
89. Increase "sin" taxes Y
90. End SBA direct loans N
91. Sell Conrail N
92. Equal Rights Amendment Y
93. Marines in Lebanon Y
94. Eminent domain-Coal comps N
95. Prohibit EPA sanctions Y
96. SS age increase/Reforms N
97. Auto domestic content req Y
98. Delete jobs program fundg N
99. Highway-Gas tax bill Y
100. Raise Medicare;Cut defnse Y
101. Emergency housing aid Y
102. Across-the-board tax cuts N
103. Gramm-Latta II targets N
104. Delete B-1 bomber funds N
105. Dsapprov Saudi AWACS sale Y
106. Disapprove oil import fee Y
107. Rail Deregulation N
108. Dsapp India nuc fuel sale Y
109. Mil draft registration X
110. Chrysler Loan Guarantees Y
111. Prohibit school busing Y
112. Nuclear plant moratorium #
113. Oil price controls Y
114. Tuition Tax Credits Y
115. Est Consumer Protect Agcy Y
116. Eliminate B-1 bomber fnds N
117. Subminimum wage for youth N
118. Delete crude oil tax N
119. Natural gas deregulation N

Presidential Support Score: 1986 - 16% 1985 - 18%

STOKES, LOUIS -- Ohio 21st District [Democrat]. County of Cuyahoga (pt.). Prior Terms: House: 1969-86. Born: February 23, 1925; Cleveland, Ohio. Education: Cleveland College of Western Reserve University (B.S.); Cleveland Marshall Law College (J.D.). Military Service: U.S. Army, 1943-46. Occupation: Attorney, Stokes, Character, Terry and Perry.

STOKES, LOUIS (Cont.)

1. Immigration Reform Y
2. Open fld-search warrants Y
3. Civil pnty-hire ill alien N
4. So Afr sanc-veto override Y
5. Tax Overhaul ?
6. South Africa sanctions Y
7. Death penalty-drug bill N
8. Evidence-warrantless srch N
9. Life term-second drug off N
10. Military use in drug war N
11. Troop reduction in Europe Y
12. Prohibit chemical weapons Y
13. Bar ASAT testing Y
14. Abide SALT II weapons ban Y
15. Follow SALT II-Soviets do N
16. Reduce SDI funding Y
17. Increase SDI funding N
18. Purchase Trident sub N
19. Delete 12 MX;Add conv wpn Y
20. Raise speed limit N
21. Textile Import Quotas(*) Y
22. Req Pentagon buy US goods Y
23. AIDS ins anti-dscriminatn Y
24. Nicaraguan refugee aid Y
25. Nicaraguan contra aid N
26. US abide by SALT II N
27. Prohibit Saudi arms sale Y
28. Military Retiremnt Reform Y
29. Nicaraguan refugee aid Y
30. Ease '68 Gun Control Act X
31. Bar intrstat handgun tran ?
32. Keep '68 Gun Control Act ?
33. Nicaraguan contra aid N
34. Bar emp polygraph testing Y
35. Tax Overhaul consideratn N
36. Bar armor-piercing ammo Y
37. Tax Overhaul consideratn N
38. Make comp emissions known Y
39. Allow toxic victims suits Y
40. Strike Superfund "VAT" Y
41. Notify emp-plant closing Y
42. Bar emp consult-plant clo N
43. Medicare cuts;Tax incres' Y
44. Delete 12 MX missiles Y
45. Spending cuts;Tax incres' Y
46. Textile Import Quotas Y
47. Cut some school lunch fds N
48. Clean Water Act Amendmnts N
49. Youth work projects Y
50. Assist military in Angola N
51. Allow US troops-Nicaragua N
52. Pentagon polygraph exams N
53. Bar ASAT testing Y
54. Suspend def pmt for abuse Y
55. Bar Pentagon-contr emplmt Y
56. Increase SDI funding N
57. Reduce SDI funding Y
58. Produce chemical weapons N
59. Bar CIA fndg in Nicaragua Y
60. South Africa sanctions Y
61. Cut SS COLAs; Raise taxes N
62. Let US invest-So Africa N
63. Approve 21 MX for 1985 N
64. Emergency Farm Credit Y
65. Awards to whistle blowers Y
66. African disaster relief Y
67. Ban bank loans to So Afr P
68. Bar coun duty-free trtmt Y
69. Steel import limits Y
70. Soc Sec COLAs=inflation Y
71. Bar haz waste vctms suits N
72. Prohibit aid to Nicaragua Y
73. Cut $-Schs bar sch prayer N
74. Raise taxes; Cut Medicare Y
75. Alien residncy-prior 1982 N
76. Alien residncy-prior 1980 N
77. Pen emp-hire illgl aliens Y
78. Lmt Persh II/cruse-Europe Y
79. Delete 34 B-1 bombers #
80. Bar purch of Pershing II Y
81. Bar purchase of Sgt York Y
82. Delete $ for Trident II Y
83. Allow 15 MX missiles N
84. Bar MX procurement-1985 Y
85. Equal Access Act N
86. Aid to El Salvador N
87. Bar Nicarag water mining Y
88. Physician/Medicare freeze N
89. Increase "sin" taxes Y
90. End SBA direct loans N
91. Sell Conrail N
92. Equal Rights Amendment Y
93. Marines in Lebanon N
94. Eminent domain-Coal comps N
95. Prohibit EPA sanctions N
96. SS age increase/Reforms N
97. Auto domestic content req #
98. Delete jobs program fundg N
99. Highway-Gas tax bill Y
100. Raise Medicare;Cut defnse Y
101. Emergency housing aid Y
102. Across-the-board tax cuts N
103. Gramm-Latta II targets N
104. Delete B-1 bomber funds Y
105. Dsapprov Saudi AWACS sale Y
106. Disapprove oil import fee ?
107. Rail Deregulation N
108. Dsapp India nuc fuel sale ?
109. Mil draft registration N
110. Chrysler Loan Guarantees Y
111. Prohibit school busing N
112. Nuclear plant moratorium ?
113. Oil price controls Y
114. Tuition Tax Credits N
115. Est Consumer Protect Agcy Y
116. Eliminate B-1 bomber fnds Y

STOKES, LOUIS (Cont.)

117.	Subminimum wage for youth	N	119.	Natural gas deregulation	N
118.	Delete crude oil tax	N			

Presidential Support Score: 1986 - 11% 1985 - 15%

OKLAHOMA

JONES, JAMES R. -- Oklahoma 1st District [Democrat]. Counties of Creek (pt.), Osage (pt.), Tulsa (pt.) and Washington (pt.). Prior Terms: House: 1973-86. Born: May 5, 1939; Muskogee, Okla. Education: University of Oklahoma (A.B.); Georgetown University Law School. Military Service: U.S. Army Counterintelligence Corps, 1964-65. Occupation: Legislative assistant (1961-64); member, White House staff; assistant to the President (1965-69).

1.	Immigration Reform	Y	41.	Notify emp-plant closing	N
2.	Open fld-search warrants	Y	42.	Bar emp consult-plant clo	Y
3.	Civil pnty-hire ill alien	N	43.	Medicare cuts;Tax incres'	Y
4.	So Afr sanc-veto override	Y	44.	Delete 12 MX missiles	Y
5.	Tax Overhaul	N	45.	Spending cuts;Tax incres'	Y
6.	South Africa sanctions	?	46.	Textile Import Quotas	N
7.	Death penalty-drug bill	Y	47.	Cut some school lunch fds	Y
8.	Evidence-warrantless srch	Y	48.	Clean Water Act Amendmnts	N
9.	Life term-second drug off	Y	49.	Youth work projects	N
10.	Military use in drug war	Y	50.	Assist military in Angola	Y
11.	Troop reduction in Europe	N	51.	Allow US troops-Nicaragua	N
12.	Prohibit chemical weapons	N	52.	Pentagon polygraph exams	Y
13.	Bar ASAT testing	Y	53.	Bar ASAT testing	Y
14.	Abide SALT II weapons ban	Y	54.	Suspend def pmt for abuse	Y
15.	Follow SALT II-Soviets do	N	55.	Bar Pentagon-contr emplmt	Y
16.	Reduce SDI funding	N	56.	Increase SDI funding	N
17.	Increase SDI funding	N	57.	Reduce SDI funding	N
18.	Purchase Trident sub	Y	58.	Produce chemical weapons	Y
19.	Delete 12 MX;Add conv wpn	Y	59.	Bar CIA fndg in Nicaragua	N
20.	Raise speed limit	Y	60.	South Africa sanctions	Y
21.	Textile Import Quotas(*)	Y	61.	Cut SS COLAs; Raise taxes	Y
22.	Req Pentagon buy US goods	N	62.	Let US invest-So Africa	N
23.	AIDS ins anti-dscriminatn	Y	63.	Approve 21 MX for 1985	N
24.	Nicaraguan refugee aid	N	64.	Emergency Farm Credit	Y
25.	Nicaraguan contra aid	Y	65.	Awards to whistle blowers	Y
26.	US abide by SALT II	N	66.	African disaster relief	Y
27.	Prohibit Saudi arms sale	Y	67.	Ban bank loans to So Afr	Y
28.	Military Retiremnt Reform	Y	68.	Bar coun duty-free trtmt	N
29.	Nicaraguan refugee aid	N	69.	Steel import limits	Y
30.	Ease '68 Gun Control Act	Y	70.	Soc Sec COLAs=inflation	Y
31.	Bar intrstat handgun tran	N	71.	Bar haz waste vctms suits	Y
32.	Keep '68 Gun Control Act	N	72.	Prohibit aid to Nicaragua	Y
33.	Nicaraguan contra aid	Y	73.	Cut $-Schs bar sch prayer	Y
34.	Bar emp polygCaph testing	Y	74.	Raise taxes; Cut Medicare	Y
35.	Tax Overhaul consideratn	N	75.	Alien residncy-prior 1982	Y
36.	Bar armor-piercing ammo	Y	76.	Alien residncy-prior 1980	N
37.	Tax Overhaul consideratn	N	77.	Pen emp-hire illgl aliens	N
38.	Make comp emissions known	N	78.	Lmt Persh II/cruse-Europe	N
39.	Allow toxic victims suits	N	79.	Delete 34 B-1 bombers	N
40.	Strike Superfund "VAT"	N	80.	Bar purch of Pershing II	N

JONES, JAMES R. (Cont.)

81.	Bar purchase of Sgt York	N	101.	Emergency housing aid	Y
82.	Delete $ for Trident II	N	102.	Across-the-board tax cuts	N
83.	Allow 15 MX missiles	N	103.	Gramm-Latta II targets	N
84.	Bar MX procurement-1985	Y	104.	Delete B-1 bomber funds	N
85.	Equal Access Act	Y	105.	Dsapprov Saudi AWACS sale	Y
86.	Aid to El Salvador	N	106.	Disapprove oil import fee	?
87.	Bar Nicarag water mining	Y	107.	Rail Deregulation	Y
88.	Physician/Medicare freeze	N	108.	Dsapp India nuc fuel sale	N
89.	Increase "sin" taxes	Y	109.	Mil draft registration	Y
90.	End SBA direct loans	N	110.	Chrysler Loan Guarantees	N
91.	Sell Conrail	N	111.	Prohibit school busing	N
92.	Equal Rights Amendment	Y	112.	Nuclear plant moratorium	N
93.	Marines in Lebanon	N	113.	Oil price controls	N
94.	Eminent domain-Coal comps	Y	114.	Tuition Tax Credits	N
95.	Prohibit EPA sanctions	Y	115.	Est Consumer Protect Agcy	N
96.	SS age increase/Reforms	Y	116.	Eliminate B-1 bomber fnds	N
97.	Auto domestic content req	N	117.	Subminimum wage for youth	Y
98.	Delete jobs program fundg	N	118.	Delete crude oil tax	Y
99.	Highway-Gas tax bill	N	119.	Natural gas deregulation	Y
100.	Raise Medicare;Cut defnse	N			

Presidential Support Score: 1986 - 34% · 1985 - 40%

SYNAR, MIKE -- Oklahoma 2nd District [Democrat]. Counties of Adair, Cherokee, Craig, Creek (pt.), Delaware, Haskell, McIntosh, Mayes, Muskogee, Nowata, Okfuskee, Okmulgee, Ottawa, Pawnee, Rogers, Sequoyah, Tulsa (pt.) and Wagoner. Prior Terms: House: 1979-86. Born: October 17, 1950; Vinita, Okla. Education: University of Oklahoma (B.B.A., LL.B.); Northwestern University (M.S.). Occupation: Real estate broker; employee, U.S. forestry service; employee, Oklahoma attorney general's office.

1.	Immigration Reform	Y	27.	Prohibit Saudi arms sale	Y
2.	Open fld-search warrants	N	28.	Military Retiremnt Reform	Y
3.	Civil pnty-hire ill alien	N	29.	Nicaraguan refugee aid	Y
4.	So Afr sanc-veto override	Y	30.	Ease '68 Gun Control Act	Y
5.	Tax Overhaul	N	31.	Bar intrstat handgun tran	N
6.	South Africa sanctions	?	32.	Keep '68 Gun Control Act	Y
7.	Death penalty-drug bill	?	33.	Nicaraguan contra aid	N
8.	Evidence-warrantless srch	?	34.	Bar emp polygraph testing	Y
9.	Life term-second drug off	?	35.	Tax Overhaul consideratn	Y
10.	Military use in drug war	N	36.	Bar armor-piercing ammo	Y
11.	Troop reduction in Europe	N	37.	Tax Overhaul consideratn	Y
12.	Prohibit chemical weapons	Y	38.	Make comp emissions known	N
13.	Bar ASAT testing	Y	39.	Allow toxic victims suits	Y
14.	Abide SALT II weapons ban	Y	40.	Strike Superfund "VAT"	N
15.	Follow SALT II-Soviets do	N	41.	Notify emp-plant closing	N
16.	Reduce SDI funding	Y	42.	Bar emp consult-plant clo	Y
17.	Increase SDI funding	N	43.	Medicare cuts;Tax incres'	Y
18.	Purchase Trident sub	Y	44.	Delete 12 MX missiles	Y
19.	Delete 12 MX;Add conv wpn	Y	45.	Spending cuts;Tax incres'	Y
20.	Raise speed limit	N	46.	Textile Import Quotas	N
21.	Textile Import Quotas(*)	Y	47.	Cut some school lunch fds	N
22.	Req Pentagon buy US goods	N	48.	Clean Water Act Amendmnts	N
23.	AIDS ins anti-dscriminatn	Y	49.	Youth work projects	N
24.	Nicaraguan refugee aid	Y	50.	Assist military in Angola	N
25.	Nicaraguan contra aid	N	51.	Allow US troops-Nicaragua	N
26.	US abide by SALT II	N	52.	Pentagon polygraph exams	N

SYNAR, MIKE (Cont.)

53. Bar ASAT testing Y
54. Suspend def pmt for abuse N
55. Bar Pentagon-contr emplmt Y
56. Increase SDI funding N
57. Reduce SDI funding N
58. Produce chemical weapons N
59. Bar CIA fndg in Nicaragua Y
60. South Africa sanctions Y
61. Cut SS COLAs; Raise taxes N
62. Let US invest-So Africa N
63. Approve 21 MX for 1985 N
64. Emergency Farm Credit Y
65. Awards to whistle blowers Y
66. African disaster relief Y
67. Ban bank loans to So Afr Y
68. Bar coun duty-free trtmt N
69. Steel import limits Y
70. Soc Sec COLAs=inflation Y
71. Bar haz waste vctms suits Y
72. Prohibit aid to Nicaragua Y
73. Cut $-Schs bar sch prayer N
74. Raise taxes; Cut Medicare Y
75. Alien residncy-prior 1982 Y
76. Alien residncy-prior 1980 N
77. Pen emp-hire illgl aliens N
78. Lmt Persh II/cruse-Europe N
79. Delete 34 B-1 bombers N
80. Bar purch of Pershing II N
81. Bar purchase of Sgt York N
82. Delete $ for Trident II N
83. Allow 15 MX missiles N
84. Bar MX procurement-1985 Y
85. Equal Access Act N
86. Aid to El Salvador N
87. Bar Nicarag water mining Y
88. Physician/Medicare freeze N
89. Increase "sin" taxes Y
90. End SBA direct loans N
91. Sell Conrail N
92. Equal Rights Amendment Y
93. Marines in Lebanon Y
94. Eminent domain-Coal comps Y
95. Prohibit EPA sanctions Y
96. SS age increase/Reforms Y
97. Auto domestic content req N
98. Delete jobs program fundg Y
99. Highway-Gas tax bill N
100. Raise Medicare;Cut defnse N
101. Emergency housing aid Y
102. Across-the-board tax cuts N
103. Gramm-Latta II targets N
104. Delete B-1 bomber funds N
105. Dsapprov Saudi AWACS sale Y
106. Disapprove oil import fee Y
107. Rail Deregulation Y
108. Dsapp India nuc fuel sale Y
109. Mil draft registration Y
110. Chrysler Loan Guarantees N
111. Prohibit school busing N
112. Nuclear plant moratorium Y
113. Oil price controls N

Presidential Support Score: 1986 - 24% 1985 - 25%

WATKINS, WES -- Oklahoma 3rd District [Democrat]. Counties of Atoka, Bryan, Carter, Choctaw, Coal, Hughes, Johnston, Latimer, Le Flore, Lincoln, Love, McCurtain, Marshall, Murray, Payne, Pittsburg, Pontotoc, Pottawatomie (pt.), Pushmataha and Seminole. Prior Terms: House: 1977-86. Born: December 15, 1938; DeQueen, Ark. Education: Oklahoma State University (B.A., M.S.). Military Service: National Guard. Occupation: Oklahoma senator (1975-76).

1. Immigration Reform N
2. Open fld-search warrants Y
3. Civil pnty-hire ill alien N
4. So Afr sanc-veto override Y
5. Tax Overhaul N
6. South Africa sanctions Y
7. Death penalty-drug bill Y
8. Evidence-warrantless srch Y
9. Life term-second drug off ?
10. Military use in drug war Y
11. Troop reduction in Europe N
12. Prohibit chemical weapons N
13. Bar ASAT testing Y
14. Abide SALT II weapons ban Y
15. Follow SALT II-Soviets do N
16. Reduce SDI funding N
17. Increase SDI funding N
18. Purchase Trident sub Y
19. Delete 12 MX;Add conv wpn Y
20. Raise speed limit Y
21. Textile Import Quotas(*) Y
22. Req Pentagon buy US goods Y
23. AIDS ins anti-dscriminatn Y
24. Nicaraguan refugee aid N
25. Nicaraguan contra aid Y
26. US abide by SALT II N
27. Prohibit Saudi arms sale Y
28. Military Retiremnt Reform Y
29. Nicaraguan refugee aid N
30. Ease '68 Gun Control Act Y
31. Bar intrstat handgun tran N
32. Keep '68 Gun Control Act N

WATKINS, WES (Cont.)

33. Nicaraguan contra aid Y
34. Bar emp polygraph testing Y
35. Tax Overhaul consideratn N
36. Bar armor-piercing ammo Y
37. Tax Overhaul consideratn N
38. Make comp emissions known N
39. Allow toxic victims suits N
40. Strike Superfund "VAT" N
41. Notify emp-plant closing N
42. Bar emp consult-plant clo Y
43. Medicare cuts;Tax incres' N
44. Delete 12 MX missiles Y
45. Spending cuts;Tax incres' N
46. Textile Import Quotas N
47. Cut some school lunch fds N
48. Clean Water Act Amendmnts N
49. Youth work projects N
50. Assist military in Angola Y
51. Allow US troops-Nicaragua N
52. Pentagon polygraph exams Y
53. Bar ASAT testing N
54. Suspend def pmt for abuse Y
55. Bar Pentagon-contr emplmt Y
56. Increase SDI funding N
57. Reduce SDI funding N
58. Produce chemical weapons N
59. Bar CIA fndg in Nicaragua N
60. South Africa sanctions Y
61. Cut SS COLAs; Raise taxes N
62. Let US invest-So Africa N
63. Approve 21 MX for 1985 Y
64. Emergency Farm Credit Y
65. Awards to whistle blowers Y
66. African disaster relief Y
67. Ban bank loans to So Afr ?
68. Bar coun duty-free trtmt N
69. Steel import limits Y
70. Soc Sec COLAs=inflation Y
71. Bar haz waste vctms suits Y
72. Prohibit aid to Nicaragua Y
73. Cut $-Schs bar sch prayer Y
74. Raise taxes; Cut Medicare Y
75. Alien residncy-prior 1982 Y
76. Alien residncy-prior 1980 N
77. Pen emp-hire illgl aliens N
78. Lmt Persh II/cruse-Europe N
79. Delete 34 B-1 bombers N
80. Bar purch of Pershing II N
81. Bar purchase of Sgt York N
82. Delete $ for Trident II N
83. Allow 15 MX missiles Y
84. Bar MX procurement-1985 N
85. Equal Access Act Y
86. Aid to El Salvador ?
87. Bar Nicarag water mining Y
88. Physician/Medicare freeze N
89. Increase "sin" taxes Y
90. End SBA direct loans ?
91. Sell Conrail N
92. Equal Rights Amendment Y
93. Marines in Lebanon N
94. Eminent domain-Coal comps Y
95. Prohibit EPA sanctions Y
96. SS age increase/Reforms Y
97. Auto domestic content req Y
98. Delete jobs program fundg N
99. Highway-Gas tax bill Y
100. Raise Medicare;Cut defnse N
101. Emergency housing aid Y
102. Across-the-board tax cuts N
103. Gramm-Latta II targets N
104. Delete B-1 bomber funds N
105. Dsapprov Saudi AWACS sale Y
106. Disapprove oil import fee Y
107. Rail Deregulation Y
108. Dsapp India nuc fuel sale N
109. Mil draft registration Y
110. Chrysler Loan Guarantees N
111. Prohibit school busing Y
112. Nuclear plant moratorium N
113. Oil price controls N
114. Tuition Tax Credits N
115. Est Consumer Protect Agcy N
116. Eliminate B-1 bomber fnds N
117. Subminimum wage for youth Y
118. Delete crude oil tax Y
119. Natural gas deregulation Y

Presidential Support Score: 1986 - 33% 1985 - 43%

McCURDY, DAVE -- Oklahoma 4th District [Democrat]. Counties of Cleveland, Comanche, Cotton, Garvin, Grady, Jackson, Jefferson, McClain, Oklahoma (pt.), Pottawatomie (pt.), Stephens and Tillman. Prior Terms: House: 1981-86. Born: March 30, 1950; Canadian, Tex. Education: University of Oklahoma (B.A., J.D.). Military Service: U.S. Air Force Reserve, 1969-72. Occupation: Attorney; assistant attorney general, Oklahoma (1975-77); member, Luttrell, Pendarvis & Rawlinson (1978-79).

1. Immigration Reform ?
2. Open fld-search warrants ?
3. Civil pnty-hire ill alien ?
4. So Afr sanc-veto override Y
5. Tax Overhaul N
6. South Africa sanctions Y

McCURDY, DAVE (Cont.)

7. Death penalty-drug bill Y
8. Evidence-warrantless srch Y
9. Life term-second drug off Y
10. Military use in drug war Y
11. Troop reduction in Europe N
12. Prohibit chemical weapons N
13. Bar ASAT testing Y
14. Abide SALT II weapons ban Y
15. Follow SALT II-Soviets do N
16. Reduce SDI funding N
17. Increase SDI funding N
18. Purchase Trident sub Y
19. Delete 12 MX;Add conv wpn N
20. Raise speed limit Y
21. Textile Import Quotas(*) Y
22. Req Pentagon buy US goods N
23. AIDS ins anti-dscriminatn Y
24. Nicaraguan refugee aid N
25. Nicaraguan contra aid N
26. US abide by SALT II N
27. Prohibit Saudi arms sale Y
28. Military Retiremnt Reform ?
29. Nicaraguan refugee aid N
30. Ease '68 Gun Control Act Y
31. Bar intrstat handgun tran N
32. Keep '68 Gun Control Act N
33. Nicaraguan contra aid N
34. Bar emp polygraph testing ?
35. Tax Overhaul consideratn N
36. Bar armor-piercing ammo Y
37. Tax Overhaul consideratn N
38. Make comp emissions known Y
39. Allow toxic victims suits N
40. Strike Superfund "VAT" N
41. Notify emp-plant closing N
42. Bar emp consult-plant clo Y
43. Medicare cuts;Tax incres' Y
44. Delete 12 MX missiles N
45. Spending cuts;Tax incres' Y
46. Textile Import Quotas N
47. Cut some school lunch fds N
48. Clean Water Act Amendmnts N
49. Youth work projects N
50. Assist military in Angola Y
51. Allow US troops-Nicaragua N
52. Pentagon polygraph exams Y
53. Bar ASAT testing Y
54. Suspend def pmt for abuse N
55. Bar Pentagon-contr emplmt Y
56. Increase SDI funding N
57. Reduce SDI funding N
58. Produce chemical weapons Y
59. Bar CIA fndg in Nicaragua N
60. South Africa sanctions Y
61. Cut SS COLAs; Raise taxes Y
62. Let US invest-So Africa N
63. Approve 21 MX for 1985 Y
64. Emergency Farm Credit Y
65. Awards to whistle blowers Y
66. African disaster relief Y
67. Ban bank loans to So Afr ?
68. Bar coun duty-free trtmt N
69. Steel import limits N
70. Soc Sec COLAs=inflation Y
71. Bar haz waste vctms suits Y
72. Prohibit aid to Nicaragua Y
73. Cut $-Schs bar sch prayer Y
74. Raise taxes; Cut Medicare Y
75. Alien residncy-prior 1982 N
76. Alien residncy-prior 1980 ?
77. Pen emp-hire illgl aliens N
78. Lmt Persh II/cruse-Europe ?
79. Delete 34 B-1 bombers N
80. Bar purch of Pershing II N
81. Bar purchase of Sgt York N
82. Delete $ for Trident II N
83. Allow 15 MX missiles Y
84. Bar MX procurement-1985 N
85. Equal Access Act Y
86. Aid to El Salvador Y
87. Bar Nicarag water mining Y
88. Physician/Medicare freeze N
89. Increase "sin" taxes Y
90. End SBA direct loans N
91. Sell Conrail N
92. Equal Rights Amendment Y
93. Marines in Lebanon N
94. Eminent domain-Coal comps Y
95. Prohibit EPA sanctions Y
96. SS age increase/Reforms Y
97. Auto domestic content req Y
98. Delete jobs program fundg Y
99. Highway-Gas tax bill N
100. Raise Medicare;Cut defnse N
101. Emergency housing aid Y
102. Across-the-board tax cuts Y
103. Gramm-Latta II targets N
104. Delete B-1 bomber funds N
105. Dsapprov Saudi AWACS sale Y

Presidential Support Score: 1986 - 32% 1985 - 44%

EDWARDS, MICKEY -- Oklahoma 5th District [Republican]. Counties of Canadian (pt.), Kay, Logan, Noble, Oklahoma (pt.), Osage (pt.) and Washington (pt.). Prior Terms: House: 1977-86. Born: July 12, 1937. Education: University of Oklahoma (B.A.); Oklahoma City University (J.D.). Occupation: Journalist; assistant city editor; editor; journalism teacher; legislative consultant (1973-76).

EDWARDS, MICKEY (Cont.)

1.	Immigration Reform	?	60.	South Africa sanctions	?
2.	Open fld-search warrants	?	61.	Cut SS COLAs; Raise taxes	N
3.	Civil pnty-hire ill alien	?	62.	Let US invest-So Africa	N
4.	So Afr sanc-veto override	?	63.	Approve 21 MX for 1985	Y
5.	Tax Overhaul	N	64.	Emergency Farm Credit	Y
6.	South Africa sanctions	Y	65.	Awards to whistle blowers	Y
7.	Death penalty-drug bill	Y	66.	African disaster relief	Y
8.	Evidence-warrantless srch	Y	67.	Ban bank loans to So Afr	N
9.	Life term-second drug off	Y	68.	Bar coun duty-free trtmt	N
10.	Military use in drug war	Y	69.	Steel import limits	N
11.	Troop reduction in Europe	N	70.	Soc Sec COLAs=inflation	Y
12.	Prohibit chemical weapons	N	71.	Bar haz waste vctms suits	Y
13.	Bar ASAT testing	N	72.	Prohibit aid to Nicaragua	N
14.	Abide SALT II weapons ban	N	73.	Cut $-Schs bar sch prayer	Y
15.	Follow SALT II-Soviets do	Y	74.	Raise taxes; Cut Medicare	N
16.	Reduce SDI funding	N	75.	Alien residncy-prior 1982	N
17.	Increase SDI funding	Y	76.	Alien residncy-prior 1980	Y
18.	Purchase Trident sub	Y	77.	Pen emp-hire illgl aliens	N
19.	Delete 12 MX;Add conv wpn	N	78.	Lmt Persh II/cruse-Europe	?
20.	Raise speed limit	Y	79.	Delete 34 B-1 bombers	N
21.	Textile Import Quotas(*)	N	80.	Bar purch of Pershing II	N
22.	Req Pentagon buy US goods	N	81.	Bar purchase of Sgt York	N
23.	AIDS ins anti-dscriminatn	N	82.	Delete $ for Trident II	N
24.	Nicaraguan refugee aid	N	83.	Allow 15 MX missiles	Y
25.	Nicaraguan contra aid	Y	84.	Bar MX procurement-1985	N
26.	US abide by SALT II	Y	85.	Equal Access Act	Y
27.	Prohibit Saudi arms sale	Y	86.	Aid to El Salvador	Y
28.	Military Retiremnt Reform	Y	87.	Bar Nicarag water mining	N
29.	Nicaraguan refugee aid	Y	88.	Physician/Medicare freeze	Y
30.	Ease '68 Gun Control Act	Y	89.	Increase "sin" taxes	N
31.	Bar intrstat handgun tran	?	90.	End SBA direct loans	N
32.	Keep '68 Gun Control Act	?	91.	Sell Conrail	N
33.	Nicaraguan contra aid	Y	92.	Equal Rights Amendment	N
34.	Bar emp polygraph testing	N	93.	Marines in Lebanon	Y
35.	Tax Overhaul consideratn	N	94.	Eminent domain-Coal comps	Y
36.	Bar armor-piercing ammo	Y	95.	Prohibit EPA sanctions	Y
37.	Tax Overhaul consideratn	N	96.	SS age increase/Reforms	Y
38.	Make comp emissions known	N	97.	Auto domestic content req	N
39.	Allow toxic victims suits	N	98.	Delete jobs program fundg	Y
40.	Strike Superfund "VAT"	N	99.	Highway-Gas tax bill	N
41.	Notify emp-plant closing	N	100.	Raise Medicare;Cut defnse	N
42.	Bar emp consult-plant clo	Y	101.	Emergency housing aid	Y
43.	Medicare cuts;Tax incres'	N	102.	Across-the-board tax cuts	Y
44.	Delete 12 MX missiles	N	103.	Gramm-Latta II targets	Y
45.	Spending cuts;Tax incres'	N	104.	Delete B-1 bomber funds	N
46.	Textile Import Quotas	N	105.	Dsapprov Saudi AWACS sale	N
47.	Cut some school lunch fds	Y	106.	Disapprove oil import fee	Y
48.	Clean Water Act Amendmnts	Y	107.	Rail Deregulation	Y
49.	Youth work projects	N	108.	Dsapp India nuc fuel sale	Y
50.	Assist military in Angola	Y	109.	Mil draft registration	N
51.	Allow US troops-Nicaragua	Y	110.	Chrysler Loan Guarantees	N
52.	Pentagon polygraph exams	Y	111.	Prohibit school busing	Y
53.	Bar ASAT testing	N	112.	Nuclear plant moratorium	Y
54.	Suspend def pmt for abuse	N	113.	Oil price controls	N
55.	Bar Pentagon-contr emplmt	Y	114.	Tuition Tax Credits	Y
56.	Increase SDI funding	Y	115.	Est Consumer Protect Agcy	N
57.	Reduce SDI funding	N	116.	Eliminate B-1 bomber fnds	?
58.	Produce chemical weapons	Y	117.	Subminimum wage for youth	Y
59.	Bar CIA fndg in Nicaragua	N	118.	Delete crude oil tax	Y

EDWARDS, MICKEY (Cont.)
119. Natural gas deregulation Y

Presidential Support Score: 1986 - 73% 1985 - 71%

ENGLISH, GLENN -- Oklahoma 6th District [Democrat]. Counties of Alfalfa, Beaver, Beckhorn, Blaine, Caddo, Canadian (pt.), Cimarron, Custer, Dewey, Ellis, Garfield, Grant, Greer, Harmon, Harper, Kingfisher, Kiowa, Major, Oklahoma (pt.), Roger Mills, Texas, Washita, Woods and Woodward. Prior Terms: House: 1975-86. Born: November 30, 1940; Cordell, Okla. Education: Southwestern State College. Military Service: U.S. Army Reserves, 1965-71. Occupation: Petroleum landman; congressional staff member.

1. Immigration Reform N
2. Open fld-search warrants Y
3. Civil pnty-hire ill alien N
4. So Afr sanc-veto override Y
5. Tax Overhaul N
6. South Africa sanctions Y
7. Death penalty-drug bill Y
8. Evidence-warrantless srch Y
9. Life term-second drug off Y
10. Military use in drug war N
11. Troop reduction in Europe N
12. Prohibit chemical weapons N
13. Bar ASAT testing N
14. Abide SALT II weapons ban Y
15. Follow SALT II-Soviets do Y
16. Reduce SDI funding N
17. Increase SDI funding N
18. Purchase Trident sub Y
19. Delete 12 MX;Add conv wpn N
20. Raise speed limit Y
21. Textile Import Quotas(*) Y
22. Req Pentagon buy US goods N
23. AIDS ins anti-dscriminatn Y
24. Nicaraguan refugee aid N
25. Nicaraguan contra aid Y
26. US abide by SALT II Y
27. Prohibit Saudi arms sale Y
28. Military Retiremnt Reform Y
29. Nicaraguan refugee aid N
30. Ease '68 Gun Control Act Y
31. Bar intrstat handgun tran N
32. Keep '68 Gun Control Act N
33. Nicaraguan contra aid Y
34. Bar emp polygraph testing Y
35. Tax Overhaul consideratn N
36. Bar armor-piercing ammo Y
37. Tax Overhaul consideratn N
38. Make comp emissions known N
39. Allow toxic victims suits N
40. Strike Superfund "VAT" N
41. Notify emp-plant closing N
42. Bar emp consult-plant clo Y
43. Medicare cuts;Tax incres' N
44. Delete 12 MX missiles N
45. Spending cuts;Tax incres' N
46. Textile Import Quotas N
47. Cut some school lunch fds N
48. Clean Water Act Amendmnts Y
49. Youth work projects N
50. Assist military in Angola Y
51. Allow US troops-Nicaragua Y
52. Pentagon polygraph exams Y
53. Bar ASAT testing N
54. Suspend def pmt for abuse N
55. Bar Pentagon-contr emplmt Y
56. Increase SDI funding N
57. Reduce SDI funding N
58. Produce chemical weapons Y
59. Bar CIA fndg in Nicaragua N
60. South Africa sanctions Y
61. Cut SS COLAs; Raise taxes N
62. Let US invest-So Africa N
63. Approve 21 MX for 1985 Y
64. Emergency Farm Credit Y
65. Awards to whistle blowers Y
66. African disaster relief Y
67. Ban bank loans to So Afr Y
68. Bar coun duty-free trtmt N
69. Steel import limits N
70. Soc Sec COLAs=inflation Y
71. Bar haz waste vctms suits Y
72. Prohibit aid to Nicaragua N
73. Cut $-Schs bar sch prayer Y
74. Raise taxes; Cut Medicare N
75. Alien residncy-prior 1982 N
76. Alien residncy-prior 1980 N
77. Pen emp-hire illgl aliens N
78. Lmt Persh II/cruse-Europe ?
79. Delete 34 B-1 bombers N
80. Bar purch of Pershing II N
81. Bar purchase of Sgt York N
82. Delete $ for Trident II N
83. Allow 15 MX missiles Y
84. Bar MX procurement-1985 N
85. Equal Access Act Y
86. Aid to El Salvador Y
87. Bar Nicarag water mining Y
88. Physician/Medicare freeze N
89. Increase "sin" taxes N
90. End SBA direct loans N

ENGLISH, GLENN (Cont.)

91. Sell Conrail N
92. Equal Rights Amendment Y
93. Marines in Lebanon N
94. Eminent domain-Coal comps Y
95. Prohibit EPA sanctions Y
96. SS age increase/Reforms Y
97. Auto domestic content req Y
98. Delete jobs program fundg Y
99. Highway-Gas tax bill N
100. Raise Medicare;Cut defnse N
101. Emergency housing aid Y
102. Across-the-board tax cuts Y
103. Gramm-Latta II targets Y
104. Delete B-1 bomber funds N
105. Dsapprov Saudi AWACS sale Y
106. Disapprove oil import fee Y
107. Rail Deregulation Y
108. Dsapp India nuc fuel sale Y
109. Mil draft registration Y
110. Chrysler Loan Guarantees N
111. Prohibit school busing Y
112. Nuclear plant moratorium N
113. Oil price controls N
114. Tuition Tax Credits N
115. Est Consumer Protect Agcy N
116. Eliminate B-1 bomber fnds N
117. Subminimum wage for youth N
118. Delete crude oil tax Y
119. Natural gas deregulation Y

Presidential Support Score: 1986 - 44% 1985 - 58%

OREGON

AuCOIN, LES -- Oregon 1st District [Democrat]. Counties of Clatsop, Columbia, Lincoln, Multnomah (pt.), Polk (pt.), Tillamook, Washington and Yamhill. Prior Terms: House: 1975-86. Born: October 21, 1942; Redmond, Ore. Education: University of the Pacific (B.A.). Military Service: U.S. Army, 1961-64. Occupation: Newsman, "Redmond Spokesman" (1960, 1964); "Portland Oregonian" (1965-66); director, public information, Pacific University (1966-73); administrator, Skidmore, Owings and Merrill (1973-74); Oregon representative (1973-75).

1. Immigration Reform Y
2. Open fld-search warrants Y
3. Civil pnty-hire ill alien Y
4. So Afr sanc-veto override Y
5. Tax Overhaul Y
6. South Africa sanctions Y
7. Death penalty-drug bill N
8. Evidence-warrantless srch N
9. Life term-second drug off Y
10. Military use in drug war N
11. Troop reduction in Europe N
12. Prohibit chemical weapons Y
13. Bar ASAT testing Y
14. Abide SALT II weapons ban Y
15. Follow SALT II-Soviets do N
16. Reduce SDI funding Y
17. Increase SDI funding N
18. Purchase Trident sub N
19. Delete 12 MX;Add conv wpn Y
20. Raise speed limit N
21. Textile Import Quotas(*) N
22. Req Pentagon buy US goods N
23. AIDS ins anti-dscriminatn Y
24. Nicaraguan refugee aid Y
25. Nicaraguan contra aid N
26. US abide by SALT II N
27. Prohibit Saudi arms sale Y
28. Military Retiremnt Reform Y
29. Nicaraguan refugee aid Y
30. Ease '68 Gun Control Act Y
31. Bar intrstat handgun tran N
32. Keep '68 Gun Control Act N
33. Nicaraguan contra aid N
34. Bar emp polygraph testing Y
35. Tax Overhaul consideratn N
36. Bar armor-piercing ammo Y
37. Tax Overhaul consideratn N
38. Make comp emissions known Y
39. Allow toxic victims suits Y
40. Strike Superfund "VAT" Y
41. Notify emp-plant closing N
42. Bar emp consult-plant clo Y
43. Medicare cuts;Tax incres' Y
44. Delete 12 MX missiles Y
45. Spending cuts;Tax incres' Y
46. Textile Import Quotas N
47. Cut some school lunch fds N
48. Clean Water Act Amendmnts N
49. Youth work projects Y
50. Assist military in Angola N
51. Allow US troops-Nicaragua N
52. Pentagon polygraph exams Y
53. Bar ASAT testing Y
54. Suspend def pmt for abuse Y
55. Bar Pentagon-contr emplmt Y
56. Increase SDI funding N

AuCOIN, LES (Cont.)

57. Reduce SDI funding Y
58. Produce chemical weapons N
59. Bar CIA fndg in Nicaragua Y
60. South Africa sanctions Y
61. Cut SS COLAs; Raise taxes N
62. Let US invest-So Africa N
63. Approve 21 MX for 1985 N
64. Emergency Farm Credit Y
65. Awards to whistle blowers Y
66. African disaster relief Y
67. Ban bank loans to So Afr Y
68. Bar coun duty-free trtmt N
69. Steel import limits Y
70. Soc Sec COLAs=inflation Y
71. Bar haz waste vctms suits N
72. Prohibit aid to Nicaragua Y
73. Cut $-Schs bar sch prayer N
74. Raise taxes; Cut Medicare Y
75. Alien residncy-prior 1982 ?
76. Alien residncy-prior 1980 Y
77. Pen emp-hire illgl aliens N
78. Lmt Persh II/cruse-Europe Y
79. Delete 34 B-1 bombers Y
80. Bar purch of Pershing II Y
81. Bar purchase of Sgt York Y
82. Delete $ for Trident II Y
83. Allow 15 MX missiles N
84. Bar MX procurement-1985 Y
85. Equal Access Act N
86. Aid to El Salvador N
87. Bar Nicarag water mining Y
88. Physician/Medicare freeze Y
89. Increase "sin" taxes Y
90. End SBA direct loans N
91. Sell Conrail N
92. Equal Rights Amendment Y
93. Marines in Lebanon N
94. Eminent domain-Coal comps N
95. Prohibit EPA sanctions ?
96. SS age increase/Reforms Y
97. Auto domestic content req N
98. Delete jobs program fundg N
99. Highway-Gas tax bill Y
100. Raise Medicare;Cut defnse Y
101. Emergency housing aid Y
102. Across-the-board tax cuts N
103. Gramm-Latta II targets N
104. Delete B-1 bomber funds Y
105. Dsapprov Saudi AWACS sale Y
106. Disapprove oil import fee ?
107. Rail Deregulation N
108. Dsapp India nuc fuel sale Y
109. Mil draft registration N
110. Chrysler Loan Guarantees N
111. Prohibit school busing N
112. Nuclear plant moratorium Y
113. Oil price controls N
114. Tuition Tax Credits ?
115. Est Consumer Protect Agcy Y
116. Eliminate B-1 bomber fnds Y
117. Subminimum wage for youth N
118. Delete crude oil tax N
119. Natural gas deregulation Y

Presidential Support Score: 1986 - 30% 1985 - 24%

SMITH, ROBERT F. (Bob) -- Oregon 2nd District [Republican]. Counties of Baker, Crook, Deschutes, Gilliam, Grant, Harney, Hood River, Jackson (pt.), Jefferson, Josephine (pt.), Klamath, Lake, Malheur, Morrow, Sherman, Umatilla, Union, Wallowa, Wasco and Wheeler. Prior Terms: House: 1983-86. Born: June 16, 1931; Portland, Ore. Education: Willamette University (B.A.). Occupation: Oregon legislator (1960-72); Oregon senator (1972-82); member, Harney County Chamber of Commerce; trustee, Willamette University.

1. Immigration Reform N
2. Open fld-search warrants Y
3. Civil pnty-hire ill alien Y
4. So Afr sanc-veto override N
5. Tax Overhaul Y
6. South Africa sanctions N
7. Death penalty-drug bill Y
8. Evidence-warrantless srch Y
9. Life term-second drug off Y
10. Military use in drug war Y
11. Troop reduction in Europe N
12. Prohibit chemical weapons Y
13. Bar ASAT testing N
14. Abide SALT II weapons ban N
15. Follow SALT II-Soviets do Y
16. Reduce SDI funding ?
17. Increase SDI funding N
18. Purchase Trident sub N
19. Delete 12 MX;Add conv wpn N
20. Raise speed limit Y
21. Textile Import Quotas(*) N
22. Req Pentagon buy US goods Y
23. AIDS ins anti-dscriminatn N
24. Nicaraguan refugee aid N
25. Nicaraguan contra aid Y
26. US abide by SALT II Y
27. Prohibit Saudi arms sale Y
28. Military Retiremnt Reform Y

SMITH, ROBERT F. (Bob) (Cont.)

29. Nicaraguan refugee aid Y
30. Ease '68 Gun Control Act Y
31. Bar intrstat handgun tran N
32. Keep '68 Gun Control Act N
33. Nicaraguan contra aid Y
34. Bar emp polygraph testing N
35. Tax Overhaul consideratn N
36. Bar armor-piercing ammo N
37. Tax Overhaul consideratn N
38. Make comp emissions known N
39. Allow toxic victims suits N
40. Strike Superfund "VAT" N
41. Notify emp-plant closing X
42. Bar emp consult-plant clo Y
43. Medicare cuts;Tax incres' N
44. Delete 12 MX missiles N
45. Spending cuts;Tax incres' N
46. Textile Import Quotas N
47. Cut some school lunch fds N
48. Clean Water Act Amendmnts Y
49. Youth work projects N
50. Assist military in Angola Y
51. Allow US troops-Nicaragua Y
52. Pentagon polygraph exams Y
53. Bar ASAT testing N
54. Suspend def pmt for abuse N
55. Bar Pentagon-contr emplmt Y
56. Increase SDI funding N
57. Reduce SDI funding N
58. Produce chemical weapons N
59. Bar CIA fndg in Nicaragua N
60. South Africa sanctions N
61. Cut SS COLAs; Raise taxes N
62. Let US invest-So Africa Y
63. Approve 21 MX for 1985 Y
64. Emergency Farm Credit N
65. Awards to whistle blowers Y
66. African disaster relief Y
67. Ban bank loans to So Afr Y
68. Bar coun duty-free trtmt N
69. Steel import limits N
70. Soc Sec COLAs=inflation Y
71. Bar haz waste vctms suits Y
72. Prohibit aid to Nicaragua Y
73. Cut $-Schs bar sch prayer Y
74. Raise taxes; Cut Medicare N
75. Alien residncy-prior 1982 N
76. Alien residncy-prior 1980 Y
77. Pen emp-hire illgl aliens N
78. Lmt Persh II/cruse-Europe N
79. Delete 34 B-1 bombers N
80. Bar purch of Pershing II N
81. Bar purchase of Sgt York N
82. Delete $ for Trident II N
83. Allow 15 MX missiles Y
84. Bar MX procurement-1985 N
85. Equal Access Act Y
86. Aid to El Salvador Y
87. Bar Nicarag water mining Y
88. Physician/Medicare freeze Y
89. Increase "sin" taxes N
90. End SBA direct loans N
91. Sell Conrail Y
92. Equal Rights Amendment N
93. Marines in Lebanon Y
94. Eminent domain-Coal comps Y
95. Prohibit EPA sanctions Y
96. SS age increase/Reforms Y

Presidential Support Score: 1986 - 66% 1985 - 63%

WYDEN, RON -- Oregon 3rd District [Democrat]. Counties of Clackamas (pt.) and Multnomah (pt.). Prior Terms: House: 1981-86. Born: May 3, 1949; Wichita, Kan. Education: University of California; Stanford University (A.B.); University of Oregon School of Law (J.D.). Occupation: Attorney; co-founder, co-director, Gray Panthers; director, Oregon Legal Services for the Elderly; instructor.

1. Immigration Reform Y
2. Open fld-search warrants Y
3. Civil pnty-hire ill alien Y
4. So Afr sanc-veto override Y
5. Tax Overhaul Y
6. South Africa sanctions Y
7. Death penalty-drug bill Y
8. Evidence-warrantless srch N
9. Life term-second drug off Y
10. Military use in drug war Y
11. Troop reduction in Europe N
12. Prohibit chemical weapons Y
13. Bar ASAT testing Y
14. Abide SALT II weapons ban Y
15. Follow SALT II-Soviets do N
16. Reduce SDI funding Y
17. Increase SDI funding N
18. Purchase Trident sub Y
19. Delete 12 MX;Add conv wpn Y
20. Raise speed limit Y
21. Textile Import Quotas(*) N
22. Req Pentagon buy US goods N
23. AIDS ins anti-dscriminatn Y
24. Nicaraguan refugee aid Y
25. Nicaraguan contra aid N
26. US abide by SALT II N
27. Prohibit Saudi arms sale Y
28. Military Retiremnt Reform Y

WYDEN, RON (Cont.)

29. Nicaraguan refugee aid Y
30. Ease '68 Gun Control Act Y
31. Bar intrstat handgun tran N
32. Keep '68 Gun Control Act N
33. Nicaraguan contra aid N
34. Bar emp polygraph testing Y
35. Tax Overhaul consideratn N
36. Bar armor-piercing ammo Y
37. Tax Overhaul consideratn N
38. Make comp emissions known Y
39. Allow toxic victims suits Y
40. Strike Superfund "VAT" Y
41. Notify emp-plant closing N
42. Bar emp consult-plant clo Y
43. Medicare cuts;Tax incres' Y
44. Delete 12 MX missiles Y
45. Spending cuts;Tax incres' Y
46. Textile Import Quotas N
47. Cut some school lunch fds N
48. Clean Water Act Amendmnts N
49. Youth work projects Y
50. Assist military in Angola N
51. Allow US troops-Nicaragua N
52. Pentagon polygraph exams Y
53. Bar ASAT testing Y
54. Suspend def pmt for abuse Y
55. Bar Pentagon-contr emplmt Y
56. Increase SDI funding N
57. Reduce SDI funding N
58. Produce chemical weapons N
59. Bar CIA fndg in Nicaragua Y
60. South Africa sanctions Y
61. Cut SS COLAs; Raise taxes N
62. Let US invest-So Africa N
63. Approve 21 MX for 1985 N
64. Emergency Farm Credit Y
65. Awards to whistle blowers Y
66. African disaster relief Y
67. Ban bank loans to So Afr Y
68. Bar coun duty-free trtmt N
69. Steel import limits N
70. Soc Sec COLAs=inflation Y
71. Bar haz waste vctms suits N
72. Prohibit aid to Nicaragua Y
73. Cut $-Schs bar sch prayer N
74. Raise taxes; Cut Medicare Y
75. Alien residncy-prior 1982 N
76. Alien residncy-prior 1980 N
77. Pen emp-hire illgl aliens N
78. Lmt Persh II/cruse-Europe Y
79. Delete 34 B-1 bombers Y
80. Bar purch of Pershing II Y
81. Bar purchase of Sgt York Y
82. Delete $ for Trident II Y
83. Allow 15 MX missiles N
84. Bar MX procurement-1985 Y
85. Equal Access Act N
86. Aid to El Salvador N
87. Bar Nicarag water mining Y
88. Physician/Medicare freeze N
89. Increase "sin" taxes Y
90. End SBA direct loans N
91. Sell Conrail N
92. Equal Rights Amendment Y
93. Marines in Lebanon N
94. Eminent domain-Coal comps N
95. Prohibit EPA sanctions Y
96. SS age increase/Reforms N
97. Auto domestic content req N
98. Delete jobs program fundg N
99. Highway-Gas tax bill Y
100. Raise Medicare;Cut defnse Y
101. Emergency housing aid Y
102. Across-the-board tax cuts N
103. Gramm-Latta II targets N
104. Delete B-1 bomber funds Y
105. Dsapprov Saudi AWACS sale Y

Presidential Support Score: 1986 - 25% 1985 - 26%

WEAVER, JAMES -- Oregon 4th District [Democrat]. Counties of Benton (pt.), Coos, Curry, Douglas, Jackson (pt.), Josephine (pt.), Lane, Linn (pt.) and Marion (pt.). Prior Terms: House: 1975-86. Born: August 8, 1927; Brookings, S.D. Education: University of Oregon (B.A.). Military Service: U.S. Navy. Occupation: Builder.

1. Immigration Reform ?
2. Open fld-search warrants Y
3. Civil pnty-hire ill alien N
4. So Afr sanc-veto override ?
5. Tax Overhaul N
6. South Africa sanctions Y
7. Death penalty-drug bill N
8. Evidence-warrantless srch N
9. Life term-second drug off ?
10. Military use in drug war ?
11. Troop reduction in Europe Y
12. Prohibit chemical weapons Y
13. Bar ASAT testing Y
14. Abide SALT II weapons ban Y
15. Follow SALT II-Soviets do N
16. Reduce SDI funding Y
17. Increase SDI funding N
18. Purchase Trident sub N
19. Delete 12 MX;Add conv wpn Y
20. Raise speed limit Y

WEAVER, JAMES (Cont.)

21. Textile Import Quotas(*)	Y	71. Bar haz waste vctms suits	N
22. Req Pentagon buy US goods	Y	72. Prohibit aid to Nicaragua	Y
23. AIDS ins anti-dscriminatn	Y	73. Cut $-Schs bar sch prayer	N
24. Nicaraguan refugee aid	Y	74. Raise taxes; Cut Medicare	Y
25. Nicaraguan contra aid	N	75. Alien residncy-prior 1982	Y
26. US abide by SALT II	N	76. Alien residncy-prior 1980	N
27. Prohibit Saudi arms sale	Y	77. Pen emp-hire illgl aliens	Y
28. Military Retiremnt Reform	Y	78. Lmt Persh II/cruse-Europe	Y
29. Nicaraguan refugee aid	Y	79. Delete 34 B-1 bombers	Y
30. Ease '68 Gun Control Act	Y	80. Bar purch of Pershing II	Y
31. Bar intrstat handgun tran	N	81. Bar purchase of Sgt York	Y
32. Keep '68 Gun Control Act	N	82. Delete $ for Trident II	Y
33. Nicaraguan contra aid	N	83. Allow 15 MX missiles	N
34. Bar emp polygraph testing	#	84. Bar MX procurement-1985	Y
35. Tax Overhaul consideratn	Y	85. Equal Access Act	Y
36. Bar armor-piercing ammo	N	86. Aid to El Salvador	N
37. Tax Overhaul consideratn	Y	87. Bar Nicarag water mining	Y
38. Make comp emissions known	Y	88. Physician/Medicare freeze	N
39. Allow toxic victims suits	Y	89. Increase "sin" taxes	Y
40. Strike Superfund "VAT"	Y	90. End SBA direct loans	N
41. Notify emp-plant closing	Y	91. Sell Conrail	?
42. Bar emp consult-plant clo	N	92. Equal Rights Amendment	Y
43. Medicare cuts;Tax incres'	Y	93. Marines in Lebanon	N
44. Delete 12 MX missiles	Y	94. Eminent domain-Coal comps	N
45. Spending cuts;Tax incres'	Y	95. Prohibit EPA sanctions	Y
46. Textile Import Quotas	Y	96. SS age increase/Reforms	N
47. Cut some school lunch fds	N	97. Auto domestic content req	Y
48. Clean Water Act Amendmnts	N	98. Delete jobs program fundg	Y
49. Youth work projects	Y	99. Highway-Gas tax bill	N
50. Assist military in Angola	N	100. Raise Medicare;Cut defnse	Y
51. Allow US troops-Nicaragua	N	101. Emergency housing aid	Y
52. Pentagon polygraph exams	?	102. Across-the-board tax cuts	N
53. Bar ASAT testing	Y	103. Gramm-Latta II targets	N
54. Suspend def pmt for abuse	Y	104. Delete B-1 bomber funds	Y
55. Bar Pentagon-contr emplmt	Y	105. Dsapprov Saudi AWACS sale	Y
56. Increase SDI funding	N	106. Disapprove oil import fee	Y
57. Reduce SDI funding	Y	107. Rail Deregulation	N
58. Produce chemical weapons	N	108. Dsapp India nuc fuel sale	Y
59. Bar CIA fndg in Nicaragua	Y	109. Mil draft registration	N
60. South Africa sanctions	Y	110. Chrysler Loan Guarantees	N
61. Cut SS COLAs; Raise taxes	N	111. Prohibit school busing	N
62. Let US invest-So Africa	N	112. Nuclear plant moratorium	?
63. Approve 21 MX for 1985	N	113. Oil price controls	Y
64. Emergency Farm Credit	Y	114. Tuition Tax Credits	N
65. Awards to whistle blowers	Y	115. Est Consumer Protect Agcy	Y
66. African disaster relief	Y	116. Eliminate B-1 bomber fnds	Y
67. Ban bank loans to So Afr	?	117. Subminimum wage for youth	N
68. Bar coun duty-free trtmt	Y	118. Delete crude oil tax	N
69. Steel import limits	Y	119. Natural gas deregulation	N
70. Soc Sec COLAs=inflation	Y		

Presidential Support Score: 1986 - 8% 1985 - 14%

SMITH, DENNY -- Oregon 5th District [Republican]. Counties of Benton (pt.), Clackamas (pt.), Linn (pt.), Marion (pt.) and Polk (pt.). Prior Terms: House: 1981-86. Born: January 19, 1938; Ontario, Ore. Education: Willamette University. Military Service: U.S. Air Force 1958-59, 1962-66; Oregon Air Guard,

SMITH, DENNY (Cont.)
1960-62. Occupation: Chairman, Board Eagle Newspapers, Inc.; pilot, Pan American World Airways.

1. Immigration Reform N
2. Open fld-search warrants Y
3. Civil pnty-hire ill alien Y
4. So Afr sanc-veto override N
5. Tax Overhaul N
6. South Africa sanctions N
7. Death penalty-drug bill Y
8. Evidence-warrantless srch Y
9. Life term-second drug off Y
10. Military use in drug war Y
11. Troop reduction in Europe Y
12. Prohibit chemical weapons N
13. Bar ASAT testing N
14. Abide SALT II weapons ban N
15. Follow SALT II-Soviets do Y
16. Reduce SDI funding N
17. Increase SDI funding N
18. Purchase Trident sub N
19. Delete 12 MX;Add conv wpn N
20. Raise speed limit Y
21. Textile Import Quotas(*) Y
22. Req Pentagon buy US goods Y
23. AIDS ins anti-dscriminatn N
24. Nicaraguan refugee aid N
25. Nicaraguan contra aid Y
26. US abide by SALT II Y
27. Prohibit Saudi arms sale Y
28. Military Retiremnt Reform Y
29. Nicaraguan refugee aid Y
30. Ease '68 Gun Control Act Y
31. Bar intrstat handgun tran N
32. Keep '68 Gun Control Act N
33. Nicaraguan contra aid Y
34. Bar emp polygraph testing N
35. Tax Overhaul consideratn N
36. Bar armor-piercing ammo Y
37. Tax Overhaul consideratn N
38. Make comp emissions known N
39. Allow toxic victims suits N
40. Strike Superfund "VAT" Y
41. Notify emp-plant closing N
42. Bar emp consult-plant clo Y
43. Medicare cuts;Tax incres' X
44. Delete 12 MX missiles N
45. Spending cuts;Tax incres' X
46. Textile Import Quotas N
47. Cut some school lunch fds Y
48. Clean Water Act Amendmnts Y
49. Youth work projects X
50. Assist military in Angola Y
51. Allow US troops-Nicaragua Y
52. Pentagon polygraph exams Y
53. Bar ASAT testing N
54. Suspend def pmt for abuse N
55. Bar Pentagon-contr emplmt Y
56. Increase SDI funding Y
57. Reduce SDI funding N
58. Produce chemical weapons Y
59. Bar CIA fndg in Nicaragua N
60. South Africa sanctions N
61. Cut SS COLAs; Raise taxes N
62. Let US invest-So Africa Y
63. Approve 21 MX for 1985 Y
64. Emergency Farm Credit N
65. Awards to whistle blowers Y
66. African disaster relief N
67. Ban bank loans to So Afr N
68. Bar coun duty-free trtmt N
69. Steel import limits N
70. Soc Sec COLAs=inflation Y
71. Bar haz waste vctms suits Y
72. Prohibit aid to Nicaragua N
73. Cut $-Schs bar sch prayer Y
74. Raise taxes; Cut Medicare N
75. Alien residncy-prior 1982 Y
76. Alien residncy-prior 1980 Y
77. Pen emp-hire illgl aliens N
78. Lmt Persh II/cruse-Europe N
79. Delete 34 B-1 bombers N
80. Bar purch of Pershing II N
81. Bar purchase of Sgt York Y
82. Delete $ for Trident II N
83. Allow 15 MX missiles Y
84. Bar MX procurement-1985 N
85. Equal Access Act #
86. Aid to El Salvador Y
87. Bar Nicarag water mining Y
88. Physician/Medicare freeze Y
89. Increase "sin" taxes N
90. End SBA direct loans Y
91. Sell Conrail Y
92. Equal Rights Amendment N
93. Marines in Lebanon N
94. Eminent domain-Coal comps Y
95. Prohibit EPA sanctions ?
96. SS age increase/Reforms Y
97. Auto domestic content req N
98. Delete jobs program fundg Y
99. Highway-Gas tax bill N
100. Raise Medicare;Cut defnse N
101. Emergency housing aid Y
102. Across-the-board tax cuts Y
103. Gramm-Latta II targets Y
104. Delete B-1 bomber funds N
105. Dsapprov Saudi AWACS sale Y

Presidential Support Score: 1986 - 75% 1985 - 76%

PENNSYLVANIA

FOGLIETTA, THOMAS M. -- Pennsylvania 1st District [Democrat]. County of Philadelphia (pt.). Prior Terms: House: 1981-86. Born: December 3, 1928; Philadelphia, Pa. Education: St. Joseph's College (B.A.); Temple University (J.D.). Occupation: Philadelphia city councilman; attorney; boardmember, St. Luke's Hospital; boardmember, Guiffre Medical Center; Labor Department regional director.

1. Immigration Reform Y
2. Open fld-search warrants Y
3. Civil pnty-hire ill alien N
4. So Afr sanc-veto override Y
5. Tax Overhaul Y
6. South Africa sanctions Y
7. Death penalty-drug bill Y
8. Evidence-warrantless srch N
9. Life term-second drug off Y
10. Military use in drug war N
11. Troop reduction in Europe N
12. Prohibit chemical weapons Y
13. Bar ASAT testing Y
14. Abide SALT II weapons ban Y
15. Follow SALT II-Soviets do N
16. Reduce SDI funding Y
17. Increase SDI funding N
18. Purchase Trident sub Y
19. Delete 12 MX;Add conv wpn Y
20. Raise speed limit N
21. Textile Import Quotas(*) Y
22. Req Pentagon buy US goods Y
23. AIDS ins anti-dscriminatn Y
24. Nicaraguan refugee aid Y
25. Nicaraguan contra aid N
26. US abide by SALT II N
27. Prohibit Saudi arms sale Y
28. Military Retiremnt Reform Y
29. Nicaraguan refugee aid Y
30. Ease '68 Gun Control Act N
31. Bar intrstat handgun tran Y
32. Keep '68 Gun Control Act Y
33. Nicaraguan contra aid N
34. Bar emp polygraph testing Y
35. Tax Overhaul consideratn Y
36. Bar armor-piercing ammo Y
37. Tax Overhaul consideratn Y
38. Make comp emissions known Y
39. Allow toxic victims suits Y
40. Strike Superfund "VAT" N
41. Notify emp-plant closing Y
42. Bar emp consult-plant clo N
43. Medicare cuts;Tax incres' Y
44. Delete 12 MX missiles Y
45. Spending cuts;Tax incres' Y
46. Textile Import Quotas Y
47. Cut some school lunch fds N
48. Clean Water Act Amendmnts N
49. Youth work projects Y
50. Assist military in Angola N
51. Allow US troops-Nicaragua N
52. Pentagon polygraph exams Y
53. Bar ASAT testing Y
54. Suspend def pmt for abuse Y
55. Bar Pentagon-contr emplmt Y
56. Increase SDI funding N
57. Reduce SDI funding Y
58. Produce chemical weapons N
59. Bar CIA fndg in Nicaragua Y
60. South Africa sanctions Y
61. Cut SS COLAs; Raise taxes N
62. Let US invest-So Africa N
63. Approve 21 MX for 1985 N
64. Emergency Farm Credit Y
65. Awards to whistle blowers Y
66. African disaster relief Y
67. Ban bank loans to So Afr ?
68. Bar coun duty-free trtmt Y
69. Steel import limits Y
70. Soc Sec COLAs=inflation Y
71. Bar haz waste vctms suits N
72. Prohibit aid to Nicaragua Y
73. Cut $-Schs bar sch prayer N
74. Raise taxes; Cut Medicare Y
75. Alien residncy-prior 1982 N
76. Alien residncy-prior 1980 N
77. Pen emp-hire illgl aliens Y
78. Lmt Persh II/cruse-Europe Y
79. Delete 34 B-1 bombers Y
80. Bar purch of Pershing II Y
81. Bar purchase of Sgt York N
82. Delete $ for Trident II N
83. Allow 15 MX missiles N
84. Bar MX procurement-1985 Y
85. Equal Access Act N
86. Aid to El Salvador N
87. Bar Nicarag water mining Y
88. Physician/Medicare freeze N
89. Increase "sin" taxes ?
90. End SBA direct loans ?
91. Sell Conrail ?
92. Equal Rights Amendment Y
93. Marines in Lebanon Y
94. Eminent domain-Coal comps Y
95. Prohibit EPA sanctions ?
96. SS age increase/Reforms N
97. Auto domestic content req Y
98. Delete jobs program fundg N
99. Highway-Gas tax bill Y
100. Raise Medicare;Cut defnse Y

FOGLIETTA, THOMAS M. (Cont.)

101. Emergency housing aid ?
102. Across-the-board tax cuts N
103. Gramm-Latta II targets N
104. Delete B-1 bomber funds Y
105. Dsapprov Saudi AWACS sale Y

Presidential Support Score: 1986 - 16% 1985 - 20%

GRAY, WILLIAM H., III -- Pennsylvania 2nd District [Democrat]. County of Philadelphia (pt.). Prior Terms: House: 1979-86. Born: August 20, 1941; Baton Rouge, La. Education: Franklin and Marshall College (B.A.); Temple University; Drew Theological Seminary; Princeton Theological Seminary; University of Pennsylvania; Mansfield College of Oxford University. Occupation: College Lecturer; pastor.

1. Immigration Reform Y
2. Open fld-search warrants Y
3. Civil pnty-hire ill alien ?
4. So Afr sanc-veto override Y
5. Tax Overhaul Y
6. South Africa sanctions Y
7. Death penalty-drug bill Y
8. Evidence-warrantless srch N
9. Life term-second drug off Y
10. Military use in drug war N
11. Troop reduction in Europe Y
12. Prohibit chemical weapons Y
13. Bar ASAT testing Y
14. Abide SALT II weapons ban Y
15. Follow SALT II-Soviets do N
16. Reduce SDI funding Y
17. Increase SDI funding N
18. Purchase Trident sub Y
19. Delete 12 MX;Add conv wpn ?
20. Raise speed limit N
21. Textile Import Quotas(*) Y
22. Req Pentagon buy US goods Y
23. AIDS ins anti-dscriminatn Y
24. Nicaraguan refugee aid Y
25. Nicaraguan contra aid N
26. US abide by SALT II N
27. Prohibit Saudi arms sale Y
28. Military Retiremnt Reform Y
29. Nicaraguan refugee aid Y
30. Ease '68 Gun Control Act N
31. Bar intrstat handgun tran Y
32. Keep '68 Gun Control Act Y
33. Nicaraguan contra aid N
34. Bar emp polygraph testing Y
35. Tax Overhaul consideratn Y
36. Bar armor-piercing ammo Y
37. Tax Overhaul consideratn Y
38. Make comp emissions known Y
39. Allow toxic victims suits Y
40. Strike Superfund "VAT" N
41. Notify emp-plant closing Y
42. Bar emp consult-plant clo N
43. Medicare cuts;Tax incres' Y
44. Delete 12 MX missiles Y
45. Spending cuts;Tax incres' Y
46. Textile Import Quotas Y
47. Cut some school lunch fds N
48. Clean Water Act Amendmnts N
49. Youth work projects Y
50. Assist military in Angola N
51. Allow US troops-Nicaragua N
52. Pentagon polygraph exams N
53. Bar ASAT testing ?
54. Suspend def pmt for abuse ?
55. Bar Pentagon-contr emplmt Y
56. Increase SDI funding N
57. Reduce SDI funding Y
58. Produce chemical weapons N
59. Bar CIA fndg in Nicaragua Y
60. South Africa sanctions Y
61. Cut SS COLAs; Raise taxes P
62. Let US invest-So Africa N
63. Approve 21 MX for 1985 N
64. Emergency Farm Credit Y
65. Awards to whistle blowers Y
66. African disaster relief Y
67. Ban bank loans to So Afr ?
68. Bar coun duty-free trtmt Y
69. Steel import limits Y
70. Soc Sec COLAs=inflation Y
71. Bar haz waste vctms suits N
72. Prohibit aid to Nicaragua Y
73. Cut $-Schs bar sch prayer N
74. Raise taxes; Cut Medicare Y
75. Alien residncy-prior 1982 N
76. Alien residncy-prior 1980 N
77. Pen emp-hire illgl aliens Y
78. Lmt Persh II/cruse-Europe Y
79. Delete 34 B-1 bombers Y
80. Bar purch of Pershing II Y
81. Bar purchase of Sgt York Y
82. Delete $ for Trident II Y
83. Allow 15 MX missiles N
84. Bar MX procurement-1985 Y
85. Equal Access Act N
86. Aid to El Salvador N
87. Bar Nicarag water mining Y
88. Physician/Medicare freeze N
89. Increase "sin" taxes Y
90. End SBA direct loans N

GRAY, WILLIAM H., III (Cont.)

91. Sell Conrail N
92. Equal Rights Amendment Y
93. Marines in Lebanon N
94. Eminent domain-Coal comps Y
95. Prohibit EPA sanctions N
96. SS age increase/Reforms N
97. Auto domestic content req Y
98. Delete jobs program fundg N
99. Highway-Gas tax bill Y
100. Raise Medicare;Cut defnse Y
101. Emergency housing aid Y
102. Across-the-board tax cuts N
103. Gramm-Latta II targets N
104. Delete B-1 bomber funds Y
105. Dsapprov Saudi AWACS sale Y
106. Disapprove oil import fee Y
107. Rail Deregulation N
108. Dsapp India nuc fuel sale Y
109. Mil draft registration X
110. Chrysler Loan Guarantees Y
111. Prohibit school busing N
112. Nuclear plant moratorium Y
113. Oil price controls Y

Presidential Support Score: 1986 - 14% 1985 - 15%

BORSKI, ROBERT A. -- Pennsylvania 3rd District [Democrat]. County of Philadelphia (pt.). Prior Terms: House: 1983-86. Born: October 20, 1948; Philadelphia, Pa. Education: University of Baltimore (B.A.). Occupation: Assistant basketball coach; stockbroker; Pennsylvania legislator (1976-82).

1. Immigration Reform Y
2. Open fld-search warrants Y
3. Civil pnty-hire ill alien N
4. So Afr sanc-veto override Y
5. Tax Overhaul Y
6. South Africa sanctions Y
7. Death penalty-drug bill Y
8. Evidence-warrantless srch Y
9. Life term-second drug off Y
10. Military use in drug war N
11. Troop reduction in Europe N
12. Prohibit chemical weapons Y
13. Bar ASAT testing Y
14. Abide SALT II weapons ban Y
15. Follow SALT II-Soviets do N
16. Reduce SDI funding N
17. Increase SDI funding N
18. Purchase Trident sub Y
19. Delete 12 MX;Add conv wpn Y
20. Raise speed limit N
21. Textile Import Quotas(*) Y
22. Req Pentagon buy US goods Y
23. AIDS ins anti-dscriminatn Y
24. Nicaraguan refugee aid Y
25. Nicaraguan contra aid N
26. US abide by SALT II N
27. Prohibit Saudi arms sale Y
28. Military Retiremnt Reform Y
29. Nicaraguan refugee aid Y
30. Ease '68 Gun Control Act N
31. Bar intrstat handgun tran Y
32. Keep '68 Gun Control Act Y
33. Nicaraguan contra aid N
34. Bar emp polygraph testing Y
35. Tax Overhaul consideratn Y
36. Bar armor-piercing ammo Y
37. Tax Overhaul consideratn Y
38. Make comp emissions known Y
39. Allow toxic victims suits N
40. Strike Superfund "VAT" N
41. Notify emp-plant closing Y
42. Bar emp consult-plant clo N
43. Medicare cuts;Tax incres' Y
44. Delete 12 MX missiles Y
45. Spending cuts;Tax incres' Y
46. Textile Import Quotas Y
47. Cut some school lunch fds N
48. Clean Water Act Amendmnts N
49. Youth work projects Y
50. Assist military in Angola N
51. Allow US troops-Nicaragua N
52. Pentagon polygraph exams Y
53. Bar ASAT testing Y
54. Suspend def pmt for abuse Y
55. Bar Pentagon-contr emplmt Y
56. Increase SDI funding N
57. Reduce SDI funding N
58. Produce chemical weapons N
59. Bar CIA fndg in Nicaragua Y
60. South Africa sanctions Y
61. Cut SS COLAs; Raise taxes N
62. Let US invest-So Africa N
63. Approve 21 MX for 1985 N
64. Emergency Farm Credit Y
65. Awards to whistle blowers Y
66. African disaster relief Y
67. Ban bank loans to So Afr Y
68. Bar coun duty-free trtmt Y
69. Steel import limits Y
70. Soc Sec COLAs=inflation Y
71. Bar haz waste vctms suits N
72. Prohibit aid to Nicaragua Y
73. Cut $-Schs bar sch prayer N
74. Raise taxes; Cut Medicare Y
75. Alien residncy-prior 1982 Y
76. Alien residncy-prior 1980 N

BORSKI, ROBERT A. (Cont.)

77. Pen emp-hire illgl aliens Y
78. Lmt Persh II/cruse-Europe N
79. Delete 34 B-1 bombers Y
80. Bar purch of Pershing II N
81. Bar purchase of Sgt York Y
82. Delete $ for Trident II N
83. Allow 15 MX missiles N
84. Bar MX procurement-1985 Y
85. Equal Access Act N
86. Aid to El Salvador N
87. Bar Nicarag water mining Y
88. Physician/Medicare freeze N
89. Increase "sin" taxes Y
90. End SBA direct loans N
91. Sell Conrail N
92. Equal Rights Amendment Y
93. Marines in Lebanon Y
94. Eminent domain-Coal comps Y
95. Prohibit EPA sanctions Y
96. SS age increase/Reforms N

Presidential Support Score: 1986 - 20% 1985 - 24%

KOLTER, JOE -- Pennsylvania 4th District [Democrat]. Counties of Armstrong (pt.), Beaver (pt.), Butler, Indiana, Lawrence (pt.) and Westmoreland (pt.). Prior Terms: House: 1983-86. Born: September 3, 1946; McDonald, Ohio. Education: Geneva College. Military Service: U.S. Army. Occupation: Accountant; teacher; councilman; Pennsylvania legislator (1968-82).

1. Immigration Reform N
2. Open fld-search warrants N
3. Civil pnty-hire ill alien N
4. So Afr sanc-veto override Y
5. Tax Overhaul N
6. South Africa sanctions Y
7. Death penalty-drug bill Y
8. Evidence-warrantless srch Y
9. Life term-second drug off Y
10. Military use in drug war Y
11. Troop reduction in Europe N
12. Prohibit chemical weapons Y
13. Bar ASAT testing Y
14. Abide SALT II weapons ban Y
15. Follow SALT II-Soviets do N
16. Reduce SDI funding N
17. Increase SDI funding N
18. Purchase Trident sub N
19. Delete 12 MX;Add conv wpn Y
20. Raise speed limit N
21. Textile Import Quotas(*) Y
22. Req Pentagon buy US goods Y
23. AIDS ins anti-dscriminatn Y
24. Nicaraguan refugee aid N
25. Nicaraguan contra aid N
26. US abide by SALT II N
27. Prohibit Saudi arms sale Y
28. Military Retiremnt Reform N
29. Nicaraguan refugee aid N
30. Ease '68 Gun Control Act Y
31. Bar intrstat handgun tran N
32. Keep '68 Gun Control Act N
33. Nicaraguan contra aid N
34. Bar emp polygraph testing Y
35. Tax Overhaul consideratn N
36. Bar armor-piercing ammo Y
37. Tax Overhaul consideratn Y
38. Make comp emissions known Y
39. Allow toxic victims suits N
40. Strike Superfund "VAT" N
41. Notify emp-plant closing Y
42. Bar emp consult-plant clo N
43. Medicare cuts;Tax incres' N
44. Delete 12 MX missiles N
45. Spending cuts;Tax incres' N
46. Textile Import Quotas Y
47. Cut some school lunch fds N
48. Clean Water Act Amendmnts N
49. Youth work projects ?
50. Assist military in Angola N
51. Allow US troops-Nicaragua N
52. Pentagon polygraph exams Y
53. Bar ASAT testing ?
54. Suspend def pmt for abuse Y
55. Bar Pentagon-contr emplmt Y
56. Increase SDI funding N
57. Reduce SDI funding Y
58. Produce chemical weapons N
59. Bar CIA fndg in Nicaragua Y
60. South Africa sanctions Y
61. Cut SS COLAs; Raise taxes N
62. Let US invest-So Africa N
63. Approve 21 MX for 1985 N
64. Emergency Farm Credit Y
65. Awards to whistle blowers Y
66. African disaster relief ?
67. Ban bank loans to So Afr Y
68. Bar coun duty-free trtmt Y
69. Steel import limits Y
70. Soc Sec COLAs=inflation Y
71. Bar haz waste vctms suits N
72. Prohibit aid to Nicaragua Y
73. Cut $-Schs bar sch prayer Y
74. Raise taxes; Cut Medicare N
75. Alien residncy-prior 1982 Y
76. Alien residncy-prior 1980 N
77. Pen emp-hire illgl aliens Y
78. Lmt Persh II/cruse-Europe ?

KOLTER, JOE (Cont.)

79. Delete 34 B-1 bombers Y
80. Bar purch of Pershing II Y
81. Bar purchase of Sgt York Y
82. Delete $ for Trident II N
83. Allow 15 MX missiles N
84. Bar MX procurement-1985 Y
85. Equal Access Act Y
86. Aid to El Salvador N
87. Bar Nicarag water mining Y
88. Physician/Medicare freeze N
89. Increase "sin" taxes Y
90. End SBA direct loans N
91. Sell Conrail N
92. Equal Rights Amendment Y
93. Marines in Lebanon Y
94. Eminent domain-Coal comps N
95. Prohibit EPA sanctions ?
96. SS age increase/Reforms N

Presidential Support Score: 1986 - 25% 1985 - 28%

SCHULZE, RICHARD T. -- Pennsylvania 5th District [Republican]. Counties of Chester (pt.), Delaware (pt.) and Montgomery (pt.). Prior Terms: House: 1975-86. Born: August 7, 1929; Philadelphia, Pa. Education: Houston University; Villanova University; Temple University Extension. Military Service: U.S. Army, 1951-53. Occupation: Retail electrical appliance businessman; Registrar, wills and clerk, Orphans Court (1967-69); Pennsylvania representative (1969-74).

1. Immigration Reform ?
2. Open fld-search warrants ?
3. Civil pnty-hire ill alien N
4. So Afr sanc-veto override Y
5. Tax Overhaul Y
6. South Africa sanctions Y
7. Death penalty-drug bill ?
8. Evidence-warrantless srch ?
9. Life term-second drug off Y
10. Military use in drug war Y
11. Troop reduction in Europe N
12. Prohibit chemical weapons N
13. Bar ASAT testing N
14. Abide SALT II weapons ban N
15. Follow SALT II-Soviets do Y
16. Reduce SDI funding N
17. Increase SDI funding N
18. Purchase Trident sub N
19. Delete 12 MX;Add conv wpn N
20. Raise speed limit N
21. Textile Import Quotas(*) Y
22. Req Pentagon buy US goods Y
23. AIDS ins anti-dscriminatn N
24. Nicaraguan refugee aid N
25. Nicaraguan contra aid Y
26. US abide by SALT II Y
27. Prohibit Saudi arms sale Y
28. Military Retiremnt Reform Y
29. Nicaraguan refugee aid Y
30. Ease '68 Gun Control Act #
31. Bar intrstat handgun tran N
32. Keep '68 Gun Control Act N
33. Nicaraguan contra aid Y
34. Bar emp polygraph testing N
35. Tax Overhaul consideratn N
36. Bar armor-piercing ammo Y
37. Tax Overhaul consideratn N
38. Make comp emissions known N
39. Allow toxic victims suits N
40. Strike Superfund "VAT" N
41. Notify emp-plant closing N
42. Bar emp consult-plant clo Y
43. Medicare cuts;Tax incres' N
44. Delete 12 MX missiles N
45. Spending cuts;Tax incres' N
46. Textile Import Quotas Y
47. Cut some school lunch fds Y
48. Clean Water Act Amendmnts Y
49. Youth work projects N
50. Assist military in Angola Y
51. Allow US troops-Nicaragua Y
52. Pentagon polygraph exams Y
53. Bar ASAT testing N
54. Suspend def pmt for abuse Y
55. Bar Pentagon-contr emplmt Y
56. Increase SDI funding N
57. Reduce SDI funding N
58. Produce chemical weapons Y
59. Bar CIA fndg in Nicaragua ?
60. South Africa sanctions Y
61. Cut SS COLAs; Raise taxes Y
62. Let US invest-So Africa N
63. Approve 21 MX for 1985 Y
64. Emergency Farm Credit N
65. Awards to whistle blowers Y
66. African disaster relief Y
67. Ban bank loans to So Afr ?
68. Bar coun duty-free trtmt N
69. Steel import limits Y
70. Soc Sec COLAs=inflation Y
71. Bar haz waste vctms suits Y
72. Prohibit aid to Nicaragua Y
73. Cut $-Schs bar sch prayer Y
74. Raise taxes; Cut Medicare Y
75. Alien residncy-prior 1982 ?
76. Alien residncy-prior 1980 Y

SCHULZE, RICHARD T. (Cont.)

77. Pen emp-hire illgl aliens N
78. Lmt Persh II/cruse-Europe N
79. Delete 34 B-1 bombers N
80. Bar purch of Pershing II N
81. Bar purchase of Sgt York N
82. Delete $ for Trident II N
83. Allow 15 MX missiles Y
84. Bar MX procurement-1985 N
85. Equal Access Act Y
86. Aid to El Salvador Y
87. Bar Nicarag water mining Y
88. Physician/Medicare freeze Y
89. Increase "sin" taxes Y
90. End SBA direct loans N
91. Sell Conrail Y
92. Equal Rights Amendment N
93. Marines in Lebanon N
94. Eminent domain-Coal comps N
95. Prohibit EPA sanctions ?
96. SS age increase/Reforms Y
97. Auto domestic content req ?
98. Delete jobs program fundg ?
99. Highway-Gas tax bill Y
100. Raise Medicare;Cut defnse N
101. Emergency housing aid Y
102. Across-the-board tax cuts Y
103. Gramm-Latta II targets Y
104. Delete B-1 bomber funds N
105. Dsapprov Saudi AWACS sale N
106. Disapprove oil import fee Y
107. Rail Deregulation N
108. Dsapp India nuc fuel sale Y
109. Mil draft registration ?
110. Chrysler Loan Guarantees N
111. Prohibit school busing Y
112. Nuclear plant moratorium Y
113. Oil price controls N
114. Tuition Tax Credits ?
115. Est Consumer Protect Agcy N
116. Eliminate B-1 bomber fnds N
117. Subminimum wage for youth Y
118. Delete crude oil tax Y
119. Natural gas deregulation Y

Presidential Support Score: 1986 - 59% 1985 - 64%

YATRON, GUS -- Pennsylvania 6th District [Democrat]. Counties of Berks, Carbon (pt.), Lancaster (pt.) and Schuylkill. Prior Terms: House: 1969-86. Born: October 16, 1927; Reading, Pa. Education: Kutztown State Teachers College. Occupation: Ice cream businessman; school board member (1955); Pennsylvania representative (1956-59); Pennsylvania senator (1960-68).

1. Immigration Reform N
2. Open fld-search warrants N
3. Civil pnty-hire ill alien N
4. So Afr sanc-veto override Y
5. Tax Overhaul Y
6. South Africa sanctions Y
7. Death penalty-drug bill Y
8. Evidence-warrantless srch Y
9. Life term-second drug off Y
10. Military use in drug war Y
11. Troop reduction in Europe N
12. Prohibit chemical weapons Y
13. Bar ASAT testing Y
14. Abide SALT II weapons ban Y
15. Follow SALT II-Soviets do N
16. Reduce SDI funding N
17. Increase SDI funding N
18. Purchase Trident sub Y
19. Delete 12 MX;Add conv wpn N
20. Raise speed limit N
21. Textile Import Quotas(*) Y
22. Req Pentagon buy US goods Y
23. AIDS ins anti-dscriminatn Y
24. Nicaraguan refugee aid Y
25. Nicaraguan contra aid N
26. US abide by SALT II N
27. Prohibit Saudi arms sale Y
28. Military Retiremnt Reform Y
29. Nicaraguan refugee aid Y
30. Ease '68 Gun Control Act Y
31. Bar intrstat handgun tran N
32. Keep '68 Gun Control Act N
33. Nicaraguan contra aid N
34. Bar emp polygraph testing Y
35. Tax Overhaul consideratn Y
36. Bar armor-piercing ammo Y
37. Tax Overhaul consideratn Y
38. Make comp emissions known Y
39. Allow toxic victims suits N
40. Strike Superfund "VAT" Y
41. Notify emp-plant closing Y
42. Bar emp consult-plant clo N
43. Medicare cuts;Tax incres' N
44. Delete 12 MX missiles N
45. Spending cuts;Tax incres' N
46. Textile Import Quotas Y
47. Cut some school lunch fds N
48. Clean Water Act Amendmnts N
49. Youth work projects ?
50. Assist military in Angola N
51. Allow US troops-Nicaragua N
52. Pentagon polygraph exams Y
53. Bar ASAT testing Y
54. Suspend def pmt for abuse Y

YATRON, GUS (Cont.)

55. Bar Pentagon-contr emplmt Y
56. Increase SDI funding N
57. Reduce SDI funding N
58. Produce chemical weapons N
59. Bar CIA fndg in Nicaragua Y
60. South Africa sanctions Y
61. Cut SS COLAs; Raise taxes N
62. Let US invest-So Africa ?
63. Approve 21 MX for 1985 Y
64. Emergency Farm Credit Y
65. Awards to whistle blowers Y
66. African disaster relief Y
67. Ban bank loans to So Afr Y
68. Bar coun duty-free trtmt ?
69. Steel import limits Y
70. Soc Sec COLAs=inflation Y
71. Bar haz waste vctms suits N
72. Prohibit aid to Nicaragua Y
73. Cut $-Schs bar sch prayer Y
74. Raise taxes; Cut Medicare N
75. Alien residncy-prior 1982 Y
76. Alien residncy-prior 1980 Y
77. Pen emp-hire illgl aliens Y
78. Lmt Persh II/cruse-Europe N
79. Delete 34 B-1 bombers N
80. Bar purch of Pershing II N
81. Bar purchase of Sgt York Y
82. Delete $ for Trident II N
83. Allow 15 MX missiles Y
84. Bar MX procurement-1985 N
85. Equal Access Act Y
86. Aid to El Salvador N
87. Bar Nicarag water mining Y
88. Physician/Medicare freeze N
89. Increase "sin" taxes Y
90. End SBA direct loans N
91. Sell Conrail N
92. Equal Rights Amendment N
93. Marines in Lebanon Y
94. Eminent domain-Coal comps N
95. Prohibit EPA sanctions Y
96. SS age increase/Reforms N
97. Auto domestic content req Y
98. Delete jobs program fundg N
99. Highway-Gas tax bill N
100. Raise Medicare;cut defnse Y
101. Emergency housing aid Y
102. Across-the-board tax cuts Y
103. Gramm-Latta II targets Y
104. Delete B-1 bomber funds N
105. Dsapprov Saudi AWACS sale Y
106. Disapprove oil import fee Y
107. Rail Deregulation N
108. Dsapp India nuc fuel sale Y
109. Mil draft registration N
110. Chrysler Loan Guarantees Y
111. Prohibit school busing Y
112. Nuclear plant moratorium ?
113. Oil price controls Y
114. Tuition Tax Credits Y
115. Est Consumer Protect Agcy Y
116. Eliminate B-1 bomber fnds N
117. Subminimum wage for youth Y
118. Delete crude oil tax N
119. Natural gas deregulation N

Presidential Support Score: 1986 - 22% 1985 - 44%

EDGAR, BOB -- Pennsylvania 7th District [Democrat]. Counties of Delaware (pt.) and Philadelphia (pt.). Prior Terms: House: 1975-86. Born: May 29, 1943; Philadelphia, Pa. Education: Lycoming College (B.A.); Drew University (M.A.). Occupation: Chaplain.

1. Immigration Reform ?
2. Open fld-search warrants ?
3. Civil pnty-hire ill alien ?
4. So Afr sanc-veto override Y
5. Tax Overhaul Y
6. South Africa sanctions Y
7. Death penalty-drug bill N
8. Evidence-warrantless srch N
9. Life term-second drug off Y
10. Military use in drug war N
11. Troop reduction in Europe N
12. Prohibit chemical weapons Y
13. Bar ASAT testing Y
14. Abide SALT II weapons ban Y
15. Follow SALT II-Soviets do N
16. Reduce SDI funding Y
17. Increase SDI funding N
18. Purchase Trident sub ?
19. Delete 12 MX;Add conv wpn ?
20. Raise speed limit N
21. Textile Import Quotas(*) Y
22. Req Pentagon buy US goods ?
23. AIDS ins anti-dscriminatn Y
24. Nicaraguan refugee aid Y
25. Nicaraguan contra aid N
26. US abide by SALT II N
27. Prohibit Saudi arms sale ?
28. Military Retiremnt Reform ?
29. Nicaraguan refugee aid Y
30. Ease '68 Gun Control Act N
31. Bar intrstat handgun tran Y
32. Keep '68 Gun Control Act Y
33. Nicaraguan contra aid N
34. Bar emp polygraph testing ?

EDGAR, BOB (Cont.)

35. Tax Overhaul consideratn Y
36. Bar armor-piercing ammo Y
37. Tax Overhaul consideratn Y
38. Make comp emissions known Y
39. Allow toxic victims suits Y
40. Strike Superfund "VAT" Y
41. Notify emp-plant closing Y
42. Bar emp consult-plant clo ?
43. Medicare cuts;Tax incres' Y
44. Delete 12 MX missiles Y
45. Spending cuts;Tax incres' Y
46. Textile Import Quotas Y
47. Cut some school lunch fds N
48. Clean Water Act Amendmnts N
49. Youth work projects Y
50. Assist military in Angola N
51. Allow US troops-Nicaragua N
52. Pentagon polygraph exams N
53. Bar ASAT testing Y
54. Suspend def pmt for abuse Y
55. Bar Pentagon-contr emplmt Y
56. Increase SDI funding N
57. Reduce SDI funding Y
58. Produce chemical weapons N
59. Bar CIA fndg in Nicaragua Y
60. South Africa sanctions Y
61. Cut COLAs; Raise taxes N
62. Let US invest-So Africa N
63. Approve 21 MX for 1985 N
64. Emergency Farm Credit Y
65. Awards to whistle blowers Y
66. African disaster relief Y
67. Ban bank loans to So Afr Y
68. Bar coun duty-free trtmt Y
69. Steel import limits Y
70. Soc Sec COLAs=inflation Y
71. Bar haz waste vctms suits N
72. Prohibit aid to Nicaragua Y
73. Cut $-Schs bar sch prayer N
74. Raise taxes; Cut Medicare Y
75. Alien residncy-prior 1982 N
76. Alien residncy-prior 1980 N
77. Pen emp-hire illgl aliens Y
78. Lmt Persh II/cruse-Europe Y
79. Delete 34 B-1 bombers Y
80. Bar purch of Pershing II Y
81. Bar purchase of Sgt York Y
82. Delete $ for Trident II Y
83. Allow 15 MX missiles N
84. Bar MX procurement-1985 Y
85. Equal Access Act N
86. Aid to El Salvador N
87. Bar Nicarag water mining Y
88. Physician/Medicare freeze N
89. Increase "sin" taxes Y
90. End SBA direct loans ?
91. Sell Conrail N
92. Equal Rights Amendment Y
93. Marines in Lebanon N
94. Eminent domain-Coal comps N
95. Prohibit EPA sanctions N
96. SS age increase/Reforms N
97. Auto domestic content req Y
98. Delete jobs program fundg N
99. Highway-Gas tax bill Y
100. Raise Medicare;Cut defnse Y
101. Emergency housing aid Y
102. Across-the-board tax cuts N
103. Gramm-Latta II targets N
104. Delete B-1 bomber funds Y
105. Dsapprov Saudi AWACS sale Y
106. Disapprove oil import fee ?
107. Rail Deregulation N
108. Dsapp India nuc fuel sale Y
109. Mil draft registration N
110. Chrysler Loan Guarantees Y
111. Prohibit school busing N
112. Nuclear plant moratorium Y
113. Oil price controls N
114. Tuition Tax Credits Y
115. Est Consumer Protect Agcy Y
116. Eliminate B-1 bomber fnds Y
117. Subminimum wage for youth N
118. Delete crude oil tax N
119. Natural gas deregulation N

Presidential Support Score: 1986 - 15% 1985 - 18%

KOSTMAYER, PETER H. -- Pennsylvania 8th District [Democrat]. Counties of Bucks and Montgomery (pt.). Prior Terms: House: 1977-80, 1983-86. Born: September 27, 1946; New York City, N.Y. Education: Columbia University. Occupation: Journalist, "The Trentonian"; press secretary to the attorney general (1972-73); deputy press secretary to the governor (1973-76).

1. Immigration Reform Y
2. Open fld-search warrants Y
3. Civil pnty-hire ill alien N
4. So Afr sanc-veto override Y
5. Tax Overhaul Y
6. South Africa sanctions Y
7. Death penalty-drug bill N
8. Evidence-warrantless srch N
9. Life term-second drug off Y
10. Military use in drug war N
11. Troop reduction in Europe Y
12. Prohibit chemical weapons Y

KOSTMAYER, PETER H. (Cont.)

13. Bar ASAT testing Y
14. Abide SALT II weapons ban Y
15. Follow SALT II-Soviets do N
16. Reduce SDI funding Y
17. Increase SDI funding N
18. Purchase Trident sub Y
19. Delete 12 MX;Add conv wpn Y
20. Raise speed limit N
21. Textile Import Quotas(*) Y
22. Req Pentagon buy US goods Y
23. AIDS ins anti-dscriminatn Y
24. Nicaraguan refugee aid Y
25. Nicaraguan contra aid N
26. US abide by SALT II N
27. Prohibit Saudi arms sale Y
28. Military Retiremnt Reform Y
29. Nicaraguan refugee aid Y
30. Ease '68 Gun Control Act Y
31. Bar intrstat handgun tran N
32. Keep '68 Gun Control Act Y
33. Nicaraguan contra aid N
34. Bar emp polygraph testing Y
35. Tax Overhaul consideratn Y
36. Bar armor-piercing ammo Y
37. Tax Overhaul consideratn Y
38. Make comp emissions known Y
39. Allow toxic victims suits Y
40. Strike Superfund "VAT" N
41. Notify emp-plant closing Y
42. Bar emp consult-plant clo N
43. Medicare cuts;Tax incres' Y
44. Delete 12 MX missiles Y
45. Spending cuts;Tax incres' Y
46. Textile Import Quotas Y
47. Cut some school lunch fds N
48. Clean Water Act Amendmnts N
49. Youth work projects Y
50. Assist military in Angola N
51. Allow US troops-Nicaragua N
52. Pentagon polygraph exams N
53. Bar ASAT testing Y
54. Suspend def pmt for abuse Y
55. Bar Pentagon-contr emplmt Y
56. Increase SDI funding N
57. Reduce SDI funding Y
58. Produce chemical weapons N
59. Bar CIA fndg in Nicaragua Y
60. South Africa sanctions Y
61. Cut SS COLAs; Raise taxes N
62. Let US invest-So Africa N
63. Approve 21 MX for 1985 N
64. Emergency Farm Credit Y
65. Awards to whistle blowers Y
66. African disaster relief Y
67. Ban bank loans to So Afr Y
68. Bar coun duty-free trtmt Y
69. Steel import limits Y
70. Soc Sec COLAs=inflation Y
71. Bar haz waste vctms suits N
72. Prohibit aid to Nicaragua Y
73. Cut $-Schs bar sch prayer N
74. Raise taxes; Cut Medicare Y
75. Alien residncy-prior 1982 N
76. Alien residncy-prior 1980 N
77. Pen emp-hire illgl aliens Y
78. Lmt Persh II/cruse-Europe Y
79. Delete 34 B-1 bombers Y
80. Bar purch of Pershing II Y
81. Bar purchase of Sgt York Y
82. Delete $ for Trident II N
83. Allow 15 MX missiles N
84. Bar MX procurement-1985 Y
85. Equal Access Act N
86. Aid to El Salvador N
87. Bar Nicarag water mining Y
88. Physician/Medicare freeze N
89. Increase "sin" taxes Y
90. End SBA direct loans N
91. Sell Conrail N
92. Equal Rights Amendment Y
93. Marines in Lebanon Y
94. Eminent domain-Coal comps Y
95. Prohibit EPA sanctions ?
96. SS age increase/Reforms N
106. Disapprove oil import fee Y
107. Rail Deregulation N
108. Dsapp India nuc fuel sale Y
109. Mil draft registration N
110. Chrysler Loan Guarantees Y
111. Prohibit school busing N
112. Nuclear plant moratorium Y
113. Oil price controls Y
114. Tuition Tax Credits Y
115. Est Consumer Protect Agcy Y
116. Eliminate B-1 bomber fnds Y
117. Subminimum wage for youth N
118. Delete crude oil tax N
119. Natural gas deregulation N

Was not in office for votes 97-105.

Presidential Support Score: 1986 - 17% 1985 - 29%

SHUSTER, BUD -- Pennsylvania 9th District [Republican]. Counties of Bedford, Blair, Cambria (pt.), Clearfield (pt.), Cumberland (pt.), Franklin, Fulton, Huntingdon, Juniata and Mifflin. Prior Terms: House: 1973-86. Born: January 23, 1932; Glassport, Pa. Education: University of Pittsburgh; Duquesne University (M.B.A.); American University (Ph.D.). Military Service: U.S. Army. Occupation: Vice president, Radio Corp.

SHUSTER, BUD (Cont.)
of America; trustee, University of Pittsburgh; operator, Shuster farms.

1. Immigration Reform N
2. Open fld-search warrants N
3. Civil pnty-hire ill alien N
4. So Afr sanc-veto override N
5. Tax Overhaul N
6. South Africa sanctions N
7. Death penalty-drug bill Y
8. Evidence-warrantless srch Y
9. Life term-second drug off Y
10. Military use in drug war Y
11. Troop reduction in Europe Y
12. Prohibit chemical weapons N
13. Bar ASAT testing N
14. Abide SALT II weapons ban N
15. Follow SALT II-Soviets do Y
16. Reduce SDI funding N
17. Increase SDI funding Y
18. Purchase Trident sub N
19. Delete 12 MX;Add conv wpn N
20. Raise speed limit N
21. Textile Import Quotas(*) Y
22. Req Pentagon buy US goods Y
23. AIDS ins anti-dscriminatn N
24. Nicaraguan refugee aid N
25. Nicaraguan contra aid Y
26. US abide by SALT II Y
27. Prohibit Saudi arms sale Y
28. Military Retiremnt Reform Y
29. Nicaraguan refugee aid Y
30. Ease '68 Gun Control Act Y
31. Bar intrstat handgun tran N
32. Keep '68 Gun Control Act N
33. Nicaraguan contra aid Y
34. Bar emp polygraph testing N
35. Tax Overhaul consideratn N
36. Bar armor-piercing ammo Y
37. Tax Overhaul consideratn N
38. Make comp emissions known N
39. Allow toxic victims suits N
40. Strike Superfund "VAT" Y
41. Notify emp-plant closing N
42. Bar emp consult-plant clo Y
43. Medicare cuts;Tax incres' N
44. Delete 12 MX missiles N
45. Spending cuts;Tax incres' N
46. Textile Import Quotas Y
47. Cut some school lunch fds Y
48. Clean Water Act Amendmnts Y
49. Youth work projects N
50. Assist military in Angola Y
51. Allow US troops-Nicaragua Y
52. Pentagon polygraph exams Y
53. Bar ASAT testing N
54. Suspend def pmt for abuse N
55. Bar Pentagon-contr emplmt Y
56. Increase SDI funding Y
57. Reduce SDI funding N
58. Produce chemical weapons Y
59. Bar CIA fndg in Nicaragua N
60. South Africa sanctions N
61. Cut SS COLAs; Raise taxes N
62. Let US invest-So Africa Y
63. Approve 21 MX for 1985 Y
64. Emergency Farm Credit Y
65. Awards to whistle blowers Y
66. African disaster relief Y
67. Ban bank loans to So Afr N
68. Bar coun duty-free trtmt N
69. Steel import limits Y
70. Soc Sec COLAs=inflation Y
71. Bar haz waste vctms suits Y
72. Prohibit aid to Nicaragua N
73. Cut $-Schs bar sch prayer Y
74. Raise taxes; Cut Medicare N
75. Alien residncy-prior 1982 Y
76. Alien residncy-prior 1980 Y
77. Pen emp-hire illgl aliens N
78. Lmt Persh II/cruse-Europe N
79. Delete 34 B-1 bombers N
80. Bar purch of Pershing II N
81. Bar purchase of Sgt York N
82. Delete $ for Trident II N
83. Allow 15 MX missiles Y
84. Bar MX procurement-1985 N
85. Equal Access Act Y
86. Aid to El Salvador Y
87. Bar Nicarag water mining N
88. Physician/Medicare freeze Y
89. Increase "sin" taxes N
90. End SBA direct loans Y
91. Sell Conrail N
92. Equal Rights Amendment N
93. Marines in Lebanon Y
94. Eminent domain-Coal comps N
95. Prohibit EPA sanctions ?
96. SS age increase/Reforms Y
97. Auto domestic content req ?
98. Delete jobs program fundg ?
99. Highway-Gas tax bill Y
100. Raise Medicare;Cut defnse Y
101. Emergency housing aid Y
102. Across-the-board tax cuts Y
103. Gramm-Latta II targets Y
104. Delete B-1 bomber funds N
105. Dsapprov Saudi AWACS sale Y
106. Disapprove oil import fee ?
107. Rail Deregulation N
108. Dsapp India nuc fuel sale Y
109. Mil draft registration ?
110. Chrysler Loan Guarantees N
111. Prohibit school busing Y
112. Nuclear plant moratorium N

SHUSTER, BUD (Cont.)

113. Oil price controls X
114. Tuition Tax Credits Y
115. Est Consumer Protect Agcy N
116. Eliminate B-1 bomber fnds N
117. Subminimum wage for youth Y
118. Delete crude oil tax Y
119. Natural gas deregulation Y

Presidential Support Score: 1986 - 76% 1985 - 66%

McDADE, JOSEPH M. -- Pennsylvania 10th District [Republican]. Counties of Bradford, Clinton (pt.), Lackawanna, Monroe (pt.), Pike, Potter, Susquehanna, Tioga, Wayne and Wyoming. Prior Terms: House: 1963-86. Born: September 29, 1931; Scranton, Pa. Education: University of Notre Dame (B.A.); University of Pennsylvania (LL.B.). Occupation: Clerk, office of chief federal judge; attorney; city solicitor, City of Scranton (1962).

1. Immigration Reform Y
2. Open fld-search warrants Y
3. Civil pnty-hire ill alien N
4. So Afr sanc-veto override ?
5. Tax Overhaul Y
6. South Africa sanctions ?
7. Death penalty-drug bill #
8. Evidence-warrantless srch ?
9. Life term-second drug off Y
10. Military use in drug war N
11. Troop reduction in Europe N
12. Prohibit chemical weapons N
13. Bar ASAT testing N
14. Abide SALT II weapons ban Y
15. Follow SALT II-Soviets do Y
16. Reduce SDI funding N
17. Increase SDI funding N
18. Purchase Trident sub N
19. Delete 12 MX;Add conv wpn N
20. Raise speed limit N
21. Textile Import Quotas(*) Y
22. Req Pentagon buy US goods Y
23. AIDS ins anti-dscriminatn Y
24. Nicaraguan refugee aid N
25. Nicaraguan contra aid Y
26. US abide by SALT II Y
27. Prohibit Saudi arms sale Y
28. Military Retiremnt Reform Y
29. Nicaraguan refugee aid Y
30. Ease '68 Gun Control Act Y
31. Bar intrstat handgun tran N
32. Keep '68 Gun Control Act N
33. Nicaraguan contra aid Y
34. Bar emp polygraph testing Y
35. Tax Overhaul consideratn Y
36. Bar armor-piercing ammo Y
37. Tax Overhaul consideratn N
38. Make comp emissions known Y
39. Allow toxic victims suits Y
40. Strike Superfund "VAT" Y
41. Notify emp-plant closing Y
42. Bar emp consult-plant clo N
43. Medicare cuts;Tax incres' Y
44. Delete 12 MX missiles N
45. Spending cuts;Tax incres' N
46. Textile Import Quotas Y
47. Cut some school lunch fds N
48. Clean Water Act Amendmnts N
49. Youth work projects N
50. Assist military in Angola Y
51. Allow US troops-Nicaragua N
52. Pentagon polygraph exams Y
53. Bar ASAT testing N
54. Suspend def pmt for abuse Y
55. Bar Pentagon-contr emplmt Y
56. Increase SDI funding N
57. Reduce SDI funding N
58. Produce chemical weapons Y
59. Bar CIA fndg in Nicaragua N
60. South Africa sanctions Y
61. Cut SS COLAs; Raise taxes N
62. Let US invest-So Africa N
63. Approve 21 MX for 1985 Y
64. Emergency Farm Credit N
65. Awards to whistle blowers Y
66. African disaster relief Y
67. Ban bank loans to So Afr Y
68. Bar coun duty-free trtmt N
69. Steel import limits Y
70. Soc Sec COLAs=inflation Y
71. Bar haz waste vctms suits N
72. Prohibit aid to Nicaragua Y
73. Cut $-Schs bar sch prayer Y
74. Raise taxes; Cut Medicare Y
75. Alien residncy-prior 1982 Y
76. Alien residncy-prior 1980 Y
77. Pen emp-hire illgl aliens Y
78. Lmt Persh II/cruse-Europe N
79. Delete 34 B-1 bombers X
80. Bar purch of Pershing II N
81. Bar purchase of Sgt York N
82. Delete $ for Trident II ?
83. Allow 15 MX missiles Y
84. Bar MX procurement-1985 N
85. Equal Access Act Y
86. Aid to El Salvador Y
87. Bar Nicarag water mining Y
88. Physician/Medicare freeze Y

McDADE, JOSEPH M. (Cont.)

89. Increase "sin" taxes Y
90. End SBA direct loans N
91. Sell Conrail N
92. Equal Rights Amendment N
93. Marines in Lebanon Y
94. Eminent domain-Coal comps N
95. Prohibit EPA sanctions N
96. SS age increase/Reforms N
97. Auto domestic content req Y
98. Delete jobs program fundg N
99. Highway-Gas tax bill Y
100. Raise Medicare;Cut defnse Y
101. Emergency housing aid Y
102. Across-the-board tax cuts Y
103. Gramm-Latta II targets Y
104. Delete B-1 bomber funds N
105. Dsapprov Saudi AWACS sale ?
106. Disapprove oil import fee Y
107. Rail Deregulation N
108. Dsapp India nuc fuel sale Y
109. Mil draft registration N
110. Chrysler Loan Guarantees Y
111. Prohibit school busing N
112. Nuclear plant moratorium N
113. Oil price controls ?
114. Tuition Tax Credits Y
115. Est Consumer Protect Agcy N
116. Eliminate B-1 bomber fnds N
117. Subminimum wage for youth N
118. Delete crude oil tax Y
119. Natural gas deregulation N

Presidential Support Score: 1986 - 50% 1985 - 59%

KANJORSKI, PAUL E. -- Pennsylvania 11th District [Democrat]. Counties of Carbon (pt.), Columbia, Luzeme, Monroe (pt.), Montour, Northumberland (pt.) and Sullivan. Prior Terms: 1985-86. Born: April 2, 1937. Education: Temple University (B.S., J.D.). Military Service: U.S. Army. Occupation: Attorney; sanitary authority commissioner; own solicitor.

1. Immigration Reform Y
2. Open fld-search warrants N
3. Civil pnty-hire ill alien N
4. So Afr sanc-veto override Y
5. Tax Overhaul Y
6. South Africa sanctions Y
7. Death penalty-drug bill Y
8. Evidence-warrantless srch Y
9. Life term-second drug off Y
10. Military use in drug war Y
11. Troop reduction in Europe N
12. Prohibit chemical weapons Y
13. Bar ASAT testing Y
14. Abide SALT II weapons ban Y
15. Follow SALT II-Soviets do N
16. Reduce SDI funding N
17. Increase SDI funding N
18. Purchase Trident sub Y
19. Delete 12 MX;Add conv wpn Y
20. Raise speed limit Y
21. Textile Import Quotas(*) Y
22. Req Pentagon buy US goods Y
23. AIDS ins anti-dscriminatn Y
24. Nicaraguan refugee aid Y
25. Nicaraguan contra aid N
26. US abide by SALT II N
27. Prohibit Saudi arms sale Y
28. Military Retiremnt Reform Y
29. Nicaraguan refugee aid Y
30. Ease '68 Gun Control Act Y
31. Bar intrstat handgun tran N
32. Keep '68 Gun Control Act N
33. Nicaraguan contra aid N
34. Bar emp polygraph testing Y
35. Tax Overhaul consideratn Y
36. Bar armor-piercing ammo Y
37. Tax Overhaul consideratn Y
38. Make comp emissions known Y
39. Allow toxic victims suits N
40. Strike Superfund "VAT" Y
41. Notify emp-plant closing Y
42. Bar emp consult-plant clo N
43. Medicare cuts;Tax incres' Y
44. Delete 12 MX missiles Y
45. Spending cuts;Tax incres' N
46. Textile Import Quotas Y
47. Cut some school lunch fds N
48. Clean Water Act Amendmnts N
49. Youth work projects Y
50. Assist military in Angola N
51. Allow US troops-Nicaragua N
52. Pentagon polygraph exams Y
53. Bar ASAT testing Y
54. Suspend def pmt for abuse Y
55. Bar Pentagon-contr emplmt Y
56. Increase SDI funding N
57. Reduce SDI funding N
58. Produce chemical weapons N
59. Bar CIA fndg in Nicaragua Y
60. South Africa sanctions Y
61. Cut SS COLAs; Raise taxes N
62. Let US invest-So Africa N
63. Approve 21 MX for 1985 N
64. Emergency Farm Credit Y
65. Awards to whistle blowers Y
66. African disaster relief Y

Presidential Support Score: 1986 - 22% 1985 -33%

MURTHA, JOHN P. -- Pennsylvania 12th District [Democrat]. Counties of Armstrong (pt.), Cambria (pt.), Somerset and Westmoreland (pt.). Prior Terms: House: 1974 (Special Election)-1986. Born: June 17, 1932; New Martinsville, W. Va. Education: University of Pittsburgh (B.A.); University of Indiana. Military Service: U.S. Marine Corps. Occupation: Pennsylvania representative (1969-74).

1. Immigration Reform Y
2. Open fld-search warrants Y
3. Civil pnty-hire ill alien N
4. So Afr sanc-veto override Y
5. Tax Overhaul Y
6. South Africa sanctions Y
7. Death penalty-drug bill Y
8. Evidence-warrantless srch N
9. Life term-second drug off N
10. Military use in drug war N
11. Troop reduction in Europe N
12. Prohibit chemical weapons N
13. Bar ASAT testing N
14. Abide SALT II weapons ban N
15. Follow SALT II-Soviets do Y
16. Reduce SDI funding N
17. Increase SDI funding N
18. Purchase Trident sub Y
19. Delete 12 MX;Add conv wpn N
20. Raise speed limit N
21. Textile Import Quotas(*) Y
22. Req Pentagon buy US goods Y
23. AIDS ins anti-dscriminatn Y
24. Nicaraguan refugee aid N
25. Nicaraguan contra aid Y
26. US abide by SALT II Y
27. Prohibit Saudi arms sale Y
28. Military Retiremnt Reform Y
29. Nicaraguan refugee aid N
30. Ease '68 Gun Control Act Y
31. Bar intrstat handgun tran N
32. Keep '68 Gun Control Act N
33. Nicaraguan contra aid Y
34. Bar emp polygraph testing Y
35. Tax Overhaul consideratn Y
36. Bar armor-piercing ammo Y
37. Tax Overhaul consideratn Y
38. Make comp emissions known N
39. Allow toxic victims suits N
40. Strike Superfund "VAT" N
41. Notify emp-plant closing Y
42. Bar emp consult-plant clo N
43. Medicare cuts;Tax incres' N
44. Delete 12 MX missiles N
45. Spending cuts;Tax incres' Y
46. Textile Import Quotas Y
47. Cut some school lunch fds N
48. Clean Water Act Amendmnts N
49. Youth work projects Y
50. Assist military in Angola Y
51. Allow US troops-Nicaragua Y
52. Pentagon polygraph exams Y
53. Bar ASAT testing N
54. Suspend def pmt for abuse N
55. Bar Pentagon-contr emplmt Y
56. Increase SDI funding N
57. Reduce SDI funding N
58. Produce chemical weapons Y
59. Bar CIA fndg in Nicaragua N
60. South Africa sanctions Y
61. Cut SS COLAs; Raise taxes N
62. Let US invest-So Africa ?
63. Approve 21 MX for 1985 Y
64. Emergency Farm Credit Y
65. Awards to whistle blowers Y
66. African disaster relief Y
67. Ban bank loans to So Afr Y
68. Bar coun duty-free trtmt Y
69. Steel import limits Y
70. Soc Sec COLAs=inflation Y
71. Bar haz waste vctms suits Y
72. Prohibit aid to Nicaragua Y
73. Cut $-Schs bar sch prayer Y
74. Raise taxes; Cut Medicare Y
75. Alien residncy-prior 1982 Y
76. Alien residncy-prior 1980 N
77. Pen emp-hire illgl aliens N
78. Lmt Persh II/cruse-Europe N
79. Delete 34 B-1 bombers N
80. Bar purch of Pershing II ?
81. Bar purchase of Sgt York N
82. Delete $ for Trident II N
83. Allow 15 MX missiles Y
84. Bar MX procurement-1985 N
85. Equal Access Act ?
86. Aid to El Salvador Y
87. Bar Nicarag water mining Y
88. Physician/Medicare freeze N
89. Increase "sin" taxes Y
90. End SBA direct loans N
91. Sell Conrail N
92. Equal Rights Amendment N
93. Marines in Lebanon Y
94. Eminent domain-Coal comps N
95. Prohibit EPA sanctions Y
96. SS age increase/Reforms N
97. Auto domestic content req Y
98. Delete jobs program fundg N
99. Highway-Gas tax bill Y
100. Raise Medicare;Cut defnse N
101. Emergency housing aid Y
102. Across-the-board tax cuts N
103. Gramm-Latta II targets N
104. Delete B-1 bomber funds Y

MURTHA, JOHN P. (Cont.)

105. Dsapprov Saudi AWACS sale Y
106. Disapprove oil import fee N
107. Rail Deregulation N
108. Dsapp India nuc fuel sale N
109. Mil draft registration Y
110. Chrysler Loan Guarantees Y
111. Prohibit school busing N
112. Nuclear plant moratorium N
113. Oil price controls N
114. Tuition Tax Credits Y
115. Est Consumer Protect Agcy N
116. Eliminate B-1 bomber fnds N
117. Subminimum wage for youth N
118. Delete crude oil tax N
119. Natural gas deregulation ?

Presidential Support Score: 1986 - 43% 1985 - 52%

COUGHLIN, LAWRENCE -- Pennsylvania 13th District [Republican]. Counties of Montgomery (pt.) and Philadelphia (pt.). Prior Terms: House: 1969-86. Born: April 11, 1929; Wilkes-Barre, Pa. Education: Yale (A.B.); Harvard (M.B.A.); Temple University Evening Law School (LL.B.). Military Service: U.S. Marine Corps. Occupation: Attorney, Saul, Ewing, Remick and Saul; Pennsylvania representative (1964); Pennsylvania senator (1966).

1. Immigration Reform Y
2. Open fld-search warrants N
3. Civil pnty-hire ill alien N
4. So Afr sanc-veto override Y
5. Tax Overhaul Y
6. South Africa sanctions Y
7. Death penalty-drug bill Y
8. Evidence-warrantless srch Y
9. Life term-second drug off Y
10. Military use in drug war N
11. Troop reduction in Europe N
12. Prohibit chemical weapons Y
13. Bar ASAT testing Y
14. Abide SALT II weapons ban Y
15. Follow SALT II-Soviets do Y
16. Reduce SDI funding N
17. Increase SDI funding N
18. Purchase Trident sub N
19. Delete 12 MX;Add conv wpn N
20. Raise speed limit N
21. Textile Import Quotas(*) Y
22. Req Pentagon buy US goods Y
23. AIDS ins anti-dscriminatn Y
24. Nicaraguan refugee aid N
25. Nicaraguan contra aid Y
26. US abide by SALT II N
27. Prohibit Saudi arms sale Y
28. Military Retiremnt Reform Y
29. Nicaraguan refugee aid Y
30. Ease '68 Gun Control Act N
31. Bar intrstat handgun tran N
32. Keep '68 Gun Control Act Y
33. Nicaraguan contra aid Y
34. Bar emp polygraph testing Y
35. Tax Overhaul consideratn N
36. Bar armor-piercing ammo Y
37. Tax Overhaul consideratn N
38. Make comp emissions known Y
39. Allow toxic victims suits Y
40. Strike Superfund "VAT" N
41. Notify emp-plant closing Y
42. Bar emp consult-plant clo N
43. Medicare cuts;Tax incres' N
44. Delete 12 MX missiles Y
45. Spending cuts;Tax incres' N
46. Textile Import Quotas Y
47. Cut some school lunch fds Y
48. Clean Water Act Amendmnts N
49. Youth work projects N
50. Assist military in Angola Y
51. Allow US troops-Nicaragua Y
52. Pentagon polygraph exams Y
53. Bar ASAT testing Y
54. Suspend def pmt for abuse N
55. Bar Pentagon-contr emplmt Y
56. Increase SDI funding N
57. Reduce SDI funding N
58. Produce chemical weapons N
59. Bar CIA fndg in Nicaragua N
60. South Africa sanctions Y
61. Cut SS COLAs; Raise taxes N
62. Let US invest-So Africa N
63. Approve 21 MX for 1985 N
64. Emergency Farm Credit N
65. Awards to whistle blowers Y
66. African disaster relief Y
67. Ban bank loans to So Afr Y
68. Bar coun duty-free trtmt N
69. Steel import limits Y
70. Soc Sec COLAs=inflation Y
71. Bar haz waste vctms suits N
72. Prohibit aid to Nicaragua Y
73. Cut $-Schs bar sch prayer N
74. Raise taxes; Cut Medicare Y
75. Alien residncy-prior 1982 Y
76. Alien residncy-prior 1980 Y
77. Pen emp-hire illgl aliens N
78. Lmt Persh II/cruse-Europe N

COUGHLIN, LAWRENCE (Cont.)

79. Delete 34 B-1 bombers Y
80. Bar purch of Pershing II Y
81. Bar purchase of Sgt York N
82. Delete $ for Trident II N
83. Allow 15 MX missiles N
84. Bar MX procurement-1985 Y
85. Equal Access Act N
86. Aid to El Salvador Y
87. Bar Nicarag water mining Y
88. Physician/Medicare freeze Y
89. Increase "sin" taxes Y
90. End SBA direct loans N
91. Sell Conrail Y
92. Equal Rights Amendment Y
93. Marines in Lebanon Y
94. Eminent domain-Coal comps N
95. Prohibit EPA sanctions N
96. SS age increase/Reforms Y
97. Auto domestic content req Y
98. Delete jobs program fundg Y
99. Highway-Gas tax bill Y
100. Raise Medicare;Cut defnse N
101. Emergency housing aid Y
102. Across-the-board tax cuts Y
103. Gramm-Latta II targets Y
104. Delete B-1 bomber funds N
105. Dsapprov Saudi AWACS sale Y
106. Disapprove oil import fee Y
107. Rail Deregulation N
108. Dsapp India nuc fuel sale Y
109. Mil draft registration N
110. Chrysler Loan Guarantees Y
111. Prohibit school busing Y
112. Nuclear plant moratorium Y
113. Oil price controls N
114. Tuition Tax Credits Y
115. Est Consumer Protect Agcy N
116. Eliminate B-1 bomber fnds N
117. Subminimum wage for youth Y
118. Delete crude oil tax Y
119. Natural gas deregulation Y

Presidential Support Score: 1986 - 47% 1985 - 50%

COYNE, WILLIAM J. -- Pennsylvania 14th District [Democrat]. County of Allegheny (pt.). Prior Terms: House: 1981-86. Born: August 24, 1936; Pittsburgh, Pa. Education: Robert Morris College. Military Service: U.S. Army, 1955-57. Occupation: Pennsylvania legislator (1970-72); Pittsburgh city councilman (1974); member, Pittsburgh Housing Authority; member, Governor's Justice Commission; chairman, Public Works Commission; board member, OIC.

1. Immigration Reform Y
2. Open fld-search warrants N
3. Civil pnty-hire ill alien N
4. So Afr sanc-veto override Y
5. Tax Overhaul Y
6. South Africa sanctions Y
7. Death penalty-drug bill N
8. Evidence-warrantless srch N
9. Life term-second drug off Y
10. Military use in drug war N
11. Troop reduction in Europe N
12. Prohibit chemical weapons Y
13. Bar ASAT testing Y
14. Abide SALT II weapons ban Y
15. Follow SALT II-Soviets do N
16. Reduce SDI funding Y
17. Increase SDI funding N
18. Purchase Trident sub N
19. Delete 12 MX;Add conv wpn Y
20. Raise speed limit N
21. Textile Import Quotas(*) Y
22. Req Pentagon buy US goods Y
23. AIDS ins anti-dscriminatn Y
24. Nicaraguan refugee aid Y
25. Nicaraguan contra aid N
26. US abide by SALT II N
27. Prohibit Saudi arms sale Y
28. Military Retiremnt Reform ?
29. Nicaraguan refugee aid Y
30. Ease '68 Gun Control Act N
31. Bar intrstat handgun tran Y
32. Keep '68 Gun Control Act Y
33. Nicaraguan contra aid N
34. Bar emp polygraph testing Y
35. Tax Overhaul consideratn Y
36. Bar armor-piercing ammo Y
37. Tax Overhaul consideratn Y
38. Make comp emissions known Y
39. Allow toxic victims suits Y
40. Strike Superfund "VAT" Y
41. Notify emp-plant closing Y
42. Bar emp consult-plant clo N
43. Medicare cuts;Tax incres' Y
44. Delete 12 MX missiles Y
45. Spending cuts;Tax incres' Y
46. Textile Import Quotas Y
47. Cut some school lunch fds N
48. Clean Water Act Amendmnts N
49. Youth work projects Y
50. Assist military in Angola N
51. Allow US troops-Nicaragua N
52. Pentagon polygraph exams N

COYNE, WILLIAM J. (Cont.)

53. Bar ASAT testing Y
54. Suspend def pmt for abuse Y
55. Bar Pentagon-contr emplmt Y
56. Increase SDI funding N
57. Reduce SDI funding Y
58. Produce chemical weapons N
59. Bar CIA fndg in Nicaragua Y
60. South Africa sanctions Y
61. Cut SS COLAs; Raise taxes N
62. Let US invest-So Africa N
63. Approve 21 MX for 1985 N
64. Emergency Farm Credit Y
65. Awards to whistle blowers Y
66. African disaster relief Y
67. Ban bank loans to So Afr Y
68. Bar coun duty-free trtmt Y
69. Steel import limits Y
70. Soc Sec COLAs=inflation Y
71. Bar haz waste vctms suits N
72. Prohibit aid to Nicaragua Y
73. Cut $-Schs bar sch prayer N
74. Raise taxes; Cut Medicare Y
75. Alien residncy-prior 1982 N
76. Alien residncy-prior 1980 N
77. Pen emp-hire illgl aliens Y
78. Lmt Persh II/cruse-Europe Y
79. Delete 34 B-1 bombers Y
80. Bar purch of Pershing II Y
81. Bar purchase of Sgt York Y
82. Delete $ for Trident II Y
83. Allow 15 MX missiles N
84. Bar MX procurement-1985 Y
85. Equal Access Act N
86. Aid to El Salvador N
87. Bar Nicarag water mining Y
88. Physician/Medicare freeze N
89. Increase "sin" taxes Y
90. End SBA direct loans N
91. Sell Conrail N
92. Equal Rights Amendment Y
93. Marines in Lebanon Y
94. Eminent domain-Coal comps N
95. Prohibit EPA sanctions N
96. SS age increase/Reforms N
97. Auto domestic content req Y
98. Delete jobs program fundg N
99. Highway-Gas tax bill Y
100. Raise Medicare;Cut defnse Y
101. Emergency housing aid Y
102. Across-the-board tax cuts N
103. Gramm-Latta II targets N
104. Delete B-1 bomber funds Y
105. Dsapprov Saudi AWACS sale Y

Presidential Support Score: 1986 - 16% 1985 - 19%

RITTER, DON -- Pennsylvania 15th District [Republican]. Counties of Lehigh, Monroe (pt.) and Northampton. Prior Terms: House: 1979-86. Born: October 21, 1940; New York City, N.Y. Education: Lehigh University (B.S.); Massachusetts Institute of Technology (M.S., SC.D.); scientific exchange fellow, U.S. National Academy of Science/Soviet Academy of Science. Occupation: Research assistant, M.I.T. (1961-66); assistant professor, California State Polytechnic University (1968-69); contract consultant, General Dynamics Pamona Division (1968-69); assistant professor, researcher, Lehigh University (1969-78).

1. Immigration Reform N
2. Open fld-search warrants Y
3. Civil pnty-hire ill alien N
4. So Afr sanc-veto override N
5. Tax Overhaul Y
6. South Africa sanctions N
7. Death penalty-drug bill Y
8. Evidence-warrantless srch Y
9. Life term-second drug off Y
10. Military use in drug war Y
11. Troop reduction in Europe N
12. Prohibit chemical weapons N
13. Bar ASAT testing N
14. Abide SALT II weapons ban N
15. Follow SALT II-Soviets do Y
16. Reduce SDI funding N
17. Increase SDI funding N
18. Purchase Trident sub N
19. Delete 12 MX;Add conv wpn ?
20. Raise speed limit Y
21. Textile Import Quotas(*) Y
22. Req Pentagon buy US goods Y
23. AIDS ins anti-dscriminatn N
24. Nicaraguan refugee aid N
25. Nicaraguan contra aid Y
26. US abide by SALT II Y
27. Prohibit Saudi arms sale Y
28. Military Retiremnt Reform Y
29. Nicaraguan refugee aid Y
30. Ease '68 Gun Control Act Y
31. Bar intrstat handgun tran N
32. Keep '68 Gun Control Act N
33. Nicaraguan contra aid Y
34. Bar emp polygraph testing Y

RITTER, DON (Cont.)

35. Tax Overhaul consideratn	Y	75. Alien residncy-prior 1982	Y
36. Bar armor-piercing ammo	Y	76. Alien residncy-prior 1980	Y
37. Tax Overhaul consideratn	N	77. Pen emp-hire illgl aliens	N
38. Make comp emissions known	N	78. Lmt Persh II/cruse-Europe	N
39. Allow toxic victims suits	N	79. Delete 34 B-1 bombers	N
40. Strike Superfund "VAT"	N	80. Bar purch of Pershing II	N
41. Notify emp-plant closing	Y	81. Bar purchase of Sgt York	Y
42. Bar emp consult-plant clo	N	82. Delete $ for Trident II	N
43. Medicare cuts;Tax incres'	N	83. Allow 15 MX missiles	Y
44. Delete 12 MX missiles	N	84. Bar MX procurement-1985	N
45. Spending cuts;Tax incres'	N	85. Equal Access Act	Y
46. Textile Import Quotas	Y	86. Aid to El Salvador	Y
47. Cut some school lunch fds	Y	87. Bar Nicarag water mining	N
48. Clean Water Act Amendmnts	Y	88. Physician/Medicare freeze	Y
49. Youth work projects	?	89. Increase "sin" taxes	Y
50. Assist military in Angola	Y	90. End SBA direct loans	?
51. Allow US troops-Nicaragua	Y	91. Sell Conrail	N
52. Pentagon polygraph exams	?	92. Equal Rights Amendment	N
53. Bar ASAT testing	N	93. Marines in Lebanon	Y
54. Suspend def pmt for abuse	Y	94. Eminent domain-Coal comps	Y
55. Bar Pentagon-contr emplmt	Y	95. Prohibit EPA sanctions	N
56. Increase SDI funding	Y	96. SS age increase/Reforms	Y
57. Reduce SDI funding	N	97. Auto domestic content req	Y
58. Produce chemical weapons	Y	98. Delete jobs program fundg	Y
59. Bar CIA fndg in Nicaragua	N	99. Highway-Gas tax bill	N
60. South Africa sanctions	N	100. Raise Medicare;Cut defnse	Y
61. Cut SS COLAs; Raise taxes	N	101. Emergency housing aid	Y
62. Let US invest-So Africa	?	102. Across-the-board tax cuts	Y
63. Approve 21 MX for 1985	Y	103. Gramm-Latta II targets	Y
64. Emergency Farm Credit	N	104. Delete B-1 bomber funds	N
65. Awards to whistle blowers	Y	105. Dsapprov Saudi AWACS sale	Y
66. African disaster relief	Y	106. Disapprove oil import fee	Y
67. Ban bank loans to So Afr	Y	107. Rail Deregulation	N
68. Bar coun duty-free trtmt	Y	108. Dsapp India nuc fuel sale	Y
69. Steel import limits	Y	109. Mil draft registration	#
70. Soc Sec COLAs=inflation	Y	110. Chrysler Loan Guarantees	N
71. Bar haz waste vctms suits	N	111. Prohibit school busing	Y
72. Prohibit aid to Nicaragua	N	112. Nuclear plant moratorium	N
73. Cut $-Schs bar sch prayer	Y	113. Oil price controls	N
74. Raise taxes; Cut Medicare	N		

Presidential Support Score: 1986 - 70% 1985 - 75%

WALKER, ROBERT S. -- Pennsylvania 16th District [Republican]. Counties of Chester (pt.), Lancaster (pt.) and Lebanon. Prior Terms: House: 1977-86. Born: December 23, 1942; Bradford, Pa. Education: Millersville State College (B.S.); University of Delaware (M.A.). Military Service: National Guard, 1967-73. Occupation: Administrative assistant (1967-77).

1. Immigration Reform	N	10. Military use in drug war	Y
2. Open fld-search warrants	Y	11. Troop reduction in Europe	N
3. Civil pnty-hire ill alien	N	12. Prohibit chemical weapons	N
4. So Afr sanc-veto override	Y	13. Bar ASAT testing	N
5. Tax Overhaul	Y	14. Abide SALT II weapons ban	N
6. South Africa sanctions	Y	15. Follow SALT II-Soviets do	Y
7. Death penalty-drug bill	Y	16. Reduce SDI funding	N
8. Evidence-warrantless srch	Y	17. Increase SDI funding	Y
9. Life term-second drug off	Y	18. Purchase Trident sub	N

WALKER, ROBERT S. (Cont.)

19. Delete 12 MX;Add conv wpn N
20. Raise speed limit Y
21. Textile Import Quotas(*) N
22. Req Pentagon buy US goods Y
23. AIDS ins anti-dscriminatn N
24. Nicaraguan refugee aid N
25. Nicaraguan contra aid Y
26. US abide by SALT II Y
27. Prohibit Saudi arms sale Y
28. Military Retiremnt Reform Y
29. Nicaraguan refugee aid Y
30. Ease '68 Gun Control Act Y
31. Bar intrstat handgun tran N
32. Keep '68 Gun Control Act N
33. Nicaraguan contra aid Y
34. Bar emp polygraph testing N
35. Tax Overhaul consideratn N
36. Bar armor-piercing ammo Y
37. Tax Overhaul consideratn N
38. Make comp emissions known N
39. Allow toxic victims suits N
40. Strike Superfund "VAT" Y
41. Notify emp-plant closing N
42. Bar emp consult-plant clo Y
43. Medicare cuts;Tax incres' N
44. Delete 12 MX missiles N
45. Spending cuts;Tax incres' N
46. Textile Import Quotas N
47. Cut some school lunch fds Y
48. Clean Water Act Amendmnts Y
49. Youth work projects N
50. Assist military in Angola Y
51. Allow US troops-Nicaragua Y
52. Pentagon polygraph exams Y
53. Bar ASAT testing N
54. Suspend def pmt for abuse N
55. Bar Pentagon-contr emplmt Y
56. Increase SDI funding Y
57. Reduce SDI funding N
58. Produce chemical weapons N
59. Bar CIA fndg in Nicaragua N
60. South Africa sanctions N
61. Cut SS COLAs; Raise taxes N
62. Let US invest-So Africa Y
63. Approve 21 MX for 1985 Y
64. Emergency Farm Credit N
65. Awards to whistle blowers Y
66. African disaster relief Y
67. Ban bank loans to So Afr Y
68. Bar coun duty-free trtmt N
69. Steel import limits Y
70. Soc Sec COLAs=inflation Y
71. Bar haz waste vctms suits Y
72. Prohibit aid to Nicaragua N
73. Cut $-Schs bar sch prayer Y
74. Raise taxes; Cut Medicare N
75. Alien residncy-prior 1982 Y
76. Alien residncy-prior 1980 Y
77. Pen emp-hire illgl aliens N
78. Lmt Persh II/cruse-Europe N
79. Delete 34 B-1 bombers N
80. Bar purch of Pershing II N
81. Bar purchase of Sgt York N
82. Delete $ for Trident II N
83. Allow 15 MX missiles Y
84. Bar MX procurement-1985 N
85. Equal Access Act Y
86. Aid to El Salvador Y
87. Bar Nicarag water mining N
88. Physician/Medicare freeze Y
89. Increase "sin" taxes ?
90. End SBA direct loans Y
91. Sell Conrail Y
92. Equal Rights Amendment N
93. Marines in Lebanon N
94. Eminent domain-Coal comps N
95. Prohibit EPA sanctions Y
96. SS age increase/Reforms Y
97. Auto domestic content req N
98. Delete jobs program fundg Y
99. Highway-Gas tax bill N
100. Raise Medicare;Cut defnse N
101. Emergency housing aid N
102. Across-the-board tax cuts Y
103. Gramm-Latta II targets Y
104. Delete B-1 bomber funds N
105. Dsapprov Saudi AWACS sale Y
106. Disapprove oil import fee Y
107. Rail Deregulation N
108. Dsapp India nuc fuel sale Y
109. Mil draft registration N
110. Chrysler Loan Guarantees N
111. Prohibit school busing Y
112. Nuclear plant moratorium Y
113. Oil price controls N
114. Tuition Tax Credits Y
115. Est Consumer Protect Agcy N
116. Eliminate B-1 bomber fnds N
117. Subminimum wage for youth Y
118. Delete crude oil tax Y
119. Natural gas deregulation Y

Presidential Support Score: 1986 - 83% 1985 - 80%

GEKAS, GEORGE W. -- Pennsylvania 17th District [Republican]. Counties of Dauphin, Lycoming, Northumberland (pt.), Perry, Snyder and Union. Prior Terms: House: 1983-86. Born: April 14, 1930; Harrisburg, Pa. Education: Dickinson College; Dickinson Law School. Military Service: U.S. Army, 1953-56. Occupa-

GEKAS, GEORGE W. (Cont.)
tion: Attorney; assistant district attorney (1960-66); Pennsylvania representative (1967-74); Pennsylvania senator (1976-82).

1.	Immigration Reform	N	49.	Youth work projects	N
2.	Open fld-search warrants	N	50.	Assist military in Angola	Y
3.	Civil pnty-hire ill alien	N	51.	Allow US troops-Nicaragua	Y
4.	So Afr sanc-veto override	Y	52.	Pentagon polygraph exams	Y
5.	Tax Overhaul	N	53.	Bar ASAT testing	N
6.	South Africa sanctions	Y	54.	Suspend def pmt for abuse	N
7.	Death penalty-drug bill	Y	55.	Bar Pentagon-contr emplmt	Y
8.	Evidence-warrantless srch	Y	56.	Increase SDI funding	Y
9.	Life term-second drug off	Y	57.	Reduce SDI funding	N
10.	Military use in drug war	Y	58.	Produce chemical weapons	Y
11.	Troop reduction in Europe	N	59.	Bar CIA fndg in Nicaragua	N
12.	Prohibit chemical weapons	N	60.	South Africa sanctions	Y
13.	Bar ASAT testing	N	61.	Cut SS COLAs; Raise taxes	N
14.	Abide SALT II weapons ban	N	62.	Let US invest-So Africa	Y
15.	Follow SALT II-Soviets do	Y	63.	Approve 21 MX for 1985	Y
16.	Reduce SDI funding	N	64.	Emergency Farm Credit	N
17.	Increase SDI funding	Y	65.	Awards to whistle blowers	Y
18.	Purchase Trident sub	N	66.	African disaster relief	Y
19.	Delete 12 MX;Add conv wpn	N	67.	Ban bank loans to So Afr	N
20.	Raise speed limit	N	68.	Bar coun duty-free trtmt	N
21.	Textile Import Quotas(*)	N	69.	Steel import limits	Y
22.	Req Pentagon buy US goods	Y	70.	Soc Sec COLAs=inflation	Y
23.	AIDS ins anti-dscriminatn	N	71.	Bar haz waste vctms suits	Y
24.	Nicaraguan refugee aid	N	72.	Prohibit aid to Nicaragua	N
25.	Nicaraguan contra aid	Y	73.	Cut $-Schs bar sch prayer	Y
26.	US abide by SALT II	Y	74.	Raise taxes; Cut Medicare	Y
27.	Prohibit Saudi arms sale	Y	75.	Alien residncy-prior 1982	Y
28.	Military Retiremnt Reform	Y	76.	Alien residncy-prior 1980	Y
29.	Nicaraguan refugee aid	Y	77.	Pen emp-hire illgl aliens	N
30.	Ease '68 Gun Control Act	Y	78.	Lmt Persh II/cruse-Europe	N
31.	Bar intrstat handgun tran	N	79.	Delete 34 B-1 bombers	N
32.	Keep '68 Gun Control Act	N	80.	Bar purch of Pershing II	N
33.	Nicaraguan contra aid	Y	81.	Bar purchase of Sgt York	Y
34.	Bar emp polygraph testing	Y	82.	Delete $ for Trident II	N
35.	Tax Overhaul consideratn	Y	83.	Allow 15 MX missiles	Y
36.	Bar armor-piercing ammo	Y	84.	Bar MX procurement-1985	N
37.	Tax Overhaul consideratn	N	85.	Equal Access Act	Y
38.	Make comp emissions known	N	86.	Aid to El Salvador	Y
39.	Allow toxic victims suits	N	87.	Bar Nicarag water mining	N
40.	Strike Superfund "VAT"	Y	88.	Physician/Medicare freeze	Y
41.	Notify emp-plant closing	N	89.	Increase "sin" taxes	Y
42.	Bar emp consult-plant clo	Y	90.	End SBA direct loans	Y
43.	Medicare cuts;Tax incres'	N	91.	Sell Conrail	N
44.	Delete 12 MX missiles	N	92.	Equal Rights Amendment	Y
45.	Spending cuts;Tax incres'	N	93.	Marines in Lebanon	Y
46.	Textile Import Quotas	Y	94.	Eminent domain-Coal comps	N
47.	Cut some school lunch fds	N	95.	Prohibit EPA sanctions	Y
48.	Clean Water Act Amendmnts	Y	96.	SS age increase/Reforms	Y

Presidential Support Score: 1986 - 75% 1985 - 73%

WALGREN, DOUG -- Pennsylvania 18th District [Democrat]. County of Allegheny (pt.). Prior Terms: House: 1977-86. Born: December 28, 1940; Rochester, N.Y. Education: Dartmouth College (B.A.); Stanford Law School (LL.B.). Occupation: Attorney,

WALGREN, DOUG (Cont.)
Neighborhood Legal Services (1967-68); private attorney (1969-72); corporate counsel, Behavioral Research Laboratories, Inc. (1973-75).

1. Immigration Reform Y
2. Open fld-search warrants N
3. Civil pnty-hire ill alien N
4. So Afr sanc-veto override Y
5. Tax Overhaul Y
6. South Africa sanctions Y
7. Death penalty-drug bill Y
8. Evidence-warrantless srch Y
9. Life term-second drug off Y
10. Military use in drug war Y
11. Troop reduction in Europe Y
12. Prohibit chemical weapons Y
13. Bar ASAT testing Y
14. Abide SALT II weapons ban Y
15. Follow SALT II-Soviets do N
16. Reduce SDI funding Y
17. Increase SDI funding N
18. Purchase Trident sub N
19. Delete 12 MX;Add conv wpn Y
20. Raise speed limit N
21. Textile Import Quotas(*) Y
22. Req Pentagon buy US goods Y
23. AIDS ins anti-dscriminatn Y
24. Nicaraguan refugee aid Y
25. Nicaraguan contra aid N
26. US abide by SALT II N
27. Prohibit Saudi arms sale Y
28. Military Retiremnt Reform Y
29. Nicaraguan refugee aid N
30. Ease '68 Gun Control Act N
31. Bar intrstat handgun tran Y
32. Keep '68 Gun Control Act Y
33. Nicaraguan contra aid N
34. Bar emp polygraph testing Y
35. Tax Overhaul consideratn Y
36. Bar armor-piercing ammo Y
37. Tax Overhaul consideratn Y
38. Make comp emissions known ?
39. Allow toxic victims suits ?
40. Strike Superfund "VAT" N
41. Notify emp-plant closing Y
42. Bar emp consult-plant clo N
43. Medicare cuts;Tax incres' Y
44. Delete 12 MX missiles Y
45. Spending cuts;Tax incres' Y
46. Textile Import Quotas Y
47. Cut some school lunch fds N
48. Clean Water Act Amendmnts N
49. Youth work projects Y
50. Assist military in Angola N
51. Allow US troops-Nicaragua N
52. Pentagon polygraph exams Y
53. Bar ASAT testing Y
54. Suspend def pmt for abuse Y
55. Bar Pentagon-contr emplmt Y
56. Increase SDI funding N
57. Reduce SDI funding Y
58. Produce chemical weapons Y
59. Bar CIA fndg in Nicaragua Y
60. South Africa sanctions Y
61. Cut SS COLAs; Raise taxes Y
62. Let US invest-So Africa ?
63. Approve 21 MX for 1985 N
64. Emergency Farm Credit Y
65. Awards to whistle blowers Y
66. African disaster relief Y
67. Ban bank loans to So Afr ?
68. Bar coun duty-free trtmt Y
69. Steel import limits Y
70. Soc Sec COLAs=inflation Y
71. Bar haz waste vctms suits N
72. Prohibit aid to Nicaragua Y
73. Cut $-Schs bar sch prayer N
74. Raise taxes; Cut Medicare Y
75. Alien residncy-prior 1982 Y
76. Alien residncy-prior 1980 N
77. Pen emp-hire illgl aliens N
78. Lmt Persh II/cruse-Europe N
79. Delete 34 B-1 bombers Y
80. Bar purch of Pershing II Y
81. Bar purchase of Sgt York Y
82. Delete $ for Trident II N
83. Allow 15 MX missiles N
84. Bar MX procurement-1985 Y
85. Equal Access Act N
86. Aid to El Salvador N
87. Bar Nicarag water mining Y
88. Physician/Medicare freeze N
89. Increase "sin" taxes Y
90. End SBA direct loans N
91. Sell Conrail N
92. Equal Rights Amendment Y
93. Marines in Lebanon N
94. Eminent domain-Coal comps Y
95. Prohibit EPA sanctions Y
96. SS age increase/Reforms N
97. Auto domestic content req Y
98. Delete jobs program fundg N
99. Highway-Gas tax bill Y
100. Raise Medicare;Cut defnse Y
101. Emergency housing aid Y
102. Across-the-board tax cuts N
103. Gramm-Latta II targets N
104. Delete B-1 bomber funds Y
105. Dsapprov Saudi AWACS sale Y
106. Disapprove oil import fee Y
107. Rail Deregulation N
108. Dsapp India nuc fuel sale Y
109. Mil draft registration Y
110. Chrysler Loan Guarantees Y

WALGREN, DOUG (Cont.)

111. Prohibit school busing Y
112. Nuclear plant moratorium Y
113. Oil price controls Y
114. Tuition Tax Credits Y
115. Est Consumer Protect Agcy Y
116. Eliminate B-1 bomber fnds Y
117. Subminimum wage for youth N
118. Delete crude oil tax N
119. Natural gas deregulation N

Presidential Support Score: 1986 - 13% 1985 - 25%

GOODLING, WILLIAM F. -- Pennsylvania 19th District [Republican]. Counties of Adams, Cumberland (pt.) and York. Prior Terms: House: 1975-86. Born: 1928; Loganville, Pa. Education: University of Maryland (B.S.); Western Maryland College (M.A.); Pennsylvania State University. Military Service: 1946-48. Occupation: High school teacher; guidance counselor; principal school superintendent.

1. Immigration Reform Y
2. Open fld-search warrants Y
3. Civil pnty-hire ill alien Y
4. So Afr sanc-veto override Y
5. Tax Overhaul Y
6. South Africa sanctions Y
7. Death penalty-drug bill N
8. Evidence-warrantless srch Y
9. Life term-second drug off Y
10. Military use in drug war Y
11. Troop reduction in Europe N
12. Prohibit chemical weapons Y
13. Bar ASAT testing N
14. Abide SALT II weapons ban N
15. Follow SALT II-Soviets do Y
16. Reduce SDI funding N
17. Increase SDI funding N
18. Purchase Trident sub N
19. Delete 12 MX;Add conv wpn Y
20. Raise speed limit N
21. Textile Import Quotas(*) Y
22. Req Pentagon buy US goods Y
23. AIDS ins anti-dscriminatn N
24. Nicaraguan refugee aid N
25. Nicaraguan contra aid Y
26. US abide by SALT II Y
27. Prohibit Saudi arms sale Y
28. Military Retiremnt Reform Y
29. Nicaraguan refugee aid Y
30. Ease '68 Gun Control Act Y
31. Bar intrstat handgun tran Y
32. Keep '68 Gun Control Act N
33. Nicaraguan contra aid Y
34. Bar emp polygraph testing N
35. Tax Overhaul consideratn Y
36. Bar armor-piercing ammo Y
37. Tax Overhaul consideratn N
38. Make comp emissions known Y
39. Allow toxic victims suits N
40. Strike Superfund "VAT" Y
41. Notify emp-plant closing N
42. Bar emp consult-plant clo Y
43. Medicare cuts;Tax incres' N
44. Delete 12 MX missiles Y
45. Spending cuts;Tax incres' N
46. Textile Import Quotas Y
47. Cut some school lunch fds N
48. Clean Water Act Amendmnts Y
49. Youth work projects N
50. Assist military in Angola Y
51. Allow US troops-Nicaragua N
52. Pentagon polygraph exams Y
53. Bar ASAT testing Y
54. Suspend def pmt for abuse N
55. Bar Pentagon-contr emplmt Y
56. Increase SDI funding N
57. Reduce SDI funding N
58. Produce chemical weapons Y
59. Bar CIA fndg in Nicaragua N
60. South Africa sanctions Y
61. Cut SS COLAs; Raise taxes Y
62. Let US invest-So Africa Y
63. Approve 21 MX for 1985 N
64. Emergency Farm Credit N
65. Awards to whistle blowers Y
66. African disaster relief Y
67. Ban bank loans to So Afr Y
68. Bar coun duty-free trtmt N
69. Steel import limits Y
70. Soc Sec COLAs=inflation Y
71. Bar haz waste vctms suits Y
72. Prohibit aid to Nicaragua Y
73. Cut $-Schs bar sch prayer Y
74. Raise taxes; Cut Medicare N
75. Alien residncy-prior 1982 Y
76. Alien residncy-prior 1980 Y
77. Pen emp-hire illgl aliens N
78. Lmt Persh II/cruse-Europe N
79. Delete 34 B-1 bombers N
80. Bar purch of Pershing II Y
81. Bar purchase of Sgt York Y
82. Delete $ for Trident II N
83. Allow 15 MX missiles Y
84. Bar MX procurement-1985 N
85. Equal Access Act Y
86. Aid to El Salvador Y

GOODLING, WILLIAM F. (Cont.)

87. Bar Nicarag water mining Y
88. Physician/Medicare freeze Y
89. Increase "sin" taxes Y
90. End SBA direct loans Y
91. Sell Conrail N
92. Equal Rights Amendment Y
93. Marines in Lebanon Y
94. Eminent domain-Coal comps N
95. Prohibit EPA sanctions Y
96. SS age increase/Reforms N
97. Auto domestic content req Y
98. Delete jobs program fundg Y
99. Highway-Gas tax bill N
100. Raise Medicare;Cut defnse N
101. Emergency housing aid N
102. Across-the-board tax cuts Y
103. Gramm-Latta II targets Y
104. Delete B-1 bomber funds N
105. Dsapprov Saudi AWACS sale N
106. Disapprove oil import fee Y
107. Rail Deregulation Y
108. Dsapp India nuc fuel sale Y
109. Mil draft registration ?
110. Chrysler Loan Guarantees Y
111. Prohibit school busing Y
112. Nuclear plant moratorium Y
113. Oil price controls N
114. Tuition Tax Credits Y
115. Est Consumer Protect Agcy N
116. Eliminate B-1 bomber fnds N
117. Subminimum wage for youth Y
118. Delete crude oil tax Y
119. Natural gas deregulation Y

Presidential Support Score: 1986 - 60% 1985 - 61%

GAYDOS, JOSEPH M. -- Pennsylvania 20th District [Democrat]. Counties of Allegheny (pt.) and Westmoreland (pt.). Prior Terms: House: 1968 (Special Election)-1986. Born: July 3, 1926; Braddock, Pa. Education: Duquesne University; University of Notre Dame Law School (LL.B.). Military Service: U.S. Naval Reserve, WW II. Occupation: Pennsylvania senator; Pennsylvania deputy attorney general; Allegheny County assistant solicitor; general counsel, United Mine Workers of America.

1. Immigration Reform N
2. Open fld-search warrants Y
3. Civil pnty-hire ill alien N
4. So Afr sanc-veto override ?
5. Tax Overhaul Y
6. South Africa sanctions Y
7. Death penalty-drug bill Y
8. Evidence-warrantless srch Y
9. Life term-second drug off ?
10. Military use in drug war Y
11. Troop reduction in Europe N
12. Prohibit chemical weapons N
13. Bar ASAT testing Y
14. Abide SALT II weapons ban Y
15. Follow SALT II-Soviets do N
16. Reduce SDI funding N
17. Increase SDI funding N
18. Purchase Trident sub Y
19. Delete 12 MX;Add conv wpn N
20. Raise speed limit N
21. Textile Import Quotas(*) Y
22. Req Pentagon buy US goods Y
23. AIDS ins anti-dscriminatn Y
24. Nicaraguan refugee aid ?
25. Nicaraguan contra aid ?
26. US abide by SALT II Y
27. Prohibit Saudi arms sale Y
28. Military Retiremnt Reform N
29. Nicaraguan refugee aid N
30. Ease '68 Gun Control Act Y
31. Bar intrstat handgun tran N
32. Keep '68 Gun Control Act N
33. Nicaraguan contra aid Y
34. Bar emp polygraph testing Y
35. Tax Overhaul consideratn N
36. Bar armor-piercing ammo Y
37. Tax Overhaul consideratn N
38. Make comp emissions known Y
39. Allow toxic victims suits N
40. Strike Superfund "VAT" N
41. Notify emp-plant closing Y
42. Bar emp consult-plant clo N
43. Medicare cuts;Tax incres' N
44. Delete 12 MX missiles N
45. Spending cuts;Tax incres' N
46. Textile Import Quotas Y
47. Cut some school lunch fds N
48. Clean Water Act Amendmnts N
49. Youth work projects Y
50. Assist military in Angola N
51. Allow US troops-Nicaragua Y
52. Pentagon polygraph exams Y
53. Bar ASAT testing N
54. Suspend def pmt for abuse N
55. Bar Pentagon-contr emplmt Y
56. Increase SDI funding ?
57. Reduce SDI funding ?
58. Produce chemical weapons N
59. Bar CIA fndg in Nicaragua Y
60. South Africa sanctions Y

GAYDOS, JOSEPH M. (Cont.)

61. Cut SS COLAs; Raise taxes N
62. Let US invest-So Africa N
63. Approve 21 MX for 1985 N
64. Emergency Farm Credit Y
65. Awards to whistle blowers Y
66. African disaster relief Y
67. Ban bank loans to So Afr Y
68. Bar coun duty-free trtmt Y
69. Steel import limits Y
70. Soc Sec COLAs=inflation Y
71. Bar haz waste vctms suits N
72. Prohibit aid to Nicaragua Y
73. Cut $-Schs bar sch prayer Y
74. Raise taxes; Cut Medicare N
75. Alien residncy-prior 1982 N
76. Alien residncy-prior 1980 N
77. Pen emp-hire illgl aliens Y
78. Lmt Persh II/cruse-Europe N
79. Delete 34 B-1 bombers N
80. Bar purch of Pershing II Y
81. Bar purchase of Sgt York N
82. Delete $ for Trident II N
83. Allow 15 MX missiles N
84. Bar MX procurement-1985 Y
85. Equal Access Act Y
86. Aid to El Salvador N
87. Bar Nicarag water mining Y
88. Physician/Medicare freeze N
89. Increase "sin" taxes Y
90. End SBA direct loans N
91. Sell Conrail N
92. Equal Rights Amendment N
93. Marines in Lebanon N
94. Eminent domain-Coal comps N
95. Prohibit EPA sanctions Y
96. SS age increase/Reforms N
97. Auto domestic content req Y
98. Delete jobs program fundg N
99. Highway-Gas tax bill Y
100. Raise Medicare;Cut defnse Y
101. Emergency housing aid Y
102. Across-the-board tax cuts N
103. Gramm-Latta II targets N
104. Delete B-1 bomber funds N
105. Dsapprov Saudi AWACS sale Y
106. Disapprove oil import fee Y
107. Rail Deregulation N
108. Dsapp India nuc fuel sale N
109. Mil draft registration Y
110. Chrysler Loan Guarantees Y
111. Prohibit school busing Y
112. Nuclear plant moratorium N
113. Oil price controls Y
114. Tuition Tax Credits Y
115. Est Consumer Protect Agcy Y
116. Eliminate B-1 bomber fnds Y
117. Subminimum wage for youth N
118. Delete crude oil tax N
119. Natural gas deregulation N

Presidential Support Score: 1986 - 34% 1985 - 28%

RIDGE, THOMAS J. -- Pennsylvania 21st District [Republican]. Counties of Crawford, Erie, Lawrence (pt.) and Mercer. Prior Terms: House: 1983-86. Born: August 26, 1945; Munhall, Pa. Education: Harvard University (B.A.); Dickinson School of Law (J.D.). Military Service: U.S. Army. Occupation: Congressional aide; legal instructor; law clerk; attorney; assistant district attorney.

1. Immigration Reform Y
2. Open fld-search warrants Y
3. Civil pnty-hire ill alien N
4. So Afr sanc-veto override Y
5. Tax Overhaul Y
6. South Africa sanctions Y
7. Death penalty-drug bill Y
8. Evidence-warrantless srch N
9. Life term-second drug off Y
10. Military use in drug war Y
11. Troop reduction in Europe N
12. Prohibit chemical weapons N
13. Bar ASAT testing Y
14. Abide SALT II weapons ban N
15. Follow SALT II-Soviets do N
16. Reduce SDI funding N
17. Increase SDI funding N
18. Purchase Trident sub Y
19. Delete 12 MX;Add conv wpn Y
20. Raise speed limit N
21. Textile Import Quotas(*) Y
22. Req Pentagon buy US goods Y
23. AIDS ins anti-dscriminatn N
24. Nicaraguan refugee aid N
25. Nicaraguan contra aid N
26. US abide by SALT II Y
27. Prohibit Saudi arms sale N
28. Military Retiremnt Reform Y
29. Nicaraguan refugee aid Y
30. Ease '68 Gun Control Act Y
31. Bar intrstat handgun tran Y
32. Keep '68 Gun Control Act N
33. Nicaraguan contra aid N
34. Bar emp polygraph testing Y
35. Tax Overhaul consideratn N
36. Bar armor-piercing ammo Y

RIDGE, THOMAS J. (Cont.)

37. Tax Overhaul consideratn	N		67. Ban bank loans to So Afr	Y
38. Make comp emissions known	Y		68. Bar coun duty-free trtmt	Y
39. Allow toxic victims suits	N		69. Steel import limits	Y
40. Strike Superfund "VAT"	N		70. Soc Sec COLAs=inflation	Y
41. Notify emp-plant closing	Y		71. Bar haz waste vctms suits	Y
42. Bar emp consult-plant clo	N		72. Prohibit aid to Nicaragua	Y
43. Medicare cuts;Tax incres'	Y		73. Cut $-Schs bar sch prayer	N
44. Delete 12 MX missiles	Y		74. Raise taxes; Cut Medicare	N
45. Spending cuts;Tax incres'	N		75. Alien residncy-prior 1982	Y
46. Textile Import Quotas	Y		76. Alien residncy-prior 1980	Y
47. Cut some school lunch fds	N		77. Pen emp-hire illgl aliens	N
48. Clean Water Act Amendmnts	N		78. Lmt Persh II/cruse-Europe	?
49. Youth work projects	Y		79. Delete 34 B-1 bombers	N
50. Assist military in Angola	Y		80. Bar purch of Pershing II	N
51. Allow US troops-Nicaragua	N		81. Bar purchase of Sgt York	Y
52. Pentagon polygraph exams	Y		82. Delete $ for Trident II	N
53. Bar ASAT testing	Y		83. Allow 15 MX missiles	N
54. Suspend def pmt for abuse	N		84. Bar MX procurement-1985	Y
55. Bar Pentagon-contr emplmt	Y		85. Equal Access Act	Y
56. Increase SDI funding	N		86. Aid to El Salvador	Y
57. Reduce SDI funding	N		87. Bar Nicarag water mining	Y
58. Produce chemical weapons	Y		88. Physician/Medicare freeze	Y
59. Bar CIA fndg in Nicaragua	N		89. Increase "sin" taxes	Y
60. South Africa sanctions	N		90. End SBA direct loans	N
61. Cut SS COLAs; Raise taxes	N		91. Sell Conrail	N
62. Let US invest-So Africa	Y		92. Equal Rights Amendment	Y
63. Approve 21 MX for 1985	N		93. Marines in Lebanon	Y
64. Emergency Farm Credit	Y		94. Eminent domain-Coal comps	N
65. Awards to whistle blowers	Y		95. Prohibit EPA sanctions	Y
66. African disaster relief	Y		96. SS age increase/Reforms	Y

Presidential Support Score: 1986 - 48% 1985 - 44%

MURPHY, AUSTIN J. -- Pennsylvania 22nd District [Democrat]. Counties of Allegheny (pt.), Beaver (pt.), Fayette, Greene and Washington. Prior Terms: House: 1977-86. Born: June 17, 1927; North Charleroi, Pa. Education: Duquesne University (B.A.); University of Pittsburgh (LL.B.). Occupation: Pennsylvania representative (1959-71); Pennsylvania senator (1971); assistant district attorney.

1. Immigration Reform	N		19. Delete 12 MX;Add conv wpn	?
2. Open fld-search warrants	N		20. Raise speed limit	N
3. Civil pnty-hire ill alien	N		21. Textile Import Quotas(*)	Y
4. So Afr sanc-veto override	Y		22. Req Pentagon buy US goods	Y
5. Tax Overhaul	N		23. AIDS ins anti-dscriminatn	Y
6. South Africa sanctions	Y		24. Nicaraguan refugee aid	N
7. Death penalty-drug bill	Y		25. Nicaraguan contra aid	N
8. Evidence-warrantless srch	N		26. US abide by SALT II	N
9. Life term-second drug off	Y		27. Prohibit Saudi arms sale	?
10. Military use in drug war	Y		28. Military Retiremnt Reform	Y
11. Troop reduction in Europe	Y		29. Nicaraguan refugee aid	N
12. Prohibit chemical weapons	N		30. Ease '68 Gun Control Act	Y
13. Bar ASAT testing	Y		31. Bar intrstat handgun tran	N
14. Abide SALT II weapons ban	Y		32. Keep '68 Gun Control Act	N
15. Follow SALT II-Soviets do	N		33. Nicaraguan contra aid	N
16. Reduce SDI funding	N		34. Bar emp polygraph testing	Y
17. Increase SDI funding	N		35. Tax Overhaul consideratn	N
18. Purchase Trident sub	N		36. Bar armor-piercing ammo	Y

MURPHY, AUSTIN J. (Cont.)

37. Tax Overhaul consideratn N
38. Make comp emissions known Y
39. Allow toxic victims suits N
40. Strike Superfund "VAT" N
41. Notify emp-plant closing Y
42. Bar emp consult-plant clo N
43. Medicare cuts;Tax incres' N
44. Delete 12 MX missiles Y
45. Spending cuts;Tax incres' N
46. Textile Import Quotas Y
47. Cut some school lunch fds N
48. Clean Water Act Amendmnts N
49. Youth work projects Y
50. Assist military in Angola N
51. Allow US troops-Nicaragua N
52. Pentagon polygraph exams Y
53. Bar ASAT testing Y
54. Suspend def pmt for abuse Y
55. Bar Pentagon-contr emplmt Y
56. Increase SDI funding N
57. Reduce SDI funding N
58. Produce chemical weapons Y
59. Bar CIA fndg in Nicaragua N
60. South Africa sanctions Y
61. Cut SS COLAs; Raise taxes N
62. Let US invest-So Africa N
63. Approve 21 MX for 1985 N
64. Emergency Farm Credit Y
65. Awards to whistle blowers Y
66. African disaster relief Y
67. Ban bank loans to So Afr ?
68. Bar coun duty-free trtmt Y
69. Steel import limits Y
70. Soc Sec COLAs=inflation Y
71. Bar haz waste vctms suits Y
72. Prohibit aid to Nicaragua Y
73. Cut $-Schs bar sch prayer Y
74. Raise taxes; Cut Medicare N
75. Alien residncy-prior 1982 Y
76. Alien residncy-prior 1980 Y
77. Pen emp-hire illgl aliens Y
78. Lmt Persh II/cruse-Europe N
79. Delete 34 B-1 bombers N
80. Bar purch of Pershing II N
81. Bar purchase of Sgt York N
82. Delete $ for Trident II N
83. Allow 15 MX missiles Y
84. Bar MX procurement-1985 Y
85. Equal Access Act Y
86. Aid to El Salvador N
87. Bar Nicarag water mining ?
88. Physician/Medicare freeze Y
89. Increase "sin" taxes N
90. End SBA direct loans N
91. Sell Conrail N
92. Equal Rights Amendment Y
93. Marines in Lebanon N
94. Eminent domain-Coal comps N
95. Prohibit EPA sanctions Y
96. SS age increase/Reforms N
97. Auto domestic content req Y
98. Delete jobs program fundg N
99. Highway-Gas tax bill N
100. Raise Medicare;Cut defnse Y
101. Emergency housing aid Y
102. Across-the-board tax cuts N
103. Gramm-Latta II targets N
104. Delete B-1 bomber funds Y
105. Dsapprov Saudi AWACS sale Y
106. Disapprove oil import fee Y
107. Rail Deregulation N
108. Dsapp India nuc fuel sale Y
109. Mil draft registration Y
110. Chrysler Loan Guarantees Y
111. Prohibit school busing Y
112. Nuclear plant moratorium N
113. Oil price controls Y
114. Tuition Tax Credits Y
115. Est Consumer Protect Agcy Y
116. Eliminate B-1 bomber fnds N
117. Subminimum wage for youth N
118. Delete crude oil tax N
119. Natural gas deregulation N

Presidential Support Score: 1986 - 20% 1985 - 36%

CLINGER, WILLIAM F., Jr. -- Pennsylvania 23rd District [Republican] Counties of Armstrong (pt.), Cameron, Centre, Clarion, Clearfield (pt.), Clinton (pt.), Elk, Forest, Jefferson, McKean, Venango and Warren. Prior Terms: House: 1979-86. Born: April 4, 1929; Warren, Pa. Education: Johns Hopkins University (B.A.); University of Virginia Law School (LL.B.). Military Service: U.S. Navy, 1951-55. Occupation: Advertiser, New Process (1954-62); attorney, Harper, Clinger and Eberly (1965-75); Pennsylvania committeeman (1968-75); chief counsel, Economic Development Administration (1975-77).

1. Immigration Reform Y
2. Open fld-search warrants Y
3. Civil pnty-hire ill alien N
4. So Afr sanc-veto override Y
5. Tax Overhaul Y
6. South Africa sanctions Y

CLINGER, WILLIAM F., Jr. (Cont.)

7. Death penalty-drug bill Y
8. Evidence-warrantless srch Y
9. Life term-second drug off Y
10. Military use in drug war Y
11. Troop reduction in Europe N
12. Prohibit chemical weapons Y
13. Bar ASAT testing Y
14. Abide SALT II weapons ban Y
15. Follow SALT II-Soviets do Y
16. Reduce SDI funding N
17. Increase SDI funding N
18. Purchase Trident sub N
19. Delete 12 MX;Add conv wpn N
20. Raise speed limit N
21. Textile Import Quotas(*) Y
22. Req Pentagon buy US goods Y
23. AIDS ins anti-dscriminatn Y
24. Nicaraguan refugee aid N
25. Nicaraguan contra aid Y
26. US abide by SALT II Y
27. Prohibit Saudi arms sale Y
28. Military Retiremnt Reform Y
29. Nicaraguan refugee aid Y
30. Ease '68 Gun Control Act Y
31. Bar intrstat handgun tran N
32. Keep '68 Gun Control Act N
33. Nicaraguan contra aid Y
34. Bar emp polygraph testing Y
35. Tax Overhaul consideratn Y
36. Bar armor-piercing ammo Y
37. Tax Overhaul consideratn N
38. Make comp emissions known Y
39. Allow toxic victims suits N
40. Strike Superfund "VAT" N
41. Notify emp-plant closing Y
42. Bar emp consult-plant clo N
43. Medicare cuts;Tax incres' Y
44. Delete 12 MX missiles N
45. Spending cuts;Tax incres' N
46. Textile Import Quotas Y
47. Cut some school lunch fds N
48. Clean Water Act Amendmnts Y
49. Youth work projects Y
50. Assist military in Angola Y
51. Allow US troops-Nicaragua N
52. Pentagon polygraph exams Y
53. Bar ASAT testing Y
54. Suspend def pmt for abuse N
55. Bar Pentagon-contr emplmt Y
56. Increase SDI funding N
57. Reduce SDI funding N
58. Produce chemical weapons N
59. Bar CIA fndg in Nicaragua Y
60. South Africa sanctions N
61. Cut SS COLAs; Raise taxes N
62. Let US invest-So Africa Y
63. Approve 21 MX for 1985 Y
64. Emergency Farm Credit Y
65. Awards to whistle blowers Y
66. African disaster relief Y
67. Ban bank loans to So Afr Y
68. Bar coun duty-free trtmt N
69. Steel import limits Y
70. Soc Sec COLAs=inflation Y
71. Bar haz waste vctms suits Y
72. Prohibit aid to Nicaragua Y
73. Cut $-Schs bar sch prayer Y
74. Raise taxes; Cut Medicare N
75. Alien residncy-prior 1982 N
76. Alien residncy-prior 1980 Y
77. Pen emp-hire illgl aliens N
78. Lmt Persh II/cruse-Europe N
79. Delete 34 B-1 bombers Y
80. Bar purch of Pershing II N
81. Bar purchase of Sgt York N
82. Delete $ for Trident II N
83. Allow 15 MX missiles Y
84. Bar MX procurement-1985 N
85. Equal Access Act Y
86. Aid to El Salvador Y
87. Bar Nicarag water mining Y
88. Physician/Medicare freeze Y
89. Increase "sin" taxes Y
90. End SBA direct loans N
91. Sell Conrail N
92. Equal Rights Amendment Y
93. Marines in Lebanon Y
94. Eminent domain-Coal comps Y
95. Prohibit EPA sanctions N
96. SS age increase/Reforms Y
97. Auto domestic content req N
98. Delete jobs program fundg Y
99. Highway-Gas tax bill Y
100. Raise Medicare;Cut defnse N
101. Emergency housing aid N
102. Across-the-board tax cuts Y
103. Gramm-Latta II targets Y
104. Delete B-1 bomber funds N
105. Dsapprov Saudi AWACS sale N
106. Disapprove oil import fee Y
107. Rail Deregulation N
108. Dsapp India nuc fuel sale Y
109. Mil draft registration Y
110. Chrysler Loan Guarantees N
111. Prohibit school busing N
112. Nuclear plant moratorium N
113. Oil price controls N

Presidential Support Score: 1986 - 53% 1985 - 50%

RHODE ISLAND

St. GERMAIN, FERNAND J. -- Rhode Island 1st District [Democrat]. Counties of Bristol, Newport and Providence (pt.). Prior Terms: House: 1961-86. Born: January 9, 1928; Blackstone, Mass. Education: Providence College (Ph.D.); Boston University Law School (LL.B.). Military Service: U.S. Army, 1949-52. Occupation: Attorney; Rhode Island representative (1952-60).

1.	Immigration Reform	Y
2.	Open fld-search warrants	N
3.	Civil pnty-hire ill alien	N
4.	So Afr sanc-veto override	Y
5.	Tax Overhaul	Y
6.	South Africa sanctions	?
7.	Death penalty-drug bill	Y
8.	Evidence-warrantless srch	N
9.	Life term-second drug off	Y
10.	Military use in drug war	Y
11.	Troop reduction in Europe	N
12.	Prohibit chemical weapons	Y
13.	Bar ASAT testing	Y
14.	Abide SALT II weapons ban	Y
15.	Follow SALT II-Soviets do	N
16.	Reduce SDI funding	Y
17.	Increase SDI funding	N
18.	Purchase Trident sub	Y
19.	Delete 12 MX;Add conv wpn	Y
20.	Raise speed limit	N
21.	Textile Import Quotas(*)	Y
22.	Req Pentagon buy US goods	Y
23.	AIDS ins anti-dscriminatn	Y
24.	Nicaraguan refugee aid	Y
25.	Nicaraguan contra aid	N
26.	US abide by SALT II	N
27.	Prohibit Saudi arms sale	Y
28.	Military Retiremnt Reform	Y
29.	Nicaraguan refugee aid	Y
30.	Ease '68 Gun Control Act	N
31.	Bar intrstat handgun tran	Y
32.	Keep '68 Gun Control Act	Y
33.	Nicaraguan contra aid	N
34.	Bar emp polygraph testing	Y
35.	Tax Overhaul consideratn	Y
36.	Bar armor-piercing ammo	Y
37.	Tax Overhaul consideratn	Y
38.	Make comp emissions known	Y
39.	Allow toxic victims suits	Y
40.	Strike Superfund "VAT"	Y
41.	Notify emp-plant closing	Y
42.	Bar emp consult-plant clo	N
43.	Medicare cuts;Tax incres'	Y
44.	Delete 12 MX missiles	Y
45.	Spending cuts;Tax incres'	Y
46.	Textile Import Quotas	Y
47.	Cut some school lunch fds	N
48.	Clean Water Act Amendmnts	N
49.	Youth work projects	?
50.	Assist military in Angola	N
51.	Allow US troops-Nicaragua	N
52.	Pentagon polygraph exams	Y
53.	Bar ASAT testing	Y
54.	Suspend def pmt for abuse	?
55.	Bar Pentagon-contr emplmt	Y
56.	Increase SDI funding	N
57.	Reduce SDI funding	N
58.	Produce chemical weapons	N
59.	Bar CIA fndg in Nicaragua	Y
60.	South Africa sanctions	Y
61.	Cut SS COLAs; Raise taxes	N
62.	Let US invest-So Africa	N
63.	Approve 21 MX for 1985	N
64.	Emergency Farm Credit	Y
65.	Awards to whistle blowers	Y
66.	African disaster relief	Y
67.	Ban bank loans to So Afr	Y
68.	Bar coun duty-free trtmt	Y
69.	Steel import limits	Y
70.	Soc Sec COLAs=inflation	Y
71.	Bar haz waste vctms suits	N
72.	Prohibit aid to Nicaragua	Y
73.	Cut $-Schs bar sch prayer	?
74.	Raise taxes; Cut Medicare	Y
75.	Alien residncy-prior 1982	N
76.	Alien residncy-prior 1980	N
77.	Pen emp-hire illgl aliens	N
78.	Lmt Persh II/cruse-Europe	N
79.	Delete 34 B-1 bombers	Y
80.	Bar purch of Pershing II	N
81.	Bar purchase of Sgt York	N
82.	Delete $ for Trident II	N
83.	Allow 15 MX missiles	N
84.	Bar MX procurement-1985	Y
85.	Equal Access Act	Y
86.	Aid to El Salvador	N
87.	Bar Nicarag water mining	Y
88.	Physician/Medicare freeze	N
89.	Increase "sin" taxes	Y
90.	End SBA direct loans	N
91.	Sell Conrail	N
92.	Equal Rights Amendment	N
93.	Marines in Lebanon	N
94.	Eminent domain-Coal comps	Y
95.	Prohibit EPA sanctions	N
96.	SS age increase/Reforms	N
97.	Auto domestic content req	Y
98.	Delete jobs program fundg	N
99.	Highway-Gas tax bill	Y
100.	Raise Medicare;Cut defnse	Y

St. GERMAIN, FERNAND J. (Cont.)

101. Emergency housing aid Y
102. Across-the-board tax cuts N
103. Gramm-Latta II targets N
104. Delete B-1 bomber funds Y
105. Dsapprov Saudi AWACS sale Y
106. Disapprove oil import fee Y
107. Rail Deregulation ?
108. Dsapp India nuc fuel sale Y
109. Mil draft registration ?
110. Chrysler Loan Guarantees Y
111. Prohibit school busing N
112. Nuclear plant moratorium Y
113. Oil price controls Y
114. Tuition Tax Credits Y
115. Est Consumer Protect Agcy Y
116. Eliminate B-1 bomber fnds Y
117. Subminimum wage for youth N
118. Delete crude oil tax N
119. Natural gas deregulation N

Presidential Support Score: 1986 - 20% 1985 - 20%

SCHNEIDER, CLAUDINE -- Rhode Island 2nd District [Republican]. Counties of Kent, Providence (pt.) and Washington. Prior Terms: House: 1981-86. Born: March 25, 1947; Clairton, Pa. Education: Rosemont College; University of Barcelona; Windham College. Occupation: Founder, Rhode Island Committee on Energy; executive director, Conservation Law Foundation; federal coordinator, Rhode Island's Coastal Zone Management Program; citizen representative, Energy Research and Development Administration.

1. Immigration Reform ?
2. Open fld-search warrants ?
3. Civil pnty-hire ill alien ?
4. So Afr sanc-veto override +
5. Tax Overhaul Y
6. South Africa sanctions Y
7. Death penalty-drug bill N
8. Evidence-warrantless srch N
9. Life term-second drug off ?
10. Military use in drug war N
11. Troop reduction in Europe N
12. Prohibit chemical weapons Y
13. Bar ASAT testing Y
14. Abide SALT II weapons ban Y
15. Follow SALT II-Soviets do N
16. Reduce SDI funding N
17. Increase SDI funding N
18. Purchase Trident sub Y
19. Delete 12 MX;Add conv wpn Y
20. Raise speed limit N
21. Textile Import Quotas(*) Y
22. Req Pentagon buy US goods Y
23. AIDS ins anti-dscriminatn Y
24. Nicaraguan refugee aid Y
25. Nicaraguan contra aid N
26. US abide by SALT II N
27. Prohibit Saudi arms sale Y
28. Military Retiremnt Reform Y
29. Nicaraguan refugee aid Y
30. Ease '68 Gun Control Act N
31. Bar intrstat handgun tran Y
32. Keep '68 Gun Control Act Y
33. Nicaraguan contra aid N
34. Bar emp polygraph testing Y
35. Tax Overhaul consideratn Y
36. Bar armor-piercing ammo Y
37. Tax Overhaul consideratn N
38. Make comp emissions known Y
39. Allow toxic victims suits Y
40. Strike Superfund "VAT" Y
41. Notify emp-plant closing Y
42. Bar emp consult-plant clo Y
43. Medicare cuts;Tax incres' Y
44. Delete 12 MX missiles Y
45. Spending cuts;Tax incres' N
46. Textile Import Quotas Y
47. Cut some school lunch fds N
48. Clean Water Act Amendmnts ?
49. Youth work projects N
50. Assist military in Angola Y
51. Allow US troops-Nicaragua N
52. Pentagon polygraph exams Y
53. Bar ASAT testing Y
54. Suspend def pmt for abuse Y
55. Bar Pentagon-contr emplmt Y
56. Increase SDI funding N
57. Reduce SDI funding Y
58. Produce chemical weapons N
59. Bar CIA fndg in Nicaragua Y
60. South Africa sanctions Y
61. Cut SS COLAs; Raise taxes N
62. Let US invest-So Africa N
63. Approve 21 MX for 1985 N
64. Emergency Farm Credit N
65. Awards to whistle blowers Y
66. African disaster relief Y
67. Ban bank loans to So Afr Y
68. Bar coun duty-free trtmt Y
69. Steel import limits Y
70. Soc Sec COLAs=inflation Y
71. Bar haz waste vctms suits N
72. Prohibit aid to Nicaragua Y

SCHNEIDER, CLAUDINE (Cont.)

73. Cut $-Schs bar sch prayer N
74. Raise taxes; Cut Medicare Y
75. Alien residncy-prior 1982 N
76. Alien residncy-prior 1980 N
77. Pen emp-hire illgl aliens Y
78. Lmt Persh II/cruse-Europe N
79. Delete 34 B-1 bombers Y
80. Bar purch of Pershing II Y
81. Bar purchase of Sgt York Y
82. Delete $ for Trident II Y
83. Allow 15 MX missiles N
84. Bar MX procurement-1985 Y
85. Equal Access Act N
86. Aid to El Salvador N
87. Bar Nicarag water mining Y
88. Physician/Medicare freeze Y
89. Increase "sin" taxes Y
90. End SBA direct loans N
91. Sell Conrail N
92. Equal Rights Amendment Y
93. Marines in Lebanon Y
94. Eminent domain-Coal comps N
95. Prohibit EPA sanctions ?
96. SS age increase/Reforms N
97. Auto domestic content req Y
98. Delete jobs program fundg Y
99. Highway-Gas tax bill N
100. Raise Medicare;Cut defnse Y
101. Emergency housing aid +
102. Across-the-board tax cuts Y
103. Gramm-Latta II targets Y
104. Delete B-1 bomber funds Y
105. Dsapprov Saudi AWACS sale Y

Presidential Support Score: 1986 - 32% 1985 - 34%

SOUTH CAROLINA

HARTNETT, THOMAS F. -- South Carolina 1st District [Republican]. Counties of Beaufort, Berkley (pt.), Charleston, Colleton, Dorchester, Hampton and Jasper. Prior Terms: House: 1981-86. Born: August 7, 1941; Charleston, S.C. Education: College of Charleston; University of South Carolina; University of Georgia. Military Service: U.S. Air Force, 1963; U.S. Air Force Reserve, 1963-69. Occupation: President, Harnett Realty Company; South Carolina representative (1965-72); South Carolina senator (1973-80).

1. Immigration Reform ?
2. Open fld-search warrants ?
3. Civil pnty-hire ill alien ?
4. So Afr sanc-veto override ?
5. Tax Overhaul N
6. South Africa sanctions ?
7. Death penalty-drug bill ?
8. Evidence-warrantless srch ?
9. Life term-second drug off Y
10. Military use in drug war Y
11. Troop reduction in Europe ?
12. Prohibit chemical weapons ?
13. Bar ASAT testing N
14. Abide SALT II weapons ban N
15. Follow SALT II-Soviets do Y
16. Reduce SDI funding N
17. Increase SDI funding Y
18. Purchase Trident sub ?
19. Delete 12 MX;Add conv wpn ?
20. Raise speed limit Y
21. Textile Import Quotas(*) Y
22. Req Pentagon buy US goods N
23. AIDS ins anti-dscriminatn ?
24. Nicaraguan refugee aid N
25. Nicaraguan contra aid Y
26. US abide by SALT II #
27. Prohibit Saudi arms sale N
28. Military Retiremnt Reform ?
29. Nicaraguan refugee aid Y
30. Ease '68 Gun Control Act Y
31. Bar intrstat handgun tran N
32. Keep '68 Gun Control Act N
33. Nicaraguan contra aid Y
34. Bar emp polygraph testing N
35. Tax Overhaul consideratn N
36. Bar armor-piercing ammo N
37. Tax Overhaul consideratn N
38. Make comp emissions known N
39. Allow toxic victims suits N
40. Strike Superfund "VAT" N
41. Notify emp-plant closing N
42. Bar emp consult-plant clo #
43. Medicare cuts;Tax incres' N
44. Delete 12 MX missiles N
45. Spending cuts;Tax incres' N
46. Textile Import Quotas Y
47. Cut some school lunch fds Y
48. Clean Water Act Amendmnts Y
49. Youth work projects X
50. Assist military in Angola Y
51. Allow US troops-Nicaragua Y
52. Pentagon polygraph exams Y

HARTNETT, THOMAS F. (Cont.)

53. Bar ASAT testing N
54. Suspend def pmt for abuse N
55. Bar Pentagon-contr emplmt Y
56. Increase SDI funding Y
57. Reduce SDI funding N
58. Produce chemical weapons Y
59. Bar CIA fndg in Nicaragua N
60. South Africa sanctions N
61. Cut SS COLAs; Raise taxes N
62. Let US invest-So Africa Y
63. Approve 21 MX for 1985 Y
64. Emergency Farm Credit N
65. Awards to whistle blowers Y
66. African disaster relief Y
67. Ban bank loans to So Afr N
68. Bar coun duty-free trtmt N
69. Steel import limits N
70. Soc Sec COLAs=inflation Y
71. Bar haz waste vctms suits Y
72. Prohibit aid to Nicaragua N
73. Cut $-Schs bar sch prayer Y
74. Raise taxes; Cut Medicare N
75. Alien residncy-prior 1982 Y
76. Alien residncy-prior 1980 Y
77. Pen emp-hire illgl aliens N
78. Lmt Persh II/cruse-Europe N
79. Delete 34 B-1 bombers N
80. Bar purch of Pershing II N
81. Bar purchase of Sgt York N
82. Delete $ for Trident II N
83. Allow 15 MX missiles Y
84. Bar MX procurement-1985 N
85. Equal Access Act Y
86. Aid to El Salvador Y
87. Bar Nicarag water mining N
88. Physician/Medicare freeze Y
89. Increase "sin" taxes N
90. End SBA direct loans Y
91. Sell Conrail Y
92. Equal Rights Amendment N
93. Marines in Lebanon Y
94. Eminent domain-Coal comps X
95. Prohibit EPA sanctions Y
96. SS age increase/Reforms Y
97. Auto domestic content req N
98. Delete jobs program fundg Y
99. Highway-Gas tax bill N
100. Raise Medicare;Cut defnse N
101. Emergency housing aid N
102. Across-the-board tax cuts Y
103. Gramm-Latta II targets Y
104. Delete B-1 bomber funds N
105. Dsapprov Saudi AWACS sale N

Presidential Support Score: 1986 - 52% 1985 - 65%

SPENCE, FLOYD -- South Carolina 2nd District [Republican]. Counties of Bamberg, Calhoun, Lexington, Orangeburg and Richland. Prior Terms: House: 1971-86. Born: April 9, 1928; Columbia, S.C. Education: University of South Carolina (B.A., LL.B.); National Defense War College. Military Service: U.S. Navy. Occupation: South Carolina representative and senator; attorney, Callison and Spence.

1. Immigration Reform N
2. Open fld-search warrants N
3. Civil pnty-hire ill alien N
4. So Afr sanc-veto override N
5. Tax Overhaul N
6. South Africa sanctions N
7. Death penalty-drug bill Y
8. Evidence-warrantless srch Y
9. Life term-second drug off ?
10. Military use in drug war Y
11. Troop reduction in Europe N
12. Prohibit chemical weapons N
13. Bar ASAT testing N
14. Abide SALT II weapons ban N
15. Follow SALT II-Soviets do Y
16. Reduce SDI funding N
17. Increase SDI funding Y
18. Purchase Trident sub Y
19. Delete 12 MX;Add conv wpn N
20. Raise speed limit Y
21. Textile Import Quotas(*) Y
22. Req Pentagon buy US goods Y
23. AIDS ins anti-dscriminatn N
24. Nicaraguan refugee aid N
25. Nicaraguan contra aid Y
26. US abide by SALT II Y
27. Prohibit Saudi arms sale Y
28. Military Retiremnt Reform Y
29. Nicaraguan refugee aid Y
30. Ease '68 Gun Control Act Y
31. Bar intrstat handgun tran N
32. Keep '68 Gun Control Act N
33. Nicaraguan contra aid Y
34. Bar emp polygraph testing N
35. Tax Overhaul consideratn N
36. Bar armor-piercing ammo Y
37. Tax Overhaul consideratn N
38. Make comp emissions known N
39. Allow toxic victims suits N
40. Strike Superfund "VAT" N
41. Notify emp-plant closing N
42. Bar emp consult-plant clo Y

SPENCE, FLOYD (Cont.)

43. Medicare cuts;Tax incres' N
44. Delete 12 MX missiles N
45. Spending cuts;Tax incres' N
46. Textile Import Quotas Y
47. Cut some school lunch fds Y
48. Clean Water Act Amendmnts Y
49. Youth work projects N
50. Assist military in Angola Y
51. Allow US troops-Nicaragua Y
52. Pentagon polygraph exams Y
53. Bar ASAT testing N
54. Suspend def pmt for abuse N
55. Bar Pentagon-contr emplmt Y
56. Increase SDI funding Y
57. Reduce SDI funding N
58. Produce chemical weapons Y
59. Bar CIA fndg in Nicaragua N
60. South Africa sanctions N
61. Cut SS COLAs; Raise taxes N
62. Let US invest-So Africa Y
63. Approve 21 MX for 1985 Y
64. Emergency Farm Credit Y
65. Awards to whistle blowers Y
66. African disaster relief Y
67. Ban bank loans to So Afr N
68. Bar coun duty-free trtmt N
69. Steel import limits N
70. Soc Sec COLAs=inflation Y
71. Bar haz waste vctms suits Y
72. Prohibit aid to Nicaragua N
73. Cut $-Schs bar sch prayer Y
74. Raise taxes; Cut Medicare Y
75. Alien residncy-prior 1982 Y
76. Alien residncy-prior 1980 Y
77. Pen emp-hire illgl aliens N
78. Lmt Persh II/cruse-Europe N
79. Delete 34 B-1 bombers N
80. Bar purch of Pershing II N
81. Bar purchase of Sgt York N
82. Delete $ for Trident II N
83. Allow 15 MX missiles Y
84. Bar MX procurement-1985 N
85. Equal Access Act Y
86. Aid to El Salvador Y
87. Bar Nicarag water mining N
88. Physician/Medicare freeze Y
89. Increase "sin" taxes Y
90. End SBA direct loans N
91. Sell Conrail Y
92. Equal Rights Amendment N
93. Marines in Lebanon Y
94. Eminent domain-Coal comps N
95. Prohibit EPA sanctions Y
96. SS age increase/Reforms Y
97. Auto domestic content req N
98. Delete jobs program fundg Y
99. Highway-Gas tax bill N
100. Raise Medicare;Cut defnse N
101. Emergency housing aid Y
102. Across-the-board tax cuts Y
103. Gramm-Latta II targets Y
104. Delete B-1 bomber funds N
105. Dsapprov Saudi AWACS sale N
106. Disapprove oil import fee Y
107. Rail Deregulation N
108. Dsapp India nuc fuel sale Y
109. Mil draft registration Y
110. Chrysler Loan Guarantees Y
111. Prohibit school busing Y
112. Nuclear plant moratorium N
113. Oil price controls N
114. Tuition Tax Credits N
115. Est Consumer Protect Agcy N
116. Eliminate B-1 bomber fnds N
117. Subminimum wage for youth Y
118. Delete crude oil tax Y
119. Natural gas deregulation Y

Presidential Support Score: 1986 - 68% 1985 - 61%

DERRICK, BUTLER -- South Carolina 3rd District [Democrat]. Counties of Abbeville, Aiken, Allendale, Anderson, Barnwell, Edgefield, Greenwood, McCormick, Oconee, Pickens and Saluda. Prior Terms: House: 1975-86. Born: September 30, 1936. Education: University of South Carolina; University of Georgia Law School (LL.B.). Occupation: Attorney; South Carolina legislator (1969-74).

1. Immigration Reform Y
2. Open fld-search warrants Y
3. Civil pnty-hire ill alien N
4. So Afr sanc-veto override ?
5. Tax Overhaul Y
6. South Africa sanctions Y
7. Death penalty-drug bill Y
8. Evidence-warrantless srch N
9. Life term-second drug off Y
10. Military use in drug war N
11. Troop reduction in Europe N
12. Prohibit chemical weapons Y
13. Bar ASAT testing Y
14. Abide SALT II weapons ban Y
15. Follow SALT II-Soviets do N
16. Reduce SDI funding N
17. Increase SDI funding N
18. Purchase Trident sub Y

DERRICK, BUTLER (Cont.)

19. Delete 12 MX;Add conv wpn Y
20. Raise speed limit N
21. Textile Import Quotas(*) Y
22. Req Pentagon buy US goods Y
23. AIDS ins anti-dscriminatn Y
24. Nicaraguan refugee aid Y
25. Nicaraguan contra aid N
26. US abide by SALT II N
27. Prohibit Saudi arms sale Y
28. Military Retiremnt Reform Y
29. Nicaraguan refugee aid Y
30. Ease '68 Gun Control Act Y
31. Bar intrstat handgun tran N
32. Keep '68 Gun Control Act N
33. Nicaraguan contra aid N
34. Bar emp polygraph testing N
35. Tax Overhaul consideratn Y
36. Bar armor-piercing ammo Y
37. Tax Overhaul consideratn Y
38. Make comp emissions known N
39. Allow toxic victims suits N
40. Strike Superfund "VAT" N
41. Notify emp-plant closing N
42. Bar emp consult-plant clo Y
43. Medicare cuts;Tax incres' Y
44. Delete 12 MX missiles N
45. Spending cuts;Tax incres' Y
46. Textile Import Quotas Y
47. Cut some school lunch fds N
48. Clean Water Act Amendmnts N
49. Youth work projects Y
50. Assist military in Angola N
51. Allow US troops-Nicaragua ?
52. Pentagon polygraph exams Y
53. Bar ASAT testing Y
54. Suspend def pmt for abuse Y
55. Bar Pentagon-contr emplmt Y
56. Increase SDI funding N
57. Reduce SDI funding N
58. Produce chemical weapons N
59. Bar CIA fndg in Nicaragua Y
60. South Africa sanctions Y
61. Cut SS COLAs; Raise taxes N
62. Let US invest-So Africa ?
63. Approve 21 MX for 1985 N
64. Emergency Farm Credit Y
65. Awards to whistle blowers Y
66. African disaster relief Y
67. Ban bank loans to So Afr ?
68. Bar coun duty-free trtmt N
69. Steel import limits N
70. Soc Sec COLAs=inflation Y
71. Bar haz waste vctms suits Y
72. Prohibit aid to Nicaragua Y
73. Cut $-Schs bar sch prayer Y
74. Raise taxes; Cut Medicare Y
75. Alien residncy-prior 1982 Y
76. Alien residncy-prior 1980 Y
77. Pen emp-hire illgl aliens N
78. Lmt Persh II/cruse-Europe N
79. Delete 34 B-1 bombers Y
80. Bar purch of Pershing II N
81. Bar purchase of Sgt York N
82. Delete $ for Trident II N
83. Allow 15 MX missiles N
84. Bar MX procurement-1985 Y
85. Equal Access Act Y
86. Aid to El Salvador N
87. Bar Nicarag water mining Y
88. Physician/Medicare freeze N
89. Increase "sin" taxes Y
90. End SBA direct loans N
91. Sell Conrail N
92. Equal Rights Amendment Y
93. Marines in Lebanon N
94. Eminent domain-Coal comps N
95. Prohibit EPA sanctions ?
96. SS age increase/Reforms N
97. Auto domestic content req N
98. Delete jobs program fundg N
99. Highway-Gas tax bill Y
100. Raise Medicare;Cut defnse Y
101. Emergency housing aid Y
102. Across-the-board tax cuts N
103. Gramm-Latta II targets Y
104. Delete B-1 bomber funds Y
105. Dsapprov Saudi AWACS sale N
106. Disapprove oil import fee Y
107. Rail Deregulation N
108. Dsapp India nuc fuel sale N
109. Mil draft registration Y
110. Chrysler Loan Guarantees Y
111. Prohibit school busing N
112. Nuclear plant moratorium N
113. Oil price controls N
114. Tuition Tax Credits N
115. Est Consumer Protect Agcy N
116. Eliminate B-1 bomber fnds Y
117. Subminimum wage for youth N
118. Delete crude oil tax N
119. Natural gas deregulation Y

Presidential Support Score: 1986 - 27% 1985 - 29%

CAMPBELL, CARROLL A., Jr. -- South Carolina 4th District [Republican]. Counties of Greenville, Spartanburg and Union. Prior Terms: House: 1979-86. Born: July 24, 1940; Greenville, S.C. Education: University of South Carolina. Occupation: President, Handy-Park Co.; vice-president, Rex Enterprises, Inc.; director, Downtown Greenville Assn. (1961-66); South Carolina

CAMPBELL, CARROLL A., Jr. (Cont.)
legislator (1971-74); executive assistant to governor (1974-76); South Carolina senator (1976).

1. Immigration Reform ?
2. Open fld-search warrants ?
3. Civil pnty-hire ill alien ?
4. So Afr sanc-veto override ?
5. Tax Overhaul Y
6. South Africa sanctions ?
7. Death penalty-drug bill Y
8. Evidence-warrantless srch ?
9. Life term-second drug off ?
10. Military use in drug war ?
11. Troop reduction in Europe ?
12. Prohibit chemical weapons ?
13. Bar ASAT testing X
14. Abide SALT II weapons ban X
15. Follow SALT II-Soviets do #
16. Reduce SDI funding X
17. Increase SDI funding #
18. Purchase Trident sub ?
19. Delete 12 MX;Add conv wpn X
20. Raise speed limit Y
21. Textile Import Quotas(*) Y
22. Req Pentagon buy US goods ?
23. AIDS ins anti-dscriminatn ?
24. Nicaraguan refugee aid N
25. Nicaraguan contra aid Y
26. US abide by SALT II #
27. Prohibit Saudi arms sale Y
28. Military Retiremnt Reform Y
29. Nicaraguan refugee aid Y
30. Ease '68 Gun Control Act Y
31. Bar intrstat handgun tran N
32. Keep '68 Gun Control Act N
33. Nicaraguan contra aid Y
34. Bar emp polygraph testing X
35. Tax Overhaul consideratn N
36. Bar armor-piercing ammo Y
37. Tax Overhaul consideratn N
38. Make comp emissions known N
39. Allow toxic victims suits N
40. Strike Superfund "VAT" N
41. Notify emp-plant closing N
42. Bar emp consult-plant clo Y
43. Medicare cuts;Tax incres' N
44. Delete 12 MX missiles N
45. Spending cuts;Tax incres' N
46. Textile Import Quotas Y
47. Cut some school lunch fds Y
48. Clean Water Act Amendmnts Y
49. Youth work projects N
50. Assist military in Angola Y
51. Allow US troops-Nicaragua Y
52. Pentagon polygraph exams Y
53. Bar ASAT testing N
54. Suspend def pmt for abuse N
55. Bar Pentagon-contr emplmt Y
56. Increase SDI funding N
57. Reduce SDI funding N
58. Produce chemical weapons Y
59. Bar CIA fndg in Nicaragua N
60. South Africa sanctions N
61. Cut SS COLAs; Raise taxes N
62. Let US invest-So Africa Y
63. Approve 21 MX for 1985 Y
64. Emergency Farm Credit Y
65. Awards to whistle blowers Y
66. African disaster relief Y
67. Ban bank loans to So Afr Y
68. Bar coun duty-free trtmt N
69. Steel import limits N
70. Soc Sec COLAs=inflation Y
71. Bar haz waste vctms suits Y
72. Prohibit aid to Nicaragua N
73. Cut $-Schs bar sch prayer +
74. Raise taxes; Cut Medicare Y
75. Alien residncy-prior 1982 Y
76. Alien residncy-prior 1980 Y
77. Pen emp-hire illgl aliens N
78. Lmt Persh II/cruse-Europe N
79. Delete 34 B-1 bombers N
80. Bar purch of Pershing II N
81. Bar purchase of Sgt York N
82. Delete $ for Trident II N
83. Allow 15 MX missiles Y
84. Bar MX procurement-1985 N
85. Equal Access Act Y
86. Aid to El Salvador Y
87. Bar Nicarag water mining N
88. Physician/Medicare freeze Y
89. Increase "sin" taxes Y
90. End SBA direct loans N
91. Sell Conrail Y
92. Equal Rights Amendment N
93. Marines in Lebanon Y
94. Eminent domain-Coal comps N
95. Prohibit EPA sanctions Y
96. SS age increase/Reforms Y
97. Auto domestic content req N
98. Delete jobs program fundg Y
99. Highway-Gas tax bill N
100. Raise Medicare;Cut defnse N
101. Emergency housing aid ?
102. Across-the-board tax cuts Y
103. Gramm-Latta II targets Y
104. Delete B-1 bomber funds N
105. Dsapprov Saudi AWACS sale N
106. Disapprove oil import fee Y
107. Rail Deregulation N
108. Dsapp India nuc fuel sale Y
109. Mil draft registration Y
110. Chrysler Loan Guarantees N
111. Prohibit school busing Y
112. Nuclear plant moratorium N

CAMPBELL, CARROLL A., Jr. (Cont.)
113. Oil price controls N

Presidential Support Score: 1986 - 33% 1985 - 63%

SPRATT, JOHN M., Jr. -- South Carolina 5th District [Democrat]. Counties of Cherokee, Chester, Chesterfield, Fairfield, Kershaw, Lancaster, Laurens, Lee, Newberry, Sumter and York. Prior Terms: House: 1983-86. Born: November 1, 1942; Charlotte, N.C. Education: Davidson College (A.B.); Oxford University, Corpus Christi College (M.A.); Yale Law School (LL.B.). Military Service: U.S. Army, 1969-71. Occupation: Private law practice (1971-82); county attorney (1973-82); banker (1973-82); president, insurance agency; chairman, hospital board.

1. Immigration Reform Y
2. Open fld-search warrants Y
3. Civil pnty-hire ill alien N
4. So Afr sanc-veto override Y
5. Tax Overhaul Y
6. South Africa sanctions Y
7. Death penalty-drug bill Y
8. Evidence-warrantless srch N
9. Life term-second drug off Y
10. Military use in drug war N
11. Troop reduction in Europe N
12. Prohibit chemical weapons N
13. Bar ASAT testing Y
14. Abide SALT II weapons ban Y
15. Follow SALT II-Soviets do N
16. Reduce SDI funding N
17. Increase SDI funding N
18. Purchase Trident sub Y
19. Delete 12 MX;Add conv wpn N
20. Raise speed limit N
21. Textile Import Quotas(*) Y
22. Req Pentagon buy US goods Y
23. AIDS ins anti-dscriminatn Y
24. Nicaraguan refugee aid N
25. Nicaraguan contra aid N
26. US abide by SALT II N
27. Prohibit Saudi arms sale N
28. Military Retiremnt Reform Y
29. Nicaraguan refugee aid N
30. Ease '68 Gun Control Act Y
31. Bar intrstat handgun tran Y
32. Keep '68 Gun Control Act N
33. Nicaraguan contra aid N
34. Bar emp polygraph testing N
35. Tax Overhaul consideratn Y
36. Bar armor-piercing ammo Y
37. Tax Overhaul consideratn Y
38. Make comp emissions known Y
39. Allow toxic victims suits N
40. Strike Superfund "VAT" N
41. Notify emp-plant closing N
42. Bar emp consult-plant clo Y
43. Medicare cuts;Tax incres' Y
44. Delete 12 MX missiles N
45. Spending cuts;Tax incres' Y
46. Textile Import Quotas Y
47. Cut some school lunch fds N
48. Clean Water Act Amendmnts N
49. Youth work projects N
50. Assist military in Angola Y
51. Allow US troops-Nicaragua N
52. Pentagon polygraph exams Y
53. Bar ASAT testing Y
54. Suspend def pmt for abuse N
55. Bar Pentagon-contr emplmt Y
56. Increase SDI funding N
57. Reduce SDI funding N
58. Produce chemical weapons Y
59. Bar CIA fndg in Nicaragua Y
60. South Africa sanctions +
61. Cut SS COLAs; Raise taxes Y
62. Let US invest-So Africa N
63. Approve 21 MX for 1985 N
64. Emergency Farm Credit Y
65. Awards to whistle blowers Y
66. African disaster relief Y
67. Ban bank loans to So Afr Y
68. Bar coun duty-free trtmt N
69. Steel import limits Y
70. Soc Sec COLAs=inflation Y
71. Bar haz waste vctms suits Y
72. Prohibit aid to Nicaragua Y
73. Cut $-Schs bar sch prayer N
74. Raise taxes; Cut Medicare Y
75. Alien residncy-prior 1982 Y
76. Alien residncy-prior 1980 Y
77. Pen emp-hire illgl aliens N
78. Lmt Persh II/cruse-Europe N
79. Delete 34 B-1 bombers N
80. Bar purch of Pershing II N
81. Bar purchase of Sgt York N
82. Delete $ for Trident II N
83. Allow 15 MX missiles Y
84. Bar MX procurement-1985 Y
85. Equal Access Act Y
86. Aid to El Salvador N
87. Bar Nicarag water mining Y
88. Physician/Medicare freeze N

SPRATT, JOHN M., Jr. (Cont.)

89. Increase "sin" taxes Y
90. End SBA direct loans N
91. Sell Conrail N
92. Equal Rights Amendment Y
93. Marines in Lebanon Y
94. Eminent domain-Coal comps N
95. Prohibit EPA sanctions Y
96. SS age increase/Reforms N

Presidential Support Score: 1986 - 28% 1985 - 41%

TALLON, ROBIN -- South Carolina 6th District [Democrat]. Counties of Berkeley (pt.), Clarendon, Darlington, Dillon, Florence, Georgetown, Horry, Marion, Marlboro and Williamsburg. Prior Terms: House: 1983-86. Born: Auigust 8, 1946; Hemingway, S.C. Education: University of South Carolina. Occupation: Owner, Robin's Men's Stores; South Carolina representative (1980-82).

1. Immigration Reform N
2. Open fld-search warrants N
3. Civil pnty-hire ill alien N
4. So Afr sanc-veto override Y
5. Tax Overhaul N
6. South Africa sanctions Y
7. Death penalty-drug bill Y
8. Evidence-warrantless srch Y
9. Life term-second drug off Y
10. Military use in drug war Y
11. Troop reduction in Europe N
12. Prohibit chemical weapons N
13. Bar ASAT testing N
14. Abide SALT II weapons ban N
15. Follow SALT II-Soviets do Y
16. Reduce SDI funding N
17. Increase SDI funding N
18. Purchase Trident sub N
19. Delete 12 MX;Add conv wpn N
20. Raise speed limit Y
21. Textile Import Quotas(*) Y
22. Req Pentagon buy US goods Y
23. AIDS ins anti-dscriminatn Y
24. Nicaraguan refugee aid N
25. Nicaraguan contra aid Y
26. US abide by SALT II Y
27. Prohibit Saudi arms sale Y
28. Military Retiremnt Reform Y
29. Nicaraguan refugee aid N
30. Ease '68 Gun Control Act Y
31. Bar intrstat handgun tran N
32. Keep '68 Gun Control Act N
33. Nicaraguan contra aid Y
34. Bar emp polygraph testing N
35. Tax Overhaul consideratn Y
36. Bar armor-piercing ammo Y
37. Tax Overhaul consideratn N
38. Make comp emissions known N
39. Allow toxic victims suits N
40. Strike Superfund "VAT" N
41. Notify emp-plant closing N
42. Bar emp consult-plant clo Y
43. Medicare cuts;Tax incres' Y
44. Delete 12 MX missiles N
45. Spending cuts;Tax incres' Y
46. Textile Import Quotas Y
47. Cut some school lunch fds N
48. Clean Water Act Amendmnts N
49. Youth work projects N
50. Assist military in Angola Y
51. Allow US troops-Nicaragua N
52. Pentagon polygraph exams Y
53. Bar ASAT testing Y
54. Suspend def pmt for abuse N
55. Bar Pentagon-contr emplmt Y
56. Increase SDI funding N
57. Reduce SDI funding N
58. Produce chemical weapons Y
59. Bar CIA fndg in Nicaragua N
60. South Africa sanctions Y
61. Cut SS COLAs; Raise taxes N
62. Let US invest-So Africa N
63. Approve 21 MX for 1985 N
64. Emergency Farm Credit Y
65. Awards to whistle blowers Y
66. African disaster relief Y
67. Ban bank loans to So Afr ?
68. Bar coun duty-free trtmt N
69. Steel import limits Y
70. Soc Sec COLAs=inflation Y
71. Bar haz waste vctms suits Y
72. Prohibit aid to Nicaragua Y
73. Cut $-Schs bar sch prayer Y
74. Raise taxes; Cut Medicare Y
75. Alien residncy-prior 1982 Y
76. Alien residncy-prior 1980 Y
77. Pen emp-hire illgl aliens ?
78. Lmt Persh II/cruse-Europe N
79. Delete 34 B-1 bombers N
80. Bar purch of Pershing II N
81. Bar purchase of Sgt York N
82. Delete $ for Trident II N
83. Allow 15 MX missiles Y
84. Bar MX procurement-1985 N
85. Equal Access Act Y
86. Aid to El Salvador Y
87. Bar Nicarag water mining Y
88. Physician/Medicare freeze N
89. Increase "sin" taxes Y
90. End SBA direct loans N

TALLON, ROBIN (Cont.)

91. Sell Conrail	N	94. Eminent domain-Coal comps	N
92. Equal Rights Amendment	Y	95. Prohibit EPA sanctions	Y
93. Marines in Lebanon	Y	96. SS age increase/Reforms	N

Presidential Support Score: 1986 - 39% 1985 - 41%

SOUTH DAKOTA

DASCHLE, THOMAS A. -- Representative at Large [Democrat]. Prior Terms: House: 1979-86. Born: December 9, 1947; Aberdeen, S.D. Education: South Dakota State University (B.A.). Military Service: U.S. Air Force, 1969-72. Occupation: Congressional legislative assistant.

1. Immigration Reform	Y	44. Delete 12 MX missiles	Y
2. Open fld-search warrants	Y	45. Spending cuts;Tax incres'	Y
3. Civil pnty-hire ill alien	N	46. Textile Import Quotas	N
4. So Afr sanc-veto override	Y	47. Cut some school lunch fds	N
5. Tax Overhaul	N	48. Clean Water Act Amendmnts	N
6. South Africa sanctions	Y	49. Youth work projects	Y
7. Death penalty-drug bill	Y	50. Assist military in Angola	N
8. Evidence-warrantless srch	Y	51. Allow US troops-Nicaragua	N
9. Life term-second drug off	Y	52. Pentagon polygraph exams	Y
10. Military use in drug war	Y	53. Bar ASAT testing	Y
11. Troop reduction in Europe	N	54. Suspend def pmt for abuse	Y
12. Prohibit chemical weapons	Y	55. Bar Pentagon-contr emplmt	Y
13. Bar ASAT testing	Y	56. Increase SDI funding	?
14. Abide SALT II weapons ban	Y	57. Reduce SDI funding	?
15. Follow SALT II-Soviets do	N	58. Produce chemical weapons	N
16. Reduce SDI funding	Y	59. Bar CIA fndg in Nicaragua	Y
17. Increase SDI funding	N	60. South Africa sanctions	Y
18. Purchase Trident sub	Y	61. Cut SS COLAs; Raise taxes	Y
19. Delete 12 MX;Add conv wpn	Y	62. Let US invest-So Africa	N
20. Raise speed limit	Y	63. Approve 21 MX for 1985	N
21. Textile Import Quotas(*)	N	64. Emergency Farm Credit	Y
22. Req Pentagon buy US goods	Y	65. Awards to whistle blowers	Y
23. AIDS ins anti-dscriminatn	Y	66. African disaster relief	Y
24. Nicaraguan refugee aid	Y	67. Ban bank loans to So Afr	Y
25. Nicaraguan contra aid	N	68. Bar coun duty-free trtmt	N
26. US abide by SALT II	N	69. Steel import limits	Y
27. Prohibit Saudi arms sale	Y	70. Soc Sec COLAs=inflation	Y
28. Military Retiremnt Reform	Y	71. Bar haz waste vctms suits	Y
29. Nicaraguan refugee aid	Y	72. Prohibit aid to Nicaragua	Y
30. Ease '68 Gun Control Act	Y	73. Cut $-Schs bar sch prayer	N
31. Bar intrstat handgun tran	N	74. Raise taxes; Cut Medicare	Y
32. Keep '68 Gun Control Act	N	75. Alien residncy-prior 1982	Y
33. Nicaraguan contra aid	N	76. Alien residncy-prior 1980	N
34. Bar emp polygraph testing	Y	77. Pen emp-hire illgl aliens	N
35. Tax Overhaul consideratn	Y	78. Lmt Persh II/cruse-Europe	Y
36. Bar armor-piercing ammo	Y	79. Delete 34 B-1 bombers	N
37. Tax Overhaul consideratn	N	80. Bar purch of Pershing II	Y
38. Make comp emissions known	Y	81. Bar purchase of Sgt York	Y
39. Allow toxic victims suits	N	82. Delete $ for Trident II	N
40. Strike Superfund "VAT"	Y	83. Allow 15 MX missiles	N
41. Notify emp-plant closing	?	84. Bar MX procurement-1985	Y
42. Bar emp consult-plant clo	N	85. Equal Access Act	Y
43. Medicare cuts;Tax incres'	Y	86. Aid to El Salvador	N

DASCHLE, THOMAS A. (Cont.)

87. Bar Nicarag water mining Y
88. Physician/Medicare freeze N
89. Increase "sin" taxes N
90. End SBA direct loans N
91. Sell Conrail N
92. Equal Rights Amendment Y
93. Marines in Lebanon N
94. Eminent domain-Coal comps Y
95. Prohibit EPA sanctions Y
96. SS age increase/Reforms Y
97. Auto domestic content req ?
98. Delete jobs program fundg Y
99. Highway-Gas tax bill N
100. Raise Medicare;Cut defnse Y
101. Emergency housing aid Y
102. Across-the-board tax cuts N
103. Gramm-Latta II targets N
104. Delete B-1 bomber funds N
105. Dsapprov Saudi AWACS sale Y
106. Disapprove oil import fee Y
107. Rail Deregulation N
108. Dsapp India nuc fuel sale Y
109. Mil draft registration N
110. Chrysler Loan Guarantees Y
111. Prohibit school busing N
112. Nuclear plant moratorium Y
113. Oil price controls Y

Presidential Support Score: 1986 - 20% 1985 - 16%

TENNESSEE

QUILLEN, JAMES H. (Jimmy) -- Tennessee 1st District [Republican]. Counties of Carter, Cocke, Greene, Hawkins, Jefferson, Johnson, Sevier, Sullivan, Unicoi and Washington. Prior Terms: House: 1963-86. Born: January 11, 1916; Gate City, Va. Military Service: U.S. Navy, WW II. Occupation: Newspaper publisher; real estate businessman; mortgage banker; insurance businessman; Tennessee representative (1955-62).

1. Immigration Reform Y
2. Open fld-search warrants N
3. Civil pnty-hire ill alien Y
4. So Afr sanc-veto override N
5. Tax Overhaul Y
6. South Africa sanctions N
7. Death penalty-drug bill Y
8. Evidence-warrantless srch Y
9. Life term-second drug off Y
10. Military use in drug war Y
11. Troop reduction in Europe N
12. Prohibit chemical weapons N
13. Bar ASAT testing N
14. Abide SALT II weapons ban N
15. Follow SALT II-Soviets do Y
16. Reduce SDI funding N
17. Increase SDI funding Y
18. Purchase Trident sub ?
19. Delete 12 MX;Add conv wpn N
20. Raise speed limit N
21. Textile Import Quotas(*) Y
22. Req Pentagon buy US goods Y
23. AIDS ins anti-dscriminatn N
24. Nicaraguan refugee aid N
25. Nicaraguan contra aid Y
26. US abide by SALT II Y
27. Prohibit Saudi arms sale ?
28. Military Retiremnt Reform Y
29. Nicaraguan refugee aid Y
30. Ease '68 Gun Control Act Y
31. Bar intrstat handgun tran N
32. Keep '68 Gun Control Act N
33. Nicaraguan contra aid Y
34. Bar emp polygraph testing Y
35. Tax Overhaul consideratn Y
36. Bar armor-piercing ammo N
37. Tax Overhaul consideratn Y
38. Make comp emissions known N
39. Allow toxic victims suits N
40. Strike Superfund "VAT" N
41. Notify emp-plant closing N
42. Bar emp consult-plant clo Y
43. Medicare cuts;Tax incres' ?
44. Delete 12 MX missiles N
45. Spending cuts;Tax incres' N
46. Textile Import Quotas Y
47. Cut some school lunch fds N
48. Clean Water Act Amendmnts Y
49. Youth work projects N
50. Assist military in Angola Y
51. Allow US troops-Nicaragua Y
52. Pentagon polygraph exams Y
53. Bar ASAT testing N
54. Suspend def pmt for abuse N
55. Bar Pentagon-contr emplmt Y
56. Increase SDI funding Y
57. Reduce SDI funding N
58. Produce chemical weapons Y
59. Bar CIA fndg in Nicaragua N
60. South Africa sanctions N
61. Cut SS COLAs; Raise taxes N
62. Let US invest-So Africa Y

QUILLEN, JAMES H. (Jimmy) (Cont.)

63. Approve 21 MX for 1985 Y
64. Emergency Farm Credit N
65. Awards to whistle blowers Y
66. African disaster relief Y
67. Ban bank loans to So Afr N
68. Bar coun duty-free trtmt N
69. Steel import limits Y
70. Soc Sec COLAs=inflation Y
71. Bar haz waste vctms suits Y
72. Prohibit aid to Nicaragua Y
73. Cut $-Schs bar sch prayer Y
74. Raise taxes; Cut Medicare Y
75. Alien residncy-prior 1982 N
76. Alien residncy-prior 1980 Y
77. Pen emp-hire illgl aliens ?
78. Lmt Persh II/cruse-Europe N
79. Delete 34 B-1 bombers N
80. Bar purch of Pershing II N
81. Bar purchase of Sgt York N
82. Delete $ for Trident II N
83. Allow 15 MX missiles Y
84. Bar MX procurement-1985 N
85. Equal Access Act Y
86. Aid to El Salvador Y
87. Bar Nicarag water mining X
88. Physician/Medicare freeze Y
89. Increase "sin" taxes Y
90. End SBA direct loans Y
91. Sell Conrail Y
92. Equal Rights Amendment N
93. Marines in Lebanon Y
94. Eminent domain-Coal comps N
95. Prohibit EPA sanctions Y
96. SS age increase/Reforms Y
97. Auto domestic content req N
98. Delete jobs program fundg Y
99. Highway-Gas tax bill N
100. Raise Medicare;Cut defnse Y
101. Emergency housing aid Y
102. Across-the-board tax cuts Y
103. Gramm-Latta II targets Y
104. Delete B-1 bomber funds N
105. Dsapprov Saudi AWACS sale N
106. Disapprove oil import fee Y
107. Rail Deregulation N
108. Dsapp India nuc fuel sale Y
109. Mil draft registration Y
110. Chrysler Loan Guarantees Y
111. Prohibit school busing Y
112. Nuclear plant moratorium N
113. Oil price controls N
114. Tuition Tax Credits N
115. Est Consumer Protect Agcy N
116. Eliminate B-1 bomber fnds Y
117. Subminimum wage for youth #
118. Delete crude oil tax Y
119. Natural gas deregulation Y

Presidential Support Score: 1986 - 63% 1985 - 68%

DUNCAN, JOHN J. -- Tennessee 2nd District [Republican]. Counties of Blount, Knox, Loudon, McMinn, Monroe and Polk. Prior Terms: House: 1965-86. Born: March 24, 1919; Scott County, Tenn. Military Service: U.S. Army, 1942-45. Occupation: Assistant state attorney general (1947-56); law director (1956-59); mayor (1959-64); president, Federal Savings and Loan Assn; director, World Service Insurance Life Co.

1. Immigration Reform N
2. Open fld-search warrants N
3. Civil pnty-hire ill alien N
4. So Afr sanc-veto override Y
5. Tax Overhaul Y
6. South Africa sanctions Y
7. Death penalty-drug bill Y
8. Evidence-warrantless srch Y
9. Life term-second drug off Y
10. Military use in drug war Y
11. Troop reduction in Europe N
12. Prohibit chemical weapons N
13. Bar ASAT testing N
14. Abide SALT II weapons ban N
15. Follow SALT II-Soviets do Y
16. Reduce SDI funding N
17. Increase SDI funding Y
18. Purchase Trident sub N
19. Delete 12 MX;Add conv wpn N
20. Raise speed limit N
21. Textile Import Quotas(*) Y
22. Req Pentagon buy US goods Y
23. AIDS ins anti-dscriminatn Y
24. Nicaraguan refugee aid N
25. Nicaraguan contra aid Y
26. US abide by SALT II Y
27. Prohibit Saudi arms sale Y
28. Military Retiremnt Reform Y
29. Nicaraguan refugee aid Y
30. Ease '68 Gun Control Act Y
31. Bar intrstat handgun tran N
32. Keep '68 Gun Control Act N
33. Nicaraguan contra aid Y
34. Bar emp polygraph testing N
35. Tax Overhaul consideratn Y
36. Bar armor-piercing ammo Y
37. Tax Overhaul consideratn Y
38. Make comp emissions known N

DUNCAN, JOHN J. (Cont.)

39. Allow toxic victims suits N
40. Strike Superfund "VAT" N
41. Notify emp-plant closing N
42. Bar emp consult-plant clo Y
43. Medicare cuts;Tax incres' N
44. Delete 12 MX missiles N
45. Spending cuts;Tax incres' N
46. Textile Import Quotas Y
47. Cut some school lunch fds Y
48. Clean Water Act Amendmnts Y
49. Youth work projects N
50. Assist military in Angola Y
51. Allow US troops-Nicaragua Y
52. Pentagon polygraph exams Y
53. Bar ASAT testing N
54. Suspend def pmt for abuse N
55. Bar Pentagon-contr emplmt Y
56. Increase SDI funding N
57. Reduce SDI funding N
58. Produce chemical weapons Y
59. Bar CIA fndg in Nicaragua N
60. South Africa sanctions Y
61. Cut SS COLAs; Raise taxes N
62. Let US invest-So Africa Y
63. Approve 21 MX for 1985 Y
64. Emergency Farm Credit N
65. Awards to whistle blowers Y
66. African disaster relief Y
67. Ban bank loans to So Afr Y
68. Bar coun duty-free trtmt N
69. Steel import limits N
70. Soc Sec COLAs=inflation Y
71. Bar haz waste vctms suits Y
72. Prohibit aid to Nicaragua Y
73. Cut $-Schs bar sch prayer Y
74. Raise taxes; Cut Medicare Y
75. Alien residncy-prior 1982 N
76. Alien residncy-prior 1980 N
77. Pen emp-hire illgl aliens N
78. Lmt Persh II/cruse-Europe N
79. Delete 34 B-1 bombers N
80. Bar purch of Pershing II N
81. Bar purchase of Sgt York N
82. Delete $ for Trident II N
83. Allow 15 MX missiles Y
84. Bar MX procurement-1985 N
85. Equal Access Act Y
86. Aid to El Salvador Y
87. Bar Nicarag water mining N
88. Physician/Medicare freeze Y
89. Increase "sin" taxes Y
90. End SBA direct loans N
91. Sell Conrail Y
92. Equal Rights Amendment N
93. Marines in Lebanon Y
94. Eminent domain-Coal comps N
95. Prohibit EPA sanctions ?
96. SS age increase/Reforms Y
97. Auto domestic content req N
98. Delete jobs program fundg Y
99. Highway-Gas tax bill N
100. Raise Medicare;Coal comps Y
101. Emergency housing aid Y
102. Across-the-board tax cuts Y
103. Gramm-Latta II targets Y
104. Delete B-1 bomber funds X
105. Dsapprov Saudi AWACS sale Y
106. Disapprove oil import fee Y
107. Rail Deregulation N
108. Dsapp India nuc fuel sale N
109. Mil draft registration Y
110. Chrysler Loan Guarantees Y
111. Prohibit school busing Y
112. Nuclear plant moratorium N
113. Oil price controls N
114. Tuition Tax Credits N
115. Est Consumer Protect Agcy N
116. Eliminate B-1 bomber fnds Y
117. Subminimum wage for youth Y
118. Delete crude oil tax Y
119. Natural gas deregulation Y

Presidential Support Score: 1986 - 68% 1985 - 65%

LLOYD, MARILYN -- Tennessee 3rd District [Democrat]. Counties of Anderson, Bradley, Grundy, Hamilton, Marion, Meigs, and Roane. Prior Terms: House: 1975-78, 1983-86. Born: January 3, 1929; Fort Smith, Ark. Education: Shorter College. Occupation: Manager, radio station WTTI.

1. Immigration Reform N
2. Open fld-search warrants Y
3. Civil pnty-hire ill alien N
4. So Afr sanc-veto override Y
5. Tax Overhaul Y
6. South Africa sanctions Y
7. Death penalty-drug bill Y
8. Evidence-warrantless srch Y
9. Life term-second drug off Y
10. Military use in drug war Y
11. Troop reduction in Europe N
12. Prohibit chemical weapons N
13. Bar ASAT testing N
14. Abide SALT II weapons ban N
15. Follow SALT II-Soviets do Y
16. Reduce SDI funding N
17. Increase SDI funding N
18. Purchase Trident sub N

LLOYD, MARILYN (Cont.)

19. Delete 12 MX;Add conv wpn N
20. Raise speed limit Y
21. Textile Import Quotas(*) Y
22. Req Pentagon buy US goods Y
23. AIDS ins anti-dscriminatn N
24. Nicaraguan refugee aid N
25. Nicaraguan contra aid Y
26. US abide by SALT II Y
27. Prohibit Saudi arms sale Y
28. Military Retiremnt Reform Y
29. Nicaraguan refugee aid N
30. Ease '68 Gun Control Act Y
31. Bar intrstat handgun tran N
32. Keep '68 Gun Control Act N
33. Nicaraguan contra aid N
34. Bar emp polygraph testing N
35. Tax Overhaul consideratn Y
36. Bar armor-piercing ammo Y
37. Tax Overhaul consideratn Y
38. Make comp emissions known N
39. Allow toxic victims suits N
40. Strike Superfund "VAT" Y
41. Notify emp-plant closing Y
42. Bar emp consult-plant clo N
43. Medicare cuts;Tax incres' N
44. Delete 12 MX missiles N
45. Spending cuts;Tax incres' Y
46. Textile Import Quotas Y
47. Cut some school lunch fds ?
48. Clean Water Act Amendmnts Y
49. Youth work projects ?
50. Assist military in Angola Y
51. Allow US troops-Nicaragua Y
52. Pentagon polygraph exams Y
53. Bar ASAT testing N
54. Suspend def pmt for abuse N
55. Bar Pentagon-contr emplmt Y
56. Increase SDI funding N
57. Reduce SDI funding N
58. Produce chemical weapons Y
59. Bar CIA fndg in Nicaragua N
60. South Africa sanctions Y
61. Cut SS COLAs; Raise taxes N
62. Let US invest-So Africa N
63. Approve 21 MX for 1985 Y
64. Emergency Farm Credit +
65. Awards to whistle blowers Y
66. African disaster relief Y
67. Ban bank loans to So Afr N
68. Bar coun duty-free trtmt N
69. Steel import limits Y
70. Soc Sec COLAs=inflation Y
71. Bar haz waste vctms suits Y
72. Prohibit aid to Nicaragua N
73. Cut $-Schs bar sch prayer Y
74. Raise taxes; Cut Medicare Y
75. Alien residncy-prior 1982 Y
76. Alien residncy-prior 1980 N
77. Pen emp-hire illgl aliens N
78. Lmt Persh II/cruse-Europe N
79. Delete 34 B-1 bombers N
80. Bar purch of Pershing II N
81. Bar purchase of Sgt York N
82. Delete $ for Trident II N
83. Allow 15 MX missiles Y
84. Bar MX procurement-1985 N
85. Equal Access Act Y
86. Aid to El Salvador Y
87. Bar Nicarag water mining N
88. Physician/Medicare freeze N
89. Increase "sin" taxes Y
90. End SBA direct loans N
91. Sell Conrail N
92. Equal Rights Amendment N
93. Marines in Lebanon Y
94. Eminent domain-Coal comps N
95. Prohibit EPA sanctions ?
96. SS age increase/Reforms Y
114. Tuition Tax Credits N
115. Est Consumer Protect Agcy N
116. Eliminate B-1 bomber fnds Y
117. Subminimum wage for youth N
118. Delete crude oil tax Y
119. Natural gas deregulation Y

Was not in office for votes 97-113.
Presidential Support Score: 1986 - 55% 1985 - 52%

COOPER, JIM -- Tennessee 4th District [Democrat]. Counties of Bedford, Bledsoe, Campbell, Claiborne, Coffee, Cumberland, Fentress, Franklin, Giles, Grainger, Hamblen, Hancock, Lawrence, Lincoln, Moore, Morgan, Rhea, Scott, Sequatchie, Union, Van Buren, Warren and White. Prior Terms: House: 1983-86. Born: June 19, 1954. Education: University of North Carolina, Chapel Hill (B.S.); Harvard Law School (J.D.). Occupation: Attorney; businessman, congressional page and assistant.

1. Immigration Reform Y
2. Open fld-search warrants N
3. Civil pnty-hire ill alien N
4. So Afr sanc-veto override Y
5. Tax Overhaul Y
6. South Africa sanctions Y
7. Death penalty-drug bill N
8. Evidence-warrantless srch N

COOPER, JIM (Cont.)

9. Life term-second drug off Y	53. Bar ASAT testing Y
10. Military use in drug war N	54. Suspend def pmt for abuse Y
11. Troop reduction in Europe N	55. Bar Pentagon-contr emplmt Y
12. Prohibit chemical weapons Y	56. Increase SDI funding N
13. Bar ASAT testing Y	57. Reduce SDI funding N
14. Abide SALT II weapons ban Y	58. Produce chemical weapons N
15. Follow SALT II-Soviets do N	59. Bar CIA fndg in Nicaragua N
16. Reduce SDI funding N	60. South Africa sanctions Y
17. Increase SDI funding N	61. Cut SS COLAs; Raise taxes Y
18. Purchase Trident sub Y	62. Let US invest-So Africa N
19. Delete 12 MX;Add conv wpn Y	63. Approve 21 MX for 1985 Y
20. Raise speed limit Y	64. Emergency Farm Credit Y
21. Textile Import Quotas(*) Y	65. Awards to whistle blowers Y
22. Req Pentagon buy US goods N	66. African disaster relief Y
23. AIDS ins anti-dscriminatn Y	67. Ban bank loans to So Afr ?
24. Nicaraguan refugee aid N	68. Bar coun duty-free trtmt N
25. Nicaraguan contra aid N	69. Steel import limits Y
26. US abide by SALT II N	70. Soc Sec COLAs=inflation ?
27. Prohibit Saudi arms sale N	71. Bar haz waste vctms suits N
28. Military Retiremnt Reform Y	72. Prohibit aid to Nicaragua Y
29. Nicaraguan refugee aid Y	73. Cut $-Schs bar sch prayer N
30. Ease '68 Gun Control Act Y	74. Raise taxes; Cut Medicare Y
31. Bar intrstat handgun tran N	75. Alien residncy-prior 1982 N
32. Keep '68 Gun Control Act N	76. Alien residncy-prior 1980 N
33. Nicaraguan contra aid N	77. Pen emp-hire illgl aliens N
34. Bar emp polygraph testing Y	78. Lmt Persh II/cruse-Europe N
35. Tax Overhaul consideratn Y	79. Delete 34 B-1 bombers Y
36. Bar armor-piercing ammo Y	80. Bar purch of Pershing II N
37. Tax Overhaul consideratn Y	81. Bar purchase of Sgt York Y
38. Make comp emissions known N	82. Delete $ for Trident II N
39. Allow toxic victims suits Y	83. Allow 15 MX missiles Y
40. Strike Superfund "VAT" Y	84. Bar MX procurement-1985 N
41. Notify emp-plant closing Y	85. Equal Access Act N
42. Bar emp consult-plant clo Y	86. Aid to El Salvador N
43. Medicare cuts;Tax incres' Y	87. Bar Nicarag water mining Y
44. Delete 12 MX missiles N	88. Physician/Medicare freeze N
45. Spending cuts;Tax incres' Y	89. Increase "sin" taxes Y
46. Textile Import Quotas Y	90. End SBA direct loans N
47. Cut some school lunch fds N	91. Sell Conrail N
48. Clean Water Act Amendmnts N	92. Equal Rights Amendment N
49. Youth work projects Y	93. Marines in Lebanon Y
50. Assist military in Angola N	94. Eminent domain-Coal comps N
51. Allow US troops-Nicaragua N	95. Prohibit EPA sanctions N
52. Pentagon polygraph exams Y	96. SS age increase/Reforms Y

Presidential Support Score: 1986 - 31% 1985 - 43%

BONER, WILLIAM HILL -- Tennessee 5th District [Democrat]. Counties of Davidson and Robertson. Prior Terms: House: 1979-86. Born: February 14, 1945; Nashville, Tenn. Education: Middle Tennessee State University (1967); George Peabody College (M.A.); Y.M.C.A Night Law School (1978). Occupation: Teacher (1969-71); senior staff assistant, Mayor's Office (1971-72); director, public relations, First American National Bank (1972-76); Tennessee representative (1970-72, 1974-76); Tennessee senator (1976-78).

1. Immigration Reform N	3. Civil pnty-hire ill alien N
2. Open fld-search warrants N	4. So Afr sanc-veto override Y

BONER, WILLIAM HILL (Cont.)

5. Tax Overhaul Y
6. South Africa sanctions ?
7. Death penalty-drug bill Y
8. Evidence-warrantless srch Y
9. Life term-second drug off ?
10. Military use in drug war Y
11. Troop reduction in Europe N
12. Prohibit chemical weapons N
13. Bar ASAT testing Y
14. Abide SALT II weapons ban Y
15. Follow SALT II-Soviets do N
16. Reduce SDI funding N
17. Increase SDI funding N
18. Purchase Trident sub Y
19. Delete 12 MX;Add conv wpn ?
20. Raise speed limit Y
21. Textile Import Quotas(*) Y
22. Req Pentagon buy US goods Y
23. AIDS ins anti-dscriminatn ?
24. Nicaraguan refugee aid N
25. Nicaraguan contra aid N
26. US abide by SALT II N
27. Prohibit Saudi arms sale Y
28. Military Retiremnt Reform Y
29. Nicaraguan refugee aid Y
30. Ease '68 Gun Control Act Y
31. Bar intrstat handgun tran N
32. Keep '68 Gun Control Act N
33. Nicaraguan contra aid N
34. Bar emp polygraph testing Y
35. Tax Overhaul consideratn N
36. Bar armor-piercing ammo Y
37. Tax Overhaul consideratn Y
38. Make comp emissions known Y
39. Allow toxic victims suits Y
40. Strike Superfund "VAT" ?
41. Notify emp-plant closing N
42. Bar emp consult-plant clo N
43. Medicare cuts;Tax incres' Y
44. Delete 12 MX missiles N
45. Spending cuts;Tax incres' Y
46. Textile Import Quotas Y
47. Cut some school lunch fds N
48. Clean Water Act Amendmnts N
49. Youth work projects Y
50. Assist military in Angola N
51. Allow US troops-Nicaragua N
52. Pentagon polygraph exams Y
53. Bar ASAT testing Y
54. Suspend def pmt for abuse N
55. Bar Pentagon-contr emplmt Y
56. Increase SDI funding N
57. Reduce SDI funding N
58. Produce chemical weapons Y
59. Bar CIA fndg in Nicaragua N
60. South Africa sanctions Y
61. Cut SS COLAs; Raise taxes N
62. Let US invest-So Africa N
63. Approve 21 MX for 1985 Y
64. Emergency Farm Credit Y
65. Awards to whistle blowers Y
66. African disaster relief Y
67. Ban bank loans to So Afr ?
68. Bar coun duty-free trtmt Y
69. Steel import limits Y
70. Soc Sec COLAs=inflation Y
71. Bar haz waste vctms suits N
72. Prohibit aid to Nicaragua Y
73. Cut $-Schs bar sch prayer Y
74. Raise taxes; Cut Medicare Y
75. Alien residncy-prior 1982 Y
76. Alien residncy-prior 1980 Y
77. Pen emp-hire illgl aliens N
78. Lmt Persh II/cruse-Europe N
79. Delete 34 B-1 bombers N
80. Bar purch of Pershing II N
81. Bar purchase of Sgt York ?
82. Delete $ for Trident II N
83. Allow 15 MX missiles Y
84. Bar MX procurement-1985 N
85. Equal Access Act Y
86. Aid to El Salvador Y
87. Bar Nicarag water mining ?
88. Physician/Medicare freeze X
89. Increase "sin" taxes Y
90. End SBA direct loans N
91. Sell Conrail N
92. Equal Rights Amendment Y
93. Marines in Lebanon Y
94. Eminent domain-Coal comps N
95. Prohibit EPA sanctions Y
96. SS age increase/Reforms N
97. Auto domestic content req Y
98. Delete jobs program fundg N
99. Highway-Gas tax bill N
100. Raise Medicare;Cut defnse Y
101. Emergency housing aid Y
102. Across-the-board tax cuts Y
103. Gramm-Latta II targets N
104. Delete B-1 bomber funds N
105. Dsapprov Saudi AWACS sale Y
106. Disapprove oil import fee Y
107. Rail Deregulation N
108. Dsapp India nuc fuel sale Y
109. Mil draft registration #
110. Chrysler Loan Guarantees Y
111. Prohibit school busing Y
112. Nuclear plant moratorium N
113. Oil price controls Y

Presidential Support Score: 1986 - 30% 1985 - 44%

GORDON, BART -- Tennessee 6th District [Democrat]. Counties of Cannon, Clay, De Kalb, Jackson, Lewis, Macon, Marshall, Maury, Overton, Pickett, Putman, Rutherford, Smith, Sumner, Trousdale, Williamson, and Wilson. Prior Terms: 1985-86. Born: January 24, 1949; Education: Middle Tennessee State University (B.S.); University of Tennessee Law School (J.D.). Occupation: Attorney.

1. Immigration Reform N
2. Open fld-search warrants N
3. Civil pnty-hire ill alien Y
4. So Afr sanc-veto override Y
5. Tax Overhaul N
6. South Africa sanctions Y
7. Death penalty-drug bill N
8. Evidence-warrantless srch N
9. Life term-second drug off Y
10. Military use in drug war N
11. Troop reduction in Europe N
12. Prohibit chemical weapons Y
13. Bar ASAT testing Y
14. Abide SALT II weapons ban Y
15. Follow SALT II-Soviets do N
16. Reduce SDI funding N
17. Increase SDI funding N
18. Purchase Trident sub Y
19. Delete 12 MX;Add conv wpn Y
20. Raise speed limit Y
21. Textile Import Quotas(*) Y
22. Req Pentagon buy US goods Y
23. AIDS ins anti-dscriminatn Y
24. Nicaraguan refugee aid Y
25. Nicaraguan contra aid N
26. US abide by SALT II N
27. Prohibit Saudi arms sale Y
28. Military Retiremnt Reform Y
29. Nicaraguan refugee aid Y
30. Ease '68 Gun Control Act Y
31. Bar intrstat handgun tran N
32. Keep '68 Gun Control Act N
33. Nicaraguan contra aid N
34. Bar emp polygraph testing Y
35. Tax Overhaul consideratn Y
36. Bar armor-piercing ammo Y
37. Tax Overhaul consideratn Y
38. Make comp emissions known Y
39. Allow toxic victims suits N
40. Strike Superfund "VAT" Y
41. Notify emp-plant closing Y
42. Bar emp consult-plant clo N
43. Medicare cuts;Tax incres' Y
44. Delete 12 MX missiles Y
45. Spending cuts;Tax incres' Y
46. Textile Import Quotas Y
47. Cut some school lunch fds N
48. Clean Water Act Amendmnts N
49. Youth work projects N
50. Assist military in Angola N
51. Allow US troops-Nicaragua Y
52. Pentagon polygraph exams Y
53. Bar ASAT testing Y
54. Suspend def pmt for abuse N
55. Bar Pentagon-contr emplmt Y
56. Increase SDI funding N
57. Reduce SDI funding N
58. Produce chemical weapons N
59. Bar CIA fndg in Nicaragua N
60. South Africa sanctions Y
61. Cut SS COLAs; Raise taxes Y
62. Let US invest-So Africa N
63. Approve 21 MX for 1985 N
64. Emergency Farm Credit Y
65. Awards to whistle blowers Y
66. African disaster relief Y

Presidential Support Score: 1986 - 26% 1985 - 33%

SUNDQUIST, DON -- Tennessee 7th District [Republican]. Counties of Cheatham, Chester, Decatur, Dickson, Fayette, Hardeman, Hardin, Henderson, Hickman, Houston, Humphreys, McNairy, Montgomery, Perry, Shelby (pt.) and Wayne. Prior Terms: House: 1983-86. Born: March 15, 1936; Moline, Ill. Education: Augustana College (B.A.). Military Service: U.S. Navy, 1957-59; Navy Reserve, 1959-63. Occupation: Advertising executive; boardmember, Mid-South Coliseum; banker.

1. Immigration Reform N
2. Open fld-search warrants N
3. Civil pnty-hire ill alien N
4. So Afr sanc-veto override N
5. Tax Overhaul N
6. South Africa sanctions N
7. Death penalty-drug bill Y
8. Evidence-warrantless srch Y
9. Life term-second drug off Y
10. Military use in drug war Y
11. Troop reduction in Europe N
12. Prohibit chemical weapons N
13. Bar ASAT testing N
14. Abide SALT II weapons ban N

SUNDQUIST, DON (Cont.)

15. Follow SALT II-Soviets do Y
16. Reduce SDI funding N
17. Increase SDI funding N
18. Purchase Trident sub N
19. Delete 12 MX;Add conv wpn N
20. Raise speed limit N
21. Textile Import Quotas(*) Y
22. Req Pentagon buy US goods N
23. AIDS ins anti-dscriminatn N
24. Nicaraguan refugee aid N
25. Nicaraguan contra aid Y
26. US abide by SALT II Y
27. Prohibit Saudi arms sale Y
28. Military Retiremnt Reform Y
29. Nicaraguan refugee aid Y
30. Ease '68 Gun Control Act Y
31. Bar intrstat handgun tran N
32. Keep '68 Gun Control Act N
33. Nicaraguan contra aid Y
34. Bar emp polygraph testing N
35. Tax Overhaul consideratn N
36. Bar armor-piercing ammo Y
37. Tax Overhaul consideratn N
38. Make comp emissions known N
39. Allow toxic victims suits N
40. Strike Superfund "VAT" N
41. Notify emp-plant closing N
42. Bar emp consult-plant clo Y
43. Medicare cuts;Tax incres' N
44. Delete 12 MX missiles N
45. Spending cuts;Tax incres' N
46. Textile Import Quotas Y
47. Cut some school lunch fds Y
48. Clean Water Act Amendmnts Y
49. Youth work projects N
50. Assist military in Angola Y
51. Allow US troops-Nicaragua Y
52. Pentagon polygraph exams Y
53. Bar ASAT testing N
54. Suspend def pmt for abuse N
55. Bar Pentagon-contr emplmt Y
56. Increase SDI funding Y
57. Reduce SDI funding ?
58. Produce chemical weapons Y
59. Bar CIA fndg in Nicaragua N
60. South Africa sanctions N
61. Cut SS COLAs; Raise taxes N
62. Let US invest-So Africa Y
63. Approve 21 MX for 1985 Y
64. Emergency Farm Credit Y
65. Awards to whistle blowers Y
66. African disaster relief Y
67. Ban bank loans to So Afr Y
68. Bar coun duty-free trtmt N
69. Steel import limits N
70. Soc Sec COLAs=inflation Y
71. Bar haz waste vctms suits Y
72. Prohibit aid to Nicaragua N
73. Cut $-Schs bar sch prayer Y
74. Raise taxes; Cut Medicare Y
75. Alien residncy-prior 1982 N
76. Alien residncy-prior 1980 Y
77. Pen emp-hire illgl aliens N
78. Lmt Persh II/cruse-Europe N
79. Delete 34 B-1 bombers N
80. Bar purch of Pershing II N
81. Bar purchase of Sgt York N
82. Delete $ for Trident II N
83. Allow 15 MX missiles Y
84. Bar MX procurement-1985 N
85. Equal Access Act Y
86. Aid to El Salvador Y
87. Bar Nicarag water mining N
88. Physician/Medicare freeze Y
89. Increase "sin" taxes Y
90. End SBA direct loans Y
91. Sell Conrail Y
92. Equal Rights Amendment N
93. Marines in Lebanon Y
94. Eminent domain-Coal comps Y
95. Prohibit EPA sanctions Y
96. SS age increase/Reforms Y

Presidential Support Score: 1986 - 74% 1985 - 75%

JONES, ED -- Tennessee 8th District [Democrat]. Counties of Benton, Carroll, Crockett, Dyer, Gibson, Haywood, Henry, Lake, Lauderdale, Madison, Obion, Shelby (pt.), Stewart, Tipton and Weakley. Prior Terms: House: 1969 (Special Election)-1986. Born: April 20, 1912; Yorkville, Tenn. Education: University of Tennessee (B.S.). Occupation: Inspector, Tennessee Department of Agriculture; member, Tennessee Dairy Products Assn. (1941-43); agricultural agent, Illinois Central Railroad (1944-49, 1953-69); Tennessee Commissioner of Agriculture (1949-52); member, Board of Trustees, and President of the Board, Bethel College; president, Yorkville Telephone Cooperative; associate farm director, radio station WMC.

1. Immigration Reform N
2. Open fld-search warrants Y
3. Civil pnty-hire ill alien N
4. So Afr sanc-veto override Y

JONES, ED (Cont.)

5. Tax Overhaul Y
6. South Africa sanctions Y
7. Death penalty-drug bill Y
8. Evidence-warrantless srch Y
9. Life term-second drug off Y
10. Military use in drug war N
11. Troop reduction in Europe N
12. Prohibit chemical weapons N
13. Bar ASAT testing Y
14. Abide SALT II weapons ban Y
15. Follow SALT II-Soviets do N
16. Reduce SDI funding N
17. Increase SDI funding N
18. Purchase Trident sub N
19. Delete 12 MX;Add conv wpn N
20. Raise speed limit Y
21. Textile Import Quotas(*) Y
22. Req Pentagon buy US goods Y
23. AIDS ins anti-dscriminatn ?
24. Nicaraguan refugee aid Y
25. Nicaraguan contra aid N
26. US abide by SALT II N
27. Prohibit Saudi arms sale N
28. Military Retiremnt Reform Y
29. Nicaraguan refugee aid Y
30. Ease '68 Gun Control Act Y
31. Bar intrstat handgun tran N
32. Keep '68 Gun Control Act N
33. Nicaraguan contra aid N
34. Bar emp polygraph testing N
35. Tax Overhaul consideratn Y
36. Bar armor-piercing ammo Y
37. Tax Overhaul consideratn Y
38. Make comp emissions known N
39. Allow toxic victims suits N
40. Strike Superfund "VAT" Y
41. Notify emp-plant closing N
42. Bar emp consult-plant clo Y
43. Medicare cuts;Tax incres' Y
44. Delete 12 MX missiles N
45. Spending cuts;Tax incres' Y
46. Textile Import Quotas Y
47. Cut some school lunch fds N
48. Clean Water Act Amendmnts N
49. Youth work projects N
50. Assist military in Angola N
51. Allow US troops-Nicaragua N
52. Pentagon polygraph exams N
53. Bar ASAT testing Y
54. Suspend def pmt for abuse N
55. Bar Pentagon-contr emplmt Y
56. Increase SDI funding N
57. Reduce SDI funding N
58. Produce chemical weapons Y
59. Bar CIA fndg in Nicaragua Y
60. South Africa sanctions Y
61. Cut SS COLAs; Raise taxes N
62. Let US invest-So Africa N
63. Approve 21 MX for 1985 Y
64. Emergency Farm Credit Y
65. Awards to whistle blowers Y
66. African disaster relief Y
67. Ban bank loans to So Afr Y
68. Bar coun duty-free trtmt Y
69. Steel import limits Y
70. Soc Sec COLAs=inflation Y
71. Bar haz waste vctms suits N
72. Prohibit aid to Nicaragua Y
73. Cut $-Schs bar sch prayer ?
74. Raise taxes; Cut Medicare Y
75. Alien residncy-prior 1982 Y
76. Alien residncy-prior 1980 Y
77. Pen emp-hire illgl aliens Y
78. Lmt Persh II/cruse-Europe N
79. Delete 34 B-1 bombers N
80. Bar purch of Pershing II N
81. Bar purchase of Sgt York N
82. Delete $ for Trident II N
83. Allow 15 MX missiles Y
84. Bar MX procurement-1985 N
85. Equal Access Act Y
86. Aid to El Salvador ?
87. Bar Nicarag water mining Y
88. Physician/Medicare freeze N
89. Increase "sin" taxes Y
90. End SBA direct loans N
91. Sell Conrail N
92. Equal Rights Amendment N
93. Marines in Lebanon Y
94. Eminent domain-Coal comps N
95. Prohibit EPA sanctions ?
96. SS age increase/Reforms N
97. Auto domestic content req Y
98. Delete jobs program fundg N
99. Highway-Gas tax bill N
100. Raise Medicare;Cut defnse Y
101. Emergency housing aid Y
102. Across-the-board tax cuts Y
103. Gramm-Latta II targets Y
104. Delete B-1 bomber funds N
105. Dsapprov Saudi AWACS sale Y
106. Disapprove oil import fee Y
107. Rail Deregulation X
108. Dsapp India nuc fuel sale N
109. Mil draft registration Y
110. Chrysler Loan Guarantees Y
111. Prohibit school busing Y
112. Nuclear plant moratorium N
113. Oil price controls N
114. Tuition Tax Credits N
115. Est Consumer Protect Agcy X
116. Eliminate B-1 bomber fnds Y
117. Subminimum wage for youth N
118. Delete crude oil tax N
119. Natural gas deregulation N

Presidential Support Score: 1986 - 30% 1985 - 45%

FORD, HAROLD E. -- Tennessee 9th District [Democrat]. County of Shelby (pt.). Prior Terms: House: 1975-86. Born: May 20, 1945; Memphis, Tenn. Education: Tennessee State University (B.S.); John Gupton College of Mortuary Science. Occupation: Tennessee representative; trustee, Rust College.

1. Immigration Reform Y
2. Open fld-search warrants Y
3. Civil pnty-hire ill alien N
4. So Afr sanc-veto override Y
5. Tax Overhaul Y
6. South Africa sanctions Y
7. Death penalty-drug bill N
8. Evidence-warrantless srch N
9. Life term-second drug off Y
10. Military use in drug war N
11. Troop reduction in Europe Y
12. Prohibit chemical weapons Y
13. Bar ASAT testing Y
14. Abide SALT II weapons ban Y
15. Follow SALT II-Soviets do N
16. Reduce SDI funding Y
17. Increase SDI funding N
18. Purchase Trident sub N
19. Delete 12 MX;Add conv wpn Y
20. Raise speed limit ?
21. Textile Import Quotas(*) Y
22. Req Pentagon buy US goods ?
23. AIDS ins anti-dscriminatn Y
24. Nicaraguan refugee aid Y
25. Nicaraguan contra aid N
26. US abide by SALT II N
27. Prohibit Saudi arms sale Y
28. Military Retiremnt Reform Y
29. Nicaraguan refugee aid Y
30. Ease '68 Gun Control Act N
31. Bar intrstat handgun tran Y
32. Keep '68 Gun Control Act Y
33. Nicaraguan contra aid N
34. Bar emp polygraph testing Y
35. Tax Overhaul consideratn Y
36. Bar armor-piercing ammo Y
37. Tax Overhaul consideratn Y
38. Make comp emissions known N
39. Allow toxic victims suits Y
40. Strike Superfund "VAT" N
41. Notify emp-plant closing Y
42. Bar emp consult-plant clo N
43. Medicare cuts;Tax incres' Y
44. Delete 12 MX missiles Y
45. Spending cuts;Tax incres' Y
46. Textile Import Quotas Y
47. Cut some school lunch fds N
48. Clean Water Act Amendmnts N
49. Youth work projects Y
50. Assist military in Angola N
51. Allow US troops-Nicaragua N
52. Pentagon polygraph exams ?
53. Bar ASAT testing Y
54. Suspend def pmt for abuse Y
55. Bar Pentagon-contr emplmt Y
56. Increase SDI funding ?
57. Reduce SDI funding Y
58. Produce chemical weapons N
59. Bar CIA fndg in Nicaragua Y
60. South Africa sanctions Y
61. Cut SS COLAs; Raise taxes ?
62. Let US invest-So Africa N
63. Approve 21 MX for 1985 N
64. Emergency Farm Credit Y
65. Awards to whistle blowers Y
66. African disaster relief Y
67. Ban bank loans to So Afr P
68. Bar coun duty-free trtmt Y
69. Steel import limits Y
70. Soc Sec COLAs=inflation Y
71. Bar haz waste vctms suits N
72. Prohibit aid to Nicaragua ?
73. Cut $-Schs bar sch prayer N
74. Raise taxes; Cut Medicare Y
75. Alien residncy-prior 1982 N
76. Alien residncy-prior 1980 N
77. Pen emp-hire illgl aliens Y
78. Lmt Persh II/cruse-Europe Y
79. Delete 34 B-1 bombers Y
80. Bar purch of Pershing II Y
81. Bar purchase of Sgt York Y
82. Delete $ for Trident II N
83. Allow 15 MX missiles N
84. Bar MX procurement-1985 Y
85. Equal Access Act N
86. Aid to El Salvador ?
87. Bar Nicarag water mining Y
88. Physician/Medicare freeze N
89. Increase "sin" taxes Y
90. End SBA direct loans N
91. Sell Conrail N
92. Equal Rights Amendment Y
93. Marines in Lebanon Y
94. Eminent domain-Coal comps ?
95. Prohibit EPA sanctions Y
96. SS age increase/Reforms N
97. Auto domestic content req Y
98. Delete jobs program fundg N
99. Highway-Gas tax bill N
100. Raise Medicare;Cut defnse Y
101. Emergency housing aid ?
102. Across-the-board tax cuts N
103. Gramm-Latta II targets N
104. Delete B-1 bomber funds Y
105. Dsapprov Saudi AWACS sale Y
106. Disapprove oil import fee ?
107. Rail Deregulation N
108. Dsapp India nuc fuel sale ?

FORD, HAROLD E. (Cont.)

109. Mil draft registration N
110. Chrysler Loan Guarantees Y
111. Prohibit school busing N
112. Nuclear plant moratorium N
113. Oil price controls ?
114. Tuition Tax Credits N
115. Est Consumer Protect Agcy Y
116. Eliminate B-1 bomber fnds Y
117. Subminimum wage for youth N
118. Delete crude oil tax N
119. Natural gas deregulation N

Presidential Support Score: 1986 - 16% 1985 - 18%

TEXAS

CHAPMAN, JIM -- Texas 1st District [Democrat]. Counties of Bowie, Camp, Cass, Cherokee, Delta, Franklin, Harrison, Henderson, Hopkins, Hunt (pt.), Lamar, Marion, Morris, Panola, Red River, Rusk, San Augustine, Shelby, Titus and Upshur. Prior Terms: 1985 (Special Election)-1986. Born: March 8, 1945. Education: University of Texas (B.B.A.); Southern Methodist University Law School (J.D.). Occupation: District Attorney, Texas (1977-85).

1. Immigration Reform N
2. Open fld-search warrants N
3. Civil pnty-hire ill alien Y
4. So Afr sanc-veto override Y
5. Tax Overhaul N
6. South Africa sanctions Y
7. Death penalty-drug bill Y
8. Evidence-warrantless srch Y
9. Life term-second drug off Y
10. Military use in drug war Y
11. Troop reduction in Europe N
12. Prohibit chemical weapons N
13. Bar ASAT testing N
14. Abide SALT II weapons ban Y
15. Follow SALT II-Soviets do N
16. Reduce SDI funding N
17. Increase SDI funding N
18. Purchase Trident sub N
19. Delete 12 MX;Add conv wpn N
20. Raise speed limit N
21. Textile Import Quotas(*) Y
22. Req Pentagon buy US goods Y
23. AIDS ins anti-dscriminatn Y
24. Nicaraguan refugee aid N
25. Nicaraguan contra aid N
26. US abide by SALT II N
27. Prohibit Saudi arms sale Y
28. Military Retiremnt Reform Y
29. Nicaraguan refugee aid N
30. Ease '68 Gun Control Act Y
31. Bar intrstat handgun tran N
32. Keep '68 Gun Control Act N
33. Nicaraguan contra aid N
34. Bar emp polygraph testing N
35. Tax Overhaul consideratn N
36. Bar armor-piercing ammo Y
37. Tax Overhaul consideratn N
38. Make comp emissions known N
39. Allow toxic victims suits N
40. Strike Superfund "VAT" N
41. Notify emp-plant closing N
42. Bar emp consult-plant clo Y
43. Medicare cuts;Tax incres' ?
44. Delete 12 MX missiles N
45. Spending cuts;Tax incres' Y
46. Textile Import Quotas Y
47. Cut some school lunch fds N

Presidential Support Score: 1986 - 35% 1985 - 42%

WILSON, CHARLES -- Texas 2nd District [Democrat]. Counties of Anderson, Angelina, Hardin, Houston, Jasper, Liberty, Montgomery (pt.), Nacogdoches, Newton, Orange, Polk, Sabine, San Jacinto, Trinity, Tyler and Walker. Prior Terms: House: 1973-86. Born: June 1, 1933; Trinity, Texas. Education: U.S. Naval Academy (B.S.). Military Service: U.S. Navy, 1956-60. Occupation: Lumber yard manager; Texas representative (1960-66); Texas senator (1966-72).

1. Immigration Reform Y
2. Open fld-search warrants N
3. Civil pnty-hire ill alien N
4. So Afr sanc-veto override Y
5. Tax Overhaul Y
6. South Africa sanctions Y

WILSON, CHARLES (Cont.)

7.	Death penalty-drug bill	Y
8.	Evidence-warrantless srch	N
9.	Life term-second drug off	Y
10.	Military use in drug war	Y
11.	Troop reduction in Europe	N
12.	Prohibit chemical weapons	N
13.	Bar ASAT testing	N
14.	Abide SALT II weapons ban	N
15.	Follow SALT II-Soviets do	Y
16.	Reduce SDI funding	N
17.	Increase SDI funding	Y
18.	Purchase Trident sub	Y
19.	Delete 12 MX;Add conv wpn	N
20.	Raise speed limit	N
21.	Textile Import Quotas(*)	Y
22.	Req Pentagon buy US goods	N
23.	AIDS ins anti-dscriminatn	Y
24.	Nicaraguan refugee aid	N
25.	Nicaraguan contra aid	Y
26.	US abide by SALT II	N
27.	Prohibit Saudi arms sale	N
28.	Military Retiremnt Reform	?
29.	Nicaraguan refugee aid	N
30.	Ease '68 Gun Control Act	Y
31.	Bar intrstat handgun tran	N
32.	Keep '68 Gun Control Act	N
33.	Nicaraguan contra aid	Y
34.	Bar emp polygraph testing	Y
35.	Tax Overhaul consideratn	N
36.	Bar armor-piercing ammo	?
37.	Tax Overhaul consideratn	N
38.	Make comp emissions known	N
39.	Allow toxic victims suits	N
40.	Strike Superfund "VAT"	N
41.	Notify emp-plant closing	Y
42.	Bar emp consult-plant clo	N
43.	Medicare cuts;Tax incres'	Y
44.	Delete 12 MX missiles	N
45.	Spending cuts;Tax incres'	Y
46.	Textile Import Quotas	Y
47.	Cut some school lunch fds	N
48.	Clean Water Act Amendmnts	N
49.	Youth work projects	Y
50.	Assist military in Angola	Y
51.	Allow US troops-Nicaragua	?
52.	Pentagon polygraph exams	?
53.	Bar ASAT testing	?
54.	Suspend def pmt for abuse	?
55.	Bar Pentagon-contr emplmt	?
56.	Increase SDI funding	Y
57.	Reduce SDI funding	N
58.	Produce chemical weapons	Y
59.	Bar CIA fndg in Nicaragua	N
60.	South Africa sanctions	?
61.	Cut SS COLAs; Raise taxes	Y
62.	Let US invest-So Africa	N
63.	Approve 21 MX for 1985	Y
64.	Emergency Farm Credit	Y
65.	Awards to whistle blowers	Y
66.	African disaster relief	Y
67.	Ban bank loans to So Afr	Y
68.	Bar coun duty-free trtmt	?
69.	Steel import limits	Y
70.	Soc Sec COLAs=inflation	Y
71.	Bar haz waste vctms suits	Y
72.	Prohibit aid to Nicaragua	Y
73.	Cut $-Schs bar sch prayer	Y
74.	Raise taxes; Cut Medicare	Y
75.	Alien residncy-prior 1982	Y
76.	Alien residncy-prior 1980	Y
77.	Pen emp-hire illgl aliens	N
78.	Lmt Persh II/cruse-Europe	?
79.	Delete 34 B-1 bombers	?
80.	Bar purch of Pershing II	N
81.	Bar purchase of Sgt York	N
82.	Delete $ for Trident II	N
83.	Allow 15 MX missiles	Y
84.	Bar MX procurement-1985	N
85.	Equal Access Act	Y
86.	Aid to El Salvador	Y
87.	Bar Nicarag water mining	?
88.	Physician/Medicare freeze	?
89.	Increase "sin" taxes	?
90.	End SBA direct loans	?
91.	Sell Conrail	N
92.	Equal Rights Amendment	Y
93.	Marines in Lebanon	Y
94.	Eminent domain-Coal comps	Y
95.	Prohibit EPA sanctions	?
96.	SS age increase/Reforms	Y
97.	Auto domestic content req	Y
98.	Delete jobs program fundg	?
99.	Highway-Gas tax bill	N
100.	Raise Medicare;Cut defnse	N
101.	Emergency housing aid	Y
102.	Across-the-board tax cuts	N
103.	Gramm-Latta II targets	Y
104.	Delete B-1 bomber funds	N
105.	Dsapprov Saudi AWACS sale	N
106.	Disapprove oil import fee	?
107.	Rail Deregulation	Y
108.	Dsapp India nuc fuel sale	Y
109.	Mil draft registration	Y
110.	Chrysler Loan Guarantees	Y
111.	Prohibit school busing	N
112.	Nuclear plant moratorium	N
113.	Oil price controls	N
114.	Tuition Tax Credits	N
115.	Est Consumer Protect Agcy	N
116.	Eliminate B-1 bomber fnds	N
117.	Subminimum wage for youth	Y
118.	Delete crude oil tax	N
119.	Natural gas deregulation	N

Presidential Support Score: 1986 - 38% 1985 - 40%

BARTLETT, STEVE -- Texas 3rd District [Republican]. Counties of Collin (pt.) and Dallas (pt.). Prior Terms: House: 1983-86. Born: September 19, 1947; Los Angeles, Calif. Education: University of Texas (B.A.). Occupation: Businessman; city councilman (1977-81).

1. Immigration Reform N
2. Open fld-search warrants Y
3. Civil pnty-hire ill alien Y
4. So Afr sanc-veto override N
5. Tax Overhaul N
6. South Africa sanctions N
7. Death penalty-drug bill Y
8. Evidence-warrantless srch Y
9. Life term-second drug off Y
10. Military use in drug war Y
11. Troop reduction in Europe N
12. Prohibit chemical weapons N
13. Bar ASAT testing N
14. Abide SALT II weapons ban N
15. Follow SALT II-Soviets do Y
16. Reduce SDI funding N
17. Increase SDI funding Y
18. Purchase Trident sub N
19. Delete 12 MX;Add conv wpn N
20. Raise speed limit Y
21. Textile Import Quotas(*) N
22. Req Pentagon buy US goods N
23. AIDS ins anti-dscriminatn N
24. Nicaraguan refugee aid N
25. Nicaraguan contra aid Y
26. US abide by SALT II Y
27. Prohibit Saudi arms sale N
28. Military Retiremnt Reform Y
29. Nicaraguan refugee aid Y
30. Ease '68 Gun Control Act Y
31. Bar intrstat handgun tran N
32. Keep '68 Gun Control Act N
33. Nicaraguan contra aid Y
34. Bar emp polygraph testing N
35. Tax Overhaul consideratn N
36. Bar armor-piercing ammo Y
37. Tax Overhaul consideratn N
38. Make comp emissions known N
39. Allow toxic victims suits N
40. Strike Superfund "VAT" N
41. Notify emp-plant closing N
42. Bar emp consult-plant clo Y
43. Medicare cuts;Tax incres' N
44. Delete 12 MX missiles N
45. Spending cuts;Tax incres' N
46. Textile Import Quotas N
47. Cut some school lunch fds Y
48. Clean Water Act Amendmnts Y
49. Youth work projects N
50. Assist military in Angola Y
51. Allow US troops-Nicaragua Y
52. Pentagon polygraph exams Y
53. Bar ASAT testing N
54. Suspend def pmt for abuse N
55. Bar Pentagon-contr emplmt Y
56. Increase SDI funding Y
57. Reduce SDI funding N
58. Produce chemical weapons Y
59. Bar CIA fndg in Nicaragua N
60. South Africa sanctions N
61. Cut SS COLAs; Raise taxes N
62. Let US invest-So Africa Y
63. Approve 21 MX for 1985 Y
64. Emergency Farm Credit N
65. Awards to whistle blowers Y
66. African disaster relief Y
67. Ban bank loans to So Afr Y
68. Bar coun duty-free trtmt N
69. Steel import limits Y
70. Soc Sec COLAs=inflation Y
71. Bar haz waste vctms suits Y
72. Prohibit aid to Nicaragua N
73. Cut $-Schs bar sch prayer Y
74. Raise taxes; Cut Medicare Y
75. Alien residncy-prior 1982 Y
76. Alien residncy-prior 1980 Y
77. Pen emp-hire illgl aliens N
78. Lmt Persh II/cruse-Europe N
79. Delete 34 B-1 bombers N
80. Bar purch of Pershing II N
81. Bar purchase of Sgt York N
82. Delete $ for Trident II N
83. Allow 15 MX missiles Y
84. Bar MX procurement-1985 N
85. Equal Access Act Y
86. Aid to El Salvador Y
87. Bar Nicarag water mining N
88. Physician/Medicare freeze Y
89. Increase "sin" taxes Y
90. End SBA direct loans Y
91. Sell Conrail Y
92. Equal Rights Amendment N
93. Marines in Lebanon Y
94. Eminent domain-Coal comps Y
95. Prohibit EPA sanctions Y
96. SS age increase/Reforms Y

Presidential Support Score: 1986 - 78% 1985 - 89%

HALL, RALPH M. -- Texas 4th District [Democrat]. Counties of Collin (pt.), Fannin, Grayson, Gregg, Hunt (pt.), Kaufman, Rains, Rockwall, Smith, Van Zandt and Wood. Prior Terms:

HALL, RALPH M. (Cont.)

House: 1981-86. Born: May 3, 1923; Fate, Texas. Education: University of Texas; Texas Christian University; Southern Methodist University (LL.B.). Military Service: U.S. Navy, 1942-45. Occupation: Attorney; Rockwall County judge (1950-62); Texas senator (1962-72); president and chief executive officer, Texas Aluminum Corp.; general counsel, Texas Extrusion Co., Inc.; banker; board chairman, Lakeside News, Inc.

No.	Issue	Vote
1.	Immigration Reform	N
2.	Open fld-search warrants	Y
3.	Civil pnty-hire ill alien	N
4.	So Afr sanc-veto override	?
5.	Tax Overhaul	N
6.	South Africa sanctions	N
7.	Death penalty-drug bill	Y
8.	Evidence-warrantless srch	Y
9.	Life term-second drug off	Y
10.	Military use in drug war	Y
11.	Troop reduction in Europe	Y
12.	Prohibit chemical weapons	N
13.	Bar ASAT testing	N
14.	Abide SALT II weapons ban	N
15.	Follow SALT II-Soviets do	Y
16.	Reduce SDI funding	N
17.	Increase SDI funding	Y
18.	Purchase Trident sub	N
19.	Delete 12 MX;Add conv wpn	N
20.	Raise speed limit	Y
21.	Textile Import Quotas(*)	Y
22.	Req Pentagon buy US goods	Y
23.	AIDS ins anti-dscriminatn	N
24.	Nicaraguan refugee aid	N
25.	Nicaraguan contra aid	Y
26.	US abide by SALT II	Y
27.	Prohibit Saudi arms sale	Y
28.	Military Retiremnt Reform	Y
29.	Nicaraguan refugee aid	N
30.	Ease '68 Gun Control Act	Y
31.	Bar intrstat handgun tran	N
32.	Keep '68 Gun Control Act	N
33.	Nicaraguan contra aid	Y
34.	Bar emp polygraph testing	?
35.	Tax Overhaul consideratn	N
36.	Bar armor-piercing ammo	Y
37.	Tax Overhaul consideratn	Y
38.	Make comp emissions known	N
39.	Allow toxic victims suits	N
40.	Strike Superfund "VAT"	N
41.	Notify emp-plant closing	N
42.	Bar emp consult-plant clo	Y
43.	Medicare cuts;Tax incres'	N
44.	Delete 12 MX missiles	N
45.	Spending cuts;Tax incres'	Y
46.	Textile Import Quotas	Y
47.	Cut some school lunch fds	Y
48.	Clean Water Act Amendmnts	Y
49.	Youth work projects	?
50.	Assist military in Angola	Y
51.	Allow US troops-Nicaragua	Y
52.	Pentagon polygraph exams	Y
53.	Bar ASAT testing	N
54.	Suspend def pmt for abuse	N
55.	Bar Pentagon-contr emplmt	Y
56.	Increase SDI funding	Y
57.	Reduce SDI funding	N
58.	Produce chemical weapons	Y
59.	Bar CIA fndg in Nicaragua	N
60.	South Africa sanctions	N
61.	Cut SS COLAs; Raise taxes	N
62.	Let US invest-So Africa	N
63.	Approve 21 MX for 1985	Y
64.	Emergency Farm Credit	Y
65.	Awards to whistle blowers	Y
66.	African disaster relief	N
67.	Ban bank loans to So Afr	N
68.	Bar coun duty-free trtmt	N
69.	Steel import limits	Y
70.	Soc Sec COLAs=inflation	Y
71.	Bar haz waste vctms suits	N
72.	Prohibit aid to Nicaragua	N
73.	Cut $-Schs bar sch prayer	Y
74.	Raise taxes; Cut Medicare	N
75.	Alien residncy-prior 1982	N
76.	Alien residncy-prior 1980	N
77.	Pen emp-hire illgl aliens	N
78.	Lmt Persh II/cruse-Europe	N
79.	Delete 34 B-1 bombers	N
80.	Bar purch of Pershing II	N
81.	Bar purchase of Sgt York	N
82.	Delete $ for Trident II	N
83.	Allow 15 MX missiles	Y
84.	Bar MX procurement-1985	N
85.	Equal Access Act	Y
86.	Aid to El Salvador	Y
87.	Bar Nicarag water mining	N
88.	Physician/Medicare freeze	Y
89.	Increase "sin" taxes	N
90.	End SBA direct loans	N
91.	Sell Conrail	Y
92.	Equal Rights Amendment	Y
93.	Marines in Lebanon	N
94.	Eminent domain-Coal comps	N
95.	Prohibit EPA sanctions	Y
96.	SS age increase/Reforms	Y
97.	Auto domestic content req	Y
98.	Delete jobs program fundg	N
99.	Highway-Gas tax bill	N
100.	Raise Medicare;Cut defnse	N
101.	Emergency housing aid	Y
102.	Across-the-board tax cuts	Y

HALL, RALPH M. (Cont.)

103. Gramm-Latta II targets	Y		105. Dsapprov Saudi AWACS sale	Y
104. Delete B-1 bomber funds	N			

Presidential Support Score: 1986 - 56% 1985 - 58%

BRYANT, JOHN -- Texas 5th District [Democrat]. County of Dallas (pt.). Prior Terms: House: 1983-86. Born: February 22, 1947; Lake Jackson, Texas. Education: Southern Methodist University (B.A., J.D.). Occupation: Attorney; chief counsel, Texas Senate subcommittee on Consumer Affairs; administrative assistant, Texas Senate; Texas representative.

1. Immigration Reform	Y	48. Clean Water Act Amendmnts	N
2. Open fld-search warrants	N	49. Youth work projects	Y
3. Civil pnty-hire ill alien	N	50. Assist military in Angola	N
4. So Afr sanc-veto override	Y	51. Allow US troops-Nicaragua	N
5. Tax Overhaul	N	52. Pentagon polygraph exams	Y
6. South Africa sanctions	Y	53. Bar ASAT testing	Y
7. Death penalty-drug bill	Y	54. Suspend def pmt for abuse	Y
8. Evidence-warrantless srch	Y	55. Bar Pentagon-contr emplmt	Y
9. Life term-second drug off	Y	56. Increase SDI funding	N
10. Military use in drug war	Y	57. Reduce SDI funding	N
11. Troop reduction in Europe	Y	58. Produce chemical weapons	Y
12. Prohibit chemical weapons	Y	59. Bar CIA fndg in Nicaragua	Y
13. Bar ASAT testing	Y	60. South Africa sanctions	Y
14. Abide SALT II weapons ban	Y	61. Cut SS COLAs; Raise taxes	N
15. Follow SALT II-Soviets do	N	62. Let US invest-So Africa	N
16. Reduce SDI funding	Y	63. Approve 21 MX for 1985	N
17. Increase SDI funding	N	64. Emergency Farm Credit	Y
18. Purchase Trident sub	Y	65. Awards to whistle blowers	Y
19. Delete 12 MX;Add conv wpn	Y	66. African disaster relief	Y
20. Raise speed limit	N	67. Ban bank loans to So Afr	Y
21. Textile Import Quotas(*)	Y	68. Bar coun duty-free trtmt	Y
22. Req Pentagon buy US goods	Y	69. Steel import limits	Y
23. AIDS ins anti-dscriminatn	Y	70. Soc Sec COLAs=inflation	Y
24. Nicaraguan refugee aid	Y	71. Bar haz waste vctms suits	N
25. Nicaraguan contra aid	N	72. Prohibit aid to Nicaragua	Y
26. US abide by SALT II	N	73. Cut $-Schs bar sch prayer	N
27. Prohibit Saudi arms sale	Y	74. Raise taxes; Cut Medicare	Y
28. Military Retiremnt Reform	Y	75. Alien residncy-prior 1982	N
29. Nicaraguan refugee aid	Y	76. Alien residncy-prior 1980	Y
30. Ease '68 Gun Control Act	Y	77. Pen emp-hire illgl aliens	Y
31. Bar intrstat handgun tran	N	78. Lmt Persh II/cruse-Europe	?
32. Keep '68 Gun Control Act	N	79. Delete 34 B-1 bombers	N
33. Nicaraguan contra aid	N	80. Bar purch of Pershing II	N
34. Bar emp polygraph testing	Y	81. Bar purchase of Sgt York	N
35. Tax Overhaul consideratn	N	82. Delete $ for Trident II	N
36. Bar armor-piercing ammo	Y	83. Allow 15 MX missiles	N
37. Tax Overhaul consideratn	N	84. Bar MX procurement-1985	Y
38. Make comp emissions known	Y	85. Equal Access Act	N
39. Allow toxic victims suits	Y	86. Aid to El Salvador	N
40. Strike Superfund "VAT"	N	87. Bar Nicarag water mining	Y
41. Notify emp-plant closing	Y	88. Physician/Medicare freeze	N
42. Bar emp consult-plant clo	N	89. Increase "sin" taxes	Y
43. Medicare cuts;Tax incres'	Y	90. End SBA direct loans	N
44. Delete 12 MX missiles	Y	91. Sell Conrail	N
45. Spending cuts;Tax incres'	Y	92. Equal Rights Amendment	Y
46. Textile Import Quotas	Y	93. Marines in Lebanon	N
47. Cut some school lunch fds	N	94. Eminent domain-Coal comps	N

BRYANT, JOHN (Cont.)

95. Prohibit EPA sanctions	Y	96. SS age increase/Reforms	N

Presidential Support Score: 1986 - 17% 1985 - 23%

BARTON, JOE -- Texas 6th District [Republican]. Counties of Brazos, Ellis, Freestone, Grimes, Hill, Hood, Johnston, Leon, Limestone, Madison, Navarro, Robertson, Dallas (pt.) and Montgomery (pt.). Prior Terms: 1985-86. Education: Texas A&M (B.S.); Purdue University (M.S.). Occupation: Engineer and consultant, major oil corp.

1. Immigration Reform	N	34. Bar emp polygraph testing	N
2. Open fld-search warrants	N	35. Tax Overhaul consideratn	N
3. Civil pnty-hire ill alien	Y	36. Bar armor-piercing ammo	Y
4. So Afr sanc-veto override	N	37. Tax Overhaul consideratn	N
5. Tax Overhaul	Y	38. Make comp emissions known	N
6. South Africa sanctions	N	39. Allow toxic victims suits	N
7. Death penalty-drug bill	Y	40. Strike Superfund "VAT"	N
8. Evidence-warrantless srch	Y	41. Notify emp-plant closing	N
9. Life term-second drug off	Y	42. Bar emp consult-plant clo	Y
10. Military use in drug war	Y	43. Medicare cuts;Tax incres'	N
11. Troop reduction in Europe	N	44. Delete 12 MX missiles	N
12. Prohibit chemical weapons	N	45. Spending cuts;Tax incres'	N
13. Bar ASAT testing	N	46. Textile Import Quotas	N
14. Abide SALT II weapons ban	N	47. Cut some school lunch fds	Y
15. Follow SALT II-Soviets do	Y	48. Clean Water Act Amendmnts	Y
16. Reduce SDI funding	N	49. Youth work projects	N
17. Increase SDI funding	Y	50. Assist military in Angola	Y
18. Purchase Trident sub	N	51. Allow US troops-Nicaragua	Y
19. Delete 12 MX;Add conv wpn	N	52. Pentagon polygraph exams	Y
20. Raise speed limit	Y	53. Bar ASAT testing	N
21. Textile Import Quotas(*)	N	54. Suspend def pmt for abuse	N
22. Req Pentagon buy US goods	N	55. Bar Pentagon-contr emplmt	Y
23. AIDS ins anti-dscriminatn	N	56. Increase SDI funding	Y
24. Nicaraguan refugee aid	N	57. Reduce SDI funding	N
25. Nicaraguan contra aid	Y	58. Produce chemical weapons	Y
26. US abide by SALT II	?	59. Bar CIA fndg in Nicaragua	N
27. Prohibit Saudi arms sale	Y	60. South Africa sanctions	N
28. Military Retiremnt Reform	Y	61. Cut SS COLAs; Raise taxes	N
29. Nicaraguan refugee aid	Y	62. Let US invest-So Africa	Y
30. Ease '68 Gun Control Act	Y	63. Approve 21 MX for 1985	Y
31. Bar intrstat handgun tran	N	64. Emergency Farm Credit	N
32. Keep '68 Gun Control Act	N	65. Awards to whistle blowers	Y
33. Nicaraguan contra aid	Y	66. African disaster relief	N

Presidential Support Score: 1986 - 75% 1985 - 85%

ARCHER, BILL -- Texas 7th District [Republican]. County of Harris (pt.). Prior Terms: House: 1971-86. Born: March 22, 1928; Houston, Texas. Education: Rice University; University of Texas (B.B.A, LL.B.). Military Service: U.S. Air Force. Occupation: President, Uncle Johnny Mills, Inc. (1953-61); attorney, Harris, Archer, Parks and Graul; Texas representative (1966-70).

1. Immigration Reform	N	5. Tax Overhaul	N
2. Open fld-search warrants	Y	6. South Africa sanctions	N
3. Civil pnty-hire ill alien	Y	7. Death penalty-drug bill	Y
4. So Afr sanc-veto override	N	8. Evidence-warrantless srch	Y

ARCHER, BILL (Cont.)

9. Life term-second drug off Y
10. Military use in drug war Y
11. Troop reduction in Europe N
12. Prohibit chemical weapons N
13. Bar ASAT testing N
14. Abide SALT II weapons ban N
15. Follow SALT II-Soviets do Y
16. Reduce SDI funding N
17. Increase SDI funding Y
18. Purchase Trident sub N
19. Delete 12 MX;Add conv wpn N
20. Raise speed limit Y
21. Textile Import Quotas(*) N
22. Req Pentagon buy US goods N
23. AIDS ins anti-dscriminatn N
24. Nicaraguan refugee aid N
25. Nicaraguan contra aid Y
26. US abide by SALT II Y
27. Prohibit Saudi arms sale Y
28. Military Retiremnt Reform Y
29. Nicaraguan refugee aid Y
30. Ease '68 Gun Control Act Y
31. Bar intrstat handgun tran N
32. Keep '68 Gun Control Act N
33. Nicaraguan contra aid Y
34. Bar emp polygraph testing N
35. Tax Overhaul consideratn N
36. Bar armor-piercing ammo Y
37. Tax Overhaul consideratn N
38. Make comp emissions known N
39. Allow toxic victims suits N
40. Strike Superfund "VAT" N
41. Notify emp-plant closing X
42. Bar emp consult-plant clo Y
43. Medicare cuts;Tax incres' N
44. Delete 12 MX missiles N
45. Spending cuts;Tax incres' N
46. Textile Import Quotas N
47. Cut some school lunch fds Y
48. Clean Water Act Amendmnts Y
49. Youth work projects N
50. Assist military in Angola Y
51. Allow US troops-Nicaragua Y
52. Pentagon polygraph exams Y
53. Bar ASAT testing N
54. Suspend def pmt for abuse N
55. Bar Pentagon-contr emplmt Y
56. Increase SDI funding Y
57. Reduce SDI funding N
58. Produce chemical weapons Y
59. Bar CIA fndg in Nicaragua N
60. South Africa sanctions N
61. Cut SS COLAs; Raise taxes N
62. Let US invest-So Africa Y
63. Approve 21 MX for 1985 Y
64. Emergency Farm Credit N
65. Awards to whistle blowers Y
66. African disaster relief N
67. Ban bank loans to So Afr Y
68. Bar coun duty-free trtmt N
69. Steel import limits N
70. Soc Sec COLAs=inflation Y
71. Bar haz waste vctms suits Y
72. Prohibit aid to Nicaragua N
73. Cut $-Schs bar sch prayer Y
74. Raise taxes; Cut Medicare N
75. Alien residncy-prior 1982 N
76. Alien residncy-prior 1980 N
77. Pen emp-hire illgl aliens N
78. Lmt Persh II/cruse-Europe N
79. Delete 34 B-1 bombers N
80. Bar purch of Pershing II N
81. Bar purchase of Sgt York N
82. Delete $ for Trident II N
83. Allow 15 MX missiles Y
84. Bar MX procurement-1985 N
85. Equal Access Act Y
86. Aid to El Salvador Y
87. Bar Nicarag water mining N
88. Physician/Medicare freeze Y
89. Increase "sin" taxes N
90. End SBA direct loans Y
91. Sell Conrail Y
92. Equal Rights Amendment N
93. Marines in Lebanon N
94. Eminent domain-Coal comps Y
95. Prohibit EPA sanctions Y
96. SS age increase/Reforms Y
97. Auto domestic content req N
98. Delete jobs program fundg Y
99. Highway-Gas tax bill Y
100. Raise Medicare;Cut defnse N
101. Emergency housing aid Y
102. Across-the-board tax cuts Y
103. Gramm-Latta II targets Y
104. Delete B-1 bomber funds N
105. Dsapprov Saudi AWACS sale Y
106. Disapprove oil import fee Y
107. Rail Deregulation N
108. Dsapp India nuc fuel sale Y
109. Mil draft registration Y
110. Chrysler Loan Guarantees N
111. Prohibit school busing Y
112. Nuclear plant moratorium N
113. Oil price controls N
114. Tuition Tax Credits Y
115. Est Consumer Protect Agcy N
116. Eliminate B-1 bomber fnds N
117. Subminimum wage for youth Y
118. Delete crude oil tax Y
119. Natural gas deregulation Y

Presidential Support Score: 1986 - 83% 1985 - 88%

FIELDS, JACK -- Texas 8th District [Republican]. Counties of Harris (pt.) and Montgomery (pt.). Prior Terms: House: 1981-86. Born: February 3, 1952; Humble, Texas. Education: Baylor University (B.A., J.D.). Occupation: Attorney; executive vice president, Rosewood Memorial Park; executive board member, Humble-Northeast Medical Center; executive board member, Small Business Advisory Assistance Council; Humble Chamber of Commerce chairman.

1. Immigration Reform N
2. Open fld-search warrants Y
3. Civil pnty-hire ill alien Y
4. So Afr sanc-veto override N
5. Tax Overhaul N
6. South Africa sanctions N
7. Death penalty-drug bill Y
8. Evidence-warrantless srch Y
9. Life term-second drug off Y
10. Military use in drug war Y
11. Troop reduction in Europe N
12. Prohibit chemical weapons N
13. Bar ASAT testing N
14. Abide SALT II weapons ban N
15. Follow SALT II-Soviets do Y
16. Reduce SDI funding N
17. Increase SDI funding Y
18. Purchase Trident sub N
19. Delete 12 MX;Add conv wpn N
20. Raise speed limit Y
21. Textile Import Quotas(*) N
22. Req Pentagon buy US goods N
23. AIDS ins anti-dscriminatn N
24. Nicaraguan refugee aid N
25. Nicaraguan contra aid Y
26. US abide by SALT II Y
27. Prohibit Saudi arms sale Y
28. Military Retiremnt Reform Y
29. Nicaraguan refugee aid Y
30. Ease '68 Gun Control Act Y
31. Bar intrstat handgun tran N
32. Keep '68 Gun Control Act N
33. Nicaraguan contra aid Y
34. Bar emp polygraph testing N
35. Tax Overhaul consideratn N
36. Bar armor-piercing ammo N
37. Tax Overhaul consideratn N
38. Make comp emissions known N
39. Allow toxic victims suits N
40. Strike Superfund "VAT" N
41. Notify emp-plant closing N
42. Bar emp consult-plant clo Y
43. Medicare cuts;Tax incres' N
44. Delete 12 MX missiles N
45. Spending cuts;Tax incres' N
46. Textile Import Quotas N
47. Cut some school lunch fds Y
48. Clean Water Act Amendmnts Y
49. Youth work projects N
50. Assist military in Angola Y
51. Allow US troops-Nicaragua Y
52. Pentagon polygraph exams Y
53. Bar ASAT testing N
54. Suspend def pmt for abuse N
55. Bar Pentagon-contr emplmt Y
56. Increase SDI funding Y
57. Reduce SDI funding N
58. Produce chemical weapons Y
59. Bar CIA fndg in Nicaragua N
60. South Africa sanctions N
61. Cut SS COLAs; Raise taxes N
62. Let US invest-So Africa Y
63. Approve 21 MX for 1985 Y
64. Emergency Farm Credit N
65. Awards to whistle blowers Y
66. African disaster relief N
67. Ban bank loans to So Afr Y
68. Bar coun duty-free trtmt N
69. Steel import limits Y
70. Soc Sec COLAs=inflation Y
71. Bar haz waste vctms suits Y
72. Prohibit aid to Nicaragua N
73. Cut $-Schs bar sch prayer Y
74. Raise taxes; Cut Medicare N
75. Alien residncy-prior 1982 N
76. Alien residncy-prior 1980 N
77. Pen emp-hire illgl aliens N
78. Lmt Persh II/cruse-Europe N
79. Delete 34 B-1 bombers N
80. Bar purch of Pershing II N
81. Bar purchase of Sgt York N
82. Delete $ for Trident II N
83. Allow 15 MX missiles Y
84. Bar MX procurement-1985 N
85. Equal Access Act Y
86. Aid to El Salvador Y
87. Bar Nicarag water mining N
88. Physician/Medicare freeze Y
89. Increase "sin" taxes N
90. End SBA direct loans Y
91. Sell Conrail Y
92. Equal Rights Amendment N
93. Marines in Lebanon N
94. Eminent domain-Coal comps Y
95. Prohibit EPA sanctions Y
96. SS age increase/Reforms Y
97. Auto domestic content req N
98. Delete jobs program fundg Y
99. Highway-Gas tax bill Y
100. Raise Medicare;Cut defnse N
101. Emergency housing aid Y
102. Across-the-board tax cuts Y

FIELDS, JACK (Cont.)

103. Gramm-Latta II targets Y
104. Delete B-1 bomber funds N
105. Dsapprov Saudi AWACS sale Y

Presidential Support Score: 1986 - 80% 1985 - 74%

BROOKS, JACK -- Texas 9th District [Democrat]. Counties of Chambers, Galveston, Harris (pt.) and Jefferson. Prior Terms: House: 1953-86. Born: December 18, 1922; Crowley, La. Education: University of Texas (B.J., J.D.). Military Service: U.S. Marine Corps, WW II. Occupation: Texas legislator (1946-50).

1. Immigration Reform ?
2. Open fld-search warrants ?
3. Civil pnty-hire ill alien ?
4. So Afr sanc-veto override Y
5. Tax Overhaul N
6. South Africa sanctions ?
7. Death penalty-drug bill Y
8. Evidence-warrantless srch N
9. Life term-second drug off Y
10. Military use in drug war N
11. Troop reduction in Europe N
12. Prohibit chemical weapons Y
13. Bar ASAT testing Y
14. Abide SALT II weapons ban Y
15. Follow SALT II-Soviets do N
16. Reduce SDI funding Y
17. Increase SDI funding N
18. Purchase Trident sub Y
19. Delete 12 MX;Add conv wpn Y
20. Raise speed limit N
21. Textile Import Quotas(*) Y
22. Req Pentagon buy US goods Y
23. AIDS ins anti-dscriminatn Y
24. Nicaraguan refugee aid Y
25. Nicaraguan contra aid N
26. US abide by SALT II N
27. Prohibit Saudi arms sale Y
28. Military Retiremnt Reform Y
29. Nicaraguan refugee aid Y
30. Ease '68 Gun Control Act Y
31. Bar intrstat handgun tran N
32. Keep '68 Gun Control Act N
33. Nicaraguan contra aid N
34. Bar emp polygraph testing Y
35. Tax Overhaul consideratn N
36. Bar armor-piercing ammo Y
37. Tax Overhaul consideratn ?
38. Make comp emissions known ?
39. Allow toxic victims suits ?
40. Strike Superfund "VAT" X
41. Notify emp-plant closing Y
42. Bar emp consult-plant clo N
43. Medicare cuts;Tax incres' Y
44. Delete 12 MX missiles N
45. Spending cuts;Tax incres' Y
46. Textile Import Quotas Y
47. Cut some school lunch fds N
48. Clean Water Act Amendmnts N
49. Youth work projects Y
50. Assist military in Angola N
51. Allow US troops-Nicaragua N
52. Pentagon polygraph exams N
53. Bar ASAT testing Y
54. Suspend def pmt for abuse N
55. Bar Pentagon-contr emplmt Y
56. Increase SDI funding N
57. Reduce SDI funding N
58. Produce chemical weapons Y
59. Bar CIA fndg in Nicaragua Y
60. South Africa sanctions Y
61. Cut SS COLAs; Raise taxes N
62. Let US invest-So Africa N
63. Approve 21 MX for 1985 N
64. Emergency Farm Credit Y
65. Awards to whistle blowers Y
66. African disaster relief ?
67. Ban bank loans to So Afr Y
68. Bar coun duty-free trtmt Y
69. Steel import limits Y
70. Soc Sec COLAs=inflation Y
71. Bar haz waste vctms suits Y
72. Prohibit aid to Nicaragua Y
73. Cut $-Schs bar sch prayer N
74. Raise taxes; Cut Medicare +
75. Alien residncy-prior 1982 Y
76. Alien residncy-prior 1980 N
77. Pen emp-hire illgl aliens Y
78. Lmt Persh II/cruse-Europe N
79. Delete 34 B-1 bombers Y
80. Bar purch of Pershing II N
81. Bar purchase of Sgt York N
82. Delete $ for Trident II N
83. Allow 15 MX missiles N
84. Bar MX procurement-1985 Y
85. Equal Access Act Y
86. Aid to El Salvador N
87. Bar Nicarag water mining Y
88. Physician/Medicare freeze N
89. Increase "sin" taxes Y
90. End SBA direct loans N
91. Sell Conrail N
92. Equal Rights Amendment Y
93. Marines in Lebanon N
94. Eminent domain-Coal comps #

BROOKS, JACK (Cont.)

95. Prohibit EPA sanctions Y
96. SS age increase/Reforms Y
97. Auto domestic content req Y
98. Delete jobs program fundg N
99. Highway-Gas tax bill Y
100. Raise Medicare;Cut defnse N
101. Emergency housing aid Y
102. Across-the-board tax cuts N
103. Gramm-Latta II targets N
104. Delete B-1 bomber funds Y
105. Dsapprov Saudi AWACS sale ?
106. Disapprove oil import fee ?
107. Rail Deregulation Y
108. Dsapp India nuc fuel sale N
109. Mil draft registration ?
110. Chrysler Loan Guarantees ?
111. Prohibit school busing N
112. Nuclear plant moratorium N
113. Oil price controls N
114. Tuition Tax Credits Y
115. Est Consumer Protect Agcy Y
116. Eliminate B-1 bomber fnds Y
117. Subminimum wage for youth Y
118. Delete crude oil tax Y
119. Natural gas deregulation Y

Presidential Support Score: 1986 - 22% 1985 - 24%

PICKLE, J. J. -- Texas 10th District [Democrat]. Counties of Bastrop, Blanco, Burnet (pt.), Caldwell, Hays and Travis. Prior Terms: House: 1963 (Special Election)-1986. Born: October 11, 1913; Roscoe, Texas. Education: University of Texas (B.A.). Military Service: U.S. Navy, WW II. Occupation: Area director, National Youth Administration (1938-41); radio station organizer; public relations businessman; advertising businessman; member, Texas Employment Commission (1961-63).

1. Immigration Reform Y
2. Open fld-search warrants Y
3. Civil pnty-hire ill alien Y
4. So Afr sanc-veto override Y
5. Tax Overhaul Y
6. South Africa sanctions Y
7. Death penalty-drug bill Y
8. Evidence-warrantless srch Y
9. Life term-second drug off Y
10. Military use in drug war Y
11. Troop reduction in Europe N
12. Prohibit chemical weapons Y
13. Bar ASAT testing Y
14. Abide SALT II weapons ban N
15. Follow SALT II-Soviets do Y
16. Reduce SDI funding N
17. Increase SDI funding N
18. Purchase Trident sub N
19. Delete 12 MX;Add conv wpn N
20. Raise speed limit Y
21. Textile Import Quotas(*) N
22. Req Pentagon buy US goods Y
23. AIDS ins anti-dscriminatn Y
24. Nicaraguan refugee aid N
25. Nicaraguan contra aid N
26. US abide by SALT II Y
27. Prohibit Saudi arms sale Y
28. Military Retiremnt Reform Y
29. Nicaraguan refugee aid N
30. Ease '68 Gun Control Act Y
31. Bar intrstat handgun tran Y
32. Keep '68 Gun Control Act N
33. Nicaraguan contra aid N
34. Bar emp polygraph testing Y
35. Tax Overhaul consideratn Y
36. Bar armor-piercing ammo Y
37. Tax Overhaul consideratn Y
38. Make comp emissions known Y
39. Allow toxic victims suits Y
40. Strike Superfund "VAT" N
41. Notify emp-plant closing N
42. Bar emp consult-plant clo Y
43. Medicare cuts;Tax incres' Y
44. Delete 12 MX missiles Y
45. Spending cuts;Tax incres' Y
46. Textile Import Quotas N
47. Cut some school lunch fds N
48. Clean Water Act Amendmnts N
49. Youth work projects Y
50. Assist military in Angola Y
51. Allow US troops-Nicaragua N
52. Pentagon polygraph exams Y
53. Bar ASAT testing Y
54. Suspend def pmt for abuse N
55. Bar Pentagon-contr emplmt Y
56. Increase SDI funding N
57. Reduce SDI funding N
58. Produce chemical weapons N
59. Bar CIA fndg in Nicaragua Y
60. South Africa sanctions Y
61. Cut SS COLAs; Raise taxes Y
62. Let US invest-So Africa N
63. Approve 21 MX for 1985 N
64. Emergency Farm Credit Y
65. Awards to whistle blowers Y
66. African disaster relief Y
67. Ban bank loans to So Afr ?
68. Bar coun duty-free trtmt N

PICKLE, J. J. (Cont.)

69. Steel import limits Y
70. Soc Sec COLAs=inflation Y
71. Bar haz waste vctms suits Y
72. Prohibit aid to Nicaragua Y
73. Cut $-Schs bar sch prayer N
74. Raise taxes; Cut Medicare Y
75. Alien residncy-prior 1982 Y
76. Alien residncy-prior 1980 N
77. Pen emp-hire illgl aliens N
78. Lmt Persh II/cruse-Europe N
79. Delete 34 B-1 bombers N
80. Bar purch of Pershing II N
81. Bar purchase of Sgt York N
82. Delete $ for Trident II N
83. Allow 15 MX missiles Y
84. Bar MX procurement-1985 N
85. Equal Access Act Y
86. Aid to El Salvador Y
87. Bar Nicarag water mining Y
88. Physician/Medicare freeze N
89. Increase "sin" taxes Y
90. End SBA direct loans N
91. Sell Conrail ?
92. Equal Rights Amendment Y
93. Marines in Lebanon Y
94. Eminent domain-Coal comps Y
95. Prohibit EPA sanctions N
96. SS age increase/Reforms Y
97. Auto domestic content req N
98. Delete jobs program fundg N
99. Highway-Gas tax bill Y
100. Raise Medicare;Cut defnse Y
101. Emergency housing aid Y
102. Across-the-board tax cuts N
103. Gramm-Latta II targets N
104. Delete B-1 bomber funds N
105. Dsapprov Saudi AWACS sale Y
106. Disapprove oil import fee Y
107. Rail Deregulation Y
108. Dsapp India nuc fuel sale N
109. Mil draft registration ?
110. Chrysler Loan Guarantees Y
111. Prohibit school busing Y
112. Nuclear plant moratorium N
113. Oil price controls N
114. Tuition Tax Credits N
115. Est Consumer Protect Agcy Y
116. Eliminate B-1 bomber fnds N
117. Subminimum wage for youth N
118. Delete crude oil tax Y
119. Natural gas deregulation Y

Presidential Support Score: 1986 - 39% 1985 - 40%

LEATH, MARVIN -- Texas 11th District [Democrat]. Counties of Bell, Bosque, Brown, Burnet (pt.), Coryell, Falls, Hamilton, Lampasas, McLennon, Milam, Mills, San Saba and Williamson (pt.). Prior Terms: House: 1979-86. Born: May 6, 1931; Henderson, Texas. Education: University of Texas. Military Service: U.S. Army, 1954-56. Occupation: Teacher; officer and director, Marlin First State Bank; congressional assistant (1972-74); founder, Central National Bank (1975); vice-president and director, Wilson Building Materials Co., Inc.

1. Immigration Reform N
2. Open fld-search warrants ?
3. Civil pnty-hire ill alien Y
4. So Afr sanc-veto override Y
5. Tax Overhaul N
6. South Africa sanctions Y
7. Death penalty-drug bill Y
8. Evidence-warrantless srch Y
9. Life term-second drug off Y
10. Military use in drug war N
11. Troop reduction in Europe N
12. Prohibit chemical weapons N
13. Bar ASAT testing N
14. Abide SALT II weapons ban Y
15. Follow SALT II-Soviets do N
16. Reduce SDI funding N
17. Increase SDI funding N
18. Purchase Trident sub N
19. Delete 12 MX;Add conv wpn N
20. Raise speed limit Y
21. Textile Import Quotas(*) Y
22. Req Pentagon buy US goods Y
23. AIDS ins anti-dscriminatn Y
24. Nicaraguan refugee aid N
25. Nicaraguan contra aid Y
26. US abide by SALT II Y
27. Prohibit Saudi arms sale Y
28. Military Retiremnt Reform Y
29. Nicaraguan refugee aid N
30. Ease '68 Gun Control Act Y
31. Bar intrstat handgun tran N
32. Keep '68 Gun Control Act N
33. Nicaraguan contra aid Y
34. Bar emp polygraph testing N
35. Tax Overhaul consideratn N
36. Bar armor-piercing ammo Y
37. Tax Overhaul consideratn N
38. Make comp emissions known N
39. Allow toxic victims suits N
40. Strike Superfund "VAT" N

LEATH, MARVIN (Cont.)

41.	Notify emp-plant closing	N	78.	Lmt Persh II/cruse-Europe	?
42.	Bar emp consult-plant clo	Y	79.	Delete 34 B-1 bombers	N
43.	Medicare cuts;Tax incres'	Y	80.	Bar purch of Pershing II	N
44.	Delete 12 MX missiles	N	81.	Bar purchase of Sgt York	N
45.	Spending cuts;Tax incres'	Y	82.	Delete $ for Trident II	N
46.	Textile Import Quotas	Y	83.	Allow 15 MX missiles	Y
47.	Cut some school lunch fds	Y	84.	Bar MX procurement-1985	N
48.	Clean Water Act Amendmnts	Y	85.	Equal Access Act	Y
49.	Youth work projects	N	86.	Aid to El Salvador	Y
50.	Assist military in Angola	Y	87.	Bar Nicarag water mining	N
51.	Allow US troops-Nicaragua	Y	88.	Physician/Medicare freeze	Y
52.	Pentagon polygraph exams	Y	89.	Increase "sin" taxes	N
53.	Bar ASAT testing	N	90.	End SBA direct loans	?
54.	Suspend def pmt for abuse	N	91.	Sell Conrail	Y
55.	Bar Pentagon-contr emplmt	Y	92.	Equal Rights Amendment	N
56.	Increase SDI funding	N	93.	Marines in Lebanon	Y
57.	Reduce SDI funding	N	94.	Eminent domain-Coal comps	Y
58.	Produce chemical weapons	Y	95.	Prohibit EPA sanctions	Y
59.	Bar CIA fndg in Nicaragua	N	96.	SS age increase/Reforms	Y
60.	South Africa sanctions	N	97.	Auto domestic content req	N
61.	Cut SS COLAs; Raise taxes	Y	98.	Delete jobs program fundg	N
62.	Let US invest-So Africa	N	99.	Highway-Gas tax bill	N
63.	Approve 21 MX for 1985	Y	100.	Raise Medicare;Cut defnse	N
64.	Emergency Farm Credit	Y	101.	Emergency housing aid	N
65.	Awards to whistle blowers	Y	102.	Across-the-board tax cuts	Y
66.	African disaster relief	Y	103.	Gramm-Latta II targets	Y
67.	Ban bank loans to So Afr	?	104.	Delete B-1 bomber funds	N
68.	Bar coun duty-free trtmt	N	105.	Dsapprov Saudi AWACS sale	N
69.	Steel import limits	N	106.	Disapprove oil import fee	Y
70.	Soc Sec COLAs=inflation	Y	107.	Rail Deregulation	Y
71.	Bar haz waste vctms suits	Y	108.	Dsapp India nuc fuel sale	N
72.	Prohibit aid to Nicaragua	Y	109.	Mil draft registration	Y
73.	Cut $-Schs bar sch prayer	Y	110.	Chrysler Loan Guarantees	Y
74.	Raise taxes; Cut Medicare	Y	111.	Prohibit school busing	Y
75.	Alien residncy-prior 1982	Y	112.	Nuclear plant moratorium	N
76.	Alien residncy-prior 1980	N	113.	Oil price controls	N
77.	Pen emp-hire illgl aliens	N			

Presidential Support Score: 1986 - 55% 1985 - 52%

WRIGHT, JIM -- Texas 12th District [Democrat]. County of Tarrant (pt.). Prior Terms: House: 1955-86. Born: December 22, 1922; Fort Worth, Texas. Education: Weatherford College; University of Texas. Military Service: U.S. Army Air Corps, 1941. Occupation: Partner, trade extension and advertising firm; mayor (1950-54); Texas legislator (1947-49); author.

1.	Immigration Reform	Y	13.	Bar ASAT testing	N
2.	Open fld-search warrants	Y	14.	Abide SALT II weapons ban	Y
3.	Civil pnty-hire ill alien	N	15.	Follow SALT II-Soviets do	N
4.	So Afr sanc-veto override	Y	16.	Reduce SDI funding	N
5.	Tax Overhaul	N	17.	Increase SDI funding	N
6.	South Africa sanctions	?	18.	Purchase Trident sub	Y
7.	Death penalty-drug bill	Y	19.	Delete 12 MX;Add conv wpn	N
8.	Evidence-warrantless srch	N	20.	Raise speed limit	N
9.	Life term-second drug off	Y	21.	Textile Import Quotas(*)	Y
10.	Military use in drug war	N	22.	Req Pentagon buy US goods	Y
11.	Troop reduction in Europe	N	23.	AIDS ins anti-dscriminatn	Y
12.	Prohibit chemical weapons	Y	24.	Nicaraguan refugee aid	Y

WRIGHT, JIM (Cont.)

25. Nicaraguan contra aid N
26. US abide by SALT II N
27. Prohibit Saudi arms sale Y
28. Military Retiremnt Reform Y
29. Nicaraguan refugee aid Y
30. Ease '68 Gun Control Act N
31. Bar intrstat handgun tran Y
32. Keep '68 Gun Control Act Y
33. Nicaraguan contra aid N
34. Bar emp polygraph testing ?
35. Tax Overhaul consideratn Y
36. Bar armor-piercing ammo Y
37. Tax Overhaul consideratn Y
38. Make comp emissions known N
39. Allow toxic victims suits N
40. Strike Superfund "VAT" N
41. Notify emp-plant closing Y
42. Bar emp consult-plant clo N
43. Medicare cuts;Tax incres' Y
44. Delete 12 MX missiles Y
45. Spending cuts;Tax incres' Y
46. Textile Import Quotas Y
47. Cut some school lunch fds ?
48. Clean Water Act Amendmnts N
49. Youth work projects Y
50. Assist military in Angola ?
51. Allow US troops-Nicaragua N
52. Pentagon polygraph exams Y
53. Bar ASAT testing Y
54. Suspend def pmt for abuse N
55. Bar Pentagon-contr emplmt Y
56. Increase SDI funding N
57. Reduce SDI funding N
58. Produce chemical weapons Y
59. Bar CIA fndg in Nicaragua Y
60. South Africa sanctions Y
61. Cut SS COLAs; Raise taxes N
62. Let US invest-So Africa ?
63. Approve 21 MX for 1985 N
64. Emergency Farm Credit Y
65. Awards to whistle blowers Y
66. African disaster relief Y
67. Ban bank loans to So Afr Y
68. Bar coun duty-free trtmt N
69. Steel import limits Y
70. Soc Sec COLAs=inflation Y
71. Bar haz waste vctms suits N
72. Prohibit aid to Nicaragua Y
73. Cut $-Schs bar sch prayer Y
74. Raise taxes; Cut Medicare Y
75. Alien residncy-prior 1982 Y
76. Alien residncy-prior 1980 N
77. Pen emp-hire illgl aliens Y
78. Lmt Persh II/cruse-Europe N
79. Delete 34 B-1 bombers N
80. Bar purch of Pershing II N
81. Bar purchase of Sgt York N
82. Delete $ for Trident II N
83. Allow 15 MX missiles N
84. Bar MX procurement-1985 Y
85. Equal Access Act Y
86. Aid to El Salvador Y
87. Bar Nicarag water mining Y
88. Physician/Medicare freeze N
89. Increase "sin" taxes Y
90. End SBA direct loans N
91. Sell Conrail N
92. Equal Rights Amendment Y
93. Marines in Lebanon Y
94. Eminent domain-Coal comps Y
95. Prohibit EPA sanctions Y
96. SS age increase/Reforms Y
97. Auto domestic content req Y
98. Delete jobs program fundg N
99. Highway-Gas tax bill Y
100. Raise Medicare;Cut defnse N
101. Emergency housing aid Y
102. Across-the-board tax cuts N
103. Gramm-Latta II targets N
104. Delete B-1 bomber funds N
105. Dsapprov Saudi AWACS sale Y
106. Disapprove oil import fee N
107. Rail Deregulation Y
108. Dsapp India nuc fuel sale Y
109. Mil draft registration Y
110. Chrysler Loan Guarantees Y
111. Prohibit school busing N
112. Nuclear plant moratorium N
113. Oil price controls N
114. Tuition Tax Credits N
115. Est Consumer Protect Agcy #
116. Eliminate B-1 bomber fnds Y
117. Subminimum wage for youth N
118. Delete crude oil tax N
119. Natural gas deregulation N

Presidential Support Score: 1986 - 19% 1985 - 23%

BOULTER, BEAU -- Texas 13th District [Republican]. Counties of Archer, Armstrong, Baylor, Briscoe, Carson, Childress, Clay, Collingsworth, Cottle, Dellam, Dickens, Donley, Floyd, Foard, Gray, Hall, Hansford, Hardeman, Hartley, Hemphill, Hutchinson, Kent, King, Knox, Lipscomb, Moore, Motley, Ochiltree, Oldham, Potter, Randall, Roberts, Sherman, Swisher, Wheeler, Wichita and Wilbarger. Prior Terms: 1985-86. Education: University

BOULTER, BEAU (Cont.)
of Texas (A.B.); Baylor University (J.D.). Occupation: Attorney; city commissioner.

1. Immigration Reform N
2. Open fld-search warrants Y
3. Civil pnty-hire ill alien Y
4. So Afr sanc-veto override N
5. Tax Overhaul Y
6. South Africa sanctions N
7. Death penalty-drug bill Y
8. Evidence-warrantless srch Y
9. Life term-second drug off Y
10. Military use in drug war Y
11. Troop reduction in Europe Y
12. Prohibit chemical weapons N
13. Bar ASAT testing N
14. Abide SALT II weapons ban N
15. Follow SALT II-Soviets do Y
16. Reduce SDI funding N
17. Increase SDI funding Y
18. Purchase Trident sub N
19. Delete 12 MX;Add conv wpn N
20. Raise speed limit Y
21. Textile Import Quotas(*) N
22. Req Pentagon buy US goods N
23. AIDS ins anti-dscriminatn N
24. Nicaraguan refugee aid N
25. Nicaraguan contra aid Y
26. US abide by SALT II Y
27. Prohibit Saudi arms sale Y
28. Military Retiremnt Reform Y
29. Nicaraguan refugee aid Y
30. Ease '68 Gun Control Act +
31. Bar intrstat handgun tran N
32. Keep '68 Gun Control Act N
33. Nicaraguan contra aid Y
34. Bar emp polygraph testing N
35. Tax Overhaul consideratn N
36. Bar armor-piercing ammo Y
37. Tax Overhaul consideratn N
38. Make comp emissions known N
39. Allow toxic victims suits N
40. Strike Superfund "VAT" N
41. Notify emp-plant closing N
42. Bar emp consult-plant clo Y
43. Medicare cuts;Tax incres' N
44. Delete 12 MX missiles N
45. Spending cuts;Tax incres' N
46. Textile Import Quotas N
47. Cut some school lunch fds Y
48. Clean Water Act Amendmnts Y
49. Youth work projects N
50. Assist military in Angola Y
51. Allow US troops-Nicaragua Y
52. Pentagon polygraph exams Y
53. Bar ASAT testing N
54. Suspend def pmt for abuse N
55. Bar Pentagon-contr emplmt Y
56. Increase SDI funding Y
57. Reduce SDI funding N
58. Produce chemical weapons Y
59. Bar CIA fndg in Nicaragua N
60. South Africa sanctions N
61. Cut SS COLAs; Raise taxes N
62. Let US invest-So Africa Y
63. Approve 21 MX for 1985 Y
64. Emergency Farm Credit Y
65. Awards to whistle blowers ?
66. African disaster relief ?

Presidential Support Score: 1986 - 66% 1985 - 78%

SWEENEY, MAC -- Texas 14th District [Republican]. Counties of Aransas, Austin, Bee, Brazoria (pt.), Burleson, Calhoun, Colorado, DeWitt, Fayette, Goliad, Gonzales (pt.), Guadalupe, Jackson, Lavaca, Lee, Matagorda, Refugio, Victoria, Waller, Washington, Wharton and Williamson (pt.). Prior Terms: 1985-86. Occupation: Administrative aide and director; congressional assistant.

1. Immigration Reform N
2. Open fld-search warrants Y
3. Civil pnty-hire ill alien Y
4. So Afr sanc-veto override N
5. Tax Overhaul N
6. South Africa sanctions N
7. Death penalty-drug bill Y
8. Evidence-warrantless srch Y
9. Life term-second drug off Y
10. Military use in drug war Y
11. Troop reduction in Europe N
12. Prohibit chemical weapons N
13. Bar ASAT testing N
14. Abide SALT II weapons ban N
15. Follow SALT II-Soviets do Y
16. Reduce SDI funding N
17. Increase SDI funding Y
18. Purchase Trident sub N
19. Delete 12 MX;Add conv wpn N
20. Raise speed limit ?
21. Textile Import Quotas(*) Y
22. Req Pentagon buy US goods N
23. AIDS ins anti-dscriminatn N
24. Nicaraguan refugee aid N
25. Nicaraguan contra aid Y
26. US abide by SALT II Y

SWEENEY, MAC (Cont.)

27. Prohibit Saudi arms sale Y
28. Military Retiremnt Reform Y
29. Nicaraguan refugee aid Y
30. Ease '68 Gun Control Act Y
31. Bar intrstat handgun tran N
32. Keep '68 Gun Control Act N
33. Nicaraguan contra aid Y
34. Bar emp polygraph testing N
35. Tax Overhaul consideratn N
36. Bar armor-piercing ammo Y
37. Tax Overhaul consideratn N
38. Make comp emissions known N
39. Allow toxic victims suits N
40. Strike Superfund "VAT" N
41. Notify emp-plant closing N
42. Bar emp consult-plant clo Y
43. Medicare cuts;Tax incres' N
44. Delete 12 MX missiles N
45. Spending cuts;Tax incres' N
46. Textile Import Quotas N
47. Cut some school lunch fds Y
48. Clean Water Act Amendmnts Y
49. Youth work projects N
50. Assist military in Angola Y
51. Allow US troops-Nicaragua Y
52. Pentagon polygraph exams Y
53. Bar ASAT testing N
54. Suspend def pmt for abuse N
55. Bar Pentagon-contr emplmt N
56. Increase SDI funding Y
57. Reduce SDI funding N
58. Produce chemical weapons Y
59. Bar CIA fndg in Nicaragua N
60. South Africa sanctions N
61. Cut SS COLAs; Raise taxes N
62. Let US invest-So Africa Y
63. Approve 21 MX for 1985 Y
64. Emergency Farm Credit Y
65. Awards to whistle blowers Y
66. African disaster relief N

Presidential Support Score: 1986 - 67% 1985 - 78%

de la GARZA, E. -- Texas 15th District [Democrat]. Counties of Atascosa, Brooks, Duval, Frio, Gonzales (pt.), Hidalgo, Jim Hogg, Jim Wells, Karnes, LaSalle, Live Oak, McMullen, Nueces (pt.), San Patricio, Starr, Wilson and Zapata. Prior Terms: House: 1963-86. Born: September 22, 1927; Mercedes, Texas. Education: Edinburg Junior College; St. Mary's University (LL.B., J.D.). Military Service: U.S. Navy, WW II; U.S. Army, 1950-52. Occupation: Attorney; Texas representative.

1. Immigration Reform N
2. Open fld-search warrants Y
3. Civil pnty-hire ill alien Y
4. So Afr sanc-veto override Y
5. Tax Overhaul N
6. South Africa sanctions Y
7. Death penalty-drug bill Y
8. Evidence-warrantless srch Y
9. Life term-second drug off Y
10. Military use in drug war Y
11. Troop reduction in Europe Y
12. Prohibit chemical weapons N
13. Bar ASAT testing N
14. Abide SALT II weapons ban Y
15. Follow SALT II-Soviets do N
16. Reduce SDI funding N
17. Increase SDI funding N
18. Purchase Trident sub Y
19. Delete 12 MX;Add conv wpn N
20. Raise speed limit Y
21. Textile Import Quotas(*) Y
22. Req Pentagon buy US goods Y
23. AIDS ins anti-dscriminatn Y
24. Nicaraguan refugee aid Y
25. Nicaraguan contra aid N
26. US abide by SALT II N
27. Prohibit Saudi arms sale Y
28. Military Retiremnt Reform Y
29. Nicaraguan refugee aid Y
30. Ease '68 Gun Control Act Y
31. Bar intrstat handgun tran N
32. Keep '68 Gun Control Act N
33. Nicaraguan contra aid N
34. Bar emp polygraph testing N
35. Tax Overhaul consideratn Y
36. Bar armor-piercing ammo Y
37. Tax Overhaul consideratn Y
38. Make comp emissions known Y
39. Allow toxic victims suits N
40. Strike Superfund "VAT" N
41. Notify emp-plant closing Y
42. Bar emp consult-plant clo N
43. Medicare cuts;Tax incres' Y
44. Delete 12 MX missiles N
45. Spending cuts;Tax incres' Y
46. Textile Import Quotas Y
47. Cut some school lunch fds N
48. Clean Water Act Amendmnts Y
49. Youth work projects Y
50. Assist military in Angola N
51. Allow US troops-Nicaragua N
52. Pentagon polygraph exams Y
53. Bar ASAT testing Y
54. Suspend def pmt for abuse N

de la GARZA, E. (Cont.)

55. Bar Pentagon-contr emplmt	Y	88. Physician/Medicare freeze	N
56. Increase SDI funding	N	89. Increase "sin" taxes	Y
57. Reduce SDI funding	Y	90. End SBA direct loans	N
58. Produce chemical weapons	Y	91. Sell Conrail	N
59. Bar CIA fndg in Nicaragua	N	92. Equal Rights Amendment	Y
60. South Africa sanctions	Y	93. Marines in Lebanon	Y
61. Cut SS COLAs; Raise taxes	N	94. Eminent domain-Coal comps	Y
62. Let US invest-So Africa	N	95. Prohibit EPA sanctions	N
63. Approve 21 MX for 1985	Y	96. SS age increase/Reforms	Y
64. Emergency Farm Credit	Y	97. Auto domestic content req	N
65. Awards to whistle blowers	Y	98. Delete jobs program fundg	N
66. African disaster relief	Y	99. Highway-Gas tax bill	N
67. Ban bank loans to So Afr	?	100. Raise Medicare;Cut defnse	Y
68. Bar coun duty-free trtmt	N	101. Emergency housing aid	Y
69. Steel import limits	Y	102. Across-the-board tax cuts	Y
70. Soc Sec COLAs=inflation	Y	103. Gramm-Latta II targets	N
71. Bar haz waste vctms suits	N	104. Delete B-1 bomber funds	N
72. Prohibit aid to Nicaragua	Y	105. Dsapprov Saudi AWACS sale	Y
73. Cut $-Schs bar sch prayer	Y	106. Disapprove oil import fee	Y
74. Raise taxes; Cut Medicare	N	107. Rail Deregulation	Y
75. Alien residncy-prior 1982	N	108. Dsapp India nuc fuel sale	?
76. Alien residncy-prior 1980	N	109. Mil draft registration	Y
77. Pen emp-hire illgl aliens	Y	110. Chrysler Loan Guarantees	N
78. Lmt Persh II/cruse-Europe	N	111. Prohibit school busing	Y
79. Delete 34 B-1 bombers	N	112. Nuclear plant moratorium	N
80. Bar purch of Pershing II	N	113. Oil price controls	N
81. Bar purchase of Sgt York	N	114. Tuition Tax Credits	Y
82. Delete $ for Trident II	N	115. Est Consumer Protect Agcy	N
83. Allow 15 MX missiles	Y	116. Eliminate B-1 bomber fnds	N
84. Bar MX procurement-1985	N	117. Subminimum wage for youth	Y
85. Equal Access Act	Y	118. Delete crude oil tax	Y
86. Aid to El Salvador	Y	119. Natural gas deregulation	Y
87. Bar Nicarag water mining	Y		

Presidential Support Score: 1986 - 27% 1985 - 34%

COLEMAN, RONALD D. -- Texas 16th District [Democrat]. Counties of Culberson, El Paso, Hudspeth, Jeff Davis, Loving, Reeves, Ward and Winkler. Prior Terms: House: 1983-86. Born: November 29, 1941; El Paso, Texas. Education: University of Texas (B.A., J.D.). Military Service: U.S. Army, 1967-69. Occupation: Attorney; teacher (1967); first assistant county attorney (1971); Texas legislator (1973-82).

1. Immigration Reform	N	16. Reduce SDI funding	N
2. Open fld-search warrants	Y	17. Increase SDI funding	N
3. Civil pnty-hire ill alien	Y	18. Purchase Trident sub	Y
4. So Afr sanc-veto override	Y	19. Delete 12 MX;Add conv wpn	Y
5. Tax Overhaul	N	20. Raise speed limit	Y
6. South Africa sanctions	Y	21. Textile Import Quotas(*)	Y
7. Death penalty-drug bill	Y	22. Req Pentagon buy US goods	Y
8. Evidence-warrantless srch	Y	23. AIDS ins anti-dscriminatn	Y
9. Life term-second drug off	Y	24. Nicaraguan refugee aid	Y
10. Military use in drug war	Y	25. Nicaraguan contra aid	N
11. Troop reduction in Europe	N	26. US abide by SALT II	N
12. Prohibit chemical weapons	N	27. Prohibit Saudi arms sale	Y
13. Bar ASAT testing	N	28. Military Retiremnt Reform	Y
14. Abide SALT II weapons ban	Y	29. Nicaraguan refugee aid	Y
15. Follow SALT II-Soviets do	N	30. Ease '68 Gun Control Act	Y

COLEMAN, RONALD D. (Cont.)

31. Bar intrstat handgun tran N
32. Keep '68 Gun Control Act N
33. Nicaraguan contra aid N
34. Bar emp polygraph testing N
35. Tax Overhaul consideratn Y
36. Bar armor-piercing ammo Y
37. Tax Overhaul consideratn Y
38. Make comp emissions known Y
39. Allow toxic victims suits Y
40. Strike Superfund "VAT" N
41. Notify emp-plant closing Y
42. Bar emp consult-plant clo Y
43. Medicare cuts;Tax incres' Y
44. Delete 12 MX missiles N
45. Spending cuts;Tax incres' Y
46. Textile Import Quotas Y
47. Cut some school lunch fds N
48. Clean Water Act Amendmnts N
49. Youth work projects Y
50. Assist military in Angola N
51. Allow US troops-Nicaragua N
52. Pentagon polygraph exams Y
53. Bar ASAT testing N
54. Suspend def pmt for abuse Y
55. Bar Pentagon-contr emplmt Y
56. Increase SDI funding N
57. Reduce SDI funding N
58. Produce chemical weapons Y
59. Bar CIA fndg in Nicaragua Y
60. South Africa sanctions Y
61. Cut SS COLAs; Raise taxes N
62. Let US invest-So Africa N
63. Approve 21 MX for 1985 N
64. Emergency Farm Credit Y
65. Awards to whistle blowers Y
66. African disaster relief Y
67. Ban bank loans to So Afr ?
68. Bar coun duty-free trtmt N
69. Steel import limits ?
70. Soc Sec COLAs=inflation Y
71. Bar haz waste vctms suits N
72. Prohibit aid to Nicaragua Y
73. Cut $-Schs bar sch prayer N
74. Raise taxes; Cut Medicare N
75. Alien residncy-prior 1982 N
76. Alien residncy-prior 1980 Y
77. Pen emp-hire illgl aliens Y
78. Lmt Persh II/cruse-Europe N
79. Delete 34 B-1 bombers N
80. Bar purch of Pershing II N
81. Bar purchase of Sgt York N
82. Delete $ for Trident II N
83. Allow 15 MX missiles Y
84. Bar MX procurement-1985 N
85. Equal Access Act Y
86. Aid to El Salvador Y
87. Bar Nicarag water mining Y
88. Physician/Medicare freeze N
89. Increase "sin" taxes N
90. End SBA direct loans N
91. Sell Conrail N
92. Equal Rights Amendment Y
93. Marines in Lebanon Y
94. Eminent domain-Coal comps N
95. Prohibit EPA sanctions Y
96. SS age increase/Reforms Y

Presidential Support Score: 1986 - 30% 1985 - 31%

STENHOLM, CHARLES W. -- Texas 17th District [Democrat]. Counties of Borden, Callahan, Coke, Coleman, Comanche, Concho, Cooks (pt.), Crosby, Eastland, Erath, Fisher, Garza, Glasscock, Haskell, Howard, Jack, Jones, Lynn, Martin, Mitchell, Montague, Nolan, Palo Pinto, Parker, Runnels, Scurry, Shackleford, Somervell, Stephens, Sterling, Stonewall, Taylor, Throckmorton, Wise and Young. Prior Terms: House: 1979-86. Born: October 26, 1938; Stamford, Texas. Education: Tarleton Junior College; Texas Tech University (B.S., M.S.). Occupation: Teacher (1962-65); partner, L. W. Stenholm & Son Farms (1961-69); executive vice president, Rolling Plains Cotton Growers; general manager, Stamford Electric Cooperative; owner-manager, Stenholm Farms (1969-76); manager, Watson Farms (1976-78); president, Double S. Farms, Inc. (1976-78); director, First National Bank of Stamford (1975-78).

1. Immigration Reform N
2. Open fld-search warrants Y
3. Civil pnty-hire ill alien Y
4. So Afr sanc-veto override N
5. Tax Overhaul N
6. South Africa sanctions N
7. Death penalty-drug bill Y
8. Evidence-warrantless srch Y
9. Life term-second drug off Y
10. Military use in drug war Y
11. Troop reduction in Europe Y
12. Prohibit chemical weapons N
13. Bar ASAT testing N
14. Abide SALT II weapons ban N
15. Follow SALT II-Soviets do Y
16. Reduce SDI funding N

STENHOLM, CHARLES W. (Cont.)

17. Increase SDI funding N
18. Purchase Trident sub N
19. Delete 12 MX;Add conv wpn N
20. Raise speed limit Y
21. Textile Import Quotas(*) Y
22. Req Pentagon buy US goods N
23. AIDS ins anti-dscriminatn N
24. Nicaraguan refugee aid N
25. Nicaraguan contra aid Y
26. US abide by SALT II Y
27. Prohibit Saudi arms sale Y
28. Military Retiremnt Reform Y
29. Nicaraguan refugee aid N
30. Ease '68 Gun Control Act Y
31. Bar intrstat handgun tran N
32. Keep '68 Gun Control Act Y
33. Nicaraguan contra aid Y
34. Bar emp polygraph testing N
35. Tax Overhaul consideratn N
36. Bar armor-piercing ammo Y
37. Tax Overhaul consideratn N
38. Make comp emissions known N
39. Allow toxic victims suits N
40. Strike Superfund "VAT" N
41. Notify emp-plant closing N
42. Bar emp consult-plant clo Y
43. Medicare cuts;Tax incres' Y
44. Delete 12 MX missiles N
45. Spending cuts;Tax incres' Y
46. Textile Import Quotas Y
47. Cut some school lunch fds Y
48. Clean Water Act Amendmnts Y
49. Youth work projects N
50. Assist military in Angola Y
51. Allow US troops-Nicaragua Y
52. Pentagon polygraph exams Y
53. Bar ASAT testing N
54. Suspend def pmt for abuse N
55. Bar Pentagon-contr emplmt Y
56. Increase SDI funding N
57. Reduce SDI funding N
58. Produce chemical weapons Y
59. Bar CIA fndg in Nicaragua N
60. South Africa sanctions Y
61. Cut SS COLAs; Raise taxes Y
62. Let US invest-So Africa N
63. Approve 21 MX for 1985 Y
64. Emergency Farm Credit Y
65. Awards to whistle blowers Y
66. African disaster relief Y
67. Ban bank loans to So Afr ?
68. Bar coun duty-free trtmt N
69. Steel import limits N
70. Soc Sec COLAs=inflation Y
71. Bar haz waste vctms suits Y
72. Prohibit aid to Nicaragua N
73. Cut $-Schs bar sch prayer Y
74. Raise taxes; Cut Medicare Y
75. Alien residncy-prior 1982 N
76. Alien residncy-prior 1980 N
77. Pen emp-hire illgl aliens N
78. Lmt Persh II/cruse-Europe N
79. Delete 34 B-1 bombers N
80. Bar purch of Pershing II N
81. Bar purchase of Sgt York N
82. Delete $ for Trident II N
83. Allow 15 MX missiles Y
84. Bar MX procurement-1985 N
85. Equal Access Act Y
86. Aid to El Salvador Y
87. Bar Nicarag water mining N
88. Physician/Medicare freeze Y
89. Increase "sin" taxes Y
90. End SBA direct loans N
91. Sell Conrail Y
92. Equal Rights Amendment N
93. Marines in Lebanon N
94. Eminent domain-Coal comps Y
95. Prohibit EPA sanctions Y
96. SS age increase/Reforms Y
97. Auto domestic content req N
98. Delete jobs program fundg Y
99. Highway-Gas tax bill N
100. Raise Medicare;Cut defnse N
101. Emergency housing aid N
102. Across-the-board tax cuts Y
103. Gramm-Latta II targets Y
104. Delete B-1 bomber funds N
105. Dsapprov Saudi AWACS sale N
106. Disapprove oil import fee Y
107. Rail Deregulation Y
108. Dsapp India nuc fuel sale N
109. Mil draft registration Y
110. Chrysler Loan Guarantees Y
111. Prohibit school busing Y
112. Nuclear plant moratorium N
113. Oil price controls N

Presidential Support Score: 1986 - 66% 1985 - 66%

LELAND, MICKEY -- Texas 18th District [Democrat]. County of Harris (pt.). Prior Terms: House: 1979-86. Born: November 27, 1944; Lubbock, Texas. Education: Texas Southern University (B.S.). Occupation: Instructor, clinical pharmacy, Texas Southern University; senior vice president, King State Bank; director, Hermann Hospital; Texas representative (1972-79).

1. Immigration Reform N
2. Open fld-search warrants Y

LELAND, MICKEY (Cont.)

3. Civil pnty-hire ill alien Y
4. So Afr sanc-veto override Y
5. Tax Overhaul N
6. South Africa sanctions Y
7. Death penalty-drug bill N
8. Evidence-warrantless srch N
9. Life term-second drug off N
10. Military use in drug war N
11. Troop reduction in Europe Y
12. Prohibit chemical weapons Y
13. Bar ASAT testing Y
14. Abide SALT II weapons ban Y
15. Follow SALT II-Soviets do N
16. Reduce SDI funding Y
17. Increase SDI funding N
18. Purchase Trident sub Y
19. Delete 12 MX;Add conv wpn Y
20. Raise speed limit Y
21. Textile Import Quotas(*) Y
22. Req Pentagon buy US goods Y
23. AIDS ins anti-dscriminatn Y
24. Nicaraguan refugee aid Y
25. Nicaraguan contra aid N
26. US abide by SALT II N
27. Prohibit Saudi arms sale Y
28. Military Retiremnt Reform Y
29. Nicaraguan refugee aid Y
30. Ease '68 Gun Control Act N
31. Bar intrstat handgun tran Y
32. Keep '68 Gun Control Act Y
33. Nicaraguan contra aid N
34. Bar emp polygraph testing Y
35. Tax Overhaul consideratn Y
36. Bar armor-piercing ammo Y
37. Tax Overhaul consideratn Y
38. Make comp emissions known Y
39. Allow toxic victims suits Y
40. Strike Superfund "VAT" N
41. Notify emp-plant closing Y
42. Bar emp consult-plant clo N
43. Medicare cuts;Tax incres' Y
44. Delete 12 MX missiles Y
45. Spending cuts;Tax incres' Y
46. Textile Import Quotas Y
47. Cut some school lunch fds N
48. Clean Water Act Amendmnts N
49. Youth work projects Y
50. Assist military in Angola N
51. Allow US troops-Nicaragua N
52. Pentagon polygraph exams N
53. Bar ASAT testing Y
54. Suspend def pmt for abuse Y
55. Bar Pentagon-contr emplmt Y
56. Increase SDI funding N
57. Reduce SDI funding Y
58. Produce chemical weapons N
59. Bar CIA fndg in Nicaragua Y
60. South Africa sanctions Y
61. Cut SS COLAs; Raise taxes N
62. Let US invest-So Africa N
63. Approve 21 MX for 1985 N
64. Emergency Farm Credit Y
65. Awards to whistle blowers ?
66. African disaster relief Y
67. Ban bank loans to So Afr P
68. Bar coun duty-free trtmt Y
69. Steel import limits Y
70. Soc Sec COLAs=inflation Y
71. Bar haz waste vctms suits N
72. Prohibit aid to Nicaragua ?
73. Cut $-Schs bar sch prayer N
74. Raise taxes; Cut Medicare N
75. Alien residncy-prior 1982 N
76. Alien residncy-prior 1980 N
77. Pen emp-hire illgl aliens Y
78. Lmt Persh II/cruse-Europe Y
79. Delete 34 B-1 bombers Y
80. Bar purch of Pershing II Y
81. Bar purchase of Sgt York Y
82. Delete $ for Trident II Y
83. Allow 15 MX missiles N
84. Bar MX procurement-1985 Y
85. Equal Access Act N
86. Aid to El Salvador N
87. Bar Nicarag water mining Y
88. Physician/Medicare freeze N
89. Increase "sin" taxes #
90. End SBA direct loans ?
91. Sell Conrail N
92. Equal Rights Amendment Y
93. Marines in Lebanon N
94. Eminent domain-Coal comps Y
95. Prohibit EPA sanctions Y
96. SS age increase/Reforms N
97. Auto domestic content req Y
98. Delete jobs program fundg N
99. Highway-Gas tax bill ?
100. Raise Medicare;Cut defnse Y
101. Emergency housing aid Y
102. Across-the-board tax cuts N
103. Gramm-Latta II targets N
104. Delete B-1 bomber funds Y
105. Dsapprov Saudi AWACS sale Y
106. Disapprove oil import fee ?
107. Rail Deregulation #
108. Dsapp India nuc fuel sale Y
109. Mil draft registration N
110. Chrysler Loan Guarantees Y
111. Prohibit school busing N
112. Nuclear plant moratorium N
113. Oil price controls Y

Presidential Support Score: 1986 - 9% 1985 - 20%

COMBEST, LARRY -- Texas 19th District [Republican]. Counties of Andrews, Bailey, Castro, Cochran, Dawson, Deaf Smith, Ector, Gaines, Hale, Hockley, Lamb, Lubbock, Parmer, Terry and Yoakum. Prior Terms: 1985-86. Born: West Texas. Education: West Texas State University. Occupation: Owner and operator wholesale electrical distributing company; legislative assistant (1971-78); rancher; wholesale oil business.

1. Immigration Reform N
2. Open fld-search warrants Y
3. Civil pnty-hire ill alien Y
4. So Afr sanc-veto override N
5. Tax Overhaul N
6. South Africa sanctions N
7. Death penalty-drug bill Y
8. Evidence-warrantless srch Y
9. Life term-second drug off Y
10. Military use in drug war Y
11. Troop reduction in Europe N
12. Prohibit chemical weapons N
13. Bar ASAT testing N
14. Abide SALT II weapons ban N
15. Follow SALT II-Soviets do Y
16. Reduce SDI funding N
17. Increase SDI funding Y
18. Purchase Trident sub N
19. Delete 12 MX;Add conv wpn N
20. Raise speed limit Y
21. Textile Import Quotas(*) Y
22. Req Pentagon buy US goods N
23. AIDS ins anti-dscriminatn N
24. Nicaraguan refugee aid N
25. Nicaraguan contra aid Y
26. US abide by SALT II Y
27. Prohibit Saudi arms sale N
28. Military Retiremnt Reform Y
29. Nicaraguan refugee aid Y
30. Ease '68 Gun Control Act Y
31. Bar intrstat handgun tran N
32. Keep '68 Gun Control Act N
33. Nicaraguan contra aid Y
34. Bar emp polygraph testing N
35. Tax Overhaul consideratn N
36. Bar armor-piercing ammo Y
37. Tax Overhaul consideratn N
38. Make comp emissions known N
39. Allow toxic victims suits N
40. Strike Superfund "VAT" N
41. Notify emp-plant closing N
42. Bar emp consult-plant clo Y
43. Medicare cuts;Tax incres' N
44. Delete 12 MX missiles N
45. Spending cuts;Tax incres' N
46. Textile Import Quotas Y
47. Cut some school lunch fds Y
48. Clean Water Act Amendmnts Y
49. Youth work projects N
50. Assist military in Angola Y
51. Allow US troops-Nicaragua Y
52. Pentagon polygraph exams Y
53. Bar ASAT testing N
54. Suspend def pmt for abuse N
55. Bar Pentagon-contr emplmt Y
56. Increase SDI funding Y
57. Reduce SDI funding N
58. Produce chemical weapons Y
59. Bar CIA fndg in Nicaragua N
60. South Africa sanctions N
61. Cut SS COLAs; Raise taxes N
62. Let US invest-So Africa Y
63. Approve 21 MX for 1985 Y
64. Emergency Farm Credit Y
65. Awards to whistle blowers Y
66. African disaster relief N

Presidential Support Score: 1986 - 78% 1985 - 75%

GONZALEZ, HENRY B. -- Texas 20th District [Democrat]. County of Bexar (pt.). Prior Terms: House: 1961 (Special Election)-1986. Born: May 3, 1916; San Antonio, Texas. Education: San Antonio College; University of Texas; St. Mary's University Law School (LL.B.). Occupation: San Antonio city councilman; mayor pro tem; Bexar County chief probation officer; Texas senator (1956-61).

1. Immigration Reform N
2. Open fld-search warrants Y
3. Civil pnty-hire ill alien Y
4. So Afr sanc-veto override Y
5. Tax Overhaul N
6. South Africa sanctions Y
7. Death penalty-drug bill N
8. Evidence-warrantless srch N
9. Life term-second drug off N
10. Military use in drug war N
11. Troop reduction in Europe Y
12. Prohibit chemical weapons Y
13. Bar ASAT testing Y
14. Abide SALT II weapons ban Y
15. Follow SALT II-Soviets do N
16. Reduce SDI funding Y

GONZALEZ, HENRY B. (Cont.)

17. Increase SDI funding N
18. Purchase Trident sub N
19. Delete 12 MX;Add conv wpn Y
20. Raise speed limit N
21. Textile Import Quotas(*) Y
22. Req Pentagon buy US goods Y
23. AIDS ins anti-dscriminatn Y
24. Nicaraguan refugee aid Y
25. Nicaraguan contra aid N
26. US abide by SALT II N
27. Prohibit Saudi arms sale Y
28. Military Retiremnt Reform N
29. Nicaraguan refugee aid Y
30. Ease '68 Gun Control Act N
31. Bar intrstat handgun tran Y
32. Keep '68 Gun Control Act Y
33. Nicaraguan contra aid N
34. Bar emp polygraph testing Y
35. Tax Overhaul consideratn Y
36. Bar armor-piercing ammo Y
37. Tax Overhaul consideratn Y
38. Make comp emissions known Y
39. Allow toxic victims suits Y
40. Strike Superfund "VAT" N
41. Notify emp-plant closing Y
42. Bar emp consult-plant clo N
43. Medicare cuts;Tax incres' N
44. Delete 12 MX missiles Y
45. Spending cuts;Tax incres' Y
46. Textile Import Quotas Y
47. Cut some school lunch fds N
48. Clean Water Act Amendmnts N
49. Youth work projects Y
50. Assist military in Angola N
51. Allow US troops-Nicaragua N
52. Pentagon polygraph exams N
53. Bar ASAT testing Y
54. Suspend def pmt for abuse N
55. Bar Pentagon-contr emplmt N
56. Increase SDI funding N
57. Reduce SDI funding Y
58. Produce chemical weapons N
59. Bar CIA fndg in Nicaragua Y
60. South Africa sanctions Y
61. Cut SS COLAs; Raise taxes N
62. Let US invest-So Africa N
63. Approve 21 MX for 1985 N
64. Emergency Farm Credit Y
65. Awards to whistle blowers Y
66. African disaster relief Y
67. Ban bank loans to So Afr N
68. Bar coun duty-free trtmt Y
69. Steel import limits Y
70. Soc Sec COLAs=inflation Y
71. Bar haz waste vctms suits N
72. Prohibit aid to Nicaragua Y
73. Cut $-Schs bar sch prayer N
74. Raise taxes; Cut Medicare N
75. Alien residncy-prior 1982 N
76. Alien residncy-prior 1980 N
77. Pen emp-hire illgl aliens Y
78. Lmt Persh II/cruse-Europe Y
79. Delete 34 B-1 bombers N
80. Bar purch of Pershing II P
81. Bar purchase of Sgt York N
82. Delete $ for Trident II P
83. Allow 15 MX missiles N
84. Bar MX procurement-1985 Y
85. Equal Access Act N
86. Aid to El Salvador N
87. Bar Nicarag water mining Y
88. Physician/Medicare freeze N
89. Increase "sin" taxes N
90. End SBA direct loans N
91. Sell Conrail N
92. Equal Rights Amendment Y
93. Marines in Lebanon N
94. Eminent domain-Coal comps Y
95. Prohibit EPA sanctions Y
96. SS age increase/Reforms N
97. Auto domestic content req Y
98. Delete jobs program fundg N
99. Highway-Gas tax bill N
100. Raise Medicare;Cut defnse Y
101. Emergency housing aid Y
102. Across-the-board tax cuts N
103. Gramm-Latta II targets N
104. Delete B-1 bomber funds N
105. Dsapprov Saudi AWACS sale Y
106. Disapprove oil import fee N
107. Rail Deregulation Y
108. Dsapp India nuc fuel sale N
109. Mil draft registration Y
110. Chrysler Loan Guarantees Y
111. Prohibit school busing N
112. Nuclear plant moratorium Y
113. Oil price controls Y
114. Tuition Tax Credits N
115. Est Consumer Protect Agcy Y
116. Eliminate B-1 bomber fnds N
117. Subminimum wage for youth N
118. Delete crude oil tax N
119. Natural gas deregulation N

Presidential Support Score: 1986 - 17% 1985 - 21%

LOEFFLER, TOM -- Texas 21st District [Republican]. Counties of Bandera, Bexar (pt.), Brewster, Comal, Crane, Crockett, Edwards, Gillespie, Irion, Kendall, Kerr, Kimble, Llano, McCulloch, Mason, Menard, Midland, Pecos, Presidio, Reagan,

LOEFFLER, TOM (Cont.)

Real, Schneider, Sutton, Terrell, Tom Green, Upton and Val Verde. Prior Terms: House: 1979-86. Born: August 1, 1946; Fredericksburg, Texas. Education: University of Texas (B.B.A., J.D.). Occupation: Senator's legislative counsel (1972-74); consultant, Economic Development Administration (1975).

1.	Immigration Reform	N
2.	Open fld-search warrants	Y
3.	Civil pnty-hire ill alien	Y
4.	So Afr sanc-veto override	N
5.	Tax Overhaul	N
6.	South Africa sanctions	X
7.	Death penalty-drug bill	Y
8.	Evidence-warrantless srch	Y
9.	Life term-second drug off	Y
10.	Military use in drug war	Y
11.	Troop reduction in Europe	N
12.	Prohibit chemical weapons	N
13.	Bar ASAT testing	N
14.	Abide SALT II weapons ban	N
15.	Follow SALT II-Soviets do	Y
16.	Reduce SDI funding	N
17.	Increase SDI funding	Y
18.	Purchase Trident sub	N
19.	Delete 12 MX;Add conv wpn	N
20.	Raise speed limit	Y
21.	Textile Import Quotas(*)	Y
22.	Req Pentagon buy US goods	N
23.	AIDS ins anti-dscriminatn	N
24.	Nicaraguan refugee aid	N
25.	Nicaraguan contra aid	Y
26.	US abide by SALT II	Y
27.	Prohibit Saudi arms sale	?
28.	Military Retiremnt Reform	?
29.	Nicaraguan refugee aid	Y
30.	Ease '68 Gun Control Act	Y
31.	Bar intrstat handgun tran	N
32.	Keep '68 Gun Control Act	N
33.	Nicaraguan contra aid	Y
34.	Bar emp polygraph testing	X
35.	Tax Overhaul consideratn	N
36.	Bar armor-piercing ammo	Y
37.	Tax Overhaul consideratn	N
38.	Make comp emissions known	N
39.	Allow toxic victims suits	N
40.	Strike Superfund "VAT"	N
41.	Notify emp-plant closing	N
42.	Bar emp consult-plant clo	Y
43.	Medicare cuts;Tax incres'	N
44.	Delete 12 MX missiles	N
45.	Spending cuts;Tax incres'	N
46.	Textile Import Quotas	Y
47.	Cut some school lunch fds	Y
48.	Clean Water Act Amendmnts	Y
49.	Youth work projects	X
50.	Assist military in Angola	Y
51.	Allow US troops-Nicaragua	?
52.	Pentagon polygraph exams	Y
53.	Bar ASAT testing	N
54.	Suspend def pmt for abuse	N
55.	Bar Pentagon-contr emplmt	Y
56.	Increase SDI funding	Y
57.	Reduce SDI funding	N
58.	Produce chemical weapons	Y
59.	Bar CIA fndg in Nicaragua	N
60.	South Africa sanctions	N
61.	Cut SS COLAs; Raise taxes	N
62.	Let US invest-So Africa	Y
63.	Approve 21 MX for 1985	Y
64.	Emergency Farm Credit	N
65.	Awards to whistle blowers	Y
66.	African disaster relief	Y
67.	Ban bank loans to So Afr	Y
68.	Bar coun duty-free trtmt	N
69.	Steel import limits	Y
70.	Soc Sec COLAs=inflation	Y
71.	Bar haz waste vctms suits	Y
72.	Prohibit aid to Nicaragua	N
73.	Cut $-Schs bar sch prayer	Y
74.	Raise taxes; Cut Medicare	N
75.	Alien residncy-prior 1982	N
76.	Alien residncy-prior 1980	N
77.	Pen emp-hire illgl aliens	N
78.	Lmt Persh II/cruse-Europe	N
79.	Delete 34 B-1 bombers	N
80.	Bar purch of Pershing II	N
81.	Bar purchase of Sgt York	N
82.	Delete $ for Trident II	N
83.	Allow 15 MX missiles	Y
84.	Bar MX procurement-1985	N
85.	Equal Access Act	Y
86.	Aid to El Salvador	Y
87.	Bar Nicarag water mining	N
88.	Physician/Medicare freeze	Y
89.	Increase "sin" taxes	N
90.	End SBA direct loans	Y
91.	Sell Conrail	Y
92.	Equal Rights Amendment	N
93.	Marines in Lebanon	Y
94.	Eminent domain-Coal comps	Y
95.	Prohibit EPA sanctions	Y
96.	SS age increase/Reforms	Y
97.	Auto domestic content req	N
98.	Delete jobs program fundg	Y
99.	Highway-Gas tax bill	N
100.	Raise Medicare;Cut defnse	N
101.	Emergency housing aid	Y
102.	Across-the-board tax cuts	Y
103.	Gramm-Latta II targets	Y
104.	Delete B-1 bomber funds	N

LOEFFLER, TOM (Cont.)

105. Dsapprov Saudi AWACS sale Y
106. Disapprove oil import fee Y
107. Rail Deregulation N
108. Dsapp India nuc fuel sale Y
109. Mil draft registration Y
110. Chrysler Loan Guarantees X
111. Prohibit school busing Y
112. Nuclear plant moratorium N
113. Oil price controls N

Presidential Support Score: 1986 - 51% 1985 - 60%

DeLAY TOM -- Texas 22nd District [Republican]. Counties of Brazoria (pt.), Fort Bend and Harris (pt.). Prior Terms: 1985-86. Education: University of Houston. Occupation: Businessman; Texas representative.

1. Immigration Reform N
2. Open fld-search warrants Y
3. Civil pnty-hire ill alien Y
4. So Afr sanc-veto override N
5. Tax Overhaul N
6. South Africa sanctions N
7. Death penalty-drug bill Y
8. Evidence-warrantless srch Y
9. Life term-second drug off Y
10. Military use in drug war Y
11. Troop reduction in Europe Y
12. Prohibit chemical weapons N
13. Bar ASAT testing N
14. Abide SALT II weapons ban N
15. Follow SALT II-Soviets do Y
16. Reduce SDI funding N
17. Increase SDI funding Y
18. Purchase Trident sub N
19. Delete 12 MX;Add conv wpn N
20. Raise speed limit Y
21. Textile Import Quotas(*) N
22. Req Pentagon buy US goods N
23. AIDS ins anti-dscriminatn N
24. Nicaraguan refugee aid N
25. Nicaraguan contra aid Y
26. US abide by SALT II Y
27. Prohibit Saudi arms sale Y
28. Military Retiremnt Reform Y
29. Nicaraguan refugee aid Y
30. Ease '68 Gun Control Act Y
31. Bar intrstat handgun tran N
32. Keep '68 Gun Control Act N
33. Nicaraguan contra aid Y
34. Bar emp polygraph testing N
35. Tax Overhaul consideratn N
36. Bar armor-piercing ammo Y
37. Tax Overhaul consideratn N
38. Make comp emissions known N
39. Allow toxic victims suits N
40. Strike Superfund "VAT" N
41. Notify emp-plant closing N
42. Bar emp consult-plant clo Y
43. Medicare cuts;Tax incres' N
44. Delete 12 MX missiles N
45. Spending cuts;Tax incres' N
46. Textile Import Quotas N
47. Cut some school lunch fds Y
48. Clean Water Act Amendmnts Y
49. Youth work projects N
50. Assist military in Angola Y
51. Allow US troops-Nicaragua Y
52. Pentagon polygraph exams Y
53. Bar ASAT testing N
54. Suspend def pmt for abuse N
55. Bar Pentagon-contr emplmt Y
56. Increase SDI funding Y
57. Reduce SDI funding N
58. Produce chemical weapons Y
59. Bar CIA fndg in Nicaragua N
60. South Africa sanctions N
61. Cut SS COLAs; Raise taxes N
62. Let US invest-So Africa Y
63. Approve 21 MX for 1985 Y
64. Emergency Farm Credit N
65. Awards to whistle blowers Y
66. African disaster relief N

Presidential Support Score: 1986 - 84% 1985 - 85%

BUSTAMANTE, A. G. -- Texas 23rd District [Democrat]. Counties of Bexar (pt.), Dimmit, Kinney, Maverick, Medina, Uvalde, Webb and Zavala. Prior Terms: 1985-86. Born: April 8, 1935. Education: Sul Ross University (B.A.). Military Service: U.S. Army, 1954-56. Occupation: County judge; county commissioner.

1. Immigration Reform Y
2. Open fld-search warrants N
3. Civil pnty-hire ill alien Y
4. So Afr sanc-veto override Y
5. Tax Overhaul N
6. South Africa sanctions Y

BUSTAMANTE, A. G. (Cont.)

7. Death penalty-drug bill Y
8. Evidence-warrantless srch N
9. Life term-second drug off Y
10. Military use in drug war N
11. Troop reduction in Europe N
12. Prohibit chemical weapons N
13. Bar ASAT testing Y
14. Abide SALT II weapons ban Y
15. Follow SALT II-Soviets do N
16. Reduce SDI funding N
17. Increase SDI funding N
18. Purchase Trident sub Y
19. Delete 12 MX;Add conv wpn N
20. Raise speed limit Y
21. Textile Import Quotas(*) Y
22. Req Pentagon buy US goods Y
23. AIDS ins anti-dscriminatn Y
24. Nicaraguan refugee aid N
25. Nicaraguan contra aid Y
26. US abide by SALT II N
27. Prohibit Saudi arms sale Y
28. Military Retiremnt Reform Y
29. Nicaraguan refugee aid N
30. Ease '68 Gun Control Act Y
31. Bar intrstat handgun tran ?
32. Keep '68 Gun Control Act N
33. Nicaraguan contra aid N
34. Bar emp polygraph testing Y
35. Tax Overhaul consideratn N
36. Bar armor-piercing ammo Y
37. Tax Overhaul consideratn Y
38. Make comp emissions known Y
39. Allow toxic victims suits N
40. Strike Superfund "VAT" N
41. Notify emp-plant closing Y
42. Bar emp consult-plant clo N
43. Medicare cuts;Tax incres' Y
44. Delete 12 MX missiles N
45. Spending cuts;Tax incres' Y
46. Textile Import Quotas Y
47. Cut some school lunch fds N
48. Clean Water Act Amendmnts N
49. Youth work projects Y
50. Assist military in Angola N
51. Allow US troops-Nicaragua Y
52. Pentagon polygraph exams Y
53. Bar ASAT testing Y
54. Suspend def pmt for abuse N
55. Bar Pentagon-contr emplmt Y
56. Increase SDI funding N
57. Reduce SDI funding N
58. Produce chemical weapons Y
59. Bar CIA fndg in Nicaragua ?
60. South Africa sanctions Y
61. Cut SS COLAs; Raise taxes Y
62. Let US invest-So Africa N
63. Approve 21 MX for 1985 Y
64. Emergency Farm Credit Y
65. Awards to whistle blowers Y
66. African disaster relief Y

Presidential Support Score: 1986 - 32% 1985 - 34%

FROST, MARTIN -- Texas 24th District [Democrat]. Counties of Dallas (pt.) and Tarrant (pt.). Prior Terms: House: 1979-86. Born: January 1, 1942; Glendale, Calif. Education: University of Missouri (B.A., B.J.); Georgetown Law Center (J.D.). Military Service: U.S. Army Reserve, 1966-72. Occupation: Staff writer, "Congressional Quarterly Weekly Report"; attorney; law clerk for federal judge.

1. Immigration Reform Y
2. Open fld-search warrants N
3. Civil pnty-hire ill alien N
4. So Afr sanc-veto override Y
5. Tax Overhaul N
6. South Africa sanctions ?
7. Death penalty-drug bill Y
8. Evidence-warrantless srch Y
9. Life term-second drug off N
10. Military use in drug war Y
11. Troop reduction in Europe N
12. Prohibit chemical weapons Y
13. Bar ASAT testing N
14. Abide SALT II weapons ban Y
15. Follow SALT II-Soviets do N
16. Reduce SDI funding N
17. Increase SDI funding N
18. Purchase Trident sub Y
19. Delete 12 MX;Add conv wpn N
20. Raise speed limit N
21. Textile Import Quotas(*) Y
22. Req Pentagon buy US goods Y
23. AIDS ins anti-dscriminatn Y
24. Nicaraguan refugee aid Y
25. Nicaraguan contra aid N
26. US abide by SALT II N
27. Prohibit Saudi arms sale Y
28. Military Retiremnt Reform ?
29. Nicaraguan refugee aid Y
30. Ease '68 Gun Control Act N
31. Bar intrstat handgun tran Y
32. Keep '68 Gun Control Act Y
33. Nicaraguan contra aid N
34. Bar emp polygraph testing ?
35. Tax Overhaul consideratn P
36. Bar armor-piercing ammo Y
37. Tax Overhaul consideratn P
38. Make comp emissions known N

FROST, MARTIN (Cont.)

39. Allow toxic victims suits Y
40. Strike Superfund "VAT" N
41. Notify emp-plant closing Y
42. Bar emp consult-plant clo N
43. Medicare cuts;Tax incres' Y
44. Delete 12 MX missiles N
45. Spending cuts;Tax incres' Y
46. Textile Import Quotas Y
47. Cut some school lunch fds N
48. Clean Water Act Amendmnts N
49. Youth work projects Y
50. Assist military in Angola N
51. Allow US troops-Nicaragua Y
52. Pentagon polygraph exams Y
53. Bar ASAT testing N
54. Suspend def pmt for abuse N
55. Bar Pentagon-contr emplmt Y
56. Increase SDI funding N
57. Reduce SDI funding N
58. Produce chemical weapons Y
59. Bar CIA fndg in Nicaragua Y
60. South Africa sanctions Y
61. Cut SS COLAs; Raise taxes N
62. Let US invest-So Africa N
63. Approve 21 MX for 1985 Y
64. Emergency Farm Credit Y
65. Awards to whistle blowers Y
66. African disaster relief Y
67. Ban bank loans to So Afr Y
68. Bar coun duty-free trtmt Y
69. Steel import limits Y
70. Soc Sec COLAs=inflation Y
71. Bar haz waste vctms suits N
72. Prohibit aid to Nicaragua ?
73. Cut $-Schs bar sch prayer N
74. Raise taxes; Cut Medicare Y
75. Alien residncy-prior 1982 Y
76. Alien residncy-prior 1980 Y
77. Pen emp-hire illgl aliens Y
78. Lmt Persh II/cruse-Europe N
79. Delete 34 B-1 bombers N
80. Bar purch of Pershing II N
81. Bar purchase of Sgt York N
82. Delete $ for Trident II N
83. Allow 15 MX missiles Y
84. Bar MX procurement-1985 N
85. Equal Access Act N
86. Aid to El Salvador N
87. Bar Nicarag water mining ?
88. Physician/Medicare freeze ?
89. Increase "sin" taxes N
90. End SBA direct loans N
91. Sell Conrail N
92. Equal Rights Amendment Y
93. Marines in Lebanon Y
94. Eminent domain-Coal comps N
95. Prohibit EPA sanctions ?
96. SS age increase/Reforms N
97. Auto domestic content req Y
98. Delete jobs program fundg N
99. Highway-Gas tax bill Y
100. Raise Medicare;Cut defnse Y
101. Emergency housing aid Y
102. Across-the-board tax cuts N
103. Gramm-Latta II targets N
104. Delete B-1 bomber funds N
105. Dsapprov Saudi AWACS sale Y
106. Disapprove oil import fee ?
107. Rail Deregulation Y
108. Dsapp India nuc fuel sale Y
109. Mil draft registration Y
110. Chrysler Loan Guarantees Y
111. Prohibit school busing N
112. Nuclear plant moratorium N
113. Oil price controls X

Presidential Support Score: 1986 - 23% 1985 - 26%

ANDREWS, MICHAEL A. -- Texas 25th District [Democrat]. County of Harris (pt.). Prior Terms: House: 1983-86. Born: February 7, 1944; Houston, Texas. Education: University of Texas (B.A.); Southern Methodist University School of Law (J.D.). Occupation: Law clerk, U.S. district judge (1971-72); assistant district attorney (1972-76); attorney (1976).

1. Immigration Reform N
2. Open fld-search warrants N
3. Civil pnty-hire ill alien Y
4. So Afr sanc-veto override Y
5. Tax Overhaul Y
6. South Africa sanctions Y
7. Death penalty-drug bill Y
8. Evidence-warrantless srch Y
9. Life term-second drug off Y
10. Military use in drug war Y
11. Troop reduction in Europe N
12. Prohibit chemical weapons N
13. Bar ASAT testing N
14. Abide SALT II weapons ban Y
15. Follow SALT II-Soviets do N
16. Reduce SDI funding N
17. Increase SDI funding N
18. Purchase Trident sub N
19. Delete 12 MX;Add conv wpn N
20. Raise speed limit N
21. Textile Import Quotas(*) Y
22. Req Pentagon buy US goods Y
23. AIDS ins anti-dscriminatn Y
24. Nicaraguan refugee aid N

ANDREWS, MICHAEL A. (Cont.)

25. Nicaraguan contra aid N
26. US abide by SALT II N
27. Prohibit Saudi arms sale Y
28. Military Retiremnt Reform Y
29. Nicaraguan refugee aid N
30. Ease '68 Gun Control Act Y
31. Bar intrstat handgun tran N
32. Keep '68 Gun Control Act N
33. Nicaraguan contra aid N
34. Bar emp polygraph testing Y
35. Tax Overhaul consideratn N
36. Bar armor-piercing ammo Y
37. Tax Overhaul consideratn N
38. Make comp emissions known N
39. Allow toxic victims suits N
40. Strike Superfund "VAT" N
41. Notify emp-plant closing N
42. Bar emp consult-plant clo Y
43. Medicare cuts;Tax incres' Y
44. Delete 12 MX missiles N
45. Spending cuts;Tax incres' Y
46. Textile Import Quotas Y
47. Cut some school lunch fds N
48. Clean Water Act Amendmnts N
49. Youth work projects ?
50. Assist military in Angola Y
51. Allow US troops-Nicaragua N
52. Pentagon polygraph exams Y
53. Bar ASAT testing N
54. Suspend def pmt for abuse N
55. Bar Pentagon-contr emplmt Y
56. Increase SDI funding N
57. Reduce SDI funding N
58. Produce chemical weapons Y
59. Bar CIA fndg in Nicaragua Y
60. South Africa sanctions Y
61. Cut SS COLAs; Raise taxes Y
62. Let US invest-So Africa N
63. Approve 21 MX for 1985 Y
64. Emergency Farm Credit Y
65. Awards to whistle blowers Y
66. African disaster relief Y
67. Ban bank loans to So Afr Y
68. Bar coun duty-free trtmt Y
69. Steel import limits Y
70. Soc Sec COLAs=inflation Y
71. Bar haz waste vctms suits Y
72. Prohibit aid to Nicaragua Y
73. Cut $-Schs bar sch prayer Y
74. Raise taxes; Cut Medicare Y
75. Alien residncy-prior 1982 N
76. Alien residncy-prior 1980 N
77. Pen emp-hire illgl aliens N
78. Lmt Persh II/cruse-Europe N
79. Delete 34 B-1 bombers Y
80. Bar purch of Pershing II N
81. Bar purchase of Sgt York N
82. Delete $ for Trident II N
83. Allow 15 MX missiles Y
84. Bar MX procurement-1985 N
85. Equal Access Act Y
86. Aid to El Salvador Y
87. Bar Nicarag water mining Y
88. Physician/Medicare freeze N
89. Increase "sin" taxes Y
90. End SBA direct loans N
91. Sell Conrail Y
92. Equal Rights Amendment Y
93. Marines in Lebanon Y
94. Eminent domain-Coal comps Y
95. Prohibit EPA sanctions Y
96. SS age increase/Reforms Y

Presidential Support Score: 1986 - 36% 1985 - 39%

ARMEY, DICK -- Texas 26th District [Republican]. Counties of Collin (pt.), Cooke (pt.), Denton and Tarrant (pt.). Prior Terms: 1985-86. Education: Jamestown College (B.A.); University of North Dakota (M.A.); University of Oklahoma (Ph.D.). Occupation: Economist; educator; chairman, Economics Dept., North Texas State University.

1. Immigration Reform N
2. Open fld-search warrants Y
3. Civil pnty-hire ill alien Y
4. So Afr sanc-veto override N
5. Tax Overhaul Y
6. South Africa sanctions N
7. Death penalty-drug bill Y
8. Evidence-warrantless srch Y
9. Life term-second drug off Y
10. Military use in drug war Y
11. Troop reduction in Europe N
12. Prohibit chemical weapons N
13. Bar ASAT testing N
14. Abide SALT II weapons ban N
15. Follow SALT II-Soviets do Y
16. Reduce SDI funding N
17. Increase SDI funding Y
18. Purchase Trident sub N
19. Delete 12 MX;Add conv wpn N
20. Raise speed limit Y
21. Textile Import Quotas(*) N
22. Req Pentagon buy US goods N
23. AIDS ins anti-dscriminatn N
24. Nicaraguan refugee aid N
25. Nicaraguan contra aid Y
26. US abide by SALT II Y
27. Prohibit Saudi arms sale Y
28. Military Retiremnt Reform Y

ARMEY, DICK (Cont.)

29. Nicaraguan refugee aid Y
30. Ease '68 Gun Control Act Y
31. Bar intrstat handgun tran N
32. Keep '68 Gun Control Act N
33. Nicaraguan contra aid Y
34. Bar emp polygraph testing N
35. Tax Overhaul consideratn N
36. Bar armor-piercing ammo Y
37. Tax Overhaul consideratn N
38. Make comp emissions known N
39. Allow toxic victims suits N
40. Strike Superfund "VAT" N
41. Notify emp-plant closing N
42. Bar emp consult-plant clo Y
43. Medicare cuts;Tax incres' N
44. Delete 12 MX missiles N
45. Spending cuts;Tax incres' N
46. Textile Import Quotas N
47. Cut some school lunch fds Y
48. Clean Water Act Amendmnts Y
49. Youth work projects N
50. Assist military in Angola Y
51. Allow US troops-Nicaragua Y
52. Pentagon polygraph exams Y
53. Bar ASAT testing N
54. Suspend def pmt for abuse N
55. Bar Pentagon-contr emplmt N
56. Increase SDI funding Y
57. Reduce SDI funding N
58. Produce chemical weapons N
59. Bar CIA fndg in Nicaragua N
60. South Africa sanctions N
61. Cut SS COLAs; Raise taxes N
62. Let US invest-So Africa Y
63. Approve 21 MX for 1985 Y
64. Emergency Farm Credit N
65. Awards to whistle blowers N
66. African disaster relief N

Presidential Support Score: 1986 - 83% 1985 - 88%

ORTIZ, SOLOMON P. -- Texas 27th District [Democrat]. Counties of Cameron, Kenedy, Kleberg, Nueces (pt.) and Willacy. Prior Terms: House: 1983-86. Born: June 3, 1937; Robstown, Texas. Education: Del Mar College. Military Service: U.S. Army, 1960-62. Occupation: Law enforcement official; constable (1964); county commissioner (1969); county sheriff (1977).

1. Immigration Reform Y
2. Open fld-search warrants N
3. Civil pnty-hire ill alien Y
4. So Afr sanc-veto override Y
5. Tax Overhaul N
6. South Africa sanctions Y
7. Death penalty-drug bill Y
8. Evidence-warrantless srch N
9. Life term-second drug off Y
10. Military use in drug war Y
11. Troop reduction in Europe N
12. Prohibit chemical weapons N
13. Bar ASAT testing N
14. Abide SALT II weapons ban Y
15. Follow SALT II-Soviets do N
16. Reduce SDI funding N
17. Increase SDI funding N
18. Purchase Trident sub Y
19. Delete 12 MX;Add conv wpn N
20. Raise speed limit Y
21. Textile Import Quotas(*) Y
22. Req Pentagon buy US goods Y
23. AIDS ins anti-dscriminatn Y
24. Nicaraguan refugee aid N
25. Nicaraguan contra aid Y
26. US abide by SALT II N
27. Prohibit Saudi arms sale Y
28. Military Retiremnt Reform Y
29. Nicaraguan refugee aid N
30. Ease '68 Gun Control Act Y
31. Bar intrstat handgun tran N
32. Keep '68 Gun Control Act N
33. Nicaraguan contra aid Y
34. Bar emp polygraph testing N
35. Tax Overhaul consideratn N
36. Bar armor-piercing ammo Y
37. Tax Overhaul consideratn Y
38. Make comp emissions known Y
39. Allow toxic victims suits Y
40. Strike Superfund "VAT" N
41. Notify emp-plant closing Y
42. Bar emp consult-plant clo X
43. Medicare cuts;Tax incres' Y
44. Delete 12 MX missiles N
45. Spending cuts;Tax incres' Y
46. Textile Import Quotas Y
47. Cut some school lunch fds N
48. Clean Water Act Amendmnts N
49. Youth work projects Y
50. Assist military in Angola N
51. Allow US troops-Nicaragua N
52. Pentagon polygraph exams Y
53. Bar ASAT testing Y
54. Suspend def pmt for abuse N
55. Bar Pentagon-contr emplmt Y
56. Increase SDI funding N
57. Reduce SDI funding N
58. Produce chemical weapons Y
59. Bar CIA fndg in Nicaragua N
60. South Africa sanctions Y
61. Cut SS COLAs; Raise taxes N
62. Let US invest-So Africa N

ORTIZ, SOLOMON P. (Cont.)

63. Approve 21 MX for 1985	Y		80. Bar purch of Pershing II	N
64. Emergency Farm Credit	Y		81. Bar purchase of Sgt York	?
65. Awards to whistle blowers	Y		82. Delete $ for Trident II	X
66. African disaster relief	Y		83. Allow 15 MX missiles	Y
67. Ban bank loans to So Afr	Y		84. Bar MX procurement-1985	N
68. Bar coun duty-free trtmt	N		85. Equal Access Act	Y
69. Steel import limits	Y		86. Aid to El Salvador	Y
70. Soc Sec COLAs=inflation	Y		87. Bar Nicarag water mining	Y
71. Bar haz waste vctms suits	N		88. Physician/Medicare freeze	N
72. Prohibit aid to Nicaragua	Y		89. Increase "sin" taxes	Y
73. Cut $-Schs bar sch prayer	N		90. End SBA direct loans	N
74. Raise taxes; Cut Medicare	Y		91. Sell Conrail	N
75. Alien residncy-prior 1982	N		92. Equal Rights Amendment	Y
76. Alien residncy-prior 1980	N		93. Marines in Lebanon	Y
77. Pen emp-hire illgl aliens	Y		94. Eminent domain-Coal comps	Y
78. Lmt Persh II/cruse-Europe	N		95. Prohibit EPA sanctions	Y
79. Delete 34 B-1 bombers	N		96. SS age increase/Reforms	Y

Presidential Support Score: 1986 - 35% 1985 - 36%

U T A H

HANSEN, JAMES V. -- Utah 1st District [Republican]. Counties of Beaver, Box Elder, Cache, Davis, Garfield, Iron, Juab, Kane, Millard, Morgan, Piute, Rich, Tooele, Washington, Wayne and Weber. Prior Terms: House: 1981-86. Born: August 14, 1932; Salt Lake City, Utah. Education: University of Utah (B.S.). Military Service: U.S. Navy, 1951-55. Occupation: Utah representative (1973-80); Farmington City councilman; acting mayor; insurance company executive.

1. Immigration Reform	N		30. Ease '68 Gun Control Act	Y
2. Open fld-search warrants	Y		31. Bar intrstat handgun tran	N
3. Civil pnty-hire ill alien	Y		32. Keep '68 Gun Control Act	N
4. So Afr sanc-veto override	N		33. Nicaraguan contra aid	Y
5. Tax Overhaul	N		34. Bar emp polygraph testing	N
6. South Africa sanctions	X		35. Tax Overhaul consideratn	Y
7. Death penalty-drug bill	Y		36. Bar armor-piercing ammo	N
8. Evidence-warrantless srch	Y		37. Tax Overhaul consideratn	Y
9. Life term-second drug off	Y		38. Make comp emissions known	N
10. Military use in drug war	N		39. Allow toxic victims suits	N
11. Troop reduction in Europe	N		40. Strike Superfund "VAT"	N
12. Prohibit chemical weapons	N		41. Notify emp-plant closing	N
13. Bar ASAT testing	N		42. Bar emp consult-plant clo	Y
14. Abide SALT II weapons ban	N		43. Medicare cuts;Tax incres'	N
15. Follow SALT II-Soviets do	Y		44. Delete 12 MX missiles	N
16. Reduce SDI funding	N		45. Spending cuts;Tax incres'	N
17. Increase SDI funding	Y		46. Textile Import Quotas	N
18. Purchase Trident sub	N		47. Cut some school lunch fds	Y
19. Delete 12 MX;Add conv wpn	N		48. Clean Water Act Amendmnts	Y
20. Raise speed limit	Y		49. Youth work projects	N
21. Textile import Quotas(*)	N		50. Assist military in Angola	Y
22. Req Pentagon buy US goods	N		51. Allow US troops-Nicaragua	Y
23. AIDS ins anti-dscriminatn	N		52. Pentagon polygraph exams	Y
24. Nicaraguan refugee aid	N		53. Bar ASAT testing	N
25. Nicaraguan contra aid	Y		54. Suspend def pmt for abuse	N
26. US abide by SALT II	Y		55. Bar Pentagon-contr emplmt	Y
27. Prohibit Saudi arms sale	N		56. Increase SDI funding	Y
28. Military Retiremnt Reform	Y		57. Reduce SDI funding	N
29. Nicaraguan refugee aid	Y		58. Produce chemical weapons	Y

HANSEN, JAMES V. (Cont.)

59. Bar CIA fndg in Nicaragua N
60. South Africa sanctions N
61. Cut SS COLAs; Raise taxes N
62. Let US invest-So Africa Y
63. Approve 21 MX for 1985 Y
64. Emergency Farm Credit N
65. Awards to whistle blowers Y
66. African disaster relief N
67. Ban bank loans to So Afr N
68. Bar coun duty-free trtmt N
69. Steel import limits Y
70. Soc Sec COLAs=inflation Y
71. Bar haz waste vctms suits Y
72. Prohibit aid to Nicaragua N
73. Cut $-Schs bar sch prayer Y
74. Raise taxes; Cut Medicare Y
75. Alien residncy-prior 1982 Y
76. Alien residncy-prior 1980 Y
77. Pen emp-hire illgl aliens N
78. Lmt Persh II/cruse-Europe N
79. Delete 34 B-1 bombers N
80. Bar purch of Pershing II N
81. Bar purchase of Sgt York N
82. Delete $ for Trident II N
83. Allow 15 MX missiles Y
84. Bar MX procurement-1985 N
85. Equal Access Act Y
86. Aid to El Salvador ?
87. Bar Nicarag water mining N
88. Physician/Medicare freeze Y
89. Increase "sin" taxes Y
90. End SBA direct loans Y
91. Sell Conrail Y
92. Equal Rights Amendment N
93. Marines in Lebanon Y
94. Eminent domain-Coal comps Y
95. Prohibit EPA sanctions ?
96. SS age increase/Reforms Y
97. Auto domestic content req N
98. Delete jobs program fundg Y
99. Highway-Gas tax bill N
100. Raise Medicare;Cut defnse N
101. Emergency housing aid ?
102. Across-the-board tax cuts Y
103. Gramm-Latta II targets Y
104. Delete B-1 bomber funds N
105. Dsapprov Saudi AWACS sale N

Presidential Support Score: 1986 - 80% 1985 - 81%

MONSON, DAVID S. -- Utah 2nd District [Republican]. County of Salt Lake (pt.). Prior Terms: 1985-1986. Occupation: Accountant; lieutenant governor.

1. Immigration Reform Y
2. Open fld-search warrants Y
3. Civil pnty-hire ill alien Y
4. So Afr sanc-veto override N
5. Tax Overhaul N
6. South Africa sanctions N
7. Death penalty-drug bill Y
8. Evidence-warrantless srch Y
9. Life term-second drug off Y
10. Military use in drug war Y
11. Troop reduction in Europe N
12. Prohibit chemical weapons N
13. Bar ASAT testing N
14. Abide SALT II weapons ban N
15. Follow SALT II-Soviets do Y
16. Reduce SDI funding N
17. Increase SDI funding N
18. Purchase Trident sub N
19. Delete 12 MX;Add conv wpn N
20. Raise speed limit Y
21. Textile Import Quotas(*) N
22. Req Pentagon buy US goods N
23. AIDS ins anti-dscriminatn N
24. Nicaraguan refugee aid N
25. Nicaraguan contra aid Y
26. US abide by SALT II Y
27. Prohibit Saudi arms sale Y
28. Military Retiremnt Reform Y
29. Nicaraguan refugee aid Y
30. Ease '68 Gun Control Act Y
31. Bar intrstat handgun tran N
32. Keep '68 Gun Control Act N
33. Nicaraguan contra aid Y
34. Bar emp polygraph testing N
35. Tax Overhaul consideratn N
36. Bar armor-piercing ammo Y
37. Tax Overhaul consideratn N
38. Make comp emissions known N
39. Allow toxic victims suits N
40. Strike Superfund "VAT" N
41. Notify emp-plant closing N
42. Bar emp consult-plant clo Y
43. Medicare cuts;Tax incres' N
44. Delete 12 MX missiles N
45. Spending cuts;Tax incres' N
46. Textile Import Quotas Y
47. Cut some school lunch fds Y
48. Clean Water Act Amendmnts Y
49. Youth work projects N
50. Assist military in Angola Y
51. Allow US troops-Nicaragua Y
52. Pentagon polygraph exams Y
53. Bar ASAT testing N
54. Suspend def pmt for abuse N
55. Bar Pentagon-contr emplmt N
56. Increase SDI funding Y
57. Reduce SDI funding N
58. Produce chemical weapons Y

MONSON, DAVID S. (Cont.)

59. Bar CIA fndg in Nicaragua N
60. South Africa sanctions N
61. Cut SS COLAs; Raise taxes N
62. Let US invest-So Africa Y
63. Approve 21 MX for 1985 Y
64. Emergency Farm Credit Y
65. Awards to whistle blowers Y
66. African disaster relief N

Presidential Support Score: 1986 - 74% 1985 - 78%

NIELSON, HOWARD C. -- Utah 3rd District [Republican]. Counties of Carbon, Daggett, Duchesne, Emery, Grand, Salt Lake (pt.), San Juan, Sanpete, Sevier, Summit, Uintah, Utah and Wasatch. Prior Terms: House: 1983-86. Born: September 12, 1924; Richfield, Utah. Education: University of Utah (B.S.); University of Oregon (M.S.); Stanford University (M.B.A., Ph.D.). Military Service: U.S. Army Air Force, 1943-46. Occupation: Statistician (1949-51); research economist (1951-57); professor (1957-76, 1978-82); Utah representative (1967-74); commissioner, Higher Education (1976-78).

1. Immigration Reform Y
2. Open fld-search warrants Y
3. Civil pnty-hire ill alien Y
4. So Afr sanc-veto override N
5. Tax Overhaul N
6. South Africa sanctions N
7. Death penalty-drug bill Y
8. Evidence-warrantless srch Y
9. Life term-second drug off Y
10. Military use in drug war N
11. Troop reduction in Europe Y
12. Prohibit chemical weapons N
13. Bar ASAT testing N
14. Abide SALT II weapons ban N
15. Follow SALT II-Soviets do Y
16. Reduce SDI funding N
17. Increase SDI funding N
18. Purchase Trident sub N
19. Delete 12 MX;Add conv wpn N
20. Raise speed limit Y
21. Textile Import Quotas(*) N
22. Req Pentagon buy US goods N
23. AIDS ins anti-dscriminatn N
24. Nicaraguan refugee aid N
25. Nicaraguan contra aid Y
26. US abide by SALT II Y
27. Prohibit Saudi arms sale N
28. Military Retiremnt Reform Y
29. Nicaraguan refugee aid Y
30. Ease '68 Gun Control Act Y
31. Bar intrstat handgun tran N
32. Keep '68 Gun Control Act N
33. Nicaraguan contra aid Y
34. Bar emp polygraph testing Y
35. Tax Overhaul consideratn N
36. Bar armor-piercing ammo Y
37. Tax Overhaul consideratn N
38. Make comp emissions known N
39. Allow toxic victims suits N
40. Strike Superfund "VAT" N
41. Notify emp-plant closing N
42. Bar emp consult-plant clo Y
43. Medicare cuts;Tax incres' N
44. Delete 12 MX missiles N
45. Spending cuts;Tax incres' N
46. Textile Import Quotas N
47. Cut some school lunch fds Y
48. Clean Water Act Amendmnts Y
49. Youth work projects N
50. Assist military in Angola Y
51. Allow US troops-Nicaragua Y
52. Pentagon polygraph exams Y
53. Bar ASAT testing N
54. Suspend def pmt for abuse N
55. Bar Pentagon-contr emplmt Y
56. Increase SDI funding N
57. Reduce SDI funding N
58. Produce chemical weapons Y
59. Bar CIA fndg in Nicaragua N
60. South Africa sanctions N
61. Cut SS COLAs; Raise taxes N
62. Let US invest-So Africa Y
63. Approve 21 MX for 1985 Y
64. Emergency Farm Credit N
65. Awards to whistle blowers Y
66. African disaster relief N
67. Ban bank loans to So Afr N
68. Bar coun duty-free trtmt N
69. Steel import limits Y
70. Soc Sec COLAs=inflation Y
71. Bar haz waste vctms suits Y
72. Prohibit aid to Nicaragua N
73. Cut $-Schs bar sch prayer Y
74. Raise taxes; Cut Medicare N
75. Alien residncy-prior 1982 Y
76. Alien residncy-prior 1980 Y
77. Pen emp-hire illgl aliens N
78. Lmt Persh II/cruse-Europe N
79. Delete 34 B-1 bombers N
80. Bar purch of Pershing II N
81. Bar purchase of Sgt York Y
82. Delete $ for Trident II N
83. Allow 15 MX missiles Y
84. Bar MX procurement-1985 N

NIELSON, HOWARD C. (Cont.)

85.	Equal Access Act	Y	91.	Sell Conrail	Y
86.	Aid to El Salvador	Y	92.	Equal Rights Amendment	N
87.	Bar Nicarag water mining	N	93.	Marines in Lebanon	Y
88.	Physician/Medicare freeze	Y	94.	Eminent domain-Coal comps	Y
89.	Increase "sin" taxes	N	95.	Prohibit EPA sanctions	+
90.	End SBA direct loans	Y	96.	SS age increase/Reforms	Y

Presidential Support Score: 1986 - 75% 1985 - 84%

VERMONT

JEFFORDS, JAMES M. -- Representative at Large [Republican]. Prior Terms: House: 1975-86. Born: May 11, 1934; Rutland, Vt. Education: Yale University (B.A.); Harvard Law School (LL.B.). Military Service: U.S. Navy. Occupation: Attorney; Vermont senator; attorney general; member, Governor's Commission on Crime Control and Prevention; member, Drug Abuse Council.

1.	Immigration Reform	Y	43.	Medicare cuts;Tax incres'	N
2.	Open fld-search warrants	N	44.	Delete 12 MX missiles	Y
3.	Civil pnty-hire ill alien	N	45.	Spending cuts;Tax incres'	Y
4.	So Afr sanc-veto override	Y	46.	Textile Import Quotas	Y
5.	Tax Overhaul	Y	47.	Cut some school lunch fds	N
6.	South Africa sanctions	Y	48.	Clean Water Act Amendmnts	N
7.	Death penalty-drug bill	Y	49.	Youth work projects	Y
8.	Evidence-warrantless srch	N	50.	Assist military in Angola	N
9.	Life term-second drug off	Y	51.	Allow US troops-Nicaragua	N
10.	Military use in drug war	N	52.	Pentagon polygraph exams	Y
11.	Troop reduction in Europe	N	53.	Bar ASAT testing	Y
12.	Prohibit chemical weapons	Y	54.	Suspend def pmt for abuse	Y
13.	Bar ASAT testing	Y	55.	Bar Pentagon-contr emplmt	Y
14.	Abide SALT II weapons ban	Y	56.	Increase SDI funding	?
15.	Follow SALT II-Soviets do	N	57.	Reduce SDI funding	?
16.	Reduce SDI funding	N	58.	Produce chemical weapons	?
17.	Increase SDI funding	N	59.	Bar CIA fndg in Nicaragua	Y
18.	Purchase Trident sub	Y	60.	South Africa sanctions	Y
19.	Delete 12 MX;Add conv wpn	Y	61.	Cut SS COLAs; Raise taxes	N
20.	Raise speed limit	N	62.	Let US invest-So Africa	N
21.	Textile Import Quotas(*)	Y	63.	Approve 21 MX for 1985	N
22.	Req Pentagon buy US goods	Y	64.	Emergency Farm Credit	Y
23.	AIDS ins anti-dscriminatn	Y	65.	Awards to whistle blowers	Y
24.	Nicaraguan refugee aid	Y	66.	African disaster relief	Y
25.	Nicaraguan contra aid	N	67.	Ban bank loans to So Afr	Y
26.	US abide by SALT II	N	68.	Bar coun duty-free trtmt	N
27.	Prohibit Saudi arms sale	N	69.	Steel import limits	N
28.	Military Retiremnt Reform	Y	70.	Soc Sec COLAs=inflation	Y
29.	Nicaraguan refugee aid	Y	71.	Bar haz waste vctms suits	N
30.	Ease '68 Gun Control Act	Y	72.	Prohibit aid to Nicaragua	Y
31.	Bar intrstat handgun tran	N	73.	Cut $-Schs bar sch prayer	N
32.	Keep '68 Gun Control Act	Y	74.	Raise taxes; Cut Medicare	Y
33.	Nicaraguan contra aid	N	75.	Alien residncy-prior 1982	Y
34.	Bar emp polygraph testing	Y	76.	Alien residncy-prior 1980	Y
35.	Tax Overhaul consideratn	N	77.	Pen emp-hire illgl aliens	N
36.	Bar armor-piercing ammo	Y	78.	Lmt Persh II/cruse-Europe	?
37.	Tax Overhaul consideratn	N	79.	Delete 34 B-1 bombers	Y
38.	Make comp emissions known	Y	80.	Bar purch of Pershing II	N
39.	Allow toxic victims suits	Y	81.	Bar purchase of Sgt York	Y
40.	Strike Superfund "VAT"	Y	82.	Delete $ for Trident II	N
41.	Notify emp-plant closing	Y	83.	Allow 15 MX missiles	N
42.	Bar emp consult-plant clo	Y	84.	Bar MX procurement-1985	Y

JEFFORDS, JAMES M. (Cont.)

85. Equal Access Act Y
86. Aid to El Salvador N
87. Bar Nicarag water mining #
88. Physician/Medicare freeze Y
89. Increase "sin" taxes Y
90. End SBA direct loans N
91. Sell Conrail N
92. Equal Rights Amendment Y
93. Marines in Lebanon Y
94. Eminent domain-Coal comps N
95. Prohibit EPA sanctions N
96. SS age increase/Reforms Y
97. Auto domestic content req N
98. Delete jobs program fundg Y
99. Highway-Gas tax bill N
100. Raise Medicare;Cut defnse Y
101. Emergency housing aid Y
102. Across-the-board tax cuts N
103. Gramm-Latta II targets Y
104. Delete B-1 bomber funds Y
105. Dsapprov Saudi AWACS sale Y
106. Disapprove oil import fee Y
107. Rail Deregulation N
108. Dsapp India nuc fuel sale Y
109. Mil draft registration N
110. Chrysler Loan Guarantees N
111. Prohibit school busing N
112. Nuclear plant moratorium Y
113. Oil price controls Y
114. Tuition Tax Credits Y
115. Est Consumer Protect Agcy Y
116. Eliminate B-1 bomber fnds #
117. Subminimum wage for youth Y
118. Delete crude oil tax N
119. Natural gas deregulation N

Presidential Support Score: 1986 - 40% 1985 - 30%

V I R G I N I A

BATEMAN, HERBERT H. -- Virginia 1st District [Republican]. Counties of Accomack, Caroline, Charles City, Essex, Gloucester, James City, King and Queen, King George, King William, Lancaster, Mathews, Middlesex, New Kent, Northampton, Northumberland, Richmond, Westmoreland and York. Cities of Hampton, Newport News, Poquoson and Williamsburg. Prior Terms: House: 1983-86. Born: August 7, 1928; Elizabeth City, N.C. Education: College of William and Mary (B.A.); Georgetown University (LL.B.). Military Service: U.S. Air Force, 1951-53. Occupation: High school teacher; law clerk (1956-57); attorney; associate legal counsel, U.S. Junior Chamber of Commerce (1962-63); general legal counsel, U.S. Junior Chamber of Commerce (1964-65); Virginia senator (1968-72).

1. Immigration Reform N
2. Open fld-search warrants N
3. Civil pnty-hire ill alien ?
4. So Afr sanc-veto override Y
5. Tax Overhaul N
6. South Africa sanctions Y
7. Death penalty-drug bill Y
8. Evidence-warrantless srch Y
9. Life term-second drug off Y
10. Military use in drug war N
11. Troop reduction in Europe N
12. Prohibit chemical weapons N
13. Bar ASAT testing N
14. Abide SALT II weapons ban N
15. Follow SALT II-Soviets do Y
16. Reduce SDI funding N
17. Increase SDI funding N
18. Purchase Trident sub N
19. Delete 12 MX;Add conv wpn N
20. Raise speed limit Y
21. Textile Import Quotas(*) N
22. Req Pentagon buy US goods N
23. AIDS ins anti-dscriminatn N
24. Nicaraguan refugee aid N
25. Nicaraguan contra aid Y
26. US abide by SALT II Y
27. Prohibit Saudi arms sale Y
28. Military Retiremnt Reform Y
29. Nicaraguan refugee aid Y
30. Ease '68 Gun Control Act Y
31. Bar intrstat handgun tran Y
32. Keep '68 Gun Control Act Y
33. Nicaraguan contra aid Y
34. Bar emp polygraph testing N
35. Tax Overhaul consideratn Y
36. Bar armor-piercing ammo Y
37. Tax Overhaul consideratn N
38. Make comp emissions known N
39. Allow toxic victims suits N
40. Strike Superfund "VAT" N
41. Notify emp-plant closing N
42. Bar emp consult-plant clo Y

BATEMAN, HERBERT H. (Cont.)

43. Medicare cuts;Tax incres' N
44. Delete 12 MX missiles N
45. Spending cuts;Tax incres' N
46. Textile Import Quotas Y
47. Cut some school lunch fds Y
48. Clean Water Act Amendmnts Y
49. Youth work projects N
50. Assist military in Angola Y
51. Allow US troops-Nicaragua Y
52. Pentagon polygraph exams Y
53. Bar ASAT testing N
54. Suspend def pmt for abuse N
55. Bar Pentagon-contr emplmt N
56. Increase SDI funding N
57. Reduce SDI funding N
58. Produce chemical weapons Y
59. Bar CIA fndg in Nicaragua N
60. South Africa sanctions N
61. Cut SS COLAs; Raise taxes Y
62. Let US invest-So Africa Y
63. Approve 21 MX for 1985 Y
64. Emergency Farm Credit N
65. Awards to whistle blowers Y
66. African disaster relief Y
67. Ban bank loans to So Afr N
68. Bar coun duty-free trtmt N
69. Steel import limits N
70. Soc Sec COLAs=inflation Y
71. Bar haz waste vctms suits ?
72. Prohibit aid to Nicaragua Y
73. Cut $-Schs bar sch prayer Y
74. Raise taxes; Cut Medicare Y
75. Alien residncy-prior 1982 +
76. Alien residncy-prior 1980 Y
77. Pen emp-hire illgl aliens N
78. Lmt Persh II/cruse-Europe N
79. Delete 34 B-1 bombers N
80. Bar purch of Pershing II N
81. Bar purchase of Sgt York N
82. Delete $ for Trident II N
83. Allow 15 MX missiles Y
84. Bar MX procurement-1985 N
85. Equal Access Act Y
86. Aid to El Salvador Y
87. Bar Nicarag water mining N
88. Physician/Medicare freeze Y
89. Increase "sin" taxes Y
90. End SBA direct loans Y
91. Sell Conrail Y
92. Equal Rights Amendment N
93. Marines in Lebanon Y
94. Eminent domain-Coal comps N
95. Prohibit EPA sanctions Y
96. SS age increase/Reforms Y

Presidential Support Score: 1986 - 68% 1985 - 69%

WHITEHURST, G. WILLIAM -- Virginia 2nd District [Republican]. Cities of Norfolk and Virginia Beach. Prior Terms: House: 1969-86. Born: March 12, 1925; Norfolk, Va. Education: Washington and Lee University (B.A.); University of Virginia (M.A.); West Virginia University (Ph.D.). Military Service: U.S. Navy, WW II. Occupation: Dean (1963-68); television news analyst (1962-68).

1. Immigration Reform N
2. Open fld-search warrants Y
3. Civil pnty-hire ill alien N
4. So Afr sanc-veto override Y
5. Tax Overhaul N
6. South Africa sanctions ?
7. Death penalty-drug bill Y
8. Evidence-warrantless srch Y
9. Life term-second drug off Y
10. Military use in drug war N
11. Troop reduction in Europe N
12. Prohibit chemical weapons N
13. Bar ASAT testing N
14. Abide SALT II weapons ban N
15. Follow SALT II-Soviets do Y
16. Reduce SDI funding N
17. Increase SDI funding Y
18. Purchase Trident sub N
19. Delete 12 MX;Add conv wpn N
20. Raise speed limit N
21. Textile Import Quotas(*) N
22. Req Pentagon buy US goods N
23. AIDS ins anti-dscriminatn Y
24. Nicaraguan refugee aid N
25. Nicaraguan contra aid Y
26. US abide by SALT II Y
27. Prohibit Saudi arms sale N
28. Military Retiremnt Reform Y
29. Nicaraguan refugee aid Y
30. Ease '68 Gun Control Act N
31. Bar intrstat handgun tran Y
32. Keep '68 Gun Control Act Y
33. Nicaraguan contra aid Y
34. Bar emp polygraph testing N
35. Tax Overhaul consideratn Y
36. Bar armor-piercing ammo Y
37. Tax Overhaul consideratn N
38. Make comp emissions known N
39. Allow toxic victims suits N
40. Strike Superfund "VAT" N
41. Notify emp-plant closing N
42. Bar emp consult-plant clo ?

WHITEHURST, G. WILLIAM (Cont.)

43. Medicare cuts;Tax incres' N
44. Delete 12 MX missiles N
45. Spending cuts;Tax incres' N
46. Textile Import Quotas N
47. Cut some school lunch fds Y
48. Clean Water Act Amendmnts Y
49. Youth work projects ?
50. Assist military in Angola Y
51. Allow US troops-Nicaragua Y
52. Pentagon polygraph exams Y
53. Bar ASAT testing N
54. Suspend def pmt for abuse N
55. Bar Pentagon-contr emplmt Y
56. Increase SDI funding N
57. Reduce SDI funding N
58. Produce chemical weapons Y
59. Bar CIA fndg in Nicaragua N
60. South Africa sanctions N
61. Cut SS COLAs; Raise taxes Y
62. Let US invest-So Africa Y
63. Approve 21 MX for 1985 Y
64. Emergency Farm Credit Y
65. Awards to whistle blowers Y
66. African disaster relief Y
67. Ban bank loans to So Afr Y
68. Bar coun duty-free trtmt N
69. Steel import limits N
70. Soc Sec COLAs=inflation Y
71. Bar haz waste vctms suits Y
72. Prohibit aid to Nicaragua Y
73. Cut $-Schs bar sch prayer Y
74. Raise taxes; Cut Medicare Y
75. Alien residncy-prior 1982 Y
76. Alien residncy-prior 1980 Y
77. Pen emp-hire illgl aliens ?
78. Lmt Persh II/cruse-Europe N
79. Delete 34 B-1 bombers N
80. Bar purch of Pershing II N
81. Bar purchase of Sgt York N
82. Delete $ for Trident II N
83. Allow 15 MX missiles Y
84. Bar MX procurement-1985 N
85. Equal Access Act Y
86. Aid to El Salvador Y
87. Bar Nicarag water mining N
88. Physician/Medicare freeze Y
89. Increase "sin" taxes Y
90. End SBA direct loans N
91. Sell Conrail Y
92. Equal Rights Amendment Y
93. Marines in Lebanon Y
94. Eminent domain-Coal comps N
95. Prohibit EPA sanctions Y
96. SS age increase/Reforms Y
97. Auto domestic content req N
98. Delete jobs program fundg Y
99. Highway-Gas tax bill Y
100. Raise Medicare;Cut defnse N
101. Emergency housing aid Y
102. Across-the-board tax cuts Y
103. Gramm-Latta II targets Y
104. Delete B-1 bomber funds N
105. Dsapprov Saudi AWACS sale ?
106. Disapprove oil import fee Y
107. Rail Deregulation N
108. Dsapp India nuc fuel sale N
109. Mil draft registration Y
110. Chrysler Loan Guarantees Y
111. Prohibit school busing Y
112. Nuclear plant moratorium N
113. Oil price controls N
114. Tuition Tax Credits N
115. Est Consumer Protect Agcy N
116. Eliminate B-1 bomber fnds N
117. Subminimum wage for youth Y
118. Delete crude oil tax Y
119. Natural gas deregulation Y

Presidential Support Score: 1986 - 61% 1985 - 70%

BLILEY, THOMAS J., Jr. -- Virginia 3rd District [Republican]. Counties of Chesterfield (pt.) and Henrico. City of Richmond. Prior Terms: House: 1981-86. Born: January 28, 1932; Chesterfield County, Va. Education: Georgetown University (B.A.). Military Service: U.S. Navy. Occupation: Richmond city councilman (1968); vice-mayor (1968); mayor (1970-77); president, Virginia Municipal League; board member, National League of Cities; board member, Metropolitan Richmond Chamber of Commerce; board member, Crippled Children's Hospital; board member, St. Mary's Hospital; board member, Board of Visitors, Virginia Commonwealth University; board member, Southern Bank and Trust Co.

1. Immigration Reform N
2. Open fld-search warrants Y
3. Civil pnty-hire ill alien Y
4. So Afr sanc-veto override Y
5. Tax Overhaul Y
6. South Africa sanctions Y
7. Death penalty-drug bill Y
8. Evidence-warrantless srch Y
9. Life term-second drug off Y
10. Military use in drug war Y

BLILEY, THOMAS J., Jr. (Cont.)

11. Troop reduction in Europe N
12. Prohibit chemical weapons N
13. Bar ASAT testing N
14. Abide SALT II weapons ban N
15. Follow SALT II-Soviets do Y
16. Reduce SDI funding N
17. Increase SDI funding N
18. Purchase Trident sub N
19. Delete 12 MX;Add conv wpn N
20. Raise speed limit Y
21. Textile Import Quotas(*) Y
22. Req Pentagon buy US goods N
23. AIDS ins anti-dscriminatn N
24. Nicaraguan refugee aid N
25. Nicaraguan contra aid Y
26. US abide by SALT II Y
27. Prohibit Saudi arms sale Y
28. Military Retiremnt Reform Y
29. Nicaraguan refugee aid Y
30. Ease '68 Gun Control Act Y
31. Bar intrstat handgun tran N
32. Keep '68 Gun Control Act N
33. Nicaraguan contra aid Y
34. Bar emp polygraph testing N
35. Tax Overhaul consideratn N
36. Bar armor-piercing ammo Y
37. Tax Overhaul consideratn N
38. Make comp emissions known N
39. Allow toxic victims suits N
40. Strike Superfund "VAT" N
41. Notify emp-plant closing N
42. Bar emp consult-plant clo Y
43. Medicare cuts;Tax incres' N
44. Delete 12 MX missiles N
45. Spending cuts;Tax incres' N
46. Textile Import Quotas Y
47. Cut some school lunch fds Y
48. Clean Water Act Amendmnts Y
49. Youth work projects N
50. Assist military in Angola Y
51. Allow US troops-Nicaragua Y
52. Pentagon polygraph exams Y
53. Bar ASAT testing N
54. Suspend def pmt for abuse N
55. Bar Pentagon-contr emplmt Y
56. Increase SDI funding Y
57. Reduce SDI funding N
58. Produce chemical weapons Y
59. Bar CIA fndg in Nicaragua N
60. South Africa sanctions Y
61. Cut SS COLAs; Raise taxes N
62. Let US invest-So Africa N
63. Approve 21 MX for 1985 Y
64. Emergency Farm Credit Y
65. Awards to whistle blowers Y
66. African disaster relief Y
67. Ban bank loans to So Afr Y
68. Bar coun duty-free trtmt N
69. Steel import limits N
70. Soc Sec COLAs=inflation Y
71. Bar haz waste vctms suits Y
72. Prohibit aid to Nicaragua N
73. Cut $-Schs bar sch prayer Y
74. Raise taxes; Cut Medicare Y
75. Alien residncy-prior 1982 Y
76. Alien residncy-prior 1980 Y
77. Pen emp-hire illgl aliens N
78. Lmt Persh II/cruse-Europe N
79. Delete 34 B-1 bombers N
80. Bar purch of Pershing II N
81. Bar purchase of Sgt York N
82. Delete $ for Trident II N
83. Allow 15 MX missiles Y
84. Bar MX procurement-1985 N
85. Equal Access Act Y
86. Aid to El Salvador Y
87. Bar Nicarag water mining N
88. Physician/Medicare freeze Y
89. Increase "sin" taxes Y
90. End SBA direct loans Y
91. Sell Conrail Y
92. Equal Rights Amendment N
93. Marines in Lebanon Y
94. Eminent domain-Coal comps N
95. Prohibit EPA sanctions Y
96. SS age increase/Reforms Y
97. Auto domestic content req N
98. Delete jobs program fundg Y
99. Highway-Gas tax bill N
100. Raise Medicare;Cut defnse N
101. Emergency housing aid Y
102. Across-the-board tax cuts Y
103. Gramm-Latta II targets Y
104. Delete B-1 bomber funds N
105. Dsapprov Saudi AWACS sale Y

Presidential Support Score: 1986 - 69% 1985 - 74%

SISISKY, NORMAN -- Virginia 4th District [Democrat]. Counties of Amelia, Brunswick, Chesterfield (pt.), Dinwiddie, Greensville, Isle of Wight, Nottoway, Powhatan, Prince George, Southampton, Surry and Sussex. Cities of Chesapeake, Colonial Heights, Emporia, Franklin, Hopewell, Petersburg, Portsmouth and Suffolk. Prior Terms: House: 1983-86. Born: June 9, 1927; Baltimore, Md. Education: Virginia Commonwealth University (B.S.). Military Service: U.S. Navy, 1945-46. Occu-

SISISKY, NORMAN (Cont.)
pation: Operated Pepsi-Cola bottling company; Virginia representative (1973-82); served on Board of Visitors for Virginia State University; commissioner, Petersburg Hospital Authority; trustee, Virginia State College Foundation.

1. Immigration Reform Y
2. Open fld-search warrants Y
3. Civil pnty-hire ill alien N
4. So Afr sanc-veto override Y
5. Tax Overhaul N
6. South Africa sanctions Y
7. Death penalty-drug bill Y
8. Evidence-warrantless srch Y
9. Life term-second drug off Y
10. Military use in drug war N
11. Troop reduction in Europe N
12. Prohibit chemical weapons N
13. Bar ASAT testing N
14. Abide SALT II weapons ban N
15. Follow SALT II-Soviets do Y
16. Reduce SDI funding N
17. Increase SDI funding N
18. Purchase Trident sub Y
19. Delete 12 MX;Add conv wpn N
20. Raise speed limit Y
21. Textile Import Quotas(*) Y
22. Req Pentagon buy US goods N
23. AIDS ins anti-dscriminatn Y
24. Nicaraguan refugee aid N
25. Nicaraguan contra aid Y
26. US abide by SALT II Y
27. Prohibit Saudi arms sale Y
28. Military Retiremnt Reform Y
29. Nicaraguan refugee aid N
30. Ease '68 Gun Control Act Y
31. Bar intrstat handgun tran N
32. Keep '68 Gun Control Act N
33. Nicaraguan contra aid Y
34. Bar emp polygraph testing N
35. Tax Overhaul consideratn Y
36. Bar armor-piercing ammo Y
37. Tax Overhaul consideratn Y
38. Make comp emissions known N
39. Allow toxic victims suits N
40. Strike Superfund "VAT" N
41. Notify emp-plant closing N
42. Bar emp consult-plant clo Y
43. Medicare cuts;Tax incres' Y
44. Delete 12 MX missiles Y
45. Spending cuts;Tax incres' Y
46. Textile Import Quotas Y
47. Cut some school lunch fds N
48. Clean Water Act Amendmnts Y
49. Youth work projects N
50. Assist military in Angola N
51. Allow US troops-Nicaragua N
52. Pentagon polygraph exams Y
53. Bar ASAT testing N
54. Suspend def pmt for abuse N
55. Bar Pentagon-contr emplmt Y
56. Increase SDI funding N
57. Reduce SDI funding N
58. Produce chemical weapons Y
59. Bar CIA fndg in Nicaragua N
60. South Africa sanctions Y
61. Cut SS COLAs; Raise taxes N
62. Let US invest-So Africa N
63. Approve 21 MX for 1985 N
64. Emergency Farm Credit Y
65. Awards to whistle blowers Y
66. African disaster relief Y
67. Ban bank loans to So Afr Y
68. Bar coun duty-free trtmt N
69. Steel import limits Y
70. Soc Sec COLAs=inflation Y
71. Bar haz waste vctms suits Y
72. Prohibit aid to Nicaragua Y
73. Cut $-Schs bar sch prayer N
74. Raise taxes; Cut Medicare Y
75. Alien residncy-prior 1982 Y
76. Alien residncy-prior 1980 Y
77. Pen emp-hire illgl aliens N
78. Lmt Persh II/cruse-Europe N
79. Delete 34 B-1 bombers N
80. Bar purch of Pershing II N
81. Bar purchase of Sgt York N
82. Delete $ for Trident II N
83. Allow 15 MX missiles N
84. Bar MX procurement-1985 Y
85. Equal Access Act Y
86. Aid to El Salvador Y
87. Bar Nicarag water mining Y
88. Physician/Medicare freeze N
89. Increase "sin" taxes Y
90. End SBA direct loans N
91. Sell Conrail ?
92. Equal Rights Amendment Y
93. Marines in Lebanon Y
94. Eminent domain-Coal comps N
95. Prohibit EPA sanctions ?
96. SS age increase/Reforms N

Presidential Support Score: 1986 - 40% 1985 - 39%

DANIEL, DAN -- Virginia 5th District [Democrat]. Counties of Appomattox, Bedford, Buckingham, Campbell, Carroll, Charlotte, Cumberland, Fluvanna, Franklin, Halifax, Henry, Lunenburg,

DANIEL, DAN (Cont.)
Mecklenburg, Nelson, Patrick, Pittsylvania, Prince Edward. Cities of Bedford, Danville, Lynchburg (pt.), Martinsville and South Boston. Born: May 12, 1914; Chatham, Va. Occupation: Assistant, board chairman, Dan River Mills, Inc.; Virginia Delegate (1959); member, President's People-to-People Committee (1956-65); vice chairman, Export Council; trustee.

1. Immigration Reform ?
2. Open fld-search warrants ?
3. Civil pnty-hire ill alien ?
4. So Afr sanc-veto override N
5. Tax Overhaul N
6. South Africa sanctions N
7. Death penalty-drug bill Y
8. Evidence-warrantless srch Y
9. Life term-second drug off Y
10. Military use in drug war N
11. Troop reduction in Europe N
12. Prohibit chemical weapons N
13. Bar ASAT testing N
14. Abide SALT II weapons ban N
15. Follow SALT II-Soviets do Y
16. Reduce SDI funding N
17. Increase SDI funding N
18. Purchase Trident sub N
19. Delete 12 MX;Add conv wpn N
20. Raise speed limit N
21. Textile Import Quotas(*) Y
22. Req Pentagon buy US goods Y
23. AIDS ins anti-dscriminatn N
24. Nicaraguan refugee aid N
25. Nicaraguan contra aid Y
26. US abide by SALT II Y
27. Prohibit Saudi arms sale Y
28. Military Retiremnt Reform Y
29. Nicaraguan refugee aid N
30. Ease '68 Gun Control Act Y
31. Bar intrstat handgun tran N
32. Keep '68 Gun Control Act N
33. Nicaraguan contra aid Y
34. Bar emp polygraph testing N
35. Tax Overhaul consideratn Y
36. Bar armor-piercing ammo Y
37. Tax Overhaul consideratn Y
38. Make comp emissions known N
39. Allow toxic victims suits N
40. Strike Superfund "VAT" Y
41. Notify emp-plant closing N
42. Bar emp consult-plant clo #
43. Medicare cuts;Tax incres' Y
44. Delete 12 MX missiles N
45. Spending cuts;Tax incres' N
46. Textile Import Quotas Y
47. Cut some school lunch fds Y
48. Clean Water Act Amendmnts Y
49. Youth work projects Y
50. Assist military in Angola ?
51. Allow US troops-Nicaragua N
52. Pentagon polygraph exams Y
53. Bar ASAT testing N
54. Suspend def pmt for abuse N
55. Bar Pentagon-contr emplmt N
56. Increase SDI funding N
57. Reduce SDI funding N
58. Produce chemical weapons Y
59. Bar CIA fndg in Nicaragua N
60. South AFrica sanctions N
61. Cut SS COLAs; Raise taxes N
62. Let US invest-So Africa N
63. Approve 21 MX for 1985 Y
64. Emergency Farm Credit Y
65. Awards to whistle blowers Y
66. African disaster relief Y
67. Ban bank loans to So Afr N
68. Bar coun duty-free trtmt N
69. Steel import limits N
70. Soc Sec COLAs=inflation Y
71. Bar haz waste vctms suits Y
72. Prohibit aid to Nicaragua Y
73. Cut $-Schs bar sch prayer Y
74. Raise taxes; Cut Medicare N
75. Alien residncy-prior 1982 Y
76. Alien residncy-prior 1980 Y
77. Pen emp-hire illgl aliens N
78. Lmt Persh II/cruse-Europe N
79. Delete 34 B-1 bombers N
80. Bar purch of Pershing II N
81. Bar purchase of Sgt York N
82. Delete $ for Trident II N
83. Allow 15 MX missiles Y
84. Bar MX procurement-1985 N
85. Equal Access Act Y
86. Aid to El Salvador Y
87. Bar Nicarag water mining N
88. Physician/Medicare freeze Y
89. Increase "sin" taxes N
90. End SBA direct loans Y
91. Sell Conrail Y
92. Equal Rights Amendment N
93. Marines in Lebanon Y
94. Eminent domain-Coal comps N
95. Prohibit EPA sanctions Y
96. SS age increase/Reforms Y
97. Auto domestic content req N
98. Delete jobs program fundg Y
99. Highway-Gas tax bill N
100. Raise Medicare;Cut defnse N
101. Emergency housing aid Y
102. Across-the-board tax cuts Y
103. Gramm-Latta II targets Y
104. Delete B-1 bomber funds N

DANIEL, DAN (Cont.)

105. Dsapprov Saudi AWACS sale N
106. Disapprove oil import fee Y
107. Rail Deregulation N
108. Dsapp India nuc fuel sale N
109. Mil draft registration Y
110. Chrysler Loan Guarantees N
111. Prohibit school busing Y
112. Nuclear plant moratorium N
113. Oil price controls N
114. Tuition Tax Credits N
115. Est Consumer Protect Agcy N
116. Eliminate B-1 bomber fnds N
117. Subminimum wage for youth Y
118. Delete crude oil tax Y
119. Natural gas deregulation Y

Presidential Support Score: 1986 - 63% 1985 - 66%

OLIN, JAMES R. (Jim) -- Virginia 6th District [Democrat]. Counties of Alleghany, Amherst, Augusta, Bath, Botetourt, Highland, Roanoke, Rockbridge and Rockingham. Cities of Buena Vista, Clifton Forge, Covington, Harrisburg, Lexington, Lynchburg (pt.), Roanoke, Salem, Staunton and Waynesboro. Prior Terms: House: 1983-86. Born: February 28, 1920; Chicago, Ill. Education: Cornell University (B.S.). Military Service: U.S. Army, 1943-46. Occupation: General Electric executive; county board of supervisors; board member, Burrell Memorial Hospital.

1. Immigration Reform N
2. Open fld-search warrants Y
3. Civil pnty-hire ill alien N
4. So Afr sanc-veto override Y
5. Tax Overhaul N
6. South Africa sanctions Y
7. Death penalty-drug bill ?
8. Evidence-warrantless srch N
9. Life term-second drug off Y
10. Military use in drug war N
11. Troop reduction in Europe N
12. Prohibit chemical weapons Y
13. Bar ASAT testing Y
14. Abide SALT II weapons ban Y
15. Follow SALT II-Soviets do N
16. Reduce SDI funding N
17. Increase SDI funding N
18. Purchase Trident sub N
19. Delete 12 MX;Add conv wpn Y
20. Raise speed limit N
21. Textile Import Quotas(*) Y
22. Req Pentagon buy US goods Y
23. AIDS ins anti-dscriminatn Y
24. Nicaraguan refugee aid Y
25. Nicaraguan contra aid N
26. US abide by SALT II N
27. Prohibit Saudi arms sale Y
28. Military Retiremnt Reform Y
29. Nicaraguan refugee aid Y
30. Ease '68 Gun Control Act Y
31. Bar intrstat handgun tran N
32. Keep '68 Gun Control Act N
33. Nicaraguan contra aid N
34. Bar emp polygraph testing Y
35. Tax Overhaul consideratn Y
36. Bar armor-piercing ammo Y
37. Tax Overhaul consideratn Y
38. Make comp emissions known N
39. Allow toxic victims suits N
40. Strike Superfund "VAT" N
41. Notify emp-plant closing N
42. Bar emp consult-plant clo Y
43. Medicare cuts;Tax incres' Y
44. Delete 12 MX missiles Y
45. Spending cuts;Tax incres' N
46. Textile Import Quotas Y
47. Cut some school lunch fds Y
48. Clean Water Act Amendmnts N
49. Youth work projects N
50. Assist military in Angola N
51. Allow US troops-Nicaragua N
52. Pentagon polygraph exams Y
53. Bar ASAT testing Y
54. Suspend def pmt for abuse N
55. Bar Pentagon-contr emplmt Y
56. Increase SDI funding N
57. Reduce SDI funding N
58. Produce chemical weapons N
59. Bar CIA fndg in Nicaragua Y
60. South Africa sanctions Y
61. Cut SS COLAs; Raise taxes Y
62. Let US invest-So Africa N
63. Approve 21 MX for 1985 N
64. Emergency Farm Credit Y
65. Awards to whistle blowers Y
66. African disaster relief Y
67. Ban bank loans to So Afr Y
68. Bar coun duty-free trtmt Y
69. Steel import limits N
70. Soc Sec COLAs=inflation Y
71. Bar haz waste vctms suits ?
72. Prohibit aid to Nicaragua Y
73. Cut $-Schs bar sch prayer N
74. Raise taxes; Cut Medicare Y
75. Alien residncy-prior 1982 N
76. Alien residncy-prior 1980 N
77. Pen emp-hire illgl aliens Y
78. Lmt Persh II/cruse-Europe N

OLIN, JAMES R. (Jim) (Cont.)

79.	Delete 34 B-1 bombers	N	88.	Physician/Medicare freeze	N
80.	Bar purch of Pershing II	N	89.	Increase "sin" taxes	Y
81.	Bar purchase of Sgt York	Y	90.	End SBA direct loans	N
82.	Delete $ for Trident II	N	91.	Sell Conrail	N
83.	Allow 15 MX missiles	Y	92.	Equal Rights Amendment	Y
84.	Bar MX procurement-1985	Y	93.	Marines in Lebanon	Y
85.	Equal Access Act	Y	94.	Eminent domain-Coal comps	N
86.	Aid to El Salvador	N	95.	Prohibit EPA sanctions	N
87.	Bar Nicarag water mining	Y	96.	SS age increase/Reforms	Y

Presidential Support Score: 1986 - 35% 1985 - 41%

SLAUGHTER, D. FRENCH, Jr. -- Virginia 7th District [Republican]. Counties of Albemarle, Clark, Culpeper, Fauquier, Frederick, Goochland, Greene, Hanover, Louisa, Madison, Orange, Page, Prince William (pt.), Rappahannock, Shenandoah, Spotsylvania, Stafford (pt.) and Warren. Cities of Charlottesville, Fredericksburg, Manassas, Manassas Park and Winchester. Prior Terms: 1985-86. Education: Virginia Military Institute; University of Virginia. Military Service: U.S. Army. Occupation: Attorney; Virginia delegate.

1.	Immigration Reform	N	34.	Bar emp polygraph testing	N
2.	Open fld-search warrants	Y	35.	Tax Overhaul consideratn	N
3.	Civil pnty-hire ill alien	Y	36.	Bar armor-piercing ammo	Y
4.	So Afr sanc-veto override	N	37.	Tax Overhaul consideratn	N
5.	Tax Overhaul	Y	38.	Make comp emissions known	N
6.	South Africa sanctions	N	39.	Allow toxic victims suits	N
7.	Death penalty-drug bill	Y	40.	Strike Superfund "VAT"	N
8.	Evidence-warrantless srch	Y	41.	Notify emp-plant closing	N
9.	Life term-second drug off	Y	42.	Bar emp consult-plant clo	Y
10.	Military use in drug war	Y	43.	Medicare cuts;Tax incres'	N
11.	Troop reduction in Europe	N	44.	Delete 12 MX missiles	N
12.	Prohibit chemical weapons	N	45.	Spending cuts;Tax incres'	N
13.	Bar ASAT testing	N	46.	Textile Import Quotas	Y
14.	Abide SALT II weapons ban	N	47.	Cut some school lunch fds	Y
15.	Follow SALT II-Soviets do	Y	48.	Clean Water Act Amendmnts	Y
16.	Reduce SDI funding	N	49.	Youth work projects	N
17.	Increase SDI funding	N	50.	Assist military in Angola	Y
18.	Purchase Trident sub	N	51.	Allow US troops-Nicaragua	Y
19.	Delete 12 MX;Add conv wpn	N	52.	Pentagon polygraph exams	Y
20.	Raise speed limit	N	53.	Bar ASAT testing	N
21.	Textile Import Quotas(*)	Y	54.	Suspend def pmt for abuse	N
22.	Req Pentagon buy US goods	N	55.	Bar Pentagon-contr emplmt	Y
23.	AIDS ins anti-dscriminatn	N	56.	Increase SDI funding	Y
24.	Nicaraguan refugee aid	N	57.	Reduce SDI funding	N
25.	Nicaraguan contra aid	Y	58.	Produce chemical weapons	Y
26.	US abide by SALT II	Y	59.	Bar CIA fndg in Nicaragua	N
27.	Prohibit Saudi arms sale	N	60.	South Africa sanctions	N
28.	Military Retiremnt Reform	Y	61.	Cut SS COLAs; Raise taxes	N
29.	Nicaraguan refugee aid	Y	62.	Let US invest-So Africa	Y
30.	Ease '68 Gun Control Act	Y	63.	Approve 21 MX for 1985	Y
31.	Bar intrstat handgun tran	Y	64.	Emergency Farm Credit	Y
32.	Keep '68 Gun Control Act	Y	65.	Awards to whistle blowers	Y
33.	Nicaraguan contra aid	Y	66.	African disaster relief	Y

Presidential Support Score: 1986 - 81% 1985 - 74%

PARRIS, STAN -- Virginia 8th District [Republican]. Counties of Fairfax(pt.), Prince William (pt.) and Stafford (pt.). City of

PARRIS, STAN (Cont.)

Alexandria. Prior Terms: House: 1973-74, 1981-86. Born: September 9, 1929; Champaign, Ill. Education: University of Illinois (B.S.); George Washington University (J.D.). Military Service: U.S. Air Force, Korean War. Occupation: Attorney; president, Woodbridge Lincoln Mercury Corp. and Flying Circus Aerodrome, Inc.; pilot.

1. Immigration Reform N
2. Open fld-search warrants N
3. Civil pnty-hire ill alien Y
4. So Afr sanc-veto override N
5. Tax Overhaul N
6. South Africa sanctions N
7. Death penalty-drug bill Y
8. Evidence-warrantless srch Y
9. Life term-second drug off Y
10. Military use in drug war Y
11. Troop reduction in Europe N
12. Prohibit chemical weapons N
13. Bar ASAT testing N
14. Abide SALT II weapons ban N
15. Follow SALT II-Soviets do Y
16. Reduce SDI funding N
17. Increase SDI funding N
18. Purchase Trident sub N
19. Delete 12 MX;Add conv wpn N
20. Raise speed limit Y
21. Textile Import Quotas(*) Y
22. Req Pentagon buy US goods Y
23. AIDS ins anti-dscriminatn N
24. Nicaraguan refugee aid N
25. Nicaraguan contra aid Y
26. US abide by SALT II Y
27. Prohibit Saudi arms sale Y
28. Military Retiremnt Reform Y
29. Nicaraguan refugee aid Y
30. Ease '68 Gun Control Act Y
31. Bar intrstat handgun tran N
32. Keep '68 Gun Control Act Y
33. Nicaraguan contra aid Y
34. Bar emp polygraph testing N
35. Tax Overhaul consideratn N
36. Bar armor-piercing ammo ?
37. Tax Overhaul consideratn N
38. Make comp emissions known N
39. Allow toxic victims suits N
40. Strike Superfund "VAT" Y
41. Notify emp-plant closing N
42. Bar emp consult-plant clo Y
43. Medicare cuts;Tax incres' X
44. Delete 12 MX missiles ?
45. Spending cuts;Tax incres' Y
46. Textile Import Quotas Y
47. Cut some school lunch fds N
48. Clean Water Act Amendmnts Y
49. Youth work projects N
50. Assist military in Angola Y
51. Allow US troops-Nicaragua Y
52. Pentagon polygraph exams Y
53. Bar ASAT testing N
54. Suspend def pmt for abuse N
55. Bar Pentagon-contr emplmt N
56. Increase SDI funding N
57. Reduce SDI funding N
58. Produce chemical weapons Y
59. Bar CIA fndg in Nicaragua N
60. South Africa sanctions N
61. Cut SS COLAs; Raise taxes N
62. Let US invest-So Africa Y
63. Approve 21 MX for 1985 Y
64. Emergency Farm Credit Y
65. Awards to whistle blowers Y
66. African disaster relief Y
67. Ban bank loans to So Afr Y
68. Bar coun duty-free trtmt N
69. Steel import limits N
70. Soc Sec COLAs=inflation Y
71. Bar haz waste vctms suits Y
72. Prohibit aid to Nicaragua Y
73. Cut $-Schs bar sch prayer Y
74. Raise taxes; Cut Medicare N
75. Alien residncy-prior 1982 Y
76. Alien residncy-prior 1980 Y
77. Pen emp-hire illgl aliens N
78. Lmt Persh II/cruse-Europe N
79. Delete 34 B-1 bombers N
80. Bar purch of Pershing II N
81. Bar purchase of Sgt York N
82. Delete $ for Trident II N
83. Allow 15 MX missiles Y
84. Bar MX procurement-1985 N
85. Equal Access Act Y
86. Aid to El Salvador Y
87. Bar Nicarag water mining N
88. Physician/Medicare freeze Y
89. Increase "sin" taxes N
90. End SBA direct loans Y
91. Sell Conrail Y
92. Equal Rights Amendment Y
93. Marines in Lebanon Y
94. Eminent domain-Coal comps Y
95. Prohibit EPA sanctions N
96. SS age increase/Reforms Y
97. Auto domestic content req N
98. Delete jobs program fundg Y
99. Highway-Gas tax bill Y
100. Raise Medicare;Cut defnse Y
101. Emergency housing aid Y
102. Across-the-board tax cuts Y
103. Gramm-Latta II targets Y
104. Delete B-1 bomber funds N

PARRIS, STAN (Cont.)
105. Dsapprov Saudi AWACS sale N

Presidential Support Score: 1986 - 69% 1985 - 64%

BOUCHER, FREDERICK C. (Rick) -- Virginia 9th District [Democrat]. Counties of Bland, Buchanan, Craig, Dickenson, Floyd, Giles, Grayson, Lee, Montgomery, Pulaski, Russell, Scott, Smyth, Tazewell, Washington, Wise and Wythe. Cities of Bristol, Galax, Norton and Radford. Prior Terms: House: 1983-86. Born: August 1, 1946; Washington County, Va. Education: Roanoke College (B.A.); University of Virginia. Occupation: Virginia senator (1975-82).

1. Immigration Reform Y
2. Open fld-search warrants Y
3. Civil pnty-hire ill alien N
4. So Afr sanc-veto override Y
5. Tax Overhaul N
6. South Africa sanctions ?
7. Death penalty-drug bill ?
8. Evidence-warrantless srch ?
9. Life term-second drug off Y
10. Military use in drug war N
11. Troop reduction in Europe N
12. Prohibit chemical weapons Y
13. Bar ASAT testing Y
14. Abide SALT II weapons ban Y
15. Follow SALT II-Soviets do N
16. Reduce SDI funding N
17. Increase SDI funding N
18. Purchase Trident sub Y
19. Delete 12 MX;Add conv wpn Y
20. Raise speed limit Y
21. Textile Import Quotas(*) Y
22. Req Pentagon buy US goods Y
23. AIDS ins anti-dscriminatn ?
24. Nicaraguan refugee aid Y
25. Nicaraguan contra aid N
26. US abide by SALT II N
27. Prohibit Saudi arms sale Y
28. Military Retiremnt Reform Y
29. Nicaraguan refugee aid Y
30. Ease '68 Gun Control Act Y
31. Bar intrstat handgun tran N
32. Keep '68 Gun Control Act N
33. Nicaraguan contra aid N
34. Bar emp polygraph testing Y
35. Tax Overhaul consideratn Y
36. Bar armor-piercing ammo Y
37. Tax Overhaul consideratn Y
38. Make comp emissions known Y
39. Allow toxic victims suits Y
40. Strike Superfund "VAT" Y
41. Notify emp-plant closing N
42. Bar emp consult-plant clo Y
43. Medicare cuts;Tax incres' N
44. Delete 12 MX missiles Y
45. Spending cuts;Tax incres' Y
46. Textile Import Quotas Y
47. Cut some school lunch fds N
48. Clean Water Act Amendmnts N
49. Youth work projects Y
50. Assist military in Angola N
51. Allow US troops-Nicaragua N
52. Pentagon polygraph exams N
53. Bar ASAT testing Y
54. Suspend def pmt for abuse Y
55. Bar Pentagon-contr emplmt Y
56. Increase SDI funding N
57. Reduce SDI funding N
58. Produce chemical weapons Y
59. Bar CIA fndg in Nicaragua Y
60. South Africa sanctions Y
61. Cut SS COLAs; Raise taxes N
62. Let US invest-So Africa ?
63. Approve 21 MX for 1985 N
64. Emergency Farm Credit Y
65. Awards to whistle blowers Y
66. African disaster relief Y
67. Ban bank loans to So Afr Y
68. Bar coun duty-free trtmt N
69. Steel import limits Y
70. Soc Sec COLAs=inflation Y
71. Bar haz waste vctms suits N
72. Prohibit aid to Nicaragua Y
73. Cut $-Schs bar sch prayer Y
74. Raise taxes; Cut Medicare N
75. Alien residncy-prior 1982 Y
76. Alien residncy-prior 1980 N
77. Pen emp-hire illgl aliens N
78. Lmt Persh II/cruse-Europe N
79. Delete 34 B-1 bombers N
80. Bar purch of Pershing II N
81. Bar purchase of Sgt York N
82. Delete $ for Trident II N
83. Allow 15 MX missiles N
84. Bar MX procurement-1985 Y
85. Equal Access Act Y
86. Aid to El Salvador N
87. Bar Nicarag water mining ?
88. Physician/Medicare freeze N
89. Increase "sin" taxes Y
90. End SBA direct loans N
91. Sell Conrail N
92. Equal Rights Amendment Y

BOUCHER, FREDERICK C. (Rick) (Cont.)

93. Marines in Lebanon Y
94. Eminent domain-Coal comps N
95. Prohibit EPA sanctions Y
96. SS age increase/Reforms N

Presidential Support Score: 1986 - 24% 1985 - 29%

WOLF, FRANK R. -- Virginia 10th District [Republican]. Counties of Arlington, Fairfax (pt.) and Loudoun. Cities of Fairfax and Falls Church. Prior Terms: House: 1981-86. Born: January 30, 1939; Philadelphia, Pa. Education: Pennsylvania State University (B.A.); Georgetown University Law School. Military Service: U.S. Army Signal Corps (Reserves). Occupation: Congressional legislative assistant (1968-71); assistant, Secretary of Interior (1971-74); deputy assistant secretary, Congressional and Legislative Affairs, Department of Interior (1974-75).

1. Immigration Reform N
2. Open fld-search warrants N
3. Civil pnty-hire ill alien N
4. So Afr sanc-veto override Y
5. Tax Overhaul N
6. South Africa sanctions Y
7. Death penalty-drug bill Y
8. Evidence-warrantless srch Y
9. Life term-second drug off Y
10. Military use in drug war Y
11. Troop reduction in Europe N
12. Prohibit chemical weapons N
13. Bar ASAT testing N
14. Abide SALT II weapons ban N
15. Follow SALT II-Soviets do Y
16. Reduce SDI funding N
17. Increase SDI funding N
18. Purchase Trident sub N
19. Delete 12 MX;Add conv wpn N
20. Raise speed limit N
21. Textile Import Quotas(*) N
22. Req Pentagon buy US goods N
23. AIDS ins anti-dscriminatn N
24. Nicaraguan refugee aid N
25. Nicaraguan contra aid Y
26. US abide by SALT II Y
27. Prohibit Saudi arms sale Y
28. Military Retiremnt Reform Y
29. Nicaraguan refugee aid Y
30. Ease '68 Gun Control Act Y
31. Bar intrstat handgun tran Y
32. Keep '68 Gun Control Act Y
33. Nicaraguan contra aid Y
34. Bar emp polygraph testing N
35. Tax Overhaul consideratn Y
36. Bar armor-piercing ammo Y
37. Tax Overhaul consideratn N
38. Make comp emissions known Y
39. Allow toxic victims suits N
40. Strike Superfund "VAT" Y
41. Notify emp-plant closing N
42. Bar emp consult-plant clo Y
43. Medicare cuts;Tax incres' N
44. Delete 12 MX missiles N
45. Spending cuts;Tax incres' Y
46. Textile Import Quotas N
47. Cut some school lunch fds N
48. Clean Water Act Amendmnts Y
49. Youth work projects N
50. Assist military in Angola Y
51. Allow US troops-Nicaragua Y
52. Pentagon polygraph exams Y
53. Bar ASAT testing N
54. Suspend def pmt for abuse N
55. Bar Pentagon-contr emplmt N
56. Increase SDI funding N
57. Reduce SDI funding N
58. Produce chemical weapons Y
59. Bar CIA fndg in Nicaragua N
60. South Africa sanctions N
61. Cut SS COLAs; Raise taxes N
62. Let US invest-So Africa Y
63. Approve 21 MX for 1985 Y
64. Emergency Farm Credit Y
65. Awards to whistle blowers Y
66. African disaster relief Y
67. Ban bank loans to So Afr Y
68. Bar coun duty-free trtmt N
69. Steel import limits N
70. Soc Sec COLAs=inflation Y
71. Bar haz waste vctms suits Y
72. Prohibit aid to Nicaragua Y
73. Cut $-Schs bar sch prayer Y
74. Raise taxes; Cut Medicare Y
75. Alien residncy-prior 1982 Y
76. Alien residncy-prior 1980 Y
77. Pen emp-hire illgl aliens N
78. Lmt Persh II/cruse-Europe N
79. Delete 34 B-1 bombers N
80. Bar purch of Pershing II N
81. Bar purchase of Sgt York N
82. Delete $ for Trident II N
83. Allow 15 MX missiles Y
84. Bar MX procurement-1985 N
85. Equal Access Act Y
86. Aid to El Salvador Y
87. Bar Nicarag water mining N
88. Physician/Medicare freeze Y

WOLF, FRANK R. (Cont.)

89. Increase "sin" taxes Y
90. End SBA direct loans N
91. Sell Conrail Y
92. Equal Rights Amendment N
93. Marines in Lebanon Y
94. Eminent domain-Coal comps Y
95. Prohibit EPA sanctions N
96. SS age increase/Reforms Y
97. Auto domestic content req N
98. Delete jobs program fundg Y
99. Highway-Gas tax bill N
100. Raise Medicare;Cut defnse Y
101. Emergency housing aid Y
102. Across-the-board tax cuts Y
103. Gramm-Latta II targets Y
104. Delete B-1 bomber funds N
105. Dsapprov Saudi AWACS sale Y

Presidential Support Score: 1986 - 66% 1985 - 70%

WASHINGTON

MILLER, JOHN -- Washington 1st District [Republican]. Counties of King (pt.), Kitsap (pt.) and Snohomish (pt.). Prior Terms: 1985-86. Occupation: Attorney; city councilman; commentator; assistant attorney general (1965-70).

1. Immigration Reform Y
2. Open fld-search warrants N
3. Civil pnty-hire ill alien N
4. So Afr sanc-veto override Y
5. Tax Overhaul Y
6. South Africa sanctions Y
7. Death penalty-drug bill N
8. Evidence-warrantless srch Y
9. Life term-second drug off Y
10. Military use in drug war Y
11. Troop reduction in Europe N
12. Prohibit chemical weapons Y
13. Bar ASAT testing Y
14. Abide SALT II weapons ban N
15. Follow SALT II-Soviets do Y
16. Reduce SDI funding N
17. Increase SDI funding N
18. Purchase Trident sub N
19. Delete 12 MX;Add conv wpn Y
20. Raise speed limit N
21. Textile Import Quotas(*) N
22. Req Pentagon buy US goods N
23. AIDS ins anti-dscriminatn Y
24. Nicaraguan refugee aid N
25. Nicaraguan contra aid Y
26. US abide by SALT II Y
27. Prohibit Saudi arms sale Y
28. Military Retiremnt Reform Y
29. Nicaraguan refugee aid Y
30. Ease '68 Gun Control Act N
31. Bar intrstat handgun tran Y
32. Keep '68 Gun Control Act Y
33. Nicaraguan contra aid Y
34. Bar emp polygraph testing Y
35. Tax Overhaul consideratn N
36. Bar armor-piercing ammo Y
37. Tax Overhaul consideratn N
38. Make comp emissions known Y
39. Allow toxic victims suits N
40. Strike Superfund "VAT" Y
41. Notify emp-plant closing N
42. Bar emp consult-plant clo Y
43. Medicare cuts;Tax incres' N
44. Delete 12 MX missiles Y
45. Spending cuts;Tax incres' N
46. Textile Import Quotas N
47. Cut some school lunch fds Y
48. Clean Water Act Amendmnts N
49. Youth work projects N
50. Assist military in Angola Y
51. Allow US troops-Nicaragua N
52. Pentagon polygraph exams Y
53. Bar ASAT testing Y
54. Suspend def pmt for abuse N
55. Bar Pentagon-contr emplmt Y
56. Increase SDI funding N
57. Reduce SDI funding N
58. Produce chemical weapons Y
59. Bar CIA fndg in Nicaragua N
60. South Africa sanctions Y
61. Cut SS COLAs; Raise taxes Y
62. Let US invest-So Africa N
63. Approve 21 MX for 1985 N
64. Emergency Farm Credit N
65. Awards to whistle blowers Y
66. African disaster relief Y

Presidential Support Score: 1986 - 56% 1985 - 64%

SWIFT, AL -- Washington 2nd District [Democrat]. Counties of Clallam, Grays Harbor (pt.), Island, Jefferson, Kitsap (pt.), Mason (pt.), San Juan, Skagit, Snohomish (pt.) and Whatcom. Prior Terms: House: 1979-86. Born: September 12, 1935; Tacoma, Wash. Education: Whitman College; Central Washington

SWIFT, AL (Cont.)
University. Occupation: Public affairs director, KVOS-TV (1962); administrative assistant (1965-69).

1. Immigration Reform Y
2. Open fld-search warrants Y
3. Civil pnty-hire ill alien Y
4. So Afr sanc-veto override Y
5. Tax Overhaul N
6. South Africa sanctions Y
7. Death penalty-drug bill N
8. Evidence-warrantless srch N
9. Life term-second drug off N
10. Military use in drug war N
11. Troop reduction in Europe N
12. Prohibit chemical weapons Y
13. Bar ASAT testing Y
14. Abide SALT II weapons ban Y
15. Follow SALT II-Soviets do N
16. Reduce SDI funding Y
17. Increase SDI funding N
18. Purchase Trident sub Y
19. Delete 12 MX;Add conv wpn Y
20. Raise speed limit N
21. Textile Import Quotas(*) N
22. Req Pentagon buy US goods N
23. AIDS ins anti-dscriminatn Y
24. Nicaraguan refugee aid Y
25. Nicaraguan contra aid N
26. US abide by SALT II N
27. Prohibit Saudi arms sale Y
28. Military Retiremnt Reform Y
29. Nicaraguan refugee aid Y
30. Ease '68 Gun Control Act Y
31. Bar intrstat handgun tran N
32. Keep '68 Gun Control Act N
33. Nicaraguan contra aid N
34. Bar emp polygraph testing Y
35. Tax Overhaul consideratn Y
36. Bar armor-piercing ammo Y
37. Tax Overhaul consideratn Y
38. Make comp emissions known N
39. Allow toxic victims suits N
40. Strike Superfund "VAT" Y
41. Notify emp-plant closing Y
42. Bar emp consult-plant clo N
43. Medicare cuts;Tax incres' Y
44. Delete 12 MX missiles Y
45. Spending cuts;Tax incres' Y
46. Textile Import Quotas N
47. Cut some school lunch fds N
48. Clean Water Act Amendmnts N
49. Youth work projects Y
50. Assist military in Angola N
51. Allow US troops-Nicaragua N
52. Pentagon polygraph exams N
53. Bar ASAT testing Y
54. Suspend def pmt for abuse ?
55. Bar Pentagon-contr emplmt Y
56. Increase SDI funding N
57. Reduce SDI funding N
58. Produce chemical weapons N
59. Bar CIA fndg in Nicaragua Y
60. South Africa sanctions Y
61. Cut SS COLAs; Raise taxes Y
62. Let US invest-So Africa N
63. Approve 21 MX for 1985 N
64. Emergency Farm Credit Y
65. Awards to whistle blowers Y
66. African disaster relief Y
67. Ban bank loans to So Afr Y
68. Bar coun duty-free trtmt N
69. Steel import limits Y
70. Soc Sec COLAs=inflation Y
71. Bar haz waste vctms suits N
72. Prohibit aid to Nicaragua Y
73. Cut $-Schs bar sch prayer N
74. Raise taxes; Cut Medicare Y
75. Alien residncy-prior 1982 Y
76. Alien residncy-prior 1980 N
77. Pen emp-hire illgl aliens Y
78. Lmt Persh II/cruse-Europe Y
79. Delete 34 B-1 bombers Y
80. Bar purch of Pershing II Y
81. Bar purchase of Sgt York Y
82. Delete $ for Trident II N
83. Allow 15 MX missiles N
84. Bar MX procurement-1985 Y
85. Equal Access Act N
86. Aid to El Salvador N
87. Bar Nicarag water mining Y
88. Physician/Medicare freeze N
89. Increase "sin" taxes Y
90. End SBA direct loans N
91. Sell Conrail N
92. Equal Rights Amendment Y
93. Marines in Lebanon N
94. Eminent domain-Coal comps N
95. Prohibit EPA sanctions Y
96. SS age increase/Reforms N
97. Auto domestic content req Y
98. Delete jobs program fundg N
99. Highway-Gas tax bill N
100. Raise Medicare;Cut defnse N
101. Emergency housing aid Y
102. Across-the-board tax cuts N
103. Gramm-Latta II targets N
104. Delete B-1 bomber funds Y
105. Dsapprov Saudi AWACS sale Y
106. Disapprove oil import fee Y
107. Rail Deregulation N
108. Dsapp India nuc fuel sale N
109. Mil draft registration N
110. Chrysler Loan Guarantees N
111. Prohibit school busing N
112. Nuclear plant moratorium Y

SWIFT, AL (Cont.)
113. Oil price controls Y

Presidential Support Score: 1986 - 19% 1985 - 26%

BONKER, DON -- Washington 3rd District [Democrat]. Counties of Clark, Cowlitz, Grays Harbor (pt.), Lewis, Pacific, Pierce (pt.), Thurston and Wahkiakum. Prior Terms: House: 1975-86. Born: March 7, 1937; Denver, Colo. Education: Lewis and Clark College (B.A.); American University. Military Service: U.S. Coast Guard, 1955-59. Occupation: Legislative assistant, senate committee (1964-66); auditor, Clark County (1966).

1. Immigration Reform Y
2. Open fld-search warrants Y
3. Civil pnty-hire ill alien N
4. So Afr sanc-veto override ?
5. Tax Overhaul N
6. South Africa sanctions Y
7. Death penalty-drug bill N
8. Evidence-warrantless srch N
9. Life term-second drug off N
10. Military use in drug war N
11. Troop reduction in Europe N
12. Prohibit chemical weapons Y
13. Bar ASAT testing Y
14. Abide SALT II weapons ban Y
15. Follow SALT II-Soviets do N
16. Reduce SDI funding Y
17. Increase SDI funding N
18. Purchase Trident sub Y
19. Delete 12 MX;Add conv wpn Y
20. Raise speed limit Y
21. Textile Import Quotas(*) N
22. Req Pentagon buy US goods N
23. AIDS ins anti-dscriminatn ?
24. Nicaraguan refugee aid Y
25. Nicaraguan contra aid N
26. US abide by SALT II N
27. Prohibit Saudi arms sale N
28. Military Retiremnt Reform Y
29. Nicaraguan refugee aid Y
30. Ease '68 Gun Control Act Y
31. Bar intrstat handgun tran Y
32. Keep '68 Gun Control Act Y
33. Nicaraguan contra aid N
34. Bar emp polygraph testing Y
35. Tax Overhaul consideratn Y
36. Bar armor-piercing ammo Y
37. Tax Overhaul consideratn Y
38. Make comp emissions known N
39. Allow toxic victims suits Y
40. Strike Superfund "VAT" Y
41. Notify emp-plant closing Y
42. Bar emp consult-plant clo N
43. Medicare cuts;Tax incres' Y
44. Delete 12 MX missiles ?
45. Spending cuts;Tax incres' Y
46. Textile Import Quotas N
47. Cut some school lunch fds N
48. Clean Water Act Amendmnts N
49. Youth work projects Y
50. Assist military in Angola N
51. Allow US troops-Nicaragua ?
52. Pentagon polygraph exams Y
53. Bar ASAT testing Y
54. Suspend def pmt for abuse Y
55. Bar Pentagon-contr emplmt Y
56. Increase SDI funding N
57. Reduce SDI funding Y
58. Produce chemical weapons N
59. Bar CIA fndg in Nicaragua Y
60. South Africa sanctions Y
61. Cut SS COLAs; Raise taxes N
62. Let US invest-So Africa N
63. Approve 21 MX for 1985 N
64. Emergency Farm Credit Y
65. Awards to whistle blowers Y
66. African disaster relief Y
67. Ban bank loans to So Afr Y
68. Bar coun duty-free trtmt N
69. Steel import limits Y
70. Soc Sec COLAs=inflation Y
71. Bar haz waste vctms suits N
72. Prohibit aid to Nicaragua Y
73. Cut $-Schs bar sch prayer N
74. Raise taxes; Cut Medicare Y
75. Alien residncy-prior 1982 Y
76. Alien residncy-prior 1980 N
77. Pen emp-hire illgl aliens ?
78. Lmt Persh II/cruse-Europe Y
79. Delete 34 B-1 bombers Y
80. Bar purch of Pershing II Y
81. Bar purchase of Sgt York Y
82. Delete $ for Trident II N
83. Allow 15 MX missiles N
84. Bar MX procurement-1985 Y
85. Equal Access Act Y
86. Aid to El Salvador N
87. Bar Nicarag water mining Y
88. Physician/Medicare freeze N
89. Increase "sin" taxes Y
90. End SBA direct loans N
91. Sell Conrail N
92. Equal Rights Amendment Y
93. Marines in Lebanon Y
94. Eminent domain-Coal comps N
95. Prohibit EPA sanctions +
96. SS age increase/Reforms N

BONKER, DON (Cont.)

97. Auto domestic content req N
98. Delete jobs program fundg N
99. Highway-Gas tax bill -
100. Raise Medicare;Cut defnse N
101. Emergency housing aid Y
102. Across-the-board tax cuts N
103. Gramm-Latta II targets N
104. Delete B-1 bomber funds Y
105. Dsapprov Saudi AWACS sale ?
106. Disapprove oil import fee Y
107. Rail Deregulation N
108. Dsapp India nuc fuel sale Y
109. Mil draft registration N
110. Chrysler Loan Guarantees Y
111. Prohibit school busing N
112. Nuclear plant moratorium Y
113. Oil price controls Y
114. Tuition Tax Credits ?
115. Est Consumer Protect Agcy N
116. Eliminate B-1 bomber fnds Y
117. Subminimum wage for youth Y
118. Delete crude oil tax N
119. Natural gas deregulation N

Presidential Support Score: 1986 - 24% 1985 - 23%

MORRISON, SID -- Washington 4th District [Republican]. Counties of Benton, Chelan, Douglas, Franklin, Grant, Kittitas, Klickitat, Okanogan, Skamania and Yakima. Prior Terms: House: 1981-86. Born: May 13, 1933; Yakima, Wash. Education: Yakima Valley College; Washington State University (B.S.). Military Service: U.S. Army, 1954-56. Occupation: Orchardist; Washington representative (1966-74); Washington senator (1974-80); chairman, Washington State Apple Commission; member, Board of Directors, Washington State Horticultural Association; board member, United Way.

1. Immigration Reform Y
2. Open fld-search warrants Y
3. Civil pnty-hire ill alien Y
4. So Afr sanc-veto override Y
5. Tax Overhaul Y
6. South Africa sanctions Y
7. Death penalty-drug bill Y
8. Evidence-warrantless srch Y
9. Life term-second drug off Y
10. Military use in drug war Y
11. Troop reduction in Europe N
12. Prohibit chemical weapons N
13. Bar ASAT testing N
14. Abide SALT II weapons ban N
15. Follow SALT II-Soviets do Y
16. Reduce SDI funding N
17. Increase SDI funding N
18. Purchase Trident sub Y
19. Delete 12 MX;Add conv wpn N
20. Raise speed limit Y
21. Textile Import Quotas(*) N
22. Req Pentagon buy US goods Y
23. AIDS ins anti-dscriminatn N
24. Nicaraguan refugee aid N
25. Nicaraguan contra aid Y
26. US abide by SALT II Y
27. Prohibit Saudi arms sale N
28. Military Retiremnt Reform Y
29. Nicaraguan refugee aid Y
30. Ease '68 Gun Control Act Y
31. Bar intrstat handgun tran N
32. Keep '68 Gun Control Act N
33. Nicaraguan contra aid Y
34. Bar emp polygraph testing N
35. Tax Overhaul consideratn N
36. Bar armor-piercing ammo Y
37. Tax Overhaul consideratn N
38. Make comp emissions known N
39. Allow toxic victims suits N
40. Strike Superfund "VAT" Y
41. Notify emp-plant closing N
42. Bar emp consult-plant clo Y
43. Medicare cuts;Tax incres' N
44. Delete 12 MX missiles N
45. Spending cuts;Tax incres' N
46. Textile Import Quotas N
47. Cut some school lunch fds N
48. Clean Water Act Amendmnts Y
49. Youth work projects N
50. Assist military in Angola Y
51. Allow US troops-Nicaragua Y
52. Pentagon polygraph exams Y
53. Bar ASAT testing N
54. Suspend def pmt for abuse N
55. Bar Pentagon-contr emplmt Y
56. Increase SDI funding Y
57. Reduce SDI funding N
58. Produce chemical weapons Y
59. Bar CIA fndg in Nicaragua N
60. South Africa sanctions Y
61. Cut SS COLAs; Raise taxes Y
62. Let US invest-So Africa Y
63. Approve 21 MX for 1985 Y
64. Emergency Farm Credit Y
65. Awards to whistle blowers Y
66. African disaster relief Y
67. Ban bank loans to So Afr Y
68. Bar coun duty-free trtmt N

MORRISON, SID (Cont.)

69. Steel import limits N
70. Soc Sec COLAs=inflation Y
71. Bar haz waste vctms suits Y
72. Prohibit aid to Nicaragua Y
73. Cut $-Schs bar sch prayer N
74. Raise taxes; Cut Medicare Y
75. Alien residncy-prior 1982 Y
76. Alien residncy-prior 1980 N
77. Pen emp-hire illgl aliens N
78. Lmt Persh II/cruse-Europe N
79. Delete 34 B-1 bombers N
80. Bar purch of Pershing II N
81. Bar purchase of Sgt York ?
82. Delete $ for Trident II N
83. Allow 15 MX missiles Y
84. Bar MX procurement-1985 N
85. Equal Access Act Y
86. Aid to El Salvador Y
87. Bar Nicarag water mining Y
88. Physician/Medicare freeze Y
89. Increase "sin" taxes Y
90. End SBA direct loans N
91. Sell Conrail Y
92. Equal Rights Amendment Y
93. Marines in Lebanon Y
94. Eminent domain-Coal comps N
95. Prohibit EPA sanctions +
96. SS age increase/Reforms Y
97. Auto domestic content req N
98. Delete jobs program fundg Y
99. Highway-Gas tax bill N
100. Raise Medicare;Cut defnse N
101. Emergency housing aid Y
102. Across-the-board tax cuts Y
103. Gramm-Latta II targets Y
104. Delete B-1 bomber funds N
105. Dsapprov Saudi AWACS sale N

Presidential Support Score: 1986 - 60% 1985 - 59%

FOLEY, THOMAS S. -- Washington 5th District [Democrat]. Counties of Adams, Asatin, Columbia, Ferry, Garfield, Lincoln, Pend Oreille, Spokane, Stevens, Walla Walla and Whitman. Prior Terms: House: 1965-86. Born: March 6, 1929; Spokane, Wash. Education: University of Washington (B.A., LL.B.). Occupation: Spokane County deputy prosecuting attorney; instructor, Gonzaga University Law School; Washington assistant attorney general.

1. Immigration Reform Y
2. Open fld-search warrants Y
3. Civil pnty-hire ill alien N
4. So Afr sanc-veto override Y
5. Tax Overhaul Y
6. South Africa sanctions Y
7. Death penalty-drug bill Y
8. Evidence-warrantless srch N
9. Life term-second drug off N
10. Military use in drug war N
11. Troop reduction in Europe N
12. Prohibit chemical weapons Y
13. Bar ASAT testing Y
14. Abide SALT II weapons ban Y
15. Follow SALT II-Soviets do N
16. Reduce SDI funding ?
17. Increase SDI funding N
18. Purchase Trident sub Y
19. Delete 12 MX;Add conv wpn N
20. Raise speed limit N
21. Textile Import Quotas(*) X
22. Req Pentagon buy US goods N
23. AIDS ins anti-dscriminatn Y
24. Nicaraguan refugee aid Y
25. Nicaraguan contra aid N
26. US abide by SALT II N
27. Prohibit Saudi arms sale Y
28. Military Retiremnt Reform Y
29. Nicaraguan refugee aid Y
30. Ease '68 Gun Control Act Y
31. Bar intrstat handgun tran N
32. Keep '68 Gun Control Act N
33. Nicaraguan contra aid N
34. Bar emp polygraph testing Y
35. Tax Overhaul consideratn Y
36. Bar armor-piercing ammo Y
37. Tax Overhaul consideratn Y
38. Make comp emissions known N
39. Allow toxic victims suits N
40. Strike Superfund "VAT" Y
41. Notify emp-plant closing Y
42. Bar emp consult-plant clo N
43. Medicare cuts;Tax incres' Y
44. Delete 12 MX missiles Y
45. Spending cuts;Tax incres' Y
46. Textile Import Quotas N
47. Cut some school lunch fds N
48. Clean Water Act Amendmnts N
49. Youth work projects Y
50. Assist military in Angola N
51. Allow US troops-Nicaragua N
52. Pentagon polygraph exams Y
53. Bar ASAT testing Y
54. Suspend def pmt for abuse Y
55. Bar Pentagon-contr emplmt Y
56. Increase SDI funding N
57. Reduce SDI funding N
58. Produce chemical weapons N

FOLEY, THOMAS S. (Cont.)

59. Bar CIA fndg in Nicaragua Y
60. South Africa sanctions Y
61. Cut SS COLAs; Raise taxes N
62. Let US invest-So Africa ?
63. Approve 21 MX for 1985 N
64. Emergency Farm Credit Y
65. Awards to whistle blowers Y
66. African disaster relief Y
67. Ban bank loans to So Afr Y
68. Bar coun duty-free trtmt N
69. Steel import limits N
70. Soc Sec COLAs=inflation Y
71. Bar haz waste vctms suits Y
72. Prohibit aid to Nicaragua Y
73. Cut $-Schs bar sch prayer N
74. Raise taxes; Cut Medicare Y
75. Alien residncy-prior 1982 Y
76. Alien residncy-prior 1980 N
77. Pen emp-hire illgl aliens Y
78. Lmt Persh II/cruse-Europe N
79. Delete 34 B-1 bombers N
80. Bar purch of Pershing II Y
81. Bar purchase of Sgt York Y
82. Delete $ for Trident II N
83. Allow 15 MX missiles N
84. Bar MX procurement-1985 Y
85. Equal Access Act N
86. Aid to El Salvador N
87. Bar Nicarag water mining Y
88. Physician/Medicare freeze N
89. Increase "sin" taxes Y
90. End SBA direct loans ?
91. Sell Conrail N
92. Equal Rights Amendment Y
93. Marines in Lebanon Y
94. Eminent domain-Coal comps N
95. Prohibit EPA sanctions Y
96. SS age increase/Reforms N
97. Auto domestic content req N
98. Delete jobs program fundg N
99. Highway-Gas tax bill Y
100. Raise Medicare;Cut defnse N
101. Emergency housing aid Y
102. Across-the-board tax cuts N
103. Gramm-Latta II targets N
104. Delete B-1 bomber funds N
105. Dsapprov Saudi AWACS sale Y
106. Disapprove oil import fee Y
107. Rail Deregulation N
108. Dsapp India nuc fuel sale N
109. Mil draft registration N
110. Chrysler Loan Guarantees Y
111. Prohibit school busing N
112. Nuclear plant moratorium N
113. Oil price controls N
114. Tuition Tax Credits Y
115. Est Consumer Protect Agcy N
116. Eliminate B-1 bomber fnds Y
117. Subminimum wage for youth N
118. Delete crude oil tax N
119. Natural gas deregulation N

Presidential Support Score: 1986 - 24% 1985 - 29%

DICKS, NORMAN D. -- Washington 6th District [Democrat]. Counties of Kitsap (pt.), Mason (pt.) and Pierce (pt.). Prior Terms: House: 1977-86. Born: December 16, 1940; Bremerton, Wash. Education: University of Washington (B.A., J.D.). Occupation: Congressional assistant (1968-76).

1. Immigration Reform Y
2. Open fld-search warrants Y
3. Civil pnty-hire ill alien ?
4. So Afr sanc-veto override Y
5. Tax Overhaul Y
6. South Africa sanctions Y
7. Death penalty-drug bill Y
8. Evidence-warrantless srch N
9. Life term-second drug off Y
10. Military use in drug war N
11. Troop reduction in Europe N
12. Prohibit chemical weapons N
13. Bar ASAT testing Y
14. Abide SALT II weapons ban Y
15. Follow SALT II-Soviets do N
16. Reduce SDI funding N
17. Increase SDI funding N
18. Purchase Trident sub Y
19. Delete 12 MX;Add conv wpn N
20. Raise speed limit Y
21. Textile Import Quotas(*) N
22. Req Pentagon buy US goods N
23. AIDS ins anti-dscriminatn Y
24. Nicaraguan refugee aid Y
25. Nicaraguan contra aid N
26. US abide by SALT II N
27. Prohibit Saudi arms sale Y
28. Military Retiremnt Reform Y
29. Nicaraguan refugee aid Y
30. Ease '68 Gun Control Act Y
31. Bar intrstat handgun tran Y
32. Keep '68 Gun Control Act Y
33. Nicaraguan contra aid N
34. Bar emp polygraph testing Y
35. Tax Overhaul consideratn N
36. Bar armor-piercing ammo Y
37. Tax Overhaul consideratn N
38. Make comp emissions known Y
39. Allow toxic victims suits N
40. Strike Superfund "VAT" Y

DICKS, NORMAN D. (Cont.)

41. Notify emp-plant closing Y
42. Bar emp consult-plant clo N
43. Medicare cuts;Tax incres' Y
44. Delete 12 MX missiles N
45. Spending cuts;Tax incres' Y
46. Textile Import Quotas N
47. Cut some school lunch fds N
48. Clean Water Act Amendmnts N
49. Youth work projects Y
50. Assist military in Angola N
51. Allow US troops-Nicaragua N
52. Pentagon polygraph exams ?
53. Bar ASAT testing Y
54. Suspend def pmt for abuse Y
55. Bar Pentagon-contr emplmt Y
56. Increase SDI funding N
57. Reduce SDI funding N
58. Produce chemical weapons Y
59. Bar CIA fndg in Nicaragua Y
60. South Africa sanctions Y
61. Cut SS COLAs; Raise taxes N
62. Let US invest-So Africa N
63. Approve 21 MX for 1985 Y
64. Emergency Farm Credit Y
65. Awards to whistle blowers Y
66. African disaster relief Y
67. Ban bank loans to So Afr Y
68. Bar coun duty-free trtmt N
69. Steel import limits Y
70. Soc Sec COLAs=inflation ?
71. Bar haz waste vctms suits N
72. Prohibit aid to Nicaragua Y
73. Cut $-Schs bar sch prayer N
74. Raise taxes; Cut Medicare Y
75. Alien residncy-prior 1982 Y
76. Alien residncy-prior 1980 N
77. Pen emp-hire illgl aliens N
78. Lmt Persh II/cruse-Europe N
79. Delete 34 B-1 bombers N
80. Bar purch of Pershing II Y
81. Bar purchase of Sgt York Y
82. Delete $ for Trident II N
83. Allow 15 MX missiles Y
84. Bar MX procurement-1985 N
85. Equal Access Act N
86. Aid to El Salvador N
87. Bar Nicarag water mining Y
88. Physician/Medicare freeze N
89. Increase "sin" taxes Y
90. End SBA direct loans N
91. Sell Conrail N
92. Equal Rights Amendment Y
93. Marines in Lebanon Y
94. Eminent domain-Coal comps N
95. Prohibit EPA sanctions Y
96. SS age increase/Reforms N
97. Auto domestic content req Y
98. Delete jobs program fundg N
99. Highway-Gas tax bill Y
100. Raise Medicare;Cut defnse N
101. Emergency housing aid Y
102. Across-the-board tax cuts Y
103. Gramm-Latta II targets N
104. Delete B-1 bomber funds N
105. Dsapprov Saudi AWACS sale Y
106. Disapprove oil import fee Y
107. Rail Deregulation Y
108. Dsapp India nuc fuel sale N
109. Mil draft registration Y
110. Chrysler Loan Guarantees Y
111. Prohibit school busing N
112. Nuclear plant moratorium N
113. Oil price controls Y
114. Tuition Tax Credits N
115. Est Consumer Protect Agcy Y
116. Eliminate B-1 bomber fnds Y
117. Subminimum wage for youth N
118. Delete crude oil tax N
119. Natural gas deregulation N

Presidential Support Score: 1986 - 27% 1985 - 35%

LOWRY, MIKE -- Washington 7th District [Democrat]. County of King (pt.). Prior Terms: House: 1979-86. Born: March 8, 1939; St. John, Wash. Education: Washington State University. Occupation: Chief fiscal analyst and staff director, Senate committee (1969-73); governmental affairs director, health cooperative (1974-75); county councilman (1975-77).

1. Immigration Reform Y
2. Open fld-search warrants Y
3. Civil pnty-hire ill alien Y
4. So Afr sanc-veto override Y
5. Tax Overhaul N
6. South Africa sanctions Y
7. Death penalty-drug bill N
8. Evidence-warrantless srch N
9. Life term-second drug off N
10. Military use in drug war N
11. Troop reduction in Europe N
12. Prohibit chemical weapons Y
13. Bar ASAT testing Y
14. Abide SALT II weapons ban Y
15. Follow SALT II-Soviets do N
16. Reduce SDI funding Y
17. Increase SDI funding N
18. Purchase Trident sub N
19. Delete 12 MX;Add conv wpn Y
20. Raise speed limit N

LOWRY, MIKE (Cont.)

21. Textile Import Quotas(*) N
22. Req Pentagon buy US goods N
23. AIDS ins anti-dscriminatn Y
24. Nicaraguan refugee aid Y
25. Nicaraguan contra aid N
26. US abide by SALT II N
27. Prohibit Saudi arms sale Y
28. Military Retiremnt Reform Y
29. Nicaraguan refugee aid Y
30. Ease '68 Gun Control Act N
31. Bar intrstat handgun tran Y
32. Keep '68 Gun Control Act Y
33. Nicaraguan contra aid N
34. Bar emp polygraph testing Y
35. Tax Overhaul consideratn Y
36. Bar armor-piercing ammo Y
37. Tax Overhaul consideratn N
38. Make comp emissions known Y
39. Allow toxic victims suits Y
40. Strike Superfund "VAT" Y
41. Notify emp-plant closing Y
42. Bar emp consult-plant clo N
43. Medicare cuts;Tax incres' Y
44. Delete 12 MX missiles Y
45. Spending cuts;Tax incres' Y
46. Textile Import Quotas N
47. Cut some school lunch fds N
48. Clean Water Act Amendmnts N
49. Youth work projects Y
50. Assist military in Angola N
51. Allow US troops-Nicaragua N
52. Pentagon polygraph exams N
53. Bar ASAT testing Y
54. Suspend def pmt for abuse Y
55. Bar Pentagon-contr emplmt Y
56. Increase SDI funding ?
57. Reduce SDI funding Y
58. Produce chemical weapons N
59. Bar CIA fndg in Nicaragua Y
60. South Africa sanctions Y
61. Cut SS COLAs; Raise taxes N
62. Let US invest-So Africa N
63. Approve 21 MX for 1985 N
64. Emergency Farm Credit Y
65. Awards to whistle blowers Y
66. African disaster relief Y
67. Ban bank loans to So Afr Y
68. Bar coun duty-free trtmt N
69. Steel import limits Y
70. Soc Sec COLAs=inflation Y
71. Bar haz waste vctms suits N
72. Prohibit aid to Nicaragua Y
73. Cut $-Schs bar sch prayer N
74. Raise taxes; Cut Medicare Y
75. Alien residncy-prior 1982 N
76. Alien residncy-prior 1980 N
77. Pen emp-hire illgl aliens Y
78. Lmt Persh II/cruse-Europe Y
79. Delete 34 B-1 bombers Y
80. Bar purch of Pershing II Y
81. Bar purchase of Sgt York Y
82. Delete $ for Trident II Y
83. Allow 15 MX missiles N
84. Bar MX procurement-1985 Y
85. Equal Access Act N
86. Aid to El Salvador N
87. Bar Nicarag water mining Y
88. Physician/Medicare freeze N
89. Increase "sin" taxes Y
90. End SBA direct loans N
91. Sell Conrail N
92. Equal Rights Amendment Y
93. Marines in Lebanon N
94. Eminent domain-Coal comps N
95. Prohibit EPA sanctions Y
96. SS age increase/Reforms N
97. Auto domestic content req N
98. Delete jobs program fundg N
99. Highway-Gas tax bill Y
100. Raise Medicare;Cut defnse Y
101. Emergency housing aid Y
102. Across-the-board tax cuts N
103. Gramm-Latta II targets N
104. Delete B-1 bomber funds Y
105. Dsapprov Saudi AWACS sale ?
106. Disapprove oil import fee Y
107. Rail Deregulation N
108. Dsapp India nuc fuel sale Y
109. Mil draft registration N
110. Chrysler Loan Guarantees N
111. Prohibit school busing N
112. Nuclear plant moratorium N
113. Oil price controls Y

Presidential Support Score: 1986 - 17% 1985 - 18%

CHANDLER, ROD -- Washington 8th District [Republican]. Counties of King (pt.) and Pierce (pt.). Prior Terms: House: 1983-86. Born: July 13, 1942; LaGrande, Ore. Education: Oregon State University (B.S.). Occupation: Political correspondent, TV news anchorman; assistant vice president, Washington Mutual Savings Bank; partner, public relations firm; Washington State representative.

1. Immigration Reform Y
2. Open fld-search warrants Y

CHANDLER, ROD (Cont.)

3. Civil pnty-hire ill alien N
4. So Afr sanc-veto override Y
5. Tax Overhaul N
6. South Africa sanctions Y
7. Death penalty-drug bill Y
8. Evidence-warrantless srch Y
9. Life term-second drug off N
10. Military use in drug war N
11. Troop reduction in Europe N
12. Prohibit chemical weapons N
13. Bar ASAT testing Y
14. Abide SALT II weapons ban N
15. Follow SALT II-Soviets do Y
16. Reduce SDI funding N
17. Increase SDI funding N
18. Purchase Trident sub N
19. Delete 12 MX;Add conv wpn N
20. Raise speed limit Y
21. Textile Import Quotas(*) N
22. Req Pentagon buy US goods N
23. AIDS ins anti-dscriminatn Y
24. Nicaraguan refugee aid N
25. Nicaraguan contra aid Y
26. US abide by SALT II ?
27. Prohibit Saudi arms sale N
28. Military Retiremnt Reform Y
29. Nicaraguan refugee aid Y
30. Ease '68 Gun Control Act Y
31. Bar intrstat handgun tran Y
32. Keep '68 Gun Control Act N
33. Nicaraguan contra aid Y
34. Bar emp polygraph testing N
35. Tax Overhaul consideratn N
36. Bar armor-piercing ammo Y
37. Tax Overhaul consideratn N
38. Make comp emissions known N
39. Allow toxic victims suits N
40. Strike Superfund "VAT" Y
41. Notify emp-plant closing N
42. Bar emp consult-plant clo Y
43. Medicare cuts;Tax incres' N
44. Delete 12 MX missiles N
45. Spending cuts;Tax incres' N
46. Textile Import Quotas N
47. Cut some school lunch fds Y
48. Clean Water Act Amendmnts N
49. Youth work projects N
50. Assist military in Angola Y
51. Allow US troops-Nicaragua Y
52. Pentagon polygraph exams Y
53. Bar ASAT testing Y
54. Suspend def pmt for abuse Y
55. Bar Pentagon-contr emplmt Y
56. Increase SDI funding N
57. Reduce SDI funding N
58. Produce chemical weapons Y
59. Bar CIA fndg in Nicaragua N
60. South Africa sanctions N
61. Cut SS COLAs; Raise taxes Y
62. Let US invest-So Africa Y
63. Approve 21 MX for 1985 Y
64. Emergency Farm Credit N
65. Awards to whistle blowers Y
66. African disaster relief Y
67. Ban bank loans to So Afr Y
68. Bar coun duty-free trtmt N
69. Steel import limits N
70. Soc Sec COLAs=inflation Y
71. Bar haz waste vctms suits Y
72. Prohibit aid to Nicaragua Y
73. Cut $-Schs bar sch prayer N
74. Raise taxes; Cut Medicare Y
75. Alien residncy-prior 1982 Y
76. Alien residncy-prior 1980 N
77. Pen emp-hire illgl aliens N
78. Lmt Persh II/cruse-Europe N
79. Delete 34 B-1 bombers N
80. Bar purch of Pershing II N
81. Bar purchase of Sgt York N
82. Delete $ for Trident II N
83. Allow 15 MX missiles Y
84. Bar MX procurement-1985 N
85. Equal Access Act Y
86. Aid to El Salvador Y
87. Bar Nicarag water mining Y
88. Physician/Medicare freeze Y
89. Increase "sin" taxes Y
90. End SBA direct loans N
91. Sell Conrail Y
92. Equal Rights Amendment Y
93. Marines in Lebanon Y
94. Eminent domain-Coal comps Y
95. Prohibit EPA sanctions Y
96. SS age increase/Reforms Y

Presidential Support Score: 1986 - 57% 1985 - 61%

WEST VIRGINIA

MOLLOHAN, ALAN B. -- West Virginia 1st District [Democrat]. Counties of Brooke, Doddridge, Hancock, Harrison, Marion, Marshall, Ohio, Pleasants, Ritchie, Taylor, Tyler, Wetzel and Wood. Prior Terms: House: 1983-86. Born: May 14, 1943; Fairmont, W. Va. Education: William and Mary (A.B.); West Virgi-

MOLLOHAN, ALAN B. (Cont.)
nia University College of Law (J.D.). Military Service: U.S. Army, U.S. Army Reserve. Occupation: Attorney.

1.	Immigration Reform	Y	49.	Youth work projects	Y
2.	Open fld-search warrants	N	50.	Assist military in Angola	Y
3.	Civil pnty-hire ill alien	Y	51.	Allow US troops-Nicaragua	N
4.	So Afr sanc-veto override	Y	52.	Pentagon polygraph exams	Y
5.	Tax Overhaul	Y	53.	Bar ASAT testing	Y
6.	South Africa sanctions	Y	54.	Suspend def pmt for abuse	N
7.	Death penalty-drug bill	N	55.	Bar Pentagon-contr emplmt	Y
8.	Evidence-warrantless srch	Y	56.	Increase SDI funding	N
9.	Life term-second drug off	Y	57.	Reduce SDI funding	N
10.	Military use in drug war	Y	58.	Produce chemical weapons	Y
11.	Troop reduction in Europe	N	59.	Bar CIA fndg in Nicaragua	N
12.	Prohibit chemical weapons	N	60.	South Africa sanctions	Y
13.	Bar ASAT testing	N	61.	Cut SS COLAs; Raise taxes	N
14.	Abide SALT II weapons ban	N	62.	Let US invest-So Africa	N
15.	Follow SALT II-Soviets do	Y	63.	Approve 21 MX for 1985	Y
16.	Reduce SDI funding	N	64.	Emergency Farm Credit	Y
17.	Increase SDI funding	N	65.	Awards to whistle blowers	Y
18.	Purchase Trident sub	Y	66.	African disaster relief	Y
19.	Delete 12 MX;Add conv wpn	N	67.	Ban bank loans to So Afr	Y
20.	Raise speed limit	N	68.	Bar coun duty-free trtmt	Y
21.	Textile Import Quotas(*)	Y	69.	Steel import limits	Y
22.	Req Pentagon buy US goods	Y	70.	Soc Sec COLAs=inflation	Y
23.	AIDS ins anti-dscriminatn	Y	71.	Bar haz waste vctms suits	Y
24.	Nicaraguan refugee aid	N	72.	Prohibit aid to Nicaragua	Y
25.	Nicaraguan contra aid	N	73.	Cut $-Schs bar sch prayer	Y
26.	US abide by SALT II	N	74.	Raise taxes; Cut Medicare	Y
27.	Prohibit Saudi arms sale	Y	75.	Alien residncy-prior 1982	N
28.	Military Retiremnt Reform	Y	76.	Alien residncy-prior 1980	N
29.	Nicaraguan refugee aid	N	77.	Pen emp-hire illgl aliens	N
30.	Ease '68 Gun Control Act	Y	78.	Lmt Persh II/cruse-Europe	N
31.	Bar intrstat handgun tran	N	79.	Delete 34 B-1 bombers	N
32.	Keep '68 Gun Control Act	N	80.	Bar purch of Pershing II	N
33.	Nicaraguan contra aid	N	81.	Bar purchase of Sgt York	N
34.	Bar emp polygraph testing	Y	82.	Delete $ for Trident II	N
35.	Tax Overhaul consideratn	Y	83.	Allow 15 MX missiles	Y
36.	Bar armor-piercing ammo	Y	84.	Bar MX procurement-1985	N
37.	Tax Overhaul consideratn	Y	85.	Equal Access Act	Y
38.	Make comp emissions known	N	86.	Aid to El Salvador	Y
39.	Allow toxic victims suits	N	87.	Bar Nicarag water mining	Y
40.	Strike Superfund "VAT"	N	88.	Physician/Medicare freeze	N
41.	Notify emp-plant closing	Y	89.	Increase "sin" taxes	Y
42.	Bar emp consult-plant clo	N	90.	End SBA direct loans	N
43.	Medicare cuts;Tax incres'	N	91.	Sell Conrail	N
44.	Delete 12 MX missiles	N	92.	Equál Rights Amendment	N
45.	Spending cuts;Tax incres'	Y	93.	Marines in Lebanon	Y
46.	Textile Import Quotas	Y	94.	Eminent domain-Coal comps	N
47.	Cut some school lunch fds	N	95.	Prohibit EPA sanctions	Y
48.	Clean Water Act Amendmnts	Y	96.	SS age increase/Reforms	N

Presidential Support Score: 1986 - 35% 1985 - 40%

STAGGERS, HARLEY O., Jr. -- West Virginia 2nd District [Democrat]. Counties of Barbour, Berkely, Fayette, Grant, Greenbrier, Hampshire, Hardy, Jefferson, Mineral, Monongalia, Monroe, Morgan, Pendleton, Pocahontas, Preston, Randolph, Summers, Tucker, Upshur and Webster. Prior Terms: House: 1983-86.

STAGGERS, HARLEY O., Jr. (Cont.)
Born: February 22, 1951; Washington, D.C. Education: Harvard University (B.A.); West Virginia University School of Law (J.D.). Occupation: Attorney; assistant attorney general; West Virginia senator (1980-82).

1. Immigration Reform Y
2. Open fld-search warrants N
3. Civil pnty-hire ill alien N
4. So Afr sanc-veto override Y
5. Tax Overhaul Y
6. South Africa sanctions Y
7. Death penalty-drug bill N
8. Evidence-warrantless srch N
9. Life term-second drug off Y
10. Military use in drug war Y
11. Troop reduction in Europe Y
12. Prohibit chemical weapons Y
13. Bar ASAT testing Y
14. Abide SALT II weapons ban Y
15. Follow SALT II-Soviets do N
16. Reduce SDI funding Y
17. Increase SDI funding N
18. Purchase Trident sub Y
19. Delete 12 MX;Add conv wpn Y
20. Raise speed limit N
21. Textile Import Quotas(*) Y
22. Req Pentagon buy US goods Y
23. AIDS ins anti-dscriminatn Y
24. Nicaraguan refugee aid Y
25. Nicaraguan contra aid N
26. US abide by SALT II N
27. Prohibit Saudi arms sale Y
28. Military Retiremnt Reform Y
29. Nicaraguan refugee aid Y
30. Ease '68 Gun Control Act Y
31. Bar intrstat handgun tran N
32. Keep '68 Gun Control Act N
33. Nicaraguan contra aid N
34. Bar emp polygraph testing Y
35. Tax Overhaul consideratn Y
36. Bar armor-piercing ammo Y
37. Tax Overhaul consideratn Y
38. Make comp emissions known Y
39. Allow toxic victims suits Y
40. Strike Superfund "VAT" N
41. Notify emp-plant closing Y
42. Bar emp consult-plant clo N
43. Medicare cuts;Tax incres' N
44. Delete 12 MX missiles Y
45. Spending cuts;Tax incres' Y
46. Textile Import Quotas Y
47. Cut some school lunch fds N
48. Clean Water Act Amendmnts N
49. Youth work projects Y
50. Assist military in Angola N
51. Allow US troops-Nicaragua N
52. Pentagon polygraph exams Y
53. Bar ASAT testing Y
54. Suspend def pmt for abuse Y
55. Bar Pentagon-contr emplmt Y
56. Increase SDI funding N
57. Reduce SDI funding N
58. Produce chemical weapons N
59. Bar CIA fndg in Nicaragua Y
60. South Africa sanctions Y
61. Cut SS COLAs; Raise taxes N
62. Let US invest-So Africa N
63. Approve 21 MX for 1985 N
64. Emergency Farm Credit Y
65. Awards to whistle blowers Y
66. African disaster relief Y
67. Ban bank loans to So Afr Y
68. Bar coun duty-free trtmt Y
69. Steel import limits Y
70. Soc Sec COLAs=inflation Y
71. Bar haz waste vctms suits N
72. Prohibit aid to Nicaragua Y
73. Cut $-Schs bar sch prayer N
74. Raise taxes; Cut Medicare Y
75. Alien residncy-prior 1982 Y
76. Alien residncy-prior 1980 N
77. Pen emp-hire illgl aliens Y
78. Lmt Persh II/cruse-Europe Y
79. Delete 34 B-1 bombers Y
80. Bar purch of Pershing II Y
81. Bar purchase of Sgt York Y
82. Delete $ for Trident II N
83. Allow 15 MX missiles Y
84. Bar MX procurement-1985 Y
85. Equal Access Act Y
86. Aid to El Salvador N
87. Bar Nicarag water mining Y
88. Physician/Medicare freeze N
89. Increase "sin" taxes Y
90. End SBA direct loans N
91. Sell Conrail N
92. Equal Rights Amendment Y
93. Marines in Lebanon Y
94. Eminent domain-Coal comps N
95. Prohibit EPA sanctions Y
96. SS age increase/Reforms N

Presidential Support Score: 1986 - 17% 1985 - 29%

WISE, ROBERT E., Jr. -- West Virginia 3rd District [Democrat]. Counties of Boone, Braxton, Calhoun, Clay, Gilmer, Jackson, Kanawha, Lewis, Lincoln, Mason, Nicholas, Putnam, Roane and

WISE, ROBERT E., Jr. (Cont.)
Wirt. Prior Terms: House: 1983-86. Born: January 6, 1948; Washington, D.C. Education: Duke University (B.A.); Tulane University College of Law (J.D.). Occupation: Attorney; consultant (1977-80); West Virginia senator (1980-82).

1.	Immigration Reform	Y	49.	Youth work projects	Y
2.	Open fld-search warrants	N	50.	Assist military in Angola	N
3.	Civil pnty-hire ill alien	N	51.	Allow US troops-Nicaragua	N
4.	So Afr sanc-veto override	Y	52.	Pentagon polygraph exams	Y
5.	Tax Overhaul	Y	53.	Bar ASAT testing	Y
6.	South Africa sanctions	Y	54.	Suspend def pmt for abuse	Y
7.	Death penalty-drug bill	N	55.	Bar Pentagon-contr emplmt	Y
8.	Evidence-warrantless srch	N	56.	Increase SDI funding	N
9.	Life term-second drug off	Y	57.	Reduce SDI funding	N
10.	Military use in drug war	Y	58.	Produce chemical weapons	N
11.	Troop reduction in Europe	N	59.	Bar CIA fndg in Nicaragua	Y
12.	Prohibit chemical weapons	Y	60.	South Africa sanctions	Y
13.	Bar ASAT testing	Y	61.	Cut SS COLAs; Raise taxes	N
14.	Abide SALT II weapons ban	Y	62.	Let US invest-So Africa	N
15.	Follow SALT II-Soviets do	N	63.	Approve 21 MX for 1985	N
16.	Reduce SDI funding	N	64.	Emergency Farm Credit	Y
17.	Increase SDI funding	N	65.	Awards to whistle blowers	Y
18.	Purchase Trident sub	Y	66.	African disaster relief	Y
19.	Delete 12 MX;Add conv wpn	Y	67.	Ban bank loans to So Afr	Y
20.	Raise speed limit	N	68.	Bar coun duty-free trtmt	Y
21.	Textile Import Quotas(*)	Y	69.	Steel import limits	Y
22.	Req Pentagon buy US goods	Y	70.	Soc Sec COLAs=inflation	Y
23.	AIDS ins anti-dscriminatn	Y	71.	Bar haz waste vctms suits	N
24.	Nicaraguan refugee aid	Y	72.	Prohibit aid to Nicaragua	+
25.	Nicaraguan contra aid	N	73.	Cut $-Schs bar sch prayer	N
26.	US abide by SALT II	N	74.	Raise taxes; Cut Medicare	Y
27.	Prohibit Saudi arms sale	Y	75.	Alien residncy-prior 1982	Y
28.	Military Retiremnt Reform	Y	76.	Alien residncy-prior 1980	N
29.	Nicaraguan refugee aid	Y	77.	Pen emp-hire illgl aliens	Y
30.	Ease '68 Gun Control Act	Y	78.	Lmt Persh II/cruse-Europe	N
31.	Bar intrstat handgun tran	N	79.	Delete 34 B-1 bombers	Y
32.	Keep '68 Gun Control Act	N	80.	Bar purch of Pershing II	N
33.	Nicaraguan contra aid	N	81.	Bar purchase of Sgt York	N
34.	Bar emp polygraph testing	Y	82.	Delete $ for Trident II	N
35.	Tax Overhaul consideratn	Y	83.	Allow 15 MX missiles	Y
36.	Bar armor-piercing ammo	Y	84.	Bar MX procurement-1985	Y
37.	Tax Overhaul consideratn	Y	85.	Equal Access Act	Y
38.	Make comp emissions known	Y	86.	Aid to El Salvador	N
39.	Allow toxic victims suits	N	87.	Bar Nicarag water mining	Y
40.	Strike Superfund "VAT"	N	88.	Physician/Medicare freeze	N
41.	Notify emp-plant closing	Y	89.	Increase "sin" taxes	Y
42.	Bar emp consult-plant clo	N	90.	End SBA direct loans	N
43.	Medicare cuts;Tax incres'	N	91.	Sell Conrail	N
44.	Delete 12 MX missiles	Y	92.	Equal Rights Amendment	Y
45.	Spending cuts;Tax incres'	Y	93.	Marines in Lebanon	N
46.	Textile Import Quotas	Y	94.	Eminent domain-Coal comps	N
47.	Cut some school lunch fds	N	95.	Prohibit EPA sanctions	Y
48.	Clean Water Act Amendmnts	N	96.	SS age increase/Reforms	N

Presidential Support Score: 1986 - 23% 1985 - 26%

RAHALL, NICK JOE, II -- West Virginia 4th District [Democrat]. Counties of Cabell, Logan, McDowell, Mercer, Mingo, Raleigh, Wayne and Wyoming. Prior Terms: House: 1977-86. Born: May

RAHALL, NICK JOE, II (Cont.)
20, 1949; Beckley, W. Va. Education: Duke University (A.B.); George Washington University. Occupation: Congressional staff member; president, Mountaineer Tour and Travel, Inc.; board member, Rahall Communications Corp.; sales representative, WWNR radio station.

1. Immigration Reform Y
2. Open fld-search warrants N
3. Civil pnty-hire ill alien Y
4. So Afr sanc-veto override Y
5. Tax Overhaul Y
6. South Africa sanctions Y
7. Death penalty-drug bill N
8. Evidence-warrantless srch Y
9. Life term-second drug off Y
10. Military use in drug war Y
11. Troop reduction in Europe ?
12. Prohibit chemical weapons Y
13. Bar ASAT testing Y
14. Abide SALT II weapons ban Y
15. Follow SALT II-Soviets do N
16. Reduce SDI funding Y
17. Increase SDI funding N
18. Purchase Trident sub N
19. Delete 12 MX;Add conv wpn Y
20. Raise speed limit N
21. Textile Import Quotas(*) Y
22. Req Pentagon buy US goods Y
23. AIDS ins anti-dscriminatn Y
24. Nicaraguan refugee aid Y
25. Nicaraguan contra aid N
26. US abide by SALT II N
27. Prohibit Saudi arms sale N
28. Military Retiremnt Reform Y
29. Nicaraguan refugee aid ?
30. Ease '68 Gun Control Act Y
31. Bar intrstat handgun tran N
32. Keep '68 Gun Control Act N
33. Nicaraguan contra aid N
34. Bar emp polygraph testing Y
35. Tax Overhaul consideratn Y
36. Bar armor-piercing ammo Y
37. Tax Overhaul consideratn Y
38. Make comp emissions known Y
39. Allow toxic victims suits Y
40. Strike Superfund "VAT" N
41. Notify emp-plant closing Y
42. Bar emp consult-plant clo N
43. Medicare cuts;Tax incres' N
44. Delete 12 MX missiles Y
45. Spending cuts;Tax incres' Y
46. Textile Import Quotas Y
47. Cut some school lunch fds -
48. Clean Water Act Amendmnts N
49. Youth work projects Y
50. Assist military in Angola N
51. Allow US troops-Nicaragua N
52. Pentagon polygraph exams Y
53. Bar ASAT testing Y
54. Suspend def pmt for abuse Y
55. Bar Pentagon-contr emplmt Y
56. Increase SDI funding N
57. Reduce SDI funding Y
58. Produce chemical weapons N
59. Bar CIA fndg in Nicaragua Y
60. South Africa sanctions Y
61. Cut SS COLAs; Raise taxes N
62. Let US invest-So Africa N
63. Approve 21 MX for 1985 N
64. Emergency Farm Credit Y
65. Awards to whistle blowers Y
66. African disaster relief Y
67. Ban bank loans to So Afr Y
68. Bar coun duty-free trtmt Y
69. Steel import limits Y
70. Soc Sec COLAs=inflation Y
71. Bar haz waste vctms suits ?
72. Prohibit aid to Nicaragua Y
73. Cut $-Schs bar sch prayer N
74. Raise taxes; Cut Medicare Y
75. Alien residncy-prior 1982 N
76. Alien residncy-prior 1980 N
77. Pen emp-hire illgl aliens Y
78. Lmt Persh II/cruse-Europe Y
79. Delete 34 B-1 bombers ?
80. Bar purch of Pershing II ?
81. Bar purchase of Sgt York ?
82. Delete $ for Trident II Y
83. Allow 15 MX missiles N
84. Bar MX procurement-1985 Y
85. Equal Access Act ?
86. Aid to El Salvador N
87. Bar Nicarag water mining Y
88. Physician/Medicare freeze N
89. Increase "sin" taxes Y
90. End SBA direct loans N
91. Sell Conrail N
92. Equal Rights Amendment Y
93. Marines in Lebanon Y
94. Eminent domain-Coal comps N
95. Prohibit EPA sanctions ?
96. SS age increase/Reforms N
97. Auto domestic content req Y
98. Delete jobs program fundg N
99. Highway-Gas tax bill N
100. Raise Medicare;Cut defnse Y
101. Emergency housing aid Y
102. Across-the-board tax cuts N
103. Gramm-Latta II targets N
104. Delete B-1 bomber funds Y
105. Dsapprov Saudi AWACS sale N
106. Disapprove oil import fee Y

RAHALL, NICK JOE, II (Cont.)

107. Rail Deregulation N
108. Dsapp India nuc fuel sale Y
109. Mil draft registration Y
110. Chrysler Loan Guarantees Y
111. Prohibit school busing N
112. Nuclear plant moratorium Y
113. Oil price controls Y
114. Tuition Tax Credits N
115. Est Consumer Protect Agcy N
116. Eliminate B-1 bomber fnds N
117. Subminimum wage for youth N
118. Delete crude oil tax N
119. Natural gas deregulation N

Presidential Support Score: 1986 - 20% 1985 - 20%

W I S C O N S I N

ASPIN, LES -- Wisconsin 1st District [Democrat]. Counties of Green (pt.), Jefferson (pt.), Kenosha, Racine, Rock and Walworth. Prior Terms: House: 1971-86. Born: July 21, 1938; Milwaukee, Wis. Education: Yale University (B.S.); Oxford University (M.A.); Massachusetts Institute of Technology (Ph.D.). Military Service: U.S. Army, 1966-68. Occupation: Assistant professor (1969-70); assistant, President Kennedy's Council of Economic Advisors; senate staff member (1964).

1. Immigration Reform Y
2. Open fld-search warrants N
3. Civil pnty-hire ill alien N
4. So Afr sanc-veto override Y
5. Tax Overhaul Y
6. South Africa sanctions ?
7. Death penalty-drug bill N
8. Evidence-warrantless srch N
9. Life term-second drug off Y
10. Military use in drug war N
11. Troop reduction in Europe N
12. Prohibit chemical weapons N
13. Bar ASAT testing Y
14. Abide SALT II weapons ban Y
15. Follow SALT II-Soviets do N
16. Reduce SDI funding N
17. Increase SDI funding N
18. Purchase Trident sub Y
19. Delete 12 MX;Add conv wpn N
20. Raise speed limit Y
21. Textile Import Quotas(*) Y
22. Req Pentagon buy US goods N
23. AIDS ins anti-dscriminatn Y
24. Nicaraguan refugee aid N
25. Nicaraguan contra aid Y
26. US abide by SALT II N
27. Prohibit Saudi arms sale Y
28. Military Retiremnt Reform Y
29. Nicaraguan refugee aid N
30. Ease '68 Gun Control Act Y
31. Bar intrstat handgun tran Y
32. Keep '68 Gun Control Act Y
33. Nicaraguan contra aid N
34. Bar emp polygraph testing ?
35. Tax Overhaul consideratn Y
36. Bar armor-piercing ammo Y
37. Tax Overhaul consideratn Y
38. Make comp emissions known Y
39. Allow toxic victims suits Y
40. Strike Superfund "VAT" Y
41. Notify emp-plant closing Y
42. Bar emp consult-plant clo N
43. Medicare cuts;Tax incres' Y
44. Delete 12 MX missiles N
45. Spending cuts;Tax incres' Y
46. Textile Import Quotas Y
47. Cut some school lunch fds N
48. Clean Water Act Amendmnts N
49. Youth work projects Y
50. Assist military in Angola N
51. Allow US troops-Nicaragua N
52. Pentagon polygraph exams Y
53. Bar ASAT testing Y
54. Suspend def pmt for abuse N
55. Bar Pentagon-contr emplmt Y
56. Increase SDI funding N
57. Reduce SDI funding N
58. Produce chemical weapons Y
59. Bar CIA fndg in Nicaragua Y
60. South Africa sanctions Y
61. Cut SS COLAs; Raise taxes N
62. Let US invest-So Africa N
63. Approve 21 MX for 1985 Y
64. Emergency Farm Credit Y
65. Awards to whistle blowers Y
66. African disaster relief Y
67. Ban bank loans to So Afr ?
68. Bar coun duty-free trtmt Y
69. Steel import limits Y
70. Soc Sec COLAs=inflation Y
71. Bar haz waste vctms suits N
72. Prohibit aid to Nicaragua Y

ASPIN, LES (Cont.)

73. Cut $-Schs bar sch prayer N
74. Raise taxes; Cut Medicare Y
75. Alien residncy-prior 1982 Y
76. Alien residncy-prior 1980 N
77. Pen emp-hire illgl aliens Y
78. Lmt Persh II/cruse-Europe N
79. Delete 34 B-1 bombers Y
80. Bar purch of Pershing II N
81. Bar purchase of Sgt York Y
82. Delete $ for Trident II N
83. Allow 15 MX missiles Y
84. Bar MX procurement-1985 N
85. Equal Access Act N
86. Aid to El Salvador N
87. Bar Nicarag water mining Y
88. Physician/Medicare freeze N
89. Increase "sin" taxes Y
90. End SBA direct loans N
91. Sell Conrail N
92. Equal Rights Amendment Y
93. Marines in Lebanon Y
94. Eminent domain-Coal comps N
95. Prohibit EPA sanctions Y
96. SS age increase/Reforms N
97. Auto domestic content req Y
98. Delete jobs program fundg N
99. Highway-Gas tax bill N
100. Raise Medicare;Cut defnse N
101. Emergency housing aid Y
102. Across-the-board tax cuts N
103. Gramm-Latta II targets N
104. Delete B-1 bomber funds Y
105. Dsapprov Saudi AWACS sale Y
106. Disapprove oil import fee N
107. Rail Deregulation N
108. Dsapp India nuc fuel sale Y
109. Mil draft registration Y
110. Chrysler Loan Guarantees Y
111. Prohibit school busing N
112. Nuclear plant moratorium ?
113. Oil price controls N
114. Tuition Tax Credits N
115. Est Consumer Protect Agcy Y
116. Eliminate B-1 bomber fnds Y
117. Subminimum wage for youth Y
118. Delete crude oil tax N
119. Natural gas deregulation N

Presidential Support Score: 1986 - 27% 1985 - 33%

KASTENMEIER, ROBERT W. -- Wisconsin 2nd District [Democrat]. Counties of Adams (pt.), Columbia, Dane, Dodge (pt.), Grant (pt.), Green (pt.), Iowa, Juneau (pt.), Lafayette, Richland (pt.) and Sauk. Prior Terms: House: 1959-86. Born: January 24, 1924; Beaver Dam, Wis. Education: University of Wisconsin (LL.B.). Military Service: U.S. Army, 1943-46. Occupation: Attorney; War Department branch office director; justice of the peace.

1. Immigration Reform Y
2. Open fld-search warrants Y
3. Civil pnty-hire ill alien N
4. So Afr sanc-veto override Y
5. Tax Overhaul Y
6. South Africa sanctions Y
7. Death penalty-drug bill N
8. Evidence-warrantless srch N
9. Life term-second drug off N
10. Military use in drug war N
11. Troop reduction in Europe Y
12. Prohibit chemical weapons Y
13. Bar ASAT testing Y
14. Abide SALT II weapons ban Y
15. Follow SALT II-Soviets do N
16. Reduce SDI funding Y
17. Increase SDI funding N
18. Purchase Trident sub N
19. Delete 12 MX;Add conv wpn Y
20. Raise speed limit Y
21. Textile Import Quotas(*) Y
22. Req Pentagon buy US goods N
23. AIDS ins anti-dscriminatn Y
24. Nicaraguan refugee aid Y
25. Nicaraguan contra aid N
26. US abide by SALT II N
27. Prohibit Saudi arms sale Y
28. Military Retiremnt Reform Y
29. Nicaraguan refugee aid Y
30. Ease '68 Gun Control Act N
31. Bar intrstat handgun tran Y
32. Keep '68 Gun Control Act Y
33. Nicaraguan contra aid N
34. Bar emp polygraph testing Y
35. Tax Overhaul consideratn Y
36. Bar armor-piercing ammo Y
37. Tax Overhaul consideratn Y
38. Make comp emissions known Y
39. Allow toxic victims suits Y
40. Strike Superfund "VAT" Y
41. Notify emp-plant closing Y
42. Bar emp consult-plant clo N
43. Medicare cuts;Tax incres' Y
44. Delete 12 MX missiles Y
45. Spending cuts;Tax incres' N
46. Textile Import Quotas Y
47. Cut some school lunch fds N
48. Clean Water Act Amendmnts N

KASTENMEIER, ROBERT W. (Cont.)

49. Youth work projects Y
50. Assist military in Angola N
51. Allow US troops-Nicaragua N
52. Pentagon polygraph exams N
53. Bar ASAT testing Y
54. Suspend def pmt for abuse Y
55. Bar Pentagon-contr emplmt Y
56. Increase SDI funding N
57. Reduce SDI funding Y
58. Produce chemical weapons N
59. Bar CIA fndg in Nicaragua Y
60. South Africa sanctions Y
61. Cut SS COLAs; Raise taxes N
62. Let US invest-So Africa N
63. Approve 21 MX for 1985 N
64. Emergency Farm Credit Y
65. Awards to whistle blowers Y
66. African disaster relief Y
67. Ban bank loans to So Afr Y
68. Bar coun duty-free trtmt Y
69. Steel import limits Y
70. Soc Sec COLAs=inflation Y
71. Bar haz waste vctms suits N
72. Prohibit aid to Nicaragua Y
73. Cut $-Schs bar sch prayer N
74. Raise taxes; Cut Medicare Y
75. Alien residncy-prior 1982 N
76. Alien residncy-prior 1980 N
77. Pen emp-hire illgl aliens Y
78. Lmt Persh II/cruse-Europe Y
79. Delete 34 B-1 bombers Y
80. Bar purch of Pershing II Y
81. Bar purchase of Sgt York Y
82. Delete $ for Trident II Y
83. Allow 15 MX missiles N
84. Bar MX procurement-1985 Y
85. Equal Access Act N
86. Aid to El Salvador N
87. Bar Nicarag water mining Y
88. Physician/Medicare freeze N
89. Increase "sin" taxes Y
90. End SBA direct loans N
91. Sell Conrail N
92. Equal Rights Amendment Y
93. Marines in Lebanon N
94. Eminent domain-Coal comps N
95. Prohibit EPA sanctions N
96. SS age increase/Reforms N
97. Auto domestic content req Y
98. Delete jobs program fundg N
99. Highway-Gas tax bill N
100. Raise Medicare;Cut defnse Y
101. Emergency housing aid Y
102. Across-the-board tax cuts N
103. Gramm-Latta II targets N
104. Delete B-1 bomber funds Y
105. Dsapprov Saudi AWACS sale Y
106. Disapprove oil import fee Y
107. Rail Deregulation Y
108. Dsapp India nuc fuel sale Y
109. Mil draft registration N
110. Chrysler Loan Guarantees Y
111. Prohibit school busing N
112. Nuclear plant moratorium Y
113. Oil price controls Y
114. Tuition Tax Credits N
115. Est Consumer Protect Agcy Y
116. Eliminate B-1 bomber fnds Y
117. Subminimum wage for youth Y
118. Delete crude oil tax N
119. Natural gas deregulation N

Presidential Support Score: 1986 - 16% 1985 - 16%

GUNDERSON, STEVE -- Wisconsin 3rd District [Republican]. Counties of Barron, Buffalo, Clark (pt.), Crawford, Dunn, Eau Claire, Grant (pt.), Jackson, La Crosse, Pepin, Pierce, Polk (pt.), Richland (pt.), St. Croix, Trempealeau and Vernon. Prior Terms: House: 1981-86. Born: May 10, 1951; Eau Claire, Wis. Education: University of Wisconsin (B.A.); Brown School of Broadcasting. Occupation: Wisconsin legislator (1975-79); legislative director for congressman.

1. Immigration Reform Y
2. Open fld-search warrants Y
3. Civil pnty-hire ill alien Y
4. So Afr sanc-veto override Y
5. Tax Overhaul Y
6. South Africa sanctions Y
7. Death penalty-drug bill Y
8. Evidence-warrantless srch Y
9. Life term-second drug off Y
10. Military use in drug war Y
11. Troop reduction in Europe N
12. Prohibit chemical weapons Y
13. Bar ASAT testing Y
14. Abide SALT II weapons ban N
15. Follow SALT II-Soviets do Y
16. Reduce SDI funding N
17. Increase SDI funding N
18. Purchase Trident sub Y
19. Delete 12 MX;Add conv wpn N
20. Raise speed limit Y
21. Textile Import Quotas(*) Y
22. Req Pentagon buy US goods Y

GUNDERSON, STEVE (Cont.)

23. AIDS ins anti-dscriminatn Y
24. Nicaraguan refugee aid N
25. Nicaraguan contra aid Y
26. US abide by SALT II Y
27. Prohibit Saudi arms sale Y
28. Military Retiremnt Reform Y
29. Nicaraguan refugee aid Y
30. Ease '68 Gun Control Act Y
31. Bar intrstat handgun tran N
32. Keep '68 Gun Control Act N
33. Nicaraguan contra aid Y
34. Bar emp polygraph testing N
35. Tax Overhaul consideratn Y
36. Bar armor-piercing ammo Y
37. Tax Overhaul consideratn N
38. Make comp emissions known N
39. Allow toxic victims suits N
40. Strike Superfund "VAT" Y
41. Notify emp-plant closing Y
42. Bar emp consult-plant clo Y
43. Medicare cuts;Tax incres' N
44. Delete 12 MX missiles Y
45. Spending cuts;Tax incres' N
46. Textile Import Quotas N
47. Cut some school lunch fds N
48. Clean Water Act Amendmnts Y
49. Youth work projects N
50. Assist military in Angola Y
51. Allow US troops-Nicaragua N
52. Pentagon polygraph exams Y
53. Bar ASAT testing Y
54. Suspend def pmt for abuse N
55. Bar Pentagon-contr emplmt Y
56. Increase SDI funding N
57. Reduce SDI funding N
58. Produce chemical weapons N
59. Bar CIA fndg in Nicaragua N
60. South Africa sanctions N
61. Cut SS COLAs; Raise taxes N
62. Let US invest-So Africa Y
63. Approve 21 MX for 1985 Y
64. Emergency Farm Credit Y
65. Awards to whistle blowers Y
66. African disaster relief Y
67. Ban bank loans to So Afr Y
68. Bar coun duty-free trtmt N
69. Steel import limits Y
70. Soc Sec COLAs=inflation Y
71. Bar haz waste vctms suits Y
72. Prohibit aid to Nicaragua Y
73. Cut $-Schs bar sch prayer N
74. Raise taxes; Cut Medicare Y
75. Alien residncy-prior 1982 Y
76. Alien residncy-prior 1980 Y
77. Pen emp-hire illgl aliens N
78. Lmt Persh II/cruse-Europe N
79. Delete 34 B-1 bombers Y
80. Bar purch of Pershing II N
81. Bar purchase of Sgt York N
82. Delete $ for Trident II N
83. Allow 15 MX missiles Y
84. Bar MX procurement-1985 N
85. Equal Access Act Y
86. Aid to El Salvador Y
87. Bar Nicarag water mining Y
88. Physician/Medicare freeze Y
89. Increase "sin" taxes Y
90. End SBA direct loans N
91. Sell Conrail Y
92. Equal Rights Amendment Y
93. Marines in Lebanon N
94. Eminent domain-Coal comps N
95. Prohibit EPA sanctions N
96. SS age increase/Reforms Y
97. Auto domestic content req N
98. Delete jobs program fundg Y
99. Highway-Gas tax bill N
100. Raise Medicare;Cut defnse Y
101. Emergency housing aid Y
102. Across-the-board tax cuts Y
103. Gramm-Latta II targets Y
104. Delete B-1 bomber funds Y
105. Dsapprov Saudi AWACS sale N

Presidential Support Score: 1986 - 52% 1985 - 50%

KLECZKA, GERALD D. -- Wisconsin 4th District [Democrat]. Counties of Milwaukee (pt.) and Waukesha (pt.). Prior Terms: House: 1984 (Special Election)-1986. Born: November 26, 1943; Milwaukee, Wis. Education: University of Wisconsin. Military Service: National Guard, 1963-69. Occupation: Wisconsin assemblyman (1968-72); Wisconsin senator (1974-84).

1. Immigration Reform N
2. Open fld-search warrants Y
3. Civil pnty-hire ill alien N
4. So Afr sanc-veto override Y
5. Tax Overhaul Y
6. South Africa sanctions Y
7. Death penalty-drug bill N
8. Evidence-warrantless srch N
9. Life term-second drug off Y
10. Military use in drug war N
11. Troop reduction in Europe N
12. Prohibit chemical weapons Y
13. Bar ASAT testing Y
14. Abide SALT II weapons ban Y

KLECZKA, GERALD D. (Cont.)

15. Follow SALT II-Soviets do N
16. Reduce SDI funding N
17. Increase SDI funding N
18. Purchase Trident sub N
19. Delete 12 MX;Add conv wpn Y
20. Raise speed limit N
21. Textile Import Quotas(*) N
22. Req Pentagon buy US goods Y
23. AIDS ins anti-dscriminatn Y
24. Nicaraguan refugee aid Y
25. Nicaraguan contra aid N
26. US abide by SALT II N
27. Prohibit Saudi arms sale Y
28. Military Retiremnt Reform Y
29. Nicaraguan refugee aid Y
30. Ease '68 Gun Control Act Y
31. Bar intrstat handgun tran Y
32. Keep '68 Gun Control Act Y
33. Nicaraguan contra aid N
34. Bar emp polygraph testing Y
35. Tax Overhaul consideratn Y
36. Bar armor-piercing ammo Y
37. Tax Overhaul consideratn Y
38. Make comp emissions known Y
39. Allow toxic victims suits Y
40. Strike Superfund "VAT" Y
41. Notify emp-plant closing Y
42. Bar emp consult-plant clo N
43. Medicare cuts;Tax incres' Y
44. Delete 12 MX missiles Y
45. Spending cuts;Tax incres' Y
46. Textile Import Quotas N
47. Cut some school lunch fds N
48. Clean Water Act Amendmnts N
49. Youth work projects N
50. Assist military in Angola N
51. Allow US troops-Nicaragua N
52. Pentagon polygraph exams Y
53. Bar ASAT testing Y
54. Suspend def pmt for abuse Y
55. Bar Pentagon-contr emplmt Y
56. Increase SDI funding N
57. Reduce SDI funding N
58. Produce chemical weapons N
59. Bar CIA fndg in Nicaragua Y
60. South Africa sanctions Y
61. Cut SS COLAs; Raise taxes N
62. Let US invest-So Africa N
63. Approve 21 MX for 1985 N
64. Emergency Farm Credit Y
65. Awards to whistle blowers Y
66. African disaster relief Y
67. Ban bank loans to So Afr Y
68. Bar coun duty-free trtmt Y
69. Steel import limits Y
70. Soc Sec COLAs=inflation Y
71. Bar haz waste vctms suits Y
72. Prohibit aid to Nicaragua Y
73. Cut $-Schs bar sch prayer N
74. Raise taxes; Cut Medicare Y
75. Alien residncy-prior 1982 N
76. Alien residncy-prior 1980 N
77. Pen emp-hire illgl aliens Y
78. Lmt Persh II/cruse-Europe N
79. Delete 34 B-1 bombers N
80. Bar purch of Pershing II N
81. Bar purchase of Sgt York Y
82. Delete $ for Trident II N
83. Allow 15 MX missiles N
84. Bar MX procurement-1985 Y
85. Equal Access Act N
86. Aid to El Salvador N
87. Bar Nicarag water mining Y
88. Physician/Medicare freeze N
89. Increase "sin" taxes Y

Presidential Support Score: 1986 - 25% 1985 - 28%

MOODY, JIM -- Wisconsin 5th District [Democrat]. Counties of Milwaukee (pt.) and Washington (pt.). Prior Terms: House: 1983-86. Born: September 2, 1935; Richlands, Va. Education: Haverford College (B.A.); Harvard University (M.B.A.); University of California (Ph.D.). Occupation: Field representatiave, CARE (1958-60); Country Director, Peace Corps (1961); economist, U.S. Department of Transportation (1967-69); assistant professor of Economics (1973-82); Wisconsin assemblyman (1977-78); Wisconsin senator (1979-82).

1. Immigration Reform Y
2. Open fld-search warrants Y
3. Civil pnty-hire ill alien N
4. So Afr sanc-veto override Y
5. Tax Overhaul Y
6. South Africa sanctions Y
7. Death penalty-drug bill N
8. Evidence-warrantless srch N
9. Life term-second drug off N
10. Military use in drug war N
11. Troop reduction in Europe Y
12. Prohibit chemical weapons Y
13. Bar ASAT testing Y
14. Abide SALT II weapons ban +
15. Follow SALT II-Soviets do N
16. Reduce SDI funding Y

MOODY, JIM (Cont.)

17. Increase SDI funding	N	57. Reduce SDI funding	N
18. Purchase Trident sub	Y	58. Produce chemical weapons	N
19. Delete 12 MX;Add conv wpn	Y	59. Bar CIA fndg in Nicaragua	Y
20. Raise speed limit	N	60. South Africa sanctions	Y
21. Textile Import Quotas(*)	Y	61. Cut SS COLAs; Raise taxes	Y
22. Req Pentagon buy US goods	Y	62. Let US invest-So Africa	?
23. AIDS ins anti-dscriminatn	Y	63. Approve 21 MX for 1985	N
24. Nicaraguan refugee aid	Y	64. Emergency Farm Credit	Y
25. Nicaraguan contra aid	N	65. Awards to whistle blowers	Y
26. US abide by SALT II	N	66. African disaster relief	Y
27. Prohibit Saudi arms sale	Y	67. Ban bank loans to So Afr	Y
28. Military Retiremnt Reform	Y	68. Bar coun duty-free trtmt	Y
29. Nicaraguan refugee aid	Y	69. Steel import limits	Y
30. Ease '68 Gun Control Act	Y	70. Soc Sec COLAs=inflation	N
31. Bar intrstat handgun tran	Y	71. Bar haz waste vctms suits	N
32. Keep '68 Gun Control Act	Y	72. Prohibit aid to Nicaragua	Y
33. Nicaraguan contra aid	N	73. Cut $-Schs bar sch prayer	N
34. Bar emp polygraph testing	Y	74. Raise taxes; Cut Medicare	Y
35. Tax Overhaul consideratn	Y	75. Alien residncy-prior 1982	Y
36. Bar armor-piercing ammo	Y	76. Alien residncy-prior 1980	N
37. Tax Overhaul consideratn	Y	77. Pen emp-hire illgl aliens	Y
38. Make comp emissions known	Y	78. Lmt Persh II/cruse-Europe	Y
39. Allow toxic victims suits	Y	79. Delete 34 B-1 bombers	Y
40. Strike Superfund "VAT"	Y	80. Bar purch of Pershing II	Y
41. Notify emp-plant closing	Y	81. Bar purchase of Sgt York	Y
42. Bar emp consult-plant clo	N	82. Delete $ for Trident II	Y
43. Medicare cuts;Tax incres'	Y	83. Allow 15 MX missiles	N
44. Delete 12 MX missiles	Y	84. Bar MX procurement-1985	Y
45. Spending cuts;Tax incres'	Y	85. Equal Access Act	N
46. Textile Import Quotas	Y	86. Aid to El Salvador	?
47. Cut some school lunch fds	N	87. Bar Nicarag water mining	Y
48. Clean Water Act Amendmnts	N	88. Physician/Medicare freeze	N
49. Youth work projects	Y	89. Increase "sin" taxes	Y
50. Assist military in Angola	N	90. End SBA direct loans	N
51. Allow US troops-Nicaragua	N	91. Sell Conrail	N
52. Pentagon polygraph exams	Y	92. Equal Rights Amendment	Y
53. Bar ASAT testing	Y	93. Marines in Lebanon	N
54. Suspend def pmt for abuse	Y	94. Eminent domain-Coal comps	Y
55. Bar Pentagon-contr emplmt	Y	95. Prohibit EPA sanctions	Y
56. Increase SDI funding	N	96. SS age increase/Reforms	N

Presidential Support Score: 1986 - 18% 1985 - 20%

PETRI, THOMAS E. -- Wisconsin 6th District [Republican]. Counties of Adams (pt.), Calumet, Fond du Lac (pt.), Green Lake, Juneau (pt.), Manitowoc, Marquette, Monroe, Sheboygan (pt.), Waupaca, Waushara, Winnebago and Wood (pt.). Prior Terms: House: 1979 (Special Election)-1986. Born: May 28, 1940; Marinette, Wis. Education: Harvard College (B.A., J.D.). Occupation: Law clerk, federal district judge; Peace Corps volunteer; director, crime and drug studies, President's National Advisory Council on Executive Organization (1969); Wisconsin senator (1972-79).

1. Immigration Reform	N	6. South Africa sanctions	Y
2. Open fld-search warrants	N	7. Death penalty-drug bill	Y
3. Civil pnty-hire ill alien	N	8. Evidence-warrantless srch	Y
4. So Afr sanc-veto override	Y	9. Life term-second drug off	Y
5. Tax Overhaul	Y	10. Military use in drug war	Y

PETRI, THOMAS E. (Cont.)

11. Troop reduction in Europe Y
12. Prohibit chemical weapons N
13. Bar ASAT testing N
14. Abide SALT II weapons ban N
15. Follow SALT II-Soviets do Y
16. Reduce SDI funding N
17. Increase SDI funding N
18. Purchase Trident sub N
19. Delete 12 MX;Add conv wpn Y
20. Raise speed limit Y
21. Textile Import Quotas(*) N
22. Req Pentagon buy US goods N
23. AIDS ins anti-dscriminatn N
24. Nicaraguan refugee aid N
25. Nicaraguan contra aid Y
26. US abide by SALT II Y
27. Prohibit Saudi arms sale N
28. Military Retiremnt Reform Y
29. Nicaraguan refugee aid Y
30. Ease '68 Gun Control Act Y
31. Bar intrstat handgun tran N
32. Keep '68 Gun Control Act N
33. Nicaraguan contra aid Y
34. Bar emp polygraph testing N
35. Tax Overhaul consideratn Y
36. Bar armor-piercing ammo Y
37. Tax Overhaul consideratn Y
38. Make comp emissions known Y
39. Allow toxic victims suits Y
40. Strike Superfund "VAT" Y
41. Notify emp-plant closing Y
42. Bar emp consult-plant clo Y
43. Medicare cuts;Tax incres' N
44. Delete 12 MX missiles Y
45. Spending cuts;Tax incres' N
46. Textile Import Quotas N
47. Cut some school lunch fds N
48. Clean Water Act Amendmnts N
49. Youth work projects Y
50. Assist military in Angola Y
51. Allow US troops-Nicaragua N
52. Pentagon polygraph exams Y
53. Bar ASAT testing N
54. Suspend def pmt for abuse Y
55. Bar Pentagon-contr emplmt Y
56. Increase SDI funding N
57. Reduce SDI funding N
58. Produce chemical weapons Y
59. Bar CIA fndg in Nicaragua N
60. South Africa sanctions N
61. Cut SS COLAs; Raise taxes N
62. Let US invest-So Africa Y
63. Approve 21 MX for 1985 N
64. Emergency Farm Credit Y
65. Awards to whistle blowers Y
66. African disaster relief Y
67. Ban bank loans to So Afr Y
68. Bar coun duty-free trtmt N
69. Steel import limits N
70. Soc Sec COLAs=inflation Y
71. Bar haz waste vctms suits Y
72. Prohibit aid to Nicaragua N
73. Cut $-Schs bar sch prayer Y
74. Raise taxes; Cut Medicare N
75. Alien residncy-prior 1982 Y
76. Alien residncy-prior 1980 Y
77. Pen emp-hire illgl aliens N
78. Lmt Persh II/cruse-Europe N
79. Delete 34 B-1 bombers Y
80. Bar purch of Pershing II N
81. Bar purchase of Sgt York N
82. Delete $ for Trident II N
83. Allow 15 MX missiles N
84. Bar MX procurement-1985 Y
85. Equal Access Act Y
86. Aid to El Salvador Y
87. Bar Nicarag water mining Y
88. Physician/Medicare freeze Y
89. Increase "sin" taxes Y
90. End SBA direct loans N
91. Sell Conrail Y
92. Equal Rights Amendment Y
93. Marines in Lebanon N
94. Eminent domain-Coal comps Y
95. Prohibit EPA sanctions N
96. SS age increase/Reforms Y
97. Auto domestic content req N
98. Delete jobs program fundg Y
99. Highway-Gas tax bill N
100. Raise Medicare;Cut defnse Y
101. Emergency housing aid N
102. Across-the-board tax cuts Y
103. Gramm-Latta II targets Y
104. Delete B-1 bomber funds Y
105. Dsapprov Saudi AWACS sale Y
106. Disapprove oil import fee Y
107. Rail Deregulation N
108. Dsapp India nuc fuel sale N
109. Mil draft registration Y
110. Chrysler Loan Guarantees N
111. Prohibit school busing N
112. Nuclear plant moratorium Y
113. Oil price controls N

Presidential Support Score: 1986 - 73% 1985 - 61%

OBEY, DAVID R. -- Wisconsin 7th District [Democrat]. Counties of Ashland, Bayfield, Burnett, Chippewa, Clark (pt.), Douglas, Iron, Lincoln, Marathon, Oneida (pt.), Polk (pt.), Portage, Price, Rusk, Sawyer, Taylor, Washburn and Wood (pt.). Prior

OBEY, DAVID R. (Cont.)

Terms: House: 1969 (Special Election)-1986. Born: October 3, 1938; Okmulgee, Okla. Education: University of Wisconsin (M.A.). Occupation: Wisconsin assemblyman.

1. Immigration Reform Y
2. Open fld-search warrants Y
3. Civil pnty-hire ill alien N
4. So Afr sanc-veto override Y
5. Tax Overhaul Y
6. South Africa sanctions Y
7. Death penalty-drug bill ?
8. Evidence-warrantless srch N
9. Life term-second drug off N
10. Military use in drug war N
11. Troop reduction in Europe Y
12. Prohibit chemical weapons Y
13. Bar ASAT testing Y
14. Abide SALT II weapons ban Y
15. Follow SALT II-Soviets do N
16. Reduce SDI funding Y
17. Increase SDI funding N
18. Purchase Trident sub N
19. Delete 12 MX;Add conv wpn Y
20. Raise speed limit N
21. Textile Import Quotas(*) Y
22. Req Pentagon buy US goods Y
23. AIDS ins anti-dscriminatn Y
24. Nicaraguan refugee aid Y
25. Nicaraguan contra aid N
26. US abide by SALT II N
27. Prohibit Saudi arms sale Y
28. Military Retiremnt Reform Y
29. Nicaraguan refugee aid Y
30. Ease '68 Gun Control Act Y
31. Bar intrstat handgun tran N
32. Keep '68 Gun Control Act N
33. Nicaraguan contra aid N
34. Bar emp polygraph testing Y
35. Tax Overhaul consideratn Y
36. Bar armor-piercing ammo Y
37. Tax Overhaul consideratn Y
38. Make comp emissions known Y
39. Allow toxic victims suits Y
40. Strike Superfund "VAT" Y
41. Notify emp-plant closing Y
42. Bar emp consult-plant clo N
43. Medicare cuts;Tax incres' Y
44. Delete 12 MX missiles Y
45. Spending cuts;Tax incres' Y
46. Textile Import Quotas Y
47. Cut some school lunch fds N
48. Clean Water Act Amendmnts N
49. Youth work projects Y
50. Assist military in Angola N
51. Allow US troops-Nicaragua N
52. Pentagon polygraph exams N
53. Bar ASAT testing Y
54. Suspend def pmt for abuse Y
55. Bar Pentagon-contr emplmt Y
56. Increase SDI funding N
57. Reduce SDI funding Y
58. Produce chemical weapons N
59. Bar CIA fndg in Nicaragua Y
60. South Africa sanctions Y
61. Cut SS COLAs; Raise taxes N
62. Let US invest-So Africa N
63. Approve 21 MX for 1985 N
64. Emergency Farm Credit Y
65. Awards to whistle blowers Y
66. African disaster relief Y
67. Ban bank loans to So Afr Y
68. Bar coun duty-free trtmt N
69. Steel import limits Y
70. Soc Sec COLAs=inflation Y
71. Bar haz waste vctms suits N
72. Prohibit aid to Nicaragua Y
73. Cut $-Schs bar sch prayer ?
74. Raise taxes; Cut Medicare Y
75. Alien residncy-prior 1982 Y
76. Alien residncy-prior 1980 N
77. Pen emp-hire illgl aliens Y
78. Lmt Persh II/cruse-Europe N
79. Delete 34 B-1 bombers Y
80. Bar purch of Pershing II Y
81. Bar purchase of Sgt York Y
82. Delete $ for Trident II Y
83. Allow 15 MX missiles N
84. Bar MX procurement-1985 Y
85. Equal Access Act N
86. Aid to El Salvador N
87. Bar Nicarag water mining Y
88. Physician/Medicare freeze N
89. Increase "sin" taxes Y
90. End SBA direct loans N
91. Sell Conrail N
92. Equal Rights Amendment Y
93. Marines in Lebanon N
94. Eminent domain-Coal comps N
95. Prohibit EPA sanctions Y
96. SS age increase/Reforms N
97. Auto domestic content req Y
98. Delete jobs program fundg N
99. Highway-Gas tax bill N
100. Raise Medicare;Cut defnse Y
101. Emergency housing aid Y
102. Across-the-board tax cuts N
103. Gramm-Latta II targets N
104. Delete B-1 bomber funds Y
105. Dsapprov Saudi AWACS sale Y
106. Disapprove oil import fee N
107. Rail Deregulation N
108. Dsapp India nuc fuel sale N
109. Mil draft registration N
110. Chrysler Loan Guarantees Y

OBEY, DAVID R. (Cont.)

111. Prohibit school busing N
112. Nuclear plant moratorium Y
113. Oil price controls Y
114. Tuition Tax Credits N
115. Est Consumer Protect Agcy N
116. Eliminate B-1 bomber fnds Y
117. Subminimum wage for youth Y
118. Delete crude oil tax N
119. Natural gas deregulation N

Presidential Support Score: 1986 - 19% 1985 - 15%

ROTH, TOBY -- Wisconsin 8th District [Republican]. Counties of Brown, Door, Florence, Forest, Kewaunee, Langlade, Mannette, Menominee, Oconto, Oneida (pt.), Outagamie, Shawano and Vilas. Prior Terms: House: 1979-86. Born: October 10, 1938; Appleton, Wis. Education: Marquette University (B.A.). Military Service: U.S. Army Reserve, 1962-69. Occupation: Realtor; Wisconsin legislator (1972-78).

1. Immigration Reform N
2. Open fld-search warrants N
3. Civil pnty-hire ill alien N
4. So Afr sanc-veto override N
5. Tax Overhaul Y
6. South Africa sanctions N
7. Death penalty-drug bill Y
8. Evidence-warrantless srch Y
9. Life term-second drug off Y
10. Military use in drug war Y
11. Troop reduction in Europe N
12. Prohibit chemical weapons N
13. Bar ASAT testing N
14. Abide SALT II weapons ban N
15. Follow SALT II-Soviets do Y
16. Reduce SDI funding N
17. Increase SDI funding Y
18. Purchase Trident sub N
19. Delete 12 MX;Add conv wpn Y
20. Raise speed limit Y
21. Textile Import Quotas(*) N
22. Req Pentagon buy US goods Y
23. AIDS ins anti-dscriminatn N
24. Nicaraguan refugee aid N
25. Nicaraguan contra aid Y
26. US abide by SALT II Y
27. Prohibit Saudi arms sale Y
28. Military Retiremnt Reform Y
29. Nicaraguan refugee aid Y
30. Ease '68 Gun Control Act Y
31. Bar intrstat handgun tran N
32. Keep '68 Gun Control Act N
33. Nicaraguan contra aid Y
34. Bar emp polygraph testing N
35. Tax Overhaul consideratn N
36. Bar armor-piercing ammo Y
37. Tax Overhaul consideratn N
38. Make comp emissions known N
39. Allow toxic victims suits N
40. Strike Superfund "VAT" Y
41. Notify emp-plant closing N
42. Bar emp consult-plant clo Y
43. Medicare cuts;Tax incres' N
44. Delete 12 MX missiles Y
45. Spending cuts;Tax incres' N
46. Textile Import Quotas ?
47. Cut some school lunch fds Y
48. Clean Water Act Amendmnts Y
49. Youth work projects Y
50. Assist military in Angola Y
51. Allow US troops-Nicaragua Y
52. Pentagon polygraph exams Y
53. Bar ASAT testing N
54. Suspend def pmt for abuse Y
55. Bar Pentagon-contr emplmt Y
56. Increase SDI funding N
57. Reduce SDI funding N
58. Produce chemical weapons N
59. Bar CIA fndg in Nicaragua N
60. South Africa sanctions N
61. Cut SS COLAs; Raise taxes N
62. Let US invest-So Africa Y
63. Approve 21 MX for 1985 Y
64. Emergency Farm Credit Y
65. Awards to whistle blowers Y
66. African disaster relief Y
67. Ban bank loans to So Afr Y
68. Bar coun duty-free trtmt N
69. Steel import limits Y
70. Soc Sec COLAs=inflation Y
71. Bar haz waste vctms suits Y
72. Prohibit aid to Nicaragua Y
73. Cut $-Schs bar sch prayer Y
74. Raise taxes; Cut Medicare N
75. Alien residncy-prior 1982 Y
76. Alien residncy-prior 1980 Y
77. Pen emp-hire illgl aliens N
78. Lmt Persh II/cruse-Europe N
79. Delete 34 B-1 bombers Y
80. Bar purch of Pershing II N
81. Bar purchase of Sgt York Y
82. Delete $ for Trident II N
83. Allow 15 MX missiles Y
84. Bar MX procurement-1985 N
85. Equal Access Act Y
86. Aid to El Salvador Y

ROTH, TOBY (Cont.)

87. Bar Nicarag water mining Y
88. Physician/Medicare freeze Y
89. Increase "sin" taxes Y
90. End SBA direct loans N
91. Sell Conrail Y
92. Equal Rights Amendment N
93. Marines in Lebanon N
94. Eminent domain-Coal comps Y
95. Prohibit EPA sanctions Y
96. SS age increase/Reforms Y
97. Auto domestic content req Y
98. Delete jobs program fundg Y
99. Highway-Gas tax bill N
100. Raise Medicare;Cut defnse N
101. Emergency housing aid Y
102. Across-the-board tax cuts Y
103. Gramm-Latta II targets Y
104. Delete B-1 bomber funds N
105. Dsapprov Saudi AWACS sale N
106. Disapprove oil import fee Y
107. Rail Deregulation N
108. Dsapp India nuc fuel sale N
109. Mil draft registration N
110. Chrysler Loan Guarantees N
111. Prohibit school busing Y
112. Nuclear plant moratorium N
113. Oil price controls N

Presidential Support Score: 1986 - 67% 1985 - 55%

SENSENBRENNER, F. JAMES, Jr. -- Wisconsin 9th District [Republican]. Counties of Dodge(pt.), Fond du Lac (pt.), Jefferson (pt.), Milwaukee (pt.), Ozaukee, Sheboygan (pt.), Washington (pt.) and Waukesha (pt.). Prior Terms: House: 1979-86. Born: June 14, 1943; Chicago, Ill. Education: Stanford University (A.B.); Wisconsin Law School (J.D.). Occupation: Wisconsin assemblyman (1968-75); Wisconsin senator (1975-78).

1. Immigration Reform N
2. Open fld-search warrants N
3. Civil pnty-hire ill alien N
4. So Afr sanc-veto override Y
5. Tax Overhaul N
6. South Africa sanctions Y
7. Death penalty-drug bill Y
8. Evidence-warrantless srch Y
9. Life term-second drug off Y
10. Military use in drug war Y
11. Troop reduction in Europe Y
12. Prohibit chemical weapons Y
13. Bar ASAT testing N
14. Abide SALT II weapons ban N
15. Follow SALT II-Soviets do Y
16. Reduce SDI funding N
17. Increase SDI funding N
18. Purchase Trident sub N
19. Delete 12 MX;Add conv wpn Y
20. Raise speed limit Y
21. Textile Import Quotas(*) N
22. Req Pentagon buy US goods Y
23. AIDS ins anti-dscriminatn N
24. Nicaraguan refugee aid N
25. Nicaraguan contra aid Y
26. US abide by SALT II Y
27. Prohibit Saudi arms sale Y
28. Military Retiremnt Reform Y
29. Nicaraguan refugee aid Y
30. Ease '68 Gun Control Act Y
31. Bar intrstat handgun tran N
32. Keep '68 Gun Control Act N
33. Nicaraguan contra aid Y
34. Bar emp polygraph testing N
35. Tax Overhaul consideratn N
36. Bar armor-piercing ammo Y
37. Tax Overhaul consideratn N
38. Make comp emissions known Y
39. Allow toxic victims suits N
40. Strike Superfund "VAT" Y
41. Notify emp-plant closing N
42. Bar emp consult-plant clo Y
43. Medicare cuts;Tax incres' N
44. Delete 12 MX missiles Y
45. Spending cuts;Tax incres' N
46. Textile Import Quotas N
47. Cut some school lunch fds Y
48. Clean Water Act Amendmnts N
49. Youth work projects N
50. Assist military in Angola Y
51. Allow US troops-Nicaragua Y
52. Pentagon polygraph exams Y
53. Bar ASAT testing N
54. Suspend def pmt for abuse Y
55. Bar Pentagon-contr emplmt Y
56. Increase SDI funding N
57. Reduce SDI funding N
58. Produce chemical weapons N
59. Bar CIA fndg in Nicaragua N
60. South Africa sanctions N
61. Cut SS COLAs; Raise taxes N
62. Let US invest-So Africa Y
63. Approve 21 MX for 1985 N
64. Emergency Farm Credit Y
65. Awards to whistle blowers Y
66. African disaster relief Y
67. Ban bank loans to So Afr Y
68. Bar coun duty-free trtmt N

SENSENBRENNER, F. JAMES, Jr. (Cont.)

69. Steel import limits Y
70. Soc Sec COLAs=inflation Y
71. Bar haz waste vctms suits Y
72. Prohibit aid to Nicaragua N
73. Cut $-Schs bar sch prayer Y
74. Raise taxes; Cut Medicare ?
75. Alien residncy-prior 1982 ?
76. Alien residncy-prior 1980 ?
77. Pen emp-hire illgl aliens ?
78. Lmt Persh II/cruse-Europe ?
79. Delete 34 B-1 bombers ?
80. Bar purch of Pershing II ?
81. Bar purchase of Sgt York N
82. Delete $ for Trident II N
83. Allow 15 MX missiles N
84. Bar MX procurement-1985 Y
85. Equal Access Act Y
86. Aid to El Salvador Y
87. Bar Nicarag water mining Y
88. Physician/Medicare freeze Y
89. Increase "sin" taxes N
90. End SBA direct loans Y
91. Sell Conrail ?
92. Equal Rights Amendment N
93. Marines in Lebanon N
94. Eminent domain-Coal comps N
95. Prohibit EPA sanctions Y
96. SS age increase/Reforms Y
97. Auto domestic content req N
98. Delete jobs program fundg Y
99. Highway-Gas tax bill N
100. Raise Medicare;Cut defnse N
101. Emergency housing aid Y
102. Across-the-board tax cuts Y
103. Gramm-Latta II targets Y
104. Delete B-1 bomber funds N
105. Dsapprov Saudi AWACS sale Y
106. Disapprove oil import fee Y
107. Rail Deregulation Y
108. Dsapp India nuc fuel sale N
109. Mil draft registration N
110. Chrysler Loan Guarantees N
111. Prohibit school busing Y
112. Nuclear plant moratorium ?
113. Oil price controls N

Presidential Support Score: 1986 - 73% 1985 - 68%

W Y O M I N G

CHENEY, DICK -- Representative-at-Large [Republican]. Prior Terms: House: 1979-86. Born: January 30, 1941; Lincoln, Neb. Education: University of Wyoming (B.A., M.A.); University of Wisconsin (1968). Occupation: Governor's staff member (1966); executive assistant, Office of Economic Opportunity (1969-70); deputy assistant to presidential counsellor (1971); assistant director, Cost of Living Council for Operations (1971-73); deputy assistant to the president (1974-75); financial consultant, Bradley, Woods and Co. (1973).

1. Immigration Reform Y
2. Open fld-search warrants Y
3. Civil pnty-hire ill alien Y
4. So Afr sanc-veto override N
5. Tax Overhaul N
6. South Africa sanctions N
7. Death penalty-drug bill Y
8. Evidence-warrantless srch +
9. Life term-second drug off Y
10. Military use in drug war N
11. Troop reduction in Europe N
12. Prohibit chemical weapons N
13. Bar ASAT testing N
14. Abide SALT II weapons ban N
15. Follow SALT II-Soviets do Y
16. Reduce SDI funding N
17. Increase SDI funding Y
18. Purchase Trident sub Y
19. Delete 12 MX;Add conv wpn N
20. Raise speed limit Y
21. Textile Import Quotas(*) N
22. Req Pentagon buy US goods N
23. AIDS ins anti-dscriminatn N
24. Nicaraguan refugee aid N
25. Nicaraguan contra aid Y
26. US abide by SALT II #
27. Prohibit Saudi arms sale N
28. Military Retiremnt Reform Y
29. Nicaraguan refugee aid Y
30. Ease '68 Gun Control Act Y
31. Bar intrstat handgun tran N
32. Keep '68 Gun Control Act N
33. Nicaraguan contra aid Y
34. Bar emp polygraph testing N
35. Tax Overhaul consideratn N
36. Bar armor-piercing ammo N
37. Tax Overhaul consideratn N
38. Make comp emissions known N

CHENEY, DICK (Cont.)

39. Allow toxic victims suits N
40. Strike Superfund "VAT" N
41. Notify emp-plant closing N
42. Bar emp consult-plant clo Y
43. Medicare cuts;Tax incres' N
44. Delete 12 MX missiles N
45. Spending cuts;Tax incres' N
46. Textile Import Quotas N
47. Cut some school lunch fds Y
48. Clean Water Act Amendmnts Y
49. Youth work projects N
50. Assist military in Angola Y
51. Allow US troops-Nicaragua Y
52. Pentagon polygraph exams Y
53. Bar ASAT testing N
54. Suspend def pmt for abuse N
55. Bar Pentagon-contr emplmt Y
56. Increase SDI funding Y
57. Reduce SDI funding N
58. Produce chemical weapons Y
59. Bar CIA fndg in Nicaragua N
60. South Africa sanctions N
61. Cut SS COLAs; Raise taxes N
62. Let US invest-So Africa Y
63. Approve 21 MX for 1985 Y
64. Emergency Farm Credit N
65. Awards to whistle blowers Y
66. African disaster relief N
67. Ban bank loans to So Afr N
68. Bar coun duty-free trtmt ?
69. Steel import limits ?
70. Soc Sec COLAs=inflation Y
71. Bar haz waste vctms suits Y
72. Prohibit aid to Nicaragua N
73. Cut $-Schs bar sch prayer Y
74. Raise taxes; Cut Medicare Y
75. Alien residncy-prior 1982 Y
76. Alien residncy-prior 1980 Y
77. Pen emp-hire illgl aliens N
78. Lmt Persh II/cruse-Europe N
79. Delete 34 B-1 bombers N
80. Bar purch of Pershing II N
81. Bar purchase of Sgt York N
82. Delete $ for Trident II N
83. Allow 15 MX missiles Y
84. Bar MX procurement-1985 N
85. Equal Access Act Y
86. Aid to El Salvador Y
87. Bar Nicarag water mining N
88. Physician/Medicare freeze Y
89. Increase "sin" taxes N
90. End SBA direct loans Y
91. Sell Conrail Y
92. Equal Rights Amendment N
93. Marines in Lebanon Y
94. Eminent domain-Coal comps Y
95. Prohibit EPA sanctions ?
96. SS age increase/Reforms Y
97. Auto domestic content req N
98. Delete jobs program fundg Y
99. Highway-Gas tax bill N
100. Raise Medicare;Cut defnse N
101. Emergency housing aid N
102. Across-the-board tax cuts Y
103. Gramm-Latta II targets Y
104. Delete B-1 bomber funds N
105. Dsapprov Saudi AWACS sale N
106. Disapprove oil import fee ?
107. Rail Deregulation N
108. Dsapp India nuc fuel sale Y
109. Mil draft registration Y
110. Chrysler Loan Guarantees N
111. Prohibit school busing Y
112. Nuclear plant moratorium N
113. Oil price controls N

Presidential Support Score: 1986 - 82% 1985 - 86%

SENATE

MEASURES

SENATE MEASURES

1. **S 1200. Immigration Reform.** Adoption of the conference report on the bill to overhaul the nation's immigration laws by creating new penalties against employers who knowingly hire illegal aliens; granting amnesty to illegal aliens who can prove they were in the country prior to Jan. 1, 1982; and creating a special farm worker program for Western agricultural growers. Adopted 63-24: R 29-16; D 34-8 [ND 25-5; SD 9-3]. Oct. 17, 1986.

2. **HR 4868. South Africa Sanctions.** Passage, over President Reagan's Sept. 26 veto, of the bill to impose sanctions against South Africa. Among the sanctions imposed by the bill were bans on imports of South African iron, steel, sugar and other agricultural products. The bill also prohibited exports to South Africa of petroleum products, banned new U.S. investments there, and banned imports of South African uranium, coal and textiles. Passed (thus enacted into law) 78-21: R 31-21; D 47-0 [ND 33-0; SD 14-0], October 2, 1986. A two-thirds majority of those present and voting (66 in this case) of both houses is required to override a veto. A "nay" was a vote supporting the president's position.

3. **HR 5484. Omnibus Drug Bill.** Cohen, R-Maine, motion to table (kill) the Mattingly, R-Ga., amendment to the Dole, R-Kan.-Byrd, D-W.Va., substitute to authorize the death penalty for anyone who knowingly causes the death of another individual during the course of a continuing criminal enterprise. Motion rejected 25-60: R 10-35; D 15-25 [ND 14-15; SD 1-10], Sept. 27, 1986. (The Mattingly amendment subsequently was withdrawn. The effect of the vote was to express the sense of the Senate that should the bill go to conference, Senate conferees should accept House-passed language -- identical to that in the Mattingly amendment --imposing the death penalty for certain offenses. The Dole-Byrd substitute subsequently was adopted by voice vote.)

4. **HR 5484. Omnibus Drug Bill.** Goldwater, R-Ariz., motion to table (kill) the Dixon, D-Ill., amendment to the Dole, R-Kan.-Byrd, D-W.Va., substitute, to require the president, within 30 days of enactment, to deploy military personnel and equipment "to the extent possible" to combat drug smuggling, and within 45 days of enactment to "substantially halt" drug smuggling across U.S. borders "to the extent possible." Motion agreed to 72-14: R 37-9; D 35-5 [ND 25-4; SD 10-1], Sept. 27, 1986. (The Dole-Byrd substitute later was adopted by voice vote.) A "yea" was a vote supporting the president's position.

5. **HR 3838. Tax Overhaul.** Adoption of the conference report on the bill to revise the federal income tax system by reducing individual and corporate tax rates, eliminating or

curtailing many deductions, credits and exclusions, repealing the investment tax credit, taxing capital gains as ordinary income and making other changes. Adopted 74-23: R 41-11; D 33-12 [ND 25-7; SD 8-5], Sept. 27, 1986. A "yea" was a vote supporting the president's position.

6. **S 2405. Omnibus Highway Authorization.** Symms, R-Idaho, amendment to allow states to raise the speed limit to 65 mph on rural Interstate highways outside urbanized areas with populations of 50,000 or more. Adopted 56-36: R 31-17; D 25-19 [ND 14-16; SD 11-3], Sept. 23, 1986.

7. **S J Res 412. Sequestration Order.** Passage of the joint resolution to affirm the Aug. 20, 1986, report of the Congressional Budget Office and the Office of Management and Budget setting out $19.4 billion in across-the-board spending cuts to bring the fiscal 1987 deficit into compliance with the target of $144 billion, as required by the Gramm-Rudman-Hollings anti-deficit law (PL 99-177). Rejected 15-80: R 11-39: D 4-41 [ND 1-31; SD 3-10], in the session that began Sept. 19, 1986. (A Dole, R-Kan., motion, to reconsider the vote by which the joint resolution was rejected, was left pending.)

8. **HR 4868. South Africa Sanctions.** Passage of the bill to impose economic and other sanctions against South Africa, including a ban on new U.S. investments in South Africa and prohibitions against importation of South African agricultural products, coal, uranium and steel. The bill also provided for modification or termination of the sanctions if South Africa met certain conditions, and gave authority to the president to impose new sanctions after a year if those conditions were not met. Passed 84-14: R 37-14; D 47-0 [ND 33-0; SD 14-0], Aug. 15, 1986. (The Senate had previously moved to strike the text of the House-passed bill and insert instead the text of S 2701, the Senate version of HR 4868.)

9. **S 2701. South Africa Sanctions.** Lugar, R-Ind., motion to table (kill) the Kennedy, D-Mass., amendment to add to the bill prohibitions on imports of South African agricultural products, iron and steel, and to prohibit exports to South Africa of crude oil and petroleum products. Motion rejected 44-55: R 41-11; D 3-44 [ND 1-32; SD 2-12], Aug. 15, 1986. (The Kennedy amendment subsequently was adopted by voice vote.)

10. **S 2701. South Africa Sanctions.** Lugar, R-Ind., motion to table (kill) the Kennedy, D-Mass., amendment to add the following sanctions: a ban on renewal of existing bank loans to South African businesses; a ban on the importation into the United States of South African agricultural products, coal and iron; and a ban on exports to South Africa of U.S. crude oil and petroleum products. Motion agreed to 51-48: R 46-6; D 5-42 [ND 1-32; SD 4-10], Aug. 14, 1986. A "yea" was a vote supporting the president's position. (*)

11. **HR 5052. Military Construction Appropriations, Fiscal 1987/Aid to Nicaraguan Rebels.** Adoption of titles II and III of the bill, to provide $100 million in aid for the Nicaraguan "contra" guerrillas and $300 million for economic aid to

the countries of Central America. Adopted 53-47: R 42-11; D 11-36 [ND 2-31; SD 9-5], Aug. 13, 1986. A "yea" was a vote supporting the president's position.

12. **HR 5052. Military Construction Appropriations, Fiscal 1987/Aid to Nicaraguan Rebels.** Kerry, D-Mass., amendment to terminate aid in the bill for the Nicaraguan "contra" guerrillas if the countries of Central America signed a peace agreement containing the principles outlined in an April 1986 declaration by Costa Rica, El Salvador, Guatemala and Honduras. Rejected 46-54: R 6-47; D 40-7 [ND 33-0; SD 7-7], Aug. 13, 1986. A "nay" was a vote supporting the president's position.

13. **HR 5052. Military Construction Appropriations, Fiscal 1987/Aid to Nicaraguan Rebels.** Lugar, R-Ind., motion to table (kill) the Biden, D-Del., amendment to prohibit use of the funds in the bill for aid to the Nicaraguan "contra" guerrillas until the administration had begun direct negotiations with the Nicaraguan government with the aim of achieving an agreement on security and other issues. Motion agreed to 54-45: R 43-9; D 11-36 [ND 3-30; SD 8-6], Aug. 13, 1986. A "yea" was a vote supporting the president's position.

14. **HR 5052. Military Construction Appropriations, Fiscal 1987/Aid to Nicaraguan Rebels.** Mattingly, R-Ga., motion to table (kill) the Leahy, D-Vt., amendment to prohibit expenditure by the CIA or any other intelligence agency of the funds in the bill for aid to the Nicaraguan "contra" guerrillas. Motion agreed to 57-42: R 43-9; D 14-33 [ND 5-28; SD 9-5], Aug. 13, 1986. A "yea" was a vote supporting the president's position.

15. **S 2638. Defense Authorization, Fiscal 1987.** Warner, R-Va., motion to table (kill) the Kerry, D-Mass., amendment to bar tests of any nuclear weapon in connection with the strategic defense initiative or "star wars." Motion agreed to 61-33: R 45-4; D 16-29 [ND 7-24; SD 9-5], Aug. 8, 1986. A "yea" was a vote supporting the president's position.

16. **S 2638. Defense Authorization, Fiscal 1987.** Warner, R-Va., motion to table (kill) the Kerry, D-Mass., amendment to bar tests against a target in space of the anti-satellite (ASAT) missile providing the Soviet Union conducts no (ASAT) tests. Motion agreed to 55-43: R 42-10; D 13-33 [ND 6-26; SD 7-7], Aug. 8, 1986. A "yea" was a vote supporting the president's position.

17. **S 2638. Department of Defense Authorization, Fiscal 1987.** Mathias, R-Md., perfecting amendment to the Kennedy, D-Mass., amendment, to call on President Reagan to submit to the Senate two nuclear test ban treaties -- the Peaceful Nuclear Explosions Treaty and the Threshold Test Ban Treaty -- and to propose an immediate resumption of negotiations with the Soviet Union toward a comprehensive nuclear test ban treaty. Adopted 64-35: R 21-32; D 43-3 (ND 32-1; SD 11-2), Aug. 7, 1986. (The Kennedy amendment subsequently was adopted by voice vote.) A "nay" was a vote supporting the president's position.

18. **S 2638. Department of Defense Authorization, Fiscal 1987.** DeConcini, D-Ariz., amendment to prohibit the sale or transfer of "Stinger" portable anti-aircraft missiles to U.S.-backed guerilla movements in foreign countries unless strict security measures were taken to guard the missiles. Rejected 37-63: R 8-45; D 29-18 [ND 23-10; SD 6-8], Aug. 7, 1986.

19. **S 2638. Department of Defense Authorization, Fiscal 1987.** Pryor, D-Ark., amendment to delete funds for production of the "Bigeye" chemical bomb. Rejected 50-51: R 14-39; D 36-11 [ND 29-4; SD 7-7], with Vice President George Bush casting a "nay" vote, Aug. 7, 1986. A "nay" was a vote supporting the president's position.

20. **S 2638. Department of Defense Authorization, Fiscal 1987.** Hatfield, R-Ore., amendment to prohibit procurement or assembly of "binary" chemical munitions until Congress gives its approval. Rejected 43-57: R 14-39; D 29-18 [ND 26-7; SD 3-11], Aug. 7, 1986. A "nay" was a vote supporting the president's position.

21. **S 2638. Department of Defense Authorization, Fiscal 1987.** Warner, R-Va., motion to table (kill) the Johnston, D-La., amendment to provide a limit of $3.24 billion for research and development on the strategic defense initiative, or "star wars" program. President Reagan had requested $5.3 billion. Motion agreed to 50-49: R 41-11; D 9-38 [ND 5-28; SD 4-10), Aug. 5, 1986. A "yea" was a vote supporting the president's position.

22. **H J Res 668. Public Debt Limit/D.C. AIDS - Insurance Law.** Mathias, R-Md., motion to table (kill) the Helms, R-N.C., amendment to the Finance Committee amendment, to disapprove the District of Columbia law banning discrimination by insurance companies against persons testing positive for the virus causing acquired immune deficiency syndrome (AIDS). Motion rejected 41-53: R 14-34; D 27-19 [ND 22-10; SD 5-9], Aug. 1, 1986. (The Helms amendment subsequently was adopted by voice vote.)

23. **H J Res 668. Public Debt Limit/Oil Import Tariff.** Heinz, R-Pa., motion to table (kill) the Hart, D-Colo., amendment to the Finance Committee amendment, to increase the existing tariff on crude oil and refined petroleum products by $10 a barrel. Motion agreed to 82-15: R 47-4; D 35-11 [ND 27-6; SD 8-5], July 31, 1986.

24. **H J Res 668. Public Debt Limit/Windfall Profits Tax.** Heinz, R-Pa., motion to table (kill) the Nickles, R-Okla., amendment to the Finance Committee amendment, to repeal the windfall profits tax on domestic crude oil. Motion rejected 47-51: R 20-31; D 27-20 [ND 24-9; SD 3-11], July 31, 1986. (The Nickles amendment later was adopted by voice vote.)

25. **H J Res 668. Public Debt Limit/Anti-Deficit Law.** Hart, D-Colo., amendment to the Finance Committee amendment, to repeal the 1985 Balanced Budget and Emergency Deficit Control Act (the Gramm-Rudman-Hollings anti-deficit law, PL 99-177).

Rejected 30-69: R 9-43: D 21-26 [ND 20-13; SD 1-13], July 31, 1986. (The Finance Committee amendment would prevent disinvestment of the Social Security trust funds.)

26. **HR 3838. Tax Overhaul.** Baucus, D-Mont., substitute for the Bumpers, D-Ark., amendment [See Vote 27 below] to reinstate provisions granting immunity from criminal prosecution, but not civil penalties, to those who confess to unpaid taxes; to make the provisions contingent on a $200 million appropriation to the Internal Revenue Service for enforcement; to make the provisions inapplicable to income from illegal sources; and to limit the immunity from criminal prosecution to two years. Rejected 40-43: R 21-21; D 19-22 [ND 12-17; SD 7-5], June 20, 1986. (The Bumpers amendment subsequently was adopted by voice vote.)

27. **HR 3838. Tax Overhaul.** Bumpers, D-Ark., motion to table (kill) the Baucus, D-Mont., substitute for the Bumpers amendment to reinstate provisions granting immunity from criminal prosecution, but not civil penalties, to those who confess to unpaid taxes; to make the provisions contingent on a $200 million appropriation to the Internal Revenue Service for enforcement; to make the provisions inapplicable to income from illegal sources; and to limit the immunity from criminal prosecution to two years. Motion rejected 41-41: R 19-21; D 22-20 [ND 16-13; SD 6-7], June 20, 1986. (The Baucus substitute subsequently was rejected [see vote 26 above], after which the Bumpers amendment, to strike the immunity and to offset the $200 million revenue loss by limiting net operating loss carry-backs by corporations, was adopted by voice vote.)

28. **HR 3838. Tax Overhaul.** Packwood, R-Ore., motion to table (kill) the Mitchell, D-Maine, amendment to add a third tax rate of 35 percent, reduce the bottom rate from 15 percent to 14 percent and retain the bill's top capital gains rate at 27 percent. Motion agreed to 71-29: R 49-4; D 22-25 [ND 14-19; SD 8-6], June 18, 1986.

29. **HR 3838. Tax Overhaul.** Wilson, R-Calif., motion to table (kill) the Metzenbaum, D-Ohio, amendment to eliminate a provision allowing Unocal, the Union Oil Co., of California, to claim foreign tax credits on interest paid on $4.4 billion in debt incurred to fight a takeover attempt. Motion rejected 33-60: R 27-22; D 6-38 [ND 2-28; SD 4-10], June 13, 1986. (The Metzenbaum amendment was subsequently adopted by voice vote.)

30. **S J Res 316. Saudi Arms Sale.** Passage, over President Reagan's May 21 veto, of a resolution blocking the sale of weapons to Saudi Arabia. Rejected (thus sustaining the president's veto) 66-34: R 24-29; D 42-5 [ND 31-2; SD 11-3], June 5, 1986. A two-thirds majority of those present and voting (67 in this case) is required to override a veto. A "nay" was a vote supporting the president's position. (+)

31. **S 1965. Higher Education Act Amendments.** Helms, R-N.C., motion to table (kill) the Helms amendment to bar federal courts from ordering school busing except in narrowly

defined circumstances. Motion rejected 45-50: R 15-37; D 30-13 [ND 26-4; SD 4-9], June 3, 1986. (Helms, who moved to table his own amendment to force a vote on the issue, subsequently withdrew his amendment.)

32. **S J Res 316. Saudi Arms Sale.** Passage of the joint resolution to prohibit the administration's proposed $354 million sale of missiles to Saudi Arabia. Passed 73-22: R 29-20; D 44-2 [ND 32-1; SD 12-1], May 6, 1986. A "nay" was a vote supporting the president's position.

33. **S J Res 283. Aid to Nicaraguan Rebels.** Lugar, R-Ind., substitute to approve use of $100 million in Defense Department funds to provide aid to the Nicaraguan "contras." Of that amount, $25 million for non-military aid and for training the "defensive" weapons would be released immediately upon enactment of the resolution; the remainder would be released at 90-day intervals after July 1, 1986. Adopted 53-47: R 42-11; D 11-36 [ND 2-31; SD 9-5], March 27, 1986. (The joint resolution was passed by voice vote.) A "yea" was a vote supporting the president's position.

34. **S J Res 283. Aid to Nicaraguan Rebels.** Kennedy, D-Mass., substitute to prohibit U.S. aid, in any form, to military or paramilitary organizations in Nicaragua. Rejected 24-74: R 5-48; D 19-26 [ND 18-14; SD 1-12], March 27, 1986. A "nay" was a vote supporting the president's position.

35. **S J Res 225. Balanced Budget Constitutional Amendment.** Passage of the joint resolution to propose a constitutional amendment to require a balanced federal budget every year unless a three-fifths majority of the total membership of both houses of Congress votes for a specific amount of deficit spending; to require that the public debt of the United States may be increased only by a law enacted by a three-fifths majority of the total membership of both houses of Congress; to require that a bill to increase revenue shall become law only if passed by a majority of the total membership of both houses of Congress; to require the president to submit annually a proposed balanced budget to Congress; and to allow Congress to waive the requirement for a balanced budget during a declared war. Rejected 66-34: R 43-10; D 23-24 [ND 10-23; SD 13-11], March 25, 1986. A two-thirds majority of those present and voting (67 in this case) is required for passage of a constitutional amendment. A "yea" was a vote supporting the president's position.

36. **S J Res 225. Balanced Budget Constitutional Amendment.** Byrd, D-W.Va., substitute for the Thurmond, R-S.C., substitute, to provide that federal expenditures may not exceed receipts in any year, except during a declared war or when three-fifths of the members of Congress vote for deficit spending. Rejected 35-64: R 6-46; D 29-18 [ND 20-13; SD 9-5], March 12, 1986.

37. **S 638. Conrail Sale.** Passage of the bill to approve the sale of the Conrail freight railroad to the Norfolk Southern Corp. Passed 54-39: R 37-12; D 17-27 [ND 6-24; SD 11-3], Feb. 4, 1986. A "yea" was a vote supporting the president's position.

38. **HR 2100. Farm Programs Reauthorization, Fiscal 1986-90.** Adoption of the conference report on the bill to revise agriculture programs and extend them through fiscal year 1990; to modify price supports by reducing loan rates in 1986 and thereafter; to maintain income supports by freezing target prices at fiscal 1985 levels through fiscal 1987 and reduce them by a total of 10 percent over the remaining three years of the bill; to provide for agricultural export, soil conservation, farm credit and agricultural research programs; and to continue food assistance to low-income persons through fiscal 1990. Adopted (thus cleared for the president) 55-38: R 33-15; D 22-23 [ND 14-18; SD 8-5], Dec. 18, 1985.

39. **S J Res 77. Compact of Free Association.** McClure, R-Idaho, motion to table (kill) the Hart, D-Colo., amendment to impose a new $10-per-barrel oil import fee. Motion agreed to 78-18: R 48-2; D 30-16 [ND 22-11; SD 8-5], Nov. 14, 1985. (The Senate subsequently moved to strike the language of H J Res 187, the House version of the joint resolution, and insert instead the provisions of S J Res 77. The Senate subsequently passed H J Res 187 by voice vote.)

40. **HR 3128. Omnibus Budget Reconciliation, Fiscal 1986.** Passage of the bill to reduce the deficit by $85.7 billion over fiscal 1986-88 through $69.9 billion in spending cuts and $15.8 billion in added revenues. Passed 93-6: R 51-1; D 42-5 [ND 28-5; SD 14-0], Nov. 14, 1985. (The Senate previously had moved to strike the text of HR 3128, the House version of the bill, and insert instead the provisions of S 1730.) A "nay" was a vote supporting the president's position.

41. **HR 1562. Textile Import Quotas.** Passage of the bill to establish a worldwide system of quotas for imports of textiles and apparel, limit shoe imports to 60 percent of the domestic shoe market and require negotiations leading to an international agreement limiting copper production. Passed 60-39: R 25-28; D 35-11 [ND 23-10; SD 12-1], Nov. 13, 1985. A "nay" was a vote supporting the president's position.

42. **H J Res 372. Public Debt Limit.** Packwood, R-Ore., motion to table (kill) the Riegle, D-Mich., amendment to the Packwood amendment to the House amendment to the Senate amendment, to exempt veterans' compensation and medical programs from any automatic spending reductions. Motion agreed to 52-44: R 46-5; D 6-39 [ND 3-28; SD 3-11], Nov. 5, 1985.

43. **HR 2965. Commerce, Justice, State and the Judiciary Appropriations, Fiscal 1986.** Rudman, R-N.H., motion to table (kill) the Helms, R-N.C., amendment to prohibit the use of funds for the federal prison system to perform abortions on pregnant inmates, except when the mother's life was in danger. Motion rejected 46-46: R 17-31; D 29-15 [ND 23-8; SD 6-7], Oct. 24, 1985.

44. **S 1730. Omnibus Budget Reconciliation, Fiscal 1986.** Thurmond, R-S.C., perfecting amendment to the Hollings, D-S.C., amendment to establish a new system of quotas on textile imports and to limit shoe imports to 60 percent of the domestic market over the next eight years. Adopted

54-42: R 22-29; D 32-13 [ND 21-11; SD 11-2], Oct. 24, 1985. A "nay" was a vote supporting the president's position. (§)

45. **HR 3244. Transportation Appropriations, Fiscal 1986.** Andrews, R-N.D., motion to table (kill) the Armstrong, R-Colo., amendment to eliminate funding for Amtrak. Motion agreed to 71-25: R 27-24; D 44-1 [ND 30-1; SD 14-0], Oct. 23, 1985.

46. **H J Res 372. Public Debt Limit.** Packwood, R-Ore., motion to table (kill) the Bradley, D-N.J., amendment to increase by 18 cents a gallon the federal excise tax on motor fuels. Motion agreed to 89-9: R 49-2; D 40-7 [ND 27-6; SD 13-1], Oct. 10, 1985.

47. **H J Res 372. Public Debt Limit.** Dole, R-Kan. (for Gramm, R-Texas, Rudman, R-N.H., Hollings, D-S.C.) amendment to set maximum allowable federal deficits for fiscal years 1986-91, declining annually to zero in 1991, and to require the president, if projected deficits exceed those allowed, to issue an emergency order reducing all federal spending except for Social Security, interest on the federal debt and existing contractual obligations, by enough to reduce deficits to the maximum established by the bill. The amendment also revises congressional budgeting procedures and removes Social Security from the unified federal budget in fiscal 1986 and thereafter. Adopted 75-24: R 48-4; D 27-20 [ND 15-18; SD 12-2], Oct. 9, 1985. A "yea" was a vote supporting the president's position.

48. **H J Res 372. Public Debt Limit.** Melcher, D-Mont., amendment to the Dole, R-Kan. (for Gramm, R-Texas, Rudman, R-N.H., Hollings, D-S.C.) amendment, to impose a 20 percent minimum alternative tax on corporations beginning in 1986. Rejected 10-88: R 0-51; D 10-37 [ND 8-25; SD 2-12], Oct. 9, 1985.

49. **S 51. Superfund Reauthorization, Fiscal 1986-90.** Roth, R-Del., amendment to strike from the bill a section establishing a new demonstration program to pay for medical expenses of victims of hazardous substance releases, and to authorize appropriations of $30 million annually during fiscal 1986-90 for that purpose. Adopted 49-45: R 40-11; D 9-34 [ND 3-28; SD 6-6], Sept. 24, 1985. A "yea" was a vote supporting the president's position.

50. **S 1200. Immigration Reform and Control Act.** Wilson, R-Calif., amendment to create a "seasonal worker" program to allow foreign workers into the country for up to nine months each year for agricultural work, with a cap allowing no more than 350,000 of these workers in the United States at any one time. Adopted 51-44: R 36-15; D 15-29 [ND 6-25; SD 9-4], Sept. 17, 1985.

51. **S 47. School Prayer.** Weicker, R-Conn., motion to table (kill) the bill to bar the federal courts, including the Supreme Court, from considering cases involving prayer in public schools. Motion agreed to 62-36: R 24-28; D 38-8 [ND 31-1; SD 7-7], Sept. 10, 1985. (The effect of the bill would have been to restore the right of states or local communities to permit prayer in public schools without being subject to challenges in the federal courts.)

52. **S 43. Line-Item Veto.** Dole, R-Kan., motion to invoke cloture (thus limiting debate) on the Dole motion to proceed to the consideration of the bill to give the president power to veto individual spending items by requiring that appropriations bills be split by paragraph or section into separate bills before being sent to the White House. Motion rejected 58-40: R 46-7; D 12-33 [ND 8-24; SD 4-9], July 24, 1985. A three-fifths majority vote (60) of the total Senate is required to invoke cloture. A "yea" was a vote supporting the president's position.

53. **HR 1460. Anti-Apartheid Act.** Passage of the bill to impose sanctions immediately against South Africa, including a ban on bank loans to the South African government, and prohibitions against the sale of computer goods and nuclear materials to that country. The bill also calls for imposition of additional sanctions, such as a ban on new U.S. investment and a prohibition on the importation into the United States of South African gold coins, if South Africa does not reform its racial policies within 18 months. Passed 80-12: R 36-12; D 44-0 [ND 31-0; SD 13-0], July 11, 1985. (Before passing the bill, the Senate substituted the text of S 995 for the House-passed version, HR 1460.)

54. **S 49. Firearm Owners' Protection.** Passage of the bill to revise the Gun Control Act of 1968 to exempt many gun collectors from licensing requirements, remove the ban on interstate sales of rifles, shotguns and handguns, require advance notice for routine compliance inspections, and impose a mandatory five-year sentence on anyone convicted of using a firearm in a violent federal crime. Passed 79-15: R 49-2; D 30-13 [ND 18-13; SD 12-0], July 9, 1985. A "yea" was a vote supporting the president's position.

55. **S 49. Firearm Owners' Protection.** McClure, R-Idaho, motion to table (kill) the Inouye, D-Hawaii, amendment to require a 14-day waiting period between the purchase of a handgun and its delivery to the buyer. Motion agreed to 71-23: R 46-5; D 25-18 [ND 14-17; SD 11-1], July 9, 1985. A "yea" was a vote supporting the president's position.

56. **S 49. Firearm Owners' Protection.** McClure, R-Idaho, motion to table (kill) the Mathias, R-Md., amendment to retain current law allowing federal authorities to conduct all inspections of gun dealers without providing notice of such inspections. Motion agreed to 76-18: R 47-4; D 29-14 (ND 18-13; SD 11-1), July 9, 1985. A "yea" was a vote supporting the president's position.

57. **S 49. Firearm Owners' Protection.** McClure, R-Idaho, motion to table (kill) the Kennedy, D-Mass., amendment to retain the ban in the Gun Control Act of 1968 on the interstate sales of handguns. Motion agreed to 69-26: R 45-6; D 24-20 [ND 12-19; SD 12-1], July 9, 1985. A "yea" was a vote supporting the president's position.

58. **S 1003. State Department Authorizations, Fiscal 1986-87.** Nunn, D-Ga., amendment to authorize $24 million for fiscal year 1986 for humanitarian assistance to the Nicaraguan rebels and to direct the National Security Council to

monitor the use of the funds. The amendment also releases the $14 million approved for fiscal 1985 for the rebels but restricts the use of those funds to humanitarian assistance, and it urges the president to lift the economic sanctions on Nicaragua if that country agrees to a cease-fire and talks with the rebels, to call upon the rebels to remove from their ranks any individuals who have engaged in human rights abuses, and to resume bilateral negotiations with the government of Nicaragua. Adopted 55-42: R 41-10; D 14-32 [ND 4-28; SD 10-4], June 6, 1985. A "yea" was a vote supporting the president's position.

59. **S 1160. Department of Defense Authorization, Fiscal 1986.** Kerry, D-Mass., amendment to bar during fiscal years 1985 and 1986 tests against a target in space of the anti-satellite (ASAT) missile, unless the Soviet Union tests an ASAT. Rejected 35-51: R 7-40; D 28-11 [ND 24-5; SD 4-6], May 24, 1985. A "nay" was a vote supporting the president's position.

60. **S 1160. Department of Defense Authorization, Fiscal 1986.** Pryor, D-Ark., amendment to delete from the bill $163 million for the procurement of binary chemical weapons munitions, to prohibit future use of funds for such procurement, and to express the sense of Congress that the president should intensify efforts to achieve an agreement with the Soviet Union for the banning of chemical weapons. Rejected 46-50: R 15-36; D 31-14 [ND 26-7; SD 5-7], May 22, 1985. A "nay" was a vote supporting the president's position.

61. **S 1160. Department of Defense Authorization, Fiscal 1986.** Hart, D-Colo., amendment to delete from the bill $2.1 billion for the production of 21 MX missiles and to prohibit use of funds authorized by the bill for the production or deployment of MX missiles. Rejected 42-56: R 6-45; D 36-11 [ND 30-3; SD 6-8], May 21, 1985. A "nay" was a vote supporting the president's position.

62. **S Con Res 32. First Budget Resolution, Fiscal 1986.** Dole, R-Kan., motion to table (kill) the Metzenbaum, D-Ohio, perfecting amendment to the Dole-Domenici, R-N.M., amendment to the instructions of the Dole motion to recommit the concurrent resolution to the Budget Committee, to impose a 15 percent minimum tax on corporate earnings in excess of $50,000 and to use the revenues to reduce the federal deficit. Motion agreed to 61-37: R 49-3; D 12-34 [ND 8-24; SD 4-10], in the session that began May 9, 1985.

63. **S Con Res 32. First Budget Resolution Fiscal 1986.** Dole, R-Kan., motion to table (kill) the Moynihan, D-N.Y., perfecting amendment to the Dole-Domenici, R-N.M., amendment to the instructions of the Dole motion to recommit the concurrent resolution to the Budget Committee, to restore the full Social Security cost-of-living adjustment (COLA) for fiscal 1986. Motion agreed to 51-47: R 49-3; D 2-44 [ND 1-31; SD 1-13], in the session that began May 9, 1985. A "yea" was a vote supporting the president's position.

64. **S Con Res 32. First Budget Resolution, Fiscal 1986.** Grassley, R-Iowa, perfecting amendment to the Dole, R-Kan.,-

Domenici, R-N.M., amendment to the instructions of the Dole motion to recommit the concurrent resolution to the Budget Committee, to freeze funding for all federal programs in fiscal 1986 at fiscal 1985 levels, with no allowances for inflation. Rejected 27-70: R 9-42; D 18-28 [ND 13-19; SD 5-9], May 9, 1985.

65. **S Con Res 32. First Budget Resolution, Fiscal 1986.** Byrd, D-W.Va., perfecting amendment to the Dole, R-Kan.-Domenici, R-N.M., amendment to the instructions of the Dole motion to recommit the concurrent resolution to the Budget Committee, to alter the Senate GOP-White House budget by, among other changes, reducing the rate of growth for defense spending, increasing taxes and reinstating existing law treatment of Social Security cost-of-living adjustments. Rejected 43-54: R 1-50; D 42-4 [ND 30-2; SD 12-2], May 8, 1985. A "nay" was a vote supporting the president's position.

66. **S Con Res 32. First Budget Resolution, Fiscal 1986.** Dole, R-Kan., perfecting amendment to the Dole-Domenici, R-N.M., amendment to the instructions of the Dole motion to recommit the concurrent resolution to the Budget Committee, to retain existing Social Security cost-of-living adjustments (COLAs). Adopted 65-34: R 19-33; D 46-1 [ND 33-0; SD 13-1], May 1, 1985. A "nay" was a vote supporting the president's position. (The Senate GOP-White House budget given preliminary Senate approval April 30 set COLAs at the greater of 2 percent or the inflation rate.)

67. **S J Res 106. Aid to Nicaraguan Rebels.** Passage of the joint resolution to approve the release of $14 million in fiscal 1985 for supporting military or paramilitary operations in Nicaragua. Passed 53-46: R 43-9; D 10-37 [ND 1-32; SD 9-5], April 23, 1985. A "yea" was a vote supporting the president's position.

68. **S J Res 75. MX Missile Appropriation.** Passage of the joint resolution to reaffirm the appropriation of $1.5 billion in the fiscal 1985 defense budget to purchase 21 MX missiles. Passed 55-45: R 45-8; D 10-37 [ND 3-30; SD 7-7], March 20, 1985. A "yea" was a vote supporting the president's position.

69. **HR 1096. African Relief/Farm Credit.** Passage of the bill to authorize $175 million in non-food aid for emergency relief to Africa, to authorize $100 million to offset interest on restructured private farm loans guaranteed by the Farmers Home Administration (FmHA), to increase the FmHA loan guarantee program by $1.85 billion and revise certain eligibility rules and to authorize advances to eligible farmers of Commodity Credit Corporation commodity price-support loans. Passed 62-35: R 16-34; D 46-1 [ND 32-1; SD 14-0], Feb. 27, 1985. A "nay" was a vote supporting the president's position.

70. **H J Res 654. Debt Limit Increase.** Baker, R-Tenn., motion to table (kill) the Kennedy, D-Mass., amendment to call for a mutual and verifiable freeze on the production, testing and deployment of nuclear weapons and a reduction in nuclear weapons stockpiles worldwide. Motion agreed to 55-42: R

46-8; D 9-34 [ND 2-29; SD 7-5], Oct. 5, 1984. A "yea" was a vote supporting the president's position.

71. **H J Res 648. Continuing Appropriations, Fiscal 1985.** Packwood, R-Ore., motion to table (kill) the Byrd, D-W.Va., amendment to overturn the Feb. 28, 1984, Supreme Court decision in *Grove City College v. Bell* narrowing the reach of Title IX of the 1972 Education Amendments, a law designed to bar sex discrimination in educational institutions receiving federal aid. Motion agreed to 53-45: R 51-4; D 2-41 [ND 2-28; SD 0-13], Oct. 2, 1984. A "yea" was a vote supporting the president's position.

72. **HR 4616. Motor Vehicle Safety/Minimum Drinking Age.** Lautenberg, D-N.J., amendment to withhold a percentage of highway funds from states whose minimum drinking ages are under 21 and to provide incentives for other actions aimed at reducing drunk driving. Adopted 81-16: R 45-10; D 36-6 [ND 25-3; SD 11-3], June 26, 1984. A "yea" was a vote supporting the president's position.

73. **S 2723. Omnibus Defense Authorization.** Tower, R-Texas, motion to table (kill) the Nunn, D-Ga., amendment to reduce the number of U.S. military personnel stationed in Europe by 30,000 per year for three years, beginning at the end of 1987, unless other NATO member nations had increased their defense spending by certain amounts. Motion agreed to 55-41: R 49-4; D 6-37 [ND 5-26; SD 1-11], June 20, 1984. A "yea" was a vote supporting the president's position.

74. **S 2723. Omnibus Defense Authorization.** Tower, R-Texas, motion to table (kill) the Kennedy, D-Mass., amendment to provide that nothing in the bill shall be construed as authorization for funds to assist insurgent military forces in Nicaragua (the so-called "contras"). Motion agreed to 58-38: R 48-6; D 10-32 [ND 2-26; SD 8-6], June 18, 1984. A "yea" was a vote supporting the president's position.

75. **S 2723. Omnibus Defense Authorization.** Tower, R-Texas, motion to table (kill) the Moynihan, D-N.Y., amendment to produce no additional MX missiles in fiscal 1985 but to keep the MX production line ready for production pending completion of a new study of the mobile, single-warhead "Midgetman" missile. Motion agreed to 49-48: R 43-10; D 5-38 [ND 2-28; SD 3-10], June 14, 1984, with Vice President Bush casting a "yea" vote to break the 48-48 tie. A "yea" was a vote supporting the president's position.

76. **S 2723. Omnibus Defense Authorization.** Tower, R-Texas, motion to table (kill) the Leahy, D-Vt., amendment to delete $2.622 billion for production of the MX missile in fiscal 1985 and transfer $1.4 billion of the savings into a variety of non-nuclear equipment and improvements in defense readiness. Motion agreed to 55-41: R 45-7; D 10-34 [ND 4-27; SD 6-7], June 14, 1984. A "yea" was a vote supporting the president's position.

77. **HR 2163. Deficit Reduction.** Baker, R-Tenn., amendment to reduce federal deficits by $140 billion through fiscal 1987 by increasing taxes, limiting the increases in military

spending, cutting federal benefit and other non-defense programs. Adopted 65-32: R 53-0; D 12-32 [ND 6-24; SD 6-8], May 17, 1984. A "yea" was a vote supporting the president's position.

78. **H J Res 492. Department of Agriculture, Fiscal 1984 Urgent Supplemental Appropriations.** Baker, R-Tenn., motion to table (kill) the Leahy, D-Vt., amendment to require congressional authorization for the introduction of combat troops in or over El Salvador. Motion agreed to 59-36; R 49-5; D 10-31 [ND 2-25; SD 8-6], April 4, 1984. A "yea" was a vote supporting the president's position.

79. **S J Res 73. Constitutional Amendment on School Prayer.** Passage of the joint resolution to propose an amendment to the Constitution to permit organized, recited prayer in public schools and other public places. Rejected 56-44: R 37-18; D 19-26 [ND 6-25; SD 13-1], March 20, 1984. A two-thirds majority of those present and voting (67 in this case) of both houses is required for passage of a joint resolution proposing an amendment to the Constitution. A "yea" was a vote supporting the president's position.

80. **S 1765. Capital Punishment.** Passage of the bill to reinstitute the death penalty for certain federal crimes, including assassination or attempted assassination of a president, treason, espionage and specified other federal crimes resulting in the death of another person. The bill requires a separate hearing on the issue of punishment after the defendant is convicted of an offense carrying the death penalty. Passed 63-32: R 43-11; D 20-21 [ND 9-19; SD 11-2], Feb. 22, 1984. A "yea" was a vote supporting the president's position.

81. **S 1762. Comprehensive Crime Control Act.** Metzenbaum, D-Ohio, amendment to prohibit government officials from tape recording their telephone conversations without consent of the other party, with exceptions permitted for law enforcement and intelligence officers. Rejected 41-51: R 10-43; D 31-8 [ND 23-4; SD 8-4], Feb. 2, 1984. A "nay" was a vote supporting the president's position.

82. **HR 3706. Martin Luther King Jr. Holiday.** Passage of the bill to declare the third Monday in January a legal public holiday honoring Martin Luther King Jr. Passed 78-22; R 37-18; D 41-4 [ND 28-3; SD 13-1], Oct. 19, 1983.

83. **S J Res 159. Multinational Force in Lebanon.** Passage of the joint resolution to provide statutory authorization under the War Powers Resolution for continued U.S. participation in the multinational peacekeeping force in Lebanon for up to 18 months after the enactment of the resolution. Passed 54-46: R 52-3; D 2-43 [ND 2-29; SD 0-14], Sept. 29, 1983. A "yea" was a vote supporting the president's position.

84. **S J Res 3. Human Life Federalism Amendment.** Passage of the joint resolution to propose an amendment to the Constitution that would overturn the 1973 Supreme Court decision, *Roe v. Wade*, which made abortion legal. Rejected 49-50: R 34-19; D 15-31 [ND 7-25; SD 8-6], June 28, 1983. A two-

thirds majority of those present and voting (67 in this case) of both houses is required for passage of a joint resolution proposing an amendment to the Constitution. A "yea" was a vote supporting the president's position.

85. **HR 6211. Transportation Assistance Act of 1982.** Passage of the bill to authorize approximately $70 billion for highways through fiscal 1987 and approximately $12 billion for transit through fiscal 1985, and increase gasoline and other highway taxes. Passed 56-34: R 35-15; D 21-19 [ND 14-12; SD 7-7], in the session which began Dec. 20, 1982. A "yea" was a vote supporting the president's position.

86. **H J Res 631. Continuing Appropriations, Fiscal 1983.** Domenici, R-N.M., amendment to delete the section of the joint resolution providing $1.2 billion for public works jobs. Rejected 46-50: R 39-12; D 7-38 [ND 3-27; SD 4-11], in the session which began Dec. 16, 1982. A "yea" was a vote supporting the president's position.

87. **HR 6590. Tobacco Program Revisions.** Baker, R-Tenn., motion to table (kill) the Eagleton, D-Mo., amendment to authorize tobacco price support loans through 1985 (thus ending permanent authorization for these loans). Motion agreed to 49-47: R 29-23; D 20-24 [ND 7-23; SD 13-1], July 14, 1982.

88. **HR 5922. Urgent Supplemental Appropriations, Fiscal 1982.** Lugar, R-Ind., amendment to establish a new subsidy program to provide mortgages at below-market interest rates for buyers of new homes. The amendment contained a fiscal 1982 appropriation of $5.1 billion. Adopted 69-23: R 29-20; D 40-3 [ND 27-1; SD 13-2], May 27, 1982. A "nay" was a vote supporting the president's position.

89. **S 573. Oil Industry Antitrust Exemption.** Metzenbaum, D-Ohio, amendment to nullify President Reagan's Jan. 28 order terminating immediately all remaining controls on oil and gasoline. Rejected 24-68: R 3-47; D 21-21 [ND 18-10; SD 3-11], March 10, 1981. A "nay" was a vote supporting the president's position. (The bill, to extend through Sept. 30, 1981, antitrust exemptions for oil companies participating in the programs of the International Energy Agency, subsequently was passed by voice vote.)

90. **H J Res 266. Tax Cuts.** Hollings, D-S.C., amendment to the Finance Committee bill limiting the size of personal tax reductions and targeting them to middle-income taxpayers in order to achieve a balanced budget by 1984. Rejected 26-71: R 0-51; D 26-20 [ND 20-12; SD 6-8], July 22, 1981. A "nay" was a vote supporting the president's position.

91. **H J Res 266. Tax Cuts.** Finance Committee amendment to require, beginning in 1985, that individual income taxes be adjusted, or indexed, annually to offset the effects of inflation. Adopted 57-40: R 43-8; D 14-32 [ND 11-20; SD 3-12], July 16, 1981.

92. **HR 3512. Fiscal 1981 Supplemental Appropriations.** Hatfield, R-Ore., motion to table (kill) the Moynihan, D-N.Y., amendment stating the sense of the Senate in opposition to

President Reagan's proposed reductions on Social Security benefits. Motion agreed to 49-48: R 48-2; D 1-46 [ND 0-32; SD 1-14], May 20, 1981. A "yea" was a vote supporting the president's position.

93. **H Con Res 194. Saudi AWACS.** Adoption of the concurrent resolution disapproving the proposal by President Reagan to sell Saudi Arabia an $8.5 billion package of military equipment consisting of five E-3A Airborne Warning and Control System (AWACS) radar planes, 1,177 AIM-9L Sidewinder air-to-air missiles, 101 sets of conformal fuel tanks for F-15 fighter planes and six to eight KC-707 tanker aircraft. Rejected 48-52: R 12-41; D 36-11 [ND 28-4; SD 8-7], Oct. 28, 1981. A "nay" was a vote supporting the president's position.

94. **S 951. Justice Department Authorization.** Johnston, D-La., motion to invoke cloture (thus limiting debate) on the Helms, R-N.C.-Johnston amendment to prohibit federal courts in most instances from ordering school busing for racial balance. Motion agreed to 61-36: R 36-16; D 25-20 [ND 11-19; SD 14-1], Sept. 16, 1981. A three-fifths vote (60) of the full Senate is required to invoke cloture.

95. **HR 7428. Oil Import Fee/Debt Limit.** Passage, over the president's June 5 veto, of the bill to extend through June 30, 1980, the existing debt limit of $879 billion and to disapprove the $4.62 fee per barrel of imported oil that President Carter imposed effective March 15. Passed 68-10: R 33-0; D 35-10 [ND 22-9; SD 13-1], June 6, 1980. A two-thirds majority vote (52 in this case) is required for passage over a veto. A "nay" was a vote supporting the president's position.

96. **HR 2977. Domestic Violence.** Passage of the bill to authorize a program of federal assistance for programs of domestic violence prevention and services to victims, and to establish a commission to study proposals for a national service program. Passed 46-41: R 11-27; D 35-14 [ND 28-4; SD 7-10], Sept. 4, 1980. A "yea" was a vote supporting the president's position.

97. **S 2245. Trucking Deregulation.** Passage of the bill to ease federal regulation of trucking, promote competition in the industry and allow greater pricing flexibility. Passed 70-20: R 36-2; D 34-18 [ND 22-13; SD 12-5), April 15, 1980. A "yea" was a vote supporting the president's position.

98. **H Con Res 432. India Nuclear Fuel.** Adoption of the resolution to overturn President Carter's decision to ship 38 tons of enriched uranium fuel to India, for use at its Tarapur nuclear power reactors. Rejected (thus completing congressional action and allowing the sale to take place), 46-48: R 22-17; D 24-31 [ND 18-20; SD 6-11], Sept. 24, 1980. A "nay" was a vote supporting the president's position.

99. **H J Res 521. Draft Registration Funding.** Passage of the bill to transfer $13.3 million from the fiscal 1980 Department of the Air Force personnel account to the Selective Service System to register 19- and 20-year-old males for a

possible military draft. Passed 58-34: R 25-16; D 33-18 [ND 15-18; SD 18-0], June 12, 1980. A "yea" was a vote supporting the president's position.

100. **HR 5860. Chrysler Loan Guarantees.** Passage of the bill to authorize $1.5 billion in federal loan guarantees, to be matched by $2.1 billion from other sources, and to establish a $175 million employee stock ownership plan. Passed 53-44: R 12-27; D 41-17 [ND 30-10; SD 11-7], Dec. 19, 1979. A "yea" was a vote supporting the president's position.

101. **S 562. Nuclear Regulatory Commission.** Hart, D-Colo., amendment to defer issuance of any new construction permits for nuclear power plants in the first six months of fiscal 1980. Rejected 35-57: R 8-31; D 27-26 [ND 25-12; SD 2-14], July 17, 1979.

102. **S J Res 28. Direct Popular Elections.** Adoption of the joint resolution to propose a constitutional amendment to abolish the electoral college and provide for direct popular election of the president and vice president. Rejected 51-48: R 12-28; D 39-20 [ND 31-9; SD 8-11], July 10, 1979. A two-thirds majority vote (66 in this case) is required for passage of a joint resolution proposing an amendment to the Constitution. A "yea" was a vote supporting the president's position.

103. **S 1753. Elementary and Secondary Education Act Amendments.** Pell, D-R.I., motion to table (kill) the Roth, R-Del., amendment to limit court-ordered busing of students only when there was a discriminatory purpose for segregated education; to require courts to determine whether a greater degree of racial segregation resulted because of the segregation policy; and to delay federal busing orders to provide time for appeals, unless the Supreme Court or a three-member appellate court denied such a delay. Motion agreed to 49-47: R 12-26; D 37-21 [ND 34-8; SD 3-13], Aug. 23, 1978.

104. **S 2493. Airline Deregulation.** Kennedy, D-Mass., amendment to direct the Civil Aeronautics Board to authorize a proposed air transportation service unless it determined that the service was not consistent with the public convenience and necessity. Adopted 69-23: R 28-6; D 41-17 [ND 30-9; SD 11-8], April 19, 1978. A "yea" was a vote supporting the president's position.

105. **S Con Res 86. Mideast Fighter Plane Sales.** Adoption of the resolution to disapprove the sale of $4.5 billion worth of jet fighter planes to Israel, Saudi Arabia and Egypt. Rejected 44-54: R 11-26; D 33-28 [ND 26-17; SD 7-11], May 15, 1978. A "nay" was a vote supporting the president's position.

106. **S 2104. Natural Gas Pricing.** Adoption of the Pearson (R-Kan.)-Bentsen (D-Texas) amendment to end federal price controls for natural gas found onshore, retroactive to Jan. 1, 1977, and cease regulation of new offshore gas after Dec. 31, 1982, but to impose a price limit equal to the price of imported No. 2 heating oil for two years and impose an incremental pricing provision to protect homeowners,

schools and hospitals by allocating lower-cost old gas for their use. Adopted 50-46: R 34-3; D 16-43 [ND 5-35; SD 11-8], Oct. 4, 1977. A "nay" was a vote supporting the president's position.

107. **HR 7553. Public Works-ERDA Appropriations, Fiscal 1978.** Hatfield, R-Ore., amendment to prohibit production of any enhanced radiation weapon (neutron bomb). Rejected 38-58: R 10-28: D 28-30 [ND 27-14; SD 1-16], July 13, 1977.

108. **S 555. Public Officials' Integrity Act.** Passage of the bill to establish a formal mechanism for appointment of a special prosecutor to investigate alleged crimes by high-level federal officials, to provide for full financial disclosure by high-level federal officials and to set up an Office of Government Crimes in the Justice Department to investigate crimes by public employees at all levels. Passed 74-5: R 23-5; D 51-0 [ND 36-0; SD 15-0], June 27, 1977.

SENATE

VOTING RECORDS

ALABAMA

DENTON, JEREMIAH [Republican]. Term Began/Expires: 1981/1986. Born: July 15, 1924, Mobile, Ala. Education: Spring Hill College; United States Naval Academy; George Washington University (M.A.). Military Service: U.S. Navy. Occupation: Military serviceman; consultant, Christian Broadcasting Network, Inc.; assistant to the president, Spring Hill College.

1. Immigration Reform N
2. So Afr Sanc-veto override N
3. Kill-Death pnlty drug bil N
4. Kill-Mil use in drug war Y
5. Tax Overhaul Y
6. Raise speed limit Y
7. Across-the-board cuts N
8. South Africa sanctions N
9. Kill-So Africa sanctions Y
10. Kill-So Africa sanct (*) Y
11. Nicaraguan contra aid Y
12. Terminate contra aid N
13. Kill-Prohibit contra fnds Y
14. Kill-Stop CIA contra fndg Y
15. Kill-Bar nuclr tsts w/SDI Y
16. Kill-Bar ASAT testing Y
17. Nuclear test ban treaty N
18. Prohibit sale of Stinger N
19. Delete Bigeye chem bomb N
20. Bar binary chem weapons N
21. Kill-SDI funding Y
22. Kill-AIDS ins dscriminatn N
23. Kill-$10 bbl oil tariff Y
24. Kill-Repl wndfl prfts tax N
25. Repeal balanced bdgt amdt Y
26. Tax amnesty provisions Y
27. Kill-Tax amnesty subst N
28. Kill-Add third tax rate Y
29. Kill-Unocal tax provsns N
30. Block Saudi arms sale (†) N
31. Kill-Bar school busing N
32. Prohibit Saudi arms sale N
33. Nicaraguan contra aid Y
34. Bar all aid to Nicaragua N
35. Balanced budget amendment Y
36. Balanced bdgt substitute Y
37. Conrail sale Y
38. Revise farm programs Y
39. Kill-New oil import fee Y
40. Spending cuts, tax incres Y
41. Textile import quotas Y
42. Kill-Exmpt vets from cuts Y
43. Kill-Bar inmate abortn $ N
44. Textile import quotas (§) Y
45. Kill-Eliminate Amtrak $?
46. Kill-Incrs motor fuel tax Y
47. Set max allow deficits Y
48. 20% minimum tax on corps N
49. Bar $ to toxic victims Y
50. Seasonal workers in US Y
51. Kill-School prayer cases N
52. Line-item veto Y
53. South Africa sanctions N
54. Ease '68 Gun Control Act Y
55. Kill-14 day handgun wait Y
56. Kill-Gun dlr inspections Y
57. Kill-Keep '68 Gun Con Act Y
58. Nicarag humanitarian aid Y
59. Bar ASAT testing N
60. Delete chemical weapons N
61. Delete 21 MX missiles N
62. Kill-15% min tax on corps Y
63. Kill-Restore Soc Sec COLA Y
64. Freeze all funding N
65. Cut def;raise taxes, COLA N
66. Keep existing SS COLAs N
67. Aid to Nicaraguan rebels Y
68. Reaffirm purch of 21 MX Y
69. African Relief/Farm Crdt Y
70. Kill-Nuclear Freeze Y
71. Kill-Void Title IX Narrow Y
72. Raise drinking age to 21 Y
73. Kill-Reduce mil in Europe Y
74. Kill-Bar $ for contras Y
75. Kill-No new MXs in 1985 Y
76. Kill-Move MX $ to non-nuc Y
77. Deficit reduction-$140b Y
78. Kill-Req auth for troops Y
79. School Prayer amendment Y
80. Cap punish-certain crimes Y
81. Bar govt off from taping N
82. Martin L. King holiday Y
83. Auth marines in Lebanon Y
84. Anti-abortion amendment Y
85. Highway-Gas tax bill N
86. Delete job creation amend Y
87. Kill-Tobacco price supprt Y
88. Emergency housing aid ?
89. Nullify oil decontrol N
90. Target tax cuts-mid class N
91. Tax Indexing Y
92. Kill-Oppose SS benft cuts Y
93. Disapprove Saudi AWACS N
94. Anti-busing rider Y

Presidential Support Score: 1986 - 85% 1985 - 75%

HEFLIN, HOWELL [Democrat]. Term Began/Expires: 1985/1990. Prior Terms: Senate: 1979-84. Born: June 19, 1921; Tuscumbia, Ala. Education: Birmingham-Southern College (B.A.); University of Alabama Law School (J.D.). Military Service: U.S. Marine Corps, 1942-1946. Occupation: Attorney; chief justice of the Alabama Supreme Court (1971-1977).

1. Immigration Reform N
2. So Afr Sanc-veto override Y
3. Kill-Death pnlty drug bil N
4. Kill-Mil use in drug war Y
5. Tax Overhaul N
6. Raise speed limit Y
7. Across-the-board cuts N
8. South Africa sanctions Y
9. Kill-So Africa sanctions N
10. Kill-So Africa sanct (*) Y
11. Nicaraguan contra aid Y
12. Terminate contra aid N
13. Kill-Prohibit contra fnds Y
14. Kill-Stop CIA contra fndg Y
15. Kill-Bar nuclr tsts w/SDI Y
16. Kill-Bar ASAT testing Y
17. Nuclear test ban treaty N
18. Prohibit sale of Stinger N
19. Delete Bigeye chem bomb N
20. Bar binary chem weapons N
21. Kill-SDI funding Y
22. Kill-AIDS ins dscriminatn N
23. Kill-$10 bbl oil tariff Y
24. Kill-Repl wndfl prfts tax N
25. Repeal balanced bdgt amdt N
26. Tax amnesty provisions Y
27. Kill-Tax amnesty subst N
28. Kill-Add third tax rate Y
29. Kill-Unocal tax provsns Y
30. Block Saudi arms sale (†) Y
31. Kill-Bar school busing Y
32. Prohibit Saudi arms sale Y
33. Nicaraguan contra aid Y
34. Bar all aid to Nicaragua N
35. Balanced budget amendment Y
36. Balanced bdgt substitute Y
37. Conrail sale N
38. Revise farm programs N
39. Kill-New oil import fee Y
40. Spending cuts, tax incres Y
41. Textile import quotas Y
42. Kill-Exmpt vets from cuts N
43. Kill-Bar inmate abortn $ N
44. Textile import quotas (§) +
45. Kill-Eliminate Amtrak $ Y
46. Kill-Incrs motor fuel tax Y
47. Set max allow deficits Y
48. 20% minimum tax on corps N
49. Bar $ to toxic victims Y
50. Seasonal workers in US Y
51. Kill-School prayer cases N
52. Line-item veto Y
53. South Africa sanctions Y
54. Ease '68 Gun Control Act Y
55. Kill-14 day handgun wait Y
56. Kill-Gun dlr inspections Y
57. Kill-Keep '68 Gun Con Act Y
58. Nicarag humanitarian aid Y
59. Bar ASAT testing N
60. Delete chemical weapons N
61. Delete 21 MX missiles N
62. Kill-15% min tax on corps Y
63. Kill-Restore Soc Sec COLA N
64. Freeze all funding N
65. Cut def;raise taxes, COLA Y
66. Keep existing SS COLAs Y
67. Aid to Nicaraguan rebels Y
68. Reaffirm purch of 21 MX Y
69. African Relief/Farm Crdt Y
70. Kill-Nuclear Freeze Y
71. Kill-Void Title IX Narrow N
72. Raise drinking age to 21 Y
73. Kill-Reduce mil in Europe Y
74. Kill-Bar $ for contras Y
75. Kill-No new MXs in 1985 Y
76. Kill-Move MX $ to non-nuc Y
77. Deficit reduction-$140b Y
78. Kill-Req auth for troops Y
79. School Prayer amendment Y
80. Cap punish-certain crimes Y
81. Bar govt off from taping N
82. Martin L. King holiday Y
83. Auth marines in Lebanon N
84. Anti-abortion amendment Y
85. Highway-Gas tax bill N
86. Delete job creation amend N
87. Kill-Tobacco price supprt Y
88. Emergency housing aid Y
89. Nullify oil decontrol N
90. Target tax cuts-mid class N
91. Tax Indexing Y
92. Kill-Oppose SS benft cuts N
93. Disapprove Saudi AWACS Y
94. Anti-busing rider Y
95. Disapprove oil import fee ?
96. Domestic violence funds N
97. Trucking Deregulation N
98. Overturn India fuel sale Y
99. Mil draft registration Y
100. Chrysler Loan Guarantees Y
101. Nuclear plant moratorium N
102. Abolish electoral college N

Presidential Support Score: 1986 - 76% 1985 - 54%

ALASKA

MURKOWSKI, FRANK H. [Republican]. Term Began/Expires: 1981/1986. Born: March 28, 1933, Seattle, Wash. Education: University of Santa Clara; Seattle University (B.A.). Military Service: U.S. Coast Guard, 1955-56. Occupation: Banker; Alaska commissioner of economic development (1966-70); president, Alaska Bankers Assn. (1972); president, Alaska Chamber of Commerce (1977); president, Alaska National Bank of the North (1971-80).

1. Immigration Reform	#	48. 20% minimum tax on corps	N
2. So Afr Sanc-veto override	Y	49. Bar $ to toxic victims	Y
3. Kill-Death pnlty drug bil	N	50. Seasonal workers in US	Y
4. Kill-Mil use in drug war	N	51. Kill-School prayer cases	N
5. Tax Overhaul	Y	52. Line-item veto	Y
6. Raise speed limit	Y	53. South Africa sanctions	?
7. Across-the-board cuts	N	54. Ease '68 Gun Control Act	Y
8. South Africa sanctions	+	55. Kill-14 day handgun wait	Y
9. Kill-So Africa sanctions	Y	56. Kill-Gun dlr inspections	Y
10. Kill-So Africa sanct (*)	Y	57. Kill-Keep '68 Gun Con Act	Y
11. Nicaraguan contra aid	Y	58. Nicarag humanitarian aid	Y
12. Terminate contra aid	N	59. Bar ASAT testing	N
13. Kill-Prohibit contra fnds	Y	60. Delete chemical weapons	N
14. Kill-Stop CIA contra fndg	Y	61. Delete 21 MX missiles	N
15. Kill-Bar nuclr tsts w/SDI	Y	62. Kill-15% min tax on corps	Y
16. Kill-Bar ASAT testing	Y	63. Kill-Restore Soc Sec COLA	Y
17. Nuclear test ban treaty	Y	64. Freeze all funding	N
18. Prohibit sale of Stinger	N	65. Cut def;raise taxes, COLA	N
19. Delete Bigeye chem bomb	N	66. Keep existing SS COLAs	N
20. Bar binary chem weapons	N	67. Aid to Nicaraguan rebels	Y
21. Kill-SDI funding	Y	68. Reaffirm purch of 21 MX	Y
22. Kill-AIDS ins dscriminatn	N	69. African Relief/Farm Crdt	Y
23. Kill-$10 bbl oil tariff	Y	70. Kill-Nuclear Freeze	Y
24. Kill-Repl wndfl prfts tax	N	71. Kill-Void Title IX Narrow	Y
25. Repeal balanced bdgt amdt	N	72. Raise drinking age to 21	Y
26. Tax amnesty provisions	?	73. Kill-Reduce mil in Europe	Y
27. Kill-Tax amnesty subst	?	74. Kill-Bar $ for contras	Y
28. Kill-Add third tax rate	Y	75. Kill-No new MXs in 1985	Y
29. Kill-Unocal tax provsns	Y	76. Kill-Move MX $ to non-nuc	Y
30. Block Saudi arms sale (†)	Y	77. Deficit reduction-$140b	Y
31. Kill-Bar school busing	N	78. Kill-Req auth for troops	Y
32. Prohibit Saudi arms sale	Y	79. School Prayer amendment	Y
33. Nicaraguan contra aid	Y	80. Cap punish-certain crimes	?
34. Bar all aid to Nicaragua	N	81. Bar govt off from taping	N
35. Balanced budget amendment	Y	82. Martin L. King holiday	N
36. Balanced bdgt substitute	N	83. Auth marines in Lebanon	Y
37. Conrail sale	?	84. Anti-abortion amendment	Y
38. Revise farm programs	?	85. Highway-Gas tax bill	Y
39. Kill-New oil import fee	Y	86. Delete job creation amend	Y
40. Spending cuts, tax incres	Y	87. Kill-Tobacco price supprt	?
41. Textile import quotas	N	88. Emergency housing aid	N
42. Kill-Exmpt vets from cuts	Y	89. Nullify oil decontrol	N
43. Kill-Bar inmate abortn $	N	90. Target tax cuts-mid class	N
44. Textile import quotas (§)	Y	91. Tax Indexing	Y
45. Kill-Eliminate Amtrak $	N	92. Kill-Oppose SS benft cuts	Y
46. Kill-Incrs motor fuel tax	Y	93. Disapprove Saudi AWACS	N
47. Set max allow deficits	Y	94. Anti-busing rider	Y

Presidential Support Score: 1986 - 80% 1985 - 82%

STEVENS, TED [Republican]. Term Began/Expires: 1985/1990. Prior Terms: House: 1965-68. Senate: 1968 (Special Appointment)-1984. Born: November 18, 1923; Indianapolis, Ind. Education: Oregon State College; University of California; Harvard Law School (LL.B.). Military Service: U.S. Air Force, 1943-46. Occupation: Attorney, Northcutt Ely (1950-52), Collins & Clasby (1953); U.S. states attorney (1953-56); legislative counselman, Department of Interior (1956-58); assistant to the secretary of Interior (1958-60); solicitor, Department of Interior (1960-61); attorney (1961-68).

1. Immigration Reform Y
2. So Afr Sanc-veto override N
3. Kill-Death pnlty drug bil N
4. Kill-Mil use in drug war Y
5. Tax Overhaul Y
6. Raise speed limit ?
7. Across-the-board cuts N
8. South Africa sanctions Y
9. Kill-So Africa sanctions Y
10. Kill-So Africa sanct (*) Y
11. Nicaraguan contra aid Y
12. Terminate contra aid N
13. Kill-Prohibit contra fnds Y
14. Kill-Stop CIA contra fndg Y
15. Kill-Bar nuclr tsts w/SDI Y
16. Kill-Bar ASAT testing Y
17. Nuclear test ban treaty N
18. Prohibit sale of Stinger N
19. Delete Bigeye chem bomb N
20. Bar binary chem weapons N
21. Kill-SDI funding Y
22. Kill-AIDS ins dscriminatn N
23. Kill-$10 bbl oil tariff Y
24. Kill-Repl wndfl prfts tax N
25. Repeal balanced bdgt amdt N
26. Tax amnesty provisions Y
27. Kill-Tax amnesty subst N
28. Kill-Add third tax rate Y
29. Kill-Unocal tax provsns Y
30. Block Saudi arms sale (†) N
31. Kill-Bar school busing N
32. Prohibit Saudi arms sale ?
33. Nicaraguan contra aid Y
34. Bar all aid to Nicaragua N
35. Balanced budget amendment Y
36. Balanced bdgt substitute Y
37. Conrail sale Y
38. Revise farm programs Y
39. Kill-New oil import fee N
40. Spending cuts, tax incres Y
41. Textile import quotas N
42. Kill-Exmpt vets from cuts Y
43. Kill-Bar inmate abortn $ Y
44. Textile import quotas (§) X
45. Kill-Eliminate Amtrak $ Y
46. Kill-Incrs motor fuel tax Y
47. Set max allow deficits Y
48. 20% minimum tax on corps N
49. Bar $ to toxic victims Y
50. Seasonal workers in US Y
51. Kill-School prayer cases Y
52. Line-item veto Y
53. South Africa sanctions Y
54. Ease '68 Gun Control Act Y
55. Kill-14 day handgun wait Y
56. Kill-Gun dlr inspections Y
57. Kill-Keep '68 Gun Con Act Y
58. Nicarag humanitarian aid Y
59. Bar ASAT testing N
60. Delete chemical weapons N
61. Delete 21 MX missiles N
62. Kill-15% min tax on corps Y
63. Kill-Restore Soc Sec COLA Y
64. Freeze all funding N
65. Cut def;raise taxes, COLA N
66. Keep existing SS COLAs N
67. Aid to Nicaraguan rebels Y
68. Reaffirm purch of 21 MX Y
69. African Relief/Farm Crdt Y
70. Kill-Nuclear Freeze Y
71. Kill-Void Title IX Narrow Y
72. Raise drinking age to 21 Y
73. Kill-Reduce mil in Europe Y
74. Kill-Bar $ for contras Y
75. Kill-No new MXs in 1985 Y
76. Kill-Move MX $ to non-nuc Y
77. Deficit reduction-$140b Y
78. Kill-Req auth for troops Y
79. School Prayer amendment Y
80. Cap punish-certain crimes Y
81. Bar govt off from taping N
82. Martin L. King holiday Y
83. Auth marines in Lebanon Y
84. Anti-abortion amendment N
85. Highway-Gas tax bill Y
86. Delete job creation amend Y
87. Kill-Tobacco price supprt Y
88. Emergency housing aid Y
89. Nullify oil decontrol N
90. Target tax cuts-mid class ?
91. Tax Indexing Y
92. Kill-Oppose SS benft cuts Y
93. Disapprove Saudi AWACS N
94. Anti-busing rider N
95. Disapprove oil import fee ?
96. Domestic violence funds ?
97. Trucking Deregulation Y
98. Overturn India fuel sale N

STEVENS, TED (Cont.)

99. Mil draft registration	Y	104. Airline Deregulation	N
100. Chrysler Loan Guarantees	Y	105. Disappr Mideast jet sales	N
101. Nuclear plant moratorium	N	106. Natural gas deregulation	Y
102. Abolish electoral college	N	107. Prohibit neutron bomb	N
103. Kill-Lmt ct-ordered bus	N	108. Financial disclosure-off	Y

Presidential Support Score: 1986 - 85% 1985 - 75%

ARIZONA

GOLDWATER, BARRY [Republican]. Term Began/Expires: 1981/1986. Prior Terms: Senate: 1953-64; 1969-80. Born: January 1, 1909; Phoenix, Ariz. Education: Staunton Military Academy; University of Arizona. Military Service: Infantry Reserve, 1930-42; Air Force, 1941-45. Occupation: Member, City Council of Phoenix (1949-53); author.

1. Immigration Reform	?	41. Textile import quotas	N
2. So Afr Sanc-veto override	N	42. Kill-Exmpt vets from cuts	Y
3. Kill-Death pnlty drug bil	?	43. Kill-Bar inmate abortn $	?
4. Kill-Mil use in drug war	Y	44. Textile import quotas (§)	N
5. Tax Overhaul	Y	45. Kill-Eliminate Amtrak $	N
6. Raise speed limit	Y	46. Kill-Incrs motor fuel tax	Y
7. Across-the-board cuts	?	47. Set max allow deficits	Y
8. South Africa sanctions	-	48. 20% minimum tax on corps	N
9. Kill-So Africa sanctions	?	49. Bar $ to toxic victims	Y
10. Kill-So Africa sanct (*)	?	50. Seasonal workers in US	Y
11. Nicaraguan contra aid	Y	51. Kill-School prayer cases	Y
12. Terminate contra aid	N	52. Line-item veto	Y
13. Kill-Prohibit contra fnds	Y	53. South Africa sanctions	-
14. Kill-Stop CIA contra fndg	Y	54. Ease '68 Gun Control Act	Y
15. Kill-Bar nuclr tsts w/SDI	Y	55. Kill-14 day handgun wait	Y
16. Kill-Bar ASAT testing	Y	56. Kill-Gun dlr inspections	Y
17. Nuclear test ban treaty	N	57. Kill-Keep '68 Gun Con Act	Y
18. Prohibit sale of Stinger	N	58. Nicarag humanitarian aid	?
19. Delete Bigeye chem bomb	N	59. Bar ASAT testing	N
20. Bar binary chem weapon	N	60. Delete chemical weapons	N
21. Kill-SDI funding	Y	61. Delete 21 MX missiles	N
22. Kill-AIDS ins dscriminatn	Y	62. Kill-15% min tax on corps	Y
23. Kill-$10 bbl oil tariff	?	63. Kill-Restore Soc Sec COLA	Y
24. Kill-Repl wndfl prfts tax	?	64. Freeze all funding	N
25. Repeal balanced bdgt amdt	N	65. Cut def;raise taxes, COLA	N
26. Tax amnesty provisions	Y	66. Keep existing SS COLAs	N
27. Kill-Tax amnesty subst	?	67. Aid to Nicaraguan rebels	Y
28. Kill-Add third tax rate	Y	68. Reaffirm purch of 21 MX	Y
29. Kill-Unocal tax provsns	Y	69. African Relief/Farm Crdt	?
30. Block Saudi arms sale (†)	N	70. Kill-Nuclear Freeze	Y
31. Kill-Bar school busing	N	71. Kill-Void Title IX Narrow	Y
32. Prohibit Saudi arms sale	N	72. Raise drinking age to 21	N
33. Nicaraguan contra aid	Y	73. Kill-Reduce mil in Europe	Y
34. Bar all aid to Nicaragua	N	74. Kill-Bar $ for contras	Y
35. Balanced budget amendment	Y	75. Kill-No new MXs in 1985	Y
36. Balanced bdgt substitute	N	76. Kill-Move MX $ to non-nuc	Y
37. Conrail sale	Y	77. Deficit reduction-$140b	Y
38. Revise farm programs	N	78. Kill-Req auth for troops	Y
39. Kill-New oil import fee	?	79. School Prayer amendment	N
40. Spending cuts, tax incres	Y	80. Cap punish-certain crimes	Y

GOLDWATER, BARRY (Cont.)

81. Bar govt off from taping N
82. Martin L. King holiday N
83. Auth marines in Lebanon Y
84. Anti-abortion amendment N
85. Highway-Gas tax bill ?
86. Delete job creation amend ?
87. Kill-Tobacco price supprt Y
88. Emergency housing aid N
89. Nullify oil decontrol N
90. Target tax cuts-mid class N
91. Tax Indexing Y
92. Kill-Oppose SS benft cuts Y
93. Disapprove Saudi AWACS N
94. Anti-busing rider Y
95. Disapprove oil import fee Y
96. Domestic violence funds -
97. Trucking Deregulation Y
98. Overturn India fuel sale #
99. Mil draft registration Y
100. Chrysler Loan Guarantees -
101. Nuclear plant moratorium N
102. Abolish electoral college N
103. Kill-Lmt ct-ordered bus N
104. Airline Deregulation ?
105. Disappr Mideast jet sales N
106. Natural gas deregulation Y
107. Prohibit neutron bomb N
108. Financial disclosure-off X

Presidential Support Score: 1986 - 70% 1985 - 72%

DeCONCINI, DENNIS [Democrat]. Term Began/Expires: 1983/1988. Prior Terms: Senate: 1976-82. Born: May 8, 1937; Tucson, Ariz. Education: University of Arizona (B.A., LL.B.). Military Service: U.S. Army, 1959-60; Army Reserves, 1960-1967. Occupation: Attorney; Pima county attorney.

1. Immigration Reform -
2. So Afr Sanc-veto override Y
3. Kill-Death pnlty drug bil N
4. Kill-Mil use in drug war N
5. Tax Overhaul N
6. Raise speed limit Y
7. Across-the-board cuts N
8. South Africa sanctions Y
9. Kill-So Africa sanctions N
10. Kill-So Africa sanct (*) N
11. Nicaraguan contra aid N
12. Terminate contra aid Y
13. Kill-Prohibit contra fnds Y
14. Kill-Stop CIA contra fndg Y
15. Kill-Bar nuclr tsts w/SDI Y
16. Kill-Bar ASAT testing Y
17. Nuclear test ban treaty Y
18. Prohibit sale of Stinger Y
19. Delete Bigeye chem bomb Y
20. Bar binary chem weapons N
21. Kill-SDI funding N
22. Kill-AIDS ins dscriminatn N
23. Kill-$10 bbl oil tariff Y
24. Kill-Repl wndfl prfts tax Y
25. Repeal balanced bdgt amdt Y
26. Tax amnesty provisions N
27. Kill-Tax amnesty subst Y
28. Kill-Add third tax rate Y
29. Kill-Unocal tax provsns N
30. Block Saudi arms sale (†) Y
31. Kill-Bar school busing N
32. Prohibit Saudi arms sale Y
33. Nicaraguan contra aid N
34. Bar all aid to Nicaragua N
35. Balanced budget amendment Y
36. Balanced bdgt substitute N
37. Conrail sale Y
38. Revise farm programs N
39. Kill-New oil import fee Y
40. Spending cuts, tax incres Y
41. Textile import quotas Y
42. Kill-Exmpt vets from cuts N
43. Kill-Bar inmate abortn $ N
44. Textile import quotas (§) Y
45. Kill-Eliminate Amtrak $ Y
46. Kill-Incrs motor fuel tax Y
47. Set max allow deficits Y
48. 20% minimum tax on corps N
49. Bar $ to toxic victims N
50. Seasonal workers in US Y
51. Kill-School prayer cases Y
52. Line-item veto #
53. South Africa sanctions Y
54. Ease '68 Gun Control Act Y
55. Kill-14 day handgun wait Y
56. Kill-Gun dlr inspections Y
57. Kill-Keep '68 Gun Con Act Y
58. Nicarag humanitarian aid Y
59. Bar ASAT testing ?
60. Delete chemical weapons Y
61. Delete 21 MX missiles N
62. Kill-15% min tax on corps Y
63. Kill-Restore Soc Sec COLA N
64. Freeze all funding Y
65. Cut def;raise taxes, COLA Y
66. Keep existing SS COLAs Y
67. Aid to Nicaraguan rebels N
68. Reaffirm purch of 21 MX Y
69. African Relief/Farm Crdt Y
70. Kill-Nuclear Freeze N
71. Kill-Void Title IX Narrow N
72. Raise drinking age to 21 Y

DeCONCINI, DENNIS (Cont.)

73.	Kill-Reduce mil in Europe	N	91.	Tax Indexing	Y
74.	Kill-Bar $ for contras	Y	92.	Kill-Oppose SS benft cuts	N
75.	Kill-No new MXs in 1985	#	93.	Disapprove Saudi AWACS	Y
76.	Kill-Move MX $ to non-nuc	Y	94.	Anti-busing rider	Y
77.	Deficit reduction-$140b	N	95.	Disapprove oil import fee	Y
78.	Kill-Req auth for troops	?	96.	Domestic violence funds	Y
79.	School Prayer amendment	N	97.	Trucking Deregulation	?
80.	Cap punish-certain crimes	Y	98.	Overturn India fuel sale	N
81.	Bar govt off from taping	N	99.	Mil draft registration	Y
82.	Martin L. King holiday	Y	100.	Chrysler Loan Guarantees	N
83.	Auth marines in Lebanon	N	101.	Nuclear plant moratorium	Y
84.	Anti-abortion amendment	Y	102.	Abolish electoral college	Y
85.	Highway-Gas tax bill	Y	103.	Kill-Lmt ct-ordered bus	N
86.	Delete job creation amend	N	104.	Airline Deregulation	Y
87.	Kill-Tobacco price supprt	N	105.	Disappr Mideast jet sales	Y
88.	Emergency housing aid	Y	106.	Natural gas deregulation	Y
89.	Nullify oil decontrol	N	107.	Prohibit neutron bomb	Y
90.	Target tax cuts-mid class	N	108.	Financial disclosure-off	Y

Presidential Support Score: 1986 - 45% 1985 - 45%

A R K A N S A S

BUMPERS, DALE [Democrat]. Term Began/Expires: 1981/1986. Prior Terms: Senate: 1975-80. Born: August 12, 1925; Charleston, Ark. Education: University of Arkansas; Northwestern University Law School (LL.B.). Military Service: Marine Corps, 1943-46. Occupation: Owner, Charleston Hardware and Furniture Co. (1951-66); owner, Angus Breeding Farm (1966-70); special justice, Arkansas Supreme Court; governor of Arkansas (1970-74).

1.	Immigration Reform	N	27.	Kill-Tax amnesty subst	Y
2.	So Afr Sanc-veto override	Y	28.	Kill-Add third tax rate	N
3.	Kill-Death pnlty drug bil	N	29.	Kill-Unocal tax provsns	N
4.	Kill-Mil use in drug war	Y	30.	Block Saudi arms sale (†)	Y
5.	Tax Overhaul	Y	31.	Kill-Bar school busing	Y
6.	Raise speed limit	Y	32.	Prohibit Saudi arms sale	Y
7.	Across-the-board cuts	N	33.	Nicaraguan contra aid	N
8.	South Africa sanctions	Y	34.	Bar all aid to Nicaragua	N
9.	Kill-So Africa sanctions	N	35.	Balanced budget amendment	N
10.	Kill-So Africa sanct (*)	N	36.	Balanced bdgt substitute	N
11.	Nicaraguan contra aid	N	37.	Conrail sale	Y
12.	Terminate contra aid	Y	38.	Revise farm programs	Y
13.	Kill-Prohibit contra fnds	N	39.	Kill-New oil import fee	Y
14.	Kill-Stop CIA contra fndg	N	40.	Spending cuts, tax incres	Y
15.	Kill-Bar nuclr tsts w/SDI	N	41.	Textile import quotas	Y
16.	Kill-Bar ASAT testing	N	42.	Kill-Exmpt vets from cuts	N
17.	Nuclear test ban treaty	Y	43.	Kill-Bar inmate abortn $	Y
18.	Prohibit sale of Stinger	N	44.	Textile import quotas (§)	Y
19.	Delete Bigeye chem bomb	Y	45.	Kill-Eliminate Amtrak $	Y
20.	Bar binary chem weapons	N	46.	Kill-Incrs motor fuel tax	Y
21.	Kill-SDI funding	N	47.	Set max allow deficits	Y
22.	Kill-AIDS ins dscriminatn	Y	48.	20% minimum tax on corps	N
23.	Kill-$10 bbl oil tariff	Y	49.	Bar $ to toxic victims	N
24.	Kill-Repl wndfl prfts tax	N	50.	Seasonal workers in US	Y
25.	Repeal balanced bdgt amdt	N	51.	Kill-School prayer cases	Y
26.	Tax amnesty provisions	N	52.	Line-item veto	N

BUMPERS, DALE (Cont.)

53.	South Africa sanctions	Y	81.	Bar govt off from taping	Y
54.	Ease '68 Gun Control Act	Y	82.	Martin L. King holiday	Y
55.	Kill-14 day handgun wait	Y	83.	Auth marines in Lebanon	N
56.	Kill-Gun dlr inspections	Y	84.	Anti-abortion amendment	N
57.	Kill-Keep '68 Gun Con Act	Y	85.	Highway-Gas tax bill	N
58.	Nicarag humanitarian aid	N	86.	Delete job creation amend	N
59.	Bar ASAT testing	Y	87.	Kill-Tobacco price supprt	N
60.	Delete chemical weapons	N	88.	Emergency housing aid	Y
61.	Delete 21 MX missiles	Y	89.	Nullify oil decontrol	Y
62.	Kill-15% min tax on corps	N	90.	Target tax cuts-mid class	Y
63.	Kill-Restore Soc Sec COLA	N	91.	Tax Indexing	N
64.	Freeze all funding	Y	92.	Kill-Oppose SS benft cuts	N
65.	Cut def;raise taxes, COLA	Y	93.	Disapprove Saudi AWACS	Y
66.	Keep existing SS COLAs	Y	94.	Anti-busing rider	N
67.	Aid to Nicaraguan rebels	N	95.	Disapprove oil import fee	Y
68.	Reaffirm purch of 21 MX	N	96.	Domestic violence funds	Y
69.	African Relief/Farm Crdt	Y	97.	Trucking Deregulation	?
70.	Kill-Nuclear Freeze	N	98.	Overturn India fuel sale	Y
71.	Kill-Void Title IX Narrow	N	99.	Mil draft registration	Y
72.	Raise drinking age to 21	Y	100.	Chrysler Loan Guarantees	N
73.	Kill-Reduce mil in Europe	N	101.	Nuclear plant moratorium	Y
74.	Kill-Bar $ for contras	N	102.	Abolish electoral college	N
75.	Kill-No new MXs in 1985	N	103.	Kill-Lmt ct-ordered bus	Y
76.	Kill-Move MX $ to non-nuc	N	104.	Airline Deregulation	Y
77.	Deficit reduction-$140b	N	105.	Disappr Mideast jet sales	N
78.	Kill-Req auth for troops	N	106.	Natural gas deregulation	N
79.	School Prayer amendment	N	107.	Prohibit neutron bomb	Y
80.	Cap punish-certain crimes	Y	108.	Financial disclosure-off	Y

Presidential Support Score: 1986 - 39% 1985 - 32%

PRYOR, DAVID [Democrat]. Term Began/Expires: 1985/1990. Prior Terms: House: 1965-72; Senate: 1979-84. Born: August 29, 1934; Camden, Ark. Education: University of Arkansas (B.A., LL.B.). Occupation: Attorney, Pryor and Barnes; publisher; Arkansas representative.

1.	Immigration Reform	Y	23.	Kill-$10 bbl oil tariff	Y
2.	So Afr Sanc-veto override	Y	24.	Kill-Repl wndfl prfts tax	N
3.	Kill-Death pnlty drug bil	?	25.	Repeal balanced bdgt amdt	N
4.	Kill-Mil use in drug war	?	26.	Tax amnesty provisions	N
5.	Tax Overhaul	?	27.	Kill-Tax amnesty subst	Y
6.	Raise speed limit	Y	28.	Kill-Add third tax rate	Y
7.	Across-the-board cuts	N	29.	Kill-Unocal tax provsns	N
8.	South Africa sanctions	Y	30.	Block Saudi arms sale (†)	Y
9.	Kill-So Africa sanctions	N	31.	Kill-Bar school busing	?
10.	Kill-So Africa sanct (*)	N	32.	Prohibit Saudi arms sale	Y
11.	Nicaraguan contra aid	N	33.	Nicaraguan contra aid	N
12.	Terminate contra aid	Y	34.	Bar all aid to Nicaragua	N
13.	Kill-Prohibit contra fnds	N	35.	Balanced budget amendment	Y
14.	Kill-Stop CIA contra fndg	N	36.	Balanced bdgt substitute	Y
15.	Kill-Bar nuclr tsts w/SDI	N	37.	Conrail sale	Y
16.	Kill-Bar ASAT testing	N	38.	Revise farm programs	Y
17.	Nuclear test ban treaty	Y	39.	Kill-New oil import fee	N
18.	Prohibit sale of Stinger	Y	40.	Spending cuts, tax incres	Y
19.	Delete Bigeye chem bomb	Y	41.	Textile import quotas	Y
20.	Bar binary chem weapons	Y	42.	Kill-Exmpt vets from cuts	N
21.	Kill-SDI funding	N	43.	Kill-Bar inmate abortn $	Y
22.	Kill-AIDS ins dscriminatn	N	44.	Textile import quotas (§)	Y

PRYOR, DAVID (Cont.)

45. Kill-Eliminate Amtrak $ Y
46. Kill-Incrs motor fuel tax Y
47. Set max allow deficits Y
48. 20% minimum tax on corps N
49. Bar $ to toxic victims N
50. Seasonal workers in US Y
51. Kill-School prayer cases Y
52. Line-item veto N
53. South Africa sanctions Y
54. Ease '68 Gun Control Act Y
55. Kill-14 day handgun wait Y
56. Kill-Gun dlr inspections Y
57. Kill-Keep '68 Gun Con Act Y
58. Nicarag humanitarian aid N
59. Bar ASAT testing Y
60. Delete chemical weapons Y
61. Delete 21 MX missiles Y
62. Kill-15% min tax on corps N
63. Kill-Restore Soc Sec COLA N
64. Freeze all funding Y
65. Cut def;raise taxes, COLA Y
66. Keep existing SS COLAs Y
67. Aid to Nicaraguan rebels N
68. Reaffirm purch of 21 MX N
69. African Relief/Farm Crdt Y
70. Kill-Nuclear Freeze ?
71. Kill-Void Title IX Narrow N
72. Raise drinking age to 21 Y
73. Kill-Reduce mil in Europe N
74. Kill-Bar $ for contras N
75. Kill-No new MXs in 1985 N
76. Kill-Move MX $ to non-nuc N
77. Deficit reduction-$140b Y
78. Kill-Req auth for troops N
79. School Prayer amendment Y
80. Cap punish-certain crimes Y
81. Bar govt off from taping Y
82. Martin L. King holiday Y
83. Auth marines in Lebanon N
84. Anti-abortion amendment N
85. Highway-Gas tax bill N
86. Delete job creation amend N
87. Kill-Tobacco price supprt ?
88. Emergency housing aid Y
89. Nullify oil decontrol N
90. Target tax cuts-mid class N
91. Tax Indexing Y
92. Kill-Oppose SS benft cuts N
93. Disapprove Saudi AWACS Y
94. Anti-busing rider Y
95. Disapprove oil import fee Y
96. Domestic violence funds Y
97. Trucking Deregulation Y
98. Overturn India fuel sale Y
99. Mil draft registration Y
100. Chrysler Loan Guarantees N
101. Nuclear plant moratorium ?
102. Abolish electoral college Y

Presidential Support Score: 1986 - 35% 1985 - 32%

CALIFORNIA

WILSON, PETE [Republican]. Term Began/Expires: 1983/1988. Born: August 23, 1933; Lake Forest, Ill. Education: Yale University (B.A.); University of California (law degree, 1962). Military Service: U.S. Marine Corps, 1955-58. Occupation: California state legislature (1966-71); mayor, city of San Diego (1971-83).

1. Immigration Reform Y
2. So Afr Sanc-veto override Y
3. Kill-Death pnlty drug bil N
4. Kill-Mil use in drug war N
5. Tax Overhaul Y
6. Raise speed limit Y
7. Across-the-board cuts Y
8. South Africa sanctions Y
9. Kill-So Africa sanctions Y
10. Kill-So Africa sanct (*) Y
11. Nicaraguan contra aid Y
12. Terminate contra aid N
13. Kill-Prohibit contra fnds Y
14. Kill-Stop CIA contra fndg Y
15. Kill-Bar nuclr tsts w/SDI Y
16. Kill-Bar ASAT testing Y
17. Nuclear test ban treaty N
18. Prohibit sale of Stinger N
19. Delete Bigeye chem bomb N
20. Bar binary chem weapons N
21. Kill-SDI funding Y
22. Kill-AIDS ins dscriminatn N
23. Kill-$10 bbl oil tariff Y
24. Kill-Repl wndfl prfts tax N
25. Repeal balanced bdgt amdt N
26. Tax amnesty provisions N
27. Kill-Tax amnesty subst Y
28. Kill-Add third tax rate Y
29. Kill-Unocal tax provsns Y
30. Block Saudi arms sale (†) Y
31. Kill-Bar school busing N
32. Prohibit Saudi arms sale Y
33. Nicaraguan contra aid Y
34. Bar all aid to Nicaragua N

WILSON, PETE (Cont.)

35. Balanced budget amendment Y
36. Balanced bdgt substitute N
37. Conrail sale Y
38. Revise farm programs N
39. Kill-New oil import fee Y
40. Spending cuts, tax incres Y
41. Textile import quotas N
42. Kill-Exmpt vets from cuts Y
43. Kill-Bar inmate abortn $ N
44. Textile import quotas (§) N
45. Kill-Eliminate Amtrak $ N
46. Kill-Incrs motor fuel tax Y
47. Set max allow deficits Y
48. 20% minimum tax on corps N
49. Bar $ to toxic victims Y
50. Seasonal workers in US Y
51. Kill-School prayer cases Y
52. Line-item veto Y
53. South Africa sanctions Y
54. Ease '68 Gun Control Act Y
55. Kill-14 day handgun wait Y
56. Kill-Gun dlr inspections Y
57. Kill-Keep '68 Gun Con Act Y
58. Nicarag humanitarian aid Y
59. Bar ASAT testing N
60. Delete chemical weapons N
61. Delete 21 MX missiles N
62. Kill-15% min tax on corps Y
63. Kill-Restore Soc Sec COLA Y
64. Freeze all funding ?
65. Cut def;raise taxes, COLA ?
66. Keep existing SS COLAs N
67. Aid to Nicaraguan rebels Y
68. Reaffirm purch of 21 MX Y
69. African Relief/Farm Crdt N
70. Kill-Nuclear Freeze Y
71. Kill-Void Title IX Narrow Y
72. Raise drinking age to 21 Y
73. Kill-Reduce mil in Europe Y
74. Kill-Bar $ for contras Y
75. Kill-No new MXs in 1985 Y
76. Kill-Move MX $ to non-nuc Y
77. Deficit reduction-$140b Y
78. Kill-Req auth for troops Y
79. School Prayer amendment Y
80. Cap punish-certain crimes Y
81. Bar govt off from taping N
82. Martin L. King holiday Y
83. Auth marines in Lebanon Y
84. Anti-abortion amendment N

Presidential Support Score: 1986 - 84% 1985 - 75%

CRANSTON, ALAN [Democrat]. Term Began/Expires: 1981/1986. Prior Terms: Senate: 1969-80. Born: June 19, 1914; Palo Alto, Calif. Education: Stanford University (B.A.). Military Service: U.S. Army, 1944-45. Occupation: Foreign correspondent, International News Service, Europe and Africa (1937-38); foreign language division, Office of War Information (1940-44); author; realtor property manager; state controller, California (1958-66).

1. Immigration Reform Y
2. So Afr Sanc-veto override Y
3. Kill-Death pnlty drug bil Y
4. Kill-Mil use in drug war Y
5. Tax Overhaul Y
6. Raise speed limit ?
7. Across-the-board cuts N
8. South Africa sanctions Y
9. Kill-So Africa sanctions N
10. Kill-So Africa sanct (*) N
11. Nicaraguan contra aid N
12. Terminate contra aid Y
13. Kill-Prohibit contra fnds N
14. Kill-Stop CIA contra fndg N
15. Kill-Bar nuclr tsts w/SDI N
16. Kill-Bar ASAT testing N
17. Nuclear test ban treaty Y
18. Prohibit sale of Stinger Y
19. Delete Bigeye chem bomb Y
20. Bar binary chem weapons Y
21. Kill-SDI funding N
22. Kill-AIDS ins dscriminatn Y
23. Kill-$10 bbl oil tariff Y
24. Kill-Repl wndfl prfts tax Y
25. Repeal balanced bdgt amdt Y
26. Tax amnesty provisions ?
27. Kill-Tax amnesty subst ?
28. Kill-Add third tax rate N
29. Kill-Unocal tax provsns Y
30. Block Saudi arms sale (†) Y
31. Kill-Bar school busing Y
32. Prohibit Saudi arms sale Y
33. Nicaraguan contra aid N
34. Bar all aid to Nicaragua Y
35. Balanced budget amendment N
36. Balanced bdgt substitute Y
37. Conrail sale N
38. Revise farm programs Y
39. Kill-New oil import fee Y
40. Spending cuts, tax incres Y
41. Textile import quotas N
42. Kill-Exmpt vets from cuts N

CRANSTON, ALAN (Cont.)

43.	Kill-Bar inmate abortn $	Y	76.	Kill-Move MX $ to non-nuc	N
44.	Textile import quotas (§)	N	77.	Deficit reduction-$140b	N
45.	Kill-Eliminate Amtrak $	Y	78.	Kill-Req auth for troops	N
46.	Kill-Incrs motor fuel tax	Y	79.	School Prayer amendment	N
47.	Set max allow deficits	N	80.	Cap punish-certain crimes	?
48.	20% minimum tax on corps	N	81.	Bar govt off from taping	?
49.	Bar $ to toxic victims	N	82.	Martin L. King holiday	Y
50.	Seasonal workers in US	N	83.	Auth marines in Lebanon	N
51.	Kill-School prayer cases	Y	84.	Anti-abortion amendment	N
52.	Line-item veto	N	85.	Highway-Gas tax bill	?
53.	South Africa sanctions	Y	86.	Delete job creation amend	N
54.	Ease '68 Gun Control Act	N	87.	Kill-Tobacco price supprt	Y
55.	Kill-14 day handgun wait	N	88.	Emergency housing aid	Y
56.	Kill-Gun dlr inspections	N	89.	Nullify oil decontrol	?
57.	Kill-Keep '68 Gun Con Act	N	90.	Target tax cuts-mid class	Y
58.	Nicarag humanitarian aid	N	91.	Tax Indexing	N
59.	Bar ASAT testing	Y	92.	Kill-Oppose SS benft cuts	N
60.	Delete chemical weapons	Y	93.	Disapprove Saudi AWACS	Y
61.	Delete 21 MX missiles	Y	94.	Anti-busing rider	N
62.	Kill-15% min tax on corps	N	95.	Disapprove oil import fee	?
63.	Kill-Restore Soc Sec COLA	N	96.	Domestic violence funds	Y
64.	Freeze all funding	N	97.	Trucking Deregulation	Y
65.	Cut def;raise taxes, COLA	Y	98.	Overturn India fuel sale	Y
66.	Keep existing SS COLAs	Y	99.	Mil draft registration	N
67.	Aid to Nicaraguan rebels	N	100.	Chrysler Loan Guarantees	Y
68.	Reaffirm purch of 21 MX	N	101.	Nuclear plant moratorium	Y
69.	African Relief/Farm Crdt	Y	102.	Abolish electoral college	Y
70.	Kill-Nuclear Freeze	N	103.	Kill-Lmt ct-ordered bus	Y
71.	Kill-Void Title IX Narrow	N	104.	Airline Deregulation	Y
72.	Raise drinking age to 21	Y	105.	Disappr Mideast jet sales	Y
73.	Kill-Reduce mil in Europe	N	106.	Natural gas deregulation	N
74.	Kill-Bar $ for contras	N	107.	Prohibit neutron bomb	Y
75.	Kill-No new MXs in 1985	N	108.	Financial disclosure-off	?

Presidential Support Score: 1986 - 21% 1985 - 25%

COLORADO

ARMSTRONG, WILLIAM L. [Republican]. Term Began/Expires: 1985/ 1990. Prior Terms: House: 1973-78; Senate: 1979-84. Born: March 16, 1937; Fremont, Neb. Education: Tulane University; University of Minnesota. Military Service: Army National Guard, 1957-63. Occupation: President, radio station KOSI AM-FM; director, Peoples Bank & Trust Co., Peoples Bank of Arapahoe County and Intermountain Network; vice president, Associated Press Broadcasters Assn; member, Colorado assemblyman (1963-64); Colorado senator (1965-72).

1.	Immigration Reform	N	11.	Nicaraguan contra aid	Y
2.	So Afr Sanc-veto override	N	12.	Terminate contra aid	N
3.	Kill-Death pnlty drug bil	N	13.	Kill-Prohibit contra fnds	Y
4.	Kill-Mil use in drug war	Y	14.	Kill-Stop CIA contra fndg	Y
5.	Tax Overhaul	Y	15.	Kill-Bar nuclr tsts w/SDI	Y
6.	Raise speed limit	Y	16.	Kill-Bar ASAT testing	Y
7.	Across-the-board cuts	Y	17.	Nuclear test ban treaty	N
8.	South Africa sanctions	N	18.	Prohibit sale of Stinger	N
9.	Kill-So Africa sanctions	Y	19.	Delete Bigeye chem bomb	N
10.	Kill-So Africa sanct (*)	Y	20.	Bar binary chem weapons	N

ARMSTRONG, WILLIAM L. (Cont.)

21.	Kill-SDI funding	Y	62.	Kill-15% min tax on corps	Y
22.	Kill-AIDS ins dscriminatn	N	63.	Kill-Restore Soc Sec COLA	Y
23.	Kill-$10 bbl oil tariff	Y	64.	Freeze all funding	N
24.	Kill-Repl wndfl prfts tax	N	65.	Cut def;raise taxes, COLA	N
25.	Repeal balanced bdgt amdt	N	66.	Keep existing SS COLAs	N
26.	Tax amnesty provisions	N	67.	Aid to Nicaraguan rebels	Y
27.	Kill-Tax amnesty subst	Y	68.	Reaffirm purch of 21 MX	Y
28.	Kill-Add third tax rate	Y	69.	African Relief/Farm Crdt	N
29.	Kill-Unocal tax provsns	Y	70.	Kill-Nuclear Freeze	Y
30.	Block Saudi arms sale (†)	N	71.	Kill-Void Title IX Narrow	Y
31.	Kill-Bar school busing	N	72.	Raise drinking age to 21	N
32.	Prohibit Saudi arms sale	Y	73.	Kill-Reduce mil in Europe	Y
33.	Nicaraguan contra aid	Y	74.	Kill-Bar $ for contras	Y
34.	Bar all aid to Nicaragua	N	75.	Kill-No new MXs in 1985	Y
35.	Balanced budget amendment	Y	76.	Kill-Move MX $ to non-nuc	Y
36.	Balanced bdgt substitute	N	77.	Deficit reduction-$140b	Y
37.	Conrail sale	Y	78.	Kill-Req auth for troops	Y
38.	Revise farm programs	Y	79.	School Prayer amendment	Y
39.	Kill-New oil import fee	Y	80.	Cap punish-certain crimes	Y
40.	Spending cuts, tax incres	Y	81.	Bar govt off from taping	?
41.	Textile import quotas	N	82.	Martin L. King holiday	Y
42.	Kill-Exmpt vets from cuts	Y	83.	Auth marines in Lebanon	Y
43.	Kill-Bar inmate abortn $	N	84.	Anti-abortion amendment	Y
44.	Textile import quotas (§)	N	85.	Highway-Gas tax bill	N
45.	Kill-Eliminate Amtrack $	N	86.	Delete job creation amend	Y
46.	Kill-Incrs motor fuel tax	Y	87.	Kill-Tobacco price supprt	Y
47.	Set max allow deficits	Y	88.	Emergency housing aid	N
48.	20% minimum tax on corps	N	89.	Nullify oil decontrol	N
49.	Bar $ to toxic victims	Y	90.	Target tax cuts-mid class	N
50.	Seasonal workers in US	Y	91.	Tax Indexing	Y
51.	Kill-School prayer cases	N	92.	Kill-Oppose SS benft cuts	Y
52.	Line-item veto	Y	93.	Disapprove Saudi AWACS	N
53.	South Africa sanctions	?	94.	Anti-busing rider	Y
54.	Ease '68 Gun Control Act	?	95.	Disapprove oil import fee	Y
55.	Kill-14 day handgun wait	?	96.	Domestic violence funds	?
56.	Kill-Gun dlr inspections	?	97.	Trucking Deregulation	Y
57.	Kill-Keep '68 Gun Con Act	?	98.	Overturn India fuel sale	Y
58.	Nicarag humanitarian aid	Y	99.	Mil draft registration	N
59.	Bar ASAT testing	N	100.	Chrysler Loan Guarantees	N
60.	Delete chemical weapons	N	101.	Nuclear plant moratorium	N
61.	Delete 21 MX missiles	N	102.	Abolish electoral college	Y

Presidential Support Score: 1986 - 95% 1985 - 72%

HART, GARY [Democrat]. Term Began/Expires: 1981/1986. Prior Terms: Senate: 1975-80. Born: November 28, 1937; Ottawa, Kan. Education: Bethany College; Yale Divinity School; Yale University Law School. Occupation: U.S. attorney; special assistant to the secretary of Interior; attorney.

1.	Immigration Reform	Y	11.	Nicaraguan contra aid	N
2.	So Afr Sanc-veto override	Y	12.	Terminate contra aid	Y
3.	Kill-Death pnlty drug bil	Y	13.	Kill-Prohibit contra fnds	N
4.	Kill-Mil use in drug war	Y	14.	Kill-Stop CIA contra fndg	N
5.	Tax Overhaul	Y	15.	Kill-Bar nuclr tsts w/SDI	N
6.	Raise speed limit	Y	16.	Kill-Bar ASAT testing	N
7.	Across-the-board cuts	N	17.	Nuclear test ban treaty	Y
8.	South Africa sanctions	Y	18.	Prohibit sale of Stinger	Y
9.	Kill-So Africa sanctions	N	19.	Delete Bigeye chem bomb	Y
10.	Kill-So Africa sanct (*)	N	20.	Bar binary chem weapons	Y

HART, GARY (Cont.)

21. Kill-SDI funding N
22. Kill-AIDS ins dscriminatn Y
23. Kill-$10 bbl oil tariff N
24. Kill-Repl wndfl prfts tax N
25. Repeal balanced bdgt amdt Y
26. Tax amnesty provisions N
27. Kill-Tax amnesty subst Y
28. Kill-Add third tax rate Y
29. Kill-Unocal tax provsns Y
30. Block Saudi arms sale (†) Y
31. Kill-Bar school busing Y
32. Prohibit Saudi arms sale Y
33. Nicaraguan contra aid N
34. Bar all aid to Nicaragua Y
35. Balanced budget amendment N
36. Balanced bdgt substitute N
37. Conrail sale N
38. Revise farm programs N
39. Kill-New oil import fee N
40. Spending cuts, tax incres Y
41. Textile import quotas N
42. Kill-Exmpt vets from cuts N
43. Kill-Bar inmate abortn $ Y
44. Textile import quotas (§) N
45. Kill-Eliminate Amtrak $ Y
46. Kill-Incrs motor fuel tax N
47. Set max allow deficits N
48. 20% minimum tax on corps N
49. Bar $ to toxic victims N
50. Seasonal workers in US N
51. Kill-School prayer cases Y
52. Line-item veto N
53. South Africa sanctions Y
54. Ease '68 Gun Control Act N
55. Kill-14 day handgun wait N
56. Kill-Gun dlr inspections Y
57. Kill-Keep '68 Gun Con Act N
58. Nicarag humanitarian aid N
59. Bar ASAT testing Y
60. Delete chemical weapons Y
61. Delete 21 MX missiles Y
62. Kill-15% min tax on corps N
63. Kill-Restore Soc Sec COLA N
64. Freeze all funding N
65. Cut def;raise taxes, COLA Y
66. Keep existing SS COLAs Y
67. Aid to Nicaraguan rebels N
68. Reaffirm purch of 21 MX N
69. African Relief/Farm Crdt Y
70. Kill-Nuclear Freeze N
71. Kill-Void Title IX Narrow N
72. Raise drinking age to 21 ?
73. Kill-Reduce mil in Europe Y
74. Kill-Bar $ for contras ?
75. Kill-No new MXs in 1985 N
76. Kill-Move MX $ to non-nuc N
77. Deficit reduction-$140b ?
78. Kill-Req auth for troops ?
79. School Prayer amendment N
80. Cap punish-certain crimes N
81. Bar govt off from taping ?
82. Martin L. King holiday Y
83. Auth marines in Lebanon N
84. Anti-abortion amendment N
85. Highway-Gas tax bill Y
86. Delete job creation amend N
87. Kill-Tobacco price supprt N
88. Emergency housing aid N
89. Nullify oil decontrol ?
90. Target tax cuts-mid class Y
91. Tax Indexing Y
92. Kill-Oppose SS benft cuts N
93. Disapprove Saudi AWACS Y
94. Anti-busing rider N
95. Disapprove oil import fee N
96. Domestic violence funds Y
97. Trucking Deregulation Y
98. Overturn India fuel sale Y
99. Mil draft registration N
100. Chrysler Loan Guarantees N
101. Nuclear plant moratorium Y
102. Abolish electoral college Y
103. Kill-Lmt ct-ordered bus Y
104. Airline Deregulation Y
105. Disappr Mideast jet sales Y
106. Natural gas deregulation N
107. Prohibit neutron bomb Y
108. Financial disclosure-off Y

Presidential Support Score: 1986 - 23% 1985 - 21%

CONNECTICUT

WEICKER, LOWELL P., Jr. [Republican]. Term Began/Expires: 1983/1988. Prior Terms: House: 1969-70; Senate: 1971-82. Born: May 16, 1931; Paris, France. Education: Yale University (B.A.); University of Virginia (LL.B.). Military Service: U.S. Army. Occupation: Connecticut representative (1963-68); attorney.

1. Immigration Reform Y
2. So Afr Sanc-veto override Y
3. Kill-Death pnlty drug bil Y
4. Kill-Mil use in drug war Y

WEICKER, LOWELL P., Jr. (Cont.)

5.	Tax Overhaul	N	57.	Kill-Keep '68 Gun Con Act	N
6.	Raise speed limit	N	58.	Nicarag humanitarian aid	N
7.	Across-the-board cuts	N	59.	Bar ASAT testing	Y
8.	South Africa sanctions	Y	60.	Delete chemical weapons	Y
9.	Kill-So Africa sanctions	N	61.	Delete 21 MX missiles	Y
10.	Kill-So Africa sanct (*)	N	62.	Kill-15% min tax on corps	N
11.	Nicaraguan contra aid	N	63.	Kill-Restore Soc Sec COLA	Y
12.	Terminate contra aid	N	64.	Freeze all funding	Y
13.	Kill-Prohibit contra fnds	N	65.	Cut def;raise taxes, COLA	N
14.	Kill-Stop CIA contra fndg	N	66.	Keep existing SS COLAs	Y
15.	Kill-Bar nuclr tsts w/SDI	?	67.	Aid to Nicaraguan rebels	N
16.	Kill-Bar ASAT testing	N	68.	Reaffirm purch of 21 MX	N
17.	Nuclear test ban treaty	Y	69.	African Relief/Farm Crdt	Y
18.	Prohibit sale of Stinger	Y	70.	Kill-Nuclear Freeze	N
19.	Delete Bigeye chem bomb	Y	71.	Kill-Void Title IX Narrow	N
20.	Bar binary chem weapons	Y	72.	Raise drinking age to 21	Y
21.	Kill-SDI funding	N	73.	Kill-Reduce mil in Europe	Y
22.	Kill-AIDS ins dscriminatn	?	74.	Kill-Bar $ for contras	N
23.	Kill-$10 bbl oil tariff	Y	75.	Kill-No new MXs in 1985	N
24.	Kill-Repl wndfl prfts tax	Y	76.	Kill-Move MX $ to non-nuc	N
25.	Repeal balanced bdgt amdt	Y	77.	Deficit reduction-$140b	Y
26.	Tax amnesty provisions	?	78.	Kill-Req auth for troops	N
27.	Kill-Tax amnesty subst	?	79.	School Prayer amendment	N
28.	Kill-Add third tax rate	Y	80.	Cap punish-certain crimes	N
29.	Kill-Unocal tax provsns	N	81.	Bar govt off from taping	Y
30.	Block Saudi arms sale (†)	Y	82.	Martin L. King holiday	Y
31.	Kill-Bar school busing	Y	83.	Auth marines in Lebanon	N
32.	Prohibit Saudi arms sale	Y	84.	Anti-abortion amendment	N
33.	Nicaraguan contra aid	N	85.	Highway-Gas tax bill	Y
34.	Bar all aid to Nicaragua	Y	86.	Delete job creation amend	N
35.	Balanced budget amendment	N	87.	Kill-Tobacco price supprt	?
36.	Balanced bdgt substitute	N	88.	Emergency housing aid	Y
37.	Conrail sale	Y	89.	Nullify oil decontrol	N
38.	Revise farm programs	?	90.	Target tax cuts-mid class	N
39.	Kill-New oil import fee	Y	91.	Tax Indexing	N
40.	Spending cuts, tax incres	Y	92.	Kill-Oppose SS benft cuts	N
41.	Textile import quotas	Y	93.	Disapprove Saudi AWACS	Y
42.	Kill-Exmpt vets from cuts	?	94.	Anti-busing rider	N
43.	Kill-Bar inmate abortn $	Y	95.	Disapprove oil import fee	?
44.	Textile import quotas (§)	Y	96.	Domestic violence funds	Y
45.	Kill-Eliminate Amtrak $	Y	97.	Trucking Deregulation	Y
46.	Kill-Incrs motor fuel tax	N	98.	Overturn India fuel sale	Y
47.	Set max allow deficits	N	99.	Mil draft registration	Y
48.	20% minimum tax on corps	N	100.	Chrysler Loan Guarantees	N
49.	Bar $ to toxic victims	Y	101.	Nuclear plant moratorium	N
50.	Seasonal workers in US	N	102.	Abolish electoral college	N
51.	Kill-School prayer cases	Y	103.	Kill-Lmt ct-ordered bus	Y
52.	Line-item veto	N	104.	Airline Deregulation	Y
53.	South Africa sanctions	Y	105.	Disappr Mideast jet sales	Y
54.	Ease '68 Gun Control Act	Y	106.	Natural gas deregulation	Y
55.	Kill-14 day handgun wait	N	107.	Prohibit neutron bomb	Y
56.	Kill-Gun dlr inspections	Y	108.	Financial disclosure-off	Y

Presidential Support Score: 1986 - 44% 1985 - 42%

DODD, CHRISTOPHER J. [Democrat]. Term Began/Expires: 1981/1986. Prior Terms: House: 1975-80. Born: May 27, 1944; Williamantic, Conn. Education: Providence College (B.A.); University of Louisville School of Law (J.D.). Military Service: U.S.

DODD, CHRISTOPHER J. (Cont.)
Army, 1969-75. Occupation: Attorney; peace corps volunteer (1966-68).

1. Immigration Reform Y
2. So Afr Sanc-veto override Y
3. Kill-Death pnlty drug bil N
4. Kill-Mil use in drug war Y
5. Tax Overhaul N
6. Raise speed limit N
7. Across-the-board cuts N
8. South Africa sanctions Y
9. Kill-So Africa sanctions N
10. Kill-So Africa sanct (*) N
11. Nicaraguan contra aid N
12. Terminate contra aid Y
13. Kill-Prohibit contra fnds N
14. Kill-Stop CIA contra fndg N
15. Kill-Bar nuclr tsts w/SDI N
16. Kill-Bar ASAT testing N
17. Nuclear test ban treaty Y
18. Prohibit sale of Stinger N
19. Delete Bigeye chem bomb Y
20. Bar binary chem weapons Y
21. Kill-SDI funding N
22. Kill-AIDS ins dscriminatn Y
23. Kill-$10 bbl oil tariff Y
24. Kill-Repl wndfl prfts tax Y
25. Repeal balanced bdgt amdt N
26. Tax amnesty provisions N
27. Kill-Tax amnesty subst Y
28. Kill-Add third tax rate Y
29. Kill-Unocal tax provsns N
30. Block Saudi arms sale (†) Y
31. Kill-Bar school busing Y
32. Prohibit Saudi arms sale Y
33. Nicaraguan contra aid N
34. Bar all aid to Nicaragua Y
35. Balanced budget amendment N
36. Balanced bdgt substitute N
37. Conrail sale N
38. Revise farm programs N
39. Kill-New oil import fee Y
40. Spending cuts, tax incres Y
41. Textile import quotas Y
42. Kill-Exmpt vets from cuts Y
43. Kill-Bar inmate abortn $ Y
44. Textile import quotas (§) Y
45. Kill-Eliminate Amtrak $ Y
46. Kill-Incrs motor fuel tax Y
47. Set max allow deficits Y
48. 20% minimum tax on corps N
49. Bar $ to toxic victims N
50. Seasonal workers in US N
51. Kill-School prayer cases Y
52. Line-item veto N
53. South Africa sanctions Y
54. Ease '68 Gun Control Act N
55. Kill-14 day handgun wait N
56. Kill-Gun dlr inspections N
57. Kill-Keep '68 Gun Con Act N
58. Nicarag humanitarian aid N
59. Bar ASAT testing Y
60. Delete chemical weapons Y
61. Delete 21 MX missiles Y
62. Kill-15% min tax on corps N
63. Kill-Restore Soc Sec COLA N
64. Freeze all funding Y
65. Cut def;raise taxes, COLA Y
66. Keep existing SS COLAs Y
67. Aid to Nicaraguan rebels N
68. Reaffirm purch of 21 MX N
69. African Relief/Farm Crdt Y
70. Kill-Nuclear Freeze N
71. Kill-Void Title IX Narrow N
72. Raise drinking age to 21 Y
73. Kill-Reduce mil in Europe Y
74. Kill-Bar $ for contras N
75. Kill-No new MXs in 1985 N
76. Kill-Move MX $ to non-nuc N
77. Deficit reduction-$140b Y
78. Kill-Req auth for troops N
79. School Prayer amendment N
80. Cap punish-certain crimes N
81. Bar govt off from taping Y
82. Martin L. King holiday Y
83. Auth marines in Lebanon N
84. Anti-abortion amendment N
85. Highway-Gas tax bill Y
86. Delete job creation amend N
87. Kill-Tobacco price supprt N
88. Emergency housing aid Y
89. Nullify oil decontrol Y
90. Target tax cuts-mid class Y
91. Tax Indexing N
92. Kill-Oppose SS benft cuts N
93. Disapprove Saudi AWACS Y
94. Anti-busing rider N

Presidential Support Score: 1986 - 26% 1985 - 34%

DELAWARE

ROTH, WILLIAM V., Jr. [Republican]. Term Began/Expires: 1983/1988. Prior Terms: House: 1967-70; Senate: 1971-82. Born: July 22, 1921; Great Falls, Mont. Education: University of Oregon

ROTH, WILLIAM V., Jr. (Cont.)
(B.A.); Harvard University (M.B.A., LL.B.). Military Service: U.S. Army, 1943-46. Occupation: Attorney.

1. Immigration Reform Y
2. So Afr Sanc-veto override Y
3. Kill-Death pnlty drug bil N
4. Kill-Mil use in drug war Y
5. Tax Overhaul N
6. Raise speed limit N
7. Across-the-board cuts N
8. South Africa sanctions Y
9. Kill-So Africa sanctions Y
10. Kill-So Africa sanct (*) Y
11. Nicaraguan contra aid Y
12. Terminate contra aid N
13. Kill-Prohibit contra fnds Y
14. Kill-Stop CIA contra fndg ?
15. Kill-Bar nuclr tsts w/SDI Y
16. Kill-Bar ASAT testing Y
17. Nuclear test ban treaty Y
18. Prohibit sale of Stinger N
19. Delete Bigeye chem bomb N
20. Bar binary chem weapons N
21. Kill-SDI funding Y
22. Kill-AIDS ins dscriminatn N
23. Kill-$10 bbl oil tariff Y
24. Kill-Repl wndfl prfts tax Y
25. Repeal balanced bdgt amdt Y
26. Tax amnesty provisions Y
27. Kill-Tax amnesty subst N
28. Kill-Add third tax rate Y
29. Kill-Unocal tax provsns Y
30. Block Saudi arms sale (†) N
31. Kill-Bar school busing N
32. Prohibit Saudi arms sale Y
33. Nicaraguan contra aid Y
34. Bar all aid to Nicaragua N
35. Balanced budget amendment Y
36. Balanced bdgt substitute N
37. Conrail sale N
38. Revise farm programs N
39. Kill-New oil import fee Y
40. Spending cuts, tax incres Y
41. Textile import quotas Y
42. Kill-Exmpt vets from cuts Y
43. Kill-Bar inmate abortn $ Y
44. Textile import quotas (§) Y
45. Kill-Eliminate Amtrak $ Y
46. Kill-Incrs motor fuel tax Y
47. Set max allow deficits Y
48. 20% minimum tax on corps N
49. Bar $ to toxic victims Y
50. Seasonal workers in US N
51. Kill-School prayer cases N
52. Line-item veto Y
53. South Africa sanctions Y
54. Ease '68 Gun Control Act Y
55. Kill-14 day handgun wait Y
56. Kill-Gun dlr inspections Y
57. Kill-Keep '68 Gun Con Act Y
58. Nicarag humanitarian aid Y
59. Bar ASAT testing N
60. Delete chemical weapons Y
61. Delete 21 MX missiles N
62. Kill-15% min tax on corps Y
63. Kill-Restore Soc Sec COLA Y
64. Freeze all funding N
65. Cut def;raise taxes, COLA N
66. Keep existing SS COLAs N
67. Aid to Nicaraguan rebels Y
68. Reaffirm purch of 21 MX Y
69. African Relief/Farm Crdt N
70. Kill-Nuclear Freeze Y
71. Kill-Void Title IX Narrow Y
72. Raise drinking age to 21 Y
73. Kill-Reduce mil in Europe N
74. Kill-Bar $ for contras Y
75. Kill-No new MXs in 1985 Y
76. Kill-Move MX $ to non-nuc Y
77. Deficit reduction-$140b Y
78. Kill-Req auth for troops Y
79. School Prayer amendment Y
80. Cap punish-certain crimes Y
81. Bar govt off from taping N
82. Martin L. King holiday Y
83. Auth marines in Lebanon N
84. Anti-abortion amendment N
85. Highway-Gas tax bill Y
86. Delete job creation amend Y
87. Kill-Tobacco price supprt N
88. Emergency housing aid N
89. Nullify oil decontrol Y
90. Target tax cuts-mid class N
91. Tax Indexing Y
92. Kill-Oppose SS benft cuts N
93. Disapprove Saudi AWACS Y
94. Anti-busing rider Y
95. Disapprove oil import fee Y
96. Domestic violence funds N
97. Trucking Deregulation Y
98. Overturn India fuel sale N
99. Mil draft registration N
100. Chrysler Loan Guarantees Y
101. Nuclear plant moratorium N
102. Abolish electoral college N
103. Kill-Lmt ct-ordered bus N
104. Airline Deregulation Y
105. Disappr Mideast jet sales Y
106. Natural gas deregulation Y
107. Prohibit neutron bomb N
108. Financial disclosure-off Y

Presidential Support Score: 1986 - 84% 1985 - 84%

BIDEN, JOSEPH R., Jr. [Democrat]. Term Began/Expires: 1985/1990. Prior Terms: Senate: 1973-84. Born: November 20, 1942; Scranton, Pa. Education: University of Delaware (A.B.); Syracuse University College of Law (J.D.). Occupation: New Castle County councilman, Delaware (1970-72).

1. Immigration Reform Y
2. So Afr Sanc-veto override Y
3. Kill-Death pnlty drug bil N
4. Kill-Mil use in drug war Y
5. Tax Overhaul Y
6. Raise speed limit Y
7. Across-the-board cuts N
8. South Africa sanctions Y
9. Kill-So Africa sanctions N
10. Kill-So Africa sanct (*) N
11. Nicaraguan contra aid N
12. Terminate contra aid Y
13. Kill-Prohibit contra fnds N
14. Kill-Stop CIA contra fndg N
15. Kill-Bar nuclr tsts w/SDI N
16. Kill-Bar ASAT testing N
17. Nuclear test ban treaty Y
18. Prohibit sale of Stinger Y
19. Delete Bigeye chem bomb Y
20. Bar binary chem weapons Y
21. Kill-SDI funding N
22. Kill-AIDS ins dscriminatn Y
23. Kill-$10 bbl oil tariff Y
24. Kill-Repl wndfl prfts tax Y
25. Repeal balanced bdgt amdt N
26. Tax amnesty provisions Y
27. Kill-Tax amnesty subst N
28. Kill-Add third tax rate N
29. Kill-Unocal tax provsns ?
30. Block Saudi arms sale (†) Y
31. Kill-Bar school busing ?
32. Prohibit Saudi arms sale Y
33. Nicaraguan contra aid N
34. Bar all aid to Nicaragua N
35. Balanced budget amendment N
36. Balanced bdgt substitute Y
37. Conrail sale N
38. Revise farm programs N
39. Kill-New oil import fee Y
40. Spending cuts, tax incres Y
41. Textile import quotas Y
42. Kill-Exmpt vets from cuts ?
43. Kill-Bar inmate abortn $ N
44. Textile import quotas (§) Y
45. Kill-Eliminate Amtrak $ Y
46. Kill-Incrs motor fuel tax Y
47. Set max allow deficits Y
48. 20% minimum tax on corps N
49. Bar $ to toxic victims N
50. Seasonal workers in US N
51. Kill-School prayer cases Y
52. Line-item veto Y
53. South Africa sanctions Y
54. Ease '68 Gun Control Act Y
55. Kill-14 day handgun wait Y
56. Kill-Gun dlr inspections Y
57. Kill-Keep '68 Gun Con Act N
58. Nicarag humanitarian aid N
59. Bar ASAT testing Y
60. Delete chemical weapons Y
61. Delete 21 MX missiles Y
62. Kill-15% min tax on corps Y
63. Kill-Restore Soc Sec COLA N
64. Freeze all funding Y
65. Cut def;raise taxes, COLA Y
66. Keep existing SS COLAs Y
67. Aid to Nicaraguan rebels N
68. Reaffirm purch of 21 MX N
69. African Relief/Farm Crdt Y
70. Kill-Nuclear Freeze N
71. Kill-Void Title IX Narrow N
72. Raise drinking age to 21 Y
73. Kill-Reduce mil in Europe N
74. Kill-Bar $ for contras N
75. Kill-No new MXs in 1985 N
76. Kill-Move MX $ to non-nuc N
77. Deficit reduction-$140b Y
78. Kill-Req auth for troops N
79. School Prayer amendment N
80. Cap punish-certain crimes N
81. Bar govt off from taping N
82. Martin L. King holiday Y
83. Auth marines in Lebanon N
84. Anti-abortion amendment N
85. Highway-Gas tax bill N
86. Delete job creation amend N
87. Kill-Tobacco price supprt N
88. Emergency housing aid Y
89. Nullify oil decontrol Y
90. Target tax cuts-mid class Y
91. Tax Indexing N
92. Kill-Oppose SS benft cuts N
93. Disapprove Saudi AWACS Y
94. Anti-busing rider Y
95. Disapprove oil import fee Y
96. Domestic violence funds Y
97. Trucking Deregulation Y
98. Overturn India fuel sale N
99. Mil draft registration ?
100. Chrysler Loan Guarantees Y
101. Nuclear plant moratorium Y
102. Abolish electoral college N
103. Kill-Lmt ct-ordered bus N
104. Airline Deregulation Y
105. Disappr Mideast jet sales Y
106. Natural gas deregulation N

BIDEN, JOSEPH R., Jr. (Cont.)

107. Prohibit neutron bomb Y
108. Financial disclosure-off ?

Presidential Support Score: 1986 28% 1985 - 31%

FLORIDA

HAWKINS, PAULA [Republican]. Term Began/Expires: 1981/1986. Born: January 24, 1927; Salt Lake City, Utah. Education: Utah State University; Occupation: Vice president, Air Florida; director, Rural Telephone Bank Board; chairman, Public Service Commission (1977-79); member, President's Commission on White House Fellowships; member, Federal Energy Administration Consumer Affairs/Special Impact Advisory Committee; member, Defense Advisory Committee on Women in the Services.

1. Immigration Reform Y
2. So Afr Sanc-veto override Y
3. Kill-Death pnlty drug bil N
4. Kill-Mil use in drug war N
5. Tax Overhaul Y
6. Raise speed limit N
7. Across-the-board cuts N
8. South Africa sanctions Y
9. Kill-So Africa sanctions Y
10. Kill-So Africa sanct (*) Y
11. Nicaraguan contra aid Y
12. Terminate contra aid N
13. Kill-Prohibit contra fnds Y
14. Kill-Stop CIA contra fndg Y
15. Kill-Bar nuclr tsts w/SDI Y
16. Kill-Bar ASAT testing Y
17. Nuclear test ban treaty N
18. Prohibit sale of Stinger N
19. Delete Bigeye chem bomb N
20. Bar binary chem weapons N
21. Kill-SDI funding +
22. Kill-AIDS ins dscriminatn N
23. Kill-$10 bbl oil tariff Y
24. Kill-Repl wndfl prfts tax Y
25. Repeal balanced bdgt amdt Y
26. Tax amnesty provisions ?
27. Kill-Tax amnesty subst ?
28. Kill-Add third tax rate Y
29. Kill-Unocal tax provsns ?
30. Block Saudi arms sale (†) Y
31. Kill-Bar school busing N
32. Prohibit Saudi arms sale +
33. Nicaraguan contra aid Y
34. Bar all aid to Nicaragua N
35. Balanced budget amendment Y
36. Balanced bdgt substitute N
37. Conrail sale Y
38. Revise farm programs Y
39. Kill-New oil import fee Y
40. Spending cuts, tax incres Y
41. Textile import quotas Y
42. Kill-Exmpt vets from cuts N
43. Kill-Bar inmate abortn $ N
44. Textile import quotas (§) Y
45. Kill-Eliminate Amtrak $ Y
46. Kill-Incrs motor fuel tax Y
47. Set max allow deficits Y
48. 20% minimum tax on corps N
49. Bar $ to toxic victims Y
50. Seasonal workers in US Y
51. Kill-School prayer cases N
52. Line-item veto Y
53. South Africa sanctions ?
54. Ease '68 Gun Control Act Y
55. Kill-14 day handgun wait Y
56. Kill-Gun dlr inspections Y
57. Kill-Keep '68 Gun Con Act Y
58. Nicarag humanitarian aid Y
59. Bar ASAT testing N
60. Delete chemical weapons N
61. Delete 21 MX missiles N
62. Kill-15% min tax on corps Y
63. Kill-Restore Soc Sec COLA Y
64. Freeze all funding N
65. Cut def;raise taxes, COLA N
66. Keep existing SS COLAs Y
67. Aid to Nicaraguan rebels Y
68. Reaffirm purch of 21 MX Y
69. African Relief/Farm Crdt Y
70. Kill-Nuclear Freeze Y
71. Kill-Void Title IX Narrow Y
72. Raise drinking age to 21 Y
73. Kill-Reduce mil in Europe Y
74. Kill-Bar $ for contras Y
75. Kill-No new MXs in 1985 Y
76. Kill-Move MX $ to non-nuc Y
77. Deficit reduction-$140b Y
78. Kill-Req auth for troops Y
79. School Prayer amendment Y
80. Cap punish-certain crimes Y
81. Bar govt off from taping N
82. Martin L. King holiday Y
83. Auth marines in Lebanon Y
84. Anti-abortion amendment Y

HAWKINS, PAULA (Cont.)

85. Highway-Gas tax bill N
86. Delete job creation amend Y
87. Kill-Tobacco price supprt Y
88. Emergency housing aid Y
89. Nullify oil decontrol Y
90. Target tax cuts-mid class N
91. Tax Indexing Y
92. Kill-Oppose SS benft cuts ?
93. Disapprove Saudi AWACS Y
94. Anti-busing rider Y

Presidential Support Score: 1986 - 66% 1985 - 73%

CHILES, LAWTON [Democrat]. Term Began/Expires: 1983/1988. Prior Terms: Senate: 1971-82. Born: April 3, 1930; Lakeland, Fla. Education: University of Florida (B.S., LL.B.). Military Service: U.S. Army. Occupation: Attorney; Florida representative (1958-66); Florida senator (1966-70).

1. Immigration Reform Y
2. So Afr Sanc-veto override Y
3. Kill-Death pnlty drug bil N
4. Kill-Mil use in drug war Y
5. Tax Overhaul N
6. Raise speed limit N
7. Across-the-board cuts N
8. South Africa sanctions Y
9. Kill-So Africa sanctions N
10. Kill-So Africa sanct (*) N
11. Nicaraguan contra aid Y
12. Terminate contra aid N
13. Kill-Prohibit contra fnds Y
14. Kill-Stop CIA contra fndg Y
15. Kill-Bar nuclr tsts w/SDI Y
16. Kill-Bar ASAT testing Y
17. Nuclear test ban treaty Y
18. Prohibit sale of Stinger N
19. Delete Bigeye chem bomb N
20. Bar binary chem weapons N
21. Kill-SDI funding N
22. Kill-AIDS ins dscriminatn Y
23. Kill-$10 bbl oil tariff Y
24. Kill-Repl wndfl prfts tax Y
25. Repeal balanced bdgt amdt N
26. Tax amnesty provisions ?
27. Kill-Tax amnesty subst Y
28. Kill-Add third tax rate Y
29. Kill-Unocal tax provsns N
30. Block Saudi arms sale (†) Y
31. Kill-Bar school busing N
32. Prohibit Saudi arms sale Y
33. Nicaraguan contra aid Y
34. Bar all aid to Nicaragua N
35. Balanced budget amendment Y
36. Balanced bdgt substitute N
37. Conrail sale N
38. Revise farm programs ?
39. Kill-New oil import fee Y
40. Spending cuts, tax incres Y
41. Textile import quotas ?
42. Kill-Exmpt vets from cuts N
43. Kill-Bar inmate abortn $ N
44. Textile import quotas (§) N
45. Kill-Eliminate Amtrak $ Y
46. Kill-Incrs motor fuel tax Y
47. Set max allow deficits N
48. 20% minimum tax on corps N
49. Bar $ to toxic victims N
50. Seasonal workers in US N
51. Kill-School prayer cases Y
52. Line-item veto N
53. South Africa sanctions Y
54. Ease '68 Gun Control Act Y
55. Kill-14 day handgun wait Y
56. Kill-Gun dlr inspections Y
57. Kill-Keep '68 Gun Con Act Y
58. Nicarag humanitarian aid Y
59. Bar ASAT testing N
60. Delete chemical weapons N
61. Delete 21 MX missiles N
62. Kill-15% min tax on corps N
63. Kill-Restore Soc Sec COLA N
64. Freeze all funding N
65. Cut def;raise taxes, COLA Y
66. Keep existing SS COLAs Y
67. Aid to Nicaraguan rebels Y
68. Reaffirm purch of 21 MX N
69. African Relief/Farm Crdt Y
70. Kill-Nuclear Freeze Y
71. Kill-Void Title IX Narrow N
72. Raise drinking age to 21 Y
73. Kill-Reduce mil in Europe N
74. Kill-Bar $ for contras Y
75. Kill-No new MXs in 1985 N
76. Kill-Move MX $ to non-nuc Y
77. Deficit reduction-$140b N
78. Kill-Req auth for troops Y
79. School Prayer amendment Y
80. Cap punish-certain crimes Y
81. Bar govt off from taping Y
82. Martin L. King holiday Y
83. Auth marines in Lebanon N
84. Anti-abortion amendment Y
85. Highway-Gas tax bill Y
86. Delete job creation amend Y
87. Kill-Tobacco price supprt Y
88. Emergency housing aid Y

CHILES, LAWTON (Cont.)

89. Nullify oil decontrol N
90. Target tax cuts-mid class Y
91. Tax Indexing N
92. Kill-Oppose SS benft cuts N
93. Disapprove Saudi AWACS Y
94. Anti-busing rider Y
95. Disapprove oil import fee N
96. Domestic violence funds Y
97. Trucking Deregulation Y
98. Overturn India fuel sale N
99. Mil draft registration Y
100. Chrysler Loan Guarantees Y
101. Nuclear plant moratorium N
102. Abolish electoral college N
103. Kill-Lmt ct-ordered bus N
104. Airline Deregulation Y
105. Disappr Mideast jet sales Y
106. Natural gas deregulation Y
107. Prohibit neutron bomb N
108. Financial disclosure-off Y

Presidential Support Score: 1986 - 58% 1985 - 40%

G E O R G I A

MATTINGLY, MACK [Republican]. Term Began/Expires: 1981/1986. Born: January 7, 1931; Anderson, Ind. Education: Indiana University (B.S.). Military Service: U.S. Air Force, 1951-55. Occupation: IBM sales representative (1958-79); owner, office supply business.

1. Immigration Reform Y
2. So Afr Sanc-veto override Y
3. Kill-Death pnlty drug bil N
4. Kill-Mil use in drug war N
5. Tax Overhaul Y
6. Raise speed limit N
7. Across-the-board cuts N
8. South Africa sanctions Y
9. Kill-So Africa sanctions N
10. Kill-So Africa sanct (*) Y
11. Nicaraguan contra aid Y
12. Terminate contra aid N
13. Kill-Prohibit contra fnds Y
14. Kill-Stop CIA contra fndg Y
15. Kill-Bar nuclr tsts w/SDI Y
16. Kill-Bar ASAT testing Y
17. Nuclear test ban treaty N
18. Prohibit sale of Stinger N
19. Delete Bigeye chem bomb N
20. Bar binary chem weapons N
21. Kill-SDI funding Y
22. Kill-AIDS ins dscriminatn N
23. Kill-$10 bbl oil tariff Y
24. Kill-Repl wndfl prfts tax N
25. Repeal balanced bdgt amdt N
26. Tax amnesty provisions N
27. Kill-Tax amnesty subst Y
28. Kill-Add third tax rate Y
29. Kill-Unocal tax provsns N
30. Block Saudi arms sale (†) Y
31. Kill-Bar school busing N
32. Prohibit Saudi arms sale Y
33. Nicaraguan contra aid Y
34. Bar all aid to Nicaragua N
35. Balanced budget amendment Y
36. Balanced bdgt substitute N
37. Conrail sale Y
38. Revise farm programs Y
39. Kill-New oil import fee Y
40. Spending cuts, tax incres Y
41. Textile import quotas Y
42. Kill-Exmpt vets from cuts Y
43. Kill-Bar inmate abortn $ N
44. Textile import quotas (§) Y
45. Kill-Eliminate Amtrak $ N
46. Kill-Incrs motor fuel tax Y
47. Set max allow deficits Y
48. 20% minimum tax on corps N
49. Bar $ to toxic victims Y
50. Seasonal workers in US Y
51. Kill-School prayer cases N
52. Line-item veto Y
53. South Africa sanctions Y
54. Ease '68 Gun Control Act Y
55. Kill-14 day handgun wait Y
56. Kill-Gun dlr inspections Y
57. Kill-Keep '68 Gun Con Act Y
58. Nicarag humanitarian aid Y
59. Bar ASAT testing N
60. Delete chemical weapons N
61. Delete 21 MX missiles N
62. Kill-15% min tax on corps Y
63. Kill-Restore Soc Sec COLA Y
64. Freeze all funding Y
65. Cut def;raise taxes, COLA N
66. Keep existing SS COLAs Y
67. Aid to Nicaraguan rebels Y
68. Reaffirm purch of 21 MX Y
69. African Relief/Farm Crdt N
70. Kill-Nuclear Freeze Y
71. Kill-Void Title IX Narrow Y
72. Raise drinking age to 21 Y
73. Kill-Reduce mil in Europe Y
74. Kill-Bar $ for contras Y

MATTINGLY, MACK (Cont.)

75.	Kill-No new MXs in 1985	Y	85.	Highway-Gas tax bill	N
76.	Kill-Move MX $ to non-nuc	Y	86.	Delete job creation amend	Y
77.	Deficit reduction-$140b	Y	87.	Kill-Tobacco price supprt	Y
78.	Kill-Req auth for troops	Y	88.	Emergency housing aid	N
79.	School Prayer amendment	Y	89.	Nullify oil decontrol	N
80.	Cap punish-certain crimes	Y	90.	Target tax cuts-mid class	N
81.	Bar govt off from taping	N	91.	Tax Indexing	Y
82.	Martin L. King holiday	Y	92.	Kill-Oppose SS benft cuts	Y
83.	Auth marines in Lebanon	Y	93.	Disapprove Saudi AWACS	N
84.	Anti-abortion amendment	Y	94.	Anti-busing rider	Y

Presidential Support Score: 1986 - 83% 1985 - 84%

NUNN, SAM [Democrat]. Term Began/Expires: 1985/1990. Prior Terms: Senate: 1972-84. Born: September 8, 1938; Perry, Ga. Education: Georgia Institute of Technology; Emory University (A.B., LL.B.). Military Service: U.S. Coast Guard, 1959-60; Reserve, 1960-68. Occupation: Attorney; farmer; Georgia representative (1968-72); president, Perry Chamber of Commerce (1964).

1.	Immigration Reform	Y	39.	Kill-New oil import fee	Y
2.	So Afr Sanc-veto override	Y	40.	Spending cuts, tax incres	Y
3.	Kill-Death pnlty drug bil	N	41.	Textile import quotas	Y
4.	Kill-Mil use in drug war	Y	42.	Kill-Exmpt vets from cuts	Y
5.	Tax Overhaul	N	43.	Kill-Bar inmate abortn $	Y
6.	Raise speed limit	Y	44.	Textile import quotas (§)	Y
7.	Across-the-board cuts	N	45.	Kill-Eliminate Amtrak $	Y
8.	South Africa sanctions	Y	46.	Kill-Incrs motor fuel tax	Y
9.	Kill-So Africa sanctions	N	47.	Set max allow deficits	Y
10.	Kill-So Africa sanct (*)	N	48.	20% minimum tax on corps	N
11.	Nicaraguan contra aid	Y	49.	Bar $ to toxic victims	Y
12.	Terminate contra aid	Y	50.	Seasonal workers in US	Y
13.	Kill-Prohibit contra fnds	Y	51.	Kill-School prayer cases	Y
14.	Kill-Stop CIA contra fndg	Y	52.	Line-item veto	Y
15.	Kill-Bar nuclr tsts w/SDI	Y	53.	South Africa sanctions	Y
16.	Kill-Bar ASAT testing	Y	54.	Ease '68 Gun Control Act	Y
17.	Nuclear test ban treaty	Y	55.	Kill-14 day handgun wait	Y
18.	Prohibit sale of Stinger	N	56.	Kill-Gun dlr inspections	N
19.	Delete Bigeye chem bomb	N	57.	Kill-Keep '68 Gun Con Act	Y
20.	Bar binary chem weapons	N	58.	Nicarag humanitarian aid	Y
21.	Kill-SDI funding	Y	59.	Bar ASAT testing	N
22.	Kill-AIDS ins dscriminatn	Y	60.	Delete chemical weapons	N
23.	Kill-$10 bbl oil tariff	Y	61.	Delete 21 MX missiles	N
24.	Kill-Repl wndfl prfts tax	N	62.	Kill-15% min tax on corps	N
25.	Repeal balanced bdgt amdt	N	63.	Kill-Restore Soc Sec COLA	N
26.	Tax amnesty provisions	Y	64.	Freeze all funding	N
27.	Kill-Tax amnesty subst	N	65.	Cut def;raise taxes, COLA	N
28.	Kill-Add third tax rate	N	66.	Keep existing SS COLAs	Y
29.	Kill-Unocal tax provsns	N	67.	Aid to Nicaraguan rebels	Y
30.	Block Saudi arms sale (†)	Y	68.	Reaffirm purch of 21 MX	Y
31.	Kill-Bar school busing	N	69.	African Relief/Farm Crdt	Y
32.	Prohibit Saudi arms sale	Y	70.	Kill-Nuclear Freeze	Y
33.	Nicaraguan contra aid	Y	71.	Kill-Void Title IX Narrow	N
34.	Bar all aid to Nicaragua	N	72.	Raise drinking age to 21	Y
35.	Balanced budget amendment	Y	73.	Kill-Reduce mil in Europe	N
36.	Balanced bdgt substitute	Y	74.	Kill-Bar $ for contras	Y
37.	Conrail sale	Y	75.	Kill-No new MXs in 1985	Y
38.	Revise farm programs	Y	76.	Kill-Move MX $ to non-nuc	Y

NUNN, SAM (Cont.)

77. Deficit reduction-$140b Y
78. Kill-Req auth for troops Y
79. School Prayer amendment Y
80. Cap punish-certain crimes Y
81. Bar govt off from taping N
82. Martin L. King holiday Y
83. Auth marines in Lebanon N
84. Anti-abortion amendment Y
85. Highway-Gas tax bill Y
86. Delete job creation amend Y
87. Kill-Tobacco price supprt Y
88. Emergency housing aid Y
89. Nullify oil decontrol N
90. Target tax cuts-mid class Y
91. Tax Indexing N
92. Kill-Oppose SS benft cuts N
93. Disapprove Saudi AWACS N
94. Anti-busing rider Y
95. Disapprove oil import fee Y
96. Domestic violence funds N
97. Trucking Deregulation Y
98. Overturn India fuel sale N
99. Mil draft registration Y
100. Chrysler Loan Guarantees N
101. Nuclear plant moratorium N
102. Abolish electoral college N
103. Kill-Lmt ct-ordered bus N
104. Airline Deregulation Y
105. Disappr Mideast jet sales Y
106. Natural gas deregulation N
107. Prohibit neutron bomb N
108. Financial disclosure-off Y

Presidential Support Score: 1986 - 59% 1985 - 58%

H A W A I I

INOUYE, DANIEL K. [Democrat]. Term Began/Expires: 1981/1986. Prior Terms: House: 1959 (Special Election)-1962; Senate: 1963-80. Born: September 7, 1924; Honolulu, Hawaii. Education: University of Hawaii (A.B.); George Washington University Law School (J.D.). Military Service: U.S. Army, WWII. Occupation: Hawaii territory representative (1954-58); Hawaii territory senator (1958-59).

1. Immigration Reform N
2. So Afr Sanc-veto override Y
3. Kill-Death pnlty drug bil Y
4. Kill-Mil use in drug war Y
5. Tax Overhaul N
6. Raise speed limit ?
7. Across-the-board cuts N
8. South Africa sanctions Y
9. Kill-So Africa sanctions N
10. Kill-So Africa sanct (*) N
11. Nicaraguan contra aid N
12. Terminate contra aid Y
13. Kill-Prohibit contra fnds N
14. Kill-Stop CIA contra fndg N
15. Kill-Bar nuclr tsts w/SDI N
16. Kill-Bar ASAT testing N
17. Nuclear test ban treaty Y
18. Prohibit sale of Stinger Y
19. Delete Bigeye chem bomb Y
20. Bar binary chem weapons Y
21. Kill-SDI funding N
22. Kill-AIDS ins dscriminatn N
23. Kill-$10 bbl oil tariff Y
24. Kill-Repl wndfl prfts tax Y
25. Repeal balanced bdgt amdt Y
26. Tax amnesty provisions N
27. Kill-Tax amnesty subst Y
28. Kill-Add third tax rate N
29. Kill-Unocal tax provsns N
30. Block Saudi arms sale (†) Y
31. Kill-Bar school busing Y
32. Prohibit Saudi arms sale Y
33. Nicaraguan contra aid N
34. Bar all aid to Nicaragua Y
35. Balanced budget amendment N
36. Balanced bdgt substitute Y
37. Conrail sale +
38. Revise farm programs Y
39. Kill-New oil import fee Y
40. Spending cuts, tax incres Y
41. Textile import quotas N
42. Kill-Exmpt vets from cuts N
43. Kill-Bar inmate abortn $ Y
44. Textile import quotas (§) N
45. Kill-Eliminate Amtrak $?
46. Kill-Incrs motor fuel tax Y
47. Set max allow deficits N
48. 20% minimum tax on corps N
49. Bar $ to toxic victims N
50. Seasonal workers in US ?
51. Kill-School prayer cases Y
52. Line-item veto N
53. South Africa sanctions Y
54. Ease '68 Gun Control Act N
55. Kill-14 day handgun wait N
56. Kill-Gun dlr inspections N
57. Kill-Keep '68 Gun Con Act N
58. Nicarag humanitarian aid N

INOUYE, DANIEL K. (Cont.)

59. Bar ASAT testing Y
60. Delete chemical weapons Y
61. Delete 21 MX missiles Y
62. Kill-15% min tax on corps N
63. Kill-Restore Soc Sec COLA N
64. Freeze all funding N
65. Cut def;raise taxes, COLA Y
66. Keep existing SS COLAs Y
67. Aid to Nicaraguan rebels N
68. Reaffirm purch of 21 MX N
69. African Relief/Farm Crdt Y
70. Kill-Nuclear Freeze N
71. Kill-Void Title IX Narrow N
72. Raise drinking age to 21 Y
73. Kill-Reduce mil in Europe N
74. Kill-Bar $ for contras N
75. Kill-No new MXs in 1985 N
76. Kill-Move MX $ to non-nuc N
77. Deficit reduction-$140b N
78. Kill-Req auth for troops N
79. School Prayer amendment N
80. Cap punish-certain crimes N
81. Bar govt off from taping Y
82. Martin L. King holiday Y
83. Auth marines in Lebanon N
84. Anti-abortion amendment N
85. Highway-Gas tax bill N
86. Delete job creation amend N
87. Kill-Tobacco price supprt Y
88. Emergency housing aid ?
89. Nullify oil decontrol Y
90. Target tax cuts-mid class Y
91. Tax Indexing N
92. Kill-Oppose SS benft cuts N
93. Disapprove Saudi AWACS Y
94. Anti-busing rider N
95. Disapprove oil import fee N
96. Domestic violence funds Y
97. Trucking Deregulation N
98. Overturn India fuel sale N
99. Mil draft registration Y
100. Chrysler Loan Guarantees Y
101. Nuclear plant moratorium N
102. Abolish electoral college Y
103. Kill-Lmt ct-ordered bus Y
104. Airline Deregulation Y
105. Disappr Mideast jet sales N
106. Natural gas deregulation N
107. Prohibit neutron bomb N
108. Financial disclosure-off ?

Presidential Support Score: 1986 - 16% 1985 - 20%

MATSUNAGA, SPARK M. [Democrat]. Term Began/Expires: 1983/1988. Prior Terms: House: 1963-76; Senate: 1977-82. Born: October 8, 1916; Kukuiula, Kauai, Hawaii. Education: University of Hawaii (Ed.B.); Havard Law School (J.D.); Northwestern University Traffic Institute; Soochow University (LL.D.). Military Service: U.S. Army, 1941-45. Occupation: Interior Department veterans counsellor (1945-47); chief, Priority Division, War Assets Administration (1947-48); assistant public prosecutor, Honolulu (1952-54); attorney, Hawaii territorial legislator (1954-59).

1. Immigration Reform Y
2. So Afr Sanc-veto override Y
3. Kill-Death pnlty drug bil Y
4. Kill-Mil use in drug war Y
5. Tax Overhaul Y
6. Raise speed limit Y
7. Across-the-board cuts ?
8. South Africa sanctions Y
9. Kill-So Africa sanctions N
10. Kill-So Africa sanct (*) N
11. Nicaraguan contra aid N
12. Terminate contra aid Y
13. Kill-Prohibit contra fnds N
14. Kill-Stop CIA contra fndg N
15. Kill-Bar nuclr tsts w/SDI N
16. Kill-Bar ASAT testing N
17. Nuclear test ban treaty Y
18. Prohibit sale of Stinger Y
19. Delete Bigeye chem bomb Y
20. Bar binary chem weapons Y
21. Kill-SDI funding N
22. Kill-AIDS ins dscriminatn N
23. Kill-$10 bbl oil tariff Y
24. Kill-Repl wndfl prfts tax N
25. Repeal balanced bdgt amdt Y
26. Tax amnesty provisions Y
27. Kill-Tax amnesty subst N
28. Kill-Add third tax rate Y
29. Kill-Unocal tax provsns N
30. Block Saudi arms sale (†) Y
31. Kill-Bar school busing Y
32. Prohibit Saudi arms sale Y
33. Nicaraguan contra aid N
34. Bar all aid to Nicaragua ?
35. Balanced budget amendment N
36. Balanced bdgt substitute Y
37. Conrail sale Y
38. Revise farm programs Y
39. Kill-New oil import fee Y
40. Spending cuts, tax incres Y

MATSUNAGA, SPARK M. (Cont.)

41. Textile import quotas	N	75. Kill-No new MXs in 1985	N
42. Kill-Exmpt vets from cuts	N	76. Kill-Move MX $ to non-nuc	N
43. Kill-Bar inmate abortn $	Y	77. Deficit reduction-$140b	N
44. Textile import quotas (§)	N	78. Kill-Req auth for troops	N
45. Kill-Eliminate Amtrak $	Y	79. School Prayer amendment	N
46. Kill-Incrs motor fuel tax	N	80. Cap punish-certain crimes	N
47. Set max allow deficits	N	81. Bar govt off from taping	Y
48. 20% minimum tax on corps	Y	82. Martin L. King holiday	Y
49. Bar $ to toxic victims	N	83. Auth marines in Lebanon	N
50. Seasonal workers in US	N	84. Anti-abortion amendment	N
51. Kill-School prayer cases	Y	85. Highway-Gas tax bill	Y
52. Line-item veto	N	86. Delete job creation amend	N
53. South Africa sanctions	Y	87. Kill-Tobacco price supprt	Y
54. Ease '68 Gun Control Act	N	88. Emergency housing aid	Y
55. Kill-14 day handgun wait	N	89. Nullify oil decontrol	Y
56. Kill-Gun dlr inspections	N	90. Target tax cuts-mid class	Y
57. Kill-Keep '68 Gun Con Act	N	91. Tax Indexing	N
58. Nicarag humanitarian aid	N	92. Kill-Oppose SS benft cuts	N
59. Bar ASAT testing	Y	93. Disapprove Saudi AWACS	Y
60. Delete chemical weapons	Y	94. Anti-busing rider	N
61. Delete 21 MX missiles	Y	95. Disapprove oil import fee	?
62. Kill-15% min tax on corps	N	96. Domestic violence funds	Y
63. Kill-Restore Soc Sec COLA	N	97. Trucking Deregulation	N
64. Freeze all funding	Y	98. Overturn India fuel sale	Y
65. Cut def;raise taxes, COLA	Y	99. Mil draft registration	N
66. Keep existing SS COLAs	Y	100. Chrysler Loan Guarantees	Y
67. Aid to Nicaraguan rebels	N	101. Nuclear plant moratorium	Y
68. Reaffirm purch of 21 MX	N	102. Abolish electoral college	Y
69. African Relief/Farm Crdt	Y	103. Kill-Lmt ct-ordered bus	Y
70. Kill-Nuclear Freeze	N	104. Airline Deregulation	Y
71. Kill-Void Title IX Narrow	N	105. Disappr Mideast jet sales	Y
72. Raise drinking age to 21	Y	106. Natural gas deregulation	N
73. Kill-Reduce mil in Europe	N	107. Prohibit neutron bomb	Y
74. Kill-Bar $ for contras	N	108. Financial disclosure-off	Y

Presidential Support Score: 1986 - 26% 1985 - 22%

IDAHO

McCLURE, JAMES A. [Republican]. Term Began/Expires: 1985/1990. Prior Terms: House: 1967-72; Senate: 1973-84. Born: December 27, 1924; Payette, Idaho. Education: University of Idaho, College of Law (J.D.). Occupation: Attorney; prosecuting attorney; Idaho senator.

1. Immigration Reform	N	14. Kill-Stop CIA contra fndg	Y
2. So Afr Sanc-veto override	N	15. Kill-Bar nuclr tsts w/SDI	Y
3. Kill-Death pnlty drug bil	N	16. Kill-Bar ASAT testing	Y
4. Kill-Mil use in drug war	Y	17. Nuclear test ban treaty	N
5. Tax Overhaul	Y	18. Prohibit sale of Stinger	N
6. Raise speed limit	Y	19. Delete Bigeye chem bomb	N
7. Across-the-board cuts	N	20. Bar binary chem weapons	N
8. South Africa sanctions	N	21. Kill-SDI funding	Y
9. Kill-So Africa sanctions	Y	22. Kill-AIDS ins dscriminatn	N
10. Kill-So Africa sanct (*)	Y	23. Kill-$10 bbl oil tariff	Y
11. Nicaraguan contra aid	Y	24. Kill-Repl wndfl prfts tax	N
12. Terminate contra aid	N	25. Repeal balanced bdgt amdt	N
13. Kill-Prohibit contra fnds	Y	26. Tax amnesty provisions	?

McCLURE, JAMES A. (Cont.)

27.	Kill-Tax amnesty subst	?	68.	Reaffirm purch of 21 MX	Y
28.	Kill-Add third tax rate	Y	69.	African Relief/Farm Crdt	N
29.	Kill-Unocal tax provsns	Y	70.	Kill-Nuclear Freeze	Y
30.	Block Saudi arms sale (†)	N	71.	Kill-Void Title IX Narrow	Y
31.	Kill-Bar school busing	N	72.	Raise drinking age to 21	N
32.	Prohibit Saudi arms sale	N	73.	Kill-Reduce mil in Europe	Y
33.	Nicaraguan contra aid	Y	74.	Kill-Bar $ for contras	Y
34.	Bar all aid to Nicaragua	N	75.	Kill-No new MXs in 1985	Y
35.	Balanced budget amendment	Y	76.	Kill-Move MX $ to non-nuc	Y
36.	Balanced bdgt substitute	Y	77.	Deficit reduction-$140b	Y
37.	Conrail sale	Y	78.	Kill-Req auth for troops	Y
38.	Revise farm programs	Y	79.	School Prayer amendment	Y
39.	Kill-New oil import fee	Y	80.	Cap punish-certain crimes	Y
40.	Spending cuts, tax incres	Y	81.	Bar govt off from taping	N
41.	Textile import quotas	Y	82.	Martin L. King holiday	N
42.	Kill-Exmpt vets from cuts	Y	83.	Auth marines in Lebanon	Y
43.	Kill-Bar inmate abortn $	N	84.	Anti-abortion amendment	Y
44.	Textile import quotas (§)	N	85.	Highway-Gas tax bill	Y
45.	Kill-Eliminate Amtrak $	N	86.	Delete job creation amend	Y
46.	Kill-Incrs motor fuel tax	Y	87.	Kill-Tobacco price supprt	Y
47.	Set max allow deficits	Y	88.	Emergency housing aid	N
48.	20% minimum tax on corps	N	89.	Nullify oil decontrol	N
49.	Bar $ to toxic victims	Y	90.	Target tax cuts-mid class	N
50.	Seasonal workers in US	Y	91.	Tax Indexing	Y
51.	Kill-School prayer cases	N	92.	Kill-Oppose SS benft cuts	Y
52.	Line-item veto	Y	93.	Disapprove Saudi AWACS	N
53.	South Africa sanctions	N	94.	Anti-busing rider	Y
54.	Ease '68 Gun Control Act	Y	95.	Disapprove oil import fee	Y
55.	Kill-14 day handgun wait	Y	96.	Domestic violence funds	N
56.	Kill-Gun dlr inspections	Y	97.	Trucking Deregulation	Y
57.	Kill-Keep '68 Gun Con Act	Y	98.	Overturn India fuel sale	N
58.	Nicarag humanitarian aid	Y	99.	Mil draft registration	N
59.	Bar ASAT testing	N	100.	Chrysler Loan Guarantees	N
60.	Delete chemical weapons	N	101.	Nuclear plant moratorium	N
61.	Delete 21 MX missiles	N	102.	Abolish electoral college	N
62.	Kill-15% min tax on corps	Y	103.	Kill-Lmt ct-ordered bus	N
63.	Kill-Restore Soc Sec COLA	Y	104.	Airline Deregulation	Y
64.	Freeze all funding	N	105.	Disappr Mideast jet sales	N
65.	Cut def;raise taxes, COLA	N	106.	Natural gas deregulation	Y
66.	Keep existing SS COLAs	N	107.	Prohibit neutron bomb	N
67.	Aid to Nicaraguan rebels	Y	108.	Financial disclosure-off	Y

Presidential Support Score: 1986 - 93% 1985 - 78%

SYMMS, STEVEN D. [Republican]. Term Began/Expires: 1981/1986. Prior Terms: House: 1972-80. Born: August 23, 1938; Nampa, Idaho. Education: University of Idaho (B.S.). Military Service: U.S. Marines, 1960-63. Occupation: Vice president, personnel and production manager, Symms Fruit Ranch; treasurer, American Conservative Union.

1.	Immigration Reform	X	8.	South Africa sanctions	N
2.	So Afr Sanc-veto override	N	9.	Kill-So Africa sanctions	Y
3.	Kill-Death pnlty drug bil	N	10.	Kill-So Africa sanct (*)	Y
4.	Kill-Mil use in drug war	Y	11.	Nicaraguan contra aid	Y
5.	Tax Overhaul	Y	12.	Terminate contra aid	N
6.	Raise speed limit	Y	13.	Kill-Prohibit contra fnds	Y
7.	Across-the-board cuts	N	14.	Kill-Stop CIA contra fndg	Y

SYMMS, STEVEN D. (Cont.)

15. Kill-Bar nuclr tsts w/SDI Y
16. Kill-Bar ASAT testing Y
17. Nuclear test ban treaty N
18. Prohibit sale of Stinger N
19. Delete Bigeye chem bomb N
20. Bar binary chem weapons N
21. Kill-SDI funding Y
22. Kill-AIDS ins dscriminatn ?
23. Kill-$10 bbl oil tariff Y
24. Kill-Repl wndfl prfts tax N
25. Repeal balanced bdgt amdt N
26. Tax amnesty provisions ?
27. Kill-Tax amnesty subst ?
28. Kill-Add third tax rate Y
29. Kill-Unocal tax provsns Y
30. Block Saudi arms sale (†) Y
31. Kill-Bar school busing N
32. Prohibit Saudi arms sale Y
33. Nicaraguan contra aid Y
34. Bar all aid to Nicaragua N
35. Balanced budget amendment Y
36. Balanced bdgt substitute N
37. Conrail sale Y
38. Revise farm programs Y
39. Kill-New oil import fee Y
40. Spending cuts, tax incres Y
41. Textile import quotas N
42. Kill-Exmpt vets from cuts Y
43. Kill-Bar inmate abortn $ N
44. Textile import quotas (§) N
45. Kill-Eliminate Amtrak $ N
46. Kill-Incrs motor fuel tax Y
47. Set max allow deficits Y
48. 20% minimum tax on corps N
49. Bar $ to toxic victims Y
50. Seasonal workers in US Y
51. Kill-School prayer cases N
52. Line-item veto Y
53. South Africa sanctions N
54. Ease '68 Gun Control Act Y
55. Kill-14 day handgun wait Y
56. Kill-Gun dlr inspections Y
57. Kill-Keep '68 Gun Con Act Y
58. Nicarag humanitarian aid Y
59. Bar ASAT testing N
60. Delete chemical weapons N
61. Delete 21 MX missiles N
62. Kill-15% min tax on corps Y
63. Kill-Restore Soc Sec COLA Y
64. Freeze all funding N
65. Cut def;raise taxes, COLA N
66. Keep existing SS COLAs N
67. Aid to Nicaraguan rebels Y
68. Reaffirm purch of 21 MX Y
69. African Relief/Farm Crdt N
70. Kill-Nuclear Freeze Y
71. Kill-Void Title IX Narrow Y
72. Raise drinking age to 21 N
73. Kill-Reduce mil in Europe ?
74. Kill-Bar $ for contras Y
75. Kill-No new MXs in 1985 Y
76. Kill-Move MX $ to non-nuc Y
77. Deficit reduction-$140b Y
78. Kill-Req auth for troops Y
79. School Prayer amendment Y
80. Cap punish-certain crimes Y
81. Bar govt off from taping N
82. Martin L. King holiday N
83. Auth marines in Lebanon Y
84. Anti-abortion amendment Y
85. Highway-Gas tax bill Y
86. Delete job creation amend Y
87. Kill-Tobacco price supprt Y
88. Emergency housing aid N
89. Nullify oil decontrol N
90. Target tax cuts-mid class N
91. Tax Indexing Y
92. Kill-Oppose SS benft cuts Y
93. Disapprove Saudi AWACS N
94. Anti-busing rider Y

Presidential Support Score: 1986 - 89% 1985 - 81%

I L L I N O I S

DIXON, ALAN J. [Democrat]. Term Began/Expires: 1981/1986. Born: July 7, 1927; Belleville, Ill. Education: University of Illinois; Washington (St. Louis) University Law School. Military Service: U.S. Navy. Occupation: Police magistrate (1949); Illinois representative (1951-63); Illinois senator (1963-71); Illinois treasurer (1971-77); Illinois secretary of state (1977-81).

1. Immigration Reform Y
2. So Afr Sanc-veto override Y
3. Kill-Death pnlty drug bil N
4. Kill-Mil use in drug war N
5. Tax Overhaul Y
6. Raise speed limit N
7. Across-the-board cuts N
8. South Africa sanctions Y

DIXON, ALAN J. (Cont.)

9. Kill-So Africa sanctions N
10. Kill-So Africa sanct (*) N
11. Nicaraguan contra aid Y
12. Terminate contra aid Y
13. Kill-Prohibit contra fnds Y
14. Kill-Stop CIA contra fndg Y
15. Kill-Bar nuclr tsts w/SDI Y
16. Kill-Bar ASAT testing Y
17. Nuclear test ban treaty Y
18. Prohibit sale of Stinger N
19. Delete Bigeye chem bomb Y
20. Bar binary chem weapons N
21. Kill-SDI funding N
22. Kill-AIDS ins dscriminatn N
23. Kill-$10 bbl oil tariff Y
24. Kill-Repl wndfl prfts tax N
25. Repeal balanced bdgt amdt N
26. Tax amnesty provisions +
27. Kill-Tax amnesty subst -
28. Kill-Add third tax rate Y
29. Kill-Unocal tax provsns N
30. Block Saudi arms sale (†) Y
31. Kill-Bar school busing Y
32. Prohibit Saudi arms sale Y
33. Nicaraguan contra aid Y
34. Bar all aid to Nicaragua N
35. Balanced budget amendment Y
36. Balanced bdgt substitute N
37. Conrail sale N
38. Revise farm programs N
39. Kill-New oil import fee Y
40. Spending cuts, tax incres Y
41. Textile import quotas Y
42. Kill-Exmpt vets from cuts N
43. Kill-Bar inmate abortn $ N
44. Textile import quotas (§) Y
45. Kill-Eliminate Amtrak $ Y
46. Kill-Incrs motor fuel tax Y
47. Set max allow deficits Y
48. 20% minimum tax on corps N
49. Bar $ to toxic victims N
50. Seasonal workers in US N
51. Kill-School prayer cases Y
52. Line-item veto Y
53. South Africa sanctions Y
54. Ease '68 Gun Control Act Y
55. Kill-14 day handgun wait Y
56. Kill-Gun dlr inspections Y
57. Kill-Keep '68 Gun Con Act N
58. Nicarag humanitarian aid Y
59. Bar ASAT testing ?
60. Delete chemical weapons N
61. Delete 21 MX missiles Y
62. Kill-15% min tax on corps Y
63. Kill-Restore Soc Sec COLA N
64. Freeze all funding Y
65. Cut def;raise taxes, COLA N
66. Keep existing SS COLAs Y
67. Aid to Nicaraguan rebels Y
68. Reaffirm purch of 21 MX N
69. African Relief/Farm Crdt Y
70. Kill-Nuclear Freeze N
71. Kill-Void Title IX Narrow N
72. Raise drinking age to 21 +
73. Kill-Reduce mil in Europe N
74. Kill-Bar $ for contras Y
75. Kill-No new MXs in 1985 N
76. Kill-Move MX $ to non-nuc N
77. Deficit reduction-$140b N
78. Kill-Req auth for troops N
79. School Prayer amendment N
80. Cap punish-certain crimes Y
81. Bar govt off from taping Y
82. Martin L. King holiday Y
83. Auth marines in Lebanon N
84. Anti-abortion amendment N
85. Highway-Gas tax bill Y
86. Delete job creation amend N
87. Kill-Tobacco price supprt N
88. Emergency housing aid Y
89. Nullify oil decontrol N
90. Target tax cuts-mid class N
91. Tax Indexing Y
92. Kill-Oppose SS benft cuts N
93. Disapprove Saudi AWACS Y
94. Anti-busing rider Y

Presidential Support Score: 1986 - 52% 1985 - 46%

SIMON, PAUL [Democrat]. Term Began/Expires: 1985/1990. Prior Terms: House: 1975-84. Born: November 29, 1928; Eugene, Ore. Education: University of Oregon; Dana College. Occupation: Teacher; newspaper editor; (1947-66); Illinois lieutenant governor (1969-73); Illinois representative (1954-62); Illinois senator (1962-69).

1. Immigration Reform Y
2. So Afr Sanc-veto override Y
3. Kill-Death pnlty drug bil ?
4. Kill-Mil use in drug war ?
5. Tax Overhaul -
6. Raise speed limit N
7. Across-the-board cuts N
8. South Africa sanctions Y
9. Kill-So Africa sanctions N
10. Kill-So Africa sanct (*) N

SIMON, PAUL (Cont.)

11. Nicaraguan contra aid N
12. Terminate contra aid Y
13. Kill-Prohibit contra fnds N
14. Kill-Stop CIA contra fndg N
15. Kill-Bar nuclr tsts w/SDI N
16. Kill-Bar ASAT testing N
17. Nuclear test ban treaty Y
18. Prohibit sale of Stinger Y
19. Delete Bigeye chem bomb Y
20. Bar binary chem weapons Y
21. Kill-SDI funding N
22. Kill-AIDS ins dscriminatn Y
23. Kill-$10 bbl oil tariff N
24. Kill-Repl wndfl prfts tax Y
25. Repeal balanced bdgt amdt N
26. Tax amnesty provisions N
27. Kill-Tax amnesty subst Y
28. Kill-Add third tax rate N
29. Kill-Unocal tax provsns N
30. Block Saudi arms sale (†) Y
31. Kill-Bar school busing Y
32. Prohibit Saudi arms sale Y
33. Nicaraguan contra aid N
34. Bar all aid to Nicaragua Y
35. Balanced budget amendment Y
36. Balanced bdgt substitute N
37. Conrail sale N
38. Revise farm programs N
39. Kill-New oil import fee N
40. Spending cuts, tax incres Y
41. Textile import quotas Y
42. Kill-Exmpt vets from cuts N
43. Kill-Bar inmate abortn $?
44. Textile import quotas (§) Y
45. Kill-Eliminate Amtrak $ Y
46. Kill-Incrs motor fuel tax Y
47. Set max allow deficits Y
48. 20% minimum tax on corps N
49. Bar $ to toxic victims N
50. Seasonal workers in US N
51. Kill-School prayer cases Y
52. Line-item veto N
53. South Africa sanctions ?
54. Ease '68 Gun Control Act ?
55. Kill-14 day handgun wait ?
56. Kill-Gun dlr inspections ?
57. Kill-Keep '68 Gun Con Act ?
58. Nicarag humanitarian aid N
59. Bar ASAT testing Y
60. Delete chemical weapons Y
61. Delete 21 MX missiles Y
62. Kill-15% min tax on corps N
63. Kill-Restore Soc Sec COLA N
64. Freeze all funding Y
65. Cut def;raise taxes, COLA Y
66. Keep existing SS COLAs Y
67. Aid to Nicaraguan rebels N
68. Reaffirm purch of 21 MX N
69. African Relief/Farm Crdt Y

Presidential Support Score: 1986 - 20% 1985 - 25%

INDIANA

LUGAR, RICHARD G. [Republican]. Term Began/Expires: 1983/1988. Prior Terms: Senate: 1977-82. Born: April 4, 1932; Indianapolis, Ind. Education: Denison University. Occupation: Businessman; Indianapolis mayor (1968-74); visiting professor, Indiana Central University.

1. Immigration Reform Y
2. So Afr Sanc-veto override Y
3. Kill-Death pnlty drug bil N
4. Kill-Mil use in drug war Y
5. Tax Overhaul Y
6. Raise speed limit Y
7. Across-the-board cuts N
8. South Africa sanctions Y
9. Kill-So Africa sanctions Y
10. Kill-So Africa sanct (*) Y
11. Nicaraguan contra aid Y
12. Terminate contra aid N
13. Kill-Prohibit contra fnds Y
14. Kill-Stop CIA contra fndg Y
15. Kill-Bar nuclr tsts w/SDI Y
16. Kill-Bar ASAT testing Y
17. Nuclear test ban treaty N
18. Prohibit sale of Stinger N
19. Delete Bigeye chem bomb N
20. Bar binary chem weapons N
21. Kill-SDI funding Y
22. Kill-AIDS ins dscriminatn N
23. Kill-$10 bbl oil tariff Y
24. Kill-Repl wndfl prfts tax N
25. Repeal balanced bdgt amdt N
26. Tax amnesty provisions N
27. Kill-Tax amnesty subst Y
28. Kill-Add third tax rate Y
29. Kill-Unocal tax provsns Y
30. Block Saudi arms sale (†) N
31. Kill-Bar school busing Y
32. Prohibit Saudi arms sale N

LUGAR, RICHARD G. (Cont.)

33. Nicaraguan contra aid Y
34. Bar all aid to Nicaragua N
35. Balanced budget amendment Y
36. Balanced bdgt substitute N
37. Conrail sale +
38. Revise farm programs Y
39. Kill-New oil import fee Y
40. Spending cuts, tax incres Y
41. Textile import quotas N
42. Kill-Exmpt vets from cuts Y
43. Kill-Bar inmate abortn $ N
44. Textile import quotas (§) N
45. Kill-Eliminate Amtrak $ Y
46. Kill-Incrs motor fuel tax Y
47. Set max allow deficits Y
48. 20% minimum tax on corps N
49. Bar $ to toxic victims Y
50. Seasonal workers in US Y
51. Kill-School prayer cases Y
52. Line-item veto Y
53. South Africa sanctions Y
54. Ease '68 Gun Control Act Y
55. Kill-14 day handgun wait Y
56. Kill-Gun dlr inspections Y
57. Kill-Keep '68 Gun Con Act Y
58. Nicarag humanitarian aid Y
59. Bar ASAT testing N
60. Delete chemical weapons N
61. Delete 21 MX missiles N
62. Kill-15% min tax on corps Y
63. Kill-Restore Soc Sec COLA Y
64. Freeze all funding N
65. Cut def;raise taxes, COLA N
66. Keep existing SS COLAs Y
67. Aid to Nicaraguan rebels Y
68. Reaffirm purch of 21 MX Y
69. African Relief/Farm Crdt N
70. Kill-Nuclear Freeze Y
71. Kill-Void Title IX Narrow Y
72. Raise drinking age to 21 Y
73. Kill-Reduce mil in Europe Y
74. Kill-Bar $ for contras Y
75. Kill-No new MXs in 1985 Y
76. Kill-Move MX $ to non-nuc Y
77. Deficit reduction-$140b Y
78. Kill-Req auth for troops Y
79. School Prayer amendment Y
80. Cap punish-certain crimes Y
81. Bar govt off from taping N
82. Martin L. King holiday Y
83. Auth marines in Lebanon Y
84. Anti-abortion amendment Y
85. Highway-Gas tax bill Y
86. Delete job creation amend Y
87. Kill-Tobacco price supprt N
88. Emergency housing aid Y
89. Nullify oil decontrol N
90. Target tax cuts-mid class N
91. Tax indexing Y
92. Kill-Oppose SS benft cuts Y
93. Disapprove Saudi AWACS N
94. Anti-busing rider Y
95. Disapprove oil import fee Y
96. Domestic violence funds N
97. Trucking Deregulation Y
98. Overturn India fuel sale Y
99. Mil draft registration Y
100. Chrysler Loan Guarantees Y
101. Nuclear plant moratorium N
102. Abolish electoral college N
103. Kill-Lmt ct-ordered bus N
104. Airline Deregulation Y
105. Disappr Mideast jet sales N
106. Natural gas deregulation Y
107. Prohibit neutron bomb N
108. Financial disclosure-off Y

Presidential Support Score: 1986 - 89% 1985 - 89%

QUAYLE, DAN [Republican]. Term Began/Expires: 1981/1986. Prior Terms: House: 1976-80. Born: February 4, 1947; Indianapolis, Ind. Education: DePauw University (B.A.); Indiana University Law School (J.D.). Occupation: Attorney; chief investigator, Consumer Protection Division, Indiana Attorney General (1971-73); director, Inheritance Tax Division, Indiana Department of Revenue (1973-74); board member and associate publisher, Huntington Herald-Press; trustee Huntington College.

1. Immigration Reform Y
2. So Afr Sanc-veto override Y
3. Kill-Death pnlty drug bil ?
4. Kill-Mil use in drug war ?
5. Tax Overhaul Y
6. Raise speed limit ?
7. Across-the-board cuts N
8. South Africa sanctions Y
9. Kill-So Africa sanctions Y
10. Kill-So Africa sanct (*) Y
11. Nicaraguan contra aid Y
12. Terminate contra aid N
13. Kill-Prohibit contra fnds Y
14. Kill-Stop CIA contra fndg Y
15. Kill-Bar nuclr tsts w/SDI Y
16. Kill-Bar ASAT testing Y

QUAYLE, DAN (Cont.)

17. Nuclear test ban treaty	N		56. Kill-Gun dlr inspections	Y
18. Prohibit sale of Stinger	N		57. Kill-Keep '68 Gun Con Act	Y
19. Delete Bigeye chem bomb	N		58. Nicarag humanitarian aid	Y
20. Bar binary chem weapons	N		59. Bar ASAT testing	N
21. Kill-SDI funding	Y		60. Delete chemical weapons	N
22. Kill-AIDS ins dscriminatn	N		61. Delete 21 MX missiles	N
23. Kill-$10 bbl oil tariff	Y		62. Kill-15% min tax on corps	Y
24. Kill-Repl wndfl prfts tax	N		63. Kill-Restore Soc Sec COLA	Y
25. Repeal balanced bdgt amdt	N		64. Freeze all funding	N
26. Tax amnesty provisions	N		65. Cut def;raise taxes, COLA	N
27. Kill-Tax amnesty subst	Y		66. Keep existing SS COLAs	Y
28. Kill-Add third tax rate	Y		67. Aid to Nicaraguan rebels	Y
29. Kill-Unocal tax provsns	Y		68. Reaffirm purch of 21 MX	Y
30. Block Saudi arms sale (†)	N		69. African Relief/Farm Crdt	N
31. Kill-Bar school busing	N		70. Kill-Nuclear Freeze	Y
32. Prohibit Saudi arms sale	N		71. Kill-Void Title IX Narrow	Y
33. Nicaraguan contra aid	Y		72. Raise drinking age to 21	Y
34. Bar all aid to Nicaragua	N		73. Kill-Reduce mil in Europe	Y
35. Balanced budget amendment	Y		74. Kill-Bar $ for contras	Y
36. Balanced bdgt substitute	N		75. Kill-No new MXs in 1985	Y
37. Conrail sale	Y		76. Kill-Move MX $ to non-nuc	Y
38. Revise farm programs	Y		77. Deficit reduction-$140b	Y
39. Kill-New oil import fee	Y		78. Kill-Req auth for troops	Y
40. Spending cuts, tax incres	Y		79. School Prayer amendment	Y
41. Textile import quotas	N		80. Cap punish-certain crimes	Y
42. Kill-Exmpt vets from cuts	Y		81. Bar govt off from taping	N
43. Kill-Bar inmate abortn $	N		82. Martin L. King holiday	Y
44. Textile import quotas (§)	N		83. Auth marines in Lebanon	Y
45. Kill-Eliminate Amtrak $	Y		84. Anti-abortion amendment	Y
46. Kill-Incrs motor fuel tax	Y		85. Highway-Gas tax bill	Y
47. Set max allow deficits	Y		86. Delete job creation amend	Y
48. 20% minimum tax on corps	N		87. Kill-Tobacco price supprt	N
49. Bar $ to toxic victims	Y		88. Emergency housing aid	Y
50. Seasonal workers in US	Y		89. Nullify oil decontrol	N
51. Kill-School prayer cases	N		90. Target tax cuts-mid class	N
52. Line-item veto	Y		91. Tax Indexing	Y
53. South Africa sanctions	Y		92. Kill-Oppose SS benft cuts	Y
54. Ease '68 Gun Control Act	Y		93. Disapprove Saudi AWACS	N
55. Kill-14 day handgun wait	Y		94. Anti-busing rider	Y

Presidential Support Score: 1986 - 91% 1985 - 88%

I O W A

GRASSLEY, CHARLES E. [Republican] Term Began/Expires: 1981/1986. Prior Terms: House: 1975-80. Born: September 17, 1933; New Hartford, Iowa. Education: University of Northern Iowa (B.A., M.A.). Occupation: Iowa legislator (1959-74); farmer.

1. Immigration Reform	Y		10. Kill-So Africa sanct (*)	Y
2. So Afr Sanc-veto override	Y		11. Nicaraguan contra aid	Y
3. Kill-Death pnlty drug bil	N		12. Terminate contra aid	N
4. Kill-Mil use in drug war	N		13. Kill-Prohibit contra fnds	Y
5. Tax Overhaul	Y		14. Kill-Stop CIA contra fndg	N
6. Raise speed limit	Y		15. Kill-Bar nuclr tsts w/SDI	Y
7. Across-the-board cuts	N		16. Kill-Bar ASAT testing	Y
8. South Africa sanctions	Y		17. Nuclear test ban treaty	Y
9. Kill-So Africa sanctions	N		18. Prohibit sale of Stinger	N

GRASSLEY, CHARLES E. (Cont.)

19. Delete Bigeye chem bomb Y
20. Bar binary chem weapons Y
21. Kill-SDI funding N
22. Kill-AIDS ins dscriminatn N
23. Kill-$10 bbl oil tariff Y
24. Kill-Repl wndfl prfts tax Y
25. Repeal balanced bdgt amdt N
26. Tax amnesty provisions Y
27. Kill-Tax amnesty subst Y
28. Kill-Add third tax rate Y
29. Kill-Unocal tax provsns N
30. Block Saudi arms sale (†) Y
31. Kill-Bar school busing N
32. Prohibit Saudi arms sale Y
33. Nicaraguan contra aid Y
34. Bar all aid to Nicaragua N
35. Balanced budget amendment Y
36. Balanced bdgt substitute N
37. Conrail sale N
38. Revise farm programs N
39. Kill-New oil import fee Y
40. Spending cuts, tax incres Y
41. Textile import quotas N
42. Kill-Exmpt vets from cuts Y
43. Kill-Bar inmate abortn $ N
44. Textile import quotas (§) N
45. Kill-Eliminate Amtrak $ Y
46. Kill-Incrs motor fuel tax Y
47. Set max allow deficits Y
48. 20% minimum tax on corps N
49. Bar $ to toxic victims Y
50. Seasonal workers in US N
51. Kill-School prayer cases N
52. Line-item veto Y
53. South Africa sanctions Y
54. Ease '68 Gun Control Act Y
55. Kill-14 day handgun wait Y
56. Kill-Gun dlr inspections Y
57. Kill-Keep '68 Gun Con Act Y
58. Nicarag humanitarian aid Y
59. Bar ASAT testing N
60. Delete chemical weapons Y
61. Delete 21 MX missiles N
62. Kill-15% min tax on corps Y
63. Kill-Restore Soc Sec COLA Y
64. Freeze all funding Y
65. Cut def;raise taxes, COLA N
66. Keep existing SS COLAs Y
67. Aid to Nicaraguan rebels Y
68. Reaffirm purch of 21 MX N
69. African Relief/Farm Crdt Y
70. Kill-Nuclear Freeze Y
71. Kill-Void Title IX Narrow Y
72. Raise drinking age to 21 N
73. Kill-Reduce mil in Europe N
74. Kill-Bar $ for contras Y
75. Kill-No new MXs in 1985 N
76. Kill-Move MX $ to non-nuc Y
77. Deficit reduction-$140b Y
78. Kill-Req auth for troops Y
79. School Prayer amendment Y
80. Cap punish-certain crimes Y
81. Bar govt off from taping N
82. Martin L. King holiday N
83. Auth marines in Lebanon Y
84. Anti-abortion amendment Y
85. Highway-Gas tax bill Y
86. Delete job creation amend Y
87. Kill-Tobacco price supprt Y
88. Emergency housing aid Y
89. Nullify oil decontrol N
90. Target tax cuts-mid class N
91. Tax Indexing Y
92. Kill-Oppose SS benft cuts Y
93. Disapprove Saudi AWACS N
94. Anti-busing rider Y

Presidential Support Score: 1986 - 68% 1985 - 66%

HARKIN, TOM [Democrat]. Term Began/Expires: 1985/1990. Prior Terms: House: 1975-84. Born: November 19, 1939; Cumming, Iowa. Education: Iowa State University (B.S.); Catholic University of America Law School. Military Service: U.S. Navy, 1962-67. Occupation: Legislative assistant; attorney.

1. Immigration Reform Y
2. So Afr Sanc-veto override Y
3. Kill-Death pnlty drug bil Y
4. Kill-Mil use in drug war Y
5. Tax Overhaul Y
6. Raise speed limit Y
7. Across-the-board cuts N
8. South Africa sanctions Y
9. Kill-So Africa sanctions N
10. Kill-So Africa sanct (*) N
11. Nicaraguan contra aid N
12. Terminate contra aid Y
13. Kill-Prohibit contra fnds N
14. Kill-Stop CIA contra fndg N
15. Kill-Bar nuclr tsts w/SDI N
16. Kill-Bar ASAT testing N
17. Nuclear test ban treaty Y
18. Prohibit sale of Stinger Y
19. Delete Bigeye chem bomb Y
20. Bar binary chem weapons Y
21. Kill-SDI funding N
22. Kill-AIDS ins dscriminatn Y

HARKIN, TOM (Cont.)

23. Kill-$10 bbl oil tariff	Y	47. Set max allow deficits	N
24. Kill-Repl wndfl prfts tax	Y	48. 20% minimum tax on corps	N
25. Repeal balanced bdgt amdt	Y	49. Bar $ to toxic victims	N
26. Tax amnesty provisions	N	50. Seasonal workers in US	N
27. Kill-Tax amnesty subst	Y	51. Kill-School prayer cases	Y
28. Kill-Add third tax rate	N	52. Line-item veto	N
29. Kill-Unocal tax provsns	N	53. South Africa sanctions	Y
30. Block Saudi arms sale (†)	Y	54. Ease '68 Gun Control Act	Y
31. Kill-Bar school busing	?	55. Kill-14 day handgun wait	N
32. Prohibit Saudi arms sale	Y	56. Kill-Gun dlr inspections	N
33. Nicaraguan contra aid	N	57. Kill-Keep '68 Gun Con Act	N
34. Bar all aid to Nicaragua	Y	58. Nicarag humanitarian aid	N
35. Balanced budget amendment	Y	59. Bar ASAT testing	+
36. Balanced bdgt substitute	Y	60. Delete chemical weapons	Y
37. Conrail sale	N	61. Delete 21 MX missiles	Y
38. Revise farm programs	N	62. Kill-15% min tax on corps	N
39. Kill-New oil import fee	Y	63. Kill-Restore Soc Sec COLA	N
40. Spending cuts, tax incres	N	64. Freeze all funding	Y
41. Textile import quotas	N	65. Cut def;raise taxes, COLA	Y
42. Kill-Exmpt vets from cuts	N	66. Keep existing SS COLAs	Y
43. Kill-Bar inmate abortn $	Y	67. Aid to Nicaraguan rebels	N
44. Textile import quotas (§)	N	68. Reaffirm purch of 21 MX	N
45. Kill-Eliminate Amtrak $	Y	69. African Relief/Farm Crdt	Y
46. Kill-Incrs motor fuel tax	Y		

Presidential Support Score: 1986 - 20% 1985 - 22%

KANSAS

DOLE, ROBERT [Republican] Term Began/Expires: 1981/1986. Prior Terms: House: 1961-68. Senate: 1969-80. Born: July 22, 1923; Russell, Kan. Education: Washburn Municipal University (A.B., LL.B.); University of Kansas. Military Service: U.S. Army, WW II. Occupation: Kansas representative (1951-53); Russell county attorney (1953-61); attorney.

1. Immigration Reform	Y	23. Kill-$10 bbl oil tariff	Y
2. So Afr Sanc-veto override	N	24. Kill-Repl wndfl prfts tax	N
3. Kill-Death pnlty drug bil	N	25. Repeal balanced bdgt amdt	N
4. Kill-Mil use in drug war	Y	26. Tax amnesty provisions	N
5. Tax Overhaul	Y	27. Kill-Tax amnesty subst	Y
6. Raise speed limit	Y	28. Kill-Add third tax rate	Y
7. Across-the-board cuts	N	29. Kill-Unocal tax provsns	N
8. South Africa sanctions	Y	30. Block Saudi arms sale (†)	N
9. Kill-So Africa sanctions	Y	31. Kill-Bar school busing	N
10. Kill-So Africa sanct (*)	Y	32. Prohibit Saudi arms sale	N
11. Nicaraguan contra aid	Y	33. Nicaraguan contra aid	Y
12. Terminate contra aid	N	34. Bar all aid to Nicaragua	N
13. Kill-Prohibit contra fnds	Y	35. Balanced budget amendment	Y
14. Kill-Stop CIA contra fndg	Y	36. Balanced bdgt substitute	N
15. Kill-Bar nuclr tsts w/SDI	Y	37. Conrail sale	Y
16. Kill-Bar ASAT testing	Y	38. Revise farm programs	Y
17. Nuclear test ban treaty	N	39. Kill-New oil import fee	Y
18. Prohibit sale of Stinger	N	40. Spending cuts, tax incres	Y
19. Delete Bigeye chem bomb	N	41. Textile import quotas	Y
20. Bar binary chem weapons	N	42. Kill-Exmpt vets from cuts	Y
21. Kill-SDI funding	Y	43. Kill-Bar inmate abortn $	N
22. Kill-AIDS ins dscriminatn	N	44. Textile import quotas (§)	N

DOLE, ROBERT (Cont.)

45. Kill-Eliminate Amtrak $ N
46. Kill-Incrs motor fuel tax Y
47. Set max allow deficits Y
48. 20% minimum tax on corps N
49. Bar $ to toxic victims Y
50. Seasonal workers in US Y
51. Kill-School prayer cases N
52. Line-item veto Y
53. South Africa sanctions Y
54. Ease '68 Gun Control Act Y
55. Kill-14 day handgun wait Y
56. Kill-Gun dlr inspections Y
57. Kill-Keep '68 Gun Con Act Y
58. Nicarag humanitarian aid Y
59. Bar ASAT testing N
60. Delete chemical weapons N
61. Delete 21 MX missiles N
62. Kill-15% min tax on corps Y
63. Kill-Restore Soc Sec COLA Y
64. Freeze all funding N
65. Cut def;raise taxes, COLA N
66. Keep existing SS COLAs N
67. Aid to Nicaraguan rebels Y
68. Reaffirm purch of 21 MX Y
69. African Relief/Farm Crdt N
70. Kill-Nuclear Freeze Y
71. Kill-Void Title IX Narrow Y
72. Raise drinking age to 21 Y
73. Kill-Reduce mil in Europe Y
74. Kill-Bar $ for contras Y
75. Kill-No new MXs in 1985 Y
76. Kill-Move MX $ to non-nuc Y
77. Deficit reduction-$140b Y
78. Kill-Req auth for troops Y
79. School Prayer amendment Y
80. Cap punish-certain crimes Y
81. Bar govt off from taping N
82. Martin L. King holiday Y
83. Auth marines in Lebanon Y
84. Anti-abortion amendment Y
85. Highway-Gas tax bill Y
86. Delete job creation amend Y
87. Kill-Tobacco price supprt Y
88. Emergency housing aid N
89. Nullify oil decontrol X
90. Target tax cuts-mid class N
91. Tax Indexing Y
92. Kill-Oppose SS benft cuts Y
93. Disapprove Saudi AWACS N
94. Anti-busing rider Y
95. Disapprove oil import fee Y
96. Domestic violence funds N
97. Trucking Deregulation Y
98. Overturn India fuel sale Y
99. Mil draft registration N
100. Chrysler Loan Guarantees Y
101. Nuclear plant moratorium N
102. Abolish electoral college Y
103. Kill-Lmt ct-ordered bus N
104. Airline Deregulation Y
105. Disappr Mideast jet sales Y
106. Natural gas deregulation Y
107. Prohibit neutron bomb N
108. Financial disclosure-off Y

Presidential Support Score: 1986 - 93% 1985 - 92%

KASSEBAUM, NANCY LANDON [Republican] Term Began/Expires: 1985/1990. Prior Terms: Senate: 1979-84. Born: July 29, 1932, Topeka, Kan. Education: University of Kansas (B.A.); University of Michigan (M.A.). Occupation: Vice president, KFH, KBRA-FM radio stations.

1. Immigration Reform Y
2. So Afr Sanc-veto override Y
3. Kill-Death pnlty drug bil N
4. Kill-Mil use in drug war Y
5. Tax Overhaul Y
6. Raise speed limit ?
7. Across-the-board cuts N
8. South Africa sanctions Y
9. Kill-So Africa sanctions Y
10. Kill-So Africa sanct (*) Y
11. Nicaraguan contra aid Y
12. Terminate contra aid N
13. Kill-Prohibit contra fnds Y
14. Kill-Stop CIA contra fndg N
15. Kill-Bar nuclr tsts w/SDI Y
16. Kill-Bar ASAT testing N
17. Nuclear test ban treaty Y
18. Prohibit sale of Stinger Y
19. Delete Bigeye chem bomb Y
20. Bar binary chem weapons Y
21. Kill-SDI funding N
22. Kill-AIDS ins dscriminatn N
23. Kill-$10 bbl oil tariff Y
24. Kill-Repl wndfl prfts tax N
25. Repeal balanced bdgt amdt Y
26. Tax amnesty provisions Y
27. Kill-Tax amnesty subst N
28. Kill-Add third tax rate Y
29. Kill-Unocal tax provsns N
30. Block Saudi arms sale (†) N
31. Kill-Bar school busing N
32. Prohibit Saudi arms sale ?
33. Nicaraguan contra aid Y
34. Bar all aid to Nicaragua N

KASSEBAUM, NANCY LANDON (Cont.)

35. Balanced budget amendment N
36. Balanced bdgt substitute N
37. Conrail sale ?
38. Revise farm programs Y
39. Kill-New oil import fee Y
40. Spending cuts, tax incres Y
41. Textile import quotas N
42. Kill-Exmpt vets from cuts Y
43. Kill-Bar inmate abortn $ Y
44. Textile import quotas (§) N
45. Kill-Eliminate Amtrak $ Y
46. Kill-Incrs motor fuel tax Y
47. Set max allow deficits N
48. 20% minimum tax on corps N
49. Bar $ to toxic victims Y
50. Seasonal workers in US Y
51. Kill-School prayer cases Y
52. Line-item veto Y
53. South Africa sanctions Y
54. Ease '68 Gun Control Act Y
55. Kill-14 day handgun wait N
56. Kill-Gun dlr inspections Y
57. Kill-Keep '68 Gun Con Act N
58. Nicarag humanitarian aid Y
59. Bar ASAT testing N
60. Delete chemical weapons Y
61. Delete 21 MX missiles Y
62. Kill-15% min tax on corps Y
63. Kill-Restore Soc Sec COLA Y
64. Freeze all funding Y
65. Cut def;raise taxes, COLA N
66. Keep existing SS COLAs N
67. Aid to Nicaraguan rebels Y
68. Reaffirm purch of 21 MX N
69. African Relief/Farm Crdt N
70. Kill-Nuclear Freeze Y
71. Kill-Void Title IX Narrow Y
72. Raise drinking age to 21 Y
73. Kill-Reduce mil in Europe Y
74. Kill-Bar $ for contras N
75. Kill-No new MXs in 1985 Y
76. Kill-Move MX $ to non-nuc Y
77. Deficit reduction-$140b Y
78. Kill-Req auth for troops Y
79. School Prayer amendment N
80. Cap punish-certain crimes Y
81. Bar govt off from taping N
82. Martin L. King holiday Y
83. Auth marines in Lebanon Y
84. Anti-abortion amendment N
85. Highway-Gas tax bill Y
86. Delete job creation amend Y
87. Kill-Tobacco price supprt Y
88. Emergency housing aid N
89. Nullify oil decontrol N
90. Target tax cuts-mid class N
91. Tax Indexing Y
92. Kill-Oppose SS benft cuts Y
93. Disapprove Saudi AWACS N
94. Anti-busing rider Y
95. Disapprove oil import fee Y
96. Domestic violence funds N
97. Trucking Deregulation Y
98. Overturn India fuel sale Y
99. Mil draft registration N
100. Chrysler Loan Guarantees N
101. Nuclear plant moratorium N
102. Abolish electoral college N

Presidential Support Score: 1986 - 70% 1985 - 76%

K E N T U C K Y

McCONNELL, MITCH [Republican] Term Began/Expires: 1985/1990. Born: February 20, 1942; Colbert County, Ala. Education: University of Louisville (B.A.); University of Kentucky Law School (J.D.). Occupation: Attorney; chief legislative assistant (1968-70); deputy assistant U.S. attorney (1974-75); elected judge/executive.

1. Immigration Reform Y
2. So Afr Sanc-veto override Y
3. Kill-Death pnlty drug bil N
4. Kill-Mil use in drug war N
5. Tax Overhaul Y
6. Raise speed limit Y
7. Across-the-board cuts N
8. South Africa sanctions Y
9. Kill-So Africa sanctions Y
10. Kill-So Africa sanct (*) Y
11. Nicaraguan contra aid Y
12. Terminate contra aid N
13. Kill-Prohibit contra fnds Y
14. Kill-Stop CIA contra fndg Y
15. Kill-Bar nuclr tsts w/SDI Y
16. Kill-Bar ASAT testing Y
17. Nuclear test ban treaty N
18. Prohibit sale of Stinger N
19. Delete Bigeye chem bomb N
20. Bar binary chem weapons N
21. Kill-SDI funding Y
22. Kill-AIDS ins dscriminatn N
23. Kill-$10 bbl oil tariff Y
24. Kill-Repl wndfl prfts tax N
25. Repeal balanced bdgt amdt N
26. Tax amnesty provisions N

McCONNELL, MITCH (Cont.)

27. Kill-Tax amnesty subst Y
28. Kill-Add third tax rate Y
29. Kill-Unocal tax provsns Y
30. Block Saudi arms sale (†) N
31. Kill-Bar school busing N
32. Prohibit Saudi arms sale N
33. Nicaraguan contra aid Y
34. Bar all aid to Nicaragua N
35. Balanced budget amendment Y
36. Balanced bdgt substitute N
37. Conrail sale N
38. Revise farm programs Y
39. Kill-New oil import fee Y
40. Spending cuts, tax incres Y
41. Textile import quotas Y
42. Kill-Exmpt vets from cuts Y
43. Kill-Bar inmate abortn $?
44. Textile import quotas (§) Y
45. Kill-Eliminate Amtrak $ N
46. Kill-Incrs motor fuel tax Y
47. Set max allow deficits Y
48. 20% minimum tax on corps N
49. Bar $ to toxic victims Y
50. Seasonal workers in US Y
51. Kill-School prayer cases N
52. Line-item veto Y
53. South Africa sanctions Y
54. Ease '68 Gun Control Act Y
55. Kill-14 day handgun wait Y
56. Kill-Gun dlr inspections Y
57. Kill-Keep '68 Gun Con Act Y
58. Nicarag humanitarian aid Y
59. Bar ASAT testing N
60. Delete chemical weapons Y
61. Delete 21 MX missiles N
62. Kill-15% min tax on corps Y
63. Kill-Restore Soc Sec COLA Y
64. Freeze all funding N
65. Cut def;raise taxes, COLA N
66. Keep existing SS COLAs Y
67. Aid to Nicaraguan rebels Y
68. Reaffirm purch of 21 MX Y
69. African Relief/Farm Crdt N

Presidential Support Score: 1986 - 88% 1985 - 85%

FORD, WENDELL H. [Democrat] Term Began/Expires: 1981/1986. Prior Terms: Senate: 1975-80. Born: September 8, 1924; Daviess County, Ky. Education: University of Kentucky; Maryland School of Insurance. Military Service: U.S. Army, WW II. Occupation: Chief administrative assistant to governor (1959); Kentucky senator (1965-67); lieutenant governor (1967-71); governor (1971-74).

1. Immigration Reform N
2. So Afr Sanc-veto override Y
3. Kill-Death pnlty drug bil N
4. Kill-Mil use in drug war Y
5. Tax Overhaul Y
6. Raise speed limit Y
7. Across-the-board cuts N
8. South Africa sanctions Y
9. Kill-So Africa sanctions Y
10. Kill-So Africa sanct (*) Y
11. Nicaraguan contra aid N
12. Terminate contra aid Y
13. Kill-Prohibit contra fnds N
14. Kill-Stop CIA contra fndg N
15. Kill-Bar nuclr tsts w/SDI Y
16. Kill-Bar ASAT testing N
17. Nuclear test ban treaty Y
18. Prohibit sale of Stinger Y
19. Delete Bigeye chem bomb Y
20. Bar binary chem weapons Y
21. Kill-SDI funding N
22. Kill-AIDS ins dscriminatn N
23. Kill-$10 bbl oil tariff Y
24. Kill-Repl wndfl prfts tax N
25. Repeal balanced bdgt amdt N
26. Tax amnesty provisions N
27. Kill-Tax amnesty subst Y
28. Kill-Add third tax rate Y
29. Kill-Unocal tax provsns N
30. Block Saudi arms sale (†) Y
31. Kill-Bar school busing N
32. Prohibit Saudi arms sale Y
33. Nicaraguan contra aid N
34. Bar all aid to Nicaragua Y
35. Balanced budget amendment Y
36. Balanced bdgt substitute Y
37. Conrail sale N
38. Revise farm programs Y
39. Kill-New oil import fee N
40. Spending cuts, tax incres Y
41. Textile import quotas Y
42. Kill-Exmpt vets from cuts N
43. Kill-Bar inmate abortn $ N
44. Textile import quotas (§) Y
45. Kill-Eliminate Amtrak $ Y
46. Kill-Incrs motor fuel tax Y
47. Set max allow deficits Y
48. 20% minimum tax on corps N
49. Bar $ to toxic victims N
50. Seasonal workers in US N
51. Kill-School prayer cases N
52. Line-item veto N

FORD, WENDELL H. (Cont.)

53. South Africa sanctions Y
54. Ease '68 Gun Control Act Y
55. Kill-14 day handgun wait Y
56. Kill-Gun dlr inspections Y
57. Kill-Keep '68 Gun Con Act Y
58. Nicarag humanitarian aid Y
59. Bar ASAT testing N
60. Delete chemical weapons Y
61. Delete 21 MX missiles Y
62. Kill-15% min tax on corps Y
63. Kill-Restore Soc Sec COLA N
64. Freeze all funding N
65. Cut def;raise taxes, COLA Y
66. Keep existing SS COLAs Y
67. Aid to Nicaraguan rebels N
68. Reaffirm purch of 21 MX N
69. African Relief/Farm Crdt Y
70. Kill-Nuclear Freeze N
71. Kill-Void Title IX Narrow N
72. Raise drinking age to 21 Y
73. Kill-Reduce mil in Europe N
74. Kill-Bar $ for contras N
75. Kill-No new MXs in 1985 N
76. Kill-Move MX $ to non-nuc N
77. Deficit reduction-$140b N
78. Kill-Req auth for troops N
79. School Prayer amendment Y
80. Cap punish-certain crimes Y
81. Bar govt off from taping Y
82. Martin L. King holiday Y
83. Auth marines in Lebanon N
84. Anti-abortion amendment Y
85. Highway-Gas tax bill N
86. Delete job creation amend N
87. Kill-Tobacco price supprt Y
88. Emergency housing aid Y
89. Nullify oil decontrol N
90. Target tax cuts-mid class Y
91. Tax Indexing N
92. Kill-Oppose SS benft cuts N
93. Disapprove Saudi AWACS Y
94. Anti-busing rider Y
95. Disapprove oil import fee Y
96. Domestic violence funds Y
97. Trucking Deregulation Y
98. Overturn India fuel sale Y
99. Mil draft registration Y
100. Chrysler Loan Guarantees Y
101. Nuclear plant moratorium Y
102. Abolish electoral college Y
103. Kill-Lmt ct-ordered bus N
104. Airline Deregulation Y
105. Disappr Mideast jet sales Y
106. Natural gas deregulation Y
107. Prohibit neutron bomb N
108. Financial disclosure-off ?

Presidential Support Score: 1986 - 35% 1985 - 39%

LOUISIANA

JOHNSTON, J. BENNETT [Democrat] Term Began/Expires: 1985/1990. Prior Terms: Senate: 1973-84. Born: June 10, 1932; Shreveport, La. Education: Washington and Lee University; United States Military Academy; Louisiana State University Law School (LL.B.). Military Service: U.S. Army, 1956-59. Occupation: Louisiana representative (1964-68); Louisiana senator (1968-1972).

1. Immigration Reform Y
2. So Afr Sanc-veto override Y
3. Kill-Death pnlty drug bil N
4. Kill-Mil use in drug war Y
5. Tax Overhaul Y
6. Raise speed limit Y
7. Across-the-board cuts N
8. South Africa sanctions Y
9. Kill-So Africa sanctions N
10. Kill-So Africa sanct (*) N
11. Nicaraguan contra aid Y
12. Terminate contra aid Y
13. Kill-Prohibit contra fnds Y
14. Kill-Stop CIA contra fndg Y
15. Kill-Bar nuclr tsts w/SDI N
16. Kill-Bar ASAT testing N
17. Nuclear test ban treaty Y
18. Prohibit sale of Stinger Y
19. Delete Bigeye chem bomb Y
20. Bar binary chem weapons N
21. Kill-SDI funding N
22. Kill-AIDS ins dscriminatn Y
23. Kill-$10 bbl oil tariff N
24. Kill-Repl wndfl prfts tax N
25. Repeal balanced bdgt amdt Y
26. Tax amnesty provisions Y
27. Kill-Tax amnesty subst N
28. Kill-Add third tax rate Y
29. Kill-Unocal tax provsns N
30. Block Saudi arms sale (†) Y
31. Kill-Bar school busing N
32. Prohibit Saudi arms sale Y
33. Nicaraguan contra aid Y
34. Bar all aid to Nicaragua N

JOHNSTON, J. BENNETT (Cont.)

35. Balanced budget amendment Y
36. Balanced bdgt substitute Y
37. Conrail sale Y
38. Revise farm programs Y
39. Kill-New oil import fee Y
40. Spending cuts, tax incres Y
41. Textile import quotas Y
42. Kill-Exmpt vets from cuts N
43. Kill-Bar inmate abortn $ N
44. Textile import quotas (§) Y
45. Kill-Eliminate Amtrak $ Y
46. Kill-Incrs motor fuel tax Y
47. Set max allow deficits N
48. 20% minimum tax on corps Y
49. Bar $ to toxic victims Y
50. Seasonal workers in US N
51. Kill-School prayer cases N
52. Line-item veto N
53. South Africa sanctions Y
54. Ease '68 Gun Control Act Y
55. Kill-14 day handgun wait Y
56. Kill-Gun dlr inspections Y
57. Kill-Keep '68 Gun Con Act Y
58. Nicarag humanitarian aid Y
59. Bar ASAT testing ?
60. Delete chemical weapons ?
61. Delete 21 MX missiles Y
62. Kill-15% min tax on corps N
63. Kill-Restore Soc Sec COLA N
64. Freeze all funding N
65. Cut def;raise taxes, COLA Y
66. Keep existing SS COLAs Y
67. Aid to Nicaraguan rebels Y
68. Reaffirm purch of 21 MX N
69. African Relief/Farm Crdt Y
70. Kill-Nuclear Freeze Y
71. Kill-Void Title IX Narrow N
72. Raise drinking age to 21 N
73. Kill-Reduce mil in Europe N
74. Kill-Bar $ for contras Y
75. Kill-No new MXs in 1985 N
76. Kill-Move MX $ to non-nuc Y
77. Deficit reduction-$140b N
78. Kill-Req auth for troops Y
79. School Prayer amendment Y
80. Cap punish-certain crimes Y
81. Bar govt off from taping N
82. Martin L. King holiday Y
83. Auth marines in Lebanon N
84. Anti-abortion amendment Y
85. Highway-Gas tax bill N
86. Delete job creation amend N
87. Kill-Tobacco price supprt Y
88. Emergency housing aid N
89. Nullify oil decontrol N
90. Target tax cuts-mid class N
91. Tax Indexing N
92. Kill-Oppose SS benft cuts N
93. Disapprove Saudi AWACS N
94. Anti-busing rider Y
95. Disapprove oil import fee Y
96. Domestic violence funds N
97. Trucking Deregulation Y
98. Overturn India fuel sale N
99. Mil draft registration Y
100. Chrysler Loan Guarantees Y
101. Nuclear plant moratorium N
102. Abolish electoral college Y
103. Kill-Lmt ct-ordered bus ?
104. Airline Deregulation Y
105. Disappr Mideast jet sales N
106. Natural gas deregulation Y
107. Prohibit neutron bomb N
108. Financial disclosure-off Y

Presidential Support Score: 1986 - 59% 1985 - 45%

LONG, RUSSELL B. [Democrat] Term Began/Expires: 1981/1986. Prior Terms: Senate: 1948 (Special Election)-1980. Born: November 3, 1918; Shreveport, La. Education: Louisiana State University (B.A., LL.B.); Military Service: U.S. Navy, WW II; U.S. Navy Reserve. Occupation: Attorney.

1. Immigration Reform Y
2. So Afr Sanc-veto override Y
3. Kill-Death pnlty drug bil N
4. Kill-Mil use in drug war N
5. Tax Overhaul Y
6. Raise speed limit Y
7. Across-the-board cuts Y
8. South Africa sanctions Y
9. Kill-So Africa sanctions N
10. Kill-So Africa sanct (*) N
11. Nicaraguan contra aid Y
12. Terminate contra aid N
13. Kill-Prohibit contra fnds Y
14. Kill-Stop CIA contra fndg Y
15. Kill-Bar nuclr tsts w/SDI Y
16. Kill-Bar ASAT testing Y
17. Nuclear test ban treaty N
18. Prohibit sale of Stinger N
19. Delete Bigeye chem bomb N
20. Bar binary chem weapons N
21. Kill-SDI funding N
22. Kill-AIDS ins dscriminatn N
23. Kill-$10 bbl oil tariff N
24. Kill-Repl wndfl prfts tax N
25. Repeal balanced bdgt amdt N
26. Tax amnesty provisions Y

LONG, RUSSELL. B. (Cont.)

27. Kill-Tax amnesty subst N
28. Kill-Add third tax rate Y
29. Kill-Unocal tax provsns Y
30. Block Saudi arms sale (†) N
31. Kill-Bar school busing N
32. Prohibit Saudi arms sale ?
33. Nicaraguan contra aid Y
34. Bar all aid to Nicaragua ?
35. Balanced budget amendment Y
36. Balanced bdgt substitute N
37. Conrail sale Y
38. Revise farm programs Y
39. Kill-New oil import fee N
40. Spending cuts, tax incres Y
41. Textile import quotas Y
42. Kill-Exmpt vets from cuts Y
43. Kill-Bar inmate abortn $ N
44. Textile import quotas (§) Y
45. Kill-Eliminate Amtrak $ Y
46. Kill-Incrs motor fuel tax Y
47. Set max allow deficits Y
48. 20% minimum tax on corps N
49. Bar $ to toxic victims Y
50. Seasonal workers in US N
51. Kill-School prayer cases N
52. Line-item veto X
53. South Africa sanctions Y
54. Ease '68 Gun Control Act ?
55. Kill-14 day handgun wait ?
56. Kill-Gun dlr inspections ?
57. Kill-Keep '68 Gun Con Act ?
58. Nicarag humanitarian aid Y
59. Bar ASAT testing ?
60. Delete chemical weapons N
61. Delete 21 MX missiles N
62. Kill-15% min tax on corps Y
63. Kill-Restore Soc Sec COLA N
64. Freeze all funding N
65. Cut def;raise taxes, COLA Y
66. Keep existing SS COLAs Y
67. Aid to Nicaraguan rebels Y
68. Reaffirm purch of 21 MX Y
69. African Relief/Farm Crdt Y
70. Kill-Nuclear Freeze Y
71. Kill-Void Title IX Narrow N
72. Raise drinking age to 21 N
73. Kill-Reduce mil in Europe ?
74. Kill-Bar $ for contras Y
75. Kill-No new MXs in 1985 N
76. Kill-Move MX $ to non-nuc Y
77. Deficit reduction-$140b Y
78. Kill-Req auth for troops Y
79. School Prayer amendment Y
80. Cap punish-certain crimes Y
81. Bar govt off from taping ?
82. Martin L. King holiday Y
83. Auth marines in Lebanon N
84. Anti-abortion amendment Y
85. Highway-Gas tax bill Y
86. Delete job creation amend N
87. Kill-Tobacco price supprt Y
88. Emergency housing aid Y
89. Nullify oil decontrol N
90. Target tax cuts-mid class N
91. Tax Indexing N
92. Kill-Oppose SS benft cuts N
93. Disapprove Saudi AWACS N
94. Anti-busing rider Y
95. Disapprove oil import fee Y
96. Domestic violence funds ?
97. Trucking Deregulation Y
98. Overturn India fuel sale N
99. Mil draft registration ?
100. Chrysler Loan Guarantees Y
101. Nuclear plant moratorium ?
102. Abolish electoral college N
103. Kill-Lmt ct-ordered bus ?
104. Airline Deregulation N
105. Disappr Mideast jet sales N
106. Natural gas deregulation Y
107. Prohibit neutron bomb ?
108. Financial disclosure-off ?

Presidential Support Score: 1986 - 79% 1985 - 52%

MAINE

COHEN, WILLIAM S. [Republican] Term Began/Expires: 1985/1990. Prior Terms: House: 1973-78; Senate: 1979-84. Born: August 28, 1940; Bangor, Maine. Education: Bowdoin College (B.A.); Boston University Law School (LL.B.) Occupation: Instructor, University of Maine; partner, Paine, Cohen, Lynch, Weatherbee and Kobritz (1965-73); assistant editor, Journal of American Trial Lawyers Assn. (1965-66); assistant county attorney (1968-70); mayor (1971-72).

1. Immigration Reform N
2. So Afr Sanc-veto override Y
3. Kill-Death pnlty drug bil Y
4. Kill-Mil use in drug war Y
5. Tax Overhaul Y
6. Raise speed limit N

COHEN, WILLIAM S. (Cont.)

7. Across-the-board cuts Y
8. South Africa sanctions Y
9. Kill-So Africa sanctions Y
10. Kill-So Africa sanct (*) Y
11. Nicaraguan contra aid Y
12. Terminate contra aid N
13. Kill-Prohibit contra fnds N
14. Kill-Stop CIA contra fndg Y
15. Kill-Bar nuclr tsts w/SDI Y
16. Kill-Bar ASAT testing Y
17. Nuclear test ban treaty Y
18. Prohibit sale of Stinger N
19. Delete Bigeye chem bomb N
20. Bar binary chem weapons N
21. Kill-SDI funding Y
22. Kill-AIDS ins dscriminatn Y
23. Kill-$10 bbl oil tariff Y
24. Kill-Repl wndfl prfts tax Y
25. Repeal balanced bdgt amdt N
26. Tax amnesty provisions N
27. Kill-Tax amnesty subst Y
28. Kill-Add third tax rate Y
29. Kill-Unocal tax provsns N
30. Block Saudi arms sale (†) Y
31. Kill-Bar school busing Y
32. Prohibit Saudi arms sale Y
33. Nicaraguan contra aid Y
34. Bar all aid to Nicaragua N
35. Balanced budget amendment N
36. Balanced bdgt substitute N
37. Conrail sale Y
38. Revise farm programs N
39. Kill-New oil import fee Y
40. Spending cuts, tax incres Y
41. Textile import quotas Y
42. Kill-Exmpt vets from cuts Y
43. Kill-Bar inmate abortn $ Y
44. Textile import quotas (§) Y
45. Kill-Eliminate Amtrak $ Y
46. Kill-Incrs motor fuel tax Y
47. Set max allow deficits Y
48. 20% minimum tax on corps N
49. Bar $ to toxic victims N
50. Seasonal workers in US N
51. Kill-School prayer cases Y
52. Line-item veto Y
53. South Africa sanctions Y
54. Ease '68 Gun Control Act Y
55. Kill-14 day handgun wait Y
56. Kill-Gun dlr inspections Y
57. Kill-Keep '68 Gun Con Act Y
58. Nicarag humanitarian aid N
59. Bar ASAT testing ?
60. Delete chemical weapons N
61. Delete 21 MX missiles N
62. Kill-15% min tax on corps N
63. Kill-Restore Soc Sec COLA Y
64. Freeze all funding N
65. Cut def;raise taxes, COLA N
66. Keep existing SS COLAs Y
67. Aid to Nicaraguan rebels Y
68. Reaffirm purch of 21 MX Y
69. African Relief/Farm Crdt N
70. Kill-Nuclear Freeze Y
71. Kill-Void Title IX Narrow N
72. Raise drinking age to 21 Y
73. Kill-Reduce mil in Europe Y
74. Kill-Bar $ for contras N
75. Kill-No new MXs in 1985 Y
76. Kill-Move MX $ to non-nuc Y
77. Deficit reduction-$140b Y
78. Kill-Req auth for troops Y
79. School Prayer amendment N
80. Cap punish-certain crimes N
81. Bar govt off from taping Y
82. Martin L. King holiday Y
83. Auth marines in Lebanon Y
84. Anti-abortion amendment N
85. Highway-Gas tax bill N
86. Delete job creation amend N
87. Kill-Tobacco price supprt N
88. Emergency housing aid N
89. Nullify oil decontrol N
90. Target tax cuts-mid class N
91. Tax Indexing Y
92. Kill-Oppose SS benft cuts Y
93. Disapprove Saudi AWACS N
94. Anti-busing rider N
95. Disapprove oil import fee Y
96. Domestic violence funds N
97. Trucking Deregulation N
98. Overturn India fuel sale Y
99. Mil draft registration N
100. Chrysler Loan Guarantees N
101. Nuclear plant moratorium Y
102. Abolish electoral college N

Presidential Support Score: 1986 - 79% 1985 - 63%

MITCHELL, GEORGE J. [Democrat] Term Began/Expires: 1983/1988. Prior Terms: Senate: 1980 (Special Election)-1982. Born: August 20, 1933; Waterville, Maine. Education: Bowdoin College; Georgetown University Law Center. Military Service: U.S. Army, 1954-56. Occupation: Justice Department attorney (1960-62); Senate staff member (1962-65); partner, Jensen, Baird, Gardner, Donovan and Henry (1965-77); assistant county attorney, Cumberland County, Maine (1971); U.S. attorney, Maine (1977-79).

MITCHELL, GEORGE J. (Cont.)

1. Immigration Reform N
2. So Afr Sanc-veto override Y
3. Kill-Death pnlty drug bil Y
4. Kill-Mil use in drug war Y
5. Tax Overhaul Y
6. Raise speed limit N
7. Across-the-board cuts N
8. South Africa sanctions Y
9. Kill-So Africa sanctions N
10. Kill-So Africa sanct (*) N
11. Nicaraguan contra aid N
12. Terminate contra aid Y
13. Kill-Prohibit contra fnds N
14. Kill-Stop CIA contra fndg N
15. Kill-Bar nuclr tsts w/SDI N
16. Kill-Bar ASAT testing N
17. Nuclear test ban treaty Y
18. Prohibit sale of Stinger Y
19. Delete Bigeye chem bomb Y
20. Bar binary chem weapons Y
21. Kill-SDI funding N
22. Kill-AIDS ins dscriminatn ?
23. Kill-$10 bbl oil tariff Y
24. Kill-Repl wndfl prfts tax Y
25. Repeal balanced bdgt amdt N
26. Tax amnesty provisions Y
27. Kill-Tax amnesty subst N
28. Kill-Add third tax rate N
29. Kill-Unocal tax provsns N
30. Block Saudi arms sale (†) Y
31. Kill-Bar school busing Y
32. Prohibit Saudi arms sale Y
33. Nicaraguan contra aid N
34. Bar all aid to Nicaragua N
35. Balanced budget amendment N
36. Balanced bdgt substitute N
37. Conrail sale Y
38. Revise farm programs N
39. Kill-New oil import fee Y
40. Spending cuts, tax incres Y
41. Textile import quotas Y
42. Kill-Exmpt vets from cuts N
43. Kill-Bar inmate abortn $ N
44. Textile import quotas (§) Y
45. Kill-Eliminate Amtrak $ Y
46. Kill-Incrs motor fuel tax Y
47. Set max allow deficits N
48. 20% minimum tax on corps N
49. Bar $ to toxic victims N
50. Seasonal workers in US Y
51. Kill-School prayer cases Y
52. Line-item veto N
53. South Africa sanctions Y
54. Ease '68 Gun Control Act Y
55. Kill-14 day handgun wait Y
56. Kill-Gun dlr inspections Y
57. Kill-Keep '68 Gun Con Act Y
58. Nicarag humanitarian aid N
59. Bar ASAT testing Y
60. Delete chemical weapons Y
61. Delete 21 MX missiles Y
62. Kill-15% min tax on corps N
63. Kill-Restore Soc Sec COLA N
64. Freeze all funding N
65. Cut def;raise taxes, COLA Y
66. Keep existing SS COLAs Y
67. Aid to Nicaraguan rebels N
68. Reaffirm purch of 21 MX N
69. African Relief/Farm Crdt Y
70. Kill-Nuclear Freeze N
71. Kill-Void Title IX Narrow N
72. Raise drinking age to 21 Y
73. Kill-Reduce mil in Europe Y
74. Kill-Bar $ for contras N
75. Kill-No new MXs in 1985 N
76. Kill-Move MX $ to non-nuc N
77. Deficit reduction-$140b N
78. Kill-Req auth for troops N
79. School Prayer amendment N
80. Cap punish-certain crimes N
81. Bar govt off from taping Y
82. Martin L. King holiday Y
83. Auth marines in Lebanon Y
84. Anti-abortion amendment N
85. Highway-Gas tax bill N
86. Delete job creation amend N
87. Kill-Tobacco price supprt N
88. Emergency housing aid Y
89. Nullify oil decontrol Y
90. Target tax cuts-mid class N
91. Tax indexing N
92. Kill-Oppose SS benft cuts N
93. Disapprove Saudi AWACS Y
94. Anti-busing rider N
95. Disapprove oil import fee Y
96. Domestic violence funds Y
97. Trucking Deregulation
98. Overturn India fuel sale N
99. Mil draft registration N

Sworn in May 19, 1980 and missed vote 97.
Presidential Support Score: 1986 - 31% 1985 - 33%

MARYLAND

MATHIAS, CHARLES McC., Jr. [Republican] Term Began/Expires: 1981/1986. Prior Terms: House: 1961-68; Senate: 1969-80. Born: July 24, 1922; Frederick, Md. Education: Haverford College

MATHIAS, CHARLES McC., Jr. (Cont.)
(B.A.); Yale University; University of Maryland (LL.B.). Military Service: U. S. Naval Reserve. Occupation: Maryland assistant attorney general (1953-54); Frederick city attorney (1954-59); Maryland delegate (1958-60).

1. Immigration Reform ?
2. So Afr Sanc-veto override Y
3. Kill-Death pnlty drug bil Y
4. Kill-Mil use in drug war Y
5. Tax Overhaul Y
6. Raise speed limit N
7. Across-the-board cuts N
8. South Africa sanctions Y
9. Kill-So Africa sanctions N
10. Kill-So Africa sanct (*) Y
11. Nicaraguan contra aid N
12. Terminate contra aid N
13. Kill-Prohibit contra fnds N
14. Kill-Stop CIA contra fndg N
15. Kill-Bar nuclr tsts w/SDI ?
16. Kill-Bar ASAT testing N
17. Nuclear test ban treaty Y
18. Prohibit sale of Stinger Y
19. Delete Bigeye chem bomb Y
20. Bar binary chem weapons Y
21. Kill-SDI funding N
22. Kill-AIDS ins dscriminatn Y
23. Kill-$10 bbl oil tariff N
24. Kill-Repl wndfl prfts tax Y
25. Repeal balanced bdgt amdt Y
26. Tax amnesty provisions N
27. Kill-Tax amnesty subst N
28. Kill-Add third tax rate N
29. Kill-Unocal tax provsns N
30. Block Saudi arms sale (†) N
31. Kill-Bar school busing Y
32. Prohibit Saudi arms sale N
33. Nicaraguan contra aid N
34. Bar all aid to Nicaragua Y
35. Balanced budget amendment N
36. Balanced bdgt substitute Y
37. Conrail sale N
38. Revise farm programs ?
39. Kill-New oil import fee N
40. Spending cuts, tax incres Y
41. Textile import quotas Y
42. Kill-Exmpt vets from cuts Y
43. Kill-Bar inmate abortn $ Y
44. Textile import quotas (§) Y
45. Kill-Eliminate Amtrak $ Y
46. Kill-Incrs motor fuel tax ?
47. Set max allow deficits ?
48. 20% minimum tax on corps ?
49. Bar $ to toxic victims N
50. Seasonal workers in US N
51. Kill-School prayer cases Y
52. Line-item veto N
53. South Africa sanctions Y
54. Ease '68 Gun Control Act N
55. Kill-14 day handgun wait N
56. Kill-Gun dlr inspections N
57. Kill-Keep '68 Gun Con Act N
58. Nicarag humanitarian aid N
59. Bar ASAT testing Y
60. Delete chemical weapons Y
61. Delete 21 MX missiles N
62. Kill-15% min tax on corps Y
63. Kill-Restore Soc Sec COLA N
64. Freeze all funding N
65. Cut def;raise taxes, COLA Y
66. Keep existing SS COLAs Y
67. Aid to Nicaraguan rebels N
68. Reaffirm purch of 21 MX Y
69. African Relief/Farm Crdt Y
70. Kill-Nuclear Freeze N
71. Kill-Void Title IX Narrow Y
72. Raise drinking age to 21 Y
73. Kill-Reduce mil in Europe Y
74. Kill-Bar $ for contras Y
75. Kill-No new MXs in 1985 N
76. Kill-Move MX $ to non-nuc N
77. Deficit reduction-$140b ?
78. Kill-Req auth for troops Y
79. School Prayer amendment N
80. Cap punish-certain crimes N
81. Bar govt off from taping Y
82. Martin L. King holiday Y
83. Auth marines in Lebanon Y
84. Anti-abortion amendment N
85. Highway-Gas tax bill Y
86. Delete job creation amend ?
87. Kill-Tobacco price supprt N
88. Emergency housing aid Y
89. Nullify oil decontrol N
90. Target tax cuts-mid class ?
91. Tax Indexing N
92. Kill-Oppose SS benft cuts ?
93. Disapprove Saudi AWACS N
94. Anti-busing rider N
95. Disapprove oil import fee Y
96. Domestic violence funds Y
97. Trucking Deregulation Y
98. Overturn India fuel sale N
99. Mil draft registration N
100. Chrysler Loan Guarantees Y
101. Nuclear plant moratorium N
102. Abolish electoral college Y
103. Kill-Lmt ct-ordered bus Y
104. Airline Deregulation Y
105. Disappr Mideast jet sales N
106. Natural gas deregulation Y
107. Prohibit neutron bomb Y
108. Financial disclosure-off Y

Presidential Support Score: 1986 - 35% 1985 - 43%

SARBANES, PAUL S. [Democrat] Term Began/Expires: 1983/1988. Prior Terms: House: 1971-76; Senate: 1977-82. Born: Feb. 3, 1933; Salisbury, Md. Education: Princeton University (A.B.); Oxford University (B.A.); Harvard Law School (LL.B.). Occupation: Attorney, Venable, Baetjer and Howard; assistant to the chairman, Council on Economic Advisers (1962-63); executive director, Baltimore City Charter Revision Committee (1963-1964); Maryland Delegate (1967-71).

1.	Immigration Reform	Y	52.	Line-item veto	N
2.	So Afr Sanc-veto override	Y	53.	South Africa sanctions	Y
3.	Kill-Death pnlty drug bil	Y	54.	Ease '68 Gun Control Act	N
4.	Kill-Mil use in drug war	Y	55.	Kill-14 day handgun wait	N
5.	Tax Overhaul	Y	56.	Kill-Gun dlr inspections	N
6.	Raise speed limit	N	57.	Kill-Keep '68 Gun Con Act	N
7.	Across-the-board cuts	N	58.	Nicarag humanitarian aid	N
8.	South Africa sanctions	Y	59.	Bar ASAT testing	Y
9.	Kill-So Africa sanctions	N	60.	Delete chemical weapons	Y
10.	Kill-So Africa sanct (*)	N	61.	Delete 21 MX missiles	Y
11.	Nicaraguan contra aid	N	62.	Kill-15% min tax on corps	N
12.	Terminate contra aid	Y	63.	Kill-Restore Soc Sec COLA	N
13.	Kill-Prohibit contra fnds	N	64.	Freeze all funding	N
14.	Kill-Stop CIA contra fndg	N	65.	Cut def;raise taxes, COLA	Y
15.	Kill-Bar nuclr tsts w/SDI	N	66.	Keep existing SS COLAs	Y
16.	Kill-Bar ASAT testing	N	67.	Aid to Nicaraguan rebels	N
17.	Nuclear test ban treaty	Y	68.	Reaffirm purch of 21 MX	N
18.	Prohibit sale of Stinger	Y	69.	African Relief/Farm Crdt	Y
19.	Delete Bigeye chem bomb	Y	70.	Kill-Nuclear Freeze	N
20.	Bar binary chem weapons	Y	71.	Kill-Void Title IX Narrow	N
21.	Kill-SDI funding	N	72.	Raise drinking age to 21	Y
22.	Kill-AIDS ins dscriminatn	Y	73.	Kill-Reduce mil in Europe	N
23.	Kill-$10 bbl oil tariff	Y	74.	Kill-Bar $ for contras	N
24.	Kill-Repl wndfl prfts tax	Y	75.	Kill-No new MXs in 1985	N
25.	Repeal balanced bdgt amdt	Y	76.	Kill-Move MX $ to non-nuc	N
26.	Tax amnesty provisions	N	77.	Deficit reduction-$140b	N
27.	Kill-Tax amnesty subst	Y	78.	Kill-Req auth for troops	N
28.	Kill-Add third tax rate	N	79.	School Prayer amendment	N
29.	Kill-Unocal tax provsns	N	80.	Cap punish-certain crimes	N
30.	Block Saudi arms sale (†)	Y	81.	Bar govt off from taping	Y
31.	Kill-Bar school busing	Y	82.	Martin L. King holiday	Y
32.	Prohibit Saudi arms sale	Y	83.	Auth marines in Lebanon	N
33.	Nicaraguan contra aid	N	84.	Anti-abortion amendment	N
34.	Bar all aid to Nicaragua	Y	85.	Highway-Gas tax bill	N
35.	Balanced budget amendment	N	86.	Delete job creation amend	N
36.	Balanced bdgt substitute	Y	87.	Kill-Tobacco price supprt	Y
37.	Conrail sale	N	88.	Emergency housing aid	Y
38.	Revise farm programs	Y	89.	Nullify oil decontrol	Y
39.	Kill-New oil import fee	N	90.	Target tax cuts-mid class	N
40.	Spending cuts, tax incres	Y	91.	Tax Indexing	N
41.	Textile import quotas	Y	92.	Kill-Oppose SS benft cuts	N
42.	Kill-Exmpt vets from cuts	N	93.	Disapprove Saudi AWACS	Y
43.	Kill-Bar inmate abortn $	Y	94.	Anti-busing rider	N
44.	Textile import quotas (§)	Y	95.	Disapprove oil import fee	Y
45.	Kill-Eliminate Amtrak $	Y	96.	Domestic violence funds	Y
46.	Kill-Incrs motor fuel tax	Y	97.	Trucking Deregulation	Y
47.	Set max allow deficits	N	98.	Overturn India fuel sale	N
48.	20% minimum tax on corps	N	99.	Mil draft registration	N
49.	Bar $ to toxic victims	N	100.	Chrysler Loan Guarantees	Y
50.	Seasonal workers in US	N	101.	Nuclear plant moratorium	Y
51.	Kill-School prayer cases	Y	102.	Abolish electoral college	N

SARBANES, PAUL S. (Cont.)

103. Kill-Lmt ct-ordered bus N
104. Airline Deregulation Y
105. Disappr Mideast jet sales Y
106. Natural gas deregulation N
107. Prohibit neutron bomb Y
108. Financial disclosure-off Y

Presidential Support Score: 1986 - 19% 1985 - 22%

MASSACHUSETTS

KENNEDY, EDWARD M. [Democrat] Term Began/Expires: 1983/1988. Prior Terms: Senate: 1962 (Special Election)- 1982. Born: February 22, 1932; Boston, Mass. Education: Milton Academy; Harvard College (A.B.); International Law School, the Hague, Holland; University of Virginia Law School (LL.B.). Military Service: U.S. Army, 1951-53. Occupation: Suffolk County assistant district attorney (1961-62).

1. Immigration Reform N
2. So Afr Sanc-veto override Y
3. Kill-Death pnlty drug bil ?
4. Kill-Mil use in drug war ?
5. Tax Overhaul Y
6. Raise speed limit Y
7. Across-the-board cuts N
8. South Africa sanctions Y
9. Kill-So Africa sanctions N
10. Kill-So Africa sanct (*) N
11. Nicaraguan contra aid N
12. Terminate contra aid Y
13. Kill-Prohibit contra fnds N
14. Kill-Stop CIA contra fndg N
15. Kill-Bar nuclr tsts w/SDI N
16. Kill-Bar ASAT testing N
17. Nuclear test ban treaty Y
18. Prohibit sale of Stinger Y
19. Delete Bigeye chem bomb Y
20. Bar binary chem weapons Y
21. Kill-SDI funding N
22. Kill-AIDS ins dscriminatn Y
23. Kill-$10 bbl oil tariff Y
24. Kill-Repl wndfl prfts tax Y
25. Repeal balanced bdgt amdt N
26. Tax amnesty provisions Y
27. Kill-Tax amnesty subst N
28. Kill-Add third tax rate Y
29. Kill-Unocal tax provsns N
30. Block Saudi arms sale (†) Y
31. Kill-Bar school busing ?
32. Prohibit Saudi arms sale Y
33. Nicaraguan contra aid N
34. Bar all aid to Nicaragua Y
35. Balanced budget amendment N
36. Balanced bdgt substitute Y
37. Conrail sale +
38. Revise farm programs ?
39. Kill-New oil import fee Y
40. Spending cuts, tax incres Y
41. Textile import quotas Y
42. Kill-Exmpt vets from cuts N
43. Kill-Bar inmate abortn $ Y
44. Textile import quotas (§) Y
45. Kill-Eliminate Amtrak $ Y
46. Kill-Incrs motor fuel tax Y
47. Set max allow deficits Y
48. 20% minimum tax on corps Y
49. Bar $ to toxic victims N
50. Seasonal workers in US N
51. Kill-School prayer cases Y
52. Line-item veto Y
53. South Africa sanctions Y
54. Ease '68 Gun Control Act N
55. Kill-14 day handgun wait N
56. Kill-Gun dlr inspections N
57. Kill-Keep '68 Gun Con Act N
58. Nicarag humanitarian aid N
59. Bar ASAT testing Y
60. Delete chemical weapons Y
61. Delete 21 MX missiles Y
62. Kill-15% min tax on corps N
63. Kill-Restore Soc Sec COLA N
64. Freeze all funding N
65. Cut def;raise taxes, COLA Y
66. Keep existing SS COLAs Y
67. Aid to Nicaraguan rebels N
68. Reaffirm purch of 21 MX N
69. African Relief/Farm Crdt Y
70. Kill-Nuclear Freeze N
71. Kill-Void Title IX Narrow N
72. Raise drinking age to 21 Y
73. Kill-Reduce mil in Europe N
74. Kill-Bar $ for contras N
75. Kill-No new MXs in 1985 N
76. Kill-Move MX $ to non-nuc N
77. Deficit reduction-$140b N
78. Kill-Req auth for troops N
79. School Prayer amendment N
80. Cap punish-certain crimes N
81. Bar govt off from taping N
82. Martin L. King holiday Y
83. Auth marines in Lebanon N
84. Anti-abortion amendment N

KENNEDY, EDWARD M. (Cont.)

85. Highway-Gas tax bill -
86. Delete job creation amend N
87. Kill-Tobacco price supprt N
88. Emergency housing aid Y
89. Nullify oil decontrol ?
90. Target tax cuts-mid class Y
91. Tax Indexing N
92. Kill-Oppose SS benft cuts N
93. Disapprove Saudi AWACS Y
94. Anti-busing rider X
95. Disapprove oil import fee Y
96. Domestic violence funds ?
97. Trucking Deregulation ?
98. Overturn India fuel sale Y
99. Mil draft registration N
100. Chrysler Loan Guarantees Y
101. Nuclear plant moratorium Y
102. Abolish electoral college Y
103. Kill-Lmt ct-ordered bus Y
104. Airline Deregulation Y
105. Disappr Mideast jet sales Y
106. Natural gas deregulation N
107. Prohibit neutron bomb Y
108. Financial disclosure-off Y

Presidential Support Score: 1986 - 29% 1985 - 27%

KERRY, JOHN F. [Democrat] Term Began/Expires: 1985/1990. Born: December 11, 1943; Denver, Colo. Education: Yale University (B.A.); Boston College Law School (J.D.). Military Service: U.S. Navy. Occupation: Attorney; assistant district attorney; lieutenant governor (1982).

1. Immigration Reform Y
2. So Afr Sanc-veto override Y
3. Kill-Death pnlty drug bil ?
4. Kill-Mil use in drug war ?
5. Tax Overhaul Y
6. Raise speed limit Y
7. Across-the-board cuts N
8. South Africa sanctions Y
9. Kill-So Africa sanctions N
10. Kill-So Africa sanct (*) N
11. Nicaraguan contra aid N
12. Terminate contra aid Y
13. Kill-Prohibit contra fnds N
14. Kill-Stop CIA contra fndg N
15. Kill-Bar nuclr tsts w/SDI N
16. Kill-Bar ASAT testing N
17. Nuclear test ban treaty Y
18. Prohibit sale of Stinger Y
19. Delete Bigeye chem bomb Y
20. Bar binary chem weapons Y
21. Kill-SDI funding N
22. Kill-AIDS ins dscriminatn Y
23. Kill-$10 bbl oil tariff Y
24. Kill-Repl wndfl prfts tax Y
25. Repeal balanced bdgt amdt N
26. Tax amnesty provisions Y
27. Kill-Tax amnesty subst N
28. Kill-Add third tax rate N
29. Kill-Unocal tax provsns N
30. Block Saudi arms sale (†) Y
31. Kill-Bar school busing Y
32. Prohibit Saudi arms sale Y
33. Nicaraguan contra aid N
34. Bar all aid to Nicaragua Y
35. Balanced budget amendment N
36. Balanced bdgt substitute Y
37. Conrail sale ?
38. Revise farm programs N
39. Kill-New oil import fee Y
40. Spending cuts, tax incres N
41. Textile import quotas Y
42. Kill-Exmpt vets from cuts N
43. Kill-Bar inmate abortn $ Y
44. Textile import quotas (§) Y
45. Kill-Eliminate Amtrak $ Y
46. Kill-Incrs motor fuel tax Y
47. Set max allow deficits Y
48. 20% minimum tax on corps N
49. Bar $ to toxic victims N
50. Seasonal workers in US N
51. Kill-School prayer cases Y
52. Line-item veto N
53. South Africa sanctions Y
54. Ease '68 Gun Control Act N
55. Kill-14 day handgun wait N
56. Kill-Gun dlr inspections N
57. Kill-Keep '68 Gun Con Act N
58. Nicarag humanitarian aid N
59. Bar ASAT testing Y
60. Delete chemical weapons Y
61. Delete 21 MX missiles Y
62. Kill-15% min tax on corps N
63. Kill-Restore Soc Sec COLA N
64. Freeze all funding N
65. Cut def;raise taxes, COLA Y
66. Keep existing SS COLAs Y
67. Aid to Nicaraguan rebels N
68. Reaffirm purch of 21 MX N
69. African Relief/Farm Crdt Y

Presidential Support Score: 1986 - 21% 1985 - 26%

MICHIGAN

LEVIN, CARL [Democrat] Term Began/Expires: 1985/1990. Prior Terms: Senate: 1979-84. Born: June 28, 1934; Detroit, Mich. Education: Swarthmore College; Harvard Law School. Occupation: Assistant attorney general and general counsel, Michigan Civil Rights Commission (1964-67); special assistant attorney general, Michigan, and chief appellate defender, Detroit (1968-69); Detroit city councilman (1970-73); instructor, University of Detroit and Wayne State University Law School.

No.	Issue	Vote	No.	Issue	Vote
1.	Immigration Reform	Y	50.	Seasonal workers in US	N
2.	So Afr Sanc-veto override	Y	51.	Kill-School prayer cases	Y
3.	Kill-Death pnlty drug bil	N	52.	Line-item veto	N
4.	Kill-Mil use in drug war	Y	53.	South Africa sanctions	Y
5.	Tax Overhaul	N	54.	Ease '68 Gun Control Act	N
6.	Raise speed limit	N	55.	Kill-14 day handgun wait	N
7.	Across-the-board cuts	N	56.	Kill-Gun dlr inspections	Y
8.	South Africa sanctions	Y	57.	Kill-Keep '68 Gun Con Act	N
9.	Kill-So Africa sanctions	N	58.	Nicarag humanitarian aid	N
10.	Kill-So Africa sanct (*)	N	59.	Bar ASAT testing	Y
11.	Nicaraguan contra aid	N	60.	Delete chemical weapons	Y
12.	Terminate contra aid	Y	61.	Delete 21 MX missiles	Y
13.	Kill-Prohibit contra fnds	N	62.	Kill-15% min tax on corps	N
14.	Kill-Stop CIA contra fndg	N	63.	Kill-Restore Soc Sec COLA	N
15.	Kill-Bar nuclr tsts w/SDI	N	64.	Freeze all funding	N
16.	Kill-Bar ASAT testing	N	65.	Cut def;raise taxes, COLA	Y
17.	Nuclear test ban treaty	Y	66.	Keep existing SS COLAs	Y
18.	Prohibit sale of Stinger	N	67.	Aid to Nicaraguan rebels	N
19.	Delete Bigeye chem bomb	Y	68.	Reaffirm purch of 21 MX	N
20.	Bar binary chem weapons	Y	69.	African Relief/Farm Crdt	Y
21.	Kill-SDI funding	N	70.	Kill-Nuclear Freeze	N
22.	Kill-AIDS ins dscriminatn	Y	71.	Kill-Void Title IX Narrow	N
23.	Kill-$10 bbl oil tariff	N	72.	Raise drinking age to 21	Y
24.	Kill-Repl wndfl prfts tax	Y	73.	Kill-Reduce mil in Europe	N
25.	Repeal balanced bdgt amdt	N	74.	Kill-Bar $ for contras	N
26.	Tax amnesty provisions	N	75.	Kill-No new MXs in 1985	N
27.	Kill-Tax amnesty subst	Y	76.	Kill-Move MX $ to non-nuc	N
28.	Kill-Add third tax rate	N	77.	Deficit reduction-$140b	N
29.	Kill-Unocal tax provsns	N	78.	Kill-Req auth for troops	N
30.	Block Saudi arms sale (†)	Y	79.	School Prayer amendment	N
31.	Kill-Bar school busing	Y	80.	Cap punish-certain crimes	N
32.	Prohibit Saudi arms sale	Y	81.	Bar govt off from taping	Y
33.	Nicaraguan contra aid	N	82.	Martin L. King holiday	Y
34.	Bar all aid to Nicaragua	Y	83.	Auth marines in Lebanon	N
35.	Balanced budget amendment	N	84.	Anti-abortion amendment	N
36.	Balanced bdgt substitute	Y	85.	Highway-Gas tax bill	Y
37.	Conrail sale	N	86.	Delete job creation amend	N
38.	Revise farm programs	Y	87.	Kill-Tobacco price supprt	N
39.	Kill-New oil import fee	N	88.	Emergency housing aid	Y
40.	Spending cuts, tax incres	Y	89.	Nullify oil decontrol	Y
41.	Textile import quotas	Y	90.	Target tax cuts-mid class	Y
42.	Kill-Exmpt vets from cuts	N	91.	Tax Indexing	Y
43.	Kill-Bar inmate abortn $	Y	92.	Kill-Oppose SS benft cuts	N
44.	Textile import quotas (§)	Y	93.	Disapprove Saudi AWACS	Y
45.	Kill-Eliminate Amtrak $	Y	94.	Anti-busing rider	N
46.	Kill-Incrs motor fuel tax	Y	95.	Disapprove oil import fee	Y
47.	Set max allow deficits	Y	96.	Domestic violence funds	Y
48.	20% minimum tax on corps	Y	97.	Trucking Deregulation	Y
49.	Bar $ to toxic victims	N	98.	Overturn India fuel sale	N

LEVIN, CARL (Cont.)

99. Mil draft registration N
100. Chrysler Loan Guarantees Y
101. Nuclear plant moratorium Y
102. Abolish electoral college Y

Presidential Support Score: 1986 - 24% 1985 - 25%

RIEGLE, DONALD W., Jr. [Democrat] Term Began/Expires: 1983/1988. Prior Terms: House: 1965-76; Senate: 1976 (Special Election)-1982. Born: February 4, 1938; Flint, Mich. Education: University of Michigan (B.A.); Michigan State University (M.B.A.); Harvard Business School. Occupation: Employee, International Business Machines Corp. (1961-64); consultant, Harvard/MIT Joint Center on Urban Studies; faculty member, Michigan State University, Boston University, Harvard; author.

1. Immigration Reform N
2. So Afr Sanc-veto override Y
3. Kill-Death pnlty drug bil N
4. Kill-Mil use in drug war N
5. Tax Overhaul Y
6. Raise speed limit Y
7. Across-the-board cuts N
8. South Africa sanctions Y
9. Kill-So Africa sanctions N
10. Kill-So Africa sanct (*) N
11. Nicaraguan contra aid N
12. Terminate contra aid Y
13. Kill-Prohibit contra fnds N
14. Kill-Stop CIA contra fndg N
15. Kill-Bar nuclr tsts w/SDI N
16. Kill-Bar ASAT testing N
17. Nuclear test ban treaty Y
18. Prohibit sale of Stinger Y
19. Delete Bigeye chem bomb Y
20. Bar binary chem weapons Y
21. Kill-SDI funding N
22. Kill-AIDS ins dscriminatn Y
23. Kill-$10 bbl oil tariff Y
24. Kill-Repl wndfl prfts tax Y
25. Repeal balanced bdgt amdt Y
26. Tax amnesty provisions N
27. Kill-Tax amnesty subst N
28. Kill-Add third tax rate N
29. Kill-Unocal tax provsns N
30. Block Saudi arms sale (†) Y
31. Kill-Bar school busing Y
32. Prohibit Saudi arms sale Y
33. Nicaraguan contra aid N
34. Bar all aid to Nicaragua Y
35. Balanced budget amendment N
36. Balanced bdgt substitute N
37. Conrail sale N
38. Revise farm programs Y
39. Kill-New oil import fee Y
40. Spending cuts, tax incres Y
41. Textile import quotas Y
42. Kill-Exmpt vets from cuts N
43. Kill-Bar inmate abortn $ Y
44. Textile import quotas (§) Y
45. Kill-Eliminate Amtrak $ Y
46. Kill-Incrs motor fuel tax Y
47. Set max allow deficits N
48. 20% minimum tax on corps N
49. Bar $ to toxic victims N
50. Seasonal workers in US Y
51. Kill-School prayer cases Y
52. Line-item veto N
53. South Africa sanctions Y
54. Ease '68 Gun Control Act Y
55. Kill-14 day handgun wait Y
56. Kill-Gun dlr inspections Y
57. Kill-Keep '68 Gun Con Act N
58. Nicarag humanitarian aid N
59. Bar ASAT testing Y
60. Delete chemical weapons Y
61. Delete 21 MX missiles Y
62. Kill-15% min tax on corps N
63. Kill-Restore Soc Sec COLA N
64. Freeze all funding N
65. Cut def;raise taxes, COLA Y
66. Keep existing SS COLAs Y
67. Aid to Nicaraguan rebels N
68. Reaffirm purch of 21 MX N
69. African Relief/Farm Crdt Y
70. Kill-Nuclear Freeze N
71. Kill-Void Title IX Narrow N
72. Raise drinking age to 21 Y
73. Kill-Reduce mil in Europe N
74. Kill-Bar $ for contras N
75. Kill-No new MXs in 1985 N
76. Kill-Move MX $ to non-nuc N
77. Deficit reduction-$140b N
78. Kill-Req auth for troops N
79. School Prayer amendment N
80. Cap punish-certain crimes N
81. Bar govt off from taping Y
82. Martin L. King holiday Y
83. Auth marines in Lebanon N
84. Anti-abortion amendment N
85. Highway-Gas tax bill N
86. Delete job creation amend N
87. Kill-Tobacco price supprt N
88. Emergency housing aid Y
89. Nullify oil decontrol Y
90. Target tax cuts-mid class N

RIEGLE, DONALD W., Jr. (Cont.)

91. Tax Indexing Y
92. Kill-Oppose SS benft cuts N
93. Disapprove Saudi AWACS Y
94. Anti-busing rider N
95. Disapprove oil import fee Y
96. Domestic violence funds Y
97. Trucking Deregulation ?
98. Overturn India fuel sale Y
99. Mil draft registration N
100. Chrysler Loan Guarantees Y
101. Nuclear plant moratorium Y
102. Abolish electoral college Y
103. Kill-Lmt ct-ordered bus Y
104. Airline Deregulation Y
105. Disappr Mideast jet sales Y
106. Natural gas deregulation N
107. Prohibit neutron bomb Y
108. Financial disclosure-off Y

Presidential Support Score: 1986 - 19% 1985 - 24%

MINNESOTA

BOSCHWITZ, RUDY [Republican] Term Began/Expires: 1985/1990. Prior Terms: Senate: 1979-84. Born: November 7, 1930; Berlin, Germany. Education: Johns Hopkins University; New York University (B.S., LL.B.). Military Service: U.S. Army Signal Corps. Occupation: Attorney; founder, Plywood Minnesota (1963).

1. Immigration Reform Y
2. So Afr Sanc-veto override Y
3. Kill-Death pnlty drug bil Y
4. Kill-Mil use in drug war Y
5. Tax Overhaul Y
6. Raise speed limit N
7. Across-the-board cuts N
8. South Africa sanctions Y
9. Kill-So Africa sanctions Y
10. Kill-So Africa sanct (*) Y
11. Nicaraguan contra aid Y
12. Terminate contra aid N
13. Kill-Prohibit contra fnds Y
14. Kill-Stop CIA contra fndg Y
15. Kill-Bar nuclr tsts w/SDI Y
16. Kill-Bar ASAT testing Y
17. Nuclear test ban treaty N
18. Prohibit sale of Stinger N
19. Delete Bigeye chem bomb N
20. Bar binary chem weapons N
21. Kill-SDI funding Y
22. Kill-AIDS ins dscriminatn Y
23. Kill-$10 bbl oil tariff Y
24. Kill-Repl wndfl prfts tax N
25. Repeal balanced bdgt amdt N
26. Tax amnesty provisions Y
27. Kill-Tax amnesty subst N
28. Kill-Add third tax rate Y
29. Kill-Unocal tax provsns Y
30. Block Saudi arms sale (†) Y
31. Kill-Bar school busing Y
32. Prohibit Saudi arms sale Y
33. Nicaraguan contra aid Y
34. Bar all aid to Nicaragua N
35. Balanced budget amendment Y
36. Balanced bdgt substitute N
37. Conrail sale Y
38. Revise farm programs Y
39. Kill-New oil import fee Y
40. Spending cuts, tax incres Y
41. Textile import quotas N
42. Kill-Exmpt vets from cuts Y
43. Kill-Bar inmate abortn $ N
44. Textile import quotas (§) N
45. Kill-Eliminate Amtrak $ N
46. Kill-Incrs motor fuel tax Y
47. Set max allow deficits Y
48. 20% minimum tax on corps N
49. Bar $ to toxic victims Y
50. Seasonal workers in US Y
51. Kill-School prayer cases Y
52. Line-item veto Y
53. South Africa sanctions Y
54. Ease '68 Gun Control Act Y
55. Kill-14 day handgun wait Y
56. Kill-Gun dlr inspections Y
57. Kill-Keep '68 Gun Con Act Y
58. Nicarag humanitarian aid Y
59. Bar ASAT testing N
60. Delete chemical weapons N
61. Delete 21 MX missiles N
62. Kill-15% min tax on corps Y
63. Kill-Restore Soc Sec COLA Y
64. Freeze all funding Y
65. Cut def;raise taxes, COLA N
66. Keep existing SS COLAs N
67. Aid to Nicaraguan rebels Y
68. Reaffirm purch of 21 MX Y
69. African Relief/Farm Crdt N
70. Kill-Nuclear Freeze Y
71. Kill-Void Title IX Narrow Y
72. Raise drinking age to 21 Y
73. Kill-Reduce mil in Europe Y
74. Kill-Bar $ for contras Y

BOSCHWITZ, RUDY (Cont.)

75. Kill-No new MXs in 1985 Y
76. Kill-Move MX $ to non-nuc Y
77. Deficit reduction-$140b Y
78. Kill-Req auth for troops Y
79. School Prayer amendment N
80. Cap punish-certain crimes N
81. Bar govt off from taping Y
82. Martin L. King holiday Y
83. Auth marines in Lebanon Y
84. Anti-abortion amendment Y
85. Highway-Gas tax bill Y
86. Delete job creation amend Y
87. Kill-Tobacco price supprt Y
88. Emergency housing aid Y
89. Nullify oil decontrol N
90. Target tax cuts-mid class N
91. Tax Indexing N
92. Kill-Oppose SS benft cuts Y
93. Disapprove Saudi AWACS Y
94. Anti-busing rider N
95. Disapprove oil import fee Y
96. Domestic violence funds Y
97. Trucking Deregulation Y
98. Overturn India fuel sale Y
99. Mil draft registration Y
100. Chrysler Loan Guarantees N
101. Nuclear plant moratorium Y
102. Abolish electoral college N

Presidential Support Score: 1986 - 85% 1985 - 87%

DURENBERGER, DAVID [Republican] Term Began/Expires: 1983/1988. Prior Terms: Senate: 1978 (Special Election) - 1982. Born: August 19, 1934; St. Cloud, Minn. Education: St. John's University (B.A.); University of Minnesota Law School (J.D.). Military Service: U.S. Army. Occupation: Attorney; executive secretary to governor (1967-71).

1. Immigration Reform Y
2. So Afr Sanc-veto override Y
3. Kill-Death pnlty drug bil Y
4. Kill-Mil use in drug war Y
5. Tax Overhaul Y
6. Raise speed limit Y
7. Across-the-board cuts N
8. South Africa sanctions Y
9. Kill-So Africa sanctions Y
10. Kill-So Africa sanct (*) Y
11. Nicaraguan contra aid N
12. Terminate contra aid Y
13. Kill-Prohibit contra fnds N
14. Kill-Stop CIA contra fndg Y
15. Kill-Bar nuclr tsts w/SDI Y
16. Kill-Bar ASAT testing Y
17. Nuclear test ban treaty Y
18. Prohibit sale of Stinger N
19. Delete Bigeye chem bomb Y
20. Bar binary chem weapons Y
21. Kill-SDI funding Y
22. Kill-AIDS ins dscriminatn Y
23. Kill-$10 bbl oil tariff Y
24. Kill-Repl wndfl prfts tax Y
25. Repeal balanced bdgt amdt N
26. Tax amnesty provisions N
27. Kill-Tax amnesty subst Y
28. Kill-Add third tax rate Y
29. Kill-Unocal tax provsns N
30. Block Saudi arms sale (†) Y
31. Kill-Bar school busing Y
32. Prohibit Saudi arms sale Y
33. Nicaraguan contra aid N
34. Bar all aid to Nicaragua N
35. Balanced budget amendment Y
36. Balanced bdgt substitute N
37. Conrail sale Y
38. Revise farm programs Y
39. Kill-New oil import fee Y
40. Spending cuts, tax incres Y
41. Textile import quotas N
42. Kill-Exmpt vets from cuts Y
43. Kill-Bar inmate abortn $ N
44. Textile import quotas (§) N
45. Kill-Eliminate Amtrak $ Y
46. Kill-Incrs motor fuel tax Y
47. Set max allow deficits Y
48. 20% minimum tax on corps N
49. Bar $ to toxic victims N
50. Seasonal workers in US N
51. Kill-School prayer cases Y
52. Line-item veto N
53. South Africa sanctions Y
54. Ease '68 Gun Control Act Y
55. Kill-14 day handgun wait Y
56. Kill-Gun dlr inspections Y
57. Kill-Keep '68 Gun Con Act Y
58. Nicarag humanitarian aid Y
59. Bar ASAT testing N
60. Delete chemical weapons Y
61. Delete 21 MX missiles Y
62. Kill-15% min tax on corps Y
63. Kill-Restore Soc Sec COLA Y
64. Freeze all funding N
65. Cut def;raise taxes, COLA N
66. Keep existing SS COLAs Y
67. Aid to Nicaraguan rebels Y
68. Reaffirm purch of 21 MX N
69. African Relief/Farm Crdt Y
70. Kill-Nuclear Freeze Y

DURENBERGER, DAVID (Cont.)

71. Kill-Void Title IX Narrow Y
72. Raise drinking age to 21 Y
73. Kill-Reduce mil in Europe Y
74. Kill-Bar $ for contras Y
75. Kill-No new MXs in 1985 N
76. Kill-Move MX $ to non-nuc N
77. Deficit reduction-$140b Y
78. Kill-Req auth for troops Y
79. School Prayer amendment N
80. Cap punish-certain crimes N
81. Bar govt off from taping N
82. Martin L. King holiday Y
83. Auth marines in Lebanon Y
84. Anti-abortion amendment Y
85. Highway-Gas tax bill Y
86. Delete job creation amend Y
87. Kill-Tobacco price supprt N
88. Emergency housing aid +
89. Nullify oil decontrol N
90. Target tax cuts-mid class N
91. Tax Indexing Y
92. Kill-Oppose SS benft cuts Y
93. Disapprove Saudi AWACS Y
94. Anti-busing rider N
95. Disapprove oil import fee Y
96. Domestic violence funds Y
97. Trucking Deregulation +
98. Overturn India fuel sale N
99. Mil draft registration Y
100. Chrysler Loan Guarantees N
101. Nuclear plant moratorium Y
102. Abolish electoral college Y

Presidential Support Score: 1986 - 65% 1985 - 70%

MISSISSIPPI

COCHRAN, THAD [Republican] Term Began/Expires: 1985/1990. Prior Terms: House: 1973-78; Senate: 1978 (Special Appointment)-1984. Born: December 7, 1937; Pontotoc, Miss. Education: University of Mississippi (B.A., J.D.); Trinity College, Dublin. Military Service: U.S. Navy, 1959-61. Occupation: Attorney, Watkins and Eager (1965).

1. Immigration Reform N
2. So Afr Sanc-veto override N
3. Kill-Death pnlty drug bil ?
4. Kill-Mil use in drug war ?
5. Tax Overhaul Y
6. Raise speed limit Y
7. Across-the-board cuts N
8. South Africa sanctions Y
9. Kill-So Africa sanctions Y
10. Kill-So Africa sanct (*) Y
11. Nicaraguan contra aid Y
12. Terminate contra aid N
13. Kill-Prohibit contra fnds Y
14. Kill-Stop CIA contra fndg Y
15. Kill-Bar nuclr tsts w/SDI Y
16. Kill-Bar ASAT testing Y
17. Nuclear test ban treaty N
18. Prohibit sale of Stinger N
19. Delete Bigeye chem bomb N
20. Bar binary chem weapons N
21. Kill-SDI funding Y
22. Kill-AIDS ins dscriminatn N
23. Kill-$10 bbl oil tariff Y
24. Kill-Repl wndfl prfts tax N
25. Repeal balanced bdgt amdt N
26. Tax amnesty provisions N
27. Kill-Tax amnesty subst Y
28. Kill-Add third tax rate Y
29. Kill-Unocal tax provsns N
30. Block Saudi arms sale (†) N
31. Kill-Bar school busing N
32. Prohibit Saudi arms sale N
33. Nicaraguan contra aid Y
34. Bar all aid to Nicaragua N
35. Balanced budget amendment Y
36. Balanced bdgt substitute N
37. Conrail sale ?
38. Revise farm programs Y
39. Kill-New oil import fee Y
40. Spending cuts, tax incres Y
41. Textile import quotas Y
42. Kill-Exmpt vets from cuts Y
43. Kill-Bar inmate abortn $ Y
44. Textile import quotas (§) Y
45. Kill-Eliminate Amtrak $ Y
46. Kill-Incrs motor fuel tax Y
47. Set max allow deficits Y
48. 20% minimum tax on corps N
49. Bar $ to toxic victims Y
50. Seasonal workers in US Y
51. Kill-School prayer cases N
52. Line-item veto Y
53. South Africa sanctions Y
54. Ease '68 Gun Control Act Y
55. Kill-14 day handgun wait Y
56. Kill-Gun dlr inspections Y
57. Kill-Keep '68 Gun Con Act Y
58. Nicarag humanitarian aid Y
59. Bar ASAT testing N
60. Delete chemical weapons N

COCHRAN, THAD (Cont.)

Vote		Vote	
61. Delete 21 MX missiles	N	82. Martin L. King holiday	Y
62. Kill-15% min tax on corps	Y	83. Auth marines in Lebanon	Y
63. Kill-Restore Soc Sec COLA	Y	84. Anti-abortion amendment	Y
64. Freeze all funding	N	85. Highway-Gas tax bill	N
65. Cut def;raise taxes, COLA	N	86. Delete job creation amend	N
66. Keep existing SS COLAs	N	87. Kill-Tobacco price supprt	Y
67. Aid to Nicaraguan rebels	Y	88. Emergency housing aid	Y
68. Reaffirm purch of 21 MX	Y	89. Nullify oil decontrol	N
69. African Relief/Farm Crdt	N	90. Target tax cuts-mid class	N
70. Kill-Nuclear Freeze	Y	91. Tax Indexing	N
71. Kill-Void Title IX Narrow	Y	92. Kill-Oppose SS benft cuts	Y
72. Raise drinking age to 21	Y	93. Disapprove Saudi AWACS	N
73. Kill-Reduce mil in Europe	Y	94. Anti-busing rider	Y
74. Kill-Bar $ for contras	Y	95. Disapprove oil import fee	?
75. Kill-No new MXs in 1985	Y	96. Domestic violence funds	N
76. Kill-Move MX $ to non-nuc	Y	97. Trucking Deregulation	Y
77. Deficit reduction-$140b	Y	98. Overturn India fuel sale	N
78. Kill-Req auth for troops	Y	99. Mil draft registration	Y
79. School Prayer amendment	Y	100. Chrysler Loan Guarantees	N
80. Cap punish-certain crimes	Y	101. Nuclear plant moratorium	N
81. Bar govt off from taping	N	102. Abolish electoral college	N

Presidential Support Score: 1986 - 89% 1985 - 80%

STENNIS, JOHN C. [Democrat] Term Began/Expires: 1983/1988. Prior Terms: Senate: 1947-82. Born: August 3, 1901; Kemper County, Miss. Education: Mississippi State University (B.S.); University of Virginia Law School (LL.B.). Occupation: Mississippi representative (1928-32); prosecuting attorney (1931, 1935); circuit judge (1937, 1938, 1942, 1946).

Vote		Vote	
1. Immigration Reform	?	29. Kill-Unocal tax provsns	Y
2. So Afr Sanc-veto override	Y	30. Block Saudi arms sale (†)	N
3. Kill-Death pnlty drug bil	Y	31. Kill-Bar school busing	Y
4. Kill-Mil use in drug war	Y	32. Prohibit Saudi arms sale	N
5. Tax Overhaul	Y	33. Nicaraguan contra aid	Y
6. Raise speed limit	Y	34. Bar all aid to Nicaragua	N
7. Across-the-board cuts	Y	35. Balanced budget amendment	Y
8. South Africa sanctions	Y	36. Balanced bdgt substitute	N
9. Kill-So Africa sanctions	Y	37. Conrail sale	Y
10. Kill-So Africa sanct (*)	Y	38. Revise farm programs	Y
11. Nicaraguan contra aid	Y	39. Kill-New oil import fee	?
12. Terminate contra aid	N	40. Spending cuts, tax incres	Y
13. Kill-Prohibit contra fnds	N	41. Textile import quotas	Y
14. Kill-Stop CIA contra fndg	Y	42. Kill-Exmpt vets from cuts	N
15. Kill-Bar nuclr tsts w/SDI	Y	43. Kill-Bar inmate abortn $	?
16. Kill-Bar ASAT testing	Y	44. Textile import quotas (§)	Y
17. Nuclear test ban treaty	?	45. Kill-Eliminate Amtrak $	Y
18. Prohibit sale of Stinger	N	46. Kill-Incrs motor fuel tax	Y
19. Delete Bigeye chem bomb	N	47. Set max allow deficits	Y
20. Bar binary chem weapons	N	48. 20% minimum tax on corps	N
21. Kill-SDI funding	Y	49. Bar $ to toxic victims	?
22. Kill-AIDS ins dscriminatn	Y	50. Seasonal workers in US	?
23. Kill-$10 bbl oil tariff	?	51. Kill-School prayer cases	N
24. Kill-Repl wndfl prfts tax	N	52. Line-item veto	N
25. Repeal balanced bdgt amdt	N	53. South Africa sanctions	?
26. Tax amnesty provisions	Y	54. Ease '68 Gun Control Act	?
27. Kill-Tax amnesty subst	N	55. Kill-14 day handgun wait	?
28. Kill-Add third tax rate	N	56. Kill-Gun dlr inspections	?

STENNIS, JOHN C. (Cont.)

57. Kill-Keep '68 Gun Con Act Y
58. Nicarag humanitarian aid Y
59. Bar ASAT testing N
60. Delete chemical weapons ?
61. Delete 21 MX missiles N
62. Kill-15% min tax on corps Y
63. Kill-Restore Soc Sec COLA Y
64. Freeze all funding N
65. Cut def;raise taxes, COLA Y
66. Keep existing SS COLAs N
67. Aid to Nicaraguan rebels Y
68. Reaffirm purch of 21 MX Y
69. African Relief/Farm Crdt Y
70. Kill-Nuclear Freeze Y
71. Kill-Void Title IX Narrow ?
72. Raise drinking age to 21 N
73. Kill-Reduce mil in Europe N
74. Kill-Bar $ for contras Y
75. Kill-No new MXs in 1985 Y
76. Kill-Move MX $ to non-nuc Y
77. Deficit reduction-$140b N
78. Kill-Req auth for troops Y
79. School Prayer amendment Y
80. Cap punish-certain crimes Y
81. Bar govt off from taping N
82. Martin L. King holiday N
83. Auth marines in Lebanon N
84. Anti-abortion amendment Y
85. Highway-Gas tax bill Y
86. Delete job creation amend N
87. Kill-Tobacco price supprt Y
88. Emergency housing aid Y
89. Nullify oil decontrol N
90. Target tax cuts-mid class N
91. Tax Indexing N
92. Kill-Oppose SS benft cuts N
93. Disapprove Saudi AWACS N
94. Anti-busing rider Y
95. Disapprove oil import fee Y
96. Domestic violence funds N
97. Trucking Deregulation Y
98. Overturn India fuel sale N
99. Mil draft registration Y
100. Chrysler Loan Guarantees N
101. Nuclear plant moratorium N
102. Abolish electoral college N
103. Kill-Lmt ct-ordered bus N
104. Airline Deregulation N
105. Disappr Mideast jet sales N
106. Natural gas deregulation Y
107. Prohibit neutron bomb N
108. Financial disclosure-off ?

Presidential Support Score: 1986 - 64% 1985 - 41%

MISSOURI

DANFORTH, JOHN C. [Republican] Term Began/Expires: 1983/1988. Prior Terms: Senate: 1977-82. Born: September 5, 1936; St. Louis, Mo. Education: Princeton University (A.B.); Yale University (B.D., LL.B.). Occupation: Attorney; Missouri attorney general (1969-76); ordained clergyman.

1. Immigration Reform Y
2. So Afr Sanc-veto override Y
3. Kill-Death pnlty drug bil Y
4. Kill-Mil use in drug war Y
5. Tax Overhaul N
6. Raise speed limit N
7. Across-the-board cuts Y
8. South Africa sanctions Y
9. Kill-So Africa sanctions Y
10. Kill-So Africa sanct (*) Y
11. Nicaraguan contra aid Y
12. Terminate contra aid N
13. Kill-Prohibit contra fnds Y
14. Kill-Stop CIA contra fndg Y
15. Kill-Bar nuclr tsts w/SDI Y
16. Kill-Bar ASAT testing Y
17. Nuclear test ban treaty Y
18. Prohibit sale of Stinger N
19. Delete Bigeye chem bomb Y
20. Bar binary chem weapons Y
21. Kill-SDI funding Y
22. Kill-AIDS ins dscriminatn N
23. Kill-$10 bbl oil tariff Y
24. Kill-Repl wndfl prfts tax Y
25. Repeal balanced bdgt amdt N
26. Tax amnesty provisions N
27. Kill-Tax amnesty subst Y
28. Kill-Add third tax rate Y
29. Kill-Unocal tax provsns Y
30. Block Saudi arms sale (†) Y
31. Kill-Bar school busing N
32. Prohibit Saudi arms sale Y
33. Nicaraguan contra aid Y
34. Bar all aid to Nicaragua N
35. Balanced budget amendment Y
36. Balanced bdgt substitute N
37. Conrail sale Y
38. Revise farm programs Y
39. Kill-New oil import fee Y
40. Spending cuts, tax incres Y
41. Textile import quotas N
42. Kill-Exmpt vets from cuts Y
43. Kill-Bar inmate abortn $ N
44. Textile import quotas (§) N
45. Kill-Eliminate Amtrak $?
46. Kill-Incrs motor fuel tax Y

DANFORTH, JOHN C. (Cont.)

47. Set max allow deficits Y
48. 20% minimum tax on corps N
49. Bar $ to toxic victims Y
50. Seasonal workers in US N
51. Kill-School prayer cases Y
52. Line-item veto Y
53. South Africa sanctions Y
54. Ease '68 Gun Control Act Y
55. Kill-14 day handgun wait Y
56. Kill-Gun dlr inspections Y
57. Kill-Keep '68 Gun Con Act Y
58. Nicarag humanitarian aid Y
59. Bar ASAT testing ?
60. Delete chemical weapons Y
61. Delete 21 MX missiles N
62. Kill-15% min tax on corps Y
63. Kill-Restore Soc Sec COLA Y
64. Freeze all funding N
65. Cut def;raise taxes, COLA N
66. Keep existing SS COLAs N
67. Aid to Nicaraguan rebels Y
68. Reaffirm purch of 21 MX Y
69. African Relief/Farm Crdt Y
70. Kill-Nuclear Freeze Y
71. Kill-Void Title IX Narrow Y
72. Raise drinking age to 21 Y
73. Kill-Reduce mil in Europe Y
74. Kill-Bar $ for contras Y
75. Kill-No new MXs in 1985 Y
76. Kill-Move MX $ to non-nuc Y
77. Deficit reduction-$140b Y
78. Kill-Req auth for troops Y
79. School Prayer amendment N
80. Cap punish-certain crimes N
81. Bar govt off from taping N
82. Martin L. King holiday Y
83. Auth marines in Lebanon Y
84. Anti-abortion amendment Y
85. Highway-Gas tax bill Y
86. Delete job creation amend Y
87. Kill-Tobacco price supprt N
88. Emergency housing aid Y
89. Nullify oil decontrol N
90. Target tax cuts-mid class N
91. Tax Indexing Y
92. Kill-Oppose SS benft cuts Y
93. Disapprove Saudi AWACS Y
94. Anti-busing rider Y
95. Disapprove oil import fee Y
96. Domestic violence funds N
97. Trucking Deregulation Y
98. Overturn India fuel sale Y
99. Mil draft registration N
100. Chrysler Loan Guarantees Y
101. Nuclear plant moratorium N
102. Abolish electoral college Y
103. Kill-Lmt ct-ordered bus N
104. Airline Deregulation N
105. Disappr Mideast jet sales N
106. Natural gas deregulation Y
107. Prohibit neutron bomb Y
108. Financial disclosure-off Y

Presidential Support Score: 1986 - 80% 1985 - 81%

EAGLETON, THOMAS F. [Democrat] Term Began/Expires: 1981/1986. Prior Terms: Senate: 1969-80. Born: September 4, 1929; St. Louis, Mo. Education: Amherst College (B.A.); Harvard University (LL.B.). Military Service: U.S. Navy. Occupation: Attorney (1953-56); circuit attorney (1957-60); attorney general (1961-65); lieutenant governor (1965-69).

1. Immigration Reform Y
2. So Afr Sanc-veto override Y
3. Kill-Death pnlty drug bil Y
4. Kill-Mil use in drug war Y
5. Tax Overhaul N
6. Raise speed limit N
7. Across-the-board cuts N
8. South Africa sanctions Y
9. Kill-So Africa sanctions N
10. Kill-So Africa sanct (*) N
11. Nicaraguan contra aid N
12. Terminate contra aid Y
13. Kill-Prohibit contra fnds N
14. Kill-Stop CIA contra fndg N
15. Kill-Bar nuclr tsts w/SDI ?
16. Kill-Bar ASAT testing ?
17. Nuclear test ban treaty Y
18. Prohibit sale of Stinger Y
19. Delete Bigeye chem bomb Y
20. Bar binary chem weapons Y
21. Kill-SDI funding N
22. Kill-AIDS ins dscriminatn Y
23. Kill-$10 bbl oil tariff N
24. Kill-Repl wndfl prfts tax Y
25. Repeal balanced bdgt amdt Y
26. Tax amnesty provisions N
27. Kill-Tax amnesty subst Y
28. Kill-Add third tax rate N
29. Kill-Unocal tax provsns ?
30. Block Saudi arms sale (†) Y
31. Kill-Bar school busing Y
32. Prohibit Saudi arms sale Y
33. Nicaraguan contra aid N
34. Bar all aid to Nicaragua N
35. Balanced budget amendment N
36. Balanced bdgt substitute Y

EAGLETON, THOMAS F. (Cont.)

37. Conrail sale Y
38. Revise farm programs Y
39. Kill-New oil import fee N
40. Spending cuts, tax incres Y
41. Textile im?ort quotas Y
42. Kill-Exmpt vets from cuts N
43. Kill-Bar inmate abortn $?
44. Textile import quotas (§) #
45. Kill-Eliminate Amtrak $?
46. Kill-Incrs motor fuel tax N
47. Set max allow deficits N
48. 20% minimum tax on corps N
49. Bar $ to toxic victims N
50. Seasonal workers in US N
51. Kill-School prayer cases Y
52. Line-item veto N
53. South Africa sanctions Y
54. Ease '68 Gun Control Act Y
55. Kill-14 day handgun wait Y
56. Kill-Gun dlr inspections Y
57. Kill-Keep '68 Gun Con Act Y
58. Nicarag humanitarian aid N
59. Bar ASAT testing Y
60. Delete chemical weapons Y
61. Delete 21 MX missiles Y
62. Kill-15% min tax on corps N
63. Kill-Restore Soc Sec COLA N
64. Freeze all funding N
65. Cut def;raise taxes, COLA Y
66. Keep existing SS COLAs Y
67. Aid to Nicaraguan rebels N
68. Reaffirm purch of 21 MX N
69. African Relief/Farm Crdt Y
70. Kill-Nuclear Freeze N
71. Kill-Void Title IX Narrow N
72. Raise drinking age to 21 Y
73. Kill-Reduce mil in Europe N
74. Kill-Bar $ for contras N
75. Kill-No new MXs in 1985 N
76. Kill-Move MX $ to non-nuc N
77. Deficit reduction-$140b N
78. Kill-Req auth for troops N
79. School Prayer amendment N
80. Cap punish-certain crimes N
81. Bar govt off from taping ?
82. Martin L. King holiday Y
83. Auth marines in Lebanon N
84. Anti-abortion amendment Y
85. Highway-Gas tax bill N
86. Delete job creation amend N
87. Kill-Tobacco price supprt N
88. Emergency housing aid Y
89. Nullify oil decontrol Y
90. Target tax cuts-mid class Y
91. Tax indexing N
92. Kill-Oppose SS benft cuts N
93. Disapprove Saudi AWACS Y
94. Anti-busing rider N
95. Disapprove oil import fee Y
96. Domestic violence funds ?
97. Trucking Deregulation N
98. Overturn India fuel sale N
99. Mil draft registration N
100. Chrysler Loan Guarantees Y
101. Nuclear plant moratorium ?
102. Abolish electoral college N
103. Kill-Lmt ct-ordered bus Y
104. Airline Deregulation Y
105. Disappr Mideast jet sales N
106. Natural gas deregulation N
107. Prohibit neutron bomb N
108. Financial disclosure-off Y

Presidential Support Score: 1986 - 29% 1985 - 30%

MONTANA

BAUCUS, MAX [Democrat] Term Began/Expires: 1985/1990. Prior Terms: House: 1975-78; Senate: 1978 (Special Appointment)-1984. Born: December 11, 1941; Helena, Mont. Education: Stanford University (B.A., LL.B.). Occupation: Attorney, Civil Aeronautics Board (1967-68); legal assistant, Securities and Exchange Commission (1968-71); private attorney (1971); Montana representative (1973).

1. Immigration Reform Y
2. So Afr Sanc-veto override Y
3. Kill-Death pnlty drug bil N
4. Kill-Mil use in drug war Y
5. Tax Overhaul Y
6. Raise speed limit Y
7. Across-the-board cuts N
8. South Africa sanctions Y
9. Kill-So Africa sanctions N
10. Kill-So Africa sanct (*) N
11. Nicaraguan contra aid N
12. Terminate contra aid Y
13. Kill-Prohibit contra fnds N
14. Kill-Stop CIA contra fndg N
15. Kill-Bar nuclr tsts w/SDI N
16. Kill-Bar ASAT testing N
17. Nuclear test ban treaty Y
18. Prohibit sale of Stinger N

BAUCUS, MAX (Cont.)

19. Delete Bigeye chem bomb Y
20. Bar binary chem weapons Y
21. Kill-SDI funding N
22. Kill-AIDS ins dscriminatn Y
23. Kill-$10 bbl oil tariff Y
24. Kill-Repl wndfl prfts tax N
25. Repeal balanced bdgt amdt N
26. Tax amnesty provisions Y
27. Kill-Tax amnesty subst N
28. Kill-Add third tax rate Y
29. Kill-Unocal tax provsns N
30. Block Saudi arms sale (†) Y
31. Kill-Bar school busing Y
32. Prohibit Saudi arms sale Y
33. Nicaraguan contra aid N
34. Bar all aid to Nicaragua N
35. Balanced budget amendment N
36. Balanced bdgt substitute Y
37. Conrail sale N
38. Revise farm programs Y
39. Kill-New oil import fee Y
40. Spending cuts, tax incres Y
41. Textile import quotas N
42. Kill-Exmpt vets from cuts N
43. Kill-Bar inmate abortn $ Y
44. Textile import quotas (§) N
45. Kill-Eliminate Amtrak $ Y
46. Kill-Incrs motor fuel tax Y
47. Set max allow deficits Y
48. 20% minimum tax on corps Y
49. Bar $ to toxic victims -
50. Seasonal workers in US Y
51. Kill-School prayer cases Y
52. Line-item veto N
53. South Africa sanctions Y
54. Ease '68 Gun Control Act Y
55. Kill-14 day handgun wait Y
56. Kill-Gun dlr inspections Y
57. Kill-Keep '68 Gun Con Act Y
58. Nicarag humanitarian aid N
59. Bar ASAT testing Y
60. Delete chemical weapons Y
61. Delete 21 MX missiles Y
62. Kill-15% min tax on corps N
63. Kill-Restore Soc Sec COLA N
64. Freeze all funding Y
65. Cut def;raise taxes, COLA Y
66. Keep existing SS COLAs Y
67. Aid to Nicaraguan rebels N
68. Reaffirm purch of 21 MX N
69. African Relief/Farm Crdt Y
70. Kill-Nuclear Freeze N
71. Kill-Void Title IX Narrow N
72. Raise drinking age to 21 N
73. Kill-Reduce mil in Europe N
74. Kill-Bar $ for contras N
75. Kill-No new MXs in 1985 N
76. Kill-Move MX $ to non-nuc N
77. Deficit reduction-$140b Y
78. Kill-Req auth for troops N
79. School Prayer amendment N
80. Cap punish-certain crimes Y
81. Bar govt off from taping Y
82. Martin L. King holiday Y
83. Auth marines in Lebanon N
84. Anti-abortion amendment N
85. Highway-Gas tax bill Y
86. Delete job creation amend N
87. Kill-Tobacco price supprt N
88. Emergency housing aid Y
89. Nullify oil decontrol N
90. Target tax cuts-mid class N
91. Tax Indexing Y
92. Kill-Oppose SS benft cuts N
93. Disapprove Saudi AWACS Y
94. Anti-busing rider N
95. Disapprove oil import fee ?
96. Domestic violence funds Y
97. Trucking Deregulation Y
98. Overturn India fuel sale N
99. Mil draft registration Y
100. Chrysler Loan Guarantees Y
101. Nuclear plant moratorium ?
102. Abolish electoral college Y

Presidential Support Score: 1986 - 30% 1985 - 30%

MELCHER, JOHN [Democrat] Term Began/Expires: 1983/1988. Prior Terms: House: 1969 (Special Election)-1976; Senate: 1977-82. Born: September 6, 1924; Sioux City, Iowa. Education: University of Minnesota, Iowa State University. Military Service: U.S. Army, 1943-45. Occupation: Partner, Yellowstone Valley Veterinary Clinic; alderman (1953); mayor (1955-60); Montana representative (1960); Montana senator (1963, 1965).

1. Immigration Reform Y
2. So Afr Sanc-veto override Y
3. Kill-Death pnlty drug bil Y
4. Kill-Mil use in drug war Y
5. Tax Overhaul N
6. Raise speed limit Y
7. Across-the-board cuts N
8. South Africa sanctions Y
9. Kill-So Africa sanctions N
10. Kill-So Africa sanct (*) N
11. Nicaraguan contra aid N
12. Terminate contra aid Y

MELCHER, JOHN (Cont.)

13. Kill-Prohibit contra fnds N
14. Kill-Stop CIA contra fndg N
15. Kill-Bar nuclr tsts w/SDI N
16. Kill-Bar ASAT testing N
17. Nuclear test ban treaty Y
18. Prohibit sale of Stinger Y
19. Delete Bigeye chem bomb Y
20. Bar binary chem weapons Y
21. Kill-SDI funding N
22. Kill-AIDS ins dscriminatn Y
23. Kill-$10 bbl oil tariff N
24. Kill-Repl wndfl prfts tax N
25. Repeal balanced bdgt amdt Y
26. Tax amnesty provisions Y
27. Kill-Tax amnesty subst N
28. Kill-Add third tax rate N
29. Kill-Unocal tax provsns N
30. Block Saudi arms sale (†) Y
31. Kill-Bar school busing Y
32. Prohibit Saudi arms sale Y
33. Nicaraguan contra aid N
34. Bar all aid to Nicaragua Y
35. Balanced budget amendment Y
36. Balanced bdgt substitute Y
37. Conrail sale N
38. Revise farm programs Y
39. Kill-New oil import fee Y
40. Spending cuts, tax incres N
41. Textile import quotas Y
42. Kill-Exmpt vets from cuts N
43. Kill-Bar inmate abortn $ N
44. Textile import quotas (§) Y
45. Kill-Eliminate Amtrak $ Y
46. Kill-Incrs motor fuel tax Y
47. Set max allow deficits Y
48. 20% minimum tax on corps Y
49. Bar $ to toxic victims N
50. Seasonal workers in US N
51. Kill-School prayer cases Y
52. Line-item veto N
53. South Africa sanctions Y
54. Ease '68 Gun Control Act Y
55. Kill-14 day handgun wait N
56. Kill-Gun dlr inspections Y
57. Kill-Keep '68 Gun Con Act Y
58. Nicarag humanitarian aid N
59. Bar ASAT testing +
60. Delete chemical weapons Y
61. Delete 21 MX missiles Y
62. Kill-15% min tax on corps N
63. Kill-Restore Soc Sec COLA N
64. Freeze all funding Y
65. Cut def;raise taxes, COLA Y
66. Keep existing SS COLAs Y
67. Aid to Nicaraguan rebels N
68. Reaffirm purch of 21 MX N
69. African Relief/Farm Crdt Y
70. Kill-Nuclear Freeze N
71. Kill-Void Title IX Narrow N
72. Raise drinking age to 21 N
73. Kill-Reduce mil in Europe N
74. Kill-Bar $ for contras N
75. Kill-No new MXs in 1985 N
76. Kill-Move MX $ to non-nuc N
77. Deficit reduction-$140b N
78. Kill-Req auth for troops N
79. School Prayer amendment Y
80. Cap punish-certain crimes N
81. Bar govt off from taping Y
82. Martin L. King holiday Y
83. Auth marines in Lebanon N
84. Anti-abortion amendment Y
85. Highway-Gas tax bill Y
86. Delete job creation amend N
87. Kill-Tobacco price supprt Y
88. Emergency housing aid Y
89. Nullify oil decontrol N
90. Target tax cuts-mid class N
91. Tax Indexing Y
92. Kill-Oppose SS benft cuts N
93. Disapprove Saudi AWACS N
94. Anti-busing rider Y
95. Disapprove oil import fee Y
96. Domestic violence funds Y
97. Trucking Deregulation N
98. Overturn India fuel sale N
99. Mil draft registration N
100. Chrysler Loan Guarantees Y
101. Nuclear plant moratorium Y
102. Abolish electoral college N
103. Kill-Lmt ct-ordered bus Y
104. Airline Deregulation N
105. Disappr Mideast jet sales Y
106. Natural gas deregulation Y
107. Prohibit neutron bomb Y
108. Financial disclosure-off Y

Presidential Support Score: 1986 - 21% 1985 - 20%

NEBRASKA

EXON, J. JAMES [Democrat] Term Began/Expires: 1985/1990. Prior Terms: Senate: 1979-84. Born: August 9, 1921; Geddes, S.D. Education: University of Omaha. Military Service: U.S. Army, 1942-45; Army Reserve, 1945-49. Occupation: Branch manager, Universal Finance Corp. (1945-53); president, Exon's Inc. (1953-71); governor (1971-78).

EXON, J. JAMES (Cont.)

No.	Vote	Vote
1.	Immigration Reform	Y
2.	So Afr Sanc-veto override	Y
3.	Kill-Death pnlty drug bil	N
4.	Kill-Mil use in drug war	Y
5.	Tax Overhaul	N
6.	Raise speed limit	Y
7.	Across-the-board cuts	N
8.	South Africa sanctions	Y
9.	Kill-So Africa sanctions	N
10.	Kill-So Africa sanct (*)	N
11.	Nicaraguan contra aid	N
12.	Terminate contra aid	Y
13.	Kill-Prohibit contra fnds	N
14.	Kill-Stop CIA contra fndg	N
15.	Kill-Bar nuclr tsts w/SDI	Y
16.	Kill-Bar ASAT testing	Y
17.	Nuclear test ban treaty	Y
18.	Prohibit sale of Stinger	N
19.	Delete Bigeye chem bomb	N
20.	Bar binary chem weapons	N
21.	Kill-SDI funding	Y
22.	Kill-AIDS ins dscriminatn	N
23.	Kill-$10 bbl oil tariff	Y
24.	Kill-Repl wndfl prfts tax	N
25.	Repeal balanced bdgt amdt	Y
26.	Tax amnesty provisions	N
27.	Kill-Tax amnesty subst	Y
28.	Kill-Add third tax rate	Y
29.	Kill-Unocal tax provsns	N
30.	Block Saudi arms sale (†)	N
31.	Kill-Bar school busing	N
32.	Prohibit Saudi arms sale	Y
33.	Nicaraguan contra aid	N
34.	Bar all aid to Nicaragua	N
35.	Balanced budget amendment	Y
36.	Balanced bdgt substitute	Y
37.	Conrail sale	N
38.	Revise farm programs	N
39.	Kill-New oil import fee	N
40.	Spending cuts, tax incres	Y
41.	Textile import quotas	N
42.	Kill-Exmpt vets from cuts	N
43.	Kill-Bar inmate abortn $	N
44.	Textile import quotas (§)	N
45.	Kill-Eliminate Amtrak $	Y
46.	Kill-Incrs motor fuel tax	Y
47.	Set max allow deficits	N
48.	20% minimum tax on corps	Y
49.	Bar $ to toxic victims	N
50.	Seasonal workers in US	Y
51.	Kill-School prayer cases	N
52.	Line-item veto	Y
53.	South Africa sanctions	Y
54.	Ease '68 Gun Control Act	Y
55.	Kill-14 day handgun wait	Y
56.	Kill-Gun dlr inspections	Y
57.	Kill-Keep '68 Gun Con Act	Y
58.	Nicarag humanitarian aid	Y
59.	Bar ASAT testing	N
60.	Delete chemical weapons	N
61.	Delete 21 MX missiles	Y
62.	Kill-15% min tax on corps	?
63.	Kill-Restore Soc Sec COLA	?
64.	Freeze all funding	?
65.	Cut def;raise taxes, COLA	?
66.	Keep existing SS COLAs	Y
67.	Aid to Nicaraguan rebels	N
68.	Reaffirm purch of 21 MX	N
69.	African Relief/Farm Crdt	Y
70.	Kill-Nuclear Freeze	Y
71.	Kill-Void Title IX Narrow	Y
72.	Raise drinking age to 21	Y
73.	Kill-Reduce mil in Europe	N
74.	Kill-Bar $ for contras	?
75.	Kill-No new MXs in 1985	N
76.	Kill-Move MX $ to non-nuc	N
77.	Deficit reduction-$140b	Y
78.	Kill-Req auth for troops	N
79.	School Prayer amendment	Y
80.	Cap punish-certain crimes	Y
81.	Bar govt off from taping	Y
82.	Martin L. King holiday	N
83.	Auth marines in Lebanon	N
84.	Anti-abortion amendment	Y
85.	Highway-Gas tax bill	N
86.	Delete job creation amend	Y
87.	Kill-Tobacco price supprt	N
88.	Emergency housing aid	Y
89.	Nullify oil decontrol	N
90.	Target tax cuts-mid class	Y
91.	Tax Indexing	Y
92.	Kill-Oppose SS benft cuts	N
93.	Disapprove Saudi AWACS	N
94.	Anti-busing rider	Y
95.	Disapprove oil import fee	Y
96.	Domestic violence funds	N
97.	Trucking Deregulation	Y
98.	Overturn India fuel sale	N
99.	Mil draft registration	Y
100.	Chrysler Loan Guarantees	N
101.	Nuclear plant moratorium	N
102.	Abolish electoral college	Y

Presidential Support Score: 1986 - 34% 1985 - 43%

ZORINSKY, EDWARD [Democrat] Term Began/Expires: 1983/1988. Prior Terms: Senate: 1977-82. Born: November 11, 1928; Omaha, Neb. Education: University of Minnesota; Creighton University; University of Nebraska (B.S.); Harvard University. Military Service: U.S. Army. Occupation: Mayor of Omaha (1973-77).

ZORINSKY, EDWARD (Cont.)

1. Immigration Reform N
2. So Afr Sanc-veto override Y
3. Kill-Death pnlty drug bil N
4. Kill-Mil use in drug war Y
5. Tax Overhaul Y
6. Raise speed limit ?
7. Across-the-board cuts N
8. South Africa sanctions Y
9. Kill-So Africa sanctions Y
10. Kill-So Africa sanct (*) Y
11. Nicaraguan contra aid N
12. Terminate contra aid Y
13. Kill-Prohibit contra fnds N
14. Kill-Stop CIA contra fndg N
15. Kill-Bar nuclr tsts w/SDI Y
16. Kill-Bar ASAT testing Y
17. Nuclear test ban treaty N
18. Prohibit sale of Stinger N
19. Delete Bigeye chem bomb N
20. Bar binary chem weapons N
21. Kill-SDI funding Y
22. Kill-AIDS ins dscriminatn N
23. Kill-$10 bbl oil tariff Y
24. Kill-Repl wndfl prfts tax N
25. Repeal balanced bdgt amdt N
26. Tax amnesty provisions N
27. Kill-Tax amnesty subst Y
28. Kill-Add third tax rate Y
29. Kill-Unocal tax provsns N
30. Block Saudi arms sale (†) N
31. Kill-Bar school busing N
32. Prohibit Saudi arms sale N
33. Nicaraguan contra aid N
34. Bar all aid to Nicaragua N
35. Balanced budget amendment Y
36. Balanced bdgt substitute N
37. Conrail sale N
38. Revise farm programs N
39. Kill-New oil import fee Y
40. Spending cuts, tax incres Y
41. Textile import quotas N
42. Kill-Exmpt vets from cuts ?
43. Kill-Bar inmate abortn $ N
44. Textile import quotas (§) N
45. Kill-Eliminate Amtrak $ Y
46. Kill-Incrs motor fuel tax Y
47. Set max allow deficits Y
48. 20% minimum tax on corps N
49. Bar $ to toxic victims Y
50. Seasonal workers in US X
51. Kill-School prayer cases Y
52. Line-item veto Y
53. South Africa sanctions Y
54. Ease '68 Gun Control Act Y
55. Kill-14 day handgun wait Y
56. Kill-Gun dlr inspections Y
57. Kill-Keep '68 Gun Con Act Y
58. Nicarag humanitarian aid N
59. Bar ASAT testing N
60. Delete chemical weapons N
61. Delete 21 MX missiles N
62. Kill-15% min tax on corps Y
63. Kill-Restore Soc Sec COLA Y
64. Freeze all funding Y
65. Cut def;raise taxes, COLA Y
66. Keep existing SS COLAs Y
67. Aid to Nicaraguan rebels N
68. Reaffirm purch of 21 MX Y
69. African Relief/Farm Crdt Y
70. Kill-Nuclear Freeze Y
71. Kill-Void Title IX Narrow Y
72. Raise drinking age to 21 Y
73. Kill-Reduce mil in Europe N
74. Kill-Bar $ for contras N
75. Kill-No new MXs in 1985 Y
76. Kill-Move MX $ to non-nuc Y
77. Deficit reduction-$140b Y
78. Kill-Req auth for troops Y
79. School Prayer amendment Y
80. Cap punish-certain crimes Y
81. Bar govt off from taping N
82. Martin L. King holiday N
83. Auth marines in Lebanon Y
84. Anti-abortion amendment Y
85. Highway-Gas tax bill N
86. Delete job creation amend Y
87. Kill-Tobacco price supprt N
88. Emergency housing aid Y
89. Nullify oil decontrol N
90. Target tax cuts-mid class N
91. Tax Indexing Y
92. Kill-Oppose SS benft cuts N
93. Disapprove Saudi AWACS N
94. Anti-busing rider Y
95. Disapprove oil import fee Y
96. Domestic violence funds N
97. Trucking Deregulation Y
98. Overturn India fuel sale N
99. Mil draft registration Y
100. Chrysler Loan Guarantees N
101. Nuclear plant moratorium N
102. Abolish electoral college Y
103. Kill-Lmt ct-ordered bus N
104. Airline Deregulation N
105. Disappr Mideast jet sales Y
106. Natural gas deregulation #
107. Prohibit neutron bomb N
108. Financial disclosure-off Y

Presidential Support Score: 1986 - 65% 1985 - 53%

NEVADA

HECHT, CHIC [Republican] Term Began/Expires: 1983/1988. Born: November 30, 1928; Cape Girardeau, Mo. Education: Washington University (B.S.). Occupation: Counter intelligence work behind the Iron Curtain; banker; proprietor, Western Emporium; Nevada senator (1966); Senate minority leader (1968)

1.	Immigration Reform	N
2.	So Afr Sanc-veto override	N
3.	Kill-Death pnlty drug bil	N
4.	Kill-Mil use in drug war	Y
5.	Tax Overhaul	Y
6.	Raise speed limit	Y
7.	Across-the-board cuts	Y
8.	South Africa sanctions	N
9.	Kill-So Africa sanctions	Y
10.	Kill-So Africa sanct (*)	Y
11.	Nicaraguan contra aid	Y
12.	Terminate contra aid	N
13.	Kill-Prohibit contra fnds	Y
14.	Kill-Stop CIA contra fndg	Y
15.	Kill-Bar nuclr tsts w/SDI	Y
16.	Kill-Bar ASAT testing	Y
17.	Nuclear test ban treaty	N
18.	Prohibit sale of Stinger	N
19.	Delete Bigeye chem bomb	N
20.	Bar binary chem weapons	N
21.	Kill-SDI funding	Y
22.	Kill-AIDS ins dscriminatn	N
23.	Kill-$10 bbl oil tariff	Y
24.	Kill-Repl wndfl prfts tax	N
25.	Repeal balanced bdgt amdt	N
26.	Tax amnesty provisions	?
27.	Kill-Tax amnesty subst	?
28.	Kill-Add third tax rate	Y
29.	Kill-Unocal tax provsns	Y
30.	Block Saudi arms sale (†)	N
31.	Kill-Bar school busing	N
32.	Prohibit Saudi arms sale	Y
33.	Nicaraguan contra aid	Y
34.	Bar all aid to Nicaragua	N
35.	Balanced budget amendment	Y
36.	Balanced bdgt substitute	N
37.	Conrail sale	Y
38.	Revise farm programs	N
39.	Kill-New oil import fee	Y
40.	Spending cuts, tax incres	Y
41.	Textile import quotas	N
42.	Kill-Exmpt vets from cuts	Y
43.	Kill-Bar inmate abortn $	N
44.	Textile import quotas (§)	N
45.	Kill-Eliminate Amtrak $	N
46.	Kill-Incrs motor fuel tax	Y
47.	Set max allow deficits	Y
48.	20% minimum tax on corps	N
49.	Bar $ to toxic victims	Y
50.	Seasonal workers in US	Y
51.	Kill-School prayer cases	N
52.	Line-item veto	Y
53.	South Africa sanctions	N
54.	Ease '68 Gun Control Act	Y
55.	Kill-14 day handgun wait	Y
56.	Kill-Gun dlr inspections	Y
57.	Kill-Keep '68 Gun Con Act	Y
58.	Nicarag humanitarian aid	Y
59.	Bar ASAT testing	N
60.	Delete chemical weapons	N
61.	Delete 21 MX missiles	N
62.	Kill-15% min tax on corps	Y
63.	Kill-Restore Soc Sec COLA	Y
64.	Freeze all funding	N
65.	Cut def;raise taxes, COLA	N
66.	Keep existing SS COLAs	N
67.	Aid to Nicaraguan rebels	Y
68.	Reaffirm purch of 21 MX	Y
69.	African Relief/Farm Crdt	N
70.	Kill-Nuclear Freeze	Y
71.	Kill-Void Title IX Narrow	Y
72.	Raise drinking age to 21	Y
73.	Kill-Reduce mil in Europe	Y
74.	Kill-Bar $ for contras	Y
75.	Kill-No new MXs in 1985	Y
76.	Kill-Move MX $ to non-nuc	Y
77.	Deficit reduction-$140b	Y
78.	Kill-Req auth for troops	Y
79.	School Prayer amendment	Y
80.	Cap punish-certain crimes	Y
81.	Bar govt off from taping	N
82.	Martin L. King holiday	N
83.	Auth marines in Lebanon	Y
84.	Anti-abortion amendment	Y

Presidential Support Score: 1986 - 90% 1985 - 89%

LAXALT, PAUL [Republican] Term Began/Expires: 1981/1986. Prior Terms: Senate: 1975-80. Born: August 2, 1922; Reno, Nev. Education: Santa Clara University; University of Denver Law School. Military Service: U.S. Army, WW II. Occupation: Ormsby County district attorney (1951-54); attorney (1954-66); lieutenant governor (1963-66); governor (1966-70); senior partner, Laxalt, Berry & Allison (1970-74).

LAXALT, PAUL (Cont.)

1. Immigration Reform ?
2. So Afr Sanc-veto override N
3. Kill-Death pnlty drug bil N
4. Kill-Mil use in drug war Y
5. Tax Overhaul Y
6. Raise speed limit Y
7. Across-the-board cuts N
8. South Africa sanctions N
9. Kill-So Africa sanctions Y
10. Kill-So Africa sanct (*) Y
11. Nicaraguan contra aid Y
12. Terminate contra aid N
13. Kill-Prohibit contra fnds Y
14. Kill-Stop CIA contra fndg Y
15. Kill-Bar nuclr tsts w/SDI Y
16. Kill-Bar ASAT testing Y
17. Nuclear test ban treaty N
18. Prohibit sale of Stinger N
19. Delete Bigeye chem bomb N
20. Bar binary chem weapons N
21. Kill-SDI funding Y
22. Kill-AIDS ins dscriminatn N
23. Kill-$10 bbl oil tariff Y
24. Kill-Repl wndfl prfts tax N
25. Repeal balanced bdgt amdt N
26. Tax amnesty provisions N
27. Kill-Tax amnesty subst ?
28. Kill-Add third tax rate Y
29. Kill-Unocal tax provsns Y
30. Block Saudi arms sale (†) N
31. Kill-Bar school busing N
32. Prohibit Saudi arms sale N
33. Nicaraguan contra aid Y
34. Bar all aid to Nicaragua N
35. Balanced budget amendment Y
36. Balanced bdgt substitute ?
37. Conrail sale Y
38. Revise farm programs Y
39. Kill-New oil import fee Y
40. Spending cuts, tax incres Y
41. Textile import quotas Y
42. Kill-Exmpt vets from cuts Y
43. Kill-Bar inmate abortn $ N
44. Textile import quotas (§) Y
45. Kill-Eliminate Amtrak $ N
46. Kill-Incrs motor fuel tax ?
47. Set max allow deficits Y
48. 20% minimum tax on corps ?
49. Bar $ to toxic victims Y
50. Seasonal workers in US Y
51. Kill-School prayer cases N
52. Line-item veto Y
53. South Africa sanctions N
54. Ease '68 Gun Control Act Y
55. Kill-14 day handgun wait Y
56. Kill-Gun dlr inspections Y
57. Kill-Keep '68 Gun Con Act Y
58. Nicarag humanitarian aid Y
59. Bar ASAT testing N
60. Delete chemical weapons N
61. Delete 21 MX missiles N
62. Kill-15% min tax on corps Y
63. Kill-Restore Soc Sec COLA Y
64. Freeze all funding N
65. Cut def;raise taxes, COLA N
66. Keep existing SS COLAs N
67. Aid to Nicaraguan rebels Y
68. Reaffirm purch of 21 MX Y
69. African Relief/Farm Crdt N
70. Kill-Nuclear Freeze Y
71. Kill-Void Title IX Narrow Y
72. Raise drinking age to 21 Y
73. Kill-Reduce mil in Europe Y
74. Kill-Bar $ for contras Y
75. Kill-No new MXs in 1985 Y
76. Kill-Move MX $ to non-nuc Y
77. Deficit reduction-$140b Y
78. Kill-Req auth for troops Y
79. School Prayer amendment Y
80. Cap punish-certain crimes Y
81. Bar govt off from taping N
82. Martin L. King holiday Y
83. Auth marines in Lebanon Y
84. Anti-abortion amendment Y
85. Highway-Gas tax bill Y
86. Delete job creation amend Y
87. Kill-Tobacco price supprt Y
88. Emergency housing aid Y
89. Nullify oil decontrol N
90. Target tax cuts-mid class N
91. Tax Indexing Y
92. Kill-Oppose SS benft cuts Y
93. Disapprove Saudi AWACS N
94. Anti-busing rider Y
95. Disapprove oil import fee Y
96. Domestic violence funds N
97. Trucking Deregulation Y
98. Overturn India fuel sale Y
99. Mil draft registration Y
100. Chrysler Loan Guarantees N
101. Nuclear plant moratorium N
102. Abolish electoral college N
103. Kill-Lmt ct-ordered bus N
104. Airline Deregulation Y
105. Disappr Mideast jet sales ?
106. Natural gas deregulation Y
107. Prohibit neutron bomb N
108. Financial disclosure-off ?

Presidential Support Score: 1986 - 89% 1985 - 82%

NEW HAMPSHIRE

HUMPHREY, GORDON J. [Republican] Term Began/Expires: 1985/1990. Prior Terms: Senate: 1979-84. Born: October 9, 1940; Bristol, Conn. Education: George Washington University; University of Maryland; Burnside-Ott Aviation Institute. Military Service: U.S. Air Force, 1958-62. Occupation: Pilot (1964-78).

1.	Immigration Reform	N	52.	Line-item veto	Y
2.	So Afr Sanc-veto override	N	53.	South Africa sanctions	N
3.	Kill-Death pnlty drug bil	N	54.	Ease '68 Gun Control Act	Y
4.	Kill-Mil use in drug war	Y	55.	Kill-14 day handgun wait	Y
5.	Tax Overhaul	Y	56.	Kill-Gun dlr inspections	Y
6.	Raise speed limit	Y	57.	Kill-Keep '68 Gun Con Act	Y
7.	Across-the-board cuts	Y	58.	Nicarag humanitarian aid	Y
8.	South Africa sanctions	N	59.	Bar ASAT testing	N
9.	Kill-So Africa sanctions	Y	60.	Delete chemical weapons	N
10.	Kill-So Africa sanct (*)	Y	61.	Delete 21 MX missiles	N
11.	Nicaraguan contra aid	Y	62.	Kill-15% min tax on corps	Y
12.	Terminate contra aid	N	63.	Kill-Restore Soc Sec COLA	Y
13.	Kill-Prohibit contra fnds	Y	64.	Freeze all funding	Y
14.	Kill-Stop CIA contra fndg	Y	65.	Cut def;raise taxes, COLA	N
15.	Kill-Bar nuclr tsts w/SDI	Y	66.	Keep existing SS COLAs	N
16.	Kill-Bar ASAT testing	Y	67.	Aid to Nicaraguan rebels	Y
17.	Nuclear test ban treaty	N	68.	Reaffirm purch of 21 MX	Y
18.	Prohibit sale of Stinger	N	69.	African Relief/Farm Crdt	N
19.	Delete Bigeye chem bomb	N	70.	Kill-Nuclear Freeze	Y
20.	Bar binary chem weapons	N	71.	Kill-Void Title IX Narrow	Y
21.	Kill-SDI funding	Y	72.	Raise drinking age to 21	N
22.	Kill-AIDS ins dscriminatn	N	73.	Kill-Reduce mil in Europe	N
23.	Kill-$10 bbl oil tariff	Y	74.	Kill-Bar $ for contras	Y
24.	Kill-Repl wndfl prfts tax	N	75.	Kill-No new MXs in 1985	N
25.	Repeal balanced bdgt amdt	N	76.	Kill-Move MX $ to non-nuc	N
26.	Tax amnesty provisions	?	77.	Deficit reduction-$140b	Y
27.	Kill-Tax amnesty subst	?	78.	Kill-Req auth for troops	Y
28.	Kill-Add third tax rate	Y	79.	School Prayer amendment	Y
29.	Kill-Unocal tax provsns	N	80.	Cap punish-certain crimes	Y
30.	Block Saudi arms sale (†)	N	81.	Bar govt off from taping	Y
31.	Kill-Bar school busing	N	82.	Martin L. King holiday	N
32.	Prohibit Saudi arms sale	?	83.	Auth marines in Lebanon	Y
33.	Nicaraguan contra aid	Y	84.	Anti-abortion amendment	Y
34.	Bar all aid to Nicaragua	N	85.	Highway-Gas tax bill	N
35.	Balanced budget amendment	Y	86.	Delete job creation amend	Y
36.	Balanced bdgt substitute	N	87.	Kill-Tobacco price supprt	N
37.	Conrail sale	Y	88.	Emergency housing aid	N
38.	Revise farm programs	N	89.	Nullify oil decontrol	N
39.	Kill-New oil import fee	Y	90.	Target tax cuts-mid class	N
40.	Spending cuts, tax incres	Y	91.	Tax indexing	Y
41.	Textile import quotas	N	92.	Kill-Oppose SS benft cuts	Y
42.	Kill-Exmpt vets from cuts	?	93.	Disapprove Saudi AWACS	N
43.	Kill-Bar inmate abortn $	N	94.	Anti-busing rider	Y
44.	Textile import quotas (§)	N	95.	Disapprove oil import fee	Y
45.	Kill-Eliminate Amtrak $	N	96.	Domestic violence funds	N
46.	Kill-Incrs motor fuel tax	Y	97.	Trucking Deregulation	Y
47.	Set max allow deficits	Y	98.	Overturn India fuel sale	Y
48.	20% minimum tax on corps	N	99.	Mil draft registration	Y
49.	Bar $ to toxic victims	N	100.	Chrysler Loan Guarantees	N
50.	Seasonal workers in US	Y	101.	Nuclear plant moratorium	N
51.	Kill-School prayer cases	N	102.	Abolish electoral college	N

Presidential Support Score: 1986 - 93% 1985 - 80%

RUDMAN, WARREN [Republican] Term Began/Expires: 1981/1986. Born: May 18, 1930; Boston, Mass. Education: Boston College of Law. Military Service: U.S. Army, 1952-54. Occupation: New Hampshire attorney general (1970-76); business manager.

1.	Immigration Reform	N	48.	20% minimum tax on corps	N
2.	So Afr Sanc-veto override	N	49.	Bar $ to toxic victims	Y
3.	Kill-Death pnlty drug bil	N	50.	Seasonal workers in US	Y
4.	Kill-Mil use in drug war	Y	51.	Kill-School prayer cases	Y
5.	Tax Overhaul	Y	52.	Line-item veto	Y
6.	Raise speed limit	Y	53.	South Africa sanctions	Y
7.	Across-the-board cuts	Y	54.	Ease '68 Gun Control Act	Y
8.	South Africa sanctions	N	55.	Kill-14 day handgun wait	Y
9.	Kill-So Africa sanctions	Y	56.	Kill-Gun dlr inspections	Y
10.	Kill-So Africa sanct (*)	Y	57.	Kill-Keep '68 Gun Con Act	Y
11.	Nicaraguan contra aid	Y	58.	Nicarag humanitarian aid	Y
12.	Terminate contra aid	N	59.	Bar ASAT testing	?
13.	Kill-Prohibit contra fnds	?	60.	Delete chemical weapons	N
14.	Kill-Stop CIA contra fndg	Y	61.	Delete 21 MX missiles	N
15.	Kill-Bar nuclr tsts w/SDI	Y	62.	Kill-15% min tax on corps	Y
16.	Kill-Bar ASAT testing	Y	63.	Kill-Restore Soc Sec COLA	Y
17.	Nuclear test ban treaty	N	64.	Freeze all funding	N
18.	Prohibit sale of Stinger	N	65.	Cut def;raise taxes, COLA	N
19.	Delete Bigeye chem bomb	N	66.	Keep existing SS COLAs	N
20.	Bar binary chem weapons	N	67.	Aid to Nicaraguan rebels	Y
21.	Kill-SDI funding	Y	68.	Reaffirm purch of 21 MX	Y
22.	Kill-AIDS ins dscriminatn	N	69.	African Relief/Farm Crdt	N
23.	Kill-$10 bbl oil tariff	Y	70.	Kill-Nuclear Freeze	Y
24.	Kill-Repl wndfl prfts tax	Y	71.	Kill-Void Title IX Narrow	Y
25.	Repeal balanced bdgt amdt	N	72.	Raise drinking age to 21	Y
26.	Tax amnesty provisions	N	73.	Kill-Reduce mil in Europe	Y
27.	Kill-Tax amnesty subst	Y	74.	Kill-Bar $ for contras	Y
28.	Kill-Add third tax rate	Y	75.	Kill-No new MXs in 1985	Y
29.	Kill-Unocal tax provsns	N	76.	Kill-Move MX $ to non-nuc	Y
30.	Block Saudi arms sale (†)	Y	77.	Deficit reduction-$140b	Y
31.	Kill-Bar school busing	Y	78.	Kill-Req auth for troops	Y
32.	Prohibit Saudi arms sale	Y	79.	School Prayer amendment	N
33.	Nicaraguan contra aid	Y	80.	Cap punish-certain crimes	Y
34.	Bar all aid to Nicaragua	N	81.	Bar govt off from taping	Y
35.	Balanced budget amendment	Y	82.	Martin L. King holiday	N
36.	Balanced bdgt substitute	N	83.	Auth marines in Lebanon	Y
37.	Conrail sale	Y	84.	Anti-abortion amendment	N
38.	Revise farm programs	N	85.	Highway-Gas tax bill	Y
39.	Kill-New oil import fee	Y	86.	Delete job creation amend	N
40.	Spending cuts, tax incres	Y	87.	Kill-Tobacco price supprt	Y
41.	Textile import quotas	Y	88.	Emergency housing aid	Y
42.	Kill-Exmpt vets from cuts	Y	89.	Nullify oil decontrol	N
43.	Kill-Bar inmate abortn $	Y	90.	Target tax cuts-mid class	N
44.	Textile import quotas (§)	Y	91.	Tax Indexing	Y
45.	Kill-Eliminate Amtrak $	N	92.	Kill-Oppose SS benft cuts	Y
46.	Kill-Incrs motor fuel tax	Y	93.	Disapprove Saudi AWACS	N
47.	Set max allow deficits	Y	94.	Anti-busing rider	N

Presidential Support Score: 1986 - 91% 1985 - 84%

NEW JERSEY

BRADLEY, BILL [Democrat] Term Began/Expires: 1985/1990. Prior Terms: Senate: 1979-84. Born: July 28, 1943; Crystal City,

BRADLEY, BILL (Cont.)

Mo. Education: Princeton University (Baccalaureate); Oxford University. Occupation: Professional athlete (1967-77); assistant to director, Office of Economic Opportunity.

No.	Issue	Vote
1.	Immigration Reform	Y
2.	So Afr Sanc-veto override	Y
3.	Kill-Death pnlty drug bil	N
4.	Kill-Mil use in drug war	Y
5.	Tax Overhaul	Y
6.	Raise speed limit	N
7.	Across-the-board cuts	N
8.	South Africa sanctions	Y
9.	Kill-So Africa sanctions	N
10.	Kill-So Africa sanct (*)	N
11.	Nicaraguan contra aid	Y
12.	Terminate contra aid	Y
13.	Kill-Prohibit contra fnds	Y
14.	Kill-Stop CIA contra fndg	Y
15.	Kill-Bar nuclr tsts w/SDI	?
16.	Kill-Bar ASAT testing	N
17.	Nuclear test ban treaty	Y
18.	Prohibit sale of Stinger	Y
19.	Delete Bigeye chem bomb	Y
20.	Bar binary chem weapons	Y
21.	Kill-SDI funding	N
22.	Kill-AIDS ins dscriminatn	Y
23.	Kill-$10 bbl oil tariff	Y
24.	Kill-Repl wndfl prfts tax	Y
25.	Repeal balanced bdgt amdt	Y
26.	Tax amnesty provisions	Y
27.	Kill-Tax amnesty subst	N
28.	Kill-Add third tax rate	Y
29.	Kill-Unocal tax provsns	N
30.	Block Saudi arms sale (†)	Y
31.	Kill-Bar school busing	Y
32.	Prohibit Saudi arms sale	Y
33.	Nicaraguan contra aid	Y
34.	Bar all aid to Nicaragua	N
35.	Balanced budget amendment	N
36.	Balanced bdgt substitute	N
37.	Conrail sale	N
38.	Revise farm programs	N
39.	Kill-New oil import fee	N
40.	Spending cuts, tax incres	Y
41.	Textile import quotas	N
42.	Kill-Exmpt vets from cuts	N
43.	Kill-Bar inmate abortn $	Y
44.	Textile import quotas (§)	N
45.	Kill-Eliminate Amtrak $	Y
46.	Kill-Incrs motor fuel tax	N
47.	Set max allow deficits	N
48.	20% minimum tax on corps	N
49.	Bar $ to toxic victims	N
50.	Seasonal workers in US	N
51.	Kill-School prayer cases	Y
52.	Line-item veto	N
53.	South Africa sanctions	Y
54.	Ease '68 Gun Control Act	?
55.	Kill-14 day handgun wait	?
56.	Kill-Gun dlr inspections	?
57.	Kill-Keep '68 Gun Con Act	?
58.	Nicarag humanitarian aid	N
59.	Bar ASAT testing	N
60.	Delete chemical weapons	Y
61.	Delete 21 MX missiles	Y
62.	Kill-15% min tax on corps	Y
63.	Kill-Restore Soc Sec COLA	N
64.	Freeze all funding	N
65.	Cut def;raise taxes, COLA	Y
66.	Keep existing SS COLAs	Y
67.	Aid to Nicaraguan rebels	N
68.	Reaffirm purch of 21 MX	N
69.	African Relief/Farm Crdt	Y
70.	Kill-Nuclear Freeze	N
71.	Kill-Void Title IX Narrow	N
72.	Raise drinking age to 21	Y
73.	Kill-Reduce mil in Europe	N
74.	Kill-Bar $ for contras	N
75.	Kill-No new MXs in 1985	N
76.	Kill-Move MX $ to non-nuc	N
77.	Deficit reduction-$140b	N
78.	Kill-Req auth for troops	N
79.	School Prayer amendment	N
80.	Cap punish-certain crimes	Y
81.	Bar govt off from taping	Y
82.	Martin L. King holiday	Y
83.	Auth marines in Lebanon	N
84.	Anti-abortion amendment	N
85.	Highway-Gas tax bill	N
86.	Delete job creation amend	N
87.	Kill-Tobacco price supprt	N
88.	Emergency housing aid	Y
89.	Nullify oil decontrol	N
90.	Target tax cuts-mid class	Y
91.	Tax Indexing	N
92.	Kill-Oppose SS benft cuts	N
93.	Disapprove Saudi AWACS	Y
94.	Anti-busing rider	N
95.	Disapprove oil import fee	N
96.	Domestic violence funds	+
97.	Trucking Deregulation	?
98.	Overturn India fuel sale	N
99.	Mil draft registration	N
100.	Chrysler Loan Guarantees	Y
101.	Nuclear plant moratorium	Y
102.	Abolish electoral college	N

Presidential Support Score: 1986 - 51% 1985 - 33%

LAUTENBERG, FRANK R. [Democrat] Term Began/Expires: 1983/1988. Born: January 23, 1924; Paterson, N.J. Education: Columbia University (B.S.). Military Service: U.S. Army, 1942. Occupation: Chief executive officer, Automatic Data Processing, Inc.; commissioner, Port Authority of New York and New Jersey.

1.	Immigration Reform	Y	43.	Kill-Bar inmate abortn $	Y
2.	So Afr Sanc-veto override	Y	44.	Textile import quotas (§)	Y
3.	Kill-Death pnlty drug bil	?	45.	Kill-Eliminate Amtrak $	Y
4.	Kill-Mil use in drug war	?	46.	Kill-Incrs motor fuel tax	Y
5.	Tax Overhaul	Y	47.	Set max allow deficits	N
6.	Raise speed limit	N	48.	20% minimum tax on corps	N
7.	Across-the-board cuts	N	49.	Bar $ to toxic victims	N
8.	South Africa sanctions	Y	50.	Seasonal workers in US	N
9.	Kill-So Africa sanctions	N	51.	Kill-School prayer cases	Y
10.	Kill-So Africa sanct (*)	N	52.	Line-item veto	N
11.	Nicaraguan contra aid	N	53.	South Africa sanctions	Y
12.	Terminate contra aid	Y	54.	Ease '68 Gun Control Act	N
13.	Kill-Prohibit contra fnds	N	55.	Kill-14 day handgun wait	N
14.	Kill-Stop CIA contra fndg	N	56.	Kill-Gun dlr inspections	N
15.	Kill-Bar nuclr tsts w/SDI	N	57.	Kill-Keep '68 Gun Con Act	N
16.	Kill-Bar ASAT testing	N	58.	Nicarag humanitarian aid	N
17.	Nuclear test ban treaty	Y	59.	Bar ASAT testing	Y
18.	Prohibit sale of Stinger	Y	60.	Delete chemical weapons	Y
19.	Delete Bigeye chem bomb	Y	61.	Delete 21 MX missiles	Y
20.	Bar binary chem weapons	Y	62.	Kill-15% min tax on corps	Y
21.	Kill-SDI funding	N	63.	Kill-Restore Soc Sec COLA	N
22.	Kill-AIDS ins dscriminatn	Y	64.	Freeze all funding	N
23.	Kill-$10 bbl oil tariff	Y	65.	Cut def;raise taxes, COLA	Y
24.	Kill-Repl wndfl prfts tax	Y	66.	Keep existing SS COLAs	Y
25.	Repeal balanced bdgt amdt	Y	67.	Aid to Nicaraguan rebels	N
26.	Tax amnesty provisions	?	68.	Reaffirm purch of 21 MX	N
27.	Kill-Tax amnesty subst	?	69.	African Relief/Farm Crdt	Y
28.	Kill-Add third tax rate	N	70.	Kill-Nuclear Freeze	N
29.	Kill-Unocal tax provsns	?	71.	Kill-Void Title IX Narrow	N
30.	Block Saudi arms sale (†)	Y	72.	Raise drinking age to 21	Y
31.	Kill-Bar school busing	Y	73.	Kill-Reduce mil in Europe	N
32.	Prohibit Saudi arms sale	Y	74.	Kill-Bar $ for contras	N
33.	Nicaraguan contra aid	N	75.	Kill-No new MXs in 1985	N
34.	Bar all aid to Nicaragua	N	76.	Kill-Move MX $ to non-nuc	N
35.	Balanced budget amendment	N	77.	Deficit reduction-$140b	N
36.	Balanced bdgt substitute	N	78.	Kill-Req auth for troops	N
37.	Conrail sale	N	79.	School Prayer amendment	N
38.	Revise farm programs	N	80.	Cap punish-certain crimes	N
39.	Kill-New oil import fee	N	81.	Bar govt off from taping	Y
40.	Spending cuts, tax incres	Y	82.	Martin L. King holiday	Y
41.	Textile import quotas	Y	83.	Auth marines in Lebanon	N
42.	Kill-Exmpt vets from cuts	N	84.	Anti-abortion amendment	N

Presidential Support Score: 1986 - 30% 1985 - 28%

NEW MEXICO

DOMENICI, PETE V. [Republican] Term Began/Expires: 1985/1990. Prior Terms: Senate: 1973-84. Born: May 7, 1932; Albuquerque, N.M. Education: University of Albuquerque; University of New Mexico (B.S.); Denver University (LL.D.). Occupation: Albuquerque city commissioner.

DOMENICI, PETE V. (Cont.)

1. Immigration Reform N
2. So Afr Sanc-veto override Y
3. Kill-Death pnlty drug bil N
4. Kill-Mil use in drug war Y
5. Tax Overhaul Y
6. Raise speed limit Y
7. Across-the-board cuts N
8. South Africa sanctions Y
9. Kill-So Africa sanctions Y
10. Kill-So Africa sanct (*) Y
11. Nicaraguan contra aid Y
12. Terminate contra aid N
13. Kill-Prohibit contra fnds Y
14. Kill-Stop CIA contra fndg Y
15. Kill-Bar nuclr tsts w/SDI Y
16. Kill-Bar ASAT testing Y
17. Nuclear test ban treaty N
18. Prohibit sale of Stinger N
19. Delete Bigeye chem bomb N
20. Bar binary chem weapons N
21. Kill-SDI funding Y
22. Kill-AIDS ins dscriminatn N
23. Kill-$10 bbl oil tariff N
24. Kill-Repl wndfl prfts tax N
25. Repeal balanced bdgt amdt N
26. Tax amnesty provisions Y
27. Kill-Tax amnesty subst N
28. Kill-Add third tax rate Y
29. Kill-Unocal tax provsns Y
30. Block Saudi arms sale (†) N
31. Kill-Bar school busing N
32. Prohibit Saudi arms sale Y
33. Nicaraguan contra aid Y
34. Bar all aid to Nicaragua N
35. Balanced budget amendment Y
36. Balanced bdgt substitute N
37. Conrail sale Y
38. Revise farm programs ?
39. Kill-New oil import fee Y
40. Spending cuts, tax incres Y
41. Textile import quotas Y
42. Kill-Exmpt vets from cuts Y
43. Kill-Bar inmate abortn $ N
44. Textile import quotas (§) N
45. Kill-Eliminate Amtrak $ N
46. Kill-Incrs motor fuel tax Y
47. Set max allow deficits Y
48. 20% minimum tax on corps N
49. Bar $ to toxic victims Y
50. Seasonal workers in US Y
51. Kill-School prayer cases Y
52. Line-item veto Y
53. South Africa sanctions Y
54. Ease '68 Gun Control Act Y
55. Kill-14 day handgun wait Y
56. Kill-Gun dlr inspections Y
57. Kill-Keep '68 Gun Con Act Y
58. Nicarag humanitarian aid Y
59. Bar ASAT testing ?
60. Delete chemical weapons N
61. Delete 21 MX missiles N
62. Kill-15% min tax on corps Y
63. Kill-Restore Soc Sec COLA Y
64. Freeze all funding N
65. Cut def;raise taxes, COLA N
66. Keep existing SS COLAs N
67. Aid to Nicaraguan rebels Y
68. Reaffirm purch of 21 MX Y
69. African Relief/Farm Crdt N
70. Kill-Nuclear Freeze Y
71. Kill-Void Title IX Narrow Y
72. Raise drinking age to 21 Y
73. Kill-Reduce mil in Europe Y
74. Kill-Bar $ for contras Y
75. Kill-No new MXs in 1985 Y
76. Kill-Move MX $ to non-nuc Y
77. Deficit reduction-$140b Y
78. Kill-Req auth for troops Y
79. School Prayer amendment Y
80. Cap punish-certain crimes Y
81. Bar govt off from taping N
82. Martin L. King holiday Y
83. Auth marines in Lebanon Y
84. Anti-abortion amendment Y
85. Highway-Gas tax bill Y
86. Delete job creation amend Y
87. Kill-Tobacco price supprt Y
88. Emergency housing aid N
89. Nullify oil decontrol N
90. Target tax cuts-mid class N
91. Tax Indexing ?
92. Kill-Oppose SS benft cuts Y
93. Disapprove Saudi AWACS N
94. Anti-busing rider Y
95. Disapprove oil import fee Y
96. Domestic violence funds N
97. Trucking Deregulation Y
98. Overturn India fuel sale N
99. Mil draft registration Y
100. Chrysler Loan Guarantees N
101. Nuclear plant moratorium N
102. Abolish electoral college N
103. Kill-Lmt ct-ordered bus N
104. Airline Deregulation Y
105. Disappr Mideast jet sales Y
106. Natural gas deregulation Y
107. Prohibit neutron bomb N
108. Financial disclosure-off Y

Presidential Support Score: 1986 - 89% 1985 - 82%

BINGAMAN, JEFF [Democrat] Term Began/Expires: 1983/1988. Born: October 3, 1943; El Paso, Texas. Education: Harvard College (B.A.); Stanford Law School. Military Service: U.S. Army Reserve, 1968-74. Occupation: New Mexico assistant attorney general (1969); private attorney (1971-73); attorney general (1979-82).

1. Immigration Reform Y
2. So Afr Sanc-veto override Y
3. Kill-Death pnlty drug bil N
4. Kill-Mil use in drug war Y
5. Tax Overhaul Y
6. Raise speed limit Y
7. Across-the-board cuts N
8. South Africa sanctions Y
9. Kill-So Africa sanctions N
10. Kill-So Africa sanct (*) N
11. Nicaraguan contra aid N
12. Terminate contra aid Y
13. Kill-Prohibit contra fnds N
14. Kill-Stop CIA contra fndg N
15. Kill-Bar nuclr tsts w/SDI Y
16. Kill-Bar ASAT testing N
17. Nuclear test ban treaty Y
18. Prohibit sale of Stinger Y
19. Delete Bigeye chem bomb N
20. Bar binary chem weapons N
21. Kill-SDI funding Y
22. Kill-AIDS ins dscriminatn N
23. Kill-$10 bbl oil tariff N
24. Kill-Repl wndfl prfts tax N
25. Repeal balanced bdgt amdt Y
26. Tax amnesty provisions Y
27. Kill-Tax amnesty subst N
28. Kill-Add third tax rate N
29. Kill-Unocal tax provsns N
30. Block Saudi arms sale (†) Y
31. Kill-Bar school busing Y
32. Prohibit Saudi arms sale Y
33. Nicaraguan contra aid N
34. Bar all aid to Nicaragua Y
35. Balanced budget amendment Y
36. Balanced bdgt substitute Y
37. Conrail sale Y
38. Revise farm programs N
39. Kill-New oil import fee N
40. Spending cuts, tax incres Y
41. Textile import quotas Y
42. Kill-Exmpt vets from cuts Y
43. Kill-Bar inmate abortn $ Y
44. Textile import quotas (§) N
45. Kill-Eliminate Amtrak $ Y
46. Kill-Incrs motor fuel tax Y
47. Set max allow deficits N
48. 20% minimum tax on corps N
49. Bar $ to toxic victims Y
50. Seasonal workers in US N
51. Kill-School prayer cases Y
52. Line-item veto N
53. South Africa sanctions Y
54. Ease '68 Gun Control Act Y
55. Kill-14 day handgun wait Y
56. Kill-Gun dlr inspections Y
57. Kill-Keep '68 Gun Con Act Y
58. Nicarag humanitarian aid N
59. Bar ASAT testing Y
60. Delete chemical weapons N
61. Delete 21 MX missiles Y
62. Kill-15% min tax on corps Y
63. Kill-Restore Soc Sec COLA N
64. Freeze all funding Y
65. Cut def;raise taxes, COLA Y
66. Keep existing SS COLAs Y
67. Aid to Nicaraguan rebels N
68. Reaffirm purch of 21 MX N
69. African Relief/Farm Crdt Y
70. Kill-Nuclear Freeze N
71. Kill-Void Title IX Narrow N
72. Raise drinking age to 21 Y
73. Kill-Reduce mil in Europe N
74. Kill-Bar $ for contras N
75. Kill-No new MXs in 1985 N
76. Kill-Move MX $ to non-nuc N
77. Deficit reduction-$140b N
78. Kill-Req auth for troops N
79. School Prayer amendment N
80. Cap punish-certain crimes N
81. Bar govt off from taping Y
82. Martin L. King holiday Y
83. Auth marines in Lebanon N
84. Anti-abortion amendment N

Presidential Support Score: 1986 - 41% 1985 - 33%

NEW YORK

D'AMATO, ALFONSE M. [Republican] Term Began/Expires: 1981/1986. Born: August 1, 1937; Brooklyn, N.Y. Education: Syracuse University (B.S., J.D.). Occupation: Attorney; public administrator (1965-68); receiver of taxes (1969); town supervisor (1971-77); presiding supervisor and vice chairman, county board of supervisors (1977-80).

D'AMATO, ALFONSE M. (Cont.)

1. Immigration Reform Y
2. So Afr Sanc-veto override Y
3. Kill-Death pnlty drug bil N
4. Kill-Mil use in drug war N
5. Tax Overhaul Y
6. Raise speed limit N
7. Across-the-board cuts N
8. South Africa sanctions Y
9. Kill-So Africa sanctions N
10. Kill-So Africa sanct (*) N
11. Nicaraguan contra aid Y
12. Terminate contra aid N
13. Kill-Prohibit contra fnds Y
14. Kill-Stop CIA contra fndg Y
15. Kill-Bar nuclr tsts w/SDI Y
16. Kill-Bar ASAT testing Y
17. Nuclear test ban treaty Y
18. Prohibit sale of Stinger Y
19. Delete Bigeye chem bomb N
20. Bar binary chem weapons N
21. Kill-SDI funding Y
22. Kill-AIDS ins dscriminatn Y
23. Kill-$10 bbl oil tariff Y
24. Kill-Repl wndfl prfts tax Y
25. Repeal balanced bdgt amdt N
26. Tax amnesty provisions Y
27. Kill-Tax amnesty subst N
28. Kill-Add third tax rate Y
29. Kill-Unocal tax provsns N
30. Block Saudi arms sale (†) Y
31. Kill-Bar school busing N
32. Prohibit Saudi arms sale Y
33. Nicaraguan contra aid Y
34. Bar all aid to Nicaragua N
35. Balanced budget amendment Y
36. Balanced bdgt substitute N
37. Conrail sale Y
38. Revise farm programs Y
39. Kill-New oil import fee Y
40. Spending cuts, tax incres Y
41. Textile import quotas Y
42. Kill-Exmpt vets from cuts Y
43. Kill-Bar inmate abortn $ N
44. Textile import quotas (§) Y
45. Kill-Eliminate Amtrak $ Y
46. Kill-Incrs motor fuel tax Y
47. Set max allow deficits Y
48. 20% minimum tax on corps N
49. Bar $ to toxic victims N
50. Seasonal workers in US Y
51. Kill-School prayer cases Y
52. Line-item veto Y
53. South Africa sanctions Y
54. Ease '68 Gun Control Act Y
55. Kill-14 day handgun wait Y
56. Kill-Gun dlr inspections Y
57. Kill-Keep '68 Gun Con Act Y
58. Nicarag humanitarian aid Y
59. Bar ASAT testing N
60. Delete chemical weapons N
61. Delete 21 MX missiles N
62. Kill-15% min tax on corps Y
63. Kill-Restore Soc Sec COLA N
64. Freeze all funding N
65. Cut def;raise taxes, COLA N
66. Keep existing SS COLAs Y
67. Aid to Nicaraguan rebels Y
68. Reaffirm purch of 21 MX Y
69. African Relief/Farm Crdt Y
70. Kill-Nuclear Freeze Y
71. Kill-Void Title IX Narrow Y
72. Raise drinking age to 21 Y
73. Kill-Reduce mil in Europe Y
74. Kill-Bar $ for contras Y
75. Kill-No new MXs in 1985 Y
76. Kill-Move MX $ to non-nuc Y
77. Deficit reduction-$140b Y
78. Kill-Req auth for troops Y
79. School Prayer amendment Y
80. Cap punish-certain crimes Y
81. Bar govt off from taping N
82. Martin L. King holiday Y
83. Auth marines in Lebanon Y
84. Anti-abortion amendment Y
85. Highway-Gas tax bill Y
86. Delete job creation amend N
87. Kill-Tobacco price supprt N
88. Emergency housing aid Y
89. Nullify oil decontrol -
90. Target tax cuts-mid class N
91. Tax Indexing Y
92. Kill-Oppose SS benft cuts Y
93. Disapprove Saudi AWACS Y
94. Anti-busing rider Y

Presidential Support Score: 1986 - 79% 1985 - 71%

MOYNIHAN, DANIEL PATRICK [Democrat] Term Began/Expires: 1983/1988. Prior Terms: Senate: 1977-82. Born: March 16, 1927; Tulsa, Okla. Education: City College of New York; Tufts University (B.A.); Fletcher School of Law and Diplomacy (M.A., Ph.D.); London School of Economics and Political Science. Military Service: U.S. Navy, 1944-47. Occupation: Assistant secretary and acting secretary to the governor of New York (1955-58); director, New York State Government Research Project (1959-61); special assistant secretary of Labor (1961-62);

MOYNIHAN, DANIEL PATRICK (Cont.)
executive assistant to secretary of Labor (1962-63); assistant secretary of Labor (1963-65); director, Joint Center of Urban Studies, MIT and Harvard (1966-69); professor, education and politics, Harvard (1966-73); assistant to president for Urban Affairs; counselor to president (1969-70); presidential consultant (1971-73); U.N. representative (1971); ambassador to India (1973-75); professor of government, Harvard (1972); author; ambassador to U.N. (1975-76).

1. Immigration Reform Y
2. So Afr Sanc-veto override Y
3. Kill-Death pnlty drug bil N
4. Kill-Mil use in drug war Y
5. Tax Overhaul Y
6. Raise speed limit N
7. Across-the-board cuts N
8. South Africa sanctions Y
9. Kill-So Africa sanctions N
10. Kill-So Africa sanct (*) N
11. Nicaraguan contra aid N
12. Terminate contra aid Y
13. Kill-Prohibit contra fnds N
14. Kill-Stop CIA contra fndg Y
15. Kill-Bar nuclr tsts w/SDI N
16. Kill-Bar ASAT testing N
17. Nuclear test ban treaty Y
18. Prohibit sale of Stinger N
19. Delete Bigeye chem bomb Y
20. Bar binary chem weapons Y
21. Kill-SDI funding N
22. Kill-AIDS ins dscriminatn Y
23. Kill-$10 bbl oil tariff Y
24. Kill-Repl wndfl prfts tax Y
25. Repeal balanced bdgt amdt Y
26. Tax amnesty provisions Y
27. Kill-Tax amnesty subst N
28. Kill-Add third tax rate Y
29. Kill-Unocal tax provsns N
30. Block Saudi arms sale (†) Y
31. Kill-Bar school busing Y
32. Prohibit Saudi arms sale Y
33. Nicaraguan contra aid N
34. Bar all aid to Nicaragua N
35. Balanced budget amendment N
36. Balanced bdgt substitute Y
37. Conrail sale Y
38. Revise farm programs N
39. Kill-New oil import fee Y
40. Spending cuts, tax incres Y
41. Textile import quotas Y
42. Kill-Exmpt vets from cuts N
43. Kill-Bar inmate abortn $ Y
44. Textile import quotas (§) Y
45. Kill-Eliminate Amtrak $ Y
46. Kill-Incrs motor fuel tax N
47. Set max allow deficits N
48. 20% minimum tax on corps N
49. Bar $ to toxic victims ?
50. Seasonal workers in US N
51. Kill-School prayer cases Y
52. Line-item veto N
53. South Africa sanctions Y
54. Ease '68 Gun Control Act N
55. Kill-14 day handgun wait N
56. Kill-Gun dlr inspections N
57. Kill-Keep '68 Gun Con Act N
58. Nicarag humanitarian aid N
59. Bar ASAT testing Y
60. Delete chemical weapons Y
61. Delete 21 MX missiles Y
62. Kill-15% min tax on corps N
63. Kill-Restore Soc Sec COLA N
64. Freeze all funding N
65. Cut def;raise taxes, COLA Y
66. Keep existing SS COLAs Y
67. Aid to Nicaraguan rebels N
68. Reaffirm purch of 21 MX N
69. African Relief/Farm Crdt Y
70. Kill-Nuclear Freeze N
71. Kill-Void Title IX Narrow N
72. Raise drinking age to 21 Y
73. Kill-Reduce mil in Europe Y
74. Kill-Bar $ for contras N
75. Kill-No new MXs in 1985 N
76. Kill-Move MX $ to non-nuc N
77. Deficit reduction-$140b N
78. Kill-Req auth for troops N
79. School Prayer amendment N
80. Cap punish-certain crimes Y
81. Bar govt off from taping Y
82. Martin L. King holiday Y
83. Auth marines in Lebanon N
84. Anti-abortion amendment N
85. Highway-Gas tax bill ?
86. Delete job creation amend N
87. Kill-Tobacco price supprt N
88. Emergency housing aid Y
89. Nullify oil decontrol Y
90. Target tax cuts-mid class N
91. Tax Indexing Y
92. Kill-Oppose SS benft cuts N
93. Disapprove Saudi AWACS Y
94. Anti-busing rider N
95. Disapprove oil import fee ?
96. Domestic violence funds Y
97. Trucking Deregulation Y
98. Overturn India fuel sale N
99. Mil draft registration Y
100. Chrysler Loan Guarantees Y

MOYNIHAN, DANIEL PATRICK (Cont.)

101. Nuclear plant moratorium N
102. Abolish electoral college N
103. Kill-Lmt ct-ordered bus Y
104. Airline Deregulation Y
105. Disappr Mideast jet sales Y
106. Natural gas deregulation N
107. Prohibit neutron bomb N
108. Financial disclosure-off Y

Presidential Support Score: 1986 - 41% 1985 - 33%

NORTH CAROLINA

BROYHILL, JAMES T. [Republican] Term Began/Expires: 1986 (appointed)-1986. Prior Terms: House: 1963-86. Born: August 19, 1927; Lenoir, N.C. Education: University of North Carolina (B.S.). Occupation: Partner, Broyhill Furniture Factories (1945-62).

1. Immigration Reform X
2. So Afr Sanc-veto override N
3. Kill-Death pnlty drug bil N
4. Kill-Mil use in drug war Y
5. Tax Overhaul Y
6. Raise speed limit Y
7. Across-the-board cuts N
8. South Africa sanctions N
9. Kill-So Africa sanctions Y
10. Kill-So Africa sanct (*) Y
11. Nicaraguan contra aid Y
12. Terminate contra aid N
13. Kill-Prohibit contra fnds Y
14. Kill-Stop CIA contra fndg Y
15. Kill-Bar nuclr tsts w/SDI Y
16. Kill-Bar ASAT testing Y
17. Nuclear test ban treaty N
18. Prohibit sale of Stinger N
19. Delete Bigeye chem bomb N
20. Bar binary chem weapons N
21. Kill-SDI funding Y
22. Kill-AIDS ins dscriminatn N
23. Kill-$10 bbl oil tariff Y
24. Kill-Repl wndfl prfts tax Y
25. Repeal balanced bdgt amdt N

Presidential Support Score: 1986 - 91%

HELMS, JESSE [Republican] Term Began/Expires: 1985/1990. Prior Terms: Senate: 1973-84. Born: October 18, 1921; Monroe, N.C. Education: Wingate Junior College; Wake Forest College. Military Service: U.S. Navy, 1942-45. Occupation: City Editor, The Raleigh Times; Senate staff member; executive director, North Carolina Bankers Assn. (1953-60); executive vice president, WRAL-TV and Tobacco Radio Network (1960-72).

1. Immigration Reform N
2. So Afr Sanc-veto override N
3. Kill-Death pnlty drug bil N
4. Kill-Mil use in drug war Y
5. Tax Overhaul N
6. Raise speed limit Y
7. Across-the-board cuts Y
8. South Africa sanctions N
9. Kill-So Africa sanctions Y
10. Kill-So Africa sanct (*) Y
11. Nicaraguan contra aid Y
12. Terminate contra aid N
13. Kill-Prohibit contra fnds Y
14. Kill-Stop CIA contra fndg Y
15. Kill-Bar nuclr tsts w/SDI Y
16. Kill-Bar ASAT testing Y
17. Nuclear test ban treaty N
18. Prohibit sale of Stinger N
19. Delete Bigeye chem bomb N
20. Bar binary chem weapons N
21. Kill-SDI funding Y
22. Kill-AIDS ins dscriminatn N
23. Kill-$10 bbl oil tariff Y
24. Kill-Repl wndfl prfts tax N
25. Repeal balanced bdgt amdt N
26. Tax amnesty provisions N
27. Kill-Tax amnesty subst Y
28. Kill-Add third tax rate Y
29. Kill-Unocal tax provsns Y
30. Block Saudi arms sale (†) N
31. Kill-Bar school busing N
32. Prohibit Saudi arms sale Y
33. Nicaraguan contra aid Y
34. Bar all aid to Nicaragua N
35. Balanced budget amendment Y
36. Balanced bdgt substitute N
37. Conrail sale Y
38. Revise farm programs Y
39. Kill-New oil import fee Y
40. Spending cuts, tax incres Y

HELMS, JESSE (Cont.)

41. Textile import quotas Y
42. Kill-Exmpt vets from cuts Y
43. Kill-Bar inmate abortn $ N
44. Textile import quotas (§) Y
45. Kill-Eliminate Amtrak $ N
46. Kill-Incrs motor fuel tax Y
47. Set max allow deficits Y
48. 20% minimum tax on corps N
49. Bar $ to toxic victims Y
50. Seasonal workers in US Y
51. Kill-School prayer cases N
52. Line-item veto Y
53. South Africa sanctions N
54. Ease '68 Gun Control Act Y
55. Kill-14 day handgun wait Y
56. Kill-Gun dlr inspections Y
57. Kill-Keep '68 Gun Con Act Y
58. Nicarag humanitarian aid Y
59. Bar ASAT testing N
60. Delete chemical weapons N
61. Delete 21 MX missiles N
62. Kill-15% min tax on corps Y
63. Kill-Restore Soc Sec COLA Y
64. Freeze all funding N
65. Cut def;raise taxes, COLA N
66. Keep existing SS COLAs N
67. Aid to Nicaraguan rebels Y
68. Reaffirm purch of 21 MX Y
69. African Relief/Farm Crdt N
70. Kill-Nuclear Freeze Y
71. Kill-Void Title IX Narrow Y
72. Raise drinking age to 21 Y
73. Kill-Reduce mil in Europe Y
74. Kill-Bar $ for contras Y
75. Kill-No new MXs in 1985 Y
76. Kill-Move MX $ to non-nuc Y
77. Deficit reduction-$140b Y
78. Kill-Req auth for troops Y
79. School Prayer amendment Y
80. Cap punish-certain crimes Y
81. Bar govt off from taping N
82. Martin L. King holiday N
83. Auth marines in Lebanon Y
84. Anti-abortion amendment P
85. Highway-Gas tax bill N
86. Delete job creation amend Y
87. Kill-Tobacco price supprt Y
88. Emergency housing aid Y
89. Nullify oil decontrol N
90. Target tax cuts-mid class N
91. Tax Indexing Y
92. Kill-Oppose SS benft cuts Y
93. Disapprove Saudi AWACS N
94. Anti-busing rider Y
95. Disapprove oil import fee Y
96. Domestic violence funds N
97. Trucking Deregulation Y
98. Overturn India fuel sale Y
99. Mil draft registration Y
100. Chrysler Loan Guarantees N
101. Nuclear plant moratorium N
102. Abolish electoral college N
103. Kill-Lmt ct-ordered bus N
104. Airline Deregulation Y
105. Disappr Mideast jet sales N
106. Natural gas deregulation Y
107. Prohibit neutron bomb N
108. Financial disclosure-off Y

Presidential Support Score: 1986 - 91% 1985 - 79%

NORTH DAKOTA

ANDREWS, MARK [Republican] Term Began/Expires: 1981/1986. Prior Terms: House: 1963 (Special Election)-1980. Born: May 19, 1926; Cass County, N.D. Education: North Dakota State University (B.S.). Military Service: U.S. Army, 1944. Occupation: President, North Dakota Crop Improvement Assn.

1. Immigration Reform Y
2. So Afr Sanc-veto override Y
3. Kill-Death pnlty drug bil Y
4. Kill-Mil use in drug war Y
5. Tax Overhaul Y
6. Raise speed limit Y
7. Across-the-board cuts N
8. South Africa sanctions Y
9. Kill-So Africa sanctions Y
10. Kill-So Africa sanct (*) Y
11. Nicaraguan contra aid N
12. Terminate contra aid Y
13. Kill-Prohibit contra fnds Y
14. Kill-Stop CIA contra fndg N
15. Kill-Bar nuclr tsts w/SDI Y
16. Kill-Bar ASAT testing N
17. Nuclear test ban treaty Y
18. Prohibit sale of Stinger N
19. Delete Bigeye chem bomb Y
20. Bar binary chem weapons Y
21. Kill-SDI funding N
22. Kill-AIDS ins dscriminatn Y
23. Kill-$10 bbl oil tariff Y
24. Kill-Repl wndfl prfts tax N
25. Repeal balanced bdgt amdt Y
26. Tax amnesty provisions Y

ANDREWS, MARK (Cont.)

27. Kill-Tax amnesty subst N
28. Kill-Add third tax rate N
29. Kill-Unocal tax provsns N
30. Block Saudi arms sale (†) Y
31. Kill-Bar school busing N
32. Prohibit Saudi arms sale Y
33. Nicaraguan contra aid N
34. Bar all aid to Nicaragua N
35. Balanced budget amendment Y
36. Balanced bdgt substitute Y
37. Conrail sale N
38. Revise farm programs Y
39. Kill-New oil import fee Y
40. Spending cuts, tax incres N
41. Textile import quotas N
42. Kill-Exmpt vets from cuts N
43. Kill-Bar inmate abortn $ N
44. Textile import quotas (§) N
45. Kill-Eliminate Amtrak $ Y
46. Kill-Incrs motor fuel tax Y
47. Set max allow deficits Y
48. 20% minimum tax on corps N
49. Bar $ to toxic victims ?
50. Seasonal workers in US N
51. Kill-School prayer cases Y
52. Line-item veto N
53. South Africa sanctions Y
54. Ease '68 Gun Control Act Y
55. Kill-14 day handgun wait Y
56. Kill-Gun dlr inspections Y
57. Kill-Keep '68 Gun Con Act Y
58. Nicarag humanitarian aid Y
59. Bar ASAT testing N
60. Delete chemical weapons Y
61. Delete 21 MX missiles Y
62. Kill-15% min tax on corps Y
63. Kill-Restore Soc Sec COLA Y
64. Freeze all funding Y
65. Cut def;raise taxes, COLA N
66. Keep existing SS COLAs Y
67. Aid to Nicaraguan rebels Y
68. Reaffirm purch of 21 MX N
69. African Relief/Farm Crdt Y
70. Kill-Nuclear Freeze N
71. Kill-Void Title IX Narrow Y
72. Raise drinking age to 21 Y
73. Kill-Reduce mil in Europe Y
74. Kill-Bar $ for contras Y
75. Kill-No new MXs in 1985 ?
76. Kill-Move MX $ to non-nuc ?
77. Deficit reduction-$140b Y
78. Kill-Req auth for troops N
79. School Prayer amendment N
80. Cap punish-certain crimes N
81. Bar govt off from taping Y
82. Martin L. King holiday Y
83. Auth marines in Lebanon Y
84. Anti-abortion amendment Y
85. Highway-Gas tax bill Y
86. Delete job creation amend N
87. Kill-Tobacco price supprt Y
88. Emergency housing aid Y
89. Nullify oil decontrol N
90. Target tax cuts-mid class N
91. Tax Indexing Y
92. Kill-Oppose SS benft cuts Y
93. Disapprove Saudi AWACS N
94. Anti-busing rider N

Presidential Support Score: 1986 - 58% 1985 - 59%

BURDICK, QUENTIN N. [Democrat] Term Began/Expires: 1983/1988. Prior Terms: House: 1959-60. Senate: 1960 (Special Election)-1982. Born: June 19, 1908; Munich, N.D. Education: University of Minnesota (B.A., LL.B.). Occupation: Attorney.

1. Immigration Reform Y
2. So Afr Sanc-veto override Y
3. Kill-Death pnlty drug bil Y
4. Kill-Mil use in drug war N
5. Tax Overhaul Y
6. Raise speed limit Y
7. Across-the-board cuts N
8. South Africa sanctions Y
9. Kill-So Africa sanctions N
10. Kill-So Africa sanct (*) N
11. Nicaraguan contra aid N
12. Terminate contra aid Y
13. Kill-Prohibit contra fnds N
14. Kill-Stop CIA contra fndg N
15. Kill-Bar nuclr tsts w/SDI N
16. Kill-Bar ASAT testing N
17. Nuclear test ban treaty Y
18. Prohibit sale of Stinger Y
19. Delete Bigeye chem bomb Y
20. Bar binary chem weapons Y
21. Kill-SDI funding N
22. Kill-AIDS ins dscriminatn Y
23. Kill-$10 bbl oil tariff Y
24. Kill-Repl wndfl prfts tax N
25. Repeal balanced bdgt amdt Y
26. Tax amnesty provisions Y
27. Kill-Tax amnesty subst N
28. Kill-Add third tax rate N
29. Kill-Unocal tax provsns N
30. Block Saudi arms sale (†) Y
31. Kill-Bar school busing Y
32. Prohibit Saudi arms sale Y
33. Nicaraguan contra aid N
34. Bar all aid to Nicaragua Y

BURDICK, QUENTIN N. (Cont.)

35. Balanced budget amendment N
36. Balanced bdgt substitute N
37. Conrail sale N
38. Revise farm programs Y
39. Kill-New oil import fee Y
40. Spending cuts, tax incres N
41. Textile import quotas N
42. Kill-Exmpt vets from cuts N
43. Kill-Bar inmate abortn $ Y
44. Textile import quotas (§) N
45. Kill-Eliminate Amtrak $ Y
46. Kill-Incrs motor fuel tax Y
47. Set max allow deficits Y
48. 20% minimum tax on corps Y
49. Bar $ to toxic victims N
50. Seasonal workers in US N
51. Kill-School prayer cases +
52. Line-item veto N
53. South Africa sanctions Y
54. Ease '68 Gun Control Act Y
55. Kill-14 day handgun wait Y
56. Kill-Gun dlr inspections Y
57. Kill-Keep '68 Gun Con Act Y
58. Nicarag humanitarian aid N
59. Bar ASAT testing Y
60. Delete chemical weapons Y
61. Delete 21 MX missiles Y
62. Kill-15% min tax on corps N
63. Kill-Restore Soc Sec COLA N
64. Freeze all funding Y
65. Cut def;raise taxes, COLA Y
66. Keep existing SS COLAs Y
67. Aid to Nicaraguan rebels N
68. Reaffirm purch of 21 MX N
69. African Relief/Farm Crdt Y
70. Kill-Nuclear Freeze N
71. Kill-Void Title IX Narrow N
72. Raise drinking age to 21 +
73. Kill-Reduce mil in Europe N
74. Kill-Bar $ for contras N
75. Kill-No new MXs in 1985 N
76. Kill-Move MX $ to non-nuc N
77. Deficit reduction-$140b N
78. Kill-Req auth for troops ?
79. School Prayer amendment N
80. Cap punish-certain crimes N
81. Bar govt off from taping Y
82. Martin L. King holiday Y
83. Auth marines in Lebanon N
84. Anti-abortion amendment N
85. Highway-Gas tax bill Y
86. Delete job creation amend N
87. Kill-Tobacco price supprt Y
88. Emergency housing aid Y
89. Nullify oil decontrol N
90. Target tax cuts-mid class N
91. Tax Indexing N
92. Kill-Oppose SS benft cuts N
93. Disapprove Saudi AWACS Y
94. Anti-busing rider N
95. Disapprove oil import fee Y
96. Domestic violence funds Y
97. Trucking Deregulation N
98. Overturn India fuel sale Y
99. Mil draft registration Y
100. Chrysler Loan Guarantees N
101. Nuclear plant moratorium N
102. Abolish electoral college Y
103. Kill-Lmt ct-ordered bus Y
104. Airline Deregulation N
105. Disappr Mideast jet sales Y
106. Natural gas deregulation Y
107. Prohibit neutron bomb N
108. Financial disclosure-off Y

Presidential Support Score: 1986 - 19% 1985 - 25%

OHIO

GLENN, JOHN [Democrat] Term Began/Expires: 1981/1986. Prior Terms: Senate: 1975-80. Born: July 18, 1921; Cambridge, Ohio. Education: Muskingum College (B.S.). Military Service: U.S. Marine Corps, 1942-65; NASA, 1959-65. Occupation: Military Serviceman; astronaut; vice president, Royal Crown (1966-68); president, Royal Crown International (1967-69); board member, Questor Corp. (1970-74).

1. Immigration Reform +
2. So Afr Sanc-veto override Y
3. Kill-Death pnlty drug bil Y
4. Kill-Mil use in drug war Y
5. Tax Overhaul Y
6. Raise speed limit N
7. Across-the-board cuts N
8. South Africa sanctions Y
9. Kill-So Africa sanctions N
10. Kill-So Africa sanct (*) N
11. Nicaraguan contra aid N
12. Terminate contra aid Y
13. Kill-Prohibit contra fnds N
14. Kill-Stop CIA contra fndg Y
15. Kill-Bar nuclr tsts w/SDI Y
16. Kill-Bar ASAT testing Y

GLENN, JOHN (Cont.)

17. Nuclear test ban treaty Y
18. Prohibit sale of Stinger N
19. Delete Bigeye chem bomb N
20. Bar binary chem weapons N
21. Kill-SDI funding Y
22. Kill-AIDS ins dscriminatn N
23. Kill-$10 bbl oil tariff Y
24. Kill-Repl wndfl prfts tax Y
25. Repeal balanced bdgt amdt Y
26. Tax amnesty provisions N
27. Kill-Tax amnesty subst Y
28. Kill-Add third tax rate Y
29. Kill-Unocal tax provsns N
30. Block Saudi arms sale (†) Y
31. Kill-Bar school busing Y
32. Prohibit Saudi arms sale Y
33. Nicaraguan contra aid N
34. Bar all aid to Nicaragua N
35. Balanced budget amendment N
36. Balanced bdgt substitute Y
37. Conrail sale N
38. Revise farm programs Y
39. Kill-New oil import fee N
40. Spending cuts, tax incres Y
41. Textile import quotas Y
42. Kill-Exmpt vets from cuts N
43. Kill-Bar inmate abortn $ Y
44. Textile import quotas (§) Y
45. Kill-Eliminate Amtrak $ Y
46. Kill-Incrs motor fuel tax Y
47. Set max allow deficits N
48. 20% minimum tax on corps N
49. Bar $ to toxic victims Y
50. Seasonal workers in US N
51. Kill-School prayer cases Y
52. Line-item veto N
53. South Africa sanctions ?
54. Ease '68 Gun Control Act Y
55. Kill-14 day handgun wait N
56. Kill-Gun dlr inspections N
57. Kill-Keep '68 Gun Con Act N
58. Nicarag humanitarian aid N
59. Bar ASAT testing N
60. Delete chemical weapons N
61. Delete 21 MX missiles Y
62. Kill-15% min tax on corps Y
63. Kill-Restore Soc Sec COLA N
64. Freeze all funding N
65. Cut def;raise taxes, COLA Y
66. Keep existing SS COLAs Y
67. Aid to Nicaraguan rebels N
68. Reaffirm purch of 21 MX N
69. African Relief/Farm Crdt Y
70. Kill-Nuclear Freeze N
71. Kill-Void Title IX Narrow ?
72. Raise drinking age to 21 Y
73. Kill-Reduce mil in Europe N
74. Kill-Bar $ for contras N
75. Kill-No new MXs in 1985 N
76. Kill-Move MX $ to non-nuc N
77. Deficit reduction-$140b N
78. Kill-Req auth for troops Y
79. School Prayer amendment N
80. Cap punish-certain crimes -
81. Bar govt off from taping ?
82. Martin L. King holiday Y
83. Auth marines in Lebanon N
84. Anti-abortion amendment N
85. Highway-Gas tax bill Y
86. Delete job creation amend ?
87. Kill-Tobacco price supprt ?
88. Emergency housing aid Y
89. Nullify oil decontrol N
90. Target tax cuts-mid class Y
91. Tax Indexing N
92. Kill-Oppose SS benft cuts N
93. Disapprove Saudi AWACS Y
94. Anti-busing rider N
95. Disapprove oil import fee ?
96. Domestic violence funds Y
97. Trucking Deregulation Y
98. Overturn India fuel sale Y
99. Mil draft registration Y
100. Chrysler Loan Guarantees Y
101. Nuclear plant moratorium N
102. Abolish electoral college Y
103. Kill-Lmt ct-ordered bus Y
104. Airline Deregulation Y
105. Disappr Mideast jet sales N
106. Natural gas deregulation N
107. Prohibit neutron bomb N
108. Financial disclosure-off Y

Presidential Support Score: 1986 - 44% 1985 - 42%

METZENBAUM, HOWARD M. [Democrat] Term Began/Expires: 1983/1988. Prior Terms: Senate: 1974 (Special Appointment); 1977-1982. Born: June 4, 1917; Cleveland, Ohio. Education: Ohio State University (B.A., LL.D.). Occupation: Ohio representative (1943-47); Ohio senator (1947-50); Ohio judicial councilman (1949-50); member, Ohio Bureau of Code Revision (1949-50); attorney, Metzenbaum, Gaines & Stern Co., L.P.A. (1941).

1. Immigration Reform Y
2. So Afr Sanc-veto override Y
3. Kill-Death pnlty drug bil Y
4. Kill-Mil use in drug war Y

METZENBAUM, HOWARD M. (Cont.)

5. Tax Overhaul Y
6. Raise speed limit N
7. Across-the-board cuts N
8. South Africa sanctions Y
9. Kill-So Africa sanctions N
10. Kill-So Africa sanct (*) N
11. Nicaraguan contra aid N
12. Terminate contra aid Y
13. Kill-Prohibit contra fnds N
14. Kill-Stop CIA contra fndg N
15. Kill-Bar nuclr tsts w/SDI N
16. Kill-Bar ASAT testing N
17. Nuclear test ban treaty Y
18. Prohibit sale of Stinger Y
19. Delete Bigeye chem bomb Y
20. Bar binary chem weapons Y
21. Kill-SDI funding N
22. Kill-AIDS ins dscriminatn Y
23. Kill-$10 bbl oil tariff Y
24. Kill-Repl wndfl prfts tax Y
25. Repeal balanced bdgt amdt Y
26. Tax amnesty provisions N
27. Kill-Tax amnesty subst Y
28. Kill-Add third tax rate N
29. Kill-Unocal tax provsns N
30. Block Saudi arms sale (†) Y
31. Kill-Bar school busing Y
32. Prohibit Saudi arms sale Y
33. Nicaraguan contra aid N
34. Bar all aid to Nicaragua Y
35. Balanced budget amendment N
36. Balanced bdgt substitute Y
37. Conrail sale N
38. Revise farm programs Y
39. Kill-New oil import fee Y
40. Spending cuts, tax incres N
41. Textile import quotas Y
42. Kill-Exmpt vets from cuts N
43. Kill-Bar inmate abortn $ Y
44. Textile import quotas (§) Y
45. Kill-Eliminate Amtrak $ Y
46. Kill-Incrs motor fuel tax Y
47. Set max allow deficits N
48. 20% minimum tax on corps N
49. Bar $ to toxic victims N
50. Seasonal workers in US N
51. Kill-School prayer cases Y
52. Line-item veto N
53. South Africa sanctions Y
54. Ease '68 Gun Control Act N
55. Kill-14 day handgun wait N
56. Kill-Gun dlr inspections N
57. Kill-Keep '68 Gun Con Act N
58. Nicarag humanitarian aid N
59. Bar ASAT testing Y
60. Delete chemical weapons Y
61. Delete 21 MX missiles Y
62. Kill-15% min tax on corps N
63. Kill-Restore Soc Sec COLA N
64. Freeze all funding N
65. Cut def;raise taxes, COLA Y
66. Keep existing SS COLAs Y
67. Aid to Nicaraguan rebels N
68. Reaffirm purch of 21 MX N
69. African Relief/Farm Crdt Y
70. Kill-Nuclear Freeze N
71. Kill-Void Title IX Narrow N
72. Raise drinking age to 21 Y
73. Kill-Reduce mil in Europe N
74. Kill-Bar $ for contras N
75. Kill-No new MXs in 1985 N
76. Kill-Move MX $ to non-nuc N
77. Deficit reduction-$140b N
78. Kill-Req auth for troops N
79. School Prayer amendment N
80. Cap punish-certain crimes N
81. Bar govt off from taping Y
82. Martin L. King holiday Y
83. Auth marines in Lebanon N
84. Anti-abortion amendment N
85. Highway-Gas tax bill N
86. Delete job creation amend N
87. Kill-Tobacco price supprt N
88. Emergency housing aid Y
89. Nullify oil decontrol Y
90. Target tax cuts-mid class Y
91. Tax Indexing N
92. Kill-Oppose SS benft cuts N
93. Disapprove Saudi AWACS Y
94. Anti-busing rider N
95. Disapprove oil import fee Y
96. Domestic violence funds Y
97. Trucking Deregulation Y
98. Overturn India fuel sale Y
99. Mil draft registration N
100. Chrysler Loan Guarantees Y
101. Nuclear plant moratorium Y
102. Abolish electoral college Y
103. Kill-Lmt ct-ordered bus Y
104. Airline Deregulation Y
105. Disappr Mideast jet sales Y
106. Natural gas deregulation N
107. Prohibit neutron bomb Y
108. Financial disclosure-off Y

Presidential Support Score: 1986 - 25% 1985 - 26%

OKLAHOMA

NICKLES, DON [Republican] Term Began/Expires: 1981/1986. Born: December 6, 1948; Ponca City, Okla. Education: Oklahoma State

NICKLES, DON (Cont.)
University (B.A.). Occupation: Oklahoma senator; vice and general manager, Nickles Machine Corp.

1.	Immigration Reform	N	48.	20% minimum tax on corps	N
2.	So Afr Sanc-veto override	N	49.	Bar $ to toxic victims	Y
3.	Kill-Death pnlty drug bil	N	50.	Seasonal workers in US	Y
4.	Kill-Mil use in drug war	N	51.	Kill-School prayer cases	N
5.	Tax Overhaul	N	52.	Line-item veto	Y
6.	Raise speed limit	Y	53.	South Africa sanctions	Y
7.	Across-the-board cuts	N	54.	Ease '68 Gun Control Act	Y
8.	South Africa sanctions	Y	55.	Kill-14 day handgun wait	Y
9.	Kill-So Africa sanctions	Y	56.	Kill-Gun dlr inspections	Y
10.	Kill-So Africa sanct (*)	Y	57.	Kill-Keep '68 Gun Con Act	Y
11.	Nicaraguan contra aid	Y	58.	Nicarag humanitarian aid	Y
12.	Terminate contra aid	N	59.	Bar ASAT testing	N
13.	Kill-Prohibit contra fnds	Y	60.	Delete chemical weapons	N
14.	Kill-Stop CIA contra fndg	Y	61.	Delete 21 MX missiles	N
15.	Kill-Bar nuclr tsts w/SDI	Y	62.	Kill-15% min tax on corps	Y
16.	Kill-Bar ASAT testing	Y	63.	Kill-Restore Soc Sec COLA	Y
17.	Nuclear test ban treaty	N	64.	Freeze all funding	N
18.	Prohibit sale of Stinger	N	65.	Cut def;raise taxes, COLA	N
19.	Delete Bigeye chem bomb	N	66.	Keep existing SS COLAs	N
20.	Bar binary chem weapons	N	67.	Aid to Nicaraguan rebels	Y
21.	Kill-SDI funding	Y	68.	Reaffirm purch of 21 MX	Y
22.	Kill-AIDS ins dscriminatn	N	69.	African Relief/Farm Crdt	N
23.	Kill-$10 bbl oil tariff	N	70.	Kill-Nuclear Freeze	Y
24.	Kill-Repl wndfl prfts tax	N	71.	Kill-Void Title IX Narrow	Y
25.	Repeal balanced bdgt amdt	N	72.	Raise drinking age to 21	Y
26.	Tax amnesty provisions	Y	73.	Kill-Reduce mil in Europe	Y
27.	Kill-Tax amnesty subst	N	74.	Kill-Bar $ for contras	Y
28.	Kill-Add third tax rate	Y	75.	Kill-No new MXs in 1985	Y
29.	Kill-Unocal tax provsns	Y	76.	Kill-Move MX $ to non-nuc	Y
30.	Block Saudi arms sale (†)	Y	77.	Deficit reduction-$140b	Y
31.	Kill-Bar school busing	N	78.	Kill-Req auth for troops	Y
32.	Prohibit Saudi arms sale	Y	79.	School Prayer amendment	Y
33.	Nicaraguan contra aid	Y	80.	Cap punish-certain crimes	Y
34.	Bar all aid to Nicaragua	N	81.	Bar govt off from taping	N
35.	Balanced budget amendment	Y	82.	Martin L. King holiday	N
36.	Balanced bdgt substitute	N	83.	Auth marines in Lebanon	Y
37.	Conrail sale	Y	84.	Anti-abortion amendment	Y
38.	Revise farm programs	N	85.	Highway-Gas tax bill	N
39.	Kill-New oil import fee	Y	86.	Delete job creation amend	Y
40.	Spending cuts, tax incres	Y	87.	Kill-Tobacco price supprt	N
41.	Textile import quotas	N	88.	Emergency housing aid	N
42.	Kill-Exmpt vets from cuts	Y	89.	Nullify oil decontrol	N
43.	Kill-Bar inmate abortn $	N	90.	Target tax cuts-mid class	N
44.	Textile import quotas (§)	N	91.	Tax Indexing	Y
45.	Kill-Eliminate Amtrak $	N	92.	Kill-Oppose SS benft cuts	Y
46.	Kill-Incrs motor fuel tax	Y	93.	Disapprove Saudi AWACS	N
47.	Set max allow deficits	Y	94.	Anti-busing rider	Y

Presidential Support Score: 1986 - 86% 1985 - 82%

BOREN, DAVID L. [Democrat] Term Began/Expires: 1985/1990. Prior Terms: Senate: 1979-1984. Born: April 21, 1941; Washington, D.C. Education: Yale Ounversity; Oxford; University of Oklahoma College of Law. Occupation: Oklahoma representative (1967-75); governor of Oklahoma (1975-77).

1.	Immigration Reform	?	3.	Kill-Death pnlty drug bil	?
2.	So Afr Sanc-veto override	Y	4.	Kill-Mil use in drug war	?

BOREN, DAVID L. (Cont.)

5. Tax Overhaul	N		54. Ease '68 Gun Control Act	Y
6. Raise speed limit	Y		55. Kill-14 day handgun wait	N
7. Across-the-board cuts	?		56. Kill-Gun dlr inspections	Y
8. South Africa sanctions	Y		57. Kill-Keep '68 Gun Con Act	N
9. Kill-So Africa sanctions	N		58. Nicarag humanitarian aid	Y
10. Kill-So Africa sanct (*)	Y		59. Bar ASAT testing	?
11. Nicaraguan contra aid	Y		60. Delete chemical weapons	Y
12. Terminate contra aid	N		61. Delete 21 MX missiles	N
13. Kill-Prohibit contra fnds	Y		62. Kill-15% min tax on corps	N
14. Kill-Stop CIA contra fndg	Y		63. Kill-Restore Soc Sec COLA	N
15. Kill-Bar nuclr tsts w/SDI	Y		64. Freeze all funding	Y
16. Kill-Bar ASAT testing	Y		65. Cut def;raise taxes, COLA	Y
17. Nuclear test ban treaty	Y		66. Keep existing SS COLAs	Y
18. Prohibit sale of Stinger	N		67. Aid to Nicaraguan rebels	Y
19. Delete Bigeye chem bomb	N		68. Reaffirm purch of 21 MX	Y
20. Bar binary chem weapons	N		69. African Relief/Farm Crdt	Y
21. Kill-SDI funding	N		70. Kill-Nuclear Freeze	?
22. Kill-AIDS ins dscriminatn	N		71. Kill-Void Title IX Narrow	N
23. Kill-$10 bbl oil tariff	N		72. Raise drinking age to 21	Y
24. Kill-Repl wndfl prfts tax	N		73. Kill-Reduce mil in Europe	N
25. Repeal balanced bdgt amdt	N		74. Kill-Bar $ for contras	Y
26. Tax amnesty provisions	Y		75. Kill-No new MXs in 1985	N
27. Kill-Tax amnesty subst	N		76. Kill-Move MX $ to non-nuc	N
28. Kill-Add third tax rate	Y		77. Deficit reduction-$140b	Y
29. Kill-Unocal tax provsns	Y		78. Kill-Req auth for troops	Y
30. Block Saudi arms sale (†)	Y		79. School Prayer amendment	Y
31. Kill-Bar school busing	N		80. Cap punish-certain crimes	Y
32. Prohibit Saudi arms sale	Y		81. Bar govt off from taping	Y
33. Nicaraguan contra aid	Y		82. Martin L. King holiday	Y
34. Bar all aid to Nicaragua	N		83. Auth marines in Lebanon	N
35. Balanced budget amendment	Y		84. Anti-abortion amendment	N
36. Balanced bdgt substitute	Y		85. Highway-Gas tax bill	N
37. Conrail sale	Y		86. Delete job creation amend	Y
38. Revise farm programs	N		87. Kill-Tobacco price supprt	Y
39. Kill-New oil import fee	N		88. Emergency housing aid	Y
40. Spending cuts, tax incres	Y		89. Nullify oil decontrol	N
41. Textile import quotas	N		90. Target tax cuts-mid class	N
42. Kill-Exmpt vets from cuts	Y		91. Tax Indexing	Y
43. Kill-Bar inmate abortn $	N		92. Kill-Oppose SS benft cuts	N
44. Textile import quotas (§)	N		93. Disapprove Saudi AWACS	N
45. Kill-Eliminate Amtrak $	Y		94. Anti-busing rider	Y
46. Kill-Incrs motor fuel tax	Y		95. Disapprove oil import fee	Y
47. Set max allow deficits	Y		96. Domestic violence funds	N
48. 20% minimum tax on corps	Y		97. Trucking Deregulation	N
49. Bar $ to toxic victims	?		98. Overturn India fuel sale	N
50. Seasonal workers in US	Y		99. Mil draft registration	Y
51. Kill-School prayer cases	Y		100. Chrysler Loan Guarantees	N
52. Line-item veto	Y		101. Nuclear plant moratorium	?
53. South Africa sanctions	Y		102. Abolish electoral college	Y

Presidential Support Score: 1986 - 69% 1985 - 47%

OREGON

HATFIELD, MARK O. [Republican] Term Began/Expires: 1985/1990. Prior Terms: Senate: 1967-84. Born: July 12, 1922; Dallas, Ore. Education: Willamette University (B.A.); Stanford University (A.M.). Military Service: U.S. Navy, WW II. Occupation: Associate professor, Willamette University (1949-56);

HATFIELD, MARK O. (Cont.)
dean of students (1950-56); Oregon representative (1950-54); Oregon senator (1954-56); secretary of state (1956-58); governor (1958-66).

1. Immigration Reform Y
2. So Afr Sanc-veto override Y
3. Kill-Death pnlty drug bil Y
4. Kill-Mil use in drug war Y
5. Tax Overhaul Y
6. Raise speed limit N
7. Across-the-board cuts N
8. South Africa sanctions Y
9. Kill-So Africa sanctions N
10. Kill-So Africa sanct (*) N
11. Nicaraguan contra aid N
12. Terminate contra aid Y
13. Kill-Prohibit contra fnds N
14. Kill-Stop CIA contra fndg N
15. Kill-Bar nuclr tsts w/SDI N
16. Kill-Bar ASAT testing N
17. Nuclear test ban treaty Y
18. Prohibit sale of Stinger Y
19. Delete Bigeye chem bomb Y
20. Bar binary chem weapons Y
21. Kill-SDI funding N
22. Kill-AIDS ins dscriminatn Y
23. Kill-$10 bbl oil tariff N
24. Kill-Repl wndfl prfts tax Y
25. Repeal balanced bdgt amdt Y
26. Tax amnesty provisions Y
27. Kill-Tax amnesty subst N
28. Kill-Add third tax rate Y
29. Kill-Unocal tax provsns Y
30. Block Saudi arms sale (†) Y
31. Kill-Bar school busing Y
32. Prohibit Saudi arms sale Y
33. Nicaraguan contra aid N
34. Bar all aid to Nicaragua Y
35. Balanced budget amendment N
36. Balanced bdgt substitute N
37. Conrail sale Y
38. Revise farm programs Y
39. Kill-New oil import fee ?
40. Spending cuts, tax incres ?
41. Textile import quotas N
42. Kill-Exmpt vets from cuts Y
43. Kill-Bar inmate abortn $?
44. Textile import quotas (§) -
45. Kill-Eliminate Amtrak $ Y
46. Kill-Incrs motor fuel tax N
47. Set max allow deficits N
48. 20% minimum tax on corps N
49. Bar $ to toxic victims Y
50. Seasonal workers in US +
51. Kill-School prayer cases Y
52. Line-item veto N
53. South Africa sanctions Y
54. Ease '68 Gun Control Act +
55. Kill-14 day handgun wait ?
56. Kill-Gun dlr inspections ?
57. Kill-Keep '68 Gun Con Act ?
58. Nicarag humanitarian aid N
59. Bar ASAT testing Y
60. Delete chemical weapons Y
61. Delete 21 MX missiles Y
62. Kill-15% min tax on corps Y
63. Kill-Restore Soc Sec COLA Y
64. Freeze all funding N
65. Cut def;raise taxes, COLA N
66. Keep existing SS COLAs Y
67. Aid to Nicaraguan rebels N
68. Reaffirm purch of 21 MX N
69. African Relief/Farm Crdt Y
70. Kill-Nuclear Freeze N
71. Kill-Void Title IX Narrow Y
72. Raise drinking age to 21 Y
73. Kill-Reduce mil in Europe Y
74. Kill-Bar $ for contras N
75. Kill-No new MXs in 1985 N
76. Kill-Move MX $ to non-nuc N
77. Deficit reduction-$140b Y
78. Kill-Req auth for troops N
79. School Prayer amendment N
80. Cap punish-certain crimes N
81. Bar govt off from taping Y
82. Martin L. King holiday Y
83. Auth marines in Lebanon N
84. Anti-abortion amendment Y
85. Highway-Gas tax bill ?
86. Delete job creation amend N
87. Kill-Tobacco price supprt N
88. Emergency housing aid Y
89. Nullify oil decontrol N
90. Target tax cuts-mid class N
91. Tax Indexing Y
92. Kill-Oppose SS benft cuts Y
93. Disapprove Saudi AWACS Y
94. Anti-busing rider N
95. Disapprove oil import fee Y
96. Domestic violence funds Y
97. Trucking Deregulation Y
98. Overturn India fuel sale Y
99. Mil draft registration N
100. Chrysler Loan Guarantees N
101. Nuclear plant moratorium Y
102. Abolish electoral college Y
103. Kill-Lmt ct-ordered bus Y
104. Airline Deregulation +
105. Disappr Mideast jet sales Y
106. Natural gas deregulation Y
107. Prohibit neutron bomb Y
108. Financial disclosure-off Y

Presidential Support Score: 1986 - 41% 1985 - 45%

PACKWOOD, BOB [Republican] Term Began/Expires: 1981/1986. Prior Terms: Senate: 1969-80. Born: September 11, 1932; Portland, Ore. Education: Willamette University (B.A.); New York University School of Law (LL.B.). Occupation: Partner, McMurry, Packwood & Stearns; Oregon representative (1962-68).

1. Immigration Reform Y
2. So Afr Sanc-veto override Y
3. Kill-Death pnlty drug bil N
4. Kill-Mil use in drug war Y
5. Tax Overhaul Y
6. Raise speed limit Y
7. Across-the-board cuts N
8. South Africa sanctions Y
9. Kill-So Africa sanctions N
10. Kill-So Africa sanct (*) N
11. Nicaraguan contra aid N
12. Terminate contra aid Y
13. Kill-Prohibit contra fnds N
14. Kill-Stop CIA contra fndg Y
15. Kill-Bar nuclr tsts w/SDI N
16. Kill-Bar ASAT testing N
17. Nuclear test ban treaty Y
18. Prohibit sale of Stinger Y
19. Delete Bigeye chem bomb Y
20. Bar binary chem weapons Y
21. Kill-SDI funding N
22. Kill-AIDS ins dscriminatn ?
23. Kill-$10 bbl oil tariff Y
24. Kill-Repl wndfl prfts tax Y
25. Repeal balanced bdgt amdt N
26. Tax amnesty provisions Y
27. Kill-Tax amnesty subst N
28. Kill-Add third tax rate Y
29. Kill-Unocal tax provsns N
30. Block Saudi arms sale (†) Y
31. Kill-Bar school busing Y
32. Prohibit Saudi arms sale Y
33. Nicaraguan contra aid N
34. Bar all aid to Nicaragua N
35. Balanced budget amendment Y
36. Balanced bdgt substitute N
37. Conrail sale Y
38. Revise farm programs Y
39. Kill-New oil import fee Y
40. Spending cuts, tax incres Y
41. Textile import quotas N
42. Kill-Exmpt vets from cuts Y
43. Kill-Bar inmate abortn $ Y
44. Textile import quotas (§) N
45. Kill-Eliminate Amtrak $ Y
46. Kill-Incrs motor fuel tax Y
47. Set max allow deficits Y
48. 20% minimum tax on corps N
49. Bar $ to toxic victims N
50. Seasonal workers in US N
51. Kill-School prayer cases Y
52. Line-item veto N
53. South Africa sanctions Y
54. Ease '68 Gun Control Act Y
55. Kill-14 day handgun wait Y
56. Kill-Gun dlr inspections Y
57. Kill-Keep '68 Gun Con Act Y
58. Nicarag humanitarian aid N
59. Bar ASAT testing ?
60. Delete chemical weapons Y
61. Delete 21 MX missiles ?
62. Kill-15% min tax on corps Y
63. Kill-Restore Soc Sec COLA Y
64. Freeze all funding N
65. Cut def;raise taxes, COLA N
66. Keep existing SS COLAs Y
67. Aid to Nicaraguan rebels N
68. Reaffirm purch of 21 MX Y
69. African Relief/Farm Crdt N
70. Kill-Nuclear Freeze N
71. Kill-Void Title IX Narrow Y
72. Raise drinking age to 21 Y
73. Kill-Reduce mil in Europe Y
74. Kill-Bar $ for contras Y
75. Kill-No new MXs in 1985 N
76. Kill-Move MX $ to non-nuc N
77. Deficit reduction-$140b Y
78. Kill-Req auth for troops Y
79. School Prayer amendment N
80. Cap punish-certain crimes Y
81. Bar govt off from taping Y
82. Martin L. King holiday Y
83. Auth marines in Lebanon Y
84. Anti-abortion amendment N
85. Highway-Gas tax bill Y
86. Delete job creation amend N
87. Kill-Tobacco price supprt N
88. Emergency housing aid Y
89. Nullify oil decontrol N
90. Target tax cuts-mid class N
91. Tax Indexing Y
92. Kill-Oppose SS benft cuts Y
93. Disapprove Saudi AWACS Y
94. Anti-busing rider N
95. Disapprove oil import fee Y
96. Domestic violence funds Y
97. Trucking Deregulation Y
98. Overturn India fuel sale N
99. Mil draft registration N
100. Chrysler Loan Guarantees N
101. Nuclear plant moratorium N
102. Abolish electoral college +
103. Kill-Lmt ct-ordered bus N
104. Airline Deregulation +
105. Disappr Mideast jet sales Y
106. Natural gas deregulation Y
107. Prohibit neutron bomb N
108. Financial disclosure-off Y

Presidential Support Score: 1986 - 49% 1985 - 72%

PENNSYLVANIA

HEINZ, JOHN [Republican] Term Began/Expires: 1983/1988. Prior Terms: House: 1971-76; Senate: 1977-82. Born: October 23, 1938; Pittsburgh, Pa. Education: Yale University (B.A.); Harvard University (M.B.A.). Military Service: Air Force, 1963-68. Occupation: Employee, H. J. Heinz Co. (1965-69); lecturer, Carnegie-Mellon University (1970).

1. Immigration Reform Y
2. So Afr Sanc-veto override Y
3. Kill-Death pnlty drug bil N
4. Kill-Mil use in drug war Y
5. Tax Overhaul Y
6. Raise speed limit N
7. Across-the-board cuts N
8. South Africa sanctions Y
9. Kill-So Africa sanctions N
10. Kill-So Africa sanct (*) N
11. Nicaraguan contra aid Y
12. Terminate contra aid N
13. Kill-Prohibit contra fnds Y
14. Kill-Stop CIA contra fndg Y
15. Kill-Bar nuclr tsts w/SDI Y
16. Kill-Bar ASAT testing N
17. Nuclear test ban treaty Y
18. Prohibit sale of Stinger N
19. Delete Bigeye chem bomb Y
20. Bar binary chem weapons Y
21. Kill-SDI funding Y
22. Kill-AIDS ins dscriminatn Y
23. Kill-$10 bbl oil tariff Y
24. Kill-Repl wndfl prfts tax Y
25. Repeal balanced bdgt amdt N
26. Tax amnesty provisions N
27. Kill-Tax amnesty subst Y
28. Kill-Add third tax rate Y
29. Kill-Unocal tax provsns N
30. Block Saudi arms sale (†) Y
31. Kill-Bar school busing Y
32. Prohibit Saudi arms sale Y
33. Nicaraguan contra aid Y
34. Bar all aid to Nicaragua N
35. Balanced budget amendment N
36. Balanced bdgt substitute N
37. Conrail sale N
38. Revise farm programs Y
39. Kill-New oil import fee Y
40. Spending cuts, tax incres Y
41. Textile import quotas Y
42. Kill-Exmpt vets from cuts Y
43. Kill-Bar inmate abortn $ Y
44. Textile import quotas (§) Y
45. Kill-Eliminate Amtrak $ Y
46. Kill-Incrs motor fuel tax Y
47. Set max allow deficits Y
48. 20% minimum tax on corps N
49. Bar $ to toxic victims N
50. Seasonal workers in US N
51. Kill-School prayer cases Y
52. Line-item veto Y
53. South Africa sanctions Y
54. Ease '68 Gun Control Act Y
55. Kill-14 day handgun wait Y
56. Kill-Gun dlr inspections Y
57. Kill-Keep '68 Gun Con Act Y
58. Nicarag humanitarian aid Y
59. Bar ASAT testing Y
60. Delete chemical weapons Y
61. Delete 21 MX missiles N
62. Kill-15% min tax on corps N
63. Kill-Restore Soc Sec COLA Y
64. Freeze all funding N
65. Cut def;raise taxes, COLA N
66. Keep existing SS COLAs Y
67. Aid to Nicaraguan rebels Y
68. Reaffirm purch of 21 MX Y
69. African Relief/Farm Crdt N
70. Kill-Nuclear Freeze Y
71. Kill-Void Title IX Narrow Y
72. Raise drinking age to 21 Y
73. Kill-Reduce mil in Europe Y
74. Kill-Bar $ for contras Y
75. Kill-No new MXs in 1985 Y
76. Kill-Move MX $ to non-nuc Y
77. Deficit reduction-$140b Y
78. Kill-Req auth for troops Y
79. School Prayer amendment N
80. Cap punish-certain crimes Y
81. Bar govt off from taping N
82. Martin L. King holiday Y
83. Auth marines in Lebanon Y
84. Anti-abortion amendment N
85. Highway-Gas tax bill ?
86. Delete job creation amend N
87. Kill-Tobacco price supprt N
88. Emergency housing aid Y
89. Nullify oil decontrol N
90. Target tax cuts-mid class N
91. Tax Indexing N
92. Kill-Oppose SS benft cuts Y
93. Disapprove Saudi AWACS Y
94. Anti-busing rider N
95. Disapprove oil import fee Y
96. Domestic violence funds N
97. Trucking Deregulation Y
98. Overturn India fuel sale Y
99. Mil draft registration N
100. Chrysler Loan Guarantees N
101. Nuclear plant moratorium Y
102. Abolish electoral college N

HEINZ, JOHN (Cont.)

103. Kill-Lmt ct-ordered bus Y
104. Airline Deregulation Y
105. Disappr Mideast jet sales Y
106. Natural gas deregulation Y
107. Prohibit neutron bomb Y
108. Financial disclosure-off Y

Presidential Support Score: 1986 - 70% 1985 - 64%

SPECTER, ARLEN [Republican] Term Began/Expires: 1981/1986. Born: February 12, 1930; Wichita, Kan. Education: Yale Law School. Occupation: Attorney, Dechert, Price and Rhoades; Philadelphia assistant district attorney.

1. Immigration Reform Y
2. So Afr Sanc-veto override Y
3. Kill-Death pnlty drug bil N
4. Kill-Mil use in drug war Y
5. Tax Overhaul Y
6. Raise speed limit ?
7. Across-the-board cuts N
8. South Africa sanctions Y
9. Kill-So Africa sanctions N
10. Kill-So Africa sanct (*) N
11. Nicaraguan contra aid N
12. Terminate contra aid Y
13. Kill-Prohibit contra fnds N
14. Kill-Stop CIA contra fndg N
15. Kill-Bar nuclr tsts w/SDI N
16. Kill-Bar ASAT testing N
17. Nuclear test ban treaty Y
18. Prohibit sale of Stinger Y
19. Delete Bigeye chem bomb Y
20. Bar binary chem weapons Y
21. Kill-SDI funding N
22. Kill-AIDS ins dscriminatn Y
23. Kill-$10 bbl oil tariff Y
24. Kill-Repl wndfl prfts tax Y
25. Repeal balanced bdgt amdt N
26. Tax amnesty provisions N
27. Kill-Tax amnesty subst Y
28. Kill-Add third tax rate N
29. Kill-Unocal tax provsns N
30. Block Saudi arms sale (†) Y
31. Kill-Bar school busing Y
32. Prohibit Saudi arms sale Y
33. Nicaraguan contra aid N
34. Bar all aid to Nicaragua Y
35. Balanced budget amendment Y
36. Balanced bdgt substitute N
37. Conrail sale N
38. Revise farm programs Y
39. Kill-New oil import fee Y
40. Spending cuts, tax incres Y
41. Textile import quotas Y
42. Kill-Exmpt vets from cuts N
43. Kill-Bar inmate abortn $ Y
44. Textile import quotas (§) Y
45. Kill-Eliminate Amtrak $ Y
46. Kill-Incrs motor fuel tax Y
47. Set max allow deficits Y
48. 20% minimum tax on corps N
49. Bar $ to toxic victims N
50. Seasonal workers in US Y
51. Kill-School prayer cases Y
52. Line-item veto Y
53. South Africa sanctions Y
54. Ease '68 Gun Control Act Y
55. Kill-14 day handgun wait Y
56. Kill-Gun dlr inspections Y
57. Kill-Keep '68 Gun Con Act Y
58. Nicarag humanitarian aid N
59. Bar ASAT testing Y
60. Delete chemical weapons Y
61. Delete 21 MX missiles N
62. Kill-15% min tax on corps Y
63. Kill-Restore Soc Sec COLA N
64. Freeze all funding N
65. Cut def;raise taxes, COLA N
66. Keep existing SS COLAs Y
67. Aid to Nicaraguan rebels N
68. Reaffirm purch of 21 MX Y
69. African Relief/Farm Crdt Y
70. Kill-Nuclear Freeze N
71. Kill-Void Title IX Narrow N
72. Raise drinking age to 21 Y
73. Kill-Reduce mil in Europe Y
74. Kill-Bar $ for contras Y
75. Kill-No new MXs in 1985 N
76. Kill-Move MX $ to non-nuc Y
77. Deficit reduction-$140b Y
78. Kill-Req auth for troops N
79. School Prayer amendment N
80. Cap punish-certain crimes Y
81. Bar govt off from taping N
82. Martin L. King holiday Y
83. Auth marines in Lebanon Y
84. Anti-abortion amendment N
85. Highway-Gas tax bill Y
86. Delete job creation amend N
87. Kill-Tobacco price supprt N
88. Emergency housing aid Y
89. Nullify oil decontrol N
90. Target tax cuts-mid class N
91. Tax Indexing Y
92. Kill-Oppose SS benft cuts Y
93. Disapprove Saudi AWACS Y
94. Anti-busing rider N

Presidential Support Score: 1986 - 33% 1985 - 61%

RHODE ISLAND

CHAFEE, JOHN H. [Republican] Term Began/Expires: 1983/1988. Prior Terms: Senate: 1977-82. Born: October 22, 1922; Providence, R.I. Education: Yale University (B.A.); Harvard Law School (LL.B.). Military Service: U.S. Marines. Occupation: Rhode Island representative (1957-63); governor (1963-69); secretary of the Navy (1969-72); attorney, Edwards and Angell.

1. Immigration Reform Y
2. So Afr Sanc-veto override Y
3. Kill-Death pnlty drug bil Y
4. Kill-Mil use in drug war Y
5. Tax Overhaul Y
6. Raise speed limit N
7. Across-the-board cuts N
8. South Africa sanctions Y
9. Kill-So Africa sanctions N
10. Kill-So Africa sanct (*) Y
11. Nicaraguan contra aid N
12. Terminate contra aid Y
13. Kill-Prohibit contra fnds N
14. Kill-Stop CIA contra fndg N
15. Kill-Bar nuclr tsts w/SDI N
16. Kill-Bar ASAT testing N
17. Nuclear test ban treaty Y
18. Prohibit sale of Stinger Y
19. Delete Bigeye chem bomb N
20. Bar binary chem weapons Y
21. Kill-SDI funding N
22. Kill-AIDS ins dscriminatn Y
23. Kill-$10 bbl oil tariff Y
24. Kill-Repl wndfl prfts tax Y
25. Repeal balanced bdgt amdt N
26. Tax amnesty provisions ?
27. Kill-Tax amnesty subst ?
28. Kill-Add third tax rate Y
29. Kill-Unocal tax provsns N
30. Block Saudi arms sale (†) N
31. Kill-Bar school busing Y
32. Prohibit Saudi arms sale N
33. Nicaraguan contra aid N
34. Bar all aid to Nicaragua N
35. Balanced budget amendment N
36. Balanced bdgt substitute N
37. Conrail sale Y
38. Revise farm programs N
39. Kill-New oil import fee Y
40. Spending cuts, tax incres Y
41. Textile import quotas N
42. Kill-Exmpt vets from cuts Y
43. Kill-Bar inmate abortn $ Y
44. Textile import quotas (§) N
45. Kill-Eliminate Amtrak $ Y
46. Kill-Incrs motor fuel tax Y
47. Set max allow deficits Y
48. 20% minimum tax on corps N
49. Bar $ to toxic victims N
50. Seasonal workers in US N
51. Kill-School prayer cases Y
52. Line-item veto Y
53. South Africa sanctions Y
54. Ease '68 Gun Control Act N
55. Kill-14 day handgun wait N
56. Kill-Gun dlr inspections N
57. Kill-Keep '68 Gun Con Act N
58. Nicarag humanitarian aid N
59. Bar ASAT testing Y
60. Delete chemical weapons Y
61. Delete 21 MX missiles N
62. Kill-15% min tax on corps Y
63. Kill-Restore Soc Sec COLA Y
64. Freeze all funding N
65. Cut def;raise taxes, COLA N
66. Keep existing SS COLAs N
67. Aid to Nicaraguan rebels N
68. Reaffirm purch of 21 MX Y
69. African Relief/Farm Crdt N
70. Kill-Nuclear Freeze N
71. Kill-Void Title IX Narrow Y
72. Raise drinking age to 21 Y
73. Kill-Reduce mil in Europe ?
74. Kill-Bar $ for contras Y
75. Kill-No new MXs in 1985 Y
76. Kill-Move MX $ to non-nuc ?
77. Deficit reduction-$140b Y
78. Kill-Req auth for troops Y
79. School Prayer amendment N
80. Cap punish-certain crimes N
81. Bar govt off from taping N
82. Martin L. King holiday Y
83. Auth marines in Lebanon Y
84. Anti-abortion amendment N
85. Highway-Gas tax bill Y
86. Delete job creation amend N
87. Kill-Tobacco price supprt N
88. Emergency housing aid Y
89. Nullify oil decontrol Y
90. Target tax cuts-mid class N
91. Tax Indexing N
92. Kill-Oppose SS benft cuts Y
93. Disapprove Saudi AWACS N
94. Anti-busing rider N
95. Disapprove oil import fee Y
96. Domestic violence funds Y
97. Trucking Deregulation Y
98. Overturn India fuel sale Y
99. Mil draft registration Y
100. Chrysler Loan Guarantees N
101. Nuclear plant moratorium Y
102. Abolish electoral college Y

CHAFEE, JOHN H. (Cont.)

103. Kill-Lmt ct-ordered bus Y
104. Airline Deregulation Y
105. Disappr Mideast jet sales N
106. Natural gas deregulation Y
107. Prohibit neutron bomb Y
108. Financial disclosure-off ?

Presidential Support Score: 1986 - 68% 1985 - 72%

PELL, CLAIBORNE [Democrat] Term Began/Expires: 1985/1990. Prior Terms: Senate: 1961-84. Born: November 22, 1918; New York, N.Y. Education: Princeton University (A.B.); Columbia University (A.M.). Military Service: U.S. Coast Guard. Occupation: Business executive; special assistant, U.N. Conference.

1. Immigration Reform Y
2. So Afr Sanc-veto override Y
3. Kill-Death pnlty drug bil Y
4. Kill-Mil use in drug war Y
5. Tax Overhaul Y
6. Raise speed limit N
7. Across-the-board cuts N
8. South Africa sanctions Y
9. Kill-So Africa sanctions N
10. Kill-So Africa sanct (*) N
11. Nicaraguan contra aid N
12. Terminate contra aid Y
13. Kill-Prohibit contra fnds N
14. Kill-Stop CIA contra fndg N
15. Kill-Bar nuclr tsts w/SDI N
16. Kill-Bar ASAT testing N
17. Nuclear test ban treaty Y
18. Prohibit sale of Stinger Y
19. Delete Bigeye chem bomb Y
20. Bar binary chem weapons Y
21. Kill-SDI funding N
22. Kill-AIDS ins dscriminatn Y
23. Kill-$10 bbl oil tariff Y
24. Kill-Repl wndfl prfts tax Y
25. Repeal balanced bdgt amdt Y
26. Tax amnesty provisions Y
27. Kill-Tax amnesty subst N
28. Kill-Add third tax rate Y
29. Kill-Unocal tax provsns N
30. Block Saudi arms sale (†) Y
31. Kill-Bar school busing Y
32. Prohibit Saudi arms sale Y
33. Nicaraguan contra aid N
34. Bar all aid to Nicaragua Y
35. Balanced budget amendment Y
36. Balanced bdgt substitute Y
37. Conrail sale N
38. Revise farm programs N
39. Kill-New oil import fee Y
40. Spending cuts, tax incres Y
41. Textile import quotas Y
42. Kill-Exmpt vets from cuts N
43. Kill-Bar inmate abortn $ Y
44. Textile import quotas (§) Y
45. Kill-Eliminate Amtrak $ Y
46. Kill-Incrs motor fuel tax N
47. Set max allow deficits N
48. 20% minimum tax on corps Y
49. Bar $ to toxic victims N
50. Seasonal workers in US N
51. Kill-School prayer cases Y
52. Line-item veto Y
53. South Africa sanctions Y
54. Ease '68 Gun Control Act N
55. Kill-14 day handgun wait N
56. Kill-Gun dlr inspections N
57. Kill-Keep '68 Gun Con Act N
58. Nicarag humanitarian aid N
59. Bar ASAT testing Y
60. Delete chemical weapons Y
61. Delete 21 MX missiles Y
62. Kill-15% min tax on corps N
63. Kill-Restore Soc Sec COLA N
64. Freeze all funding Y
65. Cut def;raise taxes, COLA Y
66. Keep existing SS COLAs Y
67. Aid to Nicaraguan rebels N
68. Reaffirm purch of 21 MX N
69. African Relief/Farm Crdt Y
70. Kill-Nuclear Freeze N
71. Kill-Void Title IX Narrow N
72. Raise drinking age to 21 Y
73. Kill-Reduce mil in Europe N
74. Kill-Bar $ for contras -
75. Kill-No new MXs in 1985 N
76. Kill-Move MX $ to non-nuc N
77. Deficit reduction-$140b N
78. Kill-Req auth for troops N
79. School Prayer amendment N
80. Cap punish-certain crimes N
81. Bar govt off from taping Y
82. Martin L. King holiday Y
83. Auth marines in Lebanon N
84. Anti-abortion amendment N
85. Highway-Gas tax bill Y
86. Delete job creation amend N
87. Kill-Tobacco price supprt N
88. Emergency housing aid +
89. Nullify oil decontrol Y
90. Target tax cuts-mid class Y
91. Tax Indexing N
92. Kill-Oppose SS benft cuts N
93. Disapprove Saudi AWACS Y
94. Anti-busing rider #

PELL, CLAIBORNE (Cont.)

95. Disapprove oil import fee N
96. Domestic violence funds Y
97. Trucking Deregulation Y
98. Overturn India fuel sale #
99. Mil draft registration +
100. Chrysler Loan Guarantees N
101. Nuclear plant moratorium Y
102. Abolish electoral college Y
103. Kill-Lmt ct-ordered bus Y
104. Airline Deregulation Y
105. Disappr Mideast jet sales Y
106. Natural gas deregulation N
107. Prohibit neutron bomb Y
108. Financial disclosure-off Y

Presidential Support Score: 1986 - 31% 1985 - 29%

SOUTH CAROLINA

THURMOND, STROM [Republican] Term Began/Expires: 1985/1990. Prior Terms: Senate: 1955-84. Born: December 5, 1902; Edgefield, S.C. Education: Clemson College. Military Service: U.S. Army, 1942-46. Occupation: Teacher, athletic coach; county superintendent of education; city and county attorney; South Carolina senator; circuit judge; governor of South Carolina (1947-51).

1. Immigration Reform Y
2. So Afr Sanc-veto override N
3. Kill-Death pnlty drug bil N
4. Kill-Mil use in drug war Y
5. Tax Overhaul Y
6. Raise speed limit Y
7. Across-the-board cuts N
8. South Africa sanctions N
9. Kill-So Africa sanctions Y
10. Kill-So Africa sanct (*) Y
11. Nicaraguan contra aid Y
12. Terminate contra aid N
13. Kill-Prohibit contra fnds Y
14. Kill-Stop CIA contra fndg Y
15. Kill-Bar nuclr tsts w/SDI Y
16. Kill-Bar ASAT testing Y
17. Nuclear test ban treaty N
18. Prohibit sale of Stinger N
19. Delete Bigeye chem bomb N
20. Bar binary chem weapons N
21. Kill-SDI funding Y
22. Kill-AIDS ins dscriminatn N
23. Kill-$10 bbl oil tariff Y
24. Kill-Repl wndfl prfts tax N
25. Repeal balanced bdgt amdt N
26. Tax amnesty provisions Y
27. Kill-Tax amnesty subst N
28. Kill-Add third tax rate Y
29. Kill-Unocal tax provsns N
30. Block Saudi arms sale (†) N
31. Kill-Bar school busing N
32. Prohibit Saudi arms sale N
33. Nicaraguan contra aid Y
34. Bar all aid to Nicaragua N
35. Balanced budget amendment Y
36. Balanced bdgt substitute N
37. Conrail sale Y
38. Revise farm programs Y
39. Kill-New oil import fee Y
40. Spending cuts, tax incres Y
41. Textile import quotas Y
42. Kill-Exmpt vets from cuts Y
43. Kill-Bar inmate abortn $ N
44. Textile import quotas (§) Y
45. Kill-Eliminate Amtrak $ N
46. Kill-Incrs motor fuel tax Y
47. Set max allow deficits Y
48. 20% minimum tax on corps N
49. Bar $ to toxic victims Y
50. Seasonal workers in US Y
51. Kill-School prayer cases N
52. Line-item veto Y
53. South Africa sanctions N
54. Ease '68 Gun Control Act Y
55. Kill-14 day handgun wait Y
56. Kill-Gun dlr inspections Y
57. Kill-Keep '68 Gun Con Act Y
58. Nicarag humanitarian aid Y
59. Bar ASAT testing N
60. Delete chemical weapons N
61. Delete 21 MX missiles N
62. Kill-15% min tax on corps Y
63. Kill-Restore Soc Sec COLA Y
64. Freeze all funding N
65. Cut def;raise taxes, COLA N
66. Keep existing SS COLAs N
67. Aid to Nicaraguan rebels Y
68. Reaffirm purch of 21 MX Y
69. African Relief/Farm Crdt N
70. Kill-Nuclear Freeze Y
71. Kill-Void Title IX Narrow Y
72. Raise drinking age to 21 N
73. Kill-Reduce mil in Europe Y
74. Kill-Bar $ for contras Y
75. Kill-No new MXs in 1985 Y
76. Kill-Move MX $ to non-nuc Y

THURMOND, STROM (Cont.)

77. Deficit reduction-$140b Y
78. Kill-Req auth for troops Y
79. School Prayer amendment Y
80. Cap punish-certain crimes Y
81. Bar govt off from taping N
82. Martin L. King holiday Y
83. Auth marines in Lebanon Y
84. Anti-abortion amendment Y
85. Highway-Gas tax bill Y
86. Delete job creation amend Y
87. Kill-Tobacco price supprt Y
88. Emergency housing aid Y
89. Nullify oil decontrol N
90. Target tax cuts-mid class N
91. Tax Indexing Y
92. Kill-Oppose SS benft cuts Y
93. Disapprove Saudi AWACS N
94. Anti-busing rider Y
95. Disapprove oil import fee Y
96. Domestic violence funds N
97. Trucking Deregulation Y
98. Overturn India fuel sale Y
99. Mil draft registration Y
100. Chrysler Loan Guarantees N
101. Nuclear plant moratorium N
102. Abolish electoral college N
103. Kill-Lmt ct-ordered bus N
104. Airline Deregulation Y
105. Disappr Mideast jet sales N
106. Natural gas deregulation Y
107. Prohibit neutron bomb N
108. Financial disclosure-off Y

Presidential Support Score: 1986 - 90% 1985 - 87%

HOLLINGS, ERNEST F. [Democrat] Term Began/Expires: 1981/1986. Prior Terms: Senate: 1966 (Special Election)-1980. Born: January 1, 1922; Charleston, S.C. Education: The Citadel (B.A.); University of South Carolina (LL.B.). Military Service: Armed Forces, 1942-45. Occupation: South Carolina representative (1948-53); lieutenant governor (1954-58); governor (1959-63).

1. Immigration Reform Y
2. So Afr Sanc-veto override Y
3. Kill-Death pnlty drug bil N
4. Kill-Mil use in drug war Y
5. Tax Overhaul Y
6. Raise speed limit N
7. Across-the-board cuts Y
8. South Africa sanctions Y
9. Kill-So Africa sanctions N
10. Kill-So Africa sanct (*) N
11. Nicaraguan contra aid Y
12. Terminate contra aid N
13. Kill-Prohibit contra fnds Y
14. Kill-Stop CIA contra fndg Y
15. Kill-Bar nuclr tsts w/SDI Y
16. Kill-Bar ASAT testing Y
17. Nuclear test ban treaty Y
18. Prohibit sale of Stinger Y
19. Delete Bigeye chem bomb N
20. Bar binary chem weapons N
21. Kill-SDI funding Y
22. Kill-AIDS ins dscriminatn N
23. Kill-$10 bbl oil tariff N
24. Kill-Repl wndfl prfts tax N
25. Repeal balanced bdgt amdt N
26. Tax amnesty provisions N
27. Kill-Tax amnesty subst Y
28. Kill-Add third tax rate N
29. Kill-Unocal tax provsns N
30. Block Saudi arms sale (†) Y
31. Kill-Bar school busing N
32. Prohibit Saudi arms sale Y
33. Nicaraguan contra aid Y
34. Bar all aid to Nicaragua N
35. Balanced budget amendment Y
36. Balanced bdgt substitute N
37. Conrail sale Y
38. Revise farm programs N
39. Kill-New oil import fee Y
40. Spending cuts, tax incres Y
41. Textile import quotas Y
42. Kill-Exmpt vets from cuts N
43. Kill-Bar inmate abortn $ Y
44. Textile import quotas (§) Y
45. Kill-Eliminate Amtrak $ Y
46. Kill-Incrs motor fuel tax Y
47. Set max allow deficits Y
48. 20% minimum tax on corps N
49. Bar $ to toxic victims Y
50. Seasonal workers in US Y
51. Kill-School prayer cases Y
52. Line-item veto Y
53. South Africa sanctions Y
54. Ease '68 Gun Control Act Y
55. Kill-14 day handgun wait Y
56. Kill-Gun dlr inspections Y
57. Kill-Keep '68 Gun Con Act Y
58. Nicarag humanitarian aid Y
59. Bar ASAT testing N
60. Delete chemical weapons N
61. Delete 21 MX missiles Y
62. Kill-15% min tax on corps N
63. Kill-Restore Soc Sec COLA N
64. Freeze all funding Y

HOLLINGS, ERNEST F. (Cont.)

65. Cut def;raise taxes, COLA Y
66. Keep existing SS COLAs Y
67. Aid to Nicaraguan rebels Y
68. Reaffirm purch of 21 MX N
69. African Relief/Farm Crdt Y
70. Kill-Nuclear Freeze N
71. Kill-Void Title IX Narrow N
72. Raise drinking age to 21 Y
73. Kill-Reduce mil in Europe N
74. Kill-Bar $ for contras Y
75. Kill-No new MXs in 1985 N
76. Kill-Move MX $ to non-nuc N
77. Deficit reduction-$140b N
78. Kill-Req auth for troops N
79. School Prayer amendment Y
80. Cap punish-certain crimes ?
81. Bar govt off from taping ?
82. Martin L. King holiday Y
83. Auth marines in Lebanon N
84. Anti-abortion amendment N
85. Highway-Gas tax bill ?
86. Delete job creation amend N
87. Kill-Tobacco price supprt Y
88. Emergency housing aid Y
89. Nullify oil decontrol Y
90. Target tax cuts-mid class Y
91. Tax Indexing N
92. Kill-Oppose SS benft cuts N
93. Disapprove Saudi AWACS Y
94. Anti-busing rider Y
95. Disapprove oil import fee Y
96. Domestic violence funds N
97. Trucking Deregulation N
98. Overturn India fuel sale N
99. Mil draft registration Y
100. Chrysler Loan Guarantees ?
101. Nuclear plant moratorium N
102. Abolish electoral college N
103. Kill-Lmt ct-ordered bus N
104. Airline Deregulation Y
105. Disappr Mideast jet sales N
106. Natural gas deregulation N
107. Prohibit neutron bomb N
108. Financial disclosure-off Y

Presidential Support Score: 1986 - 73% 1985 - 52%

SOUTH DAKOTA

ABDNOR, JAMES [Republican] Term Began/Expires: 1981/1986. Prior Terms: House: 1973-80. Born: February 13, 1923; Kennebec, S.D. Education: University of Nebraska (B.S.). Military Service: U.S. Army, WW II. Occupation: Farmer; teacher; South Dakota senator (1956-67); lieutenant governor (1968-70).

1. Immigration Reform N
2. So Afr Sanc-veto override Y
3. Kill-Death pnlty drug bil N
4. Kill-Mil use in drug war N
5. Tax Overhaul N
6. Raise speed limit Y
7. Across-the-board cuts N
8. South Africa sanctions Y
9. Kill-So Africa sanctions Y
10. Kill-So Africa sanct (*) Y
11. Nicaraguan contra aid N
12. Terminate contra aid N
13. Kill-Prohibit contra fnds Y
14. Kill-Stop CIA contra fndg Y
15. Kill-Bar nuclr tsts w/SDI Y
16. Kill-Bar ASAT testing Y
17. Nuclear test ban treaty N
18. Prohibit sale of Stinger N
19. Delete Bigeye chem bomb N
20. Bar binary chem weapons N
21. Kill-SDI funding Y
22. Kill-AIDS ins dscriminatn N
23. Kill-$10 bbl oil tariff Y
24. Kill-Repl wndfl prfts tax Y
25. Repeal balanced bdgt amdt N
26. Tax amnesty provisions N
27. Kill-Tax amnesty subst Y
28. Kill-Add third tax rate Y
29. Kill-Unocal tax provsns N
30. Block Saudi arms sale (†) Y
31. Kill-Bar school busing ?
32. Prohibit Saudi arms sale Y
33. Nicaraguan contra aid Y
34. Bar all aid to Nicaragua N
35. Balanced budget amendment Y
36. Balanced bdgt substitute N
37. Conrail sale N
38. Revise farm programs Y
39. Kill-New oil import fee Y
40. Spending cuts, tax incres Y
41. Textile import quotas N
42. Kill-Exmpt vets from cuts N
43. Kill-Bar inmate abortn $ N
44. Textile import quotas (§) N
45. Kill-Eliminate Amtrak $ Y
46. Kill-Incrs motor fuel tax Y
47. Set max allow deficits Y
48. 20% minimum tax on corps N
49. Bar $ to toxic victims Y
50. Seasonal workers in US Y

ABDNOR, JAMES (Cont.)

51. Kill-School prayer cases N
52. Line-item veto Y
53. South Africa sanctions Y
54. Ease '68 Gun Control Act Y
55. Kill-14 day handgun wait Y
56. Kill-Gun dlr inspections Y
57. Kill-Keep '68 Gun Con Act Y
58. Nicarag humanitarian aid Y
59. Bar ASAT testing N
60. Delete chemical weapons N
61. Delete 21 MX missiles N
62. Kill-15% min tax on corps Y
63. Kill-Restore Soc Sec COLA Y
64. Freeze all funding N
65. Cut def;raise taxes, COLA N
66. Keep existing SS COLAs N
67. Aid to Nicaraguan rebels Y
68. Reaffirm purch of 21 MX Y
69. African Relief/Farm Crdt Y
70. Kill-Nuclear Freeze Y
71. Kill-Void Title IX Narrow Y
72. Raise drinking age to 21 Y
73. Kill-Reduce mil in Europe Y
74. Kill-Bar $ for contras Y
75. Kill-No new MXs in 1985 Y
76. Kill-Move MX $ to non-nuc Y
77. Deficit reduction-$140b Y
78. Kill-Req auth for troops Y
79. School Prayer amendment Y
80. Cap punish-certain crimes Y
81. Bar govt off from taping N
82. Martin L. King holiday N
83. Auth marines in Lebanon Y
84. Anti-abortion amendment Y
85. Highway-Gas tax bill Y
86. Delete job creation amend Y
87. Kill-Tobacco price supprt Y
88. Emergency housing aid Y
89. Nullify oil decontrol N
90. Target tax cuts-mid class N
91. Tax Indexing Y
92. Kill-Oppose SS benft cuts Y
93. Disapprove Saudi AWACS N
94. Anti-busing rider Y

Presidential Support Score: 1986 - 75% 1985 - 77%

PRESSLER, LARRY [Republican] Term Began/Expires: 1985/1990. Prior Terms: House: 1974-78; Senate: 1979-84. Born: March 29, 1942; Humboldt, S.D. Education: University of South Dakota (B.A.); Oxford University; Kennedy School of Government (M.A.); Harvard (J.D.). Military Service: U.S. Army, 1966-68. Occupation: State Department employee; Senate staff member.

1. Immigration Reform N
2. So Afr Sanc-veto override N
3. Kill-Death pnlty drug bil ?
4. Kill-Mil use in drug war ?
5. Tax Overhaul N
6. Raise speed limit Y
7. Across-the-board cuts N
8. South Africa sanctions N
9. Kill-So Africa sanctions Y
10. Kill-So Africa sanct (*) Y
11. Nicaraguan contra aid Y
12. Terminate contra aid N
13. Kill-Prohibit contra fnds Y
14. Kill-Stop CIA contra fndg Y
15. Kill-Bar nuclr tsts w/SDI ?
16. Kill-Bar ASAT testing Y
17. Nuclear test ban treaty N
18. Prohibit sale of Stinger N
19. Delete Bigeye chem bomb N
20. Bar binary chem weapons N
21. Kill-SDI funding Y
22. Kill-AIDS ins dscriminatn N
23. Kill-$10 bbl oil tariff Y
24. Kill-Repl wndfl prfts tax Y
25. Repeal balanced bdgt amdt N
26. Tax amnesty provisions N
27. Kill-Tax amnesty subst Y
28. Kill-Add third tax rate Y
29. Kill-Unocal tax provsns ?
30. Block Saudi arms sale (†) Y
31. Kill-Bar school busing N
32. Prohibit Saudi arms sale Y
33. Nicaraguan contra aid Y
34. Bar all aid to Nicaragua N
35. Balanced budget amendment Y
36. Balanced bdgt substitute N
37. Conrail sale N
38. Revise farm programs N
39. Kill-New oil import fee Y
40. Spending cuts, tax incres Y
41. Textile import quotas N
42. Kill-Exmpt vets from cuts N
43. Kill-Bar inmate abortn $?
44. Textile import quotas (§) N
45. Kill-Eliminate Amtrak $ Y
46. Kill-Incrs motor fuel tax Y
47. Set max allow deficits Y
48. 20% minimum tax on corps N
49. Bar $ to toxic victims Y
50. Seasonal workers in US N
51. Kill-School prayer cases N
52. Line-item veto Y
53. South Africa sanctions Y
54. Ease '68 Gun Control Act Y

PRESSLER, LARRY (Cont.)

55. Kill-14 day handgun wait Y
56. Kill-Gun dlr inspections Y
57. Kill-Keep '68 Gun Con Act Y
58. Nicarag humanitarian aid Y
59. Bar ASAT testing N
60. Delete chemical weapons N
61. Delete 21 MX missiles N
62. Kill-15% min tax on corps Y
63. Kill-Restore Soc Sec COLA Y
64. Freeze all funding N
65. Cut def;raise taxes, COLA N
66. Keep existing SS COLAs Y
67. Aid to Nicaraguan rebels Y
68. Reaffirm purch of 21 MX N
69. African Relief/Farm Crdt Y
70. Kill-Nuclear Freeze Y
71. Kill-Void Title IX Narrow Y
72. Raise drinking age to 21 Y
73. Kill-Reduce mil in Europe N
74. Kill-Bar $ for contras N
75. Kill-No new MXs in 1985 N
76. Kill-Move MX $ to non-nuc Y
77. Deficit reduction-$140b Y
78. Kill-Req auth for troops N
79. School Prayer amendment Y
80. Cap punish-certain crimes Y
81. Bar govt off from taping N
82. Martin L. King holiday N
83. Auth marines in Lebanon Y
84. Anti-abortion amendment Y
85. Highway-Gas tax bill Y
86. Delete job creation amend Y
87. Kill-Tobacco price supprt Y
88. Emergency housing aid +
89. Nullify oil decontrol N
90. Target tax cuts-mid class N
91. Tax Indexing Y
92. Kill-Oppose SS benft cuts ?
93. Disapprove Saudi AWACS N
94. Anti-busing rider N
95. Disapprove oil import fee ?
96. Domestic violence funds N
97. Trucking Deregulation N
98. Overturn India fuel sale Y
99. Mil draft registration Y
100. Chrysler Loan Guarantees N
101. Nuclear plant moratorium N
102. Abolish electoral college N

Presidential Support Score: 1986 - 78% 1985 - 74%

TENNESSEE

GORE, ALBERT, Jr. [Democrat] Term Began/Expires: 1985/1990. Prior Terms: House: 1977-84. Born: March 31, 1948. Education: Harvard University; Vanderbilt Graduate School of Religion; Vanderbilt School of Law. Military Service: U.S. Army, 1969-71. Occupation: Reporter; writer; construction business.

1. Immigration Reform Y
2. So Afr Sanc-veto override Y
3. Kill-Death pnlty drug bil N
4. Kill-Mil use in drug war Y
5. Tax Overhaul Y
6. Raise speed limit N
7. Across-the-board cuts N
8. South Africa sanctions Y
9. Kill-So Africa sanctions N
10. Kill-So Africa sanct (*) N
11. Nicaraguan contra aid N
12. Terminate contra aid Y
13. Kill-Prohibit contra fnds N
14. Kill-Stop CIA contra fndg N
15. Kill-Bar nuclr tsts w/SDI N
16. Kill-Bar ASAT testing N
17. Nuclear test ban treaty Y
18. Prohibit sale of Stinger Y
19. Delete Bigeye chem bomb Y
20. Bar binary chem weapons N
21. Kill-SDI funding N
22. Kill-AIDS ins dscriminatn N
23. Kill-$10 bbl oil tariff Y
24. Kill-Repl wndfl prfts tax Y
25. Repeal balanced bdgt amdt N
26. Tax amnesty provisions Y
27. Kill-Tax amnesty subst N
28. Kill-Add third tax rate N
29. Kill-Unocal tax provsns N
30. Block Saudi arms sale (†) Y
31. Kill-Bar school busing Y
32. Prohibit Saudi arms sale Y
33. Nicaraguan contra aid N
34. Bar all aid to Nicaragua N
35. Balanced budget amendment Y
36. Balanced bdgt substitute Y
37. Conrail sale Y
38. Revise farm programs N
39. Kill-New oil import fee Y
40. Spending cuts, tax incres Y
41. Textile import quotas Y
42. Kill-Exmpt vets from cuts N
43. Kill-Bar inmate abortn $ N
44. Textile import quotas (§) Y
45. Kill-Eliminate Amtrak $ Y
46. Kill-Incrs motor fuel tax Y

GORE, ALBERT, Jr. (Cont.)

47. Set max allow deficits Y
48. 20% minimum tax on corps N
49. Bar $ to toxic victims N
50. Seasonal workers in US Y
51. Kill-School prayer cases Y
52. Line-item veto N
53. South Africa sanctions Y
54. Ease '68 Gun Control Act Y
55. Kill-14 day handgun wait Y
56. Kill-Gun dlr inspections Y
57. Kill-Keep '68 Gun Con Act Y
58. Nicarag humanitarian aid N
59. Bar ASAT testing Y
60. Delete chemical weapons Y
61. Delete 21 MX missiles N
62. Kill-15% min tax on corps N
63. Kill-Restore Soc Sec COLA N
64. Freeze all funding Y
65. Cut def;raise taxes, COLA Y
66. Keep existing SS COLAs Y
67. Aid to Nicaraguan rebels N
68. Reaffirm purch of 21 MX Y
69. African Relief/Farm Crdt Y

Presidential Support Score: 1986 - 30% 1985 - 34%

SASSER, JIM [Democrat] Term Began/Expires: 1983/1988. Prior Terms: Senate: 1977-82. Born: September 30, 1936; Memphis, Tenn. Education: University of Tennessee; Vanderbilt University (B.A., LL.B.) Military Service: U.S. Marine Corps Reserve. Occupation: Attorney, Goodpasture, Carpenter, Woods & Sasser.

1. Immigration Reform Y
2. So Afr Sanc-veto override Y
3. Kill-Death pnlty drug bil N
4. Kill-Mil use in drug war Y
5. Tax Overhaul N
6. Raise speed limit Y
7. Across-the-board cuts N
8. South Africa sanctions Y
9. Kill-So Africa sanctions N
10. Kill-So Africa sanct (*) N
11. Nicaraguan contra aid N
12. Terminate contra aid Y
13. Kill-Prohibit contra fnds N
14. Kill-Stop CIA contra fndg N
15. Kill-Bar nuclr tsts w/SDI N
16. Kill-Bar ASAT testing N
17. Nuclear test ban treaty Y
18. Prohibit sale of Stinger Y
19. Delete Bigeye chem bomb Y
20. Bar binary chem weapons Y
21. Kill-SDI funding N
22. Kill-AIDS ins dscriminatn N
23. Kill-$10 bbl oil tariff Y
24. Kill-Repl wndfl prfts tax Y
25. Repeal balanced bdgt amdt N
26. Tax amnesty provisions N
27. Kill-Tax amnesty subst Y
28. Kill-Add third tax rate N
29. Kill-Unocal tax provsns N
30. Block Saudi arms sale (†) Y
31. Kill-Bar school busing N
32. Prohibit Saudi arms sale Y
33. Nicaraguan contra aid N
34. Bar all aid to Nicaragua N
35. Balanced budget amendment Y
36. Balanced bdgt substitute Y
37. Conrail sale Y
38. Revise farm programs N
39. Kill-New oil import fee Y
40. Spending cuts, tax incres Y
41. Textile import quotas Y
42. Kill-Exmpt vets from cuts N
43. Kill-Bar inmate abortn $ Y
44. Textile import quotas (§) Y
45. Kill-Eliminate Amtrak $ Y
46. Kill-Incrs motor fuel tax Y
47. Set max allow deficits Y
48. 20% minimum tax on corps N
49. Bar $ to toxic victims N
50. Seasonal workers in US Y
51. Kill-School prayer cases N
52. Line-item veto N
53. South Africa sanctions Y
54. Ease '68 Gun Control Act Y
55. Kill-14 day handgun wait Y
56. Kill-Gun dlr inspections Y
57. Kill-Keep '68 Gun Con Act Y
58. Nicarag humanitarian aid N
59. Bar ASAT testing Y
60. Delete chemical weapons Y
61. Delete 21 MX missiles Y
62. Kill-15% min tax on corps N
63. Kill-Restore Soc Sec COLA N
64. Freeze all funding N
65. Cut def;raise taxes, COLA Y
66. Keep existing SS COLAs Y
67. Aid to Nicaraguan rebels N
68. Reaffirm purch of 21 MX N
69. African Relief/Farm Crdt Y
70. Kill-Nuclear Freeze N
71. Kill-Void Title IX Narrow N
72. Raise drinking age to 21 Y
73. Kill-Reduce mil in Europe N
74. Kill-Bar $ for contras N

SASSER, JIM (Cont.)

75. Kill-No new MXs in 1985	N	92. Kill-Oppose SS benft cuts	N
76. Kill-Move MX $ to non-nuc	N	93. Disapprove Saudi AWACS	Y
77. Deficit reduction-$140b	N	94. Anti-busing rider	Y
78. Kill-Req auth for troops	N	95. Disapprove oil import fee	?
79. School Prayer amendment	Y	96. Domestic violence funds	N
80. Cap punish-certain crimes	N	97. Trucking Deregulation	N
81. Bar govt off from taping	Y	98. Overturn India fuel sale	N
82. Martin L. King holiday	Y	99. Mil draft registration	Y
83. Auth marines in Lebanon	N	100. Chrysler Loan Guarantees	Y
84. Anti-abortion amendment	N	101. Nuclear plant moratorium	N
85. Highway-Gas tax bill	N	102. Abolish electoral college	Y
86. Delete job creation amend	N	103. Kill-Lmt ct-ordered bus	N
87. Kill-Tobacco price supprt	Y	104. Airline Deregulation	Y
88. Emergency housing aid	Y	105. Disappr Mideast jet sales	Y
89. Nullify oil decontrol	+	106. Natural gas deregulation	N
90. Target tax cuts-mid class	N	107. Prohibit neutron bomb	N
91. Tax Indexing	N	108. Financial disclosure-off	Y

Presidential Support Score: 1986 - 25% 1985 - 33%

TEXAS

GRAMM, PHIL [Republican] Term Began/Expires: 1985/1990. Prior Terms: House: 1979-84. Born: July 8, 1942; Fort Benning, Ga. Education: Georgia Military Academy; University of Georgia (B.B.A., Ph.D.). Occupation: Professor; partner, Gramm and Associates; consultant; author.

1. Immigration Reform	N	31. Kill-Bar school busing	N
2. So Afr Sanc-veto override	N	32. Prohibit Saudi arms sale	N
3. Kill-Death pnlty drug bil	N	33. Nicaraguan contra aid	Y
4. Kill-Mil use in drug war	Y	34. Bar all aid to Nicaragua	N
5. Tax Overhaul	Y	35. Balanced budget amendment	Y
6. Raise speed limit	Y	36. Balanced bdgt substitute	N
7. Across-the-board cuts	Y	37. Conrail sale	Y
8. South Africa sanctions	N	38. Revise farm programs	N
9. Kill-So Africa sanctions	Y	39. Kill-New oil import fee	Y
10. Kill-So Africa sanct (*)	Y	40. Spending cuts, tax incres	Y
11. Nicaraguan contra aid	Y	41. Textile import quotas	N
12. Terminate contra aid	N	42. Kill-Exmpt vets from cuts	Y
13. Kill-Prohibit contra fnds	Y	43. Kill-Bar inmate abortn $	N
14. Kill-Stop CIA contra fndg	Y	44. Textile import quotas (§)	N
15. Kill-Bar nuclr tsts w/SDI	Y	45. Kill-Eliminate Amtrak $	N
16. Kill-Bar ASAT testing	Y	46. Kill-Incrs motor fuel tax	Y
17. Nuclear test ban treaty	N	47. Set max allow deficits	Y
18. Prohibit sale of Stinger	N	48. 20% minimum tax on corps	N
19. Delete Bigeye chem bomb	N	49. Bar $ to toxic victims	Y
20. Bar binary chem weapons	N	50. Seasonal workers in US	Y
21. Kill-SDI funding	Y	51. Kill-School prayer cases	N
22. Kill-AIDS ins dscriminatn	N	52. Line-item veto	Y
23. Kill-$10 bbl oil tariff	Y	53. South Africa sanctions	?
24. Kill-Repl wndfl prfts tax	N	54. Ease '68 Gun Control Act	Y
25. Repeal balanced bdgt amdt	N	55. Kill-14 day handgun wait	Y
26. Tax amnesty provisions	?	56. Kill-Gun dlr inspections	Y
27. Kill-Tax amnesty subst	?	57. Kill-Keep '68 Gun Con Act	Y
28. Kill-Add third tax rate	Y	58. Nicarag humanitarian aid	Y
29. Kill-Unocal tax provsns	Y	59. Bar ASAT testing	N
30. Block Saudi arms sale (†)	N	60. Delete chemical weapons	N

GRAMM, PHIL (Cont.)

61. Delete 21 MX missiles N
62. Kill-15% min tax on corps Y
63. Kill-Restore Soc Sec COLA Y
64. Freeze all funding N
65. Cut def;raise taxes, COLA N
66. Keep existing SS COLAs N
67. Aid to Nicaraguan rebels Y
68. Reaffirm purch of 21 MX Y
69. African Relief/Farm Crdt N

Presidential Support Score: 1986 - 100% 1985 - 87%

BENTSEN, LLOYD [Democrat] Term Began/Expires: 1983/1988. Prior Terms: House: 1948 (Special Election)-1954; Senate: 1971-82. Born: February 11, 1921; Mission, Tex. Education: University of Texas (LL.B.). Military Service: U.S. Army. Occupation: Chairman, Board of Lincoln Liberty Life Insurance Co.; president, Lincoln Consolidated, Inc.; director, Continental Oil Co., Lockheed Aircraft Corp., Trunkline Gas. Co., Panhandle Eastern Pipeline Co., Bank Southwest National Assn.

1. Immigration Reform Y
2. So Afr Sanc-veto override Y
3. Kill-Death pnlty drug bil ?
4. Kill-Mil use in drug war ?
5. Tax Overhaul Y
6. Raise speed limit Y
7. Across-the-board cuts N
8. South Africa sanctions Y
9. Kill-So Africa sanctions N
10. Kill-So Africa sanct (*) N
11. Nicaraguan contra aid Y
12. Terminate contra aid N
13. Kill-Prohibit contra fnds Y
14. Kill-Stop CIA contra fndg Y
15. Kill-Bar nuclr tsts w/SDI Y
16. Kill-Bar ASAT testing N
17. Nuclear test ban treaty Y
18. Prohibit sale of Stinger N
19. Delete Bigeye chem bomb Y
20. Bar binary chem weapons N
21. Kill-SDI funding N
22. Kill-AIDS ins dscriminatn N
23. Kill-$10 bbl oil tariff N
24. Kill-Repl wndfl prfts tax N
25. Repeal balanced bdgt amdt N
26. Tax amnesty provisions ?
27. Kill-Tax amnesty subst ?
28. Kill-Add third tax rate Y
29. Kill-Unocal tax provsns N
30. Block Saudi arms sale (†) N
31. Kill-Bar school busing N
32. Prohibit Saudi arms sale Y
33. Nicaraguan contra aid Y
34. Bar all aid to Nicaragua N
35. Balanced budget amendment Y
36. Balanced bdgt substitute Y
37. Conrail sale Y
38. Revise farm programs Y
39. Kill-New oil import fee N
40. Spending cuts, tax incres Y
41. Textile import quotas Y
42. Kill-Exmpt vets from cuts N
43. Kill-Bar inmate abortn $ Y
44. Textile import quotas (§) Y
45. Kill-Eliminate Amtrak $ Y
46. Kill-Incrs motor fuel tax N
47. Set max allow deficits Y
48. 20% minimum tax on corps N
49. Bar $ to toxic victims Y
50. Seasonal workers in US Y
51. Kill-School prayer cases N
52. Line-item veto N
53. South Africa sanctions Y
54. Ease '68 Gun Control Act Y
55. Kill-14 day handgun wait Y
56. Kill-Gun dlr inspections Y
57. Kill-Keep '68 Gun Con Act Y
58. Nicarag humanitarian aid Y
59. Bar ASAT testing ?
60. Delete chemical weapons N
61. Delete 21 MX missiles N
62. Kill-15% min tax on corps N
63. Kill-Restore Soc Sec COLA N
64. Freeze all funding N
65. Cut def;raise taxes, COLA Y
66. Keep existing SS COLAs Y
67. Aid to Nicaraguan rebels Y
68. Reaffirm purch of 21 MX Y
69. African Relief/Farm Crdt Y
70. Kill-Nuclear Freeze Y
71. Kill-Void Title IX Narrow N
72. Raise drinking age to 21 Y
73. Kill-Reduce mil in Europe N
74. Kill-Bar $ for contras N
75. Kill-No new MXs in 1985 X
76. Kill-Move MX $ to non-nuc ?
77. Deficit reduction-$140b N
78. Kill-Req auth for troops N
79. School Prayer amendment Y
80. Cap punish-certain crimes N
81. Bar govt off from taping Y
82. Martin L. King holiday Y
83. Auth marines in Lebanon N
84. Anti-abortion amendment N

BENTSEN, LLOYD (Cont.)

85. Highway-Gas tax bill Y
86. Delete job creation amend N
87. Kill-Tobacco price supprt Y
88. Emergency housing aid Y
89. Nullify oil decontrol N
90. Target tax cuts-mid class -
91. Tax Indexing N
92. Kill-Oppose SS benft cuts N
93. Disapprove Saudi AWACS Y
94. Anti-busing rider Y
95. Disapprove oil import fee ?
96. Domestic violence funds Y
97. Trucking Deregulation Y
98. Overturn India fuel sale N
99. Mil draft registration Y
100. Chrysler Loan Guarantees Y
101. Nuclear plant moratorium N
102. Abolish electoral college Y
103. Kill-Lmt ct-ordered bus N
104. Airline Deregulation N
105. Disappr Mideast jet sales N
106. Natural gas deregulation Y
107. Prohibit neutron bomb N
108. Financial disclosure-off Y

Presidential Support Score: 1986 - 61% 1985 - 50%

U T A H

GARN, JAKE [Republican] Term Began/Expires: 1981/1986. Prior Terms: Senate: 1975-80. Born: October 12, 1932; Richfield, Utah. Education: University of Utah (B.S.). Military Service: U.S. Navy, 1960; Utah Air National Guard. Occupation: Insurance agent; assistant manager, Home Life Insurance Co. (1961-66); Salt Lake City commissioner (1968-72); Salt Lake City mayor (1972-74).

1. Immigration Reform N
2. So Afr Sanc-veto override ?
3. Kill-Death pnlty drug bil ?
4. Kill-Mil use in drug war ?
5. Tax Overhaul -
6. Raise speed limit ?
7. Across-the-board cuts ?
8. South Africa sanctions Y
9. Kill-So Africa sanctions Y
10. Kill-So Africa sanct (*) Y
11. Nicaraguan contra aid Y
12. Terminate contra aid N
13. Kill-Prohibit contra fnds Y
14. Kill-Stop CIA contra fndg Y
15. Kill-Bar nuclr tsts w/SDI Y
16. Kill-Bar ASAT testing Y
17. Nuclear test ban treaty N
18. Prohibit sale of Stinger N
19. Delete Bigeye chem bomb N
20. Bar binary chem weapons N
21. Kill-SDI funding Y
22. Kill-AIDS ins dscriminatn N
23. Kill-$10 bbl oil tariff Y
24. Kill-Repl wndfl prfts tax N
25. Repeal balanced bdgt amdt N
26. Tax amnesty provisions ?
27. Kill-Tax amnesty subst ?
28. Kill-Add third tax rate Y
29. Kill-Unocal tax provsns ?
30. Block Saudi arms sale (†) N
31. Kill-Bar school busing N
32. Prohibit Saudi arms sale N
33. Nicaraguan contra aid Y
34. Bar all aid to Nicaragua N
35. Balanced budget amendment Y
36. Balanced bdgt substitute N
37. Conrail sale Y
38. Revise farm programs N
39. Kill-New oil import fee Y
40. Spending cuts, tax incres Y
41. Textile import quotas Y
42. Kill-Exmpt vets from cuts Y
43. Kill-Bar inmate abortn $ N
44. Textile import quotas (§) N
45. Kill-Eliminate Amtrak $ N
46. Kill-Incrs motor fuel tax Y
47. Set max allow deficits Y
48. 20% minimum tax on corps N
49. Bar $ to toxic victims Y
50. Seasonal workers in US Y
51. Kill-School prayer cases N
52. Line-item veto Y
53. South Africa sanctions N
54. Ease '68 Gun Control Act Y
55. Kill-14 day handgun wait Y
56. Kill-Gun dlr inspections Y
57. Kill-Keep '68 Gun Con Act Y
58. Nicarag humanitarian aid Y
59. Bar ASAT testing N
60. Delete chemical weapons N
61. Delete 21 MX missiles N
62. Kill-15% min tax on corps Y
63. Kill-Restore Soc Sec COLA Y
64. Freeze all funding N
65. Cut def;raise taxes, COLA N
66. Keep existing SS COLAs N

GARN, JAKE (Cont.)

67. Aid to Nicaraguan rebels Y
68. Reaffirm purch of 21 MX Y
69. African Relief/Farm Crdt -
70. Kill-Nuclear Freeze Y
71. Kill-Void Title IX Narrow Y
72. Raise drinking age to 21 Y
73. Kill-Reduce mil in Europe Y
74. Kill-Bar $ for contras Y
75. Kill-No new MXs in 1985 Y
76. Kill-Move MX $ to non-nuc Y
77. Deficit reduction-$140b Y
78. Kill-Req auth for troops Y
79. School Prayer amendment Y
80. Cap punish-certain crimes Y
81. Bar govt off from taping N
82. Martin L. King holiday N
83. Auth marines in Lebanon Y
84. Anti-abortion amendment Y
85. Highway-Gas tax bill N
86. Delete job creation amend Y
87. Kill-Tobacco price supprt N
88. Emergency housing aid Y
89. Nullify oil decontrol N
90. Target tax cuts-mid class N
91. Tax Indexing Y
92. Kill-Oppose SS benft cuts Y
93. Disapprove Saudi AWACS N
94. Anti-busing rider Y
95. Disapprove oil import fee Y
96. Domestic violence funds N
97. Trucking Deregulation Y
98. Overturn India fuel sale N
99. Mil draft registration N
100. Chrysler Loan Guarantees N
101. Nuclear plant moratorium N
102. Abolish electoral college Y
103. Kill-Lmt ct-ordered bus N
104. Airline Deregulation Y
105. Disappr Mideast jet sales N
106. Natural gas deregulation Y
107. Prohibit neutron bomb N
108. Financial disclosure-off ?

Presidential Support Score: 1986 - 83% 1985 - 73%

HATCH, ORRIN G. [Republican] Term Began/Expires: 1983/1988. Prior Terms: Senate: 1977-82. Born: March 22, 1934; Pittsburgh, Pa. Education: Brigham Young University (B.S.); University of Pittsburgh (LL.B.). Occupation: Attorney.

1. Immigration Reform N
2. So Afr Sanc-veto override N
3. Kill-Death pnlty drug bil N
4. Kill-Mil use in drug war Y
5. Tax Overhaul N
6. Raise speed limit Y
7. Across-the-board cuts Y
8. South Africa sanctions Y
9. Kill-So Africa sanctions Y
10. Kill-So Africa sanct (*) Y
11. Nicaraguan contra aid Y
12. Terminate contra aid N
13. Kill-Prohibit contra fnds Y
14. Kill-Stop CIA contra fndg Y
15. Kill-Bar nuclr tsts w/SDI Y
16. Kill-Bar ASAT testing Y
17. Nuclear test ban treaty N
18. Prohibit sale of Stinger N
19. Delete Bigeye chem bomb N
20. Bar binary chem weapons N
21. Kill-SDI funding Y
22. Kill-AIDS ins dscriminatn N
23. Kill-$10 bbl oil tariff Y
24. Kill-Repl wndfl prfts tax N
25. Repeal balanced bdgt amdt N
26. Tax amnesty provisions N
27. Kill-Tax amnesty subst N
28. Kill-Add third tax rate Y
29. Kill-Unocal tax provsns Y
30. Block Saudi arms sale (†) N
31. Kill-Bar school busing N
32. Prohibit Saudi arms sale N
33. Nicaraguan contra aid Y
34. Bar all aid to Nicaragua N
35. Balanced budget amendment Y
36. Balanced bdgt substitute N
37. Conrail sale Y
38. Revise farm programs Y
39. Kill-New oil import fee Y
40. Spending cuts, tax incres Y
41. Textile import quotas Y
42. Kill-Exmpt vets from cuts Y
43. Kill-Bar inmate abortn $ N
44. Textile import quotas (§) Y
45. Kill-Eliminate Amtrak $ Y
46. Kill-Incrs motor fuel tax Y
47. Set max allow deficits Y
48. 20% minimum tax on corps N
49. Bar $ to toxic victims N
50. Seasonal workers in US Y
51. Kill-School prayer cases Y
52. Line-item veto Y
53. South Africa sanctions N
54. Ease '68 Gun Control Act Y
55. Kill-14 day handgun wait Y
56. Kill-Gun dlr inspections Y
57. Kill-Keep '68 Gun Con Act Y
58. Nicarag humanitarian aid Y
59. Bar ASAT testing N
60. Delete chemical weapons N

HATCH, ORRIN G. (Cont.)

61. Delete 21 MX missiles N
62. Kill-15% min tax on corps Y
63. Kill-Restore Soc Sec COLA Y
64. Freeze all funding N
65. Cut def;raise taxes, COLA N
66. Keep existing SS COLAs N
67. Aid to Nicaraguan rebels Y
68. Reaffirm purch of 21 MX Y
69. African Relief/Farm Crdt N
70. Kill-Nuclear Freeze Y
71. Kill-Void Title IX Narrow Y
72. Raise drinking age to 21 Y
73. Kill-Reduce mil in Europe Y
74. Kill-Bar $ for contras Y
75. Kill-No new MXs in 1985 Y
76. Kill-Move MX $ to non-nuc Y
77. Deficit reduction-$140b Y
78. Kill-Req auth for troops Y
79. School Prayer amendment Y
80. Cap punish-certain crimes Y
81. Bar govt off from taping N
82. Martin L. King holiday N
83. Auth marines in Lebanon Y
84. Anti-abortion amendment Y
85. Highway-gas tax bill -
86. Delete job creation amend Y
87. Kill-Tobacco price supprt N
88. Emergency housing aid Y
89. Nullify oil decontrol N
90. Target tax cuts-mid class N
91. Tax Indexing Y
92. Kill-Oppose SS benft cuts Y
93. Disapprove Saudi AWACS N
94. Anti-busing rider Y
95. Disapprove oil import fee Y
96. Domestic violence funds N
97. Trucking Deregulation Y
98. Overturn India fuel sale Y
99. Mil draft registration N
100. Chrysler Loan Guarantees N
101. Nuclear plant moratorium N
102. Abolish electoral college N
103. Kill-Lmt ct-ordered bus N
104. Airline Deregulation Y
105. Disappr Mideast jet sales N
106. Natural gas deregulation Y
107. Prohibit neutron bomb N
108. Financial disclosure-off Y

Presidential Support Score: 1986 - 93% 1985 - 82%

VERMONT

STAFFORD, ROBERT T. [Republican] Term Began/Expires: 1983/1988. Prior Terms: House: 1961-1970; Senate: 1971-82. Born: August 8, 1913; Rutland, Vt. Education: Middlebury College (B.S.); University of Michigan; Boston University Law School (LL.B.). Military Service: U.S. Navy. Occupation: Rutland city grand juror (1938-42); state's attorney (1947-51); deputy attorney general (1953-55); attorney general (1955-57); lieutenant governor (1957-59); governor (1959-61).

1. Immigration Reform Y
2. So Afr Sanc-veto override Y
3. Kill-Death pnlty drug bil ?
4. Kill-Mil use in drug war ?
5. Tax Overhaul Y
6. Raise speed limit N
7. Across-the-board cuts ?
8. South Africa sanctions Y
9. Kill-So Africa sanctions Y
10. Kill-So Africa sanct (*) Y
11. Nicaraguan contra aid N
12. Terminate contra aid N
13. Kill-Prohibit contra fnds N
14. Kill-Stop CIA contra fndg N
15. Kill-Bar nuclr tsts w/SDI ?
16. Kill-Bar ASAT testing N
17. Nuclear test ban treaty Y
18. Prohibit sale of Stinger N
19. Delete Bigeye chem bomb Y
20. Bar binary chem weapons Y
21. Kill-SDI funding N
22. Kill-AIDS ins dscriminatn Y
23. Kill-$10 bbl oil tariff Y
24. Kill-Repl wndfl prfts tax Y
25. Repeal balanced bdgt amdt Y
26. Tax amnesty provisions Y
27. Kill-Tax amnesty subst N
28. Kill-Add third tax rate Y
29. Kill-Unocal tax provsns Y
30. Block Saudi arms sale (†) N
31. Kill-Bar school busing Y
32. Prohibit Saudi arms sale N
33. Nicaraguan contra aid N
34. Bar all aid to Nicaragua Y
35. Balanced budget amendment N
36. Balanced bdgt substitute N
37. Conrail sale N
38. Revise farm programs Y
39. Kill-New oil import fee Y
40. Spending cuts, tax incres Y

STAFFORD, ROBERT T. (Cont.)

41. Textile import quotas N
42. Kill-Exmpt vets from cuts Y
43. Kill-Bar inmate abortn $ Y
44. Textile import quotas (§) N
45. Kill-Eliminate Amtrak $ Y
46. Kill-Incrs motor fuel tax Y
47. Set max allow deficits N
48. 20% minimum tax on corps N
49. Bar $ to toxic victims N
50. Seasonal workers in US N
51. Kill-School prayer cases Y
52. Line-item veto N
53. South Africa sanctions Y
54. Ease '68 Gun Control Act Y
55. Kill-14 day handgun wait Y
56. Kill-Gun dlr inspections N
57. Kill-Keep '68 Gun Con Act Y
58. Nicarag humanitarian aid N
59. Bar ASAT testing Y
60. Delete chemical weapons ?
61. Delete 21 MX missiles Y
62. Kill-15% min tax on corps Y
63. Kill-Restore Soc Sec COLA Y
64. Freeze all funding N
65. Cut def;raise taxes, COLA N
66. Keep existing SS COLAs N
67. Aid to Nicaraguan rebels N
68. Reaffirm purch of 21 MX N
69. African Relief/Farm Crdt N
70. Kill-Nuclear Freeze N
71. Kill-Void Title IX Narrow Y
72. Raise drinking age to 21 Y
73. Kill-Reduce mil in Europe Y
74. Kill-Bar $ for contras N
75. Kill-No new MXs in 1985 N
76. Kill-Move MX $ to non-nuc N
77. Deficit reduction-$140b Y
78. Kill-Req auth for troops ?
79. School Prayer amendment N
80. Cap punish-certain crimes Y
81. Bar govt off from taping N
82. Martin L. King holiday Y
83. Auth marines in Lebanon Y
84. Anti-abortion amendment N
85. Highway-Gas tax bill Y
86. Delete job creation amend Y
87. Kill-Tobacco price supprt Y
88. Emergency housing aid Y
89. Nullify oil decontrol N
90. Target tax cuts-mid class N
91. Tax Indexing Y
92. Kill-Oppose SS benft cuts Y
93. Disapprove Saudi AWACS N
94. Anti-busing rider ?
95. Disapprove oil import fee Y
96. Domestic violence funds Y
97. Trucking Deregulation Y
98. Overturn India fuel sale N
99. Mil draft registration Y
100. Chrysler Loan Guarantees Y
101. Nuclear plant moratorium N
102. Abolish electoral college Y
103. Kill-Lmt ct-ordered bus Y
104. Airline Deregulation Y
105. Disappr Mideast jet sales N
106. Natural gas deregulation Y
107. Prohibit neutron bomb N
108. Financial disclosure-off Y

Presidential Support Score: 1986 - 55% 1985 - 69%

LEAHY, PATRICK J. [Democrat] Term Began/Expires: 1981/1986. Prior Terms: Senate: 1975-80. Born: March 31, 1940; Montpelier, Vt. Education: St. Michael's College (B.A.); Georgetown University (J.D.). Occupation: Chittenden County state's attorney (1966-74).

1. Immigration Reform +
2. So Afr Sanc-veto override Y
3. Kill-Death pnlty drug bil N
4. Kill-Mil use in drug war Y
5. Tax Overhaul Y
6. Raise speed limit Y
7. Across-the-board cuts N
8. South Africa sanctions Y
9. Kill-So Africa sanctions N
10. Kill-So Africa sanct (*) N
11. Nicaraguan contra aid N
12. Terminate contra aid Y
13. Kill-Prohibit contra fnds N
14. Kill-Stop CIA contra fndg N
15. Kill-Bar nuclr tsts w/SDI N
16. Kill-Bar ASAT testing N
17. Nuclear test ban treaty Y
18. Prohibit sale of Stinger Y
19. Delete Bigeye chem bomb Y
20. Bar binary chem weapons Y
21. Kill-SDI funding N
22. Kill-AIDS ins dscriminatn Y
23. Kill-$10 bbl oil tariff Y
24. Kill-Repl wndfl prfts tax Y
25. Repeal balanced bdgt amdt N
26. Tax amnesty provisions ?
27. Kill-Tax amnesty subst ?
28. Kill-Add third tax rate N
29. Kill-Unocal tax provsns N
30. Block Saudi arms sale (†) Y
31. Kill-Bar school busing Y
32. Prohibit Saudi arms sale Y

LEAHY, PATRICK J. (Cont.)

33. Nicaraguan contra aid N
34. Bar all aid to Nicaragua Y
35. Balanced budget amendment N
36. Balanced bdgt substitute Y
37. Conrail sale N
38. Revise farm programs Y
39. Kill-New oil import fee Y
40. Spending cuts, tax incres Y
41. Textile import quotas Y
42. Kill-Exmpt vets from cuts N
43. Kill-Bar inmate abortn $ Y
44. Textile import quotas (§) Y
45. Kill-Eliminate Amtrak $ Y
46. Kill-Incrs motor fuel tax Y
47. Set max allow deficits Y
48. 20% minimum tax on corps N
49. Bar $ to toxic victims N
50. Seasonal workers in US Y
51. Kill-School prayer cases Y
52. Line-item veto Y
53. South Africa sanctions Y
54. Ease '68 Gun Control Act Y
55. Kill-14 day handgun wait Y
56. Kill-Gun dlr inspections Y
57. Kill-Keep '68 Gun Con Act Y
58. Nicarag humanitarian aid N
59. Bar ASAT testing Y
60. Delete chemical weapons Y
61. Delete 21 MX missiles Y
62. Kill-15% min tax on corps N
63. Kill-Restore Soc Sec COLA N
64. Freeze all funding N
65. Cut def;raise taxes, COLA Y
66. Keep existing SS COLAs Y
67. Aid to Nicaraguan rebels N
68. Reaffirm purch of 21 MX N
69. African Relief/Farm Crdt Y
70. Kill-Nuclear Freeze N
71. Kill-Void Title IX Narrow N
72. Raise drinking age to 21 N
73. Kill-Reduce mil in Europe N
74. Kill-Bar $ for contras N
75. Kill-No new MXs in 1985 N
76. Kill-Move MX $ to non-nuc N
77. Deficit reduction-$140b N
78. Kill-Req auth for troops N
79. School Prayer amendment N
80. Cap punish-certain crimes N
81. Bar govt off from taping Y
82. Martin L. King holiday Y
83. Auth marines in Lebanon N
84. Anti-abortion amendment N
85. Highway-Gas tax bill Y
86. Delete job creation amend N
87. Kill-Tobacco price supprt N
88. Emergency housing aid Y
89. Nullify oil decontrol Y
90. Target tax cuts-mid class Y
91. Tax Indexing N
92. Kill-Oppose SS benft cuts N
93. Disapprove Saudi AWACS Y
94. Anti-busing rider N
95. Disapprove oil import fee ?
96. Domestic violence funds Y
97. Trucking Deregulation Y
98. Overturn India fuel sale Y
99. Mil draft registration N
100. Chrysler Loan Guarantees Y
101. Nuclear plant moratorium Y
102. Abolish electoral college Y
103. Kill-Lmt ct-ordered bus N
104. Airline Deregulation Y
105. Disappr Mideast jet sales N
106. Natural gas deregulation N
107. Prohibit neutron bomb Y
108. Financial disclosure-off Y

Presidential Support Score: 1986 - 25% 1985 - 29%

V I R G I N I A

TRIBLE, PAUL S., Jr. [Republican] Term Began/Expires: 1983/1988. Prior Terms: House: 1977-82. Born: December 29, 1946; Baltimore, Md. Education: Hampden-Sydney (Va.) College (B.A.); Washington and Lee Law School (J.D.). Occupation: Law clerk, U.S. District Judge Albert Bryant, Jr. (1971-82); assistant U.S. attorney (1972-74); commonwealth's attorney (1974-76).

1. Immigration Reform Y
2. So Afr Sanc-veto override Y
3. Kill-Death pnlty drug bil N
4. Kill-Mil use in drug war Y
5. Tax Overhaul Y
6. Raise speed limit N
7. Across-the-board cuts N
8. South Africa sanctions Y
9. Kill-So Africa sanctions Y
10. Kill-So Africa sanct (*) Y
11. Nicaraguan contra aid Y
12. Terminate contra aid N
13. Kill-Prohibit contra fnds Y
14. Kill-Stop CIA contra fndg Y
15. Kill-Bar nuclr tsts w/SDI Y
16. Kill-Bar ASAT testing Y

TRIBLE, PAUL S., Jr. (Cont.)

17. Nuclear test ban treaty Y
18. Prohibit sale of Stinger N
19. Delete Bigeye chem bomb N
20. Bar binary chem weapons N
21. Kill-SDI funding Y
22. Kill-AIDS ins dscriminatn N
23. Kill-$10 bbl oil tariff Y
24. Kill-Repl wndfl prfts tax N
25. Repeal balanced bdgt amdt N
26. Tax amnesty provisions Y
27. Kill-Tax amnesty subst N
28. Kill-Add third tax rate Y
29. Kill-Unocal tax provsns Y
30. Block Saudi arms sale (†) Y
31. Kill-Bar school busing N
32. Prohibit Saudi arms sale Y
33. Nicaraguan contra aid Y
34. Bar all aid to Nicaragua N
35. Balanced budget amendment Y
36. Balanced bdgt substitute N
37. Conrail sale Y
38. Revise farm programs ?
39. Kill-New oil import fee Y
40. Spending cuts, tax incres Y
41. Textile import quotas Y
42. Kill-Exmpt vets from cuts Y
43. Kill-Bar inmate abortn $ N
44. Textile import quotas (§) Y
45. Kill-Eliminate Amtrak $ N
46. Kill-Incrs motor fuel tax Y
47. Set max allow deficits Y
48. 20% minimum tax on corps N
49. Bar $ to toxic victims Y
50. Seasonal workers in US Y
51. Kill-School prayer cases N
52. Line-item veto Y
53. South Africa sanctions Y
54. Ease '68 Gun Control Act Y
55. Kill-14 day handgun wait Y
56. Kill-Gun dlr inspections Y
57. Kill-Keep '68 Gun Con Act Y
58. Nicarag humanitarian aid Y
59. Bar ASAT testing N
60. Delete chemical weapons N
61. Delete 21 MX missiles N
62. Kill-15% min tax on corps Y
63. Kill-Restore Soc Sec COLA Y
64. Freeze all funding Y
65. Cut def;raise taxes, COLA N
66. Keep existing SS COLAs N
67. Aid to Nicaraguan rebels Y
68. Reaffirm purch of 21 MX Y
69. African Relief/Farm Crdt N
70. Kill-Nuclear Freeze Y
71. Kill-Void Title IX Narrow Y
72. Raise drinking age to 21 Y
73. Kill-Reduce mil in Europe Y
74. Kill-Bar $ for contras Y
75. Kill-No new MXs in 1985 Y
76. Kill-Move MX $ to non-nuc Y
77. Deficit reduction-$140b Y
78. Kill-Req auth for troops Y
79. School Prayer amendment Y
80. Cap punish-certain crimes Y
81. Bar govt off from taping N
82. Martin L. King holiday Y
83. Auth marines in Lebanon Y
84. Anti-abortion amendment Y

Presidential Support Score: 1986 - 84% 1985 - 86%

WARNER, JOHN W. [Republican] Term Began/Expires: 1985/1990. Prior Terms: Senate: 1979-84. Born: February 18, 1927. Education: Washington and Lee University (B.S.); University of Virginia (LL.B.). Military Service: U.S. Navy, 1944-46; U.S. Marine Corps, 1950-52. Occupation: Special assistant to U.S. attorney (1956); assistant U.S. attorney (1957-60); attorney, Hogan & Hartson; under secretary of Navy (1969-72); director of Ocean Affairs (1971-72); secretary of the Navy (1972-74); administrator, American Revolution Bicentennial Admin. (1974).

1. Immigration Reform Y
2. So Afr Sanc-veto override Y
3. Kill-Death pnlty drug bil N
4. Kill-Mil use in drug war Y
5. Tax Overhaul N
6. Raise speed limit N
7. Across-the-board cuts N
8. South Africa sanctions Y
9. Kill-So Africa sanctions Y
10. Kill-So Africa sanct (*) Y
11. Nicaraguan contra aid Y
12. Terminate contra aid N
13. Kill-Prohibit contra fnds Y
14. Kill-Stop CIA contra fndg Y
15. Kill-Bar nuclr tsts w/SDI Y
16. Kill-Bar ASAT testing Y
17. Nuclear test ban treaty N
18. Prohibit sale of Stinger N
19. Delete Bigeye chem bomb N
20. Bar binary chem weapons N
21. Kill-SDI funding Y
22. Kill-AIDS ins dscriminatn ?
23. Kill-$10 bbl oil tariff Y
24. Kill-Repl wndfl prfts tax N

WARNER, JOHN W. (Cont.)

25. Repeal balanced bdgt amdt N
26. Tax amnesty provisions Y
27. Kill-Tax amnesty subst N
28. Kill-Add third tax rate Y
29. Kill-Unocal tax provsns Y
30. Block Saudi arms sale (†) N
31. Kill-Bar school busing N
32. Prohibit Saudi arms sale N
33. Nicaraguan contra aid Y
34. Bar all aid to Nicaragua N
35. Balanced budget amendment Y
36. Balanced bdgt substitute Y
37. Conrail sale Y
38. Revise farm programs N
39. Kill-New oil import fee Y
40. Spending cuts, tax incres Y
41. Textile import quotas Y
42. Kill-Exmpt vets from cuts Y
43. Kill-Bar inmate abortn $ Y
44. Textile import quotas (§) Y
45. Kill-Eliminate Amtrak $ Y
46. Kill-Incrs motor fuel tax Y
47. Set max allow deficits Y
48. 20% minimum tax on corps N
49. Bar $ to toxic victims Y
50. Seasonal workers in US Y
51. Kill-School prayer cases N
52. Line-item veto Y
53. South Africa sanctions Y
54. Ease '68 Gun Control Act Y
55. Kill-14 day handgun wait N
56. Kill-Gun dlr inspections Y
57. Kill-Keep '68 Gun Con Act Y
58. Nicarag humanitarian aid Y
59. Bar ASAT testing N
60. Delete chemical weapons N
61. Delete 21 MX missiles N
62. Kill-15% min tax on corps Y
63. Kill-Restore Soc Sec COLA Y
64. Freeze all funding N
65. Cut def;raise taxes, COLA N
66. Keep existing SS COLAs N
67. Aid to Nicaraguan rebels Y
68. Reaffirm purch of 21 MX Y
69. African Relief/Farm Crdt N
70. Kill-Nuclear Freeze Y
71. Kill-Void Title IX Narrow Y
72. Raise drinking age to 21 Y
73. Kill-Reduce mil in Europe Y
74. Kill-Bar $ for contras Y
75. Kill-No new MXs in 1985 Y
76. Kill-Move MX $ to non-nuc Y
77. Deficit reduction-$140b Y
78. Kill-Req auth for troops Y
79. School Prayer amendment Y
80. Cap punish-certain crimes Y
81. Bar govt off from taping N
82. Martin L. King holiday Y
83. Auth marines in Lebanon Y
84. Anti-abortion amendment Y
85. Highway-Gas tax bill Y
86. Delete job creation amend Y
87. Kill-Tobacco price supprt Y
88. Emergency housing aid N
89. Nullify oil decontrol N
90. Target tax cuts-mid class N
91. Tax Indexing Y
92. Kill-Oppose SS benft cuts Y
93. Disapprove Saudi AWACS N
94. Anti-busing rider Y
95. Disapprove oil import fee Y
96. Domestic violence funds N
97. Trucking Deregulation Y
98. Overturn India fuel sale Y
99. Mil draft registration Y
100. Chrysler Loan Guarantees N
101. Nuclear plant moratorium N
102. Abolish electoral college N

Presidential Support Score: 1986 - 88% 1985 - 82%

WASHINGTON

EVANS, DANIEL J. [Republican] Term Began/Expires: 1983/1988. Born: October 16, 1925. Education: University of Washington (B.S., M.S.). Military Service: U.S. Navy. Occupation: Structural engineer; Washington representative (1956-65); governor (1965-77); president, The Evergreen State College (1977-83); chairman, Pacific Northwest Electric Power and Conservation Planning Council (1981-83).

1. Immigration Reform ?
2. So Afr Sanc-veto override Y
3. Kill-Death pnlty drug bil Y
4. Kill-Mil use in drug war Y
5. Tax Overhaul Y
6. Raise speed limit N
7. Across-the-board cuts N
8. South Africa sanctions Y
9. Kill-So Africa sanctions Y
10. Kill-So Africa sanct (*) Y
11. Nicaraguan contra aid Y
12. Terminate contra aid N

EVANS, DANIEL J. (Cont.)

13. Kill-Prohibit contra fnds Y
14. Kill-Stop CIA contra fndg Y
15. Kill-Bar nuclr tsts w/SDI Y
16. Kill-Bar ASAT testing ?
17. Nuclear test ban treaty N
18. Prohibit sale of Stinger N
19. Delete Bigeye chem bomb Y
20. Bar binary chem weapons Y
21. Kill-SDI funding N
22. Kill-AIDS ins dscriminatn Y
23. Kill-$10 bbl oil tariff Y
24. Kill-Repl wndfl prfts tax N
25. Repeal balanced bdgt amdt N
26. Tax amnesty provisions Y
27. Kill-Tax amnesty subst N
28. Kill-Add third tax rate Y
29. Kill-Unocal tax provsns ?
30. Block Saudi arms sale (†) N
31. Kill-Bar school busing Y
32. Prohibit Saudi arms sale N
33. Nicaraguan contra aid N
34. Bar all aid to Nicaragua N
35. Balanced budget amendment N
36. Balanced bdgt substitute N
37. Conrail sale N
38. Revise farm programs Y
39. Kill-New oil import fee Y
40. Spending cuts, tax incres Y
41. Textile import quotas N
42. Kill-Exmpt vets from cuts Y
43. Kill-Bar inmate abortn $ Y
44. Textile import quotas (§) N
45. Kill-Eliminate Amtrak $ Y
46. Kill-Incrs motor fuel tax Y
47. Set max allow deficits Y
48. 20% minimum tax on corps N
49. Bar $ to toxic victims Y
50. Seasonal workers in US Y
51. Kill-School prayer cases Y
52. Line-item veto Y
53. South Africa sanctions Y
54. Ease '68 Gun Control Act Y
55. Kill-14 day handgun wait Y
56. Kill-Gun dlr inspections N
57. Kill-Keep '68 Gun Con Act N
58. Nicarag humanitarian aid N
59. Bar ASAT testing N
60. Delete chemical weapons Y
61. Delete 21 MX missiles N
62. Kill-15% min tax on corps Y
63. Kill-Restore Soc Sec COLA Y
64. Freeze all funding N
65. Cut def;raise taxes, COLA N
66. Keep existing SS COLAs N
67. Aid to Nicaraguan rebels N
68. Reaffirm purch of 21 MX Y
69. African Relief/Farm Crdt N
70. Kill-Nuclear Freeze Y
71. Kill-Void Title IX Narrow Y
72. Raise drinking age to 21 N
73. Kill-Reduce mil in Europe Y
74. Kill-Bar $ for contras Y
75. Kill-No new MXs in 1985 Y
76. Kill-Move MX $ to non-nuc Y
77. Deficit reduction-$140b Y
78. Kill-Req auth for troops Y
79. School Prayer amendment N
80. Cap punish-certain crimes N
81. Bar govt off from taping N
82. Martin L. King holiday Y
83. Auth marines in Lebanon Y
84. Anti-abortion amendment
85. Highway-Gas tax bill

Sworn in Sept. 12, 1983 and missed votes 84 and 85.

Presidential Support Score: 1986 - 76% 1985 - 84%

GORTON, SLADE [Republican] Term Began/Expires: 1981/1986. Born: January 8, 1928; Chicago, Ill. Education: Dartmouth College (B.A.); Columbia University Law School (LL.B.). Military Service: U.S. Army, 1945-46; U.S. Air Force, 1953-56; U.S. Air Force Reserves. Occupation: Washington representative (1958-68); Washington attorney general (1968-80).

1. Immigration Reform #
2. So Afr Sanc-veto override Y
3. Kill-Death pnlty drug bil ?
4. Kill-Mil use in drug war ?
5. Tax Overhaul Y
6. Raise speed limit Y
7. Across-the-board cuts N
8. South Africa sanctions Y
9. Kill-So Africa sanctions Y
10. Kill-So Africa sanct (*) Y
11. Nicaraguan contra aid N
12. Terminate contra aid N
13. Kill-Prohibit contra fnds Y
14. Kill-Stop CIA contra fndg Y
15. Kill-Bar nuclr tsts w/SDI Y
16. Kill-Bar ASAT testing Y
17. Nuclear test ban treaty Y
18. Prohibit sale of Stinger N
19. Delete Bigeye chem bomb Y
20. Bar binary chem weapons N

GORTON, SLADE (Cont.)

21. Kill-SDI funding Y
22. Kill-AIDS ins dscriminatn Y
23. Kill-$10 bbl oil tariff Y
24. Kill-Repl wndfl prfts tax N
25. Repeal balanced bdgt amdt N
26. Tax amnesty provisions Y
27. Kill-Tax amnesty subst N
28. Kill-Add third tax rate N
29. Kill-Unocal tax provsns N
30. Block Saudi arms sale (†) Y
31. Kill-Bar school busing Y
32. Prohibit Saudi arms sale Y
33. Nicaraguan contra aid N
34. Bar all aid to Nicaragua N
35. Balanced budget amendment N
36. Balanced bdgt substitute N
37. Conrail sale N
38. Revise farm programs Y
39. Kill-New oil import fee Y
40. Spending cuts, tax incres Y
41. Textile import quotas N
42. Kill-Exmpt vets from cuts Y
43. Kill-Bar inmate abortn $ Y
44. Textile import quotas (§) N
45. Kill-Eliminate Amtrak $ Y
46. Kill-Incrs motor fuel tax Y
47. Set max allow deficits Y
48. 20% minimum tax on corps N
49. Bar $ to toxic victims Y
50. Seasonal workers in US Y
51. Kill-School prayer cases Y
52. Line-item veto Y
53. South Africa sanctions Y
54. Ease '68 Gun Control Act Y
55. Kill-14 day handgun wait Y
56. Kill-Gun dlr inspections Y
57. Kill-Keep '68 Gun Con Act N
58. Nicarag humanitarian aid N
59. Bar ASAT testing N
60. Delete chemical weapons N
61. Delete 21 MX missiles N
62. Kill-15% min tax on corps Y
63. Kill-Restore Soc Sec COLA Y
64. Freeze all funding N
65. Cut def;raise taxes, COLA N
66. Keep existing SS COLAs Y
67. Aid to Nicaraguan rebels N
68. Reaffirm purch of 21 MX Y
69. African Relief/Farm Crdt N
70. Kill-Nuclear Freeze Y
71. Kill-Void Title IX Narrow Y
72. Raise drinking age to 21 Y
73. Kill-Reduce mil in Europe Y
74. Kill-Bar $ for contras Y
75. Kill-No new MXs in 1985 Y
76. Kill-Move MX $ to non-nuc Y
77. Deficit reduction-$140b Y
78. Kill-Req auth for troops Y
79. School Prayer amendment N
80. Cap punish-certain crimes Y
81. Bar govt off from taping N
82. Martin L. King holiday Y
83. Auth marines in Lebanon Y
84. Anti-abortion amendment N
85. Highway-Gas tax bill Y
86. Delete job creation amend Y
87. Kill-Tobacco price supprt N
88. Emergency housing aid Y
89. Nullify oil decontrol N
90. Target tax cuts-mid class N
91. Tax Indexing Y
92. Kill-Oppose SS benft cuts Y
93. Disapprove Saudi AWACS N
94. Anti-busing rider N

Presidential Support Score: 1986 - 74% 1985 - 77%

W E S T V I R G I N I A

BYRD, ROBERT C. [Democrat] Term Began/Expires: 1983/1988. Prior Terms: House: 1953-58; Senate: 1959-82. Born: November 20, 1917; North Wilkesboro, N.C. Education: American University (J.D.). Occupation: West Virginia delegate (1946-50); West Virginia senator (1950-52).

1. Immigration Reform Y
2. So Afr Sanc-veto override Y
3. Kill-Death pnlty drug bil N
4. Kill-Mil use in drug war Y
5. Tax Overhaul Y
6. Raise speed limit N
7. Across-the-board cuts N
8. South Africa sanctions Y
9. Kill-So Africa sanctions N
10. Kill-So Africa sanct (*) N
11. Nicaraguan contra aid N
12. Terminate contra aid Y
13. Kill-Prohibit contra fnds N
14. Kill-Stop CIA contra fndg N
15. Kill-Bar nuclr tsts w/SDI Y
16. Kill-Bar ASAT testing Y
17. Nuclear test ban treaty Y
18. Prohibit sale of Stinger N
19. Delete Bigeye chem bomb Y
20. Bar binary chem weapons Y

BYRD, ROBERT C. (Cont.)

21. Kill-SDI funding Y
22. Kill-AIDS ins dscriminatn N
23. Kill-$10 bbl oil tariff Y
24. Kill-Repl wndfl prfts tax Y
25. Repeal balanced bdgt amdt Y
26. Tax amnesty provisions N
27. Kill-Tax amnesty subst Y
28. Kill-Add third tax rate N
29. Kill-Unocal tax provsns N
30. Block Saudi arms sale (†) Y
31. Kill-Bar school busing Y
32. Prohibit Saudi arms sale Y
33. Nicaraguan contra aid N
34. Bar all aid to Nicaragua N
35. Balanced budget amendment N
36. Balanced bdgt substitute Y
37. Conrail sale N
38. Revise farm programs N
39. Kill-New oil import fee Y
40. Spending cuts, tax incres Y
41. Textile import quotas Y
42. Kill-Exmpt vets from cuts N
43. Kill-Bar inmate abortn $ Y
44. Textile import quotas (§) Y
45. Kill-Eliminate Amtrak $ Y
46. Kill-Incrs motor fuel tax Y
47. Set max allow deficits N
48. 20% minimum tax on corps N
49. Bar $ to toxic victims N
50. Seasonal workers in US N
51. Kill-School prayer cases Y
52. Line-item veto N
53. South Africa sanctions Y
54. Ease '68 Gun Control Act Y
55. Kill-14 day handgun wait Y
56. Kill-Gun dlr inspections Y
57. Kill-Keep '68 Gun Con Act Y
58. Nicarag humanitarian aid Y
59. Bar ASAT testing N
60. Delete chemical weapons N
61. Delete 21 MX missiles N
62. Kill-15% min tax on corps N
63. Kill-Restore Soc Sec COLA N
64. Freeze all funding N
65. Cut def;raise taxes, COLA Y
66. Keep existing SS COLAs Y
67. Aid to Nicaraguan rebels N
68. Reaffirm purch of 21 MX Y
69. African Relief/Farm Crdt Y
70. Kill-Nuclear Freeze N
71. Kill-Void Title IX Narrow N
72. Raise drinking age to 21 Y
73. Kill-Reduce mil in Europe N
74. Kill-Bar $ for contras N
75. Kill-No new MXs in 1985 Y
76. Kill-Move MX $ to non-nuc Y
77. Deficit reduction-$140b N
78. Kill-Req auth for troops N
79. School Prayer amendment Y
80. Cap punish-certain crimes Y
81. Bar govt off from taping Y
82. Martin L. King holiday Y
83. Auth marines in Lebanon N
84. Anti-abortion amendment N
85. Highway-Gas tax bill N
86. Delete job creation amend N
87. Kill-Tobacco price supprt Y
88. Emergency housing aid Y
89. Nullify oil decontrol Y
90. Target tax cuts-mid class Y
91. Tax Indexing N
92. Kill-Oppose SS benft cuts N
93. Disapprove Saudi AWACS Y
94. Anti-busing rider Y
95. Disapprove oil import fee N
96. Domestic violence funds N
97. Trucking Deregulation N
98. Overturn India fuel sale N
99. Mil draft registration Y
100. Chrysler Loan Guarantees Y
101. Nuclear plant moratorium N
102. Abolish electoral college Y
103. Kill-Lmt ct-ordered bus Y
104. Airline Deregulation N
105. Disappr Mideast jet sales N
106. Natural gas deregulation N
107. Prohibit neutron bomb N
108. Financial disclosure-off Y

Presidential Support Score: 1986 - 38% 1985 - 37%

ROCKEFELLER, JOHN D., IV [Democrat] Term Began/Expires: 1985/1990. Born: June 18, 1937; New York City, N.Y. Education: Harvard University (A.B.) Occupation: VISTA volunteer (1964); West Virginia House of Delegates (1966-68); secretary of state (1968); governor (1976-84).

1. Immigration Reform Y
2. So Afr Sanc-veto override Y
3. Kill-Death pnlty drug bil N
4. Kill-Mil use in drug war Y
5. Tax Overhaul Y
6. Raise speed limit N
7. Across-the-board cuts N
8. South Africa sanctions Y
9. Kill-So Africa sanctions N
10. Kill-So Africa sanct (*) N
11. Nicaraguan contra aid N
12. Terminate contra aid Y

ROCKEFELLER, JOHN D., IV (Cont.)

13. Kill-Prohibit contra fnds N
14. Kill-Stop CIA contra fndg N
15. Kill-Bar nuclr tsts w/SDI N
16. Kill-Bar ASAT testing N
17. Nuclear test ban treaty Y
18. Prohibit sale of Stinger N
19. Delete Bigeye chem bomb Y
20. Bar binary chem weapons N
21. Kill-SDI funding N
22. Kill-AIDS ins dscriminatn N
23. Kill-$10 bbl oil tariff Y
24. Kill-Repl wndfl prfts tax Y
25. Repeal balanced bdgt amdt N
26. Tax amnesty provisions N
27. Kill-Tax amnesty subst Y
28. Kill-Add third tax rate N
29. Kill-Unocal tax provsns N
30. Block Saudi arms sale (†) Y
31. Kill-Bar school busing Y
32. Prohibit Saudi arms sale Y
33. Nicaraguan contra aid N
34. Bar all aid to Nicaragua N
35. Balanced budget amendment N
36. Balanced bdgt substitute N
37. Conrail sale N
38. Revise farm programs Y
39. Kill-New oil import fee N
40. Spending cuts, tax incres Y
41. Textile import quotas Y
42. Kill-Exmpt vets from cuts N
43. Kill-Bar inmate abortn $ Y
44. Textile import quotas (§) Y
45. Kill-Eliminate Amtrak $ Y
46. Kill-Incrs motor fuel tax Y
47. Set max allow deficits Y
48. 20% minimum tax on corps N
49. Bar $ to toxic victims N
50. Seasonal workers in US N
51. Kill-School prayer cases Y
52. Line-item veto N
53. South Africa sanctions Y
54. Ease '68 Gun Control Act Y
55. Kill-14 day handgun wait Y
56. Kill-Gun dlr inspections Y
57. Kill-Keep '68 Gun Con Act Y
58. Nicarag humanitarian aid +
59. Bar ASAT testing Y
60. Delete chemical weapons N
61. Delete 21 MX missiles Y
62. Kill-15% min tax on corps N
63. Kill-Restore Soc Sec COLA N
64. Freeze all funding N
65. Cut def;raise taxes, COLA Y
66. Keep existing SS COLAs Y
67. Aid to Nicaraguan rebels N
68. Reaffirm purch of 21 MX N
69. African Relief/Farm Crdt Y

Presidential Support Score: 1986 - 33% 1985 - 31%

W I S C O N S I N

KASTEN, BOB [Republican] Term Began/Expires: 1981/1986. Prior Terms: House: 1975-78. Born: June 19, 1942; Milwaukee, Wis. Education: University of Arizona (B.A.); Columbia University (M.B.A.). Military Service: U.S. Air Force; Wisconsin Air National Guard. Occupation: Wisconsin senator (1972-74); vice president, Real Estate Resources; general partner, Oliver Plunkett & Associates.

1. Immigration Reform Y
2. So Afr Sanc-veto override Y
3. Kill-Death pnlty drug bil N
4. Kill-Mil use in drug war Y
5. Tax Overhaul Y
6. Raise speed limit N
7. Across-the-board cuts N
8. South Africa sanctions Y
9. Kill-So Africa sanctions N
10. Kill-So Africa sanct (*) Y
11. Nicaraguan contra aid Y
12. Terminate contra aid N
13. Kill-Prohibit contra fnds Y
14. Kill-Stop CIA contra fndg Y
15. Kill-Bar nuclr tsts w/SDI Y
16. Kill-Bar ASAT testing Y
17. Nuclear test ban treaty Y
18. Prohibit sale of Stinger N
19. Delete Bigeye chem bomb N
20. Bar binary chem weapons N
21. Kill-SDI funding Y
22. Kill-AIDS ins dscriminatn N
23. Kill-$10 bbl oil tariff Y
24. Kill-Repl wndfl prfts tax Y
25. Repeal balanced bdgt amdt N
26. Tax amnesty provisions Y
27. Kill-Tax amnesty subst N
28. Kill-Add third tax rate Y
29. Kill-Unocal tax provsns N
30. Block Saudi arms sale (†) Y
31. Kill-Bar school busing N
32. Prohibit Saudi arms sale Y

KASTEN, BOB (Cont.)

33. Nicaraguan contra aid Y
34. Bar all aid to Nicaragua N
35. Balanced budget amendment Y
36. Balanced bdgt substitute N
37. Conrail sale Y
38. Revise farm programs N
39. Kill-New oil import fee Y
40. Spending cuts, tax incres Y
41. Textile import quotas Y
42. Kill-Exmpt vets from cuts Y
43. Kill-Bar inmate abortn $ N
44. Textile import quotas (§) Y
45. Kill-Eliminate Amtrak $ Y
46. Kill-Incrs motor fuel tax Y
47. Set max allow deficits Y
48. 20% minimum tax on corps N
49. Bar $ to toxic victims Y
50. Seasonal workers in US N
51. Kill-School prayer cases N
52. Line-item veto Y
53. South Africa sanctions Y
54. Ease '68 Gun Control Act Y
55. Kill-14 day handgun wait Y
56. Kill-Gun dlr inspections Y
57. Kill-Keep '68 Gun Con Act Y
58. Nicarag humanitarian aid Y
59. Bar ASAT testing N
60. Delete chemical weapons N
61. Delete 21 MX missiles N
62. Kill-15% min tax on corps Y
63. Kill-Restore Soc Sec COLA Y
64. Freeze all funding Y
65. Cut def;raise taxes, COLA N
66. Keep existing SS COLAs Y
67. Aid to Nicaraguan rebels Y
68. Reaffirm purch of 21 MX Y
69. African Relief/Farm Crdt Y
70. Kill-Nuclear Freeze Y
71. Kill-Void Title IX Narrow Y
72. Raise drinking age to 21 Y
73. Kill-Reduce mil in Europe Y
74. Kill-Bar $ for contras Y
75. Kill-No new MXs in 1985 Y
76. Kill-Move MX $ to non-nuc Y
77. Deficit reduction-$140b Y
78. Kill-Req auth for troops Y
79. School Prayer amendment Y
80. Cap punish-certain crimes Y
81. Bar govt off from taping N
82. Martin L. King holiday Y
83. Auth marines in Lebanon Y
84. Anti-abortion amendment Y
85. Highway-Gas tax bill N
86. Delete job creation amend Y
87. Kill-Tobacco price supprt N
88. Emergency housing aid Y
89. Nullify oil decontrol N
90. Target tax cuts-mid class N
91. Tax Indexing Y
92. Kill-Oppose SS benft cuts Y
93. Disapprove Saudi AWACS Y
94. Anti-busing rider Y

Presidential Support Score: 1986 - 83% 1985 - 74%

PROXMIRE, WILLIAM [Democrat] Term Began/Expires: 1983/1988.
Prior Terms: Senate: 1957-82. Born: November 11, 1915; Lake Forest, Ill. Education: Yale University (B.A.); Harvard Business School (M.B.A.); Harvard Graduate School of Arts and Sciences (M.P.A.) Occupation: Businessman.

1. Immigration Reform Y
2. So Afr Sanc-veto override Y
3. Kill-Death pnlty drug bil Y
4. Kill-Mil use in drug war Y
5. Tax Overhaul Y
6. Raise speed limit N
7. Across-the-board cuts Y
8. South Africa sanctions Y
9. Kill-So Africa sanctions N
10. Kill-So Africa sanct (*) N
11. Nicaraguan contra aid N
12. Terminate contra aid Y
13. Kill-Prohibit contra fnds N
14. Kill-Stop CIA contra fndg N
15. Kill-Bar nuclr tsts w/SDI N
16. Kill-Bar ASAT testing N
17. Nuclear test ban treaty Y
18. Prohibit sale of Stinger Y
19. Delete Bigeye chem bomb Y
20. Bar binary chem weapons Y
21. Kill-SDI funding N
22. Kill-AIDS ins dscriminatn Y
23. Kill-$10 bbl oil tariff Y
24. Kill-Repl wndfl prfts tax Y
25. Repeal balanced bdgt amdt N
26. Tax amnesty provisions N
27. Kill-Tax amnesty subst Y
28. Kill-Add third tax rate Y
29. Kill-Unocal tax provsns N
30. Block Saudi arms sale (†) Y
31. Kill-Bar school busing N
32. Prohibit Saudi arms sale Y
33. Nicaraguan contra aid N
34. Bar all aid to Nicaragua Y
35. Balanced budget amendment Y
36. Balanced bdgt substitute N
37. Conrail sale N
38. Revise farm programs N

PROXMIRE, WILLIAM (Cont.)

39.	Kill-New oil import fee	Y	74.	Kill-Bar $ for contras	N
40.	Spending cuts, tax incres	Y	75.	Kill-No new MXs in 1985	N
41.	Textile import quotas	Y	76.	Kill-Move MX $ to non-nuc	N
42.	Kill-Exmpt vets from cuts	Y	77.	Deficit reduction-$140b	Y
43.	Kill-Bar inmate abortn $	N	78.	Kill-Req auth for troops	N
44.	Textile import quotas (§)	Y	79.	School Prayer amendment	Y
45.	Kill-Eliminate Amtrak $	N	80.	Cap punish-certain crimes	N
46.	Kill-Incrs motor fuel tax	Y	81.	Bar govt off from taping	Y
47.	Set max allow deficits	Y	82.	Martin L. King holiday	Y
48.	20% minimum tax on corps	N	83.	Auth marines in Lebanon	N
49.	Bar $ to toxic victims	N	84.	Anti-abortion amendment	Y
50.	Seasonal workers in US	N	85.	Highway-Gas tax bill	N
51.	Kill-School prayer cases	Y	86.	Delete job creation amend	Y
52.	Line-item veto	Y	87.	Kill-Tobacco price supprt	N
53.	South Africa sanctions	Y	88.	Emergency housing aid	Y
54.	Ease '68 Gun Control Act	Y	89.	Nullify oil decontrol	Y
55.	Kill-14 day handgun wait	N	90.	Target tax cuts-mid class	N
56.	Kill-Gun dlr inspections	Y	91.	Tax Indexing	Y
57.	Kill-Keep '68 Gun Con Act	N	92.	Kill-Oppose SS benft cuts	N
58.	Nicarag humanitarian aid	N	93.	Disapprove Saudi AWACS	Y
59.	Bar ASAT testing	Y	94.	Anti-busing rider	Y
60.	Delete chemical weapons	Y	95.	Disapprove oil import fee	Y
61.	Delete 21 MX missiles	Y	96.	Domestic violence funds	N
62.	Kill-15% min tax on corps	N	97.	Trucking Deregulation	Y
63.	Kill-Restore Soc Sec COLA	N	98.	Overturn India fuel sale	Y
64.	Freeze all funding	N	99.	Mil draft registration	N
65.	Cut def;raise taxes, COLA	N	100.	Chrysler Loan Guarantees	N
66.	Keep existing SS COLAs	Y	101.	Nuclear plant moratorium	Y
67.	Aid to Nicaraguan rebels	N	102.	Abolish electoral college	Y
68.	Reaffirm purch of 21 MX	N	103.	Kill-Lmt ct-ordered bus	N
69.	African Relief/Farm Crdt	N	104.	Airline Deregulation	Y
70.	Kill-Nuclear Freeze	N	105.	Disappr Mideast jet sales	Y
71.	Kill-Void Title IX Narrow	N	106.	Natural gas deregulation	N
72.	Raise drinking age to 21	Y	107.	Prohibit neutron bomb	Y
73.	Kill-Reduce mil in Europe	N	108.	Financial disclosure-off	Y

Presidential Support Score: 1986 - 29% 1985 - 48%

W Y O M I N G

SIMPSON, ALAN K. [Republican] Term Began/Expires: 1985/1990. Prior Terms: Senate: 1979 (Special Appointment)-1984. Born: September 2, 1931; Denver, Colo. Education: University of Wyoming (B.S., LL.B.). Occupation: City attorney (1959-69); assistant attorney general (1959); U.S. commissioner (1959-69); Wyoming legislator (1964-77).

1.	Immigration Reform	Y	12.	Terminate contra aid	N
2.	So Afr Sanc-veto override	N	13.	Kill-Prohibit contra fnds	Y
3.	Kill-Death pnlty drug bil	N	14.	Kill-Stop CIA contra fndg	Y
4.	Kill-Mil use in drug war	Y	15.	Kill-Bar nuclr tsts w/SDI	Y
5.	Tax Overhaul	N	16.	Kill-Bar ASAT testing	Y
6.	Raise speed limit	Y	17.	Nuclear test ban treaty	Y
7.	Across-the-board cuts	N	18.	Prohibit sale of Stinger	N
8.	South Africa sanctions	Y	19.	Delete Bigeye chem bomb	N
9.	Kill-So Africa sanctions	Y	20.	Bar binary chem weapons	N
10.	Kill-So Africa sanct (*)	Y	21.	Kill-SDI funding	Y
11.	Nicaraguan contra aid	Y	22.	Kill-AIDS ins dscriminatn	?

SIMPSON, ALAN K. (Cont.)

23. Kill-$10 bbl oil tariff ?
24. Kill-Repl wndfl prfts tax -
25. Repeal balanced bdgt amdt ?
26. Tax amnesty provisions Y
27. Kill-Tax amnesty subst N
28. Kill-Add third tax rate Y
29. Kill-Unocal tax provsns Y
30. Block Saudi arms sale (†) N
31. Kill-Bar school busing N
32. Prohibit Saudi arms sale N
33. Nicaraguan contra aid Y
34. Bar all aid to Nicaragua N
35. Balanced budget amendment Y
36. Balanced bdgt substitute N
37. Conrail sale Y
38. Revise farm programs Y
39. Kill-New oil import fee Y
40. Spending cuts, tax incres Y
41. Textile import quotas N
42. Kill-Exmpt vets from cuts Y
43. Kill-Bar inmate abortn $ Y
44. Textile import quotas (§) N
45. Kill-Eliminate Amtrak $ N
46. Kill-Incrs motor fuel tax Y
47. Set max allow deficits Y
48. 20% minimum tax on corps N
49. Bar $ to toxic victims Y
50. Seasonal workers in US N
51. Kill-School prayer cases N
52. Line-item veto Y
53. South Africa sanctions Y
54. Ease '68 Gun Control Act Y
55. Kill-14 day handgun wait Y
56. Kill-Gun dlr inspections Y
57. Kill-Keep '68 Gun Con Act Y
58. Nicarag humanitarian aid Y
59. Bar ASAT testing N
60. Delete chemical weapons N
61. Delete 21 MX missiles N
62. Kill-15% min tax on corps Y
63. Kill-Restore Soc Sec COLA Y
64. Freeze all funding N
65. Cut def;raise taxes, COLA N
66. Keep existing SS COLAs N
67. Aid to Nicaraguan rebels Y
68. Reaffirm purch of 21 MX Y
69. African Relief/Farm Crdt N
70. Kill-Nuclear Freeze Y
71. Kill-Void Title IX Narrow Y
72. Raise drinking age to 21 N
73. Kill-Reduce mil in Europe Y
74. Kill-Bar $ for contras Y
75. Kill-No new MXs in 1985 Y
76. Kill-Move MX $ to non-nuc Y
77. Deficit reduction-$140b Y
78. Kill-Req auth for troops Y
79. School Prayer amendment Y
80. Cap punish-certain crimes Y
81. Bar govt off from taping N
82. Martin L. King holiday Y
83. Auth marines in Lebanon Y
84. Anti-abortion amendment N
85. Highway-Gas tax bill N
86. Delete job creation amend Y
87. Kill-Tobacco price supprt N
88. Emergency housing aid N
89. Nullify oil decontrol N
90. Target tax cuts-mid class N
91. Tax Indexing Y
92. Kill-Oppose SS benft cuts Y
93. Disapprove Saudi AWACS N
94. Anti-busing rider Y
95. Disapprove oil import fee Y
96. Domestic violence funds N
97. Trucking Deregulation Y
98. Overturn India fuel sale N
99. Mil draft registration Y
100. Chrysler Loan Guarantees N
101. Nuclear plant moratorium N
102. Abolish electoral college N

Presidential Support Score: 1986 - 93% 1985 - 90%

WALLOP, MALCOLM [Republican] Term Began/Expires: 1983/1988. Prior Terms: Senate: 1977-82. Born: February 27, 1933; New York, N.Y. Education: Yale University (B.A.). Military Service: U.S. Army. Occupation: Rancher; Wyoming representative; Wyoming senator.

1. Immigration Reform Y
2. So Afr Sanc-veto override N
3. Kill-Death pnlty drug bil ?
4. Kill-Mil use in drug war ?
5. Tax Overhaul N
6. Raise speed limit Y
7. Across-the-board cuts Y
8. South Africa sanctions N
9. Kill-So Africa sanctions Y
10. Kill-So Africa sanct (*) Y
11. Nicaraguan contra aid Y
12. Terminate contra aid N
13. Kill-Prohibit contra fnds Y
14. Kill-Stop CIA contra fndg Y
15. Kill-Bar nuclr tsts w/SDI Y
16. Kill-Bar ASAT testing Y
17. Nuclear test ban treaty N
18. Prohibit sale of Stinger N
19. Delete Bigeye chem bomb N
20. Bar binary chem weapons N

WALLOP, MALCOLM (Cont.)

21. Kill-SDI funding Y
22. Kill-AIDS ins dscriminatn N
23. Kill-$10 bbl oil tariff Y
24. Kill-Repl wndfl prfts tax N
25. Repeal balanced bdgt amdt N
26. Tax amnesty provisions ?
27. Kill-Tax amnesty subst ?
28. Kill-Add third tax rate Y
29. Kill-Unocal tax provsns Y
30. Block Saudi arms sale (†) N
31. Kill-Bar school busing N
32. Prohibit Saudi arms sale N
33. Nicaraguan contra aid Y
34. Bar all aid to Nicaragua N
35. Balanced budget amendment Y
36. Balanced bdgt substitute N
37. Conrail sale Y
38. Revise farm programs Y
39. Kill-New oil import fee Y
40. Spending cuts, tax incres Y
41. Textile import quotas N
42. Kill-Exmpt vets from cuts Y
43. Kill-Bar inmate abortn $ N
44. Textile import quotas (§) N
45. Kill-Eliminate Amtrak $ N
46. Kill-Incrs motor fuel tax Y
47. Set max allow deficits Y
48. 20% minimum tax on corps N
49. Bar $ to toxic victims Y
50. Seasonal workers in US Y
51. Kill-School prayer cases N
52. Line-item veto Y
53. South Africa sanctions N
54. Ease '68 Gun Control Act Y
55. Kill-14 day handgun wait Y
56. Kill-Gun dlr inspections Y
57. Kill-Keep '68 Gun Con Act Y
58. Nicarag humanitarian aid +
59. Bar ASAT testing N
60. Delete chemical weapons N
61. Delete 21 MX missiles N
62. Kill-15% min tax on corps Y
63. Kill-Restore Soc Sec COLA Y
64. Freeze all funding N
65. Cut def;raise taxes, COLA N
66. Keep existing SS COLAs N
67. Aid to Nicaraguan rebels Y
68. Reaffirm purch of 21 MX Y
69. African Relief/Farm Crdt ?
70. Kill-Nuclear Freeze Y
71. Kill-Void Title IX Narrow Y
72. Raise drinking age to 21 N
73. Kill-Reduce mil in Europe Y
74. Kill-Bar $ for contras Y
75. Kill-No new MXs in 1985 Y
76. Kill-Move MX $ to non-nuc Y
77. Deficit reduction-$140b Y
78. Kill-Req auth for troops Y
79. School Prayer amendment Y
80. Cap punish-certain crimes Y
81. Bar govt off from taping N
82. Martin L. King holiday N
83. Auth marines in Lebanon Y
84. Anti-abortion amendment N
85. Highway-Gas tax bill N
86. Delete job creation amend ?
87. Kill-Tobacco price supprt N
88. Emergency housing aid N
89. Nullify oil decontrol N
90. Target tax cuts-mid class N
91. Tax Indexing N
92. Kill-Oppose SS benft cuts Y
93. Disapprove Saudi AWACS N
94. Anti-busing rider Y
95. Disapprove oil import fee Y
96. Domestic violence funds Y
97. Trucking Deregulation Y
98. Overturn India fuel sale N
99. Mil draft registration Y
100. Chrysler Loan Guarantees N
101. Nuclear plant moratorium -
102. Abolish electoral college N
103. Kill-Lmt ct-ordered bus N
104. Airline Deregulation Y
105. Disappr Mideast jet sales N
106. Natural gas deregulation Y
107. Prohibit neutron bomb N
108. Financial disclosure-off -

Presidential Support Score: 1986 - 94% 1985 - 73%

Index